Immigration, Nationality & Refugee Law Handbook

2006 edition

Duran Seddon

Joint Council for the Welfare of Immigrants

JCWI is an independent national organisation that has been campaigning for justice in immigration, nationality and refugee law and policy for the last 38 years. It takes on challenging cases and provides expert training in this increasingly complex area of law.

The Handbook is aimed at immigration advisers and lawyers, and anyone with an interest in immigration law and practice. JCWI's unique experience is distilled in the JCWI Immigration, nationality and refugee law handbook, which has become an indispensable guide to law and practice in this area.

Duran Seddon is a barrister at Garden Court Chambers, London, specialising in immigration, human rights and welfare law. This is his second edition of the *JCWI Handbook*. Contributions to the text have also been made by Tauhid Pasha, Adrian Berry, Mark Scott, Desmond Rutledge, Navita Atreya and Peter Moss.

Editorial coordinator: Tauhid Pasha, Legal, Policy and Information Director, JCWI

© JCWI 2006

ISBN 1-874010-06-4

Cover design: Boldface
Typesetting: Boldface, 35 Eyre Street Hill, London EC1R 5ET
Printing: The Bath Press, Lower Bristol Road, Bath BA2 3BL

JCWI, 115 Old Street, London EC1V 9RT
Tel: 020 7251 8708, Fax: 020 7251 8707
Publications: 020 7608 7307
Email: info@jcwi.org.uk

Preface and acknowledgements

Welcome to the sixth edition of the *JCWI Handbook*. These continue to be challenging times for all those affected by the immigration system. The last three years have seen enormous changes and the pace of new developments keeps gathering. As well as major structural changes brought in by the 2002 and 2004 Acts, for example to the system of appeals and support, there have been over 25 statements of changes to the Immigration Rules since the last edition. Most of these contain multiple amendments to the various categories of admission and the requirements relating to them. In addition, there have been very significant changes to practice and procedure. For example, on 1 April 2003, 'humanitarian protection' and 'discretionary leave' replaced the system of asylum-based 'exceptional leave' and they have been modified again from 30 August 2005.

Routes for economic migration, regulated both by the Immigration Rules and in criteria set outside the Rules, have also been substantially developed. Further major reorganisation to these routes is being planned under the government's 'five-year strategy' – *Controlling our borders: making migration work for Britain* (February 2005). In addition, from 1 May 2004, free-movement rights have extended, with certain restrictions, to the new countries of the European Union. While the policy developed around these changes is strong on 'what migrants can do for Britain', it is short on rights and protections for individuals. Particularly for the less skilled, routes remain short-term and 'flexible'; able to be switched off when perceived economic imperatives no longer appear compatible with migration. The great playwright Arthur Miller died in 2005 but the words of his most celebrated protagonist have never been more apt:

'You can't eat the orange and throw the peel away – a man is not a piece of fruit!'[1]

As with the flaws of the American dream, so too with policy on migration. People are not to be treated as mere economic units of production. With contribution and participation, must come rights: rights of long-term residence, of family reunion and access to welfare and support when the

1 Willy Loman, *Death of A Salesman*, Act II

need arises. Similar themes are taken up in the commentary in Chapters 2 and 14.

As for asylum and human rights, in 2004 an academic at Plymouth University collected together global estimates on the appallingly high level of deaths at sea of asylum-seekers fleeing persecution or poverty.[2] The figures were constructed from interviews with refugees, records of bodies washed up on shore lines, ship-wrecks and government statistics. On the Morocco–Spain crossing alone, anywhere between 600 and 3,000 people perished during the 1990s. People resort to desperate and dangerous means of travel because there are no lawful routes to escape persecution and because prosperous states have instituted a range of mechanisms to prevent people reaching their borders: carriers' liability, the expansion of direct airside transit visas, controls and checks abroad – all measures increasingly used by the British government (▶see 701–4). In this kind of context, can it really be appropriate that the proudest (and most publicised) policy 'achievement' of our elected representatives is a 67 per cent reduction in asylum claims by 2005? Any cursory glance around the world will reveal that there has been no commensurate reduction in the level of human suffering. Until oppression and poverty are indeed made history, there is surely no point in pretending that the plight of those in genuine need of protection can be obscured by policies designed to shield them from view and to prevent their escape.

While JCWI is a campaigning and lobbying organisation, the *Handbook* is an attempt to explain the rights of those affected by immigration controls as fully as possible and to try to guide applicants and advisers through the maze of rules and regulations that now make up the immigration system. While the system continues to grow in complexity, access to advice has become increasingly difficult. While resources are poured into the regulation and accreditation of the giving of advice and representation, restrictions on the funding to actually deliver it has driven its availability down. In the light of both of these factors, the *Handbook* has once again been expanded in this edition. No book can stand as a substitute for timely, sound and experienced individual advice but we have tried to provide as many tools as we can to help applicants, advisers and lawyers to advance their cases.

The *Handbook* is divided into 14 sections, each of which is sub-divided into chapters. The main changes to the structure and content from the last edition are as follows.

- The workers and business section has been greatly expanded in line with the recent development of the 'managed migration' routes. A separate chapter is given over to the 'Immigration Employment Document' (IED) (work permits or similar documents) routes.

---

2 Pugh, 'Drowning not waving: Boat People and Humanitarianism at Sea', *Journal of Refugee Studies*, Vol. 17, No. 1 (2004).

- The EU free-movement section has also been expanded, incorporating an extra chapter on 'Accession 8' nationals and drawing also on the more recently published 'European Directorate Instructions' (EDI).

- The growth in case law and procedure has meant that, this time, asylum and human rights have been given a section each. The asylum section has five chapters with a separate chapter now given to 'third country' cases and with expanded chapters on qualifying for status, the asylum process, asylum decisions and family reunion.

- The new human rights section has four chapters. This has allowed separate treatment to be given to the ECHR itself, the use that can be made of human rights in immigration cases, the practicalities of obtaining protection and discrimination.

- Increasing dependence by the government on detention has led us to develop further the detention and enforcement section. In particular, there is greater discussion about the legality of detention, a more detailed guide on making bail applications and a separate chapter has been added on detention conditions and procedures.

- Section 11 on remedies is new to the *Handbook*. The first chapter deals with the growth area of civil claims in immigration cases. The second looks at a range of other remedies including judicial review, complaints to the Parliamentary Ombudsman and the scheme for consolatory payments.

- Inevitably, following the restructuring of the system from 4 April 2005, the appeals section has been overhauled and divided into three chapters. The first chapter looks at rights of appeal and the second deals with conducting first instance appeals before the AIT. The final chapter looks at the system for challenging decisions of the AIT and at identifying errors of law.

- The growing complexity of the welfare system means that we have created a separate chapter on social security benefits. In addition, the welfare section has separate chapters dealing with asylum support (and 'hard cases' support), appeals to the Asylum Support Adjudicator and other forms of welfare provision including housing and social services.

- The British nationality section of the *Handbook* has long been overdue for substantial revision. That has now been done. It has been expanded into three chapters with full use made of the Nationality Instructions (NI).

While the structure of the remaining sections (immigration law and advice, immigration control in practice, visitors and students, family and dependants) has remained similar, they have all been fully revised and updated.

The expanding body of important decided cases has resulted in a greater number of cases cited than in the previous edition (references for the cases cited can be found in the case index at 1551–68). In relation to those leading cases which it is particularly important to understand (for example, the decisions of the House of Lords in *Ullah*, *Razgar*, *Limbuela* and *N* and the decisions of the European Court of Justice in *Baumbast & R* and *Chen*), summary tables have been used with the important points identified. Indeed, in response to feedback from the last edition on the use of tables, I have resorted to them even more in this edition in order to give overviews, condense complex information or, in some cases, to encapsulate policies.

The *Handbook* is intended as a practical book and draws heavily on Home Office explanations of policy, practice and procedure. It uses material contained in the standard published instructions to caseworkers (the API, DSP, EDI, IDI, NI, OEM) and in the many different guidance notes and information notices published with application forms and on the main websites. It also draws on Home Office correspondence with advisers and information provided to User Panels, much of which is regularly circulated through the Immigration Law Practitioners' Association. Where a specific point has been taken from any of this material, a reference has been given.

As to the knotty issue of references to legislation, this edition is another product of the constant battle between the sophistication and detail of the subject matter and the desire to produce a book that remains true to its origins of providing a simple and accessible guide to be used by lawyers and non-lawyers alike. While the formula of providing statutory references where they may be of particular help has still informed decisions, I have also tried to respond to users' feedback asking for greater referencing. I have therefore tried to strike a balance between expanding the statutory references while still protecting the text from being submerged in them. Although it has so far been avoided, the time may be approaching for the *Handbook* to become a fully referenced, footnoted guide.

In terms of using the *Handbook*, it is intended to be used for reference rather than being read from start to finish. Immediately following this Preface there are two contents listings: a summary contents and a full contents listing. The book is also heavily cross-referenced, the intention being that, once the user has found part of the information they are looking for, they will also be directed to connected relevant information. An alternative starting point is of course the index at the end of the book.

Some users will be studying immigration law generally, or will be beginners to the area who want to gain a proper understanding of the system as a whole. In their case, the best parts of the *Handbook* to look at first are: Chapter 1 (introduction to immigration law – which also contains a guide to the contents of the book), Chapters 4–6 (system of immigration control), pages 950–7 on 'temporary admission' and Chapter 33 on the enforcement of controls. Having battled through that material, they will appreciate the skeleton on which the flesh of whole system hangs. Much of the remainder can be dipped into in any order, depending on the particular areas of interest, be it workers and business, asylum, detention, welfare etc. The sections on EU rights of free movement and British nationality, however, are best looked at separately. Although they can be crucial to a person's immigration rights, they are in essence, separate systems of law and should be approached as such.

As with previous editions, for space reasons, we have not reproduced legislation or the Immigration Rules themselves. Legislation is publicly available in electronic format and a full, consolidated version of the Rules is maintained and kept up-to-date on the Home Office website. The final part of the *Handbook* (Section 14) is therefore confined to practical information such as visas, fees, country lists for different purposes, addresses, further sources of information as well as a list of abbreviations used in the book (general and statutory) and a glossary.

The following people have made written contributions to the text and I am grateful to them all:

Tauhid Pasha, Solicitor, JCWI Legal and Policy Director

Adrian Berry, Barrister, 6 King's Bench Walk

Mark Scott, Partner, Bhatt Murphy Solicitors

Desmond Rutledge, Barrister, Garden Court Chambers

Navita Atreya, Barrister, Renaissance Chambers

Peter Moss, Bates, Wells & Braithwaite Solicitors

Tauhid Pasha has, additionally, read and commented on most of the text and has shouldered much of the burden of ensuring that it was ready for print.

I would also like to thank the following people who have helped in the production of this edition in various ways, although the omissions and errors are not theirs: Derek Beoku-Betts, Sarah Booker, Liz Davies, Andrew Eaton, Joanna Evans, Nadine Goldfoot, Maya Naidoo, Swati Patel, John Walsh, Frances Webber and Sue Willman.

Thanks are also due to staff at the Home Office who have responded to our questions and provided us with invaluable materials. I would also like to thank Kate Handforth and her colleagues at UKCOSA and Fiona Hannan at the Legal Services Commission for their help and suggestions. With thanks also to our copy-editors/proofreaders, Charles Peyton and Fiona Price for wading through a sea of material, often at late notice. Thanks again go to Carol Brickley and Paul Crittenden at Boldface Typesetters for accommo-dating our schedule and the constant changes made during production. I would like also to thank all the staff and management at JCWI for their assistance and patience. Producing this edition has been a huge project, complicated by an ever-changing environment.

Most importantly, however, the *Handbook* remains your resource and it will remain dependent upon your comments, suggestions and feedback in attempts to improve it.

In addition to stating the present law and practice, the *Handbook* also covers the proposals for change contained in the Immigration, Asylum and Nationality Bill 2005 (as it entered the committee stage in the House of Commons on 18 October 2005), the government's 'five-year strategy', its

Selective Admission: Making Migration Work for Britain paper (a consultation exercise which closed on 7 November 2005) and in other announcements. Chapter 2 looks at proposed changes but, wherever possible, where a forthcoming change is likely, this has been noted in the part of the text that is affected. It is planned to produce a supplement to this edition to cover the provisions of the 2005 Bill after they have been brought into force.

The *Handbook* is up to date as at 7 November 2005, although some later developments are referred to.

Duran Seddon
November 2005

Summary contents

Full contents listing xii

Section 1 IMMIGRATION LAW AND ADVICE

1   Introduction to immigration law and the *Handbook*   3

2   Proposed changes including the 'five-year strategy' and 2005 Bill   31

3   Immigration advice   59

Section 2 IMMIGRATION CONTROL IN PRACTICE

4   Coming to the UK   77

5   Leaving and returning   107

6   Applying to stay in the UK   123

7   Applying to 'switch' categories   159

8   Identifying immigration status   189

Section 3 VISITORS AND STUDENTS

9   Visitors   213

10   Students   249

Section 4 FAMILY MEMBERS

11   Spouses, unmarried partners, same-sex partners and fiancé(e)s   293

12   Children   357

13   Other dependent relatives   397

Section 5 WORKERS AND BUSINESS PEOPLE

14   Work for which permission is required   411

15   Permit-free employment   453

16   Business purposes   477

Section 6 EUROPEAN RIGHTS OF FREE MOVEMENT

17 Free-movement rights: background and basics 503

18 Rights of free movement in the European Economic Area 511

19 Rights of nationals of accession states 565

20 Association and cooperation agreements 577

Section 7 ASYLUM

21 Refugee status 595

22 Asylum procedures 637

23 Home Office decisions on asylum 705

24 Third country cases 737

25 Refugee family reunion 757

Section 8 HUMAN RIGHTS AND DISCRIMINATION

26 The European Convention on Human Rights 773

27 Human rights in immigration and asylum cases 785

28 Raising human rights, humanitarian protection,
discretionary leave, family reunion and travel 853

29 Discrimination 885

Section 9 DETENTION AND ENFORCEMENT

30 Detention: powers, policy and legality 897

31 Detention places, conditions and procedures 933

32 Getting people out of detention 949

33 Enforcement: port removal, illegal entry, administrative
removal, deportation and criminal offences 989

Section 10 APPEALS

34 Rights of appeal 1039

35 Conducting first instance appeals before the AIT 1085

36 Challenging decisions of the Asylum and Immigration
Tribunal 1133

Section 11 CIVIL CLAIMS, JUDICIAL REVIEW AND OTHER REMEDIES

37 Civil claims 1171

38 Judicial review, complaints, Ombudsman and *Adimi*
claims 1213

Section 12   WELFARE

39   Welfare benefits   1241

40   Housing, social services, Children Act and health care   1289

41   Asylum support and 'hard cases' support   1337

42   Asylum support appeals   1389

Section 13   BRITISH NATIONALITY

43   British nationality   1401

44   Who is a British citizen?   1425

45   Applying to be a British citizen   1447

Section 14   INFORMATION

Useful addresses and telephone numbers   1493

Visa nationals and specified nationals   1507

Fees   1509

Entry clearance posts   1511

Work-related applications   1519

Commonwealth countries   1525

Registering with the police   1527

Countries whose adoption decisions are
recognised in the UK and Hague Convention
countries   1528

Abbreviations   1530

Other sources of information   1534

Glossary   1536

CASE LIST   1551

INDEX   1569

Full contents

SECTION 1
IMMIGRATION LAW AND ADVICE

Chapter 1
Introduction to immigration law and the
Handbook 3

Structure of the Handbook 3

Other chapters in Section One 4

The development of modern immigration
law 4

Early immigration law 4

The post-Second World War period 5

Restrictions begin: the 1960s
Commonwealth Immigrants Acts 5

The foundation of present immigration
law: the Immigration Act 1971 6

Asylum and legislation in the 1990s 6

The Nationality, Immigration and Asylum
Act 2002 7

The Asylum and Immigration (Treatment
of Claimants, etc) Act 2004 8

Proposed legislation 9

What makes up the immigration law? 9

Secondary legislation 10

Immigration Rules 10

Case-law 11

Policy and practice 11

The system of immigration control 13

Immigration law and nationality law 14

'Leave' and the immigration rules 15

Asylum and human rights 19

Special groups 21

The operation of immigration controls
23

Enforcement of immigration controls 26

Appeals 27

Other rights and remedies 28

Chapter 2
Proposed changes including the 'five-
year strategy' and 2005 Bill 31

Important legislation 31

The 'five-year strategy' 33

What are the proposed changes? 33

Summary of changes under the five-year
strategy (table) 34

Making Migration Work for Britain –
Consultation 42

The five-year plan: a real strategy or a
great gamble? 44

Immigration, Asylum and Nationality
Bill 2005 50

Other proposals for change 53

Healthcare 53

Identity Cards 54

'Specified nationals' list 55

Civil Partnership Act 2004 55

Making immigration work for
everyone 55

A modern, progressive immigration
policy 55

JCWI'S recommendations for an
immigration policy (table) 56

Chapter 3
Immigration advice 59

Finding an adviser 59

Advice in England and Wales 59

Advice in Scotland and Northern Ireland 61

Where to obtain advice (table) 62

Regulation of immigration advisers 63

Those who can provide advice 63

Complaints against advisers and representatives 65

Legal aid funding in England and Wales 67

The Legal Help Scheme 69

Controlled Legal Representation (CLR) 71

Where prospects of success are poor (table) 72

Legal Representation (previously known as 'Legal Aid') 73

The Immigration and Asylum Accreditation Scheme 73

SECTION 2
IMMIGRATION CONTROL IN PRACTICE

Chapter 4
Coming to the UK 77

Entry clearance 78

Key concepts following the 1999 Act 78

When entry clearance is necessary 79

Who must get entry clearance (table) 80

When entry clearance is optional 83

Entry clearance: EEA Nationals and family members 83

Advantages and disadvantages of obtaining entry clearance 84

Other documents relating to admission to the UK 84

Entry clearances operating as leave to enter 85

Which entry clearances operate as leave to enter? 85

How do these entry clearances work? 86

How long is leave granted for when an entry clearance operates as leave 87

How many times can an entry clearance be used? 88

Applying for entry clearance 89

Delayed departures 89

Forms for applying for entry clearance (table) 90

Entry clearance decisions 93

Revocation of entry clearance by entry clearance officer 94

Granting or refusing leave to enter before arrival in the UK 94

Immigration control on arrival in the UK 95

People who do not require leave 95

People who require leave and general grounds of refusal 96

General grounds for refusal of entry clearance or leave to enter (Table) 98

People who have leave or an entry clearance when they arrive 100

Port decisions concerning entry and appeals 102

Further applications for leave to enter 103

When the immigration officer cannot make an immediate decision 104

Illegible passport stamps 104

Entry from the Republic of Ireland and through the Channel Tunnel 105

Entry through the Channel Tunnel 106

Chapter 5
Leaving and returning 107

General rules 107

Which leave does not lapse? 107

For how long does 'non-lapsing' leave stay in force 108

People who always qualify to return 109

People with the right of abode and certain British passport holders 109

People with indefinite leave 110

The 'returning residents' rule 112

What happens to returning residents on arrival? 115

People with limited leave 116

People whose leave does not lapse when they depart 116

People whose leave lapses when they depart 117

People who left the UK before 30 July 2000 118

People who wish to travel while an application or appeal is outstanding 119

Return of passports 119

Travelling before an application is decided 121

Travelling before an appeal is decided 121

Chapter 6
Applying to stay in the UK 123

This chapter 123

Further proposed changes to procedures 124

Application forms and charging 125

Charging 125

The forms 127

Which forms should be used (table) 128

Making applications in the general categories 132

Applying by post 132

Applying in person 133

Return of passports and documents 134

Ensuring the application is valid 134

Applications must be made in-time 135

Time taken for considering applications 135

Making applications in the IED, EEA, asylum and Article 3 ECHR categories 136

Extending leave in Immigration Employment Document (IED) categories 136

EEA applications 136

EEA Association Agreement applications 137

Asylum and Article 3 ECHR claims 138

Applications made outside the UK or on entry 138

Home Office decisions on applications 138

Notice of decision 139

New endorsements 139

General grounds for refusal of leave to remain (table) 140

Curtailment and other decisions made by the Home Office where no application has been made 141

Curtailment 141

Changing conditions of leave 142

Circumstances in which leave may be curtailed (table) 142

What status does a person have while waiting for a decision? 143

Decision of Home Office made before 2 October 2000 143

Decision of Home Office made on or after 2 October 2000 but before 1 April 2003 144

Decisions made after 1 April 2003 145

Applications and decisions under the provisions of the 2005 Bill 145

What happens when an application is made during a period of automatic leave? 146

Evidence of automatic extensions 146

'Exceptional leave', policies and concessions 147

Exceptional leave' and the other terms used 147

Summary of the terms used 148

The policies/concessions 148

The armed forces 150

Gurkhas discharged from the British Army 150

Foreign or Commonwealth nationals discharged from HM Forces 151

Family members of discharged Gurkhas and others discharged from HM Forces 151

The long-residence rules 151

Relevance of the old long-residence concessions 156

Chapter 7
Applying to 'switch' categories 159

Who can switch under the rules? 160

Switching categories under the immigration rules (table) 161

Switching outside the immigration rules 187

Chapter 8
Identifying immigration status 189

Conditions of leave to enter or remain 189

Summary of conditions (table) 190

Endorsements by entry clearance officers 192

On arrival in the UK 193

Endorsements by immigration officers at port 194

Endorsements by the Home Office 198

UK Residence permits 198

Endorsements no longer issued 199

Other documents 202

Asylum-seekers 203

Immigration Status Documents 204

UN travel documents and Certificates of Identity 206

Notice of temporary admission 207

Enforcement notices 208

SECTION 3
VISITORS AND STUDENTS

Chapter 9
Visitors 213

Admission as a visitor 214

Business visitors 220

Special classes of visitor 221

Visitor procedures 223

Visit entry clearances 223

Appeals 225

Applying for extensions 227

Visitors applying to change their status to another category 228

Travel outside the UK 229

Marriage visitors 229

Medical visitors 230

Extending leave as a medical visitor 231

Carers 232

The first carer application for an extension 233

Second and further carer applications for extensions 233

Working holidaymakers 235

Changes to the scheme under 2002 White Paper 235

Changes to Working Holidaymaker Scheme made in 2005 236

Changes to the Working Holidaymaker Scheme from 8 February 2005 (table) 237

Working Holidaymaker requirements under the rules from 8 February 2005 239

Transit visitors 243

Direct airside transit 243

Transit visitors entering the UK 245

Approved Destination Status Agreement with China 246

Chapter 10
Students 249

Students and prospective students 251

Additional rules for prospective
students 259

Entry clearance decisions 260

Refusal of entry at port 261

Periods of leave granted to
students 262

Conditions of leave and permission to
work while studying 263

Dependants of students 266

Extending leave as a student 268

Switching to stay as a student 274

Switching to remain as a student –
transitional arrangements 275

Breach of undertakings 276

Re-sitting, writing up theses and
sabbatical students 276

Re-sitting students 276

Postgraduate students who are writing
up a thesis 277

Students' union sabbatical officers 278

Medical and dental studies including
training 279

Student nurses 280

Postgraduate doctors and dentists 281

Medical graduates seeking to take the
PLAB test 282

Medical or dental graduates intending
to take a clinical attachment or dental
observer post 283

Fees and student grants and loans 284

Student fees: home and overseas
students 284

Student support 286

Education courses for
asylum-seekers 287

Education courses for others 287

EEA students 288

EEA students' rights to pay home fees
and receive student support 289

SECTION 4
FAMILY MEMBERS

Chapter 11
**Spouses, unmarried partners, same-sex
partners and fiancé(e)s** 293

Recent developments 295

Recent developments affecting
spouses/partners 295

Marrying in the United Kingdom –
changes made by the 2004 Act 296

Changes following the Civil Partnership
Act 2004 300

Changes to the immigration rules under
Civil Partnership Act 2004 (table) 300

The different circumstances covered in
this chapter 301

'Settled in the United Kingdom' and
'present and settled' 302

People coming to the UK as spouses,
unmarried (including same-sex) partners,
or fiancé(e)s of people settled in
the UK 303

Present and settled in the UK 305

Age of applicant and sponsor 305

Intention to live together permanently
306

Maintenance and accommodation
without recourse to public funds 308

Definition of public funds (table) 309

Additional rules for spouses or
fiancé(e)s 318

Additional rules for unmarried
partners 322

Indefinite leave to enter for couples
who have been living outside
the UK 324

The requirement for entry
clearance 325

After entry clearance is issued 325

When an application for entry clearance
is refused 328

People who have been admitted for the
'probationary period' who wish to apply
to settle in the UK 329

Claiming benefits during the
probationary period 329

Applying for settlement (indefinite leave
to remain) 330

Making the application 331

If the application is refused 332

People in the United Kingdom for other
purposes who wish to 'switch' to stay in
the UK permanently with their spouse or
partner who is settled in the UK 332

How to apply 334

Some problems which may arise 335

Can people switch to being
fiancé(e)s? 336

After the application is decided 336

People who want to stay in the UK with
their spouses or partners but who
cannot satisfy the immigration rules 337

Home Office policy in marriage cases
outside the immigration rules 338

Making the application and rights of
appeal 344

People who want to stay in the UK
although they no longer have a
relationship with a partner 344

Bereaved spouses and partners 344

Victims of domestic violence 345

Marriage or relationship breakdown
after settlement has been granted 351

Marriage and relationship breakdown in
other cases 351

People who wish to accompany or join a
spouse or partner in the UK who is here
with limited leave 352

Dependants of workers, business-
persons and others in long-term
categories 352

Dependants of students 354

Dependants of those in other temporary
categories 355

Applications for indefinite leave by
dependants of sponsors admitted in a
category leading to settlement 356

Chapter 12
Children 357

Children who have reached 18 358

Children who do not have to satisfy the
immigration rules 358

Children joining or staying with both
parents settled in the UK 360

Children applying for entry
clearance 364

Children joining one parent in
the UK 367

Children joining a person who is not a
parent 371

Children being joined by parents with
whom they have contact 372

People who apply from outside
the UK 373

People who apply when they are in
the UK 374

Parents of children at school 375

Children accompanying or joining
parents in the UK who have limited
leave 376

Children of workers and business
people 377

Children of students 378

Children of teachers and language
assistants and of people in approved
training or work experience 379

Children of working
holidaymakers 379

Adopted children 379

1) Has the adopted child become
British? 380

2) Adopted children coming to the UK
other than for settlement 381

3) Adoption rules: children who have
been adopted and who are seeking
admission for settlement or with a view
to settlement 382

Children coming to the UK for
adoption 384

Use of Article 8 ECHR 385

Children whose parents may be forced to leave 386

Removal of children and parents together 386

Enforcement against parents whose child is British 389

Unaccompanied children in the UK 390

Overall Home Office position on the welfare of the child 390

Local authority care 391

Other family court procedures 392

Children born in the UK 393

People born in the UK before 1 January 1983 393

People born in the UK on or after 1 January 1983 393

Applications under the rules for children born in the UK 394

Chapter 13
Other dependent relatives 397

Does the applicant need to use the dependent relative rules? 397

Parents and grandparents aged 65 or over 399

Parents and grandparents under 65 years and other relatives 405

Adult sons and daughters: some other considerations 407

More distant relatives 407

SECTION 5
WORKERS AND BUSINESS PEOPLE

Chapter 14
Work for which permission is required 411

Notes on using this section 412

Other work purposes not covered in this section 413

Managed migration 414

The reality of managed migration 416

Immigration employment documents 418

Charging for IEDs 419

Applying to extend leave in IED categories 420

The work permit scheme 420

Business and commercial work permits 421

End of approved employment 434

Switching 434

Supplementary work 435

Other rights of work permit holders 435

Multiple Entry work permits 435

Families of work permit holders 436

Settlement 437

Appeals and reviews 439

TWES (Training and Work Experience) work permits 440

Sportspersons' and entertainers' work permits 444

Student internship work permits 447

General Agreement on Trade in Services work permits 447

The Sectors Based Scheme 448

Seasonal Agricultural Workers' Scheme (SAWS) 450

Chapter 15
Permit-free employment 453

Long term permit-free employment under the rules 453

General common rules about entering and staying for long-term permit-free employment 454

Media representatives 455

Sole representatives 455

Private servants of diplomats 456

Domestic workers 457

Overseas government employees 459

Ministers of religion 459

Missionaries and members of religious orders 460

Operational ground staff of overseas
airlines 461

Ancestry (Commonwealth nationals
with British-born grandparents) 461

Short-term permit-free employment
under the rules 462

Au pairs 462

Teachers and language assistants 463

The Science and Engineering Graduate
Scheme 464

The Fresh Talent: Working in Scotland
Scheme 465

Permit-free employment outside the
immigration rules 467

BUNAC students 468

Film crew on location 468

'Gap-year' teachers/teaching
assistants 468

Japan Youth Exchange Scheme 469

Jewish Agency 470

Locally recruited staff of foreign
missions 470

Off-shore workers 470

Research assistants to members of
parliament 470

Representatives of overseas insurance
companies 470

Steiner establishments 471

Sportspersons 471

Technical students 472

Voluntary workers 472

People who are exempt from
immigration control 472

People with diplomatic exemption 473

Government representatives and
international officials 474

Armed forces 474

Crew of ships, trains and aircraft 475

Ceasing to be exempt and leave granted
while exempt 475

Chapter 16
Business purposes 477

Business categories 477

Business-people 478

Lawyers 480

Innovators 481

Highly Skilled Migrant Programme 483

Highly Skilled Migrant Programme
points system (table) 485

Investors 491

Writers, composers and artists 492

Retired persons of independent
means 493

Consequences of unlawful work or
business in the UK 495

Employer sanctions 496

Table 1: Documents produced to an
employer – one document option 498

Table 2: Documents produced to an
employer – two document option, first
combination 499

Table 3: Documents produced to an
employer – two document option,
second combination 499

SECTION 6
EUROPEAN RIGHTS OF FREE
MOVEMENT

Chapter 17
Free-movement rights: background and
basics 503

The development of the European
Union 503

Two systems of law 504

The European Economic Area (EEA) and
other agreements 505

Member states of the EU and the
EEA 505

European Union legislation 506

European free-movement law reflected
in UK legislation 507

European institutions 508

Chapter 18
Rights of free movement in the
European Economic Area 511

Who qualifies as a 'national' for free-movement purposes? 513

Who can use free-movement rights? 514

The important European provisions 514

UK legislation putting free-movement rights into practice 515

EEA nationals' free-movement rights to enter and remain in the UK (table) 516

Workers 518

Work-seekers 519

Self-employed people 519

Self-employed people who are no longer economically active 520

People who become unemployed involuntarily 521

People who were employed or self-employed, and are temporarily incapable of work 521

Providers and receivers of services 522

Self-sufficient persons 522

Retired persons 524

Students 524

'Posted' workers 525

Family members of EEA nationals 526

Who is a 'family member'? 527

Spouses 527

Fiancé(e)s 530

Unmarried and same-sex partners 530

Children 531

Children and parents where the EEA national is no longer in the UK, or is divorced from the other parent – Baumbast & R 531

The decision of the ECJ in Baumbast & R (table) 533

Parents and carers of EEA national children – Chen 534

The decision of the ECJ in Chen (table) 535

Family members of self-employed persons who have died 537

More distant family members 537

Home Office policy on more distant family members (table) 538

Can family members of EEA nationals use the 'ordinary' immigration law? 539

Can family members switch between EU law and the immigration rules? 540

Family members of British citizens using free-movement rights – the Surinder Singh route 541

The EEA 2000 Regulations and the Surinder Singh route 541

Can people deliberately use the Surinder Singh route in order to obtain an immigration advantage? 542

Using Surinder Singh in non-employment/self-employment cases 543

Evidence of status: residence permits and other documents 544

Residence permits and residence documents 544

Family permits 548

'Letters of acknowledgement' permitting family members to work 549

A8 nationals: registration certificates, cards and 'family-member residence stamps' 549

Entry procedures 550

EEA nationals – on entry 550

Non-EEA national family members – on entry 550

Decisions refusing or revoking rights 551

'Public policy' grounds 552

Enforcement and detention 554

Rights of appeal 556

Applicants can appeal against 'EEA decisions' 556

Documents which must be produced in order to appeal 557

Is it an in-country appeal? 558

Who is the appeal to, and what
procedures apply? 558

What if an ordinary 'immigration
decision' is made? Can an appeal be
brought? 559

Settlement 559

Rights to settlement under the
immigration rules 560

Claiming welfare 563

Chapter 19
Rights of nationals of accession
states 565

The road to restrictions 566

The five restrictions on the rights of A8
nationals 568

Impact of the restrictions on A8
nationals' and their families' immigration
rights 571

Rights of entry and enforcement 571

Rights of family members of A8
nationals 572

Settlement rights 572

Transitional arrangements 573

The Worker Registration Scheme 573

Chapter 20
Association and cooperation
agreements 577

Association Agreements with Bulgaria
and Romania 577

Entry clearance and switching to stay
under the Association Agreements 580

Application procedures and showing
that the requirements of the rules are
met 582

Settlement and family members 585

Turkey Association Agreement 585

Turkish workers 586

Turkey Association Agreement 'stand-
still' provision 588

Other Association and Cooperation
Agreements 590

SECTION 7
ASYLUM

Chapter 21
Refugee status 595

The relationship between refugees,
human rights and exceptional leave 597

Legal basis for asylum 598

The 1951 Convention and UK law 600

Qualifying for refugee status under the
1951 Convention 601

Outside country of nationality or former
habitual residence 602

Well-founded fear 602

Persecution 602

'Convention reason' for fear of
persecution 605

Membership of a particular social group:
Shah & Islam (table) 607

Unable or...unwilling to obtain the
protection of the country 610

Refugee status: common issues
(table) 610

Internal relocation 621

Standard of proof 622

Exclusion from protection under the
Refugee Convention 624

1) Refugees who do not deserve
international protection 625

2) Refugees who are a danger to the
host country 625

3) Refugees who do not need the
protection of the Convention 626

The Terrorism Act 2000 627

Ceasing to be a refugee and revocation
of indefinite leave 627

Practical use of 'cessation' and
revocation of leave 628

Does a person lose the protection of the
Refugee Convention if they are no
longer at risk of persecution but there
are 'compelling' reasons why they
should not return? 630

Refugees wishing to travel 631

Travel to Tsunami-affected areas 632

Those recognised as refugees elsewhere who wish to travel to the UK 633

Temporary protection 633

Granting temporary protection 633

Dependants of those applying for or granted temporary protection 634

Previous forms of temporary protection 635

Chapter 22
Asylum procedures 637

General background and guide to the chapter 637

Guidance from UNHCR and approach of UK courts 640

The new asylum model 641

Segmentation 642

General asylum procedures 644

Identifying asylum applicants 645

Applying on entry to the UK: 'port applicants' 645

Applying 'in-country' 647

Screening 649

Application Registration Cards and Standard Acknowledgement Letters 651

Reporting and other conditions of temporary admission for asylum-seekers 652

Home Office policy on reporting conditions for applicants granted temporary admission (table) 653

Asylum process and initial access to asylum support 654

Induction processes 655

Asylum interviews 657

One-stop procedure 662

Providing evidence in support of asylum applications 665

Evidence used in support of asylum applications (table) 666

Protection against removal and voluntary departure 667

The 'ILR family exercise' concession for asylum-seeking families who claimed asylum before 2 October 2000 668

The 'ordinary' SEF process 669

The SEF Form 670

SEF/NINO interviews 670

Submitting further evidence after the SEF interview 671

Practical problems 672

'SEF-less' procedure 672

Detained fast track processes 673

Who is likely to be put into the detained fast track? 674

Applicants who are likely to be put through a detained fast track procedure (table) 675

Access to legal representation in the detained fast track 676

Oakington fast track 677

Harmondsworth and Yarls Wood fast track 678

Accelerated non-detained procedures including the North West Project and the Dover Pilot schemes 681

'Late and opportunistic' and 'potentially NSA' claims 681

North West Project (NWP) 682

Dover Pilot 683

Prosecution for non-possession of travel document 683

'Reasonable excuse 684

Article 31 Refugee Convention and section 2 offences 684

Procedures involving section 2 cases 685

Sentences and number of cases 686

Unaccompanied minor asylum-seekers 686

Interviews 686

Home Office 'best practice' for dealing with minors 687

Refugee Council Panel of Advisers for Unaccompanied Refugee Children 688

Policy on exceptional leave where no reception facilities are available 688

Age-dispute cases 688

Home Office policy in age-dispute cases (table) 689

Dependants of asylum-seekers 691

Applying as a dependant or for family reunion? 692

Applying as dependant or claiming in own right? 692

Which family members can be dependants? 692

Permission to work 694

Before 23 July 2002 694

From 23 July 2002 to 4 February 2005 695

From 4 February 2005: new immigration rules 695

In-time asylum applicants whose leave enables them to work 696

Asylum-seekers and voluntary work 696

Special applications including those accepted while still abroad 696

Quota refugee resettlement programme ('Gateway Protection') 697

Mandate refugees 698

'Ten or more' plan 699

Group refugees 699

Transfer of refugee status 699

Applications for asylum made from abroad 701

Preventing asylum-seekers coming to the UK 701

Effect of measures to prevent asylum-seekers 702

Preventing and deterring asylum-seekers (table) 703

Chapter 23
Home Office decisions on asylum 705

Home Office country information 706

Credibility and the effect of the 2004 Act 708

Credibility under the Asylum and Immigration Act 2004 709

The immigration rules and credibility 714

'Non-compliance' refusals and 'group' decisions 715

Previous chaos in non-compliance refusals 716

Application as part of a 'group' of other asylum-seekers 716

Delays in making decisions and issuing documents 717

Backlog clearance concessions 717

Delays in issuing documents 718

The Home Office decision and reviews 719

Decisions to grant refugee status 719

New Home Office policy on the grant of refugee leave, HP and DL 720

Home Office policy on granting leave, reviewing status and cessation (table) 721

The letter recognising refugee status 727

Refusal of asylum 728

Invitations to withdraw asylum applications 730

Fresh claims for asylum 730

The immigration rules 731

Effect of new rules 732

Use of section 96 2002 Act 732

The 'fresh claim' test under the case-law 733

'Fresh claim' procedures 733

Concerns about fresh claim process 734

Refusals of asylum before 2 October 2000 735

Chapter 24
Third country cases 737

Third country cases under the
2004 Act 739

*The four categories of third country
cases under the 2004 Act (table) 739*

Challenging third country removals
under the 2004 Act 743

*Challenging removals under the
Refugee Convention 743*

*Challenging removals under the
ECHR 745*

'Clearly unfounded' certificates 745

The immigration rules 747

The Dublin agreements 748

Criteria for allocating responsibility 748

*Timetable for requests and
removals 749*

Before Dublin 749

Discretion and third country
removals 750

Family links policy 750

Other discretionary cases 751

Unusual third country cases 751

Previous third country regimes: July
1993–September 2004 752

*The 1993 Act: third country
appeals 752*

*The 1996 Act: judicial review in third
country cases 752*

*Third country cases under the 1999 and
2002 Acts 753*

Chapter 25
Refugee family reunion 757

*Family reunion – the different
options 757*

'Pre-existing' spouses and minor children
of refugees under the immigration
rules 758

Refugee family reunion outside the
immigration rules 762

*Applicants other than spouse/minor
children 762*

*Applications where a minor child is
granted refugee status in the UK 763*

*The 'principle of family unity' under the
Refugee Convention (table) 764*

Other family reunion policies 767

Refusals and appeals 768

Using the general immigration rules for
family members of settled sponsors 768

*Flexible application of rules for non
'pre-existing' spouse and minor
children 769*

Family reunion and Article 8 ECHR 769

SECTION 8
HUMAN RIGHTS AND DISCRIMINATION

Chapter 26
**The European Convention on Human
Rights** 773

*The European institutions and
incorporation 774*

The Human Rights Act 1998 775

The rights 775

How the rights work – limitations on
ECHR rights 777

Reservations and derogations 778

Limitations on ECHR rights 778

Taking a case to Europe 781

*Procedure for making an
application 782*

Procedure before the Court 783

Interim measures 783

Legal funding 784

Chapter 27
Human rights in immigration and asylum cases 785

First questions 786

'Extra-territorial effect' and 'flagrant' breaches 787

The decision in Ullah & Do (table) 788

The 'flagrant breach' requirement 790

When is a 'flagrant breach' required in Article 8 cases? 790

Claims for protection 792

The right to life (Article 2) 792

Prohibition on torture or inhuman or degrading treatment or punishment (Article 3) 794

The circumstances in which Article 3 ECHR may provide protection when the Refugee Convention does not (table) 796

Threats from 'non-state agents' and Article 3 799

Prohibition against slavery and forced labour (Article 4) 800

The right to liberty and security (Article 5) 800

The right to a fair trial (Article 6) 802

Prohibition on punishment for an act which was not a crime when it was committed (Article 7) 803

Right to respect for private life, family, home, correspondence (Article 8) 803

Article 8 'protection' claims based on sexuality 804

Freedom of thought, conscience and religion (Article 9) 807

Freedom of expression (Article 10) 807

Freedom of assembly and association (Article 11) 808

Cases where removal will have a detrimental effect on the individual 809

Health and Article 3 ECHR 809

The decision of the House of Lords in N (table) 811

Home Office policy in health cases concerning human rights 814

Health and Article 8 ECHR 816

Threats of suicide 817

Health and Article 8: the decision in Razgar (table) 817

Children and health 819

Effects of destitution 819

Right not to be denied an education 820

Family or other connections with the UK 820

The elements of Article 8 821

The Article 8 principles set out by the Court of Appeal in Mahmood (table) 822

The existence of family life 823

Does the relationship amount to family life? (table) 823

Same-sex relationships 827

Interference with the right to respect for family life 827

In accordance with the law 831

In pursuance of a legitimate aim 832

Proportionality: is the extent of the interference 'necessary' in the interests of the community? 832

The limits of the 'entry clearance' argument (table) 837

Article 8 and people wishing to come to the UK 844

Where the decision affects family life that is centred outside the UK 846

Private life connections in the UK 846

Further Article 8 case examples 847

Leave outside the rules where there is no breach of human rights 851

Chapter 28
Raising human rights, humanitarian protection, discretionary leave, family reunion and travel 853

Making human rights claims 854

Claiming as part of an asylum application 854

Independent application 855

One-stop notices 856

Claiming as part of another appeal 856

Human rights appeals and fresh claims 857

What leave is granted if a human rights claim is successful? 859

Who is granted Humanitarian Protection and and Discretionary Leave? 862

Qualifying for humanitarian protection (table) 862

Qualifying for discretionary leave (table) 864

HP and DL: periods of leave granted and settlement 866

Transitional arrangements for those granted exceptional leave 873

Family members 875

Dependants 875

Family reunion for those with HP or DL 876

Family reunion for those with ELR granted before 1 April 2003 878

Fees for entry clearance for family reunion 878

Where the family members do not possess travel documents 879

Appeals 879

Travel documents 880

'Certificate of identity' travel documents 880

Procedures for applying for travel documents 882

Chapter 29
Discrimination 885

Article 14 ECHR 885

Race discrimination 887

Ministerial authorisations 888

Independent Race Monitor 888

Ministerial authorisations for discrimination (table) 889

Appeals in race discrimination cases 890

Following through with a damages claim 891

The Roma Rights Centre case 892

SECTION 9
DETENTION AND ENFORCEMENT

Chapter 30
Detention: powers, policy and legality 897

Background to immigration detention 898

Who can be detained under the immigration legislation? 899

Recent changes to detention powers 900

Persons who may be detained (table) 902

Non-immigration reasons for detention 905

Who is likely to be detained – Home Office policy 905

Development of detention policy 906

Table 1: Detention policy: Operational Enforcement Manual 909

Table 2: Detention policy: Form IS 91R 913

Table 3: Detention policy: Other sources of policy 914

International guidelines 917

United Nations High Commissioner for Refugees 917

International Covenant on Civil and Political Rights 919

UN Convention on the Rights of the Child 919

Is the detention lawful? 919

No power to detain 920

Unlawful use of the power to detain 924

Application of the Hardial Singh principles: The case of R(I) v SSHD (table) 927

Chapter 31
Detention places, conditions and procedures 933

Expansion of detention 933

Places of detention 934

Immigration removal centres 935

Detention in prisons 936

Home Office policy on detention in prison (table) 937

Detention in police cells 938

Transfers between places of detention 938

Reasons, reviews and detention centre rules 939

Reasons for detention 939

Consular protection 940

Rules governing treatment in detention 940

Detention centre rules (table) 940

Conditions: inspection and other reports 942

Inspection 942

Other reports on aspects of detention 946

Chapter 32
Getting people out of detention 949

Temporary admission, temporary release and restriction orders 950

Applying for temporary admission 951

Conditions of temporary admission 952

'Temporary admission' conditions imposed on asylum-seekers with leave 955

End of period of temporary admission 955

If an applicant can't be removed, should they be granted leave rather than temporary admission: the case of Khadir 956

Bail from immigration authorities or police inspector 957

Bail from the Asylum and Immigration Tribunal 958

Who cannot get bail? 959

Persons who may be granted bail by the AIT (table) 960

Bail where 'appeal pending' 962

EEA cases 964

Orders for release from the criminal court 964

Repeal of automatic bail hearing provisions 964

SIAC cases 965

Applying for bail before the AIT 965

Submitting the application 966

Preparing the application for bail and grounds for bail 967

Sureties and personal recognisance 974

Procedure after the application has been submitted 977

The bail hearing before the AIT 978

Surety checklist (table) 981

The decision of the AIT on bail 983

Bail continuation or variation 984

Failure to answer to bail 985

Unlawful detention: High Court procedures 985

Two High Court procedures 986

Judicial review in detention cases 986

Habeas corpus 987

Chapter 33
Enforcement: port removal, illegal entry, administrative removal, deportation and criminal offences 989

The four basic 'enforcement' procedures and the terms used 990

Recent developments in enforcement 991

Enforcement proposals: policy and the 2005 Bill (table) 992

Taking a decision that a person must leave and policy 993

Enforcement against those aged over 65 994

Enforcement in cases where there are medical problems 995

Where there is a risk of suicide or self-harm on removal 996

Home Office policy on suicide and self-harm (table) 996

Enforcement against families 998

Port removals 1000

Administrative removal 1002

Overstaying 1003

Breach of conditions 1004

Obtaining leave to remain by deception 1007

Indefinite leave revoked because person has ceased to be a refugee 1008

Family members of those being administratively removed 1009

Deciding whether a person should be administratively removed 1009

Illegal entry 1010

Entry without seeing an immigration officer 1011

Entry without obtaining leave from an immigration officer 1012

Entry in breach of a deportation order 1012

Deception of an immigration officer 1013

Decision to treat a person as an illegal entrant 1014

Removal and return of illegal entrants 1015

Deportation 1015

Recommendations for deportation 1016

Conducive to the public good 1018

The deportation process 1021

Revocation of deportation orders 1024

Revocation of indefinite leave in deportation cases 1025

The process of removal and the possible countries of return 1026

Where can people be removed to? 1027

Travel documents 1027

Other forms of enforcement and departure 1028

How people are traced and detected 1030

Criminal offences 1031

Powers of arrest and search 1032

Criminal offences under the Immigration Acts (table) 1033

SECTION 10
APPEALS

Chapter 34
Rights of appeal 1039

Proposed changes under the 2005 Bill 1041

Proposed changes to appeals: the Immigration, Asylum and Nationality Bill 2005 (table) 1042

Appeal system – an overview 1046

The appeals structure from 4 April 2005: a ten-point overview (table) 1047

The members of the AIT and their functions 1049

Development of the appeals system and legislation 1050

When can people appeal? 1052

Table 1: Decisions against which there is a right of appeal 1053

Table 2: Exclusions from rights of appeal 1055

Table 3: Is the appeal in-country? 1059

Notice of decision 1061

Giving notice of appeal 1062

Appealing in time 1063

The appeal forms 1063

Completing the appeal form 1063

'Grounds' and 'reasons' for appeal 1064

Serving notice of appeal 1065

The 'one-stop' system 1066

Certificates under section 96 2002 Act 1067

When can section 96 certificates be issued? 1068

When will the Home Office actually need to use section 96? 1068

'Fresh claims' 1069

Appeal pending: protection from removal and immigration status 1069

Continued status while appeal 'pending' 1070

Appeals which end without being determined 1071

Family visitor entry clearance appeals 1071

Charging and oral appeals: some context 1072

Cases certified as 'clearly unfounded' 1073

Will a 'clearly unfounded' certificate exclude all in-country appeal rights? 1074

Which nationals are likely to receive 'clearly unfounded' certificates? 1074

Home Office policy on when to certify a case 1075

Legal test for deciding whether a claim is 'clearly unfounded' 1077

Steps for dealing with a 'clearly unfounded' certificate 1078

Asylum 'status' appeals under section 83 2002 Act 1079

Appeals involving 'exclusion' from refugee status 1080

No special consideration of gravity of harm 1080

Presumption that the appellant has been convicted of a particularly serious crime and is a danger to the community of the UK 1080

Special Immigration Appeals Commission 1081

Chapter 35
Conducting first instance appeals before the AIT 1085

This chapter 1085

Procedure rules and practice directions 1086

Timetable and basic procedure for appeals 1088

Timetable for first instance appeals to AIT (table) 1088

Parties to the appeal, representation and funding 1090

Representation 1090

Legal aid 1091

Preliminary decisions on notices of appeal and late appeals 1091

Late notice of appeal 1092

Late notice of appeal in 'imminent removal' cases 1093

Respondent's reasons and explanatory statements 1094

Standard appeal directions 1095

Standard directions (table) 1095

Case management review hearings and further directions 1095

General matters to be dealt with at CMR 1096

Additional matters that may be raised before hearing, including at a CMR 1097

What further directions may be requested or applications made? (table) 1098

Adjournments 1100

Procedures on adjournment applications 1101

Determining appeals in the absence of a party, without a hearing or without deciding the substance 1102

1) Appeals where a party does not attend the hearing 1102

2) Determining an appeal without a hearing 1103

3) Where the AIT makes no decision on the substance of the appeal 1104

Preparing for the full hearing 1105

Evidence generally 1105

Witnesses and witness statements 1106

Country and expert evidence 1107

Country material (table) 1109

Preparing trial bundles 1109

Using case-law 1110

How are determinations of the AIT and IAT classified? 1110

Which AIT and IAT decisions are authoritative? 1110

Which AIT and IAT decisions can be relied on before the AIT? 1111

Country guidance cases 1111

Conducting the full hearing before the immigration judge 1112

Dealing with the presenting officer and Home Office conceding appeals 1113

Preliminary matters 1114

Evidence given by the appellant and witnesses 1114

Submissions 1116

Keeping a record of proceedings 1118

After the hearing and appeal determinations 1118

Deciding appeals and the powers of the AIT 1118

What date does the AIT focus on, can it look at 'after-decision' evidence? 1119

Burden and standard of proof 1121

Previous appeals concerning the appellant 1123

When an appeal must be allowed 1124

Directions where appeal is allowed 1126

Recommendations where an appeal is dismissed 1127

Fast track appeals 1129

Fast track appeals basic procedure and timetable (table) 1130

Getting an appellant out of the fast track appeal process 1132

Chapter 36
Challenging decisions of the AIT 1133

Applying to the AIT for an order for reconsideration 1134

Cases in which it is not possible to apply for a review 1135

Time-limits for applying for a review and calculating time 1135

Procedures and guidance in applying to the AIT for a review 1137

AIT decision on application for reconsideration 1139

Applying to the High Court for an order for a review of the AIT decision 1140

Reconsideration hearings before the AIT 1143

Procedure in preparation for a reconsideration hearing 1144

Reconsideration hearings and decisions 1145

Appealing to the Court of Appeal following reconsideration determinations 1147

Renewing application to the Court of Appeal 1147

Time-limits 1148

Before the Court of Appeal 1148

The House of Lords 1149

Other routes to the Court of Appeal 1149

References by the High Court 1149

AIT sitting as a legal panel 1149

When can judicial review still be used? 1150

Decisions of the Home Office concerning appeals 1150

Decisions of the AIT that are 'procedural, ancillary or preliminary' 1150

Statutory application to the High Court not a good enough remedy 1151

Transitional appeal arrangements 1151

Public funding (Legal Aid) considerations 1153

When will funding be granted/ refused? 1154

Impact on access to justice 1155

Showing an error of law 1155

Identifying errors of law (table) 1156

Mistakes of fact and fresh evidence 1159

The test under E & R v SSHD 1159

But will the new evidence be admitted? 1160

Present practical impact of the above rules about fresh evidence 1161

Time-limits 1162

Time-limits for appealing (table) 1162

SECTION 11
CIVIL CLAIMS, JUDICIAL REVIEW AND OTHER REMEDIES

Chapter 37
Civil claims 1171

When can a civil claim be made? 1172

The law that can be used to bring a civil claim 1172

Essential approach to civil claims 1174

Unlawful detention 1174

Detention as the result of errors and incorrect information 1175

Detention by the police 1176

Places of detention and conditions of detention 1177

Places and conditions of detention: false imprisonment 1177

Places and conditions of detention: 'negligence' and other claims 1178

Places and conditions of detention: transfers 1180

Unlawful removal 1181

Unlawful family separation 1182

Assault 1182

Unlawful searches of premises 1183

Maladministration and delay in making decisions and issuing documents 1184

Claims which may be brought 1185

Discrimination 1187

Discrimination: human rights claims 1189

Discrimination: claims under the Race Relations Act and Sex Discrimination Act 1189

Dispersal and denial of adequate support 1190

Malicious prosecution 1191

Making a civil claim 1192

Which procedure? 1193

Alternatives to bringing a claim 1194

Who should the claim be made against? 1195

Time-limits 1196

Time-limits for bringing civil claims (table) 1197

Obtaining further information 1198

Public funding (legal aid) 1199

Damages 1201

The different forms of damages (table) 1202

Levels of damages: detection and/or removal cases (table) 1205

General procedures in ordinary civil claims 1210

The stages of a claim (table) 1211

Chapter 38
Judicial review, complaints, Ombudsman and *Adimi* claims 1213

Judicial review 1213

Grounds for judicial review 1214

Powers of the court in judicial review 1215

Common circumstances in which judicial review is used 1216

Before the claim: pre-action protocol 1217

Time-limits 1218

Making a claim 1218

The two stages of judicial review 1219

Imminent removals and Home Office practice where claim issued 1220

Urgent cases and injunctions 1221

Complaints to and compensation from the Home Office 1223

Home Office compensation schemes 1224

Consolatory payments for non-financial loss (table) 1226

Contacting a Member of Parliament 1227

Making contact 1228

How MPs can intervene and their effect 1228

Parliamentary Ombudsman 1229

Outcome of complaints to Ombudsman in immigration cases and compensation offered (table) 1231

Compensation for unlawful conviction of asylum-seekers under the *Adimi* principle 1235

SECTION 12
WELFARE

Chapter 39
Welfare benefits 1241

Abbreviations (table) 1242

Relationship to 'no recourse to public funds' under the immigration rules 1243

Summary of welfare benefits system 1244

General summary of welfare benefits system: what benefits are there and who is eligible for them? (table) 1244

Access to welfare benefits and immigration status: a 'ten-point' outline 1247

'Subject to immigration control' test 1249

The 'subject to immigration control' test: section 115 1999 Act (table) 1250

'Subject to immigration control': people without leave 1251

'Subject to immigration control': Condition prohibiting 'recourse to public funds' 1252

'Subject to immigration control': people given leave as a result of a maintenance undertaking 1253

'Subject to immigration control': people who have leave 'only as a result of paragraph 17 of Schedule 4' of the 1999 Act 1254

Exceptions to the 'subject to immigration control' test (table) 1255

ECSMA or CESC nationals who are 'lawfully present' 1259

The 'habitual residence' test 1259

The habitual residence test and exemptions from the test (table) 1260

Habitual residence: the general test 1262

Habitual residence: the Swaddling case 1263

The decision in Collins 1264

The 'right to reside' test 1264

Who has the right to reside? (table) 1266

'Accession 8' nationals and the right to reside 1268

Summary of the effect on A8 nationals 1268

'Accession 8' nationals and benefit entitlement (table) 1269

Additional tests for certain benefits 1273

Contributory benefits 1276

Claiming for dependants 1276

Additional benefit rights for EEA nationals and reciprocal agreements 1281

Reciprocal agreements 1282

Transferring to benefits 1282

Delays in receiving status documents 1283

National insurance number requirement 1283

Refugees and backdating claims for benefit 1284

Refugee integration loans 1286

General matters: going abroad, links between departments 1287

Effect on benefits of going abroad 1287

Links between departments 1287

**Chapter 40
Housing, social services, Children Act and health care** 1289

Housing 1289

Access to housing: three tables 1290

Table 1: General exclusion for homelessness assistance and allocation schemes 1291

Table 2: Eligibility for homelessness assistance 1293

Table 3: Qualification for allocations scheme 1294

A8 nationals and EEA nationals and eligibility for housing assistance 1295

Homelessness: local connection 1296

Homelessness: ineligible members of the household 1297

Homelessness and allocation schemes: 'lawful presence' under ECSMA and the Social Charter and the decision in Szoma 1298

Social services 1299

Turning to social services: how it arose in 1996 1299

Social services support: an overview (table) 1300

Exclusions under Schedule 3 of the 2002 Act 1301

Which forms of support are excluded under Schedule 3? 1302

Which classes of person are excluded under Schedule 3? 1302

Classes of people excluded by Schedule 3 2002 Act (table) 1303

The 'human rights' exception to exclusion under Schedule 3 1306

The human rights exception: Decision of the House of Lords in Adam, Limbuela & Tesema (table) 1307

Withholding and withdrawal of Support Regulations 1314

Restrictions under the 1999 Act 1315

Services restricted by the Immigration and Asylum Act 1999 (table) 1316

What social services support can be obtained? 1318

Community care assessments 1322

Children Act 1989 1322

The provision of support 1323

Age disputes 1324

When the child reaches the age of 18 1324

Section 9 2004 Act 'exclusion' cases and the Children Act 1325

Withdrawal of support to asylum-seeking families: Home Office guidance on Article 8 issues (table) 1327

Limitations on support under the
Children Act 1328

Health care 1328

Hospital and connected
treatment 1329

Access to free hospital treatment
(table) 1330

Primary health care – GPs and
others 1333

Education 1335

**Chapter 41
Asylum support and 'hard cases'
support** 1337

1) What other forms of support may be
available to asylum-seekers? 1337

2) What is the basic relationship
between asylum support provided by
NASS and 'interim asylum support
provided by local authorities? 1338

3) What has happened to the plan to
introduce 'accommodation
centres'? 1339

4) What are the basic materials
containing the law and policy on asylum
support? 1339

Who qualifies for asylum support? 1341

Who is an 'asylum-seeker' for asylum
support purposes? 1341

Who counts as the 'dependant' of an
asylum-seeker? 1345

Dependants of asylum-seekers
(table) 1346

'Destitute' or likely shortly to become
'destitute' 1347

Exclusions from asylum support 1350

Exclusion under section 55
2002 Act 1350

Exclusion for providing false or
incomplete information 1352

Exclusions under Schedule 3 2002 Act
(as added to by section 9
2004 Act) 1353

Exclusion of asylum-seeking families
under section 9 2004 Act: Home Office
policy and procedure (table) 1354

Exclusions under the Asylum Support
Regulations 1357

What support is provided under the
NASS scheme? 1360

NASS asylum support rates (table)
1364

NASS procedures and temporary
support 1367

The application 1367

Access to temporary (or 'emergency')
NASS support immediately after
claim 1368

Changes of circumstances 1370

Further applications for support and
appeals 1371

'Interim' asylum support 1371

Which asylum-seekers get NASS
support and which get interim
support? 1372

NASS support or interim support and
the 'interim scheme project' to move all
asylum-seekers to NASS support
(table) 1372

Deciding whether a person qualifies for
interim support 1374

Providing interim support 1375

Exclusions from interim asylum
support 1377

Procedures for getting interim support
and temporary interim support 1378

EU minimum standards for the reception
of asylum-seekers 1379

EU minimum standards for the
reception of asylum-seekers and
changes to UK regulations (table) 1380

'Hard cases' support 1381

Who can get hard cases support? 1382

'Hard cases' support: regulations and
policy (table) 1383

Applying for hard cases support and
appeals 1386

What is actually provided as hard cases
support? 1387

Chapter 42
Asylum support appeals 1389

When can a person appeal to the Asylum Support Adjudicators? 1389

Proposed changes to rights of appeal 1391

The Asylum Support Adjudicators 1391

Appeal procedures 1391

Timetable for appeals to the Asylum Support Adjudicators (table) 1392

Notice of appeal 1393

Preparation of the appeal bundle 1394

Decision of the ASA whether to hold a hearing of the appeal 1394

Further evidence before determination of the appeal 1395

Oral hearings 1395

Decisions on appeals 1396

Powers of ASA in deciding appeals 1396

Ending the appeal by withdrawal 1397

SECTION 13
BRITISH NATIONALITY

Chapter 43
British nationality 1401

This chapter 1401

Development of nationality law 1402

Types of British nationality 1404

Present types of British National status (table) 1404

Immigration advantages of British nationals who do not have the right of abode 1405

British citizens 1406

British Overseas Territories citizens (BOTCs) (formerly British Dependent Territories citizens (BDTCs)) 1406

British Overseas citizens 1408

British Nationals (Overseas) (BN(O)s) 1411

British Protected Persons 1412

British subjects 1413

British nationality law and Hong Kong 1414

British Nationals (Overseas): the Hong Kong Act 1985 1415

Acquiring British citizenship: The British Nationality (Hong Kong) Acts 1990 and 1997 and the Hong Kong (War Wives and Widows) Act 1996 1416

People from Hong Kong who are living in the UK 1417

Right of abode 1417

Right of abode under the 1948 Act –1968 Act 1418

Right of abode under the 1971 Act 1418

Right of abode under the 1981 Act 1418

Applying for a Certificate of Entitlement to the right of abode 1420

Identifying British nationality from passports 1421

Passports issued on or after 1 January 1983 1421

Passports issued before 1 January 1983 1421

Checking for British citizenship 1423

Obtaining a passport 1423

Refusal or withdrawal of a passport 1423

Chapter 44
Who is a British citizen? 1425

People who became 'British citizens' on 1 January 1983 1426

The general rule 1427

Two other categories of people who became British citizens on 1 January 1983 1427

British citizens by birth (or adoption, or found abandoned) in the UK on or after 1 January 1983 1428

Meaning of 'parent' 1428

Meaning of 'settled' 1429

What is the position of UK-born children who are not British citizens? 1430

Birth in Falkland Islands after 1 January 1983 1432

Adoption in the UK after 1 January 1983 1432

Abandoned infants 1432

BOTCs who became British citizens on 21 May 2002 1432

People born outside the UK who are British citizens by birth 1433

The meaning of British citizenship 'otherwise than by descent' and 'by descent' 1433

People born outside the UK before 1 January 1983 1434

People born outside the UK on or after 1 January 1983 1435

Persons born stateless and persons born on ships and aircraft 1437

Birth outside the UK on UK ship or aircraft 1438

Checking for British citizenship: a summary 1438

People born in the UK 1439

People born outside the UK 1439

Flowchart 1: Who is automatically a British citizen? 1440

Flowchart 2: who is a British citizen by descent? 1441

Renunciation of citizenship 1442

Registration as a British Citizen following renunciation of British Citizenship 1443

Registration as a British Citizen following renunciation of CUKC status 1443

Deprivation of citizenship 1445

Registration or naturalisation not treated as having any effect 1446

Chapter 45
Applying to be a British citizen 1447

Introduction 1447

Applications for British citizenship – general 1448

The application 1448

The decision 1450

The new oath and pledge and citizenship ceremonies 1451

Naturalisation 1453

Naturalisation based on five-years' residence 1454

Naturalisation based on marriage or civil partnership and residence 1455

Full age and capacity 1455

Absences 1456

The residence requirements 1457

'Not subject under the immigration laws to any restriction on period of stay' 1459

Not subject to any time restriction in the previous 12 months 1460

Breaches of the immigration laws during the five (or three) year residence period 1461

The 'good character' requirement 1463

Language and knowledge of life in the UK 1465

Referees 1469

Intention to make home in the UK 1469

Crown Service as an alternative to the residence requirements 1472

Registration of children 1473

Registration of children by entitlement 1474

Registration of any child by discretion 1476

Special classes of children who may register by discretion 1480

Registration of adults 1485

Those born before 1983 to British mothers 1485

Registration of BOCs, BSs, BN(O)s and BPPs 1486

Registration of stateless persons 1488

**SECTION 14
INFORMATION**

Useful addresses and telephone numbers 1493

Visa nationals and specified nationals 1507

Fees 1509

Entry clearance posts 1511

Work-related applications 1519

Commonwealth countries 1525

Registering with the police 1527

Countries whose adoption decisions are recognised in the UK and Hague Convention countries 1528

Abbreviations 1530

Other sources of information 1534

Glossary 1536

CASE LIST 1551

INDEX 1569

Section 1 **Immigration law and advice**

Chapter 1
Introduction to immigration law and the *Handbook*   3
The development of modern immigration law   4
What makes up the immigration law?   9
The system of immigration control   13
Other rights and remedies   28

Chapter 2
Proposed changes including the 'five-year strategy' and 2005 Bill   31
Important legislation   31
The 'five-year strategy'   33
Immigration, Asylum and Nationality Bill 2005   50
Other proposals for change   53
Making immigration work for everyone   55

Chapter 3
Immigration advice   59
Finding an adviser   59
Regulation of immigration advisers   63
Legal aid funding in England and Wales   67
The Immigration and Asylum Accreditation Scheme   73

1

1 Introduction to immigration law and the *Handbook*

This chapter explains the essential framework of UK immigration law and how it operates both inside and outside the UK. The chapter begins by tracing the historical development of the modern immigration system during the last century, and summarises the main Acts of Parliament which have made up the law. We then move on to look at the other main sources of immigration law: international conventions, secondary legislation, immigration rules, case-law and policy instructions and practices. We explain how we have used and referred to these materials in the book. The chapter then gives a 'bare-bones' outline of the immigration system. At the same time as outlining the different concepts and basic rules which make up the system, we indicate where in the *Handbook* you will find any particular aspect set out in detail.

This chapter is therefore intended to serve both as an overview of immigration law, and as a guide on how to use this book.

Structure of the *Handbook*

The *Handbook* as a whole is separated into both 'sections' and 'chapters'. There are 14 sections altogether, each of which contains between two and five chapters. There are 45 chapters in all. Each section begins with a brief introduction stating what is contained in the different chapters of that section. The layout of the sections and chapters at a glance is shown on ▶ix, and there is a more detailed contents listing at ▶xii. Another means of finding particular information is by checking the index at the back of the book. If the information required is very practical – for example an address, or the level of a fee for making a particular application – Section 14 on 'Information' should be checked. That section also contains dense information, including country lists of various kinds, the list of shortage occupations under the work-permit scheme, and the country income bands under the Highly Skilled Migrant Programme.

For the meaning of particular words and phrases – either that we have used or that are encountered in practice and which cause difficulty – a **glossary** can be found starting at ▶1536. Similarly, for a **list of abbreviations** we have used, including abbreviations of legislation, ▶see 1530–3. Full **references to the case-law** referred to in the text are at ▶1551–68.

Because so much of the system of immigration law is overlapping, answering one question may lead to another. We have therefore provided, throughout the text, cross-references to where connected information will be found in the book. Cross-referencing can be distracting but in an inter-connected system, unfortunately it is impossible to organise the material without it.

Other chapters in Section 1

The other chapters in this first section are as follows.

- **Chapter 2** covers the current proposals for changes to immigration law and JCWI's commentary on them. This includes legislation which is not yet in force, the government's 'five-year strategy' for immigration and the changes contained in the Immigration, Asylum and Nationality Bill 2005. Where an area of the book is subject to possible changes, we have also flagged this up in the relevant part of the text.

- **Chapter 3** looks at the availability of, and public funding for, immigration advice and representation. The chapter gives details of how to access those immigration services, and also explains how the sector is regulated so as to prevent bad advice being given. It also sets out how to make a complaint about poor service on the part of advisers.

THE DEVELOPMENT OF MODERN IMMIGRATION LAW

About 175 million people worldwide live outside the country in which they were born, according to a UN estimate. People emigrate for a variety of reasons; work, family connections and protection from oppression are prominent among them. It is undeniable that those countries with a high proportion of migrants have been enriched by them, both culturally and economically.

Developments in transport and communications systems during the last century have been among the factors which have led to increased population flows during that time. The UK system of immigration control is also a twentieth-century phenomenon. Legislation to control the circumstances in which those who are not British can enter or remain in the UK has escalated, in particular, in the last few decades. As a result, the law relating to immigration, nationality and asylum procedures has become increasingly complex and detailed over that time. Political interest in immigration and the methods used to control it, while they have always received current affairs coverage, is as high now as it has ever been, and is unlikely to diminish for the foreseeable future.

Early immigration law

Before 1905, there were no immigration laws in the UK. The entry of people who were not British subjects was technically part of the royal prerogative, and the monarch could also make decisions to expel individuals or groups of people. The Aliens Act 1905 was passed, after two decades of intermittent agitation, in order to prevent refugees – mainly Jewish, poor and fleeing from Eastern Europe – from seeking refuge in Britain. The Act only applied to boats carrying more than 20 passengers and to those travelling steerage class, who could be excluded if they were deemed 'undesirable' (usually meaning unable to properly support themselves and their dependants). The Act applied to 'aliens', which meant people who were not from any part of the British Empire. It also set up the first rudimentary machinery for checking entry, which was later expanded and developed. The year 2005 is the 100th anniversary of the Aliens Act 1905. It is depressing that there is still so much xenophobia and so many negative attitudes about immigration. We appear to be going backwards, not forwards. Why is it that, according to a British Social Attitudes Survey in December 2004, immigration is one of the only areas in which public opinion has *not* become more liberal in the last two decades?

The post-Second World War period

At the end of the Second World War, Britain had to take stock of its role in the world. The effects of the war, and the growing campaign for independence in India, made it clear that the old imperial arrangements had to change. The status of British subject, with its central notion of allegiance to the Crown, was becoming outdated, and from 1949 it was replaced by the new status of Citizen of the United Kingdom and Colonies (CUKC). The term 'British subject' was kept to refer to all the citizens of the Commonwealth. CUKCs had rights to enter and live anywhere in the Crown's dominions, and when Britain looked for labour to rebuild its war-damaged economy, the young men who arrived on the Empire Windrush in June 1948, and those who followed them, arrived as citizens. Indeed, many of the settlers who arrived aboard such ships were ex-servicemen and volunteers who had worked in Britain during the war.

Restrictions begin: the 1960s Commonwealth Immigrants Acts

It was not until the 1960s that racist agitation led the government of the day to consider restrictions on the rights of nationals outside the UK. Two statutes were introduced to bring in controls – the Commonwealth Immigrants Acts of 1962 and 1968. The 1962 Bill was implemented relatively slowly, and was opposed by Labour under the leadership of Hugh Gaitskell. However, in their 1964 election manifesto, Labour's approach was to accept the existence of the legislation, at least until new agreements with the Commonwealth governments could be negotiated.

In March 1968, with Labour in power, the second Act was rushed through parliament in three days. The effect was to deny entry to hundreds of thousands of East African Asians settled in Kenya, Uganda and Tanganyika, who were UK passport holders, unless they had a parent or grandparent born, adopted or naturalised in the UK. It constituted a shameful failure to honour assurances that had previously been provided about the rights of these passport holders. These Acts were followed by the Immigration Appeals Act 1969, which established a system of immigration appeals.

The foundation of present immigration law: the Immigration Act 1971

The structure set up by the above three Acts paved the way for the Immigration Act 1971, which was passed by a Conservative government, and came into force on 1 January 1973. It still provides the basis of immigration controls in the UK (see below) although it has been repeatedly amended in the years since then, firstly by the Immigration Act 1988. The 1971 Act put an end to major, permanent primary migration to the UK from Africa, the Indian subcontinent and the African Caribbean.

By coincidence, the 1971 Act came into force on the very day that Britain joined what was then known as the 'Common Market' – European Economic Community. The effect of this was to open up immigration controls for nationals of all the European member states at precisely the same time as the legislative curtain was being pulled down on non-white migration. The Treaty of Rome, which formed the basis for this European cooperation, had among its central principles the right of free movement of workers and the self-employed. On 1 May 2004, ten new member states, largely from Eastern Europe, joined what is now the 'European Union' (EU). The rights of free movement, although with some restrictions, have therefore also been extended to nationals of these countries.

Asylum and legislation in the 1990s

With rising numbers of people coming to the UK seeking asylum, in the early 1990s Conservative governments brought in two major pieces of legislation largely aimed at dealing with the influx of asylum-seekers. In July 1993 the Asylum and Immigration Appeals Act 1993 was introduced. Before that time, asylum was only really mentioned as an afterthought in the immigration rules. The 1993 Act effectively incorporated the 1951 Refugee Convention into the immigration rules and enabled all asylum-seekers to appeal on asylum grounds against negative decisions by the Home Office. It also, however, put the safe 'third country' removal process on to a firm footing and allowed asylum cases to be certified as being 'manifestly unfounded'. The 1993 Act also removed important rights of appeal, including those of certain visitors and students. The Asylum and Immigration Act 1996 extended the certification process to many more categories of asylum-seeker, introduced sanctions on employers who gave work to those unauthorised to take employment, and imposed severe restrictions on the welfare entitlements of both those seeking asylum and others.

The 'New' Labour government elected in 1997 set about a major review of immigration and asylum policy. In its first months, the new administration abolished the 'primary purpose' test, under which fiancé(e)s and spouses had to demonstrate that the motivating factor of their marriage was not to obtain settlement in the UK. The test had been used to discriminate in particular against those from the Asian subcontinent who sought entry in order to be with their spouses. This proved a false dawn for all those who had for long campaigned for a just immigration system.

The first major piece of immigration legislation under the new government was the Immigration and Asylum Act 1999. Although it was accompanied by new rights of appeal based on the Human Rights Act 1998, the Immigration and Asylum Act 1999 introduced a summary form of removal for those who had obtained entry to the UK and would previously have had procedural protections under the 'deportation' process. It re-cast the appeals system, with a focus on a single appeal right accompanied by draconian powers to deny appeal rights if grounds to stay in the UK were not raised at the earliest possible stage. The Act also sought to prevent asylum-seekers from arguing in a court that their removal to an EU member state may be unsafe because those countries offered less protection – arguments which many asylum-seekers had previously won. It imposed the indignity of vouchers (now abolished) and the isolation and insecurity of dispersal throughout the UK upon those seeking protection, but who had no means of financial support.

From 2000 onwards, asylum-seekers also found themselves increasingly subject to both 'fast-track' determination regimes and detention. The regimes put in place at both Oakington Reception Centre and Harmondsworth Detention Centre are described in the book (►see 673–81). While the outward justifications for these systems have been speed, efficiency and administrative necessity, the inevitable effect has been unfairness and a diminution of rights.

The 1999 Act also made substantial changes to the structure of immigration controls, imposed duties on registrars to report 'suspicious' marriages, strengthened the powers of immigration officers in the enforcement of immigration controls, extended sanctions against those carrying improperly documented passengers into the UK, and implemented a system for the regulation of immigration advice.

The Nationality, Immigration and Asylum Act 2002

At the time that the last edition of this book was being produced, the 2002 Act was progressing through parliament. Most of the changes were therefore able to be incorporated into the last edition, and JCWI's detailed views on the legislation and the thinking set out in the White Paper that preceded it, *Secure Borders, Safe Haven: Integration with Diversity in Modern Britain* (7 February 2002), were set out in Chapter 2 of the 2002 edition. In the period leading up to the White Paper, the then Home Secretary spoke increasingly about 'managed migration'. He recognised the 'positive contribution of migration to our social well-being and economic prosperity' and called for the need to encourage those resident abroad to come to the UK 'on a sensible and managed basis'. Positive new routes of economic migration have indeed been opened up in the last few years, but they owe little to legislative innovations. They are 'managed' almost entirely by policy developed at the government's discretion and, to a lesser extent, by changes made to the immigration rules (for a more detailed discussion, ▶see 414–8).

In an attempt to create a cohesive concept of 'Britishness', the nationality aspects of the 2002 Act introduced new procedures and requirements for becoming British by naturalisation. Applicants can be required to show sufficient knowledge about life in the UK, the oath of allegiance was updated, and citizenship ceremonies were introduced to make 'becoming British' a public declaration.

The 2002 Act again revised the basis for appeals and, largely in order to be able to control when people would be entitled to raise human rights appeals, introduced the concept of an underlying 'immigration decision' which could alone enable an appeal. Significant further restrictions were imposed on the appeals process. These included the formal limiting of the Immigration Appeal Tribunal's (IAT) powers to considering questions of law, preventing decisions of the IAT refusing permission to appeal from being subject to judicial review in the High Court, and replacing that procedure by a much less protective system of 'statutory review'. The Act also denied in-country appeals to asylum-seekers in cases described by the Home Office as 'clearly unfounded' and imposed new, strict deadlines by which any appeals before the appellate authority had to be completed.

New powers were enacted to 'revoke' indefinite leave to remain, and powers to deprive certain persons of British citizenship were extended. Although it has still yet to be fully implemented, the 2002 Act also laid the basis for a seamless asylum processing system involving 'induction' centres, 'accommodation' centres and then, if necessary, detention in 'removal' centres. Powers to enforce the departure of members of the family of those being removed from the UK were expanded.

The Asylum and Immigration (Treatment of Claimants, etc) Act 2004

The Asylum and Immigration (Treatment of Claimants, etc) Act 2004 obtained Royal Assent on 22 July 2004. It again imposes very significant changes on both asylum and immigration. The most significant changes are as follows.

- The 2004 Act abolishes the two-tier system of appeals – first to an adjudicator and then to the IAT – which has been in force since the time of the Immigration Appeals Act 1969 (see s26, 28–31, Schedules 1, 2, 2004 Act). The new single-tier body is the 'Asylum and Immigration Tribunal' (AIT). During the passage of the legislation, in the face of an onslaught of criticism from a wide range of people, the government drew back from its original position of isolating the AIT from any form of control by the higher courts. However, the means by which its decisions can be challenged are complex and restrictive. The Court and the AIT also have the power to determine, after the event, whether public funding should be granted. This obviously presents a disincentive for legal representatives to take on challenges to decisions of the AIT.

- A number of new criminal offences have been created (s1–7), the most controversial of which is entering the UK without a valid passport, unless there is a reasonable excuse for not having the passport. The purpose of this is to deal with people who have deliberately destroyed documents before being interviewed by the immigration authorities.

- The Act sets out various forms of conduct by asylum-seekers which the person deciding the claim (and the AIT) is required to take into account in determining the credibility of the applicant (s8).

- A number of important changes are made to the system of asylum support. These include the following: failed asylum-seeking families who do not leave the UK voluntarily can be excluded from asylum support and other help from social services; unpaid work can be imposed on those who cannot leave the UK and who are obtaining 'hard cases' support; back-dated claims of social security benefit for refugees are replaced by the ability to apply for an integration loan instead (ss9–13).

- The Act also contains provisions which prevent a registrar from registering certain marriages involving a person who requires leave to be in the UK if that person does not have a 'certificate of approval' from the Secretary of State (ss19–25).

- The 2004 Act revises again the 'third country' asylum and human rights regime by setting out three separate lists of countries, in descending order of safety, with different procedural protections attached to each. A fourth category of third-country certification may be applied to any individual case (s33, Sch 3). The ability to certify asylum and human rights claims as being 'clearly unfounded', and therefore to exclude in-country appeals, is extended by the Act (s27).

Proposed legislation

The Immigration, Asylum and Nationality Bill 2005 has been making its way through parliament during preparation of this edition of the *Handbook*. Among the new measures are some pretty severe restrictions on rights of appeal and new powers for the Secretary of State to apply a penalty to employers who employ those unlawfully in the UK. For a summary of its provisions, ▶see 50–3 (and ▶see 33–50 for the 'five-year strategy' and further consultation). For more specific details about the changes to appeals, ▶see 1041–6.

WHAT MAKES UP THE IMMIGRATION LAW?

The Acts of Parliament described above are the primary source of law in immigration, just as in other fields. Importantly, these Acts have given the force of law to certain rights contained in international conventions which are important to immigration rights. This applies to both the 1951 Refugee Convention and the European Convention of Human Rights (see below). Although, the recent Acts are very large pieces of legislation, neither the 1999 Act, the 2002 Act, nor the latest, 2004 Act, have consolidated all of the existing immigration Acts of Parliament into one, as might have been hoped. This means that some parts of all the legislation introduced from 1971 onwards are still in force, although heavily amended. In addition, separate Acts of Parliament deal with other matters – for, example, nationality is mainly governed by the British Nationality Act 1981, and appeals in national security cases are covered by the Special Immigration Appeals Commission Act 1997. This all makes the task of the immigration adviser harder, because there is no one place in which the main legal provisions can be found; they remain scattered across different pieces of legislation.

Secondary legislation

Leaving aside the main Acts of Parliament, much of the detail of immigration law and procedure is contained in what is called 'secondary' legislation. This consists of regulations, rules and orders that the government is given a power to make under the main Acts. Secondary legislation has increasingly been used to provide the nitty-gritty of many immigration processes. It is used, for example, to regulate the procedure for immigration and asylum appeals, the giving of notices of immigration decisions, requirements to register with the police, the asylum support scheme, and procedures for naturalisation as a British citizen.

Immigration Rules

The 'immigration rules', which the Home Office is given the power to make by the 1971 Act, are another essential source of immigration law. The purpose of the rules is to set out the requirements that must be satisfied in order for a person to be admitted to the UK in any particular category (▶see also 15–16, below). It should be noted that, unlike Acts of Parliament or secondary legislation, the immigration rules are not 'legislation'. They are written in a more relaxed and informal way and, accordingly, there is more room for manoeuvre when it comes to interpreting them.

The present full statement of immigration rules is called 'HC 395'. When new rules are made, usually several times a year, they either add to or amend this statement. Occasionally, rather than amend the existing statement of the rules, the Home Office issues a whole new statement of rules to replace the previous statement. This has not, however, happened since 1994, when HC 395 was issued. There have, for a long time, been repeated rumours – and also indications from the Home Office – of the production of a new, consolidated statement of immigration rules, but it has not so far emerged. Meanwhile HC 395 is dotted about with letters added to the numbers of the paragraphs in order to make way for detailed additions to the rules. For example, the category of 'Parents of a child at school' is contained in paragraphs 56A–56C HC 395.

The rules are always entitled 'Statement of Changes in Immigration Rules', and are a convenient way of making law because they can be altered so much more easily than Acts. All that is required is that a copy of the proposed new rules is laid before parliament, where they are subject to what is called the 'negative resolution' procedure. This provides that the new rules may come into force straight away (bigger changes may be postponed to take effect later), and remain in force unless MPs call for a debate, which may be in committee rather than in the main chamber of the House of Commons or Lords. In that debate it is possible for the rules as a whole either to be voted down or accepted, but they cannot be amended. A statement of immigration rules has only once been voted down in this way.

Because statements of rules all carry the same title, individual new rules are known instead by their numbers. These are prefixed by 'HC' (for 'House of Commons' paper) if the House is sitting at the time. If a change is introduced during a parliamentary recess, they are prefixed by 'Cmd' (for 'Command' paper).

Case-law

Throughout the period described above, the amount of law decided by the courts on the basis of hearing individual cases has grown immensely. This is known as 'case-law'. Case-law is especially important in the areas of asylum and human rights as will be seen from the number of cases referred to in the relevant parts of the *Handbook*, compared to the rest. One reason for this is the very broad way in which the international instruments relating to these areas are framed. When it comes to applying the rights to individual cases, careful interpretation is required, which is ultimately the job of the courts.

Since the incorporation of the European Convention of Human Rights (ECHR) by the Human Rights Act 1998, many hard-fought battles have been waged in the courts to try to secure maximum protection under the ECHR for those affected by immigration decisions. Prominent examples are the decision of the Court of Appeal in *Mahmood* (impact of Article 8 on immigration decisions which interfere with family life, ▶see 822–3), and that of the House of Lords in *Ullah & Do* ('extra-territorial' effect of the Convention rights, ▶see 788–9).

Policy and practice

Policies, practices and procedures which are not formally set out in the legislation or the immigration rules also play an important part in shaping the immigration system. They are subject to being changed unpredictably and without any real accountability. A good source of information about practice and policy are the different sets of policy instructions which the

Immigration and Nationality Directorate (IND) posts on its website (www.ind.homeoffice.gov.uk). These instructions are intended as internal documents for the benefit of Home Office staff in order to help them carry out their functions and make decisions. They were made available publicly as part of the Home Office's drive towards greater openness, and are as follows.

- **The Immigration and Nationality Directorate Instructions (IDI)** provide details about how on-entry and after-entry applications are handled. Chapters 1–13 of these instructions correspond to Parts 1–13 of the immigration rules (HC 395). So, these parts of the IDI are divided into the different categories of entry which are to be found in the rules. Chapters 14–20 of the IDI deal with additional policy and procedures.

- **The Asylum Policy Instructions (API)** contain the Home Office's policy in relation to asylum matters.

- **The Operational Enforcement Manual (OEM)** provides guidance on the various procedures under which people can be forced to leave the UK. At the time of writing, it was still in the process of being updated (▶see 908).

- **The Nationality Instructions (NI)** provide staff with guidance on making decisions relating to nationality. There are two volumes. Volume I contains the case-working instructions (divided into six parts), and Volume II contains other general and procedural information.

- **The European Directorate Instructions (EDI)** provide guidance on immigration cases involving EU free-movement rights.

Asylum support policy Policy in relation to asylum support is set out in a series of National Asylum Support service (NASS) 'Policy Bulletins' which can also be downloaded from the NASS website. Each bulletin deals with a different aspect of the NASS system – 'grace periods' and 'mixed households', for example – and they are regularly added to and replaced.

Working in the UK policy The Work Permits (UK) website (www.workpermits.gov.uk) provides a series of 'Guidance Notes' and other policy papers which set out both the criteria and policy upon which Immigration Employment Documents (IEDs), such as work permits, may be issued. Note that, in late 2005, the main Home Office website also began carrying the 'Business and Commercial Internal Caseworker Guidance' which gives guidance mainly on work permit issues.

Entry clearance policy Detailed instructions to entry clearance officers (ECOs) about dealing with applications for entry clearance can be found in the Diplomatic Service Procedures, Entry Clearance Volume I, General Instructions (DSP). They are divided into 28 chapters, which have annexes containing additional procedural and other related information and example sample documents. They can be accessed by visiting the UK Visas website (www.ukvisas.gov.uk).

While these materials provide a rich source of information, care must be taken. In particular, the instructions contained on the IND website are not always up to date. Also, some of the material is sensitive, and so is deleted from the published version. It is also not always easy to access. The IDI probably has the most complicated layout. It is broken down into 'chapters' and 'sections'. The guidance provided in the different sections is in many cases supplemented by annexes, separate from the main text. It is often these annexes that contain the really useful material. In general, where we have taken specific information from any of these materials in the book, we have provided a reference. So, for example, 'IDI, Ch1, s1, annex A para. 1' is a reference to paragraph 1 of annex A, which supplements Section 1 of Chapter 1 of the Immigration Directorates' Instructions (it concerns the 'right of abode'). But we have not generally given specific paragraph references to the Work Permits (UK) Guidance Notes, because they are reissued every six months or so with some changes. Fortunately, they contain a full contents listing, and so relevant information can be quickly identified.

Policy is not restricted to the above materials. Sometimes policies and practices exist that are not published, and advisers only come to find out about them on a case-by-case basis. As a result, a culture has grown up by which notes and letters to advisers from the Home Office are circulated among the community of immigration lawyers and advisers, often through the Immigration Law Practitioners' Association (ILPA). A willingness to cooperate and share materials is vital to immigration lawyers. Where we have drawn on this kind of material in the *Handbook*, we have generally provided a reference.

Procedures and practices often change without any legislation. For example, until recently, recognised refugees were granted indefinite leave in the UK, but they are now granted limited leave only and their status is subject to a system of review (▶see 720 onwards).

THE SYSTEM OF IMMIGRATION CONTROL

Certain people are hardly affected by immigration controls. The 1971 Act defines the class of people who have the 'right of abode' in the UK (British citizens and some Commonwealth nationals – see Glossary), and states that they may freely reside in and come and go from the UK as they please. Of course, a British citizen has to demonstrate that they are entitled to the right of abode when they come into the UK, usually by producing their British passport to the immigration officer. The main divide in immigration law is between those who enjoy the right of abode and those who do not. (There are, however, certain special groups not easily accommodated by this divide, ▶21–23 below). The majority of people who do not have the right of abode require specific permission in order to enter or remain in the UK, which they can only obtain from the immigration authorities. The technical term for this permission is 'leave', and we refer to 'leave' throughout the book.

'Subject to immigration control' For many years lawyers and Home Office officials described those who need leave as being 'subject to immigration control'. This is the definition used in the 1996 Act, and indeed it is still often used. We have not used this phrase to describe those who need leave. This is because the 1999 Act introduced a new definition – 'subject to immigration control' – in order to describe people who are excluded from various forms of welfare provision (s115). That definition does not simply refer to people who need leave to be here. There are also various other legislative provisions that impose different meanings upon the same term. To avoid confusion, we therefore only use 'subject to immigration control' when dealing with welfare entitlements. We describe those who do not have the right of abode simply as persons who 'need leave' to come to or to stay in the UK.

The system for controlling entry to the UK including applications to come to the UK, leaving and returning to the UK and applying to stay in the UK are all described in **Section 2**.

Identifying status

A selection of the multitude of different endorsements and forms that denote different kinds of immigration status is reproduced in **Chapter 8**, together with a short explanation of each. If you are simply trying to identify quickly the status which a person has from a document, you should first look here, and then follow the references given to other parts of the *Handbook* for related information. That chapter also contains the conditions that a person admitted to the UK in any particular category is likely to have attached to their leave (▶see further below, 18).

Immigration law and nationality law

'Nationality' is a branch of law in its own right. Questions of nationality or 'citizenship' are closely connected to immigration law because a person's nationality is central to determining what immigration rights they have; but nationality and immigration should still not be confused. The kind of passport which a person holds depends on their nationality. However, a passport is only evidence of a person's nationality; it is not the ultimate source of it. So the possession or absence of a passport is not always conclusive of a person's proper national status.

Unlike in most countries, nationality and citizenship are not the same thing in UK law. This is because, largely as a result of Britain's colonial past, there are various different kinds of British nationality. It is not the case that all British nationals have the right of abode – namely the right to freely enter and live in the UK free from immigration controls. Only one of the categories of British nationals, known as 'British citizens', carries that right. The link between holding a British passport and being able to come and go freely from the UK was broken by the Commonwealth Immigrants Acts in the 1960s.

The main Act of Parliament which now governs nationality is the British Nationality Act 1981 (we have referred to it as the 'BNA 1981'), although important changes were made by the 2002 Act. **Section 13** of the *Handbook* deals with British nationality law. **Chapter 43** explains the different kinds of British national and the different immigration rights which they enjoy. **Chapter 44** discusses how to check whether someone is a British citizen. **Chapter 45** explains how people can become British citizens through processes known as 'naturalisation' and 'registration'.

'Leave' and the immigration rules

As to those who need leave in order to enter or stay in the UK (▶see 13–14), the Acts of Parliament do not set out who should and should not be granted 'leave', nor for how long they should be given it, nor on what conditions. This is the role of the immigration rules made under the 1971 Act.

Categories of entry under the immigration rules

The immigration rules set out various categories in which people can be granted leave, for example 'visitor', 'student', 'work permit holder', 'investor', 'spouse', 'unmarried partner', 'sole representative', 'language assistant', 'asylum', etc. In each category, the rules indicate different requirements which need to be satisfied before a person can be granted leave. For example, a student needs to demonstrate that, among other things, they are able and intend to follow their course of study, and that it is a 'full-time' course (see para. 57(ii) HC 395). For those categories under the rules which are sometimes known as 'temporary purposes' (for example, visitors and students), applicants generally need to show that they intend to leave the UK when the purpose of their stay is over.

The vast majority of the categories under the rules require that the applicant can be 'maintained and accommodated' without recourse to public funds. We deal in detail with these requirements, often simply referred to as the **'public funds' rules**, at ▶308–318. Most of what is explained there applies to these requirements wherever they are to be found in the rules, although there are slight variations in the way in which the rules are phrased.

Note that even if the particular requirements for one of the categories of entry under the rules are all satisfied, the rules also set out general grounds upon which leave can still be refused (▶see 97–9, 140–1).

Categories of entry and the *Handbook*

We deal with the different categories in which people who need leave can enter and remain in the UK in separate sections of the *Handbook*.

- **Section 3** covers certain people who are coming to the UK for temporary purposes, including visitors of many different kinds, working holiday-makers and students. **Chapter 9** covers visitors and working holidaymakers. **Chapter 10** deals with students of all kinds and ages including, for example, school students, medical and postgraduate students and students re-sitting exams. It also looks at the arrangements for finance for students (fees, loans and grants) and it covers EEA students. This section does not, of course, cover all people coming to the UK temporarily. There are other temporary categories – for example seasonal agricultural workers – but they are more easily covered under the work and business section (see below).

- **Section 4** deals with those who seek to enter or remain as family members. Separate chapters are given to spouses and partners (**Chapter 11**), children, including adopted children (**Chapter 12**) and other relatives (**Chapter 13**). This section deals both with family members who want to join their relatives in the UK permanently, and those who are seeking to join relatives who are here for a limited period. The right to respect for private and family life, under Article 8 ECHR, is very important to immigration cases involving family members; full details are contained in **Chapter 27,** ▶820–50.

- **Section 5** concerns people who want to come to the UK for work or business purposes. There are many different categories covered in this section. Those categories that require an 'Immigration Employment Document' (IED) (for example, a work permit) to be issued before leave can be granted are dealt with in **Chapter 14**. 'Permit-free' employment, both under the rules and outside the rules, is covered in **Chapter 15**. **Chapter 16** looks at entry for business purposes, and includes details of the 'Innovators' scheme and the Highly Skilled Migrant Programme. It also covers the consequences of working or entering into business unlawfully in the UK, and sets out the law relating to the criminal offence which can be committed by an employer who employs someone who is not authorised to work (▶see 495–500). Note that discharged members of **HM Forces** are dealt with separately at ▶150–1.

Generally, when we explain the requirements of the rules in the above categories, we give details of those requirements that need to be satisfied for the particular category and an explanation of those requirements. There are also details about whether a person can extend their leave in the category, how long an applicant will be able to stay in the UK, and information about the rights of any dependants they may have. However, broader discussion of making immigration applications, whether for entry clearance or for leave to remain while in the UK, can be found in **Section 2**. **Section 4**, dealing with family members, gives fuller details on the rights of dependants.

Leave outside the immigration rules

The rules do not, however, cover every circumstance, and the immigration authorities always have discretion to grant leave outside the immigration rules. Some important issues are left as matters of practice outside the rules. Where such practices are clearly defined and written down, they are

often termed 'policies', or sometimes 'concessions'. A number of concessions have recently been brought within the immigration rules. For
example, what were formerly the 'long residence concessions' – also
known as the 'ten-year rule' and the '14-year rule' – are now part of the
rules (see paras 276A–D HC 395 and ►see 151–7).

The different concessions are dealt with in the *Handbook* in the part
where each concession is most relevant, but for a more detailed explanation of the exercise of discretion outside the immigration rules and the
terms **'exceptional leave'**, **'Humanitarian Protection'** and **'Discretionary
Leave'**, ►see 147–8, 597–8 and 859–62. For a list of the most important
concessions and where to find them in the *Handbook*, ►see 148–50.

Limited leave and indefinite leave

Under the 1971 Act, leave which is granted can be either 'limited' or
'indefinite' (s3(1)(b) 1971 Act). The immigration rules spell out what
period of leave is to be given to people either entering or extending their
stay in the UK, in the various different categories. Those who are coming
to the UK only for temporary purposes – such as visitors, students, au
pairs, and seasonal agricultural workers – may only be granted limited
leave. Others may be applying to stay in the UK permanently, and may be
granted indefinite leave. In some categories, people can be granted
indefinite leave straight away – for example, family members (other than
spouses and partners) who are applying to stay with a relative who is
already settled in the UK.

In many of the categories of entry, applicants do not immediately obtain
the right to remain permanently in the UK, but they will gain that right
after a particular period of time. In these categories, therefore, applicants
are first granted a period of limited leave, which they need to apply to
extend before they are eventually granted indefinite leave. Categories
that are work-related generally require that an applicant has been in the
UK with limited leave continuously for four years before they are eligible
for indefinite leave. This is likely to be extended to five years under
government proposals. This applies, for example, to work-permit holders
and to innovators. For how this 'continuous' period is calculated, see
438–9. Applicants for indefinite leave as a foreign spouse generally have
to serve a two-year qualification or 'probationary' year before they can
apply for indefinite leave.

'Settled' Another term with a meaning similar to 'indefinite leave' is
'settled', which is used to refer to anyone who normally resides in the UK
and who has no limitations or conditions on their right to stay here (see
para. 6 HC 395, and see s50(1)–(4) British Nationality Act 1981). All those
who have indefinite leave or the right of abode in the UK and who
ordinarily reside here, are therefore generally referred to as being 'settled'.

Returning residents Those who have indefinite leave are able to leave
and return to the UK under a special category under the immigration rules

called 'returning residents'. Anyone who has indefinite leave, regardless of the basis upon which it was granted, can use the 'returning residents' rule. This category is therefore dealt with separately, as part of our explanation of the practical arrangements of immigration control (▶see 112–16).

Conditions of leave

Where a person is granted *limited leave*, conditions may be imposed on it. The possible conditions are:

- either prohibition of all employment or business activities, or restriction of a person's employment or business activity to a particular kind;
- a requirement that the person maintain and accommodate themselves and their dependants without recourse to public funds (for the meaning of 'public funds', ▶see 308–9);
- a requirement that the person register with the police (▶see 1006–7 and 1527 for more details).

In some categories, the immigration rules indicate which conditions should be imposed on the leave. The Home Office uses a system of 'codes' for the various combinations of possible conditions. The appropriate codes for each category are set out in the IDI. For quick reference, we have set out the codes in full, and the conditions which are normally imposed on leave, for all the different categories ▶see 190–1. We also make reference to the usual conditions in the part of the book dealing with the category of entry in question.

It should be noted, however, that the usual conditions which an applicant can expect to have been given are not always the conditions which have in fact been attached. Mistakes can occur, and sometimes people are deliberately treated differently and sometimes applicants misapprehend the basis upon which they have been granted leave. Advisers can only be sure of the period of leave granted and the conditions attached to it by looking at the actual grant of leave endorsed in the passport or travel document, or set out in a written notice. Indefinite leave cannot be made subject to any conditions.

Temporary admission and detention

In most circumstances when a person who needs leave is refused leave, or where no immediate decision can be made whether to grant them leave or not, one of two things may happen. They can either be granted a form of 'temporary admission', or they may be detained. 'Temporary admission' is a technical term, but is also used loosely to describe the various bases upon which the immigration authorities can let a person stay in the UK for the time being while immigration processes are taking place – for example, while a decision is being made or arrangements for their removal are being put in place. Conditions can be attached to temporary admission, and it can be brought to an end at any time. For a fuller description of **temporary admission,** ▶see 950–7.

The powers of immigration detention under the 1971 Act are an alternative to temporary admission. Aside from the special conditions which apply to detention at Oakington Reception Centre, it is Home Office policy only to detain people where it is strictly necessary to do so – for example, if there is a risk that they will abscond. Detention is dealt with in **Section 9.** **Chapter 30** sets out the powers of detention, and includes the various legal limitations on those powers, including those imposed by Article 5 ECHR (the right to liberty and security). It also looks closely at Home Office policy on when people will be detained. **Chapter 32** contains information about how to get people out of detention and looks at the practical aspects of making bail applications and bail hearings. **Chapter 31** looks at the conditions which people face in detention and at the various reports which have been made about immigration detention. It also contains details of the Detention Centre Rules, which regulate the treatment of people while they are detained. It also deals with certain procedures connected to detention, for example the duty to give reasons for detention and to regularly review whether a person should continue to be detained.

Asylum and human rights

During the past 12 years asylum law has changed beyond recognition, and it continues to be subject to rapid change. The law on asylum stems from the United Nations Convention on the Status of Refugees of 1951, amended by a Protocol in 1967. Before 1993, it was not entirely clear what status this Convention had in UK law, and very little was written into the law about the status of refugees, how their cases should be determined, or what their rights were. The Refugee Convention became a firmer part of British law through the Asylum and Immigration Appeals Act 1993, which states that the immigration rules must not be read as allowing the immigration authorities to do anything which contravenes the UK's obligations under the Convention (s2 1993 Act). The most important obligation is that contained in Article 33 of the Convention, which prohibits the return of a person to a country in which they have a 'well founded fear of persecution' for reasons of race, religion, nationality, political opinion, or membership of a particular social group. Such people are defined as 'refugees' (Article 1 of the Convention).

The numbers claiming asylum continued to rise in the 1990s, and a large proportion of the case-loads of many solicitors and advisers consists of asylum cases. As indicated above, most of the recent legislative provisions have focused on asylum-seekers.

We deal with asylum in **Section 7**, in which there are separate chapters covering the definition of 'refugees' and what a person needs to show in order to qualify (**Chapter 21**); the detailed procedures for handling asylum claims (**Chapter 22**); Home Office asylum decision-making (**Chapter 23**);

and 'third-country' cases i.e. where an applicant may be returned to a country which is not their country of origin for their claim to be decided there (**Chapter 24**).

Chapter 22 on asylum procedures contains a range of information covering, for example, all of the various different 'segments' to which a case can be allocated in order to be processed including detained procedures; screening; 'induction' processes; conditions of temporary admission; the treatment of dependants; unaccompanied minors and age disputes; working as an asylum-seeker; prosecutions under the 2004 Act; the 'family' concession for asylum-seekers and 'special' asylum applications which may be made from abroad.

The benefits of obtaining asylum are substantial: in particular, refugees can bring certain family members to the UK without having to satisfy the rules relating to maintenance and accommodation. Rights of family reunion are dealt with in **Chapter 25**.

Human rights

The incorporation of many of the rights guaranteed by the European Convention on Human Rights (ECHR) by the Human Rights Act 1998 (HRA), has made important changes to all areas of immigration law. Advisers must now always consider whether their case involves any human rights issues. The most important rights, as far as immigration lawyers are concerned, are Article 3 (prohibition against torture and inhuman or degrading treatment or punishment) and Article 8 (right to respect for private and family life).

Human rights are covered in **Section 8**. **Chapter 26** contains general details about the way the HRA works and explains the different rights that have been brought into UK law. **Chapter 27** looks at the ways in which the ECHR can help in particular immigration cases. It considers how the ECHR can provide protection in claims for 'protection' from ill-treatment or in claims that an applicant will suffer a particular detrimental effect (often to their health) if they are required to return, and cases where the applicant has a family or other connection to the UK.

Chapter 28 looks at the way in which human rights claims can be made and how they are decided. It covers the new forms of leave which are given to those who succeed: 'Humanitarian Protection' (HP) and 'Discretionary Leave' (DL) and at Home Office policy in granting and extending that leave. It also considers family members of those applying for or granted HP and DL.

The final chapter in this section (**Chapter 29**) deals with discrimination. Provisions to prevent race discrimination form part of UK law quite independently of the ECHR. However, discrimination clearly overlaps with Article 14 ECHR, which prohibits discrimination in the rights which are guaranteed by the Convention.

When we refer to 'asylum' and 'asylum-seekers' in the *Handbook*, we generally use these terms to refer to those who are seeking 'refugee' status under the 1951 Convention. However, Article 3 has added a further firm layer of protection to the asylum system, which is important for those who might not satisfy the strict definition of 'refugee' (for the added protection provided by Article 3, in particular, ▶see the table at 796–9). In some areas of immigration law – for example, the system of asylum support – a claim for 'asylum' is now defined as including a claim under Article 3 as well as under the 1951 Convention (▶see 1342–3).

Temporary protection

From 1 January 2005, a new category of 'temporary protection' has been introduced into the rules (paras 354-356B HC 395 inserted by HC 164, December 2004). The purpose of this new category is to implement the Temporary Protection Directive (Directive 2001/55/EC), which was adopted by the Council of the European Union in July 2001 and which requires minimum protection to be granted in the event of a 'mass influx of displaced persons'. Initial limited leave of up to 12 months can be granted, which can be extended for periods of six months at a time. Temporary protection is dealt with in **Section 7**, at ▶633–5.

Special groups

We have said that the main divide in immigration law is between those who possess the right of abode in the UK and those who do not. The latter require leave to be in the UK. Certain groups of people, however, need to be considered separately from this general divide. By far the most important of these special groups is those who can benefit from European rights of free movement. The other groups are made up of those who, for specific reasons, are 'exempt' from immigration control, and Irish nationals. We now look briefly at each group.

1) European rights of free movement

Nationals of the countries of Europe have immigration rights which come not from UK law but from European law, in the form of the EC Treaty and the various directives made under it. The Home Office has had to change drastically its ways of dealing with these cases in the years since 1973, as court cases have gradually shown how far-reaching European free-movement rights are. Most recently, on 1 May 2004, another ten countries, largely from Eastern Europe, joined the EU. The rights also extend beyond the member states of what is now the EU to include three associated states from the old European Free Trade Association (EFTA) – Norway, Iceland and Liechtenstein – which, together with the EU countries, now form the European Economic Area (EEA). By a further special agreement, originally made in June 1999, the rights of free movement also extend to Swiss nationals.

EEA nationals can enter the UK without requiring leave to do so, even though they do not have the right of abode. Having entered, they are free to take up any employment (with a very few exceptions, mainly in the higher reaches of the civil service and in areas where national security is an issue), or to set themselves up in business or in self-employment.

The immigration rights of nationals of these countries are, however, dependent on their exercising the rights of free movement recognised by EU law – namely, as workers, self-employed persons, providers or recipients of services, people who are self-sufficient, retired persons, or students. They can also be excluded from exercising free-movement rights on grounds of public policy, public security or public health. If they are not exercising free-movement rights or are excluded from doing so, immigration rights can be denied to them, and their removal from the UK can be enforced. Spouses and other close family members of EEA nationals can also benefit from these free-movement rights, even if they are not themselves EEA nationals (such persons are often termed 'third-country' nationals). The government has made regulations (the Immigration (European Economic Area) Regulations 2000) which describe the EU free-movement rights, although they are not the source of them (we have referred to them as the 'EEA 2000 Regulations').

A number of Eastern European countries that are not members of the EU have concluded 'Association Agreements' with the countries of the EU which enable nationals of those countries to migrate in order to establish themselves in business or self-employment. They are sometimes called the 'Europe' Agreements. The source of these immigration rights is not domestic law, but the rights they give rise to are set out in the immigration rules. An older and somewhat different Association Agreement exists in relation to Turkey, the 'Ankara' Agreement.

Free movement rights and the *Handbook* European rights of free movement are dealt with in **Section 6**. **Chapter 17** looks at the background to the free-movement rights and the systems of law under which they operate. **Chapter 18** sets out who qualifies for free-movement rights, the rights of family members, the procedures that apply, rights of appeal, and the rights of EEA nationals to obtain permanent rights of residence. As indicated above, ten new states joined the EU on 1 May 2004. For the time being, some restrictions have been placed on the free-movement rights of eight of those countries (known as the 'Accession 8' or 'A8' countries). For details about the accession of these countries and the restrictions on the rights granted to their nationals compared to other EEA nationals, see **Chapter 19**.

Changes to benefit and related rules caused by the new accessions are covered in **Chapter 39** dealing with welfare benefits (▶see 1264–73). **Chapter 20** covers the Association Agreements. One of the advantages of the Ankara Agreement is that the 'old', less restrictive business immigration rules apply to Turkish nationals.

2) Irish nationals

Irish citizens are, of course, EEA nationals; but they already had a special status in British immigration law before the two countries joined the Common Market. There has been no passport control between the two countries ever since the formation of the Irish Republic, and Irish people have always been able to come and work in the UK freely. In effect, Irish nationals are treated as though they have indefinite leave by virtue of their nationality alone. This is not affected by European law, but the rights applying to members of their families who are not themselves Irish are now more clear-cut as a result of EU law.

3) Persons 'exempt' from immigration control

Some groups of people, although they are not British citizens, are exempt from immigration control, and therefore do not need leave to be in the UK. This applies to certain of the following: diplomats; staff and officials of embassies and high commissions; government representatives and international officials; members of foreign armed forces; crew of ships, trains and aircrafts. Certain family members are also exempt. The exemption from immigration control only continues for as long as the person keeps the status for which it was given. Because those who are exempt are largely defined by their position or employment, they are covered in the workers and business section, at ▶472–6.

The operation of immigration controls

Immigration controls operate both overseas and in the UK. The general operation of controls is dealt with in **Section 2**. It is a general section that applies to all of those who need leave to be in the UK, and who therefore have to deal with the immigration system. It explains the 'mechanics' of the system and sets out, in broad terms, matters such as what forms are used and how decisions are made. There is obviously some overlap with later sections focusing on particular categories of entry (see above). What follows below is a brief overview of the operation of controls (dealt with more substantially in **Section 2**) and an introduction to some of the concepts and terms used.

Chapter 4 covers the process of entry, and therefore explains the system of entry clearances (often referred to as 'visas') that can be obtained from posts abroad. It also deals with what happens when a person arrives at a port of entry in the UK.

Chapter 5 deals with leaving the UK and qualifying to be readmitted on return. It looks at what happens to the leave which a person has when they leave the UK, and considers also the category of 'returning residents' referred to above.

Chapter 6 deals with all aspects of applying to extend leave in the UK. It also looks at applications for settlement on the basis of long residence.

Chapter 7 deals with applications to 'switch' – i.e. to change category while remaining in the UK. This is an area which has been subject to recent change, and can only really be covered by looking at all of the categories together. Therefore, although switching is covered in part when we look at individual categories, it is in that chapter that we deal with it fully .

Immigration authorities

We use the term 'immigration authorities' as a shorthand to refer to all those officials who can make decisions about applications to come to and stay in the UK. They include the following.

Entry clearance officers (ECOs) ECOs make decisions at British posts abroad about whether people should be permitted to come to the UK (▶see 1511–18 for a list of posts abroad, the different entry clearance facilities offered by each, and the cost of making applications ▶see also 89–93). There is an inter-departmental body which straddles the Home Office and the Foreign and Commonwealth Office called 'UK Visas' (it was previously called the 'Joint Entry Clearance Unit'), which oversees the work of ECOs at the posts abroad.

Immigration officers The immigration service is generally responsible for immigration control 'on entry' – that is, when a person arrives in the UK. Immigration officers also, however, play an important part in the enforcement of immigration control, namely the detention and removal of those who are not permitted to be in the UK. The immigration service gives its officers different ranks. As well as ordinary immigration officers, there are chief immigration officers and immigration inspectors.

Officers of the Secretary of State for the Home Department These officers and case-workers are part of the 'Immigration and Nationality Directorate' (IND) of the Home Office, and they are responsible for 'after-entry' immigration controls, namely applications for extensions of leave in the UK. Asylum applications, even if made initially to an immigration officer at port, are always referred to the IND to decide whether the person actually qualifies for asylum, but they may then be referred back for the immigration officer actually to issue the grant or refusal of leave. These officers also have a significant role to play in enforcement. Work Permits (UK) is the part of IND that makes decisions about work permit applications, and indeed all applications involving 'Immigration Employment Documents' (IED) (▶see Glossary 1536). It was previously the case that the Department of Work and Pensions (previously the Department of Education and Employment) would make decisions about whether to authorise an application for a work permit, but those functions have now all been transferred.

Entry clearance

'Entry clearance' is the term given in immigration law to documents issued by ECOs which count as evidence that the person is entitled to enter the

UK under the immigration rules. Entry clearances must be applied for and obtained from an ECO while the applicant is outside the UK. 'Visa national' is the name given to a person who requires an entry clearance for entry to the UK, whatever the purpose for which they wish to come to the UK, (▶see 1507 for a list of visa national countries). Non-visa nationals may require entry clearance, depending on the purpose for which they wish to come to the UK, and sometimes it is advisable to get one even if it is not mandatory. For a full explanation of the different terms used to cover entry clearance, ▶see 78–9, 84–5.

The most important recent development relating to entry clearance is that the government has progressively implemented a system which requires *all* foreign nationals who seek to come to the UK for more than six months to obtain an entry clearance, whatever their purpose in coming here. The countries which were originally included within this are listed in Appendix 3 to HC 395, and nationals from these countries are known as 'specified nationals'. From 13 November 2005, the requirement applies to all foreign nationals (▶see 80–83).

Changes made under the 1999 Act mean that, usually, entry clearances actually operate as leave to enter the, UK as well as simply being evidence that a person is eligible for entry. This has caused a great deal of confusion – in particular in working out how long a person has been granted leave for. We explain the way in which these entry clearances operate at ▶85–9.

Leave to 'enter' and leave to 'remain'

Leave is divided into 'leave to enter' and 'leave to remain'. Naturally enough, a person who arrives in the UK and seeks entry is given or refused leave to 'enter'. A person who has already entered, whether by having been given leave to enter or having entered illegally, is given or refused leave to 'remain'. Applications for leave to remain in most categories (not, for example, asylum) have to be made on prescribed application forms (▶see 127–32).

The traditional operation of controls was always that immigration officers would grant or refuse leave to enter while the Home Office would deal with applications for leave to remain (see s4(1), 1971 Act). This division of responsibility is, however, becoming blurred. Home Office officials at IND are now able to grant or refuse leave to enter to asylum-seekers, so as to avoid the delays caused by the system whereby the asylum claim is referred by the immigration officer to IND, which considers the claim and then refers the case back to the port to implement the immigration decision. These powers are still not being fully implemented, however. Immigration officers have the power, acting on behalf of IND, to make decisions to 'vary' leave (that is, to extend it, or to add or remove conditions) when a person arrives in the UK who already has leave (see para. 31A HC 395).

Non-lapsing leave

Changes made under the 1999 Act have meant that not all leave granted to a person to be in the UK 'lapses' when a person leaves the Common Travel Area (CTA) (see below). A person may now leave and return to the UK with their leave still fully in force. The way in which this works is explained at ▶107–9, 116–8, 100–02.

The Common Travel Area

The 'Common Travel Area' (CTA) comprises the UK (England, Wales, Scotland, Northern Ireland), the Channel Islands, the Isle of Man and the Republic of Ireland. No immigration control as such operates on journeys within the CTA. Passports are generally not checked. However, because there is no passport control, complicated rules exist to control the situation of people who travel within the CTA who are not EEA nationals. It is still quite possible to enter the UK unlawfully from elsewhere in the CTA, even though a passenger had no intention of doing so and came on a commercial flight or ship perfectly openly (▶see 105–6).

Enforcement of immigration controls

We use the word 'enforcement' in the *Handbook* to refer to all the different ways in which people can be required to leave the UK. Enforcement does not have to include detention, but it often does, and therefore we include a chapter on enforcement at the end of the section which also deals with detention (**Chapter 33**). The precise procedure operated to force people to leave depends on their immigration status at the time. **Chapter 33** therefore describes the following separate enforcement procedures:

- **'port removal'** of people who have arrived and applied for and been refused leave to enter (▶1000–2);

- **'administrative' removal** of people who were granted leave, but have either breached their conditions of leave, 'overstayed' their leave (i.e. stayed longer than permitted by their leave), or obtained leave to remain by deception (▶1002–10);

- **removal of illegal entrants** – namely, those who obtained entry to the UK in breach of immigration law, and who are not permitted by the immigration authorities to remain in the UK (▶1010–5);

- **deportation** of people whose presence the Home Office decides is not 'conducive to the public good', or who have been recommended for deportation by a criminal court after they have been convicted of an offence (▶1015–26).

Most of those who, before the 1999 Act, would have been 'deported' are now subject to the much quicker process of 'administrative removal'. Deportation is only applied to the narrow group of people referred to above. **Chapter 33** also looks briefly at other forms of enforcement that are very rarely used (▶1028–30). Also covered are the various criminal offences that may be committed which are relevant to immigration control (▶1031–6).

Appeals

At the beginning of 2005 there was still a two-tier structure of immigration and asylum appeals. The first appeal was to an adjudicator, and thereafter there was an appeal to the Immigration Appeal Tribunal (IAT). As stated above, the 2004 Act has completely restructured the appeals system by creating a single-tier 'Asylum and Immigration Tribunal', with new procedures and more limited rights to challenge decisions.

Section 10 covers appeals. For a 'ten-point' overview of the new appeals system, ▶see 1047–9. Although the relevant time-limits are mentioned throughout the section, there is a table dealing fully with time-limits at ▶1162–7.

Chapter 34 discusses fully the rights of appeal that exist under the appeals system, and the restrictions and limitations which are placed on them. The system is quite complex. In order to be able to determine what appeal rights there may be, take the following steps. First, see whether there is a right of appeal in principle (Table 1 at ▶1053–5). Then see whether, in the particular circumstances of the case, the appeal right is excluded (Table 2 at ▶1055–8). Finally, look at Table 3 at ▶1059–61 to check whether the right of appeal is in-country or not.

Note that the 2005 Bill proposes to make changes to the rights of appeal. These proposals are summarised in the table at ▶1042–6. The chapter also contains details about some specific appeals: family visitor appeals; appeals to the Special Immigration Appeals Commission; appeals where the Home Office is trying to exclude a person from the Refugee Convention and 'status' appeals where an applicant is trying to upgrade their status to that of a refugee. **Chapter 34** also looks at Home Office decisions to exclude in-country appeals by issuing a decision that an asylum or human rights claim is 'clearly unfounded' or that the applicant should have raised the particular issue previously. This chapter also looks at notices of decision and giving notice of appeal.

The following chapter (**Chapter 35**), focuses on practical matters concerning the actual conducting of appeals at first instance before the AIT. It looks at all of the procedures which apply to such appeals and at the powers of the AIT in deciding appeals. It also looks at the 'fast-track' appeal process. For an overview of the basic timetable for appeals in non-fast-track cases, ▶see the table at 1088–9; and for a similar overview for fast-track cases, ▶see 1130–1.

The final chapter in the section (**Chapter 36**) deals with challenging decisions of the AIT and at all of the procedures for taking such challenges. It also looks at transitional arrangements (i.e. how the new appeal system operates in cases which were outstanding when it came into force on 4 April 2005) and at identifying errors of law. At the end of the chapter is a table dealing with all of the time-limits relevant to appeals and challenging decisions of the AIT and at the possibility of extending time (▶see 1162–7).

Other appeals

It should be noted that there are some particular, specialised areas of the appeals system that are not covered by **Section 10,** but are instead dealt with in the part of the book most appropriate to them. These are:

- the rights of appeal or challenge available (or not available) in cases where the immigration authorities are trying to remove an asylum-seeker to a **'safe' third country** (▶739–46);
- appeals against decisions in cases involving **EEA nationals** and their family members (▶556–9, 532);
- appeals (also called 'reviews') of **decisions of Work Permits (UK)** to refuse to issue an IED (▶439–40);
- appeals against **decisions of the National Asylum Support Service** (NASS) relating to asylum support (▶see Chapter 42);
- **bail applications** (although not strictly 'appeals', ▶958–85).

OTHER RIGHTS AND REMEDIES

Outside of the formal 'immigration' system, the giving of immigration advice has become increasingly connected with other aspects of the legal system. The *Handbook* seeks to provide guidance on the following further areas, which often have a direct effect on those affected by immigration control.

Welfare

The period since the mid-1990s has seen an ever-growing coordination between legislation concerned with immigration rights and access to the various forms of welfare provision. Under the 1996 Act, access to core social security benefits was restricted to those who claimed asylum 'on arrival' in the UK, and the period for which asylum-seekers could claim was severely limited. The 1999 Act took asylum-seekers largely out of mainstream support, and set up a new system of 'asylum support' for essential living needs and accommodation, which was to be administered by a new part of the Home Office, the National Asylum Support Service (NASS) and local authorities. The system also involved the 'dispersal' of asylum-seekers throughout the UK.

Both the 2002 and 2004 Acts introduced dramatic new measures relating to support, which include the denial of support to those who fail to claim asylum 'as soon as reasonably practicable' after arrival in the UK; the creation of new classes of person who are excluded from asylum support and other forms of support by their immigration status; the withdrawal of support from failed asylum-seeking families who fail to cooperate with voluntary arrangements for their departure. The systems for asylum support (including temporary or 'emergency' support) and 'hard cases' support are dealt with in **Chapter 41**. Appeals to the Asylum Support Adjudicator are covered in **Chapter 42**.

The 1999 Act also introduced a new test of being 'subject to immigration control', which restricted access to non-contributory benefits and certain social services provision. Access to housing has been subject to similar restrictions. While this is the most important provision, the rules about access to benefits, housing, social services support, Children Act support and healthcare are many and complex, and subject to many exceptions. **Chapter 39** describes access to welfare benefits and **Chapter 40** looks at access to all other forms of support (housing, social services, Children Act etc).

Civil claims

The powers of immigration detention are wide-ranging. Immigration officers often use those powers and the powers of removal in an arbitrary and oppressive way. The general civil law provides remedies for people who are unlawfully detained or removed from the UK or in some other circumstances where they are treated unlawfully in an immigration context. This enables people to claim compensation for the wrongs done to them. As far as immigration law and practice is concerned, this is a relatively new growth area. The circumstances in which a civil claim may be brought, and the basic procedures which apply, are set out in **Chapter 37**.

Judicial review and other remedies

The second chapter in **Section 11**, **Chapter 38**, looks at judicial review and other remedies that those affected by the immigration system may have recourse to. Judicial review has been gradually ousted as a means of supervising the immigration appeals system. Under the 2002 Act, it was removed as a basis for challenging decisions of the IAT to refuse to grant leave to appeal. The 2004 Act has imposed a very restrictive means of challenging the new AIT, which generally excludes the use of judicial review. **Chapter 38** looks at the circumstances in which judicial review is still used in immigration cases, notably in challenges to 'certificates' issued by the Secretary of State, in support and detention cases, and in preventing unlawful removals. The chapter also covers basic judicial review procedures ▶1213–22.

Chapter 38 also looks at other remedies including:

- complaints to the Home Office and the Home Office's 'consolatory payments' scheme (which recently came to light) (▶1223–7);

- complaining to the Parliamentary Ombudsman (▶see the table at 1229–35 dealing with financial awards made in earlier cases);
- contacting MPs (▶1227–8);
- the ability of refugees to claim compensation for wrongful prosecution concerning their entry to the UK (▶1235–8).

2 Proposed changes including the 'five-year strategy' and 2005 Bill

This chapter covers the likely future changes in immigration, asylum and nationality law. There are three aspects to the future changes.

- First we discuss the major legislation which is already in existence, but which has not yet been brought into force (below).
- Next we look at the government's 'five-year strategy' for asylum and immigration, announced in February 2005. The key anticipated changes to immigration law and procedures are summarised in the table at ▶34–42. A fuller discussion of the proposals follows, together with JCWI's views on them. We also look at the government's consultation document, *Making Migration Work for Britain*, launched on 19 July 2005 (▶42–50)
- Next we cover the latest proposed immigration legislation, the Immigration, Asylum and Nationality Bill 2005 which entered committee stage in Parliament in October 2005 (▶see 50–3).
- We then examine some other government proposals for change which do not form part of the above but are likely to have significant implications for those affected by immigration control: changes to healthcare provision; the introduction of identity cards; the expansion of the list of 'specified nationals'; and the changes to the immigration rules following the Civil Partnership Act 2004 (▶see 53–5).

JCWI's own proposals for a fair immigration policy that works for everyone are at ▶55–7.

Proposals in the five-year strategy to consolidate most of the various work-related categories into a single points-based system with five tiers are discussed briefly in this chapter. In the section on workers and business, we have set out in more detail which existing categories of workers, students, trainees and visitors are likely to be assimilated to which part of the new system (▶see 34–6).

IMPORTANT LEGISLATION

Important parts of the Nationality, Immigration and Asylum Act 2002 and the Asylum and the Immigration (Treatment of Claimants, etc.) Act 2004 have not yet been implemented.

The 2002 Act

The following significant parts of the 2002 Act have yet to be implemented.

Accommodation Centres Although section 16 of the 2002 Act, which permits the Secretary of State to set up accommodation centres, came into force on 7 November 2002, much of part 2 of the Act, which concerns the operation of these centres, is yet to be brought in. The idea of the accommodation centres is that certain asylum-seekers would be required to reside in them, where they would be subject to reporting conditions and where they may be provided with support. The further plan was to establish hearing centres close by the accommodation centres, where asylum and human rights appeals could be heard. In part, the delay in bringing in all the legislation and in setting up the centres reflects the immense opposition the government has faced in trying to establish them. Much of the opposition has come from local councils contesting planning permission for the proposed locations. In the summer of 2005, the government decided not to press ahead with accommodation centres after all.

Nationality Certain provisions concerning nationality, contained in part 1 of the Act, have yet to be implemented. The distinction drawn in nationality law between legitimate and illegitimate children (▶see 1429) is to be eliminated, but this has yet to be implemented. The minimum age requirement for registration as a British citizen by stateless children born in the UK is also to be abolished (sections 8 and 9). This is also still to be implemented. From 1 November 2005, sections 1(1) and (2) 2002 Act came into force. From that date, applicants for naturalisation have to demonstrate 'sufficient knowledge about life in the UK', by taking a special test or 'ESOL' course (for further details ▶see 1467–8).

The 2004 Act

Most of the 2004 Act has been brought into force. From 4 April 2005, a new appeals system was established incorporating the new Asylum and Immigration Tribunal ('AIT'; ▶see 1046–52). Sections 12 and 13 of the 2004 Act were due to be brought in between the summer and autumn of 2005, following the government's consultation document, *Integration Matters: A National Strategy for Refugee Integration*, which was published in March 2005. These two provisions, which are not yet in force, establish a new 'Refugee Integration Loan', and abolish the present provisions for the back-dating of income support, housing benefit and council tax benefit for refugees (▶see also 1284–87). The loans will be interest-free, and all recognised refugees will be eligible to apply for a loan. It is intended that the loan will assist a refugee in taking up vocational training, purchasing the tools of a trade, or providing a deposit for accommodation.

THE 'FIVE-YEAR STRATEGY'

In February 2005 the government produced its 'five-year strategy' for immigration and asylum, entitled *Controlling our borders: Making migration work for Britain* (Command Paper, Cm 6472). The strategy draws heavily on the assumption that there is an increasing need to regulate and control entry to the UK's labour market, to step up border control, and to enhance enforcement measures.

What are the proposed changes?

The main thrust of the strategy is a multi-pronged drive to 'crack down' on illegal entry and unlawful working, to step up fast-tracking of asylum claims and detention, and to toughen removals policy and enhance surveillance before, on and after entry. The strategy also aims to 'rationalise' the routes of entry for work purposes. It is not a new approach, but the repackaging of an old one, combined with a further hardening of measures. Three major pieces of legislation concerning asylum and immigration under the present government's time in office have successively boosted the powers of the immigration authorities to refuse entry, to detain and remove applicants, and to limit legal challenge to their decisions.

The key proposals are set out in the table below. The table sets out the proposal, the nature of the expected change in the law to give effect to the proposal, and the impact of the change on the existing system.

A key part of the five-year strategy is the introduction of a single points-based system for the existing categories of economic migration. The government has been consulting on this change and intends to announce the timetable for introduction of the new system in spring 2006. The consultation paper concerning economic migration, *Making Migration Work for Britain* was issued on 19 July 2005 and elaborates on the proposals contained in the five-year strategy. We look further at this immediately after the table (▶42–3).

SUMMARY OF CHANGES UNDER THE FIVE-YEAR STRATEGY

Proposals	Expected new legislation/rules/ procedure	Impact
ECONOMIC MIGRATION: WORKERS AND STUDENTS		
A new 'single points-based system' for the existing categories of economic migration (including workers, students, trainees and visitors). The new system will work on the basis of the tiers set out below **Note that although the five-year strategy proposed four tiers, we have set out below the position following the government's consultation paper *Making Migration Work for Britain* which incorporates five tiers.**	No primary legislation is required – simply changes to the immigration rules.	Phased withdrawal of existing structure of work permits and the various existing 'managed migration' routes. Possible phasing out of the existing student categories.
'Fresh Talent Initiative' for Scotland. This scheme enables students who qualify at Scottish universities to obtain leave to look for work (▶see 465–7 for more details).	Amendment to the immigration rules.	Introduced from 22 June 2005.
Tier 1 – highly skilled persons		
A points–based scheme for graduate-level professionals, such as doctors and engineers. They may enter and seek work without a job offer. Those admitted under Tier 1 will be able to settle in the UK, and can be joined by their dependants.	Amendments to the immigration rules. The points criteria can be decided by the Home Office without parliamentary approval.	Tier 1 will incorporate existing categories, such as the Highly Skilled Migrant Programme, Innovators, Investors.
Tier 2 – skilled persons		
Entry only with a job offer in: • a listed shortage occupation or,	Amendments to the rules and internal criteria.	Tier 2 appears to correspond with both tiers of the current Business and Commercial work-

Proposals	Expected new legislation /rules/ procedure	Impact
• where the employer is unable to recruit within the UK/EU. Those admitted under Tier 2 will be able to settle in the UK, and it is expected they will be able to be joined by their dependants.		permit system (▶see 424–6). Some intra-company transferees may come within Tier 1 or 2, or even 4. The MBA scheme is likely to fall within Tier 2 also.

Tier 3 – low-skilled persons

New schemes may be introduced on a small-scale, 'tightly managed' quota system where additional economic needs are identified. Applicants may be admitted for fixed, temporary periods only and financial bonds may be required. Those admitted under Tier 3 will not be able to settle in the UK, and they cannot be joined by their dependants.	Amendments to the rules and internal criteria.	The Home Office will phase out the existing quota-based schemes, such as the Sectors-Based Schemes and the Seasonal Agricultural Workers' Scheme (▶see further 448–52).

Tier 4 – Students

Students will be admitted under Tier 4. The existing tests under the immigration rules will be used as the basis of a points system for them. Some students will be able to move into permanent categories.	Amendments to the rules and internal criteria.	Some graduate 'students' will be accommodated under Tier 5 below. Note that, under the five-year strategy Tiers 4 and 5 were amalgamated – the government's later proposals have separated them out.

Tier 5 – Visiting workers, trainees, youth mobility schemes

Those admitted under the various Tier 5 categories will not be able to settle in the UK. However, certain graduates and health professionals will be able to	Amendments to the rules and internal criteria.	Tier 5 will incorporate: • Working Holidaymakers and some other 'working visitors'; • some existing work permit categories, such as the Training and Work Experience

Proposals	Expected new legislation /rules/ procedure	Impact
'switch' into long-term employment. It is unclear if they will be allowed to be joined by their dependants. Financial bonds may be required. Certain schemes (including the Working Holidaymaker Scheme and other cultural exchange schemes) will only be open to those who are nationals of countries that have negotiated return agreements with the UK (▶see 237).		Scheme, entertainers, footballers; • possibly some current 'permit-free' categories under the immigration rules, such as ministers of religion and sole representatives of overseas firms; • youth mobility and cultural exchange schemes; • post-graduate doctors, dentists, trainee GPs, those taking the PLAB test and clinical attachments; nurses doing supervised practice; those on a Science and Engineering Graduate Scheme; and participants in the 'Fresh Talent' Working in Scotland Scheme.
'Sponsors' (normally the employer or the educational institution) will be required for all tiers below Tier 1. They will be expected to ensure that applicants comply with the requirements of their leave.	Possible primary legislation imposing a requirement on sponsors to report to the Home Office.	
Financial bonds may have to be deposited for those applying under specific categories (possibly under Tiers 3 and 4). They will apply to those who are from 'higher-risk' countries or visa nationals. The deposit will be forfeited if they do not leave when their leave expires.	There is existing legislation in the 1999 Act which may be used.	This proposal is highly controversial. The idea has previously been raised for visitors, but it was never implemented. The main impact will inevitably be felt by those from poorer, non-white countries. It will be hugely unpopular with ethnic minority communities in the UK.

Proposals	Expected new legislation/rules/ procedure	Impact
SETTLEMENT GENERAL		
English language and 'knowledge of life in the UK' tests		
All those who apply for settlement, including family dependants, workers, and possibly refugees, will be expected to pass English language and 'knowledge of life in the UK' tests.	Immigration rules change and possible primary legislation.	These tests reflect changes that have already been made for those applying to naturalise as British citizens.
Workers		
Only highly skilled and skilled workers (Tiers 1 and 2) will be able to obtain settlement.	Amendments to the immigration rules.	Certain categories under the present work permit scheme, and certain permit-free categories under the rules, will be incorporated into Tier 5, and applicants admitted under them will not be able to obtain settlement. However, those who are sufficiently skilled and who do wish to settle may be able to qualify under Tiers 1 or 2, and will be advised to apply accordingly.
The settlement period will be raised from four to five years.	Amendments to the immigration rules.	
FAMILY		
Ending 'chain migration'		
Those who have themselves settled through family reunion cannot sponsor their own family, unless they have been settled for five years or have obtained citizenship.	Amendments to the immigration rules.	
Spouses/partners		
The minimum age for spouses/partners who wish to come to or stay in the UK may be raised from 18 to 21.	Amendments to the immigration rules.	This is the latest of a series of measures restricting the ability of those in the UK to sponsor their spouses and partners. Measures already brought in include:

Proposals	Expected new legislation/rules/ procedure	Impact
		• Raising the minimum age for spouses, partners and their sponsors from 16 to 18; • Extending the probationary period of spouses before they are granted settlement from one to two years (applicable to spouses and partners); • Preventing those admitted to the UK for a total of six months or less from applying to stay on the basis of marriage.

APPEALS

Students and workers

Proposals	Expected new legislation/rules/ procedure	Impact
The right of appeal may be abolished for those applying for entry clearance or leave to enter as students or workers. Unreasonable decisions will be 'guarded against' by extending the remit of the independent Entry Clearance Monitor.	Primary legislation will be needed. For details about proposed changes to appeal rights under the 2005 Bill, ▶see 1041–6.	ECOs are particularly prone to reach decisions that are flawed. With students and managed migration schemes forming the main plank of primary migration to the UK, this could force people to resort to judicial review of ECOs' decisions. No target date has been set for implementation.

Family visit appeals

Proposals	Expected new legislation/rules/ procedure	Impact
The only visitors who presently have a right of appeal against a refusal of entry clearance are those who are defined as 'family visitors'. It is proposed to restrict this definition to 'close' family members only (▶see 48, 1071–3 for further details).	Change to regulations.	
The right to an oral hearing will be abolished, and paper-only appeals will replace them.	Primary legislation may be needed but see existing s106(2) 2002 Act.	This change is likely to reduce greatly the number of successful family visitor appeals.

Proposals	Expected new legislation/rules/procedure	Impact
VISITORS		
Visitors will be given three months' entry instead of six months.	Amendment to the immigration rules.	No justification has been put forward for this proposal.
ASYLUM		
		The government has maintained its commitment to the 1951 Geneva Convention.
Limited leave only will be granted to recognised refugees. This change has been implemented (▶see 719 onwards). After three or five years, a reassessment of the country situation will take place before settlement is granted.	Changes to internal policy instructions. Note that, even though as a matter of policy indefinite leave has been granted to refugees since 1998, the immigration rules continued to state that they would be granted limited leave: paras 330, 335 HC 395.	Since July 1998, recognised refugees have been granted indefinite leave. The present proposal reverts to a position even more restrictive than the policy prior to July 1998, when refugees were initially granted four years' limited leave and were then able to settle. The present proposal is coupled with the threat of return should the country situation have changed.
Up to 30 per cent of all new asylum applicants will be detained and their applications fast-tracked. Detention capacity at Harmondsworth will be expanded and a new fast-track facility for females will open at Yarl's Wood in May 2005.	Changes to internal policy operation.	Fast-track processes have been subject to challenge. In a legal challenge to the Harmondsworth fast-track process, the Court of Appeal decided that, although the process itself is not unlawful, it has the potential to be operated unfairly if immigration officers do not exercise flexibility and take applicants out of fast-track in appropriate circumstances. The legality of detention at Oakington is being tested before the European Court of Human Rights.
Those asylum applicants who are not being detained will be subject to a 'tightly managed'	Changes to internal policy operation.	The new non-detained process is being tested in the 'North West Pilot', and is likely to be rolled out nationwide.

Proposals	Expected new legislation/rules/ procedure	Impact
process in which a decision will be made within one month, with speedy removals for those who fail. It is proposed that the same Home Office case manager will maintain responsibility for the case throughout. For general details about the 'New Asylum Model' ▶see 641–4. A new screening process will identify which track an applicant will be put through.		
The Home Office intends to maintain contact during the asylum process through reporting. The electronic monitoring pilot will be rolled out. For details about this ▶see 953–5.	Powers to electronically monitor those on temporary admission are contained in the 2004 Act, and have already been brought into force.	Electronic monitoring has commenced and is currently being evaluated.
IMMIGRATION CONTROL		
New-style residence permits will act as ID cards and will be issued to all those in the UK for more than three months. The permits are intended to verify identity, and to tackle illegal working and 'fraudulent access to public services'.	Changes to procedures.	This proposal is separate to the government's proposals for ID cards, and the alleged immigration justification for such cards (▶see below 54).
By 2008, all visa national applicants applying for entry clearance will be fingerprinted at the British post abroad.	There may be further primary legislation, but fingerprinting has commenced at some posts already.	Fingerprinting at posts has already begun for all nationals of Sri Lanka and certain East African countries.
The 'e-Borders' programme will expand UK databases on passengers. The information to be collated will include: fingerprints, arrival and	Probably practice and procedural changes only.	In the absence at present of ID card legislation, a database of foreign nationals is being created.

Proposals	Expected new legislation/rules/ procedure	Impact
departure information, and other biometric data such as iris patterns.		
Screening for tuberculosis of visa applicants on 'high-risk' routes.	Powers already exist in the immigration rules for an ECO to refer a visa applicant for a medical examination (paras 39, 320(7)(17) HC 395). It is possible that there will be further legislation or rules, and/or use of existing powers may be stepped up.	This proposal has been criticised by the medical profession as stigmatising and not assisting the UK's capacity to fight infectious diseases.
The regulation of gangmasters – a licensing authority will be set up.	Legislation is already in place in the form of the Gangmasters (Licensing) Act 2004.	
On-the-spot, fixed-penalty fines for employers employing those not legally permitted to work. Fines will be up to £2,000 per worker (for the existing employer sanctions, see ▶496–500).	Primary legislation needed.	This will increase fears of employing those from abroad and add to discrimination in the employment field.

REMOVALS

Bilateral returns agreements for failed asylum-seekers.

It will become the norm to detain failed asylum-seekers as more returns agreements are negotiated.

For details of the new 'memoranda of understanding' to be agreed in relation to cases of the proposed return of suspected terrorists ▶see 1019–20. | Agreements have already been negotiated with certain countries, including Afghanistan, Albania, China, India, Somaliland, Sri Lanka and Turkey. Further agreements are likely. | Failure by individual countries to agree arrangements with the UK for returns could result in access to the migration fund and to other migration schemes (e.g. Tier 3 schemes) being denied to those countries' nationals. |

Proposals	Expected new legislation/rules/procedure	Impact
By the end of 2005 the government aims to increase the monthly rate of removals to exceed the number of 'unfounded applications'.	Operation of procedures.	
Return unaccompanied asylum-seeking children (UASCs) through family-tracing projects.	Internal operation only. Likely to be announced through IDI changes. Already started for Albania.	The Albanian UASC returns project has been criticised for the unacceptable risk of danger and destitution in which it places removed minors.
Regulation of overseas advisers.	Primary legislation needed.	This proposal will widen the powers of the Office of the Immigration Services Commissioner.

Making Migration Work for Britain – Consultation document, July 2005

The single points system for all economic migration routes proposed by the five-year strategy is also set out (and slightly modified) in the government's consultation document issued on 19 July 2005, *Making Migration Work for Britain*. The government states that it will announce firm proposals for change and a timetable for implementation in the spring of 2006.

The 'five-year' strategy proposed a four-tier system. *Making Migration Work* proposes five tiers. For ease, the 'five-tier' system and certain other modifications made by the consultation document are incorporated into the five-year strategy table above.

The consultation document confirms that only applicants in Tiers 1 and 2 will have a route to permanent residence after they have resided in the UK for five years and others will not. However, it may be possible for some, to switch into Tiers 1 and 2. This is likely to apply, for example, to students graduating and finding work in a shortage area, people on the 'Fresh Talent: Working in Scotland' scheme or post-doctoral researchers and health professionals. The consultation document makes certain further proposals as set out below.

Skills Advisory Body and work shortages The government proposes a new Skills Advisory Body (SAB) which will use information available on the UK labour market and skill shortages to develop a full picture of the UK and advise the government on the state of the labour market. It will advise in particular on the shortage areas which are to be included on a UK list of shortage occupations. As a result, most applications in Tier 2 will be for shortage sectors identified by the SAB. However, provision will also be made for some employers, particularly in new areas of business, whose needs may not be picked up by the SAB. The points system will allow for an applicant whose job offer is not on the shortage list to reach the points threshold by a combination of salary, skill and need.

Work permit auctions A further possibility floated in *Making Migration Work for Britain* (at p.21) is that of auctioning work permits for non-shortage vacancies. It is suggested that employers could bid for permits which are released on a monthly basis with the highest bids securing the permits. This is intended to test the real economic value of migrant labour.

Sponsors Aside from Tier 1, it is proposed that all applicants will need a sponsor. This is intended to build on the existing responsibilities of employers to inform the Home Office if a migrant worker leaves employment and the Home Office's request that educational institutions report students who have ceased attending. Sponsors will become more actively involved in assessing an applicant's suitability for entry and telling the Home Office if an applicant is no longer fulfilling the purpose for which entry is granted. It is proposed to draw up a list of recognised sponsors. For students, it is proposed that every application is accompanied by a 'certificate of sponsorship' from a *bona fide* educational institution.

Application/appeal procedures The government proposes that applicants will be able to make an initial self-assessment online using guidance. After this, they could then be directed to the relevant set of criteria to see whether they qualify to come to the UK and, if so, under which tier. After making their self-assessment, applicants could submit their formal application. The government also proposes to abolish the present two-stage process which separates out immigration issues and employment qualifications. Hand-in-hand with this comes a withdrawal of rights of appeal:

'To reduce bureaucracy, we propose that we should replace the current two stage application scheme (immigration issues assessed by visa issuing posts abroad, employment qualifications assessed by the Managed Migration Directorate in the UK) with a single, robust pre-entry or in-country check. The criteria should be objective and verifiable. Once the criteria are objective and verifiable, it should no longer be necessary to retain a right of appeal against refusal. We propose to extend our monitoring function to help safeguard consistency and quality of decisions and propose developing a system of administrative review. People will, of course, be entitled to reapply if they can subsequently meet the criteria.' (*Making Migration Work for Britain*, para. 1.9)

The five-year plan: a real strategy or a great gamble?

The five-year strategy is intended to provide a long-term blueprint for the development of immigration policy. It continues the policy of the government's previous White Papers (*Fairer, Faster, Firmer*, 1998, and *Secure Borders, Safe Haven*, 2002) which saw immigration in the modern world as driven by the forces of globalisation, the successful harnessing of which is essential to the future prosperity and growth of the British economy. From this perspective, the government view is that migration must be required to 'work for Britain', and to this end must be tightly managed at each of its key stages. These key stages are identified as:

- controls on initial admission to the country;
- careful management of decisions on who is to be allowed to remain on a permanent basis;
- efficient enforcement of the rules covering the above;
- rigorous enforced departure of those not entitled to remain in the UK.

The government's plans are based on an assumption that it can and should closely regulate every aspect of migration, from assessing those entitled to be admitted, to closely controlling their subsequent stay in the UK and expelling those who break the rules or who no longer have a basis to remain. Ever more sophisticated and intrusive systems of surveillance are being built onto the existing databases. They will eventually hold the fingerprints of all visa nationals, and may be widened to include other biometric data such as iris prints. These measures, which are mentioned in the strategy, may be followed by a compulsory identity card registration scheme for foreign nationals (▶see 54), although the latter is not explicitly referred to in the strategy. The present pilot scheme for electronic tracking of asylum seekers and failed applicants is set to be implemented much more widely, and the removals regime will be bolstered by more detention facilities and an increased use of returns agreements, which various countries will be encouraged to sign by use of the carrot-and-stick approach.

Working in the UK

It is acknowledged that the existing schemes under which people may come to the UK for economic purposes are complex. The present government's programme of 'managed migration' has greatly added to its complexity and bureaucracy. The proposal to rid the system of the requirement to make separate applications for work permits and leave to remain would be a step forward (again, the system of separate applications for 'Immigration Employment Documents' (IEDs) was introduced by the present administration – for an assessment of existing economic migration policy and practice, ▶see 414–8). *However*, looked at in detail, the proposed multi-tier scheme to replace them is not necessarily an exercise in simplification (for example, depending on their level of skills, some applicants will have a choice as to which category to apply under); and nor will it necessarily benefit either applicants or the community.

The five tiers The establishment of five separate tiers of labour migrants, with the highly skilled at one end and visiting workers at the other, seems likely simply to 're-badge' the existing categories of work permit, highly skilled migrant, permit-free employee and the various categories of student, trainee and working visitor under each heading of the new tiers. At the present time, most of the economic routes contain requirements, either under the rules or set outside the rules, which, if satisfied, qualify a person to be admitted to the UK (of course, the HSMP and the Innovator schemes also already have a points system which has to be satisfied). The present requirements for each kind of application are carefully tailored to that category of entrant. In addition, although the categories are numerous and, not all are contained in the rules, they are at least each readily understandable for what they are: 'student intern', 'working holiday-maker', 'voluntary worker', 'sole representative', etc. The strategy contains no analysis of what impact the substitution of a points system will have on migration for those who presently qualify for admission under the existing routes. Will the numbers of those who would previously have been admitted under each of the various categories for a particular economic purpose go up or down in each category? What will be the effect on existing businesses? What are the implications for the stimulation of new business by both human and financial capital? What will be the effect on international student numbers, and thus on the viability of courses operated by the different educational institutions? What will be the implications for the policy underlying the Prime Minister's Initiative (▶see 249) as to the general desirability of encouraging international students?

Bonds The government proposes to require those applying under the low-skilled labour migration schemes to lodge a 'bond' of up to £1,000, which may be forfeited if they do not leave at the end of their stay. Inevitably, the proposal has generated hostility; it will increase the cost of migration for those migrant workers who are least able to afford it, and will operate as a disincentive to apply. The short-term nature of the schemes for which it is proposed, described as 'small tightly managed quota-based schemes for specific shortage areas and for fixed periods only', make it difficult enough for the workers concerned to obtain an adequate return on their investment.

Whose interests? The strategy in relation to economic migration continues the government's focus upon the economic needs of the UK, and is very thin on the question of the wider rights of those whom it is intended to admit to meet the need. Those in the lower tiers will be denied settlement rights and, it appears, may be denied the right to be joined by their family members. The government's consultation document, *Making Migration Work For Britain* boldly states:

'Migrant workers should be offered the opportunity to apply for permanent residence only where it is in the UK interest to do so. It will therefore be open only to Tier 1 and 2 migrant workers and their dependants, where they have satisfied a residence requirement and tests of English language and knowledge of life in the UK.' (para. 1.10)

The denial to these workers of settlement or of the ability to switch is likely to lead to many entering the undocumented labour market on the expiry of their leave, and being exploited by employers (see the TUC's *Migrant Workers: A TUC Guide*). Can it be fair that those admitted to undertake work in the most unpopular and demanding areas of employment, which the existing workforce is not prepared to do, should have the quality of their lives diminished by the denial of the admission of their family members? These workers' rights will continue to be overlooked. In addition, the settlement and family rights of others, such as domestic workers and the other permit-free categories, which are to be shoe-horned into the lower tiers, will be taken away unless the particular individuals can qualify for admission in the higher tiers.

Some conclusions Unless this initiative is very carefully thought through, it is likely to amount to an expensive exercise in label-changing, prompted by the pre-election imperative to be seen to be intervening in the vexed question of immigration and economic migration. There is a high risk that the proposals will benefit neither applicants nor the community, and that there will be no net gain in terms of simplicity. The implementation of the changes will be attended by the inevitable disadvantages caused by large-scale reorganisation. If past rule changes are anything to go by, there is also a very large potential for confusion and unfairness caused by lack of adequate thought being given to transitional arrangements.

Enforcement in the workplace

The strategy announces that the number of enforcement operations it conducted in the workplace increased more than three-fold in one year, and that 3,330 people were picked up for unlawful working. There is no response to the widespread concern that the strategy of raids and checks on workplaces by immigration officials has directly contributed to the increased levels of discrimination against and exploitation of migrant workers in the sectors of the economy targeted for these exercises.

The strategy proposes on-the-spot fines of £2,000 per undocumented employee. However, the government has been made well aware that, since their implementation, employer sanctions have been suspected of deterring employers from engaging black and minority ethnic workers, whose immigration status is frequently presumed, often without any grounds, to be problematic. A joint report published by the CRE, the Refugee Council and JCWI in 1998 described how a 'culture of suspicion' had emerged as a consequence of the employer sanctions contained in the Asylum and Immigration Act 1996 (*A Culture of Suspicion: The Impact of Internal Immigration Controls*). The CBI and other business associations have signalled their concern about this proposal. They have pointed out that employers are naturally risk-averse in such matters, and that the threat of heavy fines for making an error as to immigration status could damage the other efforts which have been made to promote anti-discrimination and equal opportunity policies in the workplace.

Asylum

The strategy paper provides reassurance that the UK is fully committed to the 1951 Refugee Convention. What it does not do is demonstrate how the government intends to ensure that its obligation to provide protection to people in fear of persecution will be met in all cases. The government's standard for judging performance on asylum matters is not the protection of the rights guaranteed under the Convention, but the quite separate question of driving down the numbers of applications – the paper boasts a 67 per cent reduction in asylum claims from their peak in 2002. It is well known that the central difficulty facing asylum-seekers is finding a way to flee to safety in order to access the rights the 1951 Convention gives them. For the last eight years, the government has worked hard at measures aimed at closing down the routes used by asylum-seekers to attempt to reach the UK (by the imposition of visa regimes and direct airside transit visas; the introduction of high-tech freight-searching equipment in places like Calais and Ostend, etc). The government now proposes to exert 'much greater control over asylum-seekers' through the increased use of detention and surveillance throughout the asylum consideration process. The paper states that the aim is that, by the end of 2005, up to 30 per cent of asylum-seekers will be subject to detention and a fast-track process based upon the existing systems at Oakington and Harmondsworth.

These proposals are made in the knowledge that the current system for assessing asylum applications in the UK is considered by leading partners, such as the UNHCR, to be flawed in many respects. Officers are often poorly trained on the requirements of the law, and they are badly resourced in terms of background information on the countries which generate refugee movements. A recent report published by the Commons Select Committee on Public Accounting criticised the quality of IND's asylum case-working, pointing out that poor decisions led to a high level of successful legal challenges to refusals and removal decisions.

Limited leave and review No proper justification is given for the government's reversal of its decision in 1998 to grant immediate settlement to those who qualify as refugees under the Convention. The government now intends to reassess each case after five years. The pre-1998 system was criticised precisely because granting limited leave only led to prolonged uncertainty and anxiety for those already traumatised, because it undermined and delayed integration, and because it imposed the additional cost of processing a later settlement application. It is unclear why, in implementing this measure, the government should wish to undermine its own policy of the early and full integration of refugees into the social and economic life of the UK through its recently launched National Strategy for Refugee Integration. Nevertheless, the policy has been introduced (▶see 720).

For full details of the 'New Asylum Model' presently being implemented, ▶see 641–4.

Appeals

The strategy proposes the abolition of rights of appeal against refusals of entry clearance and leave to enter for both students and workers. For full details of the proposals in the 2005 Bill concerning appeal rights (obviously primary legislation is needed), ▶see the table on 1042–6 and see also below, 50–1.

Previous attempts by the government to oust or limit rights of appeal have proved highly controversial. With some exceptions, immigration rights of appeal have been steadily eroded since 1993, and this proposal represents yet another attempt to place immigration decision-making beyond the realms of proper accountability. The standard of entry clearance decision-making is often poor, and with students and workers forming the main plank of primary migration to the UK, it is essential that an official's decisions are subject to effective independent scrutiny. The proposed extension of the remit of the Entry Clearance Monitor, while it may enable the practices of various ECOs to be commented upon, will not, apparently, provide a remedy for individual injustices. Of course, should appeal rights be removed, applicants will be forced to resort to judicial review, which is more expensive (for all parties); less effective, in that the circumstances in which the court can intervene are much more limited; and, even if successful, will require the decision to be taken again, rather than simply reversing the decision, as would be the case if an appeal was allowed by the AIT.

The proposal to abolish the right to an oral hearing in family visit entry clearance appeals, and to limit those relations who can qualify as 'family' visitors who are entitled to the right of appeal, is unwarranted. A report by a government review team (*Review of Family Visitor Appeals*, June 2003) found that the success rate for oral appeals was 73 per cent, compared to 38 per cent for paper appeals. The disparity only reinforces the importance of retaining the right to an oral hearing in order to challenge incorrect decisions. For more details on family visit appeals, ▶see 1071–3.

Settlement

The suggestion that new English language and 'knowledge of life in the UK' tests will have to be taken before indefinite leave is granted causes concern. These proposed new requirements are similar to the tests recently intoduced in applications for British citizenship (▶see 1467–8). The government appears to intend, for example, that the spouses and children of persons settled in the UK will be expected to pass English language and 'knowledge of life in the UK' tests before being granted settlement. Until the government clarifies its intentions, JCWI is concerned that the proposals present new barriers to family reunification in the UK, which potentially infringe the right to respect for family life under Article 8 ECHR. It appears that refugees, who have established their inability to return to their country, may also have to take these tests before being granted indefinite leave.

Secure Borders

As the core of its work on 'secure borders', the strategy proposes to continue the work done in recent years on pre-entry controls. The intention is to fingerprint all visa applicants by 2008, to screen those travellers coming from 'high-risk' areas for tuberculosis, to expand the network of Airline Liaison Officers (ALOs – UK immigration officials operating in overseas airports) and to continue to deploy immigration officers in France and Belgium. There is no attempted evaluation of the effectiveness of this work, other than the claimed success of ALOs in preventing 33,000 people boarding flights to the UK in 2003.

If the recent work is to be the basis for a continued five-year strategy, one would expect to have seen a more detailed analysis. For example, knowing that 33,000 persons were refused the opportunity to board flights to the UK is of little value without knowing who these people were, by what criteria their 'undesirability' was assessed, and what are the wider consequences of the action. Were these individuals a threat to national security? Were they asylum-seekers desperately attempting to flee and, of necessity, not properly documented? How much has the UK lost in potential tourist income by the negative perception of the UK caused by bureaucratic heavy-handedness? The strategy might also have considered the implications of the judgment of the House of Lords in the recent *European Roma Rights Centre* case, in which the Lords ruled that the actions of British immigration officials based at Prague airport in 2001 had unlawfully discriminated against ethnic Roma Czech nationals, and were contrary to their human rights (▶see further on this case 892–3). Without a serious, honest audit of the measures it has already taken, a pre-entry strategy of 'more of the same' is likely to meet with further legal challenge.

Summary: a shake of the dice

The strategy paper contains little by way of new thinking on immigration or asylum. There is no sense from the paper that the government is interested in a proper evaluation of the effect of its immigration policies over the past eight years. What the recent period has demonstrated again and again is the capacity of immigration policy to generate conflict with other declared objectives – for example, on questions of social cohesion and diversity, equality of opportunity, multiculturalism, pluralism, human rights, cooperative foreign policy and international development. None of this receives proper discussion in the strategy. It is a strategy driven only by a myopic interpretation of Britain's economic interests, and the perceived need to demonstrate that, in the UK, immigration is heavily 'controlled'.

It is accepted on all sides that migration is essential for the life of the UK. Getting immigration policies right presents both a challenge and an opportunity. Only by acknowledging the realities of migration, and properly analysing the consequences of its policy, does the government stand a chance of developing a strategy which meets both. What the government has produced is a strategy that fails to assess the impact of its proposals – including in relation to its avowed aim of using migration to promote the needs of the economy. It fails to reward responsibilities with rights, and risks depreciating yet further the confidence of the migrant community in Britain's commitment to fairness and integrity. While the government may wish to liberalise the betting laws, it should not gamble with Britain's future.

IMMIGRATION, ASYLUM AND NATIONALITY BILL 2005

After the general election in May 2005, the government announced that it would be introducing a new immigration and asylum bill to parliament. The proposals are summarised below, together with JCWI's commentary on them. Our analysis is based on the Bill as it was published prior to first reading in the House of Commons on 22 June 2005. We have also incorporated most of the government's proposed amendments as it entered Committee stage on 18 October 2005.

The 2005 Bill was introduced as 'tackling abuse and implementing change'. It is intended to provide legislative provisions for important parts of the five-year strategy set out above (▶see 34–42). Below we look at key measures in the Bill, some of which are also dealt with elsewhere in the Handbook as indicated.

A full analysis of the changes to appeal rights is contained in the tables at ▶1042–9.

Removing appeal rights

The 2005 Bill contains sweeping measures excluding important rights of appeal. The proposals include:

- removal of the current right of appeal against decisions by the Home Office to extend, vary or curtail leave. This potentially excludes appeal rights for those seeking to stay further in the UK as students, in order to work here or even to stay as family members;
- removal of the present right of appeal against entry clearance refusals except for people applying to join or visit certain family members settled in the UK.

The proposed abolition of appeal rights and the injustices this will cause are discussed in the context of the five-year strategy above (▶see 48). In her report issued in February 2005, the Entry Clearance Monitor, Fiona Lindsley, expressed concern at the 'dramatic rise' in the refusal rate for non-settlement visas which has more than doubled since 2000. She was especially concerned over refusal rates for students which, in 2003–2004, stood at over 50 per cent at 16 British posts worldwide. In the parliamentary debate when the Bill was given its second reading (5 July 2005), the Home Secretary explained the reasoning behind the removal of appeal rights, which he justified as necessary to deal with applications 'in the most effective and efficient way possible'. This was despite figures being put to him in the course of the debate that over 60 per cent of student appeals in which representation is provided by the Immigration Advisory Service are successful and that in 90 per cent of Sheffield University's challenges the refusal was withdrawn.

Despite assurances from the government that they aim to increase the transparency and quality of decisions, it is JCWI's view that the removal of judicial scrutiny is far more likely to have the opposite effect. Withdrawal of appeal rights reduces rather than enhances accountability.

A particularly damaging provision in the Bill is the removal of continuing leave provisions that will effectively make those who decide to appeal against Home Office decisions to refuse in-time in-country applications, into overstayers (▶see 1045–6). ILPA states in its briefing that this will have:

'…the appalling effect of criminalizing all people refused extensions of stay in the UK…they may be detained and removed. If they do not leave the UK, they are committing a criminal offence… This is not streamlining the appeal system as the government claims. It is subverting and stacking the appeal system.' (ILPA briefing, 10 October 2005)

The Bill does however include measures to protect 'status' appeals for those refused further leave as refugees and a new appeal right for refugees whose indefinite leave is revoked.

For full details of these proposed changes to the appeal system, ▶see 1041–6. For further commentary on the proposals as they affect family visitors in particular, ▶see 1071–3.

Strengthening penalties against employers

The new Bill aims to 'tackle illegal working' by:

- a new civil penalty for employers who employ those who are not 'legally allowed' to work in the UK;
- a code of practice to determine when the penalty should be imposed and how much it should be;
- a new criminal offence of employing someone subject to immigration control 'knowing' that they are not allowed to work in the UK.

There will be a right of appeal for employers against the proposed new penalty.

The Bill does not replace the existing criminal penalties under section 8 of the Asylum and Immigration Act 1996 which sets out the present employer sanctions (for full details about section 8 and the defences available, ▶see 496–500). The existing sanction under section 8 was substantially amended as recently as May 2004. It appears that, if the proposals are passed, they will sit alongside existing sanctions against employers. The negative effect of imposing sanctions upon those employing those subject to immigration control has been apparent since the 1996 Act. Frequently offers of employment to prospective employees whose immigration status is not adequately understood are withheld and sometimes existing employees are dismissed.

The position of migrant workers will inevitably be further eroded by the Bill which also proposes to extend employers' obligations from checking immigration status at the point of engagement, to monitoring that status throughout the entire period of employment. It is clear that this will result in the constant monitoring of non-British employees resulting in a culture of suspicion and intimidation as well as a significant disincentive to employers to take on people who, although at the time of their engagement are permitted to work, are viewed as ongoing liabilities. Groups who may be particularly affected are: asylum-seekers who had permission to work; refugees granted limited leave to remain; family members of settled persons with limited (probationary) leave; and students.

Powers to gather more information

The 2005 Bill extends the powers of immigration officers and Home Office officials to:

- retain documents from passengers and require them to provide biometric information such as iris and finger prints;
- request passengers lists of ships and aircraft;
- share information with other departments such as the Inland Revenue and Customs.

JCWI has voiced its concerns about the growth of state surveillance in the affairs of people whose activities do not give rise to concerns in the areas of protecting public order and security. If information held by, for example, the Inland Revenue and Customs, does not give rise to a prosecution for an offence under tax and customs laws, a breach of the right to privacy could be created if that department shares information on a routine basis with other departments or authorities.

Anti-terror measures

In his written statement of 12 October 2005, the Home Secretary indicated that he would add new clauses to the Bill in the Standing

Committee which would supplement anti-terror measures and which are not covered by the Terrorism Bill introduced in October 2005. He indicated that he would add new clauses to the 2005 Bill to:

- restrict the grant of asylum to those whose conduct is covered by the new list of 'unacceptable behaviours' which sets out new criteria defining when someone's presence in the UK is not 'conducive to the public good' (for details of this list, ▶see 1019–20);

- deprive a person of their British citizenship, where this is 'conducive to the public good' in accordance with the new unacceptable behaviour criteria discussed above;

- remove in-country rights of appeal against deportation orders in national security cases.

JCWI's view is that deprivation of citizenship must be a measure of last resort which cannot and should not be used lightly. The list of 'unacceptable behaviours' is so wide, that it is inevitable that this power will be misused with little prospect of redress. Excluding an asylum-seekers' rights under the Refugee Convention on similar grounds is unnecessary and unacceptable, given that the criteria for exclusion is specifically set out in the Convention itself (▶see 624–6).

OTHER PROPOSALS FOR CHANGE

Aside from the five-year strategy, there are a number of other proposals for change in the near future, set out below.

Healthcare

In May 2004, the Department of Health launched a consultation on new proposals to exclude 'overseas visitors' from primary (i.e. GPs) healthcare services. Under these proposals, both visitors and those who do not have leave to enter or remain in the UK would only have access to emergency or immediately necessary treatment. The proposals are justified in the consultation paper on the basis that,

'...the NHS is a national institution and not an international one. It is there to provide free treatment for those who live here and not for those who do not.'

Included in the proposed category of 'overseas visitors' are failed asylum-seekers and undocumented migrants, many of whom are unable to return, and are among the most excluded in British society. Although these groups are presently not expressly entitled to primary healthcare (mainly GP services), GPs have a broad discretion to give treatment to them (for further details of access to healthcare services, ▶see 1328–35). The Department of Health proposes to prevent GP and other primary care practices from registering ineligible categories of people as patients.

Undocumented migrants and failed asylum-seekers are at risk of illness associated with poor diet and poor living conditions (such as heart disease and diabetes). They will be denied all medical services until their health reaches crisis point and they are admitted to hospital as an emergency. A policy of preventing failed asylum-seekers from accessing certain services is particularly unfair.

In JCWI's response to the consultation paper (submitted in August 2004 and available on the JCWI website www.jcwi.org.uk), we identify the particularly vulnerable groups as pregnant women and nursing mothers, children, and those with HIV/AIDS, as well as others with chronic communicable diseases. Even if the present proposals are not intended to be discriminatory, JCWI is concerned that ethnic minorities in the settled community may experience discrimination, as frontline staff make judgments about eligibility based on personal perceptions of race, nationality, dress and language ability. The government has not yet provided a formal response to the consultation, and there has been no indication as to when the proposals will be implemented.

Identity Cards

The proposed restrictions on access to healthcare outlined above are designed to coincide with the commencement of new powers for public services officials, such as hospital and GP staff, to demand identification from foreign nationals. The Identity Cards Bill, which was presented to parliament in November 2004, requires specified categories of people to register themselves on a new National Identity Register. The government has indicated that the first category subject to compulsory registration will be all foreign nationals who have been in the UK for over three months. Under the Bill, the provision of public services to those who must obtain an ID card can be made conditional on the production of the card.

JCWI has been lobbying strongly against the Bill, on the grounds that the imposition of a compulsory scheme upon foreign nationals may be racially discriminatory. The Parliamentary Joint Committee on Human Rights has agreed that the scheme raises significant questions of disproportionate and discriminatory interference with private life under Articles 8 and 14 ECHR. Independent research on the effect of ID cards in other European countries shows that such a scheme risks promoting a general culture of suspicion towards the black and other ethnic communities. In Germany, officers were found to be demanding ID from ethnic-minority persons disproportionately; and in France, where carrying an ID card is completely voluntary, discrimination was found to occur in the implementation of ID checks by French senior officials.

The ID Cards Bill is due to be presented to the House of Lords in November 2005.

'Specified nationals' list

The list of countries whose nationals are 'specified' nationals was contained in Appendix 3 to the immigration rules. 'Specified' nationals require an entry clearance in order to come to the UK for more than six months for *any* purpose. The Home Office's intention has always been that this requirement will apply to all 'non-visa nationals', so that everyone coming to the UK for more than six months will need an entry clearance unless they are exempt or they claim asylum in the UK. From 13 November 2003, ten countries were designated so that their nationals were 'specified nationals' (see HC 1224). That was phase one of the changes. Phase two came into force on 13 November 2005 with a short 'grace' period to 13 January 2006 (see HC 645). This means that all non-EEA, non visa nationals coming to the UK for any purpose who intend to stay for more than six months, need entry clearance. Because all non-visa national countries are now effectively 'specified', this phrase has been dropped from the rules. It is still used in the *Handbook* because this change is just after our main cut off date but should now be read with this wide meaning (▶80–3).

Civil Partnership Act 2004

The Civil Partnership Act 2004 is in force from 5 December 2005. The Home Office recognises that couples who register their partnership should be entitled to equal treatment across a range of legal matters. It has amended the immigration rules from 5 December 2005 so as to treat civil partners and proposed civil partners in the same way as spouses and fiancé(e)s (HC 582, ▶see 3000–1).

MAKING IMMIGRATION WORK FOR EVERYONE

Although the future changes discussed in this chapter are driven by the policy objective of restricting the entry of those wishing to come to the UK, while strictly managing and controlling those who are already here, there is general agreement among all the major political parties that migration brings significant benefits to the UK. We have examined and criticised the government's strategy here. In April 2005 JCWI published its own recommendations for a just, workable immigration policy, entitled 'Making immigration work for everyone'. Its recommendations are summarised in a leaflet that can be downloaded from JCWI's website, at www.jcwi.org.uk, and are set out below.

A modern, progressive immigration policy

A bold and progressive immigration policy is required. At the heart of the policy is the need to afford migrants rights equal to the standards expected from a modern, democratic nation in the twenty-first century. This includes the following:

- Recognition of the needs of the many people fleeing persecution and other forms of harm, with a willingness to provide for those needs in practice, not just in words. They should be provided with accessible routes of entry and humane determination and integration procedures, which remedy rather than compound their previous experiences of detention, fear and stigmatism.

- A thorough appraisal of the contribution of migration to the British economy, taking account not just of existing narrow demands, but of the role that migration plays in nurturing future potential in the UK, and supporting the relief of poverty in developing countries through remittances and returning skills.

- A humane regime of rights for migrants who have become established in the UK: comprehensive rights of family reunion, unhindered access to public services such as healthcare and benefits for those who require them, and the right to qualify for permanent stay.

JCWI also believes that immigration policy should be an integral part of the government's foreign policy. Protection for those who need it, combined with flexible migration, increases mutual understanding and can promote economic prosperity, development and peace internationally. We also believe that the time has come to de-couple the immigration debate from the heat of political feuding, which results in knee-jerk measures of increasing severity that benefit no-one. It is time to establish an immigration system based on core principles, upon which it may be possible to achieve consensus, and for operational and other decision-making processes to be handled by an independent body directly responsible to parliament.

JCWI'S RECOMMENDATIONS FOR AN IMMIGRATION POLICY THAT WORKS FOR EVERYONE

Prosperity and protection

Immigration policy should be determined by four fundamental priorities:

- the obligation to provide human rights protection to those seeking refuge in the UK;

- recognition that economic migration brings benefits to the UK and promotes increased prosperity across society;

- a robust system of fundamental human and civil rights, which underpins the position of all migrants in the UK, whatever their status;

- the promotion of global economic development and peace, based on equal access to the UK.

Ten recommendations for a workable, responsible policy

The UK should:

- fulfil its obligations under international human rights treaties such as the Geneva Convention, and admit its fair share of the world's refugees;
- create an independent decision-making body on immigration, directly responsible to parliament and not the Home Office;
- end the arbitrary detention of asylum-seekers and the compulsory dispersal of asylum-seekers away from their sources of community support;
- help ensure immediate access to employment and training opportunities for asylum-seekers;
- ensure user-friendly visa procedures for all persons wishing to migrate to the UK for the purpose of work and/or business;
- offer the right to reside to anyone who is employed or running a business, and offer the right for all migrant workers to be joined by dependent family members;
- ensure that public services and social security are available to everyone living and working in the UK, and to members of their family;
- ensure a full and unhindered right to marry, found a family, and settle in the UK;
- review all immigration policies periodically to ensure that they have not become instruments of institutional discrimination;
- combat discrimination against the free movement of people from the poorer regions of the world, and ensure that the UK's immigration system promotes the economic prosperity of all countries, as well as greater international co-operation and stability.

3   Immigration advice

The need for well-trained advisers who can provide accurate immigration advice has never been greater. The pace of change in immigration legislation and its complexity makes it vital that anyone who has an immigration query seeks help from the right sources. This chapter is divided into three parts. For those seeking legal advice, the first part of the chapter (▶below) sets out how to find an immigration adviser in England and Wales, Scotland and Northern Ireland, and the different levels of advice that are currently available.

The second part of the chapter sets out the regulatory framework that has developed to govern immigration advisers (▶63–7). It sets out the regulatory mechanisms that the Office of the Immigration Services Commissioner employs, how to make a complaint against different types of adviser, and the disciplinary powers of the Immigration Services Tribunal.

The last part of the chapter looks briefly at the complex system of legal aid funding that has developed in England and Wales, including the different legal aid schemes available and the contracts under which advisers can obtain public funding from the Legal Services Commission to give out immigration advice (▶67–73). It also discusses the new mandatory Accreditation Scheme developed by the Legal Services Commission and the Law Society to accredit advisers in England and Wales (▶73–4).

FINDING AN ADVISER

Advice in England and Wales

Community Legal Service

Advisers in England and Wales who can give out free legal advice belong to the Community Legal Service (CLS) network, ▶see 61–2 for those seeking advice in Scotland and Northern Ireland and the table at ▶62–3 for a summary. The government set up the Community Legal Service (CLS) in order to improve access to, and the quality of, legal services and to base the delivery of services on local needs and priorities. The CLS Quality Mark is issued to advisers who can demonstrate that they have met certain minimum standards laid down by the Legal Services Commission (LSC), which is the statutory body that operates the CLS and also provides legal aid funding for specialist advice.

Those seeking basic immigration advice can approach organisations that form part of the CLS network and have one of two types of 'General Help' Quality mark. These organisations can give advice at the following levels:

'General Help' General Help normally constitutes one-off advice for which there is no ongoing case file. Advisers in this category can only give out very basic assistance, which may include filling in forms such as passport applications. Such providers will often refer or 'signpost' someone on to a more experienced adviser.

'General Help including Casework' Straightforward work, which may require on-going support such as naturalisation or travel document applications that require form-filling and other basic correspondence fall into this category. Organisations providing immigration advice at this level must possess a Quality Mark specifically in the immigration category. To be certified at this level, they must have at least one person conducting immigration work for at least 12 hours per week. Citizens Advice bureaux and generalist advice centres are typically funded to carry out this level of work. More complex work should be referred to a provider who has a contract with the Legal Services Commission to provide 'Specialist Help'.

'Specialist Help' Organisations with the Specialist Help Quality Mark typically include solicitors in private practice, law centres, some Citizens Advice bureaux and specialist advice agencies. Free specialist immigration advice funded by legal aid administered by the LSC may be available from those organisations that possess the Specialist Quality Mark and have entered into a contract with the LSC. All organisations that provide legally aided immigration and asylum advice must now comply with the stringent requirements of the Immigration and Asylum Accreditation Scheme and are regularly audited by the LSC. For more details about legal aid funding ▶see 67–73.

Quality Mark holders also have access to telephone consultancy lines funded by the LSC. JCWI provides such an LSC-funded consultancy line (telephone 0845 602 1020) and this line is open from 10am to 1pm Monday to Friday. Clarification on complex issues concerning immigration, asylum and nationality law is provided by this service.

These solicitors and other agencies form part of the Community Legal Service network and are listed in the CLS Directory which is organised into geographical regions across England and Wales and can be accessed via their website (www.clsdirect.org.uk). The CLS has also set up a telephone call centre, which can provide details of appropriate advisers, ▶see the table at 62–3 for details.

Other advisers

The Office of the Immigration Services Commissioner (OISC) was set up to regulate immigration advisers who do not belong to a professional body such as the Law Society, which regulates solicitors. It regulates non-solicitor advice agencies in both the private and voluntary sector. Details of how to contact private advisers and advisers in the voluntary sector who are approved by the OISC to give immigration advice can be obtained from the OISC and their website has a useful 'adviser finder' section. ▶See the table at 62–3 for details.

The OISC has divided immigration and asylum work into three levels: Initial Advice (level 1), Casework (level 2), and Specialist (level 3). These levels broadly reflect the standards set by the CLS Quality Mark scheme (▶see above). Within each level various categories of advice are identified. The competence that advisers must demonstrate in order to meet the OISC criteria at each level are set out in the OISC's 'Guidance on Competence'.

Advice in Scotland and Northern Ireland

The OISC regulatory scheme applies to advisers throughout the UK, including Scotland and Northern Ireland, and details of approved advisers can be obtained from the OISC. However, this list will not include solicitors, barristers (known as 'advocates' in Scotland) or legal executives.

Scotland

Legal aid in Scotland is provided not by the LSC but by the Scottish Legal Aid Board under the Legal Aid (Scotland) Act 1986. Provided that the person needing help is financially eligible, assistance towards solicitors' fees for advice and help can be obtained through the 'Advice and Assistance' (also known as the 'Green Form') scheme and representation before the Asylum and Immigration Tribunal can be provided under the 'Assistance By Way of Representation' (ABWOR) scheme. Civil legal aid is available for cases which reach the Scottish Court of Session and the House of Lords. Any solicitor in Scotland can provide immigration advice under the above legal aid schemes. However, only a solicitor registered with the Board to provide criminal legal assistance (criminal legal aid or advice and assistance on a criminal matter) can provide legal assistance in connection with any criminal aspect of an immigration problem.

The Law Society of Scotland regulates solicitors, some of whom may provide immigration advice. The Law Society of Scotland can be contacted for the names of solicitors who provide this type of advice (▶see the table below).

Northern Ireland

In Northern Ireland, legal aid funding is managed by the Law Society of Northern Ireland, which is the professional body for solicitors there, under the Legal Aid, Advice and Assistance (Northern Ireland) Order 1981. Provided the person requiring the advice is financially eligible, legal fees are subsidised by the 'Advice and Assistance' scheme. 'Civil legal aid' is available for actions in the High Court and above. There is no list of solicitors who provide immigration advice but the Law Society can be contacted for details of solicitors who operate the legal aid scheme, see details in the table below.

WHERE TO OBTAIN ADVICE

England and Wales

Community Legal Service (CLS)

The CLS Directory contains details of private solicitors' firms and not-for-profit advice agencies that are approved legal aid suppliers of immigration advice. A local adviser can be obtained through the:

- CLS Directory Line: telephone 0845 608 1122;
- CLS Direct website: www.clsdirect.org.uk;
- CLS Regional Directories (13 in number); these can be found in local libraries, advice centres and solicitors' firms.

Office of the Immigration Services Commissioner (OISC)

The OISC has a list of all not-for-profit sector advice agencies and private advisers (but not solicitors' firms) who are approved by them to give out immigration advice. The list is held on their website:

- www.oisc.org.uk under a useful section called 'Adviser Finder';
- or telephone their help line: 0845 000 0046.

Scotland

The OISC website and help line (see above) can be consulted for non-solicitor agencies.

For solicitors' firms, the Law Society of Scotland provides names of firms who give immigration/nationality advice. Details can be obtained from its website:

- www.lawscot.org.uk under the 'Firms and Branches' section;
- or telephone: 0131 226 7411. Ask for the Records Department, which will be able to provide contact details of three solicitors from its list at any one time.

It should be noted that the solicitors' firms on the list are not specifically approved by the OISC or the Law Society to give out immigration advice but they will usually be able to apply to the Scottish Legal Aid Board for funding.

Northern Ireland

The OISC website and help line (see above) can be consulted for non-solicitor agencies.

For solicitors' firms, there is no specific list of solicitors who specialise in immigration law, although the website of the Northern Ireland Legal Services Commission contains a list of solicitors who operate the legal aid scheme.

> The Law Society of Northern Ireland can then advise on which of these solicitors specialise in immigration law.
> - telephone 028 9023 1614.

REGULATION OF IMMIGRATION ADVISERS

There are two important control mechanisms, which ensure that advisers are sufficiently expert in immigration law:

Regulation of Immigration Advisers by the Office of the Immigration Services Commissioner (OISC) Part 5 of the Immigration and Asylum Act 1999 imposes restrictions on who is able to give immigration advice and regulates those who do provide advice. The OISC has laid down a Code of Standards and Rules and ensures that all those it regulates comply with them.

Accreditation by the Legal Services Commission (LSC) and Law Society under the Immigration and Asylum Accreditation Scheme The LSC provides publicly funded (legally aided) immigration advice through a network of solicitors and advisers in England and Wales. Advisers who did not obtain accreditation by August 2005 are not allowed by the LSC to give publicly funded advice. The Accreditation Scheme is discussed further below (▶73–4).

Those who can provide advice

Under the Immigration and Asylum Act 1999, no one may provide immigration 'advice or services' (see below for definitions) unless they are either 'qualified' to do so, or they are exempted from restriction by the OISC. Persons who are 'qualified' are:

- practising solicitors, barristers or legal executives and those acting on behalf of and under their supervision. The definition also applies to similar professionals of other EEA states;
- other advisers who do not fall into the above category but who are registered with the OISC or who are acting on behalf of and supervised by a person or body which is registered. All immigration advisers who charge privately for their services must apply for registration. They have to comply with the OISC's Rules and Code of Standards (see below) and they must pay a registration fee, the amount of which depends upon the number of individual advisers in the organisation. Registration may be restricted to carrying out particular kinds of immigration work or even to particular groups of clients.

A person who is not 'qualified' to provide the advice may be exempted from the restrictions by the OISC and therefore be able to provide advice and services. Non-qualified advisers in the not-for-profit sector who provide advice free of charge must apply for exemption. In doing so, they must show compliance with the Code of Standards but not the Rules (see below).

Applications for registration or for certificates of exemption are made by completing an OISC application pack. Applications are first considered on the papers and are then followed up by a visit to the premises in order to carry out an audit.

Immigration advice and services The definition of providing immigration advice or services under the 1999 Act is broad. The provision of general information that does not relate to an individual's case is not included. In order to constitute 'advice' the information given must relate to a particular individual. Providing immigration 'services' to a person means making representations on their behalf to a court (or to the immigration appellate authorities), to the Home Office or any other government department.

OISC Rules and Code of Standards It is the general duty of the Immigration Services Commissioner to promote good practice by those who provide immigration advice or immigration services. To assist the OISC in its regulatory functions, in October 2000, the Commissioner issued 'The Commissioner's Rules' and the 'Code of Standards'. The Rules relate to the conduct, professional practice and discipline of advisers and make requirements in terms of the fees charged and the accounting and complaints procedures, which they operate. The Code of Standards sets a benchmark for the performance of advisers against which the competence and quality of an organisation or adviser may be judged. The Code mirrors many of the CLS Quality Mark requirements.

The regulatory scheme applies to those who provide immigration advice or services to individual clients 'in the course of business, whether or not for profit'. Therefore, those who advise or represent people in a personal capacity only, such as friends and relatives, are not covered by the regulatory scheme. However, those advisory organisations which only provide immigration advice incidental to their core advice duties, for example, welfare advisers, must be aware that the regulatory scheme applies. They should therefore either refer clients who need immigration advice to an alternative provider ('signposting') rather than provide specific advice to an individual, or they should apply to the Commissioner for registration or exemption.

Advice surgeries run by Members of Parliament, the Immigration and Nationality Directorate of the Home Office and other government officials are also not required to register with the OISC.

The OISC has made it clear that those who advise solely on work permits and other employment-related immigration applications have to comply with regulation requirements because work-permit advice is inextricably linked with immigration advice. Universities and their student unions will often advise students on obtaining or extending leave in the UK to study. They are specifically exempted by ministerial order from having to register with the OISC. However, similar to not-for-profit organisations, they have to demonstrate that they can comply with the OISC's Code of Standards. Health sector bodies are also exempted but similarly have to meet set standards.

Employers on the other hand, whose human resource departments will often be advising prospective and existing employees, neither have to register nor meet any of the standards laid down by the OISC.

It is a criminal offence for any person to provide immigration advice or services unless they are either qualified or exempted. The maximum penalty for providing advice in contravention of these regulations is imprisonment for two years and a fine (s91 1999 Act). The 2004 Act now gives the OISC power to apply to a justice of the peace for a warrant to enter and search any premises which the OISC has reasonable grounds for suspecting contain material of substantial value to the investigation of such a criminal offence. The OISC can also seize such material even if it is subject to legal privilege. An offence can also now be committed if a person not allowed to provide immigration advice or services advertises their services.

Complaints against advisers and representatives

Those who are dissatisfied with the immigration advice that they have received or the way in which their case has been conducted are usually advised to pursue a complaint in the first instance in accordance with any internal complaints procedures laid down by the organisation or firm advising them. If a complaint has not been handled internally to the satisfaction of the individual, then these complaints procedures should direct them to an external body that is able to deal with the matter.

Complaints to professional bodies

Those who are being advised by practising solicitors, barristers or legal executives will be able to refer a complaint to the professional body governing their adviser. Members of these professions are all regulated by their own professional bodies; the three Law Societies, which regulate solicitors throughout the UK; the Bar Council in England, the Faculty of Advocates in Scotland and the Bar Council of Northern Ireland, which regulate barristers; and the Institute of Legal Executives.

Under powers given by the 1999 Act, certain disciplinary bodies can be given the power to review the actions of advisers specifically in relation to the provision of immigration advice and restrict, suspend or prohibit them entirely from providing such advice.

Complaints in relation to immigration advice provided by members of the professional bodies discussed above can also be made directly to the OISC. For those who wish to make a complaint against their adviser, ▶see

1500 for contact details of the OISC and the professional bodies to whom a complaint can be made.

Disciplinary action by the OISC

An important function of the OISC is to handle and monitor complaints and for this purpose it has set up a complaints scheme. Complaints can be made directly to the OISC against an adviser or representative governed by the OISC relating to their competence or fitness, or alleged breaches by them of the OISC's Rules or Code (including the level of fees charged). Complaints may also be made to the OISC against solicitors, barristers and legal executives about alleged breaches of their own professional rules. If a similar issue comes to the attention of the OISC, they do not have to wait until a complaint is actually made but may investigate it on their own initiative.

The OISC does not have the power to consider complaints about those representing government departments such as the Home Office. Such complaints should be made to the relevant section within a government department, and may be made to an MP who can forward the matter to the Parliamentary Ombudsman. ▶See Chapter 38 for full details about Home Office complaints procedures and the Ombudsman.

Powers of OISC Having decided to uphold a complaint, the OISC may:

- if the organisation is registered to advise and the matter is serious enough, require that organisation to apply for continued registration straight away so that their fitness for continued registration can be reassessed, or simply indicate that the decision on the complaint should be considered next time that organisation applies for their registration to be continued;
- if the organisation is exempt from registration, consider whether to withdraw the exemption;
- if the person is a registered or exempt adviser, lay a disciplinary charge before the Immigration Services Tribunal which has even greater powers (▶see below);
- if the adviser is a member of one of the professional bodies (solicitor, barrister, legal executive) or is supervised or employed by such, refer the complaint to their own professional body (Law Society, Bar Council, Institute of Legal Executives). The OISC must also report to the Secretary of State if it considers that a professional body is failing to provide effective regulation of its members in relation to their provision of immigration advice and services. The 2004 Act has strengthened the power of the OISC to obtain information from the professional bodies, and failure to comply with OISC requests can result in the government removing that particular professional body from the list of professional bodies whose members are deemed to be 'qualified'.

Immigration Services Tribunal

The 1999 Act created the Immigration Services Tribunal as well as the OISC. The Tribunal holds hearings to determine disciplinary charges concerning registered or exempted advisers, which are referred to it by the Commissioner. In addition to the powers of the Commissioner, the Tribunal can:

- direct the adviser to repay fees where the fee charged was unreasonable;
- fine the adviser;
- restrict the immigration advice or services, which the adviser can provide;
- suspend the adviser from providing any immigration advice or services;
- prohibit the adviser from providing immigration advice or services in the future.

The Tribunal also hears appeals against decisions by the OISC to refuse an application for registration or to renew registration by potential advisers and against decisions by the OISC to withdraw an exemption from an adviser.

LEGAL AID FUNDING IN ENGLAND AND WALES

Those who are eligible for legal aid can get free immigration advice and assistance with their cases. In England and Wales the legal aid fund is called the Community Legal Service Fund and is administered by the Legal Services Commission (LSC). The power of the LSC to provide public funding (which we also refer to as legal aid) comes from the Access to Justice Act 1999 and more specifically the Funding Code, a statutory instrument that lays down the specific criteria for the various types of legal aid mentioned below.

The LSC will only fund work done by advisers who have entered into a contract with the LSC to provide specialist immigration advice. The contract is called the 'General Civil Contract'. There are two types of contract depending on whether the adviser's organisation is a solicitors' firm or a not-for-profit body. A prerequisite to entering into a General Civil Contract with the LSC is holding a Specialist Quality Mark. The various levels of Quality Mark are discussed at ▶60. Advisers who hold contracts with the LSC to provide legally aided immigration advice are referred to by the LSC as 'suppliers'.

Different legal aid rules govern the provision of immigration advice in Scotland and Northern Ireland, ▶see 61–2 above for a brief description of the different legal aid bodies in Scotland and Northern Ireland and the types of cases they fund.

The Funding Code sets out the different levels of legal aid that are available in England and Wales, of which the following are relevant for immigration matters:

- **'Legal Help'** for initial advice and for help with immigration matters where no decisions are being appealed (▶see 69–70);
- **'Controlled Legal Representation'** for appeals before the Asylum and Immigration Tribunal (▶see 71–3);
- **'Legal Representation'** for cases before the High Court, Court of Appeal and the House of Lords (▶see 73).

The Funding Code and the two General Civil Contracts are lengthy and we do not discuss them in detail in the *Handbook*. Where necessary we have referred to legal aid restrictions, for example in relation to asylum procedures in Chapter 22 ▶see 650, 659, 676–7, 689. Below, we to give a brief overview, and practitioners who have a contract with the LSC for immigration advice should refer to the contract specification relevant to them and the Funding Code.

The Legal Help and Controlled Legal Representation schemes are funded out of a core legal aid budget allocated to the LSC for the provision of immigration advice. With the ever-growing complexity of immigration legislation, and an increasingly tight grip exerted by the government on those seeking to come into or stay in the UK, the need for expert legal advice for those with immigration problems has grown, with a consequential increase in the immigration legal aid budget over some years. However, the political position taken by the government has been to severely restrict the legal aid budget for immigration and asylum in order to 'de-rail the gravy train of legal aid' (Prime Minister's speech to the Labour Party Conference, September 2003).

In June 2003 the Department for Constitutional Affairs (DCA) consulted on proposed changes to the General Civil Contract designed to restrict the amount of time that an adviser could spend in assisting an immigration client and hence the amount of money they would get paid. Despite strong opposition, not only from practitioners' groups and professional bodies, but also from refugee organisations and immigrant welfare groups such as JCWI, the changes were brought into effect during the period March to May 2004.

From April 2000, when the LSC introduced mandatory contracts for all immigration advisers who wished to give out publicly funded advice, until the changes were implemented in 2004, immigration advisers had powers devolved to them by the LSC. These devolved powers allowed advisers to grant themselves time and cost extensions to initial limits laid down by the LSC without having to revert back to them for permission. Under the changes implemented in 2004, these devolved powers were effectively removed from all but a few suppliers and financial limits were re-drawn. The main changes are as follows.

- A financial threshold for Legal Help of five hours for asylum cases and three hours for non-asylum cases. Devolved powers to exceed these new thresholds were removed. Any more work, which needs to be carried out prior to a substantive decision by the immigration authorities, can only be carried out with the prior authority of the LSC.

- The withdrawal of funding for attendance at Home Office asylum interviews, except in certain defined circumstances, (▶see 659 for further details).

- The removal of devolved powers to grant Controlled Legal Representation to conduct legally aided appeals work (save for selected suppliers).

- The requirement for all lawyers and advisers to be 'accredited' by the LSC (initially by April 2005) if they wish to provide legally aided immigration advice.

The effect of the changes has been a withdrawal by many firms of solicitors and not-for-profit organisations such as law centres from providing legally aided immigration advice because they have found it increasingly difficult to provide good quality advice within the financial constraints imposed by the LSC. The net effect on clients (many of whom are vulnerable people in need of protection, facing removal action, or are trying to exercise fundamental family reunion rights) has been a reduction in the availability of specialist legal advice. The impact of the changes has been documented by Bail for Immigration Detainees and Asylum Aid in their report, *Justice Denied, Asylum and Immigration Legal Aid, A System in Crisis*, published in April 2005.

The Legal Help Scheme

Free legal advice under the Legal Help Scheme is available in relation to most immigration matters if two basic tests are satisfied. To find out whether or not someone qualifies for Legal Help for a particular immigration problem, the individual should contact the advice provider. Where a person does not qualify for Legal Help, they may have to pay privately for assistance.

Means and 'sufficient benefit' tests

Firstly, eligibility is restricted to those who have little or no income or savings. Financial eligibility levels are set by the LSC and are varied from time to time. Secondly, the adviser has to assess whether or not the client will benefit sufficiently by the provision of legal assistance (the 'sufficient benefit' test). This test is designed to prevent work being carried out in relation to matters which demonstrate no real legal issue. Arguably, any query related to bringing someone to the UK, staying in the UK (asylum and non-asylum) and British nationality questions should satisfy this test. However, the LSC has stated that 'simple form filling' such as passport, travel document and citizenship applications will not be legally aided, unless an issue of law arises.

When conducting the 'sufficient benefit test', advisers are instructed by the LSC to adopt the 'private client approach' set out below with the aim of preventing advisers from giving out advice in certain types of cases that in the LSC's view, do not justify public funding. The LSC's reasoning behind the sufficient benefit test is set out in their General Civil Contract (Immigration Specification):

'The test is intended to prevent you starting or continuing to carry out work where there is no real legal issue in relation to which the client will benefit from the provision of Legal Help. You should adopt the private client approach, that is, would a reasonable privately paying client of moderate means pay for this as legal advice? This means for example you should not be providing Legal Help where the client's claim is clearly hopeless, vexatious or would be an abuse of process or where the client is seeking advice on non-legal matters.' (13.2.10 para. 3(c) General Civil Contract (Immigration) (NFP spec)).

Where a case demonstrates a 'poor prospect of success', an adviser will be expected to provide initial advice to clients and advise them of their options, but not to pursue the case any further under Legal Help. Advisers are explicitly prohibited from pursuing an application or representation to the immigration authorities in such circumstances, even if this means that the client's stay in the UK is prolonged. The only exception to this rule is where the client is detained and their case is subject to a 'fast-track' process. The availability of legal advice for fast-track detainees is looked at further in Chapter 22 on asylum procedures (▶676–7).

Costs limits and extensions

Following the cost-cutting changes by the DCA described above, advisers will only be able to provide a limited amount of assistance under the Legal Help Scheme depending on whether the immigration matter is an asylum case or not. The costs limits currently in place are as follows:

Type of case	Casework time/costs
Asylum	5 hours / £262.75 (£286.75 inside London)
Non-asylum	3 hours / £157.65 (£172.05 inside London)
Detained asylum	14 hours / £700.00
Detained non-asylum	10 hours / £500.00

(The costs limits for solicitors' firms are measured financially, and for not-for-profit organisations in hours.)

The costs limits are extendable on application to the LSC. However, the LSC will only grant an extension to carry out further work under the following criteria:

'In all cases, extensions will only be granted where the further work and the time proposed appear both reasonable and necessary in order for the application to succeed. It will not be considered reasonable to apply for an extension of public funds to delay a case where the delay itself will make the application more likely to succeed.' (13.2.10 para. 5 General Civil Contract (Immigration) (NFP spec)).

Controlled Legal Representation (CLR)

Financial assistance under the Legal Help Scheme will not cover the advocacy fees of a barrister or legal representative at a hearing before the Asylum and Immigration Tribunal (AIT). Instead, CLR may be provided for an initial substantive hearing before the AIT. Under the old appeals system, CLR could be made available to appeal against an adjudicator's decision to the Immigration Appeal Tribunal. Under the new single-tier appellate structure, an initial AIT decision can only be challenged by making an application for a review to the AIT or the High Court. Save for certain exceptions, CLR is only available for this process if a costs order is granted by the High Court or AIT. Public funding for reviews and reconsideration hearings are discussed in Chapter 36 (▶see 1153–5).

The means and merits tests

CLR is available to prepare an appeal and to represent a client in an initial substantive appeal before the AIT. CLR, once granted, will also cover Case Management Review Hearings (CMRH) and bail hearings before the AIT. Unless suppliers have been granted specific devolved powers to grant themselves CLR, CLR is now only available on application to the LSC for these hearings. It will be granted in such proceedings if the financial eligibility levels set by the LSC are met and if two further tests are satisfied.

Prospects of success Firstly, the prospects of the appeal being successful must be 'moderate or better' (clearly over 50 per cent). If they are 'unclear or borderline', CLR will be granted if the case is of overwhelming importance to the client (asylum cases will usually satisfy this test) or raises significant issues of human rights, or has a 'significant public interest' such as a test case. If the prospects of appeal are judged to be poor (clearly below 50 per cent) then CLR must be refused. Examples of where the prospects of success will be poor are specified in the General Civil Contract and are set out in the table below.

The cost-benefit test Secondly, the 'likely benefits from the proceedings' must justify the legal costs. This is assessed on an estimate of whether or not a private paying client would be prepared to pay for the proceedings, bearing in mind the prospects of success. Again, most asylum appeals will satisfy this test, bearing in mind the possible consequences of return to a country of persecution if the Home Office decision is incorrect. Many entry clearance and variation of leave appeals will also satisfy this test, particularly if an appellant is seeking to join family members or is not seeking a short extension of stay.

Refusal of CLR and appeals If a client is refused CLR by the LSC then the adviser can seek a formal review of the LSC's decision. If the adviser refuses CLR to the client under devolved powers, then the client can seek a formal review. Such a review must be requested within 14 days of the date of refusal. The refusal will then be considered by an external Funding

WHERE PROSPECTS OF SUCCESS ARE POOR

Examples of where the prospects of success will be poor are set out in the General Civil Contract (Immigration Specification) and are where:

- In light of all the evidence the reasons for applying to remain in the UK are, in the case of an asylum application, outside the criteria laid down in the 1951 Refugee Convention or, in the case of a human rights application, outside the criteria in the ECHR.

- In a second or subsequent asylum or human rights application, where the same facts have already been determined before an adjudicator or AIT on a previous application and dismissed and there has been no relevant change of circumstance.

- The client's circumstances and/or the circumstances within their country of origin have changed since the initial application was made such that any claim on the basis of asylum or human rights would be likely to fail.

- The client's credibility is significantly in doubt and the client is unable to provide a satisfactory explanation for any discrepancies or provide relevant corroborative evidence of their statement.

- In light of recent case law based on similar facts the appeal is likely to fail.

- The client has unreasonably failed to provide the necessary information such as to enable the supplier to properly prepare the case despite the reasonable efforts of the supplier to obtain that information.

- The client has provided false information relating to their identity or nationality and gives no reasonable explanation for this.

- The client has resided for over three months in a safe third country and does not dispute the safety of that country on reasonable grounds.

- The client is to be removed to a safe third country and does not dispute the safety of that country on reasonable grounds (this will not be relevant to claims under Article 8 of the ECHR).

Review Committee appointed by the LSC. Following a refusal, an adviser is prevented from continuing to advise the client under Legal Help in relation to the appeal itself, save from advising them on their situation and on appealing against the CLR refusal. The strict application of this particular specification of the contract has led to the appalling situation of many clients suddenly finding themselves without representation. Where suppliers can identify alternative arguments in support of their client's case, for example – representations under specific Home Office policies (for a list of some of the Home Office concessions and policies, ▶see 148–50), then they should endeavour to continue to give advice under the Legal Help scheme.

Costs limits Although the LSC considers that only four hours is normally reasonable to prepare for an appeal before the AIT unless it is 'particularly complex' (General Civil Contract), a costs limit of 12 hours or £1600 is set by the LSC. Whether this limit includes the hearing itself, the costs of instructing a barrister to represent the client and other disbursements, is dependent on whether the adviser is a solicitors' firm or a not-for-profit organisation and the particular General Civil Contract specification that applies to them. The costs limit can only be extended by application to the LSC.

Legal Representation (previously known as 'Legal Aid')

Applications for judicial review before the High Court, and appeals to the Court of Appeal and House of Lords may be funded by the LSC as 'legal representation'. It is also known as 'certificated' work because the LSC will issue a legal aid certificate if they decide to provide funding. Strict financial eligibility criteria apply and clients will be subject to a much more rigorous set of questions than they would be under the Legal Help or CLR schemes. Financial assessments are conducted by the appropriate LSC regional office, rather than the supplier, and a monthly financial contribution may be payable by the client.

Certificated work is also subject to a two-stage merits test. Particular criteria are applicable to judicial review cases, such as the availability of other procedures to challenge the decision of an immigration authority. Furthermore, prospects of the case being successful and the 'cost-benefit test' will be assessed by the regional LSC office rather than the supplier. The criteria applicable in both tests are broadly similar to those set out in the CLR scheme i.e. the cost-benefit test will be applied and the prospects of success will be assessed. Legal Representation will be refused if the prospects of achieving a successful outcome for the client are poor. Legal Representation will also be refused if the prospects of success are unclear or borderline, save where the case has a 'significant wider public interest', is of overwhelming importance to the client or raises significant human rights issues (see Access to Justice Act 1999 and the Funding Code).

However, in an emergency, for example when challenging removal directions by way of judicial review, certain solicitors' firms may be able to grant emergency certificates in-house to fund the initial cost of legal proceedings under powers devolved to them by the LSC.

THE IMMIGRATION AND ASYLUM ACCREDITATION SCHEME

Following consultation by the DCA in 2003 on changes to the public funding of immigration advisers, a new system of accreditation was rolled out during 2004 by the LSC and the Law Society. Although there was significant support in principle for some form of accreditation of immigration advisers to ensure that they deliver high quality legal advice, concerns have been raised about the tight timescale of the rollout and the actual methods of accreditation employed.

From 1 April 2005, it became a contractual requirement that every individual adviser in a solicitors' firm or non-for-profit organisation who undertakes legally aided immigration work must be accredited at a recognised level under the LSC/Law Society Accreditation Scheme. The requirement is so strict that any work carried out by a non-accredited individual (including work on pre-existing cases) will not be reimbursed by the LSC (General Civil Contract (Immigration)). However, the pace of implementation had to be slowed down in March 2005 to allow sufficient numbers of advisers to become accredited. Coupled with concerns of inadequate numbers of publicly funded advisers in England and Wales, the LSC decided to delay full implementation of the scheme to August 2005.

The Law Society and LSC have developed a set of standards that stipulates a detailed knowledge of various areas of immigration, asylum and human rights law and practice; a knowledge of the means and merits tests for the different types of legally-aided work; and skills needed to be a competent adviser, including familiarity with the professional rules of the Law Society. Three levels of caseworker (Level 1– Accredited, Level 2 – Senior, and Level 3–Advanced) as well as a 'Supervisor' standard have been implemented. The system of accreditation is heavily exam-based, but also includes mock interviews with clients. To encourage advisers who meet Level 2 to progress to the Advanced level, the LSC pays enhanced rates of remuneration to Level 3 caseworkers. The Supervisor standard needs to be met by at least one member of a team of more than one adviser.

The speed of implementation together with the heavily exam-based form of assessment has led to widespread criticism amongst immigration practitioners, many of whom feel they have been singled out compared to practitioners in other areas of law. A recent judicial review in May 2005 mounted by a group of ethnic minority practitioners on the basis that the scheme was indirectly racially discriminatory was unsuccessful. It was nevertheless an indication of the strength of feeling on this issue among some advisers.

Section 2 Immigration control in practice

2

Chapter 4
Coming to the UK 77

Entry clearance 78

Entry clearances operating as leave to enter 85

Applying for entry clearance 89

Entry clearance decisions 93

Granting or refusing leave to enter before arrival in the UK 94

Immigration control on arrival in the UK 95

Entry from the Republic of Ireland and through the Channel Tunnel 105

Chapter 5
Leaving and returning 107

General rules 107

People who always qualify to return 109

People with indefinite leave 110

People with limited leave 116

People who left the UK before 30 July 2000 118

People who wish to travel while an application or an appeal is outstanding 119

Chapter 6
Applying to stay in the UK 123

Application forms and charging 125

Making applications in the general categories 132

Making applications in the IED, EEA, asylum and Article 3 ECHR categories 136

Home Office decisions on applications 138

Curtailment and other decisions made by the
Home Office where no application has been made   141
What status does a person have while waiting for
a decision?   143
'Exceptional leave', policies and concessions   147
The armed forces   150
The long-residence rules   151

Chapter 7
Applying to 'switch' categories   159
Who can switch under the rules   160
Switching outside the immigration rules   187

Chapter 8
Identifying immigration status   189
Conditions of leave to enter or remain   189
Endorsements by entry clearance officers   192
On arrival in the UK   193
Endorsements by the Home Office   198
Other documents   202

4 Coming to the United Kingdom

This section (four chapters) looks at the practicalities of immigration control. It is therefore relevant to all of the categories in which people can be admitted to and remain in the UK, which are set out elsewhere in the *Handbook*. Together with Chapter 33 on the enforcement of immigration controls, it deals with the machinery by which the whole immigration system operates.

This chapter covers applying for entry clearance to come to the UK and it also deals with admission to the UK on arrival. In particular we look at:

- who needs entry clearance and when entry clearance is optional (▶78–83);
- the pros and cons of applying for entry clearance (▶see the table at 84);
- the way in which entry clearances operate as leave to enter, the period of leave which they give and how many times they can be used (▶85–9);
- the process of applying for entry clearance, including the forms used and the time taken to make a decision (▶89–93);
- entry clearance decisions and revocation of entry clearance (▶93–4);
- granting or refusing an applicant leave to enter before their arrival in the UK (▶94);
- immigration control on arrival as it affects: people who do not need leave, people who need leave and people who already have leave or entry clearance; we also look at the cancellation of leave on arrival and, briefly, at appeal rights (▶95–104);
- the general grounds upon which entry clearance/leave to enter can be refused (▶97–9); and
- entry from the Republic of Ireland and through the Channel Tunnel (▶105–6).

Chapter 5 deals with people who, after they have been admitted, wish to leave and then return to the UK. It looks at issues concerning qualifying to return and non-lapsing leave. The chapter also covers returning residents.

Chapter 6 deals with applying to extend leave in the UK for a limited time or indefinitely. It looks at the different prescribed forms which are used for in-country applications for different purposes. It also deals with the status people have while waiting for applications or appeals to be decided.

This chapter also deals with applying for leave on the basis of 'long residence' in the UK and looks at the categories under the rules dealing with members (or ex-members) of the armed forces.

Chapter 7 deals with who may 'switch' from one category under the immigration laws to another without leaving the UK (▶see in particular the table at 161 onwards).

Chapter 8 is about identifying immigration status from various documents. It includes sample copies of stamps, forms, notices and endorsements issued by both ECOs and the immigration authorities in the UK. The table at ▶190–1 sets out the different conditions which may be imposed on leave for each of the different categories of admission (prohibition on access to public funds, work restrictions etc). The immigration authorities refer to the different combinations of conditions as 'codes'.

Key concepts following the 1999 Act

The Immigration Act 1971 (as amended) remains the cornerstone of immigration controls. Key changes were made to the way the system operates by the Immigration and Asylum Act 1999 and the Immigration (Leave to Enter and Remain) Order 2000 which was made under it. Important parts of the system brought in by these provisions were:

- entry clearances operate as leave to enter;
- 'leave' (permission) to be in the UK can remain in place even when a person departs – the technical change that permits this prevents the person's leave from 'lapsing' when they depart;
- leave to enter the UK can be granted to a person before they arrive;
- leave that a person has when they arrive can be 'cancelled' on their arrival;
- leave to be in the UK can remain in place when a person is appealing against a refusal to extend their leave, provided that the application was made 'in time' (although the 2005 Bill proposes to withdraw this);
- permission to enter the UK can be granted on the telephone or by fax.

ENTRY CLEARANCE

An 'entry clearance' is a document which is issued by a British post overseas (British embassy, high commission or consulate), which is evidence that the holder is eligible for entry to the UK even though they are not a British citizen (s33(1) 1971 Act). People applying for entry clearance have to satisfy officials at a British post that they qualify under the requirements in the immigration rules for entry in the category in which they are applying, or that entry clearance ought to be granted exceptionally. If entry clearance is granted, it is normally placed in the applicant's passport.

'Visas', 'entry certificates', 'entry clearances' If the applicant is a 'visa national' (see below), the legal term for the entry clearance they get is a 'visa'. If the applicant is a non-visa national, the legal term for the entry clearance they get is an 'entry certificate' (see para. 25, HC 395). Many people simply use the term 'visa' to refer to both of them but this is not technically correct. The proper way to refer to them *both* is 'entry clearance' and this is the term used throughout the *Handbook*.

Form of entry clearances Following the changes under the 1999 Act, entry clearances were redesigned (▶see 192–3 for examples of the new entry clearances). Entry clearances come in two colours. Green entry clearances are used for visitors (including transit visitors) and entry clearances for all other purposes are red. The entry clearances given to visitors are also known as Uniform Format Visas (UFVs). Confusingly, they bear the name 'visa' even if the holder is a non-visa national. Red entry clearances for all other purposes bear the words 'entry clearance'.

Effective date and date of expiry Entry clearances have a date on which they become effective and a date of expiry. The date on which the entry clearance becomes effective is given on the entry clearance as the 'valid from' date. Depending upon when the person wishes to travel, the 'valid from' date can be later than the date on which the entry clearance is actually issued. The date on which the entry clearance expires is given as the 'valid until' date. The period between these two dates is the period of the entry clearance's 'validity'. These dates are critical in determining what leave a person will get when they actually arrive in the UK (see below).

Conditions Entry clearances state the conditions that will apply to the leave that the person obtains when they arrive in the UK. These conditions are sometimes referred to by immigration officers as 'codes' for shorthand. The codes reflect the various different combinations of conditions, which a person can be given. For details of the various codes ▶see 190–1.

When entry clearance is necessary

Some people must obtain an entry clearance before they come to the UK in order to be admitted under the immigration rules. For everyone else, getting an entry clearance is optional. The table below sets out who must get an entry clearance. The list of people who need entry clearance has greatly expanded recently.

Of course, even if a person needs an entry clearance under the immigration rules but arrives without one, it is still possible to ask the immigration officers to exercise discretion to waive the entry clearance requirement. This may sometimes happen if the reason for the application arises after the person has arrived and been in the UK for some time (for example an asylum-seeker marries here) but this discretion will not often be exercised. In cases where the person arriving in the UK has simply neglected to get an entry clearance, it will be very rare – in many such cases the person will be prevented from getting onto the plane/ship to come to the UK in the first place.

WHO MUST GET AN ENTRY CLEARANCE?

The following eight groups of people must get an entry clearance to be admitted to the UK under the immigration rules *unless* they fall into any of the exceptions listed further below. Note that group (4) will only require entry clearances from 13 November 2005 and that there is a grace period for them until 13 January 2006. The phrase 'specified national' has formally been dropped from the rules from 13 November 2005 because all non-EEA, non-visa nationals coming for more than six months need entry clearance (as explained in points (3) and (4) below). Under the immigration rules, leave to enter will be refused if an entry clearance is required but is not obtained (para. 24, HC 395).

Separate rules apply for EEA nationals and their family members (▶see 83–4, 550–1).

1) **'Visa nationals'** must have an entry clearance to come to the UK *whatever* their purpose in coming. At present, there are over 110 'visa national' countries (▶see 1507 for the list). However, the Secretary of State can add and remove countries to the list very quickly. The list is given in appendix 1 to the immigration rules.

2) **'Non-visa nationals'** must have an entry clearance where they are coming to the UK for a *purpose* for which the immigration rules state they need one (and see para. 24 HC 395). So, even if a country is not on the list of visa nationals (above), its nationals will still need an entry clearance if the rules specifically state that it is required in the category in which they are seeking admission. Wherever the rules state that entry clearances are required for a particular category, this is stated in the part of the *Handbook* dealing with that category. Generally, the rules require those who are coming to the UK for settlement, or for any purpose that may lead to settlement, to obtain an entry clearance. For example, people coming to join relatives in the UK to stay permanently or those coming for work, business or self-employment will generally need entry clearance. Working holidaymakers also need to get an entry clearance although entry in that capacity does not lead to settlement. Until 13 November 2003, non-visa national work-permit holders did not need to obtain entry clearance but, from that date, almost all of those who hold work permits valid for over six months needed to obtain entry clearance (▶see 428–30). Entry clearance is not needed in order to apply for asylum and indeed it cannot generally be obtained for that purpose – that is why asylum-seekers have such difficulty in actually travelling to the UK.

3) **'Specified nationals' (phase 1)** who are coming to the UK *for more than six months* must have an entry clearance whatever their purpose in coming to the UK. This requirement was introduced from 13 November 2003 (HC 1224). The ten countries listed whose nationals are 'specified nationals' are only those contained in 'phase 1' of the process (see phase 2 below). These ten countries

were the first to be 'specified' because they are the UK's largest customers in terms of travellers coming to the UK to stay for more than six months (see the first list of countries in appendix 3 to the immigration rules). There was a concessionary 'grace period' of two months granted to phase 1 nationals who entered without entry clearance so that they would still be admitted if they arrived up until 13 January 2004 without the required entry clearance. 'Specified nationals' were introduced at the same time as the change in the immigration rules which has prevented immigration officers from 'granting' leave to enter at port for longer than six months to passengers arriving without an entry clearance (para. 23A HC 395 inserted by HC 1224 as it stood till 13 November 2005). This rule applies to those who do not need to obtain entry clearance in order to be admitted. If they don't obtain it anyway, they will only be admitted for a maximum of six months initially. If they wish to stay for longer, such applicants will have to pay to make a further application. Part of the intention seems to have been to make it more worthwhile someone applying for an entry clearance even if they do not strictly need one.

The ten 'phase 1' countries are: Australia; Canada; Hong Kong (other than British Nationals (Overseas)); Japan; Malaysia; New Zealand; Singapore; South Africa; South Korea; United States of America.

4) **'Specified nationals' (phase 2)** On 13 November 2005, 'phase 2' of the project in (3) above came into effect. From this time, new immigration rules require that *all* non-EEA, non-visa nationals coming to the UK for more than six months require an entry clearance whatever their purpose in coming (para. 24 HC 395 as substituted by HC 645). This was announced by a ministerial statement and a letter from UK Visas to User Panel members (accompanied by a series of written 'questions and answers') all of which were issued on 12 July 2005. As with phase 1, there is a grace period so that those arriving in the UK up until 23.59 hours on 13 January 2006, who do not have the entry clearance made necessary by this change, will still be granted leave to enter if they otherwise qualify under the immigration rules. They will, however, only be granted leave for six months and they will then have to apply in-country for further leave (i.e. a United Kingdom Residence Permit) (see the Ministerial Statement and see the explanatory memo issued with the new rules). After 13 January 2006, if they arrive without an entry clearance, leave to enter will be refused. British Nationals (Overseas), British Overseas Territories citizens, British Overseas Citizens, British Protected Persons and British subjects are not subject to this new requirement (paras 23A, 23B, 24 HC 395).

The 'phase 2' countries are: Andorra; Antigua and Barbuda; Argentina; Bahamas; Barbados; Belize; Bermuda; Bolivia; Botswana; Brazil; Brunei; Cayman Islands; Chile; Costa Rica; Dominica; El Salvador; East Timor; Faroe Islands; Greenland; Grenada; Guatemala; Honduras; Israel; Kiribati; Lesotho; Macao; Malawi; Maldives; Marshall Islands; Mauritius; Mexico; Micronesia; Monaco; Namibia; Nauru; Nicaragua; Palau; Panama; Papua New Guinea; Paraguay; Samoa; San Marino; Seychelles; Solomon Islands; St Kitts & Nevis; St Lucia; St Vincent & Grenadines; Swaziland; Tonga; Trinidad & Tobago; Tuvalu; Uruguay; Vanuatu; Vatican City; Venezuela.

Because the 'sixth' month rule applies to *all* non-EEA non-visa nationals, formally the term 'specified' national has been dropped from the rules.

Because this change occurred after the *Handbook*'s cut off date, we still refer to 'specified' nationals in the text. This should now be read as a reference to all non-EEA, non-visa nationals.

5) **Nationals of the territories that previously made up the Socialist Federal Republic of Yugoslavia (excluding Croatia and Slovenia)** must obtain entry clearance (para. 1(a), appendix 1 to HC 395).

6) **People who hold passports or travel documents** issued by the former Soviet Union or the former Socialist Federal Republic of Yugoslavia must obtain entry clearance (para. 1(b), appendix 1 to HC 395).

7) **Stateless people** must obtain entry clearance (para 1(c), appendix 1 to HC 395).

8) **People who do not hold national documentation** must obtain entry clearance (para. 1(d), appendix 1 to HC 395).

The exceptions

Even if a person is in one of the groups mentioned above, they still do not need an entry clearance if they are any of the following (para. 2, appendix 1, HC 395):

- a person who qualifies to be admitted to the UK in the category of 'returning resident' (those who were 'settled' in the UK when they last left). They must be returning to the UK within two years in order to be exempt from needing an entry clearance (▶see 110-16 for this category);

- those coming to the UK within a period of leave previously granted to them provided that they meet all of the following conditions:

  – the leave previously granted was for more than six months;

  – the leave has not been extended automatically (for details about automatic extensions of leave under section 3C 1971 Act, ▶see 143–6);

  – the applicant is seeking entry for the same purpose as the leave previously granted.

- nationals or citizens of the People's Republic of China who hold passports issued either by the Hong Kong Special Administrative Region or the Macao Special Administrative Region.

Notes

- **Visitors** are granted leave for a maximum of six months and so they are not entry-clearance exempt under the above rules when they depart within the time of their leave and wish to return again. *However*, a visit entry clearance is *usually* valid for multiple entry (▶see below 87–8) and so, in practice, a visitor who enters with an entry clearance and then wishes to return within their six months' leave, does not need to apply for entry clearance again because they can use their existing entry clearance again.

- **Certain refugees visiting the UK** used to be entry-clearance exempt. Until 11 February 2003, people who held refugee travel documents issued by countries which are signatories to the Council of Europe Agreement of 1959 on the Abolition of Visas for Refugees were exempt from the need to obtain entry clearance if they were coming to the UK for a visit of three months or

> less. Visitors in this category now need visas if they are visa nationals (see HC 389 deleting para. 2(c), appendix 1, HC 395).
>
> - **Asylum-seekers** can be granted asylum under the immigration rules without obtaining an entry clearance. However, because in most cases there is no possibility of applying for asylum before arriving in the UK, they usually have no basis upon which to travel to the UK and are often prevented from reaching the UK. The same is true of those who wish to come to the UK to make human rights claims which are, of course, not covered by the immigration rules.

When entry clearance is optional

People who are not visa nationals and who are not coming to settle, work or do business in the UK and who are not 'specified nationals' (the phrase should now be read to include all non-EEA non-visa nationals, see the table above) seeking entry for more than six months, do not need to get an entry clearance before travelling. They have the choice of applying for entry clearance abroad, or of travelling to the UK without it and seeking entry from the immigration officer at the port of entry (para. 24, HC 395). So, for example, a non-visa national visitor has the choice of whether to apply for entry clearance or not. From 13 November 2003, the immigration rules have imposed a limit on how long a person who 'seeks leave to enter on arrival' (i.e. a person who does not arrive with entry clearance which gives leave to enter) may be admitted for. This limit is six months (para. 23A, HC 395). In any event, from 13 November 2005 non-EEA, non-visa nationals can only obtain entry to the UK without entry clearance if they do not intend to stay longer than six months. There is an exception to this for British Nationals (Overseas), British Overseas Territories Citizens, British Overseas Citizens, British Protected Persons and British subjects. Even if they wish to stay for longer than six months they may still be admitted to the UK without an entry clearance but will only be granted leave for a maximum of six months (para. 23B HC 395).

Where a person does not need an entry clearance to be admitted to the UK, they may still choose to get one before travelling so as to be surer that they will be granted entry. For example, the immigration rules actually recommend that non-visa national intending *au pairs* obtain entry clearance (para. 90, HC 395). Among the factors to consider in deciding whether to apply for entry clearance when it is not strictly required are the additional cost and delay of getting an entry clearance balanced against the risk of being refused entry on arrival without one (▶see the table below). Even where entry clearance has been obtained however, admission to the UK on arrival is not guaranteed.

Entry clearance: EEA Nationals and family members

Different considerations relating to entry clearance apply for EEA nationals and their family members. EEA nationals do not require any form of entry

---

ADVANTAGES AND DISADVANTAGES OF OBTAINING ENTRY CLEARANCE WHERE IT IS OPTIONAL

The advantages are:

- people know in advance whether they satisfy the requirements of the immigration rules and therefore they are unlikely to have problems or delays when they arrive in the UK. This may be particularly useful for people who have previously had immigration problems;
- if they are refused entry clearance, they will have spent money only on the entry-clearance fee and not on the ticket to the UK;
- if they get entry clearance but are nevertheless refused entry when they arrive in the UK, they can usually appeal against the refusal in-country and therefore attend the appeal hearing and give evidence (►see below at 102–3 and ►see also Tables 2–3 at 1056–7, 1059–60);
- in student cases, extending leave after entry will be more straightforward (for the recent problems which have occurred, ►see 268–70);

The disadvantages are:

- in some countries, there are delays in considering applications (►see 92–3 below) and there may be further delays if the applications are referred to the Home Office;
- there is a fee for entry clearance, which is not returned if the application is refused, and an application may involve more than one long journey to the nearest British post;
- the refusal rates for entry clearance overseas have generally been higher than refusal of entry at ports in the UK (there is recent evidence of high refusal rates in family visit cases, ►see 1073).

---

clearance in order to travel and be admitted to the UK. However, a non-EEA national coming as a 'family member' of an EEA national must get an EEA 'family permit' before they come if they are:

- a visa national, or
- coming to the UK to 'install' themselves i.e. to live with the EEA national rather than just for a visit.

The family permit is therefore a form of entry clearance. It can be obtained free of charge from the entry clearance officer at British posts. For more details about EEA nationals and their family members' rights of entry, ►see 550–1.

Other documents relating to admission to the UK

Entry clearances are not the only documents that may be required in order to obtain entry in a particular capacity.

Immigration Employment Documents (IEDs) These are: work permits including training and work experience scheme (TWES) permits; documents issued under the highly skilled migrants' programme; permits issued under the sectors-based scheme and work cards issued by an approved operator under the seasonal agricultural workers' scheme. Although not technically 'entry clearances', work permits used to act as entry clearance for non-visa nationals. However, most work-permit holders now need entry clearance as well as their work permit for entry to the UK. This is also generally the case for the other IED categories except for seasonal agricultural workers who may travel to the UK using simply their work card. Full details about IEDs for all of these categories are given in Chapter 14.

Certificates of entitlement British citizens and other people with the right of abode in the UK can obtain a 'certificate of entitlement' to the right of abode by applying to the entry clearance officer at a British post overseas. The documents that need to be produced depend on the basis on which the person is entitled to the right of abode (see generally, Section 13). For instance, a person born in the UK before 1 January 1983 needs to produce their full birth certificate. However, a person born in the UK on or after that date and claiming entitlement to the right of abode by birth, also needs to produce evidence of either parent's British citizenship or settled status at the time of birth and, if claiming through their father, the parents' marriage certificate. A Commonwealth citizen woman who, before 1 January 1983, married a man with the right of abode should produce evidence of her husband's British citizenship, for example, his passport or certificate of registration or naturalisation as a British citizen, as well as producing their marriage certificate. In all cases, the person applying for the certificate should also provide their own passport. Refusal of a certificate of entitlement is an 'immigration decision' which gives a right of appeal.

ENTRY CLEARANCES OPERATING AS LEAVE TO ENTER

From 28 April 2000, the law changed to allow entry clearances to operate as leave to enter the UK. The way in which the legislation is written is not completely clear and has given rise to some confusion. The relevant legislation is the Immigration (Leave to Enter and Remain) Order 2000 which we refer to as 'the Leave to Enter Order'. The form that an entry clearance takes in terms of its period of validity, is described above (▶see 79). Immediately below, we look at which entry clearances operate as leave to enter, how long they give leave for and whether they can be used more than once. For issues about refusal of entry to those carrying entry clearances (which is complex) ▶see 100–3.

Which entry clearances operate as leave to enter?

In order for an entry clearance to operate as leave to enter it must state on it the purpose for which it is given (for example, 'fiancé', 'working holidaymaker', 'visitor') and be either (art. 3, Leave to Enter Order):

- endorsed with any conditions on which it has been granted (for example, a condition that there is 'no recourse to public funds'); or
- intended to take effect as indefinite leave to enter in which case it must contain a statement to that effect.

The immigration authorities intend that all entry clearances that are granted will operate as leave to enter. However an entry clearance, which does not in fact satisfy the above conditions, will not operate as leave to enter. Such an entry clearance would probably still be valid but leave would not be given unless the immigration officer granted it on entry.

There is one exception to the above, which is that an entry clearance issued on a Refugee Convention travel document issued abroad (i.e. not by the UK) on or after 27 February 2004 will not have effect as leave to enter (see art. 3 as amended).

How do these entry clearances work?

Entry clearances have an 'effective date' (which may be later than the period on which they are issued) and an 'expiry date'. On the entry clearance itself, the effective date is shown as 'valid from' and the expiry date is shown as 'valid until'. The 'period of validity' of the entry clearance is the period between these two dates. The conditions of the leave that is given, are the conditions that are written on the entry clearance. Applicants must arrive in the UK between these dates. Because the entry clearance itself operates as the grant of leave to enter, when the applicant arrives and is examined by the immigration officer, the officer does not 'grant' leave to enter. After examination, provided everything is in order, the officer will simply allow entry and endorse the passport with a date stamp to show the date on which the person entered.

When a passenger with entry clearance which operates as leave to enter arrives in the UK, they are 'treated' as though they have been granted leave to enter 'before' their arrival but the period of their leave 'begins' on the date of their arrival (see art. 4(2)(2B)(3)(b) Leave to Enter Order; para. 25A HC 395). This is, of course, very confusing. The legislation is badly written. The intention seems to be to ensure that, although people are treated as already having been given leave, the period over which leave is counted for the purposes of, for example, immigration rules such as the probationary period, does not begin until arrival. However, in a letter to Dexter Montague & Partners solicitors in September 2001, the Home Office stated that:

'...in calculating leave, leave to remain in the United Kingdom begins on the 'valid from' date on the entry clearance and not from the applicant's date of arrival in the UK.'

But this would mean that a spouse who arrived towards the end of the 24-month period of validity of their entry clearance (intended to be the 24-month probationary period in the UK), would be able to apply for settlement soon after their arrival even though they had not been in the UK with their spouse for anything like the 24 months required. This is unlikely, therefore, to be the correct interpretation. The more likely approach is that leave is calculated from the date of arrival, as the Leave to Enter Order indeed indicates.

It is very important that the 'effective' date is given in accordance with the applicant's plans for their arrival. For suggestions of how to deal with this issue if, for example, a spouse delays arrival, ▶see 315–7.

How long is leave granted for when an entry clearance operates as leave to enter?

The length of the leave that is given when an entry clearance operates as leave to enter depends on the purpose for which the entry clearance is given.

Visit entry clearances

In the case of visit entry clearances, leave is granted for six months from the date of arrival if the period of validity remaining on the entry clearance is six months or more on the date of arrival. If the remaining period of validity is less than six months on the date of arrival, the length of leave given is the remaining period of the validity of the entry clearance (art. 4(2) Leave to Enter Order) (▶see further 223–6).

Take, for example, a person who obtained a visit entry clearance on 15 October 2004, which had an effective date (the 'valid from' date), which was also the 15 October and an expiry date (the 'valid until' date), which was 15 April 2005. If the person arrived in the UK on 2 January 2005, they would only have been given leave until 15 April 2005. They are not given six months' leave when they arrive because the remaining period of the validity of the entry clearance is less than six months. However, if the applicant had been given a visit entry clearance which was valid for two years from 15 October 2004 and arrived in the UK on the same date (2 January 2005), the entry clearance would give them leave until 2 July 2005 i.e. six months. Note, in this last example, even though the entry clearance remains valid until 15 October 2006 (and can generally be used again – see below), the applicant would become an overstayer if they remained for more than six months on any one occasion.

Under the old system, a person could simply arrive within the period during which the entry clearance was valid and be granted six months' leave by an immigration officer from that date even if it was the last day on which the entry clearance was valid. Many people have made the mistake of thinking that they have six months from the date of entry and become overstayers as a result. It is therefore very important for applicants to explain to the entry clearance officer when they are likely to be travelling to the UK. The ECO may then be persuaded to give the entry clearance an effective date close to the departure date so that the passenger gets the maximum benefit from the entry clearance.

The normal period of validity of a visit entry clearance is six months but it is possible to obtain a long-term entry clearance (with a period of validity of up to ten years) if the ECO can be persuaded that the applicant's circumstances justify it.

Approved Destination Agreement entry clearances

On 21 January 2005, the UK signed a Memorandum of Understanding on visa and related issues concerning tourist groups from the People's Republic of China coming to the UK, the 'Approved Destination Status Agreement with China' (ADS Agreement). In order to accommodate the agreement, a new category of 'visitors seeking entry under the ADS agreement' has been added to the immigration rules from 5 April 2005 (paras 56G-J HC 395 inserted by HC 486). For further details about these new rules, see 246–7. ADS visitors are only admitted for a maximum of 30 days at a time and, on arrival, their entry clearance operates as leave to enter until the expiry date of the entry clearance, which is likely to be in 30-days' (or less) time (art. 4(3)(b), (3A)(b) Leave to Enter Order).

Entry clearances which give indefinite leave

If the entry clearance states that it is to have effect as indefinite leave to enter, then, on arrival it gives leave for an indefinite period (art. 4(3)(a), (3A)(c) Leave to Enter Order).

Other entry clearances

In the case of all entry clearances not in the above three categories, the period of leave which is given is to the date of expiry of the validity of the entry clearance (art. 4(3)(b), (3A)(c) Leave to Enter Order).

How many times can an entry clearance be used?

A visit entry clearance operates as leave to enter on an unlimited number of occasions during the period of its validity. So, a person may come and go from the UK using the same entry clearance and, provided the immigration rules remain satisfied, it will operate as leave to enter on each occasion. Visit entry clearances can therefore be described as valid for 'multiple entry' (art. 4(1)(2). There are two exceptions to this:

1) if the visit entry clearance specifically states that it is only valid for one single entry (art. 4(1)(3)(3A)(a));

2) an ADS visit entry clearance is only valid for a single entry *unless* it specifically states that it is valid for 'dual-entry', in which case it may be used on two occasions during its period of validity (art. 4(2A)(2B)).

So, in cases falling in (1) above, most ADS cases and all other cases, the entry clearance is valid for one entry only during its period of validity (art 4(3)(3A). *However*, for most non-visitors the fact that their entry clearance is not valid for multiple entries does not matter. This is because, for *most*, their leave will not lapse when they depart, which allows them to return. Again, most will also be exempt from the requirement to obtain entry clearance if returning within their existing leave. For non-lapsing leave and the ability to return ▶see 107–9; 116–8. For exemptions to the need to obtain entry clearance, ▶see 82.

Delayed departures

Where, for unforeseen reasons, a person delays their departure to the UK so that they enter the UK significantly after the effective ('valid from') date, the Home Office has indicated it will adopt a 'flexible approach' if the person applies for a short extension of stay (see letter to Dexter Montague noted above). Such applications will be considered in line with the immigration rules. So, for example, where a visitor arrives significantly after the 'valid from' date they may, if they apply, be granted an extension to allow them to stay for up to six months from their date of arrival.

APPLYING FOR ENTRY CLEARANCE

There are over 150 entry clearance posts around the world in UK embassies, high commissions and consulates. They are managed by a joint agency of the Home Office and the Foreign & Commonwealth Office called 'UK Visas'. According to official figures, there was a 14 per cent increase in entry clearance applications in 2003-2004 so that the number of applications worldwide was about 2.2 million.

Which post? A person must be outside the UK in order to make an application for entry clearance. Applications should be made to the designated British post (British embassy, high commission or consulate) in the country in which the person is 'living'. However, applications for visit entry clearances do not need to be made to the post in the country where the applicant is living. The Foreign and Commonwealth Office produces a list of designated posts (▶see 1511–18). Most will deal with all types of entry clearance applications but some are restricted to dealing with particular types of applications. Where there is no designated post in their country, applicants can apply to a designated post in another country, which accepts applications in the category in which they wish to enter (para. 28, HC 395).

Problems at particular posts From time to time there are problems in making applications at particular posts for certain categories. The posts in Lagos and Abuja (both Nigeria) were receiving approximately 23,000 applications per month altogether in April 2005, making them the busiest in the world. In order to expand the operation, the Foreign and Commonwealth Office temporarily suspended applications for visit entry clearances for first time applicants aged between 18 and 30. Capacity to accept more applications should be available around the end of 2005 (letter to all MPs from Home Secretary and Foreign Secretary dated April 2005). The government subsequently extended this restriction to Nigerians who travel to neighbouring posts in West Africa, although not to Nigerians who are legally resident in neighbouring countries.

Obtaining the forms To apply for entry clearance, it is necessary to complete the relevant forms which can be downloaded from the UK Visas website (www.ukvisas. gov.uk), or a request can be made for forms to be sent directly to a UK address by calling UK Visas in London on 0207 008 8308; or the forms can be obtained free of charge from posts overseas.

Often the entry clearance officer will interview the applicant and, in some cases, may conduct further investigations such as making enquiries of other agencies or even visiting relatives or neighbours before making a decision.

FORMS FOR APPLYING FOR ENTRY CLEARANCE

Entry clearance used to be applied for using various forms in the 'IM' series. These were replaced on 1 August 2003 by the 'VAF' forms. The forms presently in use are as follows.

- **VAF 1** The categories that should apply on this form include visitors (including transit visitors); working holidaymakers; students; work-permit holders; those taking up permit-free employment; returning residents, dependants of persons in these categories and non-EEA-national dependants of EEA nationals.

- **VAF 2** The categories which should apply on this form are: spouses, unmarried partners, fiancé(e)s, children, adopted children, elderly dependants of a person either settled in the UK, or who is going to the UK to be settled. The form should also be used to apply for family reunion with a refugee.

- **VAF 3** This form should be used to make an application for a Direct Airside Transit Visa (DATV). This is for people who intend to pass through the UK in direct transit to another country or territory. Transit visitors who will actually enter the UK (i.e. will not just stay airside) should use VAF 1. For full details about both kinds of transit ►see 243–6.

- **VAF 4** This is the form to be used when applying for a certificate of entitlement to the right of abode.

- **VAF 5** This form may be used in order to apply to go to one of the Overseas Territories.

- **VAF 6** This is the form for Bulgarian or Romanian applicants who wish to enter the UK in order to establish themselves in business under an EC Association Agreement.

Note

Special forms are also available on the UK Visas website for diplomats and members of foreign governments who are coming to or passing through the UK on official business or who are being posted to the UK.

Completing the forms

While a sponsor, relative or representative may obtain the forms, help fill them in and present them, the applicant must sign and date the 'declaration' at the end to confirm that the contents of the form are correct. Note also that, in some cases, the applicant's presence will be required for fingerprints (below) or interview. The documents that are required depend on the nature of the application and the requirements of the rules that need to be satisfied. The guidance given in the relevant chapter of the *Handbook* should help. In addition, the UK Visas website carries notes for guidance for applications in the different categories. In addition, the forms themselves contain notes both in the text and at the end of the form that indicate which documents are necessary. Once the form is completed and all the necessary accompanying documents are ready, it can be presented in a number of ways: in person, online, by courier or by post. It is best to check with the particular post about the ways in which they can accept applications.

Fees and date of application

Entry clearance applications are not treated as having been made unless the required fee has been paid (para. 30, HC 395). It is possible to ask for the fee to be waived if the applicant is 'destitute' (▶see 760, 878–9). For the current fees that are payable, quoted in sterling ▶see 1510. Fees should be paid in local currency and are not refundable.

The application is treated as made on the day the British post receives the form and the fee. The date of application is particularly important in settlement applications for children who must be under 18 on the date of application. In all other cases, it is the circumstances on the date on which the application is *decided* which matters, not those on the date of the application (para. 27, HC 395).

Fingerprinting

Some entry clearance posts have recently introduced fingerprinting of applicants. For example, fingerprinting was introduced for applicants of all nationalities applying in Kenya from 8 September 2004 – this meant all visa applicants had to apply in person at the offices of 'Visa Handling Services Ltd' to have an electronic impression of their fingerprints taken and a record attached to the visa application. Exempt from the process were minors under five, holders of diplomatic and other official passports, UN officials and holders of a certificate of entitlement to the right of abode. Prior to this date, fingerprinting had already been introduced in five other East African countries: Eritrea, Ethiopia, Tanzania, Rwanda and Uganda. The purpose is to:

'...introduce biometrics into our visa application process to combat abuse of the UK's immigration and asylum system.' (UK Visas letter to User Panel, 7 September 2004).

Effective date in delayed entry cases

For the reasons set out above (▶86–7), it is essential that applicants indicate to the post the date of their proposed travel. This is so that the ECO can issue the entry clearance with an appropriate 'effective date' for when the entry clearance becomes valid. If the applicant fails to do this, then the entry clearance may become valid straight away – this will of course mean that the expiry date is brought forward meaning that the expiry of the leave which is given will also be brought forward. UK Visas have indicated that they will normally give an effective date for the entry clearance as the same date as it is issued unless they are told otherwise. They also state that it is possible to ask that the effective date be deferred by up to three months.

Time taken to process applications

British posts vary in the time it takes them to deal with an application and there are different queues for different kinds of application. In some countries, the application can be dealt with straight away. In others, for example, the countries of the Indian subcontinent, there have been long delays for people applying for settlement and there may also be delays for visitors. For information as to the expected waiting time, the best course is to contact the post concerned. Many posts have their own websites, which provide local entry clearance information.

UK Visas states that, recently, some 91 per cent of straightforward, non-settlement applications have been dealt with within 24 hours and that, if an interview is necessary, the aim is to process a non-settlement application within ten working days. They also state that, in most settlement cases, it is possible to process the application within 13 weeks although this varies depending on the post.

Some information about present waiting times is also given on the UK Visas website. The times which UK Visas were giving as waiting times as at 31 August 2005 for some of the busiest posts were as follows.

Post	Non-settlement entry clearance (in working days)	Settlement entry clearance (in weeks)
Abuja	14	2
Accra	10	9
Addis Ababa	15	2
Bangkok	86	16
Chennai	7	2
Dhaka	5	7
Harare	24	3
Kingston	3	11
Lagos	8	10
Manila	27	9
Moscow	0	0
Mumbai	7	3

Nairobi	10	21
New Delhi	2	7
New York	2	0
Pretoria	0	0

Referrals to the UK

ECOs refer certain cases to the Home Office for advice and instructions. This often leads to delay in deciding the application. Commonly referred applications are those relating to business, adoption of children and applications that do not qualify under the rules but where there are compelling circumstances, which may justify admission. Referrals also sometimes take place where the Home Office holds papers on the person in relation to previous immigration applications. When the case has been referred, representations may be made to the Home Office instead of to the overseas post.

ENTRY CLEARANCE DECISIONS

If the ECO is satisfied that the requirements of the rules are met, the person will be given entry clearance. If the ECO is not satisfied that the requirements of the rules are met, then unless it has been shown that it is appropriate to authorise entry outside the immigration rules, the application will be refused. Like other immigration officials, ECOs must now also consider rights under the European Convention of Human Rights, which have been incorporated into UK law by the Human Rights Act 1998. The immigration rules themselves state that decisions of ECOs and others must comply with human rights (para. 2, HC 395).

General grounds of refusal It should also be noted that the immigration rules relating to each category (other than refugees) only state that leave *may* be granted if the requirements of the rules relating to the particular category in question are satisfied. Therefore, even if a person satisfies the rules for the individual category, they may still be refused an entry clearance under the 'general grounds' on which leave can be refused (▶see 97–9). The general grounds for refusal are the same for applications for entry clearance as they are for leave to enter when a person arrives at a port.

Appeals Decisions are notified in writing and the applicant should be informed of rights of appeal against the refusal and how the appeal may be brought (▶see 1061–2). Not all refusals carry a right of appeal. In particular, people refused entry clearance as visitors (other than for a 'family' visit), or as students who have not yet been accepted onto a course, or who are coming on courses for six months or less, have no right of appeal. In addition, those refused because they cannot satisfy a requirement of the rules as to age or nationality: because they do not have an 'immigration document' of a particular kind; because they ask for leave longer than the rules for that category permit; or because they are seeking to enter for a purpose not permitted by the rules; also do not have the right of appeal (▶see Table 2 at 1055–8). In all these cases, however, it is still possible to bring an appeal on human rights or race discrimination grounds.

The 2005 Bill proposes to remove rights of appeal in all non-family visits and non-dependant entry clearance cases unless the appeal is on human rights or race discrimination grounds.

Revocation of entry clearance by entry clearance officer

Before a person arrives in the UK, an ECO may revoke an entry clearance after it has been granted. The ECO can only do this if (para. 30A, HC 395):

- whether or not to the holder's knowledge, false representations were used or material facts were not disclosed for the purpose of obtaining the entry clearance;
- there has been a relevant change of circumstances since the entry clearance was issued which removes the basis of the applicant's claim to be admitted; or
- the person's exclusion is conducive to the public good.

GRANTING OR REFUSING LEAVE TO ENTER BEFORE ARRIVAL IN THE UK

A change introduced under the Immigration and Asylum Act 1999 is that, from 28 April 2000, it has been possible for an immigration officer to grant or refuse leave to enter before a person has even arrived in the UK (art. 7 Leave to Enter Order). This can happen either before a person has departed from their own country or while they are on their way to the UK. Immigration officers have the power to examine and interview people outside the UK for these purposes. These powers are used to grant leave to enter to groups the Home Office believes are at low risk of abusing immigration controls, for example, school groups and recognised reputable tour groups.

To make this easier still, although the grant and refusal of leave is normally given in a written notice or stamp, immigration officers can now also grant leave to enter by fax or email and, in the case of visitors, it can be given orally over the telephone with a written notice to follow. Decisions can also be notified to a responsible third party, for example, the tour leader of a group. In addition, immigration officers may be sent abroad and make decisions there so as to relieve certain 'pressure points' at ports of entry where there would otherwise be large queues of people waiting to be granted entry.

The reason given by the Home Office both for this change and the introduction of entry clearances operating as leave (above) is to reduce the need for routine questioning at ports of entry and therefore to avoid congestion at the ports.

IMMIGRATION CONTROL ON ARRIVAL IN THE UK

When a person arrives at a port in the UK, immigration officers examine them in order to determine whether they (s2(1)(2) and paras 2-2A, Sch 2 1971 Act):

- have the right of abode in the UK (British Citizens and some Common-wealth nationals);

- may enter the UK without being given leave to enter even if they do not have the right of abode;

- require leave to enter and, if so, whether they should be granted leave to enter the UK and for what period and on what conditions leave should be given;

- already have leave when they arrive which is given by an entry clearance or otherwise;

- should have any existing leave cancelled.

All these different situations are considered below. In order to help immigration officers, non-British citizen passengers over 16 are required to fill out a 'landing card' containing essential information about their circumstances (▶see 194 for a specimen card). In carrying out their examination, immigration officers are able to search a person, their luggage or vehicle for any documents that help to show the reasons why the person has come to the UK.

People who do not require leave

'Leave' is a technical term in immigration law for 'permission' to be in the UK. It can be given for a limited or an indefinite period. Limited leave can be made subject to conditions, for example, not to work or have recourse to public funds. Indefinite leave cannot be made subject to conditions. Some people, however, do not need leave at all. They are:

- British citizens;

- a small number of other people who have the 'right of abode' in the UK (▶see 1417–21);

- those who are 'exempt' from immigration control: diplomats and others who work for embassies, members of governments, members of the armed forces including NATO forces, persons attending Commonwealth conferences, employees of some international organisations, certain crews of ships and aircrews (▶see 472–6);

- EEA nationals and their family members exercising EU rights of free movement.

These people are still required to produce to the immigration officer a passport or travel document, which demonstrates their identity and nationality. In the case of a person with a right of abode in the UK, they prove their status by producing a passport which states that they are a

British citizen or a citizen of the United Kingdom and Colonies with the right of abode in the UK, or a certificate of entitlement (s3(9) 1971 Act; see also paras 12–14 HC 395). Once these documents are produced and appear to relate to the holder, in order to refuse admittance there is a heavy burden on the immigration officer to show that the person is not entitled to the status they claim. Therefore, entry is normally a formality if the person at port produces one of these documents.

In the case of non-EEA-national family members of EEA nationals and those exempt from control, they may also be asked for documents demonstrating their status. For details about entry procedures concerning EEA nationals and their family members, ▶see 550–1.

Those exempted from immigration control may have a letter of accredit-ation or authorisation from the government or international organisation concerned. Diplomats may have been issued, by the Foreign and Com-monwealth Office, with either a certificate issued under the Diplomatic Privileges Act 1964 to show their entitlement to immunity or they may have a simple letter of confirmation.

On entry to the UK, a person who is exempt from control will often be given an open date-stamp endorsement on their passport, which is not an endorsement for indefinite leave to enter. If no satisfactory proof of status is available for those claiming exemption but there is no reason to suspect any deception, they will often be granted temporary admission until proof of their entitlement can be shown. A person who is exempt from control can also later obtain a 'notification of exemption' from the Home Office as proof of their immigration status. An example of the open date-stamp is shown at ▶196.

For the rights of entry of the holders of British passports issued in the UK and Islands or the Republic of Ireland before 1 January 1973 and certain BOCs, ▶see 1405.

People who require leave and general grounds of refusal

All those not in the above categories require 'leave' in order to come into the UK. Many people require entry clearance (▶79–83). For those who do not, immigration officers make a decision at port whether to admit them under the immigration rules. Immigration officers at the ports, like ECOs, make their decisions as to whether to grant or refuse leave to these people by applying the immigration rules. Their decisions must also be compatible with the rights under the ECHR. Exceptionally, leave may also be granted outside the rules. For those who require leave and do not already have it (remember they may have it by having an entry clearance which operates as leave to enter), if the officer decides to grant leave the passport will be stamped to show the date, the time-limit (if any) and any conditions on their stay (▶see Chapter 8 for examples).

The time period for which leave is granted, which is stated on the stamp, runs from the date of the stamp itself. If a person wishes to obtain an extension of stay, it must be applied for before the existing leave runs out. It is worth keeping a record of the date leave expires separate from the passport so that if the passport is lost, the person knows the date until which they are allowed to remain and can make any application to stay before the leave runs out. Leave will only be granted at port to those who arrive without an entry clearance for a maximum of six months (see para. 23A, HC 395). If entry is refused, this is also endorsed on the passport.

The possible conditions that an immigration officer can impose on a limited leave (or indeed which the entry clearance giving leave may contain) are (s3(1) 1971 Act; para. 8 HC 395):

- a restriction or a prohibition on employment and business;
- a requirement to register with the police;
- a condition that the person maintains and accommodates themselves and any dependants without recourse to public funds (the ability to impose these conditions was introduced on 1 November 1996).

Immigration officers may also, if an examination by the port medical officer suggests it is necessary, only allow entry subject to the condition that the person reports for further medical tests or examination by an appointed medical officer (para. 7, Sch 2 1971 Act).

General grounds of refusal

Each category of entry under the immigration rules sets out a list of requirements which, if satisfied, may result in the grant of leave but which still allows leave to be refused on the basis of one of the 'general grounds' for refusal of leave (see part 9 HC 395).

These general grounds of refusal apply in exactly the same way to applications for entry clearance. It should be noted that some of them are themselves discretionary although the presumption is leave will be refused where they apply (leave should 'normally' be refused). Others are mandatory (leave 'is' to be refused). These general grounds are set out in the table below.

The general grounds do not apparently apply to asylum cases because they state that they are additions to the grounds of possible refusal set out in the earlier parts of the rules and the asylum rules come later, in part 11 (see paras 320, 322 HC 395). However, the decision of the High Court in *Mambakasa* suggests that the general grounds could be applied even in cases coming under part 11. It is doubtful whether this can be correct as it would be contrary to the UK's obligations under the 1951 Refugee Convention to refuse to grant asylum on the basis of the various 'general' refusal grounds. It is only possible to exclude people from the protection of the Refugee Convention on the specific 'exclusion' grounds. In addition, section 2 of the 1993 Act prevents the immigration rules from allowing anything to be done which would be contrary to the Refugee Convention.

Can the general grounds of refusal be waived?

The general grounds for refusal are contained in the immigration rules. The immigration rules themselves can always be waived. Therefore, even where the rules require a refusal, that rule itself can still be waived in an appropriate case.

For example, the mandatory rule which states that an application 'is to be refused' if the application is made for a purpose not covered by the rules, was introduced for technical reasons concerning appeals. The aim was to make sure that, in all cases, the person hearing the appeal (now an immigration judge) does not have the power to reconsider on its merits the exercise of the discretion of the immigration authorities to refuse to grant leave outside the rules. If this rule were always applied, no one would ever get exceptional leave or entry clearance issued exceptionally. Advisers and representatives must therefore not be discouraged from making representations as to why an exception should be made even where refusal is mandatory under the rules.

GENERAL GROUNDS FOR REFUSAL OF ENTRY CLEARANCE OR LEAVE TO ENTER

Paragraph 320 Immigration Rules HC 395.

Grounds on which entry clearance or leave to enter 'should normally' be refused:

- not giving all the required information to the immigration officers and, if outside the UK, failing to provide a medical report requested by an immigration officer;

- seeking leave to enter as a returning resident after being away for more than two years (though the specific rules on returning residents say that people may still be admitted, for example, if they have lived here for most of their lives – ►see 112–3) or where the person does not intend to settle in the UK once more;

- travelling on a passport issued by a state that is not recognised by the British government. In practice, people who otherwise qualify for entry may be admitted on an immigration service form;

- having previously overstayed or broken other conditions of leave;

- having previously entered by deception, or been granted an extension of leave by deception;

- if people cannot show they will be allowed into the country to which they intend to travel after their time-limited stay in the UK (this does not apply to people with entry clearance for settlement or those entering as spouses leading to settlement);

- refusal by a sponsor to sign a maintenance undertaking if requested;

- whether or not the applicant knew about it, false representations have been made or there has been a failure to disclose a material fact for the purposes of obtaining an immigration employment document;

- where children are seeking entry for any reason (except to join their parents or legal guardians) without written consent from the parents or legal guardians. This does not apply to child asylum-seekers;

- refusal of a medical examination when required. This does not apply to people settled in the UK;

- if a person has been convicted of an offence, which if committed in the UK, could be punished with imprisonment for 12 months or more. This can be waived if there are strong compassionate reasons to allow entry;

- if the immigration authorities believe refusal is justified on grounds that the person's admission is not 'conducive to the public good' – if, for example, in the light of the applicant's character, conduct and associations it is undesirable to give them leave to enter;

- failure by the applicant to comply with a requirement to provide certain physical data;

- whether or not the applicant knew about it, false documentation was submitted in support of the application.

Grounds on which entry clearance or leave to enter 'is to be' refused:

- where 'entry is being sought for a purpose not covered by these rules'. This rule is intended to cover any conceivable reason for coming to the UK by stating that the application must be refused under the rules unless it falls within one of the established categories and the rules for that category are satisfied (but ▶see 99);

- if the applicant is subject to a current deportation order;

- where the applicant does not have a valid passport or identity document;

- where a person arrives in the UK through the Channel Tunnel with the intention of continuing their journey to another part of the Common Travel Area (e.g. the Republic of Ireland), but immigration officers are not satisfied that they will be accepted in that country;

- where the person is a visa national, not having a valid entry clearance for the purpose for which they seek entry;

- where the Home Secretary has directed that the exclusion of the person from the UK is conducive to the public good (for recent policy on such exclusions, ▶see 1018–21);

- where the medical inspector has confirmed it is undesirable to admit the person. This does not apply to people who are settled in the UK or where the immigration officer is satisfied that there are strong compassionate reasons for admission.

People who have leave or an entry clearance when they arrive

If a passenger already has leave when they arrive in the UK, their entry will normally be straightforward. The immigration authorities have indicated that:

'It is not envisaged that [immigration officers] will routinely conduct detailed interviews of such persons. Immigration officers will be able to check the validity of the passport and entry clearance and that the person presenting it is the rightful holder.'

However, people may be examined by the immigration officer to determine whether or not that leave should be 'cancelled' (para. 2A Sch 2 1971 Act; paras 10–10B, 321A HC 395). This process also applies to people who arrive in the UK with an entry clearance, which operates as leave to enter. This is because, for the purposes of examining them, these people are treated as having been granted leave to enter before their arrival (art. 4 Leave to Enter Order). Those who last left with 'non-lapsing' leave are also treated as having been granted leave to enter the UK before their arrival when they return within the period of their existing leave. It matters not for these purposes whether that existing leave was granted as leave to *remain* or leave to enter (art. 13(5), Leave to Enter Order).

So, to sum up, a person may already have leave when they arrive in the UK in any of the following three situations:

1) The passenger still has leave from their previous stay in the UK because it did not lapse when they previously left (▶see 107–9 for more details about 'non-lapsing' leave).

2) The passenger has an entry clearance, which operates as leave to enter (as almost all entry clearances do, ▶see above at 85–6).

3) Leave to enter was granted by the immigration authorities before the person arrived in the UK (▶see above at 94). Where a person was only given leave orally as a visitor, the burden is upon that person to show that they were in fact given it.

Examination to decide whether to cancel leave

In most cases, examination will be swift, and the passenger will be admitted with their existing leave. The period of leave that is given when a person arrives with an entry clearance which operates as leave, is slightly complex (▶see above at 86–8).

However, the officers do have the power to examine the passenger to determine whether their leave should be 'cancelled' instead. If the officer has suspicions, they may 'suspend' the existing leave until the examination is completed. If this is done, a written notice to that effect must be given. Following the examination, the immigration officer may cancel the leave (para. 2A(1)(7)–(9), Sch 2 1971 Act; paras 10A–10B, HC 395).

Leave may be cancelled if any of the following conditions apply (para. 2A(2)(2A)(3) Sch 2 1971 Act; para. 321A HC 395):

- there has been a change of circumstances such that leave should be cancelled;
- leave was obtained by giving false information or failing to disclose material facts;
- medical reasons make it undesirable to admit the passenger (unless they are settled in the UK or there are strong compassionate factors);
- the person's exclusion is conducive to the public good – this may be, for example, in the light of the applicant's character, conduct or associations;
- the applicant's purpose in coming to the UK is different from that stated on the entry clearance.

It is very important that immigration officers distinguish between 'change of circumstances' cases and 'different reasons for coming' cases because this is relevant to rights of appeal – the Immigration Service has issued a special instruction about this (▶see below at 103).

Where an applicant arrives in the UK with leave (including with an entry clearance) and their leave is cancelled under the above powers, that 'cancellation' is treated as a 'refusal of leave to enter' the UK. It is therefore an 'immigration decision' which, *in principle*, can be appealed under section 82 2002 Act. It is also treated as a refusal of leave to enter the UK *at a time when the applicant held a current entry clearance*, which is also relevant to appeal rights (see below) (para. 2A(9), Sch 2 1971 Act).

Where leave is cancelled in these ways, the passport will be endorsed with a large 'CANCELLED' stamp (▶see 197) or endorsed in writing on the passport in either red or black ink. This stamp (or written endorsement) is placed over the leave that is being cancelled.

Cancellation of *entry clearance* Note that a person who either arrives in the UK before the date on which the entry clearance becomes effective, or who seeks to enter for a purpose other than that specified in the entry clearance, may have the *entry clearance* (i.e. not just the 'leave') cancelled (see art. 6(2) Leave to Enter Order; para. 30C HC 395). It is unclear whether, for appeal purposes, an applicant in this position would also be treated as having been refused leave to enter at a time when they had entry clearance.

Cancellation of leave while outside the UK Similar criteria as those set out above can be applied by the immigration authorities to cancel any leave which a person who is outside the UK has, which did not lapse when they left. The immigration authorities may also 'vary' that leave (art. 13(6)–(9) Leave to Enter Order; para. 321A, HC 395).

People with entry clearances that do not operate as leave

As stated, all entry clearances are intended to operate as leave. However, if an entry clearance does not satisfy the conditions to qualify as operating as leave to enter (above), or it is endorsed on a Refugee Convention travel document issued abroad, or if it is an 'old style' entry clearance given before the new entry clearances were introduced, the old rules still apply. An immigration officer must decide whether to grant leave or not and what period of leave to give. An immigration officer at port can still refuse entry on similar grounds to the rules set out above for cancelling leave, namely if (para. 321 HC 395):

- false representations were made for the purpose of obtaining the entry clearance;
- material facts were not disclosed for the purpose of obtaining the entry clearance;
- there has been a change of circumstances since the entry clearance was issued which removes the grounds for granting admission;
- the refusal is justified on the basis of the person's restricted returnability to another country, on medical grounds, on grounds of their criminal record, a previous deportation order, or because their exclusion would be conducive to the public good.

People who have leave and who apply to vary it on entry

Another possibility, which may arise for someone who has leave when they arrive, is that they may apply to the immigration officer at the port for their leave to be varied (see para. 31A, HC 395). They may ask for it to be extended in time or that the conditions be changed. Where an application of this kind is made at the port then, unlike other applications to vary leave, there is no need for it to be made on a prescribed application form. The immigration officer may (but is not required to) make a decision on this application. If the immigration officer declines to make a decision but does not cancel the existing leave then, after the person has been admitted, they may apply to the Home Office for the same variation.

Port decisions concerning entry and appeals

If leave to enter is to be refused or an existing leave cancelled on a passenger's arrival in the UK, then the immigration officer must first obtain the authority of either a chief immigration officer or an immigration inspector (para. 10, HC 395). If leave is granted, the person will receive the appropriate endorsement on their passport (▶see Chapter 8 for the type of stamps). Written notice must also be given of a negative decision, which must also inform the applicant of any appeal rights (▶see 1061–2).

In some cases, there is no in-country right of appeal and the only way of challenging the decision before removal is to make further representations or to apply for judicial review. If a person has a valid entry clearance, or otherwise arrives with leave, they will generally have an in-country right of appeal. As stated above, the 'cancellation' of leave for a person who arrives in the UK with leave granted before arrival (including leave given by an entry clearance) is treated for appeal purposes as a refusal of leave to enter at a time when the applicant had an entry clearance (para. 2A(9) sch 2 1971 Act). For full details about rights of appeal, ▶see Tables 1–3 at 1052–61. The applicant will not be able to rely on their entry clearance as giving them an in-country right of appeal if the refusal is on the grounds that the applicant has come to the UK for reasons other than those stated in their entry clearance (s92(3A)–(3C) 2002 Act as added from 1 October 2004 by s28 2004 Act). However, even in these cases, there will still be an in-country appeal on asylum and/or human rights grounds provided that the claim/s are not certified as 'clearly unfounded'.

'Change of circumstance' and 'different purpose' cases The Immigration Service has recognised that it is vital that officers carefully distinguish between 'change of circumstances' cases and cases where the person's *purpose* in coming to the UK is not as stated on the entry clearance. In the latter case, they are refused under paragraph 2A(2A) of Schedule 2 1971 Act (if they have an entry clearance which operates as leave to enter) and under paragraph 320(5) HC 395 in other cases. In cases of *change of purpose*, in-country appeal rights are denied (i.e. under either s92(3B) or (3C) 2002 Act as amended) (▶see 1059–61). On 18 May 2005, the Immigration Service issued Operational Instruction No. 03/2005, 'Refusal of leave to enter on the grounds of change of purpose'. This makes it clear that a change of *purpose* refusal should be issued where:

- the passenger admits to the fact that they are seeking entry for a purpose different to that stated on the entry clearance; or
- there is 'clear evidence' that that is the case, e.g. if a person holding a visit entry clearance is in possession of a letter of enrolment from a college or an employer's letter.

Such cases should be refused using the newly designed Form IS82B. If the case is really about circumstances changing although the purpose for entry remains the same, a change of purpose refusal should not be issued.

2005 Bill Note that, at present, there is no right of appeal *at all* (in-country or out of country) for visitors and certain students who are refused leave to enter if they do not have entry clearance (s89 2002 Act). The 2005 Bill proposes to extend the need to have entry clearance in order to have a right of appeal against refusal of leave to enter, to all categories (whether entry clearance is needed for admission under the immigration rules or not). Again, there will still be in-country appeal rights in asylum and human rights cases.

Further applications for leave to enter

If leave to enter in one category is refused, there is nothing to prevent the person from applying to enter for a different reason before leaving the

UK. Those refused entry are routinely asked whether they wish to seek entry for any other reason. Practically speaking, however, it is unlikely that a person will be able to demonstrate that they are genuinely seeking entry in the further category following a refusal on a different basis. Different considerations often apply in the case of asylum-seekers, where there are frequently very good reasons why the person does not immediately declare their intentions. Unless the asylum-seeker can be removed on 'third-country' grounds, there will also usually be a right of appeal if an asylum claim is made. After a person has been refused leave to enter the UK and they have unsuccessfully exercised any in-country rights of appeal against the decision, the immigration officer has the power to set directions for the person's removal under paragraph 8 of Schedule 2 1971 Act.

When the immigration officer cannot make an immediate decision

In many cases, in particular where the person is seeking asylum, the examination of the applicant cannot be concluded straight away. Therefore, while the examination is continuing, the immigration officer has two options. Either the person may be detained pending a decision to grant or refuse entry, or they may be granted 'temporary admission' to the UK. Temporary admission is not formal 'leave', it is a restricted licence to be in the UK and it can be terminated in favour of detention at any time. Similarly, people who are initially detained under these powers, may later be released on temporary admission by the immigration officer or may be granted bail either by a chief immigration officer or an adjudicator. Temporary admission may be granted subject to conditions (as to residence, employment, reporting to the police or an immigration officer). Those placed in the 'induction' centres are formally granted temporary admission rather than being detained. For full details about temporary admission, ▶see 950–7 and ▶see 652–4.

Illegible passport stamps

Sometimes an immigration stamp may not be fully legible. Before 10 July 1988, if a person was given an illegible stamp, they were deemed to have been granted indefinite leave to enter. This is because the Immigration Act 1971 provides that people must be given notice in writing of the time-limit and conditions on which they have been granted entry. When these could not be read, the courts decided that no valid time-limit or conditions had been imposed on the person's stay (see *Minton*). Therefore, people who last entered the UK before 10 July 1988 and had no legible time-limit placed on their stay, can apply to the Home Office for confirmation that they are settled in the UK. They should obtain specialist advice before approaching the Home Office.

Since July 1988, however, the law has been changed by the Immigration Act 1988 so that people entering since that time who are given illegible stamps are deemed to have been granted leave to enter for only six months with a prohibition on employment.

ENTRY FROM THE REPUBLIC OF IRELAND AND THROUGH THE CHANNEL TUNNEL

The UK and the Republic of Ireland, together with the Isle of Man and the Channel Islands, form what is known as the 'Common Travel Area' (CTA). There are no immigration controls operating within the CTA. Therefore most people do not require leave to enter when travelling to the UK from the Republic of Ireland (but see below). People's passports are not stamped as they are not examined by immigration officers.

The need for entry clearance

Both the UK and Ireland have their own lists of countries whose nationals require pre-clearance to enter and there is no common entry clearance for both countries. Visa nationals intending to travel to both countries should obtain entry clearances from both the embassies concerned before setting out. This is necessary even though it is unlikely that passports will be checked while travelling between the UK and Ireland. Where a person who requires a visa for the Republic of Ireland arrives in the UK intending to travel on to the Republic of Ireland but does not have such a visa, the immigration officer may contact the Department of Justice in Dublin to determine whether or not the person will be accepted for admission there. If the reply is negative, the person will normally be refused leave to enter the UK.

Travelling to the UK from Ireland

Irish citizens entering the UK automatically become settled on their arrival, as do British citizens entering the Republic of Ireland. Additionally, for EEA nationals (Ireland is an EEA state) and their family members, EU law rights of free movement apply, ▶see Section 6.

For many people who are not Irish citizens and who wish to come to the UK, the provisions of the Immigration (Control of Entry through Republic of Ireland) Order 1972 apply. There are, however, exceptions and the circumstances in which this Order does not apply are set out below. Where the Order applies, people who need leave to enter and who travel from outside the CTA and enter the UK from Ireland are treated as having leave to remain in the UK for three months from the date they arrive in the UK. The leave has a prohibition on employment and business. Nothing will be stamped on their passports and there will usually be no evidence of their date of entry other than their travel ticket, if they have kept it. If they wish to remain in the UK for more than three months they should apply to the Home Office for an extension of this stay, with any evidence they have of the date of arrival (so they will not be treated as overstayers) and showing how they fit into the immigration rules to remain longer.

A visa national who has been given an entry clearance endorsed 'short visit' to enter the UK from a British embassy or high commission and who enters through Ireland, is treated as having been given leave for one month from the date of arrival in the UK and is prohibited from entering into employment and business and must register with the police. People with entry clearances for any other purpose are treated as having been given leave for three months.

The Order does not, however, give a general means of avoiding immigration controls. Its provisions (see above) do not apply to (see art. 3 of the 1972 Order and para. 15 HC 395):

- visa nationals who do not have entry clearance;
- illegal entrants and overstayers in the UK who cross to the Republic from the UK and then return to the UK;
- people who entered the Republic of Ireland unlawfully from outside the CTA;
- people who have been deported from the UK, when the deportation order is still in force;
- people who, on their last attempt to enter the UK, were refused leave to enter;
- people who arrive by air in Ireland and simply transit by air to the UK;
- people whom the Secretary of State has directed should be excluded on the grounds that their presence is not conducive to the public good.

All these people still require leave to enter the UK. If they enter without seeing an immigration officer to grant this leave, they are deemed to have entered in breach of the immigration laws and can be treated as illegal entrants. Even if they cross from Ireland, were not examined by an immigration officer, and were unaware that they were doing something wrong, the Court of Appeal decided in the case of **Bouzagou** that people in this situation are illegal entrants. They are therefore liable to removal with no right of appeal until after they have left the UK unless they are asylum-seekers or seek to remain on human rights grounds.

The powers to give directions for the removal of persons refused leave to enter and illegal entrants who have arrived from the Republic of Ireland have been expanded by the Immigration (Entry Otherwise than by Sea or Air) Order 2002.

Entry through the Channel Tunnel

Immigration law was slightly modified to deal with the situation of immigration control when a person comes to the UK through the Channel Tunnel. Two pieces of legislation, the Channel Tunnel (International Arrangements) Order 1993 and the Channel Tunnel (Miscellaneous Provisions) Order 1994 (both made under s11 Channel Tunnel Act 1987), allow UK immigration officers to carry out the powers described in this chapter both on the trains which run between London, Paris, Lille and Brussels and in 'control zones' in France and Belgium. Further provision about these 'juxtaposed' controls are made by the Nationality, Immigration and Asylum Act 2002 (Juxtaposed Controls) Order 2003 made under the 2002 Act.

5 Leaving and returning

This chapter looks at the position where a person who has already been admitted to the UK wishes to travel and then return. The rules relating to people in this position differ depending on the basis on which they have been admitted and the length of time for which they have been allowed to stay.

We look first at the general rules before turning to see how those rules affect different categories of applicant. Then we look at the position of people who want to travel whilst they are waiting for a decision on extending their stay.

GENERAL RULES

Regulations made under the Immigration and Asylum Act 1999, which were introduced in July 2000, changed the way in which the law operates so that a person may still keep their 'leave' when they depart. This system is mainly set out in article 13, Immigration (Leave to Enter and Remain) Order 2000 (we have referred to this Order as the 'Leave to Enter Order'; and see also para. 20 HC 395). 'Leave' is the formal permission that a person is given to be in the UK, which is granted by the immigration authorities.

The reason for introducing the system of non-lapsing leave was that it did not seem right that a person who had been in the UK, for example, for three years, might leave for a few days for a trip to the continent and then have to seek leave to enter again on their return and have no right of appeal if refused. Before the changes, almost all leave to enter or remain in the UK 'lapsed' when a person left the Common Travel Area (the 'CTA' is the UK, Channel Islands, the Isle of Man and the Republic of Ireland). The exceptions to this rule were very narrow and included, for example, Commonwealth nationals who left on day excursions to France, Belgium or Holland.

Which leave does not lapse?

If a person leaves the UK on or after 30 July 2000, any leave which was given before or after that date does not lapse when a person goes out of the CTA if (art. 13 Leave to Enter Order):

- it is leave which was given by means of an entry clearance (other than a visit entry clearance) which operated as leave to enter or it is leave which was given by an immigration officer or the Home Office for a period of more than six months; *and*
- the leave has not been 'varied' (changed) by the Home Office in such a way that the leave remaining after the variation is six months or less.

Any leave that does not satisfy the above conditions, still lapses as before when the person goes out of the CTA. Therefore leave given by a visit entry clearance does still lapse when the holder leaves the CTA. However, this does not matter for most visitors who came in with an entry clearance because their visit entry clearances can usually be used on any number of occasions within the period of their validity (▶see 88). On the basis that it is not leave given by an immigration officer or the Home Office, leave which is given automatically by section 3C 1971 Act when a person makes an in-time application to extend their leave also lapses when a person leaves the CTA.

For how long does 'non-lapsing' leave stay in force?

If the leave is limited leave and it does not lapse, then it remains in force when the person departs until its natural expiry time. However, if the leave is still in force two years after a person has left and the person has not returned within that time, the leave lapses at that point. If the leave was indefinite leave, it will remain in force for a continuous period of two years but will then lapse if the person has not returned to the UK.

Where leave remains in force while a person is outside the UK, for obvious reasons, the conditions that are attached to the leave are suspended until the person returns.

Cancellation of leave that has not lapsed

Even if the leave does not lapse when a person departs, it may still be cancelled while the holder is outside the CTA (or when a person returns) if any of the following conditions apply (para. 321A, HC 395):

- there has been a change of circumstances such that leave should be cancelled;
- leave was obtained by the provision of false information or failing to disclose material facts;
- medical reasons make it undesirable to admit the person (unless the person is settled in the UK or there are strong compassionate factors);
- exclusion is conducive to the public good;
- the person has failed to provide information or documents as requested by the immigration authorities.

Where leave is cancelled in this way when a person arrives in the UK, in principle, there is an in-country right of appeal to the AIT because the decision is treated as a refusal of leave to enter at a time when the applicant held an entry clearance (see para. 2A(9), Sch 2 1971 Act). However, it is always best to check the individual circumstances of the case against the complex provisions on rights of appeal (►see Tables 1–3 at 1052–60). The immigration authorities also have the power to 'vary' leave (by adding or removing conditions or altering its length) while the person is outside the UK although this will probably be rare (art. 13(6) Leave to Enter Order).

PEOPLE WHO ALWAYS QUALIFY TO RETURN

People with the right of abode and certain British passport holders

People with the right of abode do not need leave and therefore can enter the UK at any time. This applies to British citizens and some Commonwealth nationals (►see 1417–21). Where these passengers have British passports that state they are British citizens or have the right of abode, immigration officers only have to be satisfied that the person travelling is the rightful holder of the passport. Occasionally, they make checks when they suspect that a person is travelling on a forged passport or on a passport issued to someone else and people can be refused entry for this reason. It is up to the immigration officers to prove that a person travelling on a full British passport is not entitled to do so. Certain others travelling on British passports are entitled to very preferential treatment on arrival (►see below).

Certificates of entitlement to the right of abode

People born in the UK before 1983 are automatically British citizens, as are people born in the UK from 1983 onwards if either parent was a British citizen or was settled in the UK at the time of their birth. They may also be entitled to another nationality by descent from a parent and therefore may be travelling on the passport of the other country. This may be the case when the other country, for example Malaysia, does not allow dual nationality or places restrictions on the stay of people using non-national passports. People with the right of abode need to have their passports endorsed with a 'certificate of entitlement to the right of abode', as proof of their status in order to qualify to enter the UK. These certificates of entitlement can be obtained either from the Home Office, if the person is in the UK, or from a British post if the person is abroad. There is a fee payable even for people who apply within the UK (►see 1510 for the amount). Difficulties sometimes arise in countries where the British authorities are suspicious of the documents shown.

Other Commonwealth citizens with the right of abode must obtain certificates of entitlement before travelling to the UK (see s3(9)(b) 1971 Act). They may have the right of abode through the birth of a parent in the UK or through a marriage, before 1 January 1983, to a man with the right of abode. To qualify for the right of abode people must have been Commonwealth citizens at the time the British Nationality Act 1981 came into force on 1 January 1983. So Camerounians, Mozambicans, Pakistanis, Namibians and South Africans do not qualify as their countries were not then in the Commonwealth. Commonwealth nationals who apply for certificates will need to show original documents to prove their claim to the right of abode. In some countries where there may not be contemporaneous birth or marriage certificates to prove the relationship, people may have difficulties in convincing the British authorities that they qualify, and it may be necessary, for instance, to obtain sworn statements from other people who were present at the time of the marriage or birth.

Certificates of entitlement are valid for the same length of time as the passport on which they are endorsed. When people renew their passports they can then apply to the British authorities for a new certificate of entitlement.

Holders of certain British passports

Holders of passports issued before 1 January 1973 in the UK or the Republic of Ireland showing them to be British Dependent Territories Citizens (BDTCs), British Nationals (Overseas), British Overseas Citizens, British Protected Persons or British Subjects and which are not endorsed showing that the person is subject to immigration control, are freely admitted to the UK even though they are not British citizens (para. 16, HC 395). For further details about these national statuses, ►see Chapter 43 at 1404 onwards. As a result of recent legislation, BDTCs now have full citizenship rights (►1406). British Overseas Citizens who hold a UK passport wherever and whenever it was issued, are granted indefinite leave if they can show that they have been granted indefinite leave at any time since 1 March 1968 (para. 17, HC 395).

PEOPLE WITH INDEFINITE LEAVE

Where a person who has indefinite leave in the UK leaves the CTA, their leave remains in force for two years while they are away and only lapses at that point. Therefore, if a person with indefinite leave travels away and returns within two years, they are entitled to be admitted with their leave treated as continuing unless any of the grounds upon which a person may have their leave cancelled at port applies (►see 100–3). The position before the introduction of these changes was that people who had indefinite leave lost that leave when they left. However, under the immigration rules, it was usually fairly straightforward for them to get indefinite leave again immediately when they returned provided that they returned within two years and certain other conditions were met. These conditions are known as the 'returning residents' rule and the full requirements are set out below (►112–6).

On a first impression, it seems that the introduction of 'non-lapsing' leave means that the returning residents rule is unimportant and that a person returning from abroad with indefinite leave only needs to make sure that their leave cannot be cancelled under the conditions described above.

Is the returning residents rule still important?

Another problem that some returning residents faced when they returned previously was that they might be granted only limited leave as a visitor rather than indefinite leave again which meant that they lost their ability to benefit from the returning residents rule altogether unless they got indefinite leave again in the future. Again, on first impressions, 'non-lapsing' leave would also eradicate this problem.

Despite the above, the returning residents rule remains important for the following reasons:

- the returning residents rule has not been withdrawn from the immigration rules (paras 18–20 HC 395);
- it is likely that immigration officers will consider the returning residents rule as a touchstone for deciding whether there has been a 'change of circumstances', which is one of the bases on which leave can be cancelled when a person returns. This is particularly so in relation to the requirement that the person seeks to return 'for the purposes of settlement';
- the rule is still relevant to those cases where leave has lapsed, namely where the person has been outside the UK for over two years;
- similar to the category immediately above, there may be cases where a person, who had indefinite leave, last departed before 30 July 2000 (which was when the 'non-lapsing' leave provisions came into force) – the leave of such persons lapsed straightaway and they also would have to rely on the returning residents rule.

Entry clearances for returning residents

Provided a person returns within the two years, they do not need an entry clearance in order to enter as residents. As far as visa nationals are concerned, those who qualify for admission as returning residents who have not been away for more than two years, or who are returning within a period of leave granted for more than six months, for the same purposes as previously, are exempt from requiring entry clearance. Insofar as 'specified nationals' are concerned (which includes all non-visa national countries from November 2005, ▶see 80–2), it seems that no entry clearance is required because a person returning with leave would not be seeking leave to enter the UK since they already have leave (see Appendices 1 and 3, HC 395). However, a visa national or specified national who returns after they have been away for over two years and whose leave has therefore lapsed, does need to obtain an entry clearance in order to return as a resident.

The 'returning residents' rule

WHAT THE RULES SAY

The immigration rules require that people must satisfy an immigration officer that (paras 18–20 HC395):

- they have not been away for longer than two years. However, if a person has been away from the UK for over two years, there is still a discretion to readmit them under the rules if, for example, they have lived in the UK for most of their life;
- they are returning for the purpose of settlement;
- they had indefinite leave when they last left; and
- they did not have assistance from public funds towards the cost of leaving the UK.

If the applicant who has indefinite leave left the UK to accompany their spouse or unmarried partner abroad where that spouse/partner is a member of the British armed forces serving overseas, or a permanent member of the British Diplomatic Service, or a comparable UK-based staff member of the British Council, or a staff member of the Department for International Development, then it does not matter if they have been away for over two years or that they had assistance from public funds towards the cost of leaving. Such an applicant can still qualify under the rules. This does not apply, however, if the applicant goes abroad independently and it only applies if their spouse or partner is either a British citizen or is settled in the UK (see para. 19A HC 395 as substituted from 18 September 2002 by Cm 5597).

WHAT THE RULES MEAN

'Not been away for more than two years'

Those who had indefinite leave when they left the UK should make every effort to return within two years. The leave of those who have been out of the UK for nearly two years and who are unable to return within this time will lapse after the two-year period. If they wish to return and retain their status, they should apply to the British post in the country they are in for entry clearance as returning residents or at least contact the post to express their intention of returning in the future. People who are simply unable to return within the two-year period but yet apply for an entry clearance within that time as a means of stating their intentions, are more likely to be eventually readmitted.

People who have been away for more than two years before returning or applying for entry clearance to return are in a more difficult position. The rule that an application may still be granted if, 'for example', a person has 'lived here for most of his [or her] life', gives the immigration authorities some discretion, and it is one that can be appealed if necessary. The rules do not give any other examples of the circumstances that would allow people to return to their homes. However, the Immigration Directorate's Instructions state that the specific factors, which may apply in favour of an applicant who has been away for more than two years are they have (IDI Ch 1, s3, annex K, para. 2.1):

- been working abroad for a UK government body, UK company or a United Nations organisation;
- travelled abroad to work for a particular employer and have returned with that employer;
- worked abroad in the public service of a friendly country where they could not reasonably be expected to settle in that country permanently;
- family in the UK but have travelled abroad for prolonged studies;
- had prolonged medical treatment abroad;
- contacted a post abroad within two years to express their future intention to return to the UK.

In all cases, however, where a person has been away for over two years, the following factors will be taken into account (IDI Ch 1, s3, annex K, para. 2):

- the intentions of the person when they originally left to go abroad;
- the length of the previous residence in the UK;
- the time that the person has been outside the UK;
- the reason for the delay in returning;
- the strength of family ties to the UK and the extent to which the applicant maintained them in his/her absence (Article 8 ECHR could have an impact here);
- whether the person has a home in the UK.

The longer the person has been away from the UK over the two years, the more difficult it will be for them to persuade the immigration authorities to exercise their discretion favourably. The courts have held that being too ill to travel at the relevant time, when detailed medical evidence has been provided (*Khokhar*) and having a passport detained by the authorities in connection with legal proceedings were both strong enough reasons for not returning within the two-year period. People who came to the UK as young children to join their parents and were educated in the UK but who have then spent three or four years abroad without returning home may be able to qualify because of the length of their previous residence in the UK and their family ties.

It is important for people to explain in full, with evidence, the reasons why they have not been able to return to the UK within two years and why they are doing so at the time of the application. People should be prepared to argue their case, particularly if their stay away has been prolonged for reasons outside their control.

Returning for the purpose of settlement

The rules state that a person must be returning for the purposes of settlement. The rules do not require that the person is coming back to stay indefinitely on that occasion but rather that the person intends generally to keep the UK as the place of their ordinary residence. For example, a person who has a fixed-term, five-year contract to work abroad or is engaged in a course of study overseas may only be returning for a few weeks' vacation leave, but still intends to maintain their main home in the UK and to return here permanently later. They should not be refused entry as a returning resident in these circumstances. However, where people do return to the UK for short periods like this, in particular where they have been abroad for a substantial period of time, immigration officers may question them about their future intentions. The questioning has some-times been personal and intrusive.

The IDI states:

'A person who is returning only for a limited period (e.g. as a visitor) simply to show a period of residence here within two years of departure [will not qualify];

...

However, a person returning temporarily to the United Kingdom is not necessarily a visitor. Many people who have their home in the United Kingdom may spend substantial periods overseas on short-term business contracts or for studies and return to the United Kingdom for only a short period during holidays. This will not disqualify a person from readmission as a returning resident provided:

- he is normally resident in the United Kingdom; and

- at the time of admission he considers the United Kingdom to be his permanent home; and

- he has not been away from the United Kingdom for more than two years and he intends to return to the United Kingdom for settlement in the future on completion of his employment, business or studies etc.'   (IDI, Ch 1, s3, para. 2.2).

Indefinite leave when they last left the country

People must have had indefinite leave when they last left. It is not enough to have had indefinite leave but to have lost it when they last returned and to have been granted only limited leave. People in that position will not qualify under this rule. Even if they have spent most of their lives in the UK, by being admitted for a limited period, any application to settle again is considered at the discretion of the immigration authorities. They might also qualify under some other part of the rules, for example, as the spouse and children of a British citizen if the whole family has returned after some years away.

Not had assistance from public funds to leave

Although this rule refers to 'public funds', it is not intended to mean people who claimed welfare benefits or were housed by a local authority during their previous stay in the UK. Instead it is intended to refer to people who have been voluntarily 'repatriated' at public expense. The power to provide financial assistance to persons who wish to return used to be contained in section 29 of the 1971 Act; it has been replaced by the new powers in section 58 of the 2002 Act (►see 1029). In addition, section 5(6) 1971 Act enables the Secretary of State to make payments to assist persons who are liable to be deported to leave the UK together with their families.

What happens to returning residents on arrival?

Granted entry When a person returns within two years of leaving and is readmitted as a returning resident, their indefinite leave is treated as continuing. Where a person returns to the UK after two years having obtained an entry clearance, the entry clearance operates as leave to enter. The immigration officer will simply place a date stamp over the entry clearance in the passport.

Refused entry In the case of a person who has returned within the two-year period, if the immigration officer believes that there has been a sufficient change of circumstances so as to deny entry, their leave may be 'cancelled'. Those who return after two years (whose leave has therefore lapsed) and do not qualify for entry under the rule, are simply refused leave to enter the UK.

Returning residents granted limited leave

Sometimes those seeking to return as residents find that they are given only limited leave to enter as visitors even though they were seeking entry as a returning resident. This happens, in particular, where the immigration officer is not sure whether the person satisfies the immigration rules. The immigration officer may prepare a report where this course is taken. Immigration officers have sometimes granted leave for two months and advised the person to apply in that time for their right to permanent residence to be reinstated by the Home Office (see IDI, Ch 1, s3, para. 2.3). Although there is no specific provision in the immigration rules for being granted indefinite leave as a 'returning resident' after a person has already re-entered, the Home Office will normally reinstate status if the person satisfies all of the following conditions, namely they (see IDI Ch 1, s3, para. 3.1):

- had indefinite leave when they last left the UK;
- in fact qualify under the returning residents rule;
- considered themselves to qualify for entry under the returning resident rule when they arrived;

- made the application for indefinite leave to remain in time within their initial grant of limited leave.

If a passenger who had indefinite leave when they last left the UK asks for entry as a visitor on entry, the officer should first confirm with them that they understand the implications of what they are asking for and that they will no longer have their returning resident status (IDI, Ch 1, s3, para. 2.4).

Appeals when refused entry as a returning resident

If the application for entry clearance is refused, there is at present a right of appeal. The 2005 Bill may remove the right of appeal except on human rights/discrimination grounds. The entry clearance officer will provide a notice giving reasons for the refusal together with information about how to appeal.

If a returning resident returns to the UK within the period of two years and their leave is cancelled, or it is refused at a time when the applicant had an entry clearance, then, in principle, there is an in-country right of appeal against the decision. Of course, if the applicant returned with entry clearance and the basis of the refusal was that the applicant was in fact seeking leave to enter for a reason not stated in the entry clearance (for example simply for a visit), the applicant would not be able to rely on the entry clearance to obtain an in-country right of appeal (s92(3A)–(3C) 2002 Act).

If the applicant returns after the two years and without an entry clearance then there would only be an in-country right of appeal on human rights or asylum grounds.

PEOPLE WITH LIMITED LEAVE

The rules about leaving and seeking to return to the UK for people with limited leave are different depending on whether the person's leave lapses when they depart. For the general rules about non-lapsing leave, ▶see 107–9.

People whose leave does not lapse when they depart

The following two groups of people, who have limited leave in the UK, keep that leave when they exit the CTA (art. 13(2)(3) Leave to Enter Order):

- people who were given leave by the immigration officer or the Home Office for more than six months (unless the Home Office has subsequently made a decision to change that leave so that, after that decision, the person only has six months or less remaining);
- people who obtained leave by having an entry clearance that operated as leave to enter (but this does not apply to visit entry clearances).

The leave remains valid while a person is outside the UK until the period for which it was granted comes to an end. However, if the leave is still continuing two years after a person has left the UK, it lapses at that point. If the applicant returns within the period of their leave which was granted for more than six months and seeks entry for the same purpose as the leave was originally granted, then they do not require an entry clearance even if they are a visa national or a specified national. Provided that the person returns within the period of the leave and there has been no change of circumstances or other reason to justify cancelling the leave, then the person should be readmitted to the UK.

However, if any of the grounds for cancelling leave apply (▶see 100–3), then the leave may be cancelled on arrival by the immigration officer. So, for example, a student who is still following the same full-time course of studies and who still has the financial support available to do this should be readmitted for the same time as they had before leaving. However, if that student has actually stopped studying, or was on a non-degree level course and has since married a settled or British person and has a firm intention to stay in the UK permanently with them, then leave may be cancelled on the grounds that entry is now, in reality, being sought for a different purpose. The officers may decide that there is such a change of circumstances as to justify cancellation of the leave (para. 321A, HC 395). In the case of seeking entry for marriage, of course, that would be entry for which a different entry clearance would be needed.

Leave expires before return If the leave expires before the passenger returns to the UK, then the person is treated as a fresh arrival and examined accordingly. If the person returns after leave has expired and they are a visa national, or otherwise require an entry clearance for the purpose of their entry, they must obtain a fresh entry clearance from a British post.

People whose leave lapses when they depart

From 30 July 2000, the following categories of people still lose their leave when they depart from the CTA (art. 13, Leave to Enter Order):

- those who obtained leave by a visit entry clearance;
- those granted leave by an immigration officer or the Home Office for a period of six months or less;
- those whose pre-existing leave has been 'varied' (changed) by the immigration authorities so that it is valid for a period of six months or less from the date of the variation;
- those granted automatic leave under section 3C 1971 Act i.e. while waiting for a decision following an in-time application and after their original leave has run out.

Visitors who had entry clearance Most people in this category are visitors but the fact that their leave lapses doesn't harm them if they originally came with an entry clearance. This is because, with minor exceptions, visit entry clearances operate as the grant of leave on an unlimited number of occasions within the period of the validity of the entry clearance (art. 4). On each occasion that a visitor returns to the UK within the period of the validity of the entry clearance, they are granted leave for a further period of six months if the period of validity of the entry clearance is still six months or more. If it is less when the visitor returns, they are granted leave until the end of the period of the validity of the entry clearance. Visitors, therefore, do not need to obtain a further entry clearance before returning provided that their original entry clearance remains valid. Entry can, of course, still be refused even where a person has a visit entry clearance, which acts as leave to enter, on the grounds that the leave should be cancelled (▶see 100–3). In these circumstances, there is in principle, an in-country right of appeal. However, an in-country appeal in cases of visitor refusals, may be excluded if the refusal is on the grounds that the applicant is not a genuine visitor but is seeking entry for other reasons.

Other cases In addition to visitors who entered with an entry clearance, others whose leave is likely to lapse under the rules above include:

- visitors who did not enter with an entry clearance;
- people granted extensions within the rules as visitors;
- students on short courses (up to six months);
- those coming for short-term work such as seasonal agricultural workers who may be admitted for up to six months.

Also, people are sometimes exceptionally granted a period of six months or less in order for them to fulfil a specific purpose before leaving the UK. The leave of all these people, if it was not granted by an entry clearance, lapses when they depart. These people will all need to obtain a fresh entry clearance or leave in order to re-enter the UK.

PEOPLE WHO LEFT THE UK BEFORE 30 JULY 2000

The rules about 'non-lapsing' leave apply to leave which has not expired no matter when that leave was granted, that is, whether it was granted before or after 30 July 2000. However, the new rules do not apply to the leave where the holder left the CTA before 30 July 2000. This is because the transitional provisions state that the rules about lapsing leave apply to leave which was 'in force' at the time that the new rule came into force on 30 July (see art. 15(2) Leave to Enter Order). If a person left the CTA before that time, then their leave lapsed at the point they left and was therefore no longer 'in force' on 30 July 2000.

It can be expected that the old rules relating to readmission continue to apply to a person who left the UK before 30 July 2000. In summary, those rules are:

- if the person was granted leave by the immigration authorities for more than six months and they return within that period, they do not need an entry clearance;
- if the person returns within the period of time granted by the original limited leave which was given for over six months, then although that leave has lapsed, the same time-limits and conditions will normally be applied to the leave on re-entry provided that the person returning continues to satisfy the requirements of the rules. Where, however, the person returns at a time when this rule would mean that they would get less than two months, leave will normally be granted for a period of two months to give sufficient time for the making of a further application. However, if the same person returns with an entry clearance, then the period and conditions of leave will depend on the entry clearance granted;
- if the person was not previously granted leave for more than six months, or is not returning within the period of the original leave, then they need an entry clearance to return if they would ordinarily need one;
- if they return to the UK after the period of their original leave, they will be treated as fresh arrivals and examined by immigration officers in the ordinary way. If they have an entry clearance which operates as leave, they will generally be granted leave on the basis of that entry clearance. If not, the immigration officer will apply the immigration rules to decide whether they qualify for entry.

There are unlikely, now, to be many (if any) cases in which an applicant left the UK before 30 July 2000 with limited leave, which would, but for it having lapsed, still be extant now. Of course, there may be those who left the UK with indefinite leave prior to that time and, if such applicants wanted to return as residents, they would have to satisfy the returning residents rule (above).

PEOPLE WHO WISH TO TRAVEL WHILE AN APPLICATION OR AN APPEAL IS OUTSTANDING

Travelling while an application or an appeal is outstanding is hazardous. Applicants should take careful advice on the up-to-date procedures. For details about obtaining travel documents for those who have no passports or travel documents, ▶see 631–2 and 880–3.

Return of passports

While the Home Office is considering an application for an extension of leave or variation of conditions, it is normal for it to keep the applicant's passport. The passport can be requested back at any time if the holder needs it, for example, as proof of identity for a bank, to show to a marriage registrar or to obtain a driving licence. The application will not be treated as withdrawn if return of the passport is requested for purposes like this. It takes about four weeks to return a passport by post, although sometimes it can take longer. However, passports can be picked up more quickly in person. Applicants are advised to contact the Home Office in advance about this.

It is possible to ask the Home Office to speed up their consideration of the application to extend leave itself so that an applicant can travel outside the UK. The Home Office is only likely to agree to do this if there is an emergency, such as a family illness, which means that the applicant must travel (for details of the 'urgent treatment form' in the context of work and business applications, ▶see 432). In such a case, it would be necessary to obtain a letter in English from the medical authorities concerned abroad.

The Home Office states:

'If you need to travel because there is an emergency medical reason such as family illness abroad, we will consider dealing with your application quickly. You will need to have a letter faxed in English from a doctor or hospital abroad. The fax number for this is 020 8604 5781/5782.' (IND website under 'Return of passports')

However, if a person simply asks for the return of their passport 'for the purpose of travel outside the common travel area', while an application is being considered, then the immigration rules state that the application is treated as withdrawn as soon as the passport is returned (para. 34 HC 395). This rule does now seem inconsistent with the changes in the law (see above), which prevent leave from lapsing when people leave the UK, and also the new ability of the Home Office to make decisions on whether to grant or refuse or change a person's leave when they are outside the UK.

Even if the application is treated as withdrawn when a person leaves, if the previous original grant of leave has not yet expired when a person wishes to travel, then that grant of leave is still valid and the rules dealing with a person leaving and returning, which are set out above still apply. If the leave would otherwise have expired during the period while the Home Office was considering the application, then, when the Home Office returns the passport, it may grant leave to remain for a short period to enable the person to demonstrate in future that they did not actually overstay their leave before leaving. If the person's plans change and they do not travel but instead return the passport and an application form to the Home Office to continue to apply to remain, the Home Office treats this as a new application, made on this date.

It is therefore very important that people who want their passports for any purpose other than travel should make this clear in their request to the Home Office. An application is only withdrawn if the request for the passport is for the purpose of travel. As stated above, the application remains pending if the passport is taken away from the Home Office for other purposes.

Travelling before an application is decided

If a person only has leave that is granted automatically under section 3C 1971 Act when they make an in-time application and their original leave has run out, then their leave lapses when they travel outside the CTA.

It is risky for people to travel after their leave has run out and before the Home Office has decided the application, and to expect to be able to return. They will be able to leave the UK without difficulty but when they return, they will have to satisfy immigration officers that they fit into the immigration rules. Until March 1998, it was usual for immigration officers to endorse triangular departure stamps on passports of people leaving, showing the date of departure from the UK. Comparison of the dates of previous permission to stay and the date of departure will usually lead immigration officers to ask questions and then contact the Home Office to check the position. Until recently, passports were no longer stamped on departure. However, following the bombings in London in July 2005, embarkation controls were reintroduced at 'key high profile ports' (Home Office answer to an IND User Panel question on 20 September 2005). On arrival in the UK, immigration officers will often ask about the circumstances of a previous stay.

If the application to the Home Office was a straightforward one which was likely to succeed; there were good reasons for leaving; and the applicant can satisfy the ECO/immigration officers that they qualify to enter; they may be granted leave to enter for the period they request provided the rules and any requirements concerning entry clearance are satisfied.

People who need to travel while the Home Office is considering an application sometimes believe it would be easier to obtain emergency travel documents from their own embassies or high commissions and travel on these while the Home Office continues to consider the application. This is not a safe procedure. It is unusual for a travel document to be issued in these circumstances, but if one is, it does not alter the holder's immigration status – that an application for further leave to remain had been made, but not decided, when they left. When they return, immigration officers will probably see that the document was issued from a consular office in London and will wonder what the person's status was in the UK. When they know that an application was pending, they will contact the Home Office about the application and what is happening with it. It is not safe to expect entry to be granted.

Travelling before an appeal is decided

It is obviously not safe to travel out of the UK while an in-country appeal is outstanding. Section 104(4) 2002 Act states that if an appellant leaves the UK while they have an appeal against an 'immigration decision' pending, then the appeal will be treated as abandoned. If the appeal is treated as abandoned, the AIT will take no further action on it (see rule 18, Asylum and Immigration Tribunal (Procedure) Rules 2005).

6   Applying to stay in the UK

People who have been allowed to enter or remain in the UK, can apply to the Home Office for permission to extend their leave. This chapter is mainly concerned with such applications. It is important, for a number of reasons, to make applications to extend leave before the existing leave has run out. Applications to extend leave are known as applications for leave to *remain* rather than to enter. If the application is made 'in-time', they may also be referred to as applications to 'vary' leave. Only those with limited leave need to make these applications, as those with indefinite leave have no time-limit attached to the leave and no other conditions (such as restrictions on work) can be attached to an indefinite leave.

Where applicants are applying for leave to remain in a different category to the one in which they were admitted or to the one in which they presently have leave, these are known as applications to 'switch'. The immigration rules very carefully regulate the circumstances in which applicants are permitted to switch without leaving the UK and applying to return. 'Switching' is covered in the next chapter, Chapter 7. In particular, the table at ▶161 onwards sets out which applicants may switch to which category, or categories under the immigration rules.

While no-one may be treated less favourably than the immigration rules allow, there is always the possibility of asking the Home Office to exercise discretion outside the immigration rules and the Home Office has certain policies which indicate when it will be prepared to act in this way.

This chapter

At the beginning of the chapter, we look at the various application forms, which can be used to apply for leave to remain (▶see 127–32) and at the charges that are made for such applications (▶125–7). Next we look at making applications in the general categories – applying by post/in person; the validity of the application; applying in-time; and at the time taken to decide applications (▶132–6). We then look briefly at applications for further leave in the Immigration Employment Document (IED), EEA and asylum/Article 3 ECHR categories (▶136–8) but a short overview only is given as the separate procedures for applications in these categories are dealt with elsewhere.

We go on to consider Home Office decisions on applications for leave to remain. This covers the notice of decision, the endorsements that are given and the *general* grounds upon which leave to remain may be refused (▶138–41). We then look at the curtailment of leave and at other decisions, which can be taken by the Home Office without any application having been made (▶141–3).

The chapter then deals with the question of what status a person has while waiting for an in-time application for further leave to be decided or while appealing against a negative decision on such an application. We look at the provisions in the legislation (from 'VOLO' onwards), which automatically grant leave to remain (▶143–6).

We then explain the meaning of 'exceptional leave', the various different labels given by the Home Office to leave granted outside the immigration rules (including 'ELR', 'Humanitarian Protection' and 'Discretionary Leave') and note the various different concessions, which are operated outside the rules (▶see 147–50).

The chapter finally looks at two recent additions to the immigration rules that do not fit into any other chapter of the *Handbook*:

- the rules relating to members of the armed forces and their families; in particular we cover here the recent rules for granting indefinite leave to discharged Gurkhas and foreign and Commonwealth members of the armed forces and at the rules for the families of members of the armed forces who are exempt from immigration control (▶150–1);
- the rules dealing with the grant of indefinite leave on the basis of *long residence* in the UK: the ten-year rule and the 14-year rule – we also look at those parts of the old long-residence concession (outside the immigration rules) which may still be of use in applying for the exercise of discretion (▶151–7).

Further changes to procedures proposed

It seems that the government intends to make yet further changes to the procedures with which applicants must comply in order to make immigration applications or claims. The Immigration, Asylum and Nationality Bill 2005 proposes to give the Secretary of State further powers to require that specified procedures must be followed and to set out the consequences of failing to comply. The procedures may be set out in the immigration rules or in other legislation. It seems that the new power to prescribe that certain procedures are followed will replace the existing powers in section 31A 1971 Act (procedure for applications) and section 25 2004 Act (applications for permission to marry).

APPLICATION FORMS AND CHARGING

Before November 1996, there were no special rules as to what counted as an application for an extension of leave. Any clear request to the Home Office, either in person or by letter accompanied by a passport or travel document, was acceptable. Since then, however, most non-asylum applications to the Home Office for leave to remain must be made on the appropriate Home Office prescribed application form. This is the case whether the person is making an in-time or out-of-time application.

Charging

Since the last edition of the *Handbook*, the Home Office has introduced a system of charging for non-asylum in-country applications. It began on 1 August 2003. The intention was to ensure service improvement in line with charging.

In the weeks following the introduction of charging, the Minister explained the thinking as follows:

'The principle behind charging is to ensure that those who use the service pay for it to ease the burden on the general taxpayer. The fees are set under Treasury rules to recover the full administrative cost entailed in considering applications and no more. This is calculated by taking the overall costs of processing applications divided by the number of decisions we expect to make...

We are committed to deliver our published service standards and then to improve them and the revenue generated from charging will enable us to do so. I have already invested heavily to ensure that IND is in a position to meet these standards. Indeed I can confirm that we are already meeting these targets and in some cases exceeding them. There will, however, always be cases which cannot be decided within 13 weeks but we are looking to keep these to a minimum' (Letter of Beverley Hughes MP to ILPA, 23 September 2003).

The charges themselves

The charges are set out in regulations made under section 5 of the 1999 Act. These are the Immigration (Leave to Remain) (Fees) Regulations 2003 (referred to below as 'the 2003 Regulations'). They were most recently amended by the Immigration (Leave to Remain) (Fees) (Amendment) Regulations 2005. Section 5 was amended by the 2004 Act to allow charging for the transfer of limited leave into a new passport as well as the transfer of indefinite leave. A Home Office leaflet about charging can be downloaded from its website (www.ind.homeoffice.gov.uk): 'Information about charges for general casework applications from 1 April 2005'.

We do not cover here the cost of applications in the Immigration Employment Document categories, which include work permit and HSMP applications (for the cost of applications in these categories, ▶see 418–20).

Under the above regulations, the present level of charges has been in force from 1 April 2005. Subject to the categories that are exempted from charges (see below), the rates are as follows.

Application	Cost
All postal/courier applications (except student and transfer/ no-limit applications)	£335
Student postal applications	£250
Transfer of leave/no time-limit (TOC/NTL) postal applications	£160
Certificate of Approval (Marriage) applications (post only)	£135
All 'premium service' applications (made in person)	£500

For the above purposes, a 'student' application include an application as: an 'ordinary' student, a student nurse, a student who is resitting an exam, a student who is writing up a thesis, a student union sabbatical officer and a prospective student.

Exemptions from charges

Some applications are exempt from charges. There are no charges for:

- 'asylum' and article 3 ECHR applicants (see s5(3)(6), 94(1) 1999 Act);
- dependants (spouse, unmarried partner or child under the age of 18) of those seeking either asylum or applying on Article 3 grounds (s5(3)(a)(ii) 1999 Act; reg. 6, 2003 Regulations);
- those applying for indefinite leave on the grounds of domestic violence where, at the time of the application, the applicant appears to be destitute (reg. 5(e), 2003 Regulations);
- applicants who have limited leave which was granted outside the immigration rules at the time their asylum application was rejected (this could be humanitarian protection, discretionary leave or exceptional leave) and who are applying for further leave outside the immigration rules (such applications are made on either Forms ELR or HPDL, see below) (reg. 5(f), 2003 Regulations);
- applicants who are under 18 and are being provided with accommodation or maintenance by a local authority under s17, 20 or 23 of the Children Act 1989 (or certain provisions of the Children (Scotland) Act 1995 or the Children (Northern Ireland) Order 1995) (reg. 5(d)(i), 2003 Regulations);
- applicants who have limited leave to remain which was granted to them while they were under 18 at the time that their asylum application was rejected and who are now applying for further leave to remain outside the immigration rules (reg. 5(d)(ii), 2003 Regulations);
- applicants who arrive in the UK with existing leave and, on arrival, seek to vary that leave for a period of up to six months (reg. 5(b), 2003 Regulations);
- EEA nationals and their family members who are applying for residence permits, residence documents or permanent residence based on rights of free movement – their documents simply recognise their status;

- nationals of Bulgaria, Romania and Turkey and their dependants who are applying for leave to remain under the EC Association Agreements (reg. 5(a), 2003 Regulations).

In IED cases, there is a further exemption for nationals of a country that has ratified the European Social Charter or the European Revised Social Charter (▶see 419).

The forms

The application forms can be downloaded from the Immigration and Nationality Directorate website (www.ind.homeoffice.gov.uk). Alternatively, if the applicant is unable to download them, they can be obtained by telephoning the Application Forms Unit at the Home Office (tel. 0870 241 0645). If the applicant is in any doubt about which form to use, it is possible to ask the Immigration and Nationality Enquiry Bureau (tel. 0870 606 7766). However, this Bureau is part of the Home Office and cannot offer independent advice.

New forms are issued every six months or so and applications must be made using the current forms. All applications made on or after 15 September 2005 must be made on the forms which were issued from that date (see s31A 1971 Act, the Immigration (Leave to Remain) (Prescribed Forms and Procedure) (No. 2) Regulations 2005, para. 32 HC 395). The relevant forms, as well as the non-compulsory forms are set out in the table below.

Applicants should keep copies of the application form and the documents sent so that it can be proved that an application has been made.

Dependants

If a person applying to remain has dependants who seek to remain with them, there is a place on the forms for them to be included. Only the spouse, unmarried partner and dependants under 18 can be included with the main applicant on the application forms. There is one fee per application and so if any of these dependants applies separately or at a different time on another form, they will have to pay a separate fee.

The relevant part of the *Handbook* indicates whether the immigration rules allow family members to be admitted with the main applicant and, if so, what requirements have to be satisfied. Section 4 on family members also covers these questions.

WHICH FORMS SHOULD BE USED

The forms in use as of 15 September 2005 and the purposes for which they are to be used are as follows.

General forms

Form FLR (M) This form should be used to apply for an extension of leave to remain in the UK as the spouse or unmarried partner of a person present and settled in the UK (▶see Chapter 11).

Form FLR(O) This form should be used to apply for an extension of leave to remain in the following categories: visitor; private medical visitor; doctor/dentist in post-graduate training; *au pair*; teacher or language assistant under an approved exchange scheme; representative of an overseas newspaper, news agency or broadcasting organisation; private servant in a diplomatic household; domestic worker in a private household; overseas government employee; minister of religion, missionary or member of a religious order; member of the operational ground staff of an overseas-owned airline; person of UK ancestry; member of the crew of a ship, aircraft, hovercraft, hydrofoil or international train service; writer/artist/composer; spouse or child of an armed forces member who is exempt from immigration control (▶see 474–5); *or for other purposes in the immigration rules not covered by other application forms* (▶*see Chapters 9, 10, 15, 16*).

Note that the version of Form FLR (O) issued for applications from 1 April 2005 omitted the page asking for criminal convictions. In order to rectify this the Home Office began handing FLR (O) applicants a 'stand alone' criminal convictions form to complete if they applied in person at a PEO. If the application was made by post, the applicant would be sent a copy of the additional criminal convictions form by post (see IND letter to ILPA, 13 May 2005). The FLR (O) form valid from 15 September 2005 includes the questions about criminal convictions.

Form FLR (S) This form should be used to apply for an extension of leave as a student, student nurse, to resit an examination or to write up a thesis and for sabbatical officers or prospective students (▶see Chapter 10).

Form FLR (SEGS) This form is for applications for an extension of leave under the Science and Engineering Graduate Scheme (▶see 464–5).

Form FLR (FT: WISS) This form should be used to apply for an extension of leave under the 'Fresh Talent: Working in Scotland' scheme (▶see 465–6).

Form SET (M) This form should be used by a person seeking indefinite leave to remain (settlement) as the spouse or unmarried partner of a person present and settled in the UK (▶see Chapter 11).

Form SET (F) This form should be used to apply for indefinite leave to remain in the UK as a family member (not husband, wife or unmarried partner) of a person present and settled in the UK. It is to be used by: children under the age of 18 of a parent(s) or relative present and settled in the UK; adopted children under the age of 18 of parent/s present and settled in the UK; parents, grandparents or other dependent relatives aged over 18, of a person present and settled in the UK (▶see Chapters 12-13).

Form SET (O) This form should be used to apply for *indefinite* leave to remain as a person who has been in the UK for four years as a: work-permit holder; representative of an overseas newspaper, news agency or broadcasting organisation; private servant in a diplomatic household; domestic worker in a private household; overseas government employee; minister of religion, missionary or member of a religious order; member of the operational ground staff of an overseas-owned airline; person of UK ancestry; writer/artist/ composer; and highly skilled migrant (HSMP). It can also be used to apply for indefinite leave on the grounds of long residence in the UK (▶see 151–7); as the victim of domestic violence (▶see 345–51); as a foreign or Commonwealth national who has been discharged from HM Forces (▶see 150–1); or for other purposes under the immigration rules not covered by other application forms.

Form BUS This form should be used to apply for further leave *or* indefinite leave as a business person; sole representative (▶see 455–6); retired person of independent means; investor or innovator (▶see generally Chapter 16).

Form ELR This form should now only be used to apply for *indefinite leave* in the UK if the applicant was granted exceptional leave to remain before 1 April 2003 following the refusal of asylum and has completed four years of exceptional leave and still has a fear of returning to the country of origin (▶see 873–4).

Form HPDL This form should be used to apply for further leave to remain in the UK *or* to apply for indefinite leave, for a person who was granted limited leave (humanitarian protection, or discretionary leave or exceptional leave granted for less than four years) following refusal of asylum (▶see 866–75 and ▶see 720 onwards).

Form FLR (IED) ▶See 420 and ▶see 431–4 for when this form should be used.

Transferring leave into new passport

Where an applicant does not need to extend their leave, but obtains a new passport and needs their existing leave to be endorsed in the new passport, the following forms should be used.

Form TOC This form can be used to apply to have a *limited* leave endorsed in a new passport or travel document. 'TOC' stands for 'transfer of conditions'.

Form NTL This form can be used to apply for an *indefinite* leave to be endorsed in a new passport or travel document. 'NTL' stands for 'no time-limit'. People who do not wish to have their indefinite leave transferred will have to carry their old and their new passports with them so that they have evidence of their status.

Certificate of Approval for marriage

From 1 February 2005, many non-EEA nationals who need leave to be in the UK (whether they have it or not), need to apply for a 'certificate of approval' in order to marry in the UK. For full details of who needs to apply and the new procedures ▶see 296–300. The application for a certificate is made on **Form COA (Marriage)**. Note that approval to marry does not give the applicant leave to remain in the UK – a separate application for leave must be made.

Multiple applications

From 1 April 2005, the following forms have been in use for multiple applications. They are to be used *together with* the prescribed forms above in order to make multiple applications in particular categories. The purpose of these forms is to allow groups of applicants (between two and 25) to pay for the applications together in one lump sum. Each separate applicant must still complete the relevant application form and provide the information and documents relevant to their individual application.

Special guidance notes are issued together with these forms, which should be read carefully. The Home Office website also contains a further information document dealing with the procedures for these applications: 'Information about single payment for multiple applications'. Applications made under a single payment multiple application form should take the same time to process as other leave to remain applications.

Form Postal LTR Multiple This form can be used to apply for multiple further leave to remain postal applications. It can be used with the following forms only: FLR (M); FLR (O); SET (F); SET (M); SET (O) and BUS.

Form Student Multiple This form can be used together with Form FLR (S) only to make postal multiple student applications.

Form NTL/TOC Multiple This form can be used to make multiple postal applications for 'transfer of conditions' or 'no time-limit' endorsements. It can be used together with Forms TOC and NTL only.

Form COA Multiple This form can be used to make multiple applications by post for certificates of approval for marriage. It can only be used together with Form COA.

Form Premium Multiple This enables multiple applications to be made in person at the PEO. However, those applications which cannot be made at the PEO generally (for example COA (Marriage) applications and applications made on Form BUS) (▶see below at 133) cannot be included within a premium multiple application. These premium multiple applications can only be made by recognised representatives or organisations, which have an agreement with the PEO to submit an agreed number of applications on a particular day.

EEA applications

Using the application forms is optional in EEA cases. Applications can also be made by a covering letter setting out the relevant facts and enclosing the relevant documentation (▶see further below at 136–7).

Form EEC1 This is the form on which EEA nationals can apply for a residence permit. It can also be used by family members of EEA nationals to apply for a residence permit (or a 'residence document' if the family members are not themselves EEA nationals). Accession 8 nationals can also use this form if they want to obtain recognition of their right to reside in the UK in one of the free-movement categories other than as a worker (e.g. as a self-employed person or a self-sufficient person). A8 nationals can also apply for a residence permit on Form EEC1 on the basis of employment if they have legally worked in the UK without interruption for a period of 12 months and are therefore no longer required to register (for details about this group of persons, ▶see 568, 570, 1270–2). For details about applications for registration on the Worker Registration Scheme for A8 nationals who are required to register, ▶see 573–5.

Form EEC2 This can be used by EEA nationals or their family members to apply for settlement (▶see 559–63).

Form EEC3 This form can be used by the non-EEA national dependants of persons required to register under the Accession State Worker Registration Scheme in order to apply for a 'family member residence stamp' to confirm their rights of residence in the UK (▶see 570, 572, 549).

EEA Association Agreement applications

Form ECAA Main This can be used for applications for either further leave to remain or indefinite leave to remain in the UK as a self-employed person under the EC Association Agreements with Bulgaria or Romania. Dependants who are applying for an extension of leave at the same time can be included in the application.

Form Turkish ECAA (Main) This can be used for applications for further leave or indefinite leave in the UK under the Turkish Association Agreement. Dependants who are applying for an extension of leave at the same time can be included in the application.

ECAA (Dep) This form can be used for an applicant who is applying as the dependant of a person who has been granted leave under the EC Association Agreements with either Bulgaria, Romania or Turkey but who is not applying for leave at the same time as the principal. It can be used for further leave and indefinite leave applications.

Notes

1) Details about applications for Immigration Employment Documents (IED) (work permits, HSMP etc) and applying for further leave on the basis of an IED are not covered above. Further leave is applied for using **Form FLR (IED)** (▶see below 136).

2) For details about applying for naturalisation or registration as a British citizen and the forms used for these purpose, ▶see Chapter 45.

MAKING APPLICATIONS IN THE GENERAL CATEGORIES

Below we look at making immigration applications for leave to remain in the UK in all categories *other than* the asylum/article 3 ECHR, EEA or the IED (work permit etc) categories. For applications in those latter categories ▶see further below at 136–8. The procedures set out immediately below are relevant to applications made on Forms FLR (M), FLR (O); FLR (S); FLR (SEGS); FLR (FT: WISS); SET (M); SET (F); SET (O); BUS; ELR; HPDL; TOC; NTL and COA (Marriage).

Applying by post

The correct postal address for all applications is given in the Guidance Notes in the form and must be checked when sending the application. For applications where a *payment* has to be made and processed, the address is:

Initial Consideration Unit [state type of form e.g. 'FLR (M)']
Immigration and Nationality Directorate
PO Box 3615
Walsall Road
Cannock
WS11 0WS

The Home Office recommends that applicants use recorded or special delivery post as this provides the applicant with proof of posting and also helps the Home Office to record receipt of the application. Applicants who do send in their applications by recorded delivery or special delivery should keep the number. The Home Office states that it aims to acknowledge applications within one week of receiving them.

However, once the application has been sent in, if the applicant has further information to provide, then it should be sent to the following address:

Initial Consideration Unit [state type of form e.g. 'FLR (M)']
Immigration and Nationality Directorate
Lunar House
40 Wellesley Road
Croydon
CR9 2BY

The above Lunar House address is also the address for making applications on the following forms, which do not require payment: Form ELR and Form HPDL. Applications on Form HPDL should be addressed for the attention of 'ACU 1 Active Review Team'.

As indicated above, applicants applying on Form BUS, send their initial application to the Cannock address. *However*, if they need to contact the Home Office after the application has been made, they should not write to the Lunar House address but to:

Business Case Unit
Work Permits (UK)
Home Office
PO Box 3468
Sheffield
S3 8WA

Applying in person

A same-day service is offered to people who apply in person at one of the Home Office's Public Enquiry Offices (PEOs). However, this service is only offered for straightforward applications, which do not require further enquiries. The Home Office states that applicants who wish to apply in person should make an appointment in advance with one of the PEOs. There are PEOs at Croydon, London; Dominion Court, Birmingham; Reliance House, Liverpool and Festival Court, Glasgow. The addresses are given on the forms. The forms also give the telephone numbers which can be called in order to arrange for an appointment to make an 'in person' application. Further up-to-date information on PEOs and contact numbers can be found on the PEO page of the Home Office website (▶see also 1497 for details of the PEOs).

Not all types of application can be made in person and given same-day service. As well as non-straightforward applications, the following applications cannot be given same-day service and should be made by post: EEA applications (including transfer applications); COA (Marriage) applications; applications made on Form BUS, Form ELR, Form HPDL (and see reg. 14(2) Immigration (Leave to Remain) (Prescribed Forms and Procedures) (No. 2) Regulations 2005).

If the same-day service is used, the 'premium rate' (above) is charged for the application.

Return of passports and documents

An applicant who needs the return of their passport or other document urgently should contact the Home Office at the following address:

Immigration and Nationality Directorate
Passport Hotline
15th Floor
Lunar House
40 Wellesley Road
Croydon
CR9 2BY

But note if an applicant requests the return of their passport for the purposes of travel, their application for leave will be treated as having been withdrawn. The applicant will not receive a refund of the fee in these circumstances. For further details about this and the possibility of speeding up an application in urgent cases, ▶see 119–21.

Ensuring the application is valid

The application form must be (reg. 14(1), Immigration (Leave to Remain) (Prescribed Forms and Procedures) (No. 2) Regulations 2005):

- signed and dated by the applicant (except that if the applicant is under 18, the form may be signed and dated by the parent or legal guardian of the applicant on the applicant's behalf);
- accompanied by the documents and photographs required by the form; and
- completed in full in accordance with the instructions given on the form.

The application must be made on the correct form and be accompanied by originals of all the documents requested on the form. If the original documents cannot be provided, then an explanation of when they can should be given. If certified copies are sent, they should be certified by the body that issued the original and an explanation should be provided of why those documents have not been supplied and when they will be sent. Although further information can be added in covering letters, every question asked on the form must be answered on the form itself.

If any of the above requirements are not met, the application will be treated as invalid if (reg. 15(1) of the above regulations):

- the applicant does not provide an explanation for the failure to comply with the requirements, which the Home Office considers satisfactory;
- the Home Office notifies the applicant (or representative) of the failure to comply within 28 days of the date on which the application is made (for these purposes the application is treated as being made on the date of posting or the date on which the application was submitted in person and accepted at a PEO, reg. 15(2)); and

- the applicant does not comply with the requirements within a reasonable time, which cannot be more than 28 days after being notified by the Home Office of the existing failure to comply.

The Home Office's Initial Consideration Unit decides whether the application complies with the relevant requirements and, if it does not, will send the application back marked with the parts that do not comply.

It is obviously important that a valid application is made within time in order to prevent the applicant from becoming an overstayer and in order to preserve important rights of appeal.

Applications must be made in-time

Applications for extensions should always be made to the Home Office in good time before the current leave expires. If leave has already expired, then legal advice should be obtained about making a further application without delay.

The Home Office states that normally the postmark on the envelope in which the application is submitted will determine the date the application is treated as having been submitted (see Home Office leaflet, 'Information about charges for general casework applications from 1 April 2005').

The consequences of not applying for further leave in time are serious. People who do not make an in-time application for further leave:

- become liable for administrative removal from the UK as overstayers;
- may have their application for further leave refused under the general grounds for refusal in the immigration rules (▶see below 140). In some cases, this is particularly important because the specific immigration rules in some categories require that a person has limited leave at the time that a decision is made on their application and that they have not remained in breach of the immigration laws (e.g. applications to remain as the spouse or unmarried partner of a person settled in the UK);
- will, as overstayers, be excluded from most welfare benefits, support from a local authority and local authority housing (if they are not already excluded by their immigration status);
- become liable to criminal proceedings, although prosecutions are not frequent.

Time taken for considering applications

The service standards for the time to process applications to which the Minister referred in the above quote at ▶125, up-to-date for 2005/06 are as follows.

Applications made by post The aim is to decide 70 per cent of applications within four weeks (20 working days) and 90 per cent within 14 weeks (70 working days).

Applications made in person The aim is to decide 98 per cent of applications within 24 hours.

MAKING APPLICATIONS IN THE IED, EEA, ASYLUM AND ARTICLE 3 ECHR CATEGORIES

Applications made in the Immigration Employment Document (IED), EEA, asylum and Article 3 ECHR categories are also looked at elsewhere in the *Handbook*. The information given below provides an overview.

Extending leave in Immigration Employment Document (IED) categories

The forms set out in the table above do not cover those applying to extend leave in an IED category (except those applying for *indefinite* leave after four years in the UK with a work permit or under the Highly Skilled Migrants' Programme, who should use Form SET (O)).

The IED categories are:

- work-permit holder;
- HSMP;
- sectors-based scheme (SBS);
- seasonal agricultural workers' scheme (SAWS).

Since 1 April 2004, all people who wish to extend leave in order to remain in the IED categories need to go through two procedures. They must:

- obtain an IED (work permit etc); *and*
- apply to extend their leave on a separate form (Form FLR (IED)).

General details about IEDs, charging for them and for applications for leave to remain are given at ▶418–20. More specific details about making applications are given in the part of the same chapter dealing with work permits at ▶430–5. Details about all the IED categories and applying under each of them are covered in Chapter 14, except for details about the HSMP which is covered at ▶483–91.

EEA applications

EEA nationals and their family members who are in the UK may apply for residence permits (for EEA nationals) or for residence documents (for non-EEA national 'family members' of EEA nationals). Neither EEA nationals with the right to live in the UK nor their family members need to have a residence permit or document. Their right to be in the UK exists independently of documentation but these documents can be obtained as evidence of their status in the UK.

For more details about obtaining residence permits and documents, ▶see 544–9.

The Home Office provides forms upon which applications can be made (►see the table above at 131). The forms are not compulsory although the Home Office prefers that they are used because it considers that they are the best way to ensure that all the relevant details are provided. It is possible that applications made on the forms provided will be decided more quickly. The Home Office requests that applicants mark the envelope 'European Applications'. No charge is made for the applications, which are to be submitted to:

European Applications
Immigration and Nationality Directorate
Home Office
Data Processing Team
4th Floor, Block B
Whitgift Centre
15 Wellesley Road
Croydon
CR9 1AT

The Home Office states that it can normally determine EEA applications made on Forms EEC1 and EEC2 within three weeks of receipt. However, large numbers of applications have caused delays in decisions and applications have been said to be taking up to six months.

For details about the requirements for qualifying for EU free-movement rights, ►see Chapters 17–18. For details about the rights of A8 nationals in particular, ►see Chapter 19.

EEA Association Agreement applications

There are also application forms available for applications under the European Community Association Agreements (►see table above at 131). It is not compulsory to use them (although the Home Office prefers it). There are, again, no charges.

There have been delays in processing EEA Association Agreement applications. In many cases, where applications had been outstanding for some time, the Home Office began sending out Form ECAA (Main) and asking that it be completed which would often mean repeating information already provided. In response to an enquiry by Kingsley Napley Solicitors, the Home Office confirmed that sending the form out was not an attempt to make the application form compulsory. In an email dated 4 March 2005, the ECAA Task Force Team stated:

'The detailed application form is an aid to caseworkers in helping them order and consider the key factors that they need to take into account in making a decision on a case. It is also potentially helpful to applicants as a means of organising the material in support of their application. The letter which was sent out with the application form confined itself to saying 'it would be helpful if you could complete this and provide all the information requested'. It is entirely up to the applicant if they comply with the request.'

Applications and supporting documents are to be sent to:

Home Office
PO Box 3468
Sheffield
S3 8WA

For details about the requirements for qualifying under the Association Agreements, ▶see Chapter 20.

Asylum and Article 3 ECHR claims

The immigration authorities are under a duty to treat an asylum application as having been made whenever a person indicates either in writing or orally that they will be in some sort of danger if they are returned to their country of origin. Applications do not need to be submitted on a prescribed application form and there is no charge. However, applicants who wish to make a claim after entering the UK, i.e. not port applicants, and those who are not apprehended by the immigration authorities, will be required to attend one of two Asylum Screening Units in person. They will not be able to submit a postal application except for in certain circumstances.

For further details about asylum procedures, see Chapter 22. The same applies to Article 3 ECHR claims. For details about extending HP, DL or exceptional leave ▶see 866–75 and ▶see 720 onwards.

Applications made outside the UK or on entry

Applications to vary leave made when the applicant is outside the UK or applications made to the immigration officer on arrival to the UK by someone who already has leave (e.g., because they previously had leave which did not lapse) also do not need to be made on a prescribed form (see paras 31A, 32, 33A HC 395).

HOME OFFICE DECISIONS ON APPLICATIONS

The Home Office makes decisions by applying the requirements contained in the relevant immigration rules. In addition, decisions of the Home Office must always comply with an applicant's human rights under the ECHR. The immigration rules themselves do not set out the rights which are protected and the effect which they have on applications, they simply require the immigration authorities to 'carry out their duties...in compliance with the provisions of the Human Rights Act 1998' (para. 2 HC 395).

The rules for the different categories in which leave can be granted are set out in the relevant parts of the *Handbook*. However there are also *general* grounds upon which leave to remain can be refused. The immigration rules list ten grounds on which an extension of stay 'should normally be refused'. There is also one circumstance in which the rules state that leave 'is to be refused' (see para. 322(1)–(11), HC 395). These general grounds are set out in the table below (▶140–1).

Where an application or a decision is made, the Home Office may also issue the applicant with a 'one-stop' notice requiring them to state all their additional reasons for wishing to enter or remain (or not be removed from) the UK (s120 2002 Act and ▶see 662–4, 1066–7).

Notice of decision

If the application to the Home Office to extend leave is successful, the Home Office will endorse the further leave and conditions in the passport or travel document (see below for the endorsements which are now issued).

If however, the application is unsuccessful or the Home Office has curtailed leave without an application having been made (see below), then this will also be notified in writing together with information about any right of appeal which exists against the decision. For further details about Home Office notices of decision and the requirements with which the Home Office must comply, ▶see 1061–2. In most cases, provided the application was made in-time, there is a right of appeal against the decision. There are no rights of appeal, however, if the Home Office grants further leave, although not for the length of time or on the conditions that the applicant wanted. Rights of appeal are also denied if, for example, the application was not made in-time or the application was to 'switch' into a category which the immigration rules would not allow because the applicant has not been admitted with the relevant entry clearance. Except in 'third country' asylum cases or certain other certified cases, there will always be an in-country right of appeal on asylum or human rights grounds.

The rules about appeals are complex, however. For a guide as to when there is a right of appeal in principle, when it can be excluded and when the appeal is in-country, ▶see Tables 1–3 at 1052–60. For the proposed changes to rights of appeal, ▶see the table at 1042–6.

New endorsements

The endorsements placed in applicants' passports when leave is granted have changed since the last edition of the *Handbook*. On 17 June 2003, the Minister, Beverley Hughes MP, announced the introduction of the 'UKRP' (United Kingdom Residence Permit) to replace the ink stamps previously used to confirm a person's right to stay in the UK. The UKRP is issued to all those who are granted more than six months' leave in the UK. The UKRP was introduced in order to comply with an EU regulation and takes the form of a vignette in a passport. The format is a common EU-wide one and is intended to safeguard against forged documents.

Where it is not possible (or appropriate – for example an asylum-seeker only has a national passport issued by the authorities of the country they fear) to issue the UKRP in a passport, it is to be attached to another new set of documents: the 'Immigration Status Documents' (ISDs) instead. ISDs are generally for granting leave to those successful after an asylum application, although there are different ISDs depending on whether the decision is to grant refugee status, humanitarian protection or discretionary leave.

The Home Office began issuing UKRPs in late 2003. They contain:

- the person's name, nationality, gender, date of birth, passport number;
- UKRP permit number;
- place of issue;
- date of issue;
- conditions of leave in the UK;
- the type of permit it is and the date on which leave in the UK expires.

For examples of UKRPs and ISDs, ▶see Chapter 8.

GENERAL GROUNDS FOR REFUSAL OF LEAVE TO REMAIN

Paragraph 322, HC 395

Grounds on which applications for leave to remain 'should normally be refused':

- making false representations or failing to disclose a material fact when applying for leave to enter or remain in the past;
- breaking a condition imposed on previous leave to enter or remain, for example, overstaying or working without permission;
- if people have not been able to support themselves or family members without recourse to public funds;
- if a person's character, conduct or associations make it undesirable to allow them to remain, or if they are a threat to national security;
- if a sponsor refuses to give an undertaking of support, or has not complied with such an undertaking in the past;
- if people have not complied with any undertaking or declaration about the length or purpose of their stay;
- if people cannot show that they will be allowed into another country at the end of their stay (this does not apply to those who qualify for settlement, or spouses of settled people);
- if people do not produce information, documents or evidence required by the Home Office within a 'reasonable time';

- if people fail to attend an immigration interview without a reasonable explanation;
- if a child makes an application to remain not in conjunction with his or her parents or legal guardians and does not have the written consent of a parent or guardian to do so. This does not apply to child asylum-seekers.

Grounds on which applications for leave to remain 'are to be refused':

- where the application for further leave is being made for a purpose not covered by the immigration rules.

Note

If any of these factors might apply to a person, it is important to explain in any application why they should not be used as a ground of refusal and how the person otherwise qualifies for leave to remain. Under those grounds for which leave should 'normally' be refused, there remains a discretion within the immigration rules not to refuse the application even where the ground is made out. However, the word 'normally' indicates that the presumption is that the application will be refused.

Under the final ground above, the application 'is' to be refused which means that any discretion to grant an application which is made for a purpose not covered by the rules, is a discretion that can only be exercised outside the immigration rules.

CURTAILMENT AND OTHER DECISIONS MADE BY THE HOME OFFICE WHERE NO APPLICATION HAS BEEN MADE

In certain cases, the Home Office may make a decision affecting a person's existing leave even though the person has made no application. If the Home Office decides that the applicant entered the UK by deception, then it may declare the applicant an illegal entrant and the leave which they apparently had is treated as void from that time on (s33(1) 1971 Act and ▶see 1010 onwards). A deportation order invalidates any leave granted before or during the time in which the order is in force (s5(1) 1971 Act). In addition, the Home Office has certain powers to 'revoke' an indefinite leave (▶see 627–30, 1008, 1025–6).

Below we look only at the powers of the Home Office to curtail leave and to vary the conditions imposed on leave.

Curtailment

In certain circumstances, the Home Office may 'curtail' an existing limited leave (see the table below). This means bringing the leave to an end before it is due to expire. The Home Office can do this of its own accord if certain matters come to its attention. In particular, leave can be curtailed where, although the applicant did not deceive officers on entry and is not in breach of their *conditions* of leave, they no longer satisfy the *requirements* of the rules upon which they were granted leave (see s3(3)(a) 1971 Act; paras 322–323 HC 395). So, for example, if a student stops attending their course or studies, depending on the reasons for the change in circumstance and whether they are likely to begin studying again, the Home Office might decide to curtail the leave. When leave is curtailed, the person becomes an overstayer, which means that they can be administratively removed from the UK.

'Curtailment' is a form of 'variation' of leave i.e. a decision to change the leave. Where leave is curtailed so that there is no leave remaining, this is an 'immigration decision' which gives a right of appeal. So does a decision to 'revoke' indefinite leave (s82(2)(e)(f) 2002 Act). Although these decisions cut the leave off, applicants are still treated for other purposes as having their leave while they have an appeal outstanding against the decision (s82(3) 2002 Act). Under the 2005 Bill, the right of appeal against a curtailment of leave is to be withdrawn unless the applicant's existing leave is as a refugee or in other circumstances, which are yet to be specified (▶see 1042–3). Of course, there remains a right of appeal against the next logical decision to remove the person as an overstayer but this can only be brought in-country on asylum or human rights grounds.

Changing conditions of leave

In addition to curtailment, the Home Office may add, vary or take away conditions (working, recourse to public funds etc), which are attached to a limited leave (see s3(3)(a) 1971 Act). There are no specific rules as to when this can be done but people cannot be treated less favourably in terms of conditions than the immigration rules for their particular category provide. The 1999 Act took away the right of appeal against a decision to vary conditions. Only curtailment decisions (above) carry with them the right of appeal.

CIRCUMSTANCES IN WHICH LEAVE MAY BE CURTAILED

Paragraphs 322-323, HC 395

The circumstances in which leave can be curtailed are as follows:

- where false representations are made or there was a failure to disclose a material fact for the purpose of obtaining a previous leave;
- failure to comply with any conditions attached to the grant of leave to enter or remain;
- failure to continue to meet the requirements of the rules under which leave was granted;
- failure of the person to maintain or accommodate themselves and any dependants without recourse to public funds;

- where it is undesirable to allow the person to remain in the UK in the light of their character, conduct, associations or the fact that they represent a threat to national security.

Note

If any of the above circumstances apply, a decision to curtail leave is not automatic. There is a discretion within the immigration rules as to whether to curtail the leave or not.

WHAT STATUS DOES A PERSON HAVE WHILE WAITING FOR A DECISION?

In many cases where an in-time application to extend leave is made, it is not possible for the Home Office to make a decision on the application before the leave expires. What is the person's immigration status while they are waiting for a decision in such cases? Are they in the UK unlawfully? Before 1976, applicants who had made applications in-time but were still waiting for a decision when their leave ran out became overstayers and lost the right to make an appeal against the refusal because they no longer had leave as required at the time of the appeal. The unfairness of that situation was brought out in the cases of *Subramaniam* and *Suthendran*.

As a result, the Home Office introduced the Immigration (Variation of Leave) Order 1976 (known as 'VOLO'). The effect of this was to automatically extend leave when an in-time application was made but no decision was made before the applicant's leave expired. The leave that was granted was known as 'VOLO leave'. VOLO itself is no longer in existence but the legislation has continued to operate a system of automatic grants of leave while applicants are waiting for a decision on an in-time application and this has been extended to the period while they are appealing against a negative decision on an extension of leave. Unfortunately, the government has continued to tinker with the system and proposes to do so again under the 2005 Bill. Each change has been brought in with transitional arrangements. It is often important for an applicant to be able to show continuous lawful leave over many years when they are seeking an exercise of discretion generally. It is also important to applications made under the ten-year lawful residence rules (▶below at 154–5).

Below we trace the operation of automatic leave from VOLO onwards.

Decision of Home Office made before 2 October 2000

If the decision of the Home Office on an in-time application to extend leave was made before 2 October 2000 but after leave would otherwise have expired, leave is automatically extended until 28 days after the date of the decision (see Immigration (Variation of Leave) Order 1976, 'VOLO', as amended by the Immigration (Variation of Leave) (Amendment) Order 2000). Under the old appeals legislation there was a right of appeal against a negative decision (s14 1971 Act). There was, however, no automatic extension of leave during an *appeal* against a negative decision. So, although people could not be forced to leave the UK whilst exercising their variation right of appeal, they were still technically overstayers while appealing.

Conditions of the existing leave would be treated as continuing during the extended leave. So, if there were restrictions on working, those conditions would continue to apply. There were no direct restrictions on these people to prevent them from working while appealing: if they did not have leave, the conditions of the leave also did not continue. Since 1996, however, conditions preventing people from working have only been one obstacle to being able to legally obtain work. In most cases, it is a criminal offence for an employer to give work to overstayers and so working was still prevented (▶see 496–500).

Decision of Home Office made on or after 2 October 2000 but before 1 April 2003

Where the decision of the Home Office was made on or after 2 October 2000, a person also continues to have leave if an in-time application was made (see transitional arrangements contained in art 2(2), Sch 2, Immigration and Asylum Act 1999 (Commencement No 6) Order 2000). It is not important whether the *application* to extend leave was made before or after 2 October, the new provisions applied if the *decision* came on or after 2 October. In these cases, if the Home Office refused the application, leave was still treated as continuing until the end of the time-limit for appealing against the negative decision (see s3C Immigration Act 1971 as originally inserted by the 1999 Act).

If an appeal was brought against the decision, then the leave continued for as long as the appeal took to be 'finally determined', namely until the whole appeal process had been exhausted (see para. 17, Sch 4 and s58(5)-(9) 1999 Act before repeal). This applied to both asylum and non-asylum appeals against decisions refusing to extend leave.

Again, leave was generally treated as continuing on the same conditions as it was previously granted. So, if there was a condition prohibiting work, this continued during the time of the extended leave. However, for benefit and other welfare purposes, the 1999 Act deliberately treated applicants as 'subject to immigration control' during the period of automatic extension while an appeal was outstanding even if there was no public funds condition attached to the original leave (see s115(9)(d) 1999 Act).

Decisions made after 1 April 2003

Where the application is made after 1 April 2003 (or where an application was made before 1 April 2003 but was not decided on or before that date), the new version of section 3C 1971 Act introduced by the 2002 Act regulates automatic extensions of leave (see paras 2(2), 6(4), Sch 2, Nationality, Immigration and Asylum Act 2002 (Commencement No 4) Order 2003).

The new section 3C introduced under the 2002 legislation (s118 2002 Act) has not radically changed the position. The earlier section 3C did not make allowance for automatic leave to expire when an application was withdrawn or if the applicant left the UK without formally withdrawing their application. The new section 3C makes sure that this is now the case.

Under the provisions for automatic leave in the new section 3C, the applicant has an automatic extension of leave where (s3C(1) 1971 Act):

- the applicant has existing limited leave and applies in-time to extend leave; and
- the original grant of leave expires before the application to extend leave is determined.

As to the *period* of the automatic extension of leave, leave is extended during all of the following periods (s3C(2) 1971 Act):

- the time during which the application is outstanding and has not been either determined or withdrawn;
- the time after the Home Office has refused the application but the applicant is still within time to appeal against the decision (there is no automatic extension after the time for appealing has run out or while the applicant is waiting for a decision on an application to appeal out-of-time – for appeal time-limits, ▶see the table at 1162–7); and
- the time during which the appeal (and any further application for a review, reconsideration or further appeal is outstanding – and see s104 2002 Act).

So, at present, there is an automatic extension of leave during the period while the application is outstanding and during the period while the applicant is challenging a negative decision on the extension application throughout the appeals/review process. Again, the conditions imposed on the existing leave are treated as continuing during the extended grant of leave.

For the present position regarding access to welfare during these periods of automatic leave, ▶see 1250, 1254–5.

Applications and decisions under the provisions of the 2005 Bill

The 2005 Bill proposes to amend section 3C so that the automatic extension of leave ends when the initial immigration decision on the application is made by the Home Office. Under this proposal, there will therefore be no leave during the period that the applicant is appealing. Although the 2005 Bill proposes to withdraw rights of appeal generally against refusals to extend leave, it proposes to retain them in the case of refugees who are refused further leave (and they may also be retained for those refused extensions of HP and DL). The lack of an extension of leave during the appeal for these applicants may mean that they are denied access to standard welfare support during their appeals as they will become 'subject to immigration control' under section 115 1999 Act because they have no leave.

It is not clear whether the 2005 Bill will have any transitional arrangements in relation to these changes. It is likely that regulations will be made which will state when the notice of the immigration decision will be treated as having been received by the applicant (and therefore when, precisely, the leave comes to an end).

What happens when an application is made during a period of automatic leave?

In all cases, the law only allows for one automatic extension of leave before the immigration authorities again grant leave. Technically, it is not possible to make a further application for leave during the period when leave is extended under section 3C. Instead, where further representations are made, the Home Office will treat this as a 'variation' of the existing application (s3C(1)(a)(4)(5) 1971 Act). This prevents a further automatic extension of leave coming into operation. However, the idea behind treating the further representations as a 'variation' of the application, is that the Home Office will then make a decision on all of the bases put forward for staying in the UK.

So, the Home Office will issue only one decision on the application as varied, which will result in one right of appeal. Although it is a single decision, it will cover both grounds on which the application was based unless, in the second application, the applicant clearly indicates that they are withdrawing the grounds for the original application in favour of the second one.

Evidence of automatic extensions

Passports are not endorsed and returned showing that an automatic extension of leave has come into operation. It is therefore important that evidence of an in-time application to extend leave is kept in the form of copies of the previous leave, the application form, evidence of recorded/ special delivery of an in-time application and the acknowledgment received from the Home Office. Although there is no endorsement, this evidence itself can demonstrate that the applicant is not an overstayer.

'EXCEPTIONAL LEAVE', POLICIES AND CONCESSIONS

If an applicant cannot qualify under the immigration rules, there is always a power to make a favourable decision outside the rules where the immigration authorities are satisfied that this is justified. Therefore, when a person has strong compassionate or other reasons for needing to remain in the UK, but does not fit into the immigration rules, an application outside the rules should be considered. Sometimes it will be appropriate to ask that this discretion is exercised as an alternative i.e. if the immigration authorities find that the rules are not satisfied.

'Exceptional leave' and the other terms used

Unfortunately, the different terms that the Home Office has used when exercising discretion outside the rules have made the system unnecessarily confusing. On one level, the term 'exceptional' leave is simple: it describes the grant of leave to a person who does not fit into any of the rules - they are treated 'exceptionally' because normally when an applicant cannot satisfy the rules, they are refused. People can be treated exceptionally in this way where:

- their application is for a purpose simply not covered by the rules; or
- the application is for a purpose covered by the rules but one or more requirements of the rules cannot be met and the person asks for the requirement/s to be waived.

However, the term 'exceptional leave' or 'ELR' (or 'ELE' which is simply exceptional leave to 'enter' rather than remain) has been used in a narrower sense as well. It has been used to describe the leave that is given to those who do not qualify for asylum under the Refugee Convention but who are still found to be in need of international protection. From 1 April 2003, the Home Office divided this narrower form of ELR and gave it two further labels: 'humanitarian protection' (HP) and 'discretionary leave' (DL). These forms of leave are intended to reflect the UK's obligations under the ECHR (although it seems that in compelling cases DL can also be granted on a non-human rights basis). *However*, they are still granted outside the immigration rules despite the fact that the Home Office has stated that it will bring HP within the rules. In the broad sense, therefore, they are still grants of 'exceptional' leave, although they have been given a different label. Although they are replacements for the old asylum-based ELR, HP and DL can be granted where a freestanding human rights claim, or even a non-asylum or human rights claim, is made. The term exceptional leave or ELR is no longer used to describe these grants of leave: they have firmly become known now as 'HP' and 'DL'.

At the same time as it introduced HP and DL, the Home Office stated that the other, wider sense in which 'exceptional leave' is used, i.e. where an applicant is granted leave outside the rules in a non-asylum or human rights context, would also no longer be called 'exceptional' leave. It would be called 'Leave Outside the Rules' (LOTR). Again, because it is leave granted outside the rules, applicants granted it are still being treated 'exceptionally'. The term 'LOTR' has not really caught on and indeed, when the Home Office announced it, it stated that it would take some time for the new label to percolate through the system and to amend all of the instructions in line with it. Many people have continued to refer to these grants of leave as 'exceptional leave' and this is the course we have taken in the *Handbook*.

For full details about the development of exceptional leave in the asylum/ human rights context in particular and the replacement of asylum-based ELR with HP and DL and the requirements for obtaining HP and DL, ▶see 859–75, ▶see also 597–98.

Summary of the terms used

So, in summary:

1) in any case, a person may be treated more favourably than the rules permit and may be granted leave as a 'one off' – advisers and officers may refer to this as either 'exceptional leave' or 'leave outside the rules';

2) similarly, a person may be granted leave outside the rules on the basis of a policy or concession which regulates the exercise of discretion outside the rules (see below) – such persons may also be described as having been granted 'exceptional leave' or 'leave outside the rules';

3) where leave is granted outside the rules because a person is in need of international protection (although they do not qualify for asylum under the Refugee Convention), or because it is necessary to grant them leave on human rights grounds, the 'exceptional' treatment which they are given is called either HP or DL (although it is possible that DL will be granted on non-human rights grounds).

As to (1) in the above summary, applicants and advisers need to be creative in making representations as to why in the particular circumstances of a case discretion should be exercised.

As to (3) in the above summary, the detailed circumstances in which HP and DL can be granted are set out in the tables at ▶862–5. Full details about the periods of leave which can be granted, applying for settlement in those categories and applying for further leave and settlement having been granted asylum-based ELR before 1 April 2003, are set out at ▶866–75 and ▶see 720 onwards. For details about the family members of those applying or granted leave in those categories, ▶see 875–9.

The policies/concessions

As to (2) in the above summary, the main concessions/policies that remain are those relating to:

- those caring for a friend or relative in the UK (▶242–5);
- children over the age of 18 of those who hold work permits as intra-company transferees (▶436–7);
- enforcement against people with a spouse settled in the UK (DP/2/93 and DP/3/96) (▶337–41);
- enforcement against people with an unmarried partner settled in the UK (▶342–3);
- enforcement against families with children who have long residence in the UK (DP/069/99, DP/4/95, DP/4/96) (▶386–9, 998–1000);
- enforcement against unaccompanied children (▶390–3, 688, 865, 870–1);
- enforcement against those aged over 65 (▶994–5);
- those with serious health conditions where enforcement may raise human rights issues (▶814–6, 995–6);
- family reunion with a recognised refugee for dependants who are not a spouse or a minor child (▶762–8) (family reunion with those with HP, DL or ELR is also outside the rules and is covered at ▶876–9);
- those granted a recommendation by an immigration judge (▶1127–9);
- permit free employment outside the immigration rules (▶1467–72).

The 'under-12' concession has been abolished (▶see 367–8).

On 1 August 2005, following a 'Freedom of Information' request, the Home Office supplied Wilson & Co Solicitors with a long document which gives 'instructions...to immigration officers regarding how to consider cases involving compassionate circumstances'. It is stated to be 'updated' as of 25 April 2004 and is headed 'Immigration Rules and Compassionate Circumstances'. It was circulated by the Immigration Law Practitioners' Association in their August 2005 mailing and gives commentary on the application of the enforcement criteria in the rules for administrative removal and deportation (▶1009–10); the enforcement policies which apply in cases involving family and children (above); requests to remain on health grounds and the approach to recommendations made by immigration judges.

For further details about the procedural aspects of policy on enforcement, in particular in cases involving the risk of suicide and self-harm (▶see 996–8) and in family cases, ▶see 998–1000.

Concessions incorporated into the immigration rules

Several of the concessions that the Home Office has long operated outside the rules, have recently been incorporated into the immigration rules. This applies to the rules on:

- 'long residence' in the UK (▶see below at 151–7);
- domestic violence (▶see 345–51);
- domestic servants (▶see 457–9);

- family reunion for the *spouse and minor children* of refugees (▶see 758–62).

THE ARMED FORCES

In a number of ways, the immigration rules make special provision for members of the armed forces and their families:

- under the 'returning-residents' rule, the requirement that the applicant has not been away from the UK for longer than two years is waived if the applicant is the spouse or partner of a member of HM Forces serving overseas and has been accompanying them on a tour of duty abroad (▶see 112);

- a member of HM Forces who is a British citizen or settled in the UK but who is serving overseas is treated as being *present* in the UK for the purposes of the marriage and unmarried partners rules so that their foreign spouses can obtain leave and settlement even though the sponsor is not in fact in the UK (▶see304–5);

- members of the home forces, Commonwealth forces and others undergoing training in the UK and visiting forces serving in the UK, are exempt from immigration control (▶see 474–5).

There are four recent additions to the immigration rules, which benefit the following:

1) Gurkhas who have been recently discharged from the British Army;

2) foreign or Commonwealth nationals who have been recently discharged from HM Forces;

3) family members of those in the above two categories;

4) family members of members of the home or foreign armed forces who are exempt from control.

Categories (1)–(3) are looked at in turn below. Importantly the rules for both applicants and dependants in these categories do *not* require that they satisfy the maintenance and accommodation requirements of the immigration rules.

For family members of armed forces members who are exempt from control ((4) above), ▶see 475. Those family members *do* have to be maintained and accommodated without recourse to public funds.

Gurkhas discharged from the British Army

A 'Gurkha' is a national of Nepal who has served in the Brigade of Gurkhas of the British Army. Provision for discharged Gurkhas was inserted into the immigration rules from 25 October 2004 (paras 276E-R HC 395 added by Cm 1112). The new rules allow those who have served for four years as a Gurkha and who have been discharged on completion of their period of service on or after 1 July 1997, to obtain indefinite leave in the UK. They must apply for indefinite leave within two years of their discharge. If seeking to come to the UK, they must obtain entry clearance but in-country applications for those who have leave in the UK can also be considered.

Foreign or Commonwealth nationals discharged from HM Forces

Provision for all other foreign or Commonwealth nationals discharged from HM Forces was made at the same time as for Gurkhas (above) and the requirements are similar (paras 276L-Q HC 395 added by Cm 1112). Applicants must have served for four years with HM Forces before being discharged on completion of their engagement. They must apply within two years of their discharge. Indefinite leave to enter can be granted provided the applicant arrives with the relevant entry clearance. Alternatively, indefinite leave to remain can be granted provided the applicant has leave when they make their in-country application.

Family members of discharged Gurkhas and others discharged from HM Forces

From 1 January 2005, further new rules were made to provide for the family members of discharged Gurkhas and other foreign and Commonwealth nationals who have been discharged from service (paras 276R-276AC HC 395 inserted by HC 164). Under these rules, spouses and children of those settled or seeking settlement in the above two categories can also be granted indefinite leave. Spouses must have been married for at least two years. For children joining one parent only, the 'sole responsibility' or 'exclusion undesirable' rules must be satisfied (►see 368–71) unless the other parent is deceased. Children whose exclusion is undesirable may also join a 'relative' who has indefinite leave in either of the above categories. Indefinite leave to enter can be granted provided the applicant arrives with the relevant entry clearance. Indefinite leave to remain can be granted provided the applicant has leave when they make their in-country application.

No specific provision was added to the rules for unmarried partners of those in the above two categories. However, there is no reason why the ordinary rules concerning unmarried partners of those settled in the UK should not be used (►see Chapter 11). This means that, unlike the other family members, unmarried partners would have to satisfy the maintenance and accommodation requirements.

THE LONG-RESIDENCE RULES

For many years, the Home Office operated concessions outside the rules under which people could be granted indefinite leave to remain on the basis of their long residence in the UK. The concessions were based on the principles of the European Convention on Establishment, which the UK ratified in October 1969. This Convention states that nationals of countries which are a party to the Convention should not be required to leave the host country they are in if they have lawfully resided there for over ten years unless there are particularly compelling reasons why they should be required to leave, for example, relating to national security, public order, public health or morality. However, the Home Office concessions covered the nationals of any country. In addition, those whose residence in the UK had been partly or wholly unlawful could also benefit depending on the circumstances.

From 1 April 2003, the immigration rules themselves have made provision for long residence (paras 276A-D HC 395, inserted by HC 538).

Applications on the basis of long residence should be made on Form SET (O).

Continuing importance of the old concessions The Home Office IDI still contain the old concessions outside the immigration rules (IDI, Ch 18). This is clearly out of date, especially since the opening sentence of that chapter wrongly states 'There is no provision within the immigration rules for a person to be granted indefinite leave to remain solely on the basis of the length of his or her residence'. However, applicants and advisers may still find the terms of the old concessions useful. In particular, the long-residence concession was in some respects more generous than the rules. Therefore, where the immigration rules on long residence cannot be met and representations are being made on the basis of long residence outside the square corners of those rules, the concession may still give an indication of the circumstances in which discretion may be exercised. Long residence is always a relevant factor in the exercise of discretion and, even after the new rules on long residence, the Home Office has indicated that it is willing to be flexible in this area:

'In general, the requirements of the rules on long residence will be applied, but discretion may be exercised in cases where application of the rule involves particular hardship. The decision on an individual case will be made by the caseworker dealing with the application...' (Letter of IND Policy Directorate to Wesley Gryk, Solicitors, 7 June 2005).

For details of the how the old concession may still be of use, ▶see below at 156–7. First, however, we turn to the immigration rules.

WHAT THE RULES SAY

The requirements to be granted indefinite leave under the long-residence rules (paras 276A-276D, HC 395) are that the applicant:

- has had at least ten years continuous lawful residence in the UK; *or*
- has had at least 14 years continuous residence in the UK, whether lawful or unlawful (but excluding certain periods, ▶see below).

In addition to satisfying one of the above conditions, the Home Office will also have regard to the public interest and there must be 'no reasons why it would be undesirable' for the applicant to be given indefinite leave to remain taking into account the applicant's:

- age;
- strength of connections to the UK;
- personal history, including character, conduct, associations and employment record;
- domestic circumstances;
- previous criminal record and the nature of any offence of which the person has been convicted;
- compassionate circumstances; and
- any representations received on the person's behalf.

WHAT THE RULES MEAN

'Continuous residence': ten-year and 14-year rule

Under both the ten and 14-year rules, continuous residence is not broken if an applicant is absent from the UK for any period of up to and including six months *provided* that the applicant has existing limited leave on both their departure from the UK and on their return. So, if an applicant's leave has not run out or lapsed by the time they return to the UK, continuity will not be broken (for non-lapsing leave, ▶see 107–9). This applies to the 14-year rule as well even though, if they simply remain in the UK, applicants do not need to have leave in order to qualify.

In addition, continuity of residence will be broken if any of the following circumstances apply to the case:

- the applicant is removed from the UK as a port removal (having been refused leave to enter); a seaman or aircrew member; an illegal entrant; under the administrative removal provisions or under a deportation order;
- the applicant voluntarily departed the UK having been refused leave to enter or remain;
- the applicant left the UK and, on doing so, 'evidenced a clear intention not to return';
- the applicant left the UK 'in circumstances in which he could have had no reasonable expectation...that he would be lawfully be able to return';
- having been convicted of an offence, the applicant was sentenced to imprisonment (or detained in an institution other than a prison) provided that the sentence was not a suspended one; or
- the applicant has spent a total period of 18 months absent from the UK during the period in question.

'Lawful residence': ten-year rule

Under the ten-year rule, the continuous residence must also be 'lawful residence'. This means that, in order for any period to count towards the ten years, the applicant must have had one of the following forms of status:

- existing leave to enter or remain;
- temporary admission 'within section 11 of the 1971 Act' where leave to enter or remain is subsequently granted; or
- an exemption from immigration control (▶see 472–6) including cases in which the exemption ceases to apply provided that it is immediately followed by a grant of leave.

'Existing leave to enter or remain' must include the automatic leave which is granted under section 3C 1971 Act during the period when leave would naturally have expired but an in-time application is still waiting to be decided. Similarly, it must include the automatic leave granted under the same provision during an appeal against a negative decision on such an application. However, the 2005 Bill proposes to end automatic leave at the point the decision is made so that there is no leave during the appeal against the negative variation decision. If this provision comes in, it would be unfair particularly in cases where the appeal is successful, if the immigration rules on long residence are not amended so that residence while appealing against such decisions will count under the ten-year rule, even though there is no longer any valid leave during that time. For an explanation of the operation of automatic extensions of leave since 1976 and the transitional arrangements, which have accompanied the changes in the legislation, ▶see above at 143–6.

In *R (Kungwengwe) v SSHD*, the High Court rejected the applicant's argument that time spent in the UK with a valid residence document issued to show the applicant was exercising free movement rights constituted 'lawful residence' for these purposes. However, as a matter of policy, the Home Office has accepted that, where the applicant can show a combination of time spent with leave and time spent with a residence document where the applicant can show that they fully met the requirements for the issue of the document throughout the period relied on, this will be treated as sufficient if the total period comes to ten years (see para. 17 of the High Court's decision).

Temporary admission The second form of status above needs more explanation. Temporary admission isn't actually *granted* by section 11 of the 1971 Act. The role of section 11 is to create a pretence that certain people haven't entered the UK even though they have come through immigration controls. Included in the group of people to whom section 11 applies are those who make an application to the immigration officer on arrival which cannot be decided immediately and who are granted temporary admission in the meantime. Port asylum applicants are an example of people who will generally fall into this category. It seems that this is the group of persons whose time spent on temporary admission will count under the ten-year rule, provided that they are later granted leave.

Therefore, temporary admission granted to the following people does not seem to count under the rules:

- illegal entrants who have entered the UK (because s11 does not apply to people who would enter 'otherwise' than through the grant of temporary admission);
- those who have overstayed or had their leave curtailed (because they have also entered the UK);
- those who are given a slightly different form of temporary admission under Schedule 3 1971 Act who are being deported (because they will also have entered the UK).

The above seems to be the way the rules should be read although they are not completely clear. It may be that case-law will be necessary to confirm the precise meaning. For further explanation about 'temporary admission', ▶see 950 onwards.

Periods of time excluded from the 14-year rule

The 14-year rule refers only to 'continuous residence' as opposed to 'continuous lawful residence'. This clearly indicates that the residence does not have to be lawful. So a person who needs leave to be in the UK and has stayed without it, can still count this time towards the 14-year period. *However*, certain periods are excluded from the calculation of the 14 years. Essentially, the 14-year clock stops once the applicant is given either:

- a notice of a decision to take enforcement action against them; *or*
- a notice of the person's *liability* to removal.

The notice of decision to take enforcement action can be under any of the main enforcement procedures: port removal; illegal entry; administrative removal (for overstayers etc); deportation and the removal of seamen and aircrews (para. 276B(i)(b), HC 395 as substituted by Cm 6339 from 1 October 2004). Before the rules were amended on 1 October 2004, only service of removal directions themselves (or notice of intention to deport) would stop the clock. The rules were amended so that the underlying 'immigration decision' to remove (or notice of intention to deport in deportation cases) is enough to stop the clock i.e. without removal directions having yet been given. Note also that the new rules go back a stage further than even the immigration decision because, as soon as a person is told that they are 'liable' to removal, without a decision having been taken as to whether to enforce, the clock stops. The clock stops for family members of the principal under these rules in the same way as it does for the principal applicant them self.

Public interest and the desirability of granting indefinite leave

Under both the ten and 14-year rules, there is an additional requirement that, having regard to the public interest, there must be 'no reasons why it would be undesirable' for the applicant to be given indefinite leave. The relevant factors set out above are considered. The rules are still written to suggest that there is a presumption that leave will be granted provided the primary conditions about residence are met. However, the rules are less favourable than the old concessions. Under the ten-year concession, applicants would 'normally be granted indefinite leave to remain without enquiry' if the residence condition was met (IDI, Ch 18, para. 3). Under the old 14-year concession, if the residence condition was met, indefinite leave would only be refused if there were 'serious countervailing factors' and unless those factors were 'exceptionally serious' (IDI, Ch 18, paras 2, 4). Again, in 14-year residence cases, the test in the rules makes it easier to exclude an applicant even though the residence condition is met.

Relevance of the old long-residence concessions

Although the rules are intended to replace the long-residence concessions, as stated above, the concessions continue to be published in the IDI (Ch 18). It is not clear why that is the case. In some ways the concession is more generous than the rules and where that difference has an impact in any particular case, although the rules on long residence cannot quite be met, it is still worth referring to the concession in representations asking for an exercise of discretion. Below we give four practical examples.

For yet further details of the old concessions, see pages 105–108 of the 2002 Edition of the *Handbook*.

1) Waiving certain limited periods of overstaying under the ten-year concession

Under the ten-year concession the following limited periods of overstaying were considered as lawful periods of residence (IDI, Ch 18, para. 3):

- a *short* delay in submitting an application for leave to remain provided that the application is subsequently granted;
- any period between the application and the determination of an appeal provided that the appeal is successful;
- where an appeal is unsuccessful but leave is granted later (perhaps on the recommendation of an immigration judge), the period between lodging the appeal and the appeal being decided.

At the present time, the second point above will not arise where there is an appeal against a refusal to extend an in-time application for leave to remain because leave will continue during the appeal (s3C 1971 Act). In the case of other appeals it may, however, be relevant. It will also be relevant if automatic leave during appeals against refused in-time applications is abolished as is proposed under the 2005 Bill and no accompanying modification is made to the long-residence rules.

2) Absence for longer than six months

The rules suggest that absences of longer than six months will break continuity of residence. The concessions state that short absences of up to six months would not break continuity but they also state the following:

'In some cases a lengthier absence may still not sever ties to the United Kingdom. In each case the strength of the ties to the United Kingdom, the reason for, and effect of the absence should be taken into account.' (IDI, Ch 18, para. 5).

If there has been an absence of longer than six months and the applicant needs to ask for an exercise of discretion, the criteria referred to in the above quote should be addressed.

3) Residence of between ten and 14 years, not all of which is lawful

The old concession indicated that where a person has remained in the UK for between ten and 14 years but cannot, because some of the residence was unlawful, qualify under the ten-year concession, there is still a possibility that an application will be allowed (IDI, Ch 18, para. 4). The factors that the Home Office would take into account in these circumstances are:

- the length of continuous residence;
- the proportion of the residence which was lawful; and
- the strength of ties with the UK.
  Family ties, in particular, are important in this context. Again, in such a case, where representations are being made seeking the exercise of discretion, it is worth referring to these criteria.

4) British Overseas Citizens

A long-residence concession outside the immigration rules seems to exist to benefit British Overseas Citizens (BOCs) (for a description of BOCs, ▶see 1408–11). According to a letter written by the Home Office to JCWI dated 1 August 1994, and which was referred to in the case of *ex parte Patel*, BOCs who have been in the UK with limited exceptional leave for four years, may be granted indefinite leave. This concession is not contained in Chapter 18 of the IDI.

7 Applying to 'switch' categories

This chapter explains the circumstances in which people can and cannot 'switch' to another category. 'Switching' is the common term used by both the Home Office and advisers to describe a situation where an applicant, who has leave to be in the UK in one category, wishes to apply for leave to remain in a different category without leaving the UK.

Switching under the immigration rules Most of this chapter deals with the central question: who can switch under the immigration rules? (▶160–187). For quick reference, this is mainly set out in a long table, which covers all the main categories under the rules. The first part of the table explains how the table works and it is important to look at that first. At the end of the table, there are a series of important notes on the table. It is important that users read the table together with the notes because, in some cases, the notes set out conditions, which if they are not fulfilled, prevent the switch. Where the notes are relevant to the switch in question, the main part of the table will cross-refer to them e.g. 'see **Note G**'.

Switching outside the immigration rules Even if an applicant cannot switch under the *immigration rules*, in all cases the Home Office has a discretion to allow switches outside the rules where it is satisfied that the circumstances merit it. The table does not cover switching outside the immigration rules but the final part of the chapter looks at this question (▶see 187–8). For a list of the policy concessions and where to find them in the *Handbook*, ▶see 148–9.

The traditional rules

Traditionally, the question of whether an applicant could 'switch' largely depended on whether they were seeking to remain in the UK in a 'permanent' category (i.e. one leading to settlement) or a 'temporary' category (i.e. a category in which the applicant is expected to depart the UK after their period of leave). A general, traditional rule of thumb was that a person could not switch to remain in a permanent category, although switching into a temporary category was permitted. There always were, of course, significant exceptions. For example, a person could switch from any category into the category of spouse or dependent relative of a person settled in the UK.

The modern position

Amendments to the rules mean that even the broad traditional rule (above) no longer provides a useful or reliable base from which to work. For example, specific temporary categories have been set up under the immigration rules which have as their purpose the eventual switch of applicants into other long-term, permanent categories (▶see for example the Science and Engineering Graduate Scheme (SEGS), 464–5 and the Fresh Talent: Working in Scotland Scheme, 465–6). The immigration rules on switching have been made very much more detailed throughout. The question of whether an individual can switch under the rules can no longer be reduced to a simple formula. It depends, instead, on the particular rules that apply to each situation.

WHO CAN SWITCH UNDER THE RULES?

The table below sets out the switches, which *in principle* are permitted under the immigration rules. In *all* cases, applicants must satisfy the full requirements of the category of the rules into which they wish to switch. Those requirements are set out in the relevant part of the *Handbook*. In addition, in order to obtain fresh leave, none of the general grounds of refusal must apply (▶see 140–1). So, although switching may be permitted in principle, in some cases it may also be very unrealistic. For example, nothing technically prevents a visitor switching to stay as a person with long residence. However, a person admitted for a visit for up to six months is very unlikely to have ten years' recent lawful residence in the UK. So, the table sets out what is technically possible without considering whether it might be achievable on the individual facts of different cases.

In addition, in some cases, the applicant's circumstances and history may be inconsistent with the category into which they could technically switch. For example, in certain categories, in order to be admitted in the first place, applicants have to show that they intend to leave the UK at the end of their period of leave (for example visitors or those admitted as teachers or language assistants). In other categories, applicants have to show that they intend to leave *unless* at the end of their leave, they are granted further leave in one of a number of specified categories. This is the case, for example, under the Science and Engineering Graduates Scheme (SEGS). Under SEGS, applicants must intend to leave at the end of the period they are admitted for unless they are granted further leave as a work-permit holder, a highly-skilled migrant, a business-person or as an innovator (see para. 135O(vi) HC 395).

So, in some circumstances, applications to switch may cast doubt on the genuine nature of the basis of the applicant's original entry. A classic example is the applicant who, shortly after their entry in an unrelated capacity, applies to remain permanently on the basis of marriage or partnership. At worst such applicants are vulnerable to a Home Office decision that they are an illegal entrant by deception (▶see 1013–4). In most cases, of course, it will be clear that there has been a genuine change in the applicant's circumstances and intentions after their original entry.

In all cases, applications to switch should be carefully considered in the light of the applicant's circumstances, immigration history and the rules under which they were granted their existing leave. *If in doubt, advice should always be taken on these issues.*

'SWITCHING' CATEGORIES UNDER THE IMMIGRATION RULES

Using this table

- References to 'para.' and 'paras' are to paragraphs in the immigration rules, HC 395.

- 'IED' simply refers to 'Immigration Employment Document' (work permits or other required employment documents; for an explanation of IEDs ▶see 418–9).

- We have given each category under the rules a number in bold (for example, 'Visitor' is number '**1**'). In brackets after each category are the paragraphs of the rules dealing with that category. The category numbers are listed at the foot of each page of the table.

- Listed *underneath* each category, are all of the categories into which, in principle, an applicant in that category may switch. These categories are listed using the same system of numbers. For example, the first two categories into which visitors may switch are '**2**' (visitor for private medical treatment) and '**3**' (parent of a child at school). After each reference to the categories into which the applicant can switch, are the paragraphs of the rules, which allow the applicant to make that switch. Note that, in most cases, the rules do not specifically state 'x category applicants can switch into y category' – it is usually simply the *absence* of a prohibition on switching which means that the switch is permitted.

- The switching information in the main part of the table *must* be read together with the '**Notes**', which follow at the end of the table (▶see at 184–7). The notes are listed **A** to **I**. In most cases, where there are notes, which are relevant to the particular switch, the main part of the table will give a cross-reference, for example, 'but see **Note G**'.

- The table covers the main categories under the rules – certain categories are omitted either in order to prevent over-complexity, or because they are minor categories (▶see **Note I** at 186–7).

- Switching category **19** is made up of all the 'permit-free' employment categories in the rules under the one heading. For the list of individual categories this includes, see **Note D** (▶185). While these categories can generally be treated together, there is an exception, which relates to switching to remain as a 'minister of religion'. Switching to remain in this category is therefore looked at separately; see **Note E** (▶185).

- Applicants in certain of the categories may already have been granted indefinite leave (e.g. where the spouse or partner of a person settled in the UK has already served their probationary period and been granted settlement). Such applicants will generally have no need to switch. The table still includes all such categories because: (a) some applicants will still only have limited leave in that category; and (b) it is important to show whether applicants in other categories may switch *into* the category that may lead to settlement.

Switching categories

1 Visitors (paras 40-42) can switch to:

- **2** (paras 54-56);
- **3** (paras 56A-56B);
- **4** (but see **Note A** below) (para. 60(i)(b));
- **5** (but see **Note B** below) (para. 85);
- **6** (but see **Note C** below) (paras 67-69);
- **28** but the applicant must have been permitted to remain in the UK for longer than six months in total – this excludes most (but not all) of those given short-term leave (see **Note G** below) (para. 284(i), paras 285-286);
- **30** (but see **Note H** below) (paras 295D-295F);
- **31** (paras 317-319);
- **32** (paras 327-344);
- **33** (paras 276A-276D).

2 Visitors for private medical treatment (paras 51-56) can switch to:

- **1** (paras 44-46);
- **3** (paras 56A-56B);
- **4** (but see **Note A** below) (para. 60(i)(b));
- **5** (but see **Note B** below) (para. 85);
- **6** (but see **Note C** below) (paras 67-69);

1	Visitor	12 Seasonal agricultural	23 Europe Accession
2	Medical visitor	worker	Agreements
3	Parent of school child	13 Teacher/language assistant	24 Investor
4	Student	14 TWES	25 Writer/composer/artist
5	Prospective student	15 Work-permit holder	26 Right of access to child
6	Student nurse	16 HSMP	27 Retired person
7	Postgraduate doctor/dentist	17 SBS	28 Spouse of settled sponsor
8	PLAB test	18 SEGS	29 Fiancé(e) of settled sponsor
9	Clinical attachment/ dental observer	19 'Permit-free' employment	30 Partner of settled sponsor
10	*Au pair*	20 Fresh Talent: Scotland	31 Dependent relative
11	Working holidaymaker	21 Business/self-employed	32 Refugee
		22 Innovator	33 Long residence

- **28** but the applicant must have been permitted to remain in the UK for longer than six months in total – this excludes most (but not all) of those given short-term leave (see **Note G** below) (para. 284(i), paras 285-286);
- **30** (but see **Note H** below) (paras 295D-295F);
- **31** (paras 317-319);
- **32** (paras 327-344);
- **33** paras 276A-276D).

3 Parents of a child at school (paras 56A-56C) can switch to:

- **1** (paras 44-46);
- **2** (paras 54-56);
- **4** (but see **Note A** below) (para. 60(i)(b));
- **5** (but see **Note B** below) (para. 85);
- **6** (but see **Note C** below) (paras 67-69);
- **28** but the applicant must have been permitted to remain in the UK for longer than six months in total – this excludes most (but not all) of those given short-term leave (see **Note G** below) (para. 284(i), paras 285-286);
- **30** (but see **Note H** below) (paras 295D-295F);
- **31** (paras 317-319);
- **32** (paras 327-344);
- **33** (paras 276A-276D).

4 Students (paras 57-62) can switch to:

- **1** (paras 44-46);
- **2** (paras 54-56);
- **3** (paras 56A-56B);
- **5** (but see **Note B** below) (para. 85);

1	Visitor	12	Seasonal agricultural worker	23	Europe Accession Agreements
2	Medical visitor			24	Investor
3	Parent of school child	13	Teacher/language assistant	25	Writer/composer/artist
4	Student	14	TWES	26	Right of access to child
5	Prospective student	15	Work-permit holder	27	Retired person
6	Student nurse	16	HSMP	28	Spouse of settled sponsor
7	Postgraduate doctor/dentist	17	SBS	29	Fiancé(e) of settled sponsor
8	PLAB test	18	SEGS	30	Partner of settled sponsor
9	Clinical attachment/ dental observer	19	'Permit-free' employment	31	Dependent relative
		20	Fresh Talent: Scotland	32	Refugee
10	*Au pair*	21	Business/self-employed	33	Long residence
11	Working holidaymaker	22	Innovator		

- **6** (but see **Note C** below) (paras 67-69);
- **7** (para. 73(ii)(a));
- **14** (para. 119(i));
- **15** provided the applicant has obtained a degree in the UK, has the required IED for employment and, if they are sponsored by a government or an international agency, they have their sponsor's consent (para. 131A, paras 132–133);
- **16** provided they hold an IED valid for the highly skilled migrant programme and provided they have obtained a degree in the UK and, if they are sponsored by a government or an international agency, they have their sponsor's consent (para. 135DB, paras 135E-135F);
- **18** (para. 135R(ii), paras 135S-135T);
- **20** (para. 143D(ii)(a), paras 143E-143F);
- **21** provided the applicant has obtained a degree in the UK and, if they are sponsored by a government or an international agency, they have the sponsor's consent (para. 206E, paras 207-208);
- **22** provided the applicant has obtained a degree in the UK and, if they are sponsored by a government or an international agency, they have the sponsor's consent (para. 210DB, paras 210E–210F);
- **28** but the applicant must have been permitted to remain in the UK for longer than six months in total – this excludes most (but not all) of those given short-term leave (see **Note G** below) (para. 284(i), paras 285-286);
- **30** (but see **Note H** below) (paras 295D-295F);
- **31** (paras 317-319);
- **32** (paras 327-344);
- **33** (paras 276A-276D).

5 Prospective students (paras 82-87) can switch to:

- **1** (paras 44-46);
- **2** (paras 54-56);

1 Visitor	12 Seasonal agricultural worker	23 Europe Accession Agreements
2 Medical visitor		
3 Parent of school child	13 Teacher/language assistant	24 Investor
4 Student	14 TWES	25 Writer/composer/artist
5 Prospective student	15 Work-permit holder	26 Right of access to child
6 Student nurse	16 HSMP	27 Retired person
7 Postgraduate doctor/dentist	17 SBS	28 Spouse of settled sponsor
8 PLAB test	18 SEGS	29 Fiancé(e) of settled sponsor
9 Clinical attachment/ dental observer	19 'Permit-free' employment	30 Partner of settled sponsor
	20 Fresh Talent: Scotland	31 Dependent relative
10 *Au pair*	21 Business/self-employed	32 Refugee
11 Working holidaymaker	22 Innovator	33 Long residence

- **3** (paras 56A-56B);
- **4** (but see **Note A** below) (para. (60(i)(a)(b)(c), HC 395);
- **6** (but see **Note C** below) (paras 67-69);
- **28** but the applicant must have been permitted to remain in the UK for longer than six months in total – this excludes most (but not all) of those given short-term leave (see **Note G** below) (para. 284(i), paras 285-286);
- **30** (but see **Note H** below) (paras 295D-295F);
- **31** (paras 317-319);
- **32** (paras 327-344);
- **33** (paras 276A-276D).

6 Student nurses (paras 63-69) can switch to:

- **1** (paras 44-46);
- **2** (paras 54-56);
- **3** (paras 56A-56B);
- **4** (but see **Note A** below) (para. 60(i)(b));
- **5** (but see **Note B** below) (para. 85);
- **7** (para. 73(ii)(a));
- **15** provided the applicant has an IED for employment as a nurse and, if they are sponsored by a government or an international agency, they have their sponsor's consent (para. 131B, paras 132-133);
- **18** (para. 135R(ii), paras 135S-135T);
- **20** (para. 143D(ii)(a), paras 143E-143F);
- **28** but the applicant must have been permitted to remain in the UK for longer than six months in total – this excludes most (but not all) of those given short-term leave (see **Note G** below) (para. 284(i), paras 285-286);
- **30** (but see **Note H** below) (paras 295D-295F);
- **31** (paras 317-319);

1	Visitor	12	Seasonal agricultural worker	23	Europe Accession Agreements
2	Medical visitor				
3	Parent of school child	13	Teacher/language assistant	24	Investor
4	Student	14	TWES	25	Writer/composer/artist
5	Prospective student	15	Work-permit holder	26	Right of access to child
6	Student nurse	16	HSMP	27	Retired person
7	Postgraduate doctor/dentist	17	SBS	28	Spouse of settled sponsor
8	PLAB test	18	SEGS	29	Fiancé(e) of settled sponsor
9	Clinical attachment/ dental observer	19	'Permit-free' employment	30	Partner of settled sponsor
		20	Fresh Talent: Scotland	31	Dependent relative
10	Au pair	21	Business/self-employed	32	Refugee
11	Working holidaymaker	22	Innovator	33	Long residence

- **32** (paras 327-344);
- **33** (paras 276A-276D).

7 Postgraduate doctors and dentists (paras 70-75) can switch to:

- **1** (paras 44-46);
- **2** (paras 54-56);
- **3** (paras 56A-56B);
- **4** (but see **Note A** below) (para. 60(i)(b));
- **5** (but see **Note B** below) (para. 85);
- **6** (but see **Note C** below) (paras 67-69);
- **9** (para. 75K(i)(b));
- **15** provided the applicant has an IED for employment as a doctor or dentist and, if they are sponsored by a government or an international agency, they have their sponsor's consent (para. 131B, paras 132-133);
- **16** provided they hold an IED valid for the highly skilled migrant programme and, if they are sponsored by a government or an international agency, they have their sponsor's consent (para. 135DC, paras 135E-135F);
- **22** provided that, if they are sponsored by a government or an international agency, they have their sponsor's consent (para. 210DD, paras 210E-210F);
- **28** but the applicant must have been permitted to remain in the UK for longer than six months in total – this excludes most (but not all) of those given short-term leave (see **Note G** below) (para. 284(i), paras 285-286);
- **30** (but see **Note H** below) (paras 295D-295F);
- **31** (paras 317-319);
- **32** (paras 327-344);
- **33** (paras 276A-276D).

1 Visitor	12 Seasonal agricultural worker	23 Europe Accession Agreements
2 Medical visitor		
3 Parent of school child	13 Teacher/language assistant	24 Investor
4 Student	14 TWES	25 Writer/composer/artist
5 Prospective student	15 Work-permit holder	26 Right of access to child
6 Student nurse	16 HSMP	27 Retired person
7 Postgraduate doctor/dentist	17 SBS	28 Spouse of settled sponsor
8 PLAB test	18 SEGS	29 Fiancé(e) of settled sponsor
9 Clinical attachment/ dental observer	19 'Permit-free' employment	30 Partner of settled sponsor
	20 Fresh Talent: Scotland	31 Dependent relative
10 *Au pair*	21 Business/self-employed	32 Refugee
11 Working holidaymaker	22 Innovator	33 Long residence

8 **Those intending to take the PLAB test** (paras 75A-75C) can switch to:

- **1** (paras 44-46);
- **2** (paras 54-56);
- **3** (paras 56A-56B);
- **4** (but see **Note A** below) (para. 60(i)(b));
- **5** (but see **Note B** below) (para. 85);
- **6** (but see **Note C** below) (paras 67-69);
- **7** (para. 73(ii)(c));
- **9** (para. 75K(i)(a));
- **15** provided they hold an IED valid for employment as a doctor or dentist (para. 131G, paras 132-133);
- **16** provided they hold an IED valid for the highly skilled migrant programme under the priority application process for general practitioners (GPs) (para. 135DG, paras 135E-135F);
- **28** but the applicant must have been permitted to remain in the UK for longer than six months in total – this excludes most (but not all) of those given short-term leave (see **Note G** below) (para. 284(i), paras 285-286);
- **30** (but see **Note H** below) (paras 295D-295F);
- **31** (paras 317-319);
- **32** (paras 327-344);
- **33** (paras 276A-276D).

9 **Those taking up a clinical attachment or dental observer post** (paras 75G-75M) can switch to:

- **1** (paras 44-46);
- **2** (paras 54-56);
- **3** (paras 56A-56B);

1 Visitor	12 Seasonal agricultural	23 Europe Accession
2 Medical visitor	worker	Agreements
3 Parent of school child	13 Teacher/language assistant	24 Investor
4 Student	14 TWES	25 Writer/composer/artist
5 Prospective student	15 Work-permit holder	26 Right of access to child
6 Student nurse	16 HSMP	27 Retired person
7 Postgraduate doctor/dentist	17 SBS	28 Spouse of settled sponsor
8 PLAB test	18 SEGS	29 Fiancé(e) of settled sponsor
9 Clinical attachment/ dental observer	19 'Permit-free' employment	30 Partner of settled sponsor
	20 Fresh Talent: Scotland	31 Dependent relative
10 *Au pair*	21 Business/self-employed	32 Refugee
11 Working holidaymaker	22 Innovator	33 Long residence

- **4** (but see **Note A** below) (para. 60(i)(b));
- **5** (but see **Note B** below) (para. 85);
- **6** (but see **Note C** below) (paras 67-69);
- **7** (para. 73(ii)(d));
- **15** provided they hold an IED valid for employment as a doctor or dentist (para. 131G, paras 132-133);
- **16** provided they hold an IED valid for the highly skilled migrant programme under the priority application process for general practitioners (GPs) (para. 135DG, paras 135E-135F);
- **28** but the applicant must have been permitted to remain in the UK for longer than six months in total – this excludes most (but not all) of those given short-term leave (see **Note G** below) (para. 284(i), paras 285-286);
- **30** (but see **Note H** below) (paras 295D-295F);
- **31** (paras 317-319);
- **32** (paras 327-344);
- **33** (paras 276A-276D).

10 *Au pairs* (paras 88-94) can switch to:

- **1** (paras 44-46);
- **2** (paras 54-56);
- **3** (paras 56A-56B);
- **4** (but see **Note A** below) (para. 60(i)(b));
- **5** (but see **Note B** below) (para. 85);
- **6** (but see **Note C** below) (paras 67-69);
- **28** but the applicant must have been permitted to remain in the UK for longer than six months in total – this excludes most (but not all) of those given short-term leave (see **Note G** below) (para. 284(i), paras 285-286);
- **30** (but see **Note H** below) (paras 295D-295F);

1	Visitor	12	Seasonal agricultural worker	23	Europe Accession Agreements
2	Medical visitor				
3	Parent of school child	13	Teacher/language assistant	24	Investor
4	Student	14	TWES	25	Writer/composer/artist
5	Prospective student	15	Work-permit holder	26	Right of access to child
6	Student nurse	16	HSMP	27	Retired person
7	Postgraduate doctor/dentist	17	SBS	28	Spouse of settled sponsor
8	PLAB test	18	SEGS	29	Fiancé(e) of settled sponsor
9	Clinical attachment/ dental observer	19	'Permit-free' employment	30	Partner of settled sponsor
		20	Fresh Talent: Scotland	31	Dependent relative
10	*Au pair*	21	Business/self-employed	32	Refugee
11	Working holidaymaker	22	Innovator	33	Long residence

2

- **31** (paras 317-319);
- **32** (paras 327-344);
- **33** (paras 276A-276D).

11 Working holidaymakers (paras 95-100) can switch to:

- **1** (paras 44-46);
- **2** (paras 54-56);
- **3** (paras 56A-56B);
- **4** (but see **Note A** below) (para. 60(i)(b));
- **5** (but see **Note B** below) (para. 85);
- **6** (but see **Note C** below) (paras 67-69);
- **15** provided the applicant has spent more than 12 months in total in the UK as a working holidaymaker *and* they hold an IED valid for employment in one of the 'shortage occupations' listed by Work Permits (UK) (►see 424–5; 1519–21) (para. 131D, paras 132-133);
- **16** provided they hold an IED valid for the highly skilled migrant programme (para. 135DD, paras 135E-135F);
- **21** provided the applicant has spent more than 12 months in total in the UK as a working holidaymaker (para. 206F, paras 207-208);
- **22** (para. 210DC, paras 210E-210F);
- **28** but the applicant must have been permitted to remain in the UK for longer than six months in total – this excludes most (but not all) of those given short-term leave (see **Note G** below) (para. 284(i), paras 285-286);
- **30** (but see **Note H** below) (paras 295D-295F);
- **31** (paras 317-319);
- **32** (paras 327-344);
- **33** (paras 276A-276D).

1	Visitor	12	Seasonal agricultural worker	23	Europe Accession Agreements
2	Medical visitor				
3	Parent of school child	13	Teacher/language assistant	24	Investor
4	Student	14	TWES	25	Writer/composer/artist
5	Prospective student	15	Work-permit holder	26	Right of access to child
6	Student nurse	16	HSMP	27	Retired person
7	Postgraduate doctor/dentist	17	SBS	28	Spouse of settled sponsor
8	PLAB test	18	SEGS	29	Fiancé(e) of settled sponsor
9	Clinical attachment/ dental observer	19	'Permit-free' employment	30	Partner of settled sponsor
		20	Fresh Talent: Scotland	31	Dependent relative
10	*Au pair*	21	Business/self-employed	32	Refugee
11	Working holidaymaker	22	Innovator	33	Long residence

12 Seasonal workers at agricultural camps (SAWS) (paras 104-109) can switch to:

- **1** *but* time already spent as a seasonal agricultural worker counts towards the six months' maximum leave, which a visitor may be granted (paras 44-46);
- **2** (paras 54-56);
- **3** (paras 56A-56B);
- **4** (but see **Note A** below) (para. 60(i)(b));
- **5** (but see **Note B** below) (para. 85);
- **6** (but see **Note C** below) (paras 67-69);
- **28** but the applicant must have been permitted to remain in the UK for longer than six months in total – this excludes most (but not all) of those given short-term leave (see **Note G** below) (para. 284(i), paras 285-286);
- **30** (but see **Note H** below) (paras 295D-295F);
- **31** (paras 317-319);
- **32** (paras 327-344);
- **33** (paras 276A-276D).

13 Teachers and language assistants (paras 110-115) can switch to:

- **1** (paras 44-46);
- **2** (paras 54-56);
- **3** (paras 56A-56B);
- **4** (but see **Note A** below) (para. 60(i)(b));
- **5** (but see **Note B** below) (para. 85);
- **6** (but see **Note C** below) (paras 67-69);
- **28** but the applicant must have been permitted to remain in the UK for longer than six months in total – this excludes most (but not all) of those given short-term leave (see **Note G** below) (para. 284(i), paras 285-286);

1 Visitor	12 Seasonal agricultural worker	23 Europe Accession Agreements
2 Medical visitor		
3 Parent of school child	13 Teacher/language assistant	24 Investor
4 Student	14 TWES	25 Writer/composer/artist
5 Prospective student	15 Work-permit holder	26 Right of access to child
6 Student nurse	16 HSMP	27 Retired person
7 Postgraduate doctor/dentist	17 SBS	28 Spouse of settled sponsor
8 PLAB test	18 SEGS	29 Fiancé(e) of settled sponsor
9 Clinical attachment/ dental observer	19 'Permit-free' employment	30 Partner of settled sponsor
	20 Fresh Talent: Scotland	31 Dependent relative
10 *Au pair*	21 Business/self-employed	32 Refugee
11 Working holidaymaker	22 Innovator	33 Long residence

- **30** (but see **Note H** below) (paras 295D-295F);
- **31** (paras 317-319);
- **32** (paras 327-344);
- **33** (paras 276A-276D).

14 Training and Work Experience Scheme participants (TWES) (paras 116-121) can switch to:

- **1** (paras 44-46);
- **2** (paras 54-56);
- **3** (paras 56A-56B);
- **4** (but see **Note A** below) (para. 60(i)(b));
- **5** (but see **Note B** below) (para. 85);
- **6** (but see **Note C** below) (paras 67-69);
- **28** but the applicant must have been permitted to remain in the UK for longer than six months in total – this excludes most (but not all) of those given short-term leave (see **Note G** below) (para. 284(i), paras 285-286);
- **30** (but see **Note H** below) (paras 295D-295F);
- **31** (paras 317-319);
- **32** (paras 327-344);
- **33** (paras 276A-276D).

15 Work permit holders (paras 128-135) can switch to:

- **1** (paras 44-46);
- **2** (paras 54-56);
- **3** (paras 56A-56B);
- **4** (but see **Note A** below) (para. 60(i)(b));
- **5** (but see **Note B** below) (para. 85);

1	Visitor	12	Seasonal agricultural	23	Europe Accession
2	Medical visitor		worker		Agreements
3	Parent of school child	13	Teacher/language assistant	24	Investor
4	Student	14	TWES	25	Writer/composer/artist
5	Prospective student	15	Work-permit holder	26	Right of access to child
6	Student nurse	16	HSMP	27	Retired person
7	Postgraduate doctor/dentist	17	SBS	28	Spouse of settled sponsor
8	PLAB test	18	SEGS	29	Fiancé(e) of settled sponsor
9	Clinical attachment/ dental	19	'Permit-free' employment	30	Partner of settled sponsor
	observer	20	Fresh Talent: Scotland	31	Dependent relative
10	*Au pair*	21	Business/self-employed	32	Refugee
11	Working holidaymaker	22	Innovator	33	Long residence

- **6** (but see **Note C** below) (paras 67-69);
- **7** (para. 73(ii)(e));
- **9** provided that the applicant's work permit leave was given for employment as a doctor or a dentist (para. 75K(i)(c));
- **16** provided the applicant holds an IED valid for the highly skilled migrant programme (para. 135DA, paras 135E-135F);
- **21** (para. 206A, paras 207-208);
- **22** (para. 210DA, paras 210E-210F);
- **24** (para. 227A, paras 228-229);
- **27** (para. 266A, paras 267-268);
- **28** but the applicant must have been permitted to remain in the UK for longer than six months in total – this excludes most (but not all) of those given short-term leave (see **Note G** below) (para. 284(i), paras 285-286);
- **30** (but see **Note H** below) (paras 295D-295F);
- **31** (paras 317-319);
- **32** (paras 327-344);
- **33** (paras 276A-276D).

16 Highly Skilled Migrant Programme (HSMP) participants (paras 135A-135H) can switch to:

- **1** (paras 44-46);
- **2** (paras 54-56);
- **3** (paras 56A-56B);
- **4** (but see **Note A** below) (para. 60(i)(b));
- **5** (but see **Note B** below) (para. 85);
- **6** (but see **Note C** below) (paras 67-69);
- **15** provided they hold an IED valid for employment (para. 131E, paras 132-133);

1 Visitor	12 Seasonal agricultural worker	23 Europe Accession Agreements
2 Medical visitor		
3 Parent of school child	13 Teacher/language assistant	24 Investor
4 Student	14 TWES	25 Writer/composer/artist
5 Prospective student	15 Work-permit holder	26 Right of access to child
6 Student nurse	16 HSMP	27 Retired person
7 Postgraduate doctor/dentist	17 SBS	28 Spouse of settled sponsor
8 PLAB test	18 SEGS	29 Fiancé(e) of settled sponsor
9 Clinical attachment/ dental observer	19 'Permit-free' employment	30 Partner of settled sponsor
	20 Fresh Talent: Scotland	31 Dependent relative
10 *Au pair*	21 Business/self-employed	32 Refugee
11 Working holidaymaker	22 Innovator	33 Long residence

- **21** (para. 206B, paras 207-208);
- **22** (para. 210DF, paras 210E-210F);
- **24** (para. 227B, paras 228-229);
- **27** (para. 266B, paras 267-268);
- **28** but the applicant must have been permitted to remain in the UK for longer than six months in total – this excludes most (but not all) of those given short-term leave (see **Note G** below) (para. 284(i), paras 285-286);
- **30** (but see **Note H** below) (paras 295D-295F);
- **31** (paras 317-319);
- **32** (paras 327-344);
- **33** (paras 276A-276D).

17 Sectors-based-scheme participants (paras 135I-135N) can switch to:

- **1** (paras 44-46);
- **2** (paras 54-56);
- **3** (paras 56A-56B);
- **4** (but see **Note A** below) (para. 60(i)(b));
- **5** (but see **Note B** below) (para. 85);
- **6** (but see **Note C** below) (paras 67-69);
- **28** but the applicant must have been permitted to remain in the UK for longer than six months in total – this excludes most (but not all) of those given short-term leave (see **Note G** below) (para. 284(i), paras 285-286);
- **30** (but see **Note H** below) (paras 295D-295F);
- **31** (paras 317-319);
- **32** (paras 327-344);
- **33** (paras 276A-276D).

1 Visitor	12 Seasonal agricultural worker	23 Europe Accession Agreements
2 Medical visitor	13 Teacher/language assistant	24 Investor
3 Parent of school child	14 TWES	25 Writer/composer/artist
4 Student	15 Work-permit holder	26 Right of access to child
5 Prospective student	16 HSMP	27 Retired person
6 Student nurse	17 SBS	28 Spouse of settled sponsor
7 Postgraduate doctor/dentist	18 SEGS	29 Fiancé(e) of settled sponsor
8 PLAB test	19 'Permit-free' employment	30 Partner of settled sponsor
9 Clinical attachment/ dental observer	20 Fresh Talent: Scotland	31 Dependent relative
10 *Au pair*	21 Business/self-employed	32 Refugee
11 Working holidaymaker	22 Innovator	33 Long residence

18 Science and Engineering Graduates Scheme participants (SEGS) (paras 135O-135T) can switch to:

- **1** (paras 44-46);
- **2** (paras 54-56);
- **3** (paras 56A-56B);
- **4** (but see **Note A** below) (para. 60(i)(b));
- **5** (but see **Note B** below) (para. 85);
- **6** (but see **Note C** below) (paras 67-69);
- **15** provided that the applicant holds an IED for employment (para. 131C, paras 132-133);
- **16** provided that the applicant holds an IED valid for the highly skilled migrant programme (para. 135DE, paras 135E-135F);
- **20** (but see **Note F** below) (para. 143D(ii)(b), paras 143E-143F);
- **21** (para. 206C, paras 207-208);
- **22** (para. 210DE, paras 210E-210F);
- **28** but the applicant must have been permitted to remain in the UK for longer than six months in total – this excludes most (but not all) of those given short-term leave (see **Note G** below) (para. 284(i), paras 285-286);
- **30** (but see **Note H** below) (paras 295D-295F);
- **31** (paras 317-319);
- **32** (paras 327-344);
- **33** (paras 276A-276D).

19 'Permit-free' employment category (see **Note D** below for the list of 'permit-free' categories under the rules) (paras 136-143, 144-193). Those with leave under any of the permit-free employment categories under the rules can switch to:

- **1** (paras 44-46);

1 Visitor	12 Seasonal agricultural worker	23 Europe Accession Agreements
2 Medical visitor		
3 Parent of school child	13 Teacher/language assistant	24 Investor
4 Student	14 TWES	25 Writer/composer/artist
5 Prospective student	15 Work-permit holder	26 Right of access to child
6 Student nurse	16 HSMP	27 Retired person
7 Postgraduate doctor/dentist	17 SBS	28 Spouse of settled sponsor
8 PLAB test	18 SEGS	29 Fiancé(e) of settled sponsor
9 Clinical attachment/ dental observer	19 'Permit-free' employment	30 Partner of settled sponsor
	20 Fresh Talent: Scotland	31 Dependent relative
10 *Au pair*	21 Business/self-employed	32 Refugee
11 Working holidaymaker	22 Innovator	33 Long residence

- **2** (paras 54-56);
- **3** (paras 56A-56B);
- **4** (but see **Note A** below) (para. 60(i)(b));
- **5** (but see **Note B** below) (para. 85);
- **6** (but see **Note C** below) (paras 67-69);
- **28** but the applicant must have been permitted to remain in the UK for longer than six months in total – this excludes most (but not all) of those given short-term leave (see **Note G** below) (para. 284(i), paras 285-286);
- **30** (but see **Note H** below) (paras 295D-295F);
- **31** (paras 317-319);
- **32** (paras 327-344);
- **33** (paras 276A-276D).

Separate rules apply for switching *into* the permit-free category of 'minister of religion', see **Note E** below.

20 Fresh Talent: Working in Scotland Scheme participants (FT: WSS) (paras 143A-143F) can switch to:

- **1** (paras 44-46);
- **2** (paras 54-56);
- **3** (paras 56A-56B);
- **4** (but see **Note A** below) (para. 60(i)(b));
- **5** (but see **Note B** below) (para. 85);
- **6** (but see **Note C** below) (para. 67-69);
- **15** provided that they hold an IED valid for employment in Scotland and, if the applicant's studies which led them to be granted leave under the Fresh Talent Scheme (or subsequent studies) were sponsored by a government or an international agency, the applicant has the consent of their official sponsor (para. 131H, paras 132-133);

1	Visitor	12	Seasonal agricultural worker	23	Europe Accession Agreements
2	Medical visitor	13	Teacher/language assistant	24	Investor
3	Parent of school child	14	TWES	25	Writer/composer/artist
4	Student	15	Work-permit holder	26	Right of access to child
5	Prospective student	16	HSMP	27	Retired person
6	Student nurse	17	SBS	28	Spouse of settled sponsor
7	Postgraduate doctor/dentist	18	SEGS	29	Fiancé(e) of settled sponsor
8	PLAB test	19	'Permit-free' employment	30	Partner of settled sponsor
9	Clinical attachment/ dental observer	20	Fresh Talent: Scotland	31	Dependent relative
10	*Au pair*	21	Business/self-employed	32	Refugee
11	Working holidaymaker	22	Innovator	33	Long residence

- **16** provided that they hold an IED valid for the highly skilled migrant programme and, if the applicant's studies which led them to be granted leave under the Fresh Talent Scheme (or subsequent studies) were sponsored by a government or an international agency, the applicant has the consent of their official sponsor (para. 135DH, paras 135E-135F);

- **21** provided that, if the applicant's studies which led them to be granted leave under the Fresh Talent Scheme (or subsequent studies) were sponsored by a government or an international agency, the applicant has the consent of their official sponsor (para. 206G, paras 207-208);

- **22** provided that, if the applicant's studies which led them to be granted leave under the Fresh Talent Scheme (or subsequent studies) were sponsored by a government or an international agency, the applicant has the consent of their official sponsor (para. 210DH, paras 210E-210F);

- **28** but the applicant must have been permitted to remain in the UK for longer than six months in total – this excludes most (but not all) of those given short-term leave (see **Note G** below) (para. 284(i), paras 285-286);

- **30** (but see **Note H** below) (paras 295D-295F);

- **31** (paras 317-319);

- **32** (paras 327-344);

- **33** (paras 276A-276D).

21 Business/self-employed persons (paras 200-210) can switch to:

- **1** (paras 44-46);

- **2** (paras 54-56);

- **3** (paras 56A-56B);

- **4** (but see **Note A** below) (para. 60(i)(b));

- **5** (but see **Note B** below) (para. 85);

- **6** (but see **Note C** below) (paras 67-69);

- **22** (para. 210DG, paras 210E-210F);

1 Visitor	12 Seasonal agricultural worker	23 Europe Accession Agreements
2 Medical visitor		
3 Parent of school child	13 Teacher/language assistant	24 Investor
4 Student	14 TWES	25 Writer/composer/artist
5 Prospective student	15 Work-permit holder	26 Right of access to child
6 Student nurse	16 HSMP	27 Retired person
7 Postgraduate doctor/dentist	17 SBS	28 Spouse of settled sponsor
8 PLAB test	18 SEGS	29 Fiancé(e) of settled sponsor
9 Clinical attachment/ dental observer	19 'Permit-free' employment	30 Partner of settled sponsor
10 *Au pair*	20 Fresh Talent: Scotland	31 Dependent relative
11 Working holidaymaker	21 Business/self-employed	32 Refugee
	22 Innovator	33 Long residence

- **24** (para. 227C, paras 228-229);
- **27** (para. 266C, paras 267-268);
- **28** but the applicant must have been permitted to remain in the UK for longer than six months in total – this excludes most (but not all) of those given short-term leave (see **Note G** below) (para. 284(i), paras 285-286);
- **30** (but see **Note H** below) (paras 295D-295F);
- **31** (paras 317-319);
- **32** (paras 327-344);
- **33** (paras 276A-276D).

22 Innovators (paras 210A-210H) can switch to:

- **1** (paras 44-46);
- **2** (paras 54-56);
- **3** (paras 56A-56B);
- **4** (but see **Note A** below) (para. 60(i)(b));
- **5** (but see **Note B** below) (para. 85);
- **6** (but see **Note C** below) (paras 67-69);
- **15** provided that they hold a valid IED for employment (para. 131F, paras 132-133);
- **16** provided that they hold an IED valid for the highly skilled migrant programme (para. 135DF, paras 135E-135F);
- **21** (para. 206D, paras 207-208);
- **24** (para. 227D, paras 228-229);
- **27** (para. 266D, paras 267-268);
- **28** but the applicant must have been permitted to remain in the UK for longer than six months in total – this excludes most (but not all) of those given short-term leave (see **Note G** below) (para. 284(i), paras 285-286);

1	Visitor	12	Seasonal agricultural worker	23	Europe Accession Agreements
2	Medical visitor			24	Investor
3	Parent of school child	13	Teacher/language assistant	25	Writer/composer/artist
4	Student	14	TWES	26	Right of access to child
5	Prospective student	15	Work-permit holder	27	Retired person
6	Student nurse	16	HSMP	28	Spouse of settled sponsor
7	Postgraduate doctor/dentist	17	SBS	29	Fiancé(e) of settled sponsor
8	PLAB test	18	SEGS	30	Partner of settled sponsor
9	Clinical attachment/ dental observer	19	'Permit-free' employment	31	Dependent relative
10	*Au pair*	20	Fresh Talent: Scotland	32	Refugee
11	Working holidaymaker	21	Business/self-employed	33	Long residence
		22	Innovator		

- **30** (but see **Note H** below) (paras 295D-295F);
- **31** (paras 317-319);
- **32** (paras 327-344);
- **33** (paras 276A-276D).

23 Business persons under the 'Europe' Association Agreements (Bulgaria and Romania) (paras 211-223) can switch to:

- **1** (paras 44-46);
- **2** (paras 54-56);
- **3** (paras 56A-56B);
- **4** (but see **Note A** below) (para. 60(i)(b));
- **5** (but see **Note B** below) (para. 85);
- **6** (but see **Note C** below) (paras 67-69);
- **28** but the applicant must have been permitted to remain in the UK for longer than six months in total – this excludes most (but not all) of those given short-term leave (see **Note G** below) (para. 284(i), paras 285-286);
- **30** (but see **Note H** below) (paras 295D-295F);
- **31** (paras 317-319);
- **32** (paras 327-344);
- **33** (paras 276A-276D).

24 Investors (paras 224-231) can switch to:

- **1** (paras 44-46);
- **2** (paras 54-56);
- **3** (paras 56A-56B);
- **4** (but see **Note A** below) (para. 60(i)(b));
- **5** (but see **Note B** below) (para. 85);

1	Visitor	12	Seasonal agricultural worker	23	Europe Accession Agreements
2	Medical visitor				
3	Parent of school child	13	Teacher/language assistant	24	Investor
4	Student	14	TWES	25	Writer/composer/artist
5	Prospective student	15	Work-permit holder	26	Right of access to child
6	Student nurse	16	HSMP	27	Retired person
7	Postgraduate doctor/dentist	17	SBS	28	Spouse of settled sponsor
8	PLAB test	18	SEGS	29	Fiancé(e) of settled sponsor
9	Clinical attachment/ dental observer	19	'Permit-free' employment	30	Partner of settled sponsor
		20	Fresh Talent: Scotland	31	Dependent relative
10	*Au pair*	21	Business/self-employed	32	Refugee
11	Working holidaymaker	22	Innovator	33	Long residence

- **6** (but see **Note C** below) (paras 67-69);
- **28** but the applicant must have been permitted to remain in the UK for longer than six months in total – this excludes most (but not all) of those given short-term leave (see **Note G** below) (para. 284(i), paras 285-286);
- **30** (but see **Note H** below) (paras 295D-295F);
- **31** (paras 317-319);
- **32** (paras 327-344);
- **33** (paras 276A-276D).

25 Writers, composers and artists (paras 232-239) can switch to:

- **1** (paras 44-46);
- **2** (paras 54-56);
- **3** (paras 56A-56B);
- **4** (but see **Note A** below) (para. 60(i)(b));
- **5** (but see **Note B** below) (para. 85);
- **6** (but see **Note C b**elow) (paras 67-69);
- **28** but the applicant must have been permitted to remain in the UK for longer than six months in total – this excludes most (but not all) of those given short-term leave (see **Note G** below) (para. 284(i), paras 285-286);
- **30** (but see **Note H** below) (paras 295D-295F);
- **31** (paras 317-319);
- **32** (paras 327-344);
- **33** (paras 276A-276D).

26 Persons with rights of access to a child resident in UK (paras 246-248F) can switch to:

- **1** (paras 44-46);
- **2** (paras 54-56);

1 Visitor	12 Seasonal agricultural worker	23 Europe Accession Agreements
2 Medical visitor		
3 Parent of school child	13 Teacher/language assistant	24 Investor
4 Student	14 TWES	25 Writer/composer/artist
5 Prospective student	15 Work-permit holder	26 Right of access to child
6 Student nurse	16 HSMP	27 Retired person
7 Postgraduate doctor/dentist	17 SBS	28 Spouse of settled sponsor
8 PLAB test	18 SEGS	29 Fiancé(e) of settled sponsor
9 Clinical attachment/ dental observer	19 'Permit-free' employment	30 Partner of settled sponsor
	20 Fresh Talent: Scotland	31 Dependent relative
10 Au pair	21 Business/self-employed	32 Refugee
11 Working holidaymaker	22 Innovator	33 Long residence

- **3** (paras 56A-56B);
- **4** (but see **Note A** below) (para. 60(i)(b));
- **5** (but see **Note B** below) (para. 85);
- **6** (but see **Note C** below) (paras 67-69);
- **28** but the applicant must have been permitted to remain in the UK for longer than six months in total – this excludes most (but not all) of those given short-term leave (see **Note G** below) (para. 284(i), paras 285-286);
- **30** (but see **Note H** below) (paras 295D-295F);
- **31** (paras 317-319);
- **32** (paras 327-344);
- **33** (paras 276A-276D).

27 Retired persons of independent means (paras 263-270) can switch to:

- **1** (paras 44-46);
- **2** (paras 54-56);
- **3** (paras 56A-56B);
- **4** (but see **Note A** below) (para. 60(i)(b));
- **5** (but see **Note B** below) (para. 85);
- **6** (but see **Note C** below) (paras 67-69);
- **28** but the applicant must have been permitted to remain in the UK for longer than six months in total – this excludes most (but not all) of those given short-term leave (see **Note G** below) (para. 284(i), paras 285-286);
- **30** (but see **Note H** below) (paras 295D-295F);
- **31** (paras 317-319);
- **32** (paras 327-344);
- **33** (paras 276A-276D).

1 Visitor	12 Seasonal agricultural	23 Europe Accession
2 Medical visitor	worker	Agreements
3 Parent of school child	13 Teacher/language assistant	24 Investor
4 Student	14 TWES	25 Writer/composer/artist
5 Prospective student	15 Work-permit holder	26 Right of access to child
6 Student nurse	16 HSMP	27 Retired person
7 Postgraduate doctor/dentist	17 SBS	28 Spouse of settled sponsor
8 PLAB test	18 SEGS	29 Fiancé(e) of settled sponsor
9 Clinical attachment/ dental observer	19 'Permit-free' employment	30 Partner of settled sponsor
10 *Au pair*	20 Fresh Talent: Scotland	31 Dependent relative
11 Working holidaymaker	21 Business/self-employed	32 Refugee
	22 Innovator	33 Long residence

28 Spouses of persons settled in the UK (paras 277-289C) can switch to:

- **1** (paras 44-46);
- **2** (paras 54-56);
- **3** (paras 56A-56B);
- **4** (but see **Note A** below) (para. 60(i)(b));
- **5** (but see **Note B** below) (para. 85);
- **6** (but see **Note C** below) (paras 67-69);
- **26** provided that the applicant has existing leave as the spouse of the other parent of the child they wish to exercise access rights to (para. 248A(vii), paras 248B-248C);
- **30** (but see **Note H** below) (paras 295D-295F);
- **31** (paras 317-319);
- **32** (paras 327-344);
- **33** (paras 276A-276D).

29 Fiancé(e)s of persons settled in the UK (paras 289AA-295) can switch to:

- **1** (paras 44-46);
- **2** (paras 54-56);
- **3** (paras 56A-56B);
- **4** (but see **Note A** below) (para. 60(i)(b));
- **5** (but see **Note B** below) (para. 85);
- **6** (but see **Note C** below) (paras 67-69);
- **28** and note that fiancé(e)s who are switching to stay as a spouse are *exempt* from the requirement which applies to all other categories that their leave must enable them to be in the UK for longer than six months – this, of course, is a natural switch (para. 284(i), paras 285-286 and see **Note G**);
- **30** (but see **Note H** below) (paras 295D-295F);

1 Visitor	12 Seasonal agricultural	23 Europe Accession
2 Medical visitor	worker	Agreements
3 Parent of school child	13 Teacher/language assistant	24 Investor
4 Student	14 TWES	25 Writer/composer/artist
5 Prospective student	15 Work-permit holder	26 Right of access to child
6 Student nurse	16 HSMP	27 Retired person
7 Postgraduate doctor/dentist	17 SBS	28 Spouse of settled sponsor
8 PLAB test	18 SEGS	29 Fiancé(e) of settled sponsor
9 Clinical attachment/ dental observer	19 'Permit-free' employment	30 Partner of settled sponsor
10 *Au pair*	20 Fresh Talent: Scotland	31 Dependent relative
11 Working holidaymaker	21 Business/self-employed	32 Refugee
	22 Innovator	33 Long residence

- **31** (paras 317-319);
- **32** (paras 327-344);
- **33** (paras 276A-276D).

30 Unmarried partners of persons settled in the UK (paras 295AA-295I) can switch to:

- **1** (paras 44-46);
- **2** (paras 54-56);
- **3** (paras 56A-56B);
- **4** (but see **Note A** below) (para. 60(i)(b));
- **5** (but see **Note B** below) (para. 85);
- **6** (but see **Note C** below) (paras 67-69);
- **26** provided that the applicant has existing leave as the unmarried partner of the other parent of the child they wish to exercise access rights to (para. 248A(vii), paras 248B-248C);
- **28** but the applicant must have been permitted to remain in the UK for longer than six months in total – this excludes most (but not all) of those given short-term leave (see **Note G** below) (para. 284(i), paras 285-286);
- **31** (paras 317-319);
- **32** (paras 327-344);
- **33** (paras 276A-276D).

31 Parents, grandparents or other dependent relatives of sponsors who are settled in the UK (paras 317-319) (applicants in this category should already have indefinite leave and are therefore very unlikely to want to switch) can switch to:

- **1** (paras 44-46);
- **2** (paras 54-56);

1 Visitor	12 Seasonal agricultural	23 Europe Accession
2 Medical visitor	worker	Agreements
3 Parent of school child	13 Teacher/language assistant	24 Investor
4 Student	14 TWES	25 Writer/composer/artist
5 Prospective student	15 Work-permit holder	26 Right of access to child
6 Student nurse	16 HSMP	27 Retired person
7 Postgraduate doctor/dentist	17 SBS	28 Spouse of settled sponsor
8 PLAB test	18 SEGS	29 Fiancé(e) of settled sponsor
9 Clinical attachment/ dental observer	19 'Permit-free' employment	30 Partner of settled sponsor
10 *Au pair*	20 Fresh Talent: Scotland	31 Dependent relative
11 Working holidaymaker	21 Business/self-employed	32 Refugee
	22 Innovator	33 Long residence

2

- **3** (paras 56A-56B);
- **4** (but see **Note A** below) (para. 60(i)(b));
- **5** (but see **Note B** below) (para. 85);
- **6** (but see **Note C** below) (paras 67-69);
- **28** but the applicant must have been permitted to remain in the UK for longer than six months in total – this excludes most (but not all) of those given short-term leave (see **Note G** below) (para. 284(i), paras 285-286);
- **30** (but see **Note H** below) (paras 295D-295F);
- **32** (paras 327-344);
- **33** (paras 276A-276D).

32 Asylum as a refugee (paras 327-344). Those granted asylum as a refugee can switch to:

- **1** (paras 44-46);
- **2** (paras 54-56);
- **3** (paras 56A-56B);
- **4** (but see **Note A** below) (para. 60(i)(b));
- **5** (but see **Note B** below) (para. 85);
- **6** (but see **Note C** below) (paras 67-69);
- **28** but the applicant must have been permitted to remain in the UK for longer than six months in total – this excludes most (but not all) of those given short-term leave (see **Note G** below) (para. 284(i), paras 285-286);
- **30** (but see **Note H** below) (paras 295D-295F);
- **31** (paras 317-319);
- **33** (paras 276A-276D).

1 Visitor	12 Seasonal agricultural	23 Europe Accession
2 Medical visitor	worker	Agreements
3 Parent of school child	13 Teacher/language assistant	24 Investor
4 Student	14 TWES	25 Writer/composer/artist
5 Prospective student	15 Work-permit holder	26 Right of access to child
6 Student nurse	16 HSMP	27 Retired person
7 Postgraduate doctor/dentist	17 SBS	28 Spouse of settled sponsor
8 PLAB test	18 SEGS	29 Fiancé(e) of settled sponsor
9 Clinical attachment/ dental observer	19 'Permit-free' employment	30 Partner of settled sponsor
10 *Au pair*	20 Fresh Talent: Scotland	31 Dependent relative
11 Working holidaymaker	21 Business/self-employed	32 Refugee
	22 Innovator	33 Long residence

33 Long residence (paras 276A-276D). Those with leave under the long-residence rules (applicants in this category should already have indefinite leave and are therefore very unlikely to want to switch) can switch to:

- **1** (paras 44-46);
- **2** (paras 54-56);
- **3** (paras 56A-56B);
- **4** (but see **Note A** below) (para. 60(i)(b));
- **5** (but see **Note B** below) (para. 85);
- **6** (but see **Note C** below) (paras 67-69);
- **28** but the applicant must have been permitted to remain in the UK for longer than six months in total – this excludes most (but not all) of those given short-term leave (see **Note G** below) (para. 284(i), paras 285-286);
- **30** (but see **Note H** below) (paras 295D-295F);
- **31** (paras 317-319);
- **32** (paras 327-344).

Notes on switching

Note A: Switching to student status. Where the table states that applicants may switch to student status (category **4**), they may only do so if they are *not* visa nationals and they have been accepted for a course of study at degree level or above (para. 60(i)(b)). The exception to this is those admitted with entry clearances as prospective students (category **5**) – they may switch to student status in order to study on a course whether they are visa nationals or non-visa nationals and regardless of the level of the course (para. 60(i)(a)(b)(c)).

Both switching to student status and extending leave as a student can be complex. For further details, ▶see the student chapter at 278–80, 284–6.

Note B: Switching to stay as a prospective student. Where the table states that applicants may switch to prospective student status (category **5**),

1 Visitor	12 Seasonal agricultural worker	23 Europe Accession Agreements
2 Medical visitor	13 Teacher/language assistant	24 Investor
3 Parent of school child	14 TWES	25 Writer/composer/artist
4 Student	15 Work-permit holder	26 Right of access to child
5 Prospective student	16 HSMP	27 Retired person
6 Student nurse	17 SBS	28 Spouse of settled sponsor
7 Postgraduate doctor/dentist	18 SEGS	29 Fiancé(e) of settled sponsor
8 PLAB test	19 'Permit-free' employment	30 Partner of settled sponsor
9 Clinical attachment/ dental observer	20 Fresh Talent: Scotland	31 Dependent relative
10 *Au pair*	21 Business/self-employed	32 Refugee
11 Working holidaymaker	22 Innovator	33 Long residence

they may only do so if they are *not* visa nationals (para. 85(i)). They must *also* show that they will not, as a result of the immediate extension of leave as a prospective student, spend more than six months in the UK (para. 85(iii)). The time frames are therefore very tight and so the possibilities to switch to remain as a prospective student are, in reality, very limited.

Note C: Switching to stay as a student nurse. Where the table states that applicants may switch to stay as a student nurse (category **6**), they may only do so if they are *not* visa nationals (para. 67(i)).

Note D: 'Permit-free' employment. The category of 'permit-free' employment (category **19**) covers the following individual categories: representatives of overseas newspapers, news agencies or broadcasting organisations; sole representatives of overseas firms; private servants in diplomatic households; domestic workers in private households; overseas government employees; ministers of religion, missionaries and members of religious orders; airport-based operational ground staff of overseas-owned airlines; and Commonwealth citizens with UK ancestry (paras 136-186). However, for an additional special switching rule, which applies for ministers of religion, see **Note E** immediately below.

Note E: Switching to remain as a minister of religion. Although the switching provisions are the same for the 'permit-free' employment categories (**Note D** above) and so, for ease, in the table we have consolidated them as category **19**, there is an exception for switching *into* the category of minister of religion. That exception is to the following effect (note that it only applies for ministers of religion and not for missionaries or for members of a religious order).

An applicant who has been granted leave to enter or remain in the UK in any category under the rules *other than* visitor (1), private medical visitor (2) or transit visitor (not in the table), may 'switch' to remain as a minister of religion *if* they satisfy all of the following requirements (paras 174A, 174B and 175):

- they have spent at least 12 months in the UK in their existing category immediately before their switching application is made;

- they have *either* been working for at least one year as a minister of religion in any of the five years before the date on which they make their application to switch (provided that they were not in breach of their conditions of leave by doing that work), *or* where their faith requires that they are ordained before they can become a minister, they have been ordained a minister following at least one year's full time (or two years' part-time) training for their ministry; and

- they have been appointed (or are very shortly to be appointed) to a position as a minister of religion in the UK and they are suitable for that position as certified by the leadership of their future congregation.

As with all switching applicants, those switching to stay as a minister of religion under the above rule, must also satisfy all the normal requirements of the rules relating to their new category (for ministers of religion, ▶see 459–60) although, obviously, applicants do not need to obtain entry clearance.

Note F: Switching to stay under the Fresh Talent: Working in Scotland Scheme (FT: WSS). Applicants seeking to switch from the Science and Engineering Graduate Scheme (SEGS) (category **18**) to the FT: WSS (category **20**) must not be seeking leave to remain for a period which, when added to periods of leave that they have already had under SEGS or the FT: WSS, would total more than 24 months (para. 143D(iii)).

Note G: Switching to stay as a spouse. Where the table states that applicants may switch to stay as a spouse (category **28**), they can only do so if the leave which the applicant has, means that they are entitled to be in the UK for more than six months altogether counted from the date on which they entered the UK (para. 284(i)). The rule was originally introduced on 1 April 2003 (para. 284(i) HC 395 as amended by HC 538). The rule does not apply to those admitted as fiancé(e)s (category **29**). The rule will normally prevent those in short-term categories (for example visitors – who are generally only granted leave for a maximum of six months – or short-term students), from switching to remain as spouses.

However, as a result of a further modification to the wording of the rule introduced from 25 August 2003 (see Cm 5949), it was made clear that the rule does *not* mean that applications will be refused just because the *last grant* of leave was six months or less. Time is counted from the date on which the applicant last entered the UK, and includes any later grants of leave. So, provided that the total time that the applicant is permitted to be in the UK, from the date of their last entry, is more than six months, switching is not prohibited. So, for example, a person who last entered with leave to enter as a working holidaymaker, who obtains an extension of their leave as a visitor for six months, can still make an in-country application as a spouse while they have their six-months' leave as a visitor. Of course, where applicants are marrying in the UK, most must first obtain approval from the Secretary of State, which may be another obstacle (▶see 296–300).

Note also that the existing leave, which the applicant must have in order to switch to remain as a spouse must have been leave granted under the immigration rules (i.e. not outside the rules). For more on the general requirements on switching to remain as a spouse, ▶see 332–7.

Note H: Switching to stay as an unmarried partner. As with spouses, the rules require that, in order to switch to remain as an unmarried partner (category **30**), the existing leave that the applicant has was given 'in accordance with any of the provisions of these rules' (para. 295D(i)). Therefore, in order to switch under the rules, the existing leave cannot have been given outside the rules.

Note I: Categories under the rules not covered in the table. The switching table covers most categories under the rules. To avoid over-complexity, save for the category of dependent relatives under paras 317-319, it does not separately cover the family members/dependants of those admitted under the rules (for general details, ▶see Section 4 and ▶see 352–6 for dependants of those in the UK in temporary categories), nor the children of those who are settled in the UK or non-British citizen children born in the UK (▶see Chapter 12). The table also does not include 'returning residents' (paras 18-20); this is because this is a category, which only applies *on entry* to determine whether applicants returning from abroad can be admitted because they had indefinite leave when they last left the UK. The table also does not cover crew members or EEA nationals insofar as the rules make reference to them.

The table also does not cover the following more minor categories under the rules. However, details about them are given elsewhere in the *Handbook* as indicated:

- **Transit visitors** (paras 47-50) (▶243–6);
- **Visitors seeking entry for the purpose of marriage** (paras 56D-56F) (▶229–40);
- **Students re-sitting examinations** (paras 69A-69F) (▶276–7);
- **Students writing up a thesis** (paras 69G-69L) (▶277–8);
- **Students' Union sabbatical officers** (paras 87A-87F) (▶278–9);
- **Multiple-entry work-permit holders** (paras 199A-199C) (▶435–6);
- **HM armed forces** (paras 276E-276AI) (▶150–1);
- **Those granted 'temporary protection'** (paras 354-356B) (▶633–5).

SWITCHING OUTSIDE THE IMMIGRATION RULES

As indicated above, even if switching is not permitted under the immigration rules, it is possible to ask the Home Office to exercise discretion to allow an applicant to switch outside the rules.

In some situations there is specific policy as to when the Home Office will permit a switch. However, the policies operated have been changeable and there have been problems with getting the Home Office to apply a consistent practice. Where an applicant wishes to make a particular change from one category to another and the switch is not covered by the rules, it is often worth checking the IDI in relation to the particular switch to see the latest statement concerning switching into that category. For many of the categories, the IDIs simply state that switching may be permitted in 'exceptional' or 'compelling' circumstances without defining the nature of those circumstances. This obviously gives the Home Office a broad discretion to determine for itself the circumstances, which it considers sufficiently exceptional to justify allowing a switch.

October 2004 policy The Home Office issued a general statement of policy on 1 October 2004, at the same time as the immigration rules were tightened for switching into the work permit, HSMP and Innovator categories. These changes were said to

'...form part of the government's review of immigration, designed to tackle abuses of the managed migration routes and clarify processes for legitimate businesses and individuals.' (*Changing Immigration Status While in the UK* ('*Switching*'), Home Office leaflet, September/October 2004).

The same leaflet also provides policy guidance for considering the exercise of discretion when the immigration rules prevent switching. It is not completely clear whether the policy applies to all cases of switching outside the rules or just to applications to remain as a work-permit holder, under the HSMP or in the innovator category. The policy states:

'Switching from categories other than those stated in this leaflet will not be allowed except in exceptional circumstances. These circumstances will be assessed by caseworkers on a case by case discretionary basis. Circumstances relating to the job, employment and labour market will not be accepted as exceptional circumstances. Only circumstances relating to the individual which would make it unduly harsh for them to return to their country of residence may be considered as exceptional.'

Some limited guidance about what is considered 'unduly harsh' is given in the IDIs dealing with the HSMP as follows (IDI, Ch 5, s11, para. 4):

'Whilst treating each case on its merits, not all circumstances that relate to the individual will be deemed unduly harsh and therefore compelling. Examples of circumstances that may be raised and which would *not* be deemed compelling include:

- Financial burden.
- Where the overseas visa issuing post in the applicant's country of residence is closed. In such instances an alternative visa issuing post will have been designated...
- Humanitarian grounds. If there are humanitarian concerns involved, it is open to the applicant to seek leave to remain in the UK in other more appropriate categories than for the purposes of HSMP.'

Human rights applications

Granting leave on the basis of human rights is not covered by the immigration rules. Therefore, if an applicant who has been admitted in one category under the rules, applies to remain on human rights grounds, this is a form of applying to switch outside the rules. There is nothing in the Home Office policies on granting leave on human rights grounds (i.e. humanitarian protection or discretionary leave) which prevents applicants switching from a category under the rules, to remain on the basis of humanitarian protection or discretionary leave (▶see 862–5). Note, however, that the Home Office has made it clear that it will not permit switching from humanitarian protection or discretionary leave to spouse or unmarried partner status (see **Notes G-H** in the table above ▶186 and ▶see 333).

EEA Association Agreements

The Home Office operates a specific policy, which contains criteria upon which applicants will be permitted to switch to remain as a business/self-employed person under the 'Europe' Association Agreements. For full details, ▶see 580–2.

8   Identifying immigration status

The stamps which entry clearance officers (ECOs), immigration officers and officials at the Home Office put in people's passports or travel documents denote the immigration status which that person has. This chapter gives examples of common `s used by the immigration authorities. It is intended for reference, to help advisers identify endorsements so as to determine a person's status. The immigration authorities may also mark passports when entry clearance or leave is refused. These endorsements are also covered in this chapter. For a full description of how the system of immigration control operates, see the earlier chapters of this section.

The conditions of leave attached to various categories both under and outside the immigration rules are set out in the table below (▶190–91).

The various documents issued by the authorities ranging from EEA residence documents and permits, to the recently introduced UK residence permits and immigration documents are set out in this chapter. The chapter concludes with some examples of documents used in enforcement action against certain people.

CONDITIONS OF LEAVE TO ENTER OR REMAIN

One of the most important aspects of immigration status is the conditions which can be attached to limited leave (indefinite leave cannot have conditions attached). The conditions which are likely to be imposed depend on the category under the immigration rules in which a person is admitted or granted further leave. The table below summarises the conditions imposed on people in the different categories. The immigration authorities refer to the different combinations of conditions as 'codes', although this term is not used in the immigration legislation or the rules. They are referred to instead in guidance and instructions issued to immigration officials, and sometimes immigration officials will refer to conditions of leave by a particular code number in their reports and other documents.

It should be noted that, where a person arrives with entry clearance, the conditions which their leave will be subject to, are endorsed on the entry clearance. Exceptional leave (including humanitarian protection and discretionary leave) is generally not made subject to any conditions although it can be limited or indefinite.

SUMMARY OF CONDITIONS

The text to the right of each code sets out the conditions that will be contained in the passport endorsement, followed underneath by the different categories of people under the rules who will receive that endorsement. So for example, the only condition imposed on a person who is granted leave as a spouse or unmarried partner during the probationary period will be a prohibition on public funds (Code 1). They will be permitted to take any employment.

Code   **Conditions and categories of people under the rules**

Code 1   **No recourse to public funds.**

Issued to:

spouses and unmarried partners during their probationary period;

those exercising rights of access to children; children joining or accompanying a parent with limited leave; adopted children;

dependants of students who are granted leave for 12 months or more;

dependants of work-permit holders; business people and investors; those seeking to establish themselves under EC Association Agreements;

persons with UK ancestry seeking employment;

postgraduate doctors and dentists (however, see also Code 3 below).

Code 1A   **No conditions.**

Issued to:

those coming for family reunion with sponsors who have limited exceptional leave, humanitarian protection or discretionary leave or limited leave as a refugee;

those granted limited leave as a refugee, exceptional leave, humanitarian protection or discretionary leave and their dependants.

Code 2   **No recourse to public funds.**

Work and any changes must be authorised.

Issued to:

business people and investors;

students on courses of longer than six months;

student nurses;

innovators;

those seeking to establish themselves under EC Association Agreements;

work permit (including TWES) holders;

writers, artists and composers.

Code 3   **No recourse to public funds.**

No work or engaging in business.

Issued to:

Code	Conditions and categories of people under the rules
	visitors (or may be issued with Code 5N to same effect where there is doubt over intention to return) including marriage visitors, visitors for medical treatment, transit visitors; postgraduate doctors and dentists where there is doubt over registration; dependants of students who are granted less than 12 months' leave; students on short courses (of six months or less) and their dependants; dependants of domestic workers; fiancé(e)s and their dependants; retired persons of independent means.

Code 4 **No recourse to public funds. To work as [nature of work] with [employer]. Changes must be authorised.**
Issued to:

au pairs;
domestic workers in private and diplomatic households;
ministers of religion;
overseas government employees;
representatives of overseas newspapers, news agencies and broadcasting organisations;
seasonal agricultural workers;
sole representatives of overseas firms;
working holidaymakers.

Code 5N **Leave to enter for six months. Employment and recourse to public funds prohibited.**
Issued to:

students on courses of six months or less (may also be issued with Code 3);
visitors (may also be issued with Code 3) including academic visitors and visitors for medical treatment.

ILE/R **Indefinite leave to enter/remain.**
Issued to:

those joining or staying with relatives settled in UK;
spouses/unmarried partners after probationary period;
those who have been in the UK for four years in most of the categories leading to settlement;
returning residents;
refugees who have been in the UK with limited leave for five years (if granted leave on or after 30 August 2005).

Notes

1. Leave granted under Codes 1 to 4 can also be supplemented with a condition that the holder immediately registers with the police (▶see 1006–7 and the list at 1527 for who may be required to register with the police) and immediately reports any extension of leave to the police.

2. Set out above are the conditions imposed on leave in the main categories under the immigration rules; the table is *not* exhaustive.

ENDORSEMENTS BY ENTRY CLEARANCE OFFICERS

British embassies, high commissions and consulates endorse passports when they deal with entry clearance applications from people wanting to come to the UK. The entry clearance document is a sticker ('vignette') placed into the passport and is often known as a 'visa' or an 'entry certificate' (▶see pages 78–85 for a full discussion of entry clearances and who needs to apply for them).

Two new-style entry clearances have been in use from 2 October 2000 replacing the old entry clearance stickers. They operate as 'leave to enter' provided they contain the requisite information ▶see 85–6. The entry clearance only becomes effective from the 'valid from' date which will *usually* be the date on which the entry clearance is issued. The holders' leave to enter will actually start running from this date and so it is crucial that if the holder cannot travel immediately, they inform the Entry Clearance Officer (ECO). The ECO has a discretion to defer the 'valid from' date. This is especially important for those wishing to settle in the UK, such as spouses, who have to satisfy a probationary period and work permit holders and others who have to be continuously resident for four years under the immigration rules.

The 'expiry' date signifies the date on which the leave to enter will *usually* expire and after which the entry clearance will no longer be valid for travel to the UK. For full details of entry clearance acting as leave to enter ▶see 85–9, and travelling in and out of the UK, ▶see 107–9, 116–8.

Visit entry clearances

The green Uniform Format Visa (UFV) is issued to visitors (including transit visitors) who are visa-nationals, stateless persons and refugees (see left). The conditions attached to the grant of leave to enter are printed in the 'REMARKS' section beneath the holder's name, date of birth and nationality.

Other entry clearances

The red entry clearance is issued to all those who are not entering as visitors (and possibly non-visa national visitors who decide to apply for

entry clearance). The conditions attached to the grant of leave to enter are printed in the 'Obsrv.' section of the red entry clearance (see left). The conditions which are appropriate for the different purposes for which entry clearance can be granted are summarised in the table above.

Old style entry clearances

Old-style entry clearances may still be valid. Their expiry date and whether they allow single or multiple entry should be checked (see right).

Refusal of entry clearance

When an application for entry clearance has been refused, the post may indicate this in the passport by stamping a small box (see below left) containing the name of the post, date and reference number of the application,

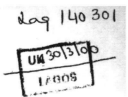

and the stamp will have a line drawn through it. If no line is drawn through it, this indicates that the application is still pending. In some instances, instead of stamping a box into the passport, the ECO may write the words 'entry clearance applied for' in the passport, followed by the date of application and the name of the post. If the application has been refused, these words may be underlined.

ON ARRIVAL IN THE UK

On arrival in the UK, immigration officers may subject all passengers to an examination to determine whether or not they are British citizens or otherwise have the right of abode. If the passenger needs leave, and does not already have it, it is the immigration officer's job to apply the immigration rules to decide whether to grant or refuse leave and, if it is granted, on what conditions.

Landing cards

Non-British national passengers can be required to fill out a landing card prior to their arrival in the UK in order to assist immigration officers (see right). The card is kept as a record and the immigration authorities may later refer to the information given on it.

Endorsements by immigration officers at port

Note For the categories of people who may be given entry under each code, ▶see the table at 190–1.

Below are examples of endorsements made to indicate a grant of leave to enter when someone arrives in the UK *without leave or an entry clearance*. The number of people who can enter without entry clearance for purposes other than a short stay of six months or less is now increasingly limited. Those who must obtain an entry clearance are set out at 80–3; they include visa nationals, and from 13 November 2005, all non-visa nationals coming to the UK for more than six months

The endorsement shows the time period for which leave is granted (in months or until a certain date) and any conditions of leave. It must be noted that, where the time period is written in words followed by the number of months in brackets e.g. THREE (3) MONTHS, then the immigration officer has written a report about that particular passenger. Any subsequent immigration officer, Home Office official or even an ECO, will then be alerted to the existence of the report.

The conditions (or 'codes') attached to the leave granted by an immigration officer depend on the category in which leave is granted (▶see 'summary of conditions' table on pages 190–191). The endorsement will also contain an arrival number at the top to facilitate any checks on embarkation.

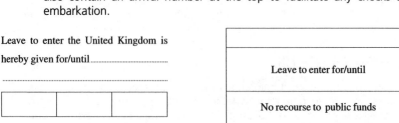

Leave to enter the United Kingdom is hereby given for/until..........................

....

CODE 1A

Leave to enter for/until

No recourse to public funds

CODE 1

Leave to enter for/until
No recourse to public funds Work (and any changes) must be authorised

CODE 2

Leave to enter for/until
No work or recourse to public funds

CODE 3

Leave to enter for/until
To work as/with
Changes must be authorised
No work or recourse to public funds

CODE 4

LEAVE TO ENTER FOR SIX MONTHS:
EMPLOYMENT AND RECOURSE TO
PUBLIC FUNDS PROHIBITED

IMMIGRATION OFFICER

· **(114)** *

- 8 NOV 2000

HEATHROW (1)

CODE 5N

Each of the above endorsements will be accompanied by a date stamp containing details of the date of endorsement and at which port and by which immigration officer it was issued. If the immigration officer has made a computer or written record of the grant, a special number will be issued in the top-most box of the endorsement which indicates the grant of leave. If someone wishes to make a complaint against an immigration officer, this number should be quoted.

Those arriving with entry clearance

If a passenger arrives with entry clearance (which operates as leave to enter), and is being admitted to the UK, then the immigration officer will not stamp their passport on arrival with the length of stay allowed or the conditions of stay. Instead, the officer will simply endorse the entry clearance vignette with a date stamp showing the date of entry as in the example given over the page.

Normally, these entry clearances will be stamped on first arrival only. However, if the person has a visit entry clearance which is valid for longer than six months and it is envisaged that they will enter the UK as a visitor on a multiple number of occasions, the passport *may* then be endorsed with a Code 5N square date stamp with conditions attached (▶see page 195 for the Code 5N stamp). Of course, all visit entry clearances can be used for any number of entries within their period of validity.

Open date stamps

A date stamp (see right) on its own which is not stamped across an entry clearance or has no conditions attached to it is called an 'open date stamp'. These may be issued to the following categories of people: those with indefinite leave, diplomatic officials and others who are 'exempt' from control, ▶see 472–6 for details of those who may be exempt.

```
IMMIGRATION OFFICER
   ·  (114)  *
   - 8 NOV 2000
   HEATHROW (1)
```

Variation of leave on entry

If a person arrives with an entry clearance which operates as leave or already has leave which has not lapsed (▶see 107–9 for non-lapsing leave), they can apply to an immigration officer to vary or extend that leave or to rectify an error made by the ECO. If they are successful, the words 'Leave varied to' will be placed above one of the code stamps (see above right).

Leave varied to:

Leave to enter for/until
No recourse to public funds

Registration with police

If immigration officers impose a requirement that the passenger registers with the police on entry (▶see 1006–7 and the list at 1527 for who may be required to register with the police), this will be endorsed as shown.

```
Register with the Police
within seven days
```

The immigration officer may use the endorsement shown to remove a condition to register.

```
The holder is no longer required
to register with the Police
```

Indefinite leave to enter

> Given indefinite leave to
> enter the United Kingdom

Those who already had indefinite leave when they last left the UK and are granted entry as returning residents will have their passports endorsed with an open date stamp (▶see 196).

When a person is travelling for the first time on a new passport, it is sensible to carry the old passport as well, so that the immigration officer can immediately see what the person's status is. The immigration officer used to endorse the passport with the indefinite leave stamp shown above. However, this practice was discontinued from November 2003. To avoid the need to carry the old passport every time that the person travels, there is now provision for them to apply for indefinite leave to be endorsed in their new passport or travel document. The fee for the application is £160 (or £500 if made in person). The endorsement will now take the form of a UK Residence Permit (▶see 198–9).

Refusals

When people are refused leave to enter the UK, their passports are still stamped with the square date stamp but an ink cross is put through this to show the refusal of leave to enter (see right).

If a refusal is withdrawn following a successful appeal, the word 'WITHDRAWN' will be written diagonally across the previously marked square date stamp (see left).

When people are refused leave to enter or their leave is cancelled, they will also be given a notice in writing or a form stating in brief the reasons for the decision and informing them of any appeal rights which they may have.

Cancellation of leave

On a person's arrival, the immigration officer has the power to cancel the leave otherwise given by an entry clearance or which the

passenger has because their leave did not lapse when they last left the Common Travel Area or were given by an immigration officer before their arrival in the UK (▶see 100–1 for a description of this process). When an immigration officer cancels leave in this way, the passport will be endorsed with a large 'CANCELLED' stamp placed over the leave which is being cancelled (see above). If the passport is not stamped in this way, it may instead be endorsed in writing in red or black ink.

While an immigration officer is examining a passenger after their arrival to decide whether to cancel their leave, they may 'suspend' their leave. A notice indicating such a suspension should be issued to the passenger.

	Code
The holder has leave to enter/remain that was granted on	
by .... and expires on	

CODE 8

Confirmation of existing limited leave in a new passport

If a person has limited leave with the conditions of the leave contained in their existing passport and a new passport is obtained to replace it, a Code 8 stamp can be issued to 'transfer' that person's existing leave to the new passport (see left). This stamp came into effect on 30 July 2000 and differs from previous practice because the Code 8 stamp acts as confirmation that leave exists in another document. The immigration service states that this is to avoid the creation of a situation where someone could end up with two periods of non-lapsing leave running concurrently. Only an immigration officer at a port of entry can grant this.

However, the Home Office has also introduced a Form TOC (transfer of conditions) on which an application can be made to have a limited leave endorsement transferred to a new passport. It is likely that a new style UK Residence Permit (see below) will be attached in the new passport or travel document.

Leaving the UK

Prior to March 1998, it was the practice of immigration officers to stamp people's passports with a triangular stamp when they left the UK (see right). The stamp showed the date, port of exit and the number of the immigration officer. Although these exit stamps were discontinued, embarkation controls were reintroduced at 'key high profile ports' following the bombings in London in July 2005.

ENDORSEMENTS BY THE HOME OFFICE

UK Residence permits

Since late 2003, the ink stamps that used to be endorsed in passports and travel documents have been progressively replaced by new 'UK Residence Permits' (UKRPs), issued to those granted more than six months' leave (▶see 199 for an example). The UKRP was introduced by the government in accordance with EU Regulation 1030/2002 which requires EU countries that have opted in to this regulation to issue uniform format vignettes to all non-EEA nationals granted more than six months' leave (excluding non-EEA national family members of EEA nationals). The new vignettes are being introduced largely as a security measure across the EU.

The new UKRP has a 'valid until' date which will usually be the date on which leave expires. The 'type of permit' and 'remarks' sections describe whether the permit gives limited leave to remain or settlement, and any

conditions attached to the leave. The wording for the conditions will reflect those stipulated under the individual codes for the various categories set out in the table on ▶190–1. UKRPs are also endorsed in Immigration Status Documents (ISDs) (▶see 204).

Endorsements no longer issued

The stamps shown below are examples of endorsements that used to be issued by the Home Office before UKRPs were phased in. Although they are no longer issued, they still remain valid. They used to be issued by the Home Office when further leave to remain was granted, ▶see the 'summary of conditions' box on 190–1 for the type of conditions attached to leave granted in the various different categories.

Leave to remain in the United Kingdom is hereby given

Until..

....
on behalf of the Secretary of State
Home Office

Date..

CODE 1A

Leave to remain in the United Kingdom on Condition that the holder maintains and Accommodates himself and any dependants Without recourse to public funds is hereby Given

Until..

....
on behalf of the Secretary of State
Home Office

Date..

CODE 1

<table>
<tr><td></td><td></td><td></td></tr>
</table>

Leave to remain in the United Kingdom, on Condition that the holder maintains and accommodates himself and any dependants without recourse to public funds, does not enter or change employment paid or unpaid without the consent of the Secretary of State for Employment and does not engage In any business or profession without the consent of the Secretary of State for the Home Department is hereby given

Until...

....

Date...

CODE 2

Leave to remain in the United Kingdom on condition that the holder maintains and accommodates himself and any dependants without recourse to public funds is hereby given

Until...

....
on behalf of the Secretary of State
Home Office

Date...

CODE 3

Despite the wording of the Code 2 stamp, responsibility for authorisation of all work has now formally transferred to the Home Office.

Leave to remain in the United Kingdom on Condition that the holder maintains and accommodates himself and any dependants without recourse to public funds is hereby given

Until...

The holder is not engaged in employment paid or unpaid other than with.........................

....

and is not to engage in any business or profession without the consent of the

....

Secretary of State for the Home Department

....
on behalf of the Secretary of State
Home Office

CODE 4

When the Home Office used to grant leave on these old-style endorsements, they used to be signed by the official who granted the leave and then stamped with a pentagonal date stamp containing the date of issue and the number of the official in brackets.

Indefinite leave to remain

The Home Office now grants indefinite leave to remain on the new UKRPs (above). Prior to that, indefinite leave used to be endorsed by sticking into the passport a green vignette (see below left) showing that there is no time limit or conditions on the person's stay. Until 1992, indefinite leave to remain was shown by a stamp rather than a vignette, the design of which was changed periodically (see below right for the last version of the stamp).

When the passport on which in-definite leave was endorsed had expired, and the person obtained a new passport, the new pass-port used to be stamped by the Home Office with the 'no time limit' stamp (see right).

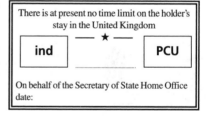

Refusals

When the Home Office refuses further leave to remain, it may underline the most recent leave to enter or remain in the passport (see right). This may not be noticed by the person but shows any other immigration official that there

has been a refusal. The person will also be notified in writing and must be given notice in writing of any appeal rights.

If the passport is a new one, with no leave to enter or remain stamped in it, the Home Office may underline the person's Home Office reference number, written on the inside back cover of the passport.

The Home Office used to write 'EMB' by the side of the last leave to enter or remain granted, or on the inside back cover of the passport. This practice has now been discontinued.

OTHER DOCUMENTS

Certificates of Entitlement

People who have the right of abode in the UK but who are not travelling on British passports need to get this right confirmed by the British embassy or high commission before travelling. They will be given a certificate of entitlement to the right of abode, which is a vignette embossed into the passport. This can also be issued by the Home Office following an application made within the UK (see right).

EEA Residence Permits and Documents

EEA nationals and their family members have rights of free movement derived from EU law, and these rights are not dependent on whether or not they possess any particular documentation. Nevertheless, they are entitled to possess documents known as 'residence permits' and 'residence documents'. These and other similar documents are discussed in greater detail at ▶544–9.

EEA residence permits Residence permits are available to EEA nationals exercising free-movement rights. They are small light-blue documents that fold into six sections, contain a photograph of the holder, and are normally valid for five years.

EEA residence documents Residence documents are issued to non-EEA national family members of EAA nationals who have the right to reside under EU law. These 'documents' take the form of an ink stamp normally endorsed into the non-EEA national's passport. They may also be endorsed into a Home Office letter.

Asylum-seekers

Application Registration Card

Application Registration Cards (ARCs) have been issued from early 2002 to asylum-seekers. An ARC is a credit-card sized form of identity issued to applicants for asylum and their dependants during the asylum screening process. Each ARC can store a good amount of detail about the holder and about the asylum claim itself. ARCs are discussed in more detail at ▶651–2.

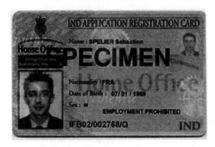

Standard Acknowledgement Letter

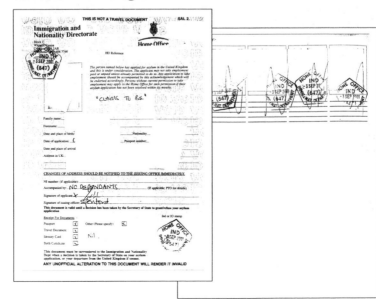

Prior to the introduction of ARCs, Standard Acknowledgement Letters (SALs) used to be issued to asylum-seekers who had not had an initial decision on their application. They are still issued to asylum applicants who cannot be issued with ARCs at screening. They will bear the applicant's and any dependants' photographs and will indicate whether or not the applicant has permission to work. There are two types of SAL. Those who applied for asylum at port on arrival may be issued with a SAL1 and in-country applicants with a SAL2.

Immigration Status Documents

Immigration Status Documents (ISDs) were phased in at the same time as UKRPs (see above) during late 2003 and early 2004. ISDs are issued to those granted refugee status, and to those given humanitarian protection or discretionary leave where it is not appropriate or possible to place a UKRP vignette in the holder's national passport. An ISD is an A4 sheet of paper folded into four, designed to hold a UKRP vignette and confirming the immigration status of the holder. Current 'status' letters (see below) can only be endorsed with ink stamps, and are often not accepted by institutions such as banks, making it difficult for the holder to open a bank account. ISDs are designed to rectify this and to be less susceptible to tampering and fraud. Nevertheless, the Home Office states on the inside cover of the ISD that it is not to be construed as 'an identity document'.

Refugees

Refugees' national passports are not stamped, because they cannot use them without forfeiting their refugee status. They will also be issued with an ISD containing a UKRP which, from 31 August 2005, will grant leave for a period of five years.

They will also be given a letter from the Home Office which explains their position as refugees and some of their rights in the UK.

Humanitarian protection and discretionary leave

The circumstances in which humanitarian protection (HP) and discretionary leave (DL) are granted are discussed in detail at ▶862–75 and ▶see 720 onwards. They will be issued with a 'status' letter (▶next page) and may be issued with an ISD (▶below). For those given HP, the ISD or national passport will contain a UKRP vignette granting leave for a period of five years (prior to 31 August 2005 it was three years). For those given DL, the ISD or national passport will contain a UKRP vignette granting leave for a maximum period of three years initially, and it may well be less. Subject to an 'active review', further periods of leave may be granted.

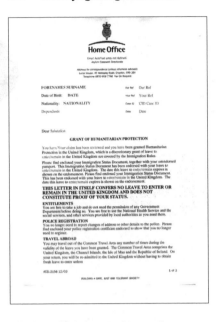

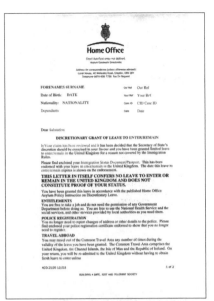

UN travel documents and Certificates of Identity

Refugees

Refugees may be given refugee travel documents, issued by the Home Office under the United Nations Convention relating to the Status of Refugees, and their leave will be endorsed in them on a UKRP vignette. The travel documents are valid for all countries except the refugee's country of origin. For more details ▶see 631–2.

Certificates of Identity

People granted HP, DL or exceptional leave (ELR) may have leave to enter or remain stamped in their national passports where possible and appropriate; otherwise they will be issued with an ISD containing a UKRP vignette (▶see above 204). However, if they wish to obtain a travel document and

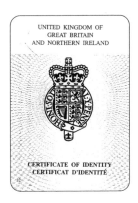

UNITED KINGDOM OF
GREAT BRITAIN
AND NORTHERN IRELAND

CERTIFICATE OF IDENTITY
CERTIFICAT D'IDENTITÉ

they do not have a passport, they may apply for a Home Office travel document called a 'Certificate of Identity' (CID) (▶shown left).

These travel documents are not recognised by all countries. For details about applying for CIDs for those with humanitarian protection, discretionary leave and exceptional leave ▶see 879–83.

One-way travel document for family reunification

When a family member wishes to travel to the UK to join someone who has sought protection, and they are unable to obtain a passport, they used to be issued with a GV3 'declaration of identity' document which was normally valid for one-way travel to the UK. These have now been replaced by a new 'Uniformed format form' issued by the British post overseas.

Notice of temporary admission

If, for example, immigration officer cannot immediately grant leave to a person on arrival, that person may be granted 'temporary admission' to the UK (▶see 652–4, 950–7). This may also be the case when a person makes an application for asylum because the decision is invariably deferred. However, asylum-seekers can also be detained on arrival. For an explanation of the circumstances in which detention may take place, ▶see Chapter 30.

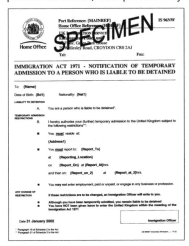

Notice of temporary admission is given on Form IS 96 (see left). It informs the person that they may be detained under Immigration Act powers, and will usually contain a condition that the person must reside at a particular address. It may also contain a condition that the person is required to report to the police, an immigration office or a reporting centre on a regular basis, or on a certain date, possibly for a further interview. For further details on how often someone may be expected to report, ▶see 653–4. Electronic monitoring may also now be imposed as a condition of temporary admission (▶see 953–5).

The form IS 96 NW contains a restriction that the person cannot work. Asylum-seekers who have waited for 12 months or more for an initial decision can be granted permission to work on request, in which case an IS 96W will be issued and the sentence containing the restriction on work is deleted or crossed out.

Enforcement notices

There are variations of the following forms, depending on the circumstances that apply at the particular time that they are issued.

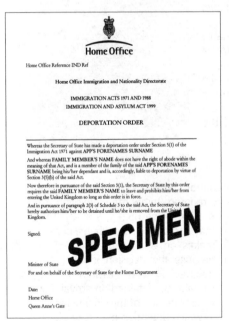

Deportation order

The circumstances under which people can be deported have been narrowed by the 1999 Act ▶see 1015–26. The notice shown (left) is a *deportation order*. A *notice of intention* to deport, which is issued before a deportation order, is issued on Forms ICD.1070 to ICD.1076 and ICD.1914.

Notice of illegal entry/ Notice to someone subject to administrative removal

An illegal entrant is someone who enters the UK in breach of the immigration laws. This may occur in a number of ways ▶see 1010–5. When the immigration authorities decide that someone is an illegal entrant, they will issue them with an IS 151A informing them of their liability to removal

Examples of the forms given to all these people are shown. There are variations of all these forms.

Removal directions for illegal entrants and those subject to administrative removal (IS 151B)

and to be detained (see left). The same form is used to notify a person that they are subject to 'administrative removal' (for example, as an over-stayer) under section 10 1999 Act. For an explanation of the circumstances in which someone may be subject to administrative removal ▶see 1002–10.

Removal directions

'Removal' is the final process in all of the standard ways in which the immigration authorities may enforce the departure of someone from the UK ▶see generally 1026–8 on enforcement. Removal directions can be given to someone who is refused leave to enter; served with notice of illegal entry; liable to be removed 'administratively' under section 10 of the 1999 Act; or a person who has had a deportation order signed against them.

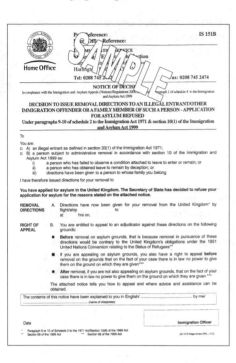

Removal directions for those refused leave to enter (IS 82)

Removal directions for those who have had a deportation order signed against them (IS118)

Section 3 Visitors and students

Chapter 9
Visitors   213
Admission as a visitor   214
Visitor procedures   223
Marriage visitors   229
Medical visitors   230
Carers   232
Working holidaymakers   235
Transit visitors   243
Approved Destination Status Agreement   246
with China

Chapter 10
Students   249
Students and prospective students   251
Re-sitting, writing up theses and sabbatical   276
students
Medical and dental studies including training   279
Fees and student grants and loans   284
EEA students   288

9 Visitors

This section deals with people who are coming to the UK for visits or to study.

This chapter deals with visitors.

Chapter 10 covers students.

The ordinary visitor rules

Those who wish to come to the UK for a short period for a particular reason, such as to see family or friends, or for a holiday, are generally classified under the immigration rules as 'visitors' (▶214-20). People who wish to come to the UK for a brief period, to conduct business only, are also seen as visitors and have to satisfy the same rules (for 'business visitors', ▶see 220–1). In addition, there are a number of 'special classes of visitor', some of whom will provide a service or do limited 'work' in the UK. The Home Office also treats these groups as visitors, and has provided specific guidance on them (▶see 221–3). It should be noted that the government's 'five year strategy' refers to 'working visitors/ visiting workers' as forming one of the tiers of the proposed new single-points-based system for entry for economic purposes (▶see 35–6). It is possible, therefore, that business visitors and some of the special classes of visitor will in the future be subsumed into that category and no longer admitted under the ordinary visitor rules. This chapter begins by looking at all the above groups – 'ordinary' visitors.

Next we look at the procedures for applying for entry as a visitor, at appeals, and at the very limited opportunities for applying for extensions (▶see 223–9).

Other visitor rules

Separate from the above, there are five distinct types of visitor for which separate provision is made in the immigration rules. This chapter then goes on to cover them. They are:

- a category of 'visitors seeking entry for the purposes of marriage' (new to the rules: para. 56D-F HC 395, inserted by HC 346 from 15 March 2005) (▶see 229–30);

- those coming to the UK for the purpose of private medical treatment – 'medical visitors' (▶see 230–2);

- those coming to the UK for an extended holiday, and who intend to work for part of the time they are here – 'working holidaymakers' (▶235–43);
- those who are simply passing through the UK en route to another country – 'transit visitors' (▶243–6); and
- Chinese nationals seeking entry as visitors under the 'Approved Destination Status Agreement' with China (▶246–7).

Carers

Note that, after dealing with medical visitors, we also look at a category which exists as a concession outside the rules for those who wish to care for a sick relative or friend – 'carers', (▶232–5).

People who need to meet parts of the visitor rules

There are certain other categories of entrant who are required to satisfy *parts* of the ordinary visitor rules, but who we deal with elsewhere, in the most appropriate parts of the *Handbook*. They are:

- parents of a child at school who is aged under 12 years (▶375–6);
- medical graduates seeking leave in order to take their 'PLAB' (Professional and Linguistic Assessment Board) test (new to the rules: para. 75A-J HC 395 inserted by HC 346 from 15 March 2005) (▶282–3);
- those seeking leave in order to undertake clinical attachments or dental observer posts (para. 75H-M HC 395 inserted by HC 346 from 15 March 2005) (▶283–4).

Note

Entry for the purposes of marriage and in order to take PLAB tests is not entirely new. They were previously dealt with in concessions outside the rules. Another related category is parents who are seeking to enter the UK in order to exercise rights of access to their children. For details about people in this situation, ▶372–5.

ADMISSION AS A VISITOR

Visitors who are visa nationals (▶see 1507) for a list of visa national countries) must obtain an entry clearance (often known as a 'visa') from a British embassy, high commission or consulate before travelling to the UK. Applicants for entry clearance must be outside the UK at the time they apply. The application can be made to any post that is designated to accept visit entry clearance applications (▶see 1511–6 for a list of posts, and ▶see 223–6, 87–8 for more details about entry clearance).

Visitors who are not visa nationals do not need to obtain entry clearance, though they may do so if they wish. Alternatively, they may apply for leave to enter at the British port. There are always advantages and disadvantages in applying for entry clearance where it is optional (▶see 84). Often the best course depends on the particular circumstances of the case, but the formal requirements of the immigration rules remain the same.

WHAT THE RULES SAY

The immigration rules state that visitors must (paras. 40–46 HC 395):

- be genuinely seeking entry for a period stated by them which is for not more than six months;
- intend to leave at the end of their visit;
- not intend to take employment, paid or unpaid, or to produce goods or provide services, including selling goods or services direct to the public, during the visit;
- not intend to study at a state school;
- maintain and accommodate themselves and any dependants from resources available to them, without working or recourse to public funds; or be maintained and accommodated by relatives or friends; and
- be able to meet the cost of their onward journey.

As is the case for other categories under the rules, even if a visitor fulfils the above specific requirements, they may still be refused entry under the general grounds of refusal which can be applied to all non-asylum cases (▶see 97–9). The period of leave given is normally six months, and will normally be granted on conditions prohibiting employment and recourse to public funds. Under the immigration rules, extensions of stay can only be granted to allow the visitor to spend a maximum total of six months in the UK, although this rule is occasionally waived (▶see below). The period of leave granted to visitors may change, as the government's five year strategy states: 'We will reduce the length of short stay visits from six to three months'.

There is no separate provision in the rules for the dependants of visitors. So family members who are also travelling will themselves need to meet the visitor rules.

WHAT THE RULES MEAN

Although the rules are the same for most visitors, whatever the purpose of the visit, the ways in which they are often interpreted for people from different countries and economic backgrounds, unfortunately, vary widely.

Genuinely seeking entry for a visit for a limited period

The immigration authorities have to be satisfied that the person is a genuine visitor. This means that their purpose in coming to the UK is for a visit and not some other purpose, such as taking employment or study. There are, however, some special classes of visitor, including 'business' visitors, in which elements of the visit include business or research (see below). If the applicant is vague about the purpose of their visit, or the officer thinks that the reason given for the visit is not believable given the person's personal circumstances, then entry is likely to be refused. For example, the Independent Entry Clearance Monitor's report for June 2004 found that lack of knowledge about tourist sites was one of the bases of refusal in over 11 per cent of cases. The IAT has held that the lack of advance planning about what places a person may visit is not necessarily a valid basis for refusal (*W (Ghana)*).

The visitor must also specify the period for which they wish to stay. This must not exceed six months, and it should be consistent with the purpose of the visit. If the visitor is vague about the purpose or the period they wish to stay for, then the officer may not be satisfied that the person in fact intends to stay for only a limited period as a genuine visitor, and admission may be refused.

The Immigration Directorates' Instructions (IDI) point out that there is no restriction on the number of visits a person may make within any given time, but people are not normally expected to stay in the UK for more than six months in any 12-month period (Ch 2, s1, annex A, para. 4). If a person appears to be spending a great deal of time (in particular, more than 50 per cent of their time) in the UK, suspicions may be raised that the person is not a genuine visitor. Past visits may be given extra scrutiny where people stay almost for the six-month visit limit and then return after a very short absence. This will particularly be so if an applicant has close family members living in the UK. The immigration authorities may suspect that the person is attempting to get round the six-month visit period and may have other reasons for seeking to remain in the UK.

No intention to work or to produce goods or provide services

The requirement is not to work or to produce goods or provide services 'including selling goods or services direct to the public'. This has been carefully drafted so as to prevent persons from being employed in the UK, or setting up and running a business here, but yet to permit the entry of 'business' visitors under the rules (▶for which see 220–1).

Intention to leave

The requirement of intention to leave, which is related to the genuineness of the visit (▶see above), is often the most difficult part of the rules to satisfy, because it relates to the applicant's state of mind, which is very difficult to prove. However, because the burden of proving that the requirements of the rules are satisfied rests on the applicant, if there is any ambiguity officers may simply refuse on the grounds that they cannot be satisfied that the requirement is met.

In assessing this requirement, the officer may go into the details of a person's life and background and ask to see evidence of their financial status and family circumstances, to determine whether they accept the applicant's account of wanting to visit the UK. If there is an interview, lots of questions may be asked: Why will you need to go back after only two weeks? Who will look after your children/farm/business while you are away? Surely you can't afford to spend this amount of money on so short a visit? Surely it will be cheaper and more convenient for your relative to come to see you? If you found a place to study, or if you found work, would you take it up? Questions might also be asked which seek to get to the bottom of an applicant's wishes, but it is important that wishes are not confused with intentions. A wish to settle in the UK if the applicant were able to do so is not the same as an intention to do so if admitted as a visitor.

On arrival, immigration officers may often search luggage and read any correspondence, including personal letters, to see if they contain any clues about the person's intentions. The IDI state that:

'…documents produced by the passenger should be assessed in conjunction with any other evidence, *however circumstantial*, which may be relevant to the case.' (Ch 2, s1, annex A, para.1, emphasis added).

Incentive to return An important factor in assessing the intention to return is whether there is an incentive to return. If there are definite reasons the applicant has for returning, they should state what they are and try to produce evidence. For example, a person in employment could have a letter from their employer confirming the length of their leave from work and when they are expected to be back; a person who is a student in their own country could have a letter from the college, confirming when the next term will begin and that the fees (if there are any) have been paid. For those who do not lead a structured life it can be more difficult, and immigration officers admit to using something they call 'nose' – their claimed sixth sense – to tell them when someone is not genuine. Officers are also encouraged to think 'Would I do that?' in connection with information they are given. However, they may not appreciate the differences in cultures which place greater importance on particular events. By the same token, officers may make assumptions about the norms of particular cultures in order to support their reasoning. The IAT has made clear on many occasions that, while officers are allowed to draw appropriate inferences, negative inferences should be based on something much more concrete than 'mere suspicion'.

Negative assumptions Some groups are more likely to be refused because assumptions are made about their intentions. For example, negative assumptions are often made about people from poorer countries, people who are relatively poor by the standards of the country from which they come and people who have relatives settled in the UK. However, as the IAT has stated, the fact that a person comes from a poor or 'third world' country does not mean that there is no incentive to return (see *Ogunkola v ECO, Lagos*), and a family history of migration does not necessarily mean that the individual applicant will not return (*Gurgur v ECO, Istanbul*). Suspicions are greatest in relation to people who are young, single or unemployed, and those who have just finished their studies. Another group targeted for refusal are those who are elderly, with family in the UK but no family members to help look after them abroad.

Sponsor's explanations After an applicant has arrived in the UK, a sponsor may sometimes be called to answer questions by an immigration officer. Suspicions about the applicant's intentions may arise in the following circumstances (IDI, Ch 2, s1, annex A, para. 1):

'...where there are material discrepancies between what the passenger and his sponsor say, when the sponsor can reasonably have been expected to know the facts, these are again grounds for doubting the passenger's credibility and not therefore being satisfied as to their intentions.'

Past immigration history Particular care needs to be taken in advising those with an adverse immigration history, which could include previous periods of overstaying, illegal entry or a previous refusal of entry clearance. If a refusal is likely on those grounds, then information should be provided to explain the earlier circumstances and to demonstrate that they will not recur. Evidence of changes of circumstances and priorities will often be important. Special attention needs to be taken to deal with a refusal based on a previous visit refusal. In 1993, the right of appeal against refusals of entry clearance to those applying as visitors was removed (it was restored under the 1999 Act, but for 'family visitors' only). Therefore, if the earlier refusal took place after July 1993 in circumstances where there was no right of appeal, reliance upon it by the officer is self-serving, since that refusal could not have been challenged on appeal.

Staying longer than stated Although leave is generally given for six months, it is not safe to stay in the UK for the full six months if the applicant originally stated that they intended to stay for a more limited period. For example, if a person stays for five months having said they intended a two-week visit for a relative's wedding, this could be taken into account in assessing their reliability when they make other applications in the future. In the worst case, the general grounds of refusal can be used to refuse applications in these circumstances. An application for leave to enter can be refused if officers judge that deception had previously been used (see paras 320(12) HC 395). Applications for extensions of stay might also be refused on the grounds that the person 'failed to honour any declaration or undertaking given orally or in writing as to the intended duration and/or purpose of [his/her] stay' (see paras 322(2)(7) HC 395). Occasionally an officer may ask for a signed written statement of the applicant's intentions about how long they will stay. Passengers must also be aware that, having arrived in the UK, when they give oral details to officers at the port, these will normally be recorded on the landing card and may be referred to later (see IDI, Ch 2, s1, annex A, paras 6-6.1).

Maintenance and accommodation

This requirement allows officers to enquire about the financial resources available to visitors and/or their friends and relatives who are supporting them. Officers will also want to know how the visitor will be accommodated in the UK. They may be staying in a hotel or guest house, in which case they need to show that they have sufficient funds to be able to pay for this. Alternatively, they may be accommodated by family and friends.

If applicants are bringing their own money, evidence such as their bank statements or a letter from their employer confirming their salary will be required. If support is being provided by others, a letter of invitation confirming willingness to support the visitor is necessary, together with the sponsor's bank statements or other supporting evidence of their resources. There is no advantage in having such letters attested by solicitors – it is the evidence itself that is important. Applicants who are relying on funds from abroad might be asked to prove that the funds can be transferred, because some countries operate quite stringent exchange controls.

Officers may decide that a person has insufficient means, and therefore is unable to support themselves. Lack of financial resources on the part of the applicant is also often taken as a sign that the applicant really intends to work in the UK and to stay for longer than the period stated. However, if a person arrives with a substantial amount of money, this is sometimes also taken as an indication that a person intends to stay for longer than stated. These calculations often depend on the circumstances. For example, what might be considered too much money for a Guyanese citizen could be thought to be perfectly adequate for a visitor from North America.

When visitors who are coming to spend time with family or friends arrive in the UK without entry clearance, it may be useful for the sponsor to come to the airport to meet them, with evidence of the financial support that is available. If the sponsor does not go to the airport, it is useful if the visitor has a telephone number for the sponsor with them, so that the immigration officer can make contact without delay, should they wish to do so.

The maintenance and accommodation requirements apply to most categories under the immigration rules. For more general details about satisfying these requirements, and the possibility of a maintenance undertaking provided by a sponsor, which are sometimes given in cases of visitors, ▶see 308 onwards.

Meeting the cost of the return journey

The requirement that the applicant can meet the cost of the return journey usually means that the visitor should have a return or onward ticket, or be able to show that they have the means to buy one. However, officials will not automatically assume that the possession of a return ticket means that a person is a genuine visitor who plans to return. They may assert that the return half of the ticket could be refunded if a person decides not to leave.

Business visitors

The purpose of some visits strains the requirements of the immigration rules and the conditions upon which admission as a visitor is normally given. This applies to some business visitors and some of the 'special classes' of visitor (see below). Nevertheless, the Home Office is prepared to admit people in these groups for a visit. As with ordinary visitors, entry clearance is not mandatory for non-visa nationals. However, if business visitors do become part of the proposed single-points system, the government has indicated that entry clearance may be mandatory.

Normal business visitors

Business visitors are dealt with in the IDI at Ch 2, s1, annex B, para. 4. Generally acceptable are those coming to the UK in order to 'transact business'. This includes: attending meetings, briefings and conferences; fact-finding or checking details of goods; negotiating or making contracts with UK businesses to buy or sell goods or services (although they must not be involved in selling goods or services directly to members of the public in the UK); purchasing trade goods. Business visitors may also come for training in techniques and work practices used in the UK, provided that the training is confined to observation, familiarisation and classroom instruction. These visitors must have their main place of business and home outside the UK, and not engage directly in business while here.

Other business visitors

The Home Office is also prepared to admit the following as business visitors – even though, strictly, they fall outside the immigration rules because they are in fact supplying a service in the United Kingdom:

- those delivering goods and passengers from abroad, such as lorry drivers and coach drivers, provided they are genuinely working an international route;
- tour group couriers contracted to a firm outside the UK, who are seeking entry to accompany a tour group and who intend to leave with that tour group;
- those coming as speakers in a conference where this is not run as a concern and the conference is a 'one-off';
- advisers, consultants, trainers, trouble-shooters etc., provided they are employed abroad by the company to which the client firm in the UK belongs;
- representatives of computer software companies coming to install, debug or enhance their products;
- representatives of foreign machine manufacturers coming to repair their company's products within the guarantee period;

- representatives of foreign machine manufacturers coming to erect, dismantle and install machinery which is too heavy to be delivered in one piece;
- '*monteurs*', who are workers coming for up to six months to erect, dismantle, install, service, repair or advise on the development of foreign machinery.

The Home Office may also exercise discretion to admit, on a one-off basis, a person who is coming to the UK for a day or so in order to take instructions or give professional advice.

Special classes of visitor

The IDI also give details of certain 'special classes' of visitor (IDI, Ch 2, s1 annex B). They are really no more than examples of persons who are coming to the UK for a short period for a specific purpose other than the 'traditional' reasons for a visit (to see relatives or for tourism) and who intend to leave when that purpose is completed. However, unlike visitors generally, those in some of these groups do intend to do some kind of work or provide services (even if they are not paid), and some of them are able to obtain admission for longer than six months in total. Subject to these modifications consistent with the purpose of their visit, these visitors must generally meet the visitor rules (above). Entry clearance is not presently mandatory for non-visa nationals. Certain special visitors who will be doing some work may be required to register with the police (for registration, ▶see 1006–7).

Academic visitors

These visitors must generally be well qualified and have been working as an academic, or in their field of academic expertise, immediately before seeking entry. Recent graduates are unlikely to qualify. If it is known at the outset that the applicant will be coming for more than 12 months or if the applicant does not meet the requirements of the academic visitor arrangements, a work permit should be arranged. Applicants fall into a number of groups:

- **Privately financed persons** coming to carry out research for their own purposes while on sabbatical leave from overseas institutions. Those who are on leave from private research companies will require a work permit (▶see in particular the category of 'sponsored researchers' under the work permit scheme, 425).
- **Academics** (including doctors) who are taking part in formal exchange arrangements with UK counterparts.
- **Eminent doctors or dentists** coming to take part in research, teaching or clinical practice.

Academic visitors must not receive funds from the UK other than those referred to above, and there must be no question of their filling a normal post in the UK. Applicants may be admitted for up to 12 months. Those admitted for only six months may apply in-country to extend their leave up to 12 months. Dependants of academic visitors may also be admitted. Switching into work permit employment will not be allowed.

Postgraduate researchers other than those studying for a UK qualification (who should enter as students) who wish to enter for the purpose of research work at a UK university or similar institution will normally need a work permit. Similarly those coming to the UK to give a series of lectures for which they will receive a fee, will normally require a work permit. Alternatively, if the academic is coming to take part in a conference or a similar single event in order to give a single address, then they may enter as a business visitor provided that the event is not a commercial venture.

Appellants seeking admission to attend appeal hearings

It is possible to seek entry for the purpose of attending an appeal hearing. Applicants have to show that they will leave the UK regardless of the outcome of their appeal. When granting leave, due account is taken of the likely duration of the appeal. Appeals are dealt with in Section 10. Those thinking of applying for this purpose should first take careful advice.

Those coming to take part in archaeological excavations

Visitors may come to the UK in order to take part in archaeological excavations, provided they will be doing unpaid work as volunteers, or will be paid only subsistence and travelling expenses. They may stay for up to a maximum of 12 months.

Child minders for relatives

Visitors may act as temporary child minders for relatives where the visitor is a close relative of the parent. Distant relatives are only acceptable if they have formed part of the family unit, or are the closest surviving relatives of the parents. It has to be shown that neither parent is able to supervise the daytime care of the child, that the arrangement is not simply to enable both parents to take gainful employment or to study, that neither parent is in a category which may lead to settlement, and that the visitor will not receive a salary. The child minder may, of course, receive board, lodging and pocket money. If it is suspected that the arrangement amounts to employment (paid or unpaid), the application will be refused.

Amateur entertainers and sportspersons

Professional entertainers and sportspersons may be admitted as visitors provided that they are not employed here. They may come for such events as personal appearances, promotions, the publication of a book, nego-tiating contracts, discussing sponsorship deals and attending an audition or a trial (provided the audition or trial is not in front of an audience). An amateur entertainer or sportsperson – i.e. one who engages in entertain-ment or sport simply for personal enjoyment rather than as a living – may be admitted as a visitor provided they can meet the ordinary requirements of the rules. These visitors may be admitted for up to six months. Note that the alternative related routes are: entry with a sportspersons'/entertainers' work permit (▶see 444–7); or entry as a sportsperson for permit-free employment outside the immigration rules (▶471–2). The line between entry for a sportsperson as a visitor and entry in the permit-free category is quite blurred, and the two almost certainly overlap.

Persons coming for job interviews

Interviewees may be admitted for six months if they can show that, if successful, they will return to their country to await the issue of a work permit or entry clearance to enter for that purpose.

Visitors seeking visas for other countries

Those seeking entry in order to obtain visas for travel to other countries may be admitted, provided they can show that they are genuinely seeking entry in order to obtain a visa, and that the duration of their visit will not exceed six months. A person seeking a settlement visa for a third country may be admitted as a visitor, provided they can show that their visa application will be decided in a short and clearly defined period, and that they are returnable to another country after their stay in the UK. Officers are likely to give careful scrutiny to applicants in this category.

Those coming for religious visits

The Diplomatic Service Procedures (DSP) (although not the IDI) continue to refer to the possibility of 'religious visits'. A religious visitor is a minister of religion or professional preacher who visits the UK on a preaching tour for not more than six months. Applicants must not engage in activity beyond preaching, and the tour must not amount to disguised employment as a minister of religion (DSP, Ch 10, para. 10.4).

VISITOR PROCEDURES

For general details about the procedures for applying for entry clearance, providing supporting evidence, the operation of entry clearances, and arrival and entry to the UK, see Chapter 4. Applications to extend leave are generally covered in Chapter 6. Appeals are also comprehensively covered in Section 10. Those parts of the *Handbook* should be read together with what follows.

Visit entry clearances

Entry clearance is compulsory for visa nationals, but non-visa nationals have a choice as to whether to get one. Visit applicants applying for entry clearance must use the non-settlement form 'VAF1', which can be downloaded from the UK Visas website. The form asks applicants to state how long they want the entry clearance to be valid for. Applicants are also asked to state whether they are applying as a 'visitor' or a 'family visitor'. This is important in relation to rights of appeal (▶see below).

Procedures introduced under the 1999 Act mean that an entry clearance is to be treated as leave to enter when the passenger arrives in the UK. In addition, visit entry clearances operate as leave on an unlimited number of occasions during the period over which they are valid. So, although the leave granted to a visitor lapses when the visitor leaves, if they return within the period of the validity of the entry clearance, then it has effect as leave to enter on each occasion (▶see 86–9).

The holder of an entry clearance must arrive in the UK during the period of the validity of the entry clearance (the time between the 'valid from' and 'valid until' dates that are on the entry clearance sticker itself, ▶see 192 for an example of an entry clearance). The period of validity for visit entry clearances will normally be six months, although they can be given for up to ten years in appropriate cases where frequent visits are likely and the immigration authorities are confident that immigration controls will not be abused. First-time applicants are very unlikely to be given an entry clearance with a long period of validity. Note that it is possible for entry clearance (or leave if the passenger arrives without an entry clearance) to be given for less than six months.

Those with entry clearance can still be refused entry, however, if there has been a fundamental change in circumstances so that they do not satisfy the visitor rules; or if it is discovered that false representations were made (or material facts were not disclosed) in order to obtain the entry clearance; or if refusal of entry is justified on medical grounds or on the grounds of the person's criminal record; or if the person is in fact the subject of a deportation order; or if their exclusion would be conducive to the public good.

Entry clearances operating as leave to enter

It is intended that all entry clearances that are granted will now operate as leave. However, if it is a visit entry clearance, in order to have this effect the law says that the entry clearance must satisfy two conditions. It must do both of the following:

- state that it is for the purpose of entry as a visitor;
- state the conditions to which the leave is subject (these conditions will normally be a prohibition on both employment and recourse to public funds).

How long is a visitor admitted for?

The period for which the visitor is actually admitted depends on the 'valid from' and the 'valid until' dates on the entry clearance.

Visitors who arrive with an entry clearance When the holder arrives in the UK with an entry clearance which operates as leave, they are treated as having been admitted for six months, beginning on the date of arrival. This is provided that, at that time, there are six months or more remaining of the validity of the entry clearance. If, at the time of entry, the remaining period of validity of the entry clearance is less then six months, the person will be admitted until the end of the period of the entry clearance's validity. If the remaining period of validity is more than six months, the visitor is still only granted leave for six months from the date of arrival.

When a person is admitted at the port with an entry clearance, a date stamp will be placed over, or to the side of, the entry clearance. It is important for people to remember that this does *not* signify a grant of leave for six months from that date. The period of leave is limited to the period of validity of the entry clearance if that is less than six months away. It is very important, therefore, for people to explain to ECOs when it is that they plan to travel, so that the 'valid from' date on the entry clearance, which is the beginning of its period of validity, is given as close as possible to the departure date. Precisely for this purpose, ECOs have been given instructions to ask all applicants when it is they will travel. The 'valid from' date can be after the date on which the entry clearance is actually issued. In this way, visitors can get the maximum benefit from their entry clearance.

Visitors who arrive without an entry clearance A non-visa national who arrives at the port and who qualifies under the immigration rules as a visitor will be granted leave by the immigration officer for up to six months. It was previously the case that the immigration rules stated that, in most cases, visitors should automatically be admitted for six months, even when they only intend to stay for a few days. However, from 1 October 1994, the rules have been less clear, stating only that people may be admitted for a period 'not exceeding' six months, subject to a condition prohibiting employment. This gives more scope for immigration officers to admit people for less than six months if they are not entirely satisfied about the applicant's intentions. Most visitors are, however, admitted for the full period of six months.

There have been reports of certain ports granting periods of 'temporary admission' to certain visitors who wish to stay for a short period, instead of granting them leave. In our view, this is unlawful. If a visitor satisfies the rules, they should be granted leave. Temporary admission may be granted to people pending a decision as to whether they satisfy the rules or not.

Visitors should keep a note of the period of the validity of the entry clearance separately so that, even if the passport is lost, they will know the length of the period they have been admitted for, and therefore the date by which they need to depart or apply for any extension of stay, if that is necessary.

Appeals

There are restrictions (set out below) on visitor appeals, both for those who have been refused entry clearance and for those refused leave to enter at the port. For full details about appeal rights, ▶see Tables 1–3 at 1052–60. For proposed changes to appeal rights ▶see the table at 1042–6. For details about family visitor cases ▶see 1071–3. In neither case can a person appeal if they have asked for entry to the UK for longer than six months, or if the Secretary of State has decided that the person's presence in the UK would not be conducive to the public good. Where there is no right of appeal, representations can be made to the ECO, or to the immigration officer, as to why they have made the wrong decision. In addition, if there are human rights reasons why the person ought to be able to come or to stay, or the person has been discriminated against and these matters are raised in representations, there will generally be a right of appeal on these grounds. The other remedy, where there is no right of appeal, is judicial review (for judicial review procedures, ▶see 1213–22). Those refused at the port who then claim asylum have a right of appeal on asylum grounds.

Appeals against family entry clearance decisions

If entry clearance is refused, the applicant will be given a notice to this effect, which explains any appeal rights. The right of appeal against refusals of entry clearance for visitors was removed in 1993. The 1997 Labour election manifesto promised 'a streamlined system of appeals for visitors denied a visa'. This promise was kept, but only in part. From 2 October 2000, there has been right of appeal against refusals of visit entry clearances but only if the applicant is applying to visit a member of their family.

Under regulation 2(1) of the Immigration Appeals (Family Visitor) Regulations 2003, a 'member of the applicant's family' is:

- their spouse, father, mother, son, daughter, grandfather, grandmother, grandchild, brother, sister, uncle, aunt, nephew, niece or first cousin (first cousin means the son or daughter of the applicant's uncle or aunt);
- the father, mother, brother or sister of the applicant's spouse;
- the spouse of the applicant's son or daughter;
- the applicant's stepfather, stepmother, stepson, stepdaughter, stepbrother or stepsister; or
- the applicant's unmarried partner with whom he or she has lived for two of the last three years before the date when the application for entry clearance is made.

For further details about family visit appeals, ▶see 1071–3. The government's five year strategy proposes to retain family visit appeals, but to:

- remove the right to an oral hearing, so that all hearings will be on paper only;
- limit the right of appeal to where the proposed visit is to a 'close family member';
- review whether to charge appellants for bringing appeals.

Appeals against refusals of entry at the port

There is generally an in-country right of appeal for visitors who are refused entry at port, provided that they have a current entry clearance. If they do not have an entry clearance, they cannot appeal (even from abroad) against a refusal of entry at the port. They are entitled to remain in the UK while the appeal is being considered. However, if a passenger arrives in the UK with an entry clearance, but the immigration officer cancels the entry clearance because the person is in fact seeking entry other than for the purpose of a visit, they will not have an in-country right of appeal (▶see 102–3, 1059–60).

Applying for extensions

There is no provision in the immigration rules for extending a visit beyond a total stay as a visitor of six months. Most visitors are admitted for six months, initially but those who were admitted for less may apply for extensions to take them up to the six-month limit. Even in these cases, applicants should show good reasons for their change of plans, otherwise the application may be refused on the grounds of a failure to 'honour any declaration or undertaking given orally or in writing as to the intended duration and/or purpose' of their visit (see para. 322(7), HC 395).

Switching to stay as a visitor Those already with leave in the UK under other categories – for example, as a student – may apply for an extension of stay as a visitor up to a maximum period of six months. However, if a person who has been admitted to the UK as a seasonal agricultural worker applies to stay after their work, the time already spent in the UK as a seasonal agricultural worker counts towards the six-month total (see para. 44 HC 395). For full details on switching ▶see Chapter 7.

Applying to stay up to six months If leave is granted for less than six months, and an application to extend the stay up to the six-month limit is made but refused, there is a right of appeal. It may be the case that by the time this appeal is processed for hearing, the purpose of seeking the extension may already have been served. If a person was originally given less than six months but seeks an extension for a period which, if granted, would mean that the total period would be in excess of six months, the Home Office should still consider granting leave for a period to bring the total period up to six months.

Applying to stay beyond six months Where a person has already been given six months in the UK as a visitor, and an application is made to remain as a visitor beyond the six-month limit, it is an application made outside the rules and is therefore dealt with at the discretion of the Home Office. There is no right of appeal against a refusal. The Home Office has stated that such applications will only be granted in the 'most exceptional compassionate circumstances' – for example if a close relative is ill (for carers, ▶see 232–5). Applications to stay for a few further weeks beyond the six-month limit because the applicant was unable to get an earlier flight may be granted, provided they are made before the expiry of the original period of leave and evidence of travel is produced (IDI, Ch 2, s1, annex A, para. 2). Some of the categories of 'special classes of visitor' listed above are examples of situations where an extension beyond six months may be granted.

Refusals and consequences of refusal People's passports may be marked to show if they have been refused an extension (▶see 201 for an example). This may make it difficult for them to return to the UK, or to travel to other countries, in the future. Even if the visitor leaves the UK when the Home Office replies, they will be on record as having been refused the extension. If they apply again in the future, officials may not be satisfied that they intend to leave the UK at the end of the next visit. Visitors should therefore be told about the possible long-term consequences of applying for extensions. It is important only to apply to extend a visit beyond the six-month period if it is really necessary.

Making the application

People must use the official Home Office form FLR(O) and send it to the Home Office, together with all the documents requested or an explanation of why the documents are not available and when they will be sent. The application must be sent in before the leave runs out. It is important to set out the reasons for wishing to stay longer – that is, why the visitor's plans have changed since the time they were admitted – and to state the further length of time required. For example, 'I want to remain as a visitor for another three months in order to help look after my sister whose baby is expected next week'.

If there is any evidence to support the reasons for staying longer and to demonstrate that the person will in fact leave the UK at the end of the further time, this should also be sent to the Home Office. The passport must be sent to the Home Office with the application. The other requirements of the rules, about maintenance and accommodation and about the visitor's intention to leave at the end of the visit, must all still be satisfied.

Visitors applying to change their status to another category

The immigration rules provide for some changes of status for people who have come to visit the UK, while prohibiting others. For example, the rules currently allow visitors:

- to apply to stay and settle with some close relatives – for example, parents coming to visit their children settled in the UK may apply to stay permanently with them;
- to apply for asylum or to remain on human rights grounds;
- if they are not visa nationals, in restricted cases, to apply to stay as students.

For full details about switching status, ▶see Chapter 7 and for visitors in particular, ▶see 162–3. Even if the rules do not allow the person to switch, this does not mean that they cannot apply for such changes, but that any application is likely to be refused. The Home Office would need to be satisfied that there were very exceptional reasons to consider granting changes of status outside the rules.

Again, before their existing leave runs out, people should make applications on the appropriate official Home Office form (▶see 127–32), asking for a change of status and showing how they fit into the relevant parts of the immigration rules concerning their new status. It is important to explain why their plans have changed since they arrived for a visit, and what has made them decide to remain for a different purpose. If the Home Office suspects that the person concealed their true reasons for wishing to be in the UK when they arrived, they may ask detailed questions to see whether the person is an illegal entrant by deception (▶see 1013–4).

Travel outside the UK

Each time a person visits the UK, their circumstances must fit the immigration rules. Visit entry clearances which count as leave to enter have that effect on an unlimited number of occasions within the period of the validity of the entry clearance. So, although the leave granted to a visitor lapses on their leaving the UK, if they return within the period of the validity of the entry clearance, it has effect as leave to enter on each occasion. So, visa nationals do not need to apply for a further entry clearance when they return within the period of validity of such an entry clearance.

This helps people who come to the UK and then intend to travel and return again for another visit – for example, those planning to go to other European countries as well as the UK; or those who want to go on Hajj with relatives living in this country and visit them both before and afterwards. Those who are planning to return to the UK successively over a long period of time should try to persuade the ECO to grant an entry clearance with a long period of validity. Frequent business visitors often need such entry clearances.

MARRIAGE VISITORS

From 15 March 2005, 'visitors seeking to enter for the purpose of marriage' has been introduced as a new category under the immigration rules (para. 56D–56F HC 395 inserted by HC 346). Previously, this category was operated as a concession outside the rules as a 'special class' of visitor. The purpose of this category is to allow people to visit in order to get married in the UK, but in circumstances where the applicant will not be staying in the UK after the marriage. There is no absolute requirement that an applicant's spouse will not remain in the UK, but obviously the intentions of both may be taken into account in judging the applicant's intentions. This rule, for example, helps couples who wish to marry in the UK, where part of their families are based, while they themselves in fact intend to set up home abroad.

All applicants are required to obtain entry clearance before travelling to the UK, and the following requirements must all be satisfied:

- the ordinary visitor rules must be met (genuine visit; intention to leave the UK; no intention to work, provide services or study at state school; support and accommodation are available; costs of onward journey can be met);
- the applicant must intend to give 'notice of marriage' (▶see 296–300 for the new requirements to give notices of marriages to registrars after 1 February 2005), or marry in the UK within the period of their visit;
- the applicant must provide evidence (where it is requested) of the arrangements both for giving notice of marriage and of the wedding ceremony that will take place during the course of the visit.

Entry will be granted for a period of up to six months. There is no provision in the rules for obtaining an extension of leave for this purpose. The previous concession stated that further leave might exceptionally be granted if there was good cause for a delay in marrying, satisfactory evidence that the marriage will take place at an early stage, and if it is still clear that the applicant intends to leave the UK after the marriage. If these circumstances arise, it is therefore worth asking for discretion to be exercised in order for a further short period of leave to be granted.

MEDICAL VISITORS

Medical visitors are covered in the immigration rules at paragraphs 51–56 HC395. Some of the requirements for entry as a medical visitor are the same as for ordinary visitors (see above). Medical visitors have to show that they do not intend to take employment, produce or provide goods and services in the UK, or study at a maintained school. They must also be able to demonstrate that they and their dependants will be maintained and accommodated without recourse to public funds, and that they are able to meet the cost of their onward journey. Entry clearance is mandatory for visa nationals. Medical visitors have, in addition, to meet both of the following requirements:

- the course of medical treatment must be of finite duration (not open-ended in length) and they must intend to leave the UK at the end of it;
- they must provide evidence of the medical condition requiring consultation or treatment in the UK, the arrangements that have been made for private medical treatment, the estimated cost and duration of the treatment (and their visit) and that they have funds available to pay for the treatment. Note that ECOs are expressly given discretion to waive the need for evidence about the arrangements for treatment, provided the

ECO is satisfied about the applicant's means and their intention to leave the UK after their treatment (DSP Ch 10, para. 10.6).

Public health considerations If the person is suffering from a communicable disease, the medical inspector at the port of arrival must be satisfied that there is no danger to public health before entry can be granted (see paras 51(ii), 320(7), HC 395). In any case, it is possible that leave will be refused if the medical inspector states that, for medical reasons, it is 'undesirable' to admit a particular person. In practice, this test is very difficult to apply because it is so vague, but the immigration authorities may seek to apply it, for example, to a person suffering from a mental disorder. There is nothing in the rules to state that immigration officials should take into account the availability of treatment in the person's own country.

Non-private treatment Note that there is no provision in the rules which allows leave to be granted for the sole purpose of obtaining free medical treatment from the NHS. This does not mean, however, that all overseas nationals in the UK are denied such treatment. For the relationship between access to NHS treatment and immigration status, ▶see 1328–34.

Medical visitors can be admitted for up to six months initially, with conditions prohibiting work and access to public funds.

Extending leave as a medical visitor

Unlike for ordinary visitors, there is no maximum time-limit for medical visits, and so it is possible to obtain extensions under the rules to stay for longer than six months. In addition, there is no requirement to have been issued with an entry clearance as a visitor or medical visitor in order to obtain an extension in this category. It is therefore possible to switch to extend stay as a medical visitor provided that the applicant was not last admitted under the 'ADS' Agreement with China (▶see 246–7 para. 54(v) HC 395). (For general details about switching ▶see Chapter 7).

Initial extension applications are readily granted if there is clear evidence of private treatment and funds. Successive extension applications are looked at with greater scrutiny. In order to get an extension, applicants still have to satisfy the above rules, and they must also do all of the following (paras 54–56, HC 395):

- produce evidence from an NHS consultant or a medical practitioner who is listed in the General Medical Council's specialist register, indicating that satisfactory arrangements have been made for private consultation/treatment, stating its length and (where treatment has begun) its progress;
- show that they have met the costs of their treatment so far;
- have sufficient funds to meet the likely future costs.

The IDI suggest that the requirement for this evidence indicates that the treatment provided must be at the level of these specialist practitioners when an applicant is seeking to *remain*, although initial entry may be sought for treatment from an ordinary GP, or an alternative medical practitioner (Ch 2, s3, annex F, para. 6). They also go into more detail than the rules as to what the letter from the doctor should contain. The list of matters which the letter should deal with is given as (Ch 2, s3, annex F, para. 1):

- the nature of the illness;
- the proposed treatment;
- the frequency of consultations;
- the likely length of the treatment;
- details of the cost of the treatment and confirmation that all expenses are being met;
- where treatment amounts to private visits to a consultant for what appears to be a relatively minor ailment, details of the progress made.

The Home Office may itself wish to write to the patient's doctor for information, in which case it should ask for the patient's consent first. In a complex case, officers might also seek their own advice from the Department of Health. The rules do not give an upper limit on the length of leave that will be granted when leave is extended. It may be expected that six months will be given, but it will depend on the nature and length of the treatment. Because the rules for extensions do not give a maximum time-limit for extensions of leave to remain, if the application is refused, as long as the application was made in time, the person will at present have an in-country right to appeal.

CARERS

There are no specific provisions in the immigration rules for carers. Where a person wants to come to the UK in order to care for a friend or relative for a short period of time only, or in order to make practical arrangements for that person's long-term care, they will be able to do so if they can satisfy the ordinary rules relating to visitors (see above). It seems that the immigration authorities are happy to treat such applications as another 'special class' of visitor (see IDI, Ch 17, s2, paras 2, 5).

Where an in-country application is made for a carer, it will be considered under a concession made outside the rules as permit-free employment (IDI, Ch 17, s2). The concession allows people who are in the UK for a temporary purpose to extend their stay in order to care for a sick relative or friend who is suffering from a 'terminal' illness, such as cancer or AIDS, or who is mentally or physically disabled. All cases are considered on their individual merits, depending on the nature of the compassionate circumstances involved. The purpose of the concession is to allow carers to enter or remain for a temporary period only, until alternative arrangements for the patient's care have been put in place (but see below for the precise requirements relating to extensions); it is not intended to enable carers to remain permanently. Because the application is being made for further limited leave outside the immigration rules, it should be made on form FLR(O).

The first carer application for an extension

The concession states that applications for extensions from carers who are *friends* of the patient should normally be refused. Applications can, however, be granted in these cases if there is an emergency – for example, where the patient has suddenly become ill and there is no time to arrange alternative care and no one else in the UK to whom the patient can turn. Applications will more readily be granted where the carer is a *relative* of the patient. In both circumstances, in addition to the compassionate features of the case, the factors taken into consideration are:

- the nature of the illness or condition;
- the kind of care that is needed;
- the care available from other sources, such as social services or other relatives and friends;
- the patient's prognosis.

Advisers should therefore obtain evidence about these matters. It will be essential to have a letter from a doctor to explain the nature of the condition, the care needs it gives rise to, and the prognosis. If leave is granted, it is likely to be for a period of three months, with a prohibition on work and recourse to public funds. The Home Office will usually make clear to the applicant by letter that leave is being given on the understanding that alternative arrangements will be made for the future care of the patient.

Second and further carer applications for extensions of leave

Applications for further extensions of leave by a carer who is a friend or relative of the patient should be supported by all of the following:

- a letter from an NHS consultant, with full details of the illness or condition and its prognosis;
- if the local social services department have been involved in the case, a letter from them setting out the benefit of the continued presence in the UK of the carer and explaining why suitable alternative care for the patient cannot be arranged;
- evidence that alternative arrangements have been or are being explored;
- details of the patient's family in the UK, how the patient was previously cared for, and why those arrangements are no longer suitable or available;
- details of the applicant's circumstances in their own country, including whether they have dependants, their employment (note that the Home Office will not generally grant leave on a longer-term basis if the carer is married or has dependants); and

- evidence to show that the applicant can be maintained and accommodated without working or recourse to public funds.

Article 8 considerations The central issue in many cases will be whether the circumstances justify the applicant being allowed to stay to care for the patient, as opposed to their being provided with what can be offered by social services. It may be that there is a case to be made under Article 8 ECHR (right to respect for private and family life) for the relative or friend being allowed to stay (▶820–51). Representatives might also want to consider the extra cost to the public of care being provided by social services instead of the carer. In deciding whether any interference in private or family life that would be caused by refusing to allow the carer to remain is justified as being proportionate under Article 8(2), the additional cost of care needs to be considered, as well as the interests of immigration control.

Case examples A Home Office refusal to grant further leave was successfully challenged in the High Court in *Zakrocki* because of strong evidence that the best care plan for an elderly, severely disabled man was for his Polish relatives to continue to look after him in his home. This was consistent with the Government's policy of 'care in the community', and the local authority regarded the help of the relatives as more appropriate and less costly than residential care. The immigration issues had to be balanced with the rights of the disabled man, a British citizen, to remain in the UK and be looked after in accordance with the policies and duties that apply to citizens of this country. A further similar case, *Green*, was unsuccessful in the High Court. The IDI (Ch17, s2, para. 4.2) relies upon the decision of the High Court in *Green*, and officers are therefore likely to quote it in their decision letters. However, the IDI fails to recognise that the Court of Appeal subsequently granted Ms Green permission to appeal against the decision of the High Court, and that the Home Office then conceded her case and granted exceptional leave before that appeal could be heard. For a recent successful 'carers' case involving Article 8, see *R (Fawad Ahmadi) v SSHD* (CA).

Leave granted and public funds In cases where there are sufficient exceptional compassionate circumstances to grant further extensions, the Home Office may grant leave for up to 12 months at a time. Again, the leave will normally be subject to conditions prohibiting work or recourse to public funds. In exceptional circumstances the Home Office may be prepared to grant leave without conditions. If there is a particular need for this, representations should be made as part of the application. However, even where a public funds condition has been imposed, it should be noted that a patient may be entitled to obtain attendance allowance in order to pay for their care. In these circumstances, the Home Office has stated that it will not treat the patient as having recourse to public funds:

'The allowance is paid to the patient rather than the carer and therefore the carer would not be considered to be in receipt of public funds. If the patient is claiming other benefits and is using these to support and accommodate the carer, provided that the patient is not claiming any extra benefit for the carer, then again this should not be considered as recourse to public funds unless the carer was to claim benefits in his own right.' (IDI, Ch17, s2, para. 6)

Of course attendance allowance is now only paid to the over-65s and the IDI is a little out of date. The logic of the above policy would also mean that where an applicant is caring for a person who is receiving the care component of disability living allowance (▶see 1245), the applicant would also not be treated as being in receipt of public funds because that benefit is also paid to the person in need of care. However, an applicant who obtained 'Carers Allowance' would be claiming public funds.

Chances of settlement Carers are not expected to obtain settlement. In certain cases, it is possible that they may do so if the length of their total residence justifies it (▶see 151 onwards), or if they manage to switch into another category which leads to settlement.

WORKING HOLIDAYMAKERS

Under the Working Holidaymaker scheme, young Commonwealth nationals (▶see 1525–6 for a list of Commonwealth countries whose nationals are able to apply to come to the UK as working holidaymakers (see paras 95–100 and Appendix 3, HC 395)) between the ages of 17 and 30 (inclusive) may come to the UK for a working holiday and stay up to a maximum of two years (paras 95–103, HC 395). Over 70,000 people made applications in the year 2004/05 (ending in January 2005) of which over 14,000 were refused. For the general range of opportunities to enter the UK in order to work, including for short periods of time and as part of a cultural exchange programme, ▶see Section 5.

Because the scheme allows entry for the purposes of work (as well as a holiday), this category has been subject to continued change over the past few years, as the government has attempted to tailor it to its economic migration policy.

Changes to the scheme under 2002 White Paper

The changes proposed by the 2002 White Paper, *Secure Borders, Safe Haven*, and their implementation, were as follows:

- extend the scheme to a range of non-Commonwealth countries – this has not yet been done;
- review the age restrictions – from 25 August 2003, the upper age limit was indeed raised from 27 to 30 (Cm 5949);
- relax the requirement that employment must be incidental to a holiday – from 25 August 2003, the requirements that employment be only 'incidental' to a holiday and that applicants must not engage in business,

provide services as a sportsman or entertainer, pursue a career in the UK and that applicants had no commitments which would require them to earn a regular income, were all relaxed so that applicants could (and should) intend 'to take employment as an integral part of a working holiday' – this change has however now been largely reversed (▶see below);

- formally allow working holidaymakers to switch to work permit employment – this was done, but the circumstances in which it is possible to switch to being a work permit holder have recently been severely limited again (▶see below);

- conduct a comprehensive review of the scheme in the light of the gross discrepancy between participants from the 'white' and 'black' Commonwealth countries, so as to make the scheme 'as inclusive as possible' – it appears clear, however, that the problems still persist (for an interesting analysis, see 'For whites only? Does the Working Holidaymaker scheme still discriminate?' INLP, 2004, Vol 18, No 2). Indeed, the most recent changes to the scheme *reverse* some of the changes made in 2003, such as removing unnecessary working restrictions, which the government had previously stated were intended to make the scheme more inclusive:

'The removal of employment restrictions will enable less affluent applicants to prove more easily to entry clearance officers their ability to support themselves without recourse to public funds. ' (Home Office letter to ILPA, 20 June 2003, concerning the 2003 changes)

The consultation document issued before the changes were made was framed in similar terms. It had stated:

'A commitment to remove certain work restrictions that disadvantage less affluent applicants should assist in this regard. Entry clearance is more likely to be granted to less affluent individuals if they have the opportunity to work for a longer period during their stay, giving a more realistic prospect of maintaining themselves without need for public funds.'

Changes to Working Holidaymaker Scheme made in 2005

On 7 February 2005, the same day that the Home Office announced its 'five year strategy', Des Browne MP, the Minister for Citizenship and Immigration, announced changes to the Working Holidaymaker scheme. These were the first changes to be made under the 'five year strategy', and they were implemented by changes in the immigration rules that took effect on the following day, 8 February 2005 (HC 302). The Minister stated:

'The main change for applicants is that we are strengthening the requirement that the work be done in support of holiday and travel intentions. It is anomalous that as a holiday and cultural exchange route it should not have attached to it any conditions that prevent migration based on long-term employment and other economic motives.'

The Minister has also expressed the view that there is abuse of the scheme by persons using it for long-term migration purposes. As indicated, many of the changes roll back the changes made in 2003. The main changes to the scheme, from February 2005, are set out in the table immediately below. The full requirements under the rules as they stand after the changes made in February 2005 (and some further, very minor changes made in July 2005) are set out at ▶239–42, below. For the transitional arrangements, ▶see below at 242–3.

CHANGES IN WORKING HOLIDAYMAKER SCHEME FROM 8 FEBRUARY 2005

The main changes to the Working Holidaymaker scheme are made by HC 302 from 8 February 2005. They are as follows.

1) The nationals who may qualify have been extended to include the following non-British citizen British nationals: British Overseas Citizens, British Overseas Territories Citizens and British Nationals (Overseas).

2) The rules no longer simply state that the scheme is open to 'Commonwealth citizens'. Instead the scheme is stated to be open to nationals of those countries 'listed in Appendix 3 of the rules'.

The Home Office intends to reach a 'Memorandum of Understanding' with each listed country. These memoranda will require co-operation from the countries concerned with efforts by the UK to return their nationals who are found to have no basis to stay in the UK. If the country fails to cooperate, the Working Holidaymaker scheme can be suspended for that country's nationals (and the country will be removed from the list). The memoranda will also allow for the scheme to be suspended in relation to any country if there is a sudden increase in the number of applications such that the entry clearance post cannot manage them.

Note that, at the outset on 8 February 2005, the list in Appendix 3 contained all the Commonwealth countries except Lesotho. There were therefore no suspensions at the outset (although at the start of 2005, the restricted service offered in Pakistan still prevented applications from being made from there). Depending on the success of the Memoranda of Understanding, future suspensions are to be expected.

On 2 April 2005, the working holidaymaker scheme was temporarily suspended in Malaysia, Sri Lanka, Namibia and Botswana. This was done because the 'rise in the number of working holidaymaker applications (at the posts in these countries) exceeded the average global increase in applications [and was] adversely affecting the ability of the visa operation to meet its Public Sector Agreement targets'. UK Visas will keep the situation under review (letter of UK Visas Policy Section to UK Visas User Panel members, 4 April 2005).

The structure of the rules means that it is possible that other, non-Commonwealth states may be added as countries participating in the Working Holidaymaker scheme. Advisers should therefore look out for changes to the list in Appendix 3 to this effect.

3) Working Holidaymakers may now only take employment which is 'incidental' to a holiday and they are restricted to working for only 12 months in total. They must also not engage in business or provide services as a professional sportsperson, and conditions will be attached to the leave to this effect.

Between 25 August 2003 and 8 February 2005, a much more relaxed rule was operated, under which applicants were permitted to take work which was 'integral to a working holiday'. This meant that there was no real restriction on the amount of work people were permitted to do, although they were still expected to take a holiday during their stay. This rule has largely changed back to how it was before 25 August 2003 (▶see further below at 239–41).

4) In the *8 February 2005 changes* references to how long a person may be admitted to the UK as a Working Holidaymaker (two years) had been deleted from the rules. The provisions of the rules allowing persons to apply for in-country extensions of stay in this category had also been deleted. However, both the Ministerial statement (above) and a letter to the UK Visas User Panel members, dated 8 February 2005, refer to 'two-year stays' being allowed. The IDI also indicate that entry clearances issued to provide two years' leave will be the norm. From 6 July 2005 the rules were amended again to reinstate the two-year period as the apparent norm (paras. 95(x), 96 HC 395 as amended by HC 104).

Provided that posts do indeed continue to grant entry clearances routinely allowing leave to enter for two years, this change will have little effect. This is because the previous rules prevented anyone from extending their stay to beyond two years from their first date of entry under this category. If, however, the immigration authorities give less than two years' leave in certain cases, then there will be a substantial negative effect. This is, firstly, because the rules no longer permit applications for in-country extensions (i.e. to bring the period up to the normal two years). Secondly, a working holidaymaker who departed after completing leave that was granted for less than two years would not be permitted to return in the same category again. This is because the on-entry rules now require that a person 'has not spent time in the United Kingdom on a previous working holidaymaker entry clearance'. Before the recent changes, a working holidaymaker granted less than two years could, under the rules, have applied to extend in-country, or returned abroad and then sought re-entry to a date up to two years from the date of their original entry.

5) Working holidaymakers who wish to switch into work permit work may now only switch into work that is listed on the Work Permits (UK) shortage occupations list. They must also have spent more than 12 months in the UK as a working holidaymaker (see rule 131D HC 395 as substituted by HC 302, and ▶see 1519–21 for the present list). For full details about working holidaymakers switching to work permit and other categories, ▶see 169.

6) The parent(s) of children seeking to be admitted as the dependant of a working holidaymaker must already be present in the UK (▶see further below, 242).

Working Holidaymaker requirements under the rules from 8 February 2005

All applicants for entry under the Working Holidaymaker scheme must obtain an entry clearance. The full list of further requirements from 8 February 2005, with further minor changes in July 2005, is as follows (paras. 95–103, HC 395) (for transitional arrangements relating to the new rules, ▶see 242–3, below).

Nationality When the changes were introduced on 8 February 2005, all Commonwealth citizens except those of Lesotho could apply. However, the formal requirement is that the country is listed in Appendix 3 to the rules. As indicated above, countries may be added or taken off the list of participating countries, and so advisers need to check updated copies of the list. Note that, confusingly, until recently there were two lists in Appendix 3, and it is only those countries specifically listed under 'list of countries participating in the Working Holidaymaker scheme' that count for these purposes. Alternatively, applicants can qualify if they are any of the following: a British Overseas Citizen, a British Overseas Territories Citizen, or British National (Overseas) (▶see 1404–12 for an explanation of these non-British citizen British nationalities).

Age The rules state that applicants must be aged between 17 and 30 (inclusive) at the date of their 'application for leave to enter'. The IDI indicate that this means they must be within this age group at the date of their application for entry clearance (IDI, Ch 4, s2 Annex C, para. 1.2). It should therefore not matter if the applicant turns 30 subsequently – for example, during the period they are waiting for their entry clearance to be issued, or while having their working holiday.

Marital status and children Applicants must be unmarried unless they are travelling with their spouse and both intend to take a working holiday together. Working holidaymakers must also not have dependent children aged five or over, or who will reach that age before the end of the working holiday.

Work Working holidaymakers must intend to take employment that is only 'incidental to their holiday', not engage in business or provide services as a professional sportsman, and they must not work for more than 12 months during their stay. The holiday must be the primary reason for the applicant coming to the UK.

Note that, although the rule prohibits business, the Home Office has confirmed that some self-employed activity may be carried out. In correspondence with Laura Devine Solicitors dated 5 July 2005, the Home Office stated that it would add the following to the IDIs (advisers should also note the definition of 'employment' in para.6 HC 395):

'The restriction on engaging in business does not rule out all self-employed activity where the latter is clearly temporary in nature, but any activity which involves commitments such as investment in premises, expensive equipment or staff is to be regarded as activity for which a person would be required to qualify under the rules relating to business.'

The rule had been relaxed by the changes made on 25 August 2003, which allowed applicants to do work that was 'integral' to their holiday (see above). The rule has now been tightened again, so that it is similar to (but not exactly the same as) the rules as they stood prior to 25 August 2003. It is not yet clear whether the same 'rule of thumb' which was then applied by the Home Office will be operated under the new rules. This general rule was that applicants could take periods of full-time employment provided that they did so for less than 50 per cent of their holiday, and that part-time work extending beyond 50 per cent of the holiday was permissible, provided it was clear that the applicant was also having a holiday. Some guidance as to how the Home Office will operate the rules is provided by the Ministerial announcement of 7 February 2005, which stated:

'…we are restricting the total length of time that can be spent in employment under the scheme to 12 months out of a two-year stay. This 12 months in employment can, however, be aggregated in any combination of periods throughout the two years.'

The guidance given by the IDI is that:

'Working holidaymakers are expected to intend to take work in the United Kingdom as an incidental part of their working holiday. Those wishing to enter in the category should treat the work they do as a purely incidental part of their holiday (which should be their primary reason for being here) rather than being the reason for which they have sought entry to the United Kingdom. Accordingly working holiday-makers must not intend to spend more than 12 months of their stay in employment, and must intend to spend the rest of their stay holidaying.

Entrants in the category may take most employment of their choice, including voluntary work.

However, they may not engage in business or provide services as a professional sportsperson, and they may only engage in work for a maximum period of 12 months in total throughout their stay. They may choose when to work and when to take their holiday breaks as they wish, but those who exceed the maximum 12 month period work permitted will be in breach of their conditions.' (Ch 4, s2, annex C, para. 2.2)

The restriction on business does not rule out all self-employed activity where the latter is temporary in nature. It should not, however, involve commitments such as investment in premises, expensive equipment or the employment of staff. Two points that remain uncertain are: whether applicants can do work for longer than 12 months if it is part-time, and whether applicants can work for the 12 months even if they are not intending to stay for the full two years. In the latter case, if the work was out of proportion to the holiday, it might well be said that it was not 'incidental' to the holiday, as is required.

The new rules have *not*, however, reverted to the previous prohibition on 'pursuing a career' in the UK. This is presumably in recognition of the switching arrangements (see below). In addition, a further flexibility is allowed for those who wish to teach in the UK as supply teachers and who have leave as working holidaymakers (see IDI, Ch 17, s12).

It should also be noted that working holidaymakers may engage in some part-time study and in short periods of full-time study. They should not, however, intend to study for the whole period for which they are in the UK, as officers are then likely to decide that they do not intend to take work incidental to a holiday (IDI, Ch 4, s2, annex C, para. 2.3).

Intentions Applicants must intend to leave the UK at the end of their holiday. It is odd that this requirement is still being kept in the rules, given that the rules allow working holidaymakers to switch to remain in certain circumstances (▶see 238 and ▶see 169). The Home Office's explanation is that it understands that plans may change during the course of the working holiday, but the entry clearance officer will simply be looking to see whether, at the time of the application, the applicant intends to leave after the working holiday. In order to satisfy the rule, applicants do not have to show that they have settled down in their own country (*K (India)* (IAT)).

Support Working holidaymakers must have the means to pay for their onward journey, and must be able to support and accommodate them-selves without recourse to public funds in the UK. Because applicants will be permitted to work, entry clearance officers will look for evidence of sufficient funds for support for at least the first two months after arrival (one month if a job has already been arranged).

What if the applicant has previously been granted leave as a working holidaymaker?

As explained above, the rules indicate that the period of leave to be expected is two years. The rules no longer permit in-country applications for extensions; nor do they allow leave to enter to be granted to those who have

'…spent time in the United Kingdom on a previous working holiday-maker entry clearance.' (para. 95(ix) HC 395)

The Home Office has confirmed that this rule will not prevent persons from being admitted if they previously obtained a working holidaymaker entry clearance but did not actually use it to come to the UK. Such persons are able to apply for and use a fresh entry clearance (IDI, Ch 4, s2, para. 2.3). Our view is that this rule does not prevent a person who has been admitted with an entry clearance that gave leave to enter as a working holidaymaker, but who departs the UK during the course of that leave, from being readmitted to continue that leave, *provided it has not expired*. This is because, firstly, the leave granted will normally not lapse on their departure from the UK (▶see 107–9), and therefore they are not seeking a fresh grant of leave to enter. Secondly, the entry clearance cannot properly be described as a 'previous' leave, since the grant of leave which it provides is still operative.

For further details about the leave that is likely to be granted to working holidaymakers and the rule about previous time spent in this category ▶see the table above at 238.

For full details about switching categories at the *end* of a period spent as a working holidaymaker, ▶see 169.

Children of working holidaymakers

Children of a working holidaymaker who are aged under five years may be admitted, provided that they can be supported and accommodated without recourse to public funds, and provided it is intended that any children will leave (usually with their parent) before reaching the age of five (paras. 101–103, HC 395). Where only one of the parents is being admitted, that parent must either be the sole surviving parent or they must have had 'sole responsibility' for the child's upbringing, or there must be serious and compelling family or other considerations which make the exclusion of the child from the UK undesirable. There must also be suitable arrangements in the UK for the child's care. These requirements are similar to those that apply where a child seeks to be admitted for settlement to join only one parent in the UK (▶see 368–71).

Children of working holidaymakers also require entry clearance. The new rules require that the parent(s) of children seeking to be admitted as the dependant of a working holidaymaker must already be 'currently present' in the UK. This suggests that children should travel after their parent(s). It is unclear how strictly the immigration authorities intend to apply this.

The rules still allow children of working holidaymakers who have been admitted with an entry clearance in that category to apply to extend their leave (although this provision has been abolished for working holidaymakers). However, children can only do this if their parent(s) have leave, and so this could only help a child who, for some reason, was initially granted less leave than their parent(s).

Transitional arrangements for working holidaymaker changes

There are no formal transitional arrangements, so the above new rules apply to all applications awaiting a decision on and after 8 February 2005. Entry clearance posts were required to advise applicants whose applications were outstanding on that date, that they could withdraw their application (with a refund of the fee paid) or continue with the application under the new rules.

However, only entry clearances issued from 8 February 2005 will be subject to formal conditions restricting work to 12 months of the total stay and prohibiting business or providing services as a sportsperson (the entry clearance vignette will contain this information). The IDI confirm that those granted entry clearance before 8 February 2005 are still not subject to any formal restrictions on the amount of work they may do during their stay (Ch 4, s2, annex C, para. 2.2). Also, a note posted on the Work Permits (UK) website on 15 February 2005 confirmed:

'All working holidaymakers who obtained entry clearance prior to 8 February will be able to work as working holidaymakers under the previous rules and conditions.'

In all cases, it is safest to check the precise conditions that the working holidaymaker has been issued with by looking at their documents. It should also be noted that the Home Office has indicated that the new *switching* arrangements (▶see 238) will only apply to applications to switch *submitted* on or after 8 February 2005.

TRANSIT VISITORS

There are two types of transit visitor. First, there are those who are not actually seeking to enter the UK. This group is not, therefore, covered in the immigration rules, since they will remain 'airside' in the transit area (immediately below). Secondly, there are those who *are* seeking to enter the UK before joining their connection in order to depart, and who are covered by the immigration rules (▶see 245–6). We look at each of these groups in turn.

Direct airside transit

Those who are transiting airside only, without entering the UK, will need a Direct Airside Transit Visa ('DATV') *if* they are nationals of one of the following countries *and* they do not fall into any of the exceptions listed immediately below (see Immigration (Passenger Transit Visa) Order 2003 as amended by further Orders in 2003, 2004 and 2005):

Afghanistan, Albania, Algeria, Angola, Bangladesh, Belarus, Burma, Burundi, Cameroon, Colombia, Congo, Democratic Republic of Congo, Ecuador, Eritrea, Ethiopia, Former Yugoslav Republic of Macedonia, Gambia, Ghana, Guinea, Guinea-Bissau, India, Iran, Iraq, Ivory Coast, Kenya, Lebanon, Liberia, Moldova, Mongolia, Nepal, Nigeria, Pakistan, Palestinian Territories, People's Republic of China, Rwanda, Senegal, Serbia and Montenegro, Sierra Leone, Somalia, Sri Lanka, Sudan, Tanzania, Turkey, Uganda, Vietnam and Zimbabwe. (Arts 2(1), 3 and Schedule, 2003 Order).

Holders of travel documents issued by the 'Turkish Republic of Northern Cyprus', the former 'Socialist Federal Republic of Yugoslavia', the former 'Federal Republic of Yugoslavia', and the former 'Zaire' also require a

DATV (art. 2(3), 2003 Order). Note that, during 2003, Croatia, Libya and Slovakia were all removed from the list of countries whose nationals require DATVs. Overall, the list of countries whose nationals require a DATV has significantly expanded in the last few years. The government's justification for this is that:

'[t]he number of people arriving at UK airports who are found to be inadmissible is unacceptably high. Certain nationals, who are required to hold a valid visa to enter the UK, may transit this country for up to 24 hours without a visa. This provides a relatively easy and inexpensive way for those who are intent on circumventing our immigration controls to do so.' (Beverley Hughes MP, Home Office Minister, 15 October 2003, written ministerial statement.)

Exemptions from need to obtain DATV

However, the above nationals will be exempted from the requirement to obtain a DATV when transiting the UK if any of the following circumstances apply (arts 2(4), 3A 2003 Order as amended):

- they are also EEA nationals or have the right of abode (▶see 1418–20) in the UK;
- they are Chinese nationals who hold a passport issued in the Hong Kong Special Administrative Region or the Macao Special Administrative Region;
- they have a diplomatic or service passport issued by the Chinese authorities;
- they have a diplomatic or official passport issued by the Indian authorities;
- they have a diplomatic or official passport issued by the Vietnamese authorities;
- they are en route to Australia, Canada, New Zealand or the US, provided they hold an airline ticket to one of those countries and the required, valid visa for one of these countries;
- they are en route from Australia, Canada, New Zealand or the US, having entered one of those countries not more than six months ago with a valid visa, and have a valid airline ticket for their country of destination;
- they are en route from Australia, Canada, New Zealand or the US to another country while they still hold a valid visa for entry to one of those four countries and a a valid airline ticket to their present country of destination;
- they have a valid US I–551 Permanent Resident Card issued on or after 21 April 1998;
- they have a valid Canadian Permanent Resident Card issued on or after 28 June 2002;
- they have a valid 'category D' visa for entry to an EEA state;
- they have a valid residence permit issued by an EEA state.

Applying for and using DATVs

If a DATV is required, an application for one should be made, using form VAF3, to an entry clearance post, for which a fee is charged. The ECO will want to confirm that the applicant has a same-day confirmed onward booking for a flight from the same airport in the UK, that the necessary visas for the country of destination are held, that the applicant intends to proceed on directly, and that the transit does not involve an overnight stay. DATVs are not actually 'entry clearances' under the 1971 Act, because they are not valid for 'entry', and therefore do not confer leave to enter, as do ordinary entry clearances. The period of their validity may be anything between one month and two years, and they are valid for multiple use. Refusal to issue a DATV does *not* lead to a right of appeal.

Passengers holding DATVs will only exceptionally be able to enter the UK – for example, if they have missed flight connections or because of the re-routing of aircraft. The immigration officer will still need to be satisfied that they are genuinely seeking entry in transit. In these circumstances, entry may be granted for up to 48 hours, as with other transit passengers entering the UK (see below).

Transit visitors entering the UK

Transit visitors are those who actually seek to enter the UK. The immigration rules require these passengers to demonstrate all of the following (paras 47–50, HC 395):

- they are in transit to another country outside the Common Travel Area (►see glossary);
- they have the means and intention of travelling there straightaway;
- they are assured of entry to their country of destination;
- they intend and are able to leave the UK within 48 hours.

This category is for people who wish to enter the UK for a very short period because they need to get to another port to continue their onward journey, or because there is a short delay before their connecting flight, or who simply wish to spend time between arrival and departure outside the transit area. Transit visitors are admitted to the UK for a maximum of 48 hours, and any application for an extension beyond that time is to be refused under the immigration rules. A person, for example, who wants to spend a few days visiting friends and family before continuing their journey, has to satisfy the ordinary rules as a visitor.

Entry clearance and entry clearance waiver

Non-visa nationals do not require entry clearance. Although normally a visa national would require an entry clearance for entry in this category, this requirement appears to be waived for transiting visa national passengers if they meet *all* of the following conditions (see IDI, Ch2, s2, annex D, para. 1):

- they are *not* a national of any of the countries listed above who require a visa for the purposes of a direct airside transit (▶243), *or*, probably, *if* they are such a national, one of the above-listed exceptions applies to them (▶244);
- they arrive by air and have a confirmed booking on an onward flight, departing within 24 hours, to their country of destination;
- they have any necessary documentation to be admitted to their country of destination, and transit visas for any other countries it will be necessary to transit through;
- their name does not appear on the immigration authorities' 'Warnings Index'.

The waiver still applies where the passenger will travel between two airports in the UK to get the connecting flight. Visa nationals who benefit from the visa waiver will only be admitted for 24 hours, rather than the usual 48 hours. This can, however, be extended to 48 hours where necessary. Note that Home Office policy on this waiver is not completely clear – the list of countries which are excluded from the entry clearance waiver given in the IDI, for example, is out of date.

If a transit visitor does obtain a visa, it will be valid for entry on any number of occasions during its period of validity. A transit passenger who arrives with an entry clearance and is refused entry is entitled to appeal.

Visa national passengers aboard a cruise ship which docks at a UK port, and who are intending to stay in the UK for no longer than 24 hours before leaving with the same cruise, do not need an entry clearance. This concession is subject to certain conditions, such as the passenger list having been passed to the immigration authorities 24 hours before the ship's arrival. Again, this concession does not apply to the nationals listed above who do not benefit from the transit visa waiver (see DSP, Vol 1, Ch 10, para. 10.3).

APPROVED DESTINATION STATUS AGREEMENT WITH CHINA

On 21 January 2005, the UK signed a Memorandum of Understanding on visa and related issues concerning tourist groups from the People's Republic of China coming to the UK. It is now known as the 'Approved Destination Status Agreement with China' or simply the 'ADS agreement'. The purpose of the agreement is to provide a special route for Chinese tourists coming to the UK with authorised travel agents. In order to accommodate the agreement, a new category of 'visitors seeking entry under the ADS agreement' has been added to the immigration rules from 5 April 2005 (paras 56G–J HC 395 inserted by HC 486).

In many ways, the requirements of the new category are similar to those for 'ordinary' visitors. The following common, standard requirements must all be met, namely that the applicant:

- intends to leave the UK at the end of the period of the visit stated by them;
- does not intend to take employment in the UK;
- does not intend to produce goods or provide services in the UK;
- does not intend to study at a maintained school;
- can be maintained and accommodated without recourse to public funds;
- can meet the cost of their return journey.

However, ADS visitors must also satisfy all of the following requirements, which make the category very different from other visitors. An applicant must:

- be a national of the People's Republic of China;
- be genuinely seeking entry as a visitor for the limited period stated by them which must not exceed 30 days;
- intend to enter, leave and travel within the UK as a member of a tourist group under the ADS agreement;
- hold a valid ADS agreement visit entry clearance.

Entry will be granted for a maximum of 30 days with a condition prohibiting work.

ADS entry clearances

Unlike other visit entry clearances, ADS entry clearances will not be valid for multiple entries. ADS entry clearances take effect as leave to enter the UK but only on the one occasion. The exception to this is if the ADS entry clearance is specifically endorsed as a 'dual-entry visa'. In that case, the entry clearance can be used for entry twice during its period of validity and, on each occasion, it will have effect as leave to enter (see art. 4 Immigration (Leave to Enter and Remain) Order 2000 as amended and for further details about this ▶see 87–8). So, in most ADS cases, the entry clearance will be valid for a single entry and will operate as leave to enter on that occasion.

Extending leave

In ordinary visitor cases, if less then six months' leave is given, the applicant can extend their leave in-country for up to the six-month maximum. In ADS visitor cases, any application for an extension of stay as a visitor under the ADS agreement is to be refused (para. 56J HC 395). In addition, specific changes have been made to the ordinary visitor, private medical visitor and 'parent of a child at school' rules to ensure that applicants admitted as ADS visitors cannot extend their leave in any of those categories (paras 44(iii), 54(v) and 56A(vi) HC 395).

10 Students

For many years, the immigration rules have allowed people to come to the United Kingdom in order to study. The British Council have reported that students from overseas contribute approximately £3 billion per year to the British economy. The 'Prime Minister's Initiative' (PMI), launched in June 1999, is intended to build long-term relations between the UK and overseas countries through providing and encouraging education and training in the UK for international students. The aim has been to make the procedures more user friendly and to increase the government scholarships which are available.

Traditionally, the immigration rules have viewed students as being a temporary category of entry. Like visitors, those coming as students normally have to show that they intend to leave the UK at the end of their proposed studies. However, as the result of a Home Office concession, certain students – in particular those wishing to take courses at degree level or higher – no longer need to demonstrate an intention to leave. It is expected that some students will go on to obtain employment in the UK and will be permitted to remain on a long-term basis and qualify for settlement (for the latest changes regarding studies in Scotland and the 'Fresh Talent' Scheme, ▶see 465–7). Switching to remain in a different capacity *after* studies is not dealt with in this chapter but is covered in part of the *Handbook* dealing with switching generally (▶see Chapter 7, in particular at 163–8 but ▶see 274–6 for switching to student status). In a further common-sense development, from June 1999, most students have been granted a general permission to enter into limited employment (▶see 263–6).

Recent developments

The most recent innovations, however, have not been positive – certain changes seem to fly in the face of the PMI. From 1 October 2004, the rules were amended to restrict both the circumstances in which applicants may extend their leave as students (▶see 268–70), and switch in order to remain as a student (▶see 274–6). (For full general details about switching ▶see Ch 7.) These rules create quite unnecessary problems for students seeking to stay in the UK in order to study. Further amendments have halved the length of time which a student may spend in the UK while studying on 'short courses' (▶see 272–3).

Students are likely to form one of the 'tiers' under the government's proposals for a five-tiered single points system.

This chapter

Most students who come to the UK for studies have already chosen and been accepted onto a particular course of study. It is also possible, however, to come to the UK as a 'prospective' student, provided the applicant will take up their course of study within six months. The chapter begins by looking at the rules for entry for both 'ordinary' students and prospective students, at all levels of the educational ladder and who may be studying on all sorts of different courses (▶251–60). We then look at the procedures for applying for entry, for extending leave in-country, the conditions attached to leave granted to students and the rights of dependants of students (▶260–76).

The immigration rules also make specific provision for certain types of student. The chapter looks at these additional classes of student in the following order.

- students who are re-sitting exams (▶276–7);
- students who are writing up their thesis (▶277–8);
- students' union sabbatical officers (▶278–9);
- student nurses (▶280–1);
- postgraduate doctors and dentists (▶281–2);
- medical graduates intending to take the 'PLAB' (Professional and Linguistic Assessment Board) test (▶282–3);
- medical or dental graduates intending to take a clinical attachment or dental observer post (▶283–4).

Re-sitting students, students writing up their thesis and sabbatical officers were added to the immigration rules from 2 October 2000. Medical graduates intending to take the PLAB test, or to take a clinical attachment or dental observer post, were added to the immigration rules from 15 March 2005 (HC 346). They were previously dealt with as concessions outside the rules.

This chapter also covers, in brief, the question of immigration status and access to student fees, grants and loans (▶see 284–8). Finally we look at the special considerations which apply to students who are EEA nationals (▶see 288–90). The chapter does not cover the requirement to register with the police which is imposed on some students. For details about who may be required to register and the procedures, ▶see 1006–7 and 1527.

Study-related or trainee categories elsewhere in the *Handbook*

There are a number of other study-related or 'trainee' categories of admission which are dealt with as a concession to the visitor rules, or as connected to work-related routes. They are covered elsewhere in the *Handbook*, as follows:

- academic visitors (▶221–2);
- *au pairs* (▶462–3);
- BUNAC students (▶468);
- sponsored researchers' work permits (▶425);
- training and work experience (TWES) work permits (▶440–3);
- student intern work permits (▶447);
- science and engineering graduates (SEGS) (▶464–5);
- technical students seeking work experience during the long vacation (▶472).

It should also be noted that the Home Office has no objection to people who are given leave as visitors taking a short course of studies that will be completed during the time of the their visit (IDI, Ch 3, s3, para. 3.10.2). During 2005 the Home Office has stated that it will introduce a special aspect of the HSMP scheme for MBA graduates from the top 50 business schools.

STUDENTS AND PROSPECTIVE STUDENTS

Entry clearance

Students and prospective students who are visa nationals (▶see 80), or who are 'specified' nationals seeking entry for more than six months (▶see 80–1), must obtain an entry clearance before travelling to the UK. (Note that, from 13 November 2005, all non-visa nationals are effectively 'specified' nationals). For others, entry clearance is not mandatory, but applicants may obtain entry clearance if they wish. They may alternatively apply for leave to enter when they arrive at a British port. For the advantages and disadvantages of applying for optional entry clearance, ▶see 84 and 261. Changes to the immigration rules made on 1 October 2004, which make it more difficult for non-visa nationals to extend their leave to stay as students (▶see 268–70), may mean that more non-visa nationals opt to obtain entry clearance before travelling.

WHAT THE RULES SAY

Students

People coming to the UK as students must show that they meet all of the following requirements (paras 57-62 HC 395):

- they have been accepted for a course of study at a publicly funded institution of further or higher education, *or* at a *bona fide* private education institution which maintains satisfactory records of enrolment and attendance, *or* an independent fee-paying school outside the maintained sector;

- the institution at which they have been accepted for a course of study is registered with the Department for Education and Skills as an education provider;
- they are able and intend to follow either:
  - a recognised full-time degree course at a publicly funded institution of further or higher education, *or*
  - a weekday full-time course involving attendance at a single institution for a minimum of at least 15 hours' organised daytime study per week of a single subject, or directly related subjects; *or*
  - a full-time course of study at an independent fee-paying school;
- if under the age of 16 years, they are enrolled at an independent fee-paying school on a full-time course of studies which meets the requirements of the Education Act 1944;
- they intend to leave the UK at the end of their studies (▶but see 258–9);
- they do not intend to engage in business or to take employment, except part-time or vacation work with the agreement of the Secretary of State (▶but see below, 264–66, for how this rule works in practice);
- they are able to meet the costs of their course and the accommodation and maintenance of themselves and any dependants without engaging in business, working or having recourse to public funds.

Prospective students

People who intend to study in the UK but who have not yet been accepted for a full-time course may be admitted as 'prospective students', for up to six months.

Prospective students have to show that they meet all of the following requirements (paras 82-87 HC 395):

- they have a genuine and realistic intention of undertaking, within six months of entry, a course of study which would meet the requirements of the student rules (above), or the requirements for leave as a student nurse (▶see below at 280–1);
- they intend to leave the UK on completion of their studies, or on completion of their leave as prospective students if they are not accepted as students;
- they can maintain and accommodate themselves and any dependants without working and without recourse to public funds.

The meaning of the rules is set out immediately below. For the meaning of the additional rules for prospective students ▶see 259–60.

WHAT THE RULES MEAN

Department for Education and Skills Register

From 1 January 2005, the immigration rules have required that the educational institution to be attended by the student is included on the Department for Education and Skills Register of education providers (para. 57(i) HC 395 substituted by HC 164). Students wanting to check whether the institution they are considering attending is on the register can view the register at www.dfes.gov.uk/providersregister. A helpline is also available for educational institutions which have not yet registered on 020 7804 9149. The Home Office is not operating any transitional arrangements in relation to this change which applies to all decisions taken on or after 1 January 2005 (IDI Ch3, s3, para. 3.4.1).

Publicly funded institutions of further or higher education

The expression 'publicly funded institution of further or higher education' is not defined in the immigration rules. Higher education is post-school education above A-level standard. Further education is post–16 education involving courses at various levels up to the standard required for entry to higher education. The institutions referred to in the rules are intended to be:

- further education and sixth-form colleges funded by the further education funding councils throughout the UK;
- institutions funded through the Learning and Skills Council;
- universities and other institutions of higher education funded by the higher education funding councils.

Bona fide private education institutions which maintain satisfactory records

Bona fide private education institutions that maintain satisfactory records of enrolment and attendance are also not defined in the rules. The words *bona fide* mean that the institution must be genuinely providing education. Private educational institutions which are often attended by international students include secretarial colleges and language schools. They may incidentally be institutions of further or higher education, but are not publicly funded. They also include American universities with campuses in the UK offering American degrees and qualifications. Because these institutions are not publicly accountable through the Department for Education and Skills, and the academic standards vary, the immigration authorities are given wide latitude to check that they are bona fide and that they keep satisfactory records of enrolment and attendance.

Recently, the Home Office announced that it was 'stepping up enforcement action to crack down on bogus establishments' (Home Secretary's statement in Home Office press release, 22 April 2004). In particular officers will check to see whether the institution (IDI Ch3, s3, para. 3.4.2.3):

- maintains satisfactory records of enrolment and attendance of students;
- provides courses which involve a minimum of 15 hours organised daytime study per week;
- ensures a suitably qualified tutor is present during the hours of study;
- offers courses leading to qualifications recognised by the appropriate accreditation bodies;
- employs suitably qualified staff to provide teaching, guidance and support to students; and
- provides adequate accommodation, facilities, staffing levels and equipment to support the numbers of students enrolled at the institution.

The British Accreditation Council for Independent Further and Higher Education (BAC), English UK (see www.englishuk.com for a list of members), The Association of British Language Schools (see www.abls.co.uk for a list of members) and the British Council all run systems for accrediting private colleges. A college does not have to be accredited in order to be regarded as *bona fide*, but accreditation will certainly help. The BAC was formed in 1984 in order to improve the standards of independent further and higher education. It publishes a list of over 100 colleges which have been inspected and accredited. Their database can be accessed at www.the-bac.org. The British Council inspects organisations in the UK which offer English language courses as a foreign language. They are accredited if they meet British Council standards. A list of the 370 or so institutions which have been accredited by the British Council can be found at www.britcoun.org/english/courses/index/htm.

The *bona fides* of a college may be the subject of a visit to the college premises by the immigration service to inspect the college and its records. This occurred in *Syed Tareq Ali v ECO, Dhaka* (IAT) in which, although the records were found to be somewhat lacking, there were explanations for this and they were found to be sufficient.

Independent fee-paying schools

Independent fee-paying schools outside the maintained sector are also not defined in the rules. They include preparatory ('prep') schools and 'public' schools. According to education law, an independent school is a school at which full-time education is provided for five or more pupils of school age, and which is *not* maintained by a local education authority. 'Maintained' schools are publicly-funded state schools. The maintained sector includes all publicly funded schools, including grant-maintained schools, voluntary-aided schools, voluntary controlled schools, sixth-form colleges attached to maintained schools and special schools. None of these schools, therefore, are 'independent' and the rules do not permit children to be granted leave in order to attend them. City Technology

Colleges and City Colleges for the Technology of the Arts not actually defined as 'maintained' but, according to the Home Office, are publicly-funded, and do not count as independent schools for the purposes of the rules. Children under five years attending nursery or pre-school classes are also not able to qualify under the rules as students.

Independent schools must be registered with the Department for Education and Skills, and an unregistered school will not enable a student to qualify. The expression 'fee-paying' describes the school rather than the parent, so that a pupil on a scholarship could presumably qualify for admission as a student under the rules.

Exchange students

As a concession to the above rule which excludes students attending a maintained school, there are some schemes for children (usually aged 16–18 years) to spend a year in a foreign school (IDI, Ch3, s3, para. 3.24.2– 3.24.1.1). Where appropriate arrangements have been put into place, leave may be granted outside the rules if all the following conditions are met:

- the organisation arranging the exchange have provided evidence that the local education authority have approved the scheme and assigned a the pupil to a school;
- suitable arrangements have been made for accommodation and there are sufficient funds for the support of the child (this will normally be assumed if a host family is confirmed);
- the pupil intends to leave the UK at the end of the exchange period.

Privately arranged exchange schemes are also acceptable provided that the local education authority has given its approval. Leave may be granted for a maximum period of a year. Public funds conditions are imposed and work is prohibited. Entry clearance is not mandatory for non-visa, non-specified nationals. Where entry clearance is issued, it will be endorsed 'exchange student'.

Full-time studies

Students will normally need a letter from the institution at which they intend to study, confirming that they have been accepted on a particular full-time course. Depending on the college and the level of studies, the immigration authorities may also ask for details of the precise number of hours per week the student will be studying.

If the student is following a recognised first, or higher level, degree course at a publicly-funded institution, it is sufficient that the institution designates the course as 'full-time'. Even though there may not be formal classes for this number of hours, it is assumed that the 15-hours requirement is met. Although, it is not stated in the rules, this also applies to those following degree courses at *bona fide* private education institutions where the degree will be awarded by a recognised university, including the Open University (IDI, Ch3, s3, para. 3.11.1). Bar students studying at the Inns of Court School of Law and who have been admitted to one of the Inns of Court are treated similarly (in addition, note that Work Permits (UK) have agreed that pupil barristers undertaking 12 months' training with a recognised Chambers, may be treated as students under the immigration rules, although trainee solicitors must obtain a TWES work permit, see IDI, Ch3, s3, para. 3.24.4.2–3.24.4.3).

All other students have to show that they will spend at least 15 hours per week in organised week-day classes. The study must be at a single institution, but it can include two or more part-time courses provided that the subjects studied are directly related. Evening classes that commence after 6 pm, (or before 6 pm if the majority of the class takes place after 6 pm) and weekend classes will not count towards the 15 hours (IDI, Ch3, s3, para. 3.11.1). Where two part-time courses are not apparently related, the student or the institution may need to explain why a particular study combination is desirable, or helps a student in their career. It has also generally been accepted by the immigration authorities that English language courses for non-English speakers can be combined with another course to meet the 15-hours requirement.

Able to meet the costs of the course

The Home Office need to know the level of fees, and whether the whole amount, or a deposit towards it, has been paid. It is not a requirement of the rules that a deposit or fees have been paid to the institution in advance, but if any money has been paid, confirmation of this is likely to help an application. Evidence to show ability to meet the cost of fees may be through cash, travellers cheques, bankers' draft, sponsorship letter or itemised bank or building society statements.

Maintenance and accommodation

The rules state that students must show that they have the money to pay their fees, and to live in the UK without needing to work and without recourse to public funds. Overseas students usually have to pay full-cost fees for their courses, often amounting to several thousand pounds (▶see 284–6). In terms of general maintenance, the British Council estimated that, in the year 2002/2003, a student living in London would need nearly £7,000 (outside London nearly £5,500) to meet their basic living expenses excluding fees.

Students may provide evidence of financial support in several ways. If they are supported by the UK Government, their home government, the British Council or another international organisation, a letter from the sponsoring body, confirming the amount of money and arrangements about fees, will probably be sufficient. If students are being privately supported, a letter from the sponsor confirming their willingness and ability to support the student is necessary. The sponsor should produce evidence of their means covering about three months, which may be recent original bank statements or pay-slips. When a friend is supporting the student, or anyone else who has no immediately obvious interest in doing so, the immigration authorities may ask questions about why the friend is helping.

Although students are able to do some work, any earnings from employment they may obtain will not be taken into consideration by the Home Office (see IDI, Ch3, s3, para. 3.15.4). Earnings from guaranteed part-time work at a publicly funded institution of further or higher education and earnings from full-time employment arranged by the institution for students on sandwich courses, will be taken into account. The Home Office's approach is probably based on the fact that the rules relating to support refer to the means available to the student 'without working'. However, given that the Home Office have issued a general approval for limited work to certain students (▶see 263–6), we suggest that those who will only have sufficient funds by working and who will be entitled to do some work, should argue that their potential earnings should be taken into account. It would seem wrong, for example, to ignore potential earnings from work where a student, who will be permitted to work, has a job offer and where the hours fit into the Home Office's general approval. Dependants of students are permitted to work where the student has been granted leave for at least 12 months (▶see 267–8), but the Home Office will only take into account their actual rather than their potential earnings.

For general details about the maintenance and accommodation requirements, ▶see 307–318. The support rules are expressed slightly differently for students than, for example, for spouses and partners. Students must be able to meet the costs of their course, accommodation and support, rather than having to show the availability of adequate accommodation which will be exclusively occupied. However, students must be able to show that there will be adequate accommodation in relation to any dependants who are also applying.

Ability to follow the course

Immigration officials also have to be satisfied that the student is academically able to follow the course. In dealing with entry clearance applications, ECOs are encouraged to check with the local British Council office if they have doubts about any foreign qualifications or certificates shown to them. The immigration authorities should not normally attempt to second-guess enrolment decisions by colleges as to the student's ability to follow a course. Where an officer is doubtful about a student's ability to follow a course, the college principal may be contacted and asked to make an assessment of the student. Immigration officials themselves have no qualifications with which to make an assessment as to the ability of a particular student to follow a particular course, and often they will base their decisions on their own appraisal of the student's proficiency in English when answering questions in interview.

It may be the case that the student has arranged to take steps to improve their English before the course begins. In the case of *Pattu-wearachchi*, the IAT decided that it was valid for a student coming to do a vocational course to decide, at entry, to follow an English language course first, and this change of plan did not invalidate the entry clearance granted. Many institutions include an English language test as part of their application process. If this has been carried out, and the college finds the student's English acceptable, this should be explained to the immigration authorities.

Intention to leave the UK and the Home Office concession

Under the immigration rules, students have to show that they intend to leave the UK at the end of their studies. In many cases, it is impossible to demonstrate at the outset of a course what a person will do at the end of it, and immigration officials therefore may make subjective decisions. If a student has any other relatives who have settled in the UK, particularly if they entered as students in the past, immigration officials may be particularly suspicious about the applicant's longer-term intentions.

Because official scholarship, or sponsoring agencies, often stipulate that a student must return, this part of the rules is rarely a problem for officially sponsored students, since they are not, without the consent of their sponsor, able to switch to privately funded studies if their sponsorship ends. However, privately funded students may have more difficulties. They may be asked what benefit the course will be to the person after returning home, or about their future career plans, and whether the course is available in his or her home country. It may be helpful to have evidence of job advertisements from the country of origin, specifying the qualification which the student hopes to obtain, or even evidence of a job offer on return. It is certainly important to relate the qualifications to be obtained to employment prospects in the home country. In particular where the applicant is from a background that is not well off, officers will sometimes weigh the cost of the course against the benefits it may bring to the student. Other evidence of commitments in the country of origin, for example having a spouse or children there, is always helpful in showing that this requirement is met.

Meaning of 'studies' The rules require that a student intends to leave the UK at the end of their 'studies', not necessarily at the end of the first course on which they enrol. If students wish to continue to follow higher-level courses after the one for which they are seeking entry, they should explain this. The immigration authorities can decide whether these plans appear to them to be realistic, either academically or financially. In the case of *Kharrazi*, concerning a 12-year-old boy's plan to progress to university from school, the Court of Appeal held that such an intention could fall within the immigration rules if it formed part of a 'coherent and definite whole which was reasonably capable of being carried out by him'.

Mere suspicion not enough In the absence of direct evidence of intentions, much will rest on the drawing of inferences from the particular circumstances of the student, including the student's academic record. The IAT has been careful to warn that inferences must be drawn only from evidence, and that 'mere suspicion' that a person will not return is not enough. As in other cases in immigration law, a distinction is to be made between a wish and an intention. Just because a student has expressed a hope of being given permission to stay on for employment after their studies, this does not automatically show that they do not intend to leave at the end those studies (see *Virendrakumar Patel v IAT*, CA).

Intention to leave concession In a concession outside the rules announced by the Home Secretary on 17 October 2001, students applying for courses at degree-level, student nurses, and postgraduate doctors and dentists no longer needed to satisfy the immigration authorities that they intend to leave the UK at the end of their studies. This concession also applied to students undertaking foundation or language courses which they needed to pass in order to be able to take up their place on a degree course. The concession was introduced in line with the change in policy to allow certain switching into work permit employment after a period of studies. For switching, ▶see Chapter 7.

The present statement of policy is contained in the IDI as follows:

'If [the immigration authorities are] satisfied that an applicant intends, and is able, to follow a chosen degree level course, it should be assumed that there is a reasonable prospect of success in their studies and consequent eligibility for employment. In such cases the intention to leave requirement should be disregarded, and considerations should concentrate on the other aspects of the Rules, with a particular emphasis on the applicant's ability and intention to follow the course of study' (Ch 3, s3, para. 3.18.2; see also DSP, Ch12, para. 12.18).

This policy is also expressly extended to those on foundation language or other courses which must be passed in order for the degree course to be commenced. There no express mention of the rule being waived for postgraduate doctors and dentists in the IDI but in practice it may well be waived. The 'intention to leave' requirement is also not presently strictly applied in relation to nurses (▶see 280).

Additional rules for prospective students

People hoping to study in the UK may not have made definite arrangements to do so before travelling. They may wish to travel to the UK in order to make arrangements to find, enrol on and then follow a suitable course. They may also need to come to the UK to attend an interview at a particular institution after which, if they are accepted, they will attend the course. So, prospective students do not actually have to be enrolled on a course, but they must have 'genuine and realistic' intentions of being accepted on to a course that fits the above student rules, and also of being able to pursue it (see *Alexander v IAT*, HL). They should therefore be able to state the kind of course they are interested in, and provide evidence of their achievements and qualifications to date to demonstrate that their goals are realistic. Prospective students must also satisfy immigration officials that if they are not successful in obtaining a place, they will leave the UK by the end of the period of leave granted (paras 82–87 HC 395).

It is important that these 'intending' students explain their plans to study to the officers and seek entry clearance, or entry, to the UK as a 'prospective student'. After they have begun their courses, they can apply to extend their leave to follow them (►see 268 onwards). Sometimes these students may feel that, as they have no specific study plans, they should seek entry as visitors. This is not advisable. In most cases it will not be possible at all because, under switching rules in force from 1 October 2004, the only people able to switch into the student category are non-visa nationals accepted for studies at degree-level or above (►see below). In addition, those who enter as visitors run the risk of being treated as illegal entrants because they concealed their true intentions, or the period for which they wished to remain (see, for example, the case of *Durojaiye*).

Prospective students also have to satisfy the immigration authorities that they have the money to support themselves for the period while they are arranging their studies, as well as during any course. Students from countries with strict foreign exchange control regulations may have problems in showing that they can fund their course before they have been accepted onto it and the funds have been transferred.

Under the rules prospective students may only be admitted for a maximum of six months, with a condition prohibiting employment. Extensions will only be permitted to bring the period of leave up to a total of six months (i.e. if less was originally granted), and provided that the rules for prospective students continue to be met. In such cases, officers will check to see whether the reasons for granting less than six months in the first place still apply.

In-country switching to remain as a prospective student is permitted for non-visa nationals (see para. 85 HC 395).

Entry clearance decisions

If entry clearance is granted, it will operate as leave to enter provided it specifies the purpose for which it has been issued and the conditions to which the leave will be subject. Unlike a visit entry clearance, a student entry clearance will act as leave to enter on one occasion during its period of validity. However, leave given to a student by an entry clearance will not lapse when the student leaves the Common Travel Area (CTA), and the student will be able to continue to re-enter with the same leave until the time it expires. The period of the leave given by the entry clearance and the conditions will generally depend on the length of the course (▶see below at 262–3).

Students applying for courses that will last for six months or less, and prospective students, do not have a right of appeal under the immigration rules against a refusal of student entry clearance (s 91 2002 Act). This has been the case since appeal rights were cut back by the 1993 Act. They may now only bring an appeal on human rights or discrimination grounds. Non-prospective students seeking entry for a course for longer than six months will have a full right of appeal against a negative entry clearance decision (but see below for future changes to appeal rights). For full details about appeal rights, ▶see Tables 1-3 at 1053–61.

Refusal of entry at port

Students with an entry clearance Students and prospective students who arrive with entry clearance generally have the right to appeal against refusal of entry, and are able to remain in the UK while the appeal is pending (ss 89, 92(3)-(3C) 2002 Act) (▶see 1059).

Students without an entry clearance Students who are not visa nationals or specified nationals seeking entry for over six months do not need to obtain entry clearance before travelling. (From 13 November 2005, all non visa nationals are, in effect, 'specified nationals'.) However, if they arrive without an entry clearance, and they cannot satisfy the immigration officer on arrival that they qualify to enter, they may be refused leave to enter, and can be sent straight back (unless, of course, they seek entry on asylum or human rights grounds). Whether they can then appeal from abroad against the refusal of leave to enter will depend on what kind of student they are (s 89 2002 Act):

- if they are seeking entry as prospective students, not yet having enrolled on a course, or if their course would last for six months or less, they will have no right of appeal at all (other than on human rights/discrimination grounds);
- students accepted onto longer courses can appeal from abroad against a refusal under the rules relating to studies.

For full details about appeal rights, ▶see Tables 1–3 at 1053–61.

Where a person has been refused entry and does not have an appeal right from within the UK, representations may still be made to immigration officers as to why they should be admitted. Unless there is important new evidence or exceptional and compelling compassionate reasons, it would be unusual for immigration officers to change their mind once a decision to refuse has been made. If the officers are not satisfied that a student is able to follow the course that they intend to take, further evidence from the academic institution may be very helpful to show that the applicant meets its admission criteria. If the reason for the refusal is lack of intention to leave at the end of studies, it will be very difficult to change the decision unless concrete evidence is produced showing that the applicant does have an incentive to return.

Future changes to appeal rights

In its 'five year strategy', the government stated that it intends to abolish appeals for both work and study routes, for those refused an entry clearance at posts overseas, those refused entry at port and those refused extensions of leave as students. The 2005 Immigration, Asylum and Nationality (IAN) Bill proposes clauses to this effect. The IAN Bill and the proposed abolition of appeal rights are set out at ▶1041–6. For JCWI's views on the proposals, ▶see 48 and 50–51.

Periods of leave granted to students

To be sure about the length of time granted to a student allowed, applicants and advisers should check what is actually endorsed on the passport both in the entry clearance sticker and on stamps showing any extensions granted. For full details about calculating the leave granted by an entry clearance, ▶see 86–9. We look at the period of leave granted to prospective students and to other specific categories of students which are covered separately in the rules, in the parts of the chapter dealing specifically with them. The following guidance applies to ordinary students.

Leave given on entry for those without an entry clearance

The immigration rules for leave to *enter*, which therefore include leave to be granted by an entry clearance, simply state that a student may be admitted for 'an appropriate period depending on the length of [the student's] course and [their] means' (para. 58 HC 395). From 13 November 2005, all non-visa nationals seeking entry for more than six months must, like visa nationals, produce an entry clearance (see paras 23A, 23B, 24 HC 395 substituted by HC 645). The only exceptions are British nationals (i.e. those without the right of abode). Non-visa nationals seeking entry for up to six months may still be granted six months' leave without having an entry clearance. British nationals may be granted leave for a longer period.

Leave given by entry clearance or in-country

The Home Office gives the following guidance in relation to leave given otherwise than above i.e. either by an entry clearance or in-country (IDI, Ch3, s1, para. 1.2.2; s3 para. 3.2.1–3.2.2; s3, para. 3.25). Mistakes are made, however, and applicants should check the leave which an ECO has given them. If it is incorrect, they may ask for it to be changed and should do this before using the entry clearance to come to the UK.

Independent fee-paying school children Children of primary school age are normally granted leave for the duration of their course of study i.e. up to age 11. Children aged 11–16 should be granted leave to complete their GCSE course. Children 16 and over (A-level) should be granted leave for the duration of their course up to age 18.

Students in further or higher education Students on courses of one year or more which follow the usual academic year from autumn to summer are normally granted leave to remain for the duration of their study until 31 October following the end of their course. For courses which do not follow the standard academic year, leave for the period of the course plus an additional four months following the end of the course should be granted. Postgraduates should also be given an extra four months at the end of the date their course formally ends (or to the date of the submission of their thesis and extra time as advised by the educational institution). In cases where the length of the course is not specified, 12 months' leave should be granted.

Short courses Students studying English or those enrolled on short courses of six months or less, should be granted leave to remain for at least six months at a time – they will often be given an extra two months. If the course is for over six months, they should normally be granted up to 12 months plus two months.

Foundation course followed by degree course Students taking a short foundation course to be followed by a degree or similar course, should normally be given leave to remain to cover the duration of *both* courses plus four months or until 31 October after the end of the degree course. This is provided that the applicant is fully enrolled on the second course. This does not apply to those taking general courses before degree level study e.g. A-levels or HNC/D. If acceptance on to the second course is conditional on passing the first course, leave will normally only be given for the duration of the foundation course plus the usual four months, or until 31 October.

Architectural students Architectural students have a complex study and training programme. They will be granted three years in order to undertake their undergraduate course (four years if they are doing a foundation year) and then three years in order to complete their practical training and postgraduate course. Applicants need to apply under the TWES scheme in order to take the professional practice and final exam.

Conditions of leave and permission to work while studying

What follows deals with ordinary students. The length of leave granted and conditions imposed on prospective students and other students which are dealt with separately in the rules are looked at in the parts where we deal with those particular students. Students will normally be given a condition prohibiting them from having recourse to public funds. Some students may be required to register with the police (▶see 1006–7). Most students are able to take some employment in the UK which is unrelated to their studies. There are two kinds of working conditions which may be imposed on student leave:

- Most students will have been granted leave with a 'working restriction' which permits them to do work as authorised by the Secretary of State. These students benefit from a deemed grant of approval to do some work as set out below. Their conditions will probably include: 'able to work as authorised by the Secretary of State'; 'work (and any changes) must be authorised' or 'leave…on condition that the holder…does not enter or change employment paid or unpaid without the consent of the Secretary of State…'

- Other students are prohibited from working which means that they must not do any work at all. Their conditions will probably include: 'no work' or 'leave…on condition that the holder…does not enter employment paid or unpaid'.

In order to be sure which applies, in all cases, students and their advisers should check the conditions of leave which the student has actually been given. As a guide, prospective students are normally prohibited from working (see paras 83, 86 HC 395) and so are many short-term students on courses of six months or less. However, Home Office guidance states that short-term (not prospective) students who indicate that they wish to take part-time employment and who 'fully meet' the student rules, will be granted leave enabling them to work as authorised like other students (IDI, Ch3, s1, para. 1.2.2.1–1.2.2.2). Short-term students should therefore indicate their intentions when applying. Those arriving at ports without an entry clearance are the most likely to be admitted with a prohibition on work – they will only be given up to six months' leave (▶see above). These applicants will therefore need to be assertive that they wish to be able to do work during their studies and therefore to be admitted with only a working restriction. The safest course for these students who really need to be able to work is to apply for entry clearance.

If an ECO makes a mistake in the conditions on which leave is granted then it is often possible to get them to correct it. However, if a prohibition against work is endorsed as a condition of the student leave in the UK, it will only be lifted by applying to the Home Office for the leave itself to be varied so as to remove the condition.

Breach of conditions and curtailment of leave If a student is caught working when not permitted, or it is established that they have exceeded their hours of permitted work, then they may be treated as breaching their conditions of leave. This is serious, it can lead to the student being administratively removed from the UK (s10 1999 Act), and/or to prosecution under the 1971 Act. A student who ceases attending their course regularly but continues to work in accordance with their conditions of leave and the general approval given to students to work, cannot be detained and removed as a person who is in breach of their conditions. Such a student continues to be a 'student' and have leave as such until such time as the Secretary of State takes action to curtail the leave (see *R (Zhou) v SSHD* (CA)), or if the circumstances allow, the person is declared to be an illegal entrant. The Home Office may curtail a leave if it determines that the person no longer fulfils the requirements of the rules under which the leave was granted (see para. 323(ii) HC 395). There is a right of appeal if leave is curtailed as it constitutes a variation of leave. Breach of conditions and possible enforcement actions are discussed in more detail at ▶1004–5.

Deemed approval for employment

Previously, students with working restrictions were required to obtain specific approval for the work they wished to do from their local Job Centre. This is no longer necessary. From 21 June 1999, to reduce administration and to provide an incentive for potential overseas students, students over the age of 16 with working restrictions are automatically authorised to take employment subject to the following restrictions which are set out in the IDI at Ch3, s3, para. 3.16. This general approval is also set out in a leaflet issued by the Department for Education and Skills in March 2002, 'International students working in the UK – what you need to know' (available on www.dfes.gov.uk/international-students/workleaflet) and in the Operational Enforcement Manual at Ch 10.6.5.

- Students may take part-time or full-time vacation work.
- They may take part-time work during term time but for not more than 20 hours per week. They may work longer hours, however, if they are working on a work placement which is part of either a 'sandwich course' or an 'internship placement' meeting description and conditions below.
- Students must not engage in business, self-employment or the provision of a service as a professional sportsperson or entertainer.
- Students must not pursue a career by filling a permanent, full-time vacancy.

Sandwich courses These are courses which include a clearly defined work placement which is approved by the educational institution providing the course. Two further conditions must be met:

- the course must lead to a degree or qualification awarded by a nationally recognised examining body; and
- the work placement must not extend beyond the end of the course.

Internship placement This is a short period of paid work which an employer may offer to a potential employee (even if the future employment might be abroad) who is studying on a first degree or higher degree course. Students will be permitted to work on the internship provided these conditions and all of the following requirements are met:

- it is for no longer than three months;
- they have not previously taken an internship with the employer;
- it forms an established part of the employer's recruitment procedures;

- it provides pay and conditions equal to those of resident workers doing the same work; and
- the internship will be completed during the student's existing period of leave as a student.

Dependants of students

The immigration rules described below allow spouses and children (under the age of 18) of the following students to be admitted to and to stay in the UK: students; prospective students; student nurses; postgraduate doctors, dentists and trainee general practitioners; those re-sitting exams and those writing up theses. The rules do not expressly provide for the dependants of sabbatical students. Nor do they include the dependants of those taking PLAB tests, or those with clinical attachments or dental observer posts (▶see 354). It is possible that the Home Office intends to make provision for the dependants of these classes of medical students, which have only recently been added to the rules.

Entry clearance for entry is not mandatory, but must be obtained if the dependant is a visa national, or a 'specified national' (▶see 80–3) seeking to remain for more than six months. Switching from another category to be a dependant of a student is permitted under the rules.

Requirements for spouses

In order to obtain leave as the spouse of a student, applicants have to show all of the following (paras 76-78 HC 395):

- they are married to a person admitted to, or allowed to remain in, the UK as a student;
- the couple intend to live together as husband and wife while the student is in the UK and the marriage is still subsisting;
- there will be adequate maintenance and accommodation for them, and any dependants, without recourse to public funds;
- they do not intend to work unless permitted to do so;
- they intend to leave the UK at the end of any leave granted.

Requirements for children

The only other family members allowed are the children of students, for whom the following requirements all apply (paras 79-81 HC 395):

- they are the child of a parent who is a student admitted to or allowed to remain in the UK;
- they are unmarried, and must not have formed an independent family unit, nor be leading an independent life;
- they will be maintained and accommodated adequately without recourse to public funds;
- they will leave the UK after any period of leave granted to the parent.

Children must be under the age of 18 when applying to enter the UK, but it doesn't matter if they turn 18 subsequently. Provided that they were admitted as the child of a student and they apply within time, they may be granted leave to remain in the same capacity, even if they are over 18.

Children of students may attend state schools while they are in the UK with leave as dependants but will not be given leave as 'students' unless they are attending a fee paying independent school and qualify under the student rules in their own right. Where a child would be required to change schools or leave the country shortly before the end of their studies or an important exam, leave may be granted outside the rules to enable the child to sit the exam or to complete the school year (IDI, Ch3, s4, para. 4.7).

Further points on dependants of students

Two further points should be noted about the rules for students' dependants:

- unlike many of the other rules relating to dependants, the student rules enable children to join one parent *without* having to demonstrate that that parent is the only living parent, or has had 'sole responsibility' for the child, or that there are reasons rendering the child's exclusion undesirable;
- as at 7 November 2005, there is no provision in the rules for leave to be granted to unmarried or same-sex partners of students with limited leave, although it is understood that the Home Office has this matter under review.

Leave and conditions for dependants of students

Dependants will normally be given the same time limit on their stay as the student themselves, and cannot be given a longer period. Public funds conditions will be imposed on the leave granted to dependants of students. If a dependant accompanies or joins a student who has leave for 12 months or more, the dependant should be given leave without conditions restricting or prohibiting work and is therefore able to work. Note that it is the length of leave which is granted to the *sponsoring student* which is crucial here. Therefore, dependants applying at a different time from their sponsor should have evidence of their sponsor's leave in order to demonstrate that they should be admitted without working conditions.

The immigration rules themselves state that dependants should be prohibited from working where less than 12 months' leave is granted to the student (para. 77, 80 HC 395). However, officers are instructed as a matter of discretion to grant leave without working conditions if (see IDI, Ch3, s4, paras 4.1, 4.4):

- the dependant's existing leave allows them to work; or
- the student was granted less than 12 months but only due to Home Office administrative delays in issuing the grant of leave, and would have been

granted 12 months or more if the application for an extension had been dealt with on the date that it was made.

Dependants who are allowed to work, and do so, do not obtain any independent claim to remain in the UK in their own right. They are still expected to leave with their sponsor.

Although the rules stipulate that family members may only come to join a student 'admitted to or allowed to remain in the UK', the Home Office confirmed in a letter to UKCOSA, dated 12 October 1994:

'Where a student wishes to bring his family to the UK with him, he can apply for entry clearance or, where appropriate, leave to enter for the whole family, at the same time. He does not need to gain entry himself first.'

Extending leave as a student

WHAT THE RULES SAY

Those who are seeking to extend their leave to the UK to continue with studies must demonstrate all of the following (paras 60-62 HC 395):

- *unless they are non-visa nationals accepted for courses at degree level or above*, they were last admitted to the UK in possession of a valid student (or prospective student) entry clearance (see below for transitional arrangements);
- they are enrolled on a full-time course and, *if the course has begun*, have regularly attended it, or any other course they have been enrolled on in the past;
- satisfactory progress on the course, including the taking and passing of any relevant examinations;
- they would not, if this extension was granted, have spent more than two years on short courses below degree level (i.e. courses of less than one year in length, or longer courses if broken off before completion);
- they have not come to the end of a period of a scholarship from a government or an international scholarship agency or, if they have, they have the written consent of their sponsor for further studies, and can show sufficient sponsorship funding.

WHAT THE RULES MEAN

The following rules apply to 'ordinary' students. For extending leave as a prospective student, ►see 260. Extensions in the other specific categories of student are dealt with in the relevant parts below.

Last admitted with student entry clearance

From 1 October 2004, this rule has been amended so that non-visa national students who wish to apply for an extension, as well as visa national students, have to show that they were last admitted with a student or prospective student entry clearance (see para. 60(i) HC 395 as substituted by Cm 6339) (▶see below for the transitional arrangements being operated). This requirement does not, however, apply to non-visa national students who have been accepted for a course of study at degree level or above (for the definition of 'degree level', ▶see 272). Here we are only looking at the ability of applicants who already have leave as students to extend their leave as students. The amendments also significantly restrict the ability of non-visa nationals to 'switch' to remain as students (for this aspect, ▶see below 274–6).

The rules require that the applicant student was 'last admitted' to the UK in possession of a valid student, or prospective student, entry clearance. The following students should not have difficulty in applying to extend their leave. They are students who, when they last entered the UK:

- did so with a student/prospective student entry clearance which, as entry clearances do, operated as leave to enter; or
- were returning to the UK from a temporary trip abroad still within the period of validity of their student/prospective student entry clearance (in which case their leave will not have lapsed).

Students who may have problems under the October 2004 rules
Examples of existing students who *may* now face difficulties in seeking to extend their leave are as follows:

- non-visa nationals (and non-specified nationals if entering for more than six months) who had been granted leave to enter as students without obtaining an entry clearance;
- those who originally entered with a student entry clearance who then extended their leave as students, and then departed and returned within the period of their extended leave i.e. so that they were re-admitted on the basis of their leave to remain after the expiry of the leave given by their student entry clearance;
- those granted leave to remain having successfully switched to stay as students (most in this category will, however, either not be caught by the rule because they are studying at degree level or above which enabled them to switch in the first place, or they may benefit from the transitional arrangements – below).

A strict application of the new rules would also prevent a non-visa national who was admitted as a prospective student, without an entry clearance, from extending their leave to remain attend a course which was below degree level. Such students will have been granted leave precisely in order for them to make arrangements to enrol on a course and then to extend their leave as students! Non-visa national prospective students may have entered without a visa or switched to remain without a visa. A further problem for non-visa nationals is that both the IDI and DSPs instruct officers that, if they arrive at the port without an entry clearance, they should not be granted leave to enter for more than six months (even if their course is for a longer period). Officers are instructed to inform such applicants that they should apply to extend their leave in-country. Such students will inevitably need to extend their leave in order to complete their existing course but the above rule apparently prevents them from doing so.

Prior to 1 October 2004, the rule relating to extensions prevented visa nationals from switching although similar wording was used and it seems that the Home Office applied the rule in a relaxed way. In practice, the Home Office may have allowed extensions provided that the applicant had *existing* leave as a student. The terms of the transitional arrangements (below) and the indications so far received by JCWI indicate that the present rules are being applied fairly strictly.

The new rule causes unnecessary problems to students and seems completely contrary to the intention behind the 'Prime Minister's Initiative' which is to simplify procedures and to make them user friendly so as to attract international students to the UK in the light of the great benefits they bring. It is to be hoped that the Home Office will either amend the new rules or relax their interpretation.

Transitional arrangements The Home Office has announced certain transitional arrangements for students who are seeking to extend their stay in the UK and who are affected by the above changes. The arrangements are that a non-visa national student who has valid leave as a student which was granted on or before 30 September 2004 will still, after that date, be able to obtain a student extension in order to study a course at below degree level even though they were not last admitted with a student entry clearance. The application to extend leave must be made while the applicant still has that existing student leave. This protection also applies to a person who entered as a prospective student on or before 30 September 2004. However, a student granted leave after 30 September 2004 will need to have been admitted with an entry clearance in order to be able to extend their leave.

The Home Office has also confirmed that, in relation to applicants who benefit from this transitional arrangement, their *later* applications to extend leave as students will also not be refused on the grounds that they do not possess an entry clearance. These transitional arrangements are set out in the IDI at Ch3, s3, para. 3.10.2 and also in a Home Office communication to UKCOSA dated 22 December 2004. For the new rules about switching to remain as a student and transitional protection for those rules, ▶see 274–6 below.

Full-time studies, maintenance and accommodation, funding, intention to leave

The Home Office requires evidence that students are still enrolled for a full-time course of study at one of the institutions referred to above, that the course and the students' abilities and intentions still meet the rules and that resources for maintenance and accommodation are still available. These things can be shown in the same way as when the student first applied to stay (above). Students who are having problems in arranging for the transfer of funds because of social or political problems at home should not be refused on this basis alone, provided that the financial difficulties are temporary (IDI, Ch3, s3, para. 3.15.7). The Home Office will look particularly hard at the question of intention to leave after their studies if the applicant: is an unsuccessful asylum applicant; has already been refused in another capacity; or appears to be moving from course to course without an intention of bringing their studies to an end.

Regular attendance

Students have to prove that they have been in regular attendance on the course they have been following. The Home Office can check attendance records with their colleges. The student application form, FLR(S), includes a section that the educational institution itself can stamp to confirm the possible number of attendances on the course, and the actual number of attendances by the student. Alternatively, the educational institution can provide a separate document confirming attendance. If the student has not attended regularly for good reasons – for example, illness – this should be explained to the Home Office and supporting evidence should be provided. If a student has been ill, a medical certificate for the period that they were unfit to attend should be obtained

Satisfactory progress including taking and passing exams

This was a new requirement in the present statement of immigration rules, HC 395. In the past, the Home Office had refused to grant extensions to students who had failed examinations on several occasions, on the grounds that they did not appear to be able to follow their course. Students who failed to sit the examinations for which they were preparing were also refused on the grounds that they did not appear to be attempting to bring their studies to an end, or did not intend to leave the UK after their studies.

Some latitude is normally given to students who can demonstrate that they are attending classes and studying, even if they are finding the course challenging. For example, where there are doubts as to progress but attendance is satisfactory and all the other requirements of the rules are met, leave may be granted with a warning that failure to produce evidence of progress may result in a refusal to grant a further extension. The Home Office will look with particular scrutiny in relation to progress at English language courses and professional courses such as accountancy, marketing and banking (detailed guidance is available to case-workers in relation to the structure of these courses, see the IDI at Ch3, s3, paras 3.6.3, 3.14.1–3.14.3). If a student has been unable to take examinations for any reason, it will be important for the institution to confirm the explanation to the Home Office.

Length of time on short courses

The rules state that extensions of leave should also not be granted to students if it would lead to a student spending more than two years on short courses. Short courses are defined as courses of less than one years' duration, but include longer courses which are abandoned before completion. Only courses 'below degree level' (see below) are caught by this rule.

Before 1 October 2004, this rule only prevented applicants from obtaining an extension if it would lead to their spending more than *four* years on short courses, and such courses were defined as those of less than *two* years' duration. There was previously, however, no exemption for courses at degree level or above (see para. 60(vi) HC 395 as amended by Cm 6339, which also inserts the definition of 'degree level' into para. 6 HC 395).

'Degree-level' study This is defined as a course which leads to a recognised UK degree at bachelor's level (BA or BSc), *or* an equivalent qualification which is at Level 6 or above of the revised National Qualifications Framework, *or* at Level 9 or above of the Scottish Credit and Qualifications Framework (para. 6 HC 395). For guidance the Home Office has produced tables which state the various 'levels' of different qualifications under both the National Qualifications Framework and the Scottish Credit and Qualifications Framework (see IDI, Ch3, s3, para. 3.17.1).

Lack of transitional arrangements and effect of the change The rules do not contain any transitional provisions relating to these changes to the 'short courses' rules and the Home Office's own notes published on the website have confirmed that there are none being operated (the IDIs also contain no transitional provisions, see Ch3, s3, para. 3.17). However, depending on how the rules are interpreted, the failure to make any transitional arrangements may mean that certain applicants cannot now be refused on the basis of the short courses rule. The rule requires that applications are refused if, 'as a result of an extension of stay', the student would spend longer than the prohibited period on short courses. It is therefore difficult to see how an extension of stay for a short course granted to a student who had *already* spent a longer period of time on short courses than is permitted would *cause* that student to remain in the UK on short courses for longer than permitted. So, arguably, granting an extension of leave, after 1 October 2004, to a student who has by that time *already* spent longer than two years on short courses, will not 'result' in them spending longer than permitted on short courses. Of course, many of the same students could not have been refused prior to 1 October 2004 because they had not spent nearly four years on short courses so as to fall foul of the rule in place then. This is because to grant such an applicant further leave after 1 October 2004, would not lead to them spending more than two years on short courses 'as a result of' an extension of leave. Students should be advised with caution but this argument is worth putting to the Home Office in the cases of students faced with a refusal in these circumstances.

Who the rule is aimed against In general terms, the aim of the short courses rule is to stop 'perpetual students', by which the Home Office means those who enrol on new courses without a properly defined study plan, without making apparent progress in their studies and students who keep breaking off one course to start another. The Home Office prefers students who follow obvious study paths to an academic goal. This rule may in particular be used against students starting a new course after they have already been studying for many years, as the Home Office may suspect that they are hoping to bring themselves within the long residence rules (▶see 151–7), in order to be able to stay permanently. In a case like this, the Home Office is also likely to doubt the student's intention to leave the UK at the end of their studies. The rule is unnecessarily restrictive for some students whose planned courses are short, or who may genuinely change their minds during courses.

If a student is changing course it is therefore important to explain in the application the reasons for abandoning a particular course, or why the student is continuing on short courses. If possible, supporting letters from course tutors or lecturers should be obtained in order to show that this is part of a regular and co-ordinated plan of studies.

Although the 'short courses' rule does not apply to applications for entry as a student, a student who had been in the UK for a long time on short courses and who then departed and, after a short absence, applied to return to do a short course, may well face refusal on the grounds of the lack of intention to leave.

How to apply to extend

Students wishing to remain in the UK longer than the initial time they have been given need to apply to the Home Office for leave before the time given runs out. As long as the application is made in time, the person applying will still be lawfully in the country while the Home Office is considering it, and during the period of any appeal.

Using the forms The application must be made on the appropriate form, FLR(S), and must be accompanied by all the documents specified on that form (or acceptable explanations as to why they are not included and an indication of when they will be). The questions asked on the form relate to: details of previous study (if the applicant was last given leave in order to study), including exams taken, qualifications obtained, course attendance; details of the proposed further studies; the time when the proposed course of studies will end; and finances. Dependants of students may be included in the application by being named on the form. From 1 August 2000, the Home Office has operated a 'Batch Postal Service for students' which enables publicly-funded institutions of further or higher education, British Council accredited English language schools, BAC accredited (see above) further and higher education institutions, independent chartered universities and students unions of all of these institutions, to submit applications on behalf of their students in 'batches'. Occasionally, some students have to apply to extend their leave because they have deferred the start or parts of their course. This will only be acceptable if there are compelling personal circumstances, for example illness or accident or as the result of a decision by the educational institution. The Home Office will expect to see documentary evidence and that the institution supports the application (IDI, Ch3, s3, para. 3.12.2.2).

Refusals If the application is made in time and is refused with the result that the applicant has no leave, there is at present an in-country right of appeal against the refusal provided the reason for the refusal is not because the applicant is seeking longer than permitted under the immigration rules (too long on short courses – see above – might be an example) (ss 88, 92 2002 Act). If the application is made late, or it has been rejected as invalid and there is no time to correct it before the initial time expires, the student will be in the UK without leave and there will also be no right of appeal at that stage. Applications to extend leave are generally covered in Chapter 6 and rights of appeal are dealt with in Chapter 34.

Switching to stay as a student

In addition to those who already have leave as a student when they wish to extend their leave (▶see 268 onwards above), the other group of 'in-country' applicants are those who wish to switch categories to stay as a student. Applications are again made using form FLR(S). The rules were changed for non-visa nationals in this group from 1 October 2004. For switching generally ▶see Chapter 7 and for switching to stay on in a different capacity after studies ▶see in particular 163–8.

The following rules only apply to 'ordinary' students. For the rules about switching to remain as a prospective student, ▶see 260. For details about switching to stay in one of the other specific categories of student, see the part below which deals directly with each of them.

Visa nationals Visa nationals may not switch to remain as students under the immigration rules. They may only seek to remain as students if they were 'last admitted' to the UK with a student, or prospective student, entry clearance (para. 60(i)(a), HC 395). As well as entry clearances for ordinary students, the Home Office has indicated that the entry clearances which count for these purposes are those for student nurses, those re-sitting exams, writing up a thesis and students' union sabbatical officers (Home Office communication to UKCOSA, 22 December 2004).

Non-visa nationals From 1 October 2004, the rules were amended so that non-visa nationals, who were not last admitted to the UK with a student or prospective student entry clearance, may now only switch to remain as students if they have been accepted on to a course of study at degree level or above (▶see 272 above for the meaning of 'degree level') (para. 60(i) HC 395 replaced by Cm 6339). The 'student entry clearances' which are acceptable for these purposes are the same as for visa nationals above. Transitional arrangements are operated for applicants who were granted a period of leave before the new rules came into force (▶see the table immediately below).

Care with switching Even if switching is permitted under the rules (or the transitional arrangements), applicants should always be wary that, if a person was admitted shortly before their decision to switch, the Home Office may investigate whether there has been a genuine change of mind. If, at the time of entry, the person had intended to remain as a student but concealed this from the immigration authorities, the Home Office could decide to treat them as an illegal entrant.

SWITCHING TO REMAIN AS A STUDENT – TRANSITIONAL ARRANGEMENTS

The Home Office is operating certain transitional arrangements for non-visa nationals who were granted leave to enter or remain in the UK before the changes in rules for switching to remain as a student which were made on 1 October 2004 (▶see 274). The arrangements are set out in a series of examples in the IDIs (IDI, ch3, s3, para. 3.10.2) and were clarified further in a Home Office communication to UKCOSA dated 22 December 2004. The relevance of the date 22 July 2004 in the transitional arrangements is that this was when the Home Office announced its intention to change the rules.

The IDI give the two following examples of those who are protected by the transitional arrangements for switching.

Example 1

A non-visa national visitor who entered the UK on or before 22 July 2004 (when the change was announced), and who makes an application for an extension of stay as a student to take a course of study below degree level, can make an in-country application within the currency of that leave.

Example 2

A non-visa national visitor who entered the UK between 23 July and 30 September 2004 could only make an application to extend leave as a student to take a course of study below degree level if the application was made on or before 30 September 2004.

The Home Office communication of 22 December 2004 gives the following further information.

1) The transitional arrangement for those granted leave before 22 July applies to those granted leave in *any* other category i.e. not just visitors (see example 1 above). It also appears to apply to anyone who has 'valid leave' granted on or before 22 July – not simply to those who 'entered' on or after that date. The switching application must, however, be made while the leave which was granted on or before 22 July is still valid.

2) The communication does not clarify whether the transitional arrangement in example 2 above applies to non-visitors but it seems likely that it does.

3) Those who benefit from the transitional arrangements on their first extension application after 1 October 2004 because they had leave in another category on or before 22 July 2004, will not be refused on *subsequent* applications which they make to extend leave on the basis of studies simply because they did not enter with a student entry clearance.

Breach of undertakings

The Home Office has recently used the general ground of refusal contained in paragraph 322(7) HC 395 to refuse switching applications. This rule gives officers discretion to refuse an application where an applicant fails to 'honour any declaration or undertaking given orally or in writing as to the intended duration and/or purpose of [his/her] stay'. Landing cards completed on arrival or ECOs notes of interview may be obtained in order to show, for example, that a visitor gave an undertaking to leave after a particular period of time.

In *Violet Tekere v SSHD*, the IAT held that a brief exchange of words with an immigration officer on arrival is normally not sufficiently formal to amount to a 'declaration or undertaking'. However, in *SSHD v Zanek Dube* (IAT), the immigration officer had only admitted the applicant on the strict understanding that she would definitely return to South Africa after her visit and she was taken to have given more than a mere statement of her present intentions. The refusal of her application to switch was therefore upheld.

RE-SITTING, WRITING UP THESES AND SABBATICAL STUDENTS

Students who need leave in order to re-sit exams or write up their thesis and sabbatical officers were added to the immigration rules from 2 October 2000. They were previously dealt with as concessions. We look at them in turn below.

Re-sitting students

WHAT THE RULES SAY

Students who wish to enter to re-sit examinations must satisfy all of the following requirements. They must (paras 69A-69F HC 395):

- meet all requirements for admission as students (see above); or alternatively, if they are no longer actually enrolled full-time on a course and attending classes, show that they met all the requirements for admission as students in the previous academic year and continue to meet the following requirements: that they intend to leave the UK at the end of their studies; that they do not intend to engage in business or take employment except authorised part-time or vacation work; that they are able to meet the costs of their course, and to maintain and accommodate themselves and any dependants without recourse to public funds;

- produce written confirmation from the education institution or independent fee-paying school that they attend, or have attended in the previous academic year, that they are required to re-sit the examination;
- provide satisfactory evidence of regular attendance during any course which has already begun, or any course which they attended in the past;
- if they have been studying with a government or international scholarship agency sponsorship that has come to an end, obtain the written consent of their official sponsor for a further period of study, and provide evidence that sufficient sponsorship funding is available;
- not previously have been granted leave to re-sit their examination.

For entry as a re-sitting student, entry clearance is mandatory for visa nationals, and for those who are specified nationals who are seeking entry for more than six months. Others do not require entry clearance. Visa nationals seeking leave to remain to re-sit exams are required to show that they were admitted to the UK with a student entry clearance (if they were visa nationals when admitted). Non-visa nationals do not need to show that they were admitted with a student entry clearance in order to extend their leave so that they can re-sit. Applications to remain should be made on FLR(S). The spouses and children of those re-sitting exams are admissible on the same terms as those of ordinary students.

Leave will be granted to cover the period of the first available re-sit with a further two months to allow the results to be received. The leave will normally be given subject to a condition restricting work to that which is generally approved. Under the rules, leave in order to re-sit an exam will only be granted once.

Postgraduate students who are writing up a thesis

WHAT THE RULES SAY

Students who wish to enter to write up a thesis must satisfy all of the following requirements (paras 69C-69L HC 395):

- meet all the requirements for admission as students (see above); or alternatively, if they are no longer actually enrolled full-time on a course and attending classes (note that most research students don't 'attend classes'), show that they met all the requirements for admission as students in the previous academic year and continue to meet the following requirements: that they intend to leave the UK at the end of their studies; that they do not intend to engage in business or take employment except authorised part-time or vacation work; that they are able to meet the costs of their course, and to maintain and accommodate themselves and any dependants without recourse to public funds;

- demonstrate that they are a postgraduate student enrolled in an educational institution as either a full-time, part-time, or writing-up student, and that their application is supported by the educational institution;

- if they have been studying with a government or international scholarship agency sponsorship that has come to an end, obtain the written consent of their official sponsor for a further period of study, and provide evidence that sufficient sponsorship funding is available;

- show that they have not previously been granted leave to write up the same thesis.

For entry as a student writing up a thesis, entry clearance is mandatory for visa nationals, and for those who are specified nationals who are seeking entry for more than six months. Others do not require entry clearance. Leave will normally be granted for a period of 12 months. Visa nationals seeking leave to remain to write up a thesis are required to show that they were admitted to the UK with a student entry clearance (if they were visa nationals when admitted). Non-visa nationals do not need to show that they were admitted with a student entry clearance in order to extend their leave so that they can complete their thesis. Applications to remain should be made on FLR(S).

Extensions beyond the 12-month period to write up the same thesis may only be granted exceptionally. Students in this position should explain why they could not complete their thesis – for example, due to prolonged illness, or where the thesis submitted needs to be rewritten because it has not reached the required standard. A letter from the institution will be required. The leave will normally be given subject to a condition restricting work to that which is generally approved. The spouses and children of those writing up a thesis are admissible on the same terms as those of ordinary students.

Students' union sabbatical officers

Sabbatical officers are elected by their student unions normally for one year, and are paid, full-time workers. The requirements for entry, or for an extension of leave, are similar to the requirements for those seeking to re-sit their examinations or write up theses, and are set out at paragraphs 87A-87F of the immigration rules (HC 395). They must currently be students (or must have been students in the year before they took up their sabbatical) and must be able to maintain and accommodate themselves. After their sabbatical they must intend to either complete their studies or leave the UK. Applicants must not intend to engage in business or to take employment except in connection with their sabbatical. If they are granted leave it will be subject to conditions permitting them to work as a sabbatical officer.

For entry as a sabbatical officer, entry clearance is mandatory for visa nationals, and for those who are specified nationals who are seeking entry for more than six months. Others do not require entry clearance. Leave will normally be granted for a period of 12 months and may be extended to up to two years from the date on which the applicant was first given leave as a student sabbatical (FLR(S) should be used). Visa nationals seeking leave to remain must show that they were admitted to the UK with a student entry clearance (if they were visa nationals when they were admitted). Non-visa nationals do not need to show that they were admitted with a student entry clearance in order to extend their leave.

Unlike other students, there is no provision in the immigration rules for the admission of the dependants of students' union sabbatical officers.

MEDICAL AND DENTAL STUDIES INCLUDING TRAINING

Some studies normally include a large amount of practical work – nursing and architecture, for example. However, studies involving a high degree of practical work are not treated consistently under the immigration rules. Medical students are generally counted as students for immigration purposes even when doing their practical work. There are specific provisions in the student rules for student nurses and midwives; doctors, dentists and general practitioners engaging in postgraduate training; medical graduates seeking to take the 'PLAB' (Professional and Linguistic Assessment Board) test; and medical or dental graduates intending to take a clinical attachment or dental observer post.

Those seeking entry for PLAB tests were previously dealt with as a special category of visitor and those wishing to do a clinical attachment or dental observer post were, until recently, covered by a concession outside the rules. All are now covered under the immigration rules in the section dealing with students. Certain other trainees who obtain a professional qualification while working as a trainee at a firm, require work permits for parts of their training, which the employer has to obtain from Work Permits (UK) under its Training and Work Experience Scheme (TWES) (►see 440–3).

Need for entry clearance for medical/dental studies

In all of the categories involving medical or dental studies, entry clearance in order to obtain entry is mandatory for visa nationals and specified nationals seeking to enter for more than six months (note that all non-visa nationals are effectively 'specified nationals' from 13 November 2005). Public funds conditions will generally be imposed on the leave granted. Those seeking entry as postgraduate doctors or dentists require entry clearance in all cases unless they are a British national without the right of abode (▶see 282).

For the rules about opportunities for switching to stay in the UK *after* the period of studies/training in these categories, ▶see 165–8.

Student nurses

WHAT THE RULES SAY

Nursing/midwifery students have to demonstrate all of the following (paras 63-69 HC 395):

- they have been accepted for training as a student nurse or midwife, leading to a recognised British qualification, or are already qualified abroad and are enrolled for an adaptation course leading to registration in the UK under the Central Council for Nursing, Midwifery and Health Visiting, and did not gain this acceptance by misrepresentation;
- they have been accepted for a course of study in a recognised nursing educational establishment offering nursing training that meets the requirements of the United Kingdom Central Council for Nursing, Midwifery and Health Visiting (NMC);
- they are able and intend to follow the course of training;
- they do not intend to work or engage in business other than their nursing training;
- they intend to leave the UK at the end of the course;
- they have sufficient funds for accommodation and maintenance in the UK of themselves and any dependants without recourse to public funds – a Department of Health bursary can contribute towards sufficient funds.

People wishing to train as nurses may also enter as prospective students, in order to come for interviews at hospitals and to finalise arrangements for their training. Although the rules specify that nurses should intend to leave at the end of their course, the IDIs state that this is not insisted upon because nurses may be able to switch to work permit employment after they have completed their courses and gained NMC registration (Ch3, s5, para. 5.2.1(5)). Visa nationals are not able to switch status while in the UK in order to stay as student nurses. They must have been last admitted to the UK with a student, or prospective student, entry clearance in order to extend their leave. Non-visa nationals may switch to stay as student nurses. Extensions of leave are permitted under the rules, but only to allow applicants up to four years to obtain their qualification, and provided that the applicant has not come to the end of a government or international scholarship – or, if they have, that they have the written consent of the official sponsor to continue their studies (form FLR(S) should be used).

Student nurses will generally be granted leave for the length of their training course and with a condition restricting the work which they may do. The general approval to work granted to them is that, before the commencement of their course, they are permitted to work for a maximum of eight weeks at the hospital at which they are to be trained. After the course has begun, they may work more than the normal 20 hours per week during term time but only in employment which is a necessary part of their course and with the agreement of their educational institution (IDI, Ch3, s5, para. 5.6). Nurses who wish to attend post-registration specialised training must qualify for a TWES permit (▶see 440–3). For switching to remain after the period granted as a student nurse, ▶see 165–6.

The spouses and children of student nurses are admissible on the same terms as those of other students.

Note that, after the cut off date for the *Handbook*, the Home Office introduced a further category of entry as an 'overseas qualified nurse or midwife' (paras 69M–69R, HC 395 inserted from 30 November 2005 by HC 645).

Postgraduate doctors and dentists

The postgraduate medical student rules were amended on 18 December 2002 (see paras 70–75 HC 395 as substituted by HC 104). They were changed yet again from 19 July 2005 (paras 70-75 HC 395 as substituted by HC 299).

WHAT THE RULES SAY

Trainee doctors and dentists must meet all of the following requirements:

- they must *either* be
  - a graduate from a medical school or dental school who has a confirmed place on a recognised Foundation Programme to continue their training as a doctor or dentist in the UK; or
  - is a doctor or dentist who has full, limited or temporary registration with the General Medical Council or General Dental Council, or who is eligible for that registration and who intends to take basic or higher specialist training in the UK in a hospital or the Community Health Services or in General Practice or in a combination of these;
- they must hold a letter from the Postgraduate Dean responsible for their training in the UK approving their training plan and recommending the period of leave that should be granted;
- they must intend to leave the UK at the end of their period of leave if they are not granted leave to remain in the UK as either:
  - a doctor or dentist undertaking a period of clinical attachment or a dental observer post;
  - a work permit holder;
  - a highly-skilled migrant;
  - a person intending to establish themselves in business or self-employment;

– an innovator; and

- if their study at medical school or subsequently was sponsored by a government or an international scholarship agency, they have the written consent of their sponsor to obtain leave as a postgraduate doctor or dentist; and

- they must be able to maintain and accommodate themselves and any dependants without recourse to public funds.

Those seeking leave to *enter* must have an entry clearance unless they are a BN(O), a BOTC, a BOC, a BPP or a British Subject under the BNA 1981. Leave will be given for up to 26 months in order to take a Foundation Programme for up to three years to train as a doctor or dentist in a hospital or the community health services or in general practice (or a combination of these).

Those seeking to extend leave to remain in this category may do so in-country if they have existing leave in this category or if they have leave as:

- a student or student nurse;
- a doctor taking the PLAB test;
- a doctor or dentist undertaking a period of clinical attachment or a dental observer post; or
- a work permit holder.

Leave will be granted for the same periods as indicated above provided all of the above rules (save for the need for entry clearance) are satisfied. Applicants who have already been granted leave under these rules will not be granted leave which, in total, would be more than:

- 26 months to complete the Foundation Programme;
- three years to complete basic specialist training if the applicant has not already completed a Foundation Programme; and
- four years to complete basic specialist training if the applicant had not already completed a Foundation Programme.

For switching to remain in a different category after the period of leave ▶see 166 and for switching generally ▶see Chapter 7.

Medical graduates seeking to take the PLAB test

The category of students seeking leave for the purposes of taking their Professional and Linguistic Assessment Board (PLAB) test was introduced into the rules from 15 March 2005 (HC 346).

WHAT THE RULES SAY

Medical graduates seeking entry to take the PLAB test have to show that they meet all of the following requirements (paras 75A-75F HC 395):

- they are a graduate from a medical school who is intending to take the PLAB test in the UK;
- they can provide documentary evidence of a confirmed test date or of their eligibility to take the PLAB test;
- they meet the following requirements of visitors to the UK: they do not intend to take employment or produce goods or provide services in the UK, do not intend to study at a maintained school, can maintain and accommodate themselves without recourse to public funds or taking employment, and can meet the outward costs of the return journey;
- they intend to leave the UK at the end of the leave granted *unless* they are successful in their PLAB tests and are granted leave to remain as a postgraduate doctor or trainee general practitioner (▶see above); to take a clinical attachment (▶see below); as a work permit holder for employment as a doctor; or under the Highly Skilled Migrant Programme as a general practitioner (▶see 487). (For further details about switching, ▶see 167.)

Students in this category will be granted entry for up to six months. It is not possible to switch into this category, but students granted entry in order to take their PLAB test may obtain extensions of up to six months at a time provided that they meet the above rules. In cases of extensions of leave, however, eligibility to take the PLAB test will not be enough, applicants must have documentary evidence of a confirmed test date. The maximum period of time a person can spend in the UK in this category is 18 months in total. Students applying for extensions for longer than this should expect to be refused.

Medical or dental graduates intending to take a clinical attachment or dental observer post

The category of students seeking leave for the purposes of taking a clinical attachment or dental observer post was introduced into the rules from 15 March 2005 (HC 346).

WHAT THE RULES SAY

Medical or dental graduates intending to take a clinical attachment or dental observer post must demonstrate all of the following in order to be granted entry (paras 75G-75M HC 395):

- they are graduates from a medical or dental school and intend to take a clinical attachment or dental observer post in the UK;
- they can provide documentary evidence of the clinical attachment or dental observer post, which must be unpaid and must involve only observation – not treatment – of patients;
- they must meet the following requirements of visitors to the UK: they do not intend to take employment or produce goods or provide services in the UK, do not intend to study at a maintained school, can maintain

and accommodate themselves without recourse to public funds or taking employment, and can meet the outward costs of the return journey;

- they intend to leave the UK at the end of their leave in this category, *unless* they are granted leave to remain as: a postgraduate doctor, dentist, or trainee general practitioner (▶see above); a work permit holder for employment as a doctor or dentist; or a general practitioner under the Highly Skilled Migrant Programme (▶see 167–8 for this switching).

The purpose of this category is to enable graduate medical and dental students to spend periods of time on unpaid attachments observing medical and dental practice in the area of their specialism. Others do not require entry clearance. Students in this category may be granted leave to enter for the period of their clinical attachment or dental observer post up to a maximum of 12 months. One of the requirements of the rules is that applicants do not intend to work. When this category appeared as a concession in the rules, officers were guided to grant leave on conditions prohibiting work (IDI, Ch3, s6, annex J, para. 6). It is likely, therefore, that those granted leave under this new category under the rules will also be given conditions prohibiting work.

Extensions may be granted to those who have leave in this category, provided the same rules as for 'on entry' applications are satisfied. If the extension application is successful, leave may be granted 'for the period of [the applicant's] clinical attachment or dental observer post' (para. 75L HC 395).

It is also possible to switch to remain *in* this category if the applicant was previously given leave to enter or remain in one of the following categories (▶see on this switching, 166–7, 172):

- for the purpose of taking the PLAB test (see above), and having passed both parts of that test;
- as a postgraduate doctor, dentist or trainee general practitioner (see above); or
- as a work permit holder for employment in the UK as a doctor or dentist.

FEES AND STUDENT GRANTS AND LOANS

It is only possible to look at fees and student grants and loans very briefly. Eligibility for home fees and student support can be complex and for full details of student fees, support, finance and funding, reference should be made to the UKCOSA (The Council for International Education) Manual 2005. A further useful guide is available from the Department for Education and Skills on their website (www.dfes.gov.uk/student support).

Student fees: home and overseas students

Overseas students normally have to meet the full cost of their courses of study in the UK. The Education (Fees and Awards) Regulations 1997 and the Education (Fees and Awards) (Scotland) Regulations 1997 allow educational institutions to charge higher fees to overseas students, and these can be several times higher than home student fees. In order to qualify as home students, students must satisfy their educational institution that they meet *all* of the following conditions:

- they have been 'ordinarily resident' (►see 1274 and 303), in the UK and Islands (i.e. the Channel Islands and the Isle of Man) throughout the three-year period preceding the 'relevant date', which will be 1 January, 1 April or 1 September closest to the beginning of the first term of their course;

- at no time during this period were they in the UK and Islands 'wholly or mainly for the purpose of receiving full-time education';

- they are 'settled' (ordinarily resident with no restrictions on the time that they are permitted to remain) in the UK on the 'relevant date' (see above). Those who are exempt from immigration control, such as diplomats, will generally not qualify. However, discretion may be exercised for those working for international organisations.

There are different requirements for refugees and others granted leave following a claim for asylum and for family members of these groups (see below). Allowances are also made, in relation to the residence period, for those who have lived or worked temporarily outside the UK and Islands for all or part of the three-year period. Separate requirements also apply to students who are EEA and Swiss nationals (►see below).

So, for example, to qualify for home student fees for a degree course which begins in October 2005, a person will need to show that they are 'settled' in the UK on 1 September 2005 (the 'relevant date') and that they have been ordinarily resident in the UK and Islands since 1 September 2002. They cannot have been here for any of that time wholly or mainly for the purpose of full-time studies. An institution is likely to conclude that someone who was in the UK with leave as a student at any point in the relevant three years cannot qualify. However, for example, a dependant who attended school in the UK and who wishes to enter higher education may satisfy the requirements because they were not necessarily here for the purpose of receiving full-time education themselves. They were here simply accompanying their parents. Those who have been granted leave under various other categories of the rules may also qualify. It is for the various educational institutions to apply these rules and make decisions about who qualifies as a home student. The guidance on fees issued to institutions in England and Wales by the Department for Education and Skills suggests that the above criteria should be strictly applied.

Exemptions

Those in any of the following groups do not have to satisfy the above requirements in order to qualify for home fees:

- those granted asylum as refugees who are ordinarily resident in the UK and Islands;

- those granted leave following rejection of an asylum application (usually exceptional leave, humanitarian protection, discretionary leave or indefinite leave under the ILR family exercise) and who are ordinarily resident in the UK and Islands;
- spouses, 'civil partners' (▶300) and children of those in the above two groups.

These separate requirements apply immediately upon grant of refugee status or other leave. So, even if the students have already started on a course, they will only have to pay home fees on the next occasion that fees are due. These separate requirements applied to refugees have become more important since August 2005 when the Home Office began granting only limited leave to refugees, so that they do not become 'settled' straight away (▶see 720 onwards). Refugees may not therefore become settled for some years, and until they do, will not be able to qualify for home status under the ordinary rules.

Student support

Support available

Student support is generally available for home students in higher education and can take the form of:

- a grant towards tuition fees, depending upon the student's income and that of their family;
- grants for low-income students towards living costs;
- student loans to help towards living costs (full-time courses only);
- grants for dependants and various other grants to help towards childcare, travel, books and equipment etc;
- grants for disabled students;
- certain other additional bursaries, grants and loans depending on the student's circumstances; for example, additional awards for those on nursing, other healthcare and teacher training courses.

For the 2004/05 academic year, the most a home student had to pay towards tuition fees was £1,150, and they may not have had to pay any tuition fees at all in Scotland.

Those required to pay home fees rather than overseas student fees (see above) are generally eligible for the above forms of student support. However, those who have been granted leave following the refusal of an asylum application, usually exceptional leave, humanitarian protection or discretionary leave, additionally need to demonstrate that they have been ordinarily resident in the UK for three years not wholly or mainly for the purpose of full-time education in order to qualify for student support.

In order to get student support, it is necessary for the student to apply to the local education authority where they live in England and Wales. In

Scotland, applications are made to the Students Awards Agency and, in Northern Ireland, the application is to the appropriate Education and Library Board.

Courses for which support is available

Student support is available for the following courses of higher education at publicly-funded institutions:

- a first degree, such as a BA, BSc or BEd;
- a Diploma of Higher Education (DipHE);
- a Higher National Diploma (HND);
- a Higher National Certificate (HNC);
- a teacher training course;
- generally all courses that are higher than 'A' level including courses that prepare students for professional examinations.

Education courses for asylum-seekers

Asylum-seekers in higher education will not qualify for home fees or student support under the above rules. The Learning and Skills Council provides funding for further education courses in England and they will fund asylum-seekers and their families, ensuring that only home fees or no fees at all are payable. In order to qualify, the asylum-seeker or their dependants must be either:

- supported through financial assistance by the National Asylum Support Service (NASS);
- in receipt of means-tested benefits;
- in receipt of assistance under the terms of the Immigration and Asylum Act 1999 or the Children Act 1989;
- assisted by a local social services department under the National Assistance Act 1948; or
- an unaccompanied minor asylum-seeker between 16 and 18 years of age and in the care of a local authority social services department.

Similar eligibility conditions apply to asylum-seekers and their dependants in Wales. In Scotland, part-time courses funded by the Scottish Further Education Funding Council may be available to asylum-seekers, their spouses and children. The only funded full-time courses available to them are English as a second or other language (ESOL) courses. There are no specific funding provisions for asylum-seekers in Northern Ireland.

Education courses for others

In addition to those covered by the fees and student support regulations, the Learning and Skills Council will fund further education courses in England for the following groups:

- those who have been living lawfully in England for three years before the start of their course, even if they are not settled, unless they have been given leave as students and their leave expires before the end of the course they plan to take;
- those who have exceptional leave to enter or remain, humanitarian protection or discretionary leave, their spouses and children, whether or not the leave was granted following an unsuccessful asylum application;
- those who have become settled within the last three years before the start of their course;
- those who have a settled spouse, to whom they have been married, and with whom they have been living in the UK for one year;
- 16–18 years olds accompanying parents who have the right of abode or leave to enter or remain in the UK;
- 16–18 year old dependants of teachers coming to the UK on a teacher-exchange scheme;
- 16–18 year olds entering the UK (where not accompanied by their parents) who hold full British citizen passports, or 16-18 year olds whose passports have been endorsed to show they have the right of abode in the UK.

EEA STUDENTS

Most EEA nationals are not subject to UK immigration law and rules but to European Community legislation ▶see Section 6 for full details. This means that they do not require leave to enter the UK when they are travelling between EEA countries to exercise their free movement rights. Swiss nationals enjoy the same rights and our references to EEA nationals are intended to include Swiss nationals. They may move in order to work, to seek work, to do business, be self-employed or to provide or receive services. Similarly, EEA nationals who are non-economically active can move between EEA countries subject to their having sufficient funds to maintain and accommodate themselves. EEA nationals are able to obtain 'residence permits', which confirm their right to live in a particular EEA country.

There are two main categories of EEA nationals who may have rights as students in the UK. The first category are those who qualify under the specific directive on students. The second category are those who have established and retained their status as workers under the terms of the European treaties.

We deal with both in turn below. However, for details about children attending educational courses (and their carers) where the EEA national is no longer in the UK, ▶see 531–4.

First category

As to the first category of EEA students, their rights are contained in EC Directive 93/96. This provides for free movement for students:

- enrolled at recognised educational establishments for the principal purpose of following vocational training courses; and
- who have declared that they have sufficient resources to avoid them or their families becoming a burden on public funds (for the test for 'becoming a burden' on public funds ▶see 522–4 dealing with 'self-sufficient persons') ; and
- who are covered by all-risk sickness insurance.

These students have a right of residence for the period of their studies, and are entitled to residence permits for that duration if they apply for them. Their spouses and children, of whatever nationality, can also stay for this period, and will be issued with residence documents, on request. The directive refers to 'vocational' courses, but in practice even those attending general courses probably have free movement rights (see the ECJ case of *D'Hoop*). EEA students' earnings or potential earnings can be considered to show that they will be able to support themselves. As EEA nationals, they are also free to work without needing separate permission.

Second category

The second category of EEA students are those who have worked here before studying. Their rights are contained within EC Regulation 1612/68, relating to the free movement of workers. They may retain the more extensive right of residence which goes with that status. This has advantages for family members, who will benefit from the usual five-year residence permits.

Students who are no longer actually working will retain their status as workers if they:

- have been in employment since last entering the UK; and
- were engaged in economic activity which was not marginal or ancillary but 'genuine and effective'; and
- intend to study on a vocational course related to their previous employment in the UK or, in the case of involuntary unemployment, intend to transfer to a new employment sector.

Students who work part-time whilst studying, provided the work is not marginal or ancillary, may argue that they are exercising their right to work and will fall within this category as workers anyway.

EEA students' rights to pay home fees and receive student support

The following EEA students may be entitled to pay home fees and are eligible to receive student support:

- EU nationals and their children of any nationality, but not their spouses. This category does not include nationals of Iceland, Liechtenstein or Norway, which are member states of the EEA but not the EU;
- EEA workers, their spouses or civil partners, and children of any nationality.

The above groups will qualify to pay home fees if:

- they have been ordinarily resident in the EEA or Switzerland for the three years leading up to the 'relevant date' (▶see 285); and
- their residence in the EEA or Switzerland was at no point during those three years wholly or mainly for the purposes of receiving full-time education.

Under the regulations governing student support, EEA workers and their dependants are entitled to the full range of student support (▶see 286–7 for the types of student support). On the other hand, only limited student support in the form of grants towards their fees are available to EU nationals and their children. Unlike EEA workers and their qualifying dependants, they are not eligible for student loans towards living costs under the regulations as drafted.

However, the European Court of Justice (ECJ) has recently ruled in the case of *Bidar* that the regulations are discriminatory. EU nationals and their children who do not fall into the second category as workers, and who have been refused grants or loans towards living costs, should invite their local education authority or funding body to reconsider any student support application, using the argument that the current regulations have been found to be unlawful. Current or former EU students who have had to abandon their studies or who were not able to take them up because they were wrongly refused funding, may be able to claim compensation and should seek advice. The Department of Education and Skills has confirmed to UKCOSA that it is considering the implications of the *Bidar* case.

Section 4 **Family members**

Chapter 11
Spouses, unmarried partners, same-sex
partners and fiancé(e)s   293

Recent developments   295

The different circumstances covered in this chapter   301

People coming to the UK as spouses, unmarried
(including same-sex) partners, or fiancé(e)s of
people settled in the UK   303

People who have been admitted for the
'probationary period' who wish to apply to settle
in the UK   329

People in the United Kingdom for other purposes
who wish to 'switch' to stay in the UK permanently
with their spouse or partner, who is settled in the UK   332

People who want to stay in the UK with their
spouses or partners but who cannot satisfy the
immigration rules   337

People who want to stay in the UK although they
no longer have a relationship with a partner   344

People who wish to accompany or join a spouse or
partner in the UK who is here with limited leave   352

Chapter 12
Children   357

Children joining or staying with both parents
settled in the UK   360

Children joining one parent in the UK   367

Children joining a person who is not a parent   371

Children being joined by parents with whom they
have contact   372

Parents of children at school   375

4

Children accompanying or joining parents in the UK
who have limited leave   376

Adopted children   379

Children whose parents may be forced to leave   386

Unaccompanied children in the UK   390

Children born in the UK   393

Chapter 13
Other dependent relatives   397

Parents and grandparents aged 65 or over   399

Parents and grandparents under 65 years, and
other relatives   405

11 Spouses, unmarried partners, same-sex partners and fiancé(e)s

This section covers the rights of members of the family of a person who already has a right to be in the United Kingdom to accompany, join and stay here with them. This chapter deals with spouses, unmarried partners, same-sex partners and fiancé(e)s. Under the immigration rules, unmarried partners, whether heterosexual or same-sex, are now treated in the same way. We have therefore used the term 'unmarried partner' to refer to both.

Chapter 12 covers the rights of children to join or stay with parents and relatives in the UK and, in some cases, to have their parents join them.

Chapter 13 looks at the rights of admission and stay of all other relatives.

Most of the rights of family members addressed in this section are set out in detail in the immigration rules. In addition, there are certain concessions that are also taken account of here; for example, enforcement policies dealing with situations where there are family members in the UK.

Since the last edition of the *Handbook*, there have been significant changes to the immigration rules affecting spouses and partners. These changes are all incorporated into this chapter, but we begin by summarising those changes (▶see the table at 295–6). We then look at the changes affecting the ability to marry in the UK made by the Asylum and Immigration (Treatment of Claimants etc.) Act 2004 (▶296–300), and then at the proposed changes to the rules that will flow from the Civil Partnership Act 2004 (▶300–1).

The main part of this chapter The main part of this chapter deals with the various circumstances in which spouses/partners may wish to enter or stay in the UK. We have divided these situations into six (▶see 301–2 below). The chapter then looks at each of those situations in turn.

Family rules elsewhere in the *Handbook*

Certain family members, although partly covered in the rules, are dealt with not in these three chapters but elsewhere in the *Handbook*:

- Family reunion with refugees is covered in Chapter 25. Chapter 28 discusses the family members of those with humanitarian protection, discretionary leave and exceptional leave (having been refused asylum) (▶875–9).

- Applications for the dependants of those *seeking* asylum are dealt with at ▶691–94.

Other rights of family members

In considering the position of family members, it is important to remember that some people may benefit from parts of the law other than the immigration rules and Home Office policies. This applies to the following family members.

Family members of EEA nationals Family members of EEA and Swiss nationals exercising rights of free movement have independent rights. This includes family members from those countries which acceded to the EU on 1 May 2004. Ireland is also an EEA country, so foreign spouses of Irish nationals who have come to the UK can generally be admitted. Some family members of UK nationals may make use of free movement rights as a result of the decision in the case of **Surinder Singh**. This establishes that British citizens who have exercised rights of free movement within the EEA and who wish to return to the UK may be accompanied by their dependants. For details about the rights of EEA family members, ▶see 526–40.

Commonwealth citizen women Some Commonwealth citizen women who married British citizen men have the 'right of abode', and therefore do not have to meet the requirements of the immigration rules. These are women who were Commonwealth citizens on 31 December 1982 (the day before the British Nationality Act 1981 came into force), and who were married on or before that date to British citizen men, or to men with the right of abode. Before they travel, these women should apply to a British post for a 'certificate of entitlement to the right of abode', for which a fee is payable.

Family members of those exempt from control Those who are exempt from immigration control (diplomats, members of the armed forces and others) and the rights of their family members are discussed together at ▶472–6. Certain family members are treated as exempt from control. Family members of armed forces members who are exempt are provided for by recent changes to the immigration rules.

Article 8 ECHR Even if a person cannot satisfy the immigration rules, they may be able to establish a right to come to or stay in the UK under Article 8 ECHR, the 'right to respect for private and family life'. Article 8 does not give all couples or other family members a right to live in the UK on the basis that one partner has a right to be in the UK. One of the most important principles under Article 8 is that it does not guarantee to a couple a choice of which country they wish to live in. However, in some cases it does benefit applicants who cannot satisfy the rules; in particular if it is not possible for them to establish their family life elsewhere. The effect of Article 8 is not covered in this section, but dealt with at ▶820–50.

RECENT DEVELOPMENTS

The recent changes to the immigration rules affecting spouses and partners are incorporated into the text of this chapter, but the most important ones are summarised in the table below. Further change is anticipated in the rules concerning dependants, because the government's 'five-year strategy' refers to the need to 'end chain migration', so that there is 'no immediate or automatic right for relatives to bring in more relatives'. What precisely is planned is not yet clear.

4

RECENT DEVELOPMENTS AFFECTING SPOUSES/PARTNERS

The *most significant* changes in the immigration rules, since the last edition of the *Handbook* (Spring 2002), affecting spouses and partners, are as follows. Several of these changes were originally proposed in the Home Office White Paper that preceded the 2002 Act, *Secure Borders, Safe Haven* (February 2002).

From 18 December 2002 (HC 104)

- The 'Domestic Violence Concession' has been incorporated as part of the immigration rules (paras 289A-C HC 395 added by HC 104, HC 538) (▶345–51). However, the kind of evidence needed to show that there has been domestic violence that has caused the relationship to permanently break down is still determined by the Home Office outside the rules.

From 1 April 2003 (HC 538)

- A specific definition of 'intention to live permanently with the other' has been introduced into the rules. It requires:

  'An intention to live together, evidenced by a clear commitment from both parties that they will live together permanently in the United Kingdom immediately following the outcome of the application in question or as soon as circumstances permit thereafter.'

- In certain cases of spouses and unmarried partners whose relationship has subsisted for at least four years, but who have been living together outside the UK, the applicant is entitled to obtain indefinite leave to enter immediately – i.e. without having to serve the 'probationary period' (paras 281(i), 282, 295A(i), 295B HC 395 as amended by HC 538) (▶see 324–5).

- The 'probationary period' served as a spouse when first admitted to, or given leave to remain in, the UK has increased from 12 months to 24 months. Through this process of 'levelling up', the probationary periods for spouses and unmarried partners are now the same.

- Those who have only been admitted to the UK for very short-term purposes (six months or less) are not able to switch to remain as spouses (▶see 333–4).

5) Applicants in heterosexual partnerships, who are free to marry, can now qualify under the rules. Previously, the unmarried partner rule had only allowed

heterosexual couples to obtain leave if they were 'legally unable to marry' under UK law, which would be the case if one party was still married to someone else. Now applicants who choose not to marry are provided for by rules (HC 538 and Cm 5949).

From 21 December 2004 (HC 164)

- In all applications as a spouse, unmarried partner or fiancé(e), both the applicant and the sponsor must be aged at least 18 years on the date the applicant arrives in the UK – or for in-country applications, on the date leave to remain would be granted (see HC 164 amending paras 277, 289AA, 295AA HC 395)

Marrying in the United Kingdom – changes made by the 2004 Act

From 1 February 2005, the Asylum and Immigration (Treatment of Claimants, etc.) Act 2004 has introduced important new measures concerning the ability of certain people actually to get married in the UK (sections 19–25). The detail is set out in the Immigration (Procedure for Marriage) Regulations 2005, which came into force on the same date (and see also, the Registration of Marriages (Amendment) Regulations 2005). The new procedures operate to prevent certain marriages from taking place in the UK.

The new procedures apply to a proposed marriage if *all three* of the following conditions are met.

1) Notice to marry is given to the Registrar on or after 1 February 2005.

2) One of the parties to the marriage is 'subject to immigration control'. For these purposes, this means that they are not an EEA national and that they require leave to be in the UK (even if they have an existing grant of leave).

3) If the marriage is in England or Wales, the marriage will be solemnised by a Registrar of Marriages. So, in England and Wales, the procedures do not apply to marriages solemnised according to the rites of a Church of England religious ceremony. This exception does not apply to marriages solemnised in Scotland and Northern Ireland – the new procedures may apply to marriages in those countries, wherever they are solemnised.

Marriage requirements

If the new procedures apply to the proposed marriage (see above), three alternative requirements must be met before the couple will be permitted to marry in the UK. *Either* the party subject to control must have an entry clearance for the purpose of marriage, *or* must have a certificate of approval for marriage issued by the Secretary of State, *or* they must be exempt from the need to obtain an entry clearance or a certificate of approval.

Entry clearance for the purpose of marriage The party to the marriage who is subject to immigration control must hold an entry clearance either as a fiancé(e) (▶see 303–4 onwards, 318 onwards), or as a marriage visitor (▶see 239–40).

Exempt groups The only people who are, at present, exempt from the need to obtain entry clearance, or a certificate of approval are those who are 'settled' in the UK. For these purposes, the same definition of 'settled' is applied as that contained in the immigration rules (▶see 302–3).

Certificate of approval If the party who is subject to immigration control does not hold one of the required entry clearances and is not settled, then specific permission, in the form of a 'certificate of approval' for marriage, will have to be obtained from the Home Office. The application is made on Form COA (Marriage), which can be downloaded from the Home Office website. A written application to the Home Office must be made accompanied by a fee of £135 (it can be paid by cheque or postal order, or debit or credit card). Where both parties are subject to control, both will require a certificate of approval, and separate fees must be paid.

The form must be sent to the Home Office Initial Consideration Unit marked 'Certificate of Approval (Marriage)'. It is not possible to apply in person at any of the Home Office's Public Enquiry Offices. The form asks for: details and nationality of the applicant; their name at birth (if different); address; daytime telephone number; Home Office reference number (if held); information on whether they have been granted leave to enter or remain for over six months; where the applicant has been granted leave to enter or remain for less than six months, details about their present immigration status, the length of their relationship, and whether there are any children by the fiancé(e); whether they have previously been married. Similar questions are asked on the form about the fiancé(e). Documentary evidence is also required: two passport-sized photographs of the applicant and fiancé(e); their passports or travel documents; where either have been married before, evidence that they are free to marry. The form must be signed by both the applicant and fiancé(e).

During the passage of the Act, the Minister explained that people granted more than six months' leave would normally be granted approval to marry (Des Browne MP, *Hansard*, 12 July 2004). The newly issued IDI state (at Ch 1, s15) that, in order to qualify for a certificate of approval, an applicant must have:

- leave that was granted for over six months; and
- at least three months of the leave remaining at the time of making the application.

This is obviously intended to permit those who would be entitled under the rules to switch to stay as a spouse to obtain approval (however, the rules on switching may be wider than the instructions on approval; ▶see 333–4 for switching to remain as a spouse). The purpose of requiring there to be at least three months of leave remaining is that the Home Office expects that all of the following will take place before leave expires: an application for a certificate of approval will be made and decided; notice of marriage will be given; the waiting period between given notice of marriage and the ceremony will pass; the marriage will take place; an application for leave to remain on the basis of marriage will be made (see Home Office letter to ILPA, 28 January 2005).

The Home Office gave further details of how leave will be calculated for these purposes in a letter to Camden Community Law Centre dated 20 July 2005. In that letter it was stated that an applicant's leave will be calculated from their original date of entry if the applicant leaves and re-enters to resume the leave already granted. However, if the applicant's leave lapses after they leave the UK or they enter with new leave because they are entering in a new capacity, the period of leave is calculated from this latest date of entry. If an applicant is granted leave in-country, the period of leave is calculated from the date of the original entry (it is assumed that this only applies if the extension application was made within time).

Even if the above conditions are met, a certificate will be refused if there is an impediment to marriage – for example, if the relationship is consanguineous, or if one of the parties is already married.

It was also originally stated by the government that, for those whose immigration status would prevent them from switching, approval might still be given if it was unreasonable to expect them to return to apply for entry clearance. The IDI state that approval may still be granted if there are 'exceptionally compassionate features, which would make it inappropriate for the person to be required to go abroad to obtain an entry clearance' (IDI, Ch 1, s15). Examples might be where the applicant is in the late stages of pregnancy and unable to travel, or if refusal of approval would result in a child having to be born out of wedlock (see statement of the Minister, Lord Rooker, *Hansard*, 28 June 2004). Further guidance about the discretionary grant of a certificate is contained in the IDI (Ch1, s15, annex NN).

The certificate of approval will be issued as valid for three months from the date on which it is issued, or it will be valid up until the date when the applicant's existing leave expires (whichever is the less). There is no right of appeal against negative decisions refusing to grant a certificate of approval, and the only remedy is by judicial review.

Marriage procedures

If the new provisions apply to the proposed marriage, then before the registrar may marry the couple the following procedures apply.

- In England and Wales, the notice of marriage must be given to a registrar of one of 76 specified registration districts. The specified registration districts for England and Wales are contained in Schedule 1 of the above

Regulations. In Scotland and Northern Ireland, notice must also be given, but all registry offices are designated.

- In England and Wales, both parties to the marriage must *together* give notice to the registrar in person of their proposed marriage. This means that both parties must attend before the registrar with evidence of: their entry clearance/settlement in the UK/certificate of approval (whichever applies – see above); identity; nationality; address; if previously married, proof of marital status and that they are free to marry.

- In England and Wales, each party must have been living in one of the registration districts for seven days before the notice is given (but the district need not be the district to which notice is actually given).

- The registrar must be satisfied that the party who is subject to immigration control has an entry clearance granted specifically for the purposes of marriage in the UK, *or* is in an exempt category (i.e. is 'settled'), *or* has a certificate of approval for the marriage issued by the Secretary of State.

Impact of the new marriage procedures

These changes go far beyond the pre-existing provisions concerning marriage, which were introduced in January 2001 by section 24 1999 Act. Those provisions require registrars to report to the Home Office if they suspect that a marriage was being entered into:

'...for the purpose of avoiding the effect of one or more provisions of the United Kingdom immigration law or the immigration rules'.

This requirement is still in force, and registrars are still expected to report these marriages.

The new procedures mean that, firstly, couples are required to go through the rigmarole of giving notice to a particular registry. Second, many will have to pay to make an application for approval. The need for specific approval applies even if the applicant's immigration status permits them to switch to remain in the UK as spouses – i.e., if they are permitted to remain in the UK for more than six months from the date of entry, and have not remained in the UK in breach of immigration laws (see para. 284(i), (iv) HC 395).

The need for the new provisions is unclear. The reason given by the government is that they are needed in order to deal with the 'increasing' number of 'sham marriages' – marriages entered into in order to get round controls. However, as will be clear from the rest of this chapter, immigration law does not allow such marriages to provide immigration rights for the non-settled partner. This is true of the rights of spouses under both EU law and the immigration rules. It is therefore not clear how preventing people actually marrying will add to the existing framework of immigration control.

Inevitably, there are likely to be human rights challenges to the operation of the new provisions. Article 12 ECHR protects the 'right to marry and to found a family'. While it is open to the state to use its laws to regulate the exercise of that right, it cannot undermine the right itself. The state may be permitted to interfere with rights to marry when the marriage is indeed a sham (see *Klip & Kurger v Netherlands*). However, the present provisions do not simply operate on sham marriages; they are an impediment to perfectly genuine proposed marriages simply because the immigration status possessed by the parties is not one of a specified kind. Given the exemption from the new procedures of marriages solemnised under the rites of the Church of England, there may also be claims that the new rules unjustifiably discriminate in respecting the right to marry (Article 12 taken with Article 14 ECHR).

Changes following the Civil Partnership Act 2004

There are further proposed changes to the immigration rules as a result of the Civil Partnership Act 2004. This legislation enables people to enter into a civil partnership agreement in the UK and so same-sex couples will be able to give their relationship a legal status. As we go to print, new immigration rules were issued (in force from 5 December 2005) the aim of which is to treat civil partners in exactly the same way as spouses (HC 582). This change is just after our cut off date and is therefore not flagged up throughout the references in the *Handbook*.

CHANGES TO IMMIGRATION RULES CIVIL PARTNERSHIP ACT 2004

The proposed changes to the immigration rules resulting from the ability to register civil partnership agreements were as follows (and see note at end of table):

- A new category of 'civil partners' will be introduced into the immigration rules. It will mirror the rules relating to spouses. 'Civil partners' will be able to apply to stay with partners who are settled in the UK or who are in the UK with limited leave, for example as students or work permit holders.

- It will be possible to apply as the equivalent of a 'fiancé(e)' in order to have a civil partnership in the UK.

- There will be an equivalent of the 'marriage visitor' rules (▶see 229–30) for people seeking to visit for the purposes of having a civil registration, but who are not proposing to stay in the UK. For such people, registering their partnership will not allow them to stay in the UK longer than normal.

- The unmarried partners rules will continue in operation as an option, both for same-sex couples who do not wish to enter into a civil partnership and for heterosexual couples.

- There will be a similar system for the granting of an approval to register a civil partnership as there is for marriage cases (see above). So a person who is

---

subject to immigration control will have to demonstrate to the registrar that they have either got an entry clearance which enables them to register a civil partnership, or they have the written permission of the Secretary of State or they have settled status in the UK. The Home Office intends to allow applicants to apply for certificates of approval *before* 5 December 2005

- Civil partnerships are to be treated in the same way as marriages for the purposes of the immigration rules relating to bereaved spouses/partners, domestic violence and the main policy on enforcement (DP/3/96).
- Civil partnerships entered into and recognised overseas will be recognised.
- The Home Office will also review whether to extend the rules to enable unmarried partners to enter and remain as dependants of sponsors in those categories under the rules which, at present, only allow spouse dependants to be admitted (▶see 352–6).

The above details are taken from information given by Home Office officials in a meeting on 10 February 2005 and also as posted on the Home Office website down to October 2005.

Note: As we go to print, the Home Office has introduced amending immigration rules (HC 582) which are in force from 5 December 2005. The amendments are fairly comprehensive. The explanatory memorandum issued with the amendments state:

'The [IND] is committed to treating civil partners in precisely the same way as it treats spouses. The immigration rules changes reflect this commitment, by amending the rules to ensure that civil partners and proposed civil partners are afforded the same treatment as spouses and fiancés throughout.'

THE DIFFERENT CIRCUMSTANCES COVERED IN THIS CHAPTER

The immigration rules concerning marriage and relationships, and the purposes of those rules, are often difficult to explain. It is widely believed that being married to a British citizen or to a person with indefinite leave to remain in the UK gives a person a 'right' to enter or remain. This is not correct. British immigration law gives no automatic rights to non-British citizen family members. The rules allow spouses, unmarried partners and fiancé(e)s of those 'settled' in the UK to be admitted and (eventually) to remain permanently with them, if certain stringent requirements are satisfied. Where a sponsor is not settled in the UK, the rules sometimes allow admission for limited periods. In very limited circumstances, where an applicant was admitted on the basis of a marriage or partnership that no longer exists, applicants may still be permitted to remain.

We have divided the different situations of people whose claim to enter or stay in the UK is based on their marriage or partnership into the following six groups. These groups are discussed in turn in the remainder of this chapter.

1) People who wish to enter the UK who are either accompanying or joining their settled partners and who intend to settle here permanently (▶see 303–29).

2) People who have been admitted as in (1) for an initial 'probationary' period and who wish to apply for settlement in the UK (▶see 329–32).

3) People in the UK for reasons unconnected with their partners – for example, as students or for work purposes – and who wish to 'switch' to remain permanently in the UK with them (▶see 332–7).

4) People as in (3) above, but who cannot satisfy the immigration rules to remain with their partners because they are illegal entrants or overstayers, or have only temporary admission to the UK – for example, as asylum-seekers (▶see 337–44).

5) People who were granted leave as the spouse or partner of a person settled in the UK, and who wish to remain in the UK permanently, but where the relationship no longer exists as a result of death (▶344–5) or domestic violence (▶345–51), or other reasons (▶351–2).

6) People who are accompanying or coming to join partners who are not settled in the UK, but who are in the UK for the time being with limited leave – for example, as students, work permit holders or business people (▶see 352–6).

From 15 March 2005, 'visitors seeking to enter for the purpose of marriage' has been introduced as a new category under the immigration rules (para. 56D–56F HC 395 inserted by HC 346). The purpose of this category is to allow people to visit in order to marry in the UK, but where the applicant will *not* be staying permanently in the UK after the marriage. Those wishing to apply under this category are therefore dealt with as visitors (for details ▶see 229–30).

'Settled in the United Kingdom' and 'present and settled'

The terms 'settled' and 'present and settled' in the UK are used a lot in this section. They are terms used to describe the status of the sponsor of the application – i.e. the family member who the applicant is attempting to join or stay with in the UK. Both terms are defined in the immigration rules (para. 6 HC 395), and it is important to understand their meaning.

Settled in the United Kingdom

'Settled in the United Kingdom' refers to a sponsor who has no restriction on the period they may stay in the UK *and* who is 'ordinarily resident' here.

Those with the right of abode (i.e. British citizens and a few Commonwealth nationals ▶see 1417–20), or who have been granted indefinite leave to enter or remain in the UK, have no restrictions on the period they may stay in the UK. If a person has been granted indefinite leave, the rules make it clear that they can still be treated as settled even though they previously entered or remained in breach of the UK laws. People with limited leave cannot be settled, as they have a limitation on the period of their stay. Those exempt from immigration control (►see 472–6) are not treated as settled, unless they are exempt as members of the home armed forces (those who are exempt and have a child born in the UK should seek advice about whether they might be treated as settled).

Those with no restrictions on their right to remain, however, also need to be 'ordinarily resident'. This generally denotes lawful presence for a settled purpose, and it describes where a person ordinarily lives. In **Shah v Barnet London Borough Council**, the House of Lords stated that ordinary residence refers to a person's abode in a particular place or country, which they have adopted voluntarily for a settled purpose (education, business, profession, employment, health or simply because they like being there) as part of the regular order of their life. The purpose might only be for a limited period; it is not necessary to have an intention to stay indefinitely. It is possible to be ordinarily resident in two places at the same time (see **Fox v Electoral Registration Officer**, CA).

'Present and settled'

This means that the sponsor is 'settled' (see above) *and* that, at the time the application under the rules is made, they are *either* physically present in the UK *or* are coming to the UK with the applicant, or to join the applicant. They must also intend to make their home in the UK with the applicant, if the application is successful. This definition was added to the rules from 1 April 2003 (para. 6 HC 395 as amended by HC 538). It is a useful addition, because it makes clear that, when the rules refer to the 'presence' in the UK of the sponsor, this includes situations where the sponsor is shortly to travel to the UK.

PEOPLE COMING TO THE UK AS SPOUSES, UNMARRIED (INCLUDING SAME-SEX) PARTNERS, OR FIANCÉ(E)S OF PEOPLE SETTLED IN THE UK

WHAT THE RULES SAY

The requirements that must be met by people seeking entry to the UK as spouses, unmarried (including same-sex) partners or fiancé(e)s include all of the following (paras. 277–283, 289AA–292, 295AA–C HC 395):

- they are seeking entry on account of their relationship to a person who is present and settled in the UK, or who is on the same occasion being admitted for settlement (►302–3, 304–5);
- both the applicant and the sponsor will be aged 18 or over on the date the applicant will arrive in the UK (►305–6);

- they and their spouse/partner/fiancé intend to live together permanently as husband and wife (or, if unmarried partners, in a relationship akin to marriage) (▶306–7);
- they will be able to maintain and accommodate themselves adequately, together with any dependants, in accommodation they own or occupy exclusively, without recourse to public funds (▶307–318).

In order to enter the UK in this category, all applicants, whether visa nationals or not, must obtain an entry clearance. Applicants may also be refused admission if any of the general grounds on which entry can be refused apply to them (▶see 97–99).

The rules for spouses and fiancé(e)s also require that they have met the other party to the marriage and, in the case of spouses, that they are seeking entry as the husband or wife, and that the marriage is subsisting (▶318–22).

The rules for fiancé(e)s require that, instead of seeking admission as a married person, applicants are seeking entry for marriage (▶318–22). The new procedures for marriage in the UK (▶see above 296–300) must be followed. It must be shown that the fiancé(e) will be adequately maintained and accommodated until the date of the marriage, and that, after the marriage, the couple will be able to maintain and accommodate themselves. The slight difference in wording simply reflects the fact that the couple may not be living together until after they are married.

Unmarried partners (we use the term to refer to both heterosexual and same-sex unmarried partners, ▶see also the proposed new rules following the Civil Partnership Act 2004, 300–1) do not have to show that they are seeking entry for marriage, but in addition to the above rules they must show that (▶see 322–3):

- they have been living together in a relationship 'akin to marriage' which has lasted for two years or more;
- any previous marriage (or similar relationship) by either partner has permanently broken down; and
- the parties are not in a 'consanguineous' relationship with each other.

Although these rules are framed with a view to the applicant settling permanently in the UK, if the application is successful, spouses and unmarried partners are normally granted an initial two years' probationary leave, after which they may apply for indefinite leave. For spouses and unmarried partners who have been living together for at least four years outside the UK, there is a separate rule enabling applicants to be granted indefinite leave to enter immediately (▶see 324–5). For entry procedure and decisions ▶see 325–9.

WHAT THE RULES MEAN

Present and settled in the United Kingdom

One partner (or spouse/fiancé(e)) must be 'present and settled' in the UK or 'on the same occasion be admitted for settlement'. The meaning of these terms is explained at ▶302–3 above, from which it will be seen that 'present' should not be read too literally.

From 18 September 2002, a modification was made to the rules as they apply to applicants whose spouses/partners are working abroad in particular capacities (see Cm 5597). From that date, sponsors of spouses and unmarried partners will be treated as 'present and settled' in the UK provided that they are either British citizens or settled in the UK *and* they are any of the following:

- a member of HM Forces serving overseas;
- a permanent member of HM Diplomatic Service or a comparable UK-based staff member of the British Council on a tour of duty abroad;
- a staff member of the Department for International Development.

This special rule does not apply to fiancé(e) applications. The rule also applies in cases where the applicant is applying in-country for the probationary period of leave, and where the application is for indefinite leave to remain. The effect of the rule is that spouses and partners of the above people are able to travel to the UK to obtain the probationary period, then depart again in order to live with their sponsor overseas and, after two years, then return to the UK in order to obtain settlement. They do not need to be accompanied by their sponsor on either occasion. The Home Office will normally expect applicants in this position to live with their sponsor overseas, unless there is clear evidence that this is not possible – for example, if the sponsor is in a war zone.

A separate modification of this rule applies for sponsors of fiancé(e)s. Sponsors of fiancé(e) applications who are EEA nationals, and who have been issued with a residence permit valid for five years, are regarded as present and settled in the UK even if they have not been granted permission to remain in the UK indefinitely (see para. 290A HC 395 as added by CM 5597 from 18 September 2002). This change has been made to provide a route of entry under the rules for fiancé(e)s of EEA nationals, because fiancé(e)s are not treated as entitled to rights of free movement until after their marriage (see Home Office letter to Northern Ireland Law Centre, 18 November 2002).

Age of applicant and sponsor

From 21 December 2004, both the applicant and the sponsor must be aged at least 18 years on the date that the applicant will arrive in the UK (see paras 277, 289AA, 295AA HC 395 as amended by HC 164 – this has further changed adjustments which were made from 1 April 2003 by HC

538). The government's stated purpose in doing this was to deal with forced marriages. In a written ministerial statement to the Commons on 27 October 2004, the Home Secretary explained: 'This is to give those who face forced marriage extra time in which to mature and resist familial pressure for them to enter a marriage that they do not want.'

The government has further stated that, if it appears necessary to deal with the same problem, it is prepared to raise the age again, to 21 years. This rule applies generally to all applications made by spouses, unmarried partners and fiancé(e)s, whether for entry, leave to remain for the probationary period, indefinite leave, or for limited leave to stay with a sponsor who also has limited leave. Where the applicant is in the UK, it is the date on which leave to remain would be granted that is the operative date. If the applicant or sponsor are within a month or two of their eighteenth birthday, the immigration authorities may be persuaded to exercise discretion. The ECO may agree to wait a short while before issuing the entry clearance, rather than refusing the application and requiring the applicant to pay a further fee to apply again (see IDI, Ch 8, s1, annex B, para. 9 – this part of the Instructions still refers to the old rules, when the applicant only had to be 16, but it can be assumed that the same discretion may be exercised).

Intention to live together permanently

The couple have to show that they intend to live together permanently as husband and wife or, for unmarried partners, in a relationship 'akin to marriage'. In practice – and particularly in relation to applications from abroad – the numbers of applicants refused under this head has increased since the abolition of the primary purpose rule in June 1997. From 1 April 2003, a specific definition was introduced to the rules to explain the meaning of this requirement (HC 538). It means:

'An intention to live together, evidenced by a clear commitment from both parties that they will live together permanently in the United Kingdom immediately following the outcome of the application in question, or as soon as circumstances permit thereafter.'

Questions may be asked about how the marriage or relationship came about, and where the couple intend to live after marriage. Information about the respective families may also be sought. However, the couple do not have to show that they have an intention to live together permanently anywhere in the world; the purpose of the rule is to ensure that that the couple intend to live together in the UK if the application is granted (see *R (Olofinusi) v IAT*, HC). So, an intention to live together that is conditional upon the application being successful could be enough, but if this is the case the parties should be prepared for detailed questioning about who imposed the condition and why (and see DSP, Ch13, para. 13.12). Plausible reasons should be given by the settled spouse if they are unwilling to live in any country other than the UK with their partner.

Certain marriages or relationships may be scrutinised more closely than others. For example, relationships between couples who have had a 'whirlwind romance', or are from strikingly different backgrounds, are of very different ages, or who do not speak the same language, may be looked at very carefully. Officers may reach subjective conclusions about such differences. Officers often unreasonably consider marriage applications from citizens of developing countries as economically motivated. But even where this is a factor, it does not of itself undermine the intention to live together on the part of the couple. Where there are doubts about the adequacy of accommodation in the UK, this is also sometimes used to argue that the couple will not be staying together. Unfortunately the ghost of the old 'primary purpose' rule which required couples to prove that the main reason they were marrying was *not* for immigration reasons, still haunts some decisions. In a case brought to light in the summer of 2005 by Dexter Montague & Partners Solicitors, the Entry Clearance Manager in Islamabad reviewed a refusal and found that 'the refusal was based on primary purpose legislation, which was abolished eight years ago'. The decision was reversed.

Previous periods of cohabitation and the birth of a child will be strong factors going to show that the rules are satisfied. However, the Home Office has indicated that it will not necessarily be satisfied that an intention to live together is demonstrated by a lengthy marriage or partnership, and that the existence of children of the relationship will not be conclusive. The Home Office gives the example that, even in a genuine marriage, there may be pressure to move children to the UK for education, but without both spouses having the intention of settling here (Home Office letter to Camden Community Law Centre, 29 October 2003).

In **Khan**, the IAT emphasised that, where a couple had been living apart after the marriage, the relevant question was their intention to cohabit in the future, and this is underlined by the new definition of the rule (see above). However, where there is to be a delay because living together is not immediately practicable, it is possible that officers will argue that there can be no present intention. Where a sponsor was in prison at the date of the decision, and still had several years of a nine-year sentence to run, the Tribunal found that the couple could not be regarded as intending to live together permanently, even though they may intend to do so at some distant time in the future (see **Shabbana Bibi v ECO, Islamabad**).

Negative decisions involving the intention to live together will often have been made following detailed questioning of the applicant and sponsor by an ECO. Inevitably, on an appeal, the Court will usually not be able to hear live evidence from the applicant. Nevertheless, the AIT must not defer to the view of the ECO simply because the officer has had first-hand knowledge of the applicant. The AIT must consider the matter independently and assess the facts for themselves, on the evidence before them (see **Kari Shahjad Miah v ECO, Dhaka**).

Maintenance and accommodation without recourse to public funds

Spouses, partners and fiancé(e)s all have to show that they can adequately maintain and accommodate themselves in the UK without recourse to public funds (paras 281(iv)(v), 290(iv)(v), 295A(v)(vi) HC 395). The maintenance and accommodation requirements as they apply to all other categories are set out separately in the immigration rules. 'Public funds' are defined in the immigration rules (para. 6 HC 395) and the list is set out in the box below. The public funds requirements are referred to throughout the immigration rules, although they are formulated slightly differently in the different places they appear. Most of what follows is of general application, although most of the cases which involve the test concern family members, which is the situation in which problems most frequently arise.

A few categories under the rules do not require that the public funds requirements are met (▶309). In addition, in certain situations people can claim public funds without being disqualified under the rules – we have referred to this as people being 'exempt' from the test (▶309–11). It is also important to recognise that it is only where the admission of the applicant will cause *additional* recourse to public funds that an application will fail under the rules (▶311). After dealing with these initial questions, we then look a the questions of 'maintenance' (▶311–13) and 'accommodation' (▶313–16) separately. Support provided by third parties is generally acceptable (▶317). Details about maintenance or sponsorship undertakings are at ▶317–18 and 403–4. For information about the consequences of claiming public funds during the probationary period, ▶see 329–30.

Which categories do the requirements apply to?

The public funds requirements apply to most categories under the rules. Only the following categories under the *rules* have *no* public funds requirements:

- refugees and their dependants;
- those seeking family reunion with refugees;
- those seeking 'temporary protection', and their dependants;
- returning residents (although they should not have caused a charge on public funds when they left the UK);
- those seeking leave on the basis of long residence in the UK;
- Gurkhas and foreign and Commonwealth citizens who have been discharged from HM forces, and their dependants;
- victims of domestic violence seeking leave to remain;
- those seeking to remain as a bereaved spouse or unmarried partner;
- non-British citizen children born in the UK who are seeking to stay with their parent(s);
- transit visitors.

DEFINITION OF PUBLIC FUNDS

'Public funds' are (para. 6 HC 395):

Income Support

Income-based Jobseeker's Allowance (JSA)

Social fund payments

Accommodation from a local authority as a homeless person

Allocation of accommodation from the housing register of a local authority (housing under part VI or VII of the Housing Act 1996 and under part II of the Housing Act 1985, Parts I or II of the Housing (Scotland) Act 1987, part II of the Housing (Northern Ireland) Order 1988)

Housing Benefit

Council Tax Benefit

State Pension Credit

Child Tax Credit

Working Tax Credit

Child Benefit

Attendance Allowance

Carers Allowance

Severe Disablement Allowance

Disability Living Allowance

Note that the above list incorporates changes made on 18 September 2002 (Cm 5597) and on 15 March 2005 (HC 346).

For the purposes of the immigration rules, 'public funds' do *not* include NHS treatment, state education or community care services, but see Chapter 31 for access to these services. In particular, as a result of amendments to social services legislation made by the 1999 Act, having a condition attached to leave which prohibits access to public funds has an impact upon whether certain community care services may be provided. Not all social security benefits are public funds. For example, a working holidaymaker who has been working and has paid sufficient contributions and is temporarily unemployed may be entitled to receive contribution-based JSA (IDI, Ch1, s7, annex W, para. 2.1).

In addition, those seeking to enter or remain on human rights grounds (humanitarian protection and discretionary leave) do not have to satisfy the public funds requirements. Others seeking to remain on a compassionate or other basis outside the rules may be granted leave even where these requirements cannot be met.

Exemptions from public funds requirement

From 15 March 2005, important exemptions have been made to the public funds test for certain classes of people. These are people whose immigration status would normally mean that they are not entitled to benefits, but who in fact are entitled to certain benefits by specific exceptions made in the benefits legislation (see para. 6B HC 395 inserted by HC 346).

Taking it in stages, s115 of the 1999 Act excludes those 'subject to immigration control' (▶1249–55) from a range of non-contributory, core social security benefits. However, the Social Security (Immigration and Asylum) Consequential Amendments Regulations 2000 re-include certain classes of people to entitlement to certain benefits (▶see the table at 1255–9 for who is re-included in respect of which benefits). Similarly, section 42 of the Tax Credits Act 2002, together with the Tax Credits (Immigration) Regulations 2003, exclude people who are subject to immigration control (the same definition as above) from obtaining child tax credit and working tax credit. Again, the same 2003 Regulations re-include certain classes of claimant (▶see the table at 1258).

The new immigration rule (i.e. para. 6B HC 395) states that these 're-included' classes are not to be regarded as having recourse to public funds if they claim them. The rule change is not well-drafted. Probably the best way to understand it is that, if a person claims or will claim a particular benefit, and they are entitled to claim that benefit because of the re-including regulations, that person will not be treated as failing the public funds test under the immigration rules for that reason. So, for example, a person who has been granted leave to enter or remain on the basis of a maintenance undertaking is entitled to claim any of the following 'public funds' benefits without that counting as having recourse to public funds: attendance allowance, carer's allowance, disability living allowance, social fund payments, child-benefit and the tax credits (▶1257, category (3); 1258, category (1)). If the same person claimed those benefits, they would not be regarded as being in breach of their conditions, and nor would their reliance on them mean that they could not satisfy the public funds test in their immigration applications. Note that such a person would not be re-included to entitlement to other benefits, such as income-based JSA, unless their sponsor died, or unless five years had passed since their entry to the UK or the date on which the undertaking was made (▶see 1256, category (1)). In practice, therefore, they would not be able to gain access to those additional benefits until that stage.

The new immigration rule is therefore an attempt to bring the immigration rules more into line with benefit entitlement. It enables certain people whose immigration status allows them to claim certain benefits to access them without their immigration position being disadvantaged. The Home Office has acknowledged that some caseworkers seemed unaware of para. 6B. It therefore undertook to re-write all affected IDIs to ensure that it is applied (Home Office letter to Devon Law Centre dated 23 August 2005).

The new exemptions and the tax credits The consequences are particularly important as far as the tax credits are concerned. We can give no more than a brief explanation of them here. The tax credits were introduced on 6 April 2003 and are administered by the Inland Revenue, and they are paid and assessed on an annual basis in line with the tax year from April to April. Child tax credit is an income-based credit for low- and middle-income families who are in or out of work, and who have responsibility for a child or children. Working tax credit is an income-based credit for working adults. It can be claimed by parents who work for 16 hours or more a week, or by those without children who work 30 hours or more a week. The 2003 Regulations *generally* (►see 1246–7, 1258) allow a couple to claim and be entitled to the tax credits as though both of them were not subject to immigration control, provided that *one* of them is either not subject to immigration control or is within one of the classes who are exempted from that test for the purposes of the tax credits (see regulation 3(2) of the 2003 Regulations).

The precise rules about who is exempted from the 'subject to immigration control' test for the purposes of the tax credits is slightly complicated (►see table at 1258). So the *general* effect of the benefit rules is that couples can obtain access to the tax credits even though one of them would otherwise be excluded from them by their immigration status. The importance of the new immigration rule is that an applicant will not be treated as having recourse to public funds where they claim, or intend to claim, the tax credits in these circumstances. The present IDI (Ch 8, s1, annex F, para. 2), although well out of date, make a similar point about the Home Office's attitude to a foreign spouse claiming 'family credit': '...where a foreign wife is married to a person present and settled in the United Kingdom, she may claim family credit on behalf of her husband and family'. Of course, family credit no longer exists; it was effectively a predecessor to working tax credit. However, it is clear from this that what was previously Home Office practice has now been put on to a firm footing in the rules.

'Additional' recourse to public funds

In October 2000, the immigration rules were amended (see para. 6 HC 395) to incorporate the long-standing Home Office policy that it is only *additional* public funds which are prohibited. This removed the doubts created by the courts' previous interpretation of the rules and the policy. The Home Office's general policy objective is not to prevent a British citizen or settled sponsor from receiving any public funds to which they are entitled in their own right. So, the settled partner may claim benefit to which they would be entitled under the social security legislation if the applicant(s) were not admitted, and this will not harm the immigration application. Indeed this independent entitlement of the sponsor can be taken into account in assessing the resources available to the family as a whole (see also IDI, ch8, s1, annex F, para. 2, and *Kaur v SSHD* (IAT)).

Adequate maintenance

In determining whether the couple can support themselves and any dependants, the immigration authorities will take into account the UK sponsor's earnings or savings. However, good evidence of this is required, and applications are often refused because of inadequate pay slips or bank statements. Sponsors are often paid in cash, and their earnings are difficult to prove. Since the introduction of the national minimum wage, it is arguable that any person in full-time employment and being paid at or above that rate would have to be regarded as in receipt of a sufficient amount, depending of course on the extent of the needs of any dependants.

Work for the applicant If the partner in the UK is on benefit but the partner abroad has the offer of a job in the UK for when he or she arrives, this may be taken into consideration. Spouses and partners seeking to enter or remain in the UK are entitled to work during the probationary period, and they can rely on their proposed earnings to meet the maintenance requirement. Fiancé(e)s may not work until they have been given leave to remain as spouses. Applicants in other categories who are prohibited from working cannot meet the requirements of the rules in this way. The spouses (and children) of students are usually permitted to work where they have been admitted for 12 months or more.

In the case of *Azam*, the IAT held that, in considering maintenance, the ECO had a duty to take into account the possibility of an applicant finding work on arrival. A letter making a job offer ought to explain why the job offer is made. It may be because of a family relationship, or because the applicant is a friend of the employee. It should also, as far as possible, be supported by some evidence of the business operation of the employer and its need for a further employee. In *Khan*, it was accepted that people may prefer to employ relatives in order to assist them to come to the UK, and that this did not necessarily undermine the genuine nature of the job offer made. The Home Office will generally reject job offers that are unrealistic in the light of the applicant's skills (which can include language), or offers that appear to have been manufactured and are unlikely to be long-term. However, the guidance states that care must be taken not to make assumptions, and the fact that unemployment is high in a particular area should not, on its own, be a good enough reason to reject the proposal that an applicant will work (IDI, Ch 8, s1, annex F, para. 5).

Date support needed The maintenance proposed does not have to be available at the date of decision, but only when the person arrives in the UK. So a woman with the right to return to work after maternity leave, for example, may rely on her future employment and earnings. The same applies to the availability of a job offer for a spouse or partner on their arrival in the UK. This also applies to the rules relating to accommodation (see below). The maintenance and accommodation requirements extend only to those who are dependants at the time of the decision. The Home Office has stated that it would not be appropriate to base a refusal on the grounds that the couple would not be able to support and accommodate any children they may have in the future. Officers are told not to ask questions about whether the couple intend to start a family.

Can the couple live off one person's benefit Although the 1999 Act prevents people from claiming public funds if they have a condition prohibiting them from doing so attached to their leave (which will be the case when probationary leave is granted), the immigration rules will not be met just because the benefit rules will stop the applicant/their sponsor from actually getting public funds. It cannot be argued that two people can live on one person's standard benefit without any additional income to support the applicant. This is because the rules require the applicant to be *adequately* maintained. The Home Office view is that the level set by income support (or income-based job-seeker's allowance) is the minimum standard of support considered to be acceptable and adequate to meet the rules. The IAT upheld this view in *Begum* (*Momotaz*). In addition, in *Uvovo*, it held that, to meet the requirements of the rules, the support must be of a level to include the equivalent of free school meals and prescription charges, because those additional facilities would be available to a person on income support or income-based JSA.

Even if a sponsor is receiving more benefit than these standard minimum levels, the additional amounts may be needed in order to cater for their special needs. The IAT made this point in *Shabir v ECO*, a case in which the sponsor was in receipt of substantial disability living allowance totalling more than the standard minimum benefit normally paid to a couple. The IAT stated that it could not be established that there would be adequate maintenance just by comparing the amount received with the basic minimum, and that all cases will depend on their own facts. On the facts in *Shabir*, the sponsor had been able to make substantial savings, which indicated that, overall, the income would be sufficient and the public funds test was satisfied. The opposite conclusion was reached on the facts of the case in *ECO v Nazia Bi*, in which the sponsor was in need of constant attention and specialised care. It was found that the applicant could not be adequately supported on the basis of the public funds geared to the sponsor's special needs. In that case the applicant's limited savings would be taken up by the cost of the airfare and wedding. In addition, the sponsor's parents were on benefit, so there were no spare resources in the household.

Adequate accommodation

If the settled or British spouse or partner is living in local authority accommodation, this does not prohibit a partner from abroad from coming to the UK, because no additional accommodation is necessarily required. However, advisers should check that the accommodation is big enough (see below) and that the landlord or local authority have no objections to any dependants residing there. People can often tell this by looking at the conditions of the tenancy agreement. The DSPs tell ECOs that:

'If possible, and especially in doubtful cases, you should ask to see a letter from the owner of the property (which may be a housing authority, housing association, landlord or a building society) confirming particulars of tenure and occupation of the dwelling, together with a description of the accommodation and, if the accommodation is rented, a copy of the lease.' (DSP, Ch 9, para 9.11)

The rules for spouses, unmarried partners and fiancé(e)s state that accommodation must be owned or occupied by them 'exclusively'. However, the Home Office (IDI, Ch 8, s1, annex F, para. 6) states:

'Accommodation can be shared with other members of a family provided that at least part of the accommodation is for the exclusive use of the sponsor and his dependants. The unit of accommodation may be as small as a separate bedroom but:

- must be owned or legally occupied by the sponsor;
- its occupation must not contravene public health regulations; and
- its occupation must not cause overcrowding as defined in the Housing Act, 1985.'

Therefore, exclusive occupation of a bedroom for a married couple should be sufficient (see IDI, Ch 8, s1, annex F, para. 6.1 and see *Zia (Raja)* and *Kasuji*).

Overcrowded accommodation Accommodation will not be adequate if it is overcrowded. The Housing Act 1985 contains statutory definitions of overcrowding, which cover both privately owned houses and those owned by local authorities. A house is overcrowded if two persons of 10 years old or more, of opposite sexes (other than partners) have to sleep in the same room (this is the 'room standard'), *or* if the number sleeping in the house exceeds that permitted in the Act (this is the 'space standard').

The Act sets out two tests for measuring the 'space standard'. In practice, however, the Home Office only uses the following test for measuring the space standard (IDI, Ch8, s1, annex F, para. 6.3). The number of persons permitted to stay in the accommodation is dependent upon the number of rooms available, as set out in the table below. It should be noted that a room only counts if it:

- has a floor area larger than 50 square feet; and
- is of a type normally used as a bedroom or a living room (kitchens and bathrooms do not count).

Number of rooms	Permitted number of persons
1	2
2	3
3	5
4	7.5
5	10

with an additional two persons for each room in excess of five.

Note: children under the age of one do not count; children aged between one and ten years only count as half a person.

There have been conflicting decisions in the IAT as to whether the fact that accommodation is not overcrowded in the terms of the Housing Act 1985 automatically means that it is 'adequate' in terms of its space and layout under the immigration rules (compare *Sultana* and *S (Pakistan)*).

Houses in multiple occupation There are separate overcrowding provisions for a house in multiple occupation (HMO), which is defined as a 'house which is occupied by persons who do not form a single household'. This is a very wide definition, and the Home Office view is that it covers not only hotels and hostels, but could also cover houses lived in by two or more couples of different generations where they do not share common facilities. The most common occurrence of this is likely to be where a couple are intending to live independently in a house which is also occupied by the settled partner's family. The definition can include a house lived in by two or more couples, even if they are related. There are no hard and fast rules to determine overcrowding in the case of HMOs. A local authority can serve a notice stating that an HMO is overcrowded, or that further residents should not be permitted to reside there. If the accommodation available is an HMO, the local authority may simply be asked to provide confirmation that they do not object to the additional person(s) residing there.

Rented accommodation As noted above, accommodation does not have to be owned. Council or privately rented accommodation is quite satisfactory. If the accommodation is owned, the property deeds, or letter from the building society or other mortgage provider confirming the ownership of the property, should be provided. If it is privately rented, the rent book and/or tenancy agreement will be required. If it is council or housing association accommodation, correspondence from the landlord is normally sufficient to show occupation. In order to show the adequacy of the accommodation, a letter from the landlord confirming the size of the accommodation and the size and number of rooms could be produced, or alternatively any other

'...description of the premises that [the Home Office] can be satisfied is accurate and genuine' (IDI, Ch8, s1, annex F, para. 6.1).

Such letters can be difficult to obtain from local authority housing departments, as they are often not regarded as urgent or as a matter of priority.

If the accommodation is privately rented, a letter from the landlord confirming the size and the tenancy, and that he or she has no objection to the extra person coming, should be submitted. The immigration authorities will usually want to see the terms of the lease or tenancy agreement for rented accommodation so that they can be sure that the letting or subletting is allowed, and that the number of people permitted to live in the property is not exceeded. This is particularly important where the landlord is a relative, and formal evidence – a rent-book, for example – may be important to show that the accommodation is actually occupied in a legal sense by the sponsor, rather than simply being provided by the relative.

Although, in our view, simple occupancy can come within the rules, it may be more difficult to show availability in the long term without a formal tenancy agreement.

Where landlords or a local authority are unwilling to write letters confirming the position, or where there is some doubt whether the requirements are met, it may be advisable to pay for a private report from an independent surveyor to confirm that the accommodation is suitable and would not be statutorily overcrowded if the applicant and any dependants were admitted.

Women sponsors It is often more difficult for women than for men in the UK to show that their partners from abroad can be maintained and accommodated in the UK. A woman looking after young children may not be able to work, and therefore may rely on benefits. If she is living with other members of her family in their accommodation, she will have to show either that this will be an adequate long-term arrangement, or that the couple have realistic plans and expectations of having their own home soon. In *Kausar*, the IAT suggested that it was easier to satisfy these requirements when a couple live in a separate family unit, rather than in joint family living arrangements.

When accommodation must be available In entry clearance cases, the accommodation (and maintenance) does not have to be available at the date of the decision of the ECO, but only when the applicant(s) arrive in the UK. This was the reason for the traditional 'rule of thumb' which has been applied that applicants must show that the necessary support will be available within about six months of the entry clearance decision. As is illustrated by the IAT case of *Olusola A Adesegun v ECO, Lagos*, the logic for this was that entry clearances used to be issued with a validity of six months, allowing applicants to travel within that period. However, the more recent entry clearances under the 1999 Act themselves give leave to enter when the applicant arrives in the UK, and they are valid for a much longer period of time – namely, for the period of leave that they will give. Nevertheless, the same principle probably applies: the question is whether, at the date of the ECO's decision, it can be said that, if the application is successful, adequate support and accommodation will be available at the point that the applicant will enter the UK. On an appeal, however, the AIT will only consider evidence of support which becomes available after the date of the decision if it was foreseeable at the date of the entry clearance decision. In most cases, this will mean that the arrangement by which the support will become available should be in existence at the time the ECO is considering the matter (see the IAT decisions in *Kazmi* and *Azad*).

Fiancé(e)s In fiancé(e) cases, accommodation for the *couple* does not need to be available on the arrival of the fiancé(e) in the UK. The Home Office has stated that it is sufficient for there to be only temporary accommodation available for the fiancé(e), perhaps with relatives and friends. However, there must a reasonable prospect that there will be adequate accommodation available for the couple after the marriage has taken place (IDI, Ch 8, s1, annex F, para. 3.2).

Children at risk For the 'adequacy' of accommodation for a child where they may be at risk of abuse, ▶see 364.

'Third-party' support

In many cases, it is proposed that other family members or friends will help to support the couple. The immigration authorities require a letter to confirm this support, as well as evidence such as recent pay slips or bank statements to prove the third party's ability to support. More generally, the continued Home Office view, as set out in the IDI (Ch8, s1, annex F, para. 5.1), is that the rules state that spouses and partners have to be able to 'maintain themselves', and that this is formulated differently to the public funds requirements in other parts of the rules. The Home Office argues that this means that the couple must support themselves from their own resources, and that 'third-party' support is only acceptable exceptionally, and as a short-term arrangement.

The Home Office approach is contrary to the case law. The rules do state that a couple need to support themselves 'from their own resources', and to insist on this is probably incompatible with the right to respect for private and family life under Article 8 ECHR. This would surely be so where, for example, the sponsor is aged or disabled and cannot work, and there are obstacles to the couple living abroad permanently. In *Arman Ali*, the High Court indicated that the Home Office approach was likely to be contrary to Article 8. However, the Home Office has not changed its guidance, even in cases where there is the offer of a maintenance undertaking, and officers will sometimes rely on some older IAT decisions setting out the restrictive approach. However, even the older IAT decisions were not all one-way. Cases which were more favourable to applicants in terms of third-party support were *Balwinder Kaur* and *Modi*. Indeed, the Tribunal accepted in *Begum (Hasna)* and *Bibi (Sonor)* that the earnings of a dependent child could be taken into account when assessing whether there would be sufficient money to maintain the family in the UK. In *Ahmed (Ishaque)* and *Begum (Zabeda)*, instead of putting its view to the higher courts, the Home Office settled cases when they were appealed to the Court of Appeal. Subsequent to *Arman Ali*, and in a determination which the IAT directed be sent to the Chief Adjudicator and the head of the Visa and Migration Department at the Foreign and Commonwealth Office, as well as to the responsible minister at the Home Office, the IAT again underlined that the fact that the rule requires the parties to maintain 'themselves' does not mean that they can only rely on their own resources (*Amjad Mahmood v ECO Islamabad*, IAT). In practice, therefore, where the question of long-term third-party support arises, the issue will be whether that support is sufficiently stable and secure for the long term (*Yousaf*).

Maintenance undertakings

Maintenance undertakings are not generally taken from spouses, fiancé(e)s or partners. This is for two reasons. First, people in this category will normally be given limited leave initially, with a condition preventing them from having recourse to public funds, which prevents access to benefits anyway. Second, the Home Office view (see above) that couples should not rely on third-party support means that it will rarely be appropriate for them to ask a third party for an undertaking. The Home Office has stated that undertakings will only 'exceptionally' be accepted in cases of marriage and partnerships – namely: 'if it is clear that it would only be in effect for a limited period and the couple have a realistic prospect of supporting themselves thereafter' (see IDI, Ch8, s1, annex F, para. 5.1).

Undertakings are more frequently taken from sponsors in other dependent relative cases where indefinite leave will be granted that would, without an undertaking, permit the applicant to obtain benefits (▶see 403–4).

Additional rules for spouses or fiancé(e)s

Spouse or fiancé(e)

A 'spouse' means someone who is legally married in a way recognised by UK law. The term does not cover common-law spouses or same-sex relationships (but ▶see 300–1 for the equality given to civil partnerships from 5 December 2005). A fiancé(e) under the rules must generally be someone who is legally able to marry under UK law. This excludes people under 16, even if they are legally free to marry in the country from which they come (although the rules now require all applicants to be 18 by the time they enter the UK). It also *appears* to exclude people who are not yet divorced, even if divorce proceedings are under way. However, the DSPs state, in relation to fiancé(e)s:

'…if the only reason for a couple not being free to marry is that one of them is awaiting a divorce, entry clearance should not be refused for this reason alone (although ECOs would normally expect to see some evidence that divorce proceedings are well under way). The reasoning behind this is that the divorce may well come through within the six months leave to enter period, thereby enabling the couple to marry… Should one of the partners still be waiting for a divorce to come through at the end of the six month period, they may apply to the Home Office for an extension of stay.' (Ch13, para. 13.9)

The rules from 5 December 2005 treat proposed civil partners in the same way as fiancé(e)s.

IAT decisions in this area have been more restrictive. For example, if an application is made for entry clearance as a *spouse* and it is found that the marriage was not valid because previous divorce proceedings had not been completed, it may be that ECOs (or the appellate authorities on appeal) may be prepared to allow the application alternatively under the fiancé(e) rules. However, this will only be done *provided* that the divorce had been completed by the time of the decision, and that the couple intend to go through a further ceremony in the UK (see the IAT decision in *Ach-Charki v SSHD*, but see the further IAT decision in *ECO, Islamabad v Mohammad Shakeel* – there is a useful discussion of the problem in the IAS Digest, Vol 8, No 2, Summer 2002, 36–7).

Polygamous spouses (i.e. where the sponsor is married to more than one person) can be admitted, *provided* the marriage is recognised as valid in the UK (▶see below). Most predominantly Muslim countries allow polygamy (except Tunisia and Turkey), as do certain other countries. These spouses can be admitted if the other spouse(s) are not in the UK and have not been in the UK since their marriage to the sponsor (entry as a visitor, illegal entry and arrival with refusal of leave to enter are not counted for these purposes). This applies irrespective of whether the applicant is a first or later spouse. So the admission of a spouse who is the second polygamous/ polyandrous spouse may prevent the admission of the first spouse, if it is the second spouse who is admitted first. Note that applications before 1 August 1988, when s2 Immigration Act 1988 came into force, are not affected by these rules. The purpose of the legislation was to prevent the formation of polygamous households in the UK.

The same rules also apply to Commonwealth women who have gained the right of abode through marriage. Most women who had the right of abode because of a polygamous marriage cannot exercise that right if another wife has already come to the UK on that basis.

Therefore, if one spouse has ever been admitted in the past to join the sponsor in the UK, another spouse can only qualify to enter if the marriage of the spouse who is in the UK has ended by divorce, or if that spouse has died. This can sometimes lead to a conflict of interest where advice is being given to more than one family member. The European Court has found that the rules relating to the admission of polygamous spouses are not in breach of the ECHR.

Marriages in other countries There is often cause for confusion in cases involving marriages overseas, where there may be very different marriage laws. Many people believe that, for example, a Ghanaian customary marriage is 'not recognised' in the UK, or that after seven years' separation a marriage in the Philippines is 'automatically' ended. Couples may then marry, in the UK or abroad, in good faith, but then the Home Office may investigate past statements and allege that the marriage is bigamous and therefore not valid. Sometimes, the police may be asked to investigate with a view to prosecution for bigamy. The whole subject is very complicated, as it involves the relationship between different countries' laws, which may be constructed on entirely different bases. We do not go into all the details here. Broadly, however, if a marriage is legally recognised and valid in the country in which it took place *and* there was nothing in the law of either party's country of 'domicile' (see below) to prevent them entering into the marriage, it will be recognised as a valid marriage under UK marriage law. This is why a polygamous marriage may be recognised by UK law as a valid marriage, even though UK law prohibits polygamy. It is the immigration law which is then used to restrict the admission of polygamous spouses to one (▶see above).

So, for example, a Nigerian customary marriage, in which there is no documentation and the ceremony is an exchange of gifts between the families, will be recognised in UK law as valid if it takes place in Nigeria, and if both parties were domiciled in Nigeria at the time of the marriage. It will not be valid if it takes place in Britain, or any other country which does not recognise this form of marriage. Another example is marriage by proxy. This is where a proxy stands in for the party to the marriage at the actual ceremony. Again, in certain countries such marriages are lawful. The first question is the lawfulness of the proxy marriage in the country in which the ceremony occurred, not whether the law of the country in which the party appointed the proxy allows such marriages.

In a press statement issued on 25 March 2004, UK Visas insisted that they would not apply the above principles to a same-sex marriage or registered relationship abroad. So, even in cases where such a marriage was valid abroad and the couple were domiciled in that country at the time of the marriage, applicants will still have to satisfy the rules relating to unmarried partners (▶322–3). The Home Office has since indicated that this situation will change and that same-sex relationships registered and recognised abroad will be recognised in the UK (▶see 301).

'Domicile' has a special meaning. It means much more than the place where a person lives or 'ordinarily resides'. It is the place that a person sees as their permanent home, where they may 'end their days'. A person's first domicile – where they were born and grew up – is their 'domicile of origin'. It is difficult to shake off the domicile of origin, but this can be done by moving to a different country and very clearly adopting it as a permanent home. Domicile is often relevant in immigration law in determining the validity of a marriage (often a polygamous marriage), of a divorce, or the legitimacy of children of polygamous marriages. The following are all relevant factors in determining a person's domicile: nationality (for example, a person may have acquired a new nationality and possibly given up a previous one); statutory declarations (for example, as to where a person intends to reside – possibly made in the course of an immigration/naturalisation application); length of residence; possession of property; employment; exercise of political rights (for example, voting); residence of family members; children's education. The Home Office has a domicile questionnaire that it may use in order to gather the information necessary to determine a person's domicile, where it does not have sufficient information on file. The questionnaire is attached to annex D of the IDI at Ch 8, s1. It is used in the majority of cases where domicile becomes an issue, and often it will be used as the basis for an interview.

Divorces overseas Divorces obtained abroad will generally be recognised in the UK if they were obtained in official proceedings, are valid in the country in which they took place and in which either spouse was habitually resident in, or if either was a national of that country. A customary divorce, on the other hand, will generally be recognised by UK law if it took place in the prescribed forms in a country that recognises the customary divorce, and in which both parties were domiciled, provided that the parties were not living in the UK for the year before the divorce. Therefore, in some cases when a person living in the UK performs a customary divorce abroad, and then marries again, the Home Office may argue that a divorce should take place in the UK before the person is free to marry again in the UK.

Immigration status, nationality and the country where the marriage took place do not affect people's ability to divorce in the UK. There may be extra delays, in that papers may have to be sent to a spouse abroad, who may be difficult to contact and unwilling to co-operate. There is no need for specialist information about the divorce laws of the country in which the marriage took place if the divorce is taking place in the UK.

If a person has gained entry to the UK on the basis of a marriage which is later found to be invalid, the person can be treated as an illegal entrant. In one example, a Filipino woman married a British man in Hong Kong when they were both working there. She had believed that because she had been separated from her husband in the Philippines (where divorce did not exist) for more than seven years, she was free to marry again, and later came to Britain. She was treated as an illegal entrant when she later tried to bring her children from her first marriage from the Philippines to join her, and it was discovered that there had been no divorce. She was able to obtain a divorce in the UK and then marry her British husband again in order to secure her status.

Guidance is provided on these questions in the IDI (Ch 8, s1, annexes B–D), but those with particular problems in this area should seek careful advice.

The couple have met each other

The parties to the marriage or proposed marriage must have met (para. 281(ii) and 290(ii) HC 395). The meeting does not have to take place before an application for entry clearance is made, but the couple must have met before the applicant is interviewed about his or her application. This requirement was intended to place an extra hurdle in the way of some arranged marriages, where the couple may not meet before the wedding day, or where the wedding is by proxy. It is only likely to be a problem for fiancé(e)s, as a married couple will almost certainly have met at the wedding. In some cases, however, it involves the extra cost of a journey abroad or to the UK before the marriage.

The IAT found, in the case of **Meharban**, that the meeting does not have to take place in the context of a marriage. It is acceptable if the couple knew each other as children, as long as they both have clear recollections of the meeting and know each other as individuals. Simply coming face to face will not be enough – there must be some mutual making of acquaintance. The fact of meeting can be proved by photographs of the couple together, by the recollections of both parties, by passport stamps showing that both were in the same country at the same time, and by supporting statements from relatives or friends who know of the meeting. ECOs are unlikely to accept that internet contact alone amounts to a meeting (see DSP, Ch13, para. 13.11).

If a couple meet after an original decision to refuse, the ECO should be invited to review the decision and – if satisfied that the couple have met and this was the only ground for the refusal – the decision should be reversed without the need for an appeal.

Additional rules for unmarried partners

Previously, a concession was operated outside the rules to provide for unmarried (including same-sex) partners. It was introduced on 13 October 1997, with a four-year living together requirement which was reduced to two years on 16 June 1999. On 2 October 2000, the concession was brought within the rules. There are to be further changes in this area following the Civil Partnership Act 2004 (▶see 300–1). The rules that unmarried partners have to satisfy, which are additional to the general rules above, are set out below.

The two-year requirement

The couple need to show that they 'have been living together in a relationship akin to marriage which has subsisted for two years or more' (para. 295A(i)(a) HC 395). The couple will generally need to show that they have been living together for the two years prior to the application. The Home Office will accept short breaks of up to six months spent living apart for good reason – for example, to work or take care of a relative – provided the relationship continued during that period (see IDI, Ch 8, s7, annex Z, para. 2). Obviously, showing that the relationship is subsisting during periods of separation by short visits will be easier for couples who have substantial financial resources.

The Home Office has stated in a letter to Cameron McKenna, dated 31 August 1999 (reported in *Legal Action* November 1999), that it is not necessary for all of the two-year period to have been spent in the UK, and that time spent here as a 'visitor' can be included in calculating the two-year period. So a person may be able to obtain entry for a visit for six months, or in order to study, and at the same time be accruing time with their partner in the UK in order to make a subsequent application for settlement. The IDI state:

'Where a couple claim that they have maintained their relationship during the two-year period by merely visiting each other as often as they can, this will not be sufficient to satisfy these provisions of the Rules. However, where a couple have been *living together* in a committed relationship for the preceding two-year period, barring short breaks, but have been dividing their time between countries (for example, by using the 'visitor' category), this will be sufficient to meet the requirement.' (Ch 8, s7, annex Z, para. 2)

When the visitor rules are used in the context of an unmarried partnership to help show that a couple are living together, there may be difficulties in demonstrating that the applicant is a genuine visitor and has an intention to leave after each trip. Nevertheless, the Home Office seems to contemplate that using these rules is possible. Therefore, although people should be advised of the strict position under the rules, when seeking entry to visit their partner, or while they are here studying in the UK and also in a relationship, they should also be aware that the general stance taken by the Home Office to this situation is a helpful one.

Living together in a relationship 'akin to marriage'

The couple must have been living together in a relationship 'akin to marriage' for two years or more (para. 295A(i)(a) HC 395). Both heterosexual and homosexual partners will be required to show their relationship is a long-term, committed one that is on the model of a marriage. Evidence going to show both 'living together' (see above) and the committed nature of the relationship may be: bank accounts, investments, tenancy agreements, domestic bills or mortgage all in joint names; correspondence linking the parties to the same address; official records of address (such as doctors' or DSS records and correspondence); letters from third parties; mutually beneficial wills; guardianship of children.

The parties are not in a 'consanguineous' relationship

Previously, the rules for unmarried partners required that the couple were legally unable to marry under UK law – other than for reason of a consanguineous relationship or age. While same-sex couples automatically qualified because they could not marry, this prevented heterosexual unmarried partners from qualifying if both parties were free to marry. From 1 April 2003, the rule requiring that the couple be unable to marry was withdrawn (HC 538). However, the parties must still not be in a 'consanguineous' relationship (see paras 295A(iii), 295D(v), 295J(iii) HC 395 inserted by Cm 5949 from 25 August 2003). This means that they must not be too closely related.

Previous marriage or similar relationship has permanently broken down

Each of the parties to the unmarried partnership is required to provide information regarding any previous marriage, or other relationship akin to marriage, which they have been in. They will be asked to specify how long ago the previous relationship was terminated, either by divorce or by separation (IDI, Ch 8, s7, annex Z, para. 1).

Indefinite leave to enter for couples who have been living outside the UK

In the case of certain spouses and unmarried partners (not fiancé(e)s) who have been living together outside the UK, the applicant may qualify for indefinite leave to enter immediately, rather than having to serve the probationary period (paras 281(i)(b),282, 295A(i)(b), 295B HC 395 as amended by HC 538 from 1 April 2003). In order to qualify, in both cases the sponsor must have the right of abode, or indefinite leave in the UK, and must be seeking to return to the UK with the applicant for the purpose of settling there. In addition:

- in the case of spouses, the couple must have married at least four years before, since which time they have been living together outside the UK;
- in the case of unmarried partners, they must have been living together outside the UK in a relationship akin to marriage which has subsisted for at least four years.

The purpose of this rule is to relieve those in well-established marital or unmarried relationships from having to undergo the probationary period. For these couples, the stability of their partnership is already proven. The rule benefits applicants who, because they have not been living with their sponsor in the UK, have not been able to qualify for settlement. The rules are clear that the marriage or relationship must have been subsisting for at least four years. However, the wording is somewhat unclear as to what the position is if the couple have not lived together outside the UK for all of that period. For example, what is the position if one or both of them lived in the UK for part of that period? The IDI assume that the rule means that the parties have

'lived together abroad...throughout that 4-year period' (Ch 8, s1, para. 2.5).

This may be too strict an interpretation. Because the rule seems aimed at assisting those applicants who have not been able to qualify for settlement earlier, but where the stability of the relationship is not in doubt, we suggest that the rules be read liberally. We would suggest that a generous reading should be given where, although one or both parties have lived for limited periods in the UK during the four-year period, their circumstances were not such as would enable the applicant to have served the probationary period and qualified for settlement at that time.

Another area that calls for consideration, but where a commonsense approach might be taken, is that of spouse applications in which the couple married less than four years before, but have been in an unmarried relationship akin to marriage for a period bringing the total period up to four years. If the rules were read very strictly an applicant in this position would only qualify for the probationary period, because the application would be as a spouse and the marriage took place less than four years before. However, it seems wrong that an applicant in this position should be disadvantaged by having got married when, had they not married, they would have been admitted with indefinite leave as an unmarried partner. It is worth applicants in this position asking for discretion to be exercised for them to be granted indefinite leave.

Note that this rule does *not* apply to in-country applications for spouses and unmarried partners. In all these cases, the rules require the probationary period to be served. This underlines the fact that the rule is intended for those couples who have been living outside the UK.

The requirement for entry clearance

All spouses, partners and fiancé(e)s must obtain entry clearance before travelling to the UK if they are planning to remain permanently under the rules described above. Applications should be made on form VAF2. For full details about applying for entry clearance, the procedures used, and waiting times (including applying in these categories), ▶see 89–94.

Spouses, partners and fiancé(e)s who are visa nationals must obtain entry clearance even if they are only planning to stay for a short time to visit their partner. A fiancé(e) coming for the purpose of getting married in the UK, after which they will leave, now always needs a visa (▶see 230). Those intending only a visit can sometimes have a hard time persuading immigration and entry clearance officers of their intentions. They may suspect that the applicant is trying to avoid either the queues abroad or the detailed interview they would face if they were to apply from there. They also later risk being declared illegal entrants if they try to stay and the immigration authorities believe that they had concealed their real intention. Officers should, however, bear in mind that there is little to gain for spouses in pretending to enter only for a visit, because the rules no longer permit switches from very short-term categories to spouse (▶see 333–4).

A passenger who arrives in the UK in order to settle with their spouse or partner but who does not have an entry clearance will generally be refused entry. Officers will attempt to remove them unless there are any compelling compassionate circumstances (IDI, Ch 8, s1, para. 2.4).

After entry clearance is issued

Law and practice about the operation of entry clearance was changed by the 1999 Act. For full details about the procedures when an entry clearance has been granted, about refusing entry to those in possession of an entry clearance, and about travelling in and out of the UK, ▶see 85–9, 93–4, 95–104 and Chapter 5.

Spouses and partners: leave given by the entry clearance

If the application is successful, the spouse or partner will be granted an entry clearance. This will operate as leave to enter beginning on the date when the person arrives in the UK. The purpose of the entry clearance is to enable the applicant to be admitted to the UK for an initial probationary period of two years, after which they can apply to settle. Until 1 April 2003 the probationary period for spouses was only one year, but from that date it has been 'levelled up' to the two years required in the case of unmarried partners (para. 282, 285 HC 395 as amended by HC 538). The transitional arrangements applied by the Home Office to this change were as follows. Applications made before 1 April 2003 (including those initially refused but successful at appeal) will be treated under the old rules. In such cases, successful applicants are still granted 12 months' probationary leave, after which they are eligible for settlement (see Home Office letter to Camden Community Law Centre, 6 May 2003).

The entry clearance will have an 'effective date' (shown as 'valid from') and an 'expiry date' (shown as 'valid until'). The entry clearance is 'valid' between these two dates. The 'valid from' date may be after the date on which the entry clearance was issued, and ECOs have been instructed to ask applicants when they propose to travel so that the 'valid from' date can be as near as possible to this time. A person must arrive in the UK during the period of validity of the entry clearance. The entry clearance then has effect as leave beginning on the date of entry and lasting until the 'valid until' date. This may well be less than the 24-month probationary period. So applicants are not simply granted 24 months by the immigration officer whenever they choose to arrive, as was the case under the old system.

Confusingly, however, the Home Office, in a letter to Dexter Montague solicitors dated 13 September 2001, suggests that the period of leave to enter is calculated from the date of validity of the entry clearance. This might mean that a person arriving in the UK 23 months after the date their entry clearance was 'valid from' would be regarded as having had leave for 23 months prior to arrival. They would then be allowed to apply for settlement after just one month of presence in the UK. This does not seem to be a sensible interpretation of the process. It also does not correspond with the Immigration (Leave to Enter and Remain) Order 2000, which states that leave 'begins' on entry to the UK.

We make the following suggestions:

- If possible, people should travel as soon as possible after the 'valid from' date and negotiate the 'valid from' date with the ECO at the time of issue of the entry clearance. If there is an unforeseen delay, applicants could try to negotiate a change of the relevant dates on the entry clearance.
- If there has been a delay between the date of validity and travel, on arrival a person can ask the immigration officer for their leave to enter to be varied up to the maximum period permitted in this situation (24 months). This can be done on arrival, although it is unlikely that many people will be

aware of this opportunity or will be advised of it by the immigration officer. This application can be made orally and without any prescribed form (see para. 31A, HC 395).

- If the immigration officer declines to deal with that application (which s/he is entitled to do), or if the person has not tried to vary their leave to enter on arrival, they may apply on form FLR(M) to the Home Office for an extension of their leave in the capacity of a spouse or partner, to complete the required probationary period in the UK before they are eligible under the rules to qualify for settlement. Alternatively, if applicants in this position apply to settle, the Home Office has indicated that it may simply grant an extension of stay to enable the probationary period to be completed, with the 24-month period being calculated from the date the applicant arrived in the UK (see IDI, Ch 8, s1, para. 4.3).

- If there is only a short delay in meeting the qualifying period, applicants can wait until near the end of the initial period of leave and make the relevant settlement application. Given the usual delays in processing such applications on the part of the Home Office, by the time the decision is actually taken, the applicant is likely to have met the qualifying probationary period, and the application sought should not be refused for this reason.

The entry clearance placed in an applicant's passport by the ECO will normally include a condition requiring them to maintain and accommodate themselves and any dependants without recourse to public funds. There is normally no other restriction, which means that they are free to take employment or run a business (▶see 193 for an example of a student entry clearance with conditions endorsed). Applicants are not normally given any further information about their rights and status by immigration officers on arrival. Only applicants who have been living together for at least four years outside the UK will be entitled to indefinite leave on entry (see above).

The above procedure is very different from the previous position, when spouses with a prior entry clearance were admitted for the probationary period, which was granted on entry to the UK provided the applicant arrived within the period of the validity of the entry clearance. If people do not understand how entry clearances now work, there is a danger that they will overstay their leave, which will make their later application for settlement much more difficult.

Fiancé(e)s

Fiancé(e)s will usually be given an entry clearance valid for six months, which operates as leave to enter from the date of arrival in the UK and ends on the expiry date, in the same way as described above. They are normally subject to a prohibition on employment and business activity, as well as a condition prohibiting them from having recourse to public funds. Once the couple have married, the applicant can apply for a variation of their leave on form FLR(M) as a spouse. If this is granted, the applicant will be given the probationary 24-month period of leave. While the application is under consideration, the prohibition on work and business continues.

Fiancé(e)s are expected to get married within the initial period of their leave. If they cannot marry within the initial period of leave, they should apply to the Home Office, on the official application form FLR(O), for further permission to remain. They should set out reasons amounting to 'good cause' why the marriage has not yet taken place, and provide satisfactory evidence that it will take place at an early date.

It is not possible to switch in-country to remain as a fiancé(e) under the rules, although the Home Office has stated that:

'where we are satisfied that there are exceptional compassionate circumstances, such as the serious terminal illness of one of the parties to the marriage, consideration may be given to granting leave on a discretionary basis' (IDI, Ch 8, s2, para. 3.2)

When an application for entry clearance is refused

If an application for entry clearance is refused, the British post has to give the spouse, partner or fiancé(e) a formal notice stating that the application has been refused, with brief reasons for the refusal and information about the right to appeal, and a form to fill in to appeal against the refusal. At the time of lodging the appeal, it may be worth making representations to the ECO to persuade them that the rules are met, or requesting the exercise of discretion, and asking for a waiver of certain aspects of the rules where there are compassionate circumstances. It is important at this stage, if not earlier, to include any human rights grounds to be argued at the appeal. Article 8 ECHR will be the most important.

When a spouse, fiancé(e) or partner is refused entry clearance and appeals against the refusal, it is the practice of officials at the British post to give a full question-and-answer record of the interview as part of their statement of the reasons for refusal. However, it will usually not be provided until the appeal has been lodged. This sometimes makes it difficult to submit detailed grounds of appeal, as the full case against the person refused may not be known. It is usually better to put in general grounds of appeal, and then supplement them later once the person refused can comment on the full details of the refusal.

If the appeal is lost, the couple can make representations to the Home Office to reconsider the case. Unless there is new information that was not available at the appeal, it is unlikely that representations will be successful. If there was new information available at the appeal, upon which the immigration judge makes a recommendation to the ECO/Home Office because of the compassionate circumstances of the case, the decision may be reconsidered on this basis. Failing any of these options, the person abroad may make a fresh application to come to the UK. If at a later point the couple have married, or the relationship has endured for a longer period, or there is a child, or the sponsor has obtained employment, depending on the basis of the refusal, these developments may make a material difference to the outcome. In order to avoid wasting time and money and risking prolonged separation, careful advice should be taken about re-applications.

PEOPLE WHO HAVE BEEN ADMITTED FOR THE 'PROBATIONARY PERIOD' WHO WISH TO APPLY TO SETTLE IN THE UK

People who are admitted as a spouse or a partner with a view to settling in the UK must normally complete the probationary period of leave before they can apply for indefinite leave. This period is two years. This applies to applicants who originally applied at a post abroad, as well as those who applied in-country. As noted above, calculating when the probationary period runs from is now more difficult, and where a person has been in the UK for a period one or two months short of the required period, it may be advisable simply to submit a settlement application on the basis that, by the time the Home Office has determined their application, they will have accumulated the necessary period of leave.

Claiming benefits during the probationary period

It is expected that the applicant will not have 'recourse to public funds'. There is, however, no objection to the sponsor, or other residents in the same household, receiving public funds to which they are entitled in their own right. The question is whether there is *additional* recourse to public funds as a result of the applicant's presence in the UK (▶see 311 above). Furthermore, in the context of the probationary period, the Home Office has stated that 'if a person has (through no fault of his or her own) had to have strictly temporary assistance from public funds, he should not be refused on this basis' (IDI, Ch 8, s1, annex F, para. 8).

In most cases, the partner from abroad will be prevented from accessing public funds because they will have a condition attached to their leave that prohibits them from obtaining public funds. The effect of the condition is to make the person 'subject to immigration control', which denies access to most welfare entitlements (see 115 1999 Act). Some applicants are exempt from the test if they claim certain benefits (▶see 309–11). In some cases, of course, applicants have been able to access benefits even though their immigration status did not allow them to obtain them. In such cases, it will be a matter for the Benefits Agency to decide whether to try to recover the benefit paid if the applicant failed to disclose or misrepresented material facts.

A couple asking about entitlements to benefit during their probationary period should therefore be informed if either of them has an entitlement to claim. However, it is important that they know about the possible immigration consequences should they need to claim for a prolonged period, or should they still be claiming at the time of the settlement application. For further details about benefit entitlement generally, ▶see 1244–7. As far as the applicant's immigration status during the probationary period is concerned, and whether there is a risk of leave being curtailed (ie. cut short) because the applicant no longer satisfies the requirements of the rules under which their leave was granted (see para. 323(ii) HC 395), the Home Office policy states:

'Curtailment of leave should only be undertaken in exceptional cases and only then if the applicant has at least six months of his leave to run. Only if there is clear evidence that, shortly after the marriage, the person who was granted leave on that basis had persistent recourse to public funds *and* there was little likelihood that the situation would change, should curtailment be considered' (IDI, Ch 8, s1, annex F, para. 9).

If settlement is refused on the grounds that a couple cannot show that they can support themselves, there is a right of appeal, provided the application is made in time. During the appeal period, the spouse or partner from abroad is allowed to work, so if one of them could then find work and they no longer needed to claim benefits, the Home Office should be invited to reconsider the matter.

Applying for settlement (indefinite leave to remain)

WHAT THE RULES SAY

The immigration rules stipulate all of the following requirements (paras 287–289, 295G–295I HC 395):

- the person was admitted, or was given an extension of stay for two years as the spouse or unmarried partner of a settled person and has completed that period;
- the person is still the spouse or partner of the same sponsor and the marriage or relationship is subsisting;
- the couple intend to live together permanently as husband and wife, or as unmarried partners in a relationship akin to marriage;
- the couple can maintain and accommodate themselves and any dependants without recourse to public funds.

WHAT THE RULES MEAN

If a person who was admitted or given an extension of leave for two years as the unmarried partner of a sponsor settled in the UK subsequently marries that sponsor, this will not affect the application for indefinite leave. The rules expressly provide that an applicant in this situation will not have to start again by applying for a probationary period as a spouse – the time as an unmarried partner and a spouse is simply combined to make up the two years (see para. 287(a) (i)(b) HC 395). For details about what to do if the applicant delayed arriving in the UK after having been granted entry clearance, so that the two-year period granted by their entry clearance has not been fully served in the UK, ▶see 326.

The Home Office may still grant settlement if an applicant has spent a limited period of the two years outside the UK – for example for employment purposes. However, if the majority of the period has been spent overseas, the Home Office may doubt that there is an intention to live together permanently, or that the couple intend to settle in the UK (IDI, Ch 8, s1, para. 4.5; Ch 8, s7, para. 5.2).

Since the change in rules on 1 April 2003 increasing the probationary period, there have been a few cases in which those applying after that date have mistakenly been granted 12 months' rather than 24 months' probationary leave. The Home Office has confirmed that, in such cases, applicants will be eligible for indefinite leave after the 12 months granted (Home Office letter to Oxfordshire Immigration and Nationality Project, 26 September 2003).

Making the application

Before the spouse or partner has completed the probationary period, they should apply to the Home Office for settlement (indefinite leave to remain) on form SET(M). The spouse or partner who is British or settled should be in the UK at the time the application is made, and must confirm that the marriage or relationship is still subsisting. If he or she is temporarily abroad, this should be explained to the Home Office. For further details about the practicalities of making in-country applications, ▶see 125–36.

It is usual for these applications to be granted routinely if the Home Office has no reason to suspect any problems. If the Home Office has been informed, either by the couple or anyone else, that they have separated, or that there have been marital problems, or if they have claimed public funds during the year, it is likely that the Home Office will ask more detailed questions. They may want to interview the couple to be sure that the immigration rules are met.

Where there is reason to doubt the lasting nature of a marriage or partnership, or where the marriage seems to have broken down but there is a real prospect of the marriage being reconciled, the Home Office occasionally grant a further probationary period instead of refusing the application outright. However, where settlement is applied for but the sponsor specifically requests a period of limited leave, settlement should generally be granted. This is probably because these circumstances might suggest that the sponsor is using their spouse or partner's immigration status as a means to exercise power over them, even though there has been no actual breakdown in the marriage or partnership (see IDI, Ch 8, s1, para. 8.1).

If the application is refused

It is possible to appeal against the refusal to grant settlement. The AIT will be able to allow the appeal where the applicant can show that the disputed aspect of the rules is met – for example, that the couple are living together in a subsisting relationship or that they can adequately maintain and accommodate themselves. Where the couple's intention to live together is in dispute, then both the applicant's and the sponsor's own live evidence in court will be crucial in addressing that as a reason for refusal.

If no appeal is lodged, then the person will become an overstayer, who is liable to administrative removal without an effective in-country right of appeal concerning the spouse/partner rules. Previously, people in this position would have had to be considered by the Home Office for deportation, in relation to which there were appeal rights. Now this procedure has been removed (except for those people who applied to regularise themselves prior to 2 October 2000). Unless a human rights or asylum claim is made, there is no opportunity for a person's circumstances to be examined independently.

PEOPLE IN THE UNITED KINGDOM FOR OTHER PURPOSES WHO WISH TO 'SWITCH' TO STAY IN THE UK PERMANENTLY WITH THEIR SPOUSE OR PARTNER, WHO IS SETTLED IN THE UK

In many cases people who are already in the UK for an unconnected purpose wish to apply to remain here with their spouse or partner. Whether they are entitled to 'switch' their status to remain permanently with them depends on whether they can satisfy the following rules. These rules also apply to those who entered as fiancé(e)s, and who have since married and wish to stay permanently. It must always be clear that there has been a genuine change of circumstances since the original leave was granted, or there may be a danger of the Home Office treating the applicant as an illegal entrant. As with applications from abroad to the ECO, if the application is successful a probationary period of two years will be granted. This is so the Home Office can be sure that the marriage or partnership will last. Those whose present immigration status means that they cannot satisfy the rules to allow them to switch will need to leave the UK and apply for entry clearance to return as a spouse. Alternatively, they could apply outside the rules – but they would have to show a very good reason preventing them from returning to obtain the necessary entry clearance.

From 1 February 2005, most potential applicants who are seeking to marry in the UK, and who then intend to apply for leave to remain, will have to obtain approval for their marriage from the Secretary of State and follow the new procedures described above (▶296–300).

WHAT THE RULES SAY

The immigration rules state that, *in addition* to the requirements (►see 303–4 onwards above) in relation to spouses or partners seeking entry to the UK, the Secretary of State must be satisfied of all of the following (paras 284–286, 295D–295F HC 395):

- the applicant has limited leave in the UK which was granted under the immigration rules;
- the applicant has not remained in the UK in breach of the immigration laws;
- the marriage – or, for unmarried partners, the beginning of the relationship – predates any decision that has been made to deport the applicant, to recommend them for deportation, to give them notice that such a recommendation is under consideration following their conviction for a criminal offence, or (for unmarried partners) any decision to give directions for removal as an overstayer, a person who has breached their conditions or obtained leave by deception;
- if the application is for leave to remain as a *spouse* (i.e. not as an unmarried partner), the leave the applicant has means that they are entitled to be in the UK for more than six months altogether, from the date on which they entered the UK – but this rule does not apply to leave granted as a fiancé(e).

WHAT THE RULES MEAN

The first requirement is that the applicant has limited leave that was 'given in accordance with any of the provisions of the [immigration] Rules'. Strictly, this means that an applicant can only switch if they have leave that was granted under the immigration rules, and not outside the rules. So, a person granted leave outside the immigration rules will not be able to switch to spouse status (see IDI, Ch 8, s1, para. 3.1). The Home Office has confirmed, for example, that it is not prepared to grant indefinite leave to an applicant who has been granted discretionary leave after they have served two years with their spouse or partner. Such a person is required to complete the usual six years' discretionary leave before being eligible for settlement. Alternatively, they could leave the UK and apply for entry clearance as a spouse/unmarried partner. In that case, if the application were granted, they would be issued with two years probationary leave, after which they could apply to settle (Home Office letter to ILPA, 24 August 2004).

Any application from a spouse or partner who has overstayed their leave, or has otherwise breached immigration laws – for example, by entering the UK illegally or breaching their conditions of leave – will be refused under the rules. Similarly, where a decision to deport a person has been made, the application will be refused under the rules. A decision to deport could have been made, for example, on 'conducive to the public good' grounds, without the person having become an overstayer or otherwise breached immigration law. These applicants may, however, still succeed in persuading the Home Office to exercise discretion in their favour (▶see 337 onwards).

A new rule prevents switching to stay for *marriage* purposes where the applicant is only in the UK for short-term purposes – six months or less. The rule was originally introduced on 1 April 2003 (para. 284(i) HC 395 as amended by HC 538). It prevents, for example, visitors (who are generally granted only up to six months) and short-term students, who are granted up to six months' leave, from switching to remain as spouses. *However*, as a result of a further modification to the wording of the rule introduced from 25 August 2003 (see Cm 5949), the rule does *not* mean that applications will be refused just because the *last grant* of leave was six months or less. Time is counted from the date on which the applicant last entered the UK, and includes any later grants of leave. So, provided the total time that the applicant is permitted to be in the UK, from the date of their last entry, is more than six months, switching is not prohibited. So, for example, a person who last entered with leave to enter as a working holidaymaker, who then obtains an extension of their leave as a visitor for six months, and who then marries a person settled in the UK, can still make an in-country application as a spouse while they have their six months' leave as a visitor. Even under the initial rule change from1 April 2003, it was not the intention of the Home Office to prevent persons in such situations from switching (see Home Office letter to Wesley Gryk Solicitors, 2 June 2003).

For details about the public funds requirements, ▶see 307–18.

How to apply

Applications may be made before the person's leave to remain runs out, on the prescribed application form FLR(M). The applicant is legally in the UK while the application is being considered provided the application was made in time (and has been accepted by the Home Office as valid). The conditions attached to the original leave remain valid until the application is decided.

The Home Office often does not subject couples making these applications to the detailed questioning carried out at some posts abroad. An interview may be carried out, or a home visit conducted, in particular in cases where the applicant has married, within a short space of time, a person who they have not known for long, or where the only evidence of the marriage comes from the applicant. The application form asks the couple a list of questions about their relationship: when and how they met, when and why they decided to marry, and their plans for the future. For unmarried partners, the requirement that the couple have been living together in a relationship akin to marriage for two years is more difficult to establish. If the relationship was conducted in the UK, the non-UK partner would have to have been in the UK in another capacity under the immigration rules for most of the two years. Formally, there needs to be a change of intention to remain as an unmarried partner after the qualifying period has been completed. However, at least in practice, where an unmarried couple have been living together and the applicant is in the UK in a temporary capacity, this issue is not usually raised by the Home Office.

The application form also requests various documents. A document specifically required for marriage applications is the civil marriage certificate. If either person had been married before, evidence of how that marriage ended is required – for example, a divorce or death certificate. Both the person applying and the settled spouse or partner have to sign declarations to confirm that the marriage or relationship has not been terminated, and that they are still living together and plan to do so permanently.

Some problems which may arise

Marrying shortly after arrival

The Home Office may be suspicious of people who marry soon after gaining entry for another purpose. For example, if an applicant gained an entry clearance as a student stating that they would be going back to their country where they have firm commitments after completing their course, and then they marry after being in Britain for a fortnight and subsequently apply as a spouse, the Home Office may suspect that this was their intention from the beginning. They may suspect that the applicant wanted to avoid the problems and delay involved in applying for a fiancé(e) entry clearance, or even that the marriage is a 'sham'. The Home Office may therefore treat the person as an illegal entrant who entered the UK by deception. For further details of illegal entry, ▶see 1010–15. It is therefore important to explain how and why the person's plans changed after arrival in the UK, as well as showing how the applicant fits into the rest of the immigration rules on marriage.

Marrying towards the end of a period of leave

The Home Office may also be suspicious of people who marry very shortly before their leave to remain runs out, and may believe that the marriage was entered into so that the applicant could stay in the UK, and that the couple have no intention of living together permanently. In these cases, evidence of the length of relationship and of the reasons why the marriage was planned for that particular date will be useful.

Duty on registrars to report 'sham' marriages

Under the 1999 Act, there is a duty on marriage registrars to report to the Home Office any suspicions they have about possible 'sham' marriage. These are defined as being marriages between any person who is not a British citizen or an EEA national and any other person (whether or not that person is a British citizen or EEA national) that have been entered into for the purposes of avoiding the effect of immigration law (▶see 1031).

Curtailment

If the probationary period of leave is granted under the above rules but it subsequently comes to the notice of the Home Office that the marriage has broken down during that time, then the non-settled partner or spouse's leave may be curtailed, exposing them to being administratively removed from the UK.

Can people switch to being fiancé(e)s?

There are no provisions in the immigration rules for people who have been allowed into the country on some other basis to apply to remain as fiancé(e)s. A person who is in the UK for a temporary purpose may have plans to marry that cannot be achieved while his or her leave to remain is still current – for example, because the British or settled partner is awaiting a divorce. It may be worth making an application as a fiancé outside the rules, at the discretion of the Home Office, using the prescribed form FLR(O). The application should explain the reasons for the delay in marrying.

If they are subsequently able to marry, having gone through the new procedures (▶296–300), after the marriage they should continue the application for leave to remain to the Home Office, by submitting form FLR(M), together with the evidence requested on it, and asking for leave to remain as a spouse.

After the application is decided

If an application is successful, a spouse or partner will be given leave to remain for a probationary period initially (two years), without any restrictions on employment, and the passport stamp will usually include a condition that the person is maintained and accommodated without recourse to public funds. Provided all is well, shortly before the end of the probationary period the applicant should apply to the Home Office for settlement (▶see 331–2 for this procedure). During the probationary period the non-settled spouse or partner may travel abroad with or without their spouse or partner and be readmitted. However, if there have been long absences abroad, there may be difficulties in satisfying the 'intention to live together' requirement later.

If the application was made while the spouse or partner from abroad had leave to remain and the application is refused, there will generally be a right of appeal against the decision. The Home Office must give the person a letter explaining the reason for refusal and the right to appeal, and forms to fill in to appeal. The applicant may remain legally in the UK while the appeal is outstanding. The person may also wish to raise human rights arguments referring to Article 8 ECHR, especially where there are children involved.

PEOPLE WHO WANT TO STAY IN THE UK WITH THEIR SPOUSES OR PARTNERS BUT WHO CANNOT SATISFY THE IMMIGRATION RULES

People who are in the UK and who wish to stay permanently with their spouse or partner, but who cannot satisfy the immigration rules explained above, can be divided into two main groups.

1) People who applied for entry at port other than on the basis of their marriage/partnership, and have been granted temporary admission or have been detained ('on entry' cases ▶see below). These people may be awaiting a decision (e.g. on an asylum application), or they may have already been refused entry.

2) People who have entered the UK but whose immigration status is such that they cannot apply within the rules to stay on the basis of their marriage or partnership. This applies to those who have entered unlawfully, have overstayed or breached immigration control, are to be deported, have been granted leave outside the rules or (if applying as spouses) have been permitted to stay in the UK for six months or less (▶see 333–4). These are all 'after entry' cases (▶see below).

In most of these cases, the applicant will be seeking to rely on Article 8 ECHR. The way Article 8 works is covered in detail in the section on human rights (▶see 820–50). Note that, after 1 February 2005, in most cases where an application cannot be made under the immigration rules to stay for the purposes of marriage, the couple will have been prevented from marriage anyway (see the new procedures for marriage in the UK, ▶296–300). If a couple have been granted approval to marry despite their immigration status, it might seem strange for the Home Office to refuse an application for leave to remain on the basis of immigration status. It is possible, however, that approval is given so as to prevent a child from being born outside of wedlock, but that the Home Office still expects the non-settled spouse to leave subsequently and apply for entry clearance.

'On entry' cases

In 'on entry' cases, the rules cannot be satisfied if the applicant has arrived without an entry clearance for marriage or partnership. Article 8 is relevant in these cases. The Home Office will often refuse to accept that Article 8 is breached, on the grounds that family life can be carried on elsewhere, or that the interests of immigration control require that the applicant applies for entry clearance like other applicants (see the decision of the Court of Appeal in *Mahmood*). There may be good reasons why applying for an entry clearance abroad is not practicable – for example, where there is no functioning post in the person's country of origin. There may also be other circumstances that make it unreasonable to expect an applicant to return even temporarily. For example, it may be unreasonable to expect nursing mothers to return to countries where there is a danger to the child's health, or risks from land-mines, or to other unsafe areas. It may be that the applicant has no means of support abroad.

Although the policies on enforcement which are referred to below formally only apply in 'after entry' cases (illegal entry, administrative removal and deportation cases), the Home Office has stated:

'Although the concessions that may apply to enforcement cases do not automatically apply to port cases, the Immigration Service will have regard to them in the context of the case under the Rules and whether it is appropriate in the circumstances of an individual to waive any Entry Clearance or visa requirement.' (para. 5, *Immigration Rules and Compassionate Circumstances*, instructions to caseworkers, 25 April 2004)

'After entry' cases

People who have breached immigration controls, or have only been granted leave outside the rules or (if applying as a spouse) have only been permitted to remain for up to six months, will not fall within the terms of the rules. The rules state that people applying to stay for marriage or partnership must not have 'remained in breach of the immigration laws', and that they must have leave granted under the rules at the time that they are applying. These applicants are therefore also making an application outside the rules. Where any of these people make an application on the basis of marriage or as unmarried partners, they are considered (under the Home Office's published policy) outside the rules (see below). Similarly, it may be possible to challenge refusals on human rights grounds under Article 8.

Home Office policy in marriage cases outside the immigration rules

The following policy applies to illegal entrants, overstayers, those who have breached conditions of their leave and deportees. It does not *formally* apply to the 'on entry' category of people described above. Although neither of the following policies refers to administrative removal (overstayers, etc), it is clear that they apply to such cases (see *Immigration Rules and Compassionate Circumstances*, Instructions to caseworkers, 25 April 2004, para. 6.3.1). The policy became much stricter from 13 March 1996, when the Home Office published new internal instructions on marriage called 'DP/3/96'. It applies to marriages which 'came to the notice' of the Home Office after that date. The Home Office has stated that civil partnerships under the Civil Partnership Act 2004 will be treated in the same way as marriage for the purposes of DP/3/96 (▶see 301). For marriages which came to the attention of the Home Office before that date, the much more generous DP/2/93 policy applies. DP/2/93 also covered unmarried partners. DP/3/96 does not expressly cover them, but the policy is based upon Article 8 and the Home Office applies a similar policy in unmarried partner cases (▶see 342).

It is important to note that, even though DP/3/96 has been accepted as being, in general, a lawful policy for the Home Office to operate, this does *not* mean that its application in all cases will be compliant with Article 8. This was made clear by the Court of Appeal in the case of *Iskio*.

Main policy DP3/96 states that action to force a foreign spouse to leave should not normally be started:

'…where the subject has a genuine and subsisting marriage with someone settled here and the couple have lived together in this country continuously since their marriage for at least two years before the commencement of enforcement action and it is unreasonable to expect the settled spouse to accompany his/her spouse on removal.'

Enforcement action This 'enforcement action' is defined as one of the following:

- a specific instruction to leave with a warning of liability to deportation if the person fails to do so (the standard letter that people receive after an appeal has been dismissed, or an out-of-time application has been refused). Since the introduction of administrative removal under section 10 of the 1999 Act, it seems that service of such a notice under this provision will also amount to enforcement action, although the policy has not been formally revised or updated. (In *MA(DD/3/96 – interpretation) Algeria*, the AIT treated service of Form IS151A being notice to a person liable to administrative removal under SID 1999 Act as well as similar notices issued on IS151A Part 2 and IS151B as sufficient to amount to the commencement of enforcement action, see paras 2, 23–24);
- service of a notice of intention to deport, or of illegal entry papers;
- a court recommendation for deportation.

If any of these actions has started, they 'stop the clock' and the person does not gain any more time by making representations or appealing.

Relocation Even if the marriage has subsisted for two years before enforcement action started, the Home Office must also believe that it is 'unreasonable' to expect the settled spouse to live abroad. It is up to the couple to make sure that the Home Office has all the information on which to make a decision; the Home Office will not necessarily ask for it. In deciding whether it is reasonable to expect the family to live abroad, the Home Office will consider whether the settled spouse:

- has very strong and close family ties with the UK, such as older children from a previous relationship who form part of the family unit; or
- has long residence in the UK; or
- has medical reasons for remaining and medical evidence conclusively showing that his or her life would be significantly impaired or endangered if he or she had to leave.

Other factors Any other matters put to the Home Office can also be considered. The instructions stress that 'each case is to be decided on its individual merits and, for instance, a particularly poor immigration history may warrant the offender's enforced departure from the UK notwithstanding the factors referred to above'. Therefore, it is important that all the background and history of the couple's relationship should be explained to the Home Office at the time of application, rather than waiting for any further questionnaire. People should not rely on the application form alone, as it does not provide space for all the exceptional or compassionate factors. It should be accompanied by a further covering letter of explanation and any documentary evidence (▶see 1009–10 for an indication of the further factors that applicants may wish to draw to the Home Office's attention).

Children Where there are children of the marriage (even those with the right of abode), this is not enough in itself. The Home Office believes that 'a child of seven years or younger could reasonably be expected to adapt to life abroad'. However, if the child suffers from 'serious ill-health for which treatment is not available in the country to which the family is going', this may be enough to enable the family to stay. The Home Office used to be of the view that a child of under 10 years could adapt, but that approach was amended by a policy statement on 24 February 1999 (DP/6/99).

Procedures For details of procedures which are applied in dealing with potential DP/3/96 and DP/2/93 cases, see the Operational Enforcement Manual at Chapter 36.3.2–36.3.3.

People who have committed criminal offences

People who would otherwise benefit from DP/3/96 (see above) but who have committed offences may be refused. The policy states: 'Serious crimes which are punishable with imprisonment, or a series of lesser crimes which show a propensity to re-offend, would normally outweigh the family ties'.

People who marry after enforcement action begins

The instructions further state that 'where a person marries after the commencement of enforcement action, removal should normally be enforced', and that 'detailed enquiries in order to ascertain whether the marriage is genuine and subsisting should not normally be undertaken'. Therefore, people who marry after the commencement of enforcement action will have the most difficulty in persuading the Home Office to allow them to remain. However, a failure to consider the nature and strength of the relationship and all the compassionate circumstances of the case, and to weigh them against the interests of immigration control, may be contrary to Article 8 ECHR in individual cases. Even under Article 8, however, it will be very hard to win such cases.

Some people may wish to try to persuade the Home Office that their situation is so exceptional as to warrant being granted leave to remain.

Others may leave the country and apply for entry clearance to return, but no guarantee can be given that this will be granted. People can be refused entry clearance on the basis of their immigration history. For example, under rule 320(11) entry can be refused for a 'failure to observe the time limit or conditions attached to any grant of leave to enter or remain in the UK'. People can also be refused if they previously entered the UK by deception (para. 320(12), HC 395). In cases of very serious immigration offending, applications can be refused if 'it seems right' to the immigration officer that, considering a person's character, conduct or association, their exclusion from the UK was 'conducive to the public good'.

There are also likely to be delays in an application from overseas being considered, as the British high commission or embassy may well refer such cases to the Home Office for instructions. The couple may therefore be separated for months, simply waiting for a decision.

People who marry before enforcement action but who have been married for less than two years

People who marry before any enforcement action is taken, but have not been married and living together for two years before the date of the enforcement action, are not directly covered by DP/3/96. In a Scottish Court of Session case, *Abdadou*, the court decided that, in these cases, the Home Office should consider the compassionate circumstances relating to the family life without any presumption, either that the application be refused or allowed. The Court of Appeal in *Mahmood* recommended that the terms of the policy be reconsidered to deal with this gap.

The strongest cases falling into this category will be those where an in-country application is made within a period of leave, but the leave does not qualify the applicant to obtain an extension as a spouse because the applicant has been admitted for only short-term purposes, or because the leave they have was granted outside the rules. In such cases the applicant may not have breached immigration controls at all, and may have entered into a completely genuine marriage in the UK. If the marriage is accepted as genuine, it will be for the Home Office to demonstrate why, in the individual case, the requirement to leave and obtain an entry clearance is a proportionate requirement of immigration control for the purposes of Article 8 ECHR.

DP/2/93 – Cases where the marriage or relationship came to the attention of the Home Office before 14 March 1996

Cases where the marriage or relationship was made known to the Home Office before 14 March 1996 are still considered under the more beneficial policy DP/2/93. In these cases, the marriage or relationship has to have subsisted for two years, but the two years do not have to have pre-dated enforcement action. This policy also applies to common law relationships 'akin to marriage'. Cases to which DP/2/93 applies will now be few and far between.

Unmarried and same-sex partners who are illegal entrants or overstayers, or have breached conditions of leave

Unmarried partners who do not have leave, who have leave granted to them outside the rules, who have breached immigration control, or who are to be deported or removed, or who have not lived together with their partners for two years, cannot make an application to remain permanently with their partners within the rules. Such applications will be considered on a discretionary basis. The Home Office in fact applies a similar policy to these cases as is set out in DP/3/96. The policy is contained in the Operational Enforcement Manual at Chapter 36.4. Enforcement action will not normally be taken if: the relationship is a genuine and subsisting one akin to marriage; the sponsor is settled; the couple have lived together in the UK for at least two years before the commencement of enforcement action; any previous marriage or relationship has permanently broken down and it is unreasonable to expect the settled partner to join the applicant on removal (see also *Immigration Rules and Compassionate Circumstances*, instructions to caseworkers at para. 7.4). The DP/3/96 policy should also be applied to civil partnership cases (▶301).

It must be remembered that non-marital relationships can amount to 'family life', and that same-sex relationships, while not necessarily amounting to family life, do involve the parties' 'private' lives (▶see 827, 846–7). The Article 8 considerations for applications by unmarried partners are, therefore, very similar to those made by those in marital relationships.

Depending on the circumstances, matters to cover in the application may include those set out below.

- The length of time the applicant has been in the UK. If there are no substantial ties in the UK, human rights applications are less likely to be successful.
- The length of time the relationship has subsisted before enforcement action. Evidence should be produced to show this – for example, that there are children of the relationship, that there has been joint purchase or renting of property, or that the couple have been together for a long time. When there is a child or children involved, particularly if they are nearly seven years old, it is worth reminding the Home Office of the internal instructions relating to them (▶see 388–9). In addition, where there is a child not of the relationship but who is resident in the UK with their other parent, and who has contact with either the applicant or his or her spouse or partner, this may be an additional factor to raise in the application, as it is relevant to the human rights of the parent and the child.
- Whether it is practicable to establish family or private life abroad. It is important to address what possibilities there are of establishing family life abroad, and what difficulties or obstacles there might be in doing this. In many countries it is very difficult for same-sex partners to live openly and freely.

- The effect on the settled partner's employment, education or career if forced to move.
- The practical difficulty the couple will have in satisfying the two-year living together requirement, and therefore of the applicant being able to apply to return the UK if the application is refused.
- The difficulty for the settled partner in gaining admission (in particular as a same-sex partner) to the other partner's country.
- Other parts of the immigration rules. Are all the other parts of the rules satisfied? For example, can the couple maintain and accommodate them-selves without recourse to public funds? The *extent* to which the Home Office is being asked to depart from the rules is relevant to whether they can be persuaded to exercise discretion favourably.
- The person's previous immigration history and any problems the applicant has had with the Home Office in the past are also relevant factors. If there have been problems, they should therefore be explained. When a marr-iage takes place at the end of a long series of applications, previous marr-iages or relationships, or other immigration problems, the Home Office will be particularly suspicious of the intentions of the applicant.

In some cases, the Home Office has treated these applications as being for settlement with a close relative, and refused them because the settled partner is not a 'relative'. The IAT held in two cases in 1994 – *Lizarzaburu* and *Livingstone* – that the Home Office should instead consider these applications on a similar basis to applications on the grounds of marriage. However, these cases occurred prior to the implementation of the un-married partners' concession and its subsequent incorporation into the immigration rules. In *Hashim*, the High Court held that there would be hardship for the gay partner of a British citizen in returning to Malaysia to seek an entry clearance because of the negative attitude towards same-sex relationships there. The fact that unmarried (including same-sex) partners are now covered within the immigration rules may in practice make it harder for applicants to succeed who do not meet the requirements of the rules.

EU free movement rights

European Union rights of free movement may be helpful to common-law, gay and lesbian couples in the light of *Reed v Netherlands*. Unmarried relationships are recognised in the immigration regulations of at least Denmark, Finland, the Netherlands, Norway and Sweden. British citizens may therefore travel to these EEA countries and be joined there by an unmarried partner. For example, a British and Ghanaian gay couple might travel to Denmark, marry and live together there (if the British partner is exercising European free-movement rights there). Some couples have been able to do this successfully in the Netherlands. Advice should be taken by applicants considering these options. The changes made to the immigra-tion rules following the Civil Partnership Act 2004 will have an impact for unmarried couples who cannot satisfy the existing rules (▶see 300–1).

Making the application and rights of appeal

The application should be made on form FLR(M) making detailed representations drawing on the factors referred to above. The Home Office may send out a further questionnaire. Any applicant and their spouse or partner may be asked to go to the Home Office or to an immigration office, where they may be interviewed together or separately. They may be asked questions about their meeting and relationship to see if they give the same answers. Sometimes the immigration service comes to a couple's home unannounced, in order to see whether they are living together and whether there is any evidence that a couple live at that address.

If the application was made when the spouse/partner or fiancé(e) from abroad did not have leave to remain and is liable to removal, there will be no right of appeal against a refusal, unless the applicant alleges that a negative decision is in breach of their human rights.

PEOPLE WHO WANT TO STAY IN THE UK ALTHOUGH THEY NO LONGER HAVE A RELATIONSHIP WITH A PARTNER

There are two important circumstances in which provision is made in the rules for an applicant to remain in the UK even though they are no longer in a relationship with their spouse or unmarried partner. These are if the sponsor has died (▶below), or if the relationship has broken down due to domestic violence (▶345 onwards). The Home Office has stated that civil partnerships under the Civil Partnership Act 2004 will be treated in the same way as marriages for the purposes of the rules relating to bereaved spouses and also domestic violence (▶300). We also consider other general circumstances of relationship breakdown.

Bereaved spouses and partners

Since 2 October 2000, there has been provision in the immigration rules for the grant of indefinite leave to spouses or unmarried partners whose settled sponsor dies during the probationary period (paras 287(b), 295M–2050 HC 395). The rules require that the applicant can show that the relationship was still subsisting at the time of death, and that the parties intended to continue to live together. The same rules apply to an unmarried partner who marries their sponsor during the probationary period, and whose spouse then dies. Applications will be granted if the sponsor dies after the formal two-year probationary period but while an application for settlement as a spouse/unmarried partner is being considered. Applications will also be looked on sympathetically if they are made out of time and there is a short period of overstaying (IDI, Ch 8, s1, para. 6.8).

It will be for the Home Office to prove that the relationship had broken down before the death and, in practice, this will be a difficult task.

Therefore, the Home Office will not normally make detailed enquiries after the death certificate of a sponsor has been produced. Bereaved spouses and unmarried partners do not have to satisfy the maintenance and accommodation requirements of the rules. Note that the bereaved spouse/unmarried partner rule does not apply to:

- spouses or partners who were granted leave as the dependants of sponsors present in the UK with *limited* leave;
- those here as family members of EEA nationals who were exercising rights of free movement before they died;
- those admitted as fiancés.

Where bereaved spouses or unmarried partners no longer wish to remain in the UK after their spouse or partner has died, the Home Office will normally grant six months' leave to enable the applicant to arrange their affairs before leaving.

Victims of domestic violence

Following a vigorous campaign fought by Southall Black Sisters and others, on 27 July 1998 the Home Office announced a concession to enable the victims of domestic violence to be granted indefinite leave to remain in the UK even though they have not completed the probationary period. From 18 December 2002, the concession was introduced into the immigration rules (paras. 289–289C HC 395 inserted by HC 104 and HC 538). However, although victims of domestic violence are now granted leave under the rules, the nature of the *evidence* required to demonstrate that a relationship broke down due to domestic violence is still set by the Home Office outside the rules.

WHAT THE RULES SAY

The rules state that a person who is the victim of domestic violence and who seeks indefinite leave to remain must:

- have been admitted to the UK, or given an extension of leave, for two years as the spouse or unmarried partner of a person present and settled in the UK;
- have been in a subsisting relationship with their spouse or unmarried partner at the beginning of the probationary period; and
- be able to produce 'such evidence as may be required by the Secretary of State' to show that the 'relationship was caused to permanently break down before the end of that period as a result of domestic violence'.

WHAT EVIDENCE IS REQUIRED BY THE HOME OFFICE?

The evidence required by the Home Office in order to satisfy the rules set out in the IDI falls into two classes (Ch 8, s1, paras 5.2-5.7). In the first class is the evidence that officers would prefer to see. If it is possible to obtain any evidence in the first class, then this should be gathered. If it is not possible to produce this, evidence in the second class should be obtained. When the concession dealing with domestic violence was first introduced, the evidence the Home Office would accept was even more restrictive – evidence in the second class was not mentioned. Nevertheless, the courts' approach to cases was still that the Home Office had at least to have regard to whatever evidence was available (see *R (McKenzie) v SSHD*, HC).

We suggest that, although the applicant's task of showing the relevant facts will be harder, the same approach must still apply. Therefore, even if the evidence doesn't meet that which is generally stated by the Home Office to be acceptable – i.e. if the evidence doesn't fall within the first or second classes – the Home Office must still consider the evidence available and determine whether, in the circumstances of the case, it is sufficient to demonstrate that the essential facts are established.

Evidence of domestic violence: first class

Evidence in the first class includes:

- a court injunction, non-molestation order or other protection order made against the sponsor (other than an 'ex parte' or 'interim' order);
- a relevant court conviction against the sponsor; or
- details of a relevant police caution issued to the sponsor.

Applicants should submit the original, or a certified copy, of the court order or convictions. 'Interim' court orders are orders which are made 'in the meantime' – i.e. pending a further hearing. 'Ex parte' orders are those made without the respondent (the sponsor) attending or being represented in order to answer the accusation. Neither of those kinds of orders is sufficient. In the case of *Ekaterina Padarina B*, in the High Court, the Home Office accepted as proof an order that was made 'ex parte', but only because the respondent/sponsor, who had the opportunity to attend to answer the case, chose not to. A final order which is time-limited, for example a prohibition on the sponsor approaching the applicant for a year, is sufficient. Where a prosecution is still pending, indefinite leave will not be granted, and instead the Home Office will wait until the case has been decided. In the meantime, the Home Office will grant leave for six months at a time. Where an applicant is awaiting a hearing in the civil court about an injunction or order, then the Home Office will probably agree to delay the decision pending the outcome of the hearing (IDI, Ch 8, s1, paras 5.5-5.6; see also parliamentary reply of Home Office Minister, 16 June 1999).

Where a caution has been issued or a prosecution is pending, it is recognised that applicants will not have documentary evidence to prove it. Instead, applicants will be asked to provide details of the sponsor's name, date of birth, nationality and address, and the date, time and place of the incident that forms the subject of the prosecution or caution. The Home Office will then make enquiries of the Criminal Records Office of the police force covering that area (the pro-forma letter of enquiry and enquiry sheet used by the Home Office for these purposes is contained in the IDI at Ch 8, s 1, annex E).

Evidence of domestic violence: second class

It is recognised by the Home Office that it is often not possible to obtain evidence in the first class because there may be an unwillingness, or insufficient evidence, to take the matter to court. Also, it often simply is not an option for many victims of domestic violence to go to the police and to have to go to court and give evidence against their abusive partner in order to try and secure a conviction in a criminal court, or to hope that their husband will admit the offence so that the police will then issue a caution. In addition, pursuing matters in the family courts and seeking final injunctions or non-molestation orders may expose women to contested applications for contact orders with children of the marriage, or for residence orders that they might otherwise have avoided.

Where it is not possible to obtain the above police or court evidence, the following evidence is acceptable. However, applicants must provide *at least two* of any of the following pieces of evidence:

- a medical report from a hospital doctor confirming that the applicant has injuries consistent with being a victim of domestic violence;
- a letter from a family practitioner who has examined the applicant and is satisfied that the applicant has injuries consistent with being a victim of domestic violence;
- an undertaking given to a court that the perpetrator of the violence will not approach the applicant who is the victim of the violence;
- a police report confirming attendance at the home of the applicant as a result of a domestic violence incident;
- a letter from a social services department confirming its involvement in connection with domestic violence;
- a letter of support or report from a women's refuge.

WHAT THE RULES MEAN

The wording of the rules restricts those who can benefit to those whose marriages or partnerships were subsisting at the beginning of the probationary period of leave, but permanently broke down within the probationary period as a result of domestic violence.

Officers will therefore look to see whether:

- the marriage or partnership was subsisting at the start of the probationary period;

- domestic violence occurred during the probationary period *and* at a time when the marriage or partnership was still subsisting (this will normally be accepted if there is evidence that the couple were living at the same address when the incident(s) took place);
- it was domestic violence that caused the marriage or partnership to break down; and
- the marriage or partnership *permanently* broke down as a result of the domestic violence.

While the rules are intended to benefit those who are the victims of domestic violence during the probationary period, and who make their applications while they still have their probationary leave, the most important point is that the above four matters all occurred during the probationary period. The reality for many people in these circumstances is that they do not immediately seek to regularise their immigration position, as they are traumatised and more concerned about protecting themselves, and often their children, from an abusive spouse or partner. There may therefore be a delay in actually making the immigration application. It is also sometimes the case that a sponsor has withheld an applicant's passport.

Therefore, if the above criteria are satisfied during the probationary period, the Home Office will look sympathetically on the application, and will generally not refuse it on the basis of a short period of overstaying (see IDI, Ch 8, s1, para. 5.8). However, the Home Office will usually reject applications from 'long-term overstayers'. So, those who stay with abusive partners and who fail to regularise their immigration position, and whose marriages or partnerships then break down, are excluded from the rules. It is still worth making detailed representations in these cases as to why leave should be granted.

Domestic violence In the Court of Appeal in *R (B) v SSHD*, the Home Office accepted that threats can come within the definition of domestic violence. It must follow that domestic violence does not necessarily have to include physical violence, and that other severe forms of abuse will qualify.

Domestic violence from other family members The immigration rules do not expressly state what relationship to the applicant the person who carried out the violence must have. Domestic violence from persons other than the sponsor may still qualify a person for settlement where the violence has been the reason for the breakdown of the marriage. This may occur, for example, '…where the persons abusing the applicant are members of the sponsor's family and against whom the sponsor offers no protection' (IDI, Ch 8, s1, para. 5.9).

Domestic violence caused the breakdown The fact that domestic violence has occurred and the marriage or partnership is no longer subsisting will not necessarily mean that the violence *caused* the permanent breakdown. Advisers and applicants must be careful to explain and show that it was the domestic violence that caused the permanent breakdown. This is sometimes difficult where a spouse or partner returns to an abusive sponsor after violence and then leaves again sometime later. However, at least where there is evidence, in the form of a court order or a conviction, confirming that the applicant was the victim of domestic violence during the probationary period while the relationship was still subsisting, indefinite leave should normally be granted without further enquiries by the Home Office (see IDI, Ch 8, s1, para. 5.3). The Court of Appeal has confirmed that 'the normal assumption would be that in those circumstances it was the violence which led to the breakdown of the marriage' (*R (B) v SSHD*).

Where the application cannot meet the rules

There will still be very strong cases which cannot fall within the specific immigration rules – for example, a spouse who has been subjected to domestic violence, but who is prevented from making an application for settlement during the probationary period by their abusive partner as a method of control, and who, due to violence, leaves their spouse after the probationary period. In such cases, it is still worth making an application, accompanied by strong representations. In other cases, there may be strong human rights, or even asylum grounds, as to why the applicant ought to be able to remain in the UK. It is possible that there may be risks of human rights abuses on return to the country of origin following the breakdown of a marriage due to domestic violence or for other reasons. The risk may come from family members or the community, against which there will not be adequate protection from the state. In such cases, the applicant may wish to refer to Article 3 ECHR (inhuman or degrading treatment), and, in some cases, to make an asylum claim under the Refugee Convention (see the House of Lords case of *Shah and Islam*, ▶607–8, 616–9).

Circumstances where the domestic violence concession does not apply

It should be noted that the concession does not apply to the spouse or partner of a sponsor who themselves only has limited leave to remain. Nor does it apply to fiancé(e)s. In both cases, the Home Office would argue that the applicants were not in the UK for the purpose of settlement. However, if a domestic violence issue arose and there were reasons why the individual could not return home, an application could still be made to the Home Office using the form SET(O), with a covering letter requesting the exercise of discretion by the Home Office, and again raising any relevant human rights arguments.

The concession also does not apply to the spouse or partner of an EEA national here exercising free movement rights. Again, if a relationship broke down on account of domestic violence, especially towards the end

of the four-year qualifying period for applying for permanent residence
(▶560), then an application could be made in the same way. It should be
remembered, however, that for EEA nationals, as long as the EEA spouse
is exercising treaty rights, their partner can generally remain as their
dependant unless they are actually divorced (▶see 529). In a letter to the
Camden Community Law Centre dated 14 March 2005, the Home Office
indicated that EEA cases involving the victims of domestic violence 'are
considered on the individual merits of the case on a discretionary basis'.
The letter also indicates that practice relating to EEA cases will change in
April 2006 when spouses and partners who have been subject to
domestic violence will be specifically protected by an EU Directive.

The position while the application is being considered

Until the applicant's status in the UK is finally resolved, she is likely to be
either an overstayer or a person who continues to have a condition on her
probationary leave prohibiting her from having recourse to public funds.
Therefore, the applicant will usually have no access to benefit, and may
only be given support through the local authority if she is determined as
having needs that arise other than only through her destitution (see s21
National Assistance Act 1948 ▶see 1315–18 for more details). This will
often be the case where the applicant is a victim of domestic violence, and
therefore vulnerable. In addition, applicants may be able to access support
under the Children Act 1989, if they have the care of a child. 'Hard cases'
support is another option – in principle it can be obtained by anyone who
is temporarily admitted to the UK (see s.4(l) 1999 Act). In cases where
leave has expired, and applicants are treated for support purposes as
unlawfully in the UK, they will need to show that it would be a breach of
their human rights if support was refused (see Sch 3, 2002 Act).

If an Article 3 or asylum claim has been made, then of course support will
be available through the National Asylum Support Service (NASS). NASS
may, however, disperse applicants away from any network of support that
the applicant has established, and advisers will need to be quick to make
any necessary representations.

How to make an application

The application should be made on the SET(O) form, with a detailed
covering letter addressing the requirements of the rules set out above.
Reference to human rights arguments, where they are relied upon, should
be included in the letter. The application should also enclose the evidence
as explained above. The form also expressly asks for a 'letter signed by the
applicant stating whether you are still living with your partner and, if the
marriage or relationship has broken down, whether domestic violence
was the reason for this'. Destitute applicants who are seeking leave on the
basis of domestic violence are exempted from the normal fee that accompanies applications for leave to remain. The Home Office has indicated
that it has given instructions to staff to 'flag up' domestic violence cases,

so that they can be processed with a degree of priority (Home Office letter to Birnberg Peirce, 16 April 2003).

What if the application is refused?

If an application is refused and the person had leave at the time of applying, then an appeal can be brought. On the appeal, the applicant can argue that the decision was not in accordance with the above rules. In cases that do not comply with the rules, but where the compassionate circumstances are strong, it may be worth asking for a recommendation (▶see 1127–9). In addition, or alternatively, an appeal raising human rights grounds can be made. Where asylum has been claimed as part of the application, then of course the appeal will also consider asylum grounds.

Marriage or relationship breakdown after settlement has been granted

If a marriage or relationship breaks down after a person has been granted settlement, this does not affect his or her immigration position. The person remains settled even if they are divorced or separated from their partner. When the separation has been difficult, it is not uncommon for the spouse who is British, or was settled first, to threaten the other partner with deportation. This is an idle threat if settlement has already been granted. The only exception to this is when the Home Office believes, and can prove, that settlement was granted through deception. This will be the case if a couple had already separated at the time settlement was granted but the Home Office was not informed about this, or indeed if the couple had never intended to remain together. It is then possible for the Home Office to begin enforcement proceedings on the grounds of that person's deception. This is rare.

Marriage and relationship breakdown in other cases

If marriages or relationships break down during the probationary period for reasons other than domestic violence or bereavement, the non-settled partner no longer has any claim to remain in the UK on the basis of that relationship. Either they will have to show that they fit into some other part of the immigration rules (for switching generally, ▶see 1127–9), or that there are strong exceptional compassionate reasons, or human rights reasons, to permit them to stay. When the marriage or partnership has ended, the person cannot use application form SET(M), but should use SET(O).

A very strong case will have to be made. The Home Office will consider the respective strength of the applicant's ties with the UK and their own country, and whether they would suffer any hardship if they were required to leave. Leave to remain will not normally be granted unless there are the most exceptional compelling or compassionate circumstances. The factors to be considered would include: the length of time the applicant was married before the breakdown; the length of time the applicant has been resident in the UK; the applicant's age and the proportion of time spent abroad before entering the UK; whether there are children of the marriage.

Applying to stay for access to children

In the past, the presence of children of the marriage was considered very significant, but the Home Office's current policy is that 'the general presumption is that a child who has spent less than seven years in the UK would be able to adapt to life abroad'. If the child or children are to stay in the UK with the settled partner, then there are specific rules enabling separated parents to be granted leave in order to obtain access to their children (for details ▶see 372–5). However, where the non-settled parent and child are living together, and the child has contact with their other parent who is settled in the UK but not residing with the child, then the parent from abroad will have to seek leave to remain in the UK outside the immigration rules, relying on the right to family life.

PEOPLE WHO WISH TO ACCOMPANY OR JOIN A SPOUSE OR PARTNER IN THE UK WHO IS HERE WITH LIMITED LEAVE

The admission of spouses and partners with a view to settlement where the sponsor is *settled* in the UK is dealt with above. However, the immigration rules also provide for the admission of the spouses and partners of those who have been granted limited leave under many (but not all) of the categories in the rules. We discuss below the various categories that enable sponsors to be joined by their spouse or partner.

For the dependants of refugees and those with temporary protection, humanitarian protection, discretionary leave or exceptional leave (having been refused asylum), see Chapter 25 on 'Family Reunion'. Where there is provision for the admission of the dependants of others granted leave outside the rules, it is mentioned in the *Handbook* where we deal with the relevant category. The admission of the dependants of those exempted from immigration control, is discussed at ▶472–6, and the dependants of Gurkhas and other foreign or commonwealth citizens who have been discharged from the armed forces are dealt with at ▶151.

For the admission of the children of those with limited leave in the UK, ▶see 376–9.

Dependants of workers, business-persons and others in long-term categories

The immigration rules allow for the admission of the spouses and unmarried (including same-sex) partners and children of people in the following long-term categories under the rules (paras 194–199, 240–245, 271–276, 295J–295L HC 395):

- work permit holders (but for TWES permit holders ▶see 355 below);
- highly skilled migrants;
- science and engineering graduates;
- representatives of overseas news media;
- sole representatives;
- private servants in diplomatic households;
- domestic workers in private households;
- overseas government employees;
- ministers of religion, missionaries and members of religious orders;
- airport-based operational ground staff of overseas-owned airlines;
- persons with UK ancestry;
- business-persons;
- innovators;
- investors;
- writers, composers, artists;
- retired persons of independent means.

Note that the rules expressly exclude the spouses and children of those admitted under the Sectors-Based Scheme (SBS) (see para. 194 HC 395). Unmarried partners of SBS participants are not expressly excluded by the rules (see para. 295J HC 395), although it may have been the intention of the government to exclude them.

All of the following common requirements for admission of these spouses and partners must be met:

- the applicant must intend to live together with their spouse or partner during their stay in the UK;
- if the applicant is married to the sponsor, the marriage must be subsisting;
- if the applicant is the unmarried partner of the sponsor: they have been living together in a relationship akin to marriage that has subsisted for two years or more, they are not in a consanguineous relationship, and any previous marriage or similar relationship has permanently broken down;
- there will be adequate maintenance and accommodation for them without recourse to public funds;
- they must not intend to stay in the UK beyond any period of leave given to their sponsor.

Applicants need an entry clearance to come to, or be allowed to remain in, the UK for this purpose. The rules do not permit switching for spouses/partners who are already in the UK in some other category. Officers may, however, waive the no-switching requirement if they are satisfied that all the other requirements are met, and that there are 'exceptional compassionate circumstances' (IDI, Ch8, s9, para. 2.2). For switching outside the rules generally, ▶see 187–8.

If the application is successful, leave to enter or remain will normally be granted for the same length of time as the spouse or partner who is a worker, business-person, etc. Home Office practice is not to restrict employment, so the dependants of the above are normally free to work. The exception to this is the dependants of retired persons of independent means, who will normally be prohibited from working.

Dependants of students

The spouses (and from 5 December 2005, civil partners) and children of students can be admitted under the immigration rules in line with the student (paras 76–81 HC 395). This applies to:

- students;
- prospective students;
- student nurses;
- postgraduate doctors, dentists and trainee GPs;
- re-sitting students;
- students writing up a thesis.

The two following points relating to the dependants of students need to be borne in mind.

- The rules do not expressly give rights to dependants of student union sabbatical officers. There is also no provision in the rules for those coming to the UK to take the 'PLAB' test, a clinical attachment, or as a dental observer (see paras 76–81 HC 395, which omit reference to paras 75A–M and 87A–F of the rules). These latter groups of medical student have only recently be added to the rules, however, and it is possible that provision will be made for their dependants in the future.

- Although there are rules relating to the admission of unmarried partners for others with limited leave (see above), as at 7 November 2005, there was no similar provision under the immigration rules for students. An application could be made outside the rules stating that the person met the other requirements of the rules for the admission of spouses and partners seeking entry in a temporary capacity (see above). Arguably, human rights discrimination grounds could also be raised, as there is no apparent justification for their omission from the rules. In June 2003 the Home Office stated that the question of allowing same-sex dependants of students to be admitted was under review.

Spouses of students seeking entry have to show that they can be maintained and accommodated without recourse to public funds, that they intend to live with the sponsor during their stay, that the marriage is subsisting, and that they intend to leave the UK at the end of any period of leave granted (▶see also 266–8). For non-visa nationals, non-specified nationals and specified nationals coming for a period of up to six months entry clearance is not required in order to obtain entry. It is also possible to switch to remain as the spouse of a student. Leave will normally be given in line with the leave given to the student and, provided that leave is for 12 months or more, it will normally permit work. If the period of leave given is less than 12 months' work will normally be prohibited. In practice, students are often only able to fund their studies with the additional income that their spouse is earning. Students' spouses should use application form FLR(O) if they are applying separately from the student, and FLR(S) if the student and spouse are applying together, in-country, for an extension of leave.

Dependants of those in other temporary categories

The immigration rules also permit the admission of the spouses and children of teachers and language assistants (under approved exchange schemes), those in approved training or work experience (i.e. TWES) (paras 122–127 HC 395) and those admitted under the 'Fresh Talent Working in Scotland' initiative (paras. 194–199 HC 395). Spouses have to satisfy the same rules as above, relating to intention to live together during their stay in the UK, subsisting marriage, maintenance and accommodation, and intention to leave after the period of leave granted. However, as with students, unmarried partners of those with leave as teachers or language assistants are not provided for under the immigration rules (but ▶see also 443 in relation to the unmarried partners of TWES permit holders). Those with leave in the 'Fresh Talent' category can, however, be joined by their unmarried partners if the normal rules for such partners are met (▶see 465–6). Entry clearance is mandatory for all those seeking entry, and switching to remain in this category is not permitted under the rules. Leave is normally granted for the same period as the sponsor.

There is no provision in the rules for the spouses and partners of working holidaymakers. Indeed, the rules require that, in the case of a working holidaymaker who is married, their spouse should intend to be admitted as a working holidaymaker with them so that they can take a working holiday together (▶see 249). Children aged under five of working holidaymakers may be admitted (▶see 239, 242).

No specific provision is made in the immigration rules for spouses, partners or children of persons in the following temporary categories contained in the rules: visitors; transit visitors; medical visitors; parents of children at school; marriage visitors; *au pairs*; seasonal agricultural workers; multiple-entry work permit holders. Dependants of people in those categories will have to qualify in their own right. In the case of visitors, dependants will usually simply qualify as visitors themselves.

Applications for indefinite leave by dependants of sponsors admitted in a category leading to settlement

Where a dependant has been admitted with limited leave as the dependant of a sponsor who is in a category leading to settlement, and that sponsor is then granted indefinite leave, the dependant may be granted indefinite leave as well. So, for example, a sponsor admitted in many of the long-term economic categories will normally be entitled to apply for indefinite leave after four continuous years in that capacity (▶see 437–9 for the relevant requirements). Their dependants, who will normally apply for indefinite leave at the same time as their sponsor, will normally be granted indefinite leave in line with them, provided all of the normal rules relating to dependants (see above) are satisfied. Since the spouse will already have lived in the UK together with their sponsor for a significant period, the formal requirement to serve the probationary period is not applied in these cases.

The rules relating to unmarried partners of sponsors in the UK for long-term economic and other purposes do not directly refer to their ability to qualify for indefinite leave at the same time as their partner obtains indefinite leave (compare paras 295J–L with para. 198 HC 395). However, the Home Office confirms that unmarried partners who were admitted and have remained in the UK as the unmarried partner of their sponsor, and who continue to satisfy the rules relating to dependants, may be granted indefinite leave at the same time as their partners (see IDI, Ch8, s17, para. 4.5). They also, therefore, do not have to wait until their partner is granted indefinite leave, and then serve the formal probationary period, before settling.

12 Children

4

This chapter covers the rights of children to come to and stay in the UK with their parents or guardians. It also covers the rights of children to be joined in the UK by their parents, where the parents do not otherwise have the right to be in the UK. It also looks at children who are in the UK on their own.

The chapter therefore covers the immigration rights of children in the following circumstances:

- children joining or staying with parents who are settled in the UK, or accompanying parents coming for settlement (▶360–7);
- children coming to join one parent in the UK, or accompanying one parent for settlement (▶367–71);
- children joining or staying with a person in the UK who is not their parent (▶371–2);
- the rights of children to have a parent, with whom they have contact, join them in the UK and remain with them (▶372–5);
- the rights of children who are under 12 and at school in the UK to be accompanied by their parent/s (▶375–6);
- children accompanying or joining parents who are in the UK with limited leave (▶376–9);
- the rights of adopted children (▶379–85);
- children whose parents may be forced to leave the UK (▶386–90);
- children in the UK on their own (▶390–3);
- children born in the UK (▶393–5).

Some matters concerning children are looked at elsewhere in the *Handbook*:

- access to welfare for children is covered in Section 12 along with all other welfare issues. For support under the Children Act specifically, ▶see 1322–8;
- for details about unaccompanied minors seeking asylum (UASCs) in the UK, ▶see 686–81;
- children applying as the dependants of asylum-seekers are covered at ▶691–4;

- for the rights of family reunion for children of parents in the UK who have been recognised as refugees ▶see Chapter 25; or if the parents have been granted HP, DL or ELR, ▶see 875–9;
- for the rights of children accepted as refugees to be joined by family members under the policy on family reunion, ▶see 763–4.

Children who have reached 18

This chapter generally concerns children who are below the age of 18. However, some children who reach 18 can still benefit from the rules set out in this chapter because:

1) The age of a child seeking to come to the UK for the purposes of settlement with parents or a relative is determined as of the date of the application rather than the date of the decision (para. 27 HC 395). So a child may have turned 18 by the date of the decision but still be granted entry clearance under the immigration rules.

2) Children who come to the UK with a view to being settled with a parent, or parents, who are settled in the UK and who are given limited leave, may subsequently be granted indefinite leave even if they reach 18 by the time they come to apply for indefinite leave. The same applies to those children who are admitted with limited leave to join a parent or parents who have limited leave in a category under the immigration rules which may lead to settlement (e.g., work or business-related purposes, ▶see 377, 436). Provided that they apply while they still have leave as a child dependant, it doesn't matter that they have subsequently become 18. They may still be granted extensions or indefinite leave in line with their parent(s).

Other children who have reached the age of 18 have to satisfy additional requirements in order to be admitted under the rules (▶see 405 onwards).

Children who do not have to satisfy the immigration rules

Some children have immigration rights which do not derive from the immigration rules. They are as follows.

Children who are British citizens People born in the UK before 1 January 1983 are British citizens and have the right of abode in the UK. Those born abroad before 1983 to British citizen fathers are automatically British citizens and are also, therefore, free to enter and remain in the UK. Children born in the UK from 1 January 1983 onwards are automatically British citizens if either parent was a British citizen or was settled here at the time of the child's birth. Most children born abroad from 1 January 1983 onwards are automatically British citizens if, at the time of the birth, either parent was a British citizen who was born, adopted, registered or naturalised in the UK. In all cases, the father's status counts only if the parents were married at the time of the birth or, in some cases, subsequently marry.

Certain changes to transmitting nationality are made by the 2002 Act but are yet to come into force (▶see 1429). To check on the nationality status of children born in the UK or children with British parents ▶see 393–4, 1438–42.

Children with the right of abode A person who is a Commonwealth citizen and who was born before 1 January 1983 to a parent who was born in the UK, has the right of abode in the UK and does not have to prove anything more than these facts to obtain a certificate of entitlement to the right of abode. If the parent relied on is the father, the parents have to have married.

People claiming these rights need to have their position confirmed abroad before travelling, by applying to a British post overseas. If they are British citizens, they may obtain British passports. If they are Commonwealth citizens with the right of abode, they have to obtain a certificate of entitlement to the right of abode. They will need the birth certificate of the parent born in the UK, the marriage certificate of their parents if the parent concerned is their father, and their own birth certificate to show who their parents are. If these certificates are not available, or not accepted as genuine, it may be difficult to satisfy the British authorities about the relationship.

Children of EEA nationals Nationals of an EEA country other than the UK who are exercising European rights of free movement in the UK are entitled to be joined here by their dependants. Normally included as dependants are children and grandchildren up to the age of 21 and beyond that age if the children are still dependent. For full details about dependants of EEA nationals, including developments as a result of the ECJ cases of *Baumbast* and *Chen,* ▶see 526–40.

Children of those 'exempt' from immigration control Children of certain people who are exempt from immigration control, may also be exempt and not have to satisfy the immigration rules. This applies, for example, to the children of diplomats who form part of their household (▶see 474).

Human rights and other considerations

In addition to the immigration rules and the Home Office policies outside the rules, which are considered in this chapter, Article 8 ECHR (right to respect for private and family life) will also be relevant in many cases involving children. Although the relationship between parents and their minor children will almost always amount to 'family life', in *Isiko* the Court of Appeal maintained the principle that immigration decisions which separate them can be justified especially where the parents' immigration history is very poor and/or criminal offences have been committed by the parent who is facing removal. For full details about whether a case can fall within the protection of Article 8, ▶see 473–6.

The Home Office tends to interpret the immigration rules on children without direct reference to other childcare legislation such as the Children Act 1989. The 1989 Act states that when a court determines any question concerning a child, the child's welfare must be the paramount consideration. The court proceeds on the basis that children should remain with their families wherever possible. Immigration law, even read together with Article 8, does not contain any of these assumptions. In *Ahmed & Patel* and in *Gangadeen*, the Court of Appeal treated the best interests of the child as a factor in immigration decisions involving family life but not as paramount. That case also confirmed that the United Nations Convention on the Rights of the Child (ratified by the UK in 1991) is not directly applicable in immigration cases.

CHILDREN JOINING OR STAYING WITH BOTH PARENTS SETTLED IN THE UK

WHAT THE RULES SAY

The rules for children coming to join settled parents state that they must (para. 297–300 HC 395):

- be the child of parents present and settled or being admitted for settlement to the UK;
- be under 18;
- be unmarried, not have formed an independent family unit and not be leading an independent life; and
- be maintained and accommodated in accommodation owned or occupied exclusively by their parents without recourse to public funds.

The child must obtain an entry clearance to come to the UK. If both parents are alive but one parent is not living in the UK and does not intend to live here, additional requirements must be satisfied. If one of the parents is dead, however, there are no additional rules to satisfy. For the circumstances where a child wishes to join a lone parent in the UK ▶see 357–61.

The following two points should be noted as applying to children in this and the other categories under the immigration rules relating to the admission of children.

1) As with most applications under the rules, children can still be refused leave if any of the general grounds for refusal apply (▶see 94–5, 140–1).
2) A child will be refused under the rules if their parent is a party to a polygamous marriage who would be refused admission for settlement under the rules denying admission to those who are polygamously married (this is generally the case where one living wife has already been admitted, ▶see 309 for further details and paras 278–278A and 296 HC 395).

Where one parent is settled and the other has leave 'with a view to settlement'

The rules are similar for a child who is accompanying, coming to join or staying with parents in the UK where one parent has limited leave with a view to settlement and the other is settled (paras. 301–303 HC 395). In those circumstances, the child will be admitted for 24 months 'with a view to settlement' and will normally be able to apply for indefinite leave at the end of those two years. This 24-month period is intended to mirror the 'probationary' period of leave, which the non-settled parent will probably have been granted.

Children of fiancé(e)s

The rules also now provide for the children of fiancé(e)s to come to the UK with the fiancé(e) and to be granted limited leave of up to six months (paras. 303A–303F, HC 395). Extensions may be granted if the fiancé(e) (their parent) is also granted an extension because the marriage has not yet taken place. The child can also obtain indefinite leave in line with the rules set out above, when their parent also seeks indefinite leave. The child must be under 18, unmarried, dependent and able to be supported without recourse to public funds. However, children coming with fiancé(e)s also have to show that there are serious and compelling family or other considerations which would make their exclusion from the UK undesirable (the 'exclusion-undesirable' rule is discussed further below at ▶370–1), that there is no other person outside the UK who could reasonably be expected to care for them and that suitable arrangements have been made for their care in the UK. Again, entry clearance is required for the child to come to the UK.

WHAT THE RULES MEAN

Parents

'Parent' obviously includes the natural parents of a child. In the immigration rules relating to the settlement of children (and for the admission of children for other purposes), the word 'parent' also includes (para. 6, HC 395):

- the stepfather of a child whose father is dead;
- the stepmother of a child whose mother is dead;
- the father as well as the mother of a non-marital child;
- in the case of a child born in the UK who is not a British citizen, a person to whom there has been a genuine transfer of parental responsibility on the ground of the original parent(s)' inability to care for the child (e.g. a foster parent or another relative).

Adoptive parents 'Parent' does *not* include an adoptive parent where the application is made under paragraphs 307–313 of the immigration rules (i.e. for settlement), that is:

- under any of the above stated rules (except, apparently the rules relating to children of fiancé(e)s); *or*
- the rules set out below at ▶367–72 for the admission of children to join one parent or relative.

Where the application is not made under paragraphs 307–313 HC 395, the definition of 'parent' includes an adoptive parent *but* only where (para. 6 HC395):

- the child was adopted in accordance with a decision taken by the competent administrative authority or court in a country whose adoption orders are recognised by the UK (▶see 1528–9 for the list of these countries and ▶see 383); or
- the child is the subject of a *de facto* adoption, which meets the requirements of the rules for such adoptions (para. 309A HC 395, ▶see 381).

For the separate rules about applications for adopted children, ▶see 379 onwards.

Although the rules define parent as 'including' the above persons, there are no other categories of person who can qualify as parent – the list is a complete list. This was the finding of the IAT in *ECO Accra v Emmanuel Attafuah* in which a man who had always thought himself to be the natural parent, discovered through DNA tests during the course of an entry clearance application, that he was in fact not the parent of the child. The IAT rejected the idea that he could be a 'parent' nevertheless, or that there were other residual classes of parent not contained in the list set out in the rules.

Where a biological relationship is relied upon and there is a dispute, DNA evidence is sometimes used (▶see 365–6).

Parents settled in the UK

The actual requirements are that either:

- both parents are present and settled in the UK; or
- both parents are coming to the UK for settlement at the same time as the child; or
- one parent is present and settled in the UK and the other is coming to the UK at the same time as the child and is being admitted for settlement.

The position where one parent is settled and the other is being admitted *with a view to settlement*, is noted above. For the definition of 'settled' and 'present and settled', see the chapter on spouses at ▶302–3.

If both parents are settled, or are being admitted for settlement and all the other requirements are satisfied, the child should be given indefinite leave.

Under 18

Children must be under 18 on the date of application to come to or remain in the UK (see para. 27, HC 395, which applies to entry clearance applications – as a matter of practice, however, the Home Office applies this to in-country cases as well, see IDI, Ch 8, s3, annex M, paras 2.1–2.3). This is an exception to the general rule that applications are decided on the circumstances existing on the date of the decision. This rule is to ensure that a child's application is not refused because a delay in determining it means that the child no longer satisfies the age requirement. To be valid, in-country extension applications have to be made on the correct Home Office application form and be accompanied by all the documents specified on the form, or an explanation of why any documents are not available and when they will be sent. It is therefore important that an in-country application is made correctly before a child reaches 18.

However, these concerns do not apply to a child who was admitted with limited leave under the rules allowing admission with a view to settlement with their parents, and who later applies for indefinite leave on the same basis. Such an applicant should be granted indefinite leave if they satisfy all the other rules, even if they have, by the date of the in-country application for settlement, reached the age of 18 (see para. 298(ii)(b), HC 395).

Refusals based simply on age where continued dependency can be shown may raise an issue under Article 8 ECHR.

Unmarried/not leading an independent life/ not formed an independent family unit

A child who is married is not eligible to be admitted under the immigration rules, even if he or she is still under 18. The marriage is taken to mean that the child has formed a closer family link with their spouse and therefore no longer qualifies to join their parents. Children who are not married but who are coming up to adulthood can be refused if immigration officials believe they have formed an 'independent family unit', or are leading an 'independent life'. These circumstances are not defined further. They possibly exclude from admission a child who has dependants of their own, even if they are not married to or living with the other parent, and children who have become self-sufficient or dependent upon someone else.

Maintenance and accommodation

The 'maintenance and accommodation without recourse to public funds' requirements apply to the vast majority of categories for admission under the immigration rules. It should be noted that the rules relating to children state that they should be maintained and accommodated 'by the parent' or parents. If third-party support is available, however, and the application is refused for this reason, this may be contrary to Articles 8 and 14 ECHR. For full details of the maintenance and accommodation requirements ▶see 308–18.

In *M & A v SSHD*, the Court of Appeal held that the fact that the rule states 'by the parent' was important because it meant that focus could be placed on the *role* of the parent in providing adequate accommodation and not just the physical nature of the accommodation. In that case, the Court dismissed the appeal of two Indian children who had been refused entry clearance to join their parents because of concerns about their safety following the death of one of the parents' other children in suspicious circumstances and injuries to two children. The Court held that the danger posed by the parents meant that the accommodation was unsafe and therefore the children could not be 'accommodated adequately'.

Note that the Home Office is cautious about refusing applications from children on maintenance and accommodation grounds alone. The particular circumstances of the case and any compassionate circumstances will be taken into account before such a refusal is issued (see IDI, Ch 8, s1, annex F, para. 10).

Children applying for entry clearance

Children have to satisfy entry clearance officers (ECOs) at the British post that they qualify. The evidence that may be required is as follows:

- proof of the child's relationship to the parents. If the child has a birth certificate showing the names of both the parents, this is very helpful. However registration of births is not universal or compulsory in some countries and a birth certificate may not exist. Also British officials are often suspicious of documents that are produced by governments in poorer countries of the world and often refuse to accept them. If the document does not exist, this should be explained and alternative evidence produced instead; for example:
  - records from the school the child is attending to show what that institution has been told about the child's age and parentage,
  - records from the hospital where the child was born,
  - information from the midwife or anyone else who knows about the birth,
  - statements or affidavits from people, preferably not related to the child and parents, confirming their knowledge of the birth and relationship;
- proof of the parent/s' status in the UK, for example, certified photocopies of his, her or their passports;
- the parents' birth certificates if either of them was born in the UK;
- evidence of financial support available to the children;
- evidence of accommodation available to the children.

Interviews and investigations

Children may well be interviewed (unless they are under ten) and the person who has been caring for them abroad is also likely to be interviewed. Questions should be confined to relatively simple matters and details of immediate family. Older children may be questioned on their own (not in the presence of a responsible adult) and in more depth. All children will need to show evidence about their relationship to their parent(s) and of maintenance and accommodation available in the UK.

Parents and children should be aware that, in certain cases, staff from the post may conduct a 'village visit'. This might happen, for example where there is no satisfactory documentary evidence to establish age or that the child is related as claimed. It may also occur in cases involving 'sole responsibility' for lone-parent applications, or if there is a question over whether a child has established an independent family unit. If a visit is made, staff may go to the place where the child lives or comes from and ask questions of people in the local community. The evidence obtained may later be produced in an appeal and may require a further independent village visit organised by the applicant in order to counter any negative conclusions – this will be time-consuming and expensive and its independence may be called into question.

For further details about entry clearance applications generally, ▶see 89–93.

DNA testing

DNA profiling can prove fairly conclusively that children are related to their parents. The test involves taking a small sample from the child and the parents and testing this for the DNA contained in it to see that the child's DNA corresponds to that of the claimed parents. The sample can now be taken by a 'buccal swab' (a mouth swab). This can of course be done in other cases where a biological relationship is unclear or disputed as well. It is a much more certain way of determining relationships than by asking family members detailed questions. However, it can also show, for example, that a father is not the father of a child whom he has always accepted and believed to be his.

Since January 1991, the government has operated a scheme under which ECOs may offer to arrange a DNA test in order to establish the claimed relationship. Procedures for DNA testing are set out in the Diplomatic Service Procedures at Chapter 14, paragraph 14.20. DNA tests can be provided for first-time applicants for settlement or the right of abode if the ECO considers 'that it would be a desirable aid to the decision-making process' (see also IDI, Ch 8, s3, annex N). The ECO must always first try to establish the relationship in the usual way by looking at documentary and other evidence. Only if 'substantial doubt' exists after this, may a test be offered. If the family agrees to take the test, arrangements will be made by the British post for the test to be done, at no extra cost to the family (the level of entry clearances fees takes account of the likely costs of these procedures). If the family refuse, this should not be a reason in itself for refusal of the application although the ECO will record the fact of the refusal together with the reason given for declining the test. The scheme does not, however, generally apply to re-applicants, namely, people who have been refused once and who are applying again.

Families not included in the scheme may still have tests carried out on their own initiative. They should get in touch with one of the companies, which the Home Office has approved to carry out DNA testing and follow the company's procedures. If the application has been refused and there is an immigration appeal pending, and the family qualifies for legal funding from the Legal Services Commission, it is possible that funding can be obtained for the test. Applicants can, of course, also pay privately.

The DNA report should state the mathematical likelihood that the applicant(s) and sponsor are related as claimed. If they are not related as claimed, the report will, where possible, state the likely nature of the relationship. Although usually conclusive, DNA evidence is not fail safe and where there is a conflict between the scientific evidence and the applicant/sponsor's evidence or other evidence, although the scientific evidence may be very difficult to dislodge, it must still be balanced against whatever other evidence exists (*Debin Bibi v ECO Dhaka*, IAT). Under 'assessing the reports', the DSPs state as follows:

'The ECO must assess the relationship(s) on the balance of probabilities from all the available evidence. Where DNA evidence is the *only* evidence available to the ECO, a report that suggests the applicants are related as claimed should be considered sufficient. Where other evidence is available to the ECO, the strength of the DNA results must be considered in conjunction with this.' (Ch 14, para. 14.20).

If the application is successful

If the ECO is satisfied that the rules are met, entry clearance will be granted to the child. Entry clearances now operate as leave to enter the UK. If the child is being admitted for settlement, the entry clearance will be endorsed with a statement that it is to have effect as indefinite leave. Otherwise, the entry clearance will be valid for a particular period (probably 24 months) and will operate as leave to enter until the expiry date of the entry clearance. After being admitted, the child is immediately entitled to state education.

If the application overseas is refused

The British post will issue a notice explaining why the application was refused, stating the child's right to appeal against the refusal, and sending forms to fill in to appeal. It does not matter if a child becomes 18 while the appeal is pending; the important date is the date of application. If the appeal is successful two years later, when a child is 19 or 20, they should be granted entry clearance provided that there is no other substantial change of circumstances. However, if an appeal fails, but a child later produces fresh evidence, for example, a DNA test result, and applies again, the application is considered to be made on the date of the second application. Advice should be taken in these cases and where possible, therefore, care should be taken not to withdraw an initial application that was made while the applicant was under 18.

Rights of appeal against entry clearance refusals are covered at ▶93, 1052–8.

CHILDREN JOINING ONE PARENT IN THE UK

WHAT THE RULES SAY

If one parent is dead, a child can join or be allowed to remain with the other parent provided that parent is present and settled in the UK, or is being admitted for settlement at the same time as the child. The same rules as for children joining both parents (see above) apply and there are no other specific requirements the child has to meet apart from proving the death of the deceased parent. The child will be given leave in line with their parent (paras. 297–300 HC 395).

However, if an application is being made for a child to join one parent where the other parent is still alive, there are further rules, which must be satisfied. It must be shown that the parent who the child is joining is either present and settled in the UK, has been admitted with a view to settlement or is being admitted for settlement/with a view to settlement at the same time as the child (paras. 297(e)–(f) and 298(i)(c)–(d) HC 395); *and*

- the parent has had 'sole responsibility' for the child's upbringing; *or*
- there are serious and compelling family or other considerations that make the child's exclusion undesirable and suitable arrangements have been made for the child's care in the UK.

The rules relating to maintenance and accommodation, age and being unmarried/not leading an independent life, which apply where both parents are being joined, must also be satisfied (see above for those requirements). Children applying to come to the UK to join one parent must also obtain entry clearance.

The 'under-12' concession

The immigration authorities used to operate a policy outside the rules to allow children who are under 12 years old to join one parent in the UK without having to satisfy the stringent 'sole responsibility' or 'serious and compelling' requirements (see pages 377–378 of the 2002 edition of the Handbook). This 'under-12' concession was withdrawn on 29 March 2003 (see IDI, Ch 8, s1, annex F, para. 10.1; Ch 8, s3, annex M, para. 12). However, there is provision in the rules to allow a *parent* to be admitted to the UK while their child, who is under 12, is attending an independent fee-paying day school (▶see below at 375–6).

Despite the withdrawal of the under-12 concession, it is possible that there remain decisions made before that date in relation to which the policy was not properly applied. This was the case in *KK*, decided in September 2004, in which the IAT considered the old IDIs in conjunction with an explanatory letter from the IND Policy Directorate, which referred to the concession. The IAT rejected the Home Office's argument that the concession was not sufficiently structured for the appellate authorities to take note of it – the decision was therefore 'not in accordance with the law' under the 2002 Act. The decision was also 'not in accordance with the law' for the purposes of Article 8(2) ECHR because it was precise enough about whether it also benefited in-country applicants.

The IDIs state that 'no applications citing the concession should be accepted after' 29 March 2003 (Ch 8, s3, annex M, para. 12). It is arguable, therefore, that if an application is made before that date but the decision is made afterwards, then the concession should still be applied.

WHAT THE RULES MEAN

A substantial amount of case law has grown up around these requirements of the rules. A parent will never literally have had 'sole responsibility' when they have been living in a different country from the child and so allowances are made. The alternative 'exclusion undesirable' requirement is notoriously difficult to satisfy.

The 'sole-responsibility' rule

The sole-responsibility rule was first introduced in 1969. The government's stated intention was to prevent the growth of all-male Pakistani families, where men who had come to work in the UK were sending for their sons, but not their wives and daughters, and it was felt that this was not in the best interests of the children. The result was that families applied to come to the UK.

The communities that continue to suffer most from the sole-responsibility rule are people from the Caribbean and from West Africa. Many women from these regions migrated in search of work, leaving young children in the care of an older relative, commonly a grandmother, for what was intended to be a short period until they could make a home for them in the UK. Money was sent for their support and close contact was maintained, but it was often not possible to say that sole responsibility for the child was with the mother. In such cases, ECOs have been known to ask many questions about contact with the child's father, who may well have remained abroad but was separated from the mother and child. It is clearly hard for children or grandparents to admit that the child has been abandoned; but if the father's contact had been kept up, even at a very low level, this could be a reason for refusing the child entry clearance.

Sole responsibility does not simply apply between parents as to who has had that responsibility but also relates to other relatives or carers who may have assumed that role in the absence of one or both parents.

In *Rudolph*, the IAT considered what should be proved in order for a child to qualify under this rule. In that case, the parents were separated and the child had been brought up in a convent in Sri Lanka while her mother was in the UK. The IAT stated:

'...we need therefore to be satisfied not only that essential financial support was provided by Mrs Rudolph but also that she was regularly consulted about and expressed a continuing and positive concern for [the child]. We agree...we should not necessarily rule out 'sole responsibility' if for a limited time during childhood it cannot be proved. It is a matter of looking at the childhood as a whole and all the actions of the mother.'

In another case, *Ramos*, the Court of Appeal gave further guidance on sole responsibility. A Filipino mother abandoned by her husband, had left her daughter with her own mother when she came to the UK to work to support them; the child's aunt and uncle lived nearby. The girl was not allowed to come to join her mother. It was stated:

'Obviously there are matters of day-to-day decision-making in the upbringing of a child which are bound to be decided on the spot by whoever is looking after the child in the absence of the parents settled here, such as getting the child to school safely and on time, or putting the child to bed...and so forth. In the present case it is not in doubt that money was provided by the mother here to support the child, and indeed the grandmother, but that again is not per se conclusive of sole responsibility... The suggestion is of course not that the father has had any responsibility or that the mother has abandoned all responsibility, but that the true conclusion on the facts is that responsibility has been shared between the mother and the grandmother and possibly also the uncle and aunt'.

The Home Office sets out the following factors as relevant to sole responsibility (IDI, Ch8, s3, annex M, para. 4.3):

- the period the parent in the UK has been separated from the child;
- the previous arrangements for the care of the child prior to the parent coming to the UK;
- who has (or has had) the day-to-day care and control of the child since the sponsor came to the UK;
- who supports the child financially;
- who takes important decisions about the child's upbringing;
- the degree of contact between the parent claiming sole responsibility and the child;

- what role the other parent and relatives outside the UK have played in the child's care and upbringing (if any).

If a court has made a residence order under the Children Act in respect of the parent whom the child is applying to join or stay with, this will normally be accepted as proving sole responsibility. This also seems to apply in the case of custody orders made overseas which are recognised in the UK. The IDI contains a list of countries whose orders are recognised for these purposes (IDI, Ch 8, s3, annex M, paras 4.4–4.5).

In general terms, the well-established principles of sole responsibility are (and see *Williams* (IAT)):

- it is not necessary for the sole responsibility to be throughout life;
- financial support is a factor but not conclusive;
- the decision maker should look at the role played by the parents but also at the part played in the upbringing by others;
- it is not fatal that others played a part in day-to-day care;
- each case depends on its own facts but the evidence must be such that it can be fairly said that the sponsor remained in sole control of the child's upbringing and responsible for the important decisions relating to the child's upbringing, such as where they live, go to school and any religious instruction.

Importantly, in the case of *Nmaju*, the Court of Appeal held that the rules allowed for circumstances where the sponsor could have had sole responsibility for a short time. In that case, the period of responsibility was for only a few months after the death of the other carer. This is important in cases where, for example, grandparents have become incapable of continuing their caring role and the parent returns to the country of origin for a short time to take charge of the child before applying to bring them to the UK.

Exclusion undesirable

The alternative to showing sole responsibility is to show that there are 'serious and compelling family or other considerations which make the child's exclusion undesirable and suitable arrangements have been made for the child's care' in the UK. This alternative can also be used where a 'relative' rather than a parent is seeking to bring a child to the UK (►see below at 371–2).

Proving that a child qualifies under this rule can often be very hard. For example, in one case where it was accepted that a father in Trinidad had sexually abused his daughter, but there was no evidence he had done anything other than beat his twin sons, the girl's appeal was allowed but her brothers' appeals were dismissed.

In deciding whether the rules are met, the conditions in the country in which the child is living are the main focus. It is incorrect, however, to weigh those conditions against the conditions available in the UK. In *Rudolph*, the IAT stated:

'we are of the opinion that such [family and other] considerations must be applied to the country in which the appellant lives and not to those pertaining in the UK...The specific example of when the general requirements will be met [is] the inability of the parent in the foreign country to look after the child. It is strongly arguable that once we have found as a fact that Mr Rudolph is incapable of looking after [her child] the appellant's case is made.'

Some cases have stressed the need for incapacity rather than just un-willingness to look after a child. A parent may be physically or mentally incapable of caring for a child. The failure of the other parent to actually look after a child can be a strong indication of their incapacity to do so (*Awuko*, IAT). Where the other parent actually abandons the child, this should be sufficient (*Haughton*, IAT).

In *Saluguo*, a child was living in comfort with her aunt and siblings in the Philippines. However, she was able to come to the UK where her mother, a domestic worker in the UK, had worked for years under very poor conditions so as to provide her children with support and an education and desperately wanted to be joined in the UK by her youngest child.

In *Ali (Iqbal)*, the High Court required a case to be reconsidered where a child had applied to accompany his mother to join his 'father' in the UK but DNA testing showed that the man, who he had always believed was his father, was not and the application was refused. However, the child had always been accepted as a child of the family and had never been involved in any deception. The court accepted that these circumstances and the presence in the UK of both people who had acted as parents could amount to serious family considerations making the child's exclusion undesirable.

The rules must now be read so far as possible as complying with ECHR rights (see s3(1) Human Rights Act 1998 (HRA)) which means that these rules must be applied so as to be consistent with the right to respect for family life under Article 8 ECHR.

CHILDREN JOINING A PERSON WHO IS NOT A PARENT

It must be remembered that, in all of the immigration rules, a 'parent' does not necessarily have to be the natural parent. It may be a step-parent replacing a parent who is dead or, in some circumstances, someone to whom there has been a transfer of parental responsibility (▶see 361–2 for the definition of 'parent' under the rules). The rules referred to above may therefore be used, in those circumstances, where the parents are not the natural parents.

However, even where the sponsor does not satisfy the definition of a parent in the immigration rules, a child can still join a 'relative' who is present and settled (or being admitted for settlement) in the UK if they can satisfy the 'exclusion undesirable' requirement of the rules referred to above (see para. 297(i)(f), HC 395). 'Other relative' for these purposes, is not defined and should, in the light of Article 8 ECHR, be read broadly. For the family relationships which can come within Article 8 ECHR, ►see the table at 823–6. The child must still, of course, satisfy the other requirements of the rules concerning age, being unmarried/not leading an independent life and be able to be supported without recourse to public funds.

Children may therefore qualify to join another relative if they are living in extremely difficult circumstances overseas. This is usually only possible if the child's parents are dead or unavailable and if there are no other relatives in the country of the child's origin who could look after them instead. An adult sibling, for example, married and settled in the UK, might be the only relative to care for a child after their parents have died. Grandparents settled in the UK might wish to care for a grandchild abandoned by his or her parents.

Any application for a child to join a relative other than a parent should be made in great detail, explaining the exceptional circumstances why the child needs to come to, or remain in, the UK and why no other arrangements could be made in the country of origin. Again, depending on the particular circumstances and family relationships involved, arguments relating to the right to respect for family life may help.

CHILDREN BEING JOINED BY PARENTS WITH WHOM THEY HAVE CONTACT

When immigration rules were introduced to provide for persons exercising rights of access to children resident in the UK, the rules were very restrictive and were essentially only for short-term access visits. From 2 October 2000, the rules were amended to enable parents to eventually settle in the UK if they have children to whom they have rights of access here. Entry clearance is still required for a parent coming to the UK. However, a parent who is in the UK when, for example, the marriage or relationship breaks down, and who has leave, can make an application to remain from within the UK. Previously, applications such as this were all made outside the rules and were often only granted after long battles with the Home Office.

The general definition of 'parent' for the purposes of the immigration rules should, in particular, be remembered in 'access' applications (►see 361–2). Most notably, there is no requirement that the parents of the child were ever married.

The purpose of these rules is to attempt to comply with the ruling of the European Court of Human Rights in **Berrehab**. This concerned a Moroccan man who was deported away from his ex-wife and their young child, with whom he had maintained very close contact. The difficulty involved in maintaining such frequent contact from abroad was held to be an infringement of the right to respect for family life under Article 8 (▶see further 831).

However, more recently, in the case of **Poku** there was found to be no violation of Article 8 when a couple, both of whom had a child from a previous relationship as well as two children of their own, had married when the wife was already threatened with deportation. The European Commission held that the couple 'must be taken to be aware of [the wife's] precarious immigration status and the probable consequential effects' when they got married. The inevitable loss of contact between the children of the previous relationships and one of their parents was, in that case, found not to be a breach of the Convention.

Parents who reside abroad with their children and who wish to bring their children to the UK to visit the partner from whom they are separated, are not specifically provided for in the rules. They, or the child on his or her own, could apply for entry as a visitor for this purpose.

For details about admission as a parent of a child at school, ▶see 375–6.

For details about the rights of children to have their parents and carers remain with them in EEA cases, ▶see 531–7.

People who apply from outside the UK

WHAT THE RULES SAY

A parent who is applying from abroad in order to enter the UK so as to exercise their rights of access to their child in the UK must satisfy all the following rules (paras 246–248 HC 395):

- the applicant must be the parent of a child who is resident in the UK;
- the parent or carer with whom the child permanently resides must be resident in the UK;
- the applicant must have evidence that they have rights of access to the child (see further below);
- the applicant must intend to continue to take an active part in the child's upbringing;
- the child must be under 18;
- there must be adequate maintenance and accommodation for the applicant without recourse to public funds.

The parent must obtain an entry clearance before coming to the UK for this purpose. As in other non-asylum cases, applications can also be refused on the basis of the general grounds for refusal.

WHAT THE RULES MEAN

The evidence of access rights that is required is either a residence or contact order, made by a court in the UK, which grants rights of access to the child who is living here. Alternatively, it is sufficient if the parent can produce a certificate from a district judge confirming their intention to maintain contact with the child. The provision in the rules for a certificate in the alternative is in line with the non-interventionist approach of the family courts not to make orders (such as for contact) where these matters can be agreed between the parents.

The Home Office acknowledged in a letter to Bates Wells & Braithwaite solicitors dated 21 December 2000 that, as the rules stand, a parental responsibility agreement registered in the High Court and signed by both parents would not be sufficient to meet the strict requirements of the rules. The Home Office agreed to review the rules in the light of this.

The Home Office has stated that it interprets the requirement that a child 'permanently reside' in the UK, as meaning that, as an absolute minimum requirement, the child should live with the settled parent/carer for 50% of the time. So, a court order which gives joint residence of a child, split equally between the parents, which results in the child staying with each for three and a half days a week would appear to enable either parent to be able to apply for leave under these rules – but only just (letter of IND Policy Directorate to Mishcon de Reya Solicitors, 17 July 2003).

The parent from abroad will have to confirm their intention to take an active role in the child's upbringing, which means playing a part and taking an interest in the child's schooling, health, social and other activities.

Parents admitted under these rules are usually given leave for 12 months and they are also able to work to support themselves, which is a welcome change from the old rules relating to access 'visits'.

People who apply when they are in the UK

WHAT THE RULES SAY

Parents can apply under these rules if they are already in the UK without having to leave to obtain entry clearance. The same rules as above apply but with the following additions/modifications (paras 248A–248F):

- the child must visit and stay with the applicant on a frequent and regular basis and the applicant must intend this to continue;
- the applicant must take and intend to continue to take an active role in the child's upbringing;
- the applicant must have limited leave to remain in the UK as the spouse or unmarried partner of a person present and settled in the UK who is the other parent of the child;

- the applicant must not have remained in breach of immigration laws; and
- as an alternative to producing evidence of a court order, the parent can provide a statement from the child's other parent (or from a supervisor where access is supervised) confirming that the applicant is maintaining contact with the child.

WHAT THE RULES MEAN

These rules are clearly aimed at the situation where the applicant's relationship with the child's other parent has broken down at a time when the applicant had limited leave and they wish to remain in the UK where they have access to their child. It will be noted that the nature of the contact between parent and child is looked at more closely as compared to out-of-country applications. This is because, in in-country cases, there is a greater opportunity to examine the nature of the ongoing contact and the role played by the applicant in the child's upbringing. Again, in the first instance, leave will be granted for 12 months and the parent is permitted to work during that time.

The Home Office has confirmed that an applicant who does not have leave but who was admitted to the UK as the family member of an EEA national (either as spouse or unmarried partner) who is settled in the UK, may also benefit from the rules allowing people to remain for the purposes of access rights to children (see above Home Office letter to Mishcon de Reya Solicitors, 17 July 2003). For details of EEA cases in which parents and carers have rights which come from EU law, ▶see 531–7.

Applications for settlement on the basis of access to a child

After a person has completed a period of 12 months, either granted on entry or in-country, as a parent exercising rights of access, they are eligible to apply for indefinite leave. The child must still be under 18 years for the parent to obtain indefinite leave.

PARENTS OF CHILDREN AT SCHOOL

A child at school may be able to remain in the UK in their own right as a student under the student rules (▶see Chapter 10). The child must be going to a private, fee-paying school and support must be available to pay the school fees and for the child to live here. If the school is not a boarding school, there should be adequate arrangements for looking after the child. The Home Office must also be satisfied that the intention is for the child to leave at the end of the studies. The immigration rules do not permit visa nationals to change their status to become students, so if the child is applying from within the UK and is a visa national, the application would be outside the rules.

There is no provision in the rules for a child to stay in the UK simply in order to attend, or to continue to attend, a state school. This can create problems when the child has been in the UK with the family for a short-term purpose, for example, if the parents are students, or diplomats or other workers posted to the UK for a term of duty, who then have to take up another post when the child is at a critical stage of education. An application to the Home Office may be made, exceptionally, for permission to continue with studies in these circumstances. For the special considerations which apply in EEA cases, ▶see 531–7.

There is specific provision in the immigration rules for leave to be granted to the parents of children under 12 who are attending an independent fee-paying day school and who satisfy the student rules (see paras 56–56C with reference to para. 41 HC 395). The parent must satisfy all of the following additional requirements. They must:

- not be seeking to make the UK their main home;
- have evidence of adequate and reliable funds for maintaining a second home in the UK;
- be able to maintain and accommodate themselves without recourse to public funds;
- intend to leave the UK when they no longer qualify under these rules;
- not intend to take employment or to produce goods or services in the UK;
- be able to meet the cost of their return journey.

Only visa nationals and specified nationals require entry clearance in order to enter the UK. The rules do not prevent 'switching' into this category except that parents last admitted to the UK under the 'Approved Destination Status Agreement with China' cannot be granted leave under these rules (see para. 56(vi) HC 395 inserted by HC 486 from 5 April 2005).

So, under these rules, a sole parent can obtain leave to be in the UK with their child and neither the 'sole responsibility' nor 'exclusion undesirable' rules need to be satisfied. Parents who make successful applications may be granted successive periods of 12 months' leave. The parent is not permitted to work. Clearly this provision is only intended to benefit the wealthy and even then there is a restriction on the age of the child, presumably because it is thought that over the age of 12, a child does not need their parents to be living in the same country as them while they attend school because they can board.

CHILDREN ACCOMPANYING OR JOINING PARENTS IN THE UK WHO HAVE LIMITED LEAVE

The situations described earlier in this chapter are generally where a child's parents are settled in the UK or are British citizens, or where the child is resident in the UK and hoping to be joined by parents. Children may also, however, be given leave to accompany their parents to the UK, join them or stay with them here where their parents have *limited* leave to be in the UK under one of the categories under the rules. If the child is allowed to come, they will be given leave for the same length of time as their parent(s). Usually, if the parent is prohibited from working (as, for example, persons of independent means are prohibited), the child will also be prohibited from working. If the parent has a restriction on working, that is, may work only with the consent of the immigration authorities, the child will usually be given no restrictions on working.

Not all categories under the rules allow child dependants to be admitted. For example, there is no provision in the rules for the children of visitors or *au pairs*. A child coming for a visit with their parents will, however, be admitted as a visitor in their own right.

For details about family reunion in the UK with those granted refugee status, ▶see Chapter 25. For processes relating to the dependants of asylum-seekers, ▶see 691–4. For details about family reunion with those granted humanitarian protection, discretionary leave or exceptional leave and dependants of those applying in those categories, ▶see 875–9. For the dependants of those admitted under the 'HM forces' rules, ▶see 151. Children of parents who have limited leave 'with a view to settlement' who may be here as spouses with a probationary period of leave, and children of fiancé(e)s are discussed earlier at (▶see 361 in particular).

For all the categories looked at below, 'parent' includes all those set out in the general definition of parent contained in the rules (▶see 361–2). 'Parent' also includes adoptive parents where:

- the adoption decision was made in accordance with the relevant country's procedures and adoption orders made in that country are recognised in the UK (▶see 383 and 1528–9); or
- the child is the subject of a *de facto* adoption, which meets the requirements of the immigration rules (para. 309A HC 395, ▶see at 381).

Children of workers and business people

The rules make provision for the admission of children whose parents have been admitted in the worker and business categories (including the children of work permit holders; highly skilled migrants; those in the permit-free employment categories; those granted leave because of their UK ancestry; business/self-employed people; innovators; investors; artists and retired persons of independent means). The rules expressly do *not* make provision for children of those granted leave to enter for employment under the sectors-based scheme (see para. 197(i) HC 305).

In order to obtain admission, children must generally show (paras 197–199 HC 395):

- they are unmarried;
- they have not formed an independent family unit and are not leading an independent life;

- there will be adequate maintenance and accommodation for them without recourse to public funds; and

- they will not remain in the UK for longer than the leave given to their parent/s.

If only one parent is in the UK and the other is still alive, the more restrictive rules about children joining lone parents must be satisfied (i.e. 'sole responsibility' or 'exclusion undesirable', ▶see 367–71).

Age In order to qualify for admission under these rules, children must be under 18 at the time of application. *However*, if a child is admitted to the UK under these rules and then seeks to extend their leave, or to be granted indefinite leave, under the same rules, it does not matter if the child has become 18 during the time they have been living in the UK. They will still be granted further leave or settlement in line with their parent(s) provided they have existing leave granted under these rules. Note that there is a separate concession, which is operated for children over the age of 18 of sponsors who are work permit holders as 'intra-company transferees' (for this and further details about the admission of families of work permit holders, ▶see 436–7).

Entry clearance All children seeking admission as dependants under these categories must obtain entry clearance abroad. In order to extend their leave, or be granted indefinite leave in line with their parents, they must also, under the rules, have been admitted with an entry clearance for entry in this same capacity.

When the parents apply to extend their leave to remain, their children should generally apply on the same form. Children can apply to be granted indefinite leave in line with their parents when the parents apply for indefinite leave.

Children of students

Students are permitted to bring their children with them. If they are visa nationals or specified nationals seeking entry for more than six months, they must obtain entry clearance from the British post overseas. If they are not, they do not need entry clearance and can apply for leave to enter at port. Children of students also have to show (paras 79–81 HC 395): that they will not remain in the UK after any period of leave granted to their parent(s); that they are under 18 and dependent; and that they can be maintained and accommodated without recourse to public funds.

The rules relating to accommodation for these children do not, however, state that it must be exclusively owned or occupied by the family. This is because the Home Office has recognised that students are likely to live in shared or college accommodation. Children will be admitted for the same length of time as the student. If this is for less than a year, they will probably be prohibited from working. Notably, a child may be admitted to join one parent where the other parent is not in the UK without having to satisfy either the sole-responsibility or exclusion-undesirable rules.

The same rule as above for the children of workers/business people applies when a child has become 18 while in the UK.

Children of teachers and language assistants and of people in approved training or work experience

Children of teachers and language assistants and of people in approved training or work experience can obtain leave to be in the UK with their parents (paras 125–127 HC 395). They must be under 18, unmarried, dependent and be supported in the UK without recourse to public funds. They must not intend to stay in the UK for longer than their parent(s). They can only be admitted to join a lone parent if their other parent is dead or if they satisfy either the 'sole-responsibility' or 'exclusion-undesirable' rule. They must obtain entry clearance to come to the UK. In order to obtain an extension of leave, they must have originally been admitted with an entry clearance in this capacity. The same rule as above for the children of workers/business people applies when a child has become 18 while in the UK.

Children of working holidaymakers

Working holidaymakers are permitted to bring their children to the UK (paras 101–103 HC 395). However, only children who are under five and who will leave the UK before reaching that age can come. This is intended to be consistent with the principle that underlies the working holiday-maker rules, which is that they are for young people (aged 17–30) who have not yet settled down. The maintenance and accommodation requirements must be satisfied. If only one parent is in the UK and the other is still alive, the more restrictive rules about children joining lone parents must be satisfied (i.e. 'sole responsibility' or 'exclusion undesirable'). All children of working holidaymakers must be granted entry clearance in order to come to the UK. In order to obtain an extension of leave in the UK, they must have been admitted with an entry clearance in this capacity.

ADOPTED CHILDREN

Determining what immigration rights exist for adopted children (or children who are to be adopted), can be approached in three steps:

1) **Has the adoption resulted in the child becoming a British citizen?** If so, the child will not need 'leave' under the immigration rules (▶see immediately below).

2) **Is the child coming to join parent/s in the UK *other than* for settlement or with a view to settlement?** If so, the definition of 'parent' under the immigration rules may be wide enough for the child to be admitted *without* the child having to satisfy the specific immigration rules dealing

with 'adopted children' for settlement purposes (i.e. paras 310–316F, HC 395) (▶see 381 and ▶see 361–2).

3) **If neither (1) nor (2) apply,** the specific immigration rules relating to adopted children will have to be satisfied (▶see 382–4).

For children who are coming to the UK *for* adoption ▶see below at 374–5.

The overlap between adoption and immigration and the various procedures that need to be complied with is complex. The Adoption (Inter-country Aspects) Act 1999 makes it a criminal offence, in certain circumstances, to bring children into the UK for adoption or to bring to the UK recently adopted children (see further the Adoption (Bringing Children into the UK) Regulations 2003 and the Inter-country Adoption (Hague Convention) Regulations 2003).

We do not give an account of all of the procedures which may apply and steps to be taken in order to properly adopt a child in the UK or abroad and in order to bring such a child to the UK for either a limited period or permanently; for example the home-study and eligibility assessments. We give an overview of the immigration considerations only. *It is recommended that applicants affected by any of the issues described below should obtain advice.* A useful point of reference is the information leaflet published by the Home Office, 'Inter-country adoption and the Immigration Rules', which is updated from time to time.

1) Has the adopted child become British?

If a British citizen parent or a married couple, one of whom is a British citizen, adopt a non-British child in a court in the UK, the child becomes British from the time the order is made (s1(5)(5A) British Nationality Act).

In addition, the UK ratified the Hague Convention on the Protection of Children and Co-operation in Respect of Inter-country Adoption on 1 June 2003. From that date where any non-British child is adopted under a 'Convention adoption' abroad by British parent/s who are 'habitually resident' in the UK, the child will become a British citizen. A 'Convention adoption' for these purposes is one which has taken place under the law of a foreign country in which the Hague Convention is in force and there are various procedures which need to have been complied with (▶see 1432 and s1(5)(5A)(8) BNA) as amended by s7 Adoption (Intercountry Aspects) Act 1999, see also the Adoption (Hague) Convention Regulations 2003 and definition of 'Convention adoption' in s72 Adoption Act 1976). The countries in which the Hague Convention is in force are listed at ▶1528.

Where prospective adoptive parents want to adopt a non-British child in the UK, they are required to inform the Home Office and the Secretary of State may apply to become a party to the proceedings and make representations to the court.

In certain other cases, although the adoption itself does not automatically mean that the child is British, the Home Office may agree to register the child as a British citizen as a matter of discretion under section 3(1) BNA (►see 1473 and, in particular, ►1481–2).

Where the above requirements are not met, the child will need leave to be in the UK and must then qualify under the immigration rules (below).

2) Adopted children coming to the UK other than for settlement

As has been seen above (►see 361–2), *except for* cases in which a child is seeking to be admitted under paragraphs 297–303 HC 395 i.e. for settlement or 'with a view to settlement' with parents who are settled (or who have been admitted with a view to settlement), adopted children may use the 'ordinary' immigration rules. This is because, apart from applications made under those paragraphs, the definition of 'parent' in the immigration rules includes an adoptive parent *provided that either* (para. 6, HC 395):

- the child was adopted in accordance with a decision taken by the competent administrative authority or court in a country whose adoption orders are recognised by the UK (►see below at 383, 1528–9); *or*
- the adoption was a *de facto* adoption in accordance with the requirements of the immigration rules (►immediately below).

A *de facto* adoption in accordance with the immigration rules means an adoption that satisfies all of the following requirements (para. 309, HC 395 inserted from 1 April 2003 by HC 538):

- for the period of at least 18 months before the application for entry clearance, the adoptive parent/s must have been living abroad (and living together if the application involves two parents);
- from the beginning of the 18-month period, the parent/s must have assumed the role of the child's parents so that there has been a genuine transfer of parental responsibility; and
- for the period of at least 12 months before the application for entry clearance, the parent/s must have been living together with the child in question and they must have been caring for the child for a minimum of 12 months.

If the above requirements are met, then the child can be admitted under the ordinary immigration rules relating to children set out earlier in this chapter. However, if the application is to bring the child under those parts of the immigration rules which apply to children of settled parents (or parents admitted with a view to settlement), the further specific 'adoption' rules will have to be met (below). The rules set out below are more difficult to satisfy. Note that the definition of *de facto* adoption is also relevant to those rules.

3) Adoption rules: children who have been adopted and who are seeking admission for settlement or with a view to settlement

The immigration rules dealing with the situation where an adoption has taken place outside the UK and where the child needs leave to enter the UK to join their adoptive parents who are settled or who have been given leave with a view to settlement, are as follows (see paras 309A–316, HC 395).

WHAT THE RULES SAY

The child must meet the general rules for children seeking to enter the UK for the purposes of settlement (►see 360–1). If only one adoptive parent is seeking to bring the child to the UK and the other parent is living, either the 'sole responsibility' or 'exclusion undesirable' rule must be satisfied (►see 368–61). However, an alternative basis for satisfying the rules in *de facto* adoption cases is for one parent to have the right of abode in the UK or indefinite leave, and to be seeking admission for the purposes of settlement.

The *additional* rules which must be satisfied are all of the following, namely that (paras 310(g)(vi)–(xii) HC 395):

- *either* the adoption took place 'in accordance with a decision taken by the competent administrative authority or court of [the child's] country of origin or the country in which [the child] is resident', that being a country whose adoption orders are recognised by the UK (►see below at 383) *or* the adoption was a *de facto* adoption (i.e. it complied with the requirements set out above at ►381);
- the adoption took place *either* when the adoptive parents were living together abroad *or* when either or both of them were settled in the UK;
- the child has 'the same rights and obligations' as any other child of the family;
- the adoption took place because of the inability of the birth parents or current carers to care for the child and there has been a genuine transfer of parental responsibility;
- the child has lost or broken ties with the family of origin; and
- the adoption was not one of convenience arranged to facilitate the child's admission to, or remaining in, the UK.

Similar rules apply for an adopted child who is seeking to be admitted to join a parent or parents who have limited leave with a view to settlement (paras 314–315 HC 395). Where children are coming to the UK in this category, they require an entry clearance. If they are already in the UK, they may be granted leave to *remain* in this category provided that they already have an existing leave. Where the parent/s are settled or are being admitted for settlement, the child will be given indefinite leave. Where the parent/s have been given only limited leave with a view to settlement, the child will be granted leave for 12 months initially but, if the rules continue to be satisfied and the parent/s settle, they will also be able to obtain indefinite leave. Again, advice should be taken on the procedural steps that should be taken in order to bring a child to the UK.

WHAT THE RULES MEAN

Adoption decision taken by the competent authority in a country whose adoption orders are recognised in the UK

The adoption rules state that the adoption must have taken place 'in accordance with a decision taken by the competent administrative authority or court of [the child's] country of origin or the country in which [the child] is resident' that being a country whose adoption orders are recognised by the UK *or* the adoption was a *de facto* (▶see below) adoption.

The adoption decision must have been taken under the proper procedures for adoption in the child's country of origin, or the country where the child is living. The country must be one whose adoption orders are legally recognised in the UK. This means that the country must be on the list of 'designated' countries set out in the Schedule to the Adoption (Designation of Overseas Adoptions) Order 1973. Alternatively, overseas Hague Convention adoption orders will also qualify as they too are recognised in the UK (see s66 Adoption and Children Act 2002) (▶see 1528–9).

De facto adoption

In the alternative to the requirement above, the adoption may be a *de facto* one. In simple terms, this means adoptions where, in reality the child has been adopted, even if the adoption is not a formal one. However, in order for there to have been a *de facto* adoption for the purposes of the rules, certain requirements need to be met. The definition of *de facto* adoption under these settlement rules is exactly the same as that which applies in order to determine whether a parent of an adopted child qualifies as a 'parent' for the purposes of the non-settlement rules for children (▶see above at 381, 361–2). However, under the settlement rules, the additional requirements (below) must also be satisfied. Previously, there was a concession outside the rules known as the '*de facto*' adoption concession but the rules now formally cover *de facto* adoptions.

Same rights and obligations

The child must have the same rights and obligations as other children of the family. This rule was introduced in 1994 and appears to be aimed against adoptions of Muslim children. A series of court cases about a Pakistani child called *Tohur Ali* had previously established that an informal adoption could qualify a child for admission. There is no official adoption procedure under Islamic law and, although it is comparatively common for a child to be brought up by another close relative, such as an uncle, there will often be no formal legal process and the child may not be considered a full child of the marriage for inheritance purposes. The rules also operate against adoptions that have taken place in countries where adoption is not recognised as a legal change of status so as to provide adopted children with the same rights as others.

Reasons for adoption

The rules state that the adoption must have come about as a result of the inability of the original parent(s) or current carer(s) to look after the child and there must be a 'genuine transfer' of parental responsibility for the adopted child. The adoption must also not be 'one of convenience' arranged to 'facilitate' the child's entry to the UK.

When an adoption takes place mainly because a couple in the UK are unable to have children, or where it reflects a family or cultural practice or tradition, for example, in cases concerning families from the Indian sub-continent, the adoption will often not qualify the child for admission under the rules. In *RS* the natural parents had two children, a boy and a girl and had been trying for another boy. When a further girl arrived, they were deeply disappointed and indeed the mother rejected the baby. The sponsor in the UK seeking to adopt was the father's brother. The IAT held that unwillingness to care for the child based upon the child's gender was not sufficient to amount to 'inability'. The Court of Appeal held that the rejection of a child on the basis of gender was not enough to show an inability to care for the child (*Sharma v ECO New Delhi*).

Lost or broken ties with family of origin

The requirement that the child has lost or broken ties with their family of origin should not be interpreted too strictly. The rule requires a loss or break of the ties of responsibility, not of affection. The 'family of origin' is not limited to natural parents, but simply identifies the family with whom an individual has been living (*Boadi v ECO*, IAT).

Children coming to the UK for adoption

From 2 October 2000, the Home Office introduced new rules to allow for the entry with a view to settlement to the UK, of children who have not yet been adopted but who will be adopted in the UK (paras 316A–316C HC 395). This reflected a previous practice outside the immigration rules. Further rules were added from 30 May 2003 to allow for the entry with a view to settlement of children to be adopted under the Hague Convention (paras 316D–316F HC 395 as added by Cm 5829). So, there are two categories under the rules under which a child for adoption may enter (below). For a reference to the Regulations which must be complied with, ▶see above at 380.

A child adopted through the courts in the UK by either of these means may become a British citizen if at least one adoptive parent is a British citizen (▶see 380–1, 1427, 1432, 1435 and summary at 1438 onwards). Otherwise, after they have been admitted, the adopted child may ask for further leave in line with their parents.

In the first category (paras 316A–C, HC 395) the rules are similar to those seeking entry as a child who has already been adopted (above) although, obviously, the child does *not* have to have already been adopted in a manner lawfully recognised by the UK. The rules state instead that the child will be adopted in the UK by their parents in accordance with UK law relating to adoption. An entry clearance must be obtained. If the application is successful, 24-months' leave to enter is given.

In the second category (paras 316D–F, HC 395) the rules relating to the reasons for adoption set out above (▶384) are not applied. Instead, the requirements are that the applicant:

- seeks leave to enter to accompany a prospective parent or parents each of whom is 'habitually resident' in the UK and wishes to adopt the applicant under the Hague Convention;
- is the subject of an 'agreement' made under Article 17(c) of the Hague Convention; and
- has been entrusted to the prospective parents by the authorities of the country from which the child is coming to the UK.

An agreement under Article 17(c) of the Hague Convention is an agreement of the 'central authorities' of both states that the adoption may proceed. The applicant must also be under 18 and the maintenance and accommodation requirements of the rules must be satisfied. The applicant must also obtain an entry clearance. Again, if the application is successful, 24-months' leave to enter is given.

Use of Article 8 ECHR

Article 8 ECHR may also be useful in cases involving adoption where the rules cannot be fully met. For example, the decision of the Court of Appeal in *Singh v ECO*, *New Delhi* shows how Article 8 may be used in the context of an adoption by relatives. A UK couple adopted their nephew in India in an adoption which was in accordance with social and cultural practices. There had been a genuine transfer of parental responsibility even though the child was not living with his adoptive parents and the child had become a member of his uncle and aunt's 'family'. The decision to refuse entry clearance to the child was an interference with the right to respect for family life under Article 8 and the Court of Appeal agreed that, in the circumstances, it was a disproportionate one.

CHILDREN WHOSE PARENTS MAY BE FORCED TO LEAVE

Below we look at two issues concerning children whose parent/s may be forced to leave the UK:

- cases in which the child's parent or parents are being force to leave the UK in which it is possible that the child may also be forced to leave as a family member (immediately below);
- cases in which the immigration authorities are considering enforcing the departure of a child's parents even though the child is British and cannot be removed (▶see 389–90).

Removal of children and parents together

As with adults, children may be removed from the UK under the powers of enforcement described in Chapter 33. However, in addition to the powers to enforce against a child because of *their own* immigration position ('overstayer' etc.), there are also powers to remove people as the *family members* of others against whom enforcement action is being taken. Where a parent's departure from the UK is being enforced under any of the four main enforcement procedures ('port removal', administrative removal, illegal entry, deportation), the child can also be removed as can a spouse. These four methods of enforcement themselves are set out and described in Chapter 33.

Powers added: port and illegal entry cases Until the 2002 Act, there was no power to remove the children of those being removed as port cases or illegal entrants simply on the basis that they were family members of a person being removed. However, the government was particularly concerned that this meant that it could not forcibly remove non-British children born in the UK to port applicants and illegal entrants (because they themselves could not be refused 'leave to enter' or declared 'illegal entrants' and then removed in their own right). So, the government passed legislation to ensure that the children of such people could also be removed (▶see 991, 1001, 1010).

Discretion whether to remove child So, if parents are being removed, the immigration authorities will generally try to ensure that the child leaves as part of the family. However, this is not automatic. Where one parent is the main subject of the enforcement action, the immigration authorities must make a decision about whether to also enforce against the other parent and child/ren as family members. Even if the child does not have another parent other than the one who is being enforced against, the immigration authorities must still consider whether it is appropriate to enforce the departure of the child. The immigration rules (▶see below) set out the factors that need to be taken into account in making such decisions.

Policy In addition to the immigration rules, the Home Office also has a policy on the approach to cases where it is considering enforcing the departure of a family in the UK. The guidance is contained in 'DP/069/99', 'DP/4/95' and 'DP/4/96' (▶below at 388–9). The position of unaccompanied children is also referred to in this guidance (▶see 390). For policy developments on the *procedures* which should be used when detaining and enforcing the departure of families ▶see 998–1000.

Article 8 ECHR may also be relevant. For example, in a case where the parents are separated and the child lives with the parent who is to be removed, enforcement may have the result of separating the child from frequent contact with the parent who will be remaining in the UK. In addition, where the circumstances of a child returning to their own or their parents' country of origin will result in health difficulties or severe hardship for the child, both Articles 3 and 8 may also be relevant (▶see 819–20).

The immigration rules

In deciding whether family members of those who are being deported or administratively removed from the UK should also have enforcement action taken against them, the immigration rules require certain factors to be taken into account (paras 364–368 and 395C, HC 395). Although those rules only directly apply to enforcement in deportation and administrative removal cases, the Home Office has stated that it considers the same general factors in enforcement cases concerning illegal entry (▶see 1009–10). There is nothing to stop representatives relying on similar factors in 'port refusal' cases.

Firstly, the immigration authorities must take into account the factors which are always relevant when enforcement is considered: age, length of residence in the UK, strength of connections with the UK, personal history (including character, conduct, employment record), domestic circumstances, any criminal record, compassionate circumstances and representations made on the person's behalf. The following additional factors must also be taken into account when considering enforcement against a spouse or child:

- the ability of spouses to maintain themselves and any children in the UK or to be maintained by relatives and friends without being a charge on public funds for the foreseeable future;
- in the case of a child of school age, the effect of removal on their education; and
- the practicability of any plans for the child's care and maintenance in the UK if one or both parents were deported or removed.

In addition, the Home Office will not normally deport or remove a child as the family member of a person being required to leave if:

- the child and their other parent are living apart from the person who is being deported or removed; or
- the child has left home and established themselves on an independent basis; or

- the child married before a decision was made to deport or remove their parent.

In addition, the Home Office will normally *not* deport or remove a spouse as a family member of a person being required to leave if:

- they have qualified for settlement in their own right; or
- they have been living apart from the person who is being deported or removed.

Home Office 'seven-year' policy

Home Office policy contained in DP/069/99 deals with cases where enforcement action is being taken against the parents of a child with long residence in the UK. The previous policy, issued in March 1996 was DP 5/96. It referred to children who had ten years or more continuous residence in the UK. This was modified to seven years in February 1999. Under the present policy, DP/069/99, enforcement action will not usually proceed against the family as a whole where the children were born in the UK and have lived here continuously until the age of seven years. The same applies to children who came to the UK at an early age and have lived in the UK for seven or more continuous years.

However, although this is the usual policy, the family's departure may still be enforced if the individual circumstances of the case justify it. The Home Office will take into account the following factors:

- the age of the children;
- the length of the parents' residence in the UK without leave;
- whether the parents have evaded immigration control and delayed removal;
- whether the children were conceived at a time when the parents had leave;
- whether removal has been delayed by repetitive representations;
- whether the parents have a history of criminal behaviour or deception;
- whether return to the country of origin would result in hardship for the children;
- whether the children's health would seriously be put at risk by return.

In *R (Dabrowski) v SSHD*, the Court of Appeal found that the return of the family to Poland where they remained for a brief interval after the refusal of an asylum claim, was enough to break the continuity of residence for the purposes of the above policy.

Even where a child has not been in the UK for seven years, the longer the child has been here, the greater weight must be placed on their residence in the UK as a compassionate factor (see Home Office guidance on enforcement sent to ILPA on 17 February 2003 and entitled 'Annex A – Regularisation Scheme for Overstayers' which gives general details about policy relating to enforcement).

Both *Dabrowski* and *Jagot* (HC) indicate that the policy should be applied in port as well as in what are technically termed 'enforcement cases'. Also, the Home Office has stated that:

'This concession does not apply to on-entry (port) cases. However, immigration service colleagues have regard to the underlying principles of this concession when deciding whether or not to grant leave to enter.' (*Immigration Rules and Compassionate Circumstances*, Instructions to Officers, 25 April 2004, para. 8.5.)

For details about Home Office policy concerning enforcement in the case of married and unmarried couples, ▶see 338–44.

Enforcement against parents whose child is British

Where a child is a British citizen but enforcement action is being considered against their non-British parents, the immigration authorities will have to think very carefully about whether it is appropriate to force the parent to leave. If the parent or parents are forced to leave then, practically speaking, this is likely to mean that the child will also have to leave and will therefore be effectively 'exiled' from their country of nationality. This situation may arise, for example, where the parents were settled with indefinite leave when the child was born in the UK (therefore giving the child British citizenship) but a decision has since been made to deport the parents on 'conducive' grounds. It might also occur where the child lives with a non-British parent who has separated from the British parent. Another example might be where the child obtained their citizenship from a British parent who is now overseas and their non-British parent, who has care of them in the UK, is being enforced against.

The decisions in *Samaroo* and *M*

The importance of the child's nationality in deciding whether enforcement should go ahead against a non-British parent is clear from the following two decisions of the Court of Appeal. In the first, *Samaroo*, the Court approved of the Home Office's decision to include within the 'compassionate circumstances', which pointed against the deportation of the parent:

'...the existence of [his son] and his age [nine years] and the fact that he is a British citizen with his own independent right to live here and his relationship to his father.' (para. 4.)

The second case, *M v London Borough of Islington and SSHD (interested party)*, was generally a case about support arrangements but it also considered the importance of a child's British citizenship in assessing the consequences for the parent's immigration status. The strong position of the British citizen child in that case was contrasted with that in the Republic of Ireland and the USA:

'The child in our case has however acquired citizenship not simply by birth, but by deliberate Parliamentary decision expressed in the British Nationality Act 1981. The child is a British citizen because she was not only born here, but born to a parent falling into a carefully limited class [i.e. born in lawful wedlock to a father with rights of permanent residence in the UK]. That careful conferment of citizenship is to be contrasted with the somewhat adventitious acquisition of citizenship in the Irish Republic that troubled the court in *Lobe*. Second, there does not appear to be in the law of either the Irish Republic or the United States, the strong and general statement of freedom to live in the UK that is to be found in section 1(1) of the Immigration Act 1971...' (para. 27.)

In the last line above, the Court of Appeal was of course referring to the fact that the right of abode gives a citizen the right to enter and live in the UK without 'let or hindrance'. Again in *M* the Court clearly felt that the implications of the child's citizenship required very careful consideration (see paras 28, 30, 57).

UNACCOMPANIED CHILDREN IN THE UK

Enforcement action against children under the age of 16 who are on their own in the UK should only be taken if their voluntary departure cannot be arranged. It must be clear that the child will be met on arrival and that they will be properly cared for afterwards. Home Office caseworkers may contact the welfare section of the foreign embassy or high commission to try to confirm this. If there is evidence that the care arrangements are seriously below the standard normally available in the country concerned, or that they are so inadequate that the child would face a serious risk of harm, enforcement will generally not proceed (see DP/4/96, paras 2–3). The text of DP/4/96 can be found in *Butterworth's Immigration Law Service* (at D83). For details about unaccompanied minors seeking asylum, ▶see 686–91 and for further details about policy where there are no adequate reception facilities, ▶see 688, 865, 870–1.

Overall Home Office position on the welfare of the child

The overall Home Office position is set out in the IDI, (Ch 8, s3 annex M, para. 6.1):

'Our aim will normally be that the child should return to his parents and/ or their country of origin. However, because we are dealing with children, it is important to take account of the welfare considerations, which may take precedence over the immigration implications of allowing a child to remain here. The welfare considerations carry more weight in relation to younger children. Where a child's parents may abuse the control by leaving a child here, the child cannot always be held responsible for this predicament.'

However, the guidance continues that the fact that the child may be 'better off' in the UK is not, of itself, sufficient for the Home Office to grant leave to remain and officers will try to establish whether there are parents or relatives who can care for the child in their own country. The Home Office may also try to return a child into the care of the welfare authorities of their own country.

In such cases, the Home Office is likely to take into account the following factors (IDI, Ch 8, s3, annex M, para. 7):

- how the child came to the UK;
- who looks after the child in the UK and what arrangements have been made with the child's family;
- the whereabouts and occupation of the child's parents/guardians;
- the child's parents/guardians' long-term plans for the child;
- the family's income;
- if the child is old enough (normally age seven or over) to express an opinion, their feelings about the situation;
- the age of the child (generally it will be more difficult to achieve the return of a younger child to the family abroad);
- the length of the child's stay in the UK (the longer the child has been in the UK, the more settled they are likely to be and the more disturbing it will be for them if they are required to leave);
- the type of care the child has in the UK – a child is more likely to have settled down if they are an integral part of a family in the UK than if they are in local authority or temporary foster care;
- the circumstances in the country of return; account will be taken of whether 'the care to be provided for the child in the country concerned would be substantially below that normally expected';
- the health of the child.

Where an application is refused, the child has not left voluntarily and attempts to enforce the departure of the child have failed, then the immigration authorities will consider granting the child leave to remain. If there is still a realistic prospect of the child returning to their parents or country of origin in the near future, the child may be granted limited leave for successive periods of 12 months (IDI, Ch 8, s3, annex M, para. 7.3).

Local authority care

If a child is unaccompanied and in need of care or for any other reason the standard of care available to them is inadequate, the social services department of a local authority has a statutory responsibility to provide for their welfare. It is therefore possible for a child who is not settled in the UK to be taken into the care of the local authority. The local authority will then have to make arrangements for the child. This may mean attempting to trace the parents in order to return the child to them abroad, or it may mean applying to the Home Office for permission for the child to remain here exceptionally. For more details about support for children under the Children Act, ▶see 1322 onwards.

For a child who is not a British citizen, being taken into care does not in itself alter the child's immigration status. Local authorities will, therefore, themselves need to take legal advice before assisting the child to make applications to the Home Office. If it appears clear that there will not be further contact with the family and that the child's long-term future will be in the UK, then if the authority applies to the Home Office for settlement on behalf of the child with full details of the circumstances, it is likely that the application will be granted. It is extremely important that any such application should be made to the Home Office before the child is 18, on form SET(O) with a covering letter setting out any legal and human rights arguments relied upon.

Home Office policy is generally to grant indefinite leave to children (IDI Ch 8, s4, annex P para. 8) where the parental rights and duties (or 'parental responsibility') have been vested solely in the local authority. This is also provided for in the immigration rules (▶see 394–5 below). However, before such a grant is made, officers will try to establish whether parental responsibility is likely to be with the local authority on a long-term or permanent basis. If it is not, perhaps because there is a possibility that the child will be returned to their parents, or will soon be 18, the immigration authorities may decide to grant only limited leave. It appears that, in relation to any child in care, whether parental responsibility has been transferred or not, the Home Office will take their lead from the local authority:

'Decisions about the future of children in the care of the local authority should be left primarily in the hands of their social services department as they will be best placed to act in the child's interests.' (IDI, Ch 8, s3, annex M, para. 8.)

Other family court procedures

It is possible that relatives or friends of children may take certain legal steps to safeguard children's welfare, such as custodianship, wardship, contact orders and residence orders. While adoption in the UK gives a child immigration and nationality rights, these other orders do not necessarily affect a child's immigration status although they often mean that the leave of a court must be obtained before a child can be removed from the UK. When making an order, for example, that a child should reside with a relative, the family courts attach more weight to the child's welfare than to irregularities surrounding the immigration status of the child or their parents. The implication is that Home Office officials should proceed with great care when court orders of this kind have been obtained. If one of these orders is applied for (or if an adoption order in the UK is applied for), the Home Office may ask to make its own representations to the family court if 'it is clear that the court proceedings are designed purely to enable the child or the parent to evade immigration control' (see DP/4/96, para. 10).

CHILDREN BORN IN THE UK

Below we look at the situation for children born in the UK before and after 1 January 1983 when the British Nationality Act 1981 came into force.

People born in the UK before 1 January 1983

Except for the children of diplomats, any person born in the UK before 1983 is automatically a British citizen by birth. This gives the child full rights to remain in the UK and to return at any time as an adult, even if he or she was taken abroad as a baby. There have been instances of people, mainly of West African origin, who have had difficulty convincing the British high commissions abroad that they were born in the UK. Others who have travelled on British passports have had difficulty in satisfying immigration officers that they are in fact British citizens on arrival. A third group are those who have been arrested in the UK as apparently having no immigration status and claim to have been born here before 1 January 1983. Often the problem is one of establishing the person's identity.

Applicants should produce their full birth certificate (the one which has details of both parents so that it can be confirmed that the father was not a diplomat). Further evidence may be needed to establish that the person applying is the child who was born in the UK and left at a very young age. DNA blood testing can establish that they are the child of their parent or parents who were in the UK at the time of their birth but it may not always be sufficient to show that the applicant is a child of that relationship, as they could be another child born abroad, in which case they may not be British. If there are close family friends or relatives living in the UK who have remained in contact with the person throughout, they may be able to make statements to confirm their continuous knowledge of the person applying. If the person had been registered with a general practitioner or there are records of childhood immunisations or other medical treatment, this might also be helpful. If he or she had lived here long enough to go to a childminder, nursery or school and records can be found, these may also be of use.

For details about obtaining passports and certificates of entitlement to the right of abode, ▶see 1420–1, 1423–4.

People born in the UK on or after 1 January 1983

Since 1 January 1983, not all children born in the UK have been born British citizens. Only a child with a British or a settled parent is automatically born British by the fact of their birth in the UK. At present, when the parents are not married, only the mother's status counts for these purposes. This is because of the special meaning given to 'parent' in nationality law (the definition of 'parent' in the immigration rules is wider). This discrimination against 'illegitimate' children should be ended by the 2002 Act but the relevant provisions are not yet in force. For full details of who is and who is not British, ▶see Chapter 44. It may also be possible for the child to register as British (▶see 1473 onwards).

So, certain children born in the UK are not British and require leave to be in the UK. However, these children are not illegal entrants because they have not entered unlawfully. They are not overstayers or in breach of their other conditions of leave because they have not had leave. They cannot be refused leave to enter the UK and then removed because they have not arrived at a port and applied for leave to enter. In principle, therefore, they could remain in the UK indefinitely, but if they left the UK, they would have to satisfy the immigration rules in order to return.

However, non-British citizen children born in the UK, can be required to leave the UK as the 'family members' of their parents if the parents' departure is being enforced under any of the main methods of enforcement. This is explained above (▶386).

Applications under the rules for children born in the UK

There is a special section in the immigration rules to cover children who are born in the UK but who are not British citizens (paras 304–309, HC 395). In order to get the benefit of these rules, the child must be under 18, born in the UK, unmarried and not be leading an independent life or have formed an independent family unit. If parents wish to obtain leave to remain for such a child, the Home Office will grant this if one parent has leave to enter or remain or if one of them has the right of abode or is a British citizen. The child will be given the same leave as the parents. If the parents' leave differs, the child will be given leave for whichever is the longer of the two. However, if the parents are living separately, the child will be given leave in line with that parent who has day-to-day care. Remember, 'parent' has a fairly broad definition under the immigration rules (▶see 361–2).

If one parent is settled, or has British citizenship, the child can be given indefinite leave. This would presently apply (i.e. until the 2002 Act equalises the position for 'illegitimate' children – see above) for example, to a child whose parents were not married and whose mother was an overseas student with limited leave so that the child was not born British. If the child's father were a refugee with indefinite leave or a British citizen, the child, at present, would obtain indefinite leave in line with their father.

Provided the same requirements as above are met, these rules also permit a child born in the UK to be given indefinite leave if they are a child 'in respect of whom the parental rights and duties are vested solely in a local authority' (para. 305(i)(c), HC 395).

Where neither parent has leave

If *neither* parent has leave, the Home Office may grant successive periods of three months' leave to a child born in the UK if the following conditions are satisfied (see para. 307, HC 395):

- *both* parents of the child are in the UK;
- it appears unlikely that the parents will be removed in the immediate future; and
- there is no other person outside the UK who could reasonably be expected to care for the child.

These circumstances might arise, for example, in the case of an asylum-seeking couple whose application is at its early stages or which is taking some time to determine.

Evidence required and rules which do not apply

For these applications, the Home Office will only require evidence that the child is the child of the parent(s) and of the parents' immigration status. Importantly, it does not have to be shown that the child can be maintained and accommodated in the UK without recourse to public funds. In addition, children making applications under these rules to remain with a sole parent do not have to satisfy the 'sole-responsibility' or 'exclusion-undesirable' rules.

Can children travel abroad and still benefit from these rules?

If children travel overseas at a time when they have not yet been granted leave to remain in the UK, they may be granted leave to enter the UK under these rules when they return *provided* that they have not been away from the UK for more than two years and they satisfy the above requirements – importantly they will need to still be under 18 and have a parent with leave in the UK, or who is travelling with them and is being admitted. However, the IDIs state that, although the immigration rules formally set out this 'two year' rule:

'The location of family members will strongly influence the deciding [of] cases in practice, and in general there will be a good case for granting leave to enter if the child is joining or travelling with a parent or other close relative here.' (IDI, Ch 8, s4, annex P, para. 10).

Where a child travelling to the UK to seek entry is a visa national, or a 'specified national' entering for more than six months, entry clearance will be required.

13 Other dependent relatives

Aside from spouses, partners and children, there are many other relatives who may need or want to come to stay permanently with family members settled in the UK. This chapter looks at those other relatives, which include sons and daughters who are aged 18 and over. The rules enable dependent relatives to come to the UK for settlement with relatives who are settled in the UK. Successful applicants are given indefinite leave. There is no provision in the immigration rules for relatives – other than spouses, unmarried partners and children – to come to the UK with, or to join, a family member who is here with limited leave – for example, as a work permit holder. Such a relative could, of course, enter as a visitor in order to visit the relative.

The immigration rules concerning these other dependent relatives are very restrictive. The relatives provided for in the rules can be divided into two groups:

1) Parents and grandparents aged 65 and over (▶399–404);

2) Parents/grandparents aged under 65, adult sons, daughters, sisters, brothers, aunts and uncles (▶405–7).

The rules are most restrictive in relation to the second group. More distant relatives are not mentioned at all by the rules, but could, of course, be admitted at the discretion of the Home Office outside the immigration rules (▶407–8).

Depending on the strength of the family ties and the circumstances of the case, it is possible that relatives who wish to come to the UK might benefit from Article 8 ECHR (▶see 820–50). Article 8 may help in those cases where the family relationship is not one covered by the rules. It may also be of use where, in principle, the relationship is covered by the rules (e.g., a grandparent over the age of 65) but where the applicant cannot in practice satisfy the rules, yet it would still be an unjustifiable interference with family life to refuse the application.

Does the applicant need to use the dependent relative rules?

Because of the restrictive nature of the dependent relative rules, it is worth checking first of all that the relative actually needs to rely on the rules for the settlement of dependent relatives.

Relatives of EEA nationals EU law gives rights to family members to come to the UK without having to satisfy the immigration rules. In addition to spouses and minor children, the following relatives may benefit from EU free-movement rights: dependent grandparents and great-grandparents of the EEA national or their spouse; grandsons and grand-daughters (and great-grandchildren) of the EEA national or of their spouse; sons, daughters, grandchildren and great-grandchildren up to the age of 21, and 21 and over if they are still dependent. In certain cases, parents of minor children have free-movement rights. The rights of the family members of EEA national students are, however, more restrictive. Other relatives may be admitted depending on their own individual circumstances. For more details about the rights of family members of EEA nationals, ▶see 526–40.

These rights do not apply to relatives of most British citizens who have not travelled between countries exercising free-movement rights themselves, but they may apply to relatives of many Irish nationals in the UK, or to those of other EEA nationals in the UK. The relatives themselves do not have to be EEA nationals and, as indicated above, they can be directly related to the EEA national's spouse, rather than directly to the EEA national. So, for example, the dependent Colombian parents of a Colombian woman married to a German man working in the UK would qualify. Although the immigration rules do not need to be satisfied, for some people the effect of becoming a charge on public funds may terminate their free-movement rights. Workers and work-seekers must have a genuine chance of obtaining work, which means that they are less likely to require public funds.

Visitors It may be that the applicant does not in fact want to live in the UK, but only to be able to visit their relatives in the UK on a frequent basis. In that case, the appropriate application is for admission as a visitor (▶Chapter 9). Care needs to be taken – if the first application that is made is for settlement as a dependent relative, and that is refused, it will be extremely difficult subsequently to persuade an ECO that a genuine visit is intended, and that the person will leave when the visit is over. However, ECOs are often reluctant to grant visit entry clearances to elderly parents who appear to be alone or in need of care overseas, because they believe that they may seek to remain permanently in the UK after they have been admitted.

Retired persons of independent means People with 'close connections' to the UK, who are 60 or over, have a guaranteed private annual income of at least £25,000 available to them in the UK, and who are no longer intending to work, can be admitted as 'retired persons of independent means', ▶493–5. They will normally be given four years' leave in the first instance, and can apply for indefinite leave after that. This will be a possible alternative route for some parents or grandparents.

PARENTS AND GRANDPARENTS AGED 65 OR OVER

The immigration rules make separate provision for parents and grandparents who are aged 65 or over (see below) and those who are under 65 (see ▶405 onwards).

WHAT THE RULES SAY

Parents or grandparents aged 65 or over, and who are coming to the UK in order to live with their adult children or grandchildren, must be (paras 317–319 HC 395):

- widows or widowers aged 65 or over; or
- travelling together as a couple, and at least one of them is 65 or over; or
- if they have married again, 65 or over and unable to look to the spouse or children of the second marriage for financial support (in these cases, the sponsor must be able and willing to maintain the applicant, as well as any spouse or child of the second marriage who would be admissible as a dependant).

Applicants have to satisfy all of the following rules:

- they must be wholly or mainly financially dependent on a sponsor who is settled in the UK, who they are seeking to join;
- they must have no other close relatives in their own country to whom they could turn for financial support;
- the relative they are joining must be present and settled in the UK, or travelling with the applicant(s), and must be admitted for settlement;
- they must be accommodated, together with any dependants, in accommodation which the sponsor owns or occupies exclusively, without recourse to public funds;
- they must be able to be maintained in the UK without recourse to public funds.

As usual, applicants can be refused if any of the general grounds for refusal apply (▶97–9, 140–1). Those who are coming to the UK must obtain an entry clearance whether or not they are visa nationals. For general details about applying for entry clearance as a dependent relative and in other categories, ▶see 89–93. Where an applicant arrives without an entry clearance, they will not be admitted unless there are exceptional compassionate circumstances that justify the exercise of discretion. The Home Office accepts that this may arise more frequently in this category of case, because the majority of the passengers will be 'elderly or distressed relatives' (IDI, Ch 8, s6, para. 2.2).

However, applications under the dependent relatives rules may also be submitted in-country by applicants who entered in a different capacity. For

Home Office policy on enforcement when an applicant is over-65 ▶see 994–5. Often the immigration authorities will require a maintenance undertaking to be given ▶403–5. In-country applications are made on form SET(F). Although switching is permitted, if an in-country application is being made it should be clear that there has been a change of circumstances since the applicant entered – otherwise the Home Office may decide that the person always intended to settle and is an illegal entrant, having obtained entry, for example, as a visitor.

If the application for entry clearance is granted, the parents or grand-parents should be given an entry clearance that operates as indefinite leave to enter. Similarly, if an in-country application is accepted, indefinite leave to remain should be given. If the entry clearance application is refused, there is a right of appeal. There is also a right of appeal against a refusal of an in-country application provided the application was made in time. There is always a right of appeal on human rights grounds, if the applicant alleges that the decision is in breach of their human rights.

WHAT THE RULES MEAN

Age requirement

The age requirement (see above) is interpreted strictly, and it is important to show the age of the applicant by a birth certificate if possible. There can be serious problems in countries where there was no system of registration of births when the parents or grandparents were born. Elderly people may not know exactly when they were born, and may date their age from local events that are also unrecorded. When they obtained their passports, they may have given an approximate age for this purpose. The British authorities may take this as the only official evidence of age, and it may be very difficult for the parents or grandparents to prove, at the time of their applications for entry clearance or to remain, that a different date of birth is more accurate.

Prior to 1 October 1994, the rules exempted widowed mothers and grand-mothers from the age requirement. Now they have to satisfy the age requirement as well. Younger parents or grandparents can still qualify, but they need to show that they are 'living alone outside the UK in the most exceptional compassionate circumstances' (see below) as well as satisfy-ing the other rules.

It is important to note that, where one parent or grandparent is over 65 and one is under 65, they must be travelling together in order to satisfy these rules. It was recognised by the IAT in *Yambos* that this creates an unnecessary gap in the rules, because they do not provide for the situation where one parent comes to the UK alone for a visit and then decides to apply for settlement, while his or her spouse also applies for an entry clearance to come to the UK. Even though they meet all the other require-ments of the rules, they could be refused on the basis that they are not travelling together. If Article 8 was raised in such a case, it would be for the Home Office to show the justification for this gap in the rules.

Wholly or mainly financially dependent on the UK relative

The words 'financially dependent' do not mean that money actually has to be changing hands. In *Bibi*, the Court of Appeal ruled that, if accommodation, clothing, food and other needs are met by the relative, then that is sufficient. If the relatives are in the UK, however, the Home Office will generally expect to see evidence of money being remitted in the form of international money orders, or a letter from the bank confirming that money is transferred on a regular basis. It is possible, however, that the applicant is being supported by the sponsor's assets abroad. The kind of evidence required will therefore depend on the circumstances. It is possible, of course, that the applicant will have received monies from relatives outside their own country but not from the UK. That will count against showing dependence on the UK relative.

Necessary dependency Dependency must be of necessity, and not created. For example, if the parent or grandparent gives away their income to other relatives, and therefore relies on money sent over by relatives in the UK, this will not satisfy the rules. Applicants may also have problems qualifying if they pass on property or capital to their children and no longer own it. The Court of Appeal held in *Desai* that the question of whether a person is 'mainly' financially dependent does not depend upon precise calculations; all of the circumstances have to be taken into account.

Emotional dependency Although the focus of the rules is on financial dependency, other kinds of dependency – for example, emotional – may be taken into account in deciding whether the rules are met. Where there are strong and long-lasting emotional ties between the sponsor in the UK and the parent, this may help to show why the parent should not be expected to turn to other relatives for support. Support provided by a sponsor over and above that necessary to enable the parent or grandparent to have a reasonable standard of living, may not be taken into account in deciding whether a person is wholly or mainly dependent on the relatives.

The IAT has indicated that the rules are intended to look at the situation when the relatives are in their own country (*Kartar Kaur*). If the relatives are dependent while they are visiting the UK and make an application while here, but are not, or would not be, dependent when they are in their own country, the requirements will generally not be satisfied.

General It is demeaning for elderly people to have to show that they cannot maintain themselves. It can also be difficult to prove, as many people do not keep records of all the money they have sent to their families abroad. If money has been sent through postal orders or international money transfer agencies, people may have kept at least some of the counterfoils. If it has been sent through a bank account, the bank may have records. Registered letter slips, showing at least that something valuable was sent, can be useful. Also of use are letters from the parents which mention the receipt of remittances, and which date as far back as possible.

If money was taken in cash by visiting relatives or friends, it may be difficult to do anything more than assert this fact. It may be helpful to have letters from the carriers, confirming when and how much money they took, or letters from the parents confirming that they received the money. It may be that the money was converted into a different currency, and that there are regular receipts which show this. Passport stamps can also show that the person carrying the money travelled at the various relevant times. When parents or grandparents have another regular income – for example, from an occupational pension – it should be shown that the money they receive from their children is more than the pension, so that they can show they are mainly, if not wholly, dependent on them.

This requirement of the rules discriminates against people who have been thrifty, or people who live in a country where an adequate old-age pension is paid. Retired people in the United States, for example, are unlikely to be financially dependent on their children rather than on any pension or insurance. It also means that parents or grandparents who own property – their own home, for example – may not be considered dependent, even though they intend to leave the home to their children.

No other close relatives to turn to for financial support

Generally, those relatives who the immigration authorities may expect to be able to provide support to the applicant include sons, daughters, brothers, sisters, grandchildren, uncles, aunts and even (but less probably) nephews, nieces and in-laws. If there is a relative living in the applicant's own country who is able and willing to support the applicant, then the Home Office position is that it would not be unreasonable for the applicant to turn to that relative for support, even if the sponsor in the UK is financially in a better position to help. This requirement is therefore often difficult to meet if there is such a relative. The Home Office may also rely on the collective ability among relatives to support the applicant.

Account must, however, be taken of cultural conditions. In parts of the Indian subcontinent, for example, it is generally accepted that it is a son's responsibility to care for his aged parents and not the responsibility of married daughters, because they have a corresponding responsibility to their husband's parents. So, for example, when the sons are in the UK but the daughters are in India, it can be argued that the daughters cannot usually be expected to care for their parents. The Home Office recognises this: 'For example, in the Indian sub-continent, married women are unlikely to be *able* to provide support'. (IDI Ch 8, s6, annex V, para. 2).

The other close relatives must be both able and willing to provide for the applicants (see the High Court cases of **Bastiampillai** and **Dadibhai**). Close relatives who do not particularly care about the applicants and who are not interested in supporting them cannot be considered as relatives to whom the applicants can 'turn'. Account should be taken of the age and health of the applicants, as well as the ability of other relatives to visit them regularly. The needs of the parents must be compared against what support is on offer. Also, the support available from the other relative should be a permanent commitment, rather than just help in an emergency (DSP, Ch15, para. 15.3).

It must also be remembered that the rule requires the close relative to be one who can be turned to for *financial* support. The IAT emphasised this point in **Sinnasamy Ramalingathathevar**, in which the adjudicator and the ECO had wrongly relied upon a young daughter who could not necessarily provide financial support. This line has also been successful, for example, in some Filipino cases, where there were other adult children still living in the country. Applications have succeeded by showing that the economic circumstances of the other sons or daughters are such that they cannot manage to look after their parents, or even their own families, without the financial support received from the UK. The Home Office does generally accept that applications from married couples should not be refused solely on the basis that they have each other to turn to (IDI, Ch 8, s6, annex V, para. 2). If other close relatives with whom the parents previously lived have died, their death certificates should be produced. If circumstances have changed, so that other relatives are no longer able to care for the parents, this should also be explained.

It is important to remember that an ECO may make local enquiries through unannounced 'village visits' to the parents' or grandparents' community. The immigration authorities are careful not to give applicants or sponsors any warning that such a visit might take place. This has been a feature of out-of-country immigration control by posts in the Indian subcontinent.

Maintenance and accommodation requirements and undertakings

The maintenance and accommodation requirements for dependent relatives are similar to those for spouses and children (►see 308–318), and similar evidence should be provided. However, dependent relatives are given indefinite leave straight away, rather than limited leave for an initial probationary period. This means that no condition can be attached to their leave which prevents them from having access to public funds (this is because no conditions can be attached to an indefinite leave). In addition, there is no other general legal liability in British law for an adult to maintain his or her parents or grandparents (unlike for spouses and children). For these reasons, the immigration authorities are likely to request that the sponsor enter into a maintenance undertaking to provide support for the applicant(s). Failure to provide an undertaking, if one is requested by the immigration authorities, is a ground for refusing the application (para. 320(14), 322(6) HC 395).

In an entry clearance application, sponsors are requested to make the undertaking on form RON 112, the significance of which should be explained to the sponsor/applicant by the ECO (DSP, Ch 8, para. 8.11 and 'sponsorship undertaking' attached to Ch 8). In an in-country application, the undertaking should be made on the form attached to the prescribed form SET(F). In both entry clearance and in-country applications, the form of undertaking will be both kept on file and sent to the DSS in Leeds. This is a formal legal undertaking by the sponsor to be responsible for the maintenance and accommodation of the applicant(s) in the UK when they are admitted. At the time of the undertaking, a further form is completed by an officer on behalf of the Secretary of State, which certifies that the undertaking is indeed a formal one given under the immigration rules.

An effective 'maintenance undertaking' is defined as one which is given 'in pursuance of the immigration rules' (see s115(10) 1999 Act). Although sponsors are requested to complete the particular forms referred to above, an undertaking *not* made on one of those forms may still be effective (▶see 1253–4). The Home Office will generally reject attempts by joint sponsors to support the application, and will ask the applicant to nominate one sponsor who will sign the undertaking (IDI, Ch 8, s6, para. 3.2).

The effect of the undertaking is to deny the applicant access to social security benefits (e.g. income support, income-based job-seekers' allowance, housing benefit, etc) for five years, or until the sponsor dies (but for full details ▶see 1250, 1253–4, 1256 category (2), 1257 category (3), 1258 categories (1) and (2)). It is also a criminal offence if a sponsor who has signed an undertaking refuses or neglects to provide support, as a result of which the applicant becomes entitled to asylum support (see s108 1999 Act). Also, under the 1999 Act, the Home Office may recoup from the sponsor amounts which are later paid to the applicant as asylum support (see also para. 35 HC 395). The DSS may also seek to recover from the sponsor any benefit paid to the applicant as a result of their failure to honour the undertaking.

The rules themselves are contradictory about whether the dependent relative has to be dependent on one relative, or whether they can be dependent on more than one relative (compare paras 317(i)(e), (f) with 317(iii)). While it may be justifiable to require one sponsor to sign the form, we suggest that support from other relatives must be taken into account in determining whether the applicant can be maintained without recourse to public funds (▶see also 317). To read the rules otherwise would not be compatible with article 8 ECHR, which requires a rational justification for decisions that interfere with family life.

The Home Office is cautious about refusing applications from dependent relatives where maintenance and accommodation is the only basis for a refusal. The particular circumstances of the case and any compassionate features will always be taken into account before such a refusal is issued (see IDI, Ch 8, s1, annex F, para. 10).

PARENTS AND GRANDPARENTS UNDER 65 YEARS, AND OTHER RELATIVES

The rules for parents and grandparents who are under 65, and for other dependent relatives, are more than those set out above. Other than the age requirement, applicants must satisfy the same requirements as above; but in addition, they must show that they are 'living alone outside the United Kingdom in the most exceptional compassionate circumstances'.

WHAT THE RULES SAY

Applicants must demonstrate all of the following (paras 317–319 HC 395):

- they are the parent or grandparent (aged under 65); son, daughter, sister, brother, aunt, uncle (all aged 18 or over) of the relative they wish to join in the UK;
- they are living alone outside the UK in the most exceptional compassionate circumstances;
- they are wholly or mainly financially dependent on their relative or relatives in the UK;
- they have no other close relatives in their own country to whom they could turn for financial support;
- the relative they are joining is present and settled in the UK, or is travelling with the applicant(s) and will be admitted for settlement;
- they will be accommodated, together with any dependants, in accommodation which their relative owns or occupies exclusively, without recourse to public funds;
- they can be maintained in the UK without recourse to public funds.

WHAT THE RULES MEAN

For details of the meaning of most of these rules, and for maintenance undertakings, see above.

Living alone in the most exceptional compassionate circumstances

This requirement is one which is notoriously difficult to satisfy. It is essentially intended to allow the admission of family members who cannot manage without the rest of their family, and who are completely isolated without them. Where the application is being made in-country, the Home Office should consider the situation of the applicant as if they were in their own country, rather than the UK. The case of *Begum* (*Manshoora*) struck out a previous requirement of this rule: that the relative had to have a standard of living lower than the average in his or her own country. The Divisional Court agreed that this requirement was unreasonable, since the fact of receiving money from abroad at all (another requirement of the rules) could bring people above the average standard of living in several countries. Nevertheless, the fact that the relative is able to send money over can still be taken into account in deciding whether the person is living in the most exceptional circumstances.

The requirement of 'living alone' does not always need to be taken literally (see *Paw*, IAT). A mother living with her young baby, for example, could be counted as 'living alone'. However, in *Ibraheem*, a father applying to join his son in the UK lived with his other son who was a violent drug addict. The IAT nevertheless found that, although his circumstances were compassionate, he was not living alone.

Depending on the precise cultural circumstances, a young, single, un-married woman living on her own, in certain countries, may satisfy the rules (see *Bayar*, IAT). Before 1 October 1994, the position under the immigration rules for such young women was better. Unmarried daugh-ters between the ages of 18 and 21 might be given 'special consideration' in coming to the UK to join their parents for settlement. They had to show they were financially dependent on their parents; that they formed part of the family unit overseas; that they would be left entirely on their own in the country in which they were living, without any other close relatives to turn to for help; and that they could be maintained and accommodated in the UK. In many countries, a young, unmarried woman living on her own is not socially acceptable, and she may incur a great deal of stigma from the rest of the community.

When family members are applying to join a parent in the UK and the applicants include sons or daughters who are over 18, it is likely that ECOs will ask more questions about them than other members of the family. More checks will be made to be sure that they remain, of necessity, dependant on the sponsor. The decision of the Court of Appeal in *Begum* (*Husna*) indicates that the rule should be interpreted consistently with Article 8 ECHR – the decision of the family to migrate to the UK cannot undermine the relevance of the circumstances which a son or daughter would be in if left alone.

Home Office instructions state as follows (IDI, Ch 8, s6, annex V):

'Each application must be considered on the individual merits of the case. It is therefore not possible to list every possible circumstance which may arise. However, illness, incapacity, isolation and poverty are all compassionate circumstances which should be considered.'

Applications are decided on a case-by-case basis, and all of the various elements of the case can be considered together to see whether they amount in combination to 'the most exceptional compassionate circumstances'. It is therefore important that the relatives applying give the fullest possible details of their circumstances to the immigration official dealing with the case, along with any evidence they can produce.

Adult sons and daughters: some other considerations

Adult sons and daughters may be able to avoid having to satisfy the restrictive rules set out above if they fall into any of the following groups although the policy relating to the second group has now been withdrawn.

Treated as minors under the immigration rules

Sons and daughters who have reached the age of 18 are still able to qualify under the rules relating to children if their application is made (but not decided) before they are 18. In some circumstances, sons and daughters who are 18 at the time of the application itself can also qualify under those rules. For details, ▶see 358.

Relationship subsequently proved by DNA

There was particular controversy about children who applied in the past to come to join their parents before they were 18 but who were refused as the authorities were not then satisfied that they were related to their parents as claimed. Some were later able to make use of DNA-testing technology to conclusively prove the disputed relationship. However, by this time they were over 18 and unable to fit into the immigration rules relating to children. The Home Office operated a policy from 14 June 1989, that it would consider giving entry to these 'overage dependants' if they could demonstrate 'some' compassionate circumstances over and above the basic injustice of having been wrongly separated from family members. Applicants also had to show that they had remained 'necessarily' dependent on their parents, rather than dependent 'by choice' and were unmarried. The policy was withdrawn on 24 August 2002.

More distant relatives

More distant relatives than those covered by the immigration rules (see above) may still make applications to come to and settle in the UK with family members. For example, cousins, nephews, nieces, half-brothers and half-sisters, or step-mothers where there is a mother still living, are all not covered by the rules.

The Home Office can grant applications outside the rules, so it may be worth trying if there are exceptional circumstances. It is important to show the immigration authorities what the strong exceptional compassionate reasons for the application are – for example, that there is a close emotional relationship between the relative and the person settled in the UK. A person who had been brought up by a great-aunt or a cousin, and who had a quasi-parental relationship with that person, would need to explain this family history and background, how the family tie developed, and why there are/were no other closer relatives who could support the person in the country of origin. If the applicant is elderly, it is more likely that exceptional compassionate reasons will be accepted. If the person has physical or mental disabilities, medical evidence to show this is required.

Although applications for other relatives are not specifically covered in the rules, it is wrong to think of them as purely discretionary, since in all cases the immigration authorities will have to apply Article 8 ECHR, which does not rigidly define which relationships fall within family life (▶see table at 823–6). It may be that if the sponsor in the UK is in need of care from the relative, the Home Office policy relating to carers can also be used (▶232–5).

Section 5 **Workers and business people**

Chapter 14
Work for which permission is required   411

Managed migration   414

Immigration Employment Documents   418

The work permit scheme   420

The Sectors-Based Scheme   448

Seasonal agricultural workers' scheme   450

Chapter 15
Permit-free employment   453

Long-term permit-free employment under
the rules   453

Short-term permit-free employment under
the rules   462

Permit-free employment outside the immigration
rules   467

People who are exempt from immigration control   472

Chapter 16
Business purposes   477

Business categories   477

Consequences of unlawful work or business
in the UK   495

5

14 Work for which permission is required

This section contains three chapters covering people who wish to come to the UK for either employment or business. This first chapter deals with categories for which a specific document issued by the immigration authorities granting permission to work in the UK must be obtained. These documents are now known by the new collective term 'Immigration Employment Documents' (IEDs) (▶see further below) and are required *in addition* to the need to obtain leave. The terms can be confusing because sometimes the individual IEDs are referred to simply as 'permits', although a 'work permit' is one kind of IED. IEDs are part of the bureaucracy associated with the government's policy of 'managed migration', which is the banner under which most of the recent changes relating to work and business have been made.

This chapter begins with an overview of managed migration and the changes to procedure connected to IEDs. The chapter goes on to cover the following IED categories: the work permit scheme (including Training or Work Experience permits); the Sectors-Based Scheme (SBS); and the Seasonal Agricultural Workers Scheme (SAWS). The Highly Skilled Migrant Programme (HSMP) is also an IED category, but because it allows entry for business as well as employment it is dealt with in the business chapter (▶483–91).

Chapter 15 covers employment for which an IED is *not* required. These categories are generally referred to as 'permit-free' or 'non-work permit' employment. The chapter looks at permit-free employment under the immigration rules in short-term categories and those which lead to settlement. It also deals with permit-free employment outside the rules, and it covers those who are exempt from immigration control and who therefore do not need either leave or any specific permission to work. People in this class generally fall into one of the exempt categories because of the work they do, or their position.

Chapter 16, deals with those coming to the UK for 'business' purposes, as opposed to being employed here. It covers business-people including the self-employed; innovators; HSMP applicants; investors; writers, composers and artists; and retired persons of independent means.

Notes on using this section

The following notes give a guide to finding information connected to the areas covered in this section. There are also important explanations of how we have used some phrases.

Appeals As with other categories of admission, decisions made under the worker and business categories will give rise to rights of appeal if an 'immigration decision' (▶1053–4) has been made and the right of appeal is not excluded. Full details are to be found in Chapter 34. For these categories, the main exclusion arises where the immigration decision is taken on the grounds that the applicant has not been issued with an IED (see s88(2)(b), (3)(c) 2002 Act). There is no ordinary right of appeal against a decision to refuse an IED, because it is not defined as an 'immigration decision'. However, there is a right to request an internal review where an IED is refused (▶see 439–40).

Entry clearance The general procedures relating to entry clearance are dealt with at ▶85–94. Where, under certain categories, we refer to entry clearance as not mandatory or as not compulsory, this means that the category of admission itself does not require an entry clearance. It does *not* mean that 'visa nationals' or any foreign national seeking entry for more than six months may arrive without an entry clearance. People in either of those two groups still generally need an entry clearance. For more detailed explanation of these terms, and of when entry clearance is required, ▶see 78–83.

Dependants Although this section gives brief details of who may be admitted as the dependants in each category, this is more fully dealt with in Section 4 (and ▶see 352–4, 355–6 for dependants of those admitted to the UK for work and business).

Leave to remain For each of the work and business categories, we give some information about applications for leave to remain. However, broader information – about procedures, documents, the forms which must be used by main applicants and dependants, and whether the application can be processed through the Home Office Public Enquiry Office (PEO) – is dealt with in Chapter 5. Where the procedures and forms are very specific to those applying for work and business, they are dealt with in the present section. For example, IED procedures and applications for leave to remain on the recent form FLR(IED) are covered below, at 430–4.

Registration Some people who come to the UK for work and business are required to register with the police. For an explanation of who is required to register and of the registration process, ▶see 1006–7, and ▶see 1527 for the list of 'relevant foreign nationals'.

Settlement Many of the work and business categories allow people to apply for settlement after they have 'spent a continuous period of four years' in the UK in a particular capacity. The interpretation of 'continuous period' is looked at as we deal with settlement for work permit holders (▶see 437–9), but the same general approach can be applied to other categories.

'Switching' 'Switching' (changing immigration status while in the UK) has become an area of particular activity and complexity in the work and business context. New immigration rules to tighten up switching in these areas were introduced on 1 October 2004. A full explanation of the possibility of switching as it applies in immigration categories generally is provided in Chapter 7. This explanation sets out when it is possible to switch under the immigration rules, but it also deals with the possibility of switching outside the rules and gives details of relevant Home Office policy. Switching is not therefore dealt with in detail, as we consider each worker and business category individually.

Unlawful work/business in the UK At the end of the section (▶495–500), we look at the consequences, for workers and employers, of working or entering into business unlawfully while in the UK. The law relating to criminal sanctions for employers changed on 1 May 2004.

Other work purposes not covered in this section

The economic activities and immigration rights of nationals of the European Economic Area (EEA) are governed by the law of the European Union (EU). This provides for the free movement of the economically active and of other categories of people. Since 1 June 2002, Swiss nationals have had the same rights within the UK as EEA nationals. From 1 May 2004, ten new states joined the EU, and benefit from certain free-movement rights. Association Agreements (sometimes known as the 'Europe Agreements') between the EU and other countries, which enable persons from those countries to come to the UK for self-employment or business, are also governed by EU law. The free-movement rights of all these nationals and their family members are fully described in Section 6.

Aside from those described in this section and those with EU free-movement rights, there are certain other people who may be admitted to the UK for work-related purposes, or who can do some work while here. Although these groups may be economically active, they have grown out of the visitor or student categories and are dealt with in the appropriate parts of the book as follows:

- certain people may be admitted as 'business visitors' in order to do very limited forms of business in the UK (▶see 220–3);
- those seeking to remain in the UK in order to provide care for a relative or friend who is ill may be allowed to stay as 'carers' (▶see 232–5);
- those coming to the UK for a 'working holiday' may obtain employment provided that their work is 'incidental' to their holiday (▶see 235–43);
- most students may now work part-time during the term-time and full-time during the vacation (▶see 263–6 for details). Chapter 10 dealing

with students also covers the rules relating to student nurses, postgraduate doctors, dentists and trainee GPs, those coming to take their PLAB tests, those with clinical or dental attachments, and students' union sabbatical officers.

In addition, the following groups of people, although their purpose for being in the UK is not necessarily work-related, are generally able to work without obtaining specific permission to do so (although the conditions endorsed in the passport, or on the grant of leave contained in a letter, should always be checked):

- people who have indefinite leave (no conditions can be attached to an indefinite leave);
- people granted refugee status;
- generally, people granted leave exceptionally – of which the largest category are those granted discretionary leave, or humanitarian protection (▶see 147–50);
- people who have been allowed to enter or remain to be with close relatives settled in the UK – for example, spouses or unmarried partners – and have been granted leave for an initial two years;
- those allowed to enter or remain in order to exercise rights of access to their children;
- any other people who have no restriction or prohibition on working contained in the endorsement on their passports or on their documents granting leave.

Those granted 'temporary admission' to the UK while their immigration status is resolved are normally subject to conditions preventing them from working. However, it is still possible in certain circumstances to ask that the conditions be relaxed to allow work. The previous practice of lifting working restrictions for asylum-seekers who have waited six months or more for an initial decision on their claim has now ended. For the present position, ▶see 695–6.

MANAGED MIGRATION

Historically, the immigration rules placed large barriers in the way of non-EEA nationals coming to the UK in order to take up work or establish businesses. UK immigration law and rules are designed to protect jobs in the UK for people already permitted to live and work in this country, and to encourage investment in businesses only from people with substantial amounts of money to invest. The process of change began towards the end of 1998 with a White Paper issued by the Department of Trade and Industry entitled *Our Competitive Future: Building the Knowledge Driven Economy*. The Paper referred to the need to attract 'bright people with scarce skills to work for UK businesses and to set up businesses of their own which create jobs'. It further stated that 'this requires a positive attitude to immigration'.

In October 2000, the skills threshold for those seeking work-permit employment was lowered to Level 3 S/NVQ. In 2002, the Home Office White Paper *Secure Borders, Safe Haven* recognised that there were recruitment difficulties and skills shortages within the resident and EEA workforces. The government has also argued that most asylum seekers are economic migrants, and that one way to deal with this 'abuse' is to provide legal opportunities for obtaining access to the UK in order to work. In a recent speech on managed migration, the former Home Secretary described the programme as a 'balanced policy about sensible, legal economic migration', and pointed to 600,000 current vacancies in the economy with shortages in particular sections and regions, especially in Scotland (Home Secretary's speech, 24 November 2004). The new routes for economic migration mapped out in the 2002 White Paper have largely been implemented.

The principal innovations are as follows:

- the Highly Skilled Migrant Programme (HSMP) (▶483–81); a new aspect of the HSMP for MBA graduates was introduced in 2005 (▶488);
- new provision for the admission of 'Innovators' (▶481–3);
- introduction of the 'Sectors Based Scheme' for the less skilled (SBS) (▶448–50);
- introduction of the Science Engineering and Graduate Scheme (SEGS) (▶464–5);
- allowing graduate-level students to 'switch' into employment (▶163–4, 259);
- changes to the Seasonal Agricultural Workers Scheme (SAWS) (▶450–2);
- changes to the Working Holidaymaker Scheme (WHS) working holidaymaker rules, including allowing applicants to switch to work-permit employment after a year and to other of the economic migration categories (▶169, 238);
- incorporation into the immigration rules of the previous concession allowing domestic workers who form part of the household overseas to enter the UK with their employer. Domestic workers are also now able to remain in the UK if they change their employer, but are still providing domestic work (▶457–9);
- the old Work Permits UK website has been replaced by a new website, 'Working in the UK', which went live on 1 December 2003. The site is intended to explain legal routes of economic migration to both businesses and foreign nationals, and can be found at www.workingintheuk.gov.uk;
- in early December 2004 the Home Office and the Scottish Executive had agreed that overseas students who complete their courses at one of Scotland's 46 further education colleges (as well as foreign graduates from Scottish universities) would be eligible to remain in the UK and work. The purpose was to address Scotland's depopulation crisis. It was thought that the scheme would benefit up to 4,000 foreign students graduating from

the universities, as well as 4,500 students studying at FE colleges. The result is the 'Fresh Talent: Working in Scotland Scheme' which was introduced into the immigration rules from 22 June 2005 (▶465–7).

Five-year strategy and consultation The latest government proposals concerning economic migration are set out in a Command Paper issued in February 2005, the 'five-year strategy'. The main proposal is to consolidate all the existing economic and semi-economic categories into a new points system. On 19 July 2005, the government launched a 16-week consultation exercise for its latest proposals on this issue. They are contained in the document issued on that date, *Making Migration Work for Britain – Consultation Launched on Managed Migration Routes to the UK*. Details of and commentaries on the five-year strategy and the consultation document are provided at ▶33–50, 51–52.

The reality of managed migration

The rhetoric and the reality concerning managed migration are two separate matters. On the one hand, the various schemes and initiatives referred to above have undoubtedly opened up opportunities for economic migration that were not previously available. This is welcome. Indeed, even the already established routes of economic migration have been expanded. For example, in the early 1990s the number of work permits issued annually was around 30,000. In the financial year ending 2004, the Home Office was expecting to issue some 200,000 work permits. No doubt the reduction of the skills threshold for work permits to N/SVQ level 3 from October 2000 has contributed to this.

Restrictions However, the economic routes for migration for those outside the EEA still remain very carefully and strictly controlled. Certain of the innovations have been restricted since their introduction. This applies to both the Sector Based Schemes and the Seasonal Agricultural Workers Schemes. Additionally, for applications made on or after 1 October 2004, the Home Office introduced stringent new measures restricting 'switching' into the work permit, HSMP and Innovator categories (▶as incorporated into Chapter 7). The government's justification for this is that these restrictions are necessary in order to 'tackle abuses of the managed migration routes' and 'clarify processes' for 'legitimate businesses and individuals'. Another backward step has been the introduction of compulsory entry clearance for those coming to the UK for work-permit employment. Whereas previously non-visa nationals who held a work permit did not also require an entry clearance, most persons coming to the UK for this purpose must now obtain one (▶see 428–9). Of course, from 13 November 2005 the system requiring visas for everyone coming to the UK for longer than six months applies to all foreign nationals requiring leave (▶see 78–83).

Flexibility? It has also become very difficult to persuade Work Permits (UK) to exercise flexibility in the application of the criteria set out in their

Guidance Notes, which describe the requirements for obtaining work permits. Employers and employees are having to be careful that they comply strictly with the criteria. A good commercial argument no longer seems to be sufficient to obtain the favourable exercising of discretion. Indeed, there was an indication in 2004 that Work Permits (UK) had been told not to exercise discretion in the operation of the work permit scheme.

Charging and service standards Another aspect of managed migration has been the introduction of charges for processing IEDs. The Home Office has asserted that it aims to deliver a 'flexible, self-financing managed migration programme that meets the UK's economic needs'. As will be seen below, these charges and charges for the associated application for leave are on an ever-upward course. In the 2003/04 financial year, the Home Office states that it obtained over £70 million through charging. Despite the introduction of charging, the standards of service in processing applications in worker and business categories have declined. For example, when it began as a pilot scheme in 2002, applications under the HSMP were routinely resolved within a day or two. By the end of 2004, applications were taking some 26 weeks to resolve. Applicants and their representatives have complained that relatively simple applications have been wrongly dealt with by inexperienced staff. The need to apply separately for an IED, as well as for further leave (on form FLR(IED), ▶see 430 onwards), has inevitably made applying for extensions more complex and expensive. Again, there have been serious delays. Although it has since improved, experience of practitioners towards the end of 2004 was that applications made on FLR(IED) were taking some 10 to 15 weeks to be determined. Work Permits (UK) has begun to maintain a weekly update on its website as to the length of time taken to process applications in employment-related categories.

The present 'service standards' target times for 2005/06 are to determine 70% of FLR(IED) applications within 20 working days and 90% of them within 45 working days. It is intended to deal with 98% of FLR(IED) applications made in person at the Croydon PEO within 24 hours. The HSMP targets are to deal with 50% of applications within 25 working days and 90% within 70 working days (see Home Office leaflet 'Revised Charges for Limited Leave to Remain for IED Holders and Highly Skilled Migrant Programme Applications from 1 April 2005', 1 April 2005).

What 'they' can do for 'us' The focus of the managed migration policy is to carve out two groups from those who wish to come to the UK: first, a group of persons with substantial skills, expertise or capital from which the UK can benefit; second, a group of unskilled workers who are prepared to do the kind of work which the resident labour force increasingly will not do for the level of wages which employers are willing to pay. Those in the second group do not generally obtain rights that will lead to settlement. Managed migration is a policy which asks: what use can this person presently be to the UK and its economy? By keeping the main requirements of the various schemes outside the immigration rules, the policy then maintains the flexibility to quickly open up and then close down immigration rights depending upon the answers to that question. The policy does not speak in terms of the rights of individuals. The latest statement of the government's proposals on managed migration again underlines this theme:

'The purpose of the reforms is to admit people selectively in order to maximise the economic benefit of migration to the UK... Migration makes a substantial contribution to economic growth, helps fill gaps in the labour market, including key public services... However, migration can have an adverse impact on public services and community life if it is not properly managed. The system should therefore be focussed primarily on bringing migrants to do key jobs that cannot be filled from the domestic labour force.' (From the Introduction to *Making Migration Work for Britain*, 19 July 2005).

At the same time, routes of migration which are based upon the rights and interests of the individual (asylum, human rights, family members) are subject to ever-increasing restriction. The latest proposals contained in the 'five year strategy' represent an intensification of this policy (for discussion on those proposals ▶see 42–5, 47–8). For more generally on this theme and the need to assess government immigration taken as a whole rather than in parts, see the discussion paper sponsored by JCWI, *Tough as Old Boots? Asylum, immigration and the paradox of New Labour policy*, available from JCWI, and JCWI's analysis of the five-year plan, *Recognise Rights, Realise Benefits*.

IMMIGRATION EMPLOYMENT DOCUMENTS

The term 'Immigration Employment Document' (IED) was introduced by the 2002 Act and refers to any document which 'relates to employment and is issued for a purpose of immigration rules' or 'in connection with leave to enter or remain in the UK' (see s122 2002 Act; the same definition is given in the immigration rules, para. 6 HC 395). The IEDs are:

- work permits (in any of the categories referred to below, including Training or Work Experience permits);
- documents issued by the Home Office confirming that the person meets the criteria under the HSMP;
- a permit issued under the SBS;
- a Home Office 'work card' issued by an approved operator under the SAWS.

Despite the new label, the documents themselves are, of course, not all new, and nor are all of the procedures connected with them. It should be noted, however, that from 1 April 2003 section 82 of the 1999 Act was amended to make it very clear that representatives acting on behalf of employers who are offering advice and services in relation to an IED must be registered with the Office of the Immigration Services Commissioner (OISC), ▶see 65. There are four other important points to note about IEDs:

1) The Home Office may charge a fee for processing applications for IEDs (▶see below).

2) Holders of IEDs must use the new form FLR(IED) ('further leave to remain – immigration employment document') in order to apply to extend their leave in the UK (▶see below at 430 onwards).

3) If the Home Office makes a decision about a person's immigration status which is based upon their not having an IED, certain appeal rights are denied (▶see 439, 1052–60).

4) Some of the immigration rules relating to 'switching' into work and business categories require that the applicant holds an IED (see paragraphs 131A-134 HC 395; for work and business switching, ▶see generally Chapter 7).

Charging for IEDs

Fees for considering an application for an IED are levied under the Immigration Employment Document (Fees) Regulations 2003 (as amended). Under those regulations, Work Permits (UK) began charging fees on 1 April 2003, when the charge for a work permit was set at £95. The level of the charge was said to be calculated by dividing the overall cost of processing work permit applications divided by the number of applications received. From 2 July 2004, the cost of applying for any IED (or to extend an IED or to change employment) has been £153 and this remains the standard fee. There are, however, exceptions to this rule. As at 1 April 2005, the exceptions are as follows:

• There is no fee, payable by the applicant, either to the approved operator or the Home Office for applications made under SAWS.

• The fee for applications made under the HSMP is £315.

• If the worker is a national of a country which has ratified either the Council of Europe Social Charter (Turin, 18 October 1961), or the Council of Europe Revised Social Charter (Strasbourg, 3 May 1996), no fee is charged. The non-EEA countries which this applies to are: Albania, Andorra, Armenia, Azerbaijan, Bulgaria, Croatia, Macedonia, Moldova, Romania and Turkey. (EEA nationals, of course, do not need to apply under IED categories).

• A single fee only is charged for group applications in the Sportspersons and entertainers category (for group applications ▶see 446).

• The fee for a schoolteacher employed in England is met by the Department of Education and Skills.

During 2004 there was a consultation exercise on proposed fees which included the possibility of charging to recover the costs of appeals and enforcement. HSMP applications have apparently taken much more time and resources to deal with than was originally envisaged which accounts for the increase in the fee payable to £315. (*Consultation: Review of Charges for Immigration Applications*, Home Office, September 2004; Home Office press release, 8 September 2004). For fees generally, ▶see 1509–1510.

Applying to extend leave in IED categories

Since 1 April 2004, all persons who wish to extend their leave in-country so as to remain in the above categories need to go through two procedures. *First*, their employer must obtain an IED (or an extension to the existing IED) as above; *then* the employee must apply to extend their leave on form FLR(IED) (▶see generally 430–4), the fee for which from 1 April 2005, has increased from £121 to £335 (£500 for 'premium' rate applications). The same exemption as that identified above for IEDs applies for nationals of countries which have ratified the Social Charter or the revised Social Charter. These administrative procedures have added to the time, inconvenience and cost incurred by the process. Previously, for example, an application which was made to extend a work permit on form WP1 was *also* treated as an application to extend the leave granted to a work permit holder.

From 1 April 2005, holders of work permits have been able to apply for leave to remain by booking an appointment at the Croydon PEO.

We now look at the IED categories in turn: the work permit scheme (immediately below); the SBS (▶448–50) and the SAWS (▶450–2). HSMP is dealt with at ▶483–91.

THE WORK PERMIT SCHEME

The work permit scheme is just one of the many ways in which non-EEA nationals can lawfully work in the UK. The other routes to working in the UK are set out in the rest of this chapter and the following two chapters. Contrary to what many people believe, it is the employer who must apply for and obtain a work permit. The permit then enables them to employ a particular person to do particular work in the UK, normally on a full-time basis. Work permits are issued by Work Permits (UK) which, from mid 2001, has been part of the Home Office Immigration and Nationality Directorate although it is based in Sheffield. Work Permits (UK) also administers the SBS and the HSMP.

The requirements for obtaining a work permit are not set down in the immigration rules, but instead described in detailed 'Guidance Notes', available on the Work Permits (UK) website at www.workpermits.gov.uk. The Notes describe both the conditions that must be satisfied in order for a work permit to be issued, and the procedures for applying for them; in what follows we have used much of the information they provide. The

Guidance Notes are re-issued every six months or so, obviously with some changes. In what follows, we have generally not given paragraph references to the Notes because the paragraphs are likely to change as the Notes are modified although the information remains very similar. Applicants can also keep up to date by consulting 'Insight', which is the Home Office newsletter for Work Permits (UK) customers. However, there is a full index at the front of each set of Notes to provide easy access to the material contained. All the relevant work permit application forms (both e-mail and postal versions) can be downloaded from www.workingintheuk.gov.uk. The forms and Notes are also available from the Work Permits (UK) distribution centre (tel. 08705 210224). Note that, in late 2005, the main Home Office website also began carrying the 'Business and Commercial Internal Caseworker Guidance' which gives guidance mainly on work permit issues.

Up-to-date processing times are posted on the Work Permits (UK) website.

Obtaining a work permit does not, by itself, grant the worker leave to be in the UK. Work permit holders must still apply to the immigration authorities in order to obtain leave. As with all such decisions, the requirements that work permit holders must meet in order to obtain entry clearance, leave, extensions of leave and indefinite leave to remain in the UK are set out in the immigration rules.

There are three main types of work permit:

- **business and commercial work permits** (▶see below)
- **training and work experience work permits** ('TWES' permits) (▶440–4)
- **sportspeople and entertainer work permits** (▶444–7)

There are two other, lesser categories of work permits. These are work permits granted to student interns (▶see 447) and those granted under the General Agreement on Trade in Services (GATS) (▶447–8).

Much of the general procedure which applies to the processing and operation of work permits is common to all work permits. We describe much of this in the following part, dealing with business and commercial work permits, which are the most common work permits. It is always, of course, worth checking the most up-to-date Guidance Notes published on the website.

Business and commercial work permits

These are the most common type of work permit, and they can be granted for up to five years. However, particularly if the employer is only recently established, the length of the permit is likely to be restricted, often to an initial 18 months. Multiple entry work permits (▶435–6) are issued for a minimum of six months and a maximum of two years. Business and commercial work permits are best understood by looking first at their general conditions. We then look at the specific categories in which applications are actually made, which are divided into two 'tiers'.

General conditions

The general conditions for eligibility are as follows. First of all, the employer must establish that they are based, and have a presence in, the UK. If the employer has not applied for a work permit in the preceding five years, Work Permits (UK) will have to see documents which show that they are UK-based and in a position to offer genuine employment here. These documents should include the latest audited accounts and a copy of the latest annual report, and might include other documents such as lease of premises, VAT returns, invoices, utility bills or registration documents.

Employees It must also be clear that the person coming to the UK is to be the employee of the employer in the UK, and that a contract of employment will exist between the two. Permits will not be issued if the stated 'employer' is really a middle-person who is providing workers to another employer, who will then actually control the work which the employee is going to do. So, although an employer can legitimately use an employment agency in order to recruit staff, permits will not be issued to employment and recruitment agencies in order carry out their functions. This policy of only issuing work permits to those employers who have direct responsibility for a post was reviewed and maintained in 2002. The only exception is that the policy is relaxed for teachers (Work Permits UK letter to ILPA, 30 October 2002). A very high proportion of overseas teachers in the UK are supplied via agencies, and these teachers are particularly important in servicing schools in the London area.

Genuine vacancy There must also be a genuine vacancy for the employment in question. A permit will not be issued if it appears that a vacancy has been contrived in order to employ a particular person. For example, persons who have a substantial interest in the company with which the employment will be held will not be eligible. This rule will not necessarily be broken, however, if the employee has only a minor interest in the business, of less than 10 per cent, which is given to them as part of the package of their employment.

Equal conditions In order to prevent employers from taking advantage of overseas labour and depressing pay and conditions in the UK, the pay and other conditions of employment must be at least equal to those which would be enjoyed by a 'resident worker' doing the same work. By referring to 'resident workers', the work permit scheme means EEA nationals and those settled in the UK.

Specific conditions

The remaining criteria can be divided into the following three requirements, all of which must be satisfied:

1) The proposed employment requires that the employee has a particular level of qualifications, skills and experience in order to do the job (the 'skills threshold').

2) The employee must have the appropriate qualifications, skills and experience in order to perform the job.

3) There must be no suitably qualified or experienced 'resident workers' available to fill the employment.

We look at each of these criteria in turn.

The skills threshold In order to satisfy the skills threshold, the employment must require that the employee has *one* of the following:

- a UK degree-level qualification;
- a Higher National Diploma (HND)-level qualification which is relevant to the employment in question;
- an HND-level qualification which is not relevant to the employment in question plus one year's full time work experience which is relevant to the employment for which the permit is sought, and which is at National/Scottish Vocational Qualification (N/SVQ) level 3 or above;
- at least three years' full-time specialist experience using the skills acquired through doing the type of job for which the permit is sought. The level at which this specialist experience must have been gained is again at N/SVQ level 3 or above. Examples of those likely to fall into this group are head or second chefs, specialist chefs, paramedics, dental technicians, and those with occupational skills or language or cultural skills not readily available in the EEA. Further information about N/SVQ level 3 jobs is available on the Qualifications and Curriculum Authority website (www.qca.org.uk).

If the skill level of the job is questioned, an employer may wish to obtain a specialist report on the NVQ level of the particular job. Such reports have been produced as evidence where decisions of Work Permits (UK) concerning the skills threshold have been disputed.

Qualifications, skills and experience of employee The employee in question must have the relevant qualifications, skills and experience referred to above so that they are able to do the job. Work Permits (UK) will not take into account any experience gained in the UK during a period when the employee was working unlawfully. For some jobs, a person who has obtained qualifications overseas may, under UK law, be required to do some conversion, training or supervised work before they are able to work in their own right. Applications can still be made in the business and commercial capacity for such employees, rather than for a TWES permit. However, if the employer is taking on a trainee above and beyond the ordinary workforce, and the person will return overseas after their traineeship, then they should apply for a TWES permit (▶see below, 440–4).

No suitably qualified resident worker available The purpose of this requirement is to protect the 'resident' workforce, on the basis that it is they who should be first in line for vacancies if any of them is suitably qualified or experienced to fill the post. As indicated above, the 'resident' workforce is made up of EEA nationals and those who are settled in the UK. For obvious reasons, this requirement is much easier to satisfy in 'Tier 1' applications. However, for 'Tier 2' applications, detailed consideration is given to the recruitment search carried out by the employer, and to the reasons given for not hiring a resident worker.

Categories of applications

From 1 October 1991, there has been a two-tier system for business and commercial work permit applications. The application form itself has separate sections relating to the different types of application. Tier 1 applications are clearly defined, and if an application falls within the first tier it is relatively straightforward to show that the above requirements are satisfied. However, if the application falls within Tier 2, the evidence that must be produced to show that the above requirements are met is much more detailed.

Tier 1 applications These are the most straightforward applications, and no recruitment search is required. Tier 1 applications are:

- *Intra-company transfers.* This group forms the bulk of Tier 1 applications. These are transfers within multinational companies. The key to applications under this category is that the employee overseas has obtained knowledge and experience of the company which is essential in order to carry out the duties required by the vacancy in the UK. The employee should have been employed abroad for not less than six months, and the British-based company should have a direct link with the overseas company by common ownership. This means that one company owns the other, or both are part of a group of companies controlled by the same holding company. If the link between the companies is not obvious, then proof may be required, for example by producing the international corporate brochure for the parent company.

- *Senior board-level posts* (or posts at an equivalent level). In order to qualify, the employee must have substantial board-level experience. Normally, applicants need three years' experience at the level of the post on offer.

- *Inward investment posts*. These are new posts essential to an inward investment project by the company that will bring substantial jobs and money to the UK. The minimum level of investment is generally £250,000. When the company is making its first application under this category, Work Permits (UK) will expect to see a business plan giving full details of the investment.

- *Shortage occupations*. These are jobs for which Work Permits (UK) readily acknowledges that suitably qualified or skilled people are in very short supply among the resident workforce. The occupations that are included in this category change frequently, and are set out in a list which is kept up to date on the Work Permits (UK) website. Presently, these occupations are generally in the healthcare and engineering sectors. As of the end of 2005, other occupations listed were: actuaries, Civil Aviation Authority Licensed Aircraft Engineers, teachers (all posts in England) and veterinary surgeons. We set out the complete list as at November 2005, including the full breakdown of occupations in the healthcare and engineering sectors at ▶1519–21. Note that, for some of the occupations, the employee is expected to have higher-level qualifications and experience than those referred to in the skills threshold (▶see above, 423).

- **Sponsored researchers**. This category is generally for people who are coming to the UK in order to undertake a period of research at an employer/host organisation. They will have a job overseas for which they are still being paid, or from which they are taking a paid or unpaid sabbatical. There is some flexibility in the operation of this category. Those considering applying might also consider applying through the academic visitor (▶see 221–2) or business visitor (▶see 220–1) routes. Among other matters, the application form (SR1) asks for details of the host employer/organisation, the qualifications and professional memberships of the person concerned, and the qualifications and skills required to do the research.

In order to succeed in a Tier 1 application, the employer needs to explain how the job falls into one of the above Tier 1 categories. The job does not have to be advertised, but the employer should explain the commercial reasons why they need to employ the person.

Tier 2 applications If the job does not fall within any of the above descriptions for Tier 1, then the Tier 2 part of the application form should be completed. Unless the employee is presently in work permit employment for a similar type of work (in which case job descriptions of the last post and the new post should be produced), the employer has to fully justify filling the post with a non-resident worker. This means providing full details of the recruitment methods. First, the employer is well advised to draw up a clear list of essential criteria and optional criteria for filling the post. If an overseas employee is recruited, then, in order to obtain a work permit, the employer should be able to demonstrate that the overseas worker achieves the highest score.

The prospective employer is expected to trawl the domestic labour market by advertising in the most appropriate media. This will usually be a national newspaper and/or a professional journal relevant to the position. Internet advertising is becoming more widely accepted, but the employer should check with the provider of the advertising space whether it is considered an appropriate place in which a person seeking employment in the field but resident in another EEA country would look. Work Permits (UK) will also expect an explanation as to why internet advertising is thought to be the best means of recruitment, and the internet advert should have been maintained for a minimum period of a week. Advertising in a Jobcentre may also be acceptable in certain occupations. A copy of the 'Jobcentre Plus' letter confirming details of the advertisement will be required. Where and how prominently the advert is displayed should reflect the level and nature of the position.

The employer will need to produce the original of a newspaper advertisement bearing the date, or correspondence showing when the advertisement was placed. The advert itself should give the details of the post (including job description), the location of the job, the qualifications and experience needed, and the closing date for applications. Work Permits (UK) state that the salary, or the salary scale, must be indicated. However, many employers do not wish to do so, and it may be sufficient for the employer to indicate that all applicants will be treated equally as to the salary offered. The advertisement should not have been placed more than six months before the work permit application is submitted. This is to ensure that there is a lack of the skills required at the time that a work permit is issued. The advert should also give sufficient time for applicants to respond; a closing date of at least four weeks from the date of the advert is recommended.

For certain senior-level or specialist posts, Work Permits (UK) may accept the use of head-hunters as the best means of recruitment. However, they will not normally accept recruitment carried out by an executive search agency that merely selects from a pre-existing list of people registered with that agency. It is possible for an employer to ask Work Permits (UK) to waive the requirement to carry out a recruitment search using any of the above methods, but the employer will have to put a strong case forward, supported by some external evidence that the employer has correctly judged that there are no suitable resident workers available.

Finally, in order to demonstrate the outcome of their recruitment searches, the employer will need to provide information on the application form which shows the total number of people who applied, the number short-listed for interview, and the reasons why each resident worker who applied was not employed. This should include an explanation of why, even with suitable extra training, the resident workers were not suitable. Employers should normally produce the CVs and written applications of all those short-listed, and the notes taken on those who have been interviewed.

Applying for the work permit

All the relevant application forms can be downloaded from the Work Permits (UK) website. Form WP1 is the basic application form used for business and commercial work permits. It should be used to apply for the initial permit, a multiple-entry work permit (▶see below, 435–6), or for a permit by which the employee is changing their employment. A different style of WP1 is used depending on whether it is intended to send the application by post or email. Applications to extend an existing permit should be made on form WP1X. (For further details about extensions, ▶see 430, and for changes of employment, ▶see 430.) However, applications for sponsored researchers should be made using form SR1, whether the application is for an initial permit, an extension, or for a change of employment. If the worker is outside the UK, the application should not be made more than six months before it is intended that they will come to the UK to start their employment. (For in-country applications, ▶see 432–3.)

Work Permits (UK) like to receive the application packaged in the following order: application form (with cheque attached, if applicable), covering letter and any representations, passports, supporting documentation. The payment slip on the application forms should be completed. Payment can be by cheque, postal order, or by credit or debit card (credit or debit card only in the case of an e-mailed application). A maximum of ten applications can be submitted for each payment slip, with one total payment (of £153 x the number of persons) being made. Applications should be sent to Work Permits (UK) at their Doncaster address (▶see 1494), indicating on the envelope which scheme the application is being made under – whether the 'business and commercial' category, the 'sports and entertainment' category, and so on. Applications can also be made by courier, although applicants are recommended to contact the team that will deal with the application about this. The number of the relevant team can be identified by looking at the Guidance Notes on the website, where the teams are listed according to the alphabetical name of the employer. Faxed applications to Doncaster can also be made, but only in very urgent cases (fax 01302 386013). A faxed application should be followed up with a hard copy of the original declaration pages of the application only (the full form should not be sent), together with a covering letter of explanation. This is so that Work Permits (UK) have a copy of the original signature of the employer. Payments with faxed applications must be by credit or debit card.

Check for mistakes After a work permit has been issued, it should be checked to ensure there are no mistakes on it. Mistakes for which Work Permits (UK) are responsible, or which are only minor, can be corrected by returning the permit and explaining the difficulty. This commonly happens with names spelt incorrectly, or if the worker's passport or personal details have been incorrectly recorded. Errors in the period of time granted by the work permit should also be notified and dealt with before entry clearance or leave is granted. This is because the period of leave granted will generally follow the period of approval given in the work permit. If there is a major error on the application form – for example a mistake in the job title or salary – then it is likely that the process will have to start again with a fresh application.

Work Permits (UK) checking procedures

Before issuing a work permit, Work Permits (UK) may ask for various additional information in order to verify that what they have been told is correct. This applies particularly if it is the employer's first work permit application. It is possible that Work Permits (UK) will visit the company before making a decision. If the worker is abroad, the entry clearance post where they are likely to apply may be asked to verify details relating to references or experience. Work Permits (UK)'s 'Compliance and Validation Team' may also carry out checks at any time after the work permit has been issued, which may also include visits to the work-place. If a compliance check is carried out prior to the work permit being issued, there will be some inevitable delay in processing the application. However, even in such cases, Work Permits (UK) state that a decision should still be made within four weeks of the application.

If difficulties arise following a check then Work Permits (UK) may work with the employer, representative and worker in order to bring the work into line with the requirements, if that is possible. But where there is deception, or where the matters alleged simply cannot be verified, the application will be refused. If the work permit has already been granted, Work Permits (UK) state that they may revoke the permit, which may result in the worker's leave being curtailed.

Coming to the UK after a permit has been granted

After it has been issued, the work permit is sent to the employer or to their legal representative. The permit must be presented to an immigration officer on the employee's entry to the UK, not later than six months from its date of issue. If the employee does not enter the UK within six months of the date of issue (stated on the permit), the permit will no longer be valid. The permit is valid to enable the employee to work in the employment which is stated in the permit from the date the employee enters the UK. The permit authorises work for a particular period, for example 'eighteen months' or 'five years'.

Entry clearance However, like all IEDs, work permits do not themselves amount to leave to be in the UK. Leave must be obtained separately, and most employees are now required to obtain an entry clearance before they arrive in the UK. Obviously all visa and specified nationals need an entry clearance. From 13 November 2003, this applied in all cases where the work permit is valid for longer than six months, although it did not apply to nationals of the ten EU accession countries which were due to become members of the EU on 1 May 2004 (see para. 128(vii) HC 395 as amended by HC 1224). The following British nationals were exempted from this rule, and therefore still do not need an entry clearance to enter for work permit employment: British National (Overseas), British Overseas Territories Citizen, British Overseas Citizen, British Protected Person or a person who, under the British Nationality Act 1981, is a British Subject (▶see 1404, 1406–14 for a description of these British nationals). In practice, the new rule was not operated until after a grace period of two months – namely, until midnight on 13 January 2004. This concession was granted in order to allow employers and applicants to become aware of the new arrangements. Those who arrived between 13 November 2003 and 13 January 2004, and who would require an entry clearance under the new rules, were granted leave to enter for six months, provided they satisfied all the other requirements. During that time they could apply for an extension of leave up to the length of their work permit without having to obtain another work permit (Work Permits (UK) circular, November 2003). From 13 November 2005, all foreign nationals coming to the UK for more than six months need entry clearance (for details ▶see 80–1).

Even in cases where an entry clearance is not formally required, Work Permits (UK) still recommends that employees obtain them before travelling. The original work permit should be sent to the worker in order to be produced to the entry clearance officer (ECO), as copies will normally not be accepted. For the general procedures relating to entry clearance, ▶see 85–94.

Meeting the immigration rules In order for an applicant to obtain entry clearance, and to be admitted to the UK on arrival, the immigration authorities must be satisfied that the immigration rules are met. They are that the employee (paras 128–130 HC 395):

- is not of an age which puts them outside the limits for employment. Children under the age of 13 are prohibited from taking employment by the Children and Young Persons Act. Those over the age of 13 are normally issued with permits in relation to entertainment performances, but only after a licence has been obtained from the child's education authority;
- is capable of taking the employment which is named in the work permit, and does not intend to take work in the UK other than the work named in the permit;
- is able to maintain and accommodate themselves and any dependants adequately, without recourse to public funds;
- in the case of a person in possession of a work permit which is valid for a period of 12 months or less, intends to leave the UK at the end of the period of employment.

It will be noted that, although there is some overlap, the requirements that need to be satisfied in order to obtain entry clearance and leave as a work permit holder are different to those for obtaining the permit in the first place. If the work permit holder satisfies all of the above conditions, then they should be admitted to the UK unless any of the general grounds for refusing admission apply (▶see 97–9). One general ground which specifically applies to holders of IEDs is where – whether or not with the holder's knowledge – false representations were made or material facts not disclosed in order to obtain it (para. 320(15) HC 395). If this is the case, entry clearance or leave to enter will 'normally' be refused.

Entry to the UK When they arrive in the UK and show their work permit and entry clearance, work permit holders will be admitted for a period in accordance with their entry clearance. This will usually be for the period approved for employment stated on the work permit, which can be up to five years. The entry clearance itself operates as leave to enter from the date of entry. Those who can arrive without an entry clearance (the British nationals referred to above, and those with work permits valid for less than six months) need to ask the immigration officer for leave to enter on their arrival. The immigration officer considers the same requirements as the entry clearance officer, described above. Provided everything is satisfactory, they will normally be granted leave for the period shown on the work permit. If a person arrives without a work permit, but it can be confirmed that a work permit has been issued, then the immigration officer may still grant leave to enter (IDI, Ch 5, s1, annex A, para. 7.1). Whether the leave is granted by the entry clearance or by the immigration officer at the port, it will be subject to a condition restricting work to that specified in the work permit.

Applying to extend the work permit

Extensions of business and commercial work permits are applied for using form WP1X, enclosing the documents requested and stating why and for how much longer the worker is required. If applying by e-mail, the employer uses the e-mail version of form WP1, stating at the appropriate part of the form that the application is for an extension. Work Permits (UK) generally do not require another recruitment search for a continuation of the same employment. Provided that the extension applications are made before both the existing permit and the worker's leave expires (but not otherwise), the worker can continue to work while the application is being considered. If the application is successful, the document that is actually issued, where the application is in-country, is a letter of approval for work permit employment, rather than a 'work permit' in the form referred to above. (For the timing of the application, ▶see 432–3.)

Changing employment

Unless the change in employment is strictly technical, approval must be obtained if a person in work permit employment wishes either to change the job they are doing for their existing employer, or to change employers. An example of a technical change is if the worker is to be employed at a different address. A change such as this should nevertheless be notified to Work Permits (UK), to prevent problems arising if a check of the workplace is carried out. If there is a change in the ownership of the business which employs the worker, this should also be notified, and Work Permits (UK) will decide whether a new work permit application is required.

Other changes require approval, which should be applied for using form WP1. The worker cannot begin the new employment until approval has been granted. If the worker is changing employers but is going to do the same type of work, then a recruitment search will not be necessary. However, if it is a completely new job, then the usual approval process will have to be gone through. Procedures relating to change of employment and other matters have been under review (▶see 433–4).

Applying to extend leave on FLR(IED)

Here we are still mainly discussing those in the business and commercial work permit category. *However, form FLR(IED), which is used for extending leave, is common to IED employment, and therefore much of the following information is relevant to IED categories generally.* For further details about applying to extend leave, ▶see also 132–41. The specific requirements of the immigration rules that need to be satisfied in each IDI category are examined as we deal with the category concerned. Under the rules for work permit holders, an employee needs to show that (para. 131, 132–133 HC 395):

- they entered the UK with a valid work permit (but for switching applications, ▶see 434);
- they have written approval (see above) to remain in the UK in order to continue to work;
- as with the 'on entry' rules discussed above, they are within the relevant age limits, capable of doing the work stated in the permit, and able to maintain and accommodate themselves and any dependants without recourse to public funds.

In all cases, after the employer has obtained an IED (or an extension of the IED), the employee must then apply to extend their leave on form FLR(IED). This form was introduced on 1 April 2004. A fee of £335 is charged for applications. Unlike the fee for the IED, this fee is demanded from the employee, although an employer may of course pay it. Nationals of the countries listed at ▶419 are exempt from this charge.

The form The form is similar to the forms relating to other in-country applications to extend leave (▶see 127–32). As well as personal details and details of employer, questions are asked concerning family, home and finances. The form also provides a list of the documentary evidence that is required, which varies slightly depending upon the category of applicant. Broadly, the list includes photographs; police registration certificate (if asked to register with the police); passport (but see ▶439–40 for details of a possible review); and evidence that the applicant and any dependants can be maintained and accommodated in the UK together without recourse to public funds. Evidence relating to support is to be in the form of formal documents such as bank statements, building society passbook or wage-slips, and it should cover at least the preceding three months. Dependants may be included in applications made on the form at no additional fee, but if they apply at a different time and on a separate form, then they will have to pay the fee appropriate to the application they are making. Sons and daughters aged 18 or over will also have to apply separately on form FLR(O). The FLR(IED) form and accompanying documents must be sent to the Work Permits (UK) address in Cannock (*not* Sheffield or Doncaster – for address ▶see 1494). Applicants are recommended to use recorded or special delivery. Emailed or faxed applications are not accepted.

Payment The form includes a payment slip enabling payment by postal order, cheque (personal or business), debit card (Delta or Switch) and credit card (Visa or MasterCard). Unless the application falls into the exempt category, payment should accompany the application. If an application is made on form FLR(IED) but without payment or sufficient payment, then Work Permits (UK) will send out a notification and require that payment is made within 28 days, or else it will treat the application as having been withdrawn. If payment is included but relevant documents required by the form are not provided, a letter will be sent out stating that, unless the documents are received within 28 days, the application will be treated as invalid (and the fee will be refunded).

Urgent need to travel However, if the applicant withdraws the application before a decision is issued, the fee will not be refunded. If an applicant asks for their passport back in order to travel while the application is still outstanding, then the application will be treated as withdrawn. Applicants are therefore advised not to make any non-urgent travel plans until passports have been returned. If the circumstances are exceptional – if, for example, a relative is ill and there is an urgent need to travel – it is possible to ask for the application to be dealt with urgently by completing an 'Urgent Treatment Form', which can be sent by fax. Other examples of a need for urgent treatment indicated on the form are family bereavement, urgent business and pre-booked holidays. If the applicant is in need of urgent medical treatment, this may also qualify (▶see also 119–20). The form can be downloaded from the Work Permits (UK) website. Note that the work permit application will not be treated as withdrawn just because the FLR(IED) application is withdrawn. Work Permits (UK) will continue to consider the work permit application – although, if a work permit is granted, the question of granting entry clearance and leave to enter will then be decided by the entry clearance officer and immigration officer when the worker wishes to be re-admitted.

Multiple applications It is possible for an employer or representative to submit up to ten IED applications together, covered by one payment slip.

Timing of applications Both the application to extend the IED and to extend leave *must* be made before the existing leave runs out. Beyond this, the following guidance can be given:

- If the applicant is extending an existing IED, then the extension application should be made between one month and three months before leave runs out. Work Permits (UK) will not generally consider the application if it is made more than three months before leave runs out. The worker should then apply to extend their leave on FLR(IED) not more than four weeks before the existing leave runs out.

- If the applicant is seeking an initial IED, and if they need to start work as soon as possible and their existing conditions do not allow them to work, then Work Permits (UK) may be prepared to deal with the application at an earlier stage. Once the IED is issued, the FLR(IED) application to extend leave should also be made as soon as possible.

In both cases, the application made on FLR(IED) must always be made within six months of the IED approval. If the application is not made within this period, then the IED will become invalid and the application will be refused.

As indicated above, applications to extend leave are to be made after the relevant IED has been issued or extended. However, if the circumstances of the case are that the applicant's leave to be in the UK is likely to expire before an IED can be obtained from Work Permits (UK), an application should be made anyway, even without the IED. This is sometimes the case if there is a delay at Work Permits (UK). In such cases, Work Permits (UK) have recently stated that those who issue work permit approval will let the section dealing with FLR(IED) extensions know their decision on the IED. We would recommend: first, if possible, time the application so that it is not necessary to rely upon this; second, if the FLR(IED) is sent without an IED, still send the document on to be linked up with the FLR(IED).

Period of leave granted If the application is successful, then leave will be granted for a period up to that authorised by the work permit. The leave will be subject to a condition restricting work to that specified in the permit.

Review of procedures In 2005, the Home Office were continuing to review procedures, including those relating to IED leave to remain applications. In particular, they were reviewing:

- whether a further leave application is necessary where there has been a *change* of employment which has been approved, and where the existing leave covers the period of the new employment (▶see 430 for work permit change of employment applications);
- what changes can be made so that people can travel while waiting for their applications to be decided.

A number of solutions to the travel problem have been suggested to Work Permits (UK). For example, applicants could submit certified copies of their passports until the application is ready for a decision, or passports could be immediately returned after being examined. Another idea being considered is that applicants could be granted an immediate three-month 'travel extension' pending the decision on the application (at present an urgent treatment request can be made ▶see 432).

Pending a review, at the Work Permits (UK) conference on 5 November 2004, the Home Office stated that it would operate an interim arrangement which allows work permit holders to start work on the basis of work permit approval for a change in their employment while they are awaiting the decision on the FLR(IED) application. This is provided that their existing period of leave covers the period of the new employment. The Home Office accepts that a non-work permit holder whose conditions of leave allow them to do any work may commence new work while awaiting the outcome of their FLR(IED) application (Home Office letter to Cameron McKenna, 23 July 2004).

Applications may be submitted by post or courier to Work Permits (UK) or in person at the *Croydon* PEO. The exception to this is applications under the HSMP which can only be sent by post or courier to Work Permits (UK) (see reg. 14(2)(b) Immigration (Leave to Remain) (Prescribed Forms and Procedures) (No. 2) Regulations 2005).

Switching

If the worker did not enter the UK with a work permit, but if approval has been granted in-country, applicants will be applying to 'switch'. This will only be permitted in certain circumstances. Broadly, the immigration rules allow those previously granted leave in the following categories to switch into work permit employment, provided that they meet the other work permit rules (paras 131A–133 HC 395); presently completed students who have a degree qualification in the UK; student nurses; postgraduate doctors; postgraduate dentists, those given leave in order to take the PLAB test or a clinical attachment or dental observer post; those granted leave under SEGS, the HSMP, the Fresh Talent: Working in Scotland Scheme, or as innovators. Postgraduate doctors and dentists may only switch for the purpose of approved work in their area of practice. The rules also allow certain working holidaymakers to switch after they have spent 12 months in the UK as working holidaymakers. For full details about this switching, and about switching outside the rules, ▶see 161–88.

If the worker did not actually enter the UK with a work permit but has already switched to work permit employment, and is now seeking a limited extension to remain in the UK to continue the work they have switched into, then strictly their applications may be outside the immigration rules. This is because they are no longer in the category from which switching is allowed ('student', or whatever) and they did not enter the UK with a work permit. Commonsense requires – and experience shows – that such applications should be granted, provided all other requirements are met.

End of approved employment

If the worker stops working before the expiry of the work permit, whether voluntarily or through redundancy, the employer is asked to notify Work Permits (UK) of this using form NPEE (Notice of Premature End of Employment). Because the worker is no longer meeting the requirements of the rules for which they were admitted, the Home Office may then curtail (bring to an end) the worker's leave and that of their dependants (see para. 323(ii) HC 395). In practice, practitioners have noticed that notice of curtailment tends to arrive a few months after the NPEE is sent in. This leaves applicants liable to be removed from the UK. Unless and until the Home Office take this action, the person's leave remains valid and they remain entitled to stay in the UK until the end of the leave granted, although they cannot take other work unless approval is given. Of course, if the worker can find alternative work permit employment, a change of employment application may be made (▶see above, 430). A worker in this position who wishes to stay in the UK in work permit employment should not delay in looking for alternative employment and getting the new employer to submit the further application.

Supplementary work

Although the leave granted to work permit holders is subject to a condition restricting the work to that specified in the permit for a particular employer, Work Permits (UK) do not object to workers taking on some additional work without obtaining specific permission. The work must be performed outside normal working hours, must amount to no more than 20 hours per week, and must be of a similar nature to that specified in the work permit – i.e. in the same profession and at the same level. Work permit holders are not, however, permitted to enter into business or self-employment. The option of supplementary work is not open to multiple-entry work permit holders. As of summer 2005, the ability of work permit holders to do supplementary work was, however, under review.

Other rights of work permit holders

Work permit holders pay national insurance contributions and income tax. They are generally prevented from access to non-contributory benefits, as they are normally admitted with a condition that they will not have recourse to public funds and are therefore 'subject to immigration control' (►see, however, the exceptions at 1255–9 and ►see 309–11). They are not, however, prevented from obtaining access to contribution-based benefits, for which they may qualify as a result of their contributions – for example, contribution-based Job-Seekers' Allowance and Incapacity Benefit (►see further 1276). Neither of these benefits counts as 'public funds' under the definition given in the immigration rules (►308–9), and so the worker would not be in breach of their conditions of leave either. However, if a person was incapacitated or made redundant so as to obtain these benefits, they would no longer be in the UK for the purpose for which leave was granted. They could then face having their leave curtailed and, depending on the circumstances, would be unlikely to obtain an extension of their leave on the basis of work.

Work permit holders also have the same rights under employment law as any other workers. The work permit does not alter any contract of employment or remove any trade union, employment or negotiating rights. However, workers who wish to continue to live in the UK are often deterred from getting into disputes with their employer because their immigration status often depends on the willingness of the employer to apply for an extension to the existing work permit.

Multiple Entry work permits

The Multiple Entry work permit is a new category under the immigration rules, introduced from 18 September 2002 (see paras 199A–199C HC

395, inserted by Cm 5597). The purpose is to allow employees who are themselves based *overseas* to enter the UK regularly in order to work for the employer in the UK, without having to obtain a new work permit on each occasion. Accordingly, on each occasion they are admitted, applicants must intend to leave the UK when they have completed their work. Of course, the ordinary work permit holder is based in the UK and will be able to travel in and out of the UK within the period of leave granted to them. Obtaining a multiple-entry permit is an alternative for employees who, because of the nature of the activity they will be carrying out in the UK, cannot make use of the business visitor rules (▶see 220–3). Multiple-entry permits are issued for between six months and two years, but they cannot be extended and nor can a change of employment be applied for. Leave is granted for a maximum of two years at a time, without any expectation of settlement. If a further period or a change of employment is required, a fresh permit must be obtained. The rules relating to entry clearance are the same as for other work permits (para. 199A(vii) HC395 as inserted from 13 January 2004 by HC176 and amended from 1 May 2004 by HC523 and ▶see 429).

Families of work permit holders

The spouse, unmarried partner and children of a work permit holder may qualify under the immigration rules to accompany or join the work permit holder in the UK (see paras 194–199, 295J–295L HC 395). Family members applying to come to the UK must obtain entry clearance from a British post overseas before travelling and, if they are applying to extend their stay, the rules require that they have been granted entry clearance to come as dependants. However, if the main applicant is permitted to switch, their dependants who are included in the same application will also be allowed to switch. Spouses and partners will have to prove their relationship to the work permit holder, that they intend to live together as partners in the UK with the work permit holder, and that they do not intend to remain longer than him or her. There must be adequate maintenance and accommodation for the family members, in accommodation that the family own or occupy exclusively without recourse to public funds (▶see 308–18).

Children Unmarried children under the age of 18 may also be admitted with the work permit holder, provided both parents live, or come to live, in the UK. If only one parent is in the UK, children have to meet either the 'sole responsibility' or 'exclusion undesirable' criteria. Once a child has been given leave to enter or remain in the UK as the dependant child in this category, they are able to apply for extensions and settlement in line with their parent even if they have subsequently reached the age of 18. This is because the immigration rules require the child either to be 'under the age of 18' *or* to have 'current leave to enter or remain in this capacity' (para. 197(ii), 198 HC 395). ECOs may exercise discretion outside the rules to grant entry clearance to children over the age of 18 to come to the UK as dependants of a parent who is a work permit holder as an intra-company transferee (▶see 424 for this category). This discretion may be exercised provided that the son or daughter is genuinely dependant on the work permit holder, is and intends to remain part of the family unit, and will not seek to remain in the UK beyond the period of leave granted to their parent. This concession is generally only applied to entry clearance applications (IDI, Ch 5, s9, para. 1.1).

Multiple-entry dependants The dependants of multiple-entry work permit holders cannot be admitted or granted leave to remain as dependants. They must qualify for entry in their own right under the immigration rules if they wish to accompany their principal.

Rights of family members Persons admitted as family members of work permit holders are generally granted leave for the same period of time as their principal. They are also free, under their conditions of leave, to take any lawful employment and to enter into business without themselves requiring work permits. No other relatives have any claim under the rules to join a work permit holder before he or she is granted settlement. For detailed rules about family members – in particular the additional requirements that apply for unmarried partners, ▶see Section 4. Family members of those in the work and business categories are dealt with at 352–4, 355–6, and further details about their maintenance and accommodation requirements are to be found at ▶307–318.

Settlement

After four continuous years of leave, while living in the UK in the capacity of a work permit holder, and during which time all requirements of the rules have been met, the work permit holder will be eligible to apply for indefinite leave to remain in the UK. The Home Office have been firm that they will not generally act outside the immigration rules to allow applicants seeking to settle as work permit holders to combine periods spent under other categories to make up the four-year period (Business User Panel, 18 March 2003). A concession is, however, made outside the rules for those seeking to combine time spent as a work permit holder and as a sole representative (▶see 456). Amalgamation of time is possible, however, under the rules in HSMP settlement applications (▶see 490–1).

In order to apply, the worker should make an application near the end of their four continuous years in the UK. The application is made to the Home Office using form SET(O), enclosing his or her passport, confirmation from the employer that the job is still continuing, and all other documents requested on the form. If there have been periods of unemployment, or periods when the person was working without a permit, these may not count towards the four years. Dependants may, on the same form, apply for settlement in line with the principal. Again, sons and daughters who have turned 18 since being granted leave as dependants in the same category, may also be settled with the work permit holder. They must be still unmarried, and not leading an independent life.

Continuous period of four years

The requirement that applicants for settlement have spent 'a continuous period of four years in the UK' in the relevant capacity (see para. 134(i) HC 395) is common to many of the work and business categories. The way in which the Home Office interprets continuity for these purposes was at one stage published at IDI Ch 5, s1, annex D. That annex was then deleted, and the subsequent annex which apparently contained the relevant guidance (IDI, Ch 5, s1, annex F) was 'not disclosed'.

In the case of *Gurung*, decided in June 2002, the IAT held that the words 'continuous period' should not be read literally. The 'rule of thumb' applied by the Home Office had not been specifically adopted in relation to private servants of diplomats, which *Gurung* concerned. Nevertheless, the Home Office representative accepted that the general rule, that absences not exceeding three months in any one year did not break continuity, should be applied to the settlement rules for private servants as well.

However, in March 2005, it came to light that the Home Office was operating on the basis of an undisclosed IDI (i.e. an IDI which was not posted on the website). This IDI stated that short absences abroad, for example for holidays (consistent with annual paid leave) or business trips (consistent with maintaining employment or self-employment in the UK), might be disregarded, provided that the applicant has clearly continued to be based in the UK. It went on to:

'In addition, time spent here in this capacity may *exceptionally* be aggregated, and continuity not insisted upon, in cases where:

- there have been no absences abroad (apart from those described [above]) and *authorised employment or business* here has not been broken by any interruptions of more than 3 months or amounting to more than 6 months in all; or

- there have been *longer absences abroad*, provided the absences were for compelling grounds either of a compassionate nature or for reasons related to the applicant's employment or business in the United Kingdom. None of the absences abroad should be of more than 3 months, and they must not amount to more than 6 months in all.'

Judicial review challenge This radical new policy would mean that applicants would not be able to be out of the UK for more than six weeks a year over the four year period. It would pin applicants to the UK for all but 12.5% of their time – much more than is required for naturalisation purposes! This would greatly undermine the competitiveness of the UK as a destination for economic migrants and fly in the face of the government's expressed intention to attract skilled and talented employees and business to the UK, which has formed part and parcel of its 'managed migration' strategy. The policy was challenged in a judicial review during the summer of 2005. In the face of challenge, the Home Office accepted that 'our current policy for investors on the calculation of the four year period for settlement purposes is that periods of absence of up to 25 per cent in total will be tolerated (provided that none of the individual trips is more than three months). As far as all the other categories of the immigration rules were concerned, the Home Office stated that it would review how the four-year residence rule operated and would publish revised guidelines (see statement reported in the *Financial Times*, 1 August 2005, page 1 and circulated letter to ILPA dated 1 September 2005).The revised guidelines have, as at the time of writing, not been published.

If, for any reason, the four-year period is found not to have been reached, an extension for a year will normally be granted by the Home Office, with a note advising the applicant to resubmit the settlement application the following year.

Appeals and reviews

As with other categories of leave, if a negative 'immigration decision' (▶1053–4) is made in relation to those who seek to enter or remain for work permit employment – for example, to refuse entry clearance or to refuse to extend leave – then there will be rights of appeal to the new Asylum and Immigration Appeal Tribunal (previously the adjudicator and the IAT). The rights of appeal are severely restricted, however, if a person is refused on the grounds that they do not have an IED. If this is the basis of the refusal, then appeals will generally be restricted to asylum, human rights and discrimination grounds, and grounds of entitlement to work under the immigration rules will be excluded (s88 2002 Act). For full details ▶see 1052–60.

IED 'appeals'

However, if an IED is refused, Work Permits (UK) operate their own internal 'review' system, for which there is no formal legal basis. Following a refusal, Work Permits (UK) should write to the employer or representative setting out the reasons why the application has been refused. In order to ask that the matter be reviewed, it is necessary to write back within 28 days of the decision, explaining why it is considered that the decision is wrong. Clearly, the review is internal, but Work Permits (UK) state that it is given 'independent consideration'. Most appeals concern disputes about whether the worker – frequently in the hotel and catering industry – has the appropriate skills to do the work.

If the team dealing with the review thinks that the original case-worker should perhaps not have accepted that *other* aspects of the criteria were met, they will not usually maintain the refusal on new grounds without giving the applicant the opportunity to provide further information. However, the review team may refuse on new grounds if either (1) it was obvious that the further information should have been provided in the first place; or (2) further information would make no difference to the decision (email correspondence between the Managed Migration Directorate of Work Permits (UK) and Laura Devine Solicitors, 10 December 2004 and 26 January 2005). Work Permits (UK) confirmed in Issue 5 of its newsletter for applicants, 'Insight' (April 2005), that if a review results in new grounds for refusal, the decision to refuse will stand even if the original ground of refusal has been overturned. It was also confirmed that only two reviews per application can be applied for after that, the applicant must submit a new application with a further fee.

TWES (Training and Work Experience) work permits

Work permits may also be issued to employers in respect of those wishing to come to the UK for training or work experience (paras 116–121 HC 395). The purpose of the scheme is to enable applicants to gain skills and experience through work-based learning which builds on their previous education and training, and which they intend to use on their return to their home countries. The age restriction that was previously contained in the rules relating to TWES was removed on 1 April 2003 (HC 538). A TWES permit is not appropriate for those who wish to enter or stay in the UK in order to obtain a qualification that can be obtained on a full-time study basis. In those cases, the person should seek admission as a student (▶see Chapter 10).

Under the TWES, persons may come to the UK for either:

* **approved training** (▶441), which is work-based training for a professional or specialist qualification; or
* **approved work experience** (▶441–2).

Basic requirements

The basic requirements for a TWES permit to be issued are that the person must be taken on as an addition to the employer's normal staffing requirements, so they must not be filling a vacancy that would otherwise be taken by a resident worker. An employer–employee relationship must exist between the worker and the UK-based employer, and the pay and conditions must be similar to those normally provided to a resident worker. The person must be working/training for a minimum of 30 hours per week (excluding any time for associated studies), and the person should have sufficient English to enable them to complete the training or work experience.

Further requirements

In addition to the basic requirements, the following two requirements must also be met:

* the entry level to qualify for the training or experience in question must be at N/SVQ level 3 or equivalent (the 'skills threshold');
* the person must have the suitable qualifications, skills and/or experience for the training or work experience in question.

In applying the above two requirements, there are separate considerations for approved training, on the one hand, and approved work experience, on the other (see below). Because the purpose of the scheme is to provide additional training to individuals, and not simply to fill vacancies, there is no requirement to satisfy the resident labour test, as there is under the business and commercial scheme. So the employer does not have to demonstrate that there are no suitable resident workers available by carrying out a recruitment search. After the skills threshold in the main work permit scheme was lowered in October 2000, many applications which might previously have been made under TWES came to be considered under the business and commercial work permit arrangements. This applies to graduate trainees and qualified professionals who require conversion/adaptation training.

It is not generally intended that those admitted under TWES will settle in the UK. On their admission to the UK, and each time they seek an extension, applicants need to demonstrate that they intend to leave the UK on the completion of their training or work experience. The length of time they will be given depends on the circumstances (▶see below). They will not normally be allowed to transfer to business and commercial work permit employment (for switching, ▶see 171). Additionally, there are restrictions on persons who have been employed under a TWES permit returning to the UK for work permit employment, until they have completed a period of time working overseas. If the person held a TWES permit for up to 12 months, they would be required to spend at least 12 months outside the UK. However, if the permit was for over 12 months, they would not normally be considered until they have spent 24 months outside the UK. Unlike in the business and commercial category, TWES work permit holders are not permitted to take any supplementary employment.

Approved training

The training should lead to a recognised professional or specialist qualification that requires an applicant to have already achieved at least N/SVQ Level 3, or its equivalent, before starting the training. Normally, the person should have an academic or vocational qualification at this level or above. The prospective employer should obviously be competent to provide the training – which will normally mean registration or approval by the relevant professional body. The training should be completed in the shortest possible time, and the person will be expected to have taken any exams at the earliest possible sitting, and they are normally allowed two attempts for each exam (three in exceptional circumstances). The permit will be issued to enable the person to achieve a single qualification only.

Work experience

Work experience should be at N/SVQ level 3 or equivalent. A person should normally have a qualification at N/SVQ level 3 or equivalent, or have 12 months' relevant experience at that level. Alternatively, applicants may be students studying at a college overseas for a qualification which is relevant to the proposed work experience, and who have reached a level of study at N/SVQ level 3 or above. A work experience programme provided by a prospective employer should describe the type and level of experience to be gained and how it will be supervised. It is necessary to set out a detailed timetable for each stage of the programme, including a description of the tasks to be undertaken.

Coming to and staying in the UK for TWES employment

As with the business work permit scheme, a TWES work permit application must be made by an employer based in the UK, and initial applications are made on Form WP1. The same rules also apply to determine who needs entry clearance (▶see 428–9). After the TWES permit has been issued, in order to obtain entry to the UK under the immigration rules the person must (paras 116–118 HC395):

- hold a valid TWES work permit;
- be capable of undertaking the training or work experience specified in the permit;
- intend to leave the UK on completion of the training or work experience;
- not intend to take employment except as specified in the permit;
- be able to maintain and accommodate themselves without recourse to public funds.

TWES permit holders are admitted subject to conditions restricting them from working, other than as stated in the permit. In some cases, an alternative to a TWES permit, will be to come as a business visitor. This applies to employees of overseas companies who wish to come to the UK for less than six months for a period of training in techniques or work practices used in the UK. Such applicants must only receive classroom instruction, and they must not do any 'hands-on' work (IDI, Ch 4, s5, annex J, para. 4; ▶see 220–1 for business visitors).

Period for which permits and leave is granted From 18 September 2002, the formal restrictions on the periods for which leave is granted under the immigration rules to TWES holders have been removed (para. 117 HC 395 as substituted by Cm 5597). However, in normal circumstances, Work Permits (UK) will grant a permit and corresponding leave according to the following guidelines:

- **Approved training** Work Permits (UK) will normally issue a permit for the average time expected to complete the training, up to a maximum period of five years. Those in approved training will normally be given leave for the period of the permit. If a permit is required for longer than this period, extensions may be obtained.
- **Work experience** Work Permits (UK) expects work experience programmes to be for not longer than 12 months; permits and leave are

granted accordingly. If there is a need for a longer period, this should be carefully explained in the original application. Extensions beyond 12 months are only exceptionally approved, and usually only up to a maximum total of 24 months.

Applying for extensions TWES permits can be extended using form WP1X. The employer should explain how much longer the person is required for and why. However, the person receiving training or experience will also need to apply to extend their leave using form FLR(IED) (▶see 430 onwards). The conditions that must be met under the immigration rules in order to obtain an extension of leave to remain in TWES employment are that the person (paras 119–121 HC395):

- entered the UK with a valid TWES work permit;
- has a letter of approval from the Home Office to continue their training or work experience;
- continues to meet the rules stated earlier – that they are capable of undertaking the training or work experience, intend to leave the UK after it has been completed, and can adequately support themselves and any dependants.

Provided that an extension application is made in time, the person may continue to work while it is being considered.

Applying to change training/work experience Form WP1 should be used to apply for changes of employment for persons who already have a TWES permit, but who wish to work for a different employer. Work Permits (UK) have said that they will accept only one change of employment in the TWES category, and only if it is made within three months of the start of the original permit. Permission will only be given if the training or work experience programme is one that Work Permits (UK) have already approved, and the person will only be given time to pick up where they left off so as to complete their existing training or experience. The person should not start working for the new employer until permission has been granted.

Families of TWES permit holders

The spouse and children of TWES permit holders may be admitted to the UK to join the TWES permit holder under the immigration rules (see paras 122–7 HC 395). The requirements for those dependants are the same as for the business and commercial scheme, and entry clearance is required (▶see 436–7). There is no provision in the rules for admitting unmarried partners, but the Guidance Notes state that unmarried partners may be admitted and so it appears that applications made for them outside the rules will be favourably considered (see TWES Guidance Notes, 3 October 2005 – 2 April 2006, para. 129). Spouses and partners are not prevented from working or from entering into business. As is the case with the main TWES holder, there is no provision in the rules for obtaining settlement.

Sportspersons' and entertainers' work permits

The Sportspersons and Entertainers work permits scheme allows employers to employ non-EEA nationals who are established sportspersons, entertainers or cultural artists. It is also possible for some technical and support staff to obtain permits in this category. The two essential conditions for qualifying are that the applicant is established and performs at a very high level, and that the resident workforce test is satisfied (for this test and the evidence needed to meet it, ▶see 423–4, 425–6).

The work permit route is not the only option for sportspeople and entertainers. Sportspeople who are coming for specific or charitable events, or who are amateurs, may be granted leave outside the immigration rules without a permit (▶471–2). Entertainers who are invited to perform at a specific event or events may be treated the same way. A specific concession outside the rules is also made for film crews filming on location (▶468). As a rule of thumb, sportspersons will require a work permit if they intend to base themselves in the UK for a sporting season, join or represent a British team and receive pay, give coaching (other than to a sportsperson or team at a specific event), or stay for longer than six months. Another alternative, depending on exactly what the applicant will be doing in the UK, is to seek entry as a business visitor (▶220–1) or as a 'special class' of visitor (▶see 222–3). There is also a category under the rules for self-employed creative artists who are basing themselves in the UK (▶492–3).

The Work Permits (UK) website (in addition to the Guidance Notes) contains extremely detailed and lengthy information about the various sports. This should be consulted in relation to applications made within a particular sport, both for the level of performance which needs to be demonstrated and on the question of conducting a recruitment search. In some sports, it is accepted that there are likely to be shortages, and Work Permits (UK) have agreed with the sports' governing bodies and players' representatives that applications do not need to be supported by evidence of a recruitment search. Similarly, where entertainers and cultural artists are performing a unique act in their own right, it will not normally be necessary to provide evidence to satisfy the resident workforce test. However, where the application is for a month or more, the performances are at the same venue or at a series of venues, and the audience is drawn to the venue rather than specifically to the applicant, evidence to satisfy the resident workforce test will be required to support an entertainer's application.

Applying the above criteria, the recognised categories under which sportspersons' and entertainers' work permits can be issued are as follows.

Sportspersons These are people who are internationally established 'at the highest level' and 'whose employment will make a significant contribution to the development of that particular sport in this country at the highest level'. Aside from the Guidance Notes, specific criteria are provided on the Work Permits (UK) website which includes the following sports: baseball and softball; basketball (players and coaches); boxers (and boxing trainers); cricket; field hockey; footballers; jockeys and trainers; ice hockey; circle kabaddi; lacrosse; polo; rugby; rugby union; and speedway riders.

Entertainers To qualify, the entertainer must have 'performed at the highest level and have established a reputation in their profession' and be engaged to 'perform or do work which only they can do'. Groups of entertainers are permitted, but the role of each member of the group should be made clear in the application. Separate from the Guidance Notes, specific criteria are provided on the Work Permits (UK) website relating to ballet, classical musicians and orchestras, dancers (including teachers and choreographers), and pantomime artists.

Unit companies These are large groups of entertainers who have regularly performed together in their own country and have toured as part of an established production. This will normally include groups such as orchestras, ballet companies and theatre productions with a history of performing together. A production specifically arranged for the purposes of a UK tour will therefore not be classed as a unit company. Evidence of the performance history of a unit company should be submitted with the application. The evidence should identify all the performers as being a permanent part of the production, and may include artist engagement contracts or publicity material.

Cultural artists This category relates to people who are 'skilled in foreign arts that are rare or unavailable in this country and can make a contribution to the arts, cultural relations and cultural awareness'. Again, groups are permitted.

Technical/support staff This category is for people whose work is directly related to the employment of those in the above categories. Applicants should have 'proven technical or other specialist skills'.

Actors Film and theatre actors who are not established will need to demonstrate their abilities by producing press reviews, recordings of their work, or material from official websites. It should be noted that all work permit applications for actors will be referred by Work Permits (UK) to the actor's union, Equity, for consultation, unless:

- the actor has international status – i.e. is a 'star';
- the application is for theatre actors who form part of a unit company;
- the work they wish to do in the UK is part of work which has already begun (for example, a film that has partly been filmed overseas);
- the role appears unlikely to be possible to fill by a member of the resident workforce;
- a thorough recruitment search has been carried out; or
- (for film actors) the work consists of location shooting.

Coming to and staying in the UK with a sportsperson's or entertainer's work permit

Initial applications for a work permit in this category should be made on form WP3. The immigration rules requiring entry clearance, which set out the requirements that must be satisfied in order for a person to be admitted or to be granted leave to remain, are the same as those that apply for the business category of work permits (▶428–30). Applications for extensions of leave must be made using form FLR(IED) (▶430–4).

Applications for sportspersons' and entertainers' work permits for a group can be made both for 'unit companies' (▶see 445) and for other groups of musicians, sports teams, theatre groups, and so on. Only one WP3 needs to be completed, with each member of the group listed on the form. If there are fewer than 20 in the group, a work permit will be issued for each member. For groups of 20 or more who are travelling together, a letter of permission will be sent to the employer or representative, instead of work permits being issued to each member of the group. Where the group members are travelling separately, however, a work permit will still be issued for each of them. Note that, although the fee payable for multiple applications usually reflects the number of persons in the group, a group application in the sportspersons and entertainers category will attract only one fee of £153 (▶see 419).

Period for which permits and leave are granted Generally, sportspersons are issued with work permits for the length of their contracts, up to a maximum of five years. Under the immigration rules, leave may then be granted for the length of the approval given. Entertainers are also issued approval for the period of their engagement in the UK, which tends to be shorter than that for sportspersons. In order to satisfy the rules for obtaining leave as a work permit holder where the permit has been granted for 12 months or less, it is necessary to show that the person intends to leave the UK at the end of the period of leave granted. If it is possible that the entertainer may wish to remain to do extra dates, this should be indicated on the original application. The leave granted will be subject to a condition restricting the work that may be done to that specified in the permit. However, sportspersons and entertainers may take certain work which is supplementary to that stated in their work permit, on the same conditions as those governing the business and commercial category (▶435).

Applying for extensions and changes of employment Applications for extensions of the permit should be made on form WP3X. Applications to change employment should be made on form WP3. If an extension application is made before leave expires, then the person can continue working while it is being considered, but permission must be obtained before a person changes the nature of their employment.

Multiple-entry work permits These permits (▶see also 435–6) are available for entertainers, but not for sportspersons. They are issued for a period of between six months and two years. They should be applied for using form WP3. Supplementary employment is not permitted if an entertainer is in the UK with a multiple-entry permit, although carrying out additional promotional activities aimed at supporting the main work for which the permit has been issued is allowed.

Settlement and dependants in the sportspersons' and entertainers' category

The rules for dependants are the same as for those with work permits in the business category (▶436–7). Indefinite leave may also be granted on the same basis as for holders of business work permits (▶see 437–9). However, owing to the seasonal nature of their work, many in the sportspersons' and entertainers' category may obtain only short-term work permits and leave for short periods at a time. Therefore, because they have not been in the UK with continuous leave and in continuous employment, indefinite leave often cannot be obtained. However, the Home Office (IDI Ch 17, Section 8, para. 9) may still grant settlement outside the immigration rules to sportspersons who meet all of the following requirements:

- they have achieved international status;
- they have, or intend to have, a home in the UK;
- they have spent at least four of the preceding eight years in the UK on short work permits.

Student internship work permits

Under the student internship work permit scheme, employers may offer an internship to a graduate or post-graduate student who is studying abroad, so that they can work in the UK as a trainee. The level of the work must be at N/SVQ level 3 or above. The period granted is short – a maximum of three months, to be taken up on completion of the student's course of studies. Internships will only be approved with companies or organisations which have a significant trading presence in the UK and elsewhere. Applications must be made on form WPSI. Because admission is only granted for three months, entry clearance is only required if the person is a visa national. Plainly, settlement is very unlikely.

General Agreement on Trade in Services work permits

General Agreement on Trade in Services (GATS) work permits are issued to employers who do not have a commercial presence in the EU, in order to enable their employees to work in the UK on service contracts awarded by British organisations. The non-European employer must be based in a country that is a member of the World Trade Organisation (WTO), and that has signed up to the GATS agreement with the WTO. Further information on these countries can be checked on the WTO website, www.wto.org. Employees must have high-level skills, and must also have all of the following:

- a recognised degree-level qualification;
- professional qualifications;
- three years' professional experience in the relevant sector;
- 12 months of employment by the overseas company, leading up to the application (this year counts as the last of the three years' professional experience).

This level of qualifications (but not professional experience) is relaxed slightly for advertising, translation and management-consulting services.

The services must also be provided in the particular service sectors specified in the Guidance Notes under the GATS scheme. These service sectors are: law; accountancy; book-keeping; taxation advice; architecture, urban planning and landscape architecture; engineering; integrated engineering; advertising; management consultancy; technical testing and analysis; translation and site investigation. For the last seven of those service sectors, Work Permits (UK) need to be satisfied that the contract meets an 'economic needs test'. This is similar to the 'resident workforce test' (▶see 423–4, 425–6), except that it is applied to the provision of services. The UK contractor has to demonstrate the need to award the contract to an organisation outside the EU. The contract must have been awarded on the basis of an open tendering procedure.

In order to apply for a work permit, the overseas employer must complete form GATSA. Once this is received, Work Permits (UK) will send form GATSB to the UK contractor for them to complete. A work permit and leave will be granted for the length of the service contract, up to a maximum of three months in any 12-month period. The worker will be expected to leave the UK at the end of the contract. Permits may be extended, in total, for up to the three-month period. Within this total period, it is possible to ask for extensions based upon changes of contract. Extensions beyond that time will not be permitted. Again, because admission is only granted for three months, entry clearance is only required if the applicant is a visa national.

THE SECTORS BASED SCHEME

The Sectors Based Scheme (SBS) was introduced as a category under the immigration rules on 30 May 2003 (paras 135I–135M HC 395 inserted by Cm 5829). The purpose of the SBS is to allow workers from outside the EEA to enter the UK in order to take less-skilled, short-term or casual jobs in areas of the employment market ('sectors') where there is a shortage of resident labour. The sectors in which work has been available are as follows. Under the 'five year' strategy the Sectors Based Scheme will be phased out. It may be replaced by a new low-skilled scheme(s) if the Home Office believes that there is a case for further such schemes.

Hotel and catering work The main areas are: bar staff, chefs at N/SVQ level 2 and below, cleaners, workers for staff canteens and restaurants, concierge staff, food-service operatives, housekeepers, kitchen assistants, room attendants, reception staff, and waiting staff. The hospitality sector closed with effect from 31 July 2005.

Food manufacturing: meat and fish processing and mushroom production The main areas are: fish filleters, fish packers, fish process operatives, animal gut removers, meat bone-breakers, meat bone-extractors, meat cold-store operatives, meat cutters, meat packers, meat process operatives, meat slaughterers, meat trimmers, mushroom processors. The food processing sector was last extended until May 2006.

The scheme is subject to specific quotas. When the scheme was introduced in 2003, there were 20,000 places available. For the year from June 2004, that number has been reduced to 15,000, with 9,000 in the hospitality sector and 6,000 in the food processing sector. The quotas are released in two half-yearly stages. So, for the half-year from 1 December 2004, there were 4,500 permits available for the hospitality sector and 3,000 for the food-processing sector. There is also a 20 per cent limit on the number of permits issued to any single nationality for each of the sectors. When the quota limits are close to being reached, notice to this effect is issued on the Work Permits (UK) website.

In order to qualify for a place on the scheme, so that an IED under the scheme can be granted, the following conditions should be satisfied:

- the worker must be a national of a non-EEA country, and aged between 18 and 30 years throughout the IED application process and at the time they enter the UK (and see amendment to the immigration rules confirming the age range, para. 135I(ii) HC 395 substituted from 30 NOvember 2005 by HC 645). It does not matter if the applicant becomes 31 after they enter the UK;
- there must be a genuine full-time vacancy for the worker in one of the above sectors offered by a UK employer;
- pay and conditions must be equal to those normally given to a resident worker doing similar work;
- suitable arrangements must have been made to accommodate the worker;
- there should be no suitable resident workers available.

Coming to the UK under the SBS

The worker must apply to an employer advertising outside the UK and obtain a job offer. The employer will then make an application on form SB1 for an IED under the SBS. After the IED has been issued, entry clearance must be obtained in all cases. The immigration rules for obtaining the entry clearance are essentially the same as for the business and commercial work permit category (▶see 429–30), save that in all cases the worker must intend to leave at the end of the approved employment. The entry clearance will usually grant a period of leave in line with the length of the permit, up to a maximum of 12 months.

If a person wishes to extend their stay in the UK under the SBS, form SB1X must be completed. However, extensions will only be granted to approve work up to the above maximum total of 12 months. If the SBS IED is extended, the applicant must then apply on form FLR(IED) to extend their leave (▶see 430–4 for applying to extend on form FLR(IED)). Provided the applications are made in time, the person may continue to work. However, Work Permits (UK) have said that the person should not continue to work if the 12-month maximum period for leave under the SBS is within 28 days of expiring. Changes of employment applications can be submitted on form SB1, but will similarly only be granted up to the 12-month maximum period. Such applications must be for new work in the same industrial sector as the worker has been employed in. A person should not change their work until permission has been granted.

Those who have been admitted under the SBS may apply to come back to the UK for any number of further stints. The only limitation is that Work Permits (UK) will not issue an IED to allow a further period under the SBS unless the applicant has been out of the UK for at least two months. But there is nothing to stop a further application being made during the two-month period, provided the worker does not intend to re-enter before two months have elapsed.

Dependants, settlement and other rights under the SBS

It goes without saying that the SBS does not of itself lead to settlement in the UK. Spouses and children cannot be admitted as dependants of someone coming to the UK under the SBS (see para. 194 HC 395, which excludes the SBS from the rules relating to dependants that apply to work permit holders and others). Family members who wish to join someone coming under the SBS have to seek leave under the immigration rules in their own right. Strangely, though, the rules appear to allow the admission of dependants who are unmarried partners (see para. 295J–L HC 395, which applies the same criteria to unmarried partners of those under the SBS as for work permit holders and other categories). Supplementary work is permitted under the SBS, provided the additional work is done outside normal working hours, is in the same industrial sector, and is in one of the jobs listed above. If an IED is refused under the SBS, the same informal review procedure applies as to other IEDs (▶see 439–40).

SEASONAL AGRICULTURAL WORKERS' SCHEME (SAWS)

The SAWS allows for non-EEA full-time overseas students aged 18 or over to come to the UK for a short period to do seasonal agricultural work. From 13 November 2003 the rules were amended to abolish the upper age limit, and to allow applicants to stay for six months at a time, rather than until 30 November of the year in question (paras 104–9 HC 395 amended by HC 1224). The purpose of the scheme is to allow farmers to recruit overseas seasonal labour to meet shortfalls in the resident work-force. The work generally involves planting and gathering crops, on-farm processing, packing crops and handling livestock. Demand among appli-cants is very high, and there is an annual quota fixing the numbers who may come in any one calendar year. Although the SAWS was expanded in 2003, and the quota was set at 25,000 places for 2004, for 2005 it has been reduced to 16,250. The justification given for this by the Immigra-tion Minister, Des Brown, on 19 May 2004, was that the SAWS

'…serves a valuable role in helping UK employers to recruit workers in sectors where there are difficulties in meeting labour needs from the resident workforce. At the same time it is important that these schemes should now reflect the fact that workers from the countries that joined the EEA [on 1 May 2004] are now free to seek work in these sectors. Most important of all it is important that these schemes are protected from abuse.'

The Minister further reaffirmed the importance of preventing SAWS workers staying beyond the period for which they have been recruited.

Coming to the UK under the SAWS

Although the scheme is subject to the overall management of Work Permits (UK), it is actually run by 'operators' who recruit suitable workers and place them on farms. Indeed, an operator may transfer a worker between different farms while they are in the UK. Operators offering places on the SAWS may recruit students by visiting universities and coll-eges overseas, by making contacts through employment agencies, or simply from applications sent to them. Work Permits (UK) has stated that it does not intend to tender for further operators before 2007.

It is the operator who then provides the applicant with a 'work card' (the relevant IED for this category). These are similar in size and appearance to normal work permits, but contain the worker's photograph and details of their placement in the UK. Before the person comes to the UK, the operator should provide him or her with information about the nature of the work and conditions, holiday and sick pay, employment rights and the minimum standards of accommodation that will be provided. The operator should also inspect the farm to ensure that the conditions are suitable.

Once the applicant has their work card, no entry clearance is required. In order to be admitted to the UK, in addition to seeing the work card, the immigration officer, acting under the immigration rules, will need to be satisfied that the applicant: intends to leave the UK at the end of the period of work; does not intend to take work other than that permitted by the work card; and can maintain and accommodate themselves adequately. There is a further requirement that any earlier leave that the person had obtained under this category expired at least three months before the date of re-entry. This is to prevent applicants from immediately returning to the UK after being here under the SAWS. There must be a gap of at least three months before the person may re-enter.

Applicants are admitted for a maximum period of six months, and subject to a condition that they will not take work other than that permitted by their work card. Those admitted under the SAWS must take part in the scheme for a minimum of five weeks. They are expected to leave the UK when their leave has expired. If less than six months were granted, an extension application can be made on form FLR(IED), up to a maximum total of six months (▶see 430–4 for applications on form FLR(IED)). First, of course, a further work card will have to be issued by the operator. Changes of work will only generally be permitted with the operator's consent.

Rights under the SAWS

There is no provision in the immigration rules for the admission of dependants of seasonal workers, and so family may not be admitted unless they can qualify under the rules in their own right. Because of the short period of leave granted, and the gaps in between any possible grants of leave, there is no expectation of settlement. Time spent as a seasonal agricultural worker also counts as time spent as a visitor, so applicants cannot stay longer than six months in total by applying to stay on as a visitor at the end of their agricultural work.

15 Permit-free employment

This chapter deals with the range of immigration employment opportunities for which an Immigration Employment Document (IED) is not required. In the categories dealt with in this chapter, the ability to work in the UK comes hand in hand with the grant of leave to be here: there is no need to make a separate application for permission to work. These categories are generally known as 'permit-free' or 'non-work permit' categories. The immigration rules contain most of these categories, but some of them still exist as concessions operated outside the rules. This chapter deals with all of the permit-free categories, beginning with those under the rules (►see below), then looking at those outside the rules (►467–72).

This chapter also covers those who are exempt from immigration control and, as a consequence, do not need specific permission to work (►472–6). Those who are exempt are generally defined by their position or employment.

For a list of work and business categories not dealt with in this section but covered elsewhere in the book, ►see 413–4.

Permit-free employment under the rules: general

It is possible to divide permit-free employment under the rules into two groups: long-term workers (below) and short-term workers (►see 462–7). Leave granted in any of the long-term worker categories eventually leads naturally on to settlement, but leave granted as a short-term worker does not. Note, however, that under the Science and Engineering Graduate (SEGs) Scheme and the Fresh Talent: Working in Scotland Scheme, in particular, applicants may qualify to switch into longer term employment which leads to settlement.

LONG TERM PERMIT-FREE EMPLOYMENT UNDER THE RULES

The various categories of long-term employment under the rules are set out below, in the order in which they appear in the immigration rules. First we look at considerations which are common to the long-term categories.

General common rules about entering and staying for long-term permit-free employment

In what follows, we set out the general common rules. There are some exceptions, which we address immediately below. In all cases, entry clearance is mandatory. In order to obtain entry clearance and leave to enter, the following general requirements need to be satisfied:

- applicants must intend to work in the particular capacity for which leave is granted, and not to take any other form of employment;
- applicants must be able to maintain and accommodate themselves and any dependants without claiming public funds (►see 308–318 for full details about these requirements).

Applicants will need to obtain confirmation of their job offer, and then submit those details to the entry clearance officer in support of their application for entry clearance. In some cases, the ECO may refer the application to the Home Office in the UK to confirm details of the job or other details before making a decision about granting entry clearance (►see 93).

Entry clearance will be issued enabling leave to enter to be granted for 12 months in the first instance. That leave may then be extended for a further three years, provided the person is still engaged in the employment in question and is required for that employment as confirmed by their employer. Applicants must also continue to meet both the specific rules relating to their category and the common rules outlined above. The applicant for an extension must have been originally admitted in the category in which they seek the extension. With one exception relating to ministers of religion (►see 459–60 and ►see 185 'Note E'), the rules prohibit switching into permit free categories. For switching generally and the exercise of discretion outside the rules, see Chapter 7. Leave will be granted subject to conditions prohibiting access to public funds and restricting work to that for which leave was originally granted.

Settlement After four continuous years' leave in the relevant qualifying category, during which time the requirements of the rules have been met, and provided the applicant is still working and their employer confirms that they are still required, the worker can be granted settlement. Applications to extend leave and for settlement are made on the general Home Office forms (►see 128–32), except for sole representatives, who should use Form BUS for these purposes. For more details about the calculation of the four-year continuous period, ►see 437–9.

Family Spouses, children and unmarried partners may be admitted to, stay and obtain settlement in the UK as dependants upon the principal worker, in the same way as for dependants of work permit holders (►see above at 436–7). Persons admitted as family members will generally be admitted without any working or business restrictions.

Exceptions to common rules

There are certain exceptions to the above rules, as follows:

- As an alternative to obtaining entry clearance, applicants in the 'overseas government employee' category can be admitted if they carry 'satisfactory documentary evidence of [their] status as an overseas government employee' (para. 161(i) HC 395). This will presumably include letters of introduction from the government employer in question, letters of appointment, or contracts of service.

- The rules allow for some applications to switch into the category of minister of religion (▶see 185 'Note E', 450).

- Ministers of religion who switched into that category, domestic workers and private servants in diplomatic households are granted extensions of leave of not more than 12 months at a time (rather than three years). However, they are still eligible for settlement after four years.

- Those admitted on the grounds of UK ancestry can be granted leave to enter initially (or given an extension) for up to four years. In addition, they also do not have to seek work of any particular kind, their conditions of leave do not restrict the work they can do, and they do not have to demonstrate that they are needed by a particular employer when they apply for settlement.

Media representatives

Representatives of overseas newspapers, news agencies and broadcasting organisations who have been posted to the UK for long-term assignments may be admitted under this category (paras 136–143 HC 395. Those coming for less than six months may apply as business visitors instead (IDI, Ch 5, s2, para. 1, and ▶see 220–1). The permanent employment of these representatives will be with the organisation abroad, and they must have been engaged outside the UK. The IDI states that employees other than journalists may be considered, and gives the examples of producers and news camera operators. It is stated, however, that administrative staff not directly involved in newsgathering require work permits (IDI, Ch 5, s2, para. 1).

Sole representatives

'Sole representatives' (paras 144–151 HC 395) are representatives of overseas firms which have no branch, subsidiary or other representative in the UK. The company must be based overseas, and the representative must have been recruited or taken on as an employee outside the UK. If a UK company exists, but as a legal entity only – for example if it was set up in anticipation of the company expanding to the UK, but it employs no staff and transacts no business – then a sole representative will still be admissible (IDI, Ch 5, s3, para. 1). The sole representative must be seeking entry as a senior employee with the power to make decisions and negotiate on behalf of the company. The representative must be a full-time employee, and must not be a majority shareholder in the firm. This is to ensure that the application is not being made to get round the strict requirements of the business rules (►see 478–80). The ECO will require documentary evidence confirming the legal, physical and trading existence of the overseas firm, and a detailed explanation of why the company requires a permanent presence in the UK, and why the proposed sole representative is suited for that role.

During the first year, the representative is expected to set up a registered branch or a wholly-owned subsidiary of the company in the UK, and to continue to run it. The ECO will expect the sole representative to be intending to spend at least nine months of the year in the UK but, exceptionally, will be prepared to admit some applicants who will spend considerably less than this time in their first year, and who will continue to be based abroad. This discretion will typically be exercised in the case of full-time senior employees of the parent company who continue to work overseas, but who have been given responsibility for setting up a limited operation in the UK to test the market (IDI, Ch 5, s3, annex J, para. 3). The sole representative can also hire local staff, or apply for work permits for prospective employees overseas to join them in the UK as employees of the company.

There is some flexibility applied in the settlement rules. First, when calculating the four years required for settlement, the Home Office operates a concession outside the rules which allows the combination of time spent as a work permit holder and as a sole representative (Home Office letter to representative of 22 November 2002; Business User Panel, 18 March 2003). Second, a sole representative who has already been given leave to bring their total period up to four years may remain and still qualify for settlement, even if in the meantime the overseas company has appointed a more senior person. This will, however, only be the case if the applicant continues to fill a genuine vacancy in the UK (IDI, Ch 6, s3, annex J, para. 2.4).

Private servants of diplomats

Private servants of diplomats (paras 152–159 HC 395) must be at least 18 years old. They must be employed full-time as a private servant of a diplomat, or of a family member who forms part of the household of a diplomat. The diplomat must be a person who has diplomatic privileges and immunity. The employer will be asked to provide and sign a statement of the main terms and conditions of the servant's employment. Frequently, servants falling into this category are housemaids or chauffeurs. They are not usually exempt from immigration control because, unlike others who work in embassies (►see 473–4 below), they are working directly for an individual diplomat, and not for the foreign mission itself. The Home Office has indicated, however, that a private servant of the head of a diplomatic mission will be treated as exempt from control provided they are employed and paid directly by the sending State (IDI, Ch 14, s1, annex

B, para. 2). It is not possible for someone who is exempt from control through a job at an embassy or high commission to change status within the UK to work for an individual diplomat, since entry clearance was not granted for this purpose. It is possible, however, for a private servant of a diplomat to change employers within the same mission; but the Home Office should be notified and the employer and servant will normally again have to sign a statement of terms and conditions (IDI, Ch 5, s4, annex M, para. 8.3).

Applicants for entry clearance in this category should be interviewed on their own, in order to confirm that they understand the terms and conditions of their employment and that they are willing to go to the UK. They should also be given an information leaflet which explains their rights (these are available in different languages including Arabic, Tagalog, Urdu, Punjabi, Bengali, Hindi, Tamil, Thai and Spanish) (IDI, Ch 5, s4, annex M, paras 1, 9.1). The employer will usually be required to provide a maintenance undertaking, including a requirement to provide the servant with their own, separate bedroom (IDI, Ch 5, s4, annex M, para. 5 and annex N).

Domestic workers

For over 20 years, beginning in 1980, this category was operated as a concession outside the immigration rules. It was finally brought within the rules on 18 September 2002 (paras 159A-159H HC 395 inserted by Cm 5597). Domestic workers in private households must be aged between 18 and 65 years. For a period of at least a year before the entry clearance application is made, they must have been employed under the same roof as the employer, or in a household that the employer uses regularly. The purpose of this is to ensure that there is a genuine existing employer/employee relationship.

The work the domestic worker will do does not, as was once the case, need to be at any particular level. Typically, domestic workers will include cleaners, chauffeurs, gardeners, cooks and some nannies and carers. It must be intended that in the UK the domestic worker will be working full-time under the same roof as his/her employer, or in a household the employer regularly uses. Accordingly, the employer must normally be present in the UK. However, it is possible for applications to be successful even if the employer spends a substantial amount of time abroad. The Home Office give the example of a housekeeper who is looking after property in the absence of their employers, and of a cook who works for the employer's family while they are travelling. In all cases, it will be necessary to show that the employer is in the UK for some of the time, and applicants should expect to have to explain their circumstances clearly if the employer's absences are for more than six months in a year (see IDI, Ch 5, s12, para. 5.1).

Applicants coming initially must intend to travel to the UK in the company of their employer or the employer's spouse or child. Some flexibility is applied here so that domestic workers may be admitted if travelling alone, provided that the time-lapse is not excessive. In such cases, they should also carry a letter from their employer explaining why they are travelling alone (IDI, Ch 5, s12, para. 2.5).

The ECO will normally require a written undertaking from the employer that they will provide adequate maintenance and accommodation (with a separate bedroom if the domestic worker is living in) for the applicant, and set out the main terms and conditions of employment in writing. The worker must be given a copy of this statement and must confirm that they agree with it. The British post should check the type and hours of work, and that the worker wants to come to the UK. The British post must interview the worker on their own, at least on the first application for entry clearance, to ensure that the worker understands the position. Again, they should also be provided with an information leaflet explaining their rights in the UK. Experience shows, however, that these procedures are frequently not implemented properly. All too often, workers ask for advice after having arrived in the UK, unaware of their immigration status and without their passport, which has been retained by abusive employers whom they have fled. The ECO who issued entry clearance may need to be contacted in these circumstances in order to establish when and on what terms the worker was admitted.

Length of leave If the employer is being admitted to the UK as a visitor, the domestic worker will normally be granted leave for up to six months, in accordance with the period granted to the employer. If the employer is admitted in any other capacity, leave will normally be given to the domestic worker for up to 12 months at a time (IDI, Ch 5, s12, para. 4.3).

Changes of employment The entry clearance should not generally state the name of the employer, and the domestic worker may obtain new employment, without obtaining approval, in other domestic work. They may obtain extensions of leave on the basis of their new employment (note that the rule relating to extensions of stay states simply that the applicant's employment must be certified by their 'current employer' – para. 159D(iii) HC 395). Although the Home Office has been issuing endorsements to domestic workers which state that 'changes must be authorised by the Secretary of State', it has nevertheless confirmed that this relates to changes to do work other than domestic work, and not changes of employer (letter to Bates, Wells and Braithwaite Solicitors, 7 June 2004). Domestic workers are able to change their employer, regardless of the reason for leaving their original employment. Nevertheless, they should notify the Home Office by letter of changes of employment (IDI, Ch 5, s12, paras 1.1, 5.2). It is desirable for domestic workers to do this, because they will need to prove that they have been in employment as a domestic worker under the rules when they seek an extension of stay. The fact that a domestic worker has changed employers will not 'stop the clock' for the purposes of calculating the four years after which they may apply for settlement. However, the domestic worker is likely to need letters from employers to show that they have spent four years in that type of employment.

Withholding of passports An ongoing problem for domestic workers is the withholding of passports by their ex-employers. In January 2003, Kalayaan, the organisation fighting for justice for migrant domestic workers, reported that some 63 per cent of migrant domestic workers' passports are withheld by their employers. The organisation may be able to provide support and practical assistance in such cases (▶see 1503 for contact details).

Overseas government employees

These are people who are not diplomats, and are not exempt from immigration control (▶see 473–4), but have formal contracts of employment with an overseas government, the United Nations Organisation, or another international organisation of which the UK is a member. They may be admitted in order to carry out full-time work for the particular government or overseas body in the UK (paras 160–168 HC 395).

Ministers of religion

The rules relating to ministers of religion (paras 169–177 HC 395) have been amended from 23 August 2004 (see Command Paper Cm 6297). According to the rules, a minister of religion is a 'religious functionary whose main regular duties comprise the leading of a congregation in performing the rites and rituals of the faith and in preaching the essentials of the creed' (para. 169(i) HC 395). The Home Office does not accept every organisation which is named as a church to qualify as a religion under the immigration rules. For example, it rejects the Church of Scientology and the Unification Church ('Moonies') for these purposes. The IDI provides notes on six of the major world religions, which give rise to frequent applications made under this category (Buddhism, Christianity, Hinduism, Islam, Judaism, Sikhism). They are not, however, the only religions which are accepted under the rules (IDI, Ch 5, s6, annex T).

Applicants have to show that they will be working full-time as ministers, and will be asked for evidence of any formal qualifications and of past experience of work as a minister. They must have worked as a minister for at least one year in the last five years. Alternatively, if ordination as a minister is the only means of entering the ministry for their particular faith, they must have been ordained as a minister after training lasting at least one year full-time, or two years part-time. The ECO will usually require a letter from the religious group giving full details of the position offered, including the pay and conditions. A list of the kinds of duties which the minister will be expected to perform is contained in the IDI and includes: leading worship, providing religious education, officiating at marriages and other such occasions, offering counselling and support to members of a congregation, and co-ordinating the work of local volunteers and lay preachers (IDI, Ch 5, s6, annex S). Pay, fringe-benefits such as accommodation, and whatever other resources are available to the minister themselves must be sufficient to show that they and their dependants can be maintained and accommodated without recourse to public funds.

The 2002 White Paper (*Secure Borders, Safe Haven*) had indicated that 'those who have already spent some time in the UK will be able to speak some English and have absorbed some of our culture and are, therefore, better able to relate their faith to the context of the UK'. This theme is taken up in the amendments to the rules made in 2004 (paras 170, 173–6 HC 395 amended by Cm 6297 from 23 August 2004). The new rules require that applicants have an International English Language Testing System (IELTS) certificate showing that they have achieved Level 4 competence in spoken English. This additional requirement applies to those seeking to enter the UK from 23 August 2004. From the same date, it also applies to those applying to switch to being a minister (▶see below), and to those seeking extensions who have already switched under the new rules. So, the new language requirement does not apply to those who entered the UK as a minister before 23 August 2004, and who are now applying to extend their leave in that capacity.

The same new rules allow applicants to switch in order to stay as a minister of religion. The requirements are that, immediately before the application to switch is made, the applicant has spent a continuous period of 12 months in the UK pursuant to leave granted to them other than as a visitor or, obviously, as a minister. The applicant must satisfy all of the requirements for ministers described above, including that relating to their length of experience. Experience gained while in breach of a condition of leave, however, will not be counted. The applicant must be at the point of being appointed to a position as a minister in the UK, and must have evidence from the leadership of the congregation that they are suitable as a minister (▶see also at 185 'Note E'). It is also possible for ministers to apply for further leave in order to work for a different employer, provided the rules continue to be met (IDI, Ch 5, s6, para. 3.1).

On 19 December 2005, the Home Office minister announced that, in January 2006, a new category of 'religious worker' would be introduced into the immigration rules, and that there would be a 'pre-entry qualification' requirement for them.

Missionaries and members of religious orders

Two other categories are lumped together in the immigration rules with the rules relating to ministers of religion (▶see above). These categories are 'missionaries' and 'members of religions orders'. The new language requirement relating to ministers of religion does not apply to either of these two categories, and nor do the new rules permitting switching.

A missionary is defined as 'a person who is directly engaged in spreading a religious doctrine and whose work is not in essence administrative or clerical'. A missionary has to show evidence of previous experience or training in missionary work, and must be sent to the UK by an overseas organisation. Applicants may also come to live in a community maintained by the religious order of which they are a member. If the person is intending to teach, this must only be at an establishment maintained by the order. If they are teaching in an outside school, the school must obtain a work permit to employ them. It is assumed that the religious order will be providing board and lodging for its members within their community.

Operational ground staff of overseas airlines

In order to qualify under this category (paras 178–185 HC 395), the applicant must have been transferred to the UK by an overseas-owned airline which operates services to and from the UK. The duties of the applicant must be to work at an international airport as a station manager, security manager or technical manager. As a concession, it may be possible for additional, less senior security staff to be admitted if a clear case can be made that they are needed, as has been the case for El Al Airlines (IDI, Ch 5, s7, para. 1.1). Staff admitted on this exceptional basis will not usually be able to stay for more than three years. Crew members of airlines are dealt with differently (▶see under the 'exempt' categories, 475). Other airline staff who are to be based in the UK require work permits.

Ancestry (Commonwealth nationals with British-born grandparents)

Commonwealth citizens aged 17 or over with a British-born grandparent (paternal or maternal) can come to the UK to work and to seek work (paras 186–193 HC 395). (For a list of Commonwealth countries, ▶see 1525–6.) Applicants must be able to show that their grandparent was born in either the UK, Channel Islands, Isle of Man or – if born before 31 March 1922 – in what is now the Republic of Ireland (see IDI, Ch 5, s8, para. 3.2). They need to prove their descent from the person born in the UK, usually by producing the grandparent's birth certificate or marriage certificate, the birth certificate of their parent descended from the grandparent, their parents' marriage certificate, and their own birth certificate. Documents are likely to be carefully scrutinised, as the immigration authorities are particularly concerned about false documentation in this area.

If the parents or grandparents were not married, any other evidence to show the relationship would be helpful, such as statements from people who knew them to confirm that they are the grandparents and parents of the applicant, or any evidence from school or medical records showing the family connections. An adoptive relationship with the grandparent, provided it is an adoption recognised by UK law, is accepted. The parent of an illegitimate child includes the father, provided he is proved to be the father. Applicants must be able to show that they either have a job lined up or that they have realistic chances of obtaining work. Account will be taken of their age and state of health.

Prior to 25 October 2004, it was possible for those who qualified to switch into this category. So, for example, a Commonwealth national with close UK ancestry could, during a visit, decide to stay in the UK to work, rather than having to return home and make the application again. The rules have now been closed off to prevent switching (para. 189 HC 395 as amended by HC 1112). It is extremely unclear why the government should have wanted to tighten its switching rules to the extent of catching straightforward applications in this category, where a person's entitlements are based on their nationality and heritage.

SHORT-TERM PERMIT-FREE EMPLOYMENT UNDER THE RULES

Those admitted under the immigration rules in order to work in the UK as au pairs, teachers or language assistants under an exchange scheme under the Science and Engineering Graduate Scheme (SEGS) or under the Fresh Talent: Working in Scotland Scheme, are not given leave with a direct expectation of settlement after they have completed a period of leave in these capacities. *For the reasons explained below, the Fresh Talent Scheme and SEGS are the closest of these categories to the long-term categories.*

A further similar category to these three groups are 'working holiday-makers', who are young Commonwealth nationals who may do some work in the UK during an extended 'holiday' of a maximum of two years. Since their work is intended to be an 'integral part of a working holiday', we look at this group in Chapter 9, dealing with visitors.

Au pairs

Young people between the ages of 17 and 27, who are unmarried and have no dependants, may apply as *au pairs* (paras 88–94 HC 395) Provided the applicant is under 28 at the time they apply for entry clearance, it does not matter if they become 28 before arriving in the UK or while here as an *au pair*. Also, discretion may be exercised where an applicant who is aged up to 28 years and six months was prevented from applying earlier by an unexpected domestic crisis, illness or the completion of a long-term course of study (IDI, Ch 4, s1, annex A, para. 1). Applicants must be nationals of either Andorra, Bosnia-Herzegovina, Bulgaria, Croatia, the Faroes, Greenland, Macedonia, Monaco, Romania, San Marino, or Turkey. It should be noted that the list of eligible countries has changed regularly. This list was provided in an amendment to the rules which took effect on 1 May 2004 (see para. 2 HC 523, April 2004). Many people from EEA countries also come to the UK as *au pairs*, but do not have to qualify formally under the immigration rules.

Au pairs may come to take up arranged placements for up to two years, and must intend to leave after their stay as an *au pair*. This two-year period cannot be aggregated over time, but instead runs for two years from the date that the *au pair* is first admitted. No allowance is made for any time spent outside the UK during that period. If leave is initially granted for less than the two years, it may be extended up to a maximum of two years from the date of entry.

The central reason why the *au pair* is coming to the UK must be in order to learn English, although there is no absolute obligation for an *au pair* to enrol on an English language course during their stay. They are required to be living as part of an English-speaking family with appropriate opportunities for study. A 'family' does not need to contain a husband, wife and children, but a person living alone is not a family (IDI, Ch 4, s1, annex A, para. 2). It is intended that the *au pair* will help in the home for not more than five hours per day, with two free days per week. As with most other categories, there is a requirement that the *au pair* is able to maintain and accommodate themselves without recourse to public funds, but in most cases this will be through the family they are staying with, who are expected to provide a reasonable allowance (at present, up to £55 per week) plus board and lodging.

Entry clearance is not compulsory, although it is advisable to obtain it even if the applicant is not a visa national or a specified national. In fact, the immigration rules actually advise potential *au pairs* wishing to know whether they are likely to be admitted to apply for entry clearance (see para. 90, HC 395). *Au pairs'* conditions of leave will prevent work other than as an *au pair*. It is possible for an *au pair* to change their host family, provided the new arrangement also meets the requirements of the au pair category. The Home Office should be notified by letter if there is such a change (IDI, Ch 4, s1, annex A, para. 2). There is no provision in the rules for the admission of the dependants of *au pairs*.

Teachers and language assistants

Teachers and language assistants may come to schools in the UK under official exchange schemes which have been approved by the Department for Education and Skills, the Scottish or Welsh Office of Education, or the Department of Education of Northern Ireland (paras 110–115 HC 395). The scheme may also be one which is administered by the British Council's Education and Training Group or the League for the Exchange of Commonwealth Teachers. Entry clearance must always be obtained, and leave will initially be granted for a maximum of 12 months, which may be extended up to a maximum of two years from the date on which the applicant was first given leave to enter in this category. Applicants must intend to leave the UK at the end of their exchange period. There is provision in the immigration rules for the admission of the spouses (but not unmarried partners) and minor children of those granted leave in this category, all of whom must obtain entry clearance. The maintenance and accommodation requirements must be satisfied both for the teacher/language assistant and their dependants.

The Science and Engineering Graduate Scheme

The Science and Engineering Graduate Scheme (SEGS) was introduced into the immigration rules on 25 October 2004 (see para. 10 Cm 6339 inserting paras 135O–135T into HC 395). It allows non-EEA nationals who have recently graduated from publicly funded UK higher or further education institutions (or *bona fide* private institutions) to enter or remain in the UK for up to 12 months in order to seek work.

Applicants must have obtained either a degree (class 2.2 or above), a Masters degree, or a Ph.D in certain physical science, maths and engineering subjects. The subjects which are eligible are those which are approved by the Department for Education and Skills (DfES), and a list is maintained on the Work Permits (UK) website. The particular courses cover areas within which Sir Gareth Roberts' review, 'The Supply of People with Science, Technology, Engineering and Mathematics Skills', indicated that the UK has a shortage, in terms of students and skilled workers. The subjects which are eligible are defined by the coding given to them by the Joint Academic Coding System (JACS), which was a system developed jointly by the Universities and Colleges Admissions Service (UCAS) and the Higher Education Statistics Agency (HESA). Applicants will need to provide evidence of their course's JACS code at the time of the application

In addition to the list of approved courses, the Work Permits (UK) website also carries guidance on when 'B Ed.' (teachers' degree courses) will qualify. If the applicant's studies in the UK were sponsored by a government or an international scholarship agency, the written consent of the sponsor for the person to stay in the UK must be obtained.

Making applications Applicants may either switch in-country from student status to SEGS or return to the UK, but they must have completed their approved course (not later studies) in the UK within the last 12 months. In-country applications should be made on the specific form provided on the website, and will cost £335 for a postal application (£500 for the premium service – ▶see 133). If an applicant leaves the UK after completing their approved course, then entry clearance is mandatory in order to return under SEGS unless the applicant is a British National (Overseas), a British Overseas Territories Citizen, a British Overseas Citizen, a British Protected Person or a British Subject under the 1981 Act. If the applicant is switching from student status, the application must be made before the student leave runs out.

Leave granted Leave may be granted for up to a maximum of 12 months and, under the rules, extensions can only be granted to bring the period up to 12 months in total (see paras 135O(v), 135R(iii) HC 395). The clock runs continuously from the date of the first grant of leave under SEGS, even if the applicant is granted less than 12 months or does not remain in the UK for the entire period of their leave. So it seems, for example, that if an applicant is granted a six-month period of leave under

SEGS, after which they leave the UK for six months, they would not be eligible to apply to be admitted under SEGS again, as the 12-month period since the initial grant of leave has expired. Those granted leave under SEGS may undertake any type of employment or self-employment, and may later switch to remain as a work permit holder, under the HSMP, as a business-person, or as an innovator (for full details ▶see 174).

General The scheme will be particularly attractive to young science and engineering graduates who have no definite offers of employment. There is no requirement to have actually secured employment before leave can be granted, which allows these graduates to shop around and make themselves eligible for a work permit. In addition, SEGS applicants only need to show that they intend to leave after their 12 months if they have not been permitted to extend their stay in any of the above four categories. So, although a person cannot stay in the UK in the long-term under SEGS itself, the scheme offers a route into long-term employment and eventual settlement. The spouse, unmarried partner and children of those granted leave under SEGS are eligible to be granted leave in line with the graduate on the basis of the same rules as apply to work permit holders ▶(see 436–7). The maintenance and accommodation requirements must be satisfied for both the principal and any dependants.

The Fresh Talent: Working in Scotland Scheme

On 22 June, the Home Office introduced the 'Fresh Talent: Working in Scotland scheme' into the immigration rules (paras 143A-143F HC 395 inserted by HC 104). The initiative for this dates back at least to the speech by Scotland's First Minister on 25 February 2003 in which he set out his policy to attract 'fresh talent' to Scotland. It supports the Scottish Executive's 'Fresh Talent Initiative' which is intended to encourage people to consider living and working in Scotland and is an attempt to address Scotland's depopulation crisis. In essence, the scheme makes it easier for non-EEA nationals who have studied in Scotland to stay on after their studies and also to switch into an immigration category to start or continue working in Scotland.

Requirements under the scheme

In order to qualify, applicants must:

- have, in the last 12 months, completed and been awarded an HND, UK recognised undergraduate degree, Master's degree or a PhD by a Scottish publicly funded institution or a Scottish *bona fide* private educational institution;
- have lived in Scotland for an 'appropriate period of time' while studying; and
- intend to seek and take employment in Scotland.

Home Office guidance sets out the postcodes for which an applicant's address will qualify them as having lived in Scotland (the postcodes are: AB, DG, DD, EH, FK, TD, G, IV, KA, KY, KW, ML, HS, PA, PH, ZE) (see IDI, Ch 5, s14). As to what counts as an appropriate period of time, the same guidance states:

'The applicant does not need to have lived in Scotland throughout the entire period of their study. It is reasonable to expect that an overseas student may have returned to their country of origin during their vacations. Students may have also spent a period studying or working abroad during their studies.

Applicants should have lived in Scotland for an appropriate period of time. The suitability of the period of time spent living in Scotland should be assessed by the caseworker on the facts of each application, but the following should be used as general guidance:

- for courses lasting one academic year, the student can normally be expected to have lived in Scotland for at least 3 months;
- for courses lasting two academic years, the student can normally be expected to have lived in Scotland for at least 6 months;
- for courses lasting two academic years, the student can normally be expected to have lived in Scotland for at least 12 months.'

If the applicant's previous studies were sponsored by a government or an international scholarship agency, the sponsor's consent for the applicant to remain under the Fresh Talent scheme must be obtained. The maintenance and accommodation requirements must also be met.

Entry clearance, grant of leave and switching

Entry clearance is required in order to come to the UK in this capacity unless the applicant is a BN(O), a BOC, a BOTC, a BPP or a British subject under the BNA 1981 (▶see 1404, 1406–1414). However, applicants can switch in order to remain in this capacity i.e. without returning to get an entry clearance if they presently have leave as a student (including student nurses and those given leave to re-sit exams or write up a thesis) or under the Science and Engineering Graduate Scheme (SEGS).

Applicants can be granted leave under the scheme for up to a maximum of 24 months (which includes any time spent under SEGS). During their period of leave under the scheme, applicants can take any type of employment, self-employment or business without having to apply for a work permit or obtain other permission. At any time during their period of leave under the scheme, applicants may switch to remain:

- as work permit holders;
- under the HSMP;
- as business-persons; or
- as innovators.

Obviously, all of the relevant requirements of the rules for the above category must be satisfied before a Fresh Talent participant can switch into that category. Indeed, in order to get their leave under the Fresh Talent scheme in the first place, the applicant must intend to depart after their Fresh Talent leave if they do not later obtain leave in any of these categories.

PERMIT-FREE EMPLOYMENT OUTSIDE THE IMMIGRATION RULES

There are a number of other categories of person who can obtain admission to the UK in order to work without an IED, but which are *not* contained in the immigration rules. We set them out in turn below. Generally, in these categories applicants have to show an intention to work in the capacity for which they are granted leave, and their terms of leave prevent them from doing other work. They need to satisfy the maintenance and accommodation requirements, although normally these will be satisfied by showing that they are going to work in the relevant employment. Those coming as voluntary workers (▶see below) will obviously have to provide additional evidence of support.

Generally, where the period of stay is subject to an upper limit in the particular category, the applicant must intend to leave the UK at the end of the period granted to them. The short-term nature of the work will usually prevent opportunities for settlement (but see, in particular, the case of Steiner teachers, outlined below). In those cases where the published policy provides information about the admission of dependants, we have given details. Where no information is given, it is best to assume that dependants will have to obtain leave in their own right under the rules. In most cases, this is likely to be as visitors.

Entry clearance It will be noted that for several of the categories the Home Office has stated that entry clearance is mandatory (there are of course no immigration rules to provide for entry clearance which are specific to these categories). This means that all applicants must obtain entry clearance in order to be granted leave to enter or remain in that particular category. Of course, even where we have indicated that entry clearance is 'not mandatory', visa nationals still need entry clearance, as do all foreign nationals who are seeking entry for more than six months (▶see 80–3). Even if entry clearance is not strictly required, applicants should always consider whether it is best to obtain it (▶see 84).

Finding the concession Because these categories exist as concessions outside the immigration rules, the requirements under them can be changed quickly and without any amendments being made to the rules. For this reason, and also so that the further details of each scheme can be checked, at the end of each description we have given references to where the existing published policy can be found.

BUNAC students

'BUNAC' is the British Universities North America Club, and it arranges overseas visits for students studying at American and British Universities. The scheme allows both American students studying in America (or on study programmes abroad), and non-US-national US green card holders studying in America, to enter the UK on two separate occasions for a maximum of six months at a time. During their time in the UK they may take any employment, and indeed are expected to for at least part of their time. Before August 1999, BUNAC students who had been admitted had to get approval from a local Jobcentre before starting work, but this is no longer the case and approval is automatically deemed to have been given (letter of Department of Education and Employment to BUNAC, 26 August 1999). Applicants must be at least 18 years old and must obtain a BUNAC card before travelling, but entry clearance is not mandatory for entry for this purpose. Extensions beyond each six-month period will not be granted in the same capacity (see IDI, Ch 17, s1).

Film crew on location

Members of a film crew shooting on location in the UK are entitled to come to the UK for up to 12 months. Those who can benefit from this concession are those who are essential to the production of the film: actors, directors, producers and technicians. They must, however, be both employed and paid outside the UK. Entry clearance is mandatory, and extensions may be granted beyond the initial 12 months if there is further location work to be done. Admission is only permitted for location work. If there is to be some studio work, other pre- or post-production work, or if the person will actually be employed or paid in the UK, then a work permit will be required in the entertainers' category (▶see 444–7), and the immigration rules will have to be satisfied. Some amateur and professional entertainers may also be admitted as visitors (▶see 222–3). In September 2003 the Home Office stated that it intended to incorporate this concession into the rules, as part of the commitment made by ministers to parliament to incorporate all concessions into the rules (Home Office letter to ILPA, 5 September 2003); but at the time of writing this has not happened. (See the Work Permits (UK) website – 'Information about film crew on location'.)

'Gap-year' teachers/teaching assistants

This category enables non-EEA nationals to come to the UK in order to work in schools during a gap-year between their secondary and degree-level education. Until recently applicants had to be either 18 or 19 years old but this age-range has been widened to include 17-year-olds because, otherwise, some Australian young people who complete secondary education at 17 were excluded (Home Office letter to the Association of Regulated Immigration Advisers, dated 20 July 2005, which confirms that the IDI will be amended). Applicants must have completed their secondary education within the 12 months before the date on which they intend to enter the UK, and must have an unconditional offer of a place on a degree course overseas, and a written offer of employment for the whole academic year either as a teacher or a teaching assistant in a school in the UK. The work must involve the person in the teaching process in the classroom. Provided it is clear that the applicant will be able to support themselves and that they intend to leave at the end of the year, the applicant will be granted 12 months' leave in order to take up the post in the school. Extensions beyond this time in the same capacity will not be granted. Entry clearance is mandatory. There is no provision for dependants to be admitted. Others who are considering a gap-year in the UK might consider applying under the working holidaymakers' rules if they are Commonwealth nationals (▶see 235–43), or as voluntary workers if they are able to support themselves without paid work (▶see 472, and IDI, Ch 17, s11).

Japan Youth Exchange Scheme

This scheme enables young Japanese nationals aged between 18 and 25 at the time they are admitted to the UK to come for an extended holiday of up to 12 months. Extensions beyond 12 months will generally not be granted. Applicants up to the age of 30 will exceptionally be considered, if there was a 'genuine and compelling' reason which prevented them from applying earlier. The scheme has been running since 2001 and its purpose is to enable young people of British and Japanese nationality to experience and understand each other's countries. A maximum of 400 participants per year are permitted. During the time that they are here, the young Japanese nationals may take work which is incidental to their holiday. As a rule of thumb, this means that they may work full-time (which means anything more than 25 hours per week) for half the time they are here, or they can work part-time for more than half of the time they are in the UK.

Applicants may not set up their own businesses, work in a professional capacity, or do other work which is in pursuit of their careers. This does not, however, prevent all professional activity if it is at a junior level, or is temporary self-employed work with small outlay. So, window cleaning, for example, would not be excluded. Participants must also not provide services as professional sportspersons or entertainers. Some study is permitted, provided that it does not prevent the person from taking a holiday. Entry clearance is mandatory, and applicants will only be admitted once in this capacity. Children of people coming under the scheme will not be admitted and a spouse will only qualify if they are also granted admission under the scheme, or some other part of the immigration rules. Indeed, if the applicant is married, they must intend to come to the UK together with their spouse (see IDI, Ch 17, s10; Work Permits (UK) website – 'Information about the Japan Youth Exchange Scheme').

Jewish Agency

The purpose of the Jewish Agency is to promote settlement of Jews in Israel. Overseas nationals who are employees of the Jewish Agency in the UK will normally be granted leave to enter for 12 months, and will be expected to work in the office of the agency. (See IDI, Ch 17, s5, para. 2.)

Locally recruited staff of foreign missions

Provided that they were recruited abroad, the staff of embassies and foreign missions will normally be exempt from immigration control (►see 473–4). If the foreign national was either living in the UK or was physically present in the UK at the time they were offered their post, then they are not exempt and require leave to be in the UK. The Home Office has indicated that they may be granted leave outside the rules to work at the mission. Reference will first be made to the Foreign and Commonwealth Office, to confirm the acceptability of the person and the work which they are going to do. Leave will normally be granted for up to 12 months at a time, but this will not lead to settlement after four years. (See IDI, Ch 14, annex A, para. 3.2.)

Off-shore workers

Those working on installations at sea are not covered by UK immigration legislation, and therefore overseas nationals may take up work on off-shore installations without permission. However, these workers usually spend their shore-leave in the UK, and wish to base their family here. For this purpose they and their dependants do need leave, and will usually be given entry for 12 months at a time. The immigration officer must be satisfied that the only work that the applicant intends to do is offshore. (See IDI, Ch 17, s4.)

Research assistants to members of parliament

These people are normally students coming to the UK to learn about British government and politics, before returning abroad to resume their studies or their careers. Research assistants are given a maximum of 12 months' leave. Entry clearance is not mandatory for this purpose. (See IDI, Ch 17, s6.)

Representatives of overseas insurance companies

Representatives of overseas insurance companies will normally be given 12 months' leave in order to sell insurance to clients in the UK. The immigration authorities will need to be satisfied that the person is indeed representing an overseas insurance company, and that the actual processing and issuing of the policy will take place abroad. (See IDI Ch 17, s5, para. 1.)

Steiner establishments

These establishments (about 70 in number) are concerned with the teaching and development of children and adults, some of whom have learning difficulties. Overseas Steiner teachers at these institutions will normally be granted entry for 12 months at a time. A qualified teacher who has completed four years in this capacity is eligible to apply for settlement if the employer confirms that they still wish to employ the person concerned. Entry clearance is not mandatory for this purpose, but is recommended.

Those who wish to do training or voluntary work at a Steiner establishment can do so if the establishment is a registered charity and the period of their work will not be more than 12 months. They will then be admitted as voluntary workers (see 462). If, however, the Steiner establishment is not a charity, or if the employment is for over 12 months, the applicant should apply for a TWES permit. Even if the permit is refused, however, leave is still likely to be granted outside the rules, provided the application is bona fide. (See IDI, Ch 17, s7; IDI, Ch 17, annex A.)

Sportspersons

Sportspersons who will be based in the UK (even for only a season), or who are coming to join a British team, will require a work permit in the sportspersons' category (▶see 444–7). Other sportspersons may simply be coming for promotional reasons, to discuss contracts, or to take part in trials. They may be admitted as business visitors (▶see 220–1). Between these two groups, there is a further group who may be admitted under this category in permit-free employment outside the immigration rules for up to six months. Applications for any of the following will fit into this group:

- professional and amateur sportspersons coming to the UK to take part in a specific event, tournament or series of events as individual competitors or as members of overseas teams (the key is that they are coming for a visit rather than to be based in the UK);
- professional and amateur sportspersons coming to the UK to take part in one-off charitable sporting events such as testimonials and exhibition matches, but without receiving payment other than for expenses;
- amateur sportspersons may be admitted to join amateur clubs in the UK. They are permitted to receive board and lodging and reasonable expenses from the club only, and are not to provide coaching.

None of the above must take any work (paid or unpaid) outside of the sporting activity for which they are admitted, although the government has indicated that, in the case of amateurs, there should be a flexible approach to this requirement, in particular in relation to unpaid coaching. Entry clearance for this purpose is not mandatory but is recommended, particularly where a person is coming for a season. Extensions beyond six months will not normally be granted. Dependants of people admitted under this category who want to accompany them, should seek entry as visitors. (See IDI Ch 17, s8.)

Technical students

The International Association for the Exchange of Students of Technical Experience (IAESTE – which is linked to UNESCO) sponsors students so that they can obtain practical experience in industry during long vacations. In the UK, work placements are with public and private companies, local authorities and universities. The scheme generally benefits students in agriculture, architecture, commerce, economics, engineering, forestry, industrial design and technology. Leave will be given for up to a maximum of three months, usually during the summer vacation. Entry clearance is not mandatory under this category, but the student should carry an IAESTE permit. (See IDI, Ch 17, s5, para. 3.)

Voluntary workers

The Home Office allows people to come to the UK in order to do voluntary work for charitable organisations for up to 12 months. (For the ability of asylum seekers to carry out voluntary work, ▶see 696.) The work must be for a registered charity (including some religious organisations that are registered) and certain other recognised charitable bodies referred to in the IDI. These workers must provide their services on a purely voluntary basis, and the work, by its nature, must not be of a kind that would normally be offered at a wage. The work the volunteer does must be 'directed towards a worthy cause' and closely related to the aims of the organisation, and must involve the volunteer giving direct assistance to the beneficiaries of the work of the organisation. So the volunteer must not be simply doing clerical, administrative or maintenance work. While volunteers may not be paid, they may receive amounts for expenses and subsistence and be provided with accommodation as a benefit in kind. These benefits must be within the exemptions from the national minimum wage legislation. The maximum period allowed at any one time is 12 months. Those here as volunteers are not able to take or seek long-term employment, but there is nothing to prevent them returning as many times as they like for voluntary work. If a volunteer does intend to return, the Home Office would normally expect to see some gap between trips. Entry clearance is not mandatory. (See IDI, Ch 17, s9; IDI, Ch 17, annex B.)

PEOPLE WHO ARE EXEMPT FROM IMMIGRATION CONTROL

Certain special groups of people are 'exempt' from immigration control, which means that, although they are not British citizens, they do not need leave to enter or remain in the UK. These groups are mainly defined by the work they will do, which is why we include them here. Provided that they are recognised as being exempt, they may enter and remain in the UK and carry out their duties without an IED, without leave, and without having to fall into any of the categories of admission in the immigration rules. Proof of entitlement may be in the form of a letter of accreditation or authorisation from the government or organisation concerned. In relation to diplomats, it may be that the Foreign and Commonwealth Office will have issued the person with a certificate under the Diplomatic Privileges Act showing that the person is entitled to diplomatic immunity. Entry clearances are issued stating that the person is 'exempt' from immigration control and, on their first arrival, their passport may be endorsed with a stamp showing the entry. Where a person arrives claiming an exemption but does not have a satisfactory form of proof, provided there is no reason to suspect them of deception, temporary admission would normally be granted until their status can be confirmed.

It is sometimes the case that a person who is in the UK and who is exempt from control seeks some form of evidence to demonstrate their status. If so, it is possible to ask the Home Office to issue a letter of notification of exemption (specimen letters can be seen at IDI, Ch. 14, annex E). The Protocol Department of the Foreign and Commonwealth Office also issues identity cards to those based at diplomatic missions in the UK, and can be used as confirmation of status. Note that people are generally only exempt for as long as they continue to have the status which gave them the exemption (for this and grace periods, ▶see 475–6).

The main groups of those who are exempt are listed below. We have excluded less significant groups and small groups such as Heads of State and their families. The specific details relating to exempt groups are contained in section 8 1971 Act and the Immigration (Exemption from Control) Order 1972, SI 1972/1613. For details about whether periods spent in the UK while exempt from immigration control count under the rules relating to long residence, ▶see 154.

People with diplomatic exemption

Those within this group are fully exempt from immigration control, including being exempt from deportation during the period they qualify. It is this group which most frequently gives rise to immigration issues or problems. Generally, in order to qualify for this exemption, the person needs to be classed as a 'member of a diplomatic mission', although high-ranking officers of organisations such as the UN also have diplomatic exemption.

The 'members' of a diplomatic missions are: the head of the mission; the diplomatic staff; the administrative, technical and service staff of the mission (such as chauffeurs, cleaners and cooks). It should be noted that the Foreign and Commonwealth Office is given lists of their diplomatic staff by the countries concerned. Not all people working for embassies will be exempt. For example, if an employee is paying local taxes, they may not be exempt from control. Another important requirement in order to qualify for the exemption, for employees who are not part of the diplomatic staff, is that that they must have been recruited to work for the mission while they were living abroad. However, locally recruited staff who are not exempt may still be granted leave in a permit-free capacity outside the immigration rules (▶see 470). Private servants of individual diplomats are usually not exempt from control, unless they are a servant of the head of the mission and are employed and paid directly by the sending state (see IDI, Ch 14, s1, annex B, para. 2). Otherwise, private servants of diplomats can qualify under the rules (▶see 456–7).

Family members Members of diplomats' families who form part of the household are also exempt from control. This includes spouses, children under 18 and dependent children over 18 who are in full-time education, other relatives who formed part of the household abroad, and other close relatives who have no one else to look after them. Unmarried partners are not exempt, but the Home Office has said that it will consider applications from them under the requirements of the immigration rules relating to unmarried partners, provided that the relationship is recognised as durable by the sending state, the relationship is akin to marriage, and the couple intend to live together in the UK for the duration of the posting (see IDI, Ch 14, s1, para. 9 and, for the unmarried partners' rules, ▶see 322–3 with reference also to 293–4 onwards).

Government representatives and international officials

Certain government representatives and other international officials are also exempt. This group includes: consular officers and employees (different from diplomats) who are appointed by their government to be based in a foreign state to represent their countries' commercial interests; members and representatives of foreign governments visiting the UK on official business; senior officials of international organisations such as the International Bank for Reconstruction and Development, and certain senior officials attending conferences in the UK. If they are not exempt, certain overseas government employees may be admitted under the immigration rules (▶see 459).

Family members who form part of the exempt person's household are also exempt. As with diplomatic exemption (▶see above), consular officers and employees of countries that have agreed a consular convention with the UK are exempt from all controls, including deportation, while the exemption is in place (the countries concerned are listed in the Schedule to the Exemption from Control Order, referred to above, and a list is maintained at IDI Ch 14, s1, para. 2.2). None of the other persons in this group is exempt from deportation.

Armed forces

Members of the UK armed forces, members of a Commonwealth force undergoing training in the UK with UK armed forces, and members of visiting armed forces coming to the UK at the invitation of the government, are exempt. These armed forces members are not exempt from deportation, however. Dependants are not exempt, and must seek leave to be in the UK. Before 15 March 2005, dependants had to apply outside the immigration rules but, from that date, specific provision has been made within the rules (paras 276AD–276AI HC 395 inserted by HC 346). Applicants must not intend to stay beyond the entitlement to remain in the UK of their principal and the maintenance and accommodation requirements must be met. In cases of children joining one parent only, the 'sole responsibility' or 'exclusion undesirable' rules must be met unless the other parent is dead. Leave will be granted for up to four years at a time.

Crew of ships, trains and aircraft

The law relating to crew members varies slightly, depending on whether they belong to a ship, aircraft or train. They are also complex. However, in very general terms, a person who arrives in the UK as part of a crew aboard one of these vessels, and who also intends to leave within a short period of time as a crew member, will be exempt from control. This exemption does not apply to those who are subject to deportation orders, or who were refused leave to enter on their last arrival in the UK, or who the immigration officer decides to subject to examination. Crew members who 'jump ship', and do not return as crew members aboard their own or another vessel, can be detained and removed from the UK under the 1971 Act.

Ceasing to be exempt and leave granted while exempt

Generally, an exemption from immigration control only continues for as long as the person keeps the status for which it was given. So, for example, when a person who is exempt from control leaves their job at an embassy, they cease to be exempt from immigration control. They then require leave to remain in the UK.

In order to prevent these people from being in 'limbo' at the point at which their job ends, from 1 March 2000 the 1999 Act made special provision for what happens to them (inserted as s8A 1971 Act). When such persons cease to be exempt from control, they are automatically treated as though they have been granted leave to remain in the UK for 90 days, beginning on the day that they ceased to be exempt. If they wish to stay longer in the UK after this period, they must apply to the Home Office within this time, and will be considered under the immigration rules. If they are refused, they will have a full right of appeal. If they do not apply within the 90-day period, they will become overstayers, and can be removed. These special provisions do not, however, apply to those who are exempt as crew members or members of armed forces.

Leave granted while exempt It may be that, either before a person became exempt or during the period of their exemption, they have been granted limited, or even indefinite, leave. If a person was granted leave during the period of their exemption, this will have been by mistake, and the Home Office acknowledges that this happens from time to time. If the leave was granted before the person became exempt, then our view is that, if it has not expired already by the end of the period of exemption, it must still be valid. If the leave was granted during the period of the exemption and is still unexpired after it, it is arguable that it is still valid. However, failing this, the Home Office has accepted that such erroneous grants are 'normally to be regarded as a pledge of public faith', and that, on an application after the person has ceased to be exempt, the leave will if necessary be endorsed again in the applicant's passport (see IDI, Ch 14, s1, para. 8.4). If the leave granted was limited leave and it will run out before the automatic 90-day extension (▶see above), then the person will still be treated as having leave until the end of the 90-day period (see s8A(3) 1971 Act).

16 Business purposes

As with employees (see Chapters 14 and 15), the immigration rules allow people to come to the UK for business purposes in carefully restricted circumstances. This chapter covers those circumstances. We look at:

- business-people (immediately below);
- lawyers (▶480–1);
- innovators (▶481–3);
- the Highly Skilled Migrant Programme (▶483–91);
- investors (▶491–2);
- writers, composers and artists (▶492–3); and
- retired persons of independent means (▶493–5).

The chapter also deals with the consequences, for both workers and their employers, of unlawfully working or entering into business in the UK (▶see 495–500).

Several further aspects of 'business' immigration are dealt with elsewhere in the book:

- The rights of EEA nationals, and also nationals of those countries which have concluded an 'Association Agreement' with the European Union to come to the UK, for self-employment or other business purposes, are covered in Section 6, which deals with free-movement rights (▶see 516–7 for a summary and Chapter 20).

- Section 6 also covers the less restrictive 'old' business immigration rules, which may be applied to Turkish nationals as a result of the 'Ankara Agreement' (Association Agreement with Turkey) (▶see 588–9).

- Persons coming to the UK for very limited business purposes may be admitted as 'business' visitors (▶see 220–3).

BUSINESS CATEGORIES

The business categories in which people may be admitted to the UK that are considered below are: general business-people; lawyers; innovators; highly skilled migrants; investors; writers, composers or artists; retired persons of independent means. We have considered the Highly Skilled

Migrants' Programme (HSMP) as part of the business categories because it enables people to set up in business as well as to take employment.

Applications for leave to remain, or for settlement for those applying under the categories dealt with in this chapter, should be made using form BUS and sent to the Business Case Unit (BCU, ►see 133 for contact details), which transferred from Croydon to Sheffield in February 2004 and became part of Work Permits (UK). There are two exceptions to this. Firstly, applications for leave to remain under HSMP should be made using form FLR(IED), and HSMP settlement applications on the ordinary SET(O) form. Secondly, applications to remain and for settlement made by writers, composers or artists are made on the general Home Office forms (►see 128, 129), as that category has not (at least as yet) transferred with the BCU to Sheffield.

Business-people

The immigration rules dealing with business-people cover those seeking to establish themselves in the UK as 'sole traders' (i.e. self-employed), or in partnerships, or as part of a UK-registered company (paras 200–210 HC 395). Not many applications are now made under these rules, because the requirements concerning the amount of investment and the need to show minimum levels of employment are very demanding. Significant work is also required in order to prepare applications. Most of those who would qualify to enter the UK under these rules will also be able to qualify under HSMP, or under the Innovator rules, and many have opted for those alternative routes. By contrast, applications by business-people under the less demanding rules of the EU Association Agreements have continued to run at high levels (►see Chapter 20).

Entry clearance is compulsory in order for people to establish themselves as business-people in the UK. In addition, all of the following requirements must be met in order for an application to succeed.

- Applicants must have at least £200,000 capital of their own to put into the business. The business should also need this amount of new financial investment. This has to be readily available capital, either in the UK already or easily transferable to the UK. The immigration authorities are entitled to ask about the origin of the funds. So borrowing money on a short-term basis from a wealthy friend will not be adequate. If the money is given by someone else, then an irrevocable deed of gift should be provided.

- Applicants should be involved full-time in running the business, and should be able to meet their share of any liabilities and show that there is a genuine need for their time and investment in the business. This means that they should not have any other time-consuming activities either in or outside the UK. They will not be allowed to engage in ordinary employment. This is intended to ensure that this part of the rules is not simply being used as a way for wealthy people who would not otherwise qualify under the rules to come to the UK, for example to join their relatives.

- Applicants must have either a controlling or an equal interest in the business, with a proportionate financial investment in it. This means that the applicant must either have more than a 50 per cent interest in the business, or else be one of a number of partners or directors with an equal interest in it (although the applicant's interest must not be too diluted). This is to make clear that the applicant is the genuine owner of the business, rather than one of its employees.

- The share of the profits that the business-person will receive must be adequate to support them and any of their dependants without recourse to public funds, and without the business-person working other than for the business. There must be no intention to work except for the business. If the applicant is setting up a new business, then plainly, in addition to the funds they are bringing to establish the business, they must have enough left over to support themselves and their family until the business can expected to make a profit.

- The business must create two full-time posts for people already settled here. If the business is an existing one, the services and investment provided by the new business-person must create these posts. If it is proposed to establish a new business, the new business must create the posts.

Business plan If the business is a new one, applicants are required to produce a detailed business plan setting out the objectives of the business and the investment and employment involved. The plan should also include the following financial projections: opening balance sheet, trading and profit/loss account, overhead expenses. If the applicant is joining an existing business, they must be able to produce the audited accounts of the business for the previous two years, and a written explanation of the terms on which they will be joining – this may also involve a business plan to show how the applicant's contribution is going to be used.

Grant of leave and extensions Business-people are normally granted leave to enter for a year initially, on conditions restricting work so that they can only work for the business. Towards the end of the year, the business-person may apply to extend their leave. There must be evidence that the business is continuing with the applicant's active and full-time involvement (without their taking other employment), that it is sufficient to support the business-person and any dependants, that the required investment has been made, and that the required new employment has been created. The immigration rules also require the production of audited accounts at the 12-month stage, but this will not be insisted upon in the case of a person who has set up a new business. In such a case, draft or management accounts will be enough (IDI, Ch 6, s1, para. 4.3). Provided the rules are met, an extension of three years will normally be granted.

It may be the case, however, that the applicant is not able to meet the full requirements of the rules at the 12-month stage, but that there is every chance that these will be met in due course. For example, it may be that only one new employee has so far been taken on, but there are plans to take on a further employee shortly when the business allows. In such cases, caseworkers can be asked to exercise some discretion and, if they are not prepared to grant the ordinary three-year extension, at least to grant a further 12 months. This will give a further opportunity to satisfy what are fairly stringent rules. It should be noted that, in such cases, the Home Office will treat the four-year period for qualifying for settlement as beginning again (IDI, Ch 6, s1, para. 4.6).

For the rules about switching to stay in the UK under the business rules, ▶see Chapter 7.

Dependants The spouse, unmarried partner and children under 18 of the business-person may be granted leave to enter and settlement in line with the business-person, provided they obtain entry clearance. They may also be granted an extension of stay in line with the business-person. Sons and daughters who reach the age of 18 after being admitted as the dependants of a business-person are still able to obtain extensions while in the UK. (For full details relating to the dependants of workers and business people, ▶see 352–4, 356.)

Settlement Settlement may be granted to the business-person and their dependants after four continuous years in the UK in this category. The business must be continuing with the business-person's active involvement, and it must be making enough profit to support them. Full yearly accounts must be provided. (For details about the calculation of the four-year period, ▶see 437–9.)

Lawyers

Earlier versions of the immigration rules provided for a separate category of self-employed people. It was intended in part to provide a route for people who wanted to set up as self-employed professionals – for example, as architects, accountants or doctors in private practice. These self-employed groups are now covered by the above business category, and it may be hard for them to meet the financial and investment requirements. Some, however, may now qualify under the HSMP. Those wishing to enter as General Medical Practitioners should certainly apply under the HSMP where they receive favourable treatment (▶487).

However, there is a concession outside the rules for self-employed overseas lawyers who are entering in order to establish a new practice, or to be a partner or a tenant in an existing one (see IDI Ch 6, s1, annex D). They do not need to have £200,000 capital to invest, nor do they have to create employment for anyone else, although they do have to show that they have sufficient funds to establish the business (if it is a new one) and to maintain themselves. Applicants may be either solicitors or barristers, provided that they can show that they have been admitted by the relevant UK professional body. Alternatively, applicants may be consultants in overseas law who are specialists in a foreign legal system. Entry clearance is mandatory, and leave will initially be given for 12 months, with the prospect of extending for 12 months at a time and settlement being granted after four years.

Innovators

On 4 September 2000 the government introduced a pilot scheme outside the immigration rules aimed at attracting outstanding entrepreneurs from overseas who will set up in business in the UK, bringing significant economic benefits to this country. The scheme is open to those who wish to set up in business in any sector, but the category was largely designed for talented entrepreneurs in the science and new technology fields – for example, those involved in the area of 'e-business'. The purpose of the scheme is to import human ideas and potential, rather than capital. There is thus no minimum level of investment required, and third-party funding for the business project is permitted.

The Home Office was happy with the scheme during its pilot period, and on 16 September 2002 it announced that the scheme would be extended indefinitely, stating that during the two-year pilot '112 of the most talented people in the world have come to Britain to set up high-tech businesses in areas such as e-commerce, electronic share dealing and music industry technology'. On 1 April 2003 the scheme was brought within the immigration rules (see paras 210A-210H HC 395 inserted by HC 538).

Qualifying as an innovator

The first requirement under the rules is that the applicant 'is approved by the Home Office as a person who meets the criteria specified by the Secretary of State for entry under the innovator scheme at the time that approval is sought'. So, as with the Immigration Employment Document (IED) categories (work permits, etc.), the actual requirements for qualifying as an innovator are only partly set by the immigration rules. The specific criteria continue to be set outside the rules (see, in addition to the above rules, 'Innovators – guide for applicants', on the Work Permits UK website). Unlike the IED categories, however, no separate application is required for a particular employment document or 'approval'. Only one application is necessary, and the immigration authorities then consider both whether the applicant can be approved as an innovator and whether the rules are satisfied.

The requirements contained in the guidance outside the rules overlap with the rules themselves. For this reason, and because they are considered in one process, it is easiest here to roll both together. So, in order to qualify for admission as an innovator, applicants are required to show all of the following:

- their proposed business will bring exceptional economic benefits to the UK;

- they have the skills, experience and formal qualifications necessary to the proposed business;
- there is sufficient initial funding in place for the business, at least for the first six months;
- the business will lead, within 12 months, to the creation of at least two full-time jobs for people settled in the UK;
- the applicant will maintain a minimum five per cent shareholding of the equity capital in the business throughout their stay in the UK as an innovator;
- the applicant will be able to support themself and any dependants without recourse to public funds, and without taking employment other than for the business.

Evidence for innovators In order to show that the above requirements are met, applicants should submit all of the following basic documents:

- a full curriculum vitae setting out their business experience, educational qualifications and personal experience;
- a business plan dealing both with the viability of the business and its economic benefit to the UK;
- a management plan explaining the proposed management team structure necessary to run the business;
- a completed self-assessment form (available on the Work Permits UK web-site) (see below).

Self-assessment form The innovators' self-assessment form is not compulsory, but it is intended to help applicants see for themselves whether they are likely to qualify. The BCU will verify the scores against the evidence submitted. The form is divided into three sections (personal characteristics, business viability, economic benefit to the UK). Each section has a minimum score that must be reached and, in addition, applicants must score an overall total of at least 100 points. All the above basic documents must themselves be supported by further evidence. For example, previous business experience should be demonstrated by registered accounts, and financial references are required to show details of outside investments which will be made into the business. Detailed guidance is given in annexes which are attached to the 'Guide for applicants' referred to above, and also on the self-assessment form. Entry clearance is mandatory in order to be admitted. After the application has been submitted to the ECO, it will be referred back to the BCU in the UK to be considered. The BCU aims to deal with applications within two weeks of receipt, but they may take longer to find their way physically to and from the entry clearance post.

Grant of leave and extensions If the above requirements are satisfied, entry clearance will be granted giving leave to enter for up to 18 months. At the end of this period, extensions may be granted for up to 30 months at a time, provided that applicants can demonstrate, by producing accounts and other trading materials, all of the following:

- they have established a profitable trading business which is sufficient to support them;
- the business continues to meet the requirements for approval by the Home Office under the scheme;
- the two full-time posts have been created;
- they have kept their minimum required shareholding in the business.

Settlement After four continuous years in the UK in this capacity (▶see 438–9), during which all of these requirements are met, innovators are eligible to apply for settlement. Dependants of innovators may be granted leave in line with them on the same basis as for business-persons (▶see above, 352–4).

Switching Those already in the UK who obtain approval under the innovator scheme, and who satisfy the other requirements above, may switch to innovator status if they were previously granted leave as work permit holders (not including TWES permits); as students (who graduated in the UK): as working holidaymakers; as postgraduate doctors, dentists or trainee general practitioners; under the Science and Engineering Graduate Scheme (SEGS) under the Fresh Talent: Working in Scotland Scheme; under the HSMP or as a business person. See Chapter 7 for full details about switching.

Highly Skilled Migrant Programme

In January 2002, the government introduced the Highly Skilled Migrant Programme (HSMP). It formed a central part of the economic migration policy set out in the 2002 White Paper, *Secure Borders, Safe Haven*, which stated that the overall aim of the Programme was to attract 'high human capital individuals, who have the qualifications and skills required by UK businesses to compete in the global marketplace'.

Note it is included in this chapter because it covers both employees and those who wish to set up in business.

Initially, the HSMP was operated as a policy outside the immigration rules, but from 1 April 2003 it has been a category of admission under the rules (paras 135A–135H HC 395 inserted by HC 538). The main requirement of the rules is that the applicant has a 'document issued by the Home Office confirming that he meets . . . the criteria specified by the Secretary of State for entry to the United Kingdom under the [HSMP]'. That document is an 'Immigration Employment Document' (IED) and so the procedures operated under the HSMP are in many ways similar to those for the other IEDs (▶see 418–20, 430–4, 439–40). So the real meat of the scheme setting out the requirements for qualifying continues to be set outside the rules, and can be found in Guidance Notes contained with the application forms on the Work Permits (UK) website. The scheme is also dealt with in the IDI (Ch 5, s11 and annexes Z1–Z8).

The HSMP has proved highly popular. It is flexible, covering people who want either to take employment or to set up in business as self-employed persons or otherwise. It has the advantage over work permits that applicants do not need a specific job offer; and it has the advantage over the main business categories (see above) that no detailed business plan is required, and it is not necessary to create jobs or to invest a minimum sum in the UK. As a result, the number of applications has been high, which has resulted in significant delays. Between January and October 2002, there were 2,041 applications of which 953 were approved and 14 had been successful on review. When the scheme began, applications were often processed within a day or so. Subsequently, the system suffered from very serious delays.

Work Permits (UK) state that they will prioritise applications which are urgent, often because a job has been offered. There is an 'urgent request' *pro forma* on the 'Working in the UK' website which can be used to make requests. Note that, although it was previously the case that urgent requests would not be considered until an application had been outstanding for six weeks, this is no longer applied. Urgent requests will be considered at any time within the case-working process (letter to Pennington's Solicitors from Work Permits UK, 16 May 2005). Because of the delays, some people have opted to pursue the work permit route, with the possibility of a switch to HSMP (which is possible under the rules) at a later stage, once the efficiency of the scheme has improved.

The HSMP criteria

Like the innovator scheme, the HSMP criteria operate largely on a 'points scored' basis. After its first year of operation, in which many of the successful applications had come from professionals working in finance in North America and Europe, significant changes were made to the scoring criteria. The intention of these changes, which were made on 28 January 2003, was to attract applications from people in more diverse sectors and from low-income countries. The criteria were significantly changed again on 31 October 2003, as follows:

- the introduction of a less demanding scoring regime for those aged under 28 (referred to as 'young persons');
- the reduction of the overall points required from 75 to 65;
- the granting of additional points where the principal applicant has a suitably qualified spouse or unmarried partner.

The number of HSMP applications increased dramatically after the reduction in the number of points required. The Home Office has stated in a series of 'questions and answers' published on its website that the new criteria will not affect those who have already been admitted on the basis of the old scoring system.

HSMP applicants are allocated points according to six criteria. The number of points that are awarded – dependent on how the applicant scores on each criterion – are set out in the table below. The first column applies to those aged 28 or over on the date that the application is received. The second column applies to those aged under 28 on that date. Further notes on each of the criteria and the terms used in the table follow below.

HIGHLY SKILLED MIGRANT PROGRAMME POINTS SYSTEM

A minimum of 65 points needs to be scored in total by adding together the scores under the six criteria. Note that, provided at least 65 points are scored in total, it is not necessary to score under each of the criteria.

	Points (applicants aged 28 years or over)	*Points (applicants aged under 28 years)*
1 Educational qualifications		
• PhD	30	30
• Master's degree	25	25
• Graduate degree (eg BA, BSc)	15	15
2 Work Experience		
• Five years in graduate level job	25	–
• PhD and three years in graduate level job	25	–
• Five years in graduate level job including two years in a senior or specialist role	35	–
• Ten years in graduate level job with five years in senior or specialist role	50	–
• Two years graduate level experience	–	25
• Four years graduate level experience	–	35
• Four years graduate level experience including one year at senior or specialist role	–	50
3 Past Earnings (per annum) (for a further explanation of this criterion, ▶see 487 and see also 1522–4)		
Income band 1 (ranging from £3,500 for code E countries to £40,000 for code A countries)	25	–
Income band 2 (ranging from £8,750 for code E countries to £100,000 for code A countries)	35	–
Income band 3 (ranging from £21,875 for code E countries to £250,000 for code A countries)	50	–

continued...

HIGHLY SKILLED MIGRANT PROGRAMME POINTS SYSTEM cont.

	Points (applicants aged 28 years or over)	Points (applicants aged under 28 years)
Income band 1 (ranging from £2,350 for code E countries to £27,000 for code A countries)	–	25
Income band 2 (ranging from £3,500 for code E countries to £40,000 for code A countries)	–	35
Income band 3 (ranging from £5,250 for code E countries to £60,000 for code A countries)	–	50
4 Achievement in Chosen Field		
• Significant achievement (having contributed significantly to development in field of work)	15	15
• Exceptional achievement (recognised beyond field of expertise, and having obtained international recognition)	25	25
5 Priority Applications		
The only category of applicants who can currently be deemed to have a 'priority application' are those who are legally entitled to work in general medical practice in the UK	50	50
6 Spouse or unmarried partner		
If qualified to degree level or is presently or has previously been in employment in a graduate-level job	10	10

Educational qualifications Qualifications must be equivalent to the recognised British degree standards. It will be necessary to produce evidence to show that the courses have been completed and the relevant qualifications awarded. In order to check qualifications, Work Permits (UK) use an external company called UK Naric which has a complete database of equivalent qualifications for all other countries outside the UK. Naric themselves can be contacted at UK NARIC, ECCTIS Ltd, Oriel House, Oriel Road, Cheltenham GL50 1XP. Their website address is www.naric.org.uk. This enables applicants to check their position before submitting their applications.

Work experience Where 'graduate-level' experience is referred to, it is not necessary that the person actually had a degree at the time the work was done, but simply that the level of the work would normally require the person to have a degree. Where 'senior' level experience is referred to, this generally includes a person who is running their own business and who employs several staff, or a board-level position in a small company, or a departmental head in a large business. Where a 'specialist' role is referred to, this means work requiring a high level of technical or artistic expertise.

Past earnings The points scored here depend upon the applicant's income earned over the preceding 12 months. Because income levels differ from country to country, the points that can be earned are weighted depending upon the country in which the applicant has been working (note *not* their country of nationality). Countries are categorised into four codes (A to E). There are then three income bands, to which separate points are allocated. Each country code has a different threshold minimum income level in order for a salary to come within each of the income bands. Obviously, the points system here is liable to change, but for a current full list of the countries and the codes assigned to them, together with a full list of the applicable income band for each code, ▶see 1522–4. The up-to-date information can also be found annexed to the HSMP Guidance Notes, published on the Work Permits (UK) website. Note that the country code applied depends on the country in which the applicant has been living and working, rather than on their country of nationality. The country list was designed by the Home Office in consultation with the Treasury and an external consultant and is apparently based on World Bank data of Gross Domestic Product per capita. Only earned income counts – applicants are not able to include private incomes from investments unless they help to manage the company from which the dividends are received.

Achievement in a chosen field A 'significant' achievement is shown by those who are known within their field to have made an important contribution. 'Exceptional' achievement covers those who are at the top of their profession, and are recognised beyond their own field of expertise. People can score by producing evidence to show how their work has been acknowledged and contributed to the development of their field. Where possible the evidence should be from an independent source. Annex Z4 to the IDI at Chapter 5, section 11 provides some examples. It is clear from this that the 'exceptional achievement' category is for those who have obtained awards such as the Nobel Prize or *Palme D'Or*. An example of 'significant achievement' given in the guidance is a leading computer architect who took a year out to write a book on computing architecture which received industry critical acclaim.

Priority applications The only priority applications so far recognised are for General Medical Practitioners. Applicants must hold full GMC registration as well as other relevant certificates, and must intend to work as GPs in the UK. Full details of how an applicant can obtain the evidence required to qualify in this area is contained in section one of the *GP Registrar Scheme: Vocational Training for General Medical Practice*. This can be found at www.doh.gov.uk/medicaltrainingintheuk/gptraining.htm.

Qualified spouse/partner In order to score additional points, the applicant's spouse or partner must either be educated to degree level, or have past or present experience of employment at graduate level. The spouse/partner must be intending to accompany the applicant to the UK, and must not already be settled in the UK. If the couple are unmarried, they must have been living together in a relationship akin to marriage that has subsisted for two years or more, and previous marriages/relationships must have permanently broken down.

Further requirements A further requirement (although no specific points are awarded) is that applicants must show that they will be able to continue their careers in the UK. In order to determine this, the application form asks what type of work is intended, for evidence of proficiency in English (where this is necessary to the work), and for evidence that the applicant has the necessary qualifications and/or professional memberships to work in their chosen area. The form also requests details of existing efforts to find work and offers of work.

MBA Graduates under the HSMP Scheme

From 13 April 2005, the Home Office introduced a further aspect of the HSMP specially designed for MBA graduates from 50 top business schools. This announcement was made in the 2004 Budget, and the initiative was intended to attract talented managers to the UK. The list of schools will be reviewed and published annually. The list was compiled by the Treasury. The details of the 'MBA Provision' are set out in the IDIs at Chapter 5, section 11, annex Z7. The list of eligible MBA programmes is contained at annex Z8. Harvard Business School tops the list and many of the schools on the list are American. Ten of the programmes are offered in the UK. The Treasury will review the list annually. The list is based on (1) the salary that graduates earn three years after graduation; (2) the employability of graduates three months after graduation. Successful applicants are automatically awarded the minimum (65) points necessary to qualify under the HSMP. In order to qualify under the MBA provision, applicants must:

- have graduated from an MBA course on the list of eligible programmes at the time that MBA course is on the list; and
- show that they will be able to continue their chosen career in the UK.

Applicants who did an MBA on a programme which is not on the eligible list may still qualify by applying under the HSMP but they will have to qualify under the normal point-scoring criteria.

Where an applicant qualifies under the MBA provision, as with other HSMP applicants, they must also satisfy the immigration rules relating to the HSMP in order to be admitted (►see below).

How to apply under HSMP

HSMP is an IED category (►see 418–9), and therefore the first stage is for applicants to obtain approval under the HSMP from Work Permits (UK).

Applications should be made by submitting form HSMP 1 (for those aged 28 years or over at the date of application) or form HSMP 1 (28) (for those aged under 28 years) to the Doncaster HSMP office. The correct fee must be paid and the form should be accompanied by the supporting evidence indicated on the form and in the Guidance Notes. The IDI provides the following list as *examples* of evidence which is required but stresses that the particular evidence needed will depend upon the application: academic certificates, academic references, employer references, evidence of ownership of business, wage slips, income tax returns, audited company accounts showing personal income, CV with supporting testimonials, published work, press articles, scholarship/research awards, industry awards/prizes, research output, (IDI, Ch 5, s11, annex Z1, para. 4 and see further documents at para. 4.1). Separate evidence will obviously be required to satisfy the immigration rules (below).

As with other IED categories, there is a right to request a review if Work Permits (UK) refuse to approve the HSMP application (▶see 439–40). Review applications should be made on form HSMP (Rev). Entry clearance is mandatory for those who are abroad (▶see below for others), and so after the applicant has received an official HSMP approval letter (the IED), they should within three months apply for entry clearance (for applications for entry clearance generally, ▶see 78–94).

The immigration rules In order to qualify for entry clearance under the immigration rules, in addition to producing the approval from Work Permits (UK), applicants need to demonstrate both of the following (paras 135A–135H HC 395):

• The ability to support themselves and any dependants without recourse to public funds. Applicants will need to show that their potential income will be enough to meet their needs and, if necessary, that they have enough savings or other resources to support themselves while seeking work or setting up in business. Correspondence between Eversheds Solicitors and Work Permits (UK) dated 4 July 2002 confirmed that the funds relied on do not have to be held directly by the applicant in the UK; they could be held overseas or provided by a sponsor. The existence of an offer of employment will clearly be taken into account.

• The intention to make the UK their main home. Note that the HSMP forms themselves contain a declaration to this effect, which applicants are asked to sign.

Leave, dependants, extensions Leave is initially granted for a period of 12 months. Spouses, unmarried partners and children of those admitted under the HSMP may be granted leave and indefinite leave in line with their sponsor. They will also be permitted to work.

A person who was granted entry to the UK under the HSMP may apply to extend their stay under this category by completing Form FLR (IED) (▶see 430–4 for this process). As well as continuing to meet all of the above rules, these applicants will need to show that, during the time they have been here under the HSMP, they have taken all reasonable steps to become economically active in employment, self-employment or both. Note that there is no absolute requirement to have actually become economically active during the 12-month period, although a good explanation will be required if an applicant has not become active. Additionally, if a person has not yet obtained employment or established a business, it may be more difficult for them to show that they have sufficient funds to support themselves. Where an extension is granted, it will be for a period of up to three years.

HSMP switching

'Switching' to remain in the UK on the basis of the HSMP is allowed for certain categories of people. Those permitted to switch under the immigration rules are, firstly, people who were granted entry as a working holidaymaker. Secondly, those who either entered as or were granted leave to remain as: work permit holders (although not those granted leave under the TWES scheme); students (who have graduated in the UK); certain postgraduate doctors, postgraduate dentists and trainee medical practitioners; as a working holidaymaker; in order to take the PLAB test or to undertake a clinical attachment under the Science and Engineering Graduate Scheme (SEGS); as innovators or under the Fresh Talent: Working in Scotland scheme. (For full details about switching, ▶see 161–87.) Switching applicants are also required to apply both for approval (using the HSMP forms) and for an extension of leave on form FLR(IED), and to pay the appropriate fees.

Settlement under HSMP

Applications for settlement may be made after four continuous years of leave (▶see 438–9 for the interpretation of 'continuous') under the HSMP, during which all of the HSMP requirements were met. Applicants must be lawfully economically active in the UK in either employment, self-employment, or both.

In August 2002, the Home Office confirmed that it would permit those applying to settle under the HSMP to combine time spent in other categories leading to settlement to make up the four years. When the HSMP was brought within the rules on 1 April 2003, the settlement rules themselves were drafted so as to allow a person who presently has leave under the HSMP to add together time spent in a whole range of categories so as to make up the four years required (see para. 135G(i), (iii) inserted by HC 538). Under these rules, time can be added together where other leave was granted in any of the following (i.e. any category under paras 128–319 HC 395):

- in any of the business categories under the rules referred to in this chapter;
- as a work permit holder (although not under TWES);

- in any of the long-term permit-free categories under the immigration rules referred to in Chapter 15;
- under SEGS;
- as a person exercising rights of access to a child resident in the UK (►see 372–5);
- as a family member of a person in the UK under any of the categories dealt with in Section 4 (family members).

If an application is made for settlement that relies upon a period during which the applicant was not here under the HSMP, then, as with the HSMP requirements, there must have been no recourse to public funds during the non-HSMP period.

Investors

The 1994 immigration rules created the category of 'investor' to attract to the UK persons of high net worth prepared to invest at least £750,000 in the UK. They are permitted to enter into business in the UK, but they must not take employment. While the government insists that the UK is competing for these persons of high net worth, it is significant that an average of only 26 investors per year have been admitted under this category since 1994. The rules have been amended from 13 January 2004 so as to allow investors in certain circumstances to rely upon funds which have been loaned to them (paras 224–31 HC 395 as amended by HC 176). These changes are again intended to enable the UK to compete to with other countries. The change is apparently based upon the Canadian experience, where investors have made a significant contribution to the economy.

Two options Therefore, there are now two ways of satisfying the investor rules. Under the first option, the investor must have at least £1 million of their own money under their control in the UK. Under the second option, the investor must own personal assets which have a value of over £2 million and have at least £1 million under their control in the UK, which may include money which has been loaned. Liabilities will of course be deducted to arrive at a net value. In the second option, the loaned money must have come from an authorised financial institution ('AFI'), which means that it is regulated by the Financial Services Authority. An AFI's letterhead will normally state that it is regulated. The Home Office have stated that the 'calculation of the applicant's personal net worth will include illiquid assets such as property, off-shore trusts and assets held by the applicant's spouse, either jointly or in the spouse's own name if they are both coming to the United Kingdom' (Home Office letter to ILPA announcing the rule change, 13 January 2004, but see also IDI, Ch 6, s3, annex G, para. 1.1).

Further requirements Under both options, the following further requirements must be satisfied. Applicants must intend to invest not less than £750,000 of their capital in the UK by way of UK Government bonds, or share or loan capital in active and trading UK registered companies (other than those mainly involved in property investment). Ordinary deposits with banks and building societies are not counted for the purpose of this investment. Investors must also intend to make the UK their main home. Provided the UK will be the applicant's main home, investors are permitted to spend time abroad and to have other residences overseas, and they do not have to intend to live in the UK for the rest of the lives (IDI, Ch 6, s3, annex G, para. 2). Also, they must be able to support themselves and any dependants without taking employment other than self-employment.

Grant of leave, extensions and settlement Entry clearance is mandatory in order to come to the UK as an investor (for details about switching into investor status ▶see Chapter 7). Investors are granted leave to enter for 12 months initially, and they may then extend that by up to three years at a time, provided they continue to satisfy the above rules. In particular, they must be able to show that, since they were admitted, they have in fact made the required investment, intend to maintain that investment, and have made the UK their main home. After four continuous years (▶see 438–9) as an investor, and provided that the requirements relating to investors continue to be met, the investor may apply for settlement. If an investor suffers losses that mean they no longer have £1 million, their extension applications will be looked at carefully. Representations should be made in these cases, as the Home Office may be prepared to grant a shorter extension (of 12 months) and to keep the case under review (IDI, Ch 6, s3, annex G, para. 4.1).

Dependants The rules relating to dependants of investors are the same as for business-persons (▶see 480, above). Spouses, unmarried partners and children may all be granted leave and settlement in line with the principal. They also require entry clearance.

Writers, composers and artists

The rules make specific provision for self-employed writers, composers and artists to come to the UK to base themselves here (paras 232–239 HC 395). The core requirement is that they must have established themselves outside the UK as a writer, composer or artist primarily engaged in producing original work which has been published (other than exclusively in newspapers or magazines), performed or exhibited for its literary, musical or artistic merit. This category is for creative people who support themselves directly from their art, with or without a private income. Examples of those who are able to qualify are: authors, essayists, playwrights, poets, freelance journalists who are established in the literary world, composers of music, painters, sculptors, photographers of international standing, cartoonists and other illustrators. The category does not cover those who are paid a salary for their work by a company. Performers such as actors, musicians, dancers and singers will not qualify. Nor, usually, will television and radio scriptwriters, publicity writers, or technicians and support staff (IDI, Ch 6, s 4, annex J, paras 1–3; see also *Stillwaggon* (IAT)). Those not basing themselves in the UK will not qualify either. Those who do not qualify may consider a work permit in the entertainers category (▶see 444–7) or applying as a business visitor (▶see 220–1) or under the HSMP (▶see 483 onwards).

There is no need to demonstrate a minimum level of investment, or to employ people in the UK. Those admitted are not able to take any other employment in the UK, but if they also have savings or private means, they may use these funds to support themselves in addition to income derived from their art, composing or writing. They must be able in this way to support themselves and any dependants without recourse to public funds. Applicants must be able to show that for the previous 12 months they have been able to support themselves and any dependants without working except as a writer, composer or artist.

Entry clearance is required, and successful applicants will be granted entry for an initial period of 12 months, and will thereafter be eligible to apply for a three-year extension. The spouses, unmarried partners or children of writers, composers and artists may be admitted and granted extensions in line with the principal applicant on the same basis as business-people (▶see 352–4, 356). As with the other business categories, settlement is also available after four continuous years (▶see 437–9).

Retired persons of independent means

Persons who are aged 60 or over, who have a guaranteed income under their control of at least £25,000 per year, net of overseas tax, and which is disposable in the UK, may be eligible to enter the UK as retired persons (paras 263–270 HC 395). 'Guaranteed' and 'under their control' means that applicants should have a right to the funds which they can legally enforce if necessary (see the decision of the High Court in *Chiew*). The Home Office will only count income which belongs to a spouse of the applicant, or held by the applicant and spouse jointly, if both are coming to the UK (IDI, Ch 7, s4, annex G, para. 2.2). In the past, there was no age limit for persons of independent means. Younger people with substantial funds must now try to qualify either as investors or business-persons.

Support and business interests Retired persons must demonstrate that they can maintain and accommodate themselves and any dependants without taking employment or obtaining help from anyone else, or claiming public funds. The Home Office interprets this as meaning that the applicant must not work in the UK or abroad. However, it is accepted that retired persons are entitled to conduct limited business. A distinction is drawn between continuing to make short trips abroad in order to 'oversee business interests', which is permitted, and 'taking an active interest' in a business, which is not (IDI, Ch 7, s4, annex G para. 2.5–2.6). The distinction may be difficult to draw in some cases. Moreover, the specific wording of the rules appear to exclude reliance on third-party support and this may, in some cases where family members based in the UK are involved, conflict with Article 8 of the ECHR (▶see also 317).

Close connection with UK Applicants also have to show that they have a 'close connection' with the UK. Examples where it will generally be accepted that the applicant has a close connection with the UK are the applicant having spent a substantial period of time in the UK in the recent past, or having close relatives settled here. Other factors which will be taken into account are: owning substantial property in the UK, long periods of Crown employment, employment with a British company, working with other British nationals and letters of support from 'eminent British citizens' (IDI, Ch 7, s4, annex H, para. 2).

Main home in UK A further requirement is that applicants must intend to make their main home in the UK. A written statement of intention is generally enough to satisfy the immigration authorities on this point. However, after the person has been admitted, extensions may be refused if the circumstances suggest that the applicant has not made the UK their main home. This may apply if, for example, they have spent substantial periods outside the UK. Applicants should expect the Home Office to check their absences.

Flexibility In general terms, this is a category which the Home Office has stated that it is prepared to operate with flexibility if the rules cannot be fully met:

'There may be cases which arise where the applicant does not meet all the requirements of the Rules, but where there are exceptional compelling grounds which would warrant the exercise of discretion... Occasionally, a person may seek to qualify on various grounds, none of which, when looked at individually, meets the requirements of the Rules. Where such a situation arises caseworkers should consider the case 'in the round' to see whether these grounds meet the spirit of the rules when taken together...' (IDI, Ch 7, s4, annex I, paras 1–2.)

The only example given is that of a person of high international standing in their own field whose presence here would reflect well on the UK, or whose abilities are likely to be of direct benefit to the people of the UK. However, it seems clear that in other cases as well, applicants can expect a sympathetic exercise of discretion. Another example might be a person who has been forced to retire early for health reasons but cannot yet meet the age requirement. It is clear, however, that the maintenance and accommodation requirements are very unlikely to be waived.

Leave, family, settlement Those intending to come to the UK under this category must obtain entry clearance. They will normally be granted leave to enter for four years straight away, with a prohibition on employment.

Holders of British passports who do not have the right of abode but who meet the rules under this category are immediately admitted with indefinite leave (IDI, Ch 7, s4, para. 2.3). For details about switching to remain as a retired person of independent means ▶see Chapter 7.

If less than four years was initially granted, provided the rules continue to be met and that the applicant has made the UK their main home, in-country extensions may be granted so as to bring the total stay up to a maximum of four years. Applicants who have remained in the UK in this capacity for four continuous years (▶see 437–9) are eligible for settlement provided the requirements of the rules are still met. The spouse, unmarried partner and children of a retired person may be admitted as dependants on a similar basis as for business-persons (▶see 352–4, 356). They will also be prohibited from working. Entry clearance is required, and their leave will also generally be subject to a condition prohibiting employment.

CONSEQUENCES OF UNLAWFUL WORK OR BUSINESS IN THE UK

Where non-EEA nationals, in breach of the law, work or enter into business other than in the ways described or referred to in Chapters 14–15 and this chapter, then the consequences can be very severe. People who work or enter into business unlawfully:

- may be administratively removed (▶1004–7, 1009–10) from the UK if they are in breach of their conditions of leave which either prohibit or restrict (▶see 18, 189–91) employment and business (s10 1999 Act);
- may have any remaining leave curtailed on the grounds that they have breached their conditions of leave, or that they no longer satisfy the rules under which leave was given (see para. 322(3) read with para. 323(i), and see para. 323(ii) HC 395) (▶141–3, 1005);
- may, if their leave is curtailed, then be administratively removed from the UK as overstayers (s10 1999 Act);
- may, if they were admitted in a category for which they had to show that they did not intend to take work, be declared illegal entrants and removed from the UK, if the immigration authorities can prove that they intended to work in the UK at the time that they were originally admitted (s33 and para. 9 Sch 2 1971 Act) (▶1013–4);
- may be refused leave to enter or remain in the future on the grounds that they have previously breached their conditions of leave (see para. 320(11) and 322(3) HC 395) (▶98–9, 140–1);
- may be committing a criminal offence (s24 Immigration Act 1971) (▶1033–4).

These possible consequences apply equally to those who work while prohibited, and also to those who are restricted from working other than in the capacity for which they were admitted, and who then do different work. Persons who have no leave and who are granted temporary admission are likely to have a condition restricting them from working (►see 695–6 for when conditions may be lifted). The immigration authorities are more likely to detain a person who breaches their conditions of temporary admission. A breach of temporary admission is also a criminal offence (s24(1)(e) 1971 Act). Moreover, a person who has been granted temporary admission at the port and who has not formally 'entered' the UK may be treated as an illegal entrant (►1011).

Employer sanctions

Specific criminal sanctions against employers who employ persons who are not permitted to work in the UK were introduced by section 8 of the 1996 Act from 27 January 1997. Many of the details were contained in the Immigration (Restrictions on Employment) Order 1996. From 1 May 2004, Section 8 was amended and the 1996 Order was replaced by the Immigration (Restrictions on Employment) Order 2004, SI 2004 No 755. Below we set out the position from 1 May 2004. In April 2004, all PAYE-registered employers in the UK should have received a copy of guidance on the new rules issued by the Home Office and entitled 'Changes to the law on preventing illegal working: short guidance for United Kingdom employers'.

Under the 2005 Bill, the government intends to introduce:

- a new civil penalty under which employers may be fined 'on the spot'; and
- a further criminal offence of employing a person who is subject to immigration control, 'knowing that they are not permitted to work'.

For further details about these proposals ►see 46–7, 51–2.

Below, we look solely at the present legislation under section 8 (and the secondary legislation made under it.) Under these provisions there are two stages in determining whether the employer is criminally liable. First, look to see whether an offence has been committed in principle. If so, stage two is to see whether there is a defence to any charges.

The offence

It is an offence for an employer to employ someone aged 16 or above who needs leave to be in the UK and who falls into any of the following categories:

- has not been granted leave to enter or remain;
- has overstayed their leave and not been granted further leave;
- has been determined to be an illegal entrant and has not been granted leave;
- is subject to a deportation order which has not been revoked;
- has leave containing a condition prohibiting them from taking employment;
- has leave containing a condition which prevents them from taking the job in question.

An example of the last situation would be a person who has a work permit enabling them to work for a particular employer as a chef, and a condition of leave restricting them to working as stated in the permit, who then takes a job on a building site (but see the defences below).

However, there will still be no offence committed if the employee was previously granted limited leave to remain in the UK which enabled them to take the employment in question, then applied in time for further leave and is still within time to appeal against a refusal, or has an appeal outstanding against the refusal (see article 3 2004 Order). At present, such a person still has their leave intact (▶see also 145–6). We suggest it must also follow that no offence is committed during the period between when an in-time application to vary leave and the decision on the application. There will also not be an offence committed if the employee is permitted to work under the immigration rules.

Before 1 May 2004, if an asylum-seeker was given written permission to work, it would not be an offence to employ them. The position since 1 May is that there will still be no criminal liability in employing such a person, provided that the relevant Application Registration Card (ARC) has been produced to and recorded by the employer, as described below. The change is that the fact that an ARC was produced and copied has now become a *defence* to the charge. The position of people on bail is not directly covered in the defences, but in a letter to Gill & Co solicitors of December 2000, the Home Office stated that an employer can employ someone granted bail by an Adjudicator whose bail conditions do not prevent employment.

Finally, it is only an offence actually to employ someone under a 'contract of employment'. Although the contract can be implicit in the circumstances, and does not have to be written, there must be an employer/employee relationship. It is not an offence to obtain the services of a self-employed person. So, if a householder hires a self-employed plumber to fix some frozen pipes, there is no offence under Section 8 even if the plumber is not entitled to enter into business in the UK.

Defences

It will be a defence to any charge under section 8 if the employer can prove that, before the 'offence' was committed, all of the following applied:

- particular document/s relating to the employee were produced to the employer (see below for the document/s which must have been produced);
- the employer either took copies of, or scanned into a database using 'Write Once Read Many' technology, all the relevant documents (strictly, only certain parts of passports and travel documents must be copied or scanned, but it is safest to keep a record of the entire document);
- the employer was satisfied that the documents appeared to relate to the particular employee (for example, any photographs appeared to be of the

employee and the date of birth given on the documents reflected the apparent age of the employee);

- where it is necessary that two documents were produced (see below), discrepancies as to the names on the document are explained by another document which was produced to the employer.

The original document/s which must have been produced are those shown in either Table 1, Table 2 or Table 3, below. The requirements contained in only one table need to be satisfied. Note that Table 1 only requires that one document had been produced, whereas Tables 2 and 3 both require that a combination of documents were produced.

It should be noted that, if the employer knew that it would be an offence to employ the person in question, then the defence will not be available.

TABLE 1 DOCUMENTS PRODUCED TO AN EMPLOYER – ONE DOCUMENT OPTION

The employer must have seen and copied or scanned any one of the following documents:

- a UK passport showing that the holder is a British citizen or a CUKC (►see 1421–2) with the right of abode in the UK;
- a passport containing a certificate of entitlement issued by the UK authorities stating that the holder has the right of abode in the UK;
- a passport or national ID card showing that the holder is an EEA National;
- a UK residence permit issued to an EEA national or to a Swiss national;
- a passport, travel document or residence document issued by the Home Office which states that the holder has a current right of residence in the UK as the family member of a named EEA national or Swiss national who is resident in the UK;
- a passport or other travel document endorsed to show that the holder has indefinite leave to enter or remain in the UK, has no time limit on their stay, or is exempt from immigration control;
- a passport or other travel document endorsed to show that the holder has current leave to enter or remain in the UK and is permitted to do the type of work in question (provided it does not require a work permit);
- an ARC issued by the Home Office to an asylum-seeker stating that the holder is permitted to take employment in the UK.

Changes to employer sanctions made by 2004 Act

From 1 October 2004, the Asylum and Immigration (Treatment of Claimants, etc) Act 2004 made further changes to the operation of employer sanctions:

- Employers can now also be tried on indictment in the Crown Court, whereas previously they could only be tried summarily in the Magistrates Court. The offence is still punishable with a fine only.

- Because the offence is now triable in either court, there is no longer a time limit for the bringing of criminal proceedings against an employer. Proceedings in the Magistrates Court must normally be brought within six months, but the Section 8 offence contained provisions enabling an extension to this time limit. The extension is abolished by the 2004 Act, but only because it is no longer needed.

TABLE 2 DOCUMENTS PRODUCED TO AN EMPLOYER – TWO DOCUMENT OPTION, FIRST COMBINATION

The employer must have seen and copied or scanned one document which meets the description in (a) below *and* any one of the documents listed in (b) below.

a) A document issued by a previous employer, the Inland Revenue, Department for Work and Pensions, Jobcentre Plus, the Employment Service, the Training and Employment Agency (Northern Ireland) or the Northern Ireland Social Security Agency and which contains the person's name and national insurance number – e.g. P45, P60, NI card;

b) One of the following documents:

- a birth certificate issued in the UK which includes the names of the holders' parents;
- a birth certificate issued in the Channel Islands, the Isle of Man, or Ireland;
- a certificate of registration or naturalisation as a British Citizen;
- a letter issued by the Home Office to the holder which indicates that the person named in it has been granted indefinite leave in the UK;
- an 'Immigration Status Document' (▶204–5) issued by the Home Office to the holder with a UK Residence Permit (▶198–9) indicating that the holder has been granted indefinite leave in the UK;
- a letter issued by the Home Office to the holder which indicates that the person named in it has current leave to be in the UK, and which allows them to do the type of work in question;
- an Immigration Status Document issued by the Home Office to the holder with a UK Residence Permit which indicates that the holder has been granted limited leave allowing them to do the type of work in question.

TABLE 3 DOCUMENTS PRODUCED TO AN EMPLOYER – TWO DOCUMENT OPTION, SECOND COMBINATION

The employer must have seen and copied or scanned both of the following:

a) a work permit or other approval to take employment issued by Work Permits (UK) (i.e. an IED);

b) either a passport or other travel document endorsed to show that the holder has current leave to be in the UK and is permitted to take the work in question, or a letter issued by the Home Office to the holder which confirms the same details.

5

Avoiding discrimination

While employers must take care not to commit an offence under Section 8 of the 1996 Act by employing those not entitled to work in the UK, they must also ensure that the procedures they adopt do not discriminate against potential employees on racial grounds. The Secretary of State has issued a specific code of practice that employers should follow, which came into operation on 2 May 2001: 'Immigration and Asylum Act 1999 – Section 22: Code of Practice for all employers on the avoidance of race discrimination in recruitment practice while seeking to prevent illegal working'.

EEA family members

Non-EEA national family members of EEA nationals who are exercising free-movement rights are permitted to work and enter into business in the UK. Employees who employ them are not commiting an offence. In order to deal with their lack of documentation while they are awaiting the issue of a residence document, they will be issued with acknowledgement letters confirming permission to take employment ▶see 549.

Section 6 **European rights of free movement**

Chapter 17
Free-movement rights: background and basics 503

Chapter 18
Rights of free movement in the EEA 511

Who qualifies as a 'national' for free-movement
purposes? 513

Who can use free-movement rights? 514

'Posted' workers 525

Family members of EEA nationals 526

Can family members of EEA nationals use the
'ordinary' immigration law? 539

Family members of British citizens using free-
movement rights – the *Surinder Singh* route 541

Evidence of status: residence permits and other
documents 544

Entry procedures 550

Decisions refusing or revoking rights 551

Rights of appeal 556

Settlement 559

Claiming welfare 563

Chapter 19
Rights of nationals of accession states 565

The road to restrictions 566

The five restrictions on the rights of A8 nationals 568

Impact of the restrictions on A8 nationals' and
their families' immigration rights 571

The Worker Registration Scheme 573

6

Chapter 20

Association and Cooperation agreements 577

Association agreements with Bulgaria and Romania 577

Turkey Association Agreement 585

Other Association and Cooperation agreements 590

17 Free-movement rights: background and basics

This section deals with immigration rights provided by the laws of the European Union. This is quite different from human rights law under the European Convention of Human Rights, which is covered in Section 8.

This chapter gives a basic background to free-movement rights by identifying the countries of the European Union (including those that 'acceded' to the EU on 1 May 2004) and the European Economic Area. We also look briefly at how the various European institutions work, and at how free-movement rights have been incorporated into UK immigration legislation and immigration rules.

Chapter 18 looks at the actual rights of free movement within the European Economic Area, and who qualifies for them, including which family members qualify. That chapter also considers how the rights work in practice, and looks at appeals against negative 'EEA decisions' made by the immigration authorities. It also deals with obtaining documents to prove status where free-movement rights are being relied on and looks at rights to settlement in EEA cases. It further looks at detention and enforcement in EEA cases.

Chapter 19 deals with the *particular restrictions* on A8 nationals and looks at the worker registration scheme. Of course, Chapter 18 generally covers the rights of Accession 8 nationals as well as all other EEA nationals.

Chapter 20 covers the immigration rights provided by the Association Agreements and Cooperation Agreements made between the EU states and certain other countries.

The development of the European Union

The European Economic Community (EEC) was set up in 1957 by the Treaty of Rome, which provided for the gradual reduction of barriers to the free movement of workers, capital, goods and services between European Community countries. An amendment to the Treaty, the Single European Act (SEA), came into force in 1986. The intention of this Act was to create a single, internal market in goods and services, and the free movement of people within the whole European Community area, by harmonising the laws of the individual countries in specific areas.

The next European agreement, the Maastricht Treaty on European Union (TEU), was ratified and came into force on 1 November 1993. Under this treaty, the EC is called the 'first pillar' of the European Union, alongside two other pillars dealing with common security (the 'second pillar'), and justice and home affairs (the 'third pillar').

Under the terms of the justice and home affairs pillar of the TEU, common policies on immigration and refugee issues were negotiated under a procedure known as 'intergovernmental co-operation', which requires the unanimous agreement of all of the member states. However, this position was revised by the terms of the Treaty of Amsterdam in 1997. The Treaty of Amsterdam amended the European Communities (EC) Treaty (the first pillar) by putting into it a new 'Title IV', dealing with visas, asylum, immigration and other matters relating to the free movement of persons. By these means, the immigration and asylum provisions of the justice and home affairs pillar were transferred to the EC pillar. Although provisions were made for certain countries (including the UK) to 'opt out' of this, the general effect of this was to make asylum and immigration policies subject to agreement by qualified majority voting, rather than to unanimous agreement.

The EU began work in earnest on the adoption of common immigration and refugee policies at a meeting of the European Council in the Finnish city of Tampere in October 1999. The Council committed itself to the adoption of a policy based on 'a full and inclusive application of the Geneva Convention', and, in particular, to 'ensuring that nobody is sent back to persecution'. For the EU Directive concerning minimum standards of conditions of reception and procedures for refugees, ▶see 656, 1379–81.

From 1 May 2004, as a result of a 'Treaty of Accession' signed on 16 April 2003 between the 15 then-existing member states of the EU and ten further states, the EU grew to 25 member-states.

For a summary of the relevant European institutions, ▶see the table at 508–9.

Two systems of law

European Union legislation and British immigration law are not always compatible. This is not surprising, because they are based on completely different premises. One of the aims of the European Union (note that the 'European Union' or 'EU' is the term more commonly used for the European Community since the Maastricht treaty) is to minimise barriers for EU citizens travelling between EU countries for certain purposes. However, one of the aims of British immigration law is to control strictly, and in many cases deter, economic migration by people who are not EU nationals.

Nationals of the EU and their family members have very extensive rights of free movement within the EU. By and large, they are able to move freely between all other EU countries, and the various national immigration laws do not apply to them.

Where these two systems of law clash, EU legislation overrides individual national laws, because most of the EU rules about freedom of movement have what is called 'direct effect'. This means that they are automatically part of the law of all the member-states.

The European Economic Area (EEA) and other agreements

From 1 January 1994, as a result of the Agreement on the European Economic Area of 1992, the rights of free movement enjoyed in the EU have been available in what is known as the 'European Economic Area' or 'EEA'. These rights extend to nationals of countries that are part of the EEA but not member states of the EU (▶see below).

In addition to the EEA, there are a number of agreements that exist between the EU and other countries. There are:

- 'Association Agreements' with Bulgaria, Romania and Turkey that give rise to certain free-movement rights (▶see Chapter 20);
- 'Association Agreements' or 'Cooperation Agreements' with: Croatia, Macedonia (Stabilisation and Association Agreements); Algeria, Morocco and Tunisia (Cooperation Agreements); Chile; 13 countries of Eastern Europe and Central Asia, and a large number of African, Caribbean and Pacific (ACP) countries. These agreements provide, among other things, largely for rights of non-discrimination in conditions of work, rather than rights of free movement (▶see 590–1).

There is also an agreement between the EU and Switzerland, which is referred to below.

Member states of the EU and the EEA

Before 1 May 2004, the 15 countries of the EU were:

Austria	Germany	Netherlands
Belgium	Greece	Portugal
Denmark	Ireland	Spain
Finland	Italy	Sweden
France	Luxembourg	United Kingdom

Following the 'Treaty of Accession' (16 April 2003), on 1 May 2004 the following ten countries joined (or 'acceded to') the EU:

Cyprus	Lithuania
Czech Republic	Malta
Estonia	Poland
Hungary	Slovakia
Latvia	Slovenia

6

Nationals of Cyprus and Malta have the same free-movement rights as other EU nationals. However, the rights of nationals of the other eight countries (known as 'A8' countries) to reside in another member state can be limited by national laws until the end of a 'transitional period' in 2011. The UK has taken advantage of this to place certain limitations on the rights of A8 nationals, which include restricting their rights to reside in the UK in order to look for work. This has been done mainly in order to prevent their access to forms of welfare support.

Bulgaria and Romania are expected to join the EU in 2007. The EU has agreed to commence full membership talks with Turkey and Croatia, which may take many years in the case of the former.

EEA From 1 January 1994, five of the European Free Trade Association (EFTA) countries – Austria, Finland, Iceland, Norway and Sweden – joined with the EU to form the 'European Economic Area' (EEA). Of these countries, Austria, Finland and Sweden joined the EU from 1 January 1995 anyway, and they are therefore listed above. Iceland, Liechtenstein and Norway did not, so the EEA remains a separate entity. Liechtenstein joined the EEA in May 1995. Switzerland decided not to join the EEA; however, in June 1999 and June 2002, the Swiss concluded agreements with the EU giving free-movement rights to Swiss nationals that are similar to those of other EEA states.

So, although they are not EU states, nationals of the following countries and their family members have similar rights of free movement to those of (non-accession) EU nationals:

Iceland
Liechtenstein
Norway
Switzerland

Terms used in the *Handbook*

In the *Handbook* we have referred to nationals of all the above countries (i.e. EU nationals, including nationals of all of the accession states, *plus* nationals of Iceland, Norway, Liechtenstein and Switzerland) as 'EEA nationals'. Because of the restrictions on the rights of nationals of eight of the 'accession countries' (listed above), we have obviously sometimes had to refer to them separately. Where that is the case, they are referred to as 'Accession 8' or 'A8' nationals.

European Union legislation

EU policies are given effect in legislation known as 'regulations' and 'directives'. Regulations are 'binding in their entirety and take direct effect in each member state'. This means that each country has to take immediate measures to bring them into force. There are regulations on the freedom of movement of workers, and the rights of workers to remain in a member-state after finishing employment there. Directives are 'binding as to the result to be achieved', meaning that countries may use different means to bring them into force. There are directives on the right of establishment for the self-employed and service-providers, and on limitations on the right of free movement for reasons of public policy, public security and public health (▶see 514–5).

European free-movement law reflected in UK legislation

Although EU law is intended to be binding on member-states, it has also been implemented by legislation (▶see below and also 515–6).

Acts of parliament

The Treaty of Rome and the directives and regulations made under it have the force of law in the UK under the European Communities Act 1972. This was amended by the European Economic Area Act 1993 in the light of the Agreement on the European Economic Area 1992. The rights of free movement were given specific recognition by section 7(1) of the Immigration Act 1988, which states that a person does not require 'leave' to enter and stay in the UK if they have rights to do so given to them by EU law. The delay was due to the Home Office working out a way of doing this that was compatible with the rest of the immigration control system. The accession of the new member-states on 1 May 2004 is implemented in UK law by the European Union (Accession) Act 2003.

The 'EEA 2000 Regulations'

European law concerning immigration is mainly contained in the Immigration (European Economic Area) Regulations 2000 (in the *Handbook* we refer to these as the 'EEA 2000 Regulations' or sometimes in this section, just to 'reg.'). However, these Regulations are not an exhaustive statement of the legal position, as they were prepared to reflect and describe the rights granted by EU law. They are not, therefore, the ultimate source of those rights. The EEA Regulations describe those who benefit from rights of free movement as 'qualified persons'. In some limited cases, therefore, EU law may give greater rights than those described in the Regulations. In cases of uncertainty, advice should be obtained.

As a result of the agreement with Switzerland (▶506), the EEA 2000 Regulations apply (with certain modifications) to Swiss nationals (see Immigration (Swiss Free Movement of Persons) (No 3) Regulations 2002 which came into force on 1 June 2002).

Accession 8 nationals The EEA 2000 Regulations also apply to Accession 8 nationals, but with restrictions on the right to reside in the UK in order to seek work and access to the issue of residence permits and, for family members, residence documents (see Regulations 4–5, Accession (Immigration and Worker Registration) Regulations 2004).

Immigration rules

Some aspects of European law are also described in the immigration rules. In particular the rules refer to:

- the immigration rights of nationals of Bulgaria and Romania, with whom the EU has an Association Agreement (paras 211–223, HC 395). Importantly, however, the immigration rules do not yet reflect the Association Agreement with Turkey (however, following certain cases, rules covering Turkish nationals may now be brought in ▶see 587);
- the right of EEA nationals to obtain settlement in the UK (paras 255–257B, HC 395);
- rights to enter and remain in the UK as the primary carer or relative of an EEA national self-sufficient child (paras 257C–257E, HC 395).

European institutions

There are several European institutions that debate proposed changes within the Union and provide for their implementation. They are set out in the following table.

EUROPEAN UNION INSTITUTIONS

The European Parliament

The Parliament sits in Strasbourg, but also has offices in Brussels. It has directly elected members (MEPs) from each EU country, and debates proposals for change in European legislation and resolutions on particular areas. It can investigate specific aspects of policy and produce reports. The Parliament has limited powers to initiate new legislation or to propose amendments to policies recommended by the European Commission. It can receive complaints from individuals about EU policies and laws and, if necessary, make references to the European Court of Justice (ECJ).

The European Commission

The Commission is based in Brussels, and is the executive wing of the EU. It has appointed members representing all the EU countries, and prepares legislation for the EU. It has its own supporting bureaucracy, also recruited from all the different EU countries. The Commission is powerful because it has responsibility for proposing and drafting the majority of new EU legislation (regulations and directives). The Commission can also receive – and is empowered to investigate – individual complaints. It is particularly useful where the complaints cover the activities of member-states as to the application of EU law.

The European Council

This is also called the 'Council of Ministers'. It consists of ministers from the EU member-states, and takes the final decisions on most legislation, having taken account of the views of the European Parliament.

The European Court of Justice

The ECJ sits in Luxembourg, and decides on legal cases brought under European law. Its interpretation of Community legislation has to be followed by individual countries. Under Article 177 of the Treaty of Rome, national courts and tribunals at any level can refer cases to the ECJ for a ruling on questions of European law. Governments of member-states may also seek rulings from the Court.

The Office of the European Ombudsman

The Ombudsman was established in 1995, and is empowered to receive complaints concerning maladministration by the European institutions. Complaints might cover such issues as wrongful application of rules, abuse of power, discrimination, or negligence. The right to complain is not limited to EU citizens, but extends to anyone living in a member-state. However, the Ombudsman's powers are limited to investigating the European institutions, and do not cover complaints against national or local administrations, even on matters concerning the application of European law.

6

18 Rights of free movement in the European Economic Area

This chapter deals with the rights of free movement enjoyed within the European Economic Area. *The overall structure, membership (the relevant states) and development of the EU and the EEA are explained in ▶Chapter 17.* Those who are unsure of the background to free-movement rights, and of which countries' nationals can qualify, should look briefly at that chapter first.

The rights under the 'Association Agreements' agreed with other countries (in particular, Bulgaria, Romania and Turkey) are dealt with in ▶Chapter 20.

Although this chapter covers rights enjoyed by the 'Accession 8' nationals, because they are EEA nationals too, for the particular considerations that apply to them and the restrictions on their rights, see ▶Chapter 19

This chapter, therefore, covers the following topics:

- who counts as a 'national' for free-movement purposes – the UK has set down which of its nationals qualify (▶see immediately below);

- the categories of people who can make use of rights of free movement (▶beginning at 514). This is probably the most important part of the chapter. We look briefly at the most important European and UK provisions, and then summarise the categories of persons who can qualify, in the table at ▶516–7. Each category is then examined in more detail from ▶518 onwards. Note that the test for not becoming a burden on 'the social assistance system of the UK' that applies to self-sufficient persons, retired persons and self-sufficient students, is looked at when self-sufficient persons are discussed, at ▶522–4;

- the rights of 'posted workers' – in other words, non-EEA national employees of businesses where it is the *business* that is exercising rights of free movement (▶525–6);

- the rights of family members of EEA nationals exercising free-movement rights (▶526–40). We discuss the different categories of family member (note that under 'spouses', we look at the position of those irregularly in the UK), which includes looking at the rights identified by the ECJ cases of **Baumbast & R** and **Chen**. We also deal with the question of whether family members of EEA nationals can use the ordinary immigration rules, and we discuss the '**Surinder Singh**' route – i.e. the issue of family members of UK nationals using free-movement rights (▶541–4);

- documents providing evidence of status and the procedures that apply in relation to them: residence permits, residence documents, family permits, 'letters of acknowledgement', and documents issued to A8 nationals (▶544–9);

- the procedures that apply on entry to the UK for EEA nationals and their family members (▶550–1);

- decisions refusing or revoking EEA rights, including exclusions from free-movement rights on the grounds of public policy. We also look here at enforcement and detention in EEA cases, both on arrival and after entry (▶551–6).;

- rights of appeal against negative 'EEA decisions' (▶556–9);

- obtaining rights to permanent residence ('settlement') in the UK in EEA cases (▶559–63);

- finally, we briefly discuss claiming welfare in EEA cases (▶563–4); but full details about this are given in the welfare section at the cross-references provided.

Abbreviations

In this chapter:

- references to the Immigration (European Economic Area) Regulations 2000 are either given as the 'EEA 2000 Regulations' or, in many cases where we have given a reference in brackets, simply as 'reg.';

- references to the 'EDI' are to the Home Office's 'European Directorate Instructions'. These fulfil a similar purpose to the IDI, and have recently been made available on the IND website. We have referred to them as follows: 'EDI, Ch, s, para.', to refer to the chapter, section and paragraph of each reference.

Note on accession and use of the term 'EEA national'

Of course, the most important recent development in free-movement rights is the 'accession' to the EU of ten new member-states, to join the then-existing 15, on 1 May 2004. The member-states, new and old, are listed at ▶505–6. Of the accession states, nationals of Cyprus and Malta have the same free-movement rights as other EEA nationals. Restrictions are, however, imposed on the other eight ('Accession 8' or 'A8') countries. These modifications of free-movement rights for A8 nationals are dealt with in Chapter 19.

In this chapter, as elsewhere, we have used the phrase 'EEA nationals' to refer to all the member-states of the EU (including the ten accession countries) *plus* nationals of Iceland, Norway, Liechtenstein and Switzerland. Nationals of the last four countries have free-movement rights similar to EU nationals, as a result of agreements between them and the

EU (►see 506). So, although 'EEA national' is used in this chapter broadly to include A8 nationals, this should always be read alongside the restrictions upon their rights dealt with in Chapter 19.

WHO QUALIFIES AS A 'NATIONAL' FOR FREE-MOVEMENT PURPOSES?

Rights of free movement generally extend only to nationals of EEA countries and their family members. People who are not nationals of an EEA country are known in EU terminology as 'third-country nationals'.

The Maastricht 'Treaty on European Union' of 1992 established the status of 'citizen of the European Union'. It did this by amending the Treaty of Rome, which has since been known as the 'Treaty establishing the European Community' ('EC Treaty'). This status of citizenship of the Union automatically exists for all people who are nationals of a member-state (Article 17(1) EC Treaty).

States are left to define for themselves who are their 'nationals' for these purposes. In most cases, this is straightforward. However, in the case of the UK the structure of nationality law is very complex – there are different categories of national (►see 1404 onwards). The UK entered a declaration that came into effect on 1 January 1983, which states that only the following categories of person are UK nationals for the purposes of EU law:

- British citizens;
- British subjects with the right of abode in the UK;
- British Dependent Territories citizens (now British Overseas Territories citizens) who acquire that citizenship from a connection with Gibraltar.

In the case of *Manjit Kaur*, the European Court of Justice (ECJ) firmly held that the UK was entitled to determine which of its nationals were EU citizens for the purposes of EU law. Therefore, Mrs Kaur's status as a British Overseas Citizen (BOC) did not mean that she was entitled to EU rights. There are several other categories of people whose status gives them a strong connection to the UK, but who are still not treated as EU citizens because of that status:

- British nationals other than those stated above;
- citizens of the Isle of Man and the Channel Islands living in those islands – they have their own immigration and citizenship laws (although many may be British citizens as well);
- Commonwealth citizens, even if they do have the right of abode in the UK;
- those with indefinite leave who are 'settled' in the UK.

So, if any of the above persons wish to travel to another EEA country, they have to fit into that country's immigration rules and regulations.

Only the UK nationals in the first list above are able to qualify for free-movement rights when they travel in the EEA. Note, however, that unless they are dual nationals with another EEA state, British citizens will only benefit from free-movement rights if they actually exercise them elsewhere in the EEA – i.e. if they move to another state. A British citizen who simply stays in the UK cannot use free-movement rights to bring family members to join them. This is because free-movement law will not operate in a 'purely internal' situation (▶see further 541 onwards).

WHO CAN USE FREE-MOVEMENT RIGHTS?

Article 18(1) of the EC Treaty provides for the right to move and reside freely in the territories of member states. However, that general right has be read together with the specific free-movement rights, and the limitations and conditions on those rights set out elsewhere in the EC Treaty and in the Regulations and Directives made under it.

The table below, ▶at 516–7, summarises the rights of free movement for EEA nationals. It also summarises some of the rights to obtain permanent residence. Further descriptions of the categories set out in the table then follow from ▶518.

The growing importance given by the European Court of Justice (ECJ) to Article 18 in particular means that the categories of person who have free-movement rights, which we have summarised in the table, should not be seen as closed. Article 18 may be used to strengthen rights and to demonstrate the existence of rights in circumstances where they have not previously been recognised – in particular, when used together with Article 8 ECHR (▶see *Baumbast & R* below at 531–4, and *Chen* at 534–7).

The important European provisions

For free-movement purposes, in addition to Article 18, the most important provisions of the EC Treaty are:

- Articles 39–42, on the free movement for workers;
- Articles 43–48, on the 'right of establishment' (for the self-employed and those with businesses);
- Articles 49–55, on those providing services.

The most important Regulations and Directives relating to free-movement rights are as follows:

- Regulation (EC) No 1612/68, on the free movement of workers and their families;
- Council Directive 73/148/EEC, on the free movement of persons for the purposes of self-employment and for providing or receiving services.

From 30 June 1992, three additional EU directives extended the rights of free movement to the following categories of economically inactive people: self-sufficient persons, retired persons, and students. These Directives are:

- Council Directive 90/364/EEC, on self-sufficient persons;
- Council Directive 90/365/EEC, on retired persons;
- Council Directive 93/96/EEC, on students.

In addition, EU law gives certain rights of permanent residence or 'settlement' (see Regulation (EC) No 1251/70, Council Directive 75/34/EEC), and Council Directive 68/360/EEC deals additionally with residence permits and documents.

Free-movement rights can be excluded on grounds of 'public policy' – meaning public policy, public security or public health. This is dealt with in Council Directive 64/221/EEC. From 30 April 2006, most of the above provisions will be repealed and consolidated instead in Directive 2004/38/EC (the Citizens' Directive). This brings together the existing rights, but there are some changes, and we have flagged up the important ones.

UK legislation putting free-movement rights into practice

Although member-states are bound by EU law, and ultimately applicants can usually rely directly on the provisions of EU law, the UK has passed specific legislation to put the EU free-movement rights into practice (▶see 507–8). Most importantly, this is achieved in the Immigration (European Economic Area) Regulations 2000 ('EEA 2000 Regulations' or simply 'regs'). The EEA 2000 Regulations apply to A8 nationals as they do to other EEA nationals, but with modifications as a result of the restrictions on their rights (Accession (Immigration and Worker Registration) Regulations 2004; see Chapter 19). They also apply to Swiss nationals but, again, with certain modifications (Immigration (Swiss Free Movement of Persons) (No. 3) Regulations 2002).

The EEA 2000 Regulations describe EEA nationals who are exercising free-movement rights as 'qualified persons', and state that they have a right to 'reside' in the UK. Unlike other foreign nationals, such people do not need 'leave' to be here (regs 5, 14; see also s7 Immigration Act 1988). There are also some provisions of the immigration rules that are intended to implement free-movement rights (see paras 257–257E, HC 395).

Advantages and disadvantages of UK legislation

In one sense, having additional UK legislation is very useful, because it collects together the effects of EU law in one place. UK legislation also defines and describes the rights of free movement in a way UK lawyers and advisers can better understand. In addition, it allows the free-movement rights to be practically applied to the UK system of immigration control.

However, because the EEA 2000 Regulations are the government's attempt to implement rights, rather than being the source of those rights, they may not always fully cover, or accurately describe, the rights themselves. They do not, for example, deal with 'posted' workers (▶see 525–6), except in relation to Swiss nationals. The flexibility required as a result of Article 18 (above) also finds no place in the Regulations. Indeed, in cases where the ECJ has explained the true extent of certain rights, the Regulations have had to be amended. If difficult questions arise as to the extent of free-movement rights in any case, careful advice may need to be taken.

The table below summarises the essential free-movement rights, and rights to obtain permanent residence.

EEA NATIONALS' 'FREE MOVEMENT' RIGHTS TO ENTER OR REMAIN IN THE UK

Rights to enter and remain

Any of the following people may travel to *and* stay in the UK:

- people who have a job to go to or to continue in the UK ('workers') (▶518–9);
- people who, although they are not actually employed, are genuinely looking for work in the UK with a realistic chance of getting it – i.e. work-seekers (▶519);
- those who are self-employed or are establishing a business in the UK (▶519–20);
- certain self-employed people who have stopped being economically active (▶520–21);
- people who wish either to provide or to receive services in the UK (▶522);
- self-sufficient persons (▶522–4);
- retired persons (▶524);
- students (for the two main categories of EEA students, ▶see Chapter 10, at 288–90 – they are also mentioned below, at ▶524–5. For children attending educational courses where the EEA national is no longer in the UK, ▶see below at 531–4).

Rights to remain

The following people have the right to stay in the UK after they have been admitted:

- people who become involuntarily unemployed (▶521);
- people who were employed or self-employed, and who stop their economic activity because they become temporarily incapable of work (▶521).

Family members

Family members of those above who have rights to enter and/or remain in the UK also have free-movement rights. In some cases, rights have been recognised for carers of children. Rights of family members are not summarised here, but are dealt with at ▶526–38.

Rights of permanent residence ('settlement')

Those in the following two groups have permanent rights of residence in the UK. The source of the rights of those in the first group is the immigration rules. Those in the second group have specific rights under Regulation (EC) No 1251/70, although these rights are also referred to in the immigration rules.

1) *Settlement under the immigration rules*

Settlement may be granted to anyone, other than a student, who has remained in the UK for four years lawfully in accordance with the EEA 2000 Regulations (or the equivalent regulations which came before them). This means that the applicant must have remained in the UK exercising rights in any of the above categories (or a combination of them), and must continue to be in the UK in any of those categories. Applicants must also have been issued with a residence permit or document that is valid for five years. Family members can also benefit. Note that special transitional arrangements have been made for Swiss nationals and A8 nationals who were previously living in the UK with leave (paras 255-255B, 257A-257B HC 395).

For further details ▶see 559–63.

2) *Settlement as a result of rights under Regulation (EC) No 1251/70*

The following groups of people may be granted settlement in accordance with rights under the above EC Regulation (see also para. 257 HC 395):

- EEA nationals who have been continuously resident in the UK for at least three years, who have been employed in the UK, or any other EEA state, for the last 12 months, and who have reached pensionable age;
- EEA nationals who have stopped working because they are permanently incapable of work because of an accident at work, or an occupational disease, which entitles them to a state disability pension;
- EEA nationals who have stopped working because they are permanently incapable of work, and who have been continuously resident in the UK for at least two years;
- family members of EEA nationals in the last three categories. (These family members can still benefit if the EEA national died during his or her working life, provided the EEA national lived in the UK for at least two years, or the EEA national died because of an accident at work or an occupational disease.)

Note

1) The table is not comprehensive as to those categories with permanent rights of residence. For full details (and cross-references to full details) concerning all the relevant categories, ▶see 559–63.

2) Rights that flow to employees of *businesses* exercising free-movement rights – i.e. 'posted' workers – are not referred to above. For details, ▶see 525–6.

Workers

The ECJ has ruled that the essential requirements for qualifying as a 'worker' are: employment for a period of time in the provision of services for and under the direction of another, in return for remuneration (payment) (see *Lawrie-Blum*). In the case of *Steymann*, the ECJ held that the provision of services in return for work was an acceptable form of payment. That case concerned a person who was living as part of a religious community, who received food and lodging in return for their work as a 'handy-man' for the community. There is no minimum level of payment that must be received.

Certain retired workers, and workers who have become incapable of work, are entitled to *permanent* rights of residence (▶see table above at 517).

Note also that EEA nationals who are studying and working at the same time can qualify as workers (▶see 288–9, 524–5).

Nature of the employment

Is the status of 'worker' affected by the kind of employment that the person has? Does employment need to be continuous, or can it be temporary or casual? The following cases give useful answers to these kinds of questions.

- In the case of *Raulin*, the ECJ considered the position of those who were on 'on-call' contracts, with a guarantee of the number of hours they would get, and who were paid by the hour. The Court held that such people could still be 'workers'.

- In *Levin*, the Court considered whether a person with a part-time contract, earning a net income below the social security norm, could qualify. Again, the Court said that, provided the work done was 'effective and genuine', as opposed to being 'marginal and ancillary', a person on a part-time contract was also entitled to free-movement rights. This was still the case even where the work was taken in order to get immigration status for the worker's spouse.

- Provided the basic conditions are met, it also does not matter that the work is done as part of training (*Lawrie-Blum*). An Irish national who spent a period of six months in vocational training in France could be a worker provided that he was engaged in effective activities, and the essential requirements of an employment relationship were fulfilled (*Ursaff*).

Top-up benefit

Obtaining benefit to top up earnings does not prevent an EEA national from qualifying as a worker. In *Kempf*, a German part-time music teacher living in the Netherlands who was giving 12 hours of lessons a week was a worker even though he was also receiving some public funds. For details about 'in-work' benefits in the UK, ▶see 1244–7 (summary of benefits system), 1265 (penultimate para.), 1268–9.

Restrictions

States have the right to restrict some jobs to their own nationals. Some public service jobs, for example, may be restricted, but only those that involve the exercise of public powers, or which concern national security. From 1 June 1996 the UK has restricted recruitment for higher-level civil service jobs to British nationals.

Work-seekers

Although, for convenience, we have categorised them separately, work-seekers who are not in work but who are genuinely looking for work with a realistic chance of getting it are also classified as 'workers'. They also, therefore, have free-movement rights. So, those who enter the UK with no offer of employment, and who are then in search of work, have a right to reside while they look for work (most A8 nationals, however, do not have rights of residence as work-seekers; ▶see 568 and, for the exceptions, ▶see categories (1)–(7) at 1270–2).

The 'six months' rule of thumb

The position may change, however, if the period during which the EEA national is out of work and looking for work without finding it becomes prolonged. This point was dealt with in *Antonissen*, in which the ECJ had to consider at what point the national authorities of a member state might decide that prolonged unemployment showed that the person had ceased to be active in the labour market. The Court ruled that a period of six months' unemployment should not undermine the status of a worker. However, at the end of six months, the onus would be on the individual to show that they are 'continuing to seek employment and that [they have] genuine chances of being engaged'. So, in general, a period of six months' unemployment will not put an end to a person's rights. Beyond that, the applicant will have to provide evidence of continuing efforts to place themselves in work for which they are suitably qualified.

Although the EEA 2000 Regulations state that the unemployed person must be 'registered', there is no actual requirement in EU law that unemployed workers should register with the employment services of the state in which they live. The benefit of registering, however, is that the acceptance by the employment service for registration as a person available for work will help in demonstrating that the person is making continued efforts to find work. Other evidence would include copies of correspondence with possible employers, or evidence of having attended job interviews.

Self-employed people

Articles 43–48 of the EC Treaty refer to the 'right of establishment', and this is the term often used by lawyers as well. This refers to rights to take up self-employment and the right to set up and run businesses and

6

companies. For convenience, we have simply used the term 'self-employ-ment' to cover all of these forms of economic activity. EEA nationals who are self-employed – or who seek to be self-employed – in the UK have free-movement rights. Of course, another way of viewing this economic activity is as providing or receiving services (see the category below). Those carrying out business activities on a temporary basis only are more likely to be seen in that category. This category is for those who are running businesses 'established' in the UK.

As with the employed, the self-employed must be involved in genuine and effective (not 'marginal and ancillary') activity, and the services must be provided in return for payment of some sort.

Special provision is made for the family members of self-employed people who die (▶see 537).

Employed or self-employed?

The central feature of being in employment is that the worker is in a position of 'subordination' to the employer. For most, the distinction between being employed as a worker (see above) and self-employed will not be important. The distinction is, however, important for A8 nationals, because their rights as self-employed persons are not as restricted – they do not have to register. Accordingly, the Home Office has issued guidance to case-workers in order for them to identify 'disguised' employment (EDI, Ch 14, annexes C–E). The distinction is also important, of course, for Bulgarian and Romanian nationals applying under the Association Agree-ments, who have to be self-employed. Guidance is also, therefore, issued to staff dealing with Association Agreement applications, so that they understand the factors that indicate self-employment rather than employ-ment (for details, ▶see 583–5).

Self-employed people who are no longer economically active

This category is similar that of EEA nationals who are able to remain per-manently under Regulation (EC) No 1251/70 (▶see table above at 517, and see also Council Directive 75/34/EEC). Indeed, people in this category are treated not only as qualified persons, but also as settled in the UK (reg. 8, EEA 2000 Regulations).

Those in any of the following groups who have stopped their business act-ivities in the UK qualify for free-movement rights under this category (reg. 4):

- people of pensionable age when they stop their self-employed activity who have been in the UK for the last 12 months before they stopped and who have lived continuously in the UK for more than three years;
- those who have lived in the UK continuously for more than two years, and who stopped their self-employed activity in the UK because they became permanently incapable of work;

- those who have lived and had self-employed activity in the UK, and who stopped being active because they became permanently incapable of work as a result of an accident at work or an occupational illness that entitles them to a state pension;
- those who have been continuously resident and active in their self-employed activity in the UK for three years, and who continue to be active in their self-employed business in another EEA state, but whose normal place of residence remains the UK, and who return home at least once a week.

For the above purposes, periods of absence of not more than three months in any year are not counted as breaking continuity of residence. In addition, periods of inactivity caused by circumstances outside the control of the self-employed person, and inactivity caused by illness or accident, count as periods of activity. Note that special further provisions are made relating to the above categories for those who are married to British citizens and also, for the first three categories, for those who carried out activities in another EEA state, but who resided in the UK during that time and returned here at least once a week (reg. 4(2)(3)).

Special provision is made for the family members of deceased 'self-employed people who have ceased activity' (▶see 537).

People who become unemployed involuntarily

Those who have been employed in the UK and become involuntarily unemployed do not lose their free-movement rights unless their unemployment becomes too prolonged and they do not have a real chance of getting further work (see under 'work-seekers', above). The EEA 2000 Regulations state that a person who is 'involuntarily unemployed' does not cease to qualify, provided that they are registered with the 'relevant employment office' (reg. 5(2)(b)).

People who were employed or self-employed, and are temporarily incapable of work

Those who were employed or self-employed in the UK, and who stop their economic activity because they become temporarily incapable of work as a result of illness or accident, still have the right to reside while they are temporarily incapable of work (reg. 5(2)(a), (3) EEA 2000 Regulations). This includes people who temporarily cease work as a result of pregnancy, or the birth of a child (see EDI, Ch 1, s2, para. 2.4; Ch 1, s3, para. 3.4). Appropriate evidence to show that a person is incapable of work, and that the incapacity is not permanent, is best obtained from a doctor. Those who become permanently incapable of work may still benefit from free-movement rights in certain circumstances (▶see table at 517).

6

Providers and receivers of services

Article 50 of the EC Treaty defines 'services' as activities of an industrial, commercial, craft or professional character that are normally 'provided for remuneration'. Regulation 3(1)(c)(d) of the EEA 2000 Regulations defines providers and receivers of services as those who provide or receive (or seek to provide or receive) these services as defined in the EC Treaty.

Because an important characteristic of providing or receiving services is that there is remuneration, a person will not be able to say that they are a receiver of services if, for example, they are receiving free healthcare from the NHS. In *Belgium v Humbel*, the ECJ held that state school education did not count, because it was not normally provided for remuneration. This was the case even though the parents did make some financial contribution to the school. Tourists are generally regarded as receivers of services, as are those receiving private healthcare (*Luisi & Carbone*, ECJ).

Providers and receivers of services are treated differently to workers and self-employed persons in the form of the residence permit they get. This is because of the generally temporary nature of this free-movement right. The worker and self-employed person is normally entitled to a residence permit of not less than five years' duration. The validity of the residence permit issued to service providers or receivers 'may be limited to the period during which the services are to be provided' (reg. 18(4)).

Self-sufficient persons

'Self-sufficient persons' are people who have the resources to support themselves and their families without becoming a burden on 'the social assistance system of the United Kingdom' (reg. 3(1)(e), (2), (5)). Self-sufficient persons (and their family members) must also be covered by sickness insurance to protect them against 'all risks' in the host country. Insurance against general health risks is probably enough for these purposes. Self-sufficient persons and retired persons (see below) must have clearer evidence that they are self-supporting than self-sufficient students. This is because, for students, the Regulations simply require them to 'assure' the Home Office, by a declaration or other means, that they have sufficient resources (see reg. 3(1)(g)(ii)).

For the recent developments giving rights to the parents and carers of self-sufficient EEA national children, ▶see below at 534–7.

Level of resources required to avoid being a burden

The EEA 2000 Regulations state that the applicant must have:

'...sufficient resources to avoid...becoming a burden on the social assistance system of the United Kingdom.' (reg. 3(1)(e)(i))

They will be 'sufficient' if they are more than the 'level below which social assistance might be granted under the United Kingdom benefit system' to a UK national in the same circumstances (see reg. 3(5)). So, in order to see whether the resources will be enough, applicants can compare what they have available with the means-tested benefits that persons in their position might get for themselves and their dependants. For a general overview of the benefits system (what benefits are paid to whom), ▶see 1244–7. Benefit rates themselves change frequently, and so they would have to be separately checked (▶see sources of information at 1535).

The Home Office has also provided guidance on the level of funds needed in order to be self-sufficient. The figures it has provided are for guidance purposes only; it is possible that some applicants may be able to support themselves with less. The EDI state that self-sufficient persons include: EEA nationals who have an income of £8,000 per annum (single person), £10,000 per annum (couple), plus £1,000 per annum per child (Ch 1, s5, para. 5.1).

Can self-sufficient persons, retired persons and self-sufficient students have any access to welfare support?

As with retired persons and self-sufficient students (see below), a person should not automatically lose their rights of residence because they become temporarily dependent on public funds. The Home Office should look at the person's circumstances in the round to see whether it would be proportionate to deny them a continuing right to reside. In *Grzelczyk*, which concerned a student who had applied for social assistance, the ECJ held that his removal could not be the automatic result of his having recourse to social assistance. The EDI state:

'EEA nationals who are in the UK as self-sufficient persons, students or retired persons should be able to support themselves without public funds. Such persons are only able to claim public funds without losing their right of residence if they are able to demonstrate that they are not an unreasonable burden on the state. To establish whether an EEA national is an *unreasonable burden* on the state each case would need to be assessed on an individual basis. If the EEA national is claiming public funds, after having been in the UK for some time, the fact that they *had been* self sufficient would be a factor in determining whether the burden is reasonable, as would the length of time that they are likely to be in receipt of public funds.' (Ch 1, s1, para. 1.2; Ch 9, s1, para. 1.3)

Although the Home Office refers here to people not losing their rights of residence by claiming public funds, the EDI also state that it would not be appropriate to issue a residence permit to an EEA national who is claiming public funds.

It seems that, in defining public funds for these purposes, the Home Office counts:

- income support;
- income-based JSA;
- housing and homelessness assistance;
- housing benefit;
- council tax benefit;
- working families' tax credit;
- social fund payments;
- child benefit;
- 'any disability allowance'.

The Home Office does not, however, count contributory benefits or 'social care support'. Unfortunately, it has not defined the latter term (see EDI, Ch 1, s1, para. 1.2; Ch 9, s1, para. 1.2).

For brief details about EEA nationals claiming welfare, ▶see 563–4 below. For the rules about eligibility for support for EEA nationals and others generally, see Section 12. In particular, the 'right to reside' test for access to core benefits, and its particular impact on A8 nationals, is covered at ▶1264–73.

Need for sufficient resources for family members

Both under this category and for retired persons and students (see below), the EEA 2000 Regulations were amended from 1 May 2004, so that the EEA national will only meet the resources requirement if the resources available are enough to prevent the EEA national *and* their family members who are residing in the UK from becoming a burden on the system. For the self-employed and retired categories, the family members must also have sickness insurance (see reg. 3(2)-(4) as substituted by the Immigration (European Economic Area) and Accession (Amendment) Regulations 2004).

Retired persons

'Retired persons' are people who were previously employed, or self-employed, and who are receiving an invalidity, early retirement or similar pension that is enough to support them and their families without their becoming a burden on the social-assistance system (see above under 'self-sufficient persons' for this definition). They and their family members must also be covered by all-risk sickness insurance. Retired persons do not have to have carried out their previous economic activity in the UK (see EDI, Ch 1, s7, para. 7.1). Retired Swiss nationals do not have a right of residence, but they may well qualify as self-sufficient persons instead.

Students

There are two main categories of EEA student:

- **self-sufficient students** who qualify under the EC Directive on students (93/96/EEC) – they must 'assure' the Secretary of State that they have sufficient resources to prevent them and their families being a burden on the social-assistance system (see 'self-sufficient persons' above for the test for this);
- **students who have worked, or are still working**, in the UK during their studies, and are able to maintain their status as workers – their rights are contained in Regulation (EC) No 1612/68.

For more detail about these two categories, ▶see Chapter 10, at 288–9.

For the rights of children of EEA nationals (and their primary carers – often the other parent) who are in education when the EEA national stops residing in the UK, ▶see below at 531–4.

'POSTED' WORKERS

The rights of free movement described above only apply to EEA nationals. The rights of non-EEA national family members are covered below. In certain cases, non-EEA national workers can benefit from free-movement rights. Where a business that is established in the EEA carries out a contract to provide services in another member state, it is entitled to take its employees with it, even if the employees are not EEA nationals. This is because EU law sees the company as the entity that is exercising free-movement rights by providing services. This means that the *non-EEA national*, as well as the EEA national, employees of the company benefit from rights of admission and residence in the other EEA state for a temporary period while the service is being provided. These workers are known as 'posted' workers.

Rush Portuguesa This principle was first established in the case of *Rush Portuguesa*, which concerned the residence status of Portuguese national employees of a Portuguese firm with a contract for civil engineering works in France. At the time, the transitional conditions dealing with the admission of Portugal to the EU allowed freedom of movement for the self-employed and service providers, but not for Portuguese *workers* seeking employment with employers based in France. The ECJ ruled that the status of the company as an undertaking lawfully entitled to provide services on a commercial basis in another member-state was enough to secure a residence status for its employees who were providing those services.

Vander Elst In this further case, a Belgian employer won recognition from the ECJ that the firm's Moroccan employees, who had been directed to provide services on its behalf in France, were entitled to consideration for their position in France under EU law, rather than French domestic employment law.

The Home Office has stated that the family members of employees of companies who benefit from these rights can also be admitted in exactly the same way as other family members of EEA nationals (letter from Joint Entry Clearance Unit to Kingsley Napley solicitors, 18 May 2001).

EEA 2000 Regulations and posted workers

Unfortunately, the EEA 2000 Regulations do not say anything about the rights of posted workers, *except* for posted employees where the employer is a Swiss national or a Swiss company. For Swiss cases, special provision is made for its nationals to be issued with a 'posted worker authorisation' (a kind of entry clearance), and the EEA 2000 Regulations are generally modified to regulate their rights (see Immigration (Swiss Free Movement of Persons) (No 3) Regulations 2002; in particular see para. 2 of the Schedule, which inserts the definition of 'posted' worker into reg. 3 of the EEA 2000 Regulations; see also, for guidance, EDI, Ch 13, s2).

The fact that the Regulations do not expressly deal with non-Swiss cases does not mean that the rights set out above do not apply in other cases. As stated previously, the UK's own regulations only describe the EU free-movement rights that exist already.

FAMILY MEMBERS OF EEA NATIONALS

'Family members' of EEA nationals who are exercising rights of free movement (i.e. family members of 'qualified persons') are also entitled to be admitted to and stay in the UK with the EEA national. They also have the right to reside in the UK, and do not need leave (see regs 13–14). Obviously, this is of great benefit to family members who are not themselves EEA nationals – often known as 'third-country' nationals – who would otherwise have to qualify to be admitted under the immigration rules.

There are of course a number of different ways in which a family member can lose their rights to freedom of movement derived from an EEA national. Firstly, a person may cease to be a 'family member'. For example, a person married to an EEA national would cease to be their family member on pronouncement of a decree absolute dissolving the marriage. A son who reached the age of 21 and who was no longer dependent would also cease to be a family member. In most cases, free-movement rights will also be lost when the EEA national themselves ceases to be a 'qualified person' by no longer living and working in the UK. This should not affect a family member where the EEA national leaves temporarily (for less than six months).

However, the case of **Baumbast & R** has modified the position – there are now at least some cases in which non-EEA national family members keep their rights even if the EEA national stops living in the UK, or if there is a divorce (▶see below 531–4).

For the possibility of using the immigration rules as an alternative to the EU route for family members, ▶see below at 539–41.

Who is a 'family member'?

The general definition of 'family member' of an EEA national is as follows (see reg. 6(4) EEA 2000 Regulations):

- a spouse;
- children, grand-children and great grand-children up to the age of 21 (and those over 21 *if* they are still dependent) of the EEA national or their spouse;
- dependent parents, grandparents and great-grandparents of either the EEA national or their spouse;
- other relatives may also qualify, on a discretionary basis, in certain circumstances (▶see 537–8).

Under current rules family members of EEA nationals who only qualify for rights of free movement as self-sufficient students are more narrowly defined. For them, only their spouse and dependent children qualify (reg. 6(1)). We now discuss some of these family members in more detail. For the practicalities of entry, ▶see 550–1, and for obtaining 'family permits', ▶see 548–9.

Note that there are specific provisions dealing with the family members of self-employed persons who have died (▶see below at 537), and with settlement rights for family members of retired workers and workers who have died (▶see table at 517). Art 12, Citizens' Directive (▶see 515) extends rights to family members of deceased EEA nationals provided the family member had resided as such for at least a year. For the position of unmarried partners, ▶see 530–1 below.

Meaning of 'dependency'

The Home Office view is that, for the purposes of the categories of family member above, 'dependency' can be by choice rather than necessity, but that it is only financial dependency and not emotional dependency that counts (EDI, Ch 2, s2, para. 2.3). This may be too narrow. If an application is refused on this basis where there is significant emotional or practical dependency, the decision should be challenged.

Spouses

A 'spouse' in this context means a person who is formally contracted in a legal marriage (see below for unmarried partners). As regards the genuineness of a marriage, there is no equivalent in EU law to the old 'primary purpose' test. The production of a valid marriage certificate is the only requirement laid down. The Home Office view is that it is entitled to investigate a marriage between an EEA national and a third-country national, to determine whether it has been entered into purely for immigration purposes, as a 'marriage of convenience'. In a statement in May 1994 explaining the government's attitude on this question, the then Home Office minister, Lord Annaly, stated that:

'A marriage of convenience is regarded as a sham marriage which is entered into solely for immigration purposes where the partners have no intention of living with each other as man and wife in a settled and genuine relationship.'

The EEA 2000 Regulations reflect this position by stating that a person cannot be a 'spouse' if the marriage was one of 'convenience' (reg. 2(1)). The IAT has adopted the same line (see *Kwong*). In order to be a marriage of convenience, the marriage must be shown to be a sham in the sense that the couple do not intend to pursue any kind of married life together.

In most EEA states, once it is accepted that a marriage is legally valid, there is no further enquiry into the nature of the marriage. In order to exclude free-movement rights in these circumstances, it is probable that EU law would require the Secretary of State to demonstrate that the marriage constituted a fraud that was sufficient to justify the exclusion of the person on public policy grounds (▶552–3).

Immigration rules as to maintenance and accommodation without recourse to public funds do not have to be met. However, for the self-sufficient categories (self-sufficient persons, retired persons, self-sufficient students), the Regulations have recently been amended to ensure that rights of residence are only recognised where the family members, as well as the sponsor, will not become a burden on the social assistance system (▶see 524 and ▶see 522–4 for the definition).

Spouses: overstayers and others irregularly in the UK

A non-EEA national overstayer who marries an EEA national should generally still be able to benefit from EU free-movement rights and can apply for a residence document, provided of course that the marriage is not a sham. In *MRAX*, the ECJ indicated that expelling an applicant who fulfilled the requirements for free movement on the basis of marriage, for the sole reason that their visa (in UK terms 'leave') had expired, may not be proportionate. The same applied to others who marry after having entered the country irregularly. Exclusion decisions should not generally be based solely on failures to comply with formalities of immigration control.

Spouses: 'port' cases and those temporarily admitted at port

As will be seen below (▶550–1), non-EEA visa national family members *and* non-EEA national family members seeking to 'install' themselves in the UK need to produce a family permit or residence document in order to be granted entry to the UK on arrival. What if, as often happens, the applicant is an asylum-seeker who is granted temporary admission, and then, while on temporary admission, marries an EEA national? Where the applicant has been in the UK for less than six months, officers at the port itself will consider the application. The following policy should be applied:

'If, in the case of a non-EEA national who has married an EEA national while on temporary admission, the port are satisfied that:

- the relationship is genuine, and
- the EEA principal is exercising Treaty rights in the United Kingdom,

the EEA family permit requirement may be waived, and the passenger admitted to the United Kingdom for six months on Code 1A. It is IS practice to advise the person concerned to apply for a residence document after entry.' (EDI, Ch 4, annex A, paras 1.2, 4-5)

Officers seem to apply the same approach to applicants who are already married to EEA nationals when they arrive in the UK without the required family permit or residence documents (indeed, it may be disproportionate for the authorities to send back an applicant who can demonstrate that they satisfy the relevant conditions, but who arrives without these documents, see **MRAX** which is itself reflected in Art 5, Citizens' Directive (▶515). The same guidance continues:

'If [the Immigration Service] establish that the passenger has no entitle-ment to admission under EC law, admission will be refused after [a referral]. This applies both to cases encountered on arrival in the United Kingdom, and in cases where a marriage took place after arrival in the United Kingdom, while the passenger was on temporary admission, but had been in the UK for less than six months.'

Where the applicant has been in the UK for more than six months, the application will be considered by the European Casework Group at the Home Office instead. It is assumed that an approach similar to the above will be applied.

Breakdown of marriage, or EEA national spouse leaves the UK

The 'spouse' relationship only breaks down for the purposes of EU law when there is a divorce (in the UK this means a decree absolute). A non-EEA national can still rely on his or her marriage to an EAA national, even if they are separated or living in different houses, and even if they are progressing with a divorce (**Diatta**, ECJ). Under Art 13 Citizens' Directive (▶515), EU family members keep their rights even after a divorce. Others *may* keep their rights depending on the length of the marriage, child arrangements or domestic violence issues. Of course, if the EEA national leaves the UK permanently, the spouse will also lose their free-movement rights. However, in both situations divorced spouses and spouses remain-ing in the UK who are the parents of children of the couple who are in education here still may have rights if the children are in education. This is the case even if the children are not EEA nationals. If the children are non-British EEA nationals, the parent may have rights drawn from the child, if the child can be said to be exercising free-movement rights as a self-sufficient person. For details of all of this, ▶see under both *Baumbast & R* and *Chen*, below at 531–7.

Domestic violence

In a letter to Camden Community Law Centre of 14 March 2005, the Home Office confirmed that it did not apply the domestic violence immigration rules to the family members of EEA nationals exercising free-movement rights. *However*, the Home Office letter continued:

'However, provisions have been made for victims of Domestic Violence under Article 13(2)(c) of the new Free Movement Directive, which comes into force in April 2006. It states that:

"Without prejudice divorce, annulment of marriage or termination of the registered partnership referred to in point 2(b) of Article 2, shall not entail the loss of the right of residence of a Union citizen's family members who are not nationals of a Member state where:
...(c) this is warranted by particularly difficult circumstances, such as having been a victim of domestic violence while the marriage or registered partnership was subsisting..." '

The Home Office letter to the law centre does not make any further direct comment on the Directive. However, even before this Directive comes into force, it seems it is worth referring to it in EEA domestic violence cases when making any representations to the Home Office, in cases where the family member cannot still benefit from free-movement rights.

Fiancé(e)s

Fiancé(e)s are not automatically 'family' members, unless discretion is exercised under regulation 10 EEA 2000 Regulations (▶see below). However, from 18 September 2002 the immigration rules on fiancé(e)s were specifically amended to allow for the admission of fiancé(e)s of EEA nationals who have been issued with a residence permit (see para. 290A HC 395).

The change in the rules means that an EEA national who has been issued with a residence permit that is valid for five years will, for the purposes of the fiancé(e) rules, be treated as 'present and settled' in the UK *even though* they have not actually been granted settlement. The fiancé(e) of such a person can then be granted leave to enter (and, in limited circumstances, extensions of leave) in exactly the same way as other fiancé(e) cases. Entry clearance must be obtained (for general details about fiancé(e)s, ▶see 303–4 onwards and 318–22). Once the couple have married, and provided the EEA national spouse is exercising free-movement rights, the applicant can then be treated as the family member of an EEA national, and granted a residence document showing that they are exercising rights of free movement (letter of IND International Policy Directorate to Northern Ireland Law Centre, 18 November 2002).

Unmarried and same-sex partners

In the case of cohabitees, the ECJ has ruled that cohabiting but unmarried couples cannot be included in the definition of 'spouse' (*Reed*). However, that case also states that, where the national law allows unmarried but cohabiting partners of its *own* nationals to obtain residence in the country, it would be discriminatory not to give that same benefit to the cohabiting partners of EEA nationals. In the UK, the immigration rules allow unmarried partners to be granted permission to enter and remain, and so unmarried partners of EEA nationals should be treated in the same way.

Although, in relation to discrimination, EU law is strongest in these circumstances where the EEA national is a *worker*, the EDI indicate that the Home Office applies this equal treatment approach to 'EEA nationals' whichever free-movement rights they are exercising (see Ch 11). In addition, in a letter of 15 August 2000 to Warner Cranston solicitors, the Home Office confirmed that unmarried partners of EEA nationals can be treated in the same way as the unmarried partner of a British citizen or person settled in the UK, even though the EEA national does not have a permanent right of residence in the UK.

Of course, the immigration rules on unmarried partners apply to same-sex as well as heterosexual relationships. A letter of the IND International Policy Directorate to Clifford Chance Solicitors, dated 16 July 2002, confirms that the same approach will be applied in EEA same-sex cases:

'These principles also apply to same sex relationships. The applicant would be required to fulfil all of the criteria under the immigration rules providing for the admittance of an unmarried partner into the United Kingdom.'

For the requirements of the immigration rules on unmarried partners, ▶see 303–4 onwards and 322–3. Under the Citizens' Directive (▶515), unmarried partners who are in a registered partnership with the EEA national that is treated by the member state as equivalent to marriage, will be treated as 'family members'.

Children

For the purposes of free-movement law, 'children' is broadly interpreted to include step-children and adopted children. The Home Office will accept adopted children provided that the adoption is recognised by the UK (EDI, Ch 2, s2, paras 2.1, 2.4.1 and ▶see 383, 1528–9).

Children and parents where the EEA national is no longer in the UK, or is divorced from the other parent – *Baumbast & R*

The children (and parents) of EEA nationals have important rights under EU law if the children are in education. These rights come from Regulation (EC) No 1612/68. Of course, they would normally have rights as ordinary family members anyway, but the important point here is that, even if the EEA worker *stops* residing or working in the UK, or divorces the other parent, the non-EEA national child *and* their parent who is their primary carer still have certain rights. This was established by the cases of *Baumbast & R v SSHD*, decided in September 2002 (▶see table below)

The EEA 2000 Regulations have been amended in order to respond to this decision.

EEA 2000 Regulations implementing *Baumbast & R*

From 1 April 2003, the EEA 2000 Regulations were amended in order to reflect the decision in *Baumbast & R* (reg. 6(2A)-(2D). The Regulations recognise rights to reside as family members for any of the following *three* groups of people:

1) the children and grandchildren of an EEA national (or their spouse) who is no longer a 'qualified person' (see below) because they have stopped residing in the UK, provided that: (i) those children/grandchildren are either under 21, or are dependent on the EEA national or their spouse; *and* (ii) they were attending an educational course (see below) in the UK when the EEA national was still residing there as a qualified person, and they are still attending such a course;

2) the divorced spouse of an EEA national if they are the primary carer of their dependent child who is under 19 and attending an educational course in the UK;

3) the spouse, or divorced spouse, of an EEA national who is no longer a 'qualified person' because that EEA national has stopped residing in the UK, where the spouse – or divorced spouse – is the primary carer of their dependent child who is under 19 and attending an educational course in the UK.

'Qualified person' Under the Regulations quoted above, it does not matter in what free-movement capacity the EEA national is or was a 'qualified person'.

Meaning of 'educational course' and applying for permanent residence For the above purposes, 'educational course' means a course within the meaning of Article 12 of Regulation (EEC) No 1612/68. This obviously includes school education. Home Office policy is:

'"Educational course" is broadly construed and will include apprenticeship and vocational training courses. It would not include nursery education unless the child was aged three or over (local authorities are only obliged to provide nursery places to three and four year olds. As there is no automatic entitlement for children under the age of three to attend nursery, such education would not fall within the definition of an educational course within the meaning of EC Directive 1612/68).' (EDI, Ch 2, s2, para. 2.10)

In a letter to the Ethnic Minorities Law Centre dated 18 August 2004, the International Policy section of the IND confirmed that, following *Baumbast*, a family member of an EEA national continues to have a right of residence in the UK even after the divorce, provided that they are the principal carer of their EEA national child and that that child is attending school. In this letter, the Home Office confirmed that they mean education up to the age of 18. In relation to applying for permanent residence, it was also stated (see also EDI, Ch 7, s2, para. 2.6):

'The applicant may accumulate periods of residence they have spent as the family member of a qualified EEA national and periods of residence they have spent in the UK in accordance with the provisions of *Baumbast.*'

THE DECISION OF THE ECJ IN *BAUMBAST & R*

Facts in *Baumbast*

Mrs Baumbast was a Columbian national who married an EEA national (a German) who worked in the UK. They had two children – one was a Columbian national, the other a dual Colombian and German national. In 1990 the family was given residence permits for five years. In 1993, Mr Baumbast's business failed, and he went to work abroad, returning only to visit the family, who remained in the UK with the children attending school.

Facts in *R*

Mrs R was a US national who married an EEA national (a Frenchman). They had two children, both of whom were dual US and French nationals. In 1990, Mrs R came to the UK as the spouse of an EEA national. The couple divorced in 1992, but remained living in the UK. The divorce settlement stated that the children should continue to live with their mother in the UK. The children retained contact with their father, who lived and worked in the UK. Mrs R began her own business in the UK.

Decision of the court

The ECJ found as follows.

1) Children of an EEA national worker who have installed themselves in an EEA state while their parent exercises free-movement rights as a worker in that state have rights of residence – not simply as family members, but in order to attend general educational courses under Regulation (EC) No 1612/68.

2) Children in the above category continue to have those rights even if the parents divorce, or if the parent who is an EEA national stops working in the host state concerned.

3) Children in the above category can still have rights to reside in the host state, even though it may be possible for them to continue their education in another EEA state.

4) Parents (including non-EEA national parents) who are the primary carers of children in the above category have the right to reside with them in order to 'facilitate' the children's exercise of their rights. This remains the case even if the parents divorce, or the EEA national parent stops working in the host state concerned. As well as the above Council Regulation, the ECJ relied on Article 8 ECHR for this finding.

5) An EEA national who has stopped exercising free-movement rights in an EEA state as a worker can still enjoy a right of residence there as a result of Article 18(1) EC Treaty (the rights of citizens of the Union 'to move and reside freely in the territory of the Member States, subject to the limitations and conditions laid down in [the] Treaty…'). States have to consider the facts of any such case to determine whether it would be proportionate to deny a right of residence. As Mr Baumbast had sufficient resources to support himself in the UK, it would be disproportionate to deny his right of residence.

Notes

1) All the family members in *Baumbast* & *R* had in fact been granted leave in the UK before the ECJ considered the matter. However, this was granted under domestic law, and so the Court considered the important question of the applicants' rights under EU law anyway.

2) The decision of the ECJ in these cases, building on the decision in the earlier case of *Echternach* & *Moritz*, is reflected in regulations 6(2A)–(2D) of the EEA 2000 Regulations (described at ▶532–3).

Parents and carers of EEA national children – *Chen*

In its decision in *Chen* in October 2004, the ECJ gave important recognition to the rights of non-EEA national parents with care of their *EEA national child* who is exercising rights as a self-sufficient person. The UK has responded to the decision by inserting a new category in the immigration rules from 1 January 2005, which allows applicants to be granted leave as the 'primary carer or relative of an EEA national self-sufficient child' (see paras 257C–257E HC 395 inserted by HC 164). Before *Chen*, the Home Office view was that children under the age of 16 were not capable of exercising EC Treaty rights. For the decision in *Chen* ▶see the table below, and for the immigration rules ▶see immediately below.

Immigration rules implementing *Chen*

From 1 January 2005, the new rules state that leave to enter or remain in the UK may be granted if the applicant meets all of the following requirements. The applicant (paras 257C–257E HC 395):

- must be the 'primary carer', parent or sibling (including half-siblings and step-siblings) of a child who is an EEA national who is under 18 and has a right of residence in the UK under the EEA 2000 Regulations as a self-sufficient person (for qualifying as a self sufficient person, ▶see above at 522–3);
- must be living with the EEA national child, or be seeking entry in order to live with them;
- must, *if* they are the sibling, be under 18 (unless they are applying for an extension to an existing leave under this same rule), unmarried, not have

formed an independent family unit, and not be leading an independent life;

- must be maintained and accommodated without taking employment or having recourse to public funds.

Note that these rules do not apply to carers, parents and siblings of a British citizen. 'EEA national' for these purposes excludes British citizens (see paras 6 and 257 HC 395).

If the applicant is seeking leave to enter, entry clearance is required. If an applicant arrives without the required entry clearance, officers will examine the case to see if there are any 'exceptional compassionate circumstances' justifying the exercise of discretion (EDI, Ch 1, s9, para. 9.5). If the applicant is seeking to *remain* in this capacity, having already been admitted, no entry clearance is required. Applicants may therefore 'switch' into this category. Leave can be granted for up to five years at a time, with a condition prohibiting employment and recourse to public funds. If the EEA national child has an existing residence permit, leave is likely to be given until the expiry of that permit. Extensions may be granted.

Sufficient resources available to the child In assessing whether the EEA national child has sufficient resources available to it, officers will check that the resources are enough for the proposed length of residence. Non-EEA nationals granted leave under these rules are not permitted to work. If they need to work in order for there to be sufficient resources available to support the child, or if they are working unlawfully, the child will be denied a residence permit, and an application under these rules will be refused (see EDI, Ch 1, s9, para. 9.2).

Settlement There is no direct provision in the rules for granting settlement in this category. Because the category allows leave to be granted under the immigration rules, the Home Office view is that applicants cannot benefit from the normal settlement rights for those residing in the UK under the EEA 2000 Regulations. Instead, non-EEA national applicants will have to wait until they qualify for indefinite leave under the long-residence rules (see EDI, Ch 1, s9, para. 9.6.1).

THE DECISION OF THE ECJ IN *CHEN*

Facts of *Chen*

The parents were both Chinese. They had one child born in China. Contrary to China's 'one child' policy, they wished to have another. Having taken legal advice, they decided to have their second child born in Ireland, so that it would be a citizen of the Republic of Ireland, with community rights and immigration rights of free movement. The second child was born in Belfast, Northern Ireland, in September 2000 and was, accordingly, an Irish national. Mother and child then moved to Cardiff and applied for long-term residence permits in the UK.

The question was whether the child and her non-EEA national mother had EU rights of residence in the UK, in circumstances where they had sufficient resources to maintain themselves. Importantly, although mother and daughter relocated to Cardiff, they had not moved between member-states because they had moved from *Northern Ireland* (i.e. the UK). The element of the case that connected it to EU rights, rather than it being a situation 'purely internal' to the UK, was the fact of the child's nationality of a separate EEA state.

Decision of the Court

The ECJ:

1) rejected the argument that there could be no free-movement rights because the applicants had not moved between member states – the child's nationality meant it was not a purely internal situation;

2) rejected the argument that the child lacked the capacity to exercise EU free-movement rights;

3) rejected the argument that it was an abusive situation which could give rise to no rights because the mother had deliberately given birth in Northern Ireland in order that her daughter would be Irish and get immigration rights within the EEA;

4) rejected the argument that a person could only be self-sufficient if they had their own resources to rely on – there is no requirement as to the *origin* of the resources;

5) found that the daughter did have rights as a self-sufficient person, given that she had enough resources available to her (through her mother) so as not to need to make claims on the UK's social-assistance system, and that she was covered by sickness insurance;

6) rejected the argument that the child could have long-term residence rights as a receiver of services (child-care and medical services) – free movement for the receipt of services is intended to be for a temporary period only;

7) rejected the idea that the mother could have a right of residence as a family member because only *dependent* relatives in the ascending line could have such rights – the child was obviously dependent on the mother, not the other way around;

8) found that the mother (who was also self-supporting) nevertheless had rights *derived* from the child's rights of residence as the child's primary carer – this was because to refuse to allow the mother to stay would 'deprive the child's right of residence of any useful effect'.

This finding in relation to the mother/carer is similar to the basis on which the ECJ in *Baumbast* found that a primary carer of a child in education ought to be allowed to reside with them, even where the worker is working outside the EU (▶see above at 533–4). As with *Baumbast*, the court relied on the fundamental rights of nationals of member states to move and reside freely contained in Article 18 EC Treaty.

Notes

1) The decision of the ECJ has been implemented by the UK in the form of immigration rules allowing primary carers or relatives of self-sufficient children

to be granted leave (paras 257C–257E HC 395). The self-sufficient child themselves may apply for a residence permit as a self-sufficient person.

2) The Irish Nationality and Citizenship Act, which came into force on 1 January 2005, made changes to Irish nationality law. Before that date, citizenship came automatically from birth. It now depends also on the status of the parents at the time of the birth. Nevertheless, *Chen* remains an important case in circumstances where a child is a national of any other EEA state. In many cases, the relevant children may be dual nationals.

Family members of self-employed persons who have died

Special provision is made for certain family members of EEA nationals who exercised rights as self-employed persons but who have since died.

The EEA 2000 Regulations recognise rights to reside for family members in either of the following two groups (reg. 5(4)(5)):

1) family members of self-employed EEA nationals who have died, where the family member was living with them immediately before they died and *either*:

- the EEA national lived continuously (ignoring absences of less than three months in any one year and absences due to military service) in the UK for at least two years before their death; *or*

- their death was the result of an accident at work or an occupational disease; *or*

- the EEA national's surviving spouse is a British national able to exercise free-movement rights (▶see 513–4 for this definition);

2) family members of self-employed EEA nationals who have ceased economic activity (▶see 520–21 above for the definition of this group), where that person has died and the family member was living with them immediately before they died.

The Regulations give these family members rights as 'qualified persons' in their own right, and they are also treated as settled in the UK (reg. 8).

For family members of *workers* who have died, see the table at ▶517.

More distant family members

EU law also gives rights to other relatives who are not included in the above categories, but who have been living 'under the same roof' of the EEA national or their spouse, and who are dependent on them. 'Other relatives' is not defined in EU law, but needs to be interpreted broadly, giving practical effect to the core principles of free movement. So the definition must go beyond formal and legal relationships.

These additional rights are reflected in regulation 10 of the EEA 2000 Regulations. This states that the immigration authorities may give family permits or residence permits and documents to other relatives if 'in all the circumstances, it appears appropriate to do so', provided that they are dependent and either were living in the EEA national's household before the EEA national came to the UK, or are still living as part of that household outside the UK. This implies a wide degree of discretion for the immigration authorities. For how the Home Office exercises this discretion, see the table below. EU law itself is expressed in more positive terms, stating that the admission of other relatives shall be 'facilitated' where they are dependent on the EEA family member (see Article 10(2), (EC) No 1612/68). Under the Citizens' Directive (▶515), unmarried partners in a 'durable relationship' may also be considered.

The extension of 'family member' to these other relatives does *not* currently apply where the EEA national is a 'qualified' person on the basis of being a self-sufficient person, a retired person, or a self-sufficient student. However, if the sponsor is a Swiss national, the extension still applies where the EEA national is a self-sufficient person or a student.

HOME OFFICE POLICY ON MORE DISTANT FAMILY MEMBERS

Home Office policy on applying regulation 10 of the EEA 2000 Regulations to recognise the rights of more distant family members is summed up as follows:

'When deciding whether is it appropriate in all the circumstances to issue a residence permit/document, case-workers will need to assess whether refusing the family member would deter the EEA national from exercising his/her Treaty rights or would create an effective obstacle to the exercise of Treaty rights. Each case must be assessed on an individual basis but an example of where it might be appropriate to issue a residence permit/document would be if the family member were very elderly or incapacitated. In assessing such cases, it would be important to consider whether there were any relatives to care for them in their home country.' (EDI, Ch 2, s2, para. 2.4)

Case-workers may also consider whether financial dependence can continue just as well with the sponsor sending money back to the third country. Applicants are likely to be refused if they have:

• lived in a third country while the EEA national was previously living in another EEA state;

• only lived as part of the EEA national's household many years ago; or

• have their own family unit (unless there are 'sufficient compassionate circumstances').

CAN FAMILY MEMBERS OF EEA NATIONALS USE THE 'ORDINARY' IMMIGRATION LAW?

As we have seen above, British citizens (who are not dual nationals) who have remained living in the UK do not count as EEA nationals for the purpose of family reunion. EU law only permits family reunion where the EEA national has actually exercised free-movement rights. Therefore, family members seeking to join British citizens and other non-EEA nationals settled in the UK usually have to use the immigration rules.

However, an EEA national may, in certain circumstances, also opt to use the immigration rules rather than free-movement rights for family reunion purposes. In many cases, whether they can do this will depend on whether they are treated as 'settled' – i.e. in the UK without any restriction on the period for which they can remain. This is because, in order to bring a family member permanently to the UK, the rules generally require the sponsor to be settled.

The EEA nationals who are treated as settled for the purposes of the 1971 Act (and therefore the immigration rules) are set out in regulation 8 of the EEA 2000 Regulations. For this list, ▶see 559–60. In addition, special provision has been made for EEA nationals who are the sponsors of fiancé(e)s (▶see 530). Other EEA nationals are not treated as settled.

So, a non-EEA national spouse of an EEA national who is settled can choose whether to apply for a residence document or for leave under the immigration rules. Below we discuss the different advantages of these two options. Remember, though, that under the immigration rules an in-country application to remain as a spouse must be made by a person with present leave. If the applicant has no leave, the application for leave under the rules is likely to be refused, and the applicant's case will have to be considered as an EEA application instead (EDI, Ch 8, s1, para. 1.1).

Advantages of using EU law

If a person has a choice whether to use EU law or domestic law, advice should be obtained. The advantages of using EU law are:

- entry clearance (in this case, the 'EEA family permit') is issued free of charge;
- it is possible to be reunited with children and grandchildren of any age (although for those aged 21 and above, it is necessary to show dependence), dependent parents and grandparents of any age and, sometimes, other dependent relatives;
- there may be additional requirements of the immigration rules that the family member may not be able to satisfy – for example, the 'sole responsibility' rule where there is another living parent who is not settled in the UK, or the requirement to show that the family member is 'living alone in the most exceptional compassionate circumstances', where, for

example, they are a parent or grandparent under 65, or son or daughter over 18.

Advantages of using the immigration rules

Where the person can qualify under the immigration rules, there are also some advantages of using them: applicants will generally obtain indefinite leave either on entry or (with spouses) after a probationary period of 24 months. It takes longer to obtain permanent rights of residence if EU law is being relied on (▶560–2).

Can family members switch between EU law and the immigration rules?

Is it possible for a person who has entered exercising free-movement rights to 'switch' to claim the benefit of the immigration rules, where they give greater benefit? For example, can the spouse of an EEA national who is exercising EU rights suddenly apply for indefinite leave to remain after completing 24 months of residence, rather than waiting the usual four-year period? After all, EU law does require equality of treatment between EEA nationals and members of their families with nationals of the country in which they reside. This point was rejected by the Court of Appeal in *Boukssid* on the grounds that the domestic law status of indefinite leave to remain did not confer a 'social advantage' for the purposes of EU law.

In the case of *Kaba*, an immigration adjudicator made a reference to the ECJ for clarification of a related legal issue. The ECJ decided that the UK was entitled to refuse to allow the spouse of an EEA national to claim the benefit of the immigration rules where the EEA national is not 'settled' (▶see 559–60 for EEA nationals who are treated as settled). It held that it was not discriminatory to require spouses of non-settled EEA nationals (who themselves have conditional rights before they are granted settlement) to wait four years before obtaining settlement – i.e. longer than the spouse of someone in the UK who has unconditional rights to reside (British citizens and those otherwise 'settled' here). The Home Office has maintained its policy of requiring spouses who have entered using free-movement rights to serve the full four years before allowing access to permanent residence (EDI, Ch 5, s4, para. 4.4). However, where the EEA national is settled, denial of rights of permanent residence to their spouses for a period of four years may be discriminatory.

Using EU rights after being admitted under the immigration rules

A person originally admitted under the immigration rules can subsequently use free-movement rights. This will often occur where a third-country national is admitted in some other capacity, and is later able to claim a free-movement right. For example, a person admitted as a student under the rules might marry an EEA national who is in the UK exercising free-movement rights. That student would then be entitled to assert their rights of residence as a family member, and could apply for a residence document as proof of their status.

FAMILY MEMBERS OF BRITISH CITIZENS USING FREE-MOVEMENT RIGHTS – THE *SURINDER SINGH* ROUTE

It follows from the above that, in many cases, family reunion is easier under EU law than under the immigration rules. The rights are more extensive, and the procedures easier. Family members of British citizens, however, cannot take advantage of this unless they themselves exercise free-movement rights (or unless they are dual nationals with another EEA state – see for example *Chen*, above, where the child was an Irish national although she had not moved between member-states). This situation has given rise to a strategy for family reunion that has become known as the *Surinder Singh* route.

The case of *Surinder Singh* was decided in the ECJ. It concerned the status of an Indian citizen who had previously lived in Germany with his British-citizen wife, who was working there. His residence in Germany had been squarely within the provisions of free-movement law. After a couple of years, however, the couple moved to the UK, where they intended to be involved in business. At the time of his admission to the UK, Mr Singh was granted leave to enter under the immigration rules. After a period, the marriage got into difficulty and the couple separated. The UK then began action to remove Mr Singh on the grounds that he no longer had a right of residence in the UK. Mr Singh countered this by arguing that he was in fact covered by the provisions of EU law by virtue of his former residence in Germany with his British wife, and that he had retained the benefit of EU law provisions when entering the UK. The ECJ agreed and held that, while the marriage was not dissolved, Mr Singh could remain.

A principle was therefore established which allows the third-country national family member of a British citizen who has lived with the British citizen in another member-state to retain their rights to benefit from EU law on moving to the UK. However, the British citizen must have been genuinely exercising rights of free movement in the other state.

The EEA 2000 Regulations and the *Surinder Singh* route

The government was not easily reconciled to the implications of the *Surinder Singh* case. Regulation 11 of the EEA 2000 Regulations des-cribes the family members of British citizens who, in the government's view, can benefit. It states that family members of British citizens will be treated in the same way as a family member of another EEA national, provided all the following conditions are met:

1) after leaving the UK, the British citizen resided in an EEA country and was employed there (other than on a transient or casual basis), or was estab-lished there as a self-employed person;

2) the family member of the British citizen is lawfully resident in another EEA state;

3) on returning to the UK, the British citizen is exercising free-movement rights (in the same way as a national of another EEA state would be a 'qualified person' under the EEA 2000 Regulations on coming to the UK);

4) if the family member is a spouse, the marriage took place, and the parties lived together in the other EEA state, before the British citizen returned to the UK.

With regard to condition (1), the EDI advise immigration officials that the period over which the rights should have been exercised is 'at least 6 months (not necessarily continuously)'. They further state that:

'An exception to this rule would be where the British national has genuinely worked abroad but must return to the United Kingdom for unforeseen reasons before the 6 months are completed' (EDI, Ch 5, s2, para. 2.2.1).

Condition (2) was recently added to the Regulations, probably as the result of the decision in *Akrich* (see below for further discussion). It is a controversial addition, and those refused on this basis should take advice. For details of the meaning of 'lawfully residing', ▶see under 'family permits', below at 548–9.

Condition (4), requiring that the marriage took place before return to the UK, reflects the fact that the rights of free movement do not generally cover the admission of fiancé(e)s.

Family members admitted under the *Surinder Singh* route have a right to reside in the UK without being granted leave under the immigration rules.

Can people *deliberately* use the *Surinder Singh* route in order to obtain an immigration advantage?

Initially the government position was that, if a British citizen had left the UK 'in order to enable his family member to acquire rights', the *Surinder Singh* route was not available. Until amended, the EEA 2000 Regulations had a specific condition reflecting this. The ECJ has made clear on many occasions that, provided applicants are in fact genuinely exercising free-movement rights, the *reason* they have chosen to do so is not relevant. In the JCWI case of *Akrich*, the IAT referred to the ECJ the question of whether EU law allows free-movement rights to be restricted on the basis of the motivation that the EEA national has for moving from one state to another. In order to avoid the effect of a deportation order made against Mr Akrich, a Moroccan who had been convicted of a criminal offence, Mr and Mrs Akrich had gone to live in Dublin temporarily. They intended to return to the UK some time later with the protection of free-movement rights. The ECJ held that

'...the motives which may have prompted a worker of a Member State to seek employment in another Member State are of no account as regards his right to enter and reside in the territory of the latter State provided that he there pursues or wishes to pursue an effective or genuine activity... Nor are such motives relevant in assessing the legal situation of the couple at the time of their return to the Member State of which the worker is a national. Such conduct cannot constitute an abuse within the meaning of paragraph 24 of the *Singh* judgment even if the spouse did not, at the time when the couple installed itself in another Member State, have a right to remain in the Member State of which the worker is a national.'

The Court confirmed that there would be an 'abuse' if the marriage was one of convenience. The government seems to have finally accepted the above by removing this 'motivation' requirement from regulation 11 (removed from 7 February 2005). The condition was never too strictly enforced anyway. If it had been, it would have closed off the *Surinder Singh* route to many families.

However, more controversially, the ECJ in **Akrich** also stated that a spouse of an EEA national who is not lawfully residing in an EEA state does not have to be admitted by the other state when they move with their family member – although in making any such decision to refuse admission, the state must have regard to the right to respect for family life under Article 8 ECHR. This part of the judgment has been criticised as being out of step with free-movement law. Nevertheless, the government has reflected it in regulation 11 (see condition (2) above).

Using *Surinder Singh* in non-employment/self-employment cases

The EEA 2000 Regulations make no reference to the situation in which a British citizen is exercising free movement in the other EEA state other than in an employed or self-employed capacity. They appear to exclude the possibility, for example, of free-movement rights applying to the case of a British citizen who has resided in another EEA country as a student, marries a third-country national, and then brings their spouse to join them in that country, then seeking the protection of EU law when returning together to the UK. Although *Surinder Singh* did not expressly cover other categories as such, the judgment does not exclude the possibility. The Home Office has expressly stated that 'non-economically active categories of Treaty right do not qualify for treatment under *Surinder Singh*' (EDI, Ch 5, s2, para. 2.2.2).

Carpenter In the *Carpenter* case in the ECJ, *Surinder Singh*-type principles were applied to a situation where the British citizen had been providing or receiving services in other EEA states. Mr Carpenter was resident in the UK, where he ran a business selling advertising space in medical and scientific journals. Because many of the advertisers were located abroad, he travelled to other EEA states for business. However, he only stayed for a few days at time on business trips to other member-states. Even so, his wife, a national of the Philippines – an overstayer who could not benefit from the policy on overstaying spouses (DP/3/96) – was found to have rights under EU law. Of importance also is the fact that, in deciding for the Carpenters, the ECJ relied heavily on Article 8 ECHR. The case also, therefore, shows the developing relationship between EU free-movement rights and the ECHR.

EVIDENCE OF STATUS: RESIDENCE PERMITS AND OTHER DOCUMENTS

In EU free-movement law, rights are not created by stamps and pieces of paper. If in fact the person fits into the categories described above, they have free-movement rights automatically, regardless of whether the Home Office has yet issued them with documents (see *Royer*, ECJ).

Nevertheless, it is generally useful for EEA nationals to have documents as *evidence* of their status because:

- they are useful evidence for those who want to be joined by family members;
- non-EEA family members who are also visa nationals, or who are residing in the UK with their family member, can use them in order to return to the UK, instead of obtaining a family permit from abroad;
- they provide useful evidence to show to employers, given the employer sanctions on employing those not permitted to work;
- they are necessary when applicants want to apply for settlement (▶560), or if they want to bring a fiancé(e) to the UK (▶530).

If a document is applied for, the applicant will obviously have to show that they are entitled to the status claimed. Even if the applicant fits one of the categories described above, they can still be excluded from free-movement rights (and denied documents) on 'public policy' grounds (▶see 552–4). We now examine the various documents that may be issued, and the procedures for obtaining them (although the sysem may be modified by the Citizens' Directive (▶515)).

Residence permits and residence documents

'**Residence permits**' are available to those who have a 'right to reside' because they are:

- EEA nationals exercising free-movement rights, and therefore 'qualified persons' under the EEA 2000 Regulations;
- family members of EEA nationals who are qualified persons, where the family member is *also* an EEA national (for non-EEA national family members, see 'residence documents' below).

'**Residence documents**' are available as evidence of the right to reside for the non-EEA national family members of EEA nationals, where the EEA national sponsor is exercising free-movement rights. Where a family member has been issued with a residence document and travels out of the UK and returns, provided it is still valid, the residence document can be produced at the port as an alternative to applying for and obtaining a 'family permit' (for which, ▶see below).

Making applications and evidence needed

Applications for residence permits and residence documents are usually made on Form EEC1, which can be obtained from the Home Office website. Guidelines for completing the form are attached to it. It is not compulsory to use this form – an application will be equally valid if it is made by letter, enclosing the relevant documents. The evidence required will depend on the nature of the application. For example, *Baumbast*-type applications will obviously require evidence of the child's education.

If the following requirements are not met, or if the Home Office believes that the applicant should be excluded from free-movement rights on grounds of public policy, then the application will be refused.

Residence permits Regulation 15 of the EEA 2000 Regulations states that a residence permit 'must' be issued to an EEA national who applies for one, provided that they produce valid identity (a valid identity card or passport issued by an EEA state), and proof that they are a qualified person. The form of proof requested will often be evidence of employment, of self-employment, or of being engaged in business activity. For those in employment, evidence from the employer will normally be required. If the person is self-employed, evidence of the state of the business will be required. If the applicant is studying, confirmation should be obtained from the relevant educational institution. In other cases, evidence of self-sufficiency will be required. The Home Office also requires two passport-size photos. A check-list of documents needed for residence permit applications is provided at Annex A to Chapter 1 of the EDI.

A family member who is an EEA national themselves must be issued with a residence permit if they have a valid ID card or passport issued by an EEA state, and proof that they are the family member of a qualified person (reg. 15).

Residence documents Non-EEA nationals who are family members of EEA nationals applying for residence documents require a valid passport, and either a family permit or other proof that they are related as claimed – such as a marriage certificate (for a spouse), full birth certificate (for a child) – to the person exercising free-movement rights in the UK. If the family member needed to get a family permit before they came to the UK – because they are a visa national, or came to reside indefinitely with the EEA national – then the EEA 2000 Regulations state that they also need to produce their family permit (reg. 15(2)(b)). This may be unlawful as EU law relating to residence permits and documents contains no requirement that an applicant be in possession of a 'visa' which is, effectively, the function of a family permit. It seems that the general practice is more generous than the Regulations suggest; for the general approach to spouse applications where formalities have not been complied with, or people are in the UK in an irregular position, ▶see 528–9 above.

Also, where applicants do not have passports or identity cards as proof of identity, Home Office guidance states that case-workers are permitted to exercise their discretion to issue a residence document where the applicant produces a Home Office-issued identity card (for example an ARC). The same is true 'where the applicant produces another form of conclusive evidence that they are a family member of the EEA national'. This may even involve submitting a wedding video to show that it is in fact the applicant who married the EEA national (EDI, Ch 2, s2, para. 2.5.1).

A third-country national family member will be issued with a 'letter of acknowledgement' while awaiting the issuing of a residence document (▶see below).

Delay in issuing permits and documents

EU law requires that residence permits are issued 'as soon as possible', and in all cases no later than six months after the date they are applied for (see Article 5, Council Directive 64/221/EEC). The Home Office states that it makes 'every effort' to comply with this, particularly where an applicant 'draws our attention to the alleged breach of this requirement' (EDI, Ch 1, s1, para. 1.4). In some cases there have been delays in issuing permits. Where the delay obstructs the exercise or enjoyment of any rights that the person is otherwise entitled to under EU law, or where the delay exceeds six months, the Home Office is arguably in breach of its legal obligations, and may be open to claims for damages.

Duration of permits and documents

Residence permits and documents are normally valid for five years from the time of issue (see regs 18–20). Permits and documents issued to family members are given on the same terms as those for the EEA national whose rights they are relying on (reg. 20(1)). However, in the cases of:

- students, they may be limited to the duration of the course (or one year if the course is for longer than a year);
- those in seasonal or short-time contract work, they may be limited to the length of the intended work or contract;
- providers or receivers of services, they may be limited to the period during which the services are to be provided;
- retired or self-sufficient persons, they are sometimes limited by the Home Office to two years, depending on whether the applicant is likely to continue to meet the relevant requirements after that time;
- primary carers of children in education who have continued rights of residence following the decision in *Baumbast* (▶above 531–4), they may be limited to the time that they are likely to continue to care for the child while they are in education.

There are also certain circumstances in which the Home Office is not required to issue a residence permit at all (▶see below).

Residence permits and documents are only evidence of status. Even if a permit or document is still valid according to its date of issue, it cannot give a status which does not exist. So, a person who is in fact no longer entitled to the status shown on the document cannot rely on it as giving them a right to reside where they very clearly have no such right. Permits and documents may also be revoked where the holder is no longer entitled to the status they show (▶see 551 onwards).

Residence permits and documents can be renewed on application (reg. 19). Family members may renew their residence permits or documents on the same terms as the qualified person who is their family member.

Validity of a residence permit if the holder leaves the UK

The Regulations state that the 'validity' of a residence permit is 'not affected' by absence from the UK for a period of no more than six consecutive months (reg. 18(7) EEA 2000 Regulations). The Home Office may, therefore, treat a permit as no longer valid if the person's absence is in excess of this period.

When the applicant has free-movement rights but a residence permit does not have to be issued

The Home Office does not have to issue a residence permit to any of the following (regs 15–16 EEA 2000 Regulations):

- a worker on a contract of employment that is limited to three months or less;
- a worker who is employed in the UK but who actually lives in another EEA country and who returns there at least once a week;
- a seasonal worker in approved employment;
- a provider or receiver of services if the services are to be provided for no more than three months.

A8 nationals (and their family members) claiming rights as workers, who are required to register on the worker registration scheme, will also not be issued with residence permits (▶see 570, and for the exceptions 1270–2).

Note also that the Home Office states that it may not issue a residence permit to a self-sufficient person who, although they still have the right to reside, are having some access to public funds. Similarly, it states that it may not issue a permit to a work-seeker (EDI, Ch 1, s1, para. 1.2; Ch 1, s2, para. 2.6). The denial of a permit to a work-seeker – even if they have had a lengthy record of employment in the UK, are genuinely seeking work and are registered with the employment authorities – may be contrary to EU law under principles taken from the ECJ case of *Hoekstra*.

Although it is not referred to in the EEA 2000 Regulations, EEA nationals who are resident for a limited period, in order either to receive or provide services on a commercial basis, are entitled to a special form of residence permit, which is known confusingly as a 'right of abode' certificate (Article 4, Directive 73/148).

Family permits

'Family permits' are effectively entry clearances for the family members of EEA nationals. They can be obtained from posts abroad free of charge. Applicants can get them from any issuing post – they do not have to travel to their country of origin in order to apply. Unless they already have a residence document, a non-EEA national who wishes to be admitted to the UK as the family member of an EEA national must obtain a family permit before travelling, if they are (reg. 12(2)(b)):

- a visa national (►see 1507 for list of visa-national countries); or
- seeking to 'install' themselves in the UK with their EEA national family member.

'Installing' themselves is not defined, but probably means seeking to reside in the UK as their ordinary home together with their EEA national family member. It means that the applicant is coming for more than just a visit, or some other limited purpose. The Home Office interpretation of 'install' is that it means 'they are coming on a permanent or semi-permanent basis' (EDI Ch 6, s1, para. 1.2).

Other family members do not need family permits, but they should at least have documents proving that they are family members of an EEA national who is exercising free-movement rights. On their arrival, such applicants will normally be advised by the immigration officer to contact the Home Office to obtain a 'residence document' (►see above). They are not obliged to do so but, again, it will give them useful evidence of status.

Requirement to issue family permit

When an application is made to a post abroad, the ECO is required to issue a family permit to the applicant if they are the family member of an EEA national who (reg. 13):

- is exercising free-movement rights at that time; or
- will be travelling to the UK with the applicant within six months (from 7 February 2005, this period was reduced from 12 months) of the time of the application, and will at that time be exercising free-movement rights.

Even if the above requirements are met, applications can be refused on public policy grounds. From 7 February 2005, the Regulations have been amended so that applications can *also* be refused if the applicant is not lawfully residing in the other EEA state (reg. 13(3)). This rule has been introduced as a result of the decision of the ECJ in *Akrich*. The Home

Office interpretation is that the applicant must have the local equivalent in that EEA state of leave, or an EEA residence document. Evidence of an outstanding application to the authorities of the EEA state will not be enough (EDI, Ch 6, s2, para. 2.2). This application of *Akrich* is controversial.

Only exceptionally are family permit applications referred back to the Home Office for further consideration. The family permit takes the form of a vignette that is placed in the passport, and is endorsed to show that it is an EEA family permit. It will state either that the family member will be travelling with the EEA national, or that they are joining the EEA national in the UK. Family permits issued after 7 February 2005 are valid for six months (those issued before that date were valid for 12 months). They can be used for the purpose of entry on an unlimited number of occasions during the period of validity.

'Letters of acknowledgement' permitting family members to work

Non-EEA national family members of EEA nationals who are exercising free-movement rights have the right to take up economic activity themselves. As with other rights in this area, that right does not depend upon their being issued with a residence document. But a problem arises because, while they are waiting for their documents to be issued, employers may be reluctant to employ them for fear of committing an offence under section 8 of the 1996 Act (criminal sanctions against employers, ▶see 496–500).

In a letter to Kingsley Napley Solicitors dated 4 July 2005, the Home Office confirmed that it will issue 'all third-country nationals who apply for a residence document' with a 'letter of acknowledgement' immediately on receiving their application. These letters will confirm that the named individual is permitted to take employment for a period while their residence document application is decided. The letters will give the employer a contact number for the IND Employers' helpline so that employers can check the position.

A8 nationals: registration certificates, cards and 'family-member residence stamps'

Separate documents are available for A8 nationals and their family members where they are not, for the time being, able to obtain residence permits and documents. A8 nationals who are workers may register under the worker registration scheme and be issued with a registration certificate and card (▶see 573–5). Their non-EEA national family members can apply, using Form EEC3, for a 'family member residence stamp' (and see reg. 33(1A), (5) EEA 2000 Regulations).

ENTRY PROCEDURES

No formal time-limit can be placed on the stay of EEA nationals or their family members when they are exercising free-movement rights. Their passports should not be endorsed with any conditions of entry. They are free to remain in the UK, to work or to study, and do not need to apply for any further permission to stay, as this is an automatic right.

The position regarding procedures on entry is somewhat different between EEA nationals and non-EEA nationals seeking admission as family members. For the powers of detention and enforcement on entry, ▶see 554–5.

EEA nationals – on entry

When an EEA national arrives in the UK, provided that they produce a valid identity card or passport issued by an EEA state, they 'must' be admitted by the immigration officer without the need to obtain formal permission or 'leave' to enter. They can only be refused admission if their exclusion is justified on public policy grounds (reg. 12(1), and ▶see below). Beyond this, the checking of EEA nationals at the internal borders of the EEA, other than an examination of their passports or national identity documents which show their nationality, is not permitted under EU law (Council Directive 68/360/EEC).

It is therefore very unusual for EEA nationals to be refused entry. In the case of *Commission v Netherlands*, the ECJ ruled that the Dutch authorities had no right to demand any further information from a German national crossing its frontier once that person had established that they were an EEA national. So, although under the EEA 2000 Regulations a person can later be removed from the UK on the ground that they are not in fact exercising free-movement rights, and are therefore not 'qualified persons', this will not generally arise on their entering the UK. For the revocation of status, ▶see 551 onwards, and for detention and enforcement of controls against EEA nationals and their family members on arrival or otherwise, ▶see 554–6.

Non-EEA national family members – on entry

In order to be admitted on entry, non-EEA nationals who are family members of EEA nationals must produce either an identity card issued by an EEA state or a valid passport (reg. 12(2)). What further documentation they need depends on their circumstances, as follows.

1) If they are a visa national, or they are coming intending to 'install' (▶see above 548) themselves with their family member, they should also have a valid EEA family permit or a residence document (from when previously in the UK).

2) In any other case they should have with them documents demonstrating that they are the family member of an EEA national who is exercising free-movement rights.

It *may* be disproportionate for the authorities to send back an applicant in (1) above who can demonstrate that they qualify for free-movement rights as the family member of an EEA national, but who arrives without a family permit or a residence document (*MRAX*). For the on-entry policy applied in spouse cases, ▶see 528–9.

The types of documents required for applicants in (2) above are not stated, and indeed the Regulations indicate that the immigration officer may not require to see any further documents. For applicants in (2) who do not have a family permit or residence document, it is still safer for them to carry other documents that will confirm their status. For example, if they are a spouse, they should have their marriage certificate. If their family member is working, the applicant should have with them some documentation showing that their family member is indeed in employment.

Both the decision of the IAT in *Chang* and the EEA 2000 Regulations indicate that the examination of non-EEA national family members can be more extensive than for EEA nationals, and can include questioning to see whether a marriage is one of convenience (▶see further 527–8).

Again, entry may be refused on public policy grounds. If the EEA family member holds a family permit when they arrive, the family permit can be revoked by the immigration officer if revocation is justified on these grounds – or if, in fact, the person is not at that time the family member of a qualified EEA national. Residence documents can also be revoked on a person's arrival if the applicant is not at that time the family member of an EEA national (reg. 22(3)(4)).

DECISIONS REFUSING OR REVOKING RIGHTS

After an EEA national or their family member has entered the UK, and even after they have been issued with one of the documents described above, the immigration authorities can make decisions withdrawing their ability to exercise free-movement rights (regs 15, 21–22).

Rights can be refused or withdrawn in either of the following two situations.

1) When an EEA national is not or has ceased to be a 'qualified' person – i.e. is not or is no longer exercising rights of free movement, *or* when the person has ceased to be the 'family' member of such a person. So, a person who bases their rights on being a worker, who is out of work and is no longer genuinely seeking work with a realistic chance of finding it, will no longer qualify. A son or daughter of a worker who is over 21 and no longer dependent will no longer qualify as a family member.

2) When the EEA national or family member qualifies for free-movement rights in that they are within one of the categories described above, *but*

the Home Office decides to exclude them from the UK on 'public policy' grounds (see below).

In either of the two above situations, the immigration authorities in the UK can:

- refuse to issue or renew a residence permit or a residence document;
- revoke a residence permit, a residence document or an EEA family permit; or
- remove the person from the UK.

'Public policy' grounds

We have used 'public policy' to refer to situations where the Home Office is justified in excluding the rights of EEA nationals or their family members on grounds of 'public policy, public security and public health'. These exclusions are interpreted tightly and narrowly. The ECJ has repeatedly held that free movement is a fundamental principle, and that the 'public policy proviso' is an exception to it which must be interpreted strictly and in favour of the continued exercise of rights. The main EU provision dealing with exclusion on this basis is Council Directive 64/221/EEC (this will be consolidated in the Citizens' Directive (▶515) with some changes).

It was decided by the ECJ in *Rutili* that, while states are free to determine their own requirements of public policy, they cannot do so in a way which would undermine the fundamental principles of equality of treatment and freedom of movement for workers. In that case, the French authorities had sought to exclude an Italian trade unionist from entering the country. In addition, public policy grounds cannot be based on economic reasons (reg. 23(a) EEA 2000 Regulations).

Where, in an in-country case, the Home Office decides to remove an EEA national or their family member on public policy grounds, it will proceed using the deportation mechanism (▶see 555).

Exclusions based on conduct

As to decisions based on a person's conduct, the exclusion of an EEA national cannot be justified on grounds of general deterrence. In *Bouchereau*, the ECJ held that the person themselves must pose a 'genuine and sufficiently serious threat to the requirements of public policy affecting one of the fundamental interests of society'. A person's past conduct, including their previous criminal convictions, are relevant only if they indicate that that person is a *present* threat to the requirements of public policy. Although the Advocate General in that case thought that extremely severe past offending could alone be enough, the ECJ itself has not found that past conduct alone is enough, but has always referred to the need for there to be some future risk of re-offending. However, Home Office policy, supported by decisions of the Court of Appeal in cases such as *Marchon* and *Schmelz*, takes a different view (▶see under 'Home Office policy' below).

In *Adoui & Cornuaille*, which concerned French nationals who were prostitutes working in Belgium, the ECJ decided that member-states could not say that conduct was contrary to public policy if it did not enforce genuine and effective measures against its own nationals for the same conduct. The court in that case also ruled that an application for re-admission after expulsion on public policy grounds could be made after a 'reasonable period'. The national authorities would be required to take into account any material change in the circumstances of the applicant that would be relevant to an assessment of the threat they posed.

The essential points about conduct that might raise public policy or public security grounds, as taken from EU law and the EEA 2000 Regulations, can be summarised as follows (see reg. 23).

- It is personal conduct on the part of the person concerned that counts, not merely that which they might be presumed to be involved with by virtue of their membership of a particular group (such as football support-ers, or those of a particular religious persuasion).
- The conduct must be sufficiently serious to pose a genuine threat to society.
- Mere failure to comply with formalities of domestic law is not enough to justify exclusion (*Royer*).
- A person's previous criminal convictions do not in themselves justify a decision on public policy or public security grounds.
- The same conduct must be dealt with in relation to nationals of the state in a way which is comparable to the serious step of denying free-move-ment rights.

Home Office policy on exclusion based on criminal offences The policy, as set out in the EDI, on deportation in cases involving EEA nat-ionals and their family members who are convicted of criminal offences appears to be as follows (Ch 3, s1, paras 1.2–1.3; Ch 3, s2; Ch 3, s9, para. 9.3).

1) If the offence is a 'minor' one, deportation action is unlikely to be appropriate.

2) Where the offence is not a minor one and a border-line decision is taken not to deport, or the applicant has offended previously but still a decision not to deport is taken, the Home Office may send the person a 'warning' letter making it clear that the conduct is not acceptable to the UK and that, if repeated, consideration may be given to deportation.

3) Where the offence is a 'serious' one (normally resulting in a prison sentence of two years or more) *and* the 'subject's history and previous convictions provide evidence of a propensity to re-offend', deportation action may be taken.

4) Where the offence is 'particularly serious' (such as drug smuggling, facilitating entry of illegal immigrants, rape, murder, and so on) deporta-

tion may be considered 'even though there is no firm evidence of a propensity to re-offend'.

The Home Office provides a list of offences as follows, but unfortunately the guidance is contradictory as to whether the following offences are the 'serious' offences (as in (3) above) or the 'particularly serious' offences (as in (4) above) (see EDI at Ch3, s2, para. 2.1.1 and s9, para. 9.3):

- violence against the person (murder, attempted murder, threat or conspiracy to murder, manslaughter, inflicting GBH, inflicting ABH);
- sexual offences (offences against children, rape, indecent assault, procurement, pornography);
- burglary, robbery, theft (armed robbery, persistent and/or large-scale case of theft or burglary);
- other offences (blackmail, counterfeiting, forgery, trafficking forged passports, trafficking dangerous drugs, public order offences, assisting unlawful immigration, trafficking in prostitution).

Public health/security/policy grounds based on disabilities and diseases

Among the conditions that a person may have that would justify their being refused entry or refused a first residence permit or document are: active TB, syphilis, an infectious or parasitic disease that threatens public health, drug addictions, and serious mental conditions. However, if a person first begins suffering from a disease or disability *after* they have been issued with their first residence permit or residence document, they cannot be removed on these grounds (reg. 23(d)(e) and Sch 1).

Enforcement and detention

The powers to enforce the departure of, and to detain, EEA nationals who do not have rights of free movement are similar to the ordinary immigration powers of enforcement and detention (▶see Section 9). Indeed, the powers given in the EEA 2000 Regulations cross-refer to and apply the general immigration powers.

Note that the 2002 Act (and regulations made under it) provide for the temporary accommodation of EEA nationals and their dependants while arrangements are made for them to leave the UK, and for assistance with travel (▶see 1314).

On arrival

A person arriving in the UK may be examined and detained while awaiting a decision as to whether to admit them, if they are either (reg. 24):

- a non-EEA national who is claiming the right to be admitted to the UK as the family member of an EEA national; or

- an EEA national who the immigration authorities suspect may be refused on public policy grounds.

If, after their arrival in the UK, a person is refused entry because (reg. 25):

- they are excluded on public policy grounds;
- they cannot demonstrate that they are an EEA national; or
- if they are not an EEA national, they cannot show that they are the family member of an EEA national exercising rights of free movement;

then they are treated in the same way as if they had been refused 'leave' to enter. They may therefore be detained and, subject to appeals, removed from the UK. For rights of appeal, ▶see 556–9.

Decisions about whether to detain are made on the basis of policy criteria similar to those applied in non-EEA cases (▶see 905 onwards, and see the policy set out at EDI, Ch 3, s5).

After entry

When the immigration authorities decide that a person who has been admitted to the UK does not fall into any of the categories of persons exercising free-movement rights, as either an EEA national or their family member, they are treated in the same way as an overstayer or a person who has breached their conditions of leave. They may therefore be detained and, subject to appeal rights, removed from the UK (reg. 26(1)(2)).

When the immigration authorities decide that a person who has been admitted is to be excluded from exercising free-movement rights on public policy grounds, they are treated in the same way as people who are being 'deported' (reg. 26(1)(3)). Apparently, in order to ensure that they have full rights of appeal against such decisions, EEA nationals and their family members against whom this action is taken will actually be issued with a notice of intention to deport. This is done in the same way as deportation proceeds in non-EEA cases. If the notice of intention to deport is not overturned on appeal, the Home Office can proceed to making the deportation order (for the deportation process, ▶see 1015–26). It appears that the Home Office will also issue a notice of intention to deport if it intends to deport after a recommendation for deportation is made by a criminal court (see ss82(2)(j), 92(2) 2002 Act; EDI, Ch 3, s1; articles 8-9, Council Directive 64/221/EEC). People subject to this action can also be detained during the process.

Detention while appealing

A person may still be detained while appealing against a decision to refuse to admit them into, or to remove them from, the UK (see the above provisions and reg. 32(3)).

Temporary admission and bail

Those who are detained while being examined on arrival to the UK, after being refused admission to the UK, or while being removed or deported from the UK, have similar rights to apply for temporary admission and bail from the immigration authorities or the AIT as in other cases (regs 24(2), 25(3), 26(2)(3), which apply the relevant parts of the 1971 and 1999 Acts to EEA cases). They may also apply for bail while appealing against an EEA decision (reg. 32(6)).

RIGHTS OF APPEAL

The rights of appeal for EEA nationals and members of their families are set out in regulations 27–33 and Schedule 2 to the EEA 2000 Regulations. In most cases the appeal is to the Asylum and Immigration Tribunal (AIT).

In addition to relying upon their rights of free movement, appellants may also argue that an adverse decision is in breach of their human rights, or that they have been discriminated against. There is also nothing to prevent EEA nationals claiming asylum, although claims are likely to be treated as 'clearly unfounded'.

Applicants can appeal against 'EEA decisions'

Those who have, or who claim to have, rights of free movement (including A8 nationals) can appeal against what are defined in the regulations as 'EEA decisions'. EEA decisions are decisions under the EEA 2000 Regulations (or under regulation (EC) No 1251/70) which concern a person's (regs 2(1), 28, 29(1)):

- right to be admitted to the UK;
- right to be issued with, to renew, or not to have revoked, a residence permit or residence document;
- removal from the UK.

Decisions under Regulation (EC) No 1251/70 are decisions concerning the rights of permanent residence in the UK, which are set out in the table at 517 (▶see also below).

A refusal of an EEA family permit is an 'EEA decision' because it concerns an applicant's 'right to be admitted', just as does a refusal to grant entry on arrival. The Home Office accepts this (EDI, Ch 6, s3, para. 3.3). Note that where, in an in-country case, an EEA national or their family member are to be removed on public policy grounds, the Home Office will proceed by using deportation action (see above).

Although appeals can be brought against decisions that 'concern' the above matters, as with other immigration appeals, there will be no right of appeal where the Home Office is permitting the applicant to remain in the UK (see reg. 33). For EEA decisions specifically, this means that there will be no appeal if the Home Office recognises the applicant's right to reside by issuing them with:

- a residence permit;
- a residence document;
- a registration certificate under the Accession Regulations; or
- a 'family member residence stamp' (these are documents which can be issued to the non-EEA national family members of A8 nationals who are required to register).

There is thus no right of appeal, for example, against the length of validity of the document issued. In addition, if one of these documents is issued while the appeal is pending, the appeal will be treated as abandoned. *However*, despite this restriction on appeal rights, the following two points should be noted.

- The Home Office seems to accept that 'any refusal to grant indefinite leave to remain which has been requested in accordance with the criteria in para. 257' of the immigration rules (i.e. under Regulation (EC) No 1251/70) is an 'EEA decision which attracts a right of appeal' (EDI, Ch 12, s16-17). So, on the Home Office view, it seems that any refusal to accept rights of permanent residence under this regulation – even if the Home Office accepts a limited right of residence – will give rise to an appeal right. While this is a little hard to square with the language of the legislation, it does indeed seem to be the intention of the EEA 2000 Regulations to give rights of appeal in all cases where settlement is refused under that EC regulation (contrast the position in other settlement cases).
- The restriction does not prevent an EEA national or family member making an asylum 'status' appeal, even if their right to reside on other grounds has been recognised. This is the case provided that the asylum claim is not certified as 'clearly unfounded' which, in the case of an EEA national, it is likely to be (reg. 33(1B)–(1D).

There is also no right of appeal unless certain documents can be produced (immediately below).

Documents which must be produced in order to appeal

In order to be able to bring an EEA appeal at all, a person must first be able to produce either:

- a valid national identity card or a valid passport, if they are claiming to be an EEA national; or
- an EEA family permit, or some other proof that they are related as claimed to the EEA national (such as a marriage certificate or birth certificate), if they are claiming to be a family member of an EEA national.

A person will not be denied the right of appeal provided it is 'reasonably apparent' that such documents they produce are both genuine and relate to the holder.

Is it an in-country appeal?

The general rule is that appeals against EEA decisions are in-country. However, appeals against any of the three following EEA decisions are out-of-country *unless* they fall within the exceptions mentioned immediately below (reg. 30):

1) decisions to refuse to admit an applicant to the UK (*including* decisions to remove a person as a result of refusing to admit them);

2) decisions to refuse to revoke a deportation order made against an applicant;

3) decisions to refuse to issue a person with an EEA family permit.

The exceptions are that appeals against decisions in (1) above are still in-country where:

- the appellant seeks to raise human rights or asylum grounds; *or*
- when the appellant arrived in the UK, they held either a residence permit, a residence document or an EEA family permit.

There also appears to be a further exception, as follows. In (1) above, removals following on from a refusal to admit are seen simply as denials of admission, and there is generally no in-country appeal. However, *if* in reality an applicant has been in the UK for more than six months, on temporary admission waiting for a decision on their status, the Home Office seems to accept that they should then be treated as though they have been admitted (EDI, Ch 4, s1). Decisions to remove such applicants, as with other decisions to remove, should therefore give an in-country right of appeal. The basis for this would be the case of *Yiadom*. In that case the ECJ held that a decision to remove the applicant, who had been on temporary admission for seven months waiting for a decision on leave to enter, had to be seen as an expulsion decision, which carried with it appeal safeguards. It could not, in reality, still be seen as a decision simply concerning admission.

While a person is exercising an in-country right of appeal against an EEA decision, they cannot be removed from the UK, and neither can a deportation order be made against them (reg. 32(1)(2)(5)).

Who is the appeal to, and what procedures apply?

In most cases, the appeal is to the AIT, as in other immigration cases. The appeal system is essentially the same as it is for those appealing against 'immigration decisions' described in Section 10. The same procedure rules and notice regulations apply (Asylum and Immigration Tribunal (Procedure) Rules 2005, Immigration (Notices) Regulations 2003). In addition, in EEA cases, the same system of challenging decisions of the AIT (review, reconsideration, appeals to the Court of Appeal) applies in the same way as in other immigration cases (reg. 29(7) and Sch 2 EEA 2000

Regulations). Note, however, that an appeal against an EEA decision is not to be treated as abandoned just because an appellant leaves the UK (reg. 27(4)).

EEA appeals to SIAC

Appeals against EEA decisions are to the Special Immigration Appeals Commission (SIAC) if: the Secretary of State states that the decision was taken at least partly on the grounds of national security, or in the interests of the UK's international relations; or the information on which the decision was based should not be made public for similar reasons. If the appeal is to SIAC, then the ordinary provisions that apply to SIAC apply to it. For SIAC appeals (▶see 1081–3).

What if an ordinary 'immigration decision' is made? Can an appeal be brought?

If the immigration authorities have issued an ordinary 'immigration decision' – i.e. normally made in relation to those who do not have and who are not claiming free-movement rights (▶see 1053–4), the applicant can still appeal against it on free-movement grounds. This is because one of the grounds of appeal in ordinary immigration appeals is (s84(1)(d) 2002 Act):

'that the appellant is an EEA national or a member of the family of an EEA national and the decision breaches the appellant's rights under the Community Treaties in respect of entry to or residence in the United Kingdom...'

However, there are provisions aimed at preventing applicants from appealing on EEA grounds against an immigration decision where they have already had a right of appeal against an EEA decision (see reg. 33(3)(4)).

SETTLEMENT

The EEA nationals and their family members who are treated as 'settled' in the UK are (reg. 8 EEA 2000 Regulations):

1) those recognised as having a right of settlement under Regulation (EC) No 1251/70 (▶see table at 517);

2) self-employed persons who have stopped economic activity (▶see 520–21) and their family members who were living with them immediately before they stopped their economic activity in the UK;

3) family members of self-employed persons and self-employed persons who have stopped economic activity, where that person has died (▶see 537);

4) those granted permission to remain in the UK indefinitely under the immigration rules (▶see below).

Other EEA nationals are not treated as settled even though they may have a right to reside. Settlement is important because it means that the person's status is secure, even if they cease being entitled to exercise free-movement rights. This is particularly important for non-EEA national family members of EEA nationals. Also, children born in the UK to an EEA national who is treated as settled are automatically British citizens.

Categories (1)–(3) are all described earlier in this chapter. Below, we discuss solely those granted settlement under the immigration rules.

Rights to settlement under the immigration rules

The immigration rules allow all persons who have been admitted under the various 'economic' categories in the rules (workers, self-employed persons, business-people, etc.) to be given indefinite leave after four years. The immigration rules have extended the same principle to EEA nationals and members of their families who have been in the UK for four years (paras 255–255B, 257A–257B HC 395). (Note that the right to permanent residence will arise after five years' continuous lawful residence under Art 16 Citizens' Directive.)

Under these rules, EEA nationals and their family members may have their residence permit or document 'endorsed to show permission to remain in the UK indefinitely' if they meet all the following conditions:

1) they have remained in the UK for four years 'in accordance with the provisions' of the EEA 2000 Regulations (or the previous Immigration (European Economic Area) Order 1994);

2) they continue to be in the UK in accordance with those Regulations;

3) they have been issued with a residence permit or document which is valid for five years.

Students are, however, not entitled to obtain settlement under these rules.

Because the EEA 2000 Regulations are intended to reflect EU rights, 'in accordance with the Regulations' is intended to benefit those who have been in the UK exercising free-movement rights. So a person who has had some breaks in their employment while in the UK, but has continued to search for employment with a genuine chance of getting it, or who has been sick or on maternity leave, may still count the time when they were not working as part of the qualification period. The Home Office accepts that

'…periods of temporary unemployment may count towards the qualifying period if the EEA national was either incapacitated (sick, maternity leave etc.) or if involuntarily unemployed (e.g. made redundant and actively seeking new employment)' (EDI, Ch 7, s2, para. 2.1).

The four years do not have to be spent exercising free-movement rights in the same category. Applicants may combine periods spent in different categories, including any time spent exercising rights as a result of the decision in *Baumbast* (see above; EDI, Ch 7, s2, para. 2.6). In addition, a spouse who has ceased to live with, but has not divorced, the EEA national, can still count that time as part of the four-year qualification period.

Although the rules state that a residence permit or document must be held, in practice it is possible to apply for a residence permit or document at the same time as applying for permanent residence. In this case, the residence permit may be issued simultaneously, and endorsed with permission to remain indefinitely. But it is easy to see how holding a residence permit or document throughout the period will help an applicant to demonstrate that they have been exercising free-movement rights for four years.

Absences from the UK

According to a Home Office letter to Clifford Chance solicitors about these applications (dated 4 December 2001):

'Absences from the United Kingdom do not penalise an application. Periods spent here in exercise of a treaty right may be amalgamated. Only in the case of very long absences would consideration be given to refusing the application.'

A good yard-stick is probably the fact that the EEA 2000 Regulations do not treat the validity of a residence permit as being affected by absences unless they are for more than six consecutive months (absences for military service are also discounted; reg. 18(7)).

Making applications

Applications by EEA nationals and their family members can be made by using Form EEC2. It is available on the IND website. Using the form is not, however, compulsory (see para. 32 HC 395). The applicant should produce any residence permit or document, their passport, and evidence of their having been in the UK exercising free-movement rights for four years. This could include such evidence as: wage-slips across the relevant period, a letter or letters from employers confirming the length of the period of employment, or a statement of the applicant's national insurance contributions record.

Granting settlement

Those granted settlement under these provisions of the rules used to be given an 'indefinite leave to remain' vignette in their passports. The practice now is to place an endorsement in the passport stating that there is no time-limit on the holder's stay in the UK.

Family members

Home Office decision-making in relation to family members can be inconsistent. Sometimes the passports of family members are endorsed to show permission to remain permanently at the same time as is that of the EEA national, even if the family members have not been in the UK for the four-year period. On other occasions, the Home Office requires that the family members themselves have completed four years' residence.

Appeals

There is no right of appeal to the AIT against refusal to grant settlement for those whose rights come simply from the immigration rules *unless*, at the same time, the Home Office is denying any right of residence by refusing to issue a residence permit or document, and/or makes a decision to remove. In this case the decision will amount to an 'EEA decision' (see above), and there is a right of appeal (see also EDI, Ch 12, s17). In some cases, a refusal may simply be based on the fact that the Home Office does not accept that the applicant has yet spent four years in the relevant capacity, in which case there will be no appeal right.

Transitional arrangements for Swiss nationals and A8 nationals seeking settlement

Transitional arrangements are made to allow time to count towards settlement, where a Swiss or A8 national was here lawfully under the immigration rules in certain categories, before nationals of those countries obtained free-movement rights – 1 June 2002 for Swiss nationals, and 1 May 2004 for A8 nationals. These transitional arrangements are contained in paragraphs 255A-255B and 257A-257B of HC 395.

Swiss nationals Swiss nationals can add the time they spent before 1 June 2002 in the UK, with leave in any category which allows applicants to obtain indefinite leave after four continuous years (i.e. all the main economic categories under the Rules), to time spent after that date, in accordance with the EEA 2000 Regulations. So a Swiss national who had spent two years with leave as a work-permit holder before 1 June 2002 would still be able to obtain settlement in June 2004 if they remained in the UK in accordance with the EEA 2000 Regulations between June 2002 and June 2004.

In addition, a Swiss national who, before 1 June 2002, was granted a probationary period of leave as a spouse, and who, after that date, was exercising free-movement rights under the EEA 2000 Regulations (as a family member or otherwise), may be granted settlement straightaway – i.e. without having to wait for the expiry of the probationary period. In order to be granted settlement under this rule, the applicant would, however, have to meet the other normal requirements of the rules for settlement as a spouse (marriage subsisting, intention to live together, maintenance and accommodation, etc.). Most Swiss nationals who benefit from this will probably already have made their applications.

Accession 8 nationals The same transitional arrangements apply to A8 nationals as to Swiss nationals (▶see above). Obviously, the modification is that the relevant 'transitional' date is the date of accession – 1 May 2004 (▶see 573).

CLAIMING WELFARE

EEA nationals are not 'subject to immigration control' under the 1999 Act – i.e. for benefits and other welfare purposes. However, like all claimants, from 1 August 1994 EEA nationals have to be 'habitually resident' in order to claim the core means-tested benefits (for the habitual residence test and the exemptions from it, ▶see 1259–64).

From 1 May 2004, in order to be habitually resident it is necessary to have a 'right to reside' in the UK. For EEA nationals and their family members who do not have leave in the UK, this means a right to reside on the basis of EU free-movement rights (see reg. 14). While this chapter has set out who is entitled to free-movement rights, for specific details about the right-to-reside test in the context of benefits, ▶see 1264–8. The main aim of this new test for benefits was to exclude A8 nationals who had come to the UK (or who were still in the UK at accession) and who did not have employment or other means of support. For the application of the test to A8 nationals, ▶see 1268–73. However, the new test obviously has implications for non-A8 EEA nationals as well. For example, a work-seeker still looking for work after six months might be refused benefit on the grounds that they no longer have a right to reside (and are therefore not habitually resident). So might a person intending to be self-employed, or a business-person who has not been able to set up their own business.

Those in the 'self-sufficient' categories (self-sufficient persons, retired persons and some students) might lose the right to reside by claiming benefits – i.e. by becoming a 'burden on the social assistance system'. As set out above, however, claiming benefits should not be enough on its own to exclude the right to reside, because excluding a person on these grounds is only permitted if it is proportionate to do so (▶see 523–4). Questions such as how long the person is likely to be claiming for, and how long they have been self-sufficient, would be relevant. Of course, a 'chicken-and-egg' situation arises here: if the right to reside is lost by claiming benefit, then the claimant will, at the same time, no longer be able to pass the habitual residence test to claim core means-tested benefits, and will no longer be a burden on at least this part of the social assistance system.

Workers, the self-employed and non-A8 EEA national work-seekers may claim benefits without ceasing to lose their rights under EU law. Workers may receive the 'in-work' benefits, such as housing and council tax benefit, the tax credits and child benefit. Of course, prolonged claiming by work-seekers may indicate that they are not in fact genuinely seeking work.

Social services, Children Act, asylum support, 'hard cases' support, housing

From 8 January 2003, support for EEA nationals and their family members from other sources – social services, the Children Act, asylum support and 'hard cases' support – has been severely restricted by Schedule 3 to the 2002 Act. Support may still be claimed if denying it would be a breach of the applicant's human rights or rights under the EC Treaties (see paras 1-3, 5, Sch 3 2002 Act). For further details about this, ▶see 1306 (and follow the further cross-references). For details about access to local authority housing for A8 and EEA nationals ▶see 1295–6 and ▶see generally 1290–8.

The 2002 Act (and regulations made under it) provide for the temporary accommodation of EEA nationals and their dependants while arrangements are made for them to leave the UK, and for assistance with travel (▶see 1314).

19 Rights of nationals of accession states

The overall structure, membership and development of the EU/EEA is explained in Chapter 17.

On 16 April 2003, a Treaty of Accession was signed in Athens between the 15 existing states of the EU and ten new states. This led to those new states joining the EU on 1 May 2004. The ten states are: Cyprus, the Czech Republic, Estonia, Hungary, Latvia, Lithuania, Malta, Poland, Slovakia and Slovenia. The European Union (Accession) Act 2003 allowed the Accession Treaty to be implemented in UK law. The important regulations made under that Act are the 'Accession (Immigration and Worker Registration) Regulations 2004'. Throughout this chapter and elsewhere we have referred to them simply as the 'Accession Regulations'.

Note that many of the restrictions on the rights of 'Accession 8' nationals referred to in this chapter are intended to affect their access to welfare entitlement. The right to reside test as it affects access to benefit is discussed more fully in Chapter 39, at ▶1264–8. The particular effect of the 'right to reside' test on A8 nationals and information about those who are exempt from the requirement to register under the worker registration scheme are also fully set out in that chapter, at ▶1268–73. For the effect on access to housing provided by a local authority, ▶see 1295–6 and ▶see generally 1290–8.

All ten of the accession states are included in the new definition of 'EEA State' contained in the EEA 2000 Regulations (see reg. 3, Accession Regulations, which amends the EEA 2000 Regulations). On the face of it, the effect of this is to give nationals of accession countries exactly the same rights as other EEA nationals. Accession nationals can become 'qualified persons' and have the 'right to reside' in the UK (regs 5 and 14 EEA 2000 Regulations), just like other EEA nationals.

Nationals of Cyprus and Malta As far as nationals of Cyprus and Malta (and their family members) are concerned, the following applies: they have the same rights of free movement as other EEA nationals, and can obtain residence permits and documents for themselves and their family members, just as other EEA nationals do. For the other eight states, rights are more restricted (►see below). Note that by 'Cyprus' is meant the Republic of Cyprus, not the 'Turkish Republic of Northern Cyprus' (TRNC), which is not recognised by the British government. Only documents issued by the Republic of Cyprus will be accepted as showing that the holder is an EEA national.

'Accession 8' nationals Nationals of the other eight states (who have become known as 'Accession 8' or 'A8' nationals) do not automatically have the same rights as other EEA nationals. Member states are permitted to impose restrictions on them during a transitional period. Technically, the Treaty permits member states to 'derogate from' (which really just means 'not apply') the rights in Articles 1–6 of EC Regulation 1612/68, and certain rights under Directive 68/360. Importantly, this allows restrictions to be placed on the rights of workers and work-seekers, and on access to residence permits/documents. The UK's Accession Regulations have indeed made use of these 'derogation' powers, so that the EEA 2000 Regulations apply to A8 nationals with restrictions. As a result of the restrictions, not all A8 workers and work-seekers are 'qualified persons' with the 'right to reside' under the EEA 2000 Regulations. A8 nationals can exercise all *other* EU free movement rights without restrictions. So A8 nationals in the following categories have the same free movement rights as other EEA nationals: self-employed, providers of services, recipients of services, self-sufficient persons, retired persons, students, and self-employed people who have ceased economic activity.

Period for restrictions on Accession 8 nationals The restrictions can initially be applied for five years (i.e. until 1 May 2009) and, exceptionally, for a further two years (until 1 May 2011). The present Accession Regulations impose restrictions under UK law until 30 April 2009 (see reg. 1(2)(c)). Under those Regulations, this period is defined as the 'accession period'.

In what follows below, we:

- briefly examine the policy background in relation to how restrictions came to be imposed (►immediately below);
- discuss the *five* important restrictions imposed on the rights of A8 nationals (►568–71);
- discuss the actual impact of the above restrictions on the immigration rights of A8 nationals. This includes looking at: rights of entry and settlement, the rights of family members of A8 nationals, and the possibility of removal (►571–3);
- discuss the Worker Registration Scheme and its practicalities (►573–5).

THE ROAD TO RESTRICTIONS

In December 2002 the government announced that it would, from the time of accession, grant nationals of the A8 countries the same rights to work in the UK as are guaranteed by EU law to nationals of other member states. This remained the government's intention at the time of the passing of the Accession Act (see above). It stated that it would keep the ability to impose restrictions as a 'safeguard'. The Explanatory Notes that accompanied the Accession Act issued in November 2003 stated:

'The Government does not expect that safeguards will be necessary, but intends to monitor closely the application of regulations made under the Act. As far as possible, this will be done through existing means of monitoring the labour market...'

An about-turn

Following intense media speculation about the effects of accession and the demands that it would make on the benefits system, there was an abrupt change of approach, signalled by an announcement by the Home Secretary on 23 February 2004. The Home Office's own consultation material concerning the implementing Regulations stated that they were intended to:

'...modify the application of the [EEA Regulations 2000] in relation to workers and work seekers from the accession States...in accordance with the Accession Treaty derogation on regulating access to the United Kingdom labour market. Workers from the [A8 states] will generally only have a right to reside in the United Kingdom as workers if they are working for an employer who is authorised to employ them under the worker registration scheme set out in the draft regulations...'

It soon became clear that, in large part, the purpose of denying certain A8 nationals this 'right to reside' was in fact to exclude them from access to *welfare support*. On the eve of accession, 25 March 2004, the Home Office put out a press release stressing the benefit to the economy of further migrant workers, but making clear that it would severely restrict access to benefits:

'They will help to fill half a million job vacancies and we will benefit from this, whether they are plumbers, plasterers or paediatricians. Hard working immigrants are welcome. Benefit tourists are not. That is why the Government is putting in place a package of measures to prevent people who are not working from accessing benefits.

The UK has one of the most dynamic economies in the world with record employment levels. Our economy can only benefit from freedom of movement of workers from the new member states. They too will benefit from a boost to their economies, with fast growth and a likely flood of foreign investment – ultimately creating jobs and opportunity in their own countries...' (138/2004, 25 March 2004)

Numbers registering and claiming benefit

According to Home Office figures, 91,000 A8 nationals registered for work between May and September 2004 (about 45 per cent of these people were definitely in the UK before 1 May 2004). This represents about 0.3 per cent of the UK workforce. Ninety-five per cent of those who registered had no dependants. Only about 500 attempted to claim out-of-work benefits, of which 97 per cent were refused. Many more claimed child benefit. (Figures from Home Office press release, 10 November 2004).

THE FIVE RESTRICTIONS ON THE RIGHTS OF A8 NATIONALS

There are five areas in which A8 nationals' rights are restricted in comparison to those of other EEA nationals. We set them out in turn below. Some parts of the restrictions are controversial – they may be contrary to EU law. We do not discuss those issues here, as they are complex. We set out the position as the government has established it in legislation.

1) No 'right to reside' as a work-seeker

Regulation 4 of the Accession Regulations specifically restricts rights granted under EU law. It states that A8 nationals who are non-self-sufficient *work-seekers* do not have the 'right to reside' in the UK. Of course, non-A8 EEA nationals generally have the right to reside while they are genuinely and realistically looking for work (this normally covers them for at least six months, ▶see 519 above). This restriction applies to A8 work-seekers who, in order to work in the UK, would need to register under the Worker Registration Scheme.

However, not all A8 nationals who work in the UK during the 'accession period' (which lasts until 30 April 2009) need to register. Regulation 2 of the Accession Regulations sets out a number of categories of people who are not 'accession state workers requiring registration'. These groups are set out as categories (1)–(7) in the table in Chapter 39, at ▶1270–2 (as indicated, the 'right to reside' relates mostly to access to welfare). A8 nationals who are within any of those categories can still have the right to reside, even if they are work-seekers. A very limited further exception is made to allow certain A8 nationals who lose their employment to keep their right to reside until the end of the month (▶see 1273). A8 nationals who are not in any of those categories do not have the right to reside while seeking work. Note that category (8) refers to those who are *working* and who do not have a registration certificate (▶1272–3).

The best known of the exempt categories is A8 nationals who have legally worked in the UK without interruption for a minimum 12-month period which ends after 30 April 2004 (category (4) ▶at 1271–2). A8 nationals in this position who stop working may have the right to reside while looking for further work.

This restriction on the right to reside does not apply to those who are entitled to reside as self-sufficient persons (▶see 522, reg. 4(3) Accession Regulations), even though they may also be work-seekers.

2) Requirement to work for an 'authorised employer' (in most cases this means registering under the Worker Registration Scheme)

An A8 national who is an 'accession state worker requiring registration' (i.e. who is not in any of the exceptions referred to in (1) above) will still not have the right to reside in the UK when they work, *unless* they are working for an 'authorised employer' (regs 4(4) and 5, Accession Regulations). Non-A8 EEA workers, of course, have the right to reside without having to work for an authorised employer.

Who is working for an authorised employer? An A8 national who is validly registered under the 'Worker Registration Scheme', and who has a certificate authorising them to work for their employer, is working for an authorised employer (see below for details of the scheme and certificates, etc). However, some accession state workers who require registration are *still* treated as working for authorised employers *even though* they do not hold a valid registration certificate. This applies to the groups set out in category (8), at ▶1272–3 (essentially, this includes: those legally working on 30 April 2004 who are still working for the same employer; those who apply to register within a month of beginning work, and who are still waiting for a decision on the application; certain seasonal agricultural workers, but only to the end of 2004 (reg. 7, Accession Regulations)).

As with (1) above, this restriction does not apply to those exercising free-movement rights in other capacities. Sometimes the line between employment and self-employment can be blurred. The Home Office is alive to the possibility of people calling themselves self-employed in order to get around the restrictions and inconvenience imposed on workers. It has issued detailed guidance to caseworkers identifying factors to help them distinguish between A8 nationals who are:

'...genuinely self-employed, and those where the applicant is in disguised employment and who is therefore required to register under the Worker Registration Scheme...'

Where there may be any question of a self-employed A8 national being treated as an employee, applicants and advisers should check this guidance, as it will help where the self-employed person wishes to apply for a residence permit. The guidance is contained in the European Directorate Instructions ('EDI'), Ch. 14, annexes C–E.

3) Narrow definition of 'family member' for the purposes of deciding which A8 national family members do not need to register

A8 nationals who are family members of non-accession EEA nationals who are exercising free-movement rights do not need to register under the Worker Registration Scheme in order to work. They also do not need to register if they are family members of an A8 national who is exercising free movement rights *and* who does not need to register. Other A8 nationals who are family members do need to register. The exempt group of A8 nationals who are family members is one of the categories referred to in (1) above who are excepted from the requirement to register (▶see category (7) at 1272).

However, the definition of 'family member' for the purposes of defining who falls into this exempt category is narrower than the normal EU definition of a family member. It covers the following family members: the EEA national's spouse, and children who are under 21 or dependent on them (for workers and the self-employed); the EEA national's spouse, and children who are dependent on them (for all other cases) (see reg. 2(6)(b), (9)(c), Accession Regulations). Compared to the usual EU definition, this definition misses out: (1) dependent relatives in the *ascending* line (grandparents); (2) children of the EEA national's *spouse* (see reg. 6, EEA 2000 Regulations). On the face of it, these latter family members will have to register if they wish to work. It should be noted, however, that the law on these aspects is not straightforward.

4) Restricted access to residents' permits/documents

A8 nationals who are 'accession state workers requiring registration' (see (1) above) are not entitled to residence permits or documents issued either for themselves or their family members (including the more distant family members who may sometimes be admitted on the basis of discretion) (see reg. 5(5)(6), Accession Regulations). A8 nationals who do not need to register (i.e. the exempted categories referred to in (1) above, being categories (1)–(7) in the table at ▶1270–2) and their family members are entitled to residence permits/documents. So, where an A8 national does not need to register – for example, after they have 'legally worked' (this will usually be work done while registered under the scheme) for 12 continuous months – they and their family members are entitled, like other EEA nationals, to residence permits and documents (▶see 1271–2 for the calculation of the 12 continuous months).

Presumably, the thinking of the government here is that, for A8 nationals who need to register, a registration card and certificate is enough to demonstrate their status.

As for family members of A8 nationals who are required to register, the Home Office has stated that their rights can be demonstrated by getting a stamp in their passport stating that they are the family member of a person working for an 'authorised employer' under the Accession Regulations. These are referred to as 'family member residence stamps' (see EDI, Ch 14, paras 5, 5.1). They can be applied for using form EEC3 (and see reg. 33 (1A)(S) EEA 2000 Regulations).

5) Denial of access to welfare for those who do not have the 'right to reside'

The 'habitual residence' test was amended so that, unless a person has the 'right to reside', they *cannot* be habitually resident, regardless of how long they have been in the UK or their reasons for being here (see Social Security (Habitual Residence) Amendment Regulations 2004). A person who is not habitually resident is excluded from many welfare benefits, as well as from access to homelessness assistance. It will be clear from the above restrictions on the 'right to reside' that this amendment to the habitual residence test severely affects A8 nationals. Although the 'right to reside' test is aimed mainly at A8 nationals, it applies to everyone, and will in particular affect other EEA nationals as well. We deal fully with the 'right to reside test' as it affects welfare rights in Chapter 39, at ▶1264–8. For the particular effect of the 'right to reside' test on A8 nationals, ▶see 1268–73. For the effect on access to housing provided by a local authority, ▶see 1295–6 and ▶see generally 1290–8.

IMPACT OF THE RESTRICTIONS ON A8 NATIONALS' AND THEIR FAMILIES' IMMIGRATION RIGHTS

Although the above restrictions relate to who has the 'right to reside' in the UK, and although formal residence permits/documents are denied to many A8 nationals in the short term, the main intentions of the restrictions are: (1) to deny access to welfare rights, and (2) to allow the government to monitor numbers of A8 nationals entering the labour force and claiming benefits (see the statistics quoted above, ▶567–8). Of course, exclusion from benefits and housing can have an indirect effect on immigration rights. Below, however, we look at the direct implications for the immigration rights of A8 nationals.

Rights of entry and enforcement

Although A8 nationals' rights to reside are restricted, there is no additional restriction on their rights to enter the UK. As with other EEA nationals, A8 nationals have a right to be admitted to the UK under Regulation 12 EEA 2000 Regulations, provided that they produce a valid national ID card or a passport. As with other EEA nationals, of course, this right can be denied on public policy grounds. So, an A8 national will not be prevented from entering the UK simply because, at the time of entry, they have no offer of employment.

Removal

The Home Office does not intend to enforce the removal of A8 nationals simply because they are in the UK with no right to reside. At the time the Accession Regulations were being brought in, the responsible minister was asked at the House of Commons Home Affairs Committee whether a non-self-financing, unemployed A8 national would be 'deported'. She stated:

'Not unless they are causing a nuisance or committing offences. If they are self-sufficient and they then become not self-sufficient because their money runs out, they will either have to go home or they can, if they have got any resources, start a business and become self-employed but they cannot, as a work-seeking person who has not got work, access support from the state.'

She added:

'It really does not make any sense to mobilise any special removal process because we could not implement it...' (Beverley Hughes MP, Minister of State, 9 March 2004)

It seems likely that A8 nationals – even those who have no rights of residence – will only be removed on public policy grounds (▶see 552–4).

Rights of family members of A8 nationals

The EEA 2000 Regulations implement the rights under EU law given to family members of EEA nationals, as well as to EEA nationals themselves (for these rights generally, ▶see 526–40). Because the accession states are now 'EEA States' for the purposes of the EEA 2000 Regulations, this of course means that those regulations cover non-EEA national family members of *A8* nationals as well.

However, as with other EEA nationals, the rights of an A8 national's family member depend on the rights of the A8 national themselves. Where the A8 national has no 'right to reside' in the UK as a 'qualified person' under the EEA 2000 Regulations as modified by the Accession Regulations (i.e. because they are a work-seeker or are not working for an authorised employer), their family members will also have no rights to reside in the UK. Where the A8 national does have a right to reside, so will their family members (see regs 6 and 14(2), EEA 2000 Regulations).

The Regulations are not absolutely clear as to whether the family member of an A8 national who themselves needs to register, and has registered, *also* needs to register *if* they also want to work (see the above Regulations, but see also reg. 2(6)(b)(i) of the Accession Regulations). The intention seems to be that such a family member will also need to register for as long as the principal needs to register. When the principal no longer needs to register, the family member will not need to either (see also EDI, Ch 14, para. 5).

Settlement rights

As with other EEA nationals, A8 nationals can qualify for settlement after four years spent in the UK with the right to reside under the EEA Regulations. Periods during which an A8 national does not have the 'right to reside' in the UK (i.e. because they are a work-seeker, or because they are working but not for an 'authorised employer'), will not count towards the four-year qualifying period to obtain the right of permanent residence. This is because such periods are not periods during which the A8 national is in the UK 'in accordance with the provisions of the EEA 2000 Regulations' (para. 255 HC 395). For rights to settlement for EEA nationals generally, ▶see 559–63. Two further points about settlement rights for A8 nationals should be noted:

Does time spent before 1 May 2004 count for settlement purposes?
Yes. A8 nationals can add the time they spent, before 1 May 2004, in the UK with leave in any capacity that allows applicants to obtain indefinite leave after four continuous years (i.e. all the main economic categories under the Rules) to time spent after 1 May 2004 in the UK in accordance with the EEA 2000 Regulations (see para. 255B HC 395). So, an A8 national who spent two years with leave as a work permit holder before 1 May 2004 would still be able to obtain settlement in May 2006. This prevents such a person from losing out on their rights to settlement as a result of accession.

Accession nationals and the asylum family concession A8 nationals who were already in the UK on 1 May 2004, and had claimed asylum, can benefit from the backlog clearance concession for asylum-seeking families on the same terms as non-A8 nationals (see letter of NASS Director at Home Office to Chief Executives of local authorities, 7 May 2004). Obviously, the A8 national and their family would have to qualify under the terms of the concession. (For further details about the family concession, ▶see 668–9.) Immediate indefinite leave is obviously a better status than the restricted free movement rights enjoyed by A8 nationals until they are eligible for settlement.

Transitional arrangements

There are transitional arrangements for accession nationals and their family members who become entitled to free-movement rights after 1 May 2004 (reg. 6, Accession Regulations). For accession nationals and their family members who qualify for the *right to reside* after 1 May 2004:

- any conditions which attached to leave given to them before 1 May 2004 ceased to exist on 1 May 2004;

- any directions given before 1 May 2004 for their removal as port removals, illegal entrants or as 'administrative removal' cases (overstayers, etc) cease to have any effect on 1 May 2004;

- *however*, where the Home Office made a decision to deport before 1 May 2004, that decision will be treated as a decision to remove on public policy grounds, and there will be a right of appeal against it as though it were an 'EEA decision' (▶see 556 onwards).

THE WORKER REGISTRATION SCHEME

As indicated above, on 23 February 2004 the Home Office announced the introduction of the 'Worker Registration Scheme'. It is worth noting that the Home Secretary indicated that it would be the beginning of a national identity card scheme for non-nationals:

'This will provide a platform for a national ID scheme under which, in time, all non-UK nationals will be required to register...' (23 February 2004)

A8 nationals who do not fall within any of the exceptions referred to above are required to apply to register their work under the scheme (for the exceptions in detail, ▶see 1270–2). They must apply within a month of starting work and, provided they do this, they will be treated as having the right to reside while they are waiting for a decision (see reg. 7(2)(b), Accession Regulations, and above).

How to apply

In order to apply to register, applicants must submit an application form (Form WRS) as well as a passport/ID card, two passport-sized photographs and a letter from their employer confirming when the employment began. It seems that an employment agency can provide the relevant evidence if it can show that they are providing work to the applicant. Forms can be obtained by contacting the Application Forms Unit on 0870 241 0645, or from the website (www.workingintheuk.gov.uk).

The application should be sent to:

Work Permits (UK) – Workers Registration Team
Home Office
Walsall Road
Cannock
WS11 0WS

The cost for first-time applicants is £50, but there are no subsequent charges. The Home Office has recommended that the employer should take a copy of the application form before it is sent off, and keep it in order to protect themselves from prosecution.

Documents issued when a person registers

If the application is successful, the applicant is sent both a worker 'registration card' and a 'registration certificate'. The applicant's passport/ID card should be returned. The certificate is particular to the employment with the stated employer, and the employer is also sent a copy. The certificate expires as soon as the worker stops working for that employer. So, if the applicant changes jobs, or takes an additional job, they must register the new job, and a further certificate will be issued authorising the applicant to work for the new employer. However, where the worker has already registered once, no further registration card will be issued, and there is also no charge for registering new or additional employment after the first registration charge.

Registration cards contain the name, nationality, date of birth and photograph of the applicant. They also have a reference number.

Registration certificates contain the name of the applicant, the reference number of the applicant's registration card, the name and address of the head or main office of the employer as stated in the application, the date on which the applicant began working for the employer, and the date of issue of the certificate.

Time for determining applications

The Home Office initially indicated that a dedicated team would deal with applications, and that 80 per cent of applications would be processed within 24 hours after the payment had cleared (Work Permits (UK) User Panel, 29 April 2004).

Refusals

If the Home Office is not satisfied that the applicant is an accession state worker eligible to register, or that the applicant began working for the particular employer on the date stated in the application, a notice of refusal will be sent out. There is no right of appeal to the AIT against such a decision. If a refusal has been received, it may be appropriate to make further representations or a re-application. Ultimately, the means of challenging the refusal would be judicial review.

Employer sanctions

It is a criminal offence for an employer to employ an accession state worker who requires registration if that employer is not an 'authorised employer' (see reg. 9, Accession Regulations). No offence will be committed if the A8 national does not in fact need to register; and note also that, in some cases, an employer is 'authorised' even if no valid certificate has (yet) been issued (▶see 569 above).

In addition, it is a defence to any criminal charge if the employer did not know that the employment of the worker in question was an offence *and*, in the first month of employment, the employer was shown a document, which appeared to the employer to show *either*:

- that the worker was not an accession worker who needed to register; *or*
- that the worker had applied for a registration certificate (in this case, the employer must also not have received either a copy of the certificate or a notice of refusal of the certificate).

In either case, in order for the defence to succeed, the employer must have kept a copy of the relevant document. This offence is separate from the criminal sanctions which can apply to employers under section 8 of the 1996 Act (s8 and the defences are covered at ▶496–500).

6

20 Association and Cooperation agreements

In addition to the rights of free movement that apply within the European Economic Area (▶see Chapter 18), the European Community has agreements with some non-EEA states providing certain immigration rights to nationals of those non-EEA countries. This chapter is concerned with those rights. The most important agreements are the Association Agreements with Bulgaria and Romania (▶see immediately below). The immigration rights under those agreements are for those who want to establish themselves in business, and they are written into the immigration rules. The EC had made similar agreements with some of the countries that joined the EU on 1 May 2004. However, nationals of the accession states now have free-movement rights as EEA nationals.

Further important rights are contained in a very different Association Agreement with Turkey. This is also known as the 'Ankara Agreement'. This agreement provides rights for some Turkish workers who have *already* entered and lawfully worked in the UK for certain periods. It also gives Turkish nationals who wish to establish themselves in business the right to have their application determined in accordance with older (and more generous) immigration rules (▶see 585–9).

Finally, we note briefly the agreements with certain other countries, which essentially give rise to 'non-discrimination' rights in employment and other areas, rather than specifically giving immigration rights (▶590–1).

ASSOCIATION AGREEMENTS WITH BULGARIA AND ROMANIA

Over time, the European Community negotiated agreements with ten 'Central and Eastern European Countries' (CEECs), which gave rise to rights to move for the purposes of establishment in business. This set of Association Agreements became known collectively as the 'Europe Agreements'. In *Gloszczuk*, the ECJ confirmed that the EU rights of establishment under the Europe Agreements are 'directly effective'. This means that they are directly part of the law of the member states. However, just as the EEA 2000 Regulations set out and describe rights of free movement in the EEA; the immigration rules set out rights under the Association Agreements (see paras 211–223, HC 395).

As stated above, many of the countries with whom the Europe Agreements were made have now acceded to the EU, and their nationals benefit from free-movement rights as a result. Until 1 May 2004, the immigration rules covered the Association Agreements with Bulgaria, the Czech Republic, Estonia, Hungary, Latvia, Lithuania, Poland, Romania, Slovakia and Slovenia. *However*, from that date, it is only the Association Agreements with Bulgaria and Romania, reached on 1 February 1995, that are of importance. Therefore, the immigration rules dealing with Association Agreements now refer only to nationals of those two countries (see amendments to rules, from 1 May 2004, made by HC 523).

The Agreements allow nationals of Bulgaria and Romania to establish themselves in the UK (and other member states) as business-persons – either as self-employed, owners of companies, or those in partnerships. Of course, the immigration rules themselves provide rights for such business-persons (▶see 478–80), but the rights under the Association Agreements give significant advantages: there is no minimum capital investment requirement, nor does the business have to employ a minimum number of people. A person with a viable business as a self-employed window cleaner can therefore succeed.

Applicants may initially be given leave to enter for a year, and then extensions of stay for a further three years. After four continuous years, they are eligible to apply for settlement. It is essential to note that both the Agreements and the rules relate to establishment in business – they do *not* give movement rights to those in employment.

Entry clearance

The immigration rules require all applicants to obtain an entry clearance in this capacity. Those seeking entry must hold a valid entry clearance, and those seeking to extend their leave in-country must have originally entered with a valid entry clearance for admission under the Association Agreements. For the circumstances in which these requirements may be waived, ▶see 580–2 below.

WHAT THE RULES SAY

The rules provide separately for (paras 211–223):

- people who intend to 'establish themselves in a company'; and
- people who intend to 'establish themselves in self-employment or in partnership'.

The requirements for both are, however, very similar, and there are some common requirements that apply to both.

Persons establishing themselves in a company

In order to be admitted as a person intending to establish themselves in a company in the UK which he or she 'effectively controls', all of the following requirements must be met:

- the applicant must be a national of Bulgaria or Romania;
- the applicant must have a controlling interest in the company;
- the applicant must be actively involved in the promotion and management of the company;
- the company must be registered in the UK, and must be trading or providing services in the UK;
- the company must own the assets of the business;
- where the applicant is taking over an existing company, they must produce a written statement of the agreement on which they are taking it over, and the company's previous annual audited accounts;
- the common requirements (▶see below) must be met.

Persons establishing themselves in self-employment or partnership

In order to be admitted as a person intending to establish themselves in self-employment or in partnership in the UK, all of the following requirements must be met:

- the applicant must be a national of Bulgaria or Romania;
- the applicant must be actively involved in trading or providing services on their own or as part of a partnership in the UK;
- the applicant, alone or with their partners, will be the owners of the assets of the business;
- if the business is a partnership, the applicant's part in the business must not be employment 'in disguise';
- where the applicant is taking over or joining an existing business, they must produce a written statement of the agreement on which they are taking it over or joining it, and the business' previous annual audited accounts;
- the common requirements (▶see below) must be met.

Common requirements

The common requirements, which all the above applicants must meet, are that:

- the money they are putting into the business must be under their control, and must be enough to establish the business in the UK;
- until the business provides the applicant with an income, they must have sufficient funds to maintain and accommodate themselves and

their dependants without taking employment (other than working for the business) or having recourse to public funds;

- the applicant's profits from the business must be sufficient to maintain and accommodate themselves and their dependants without taking employment (other than working for the business) or having recourse to public funds;

- the applicant must not intend to seek or take any other employment in the UK other than their work for the business.

When a person is admitted to the UK under the Association Agreements, they will be given leave to enter initially for 12 months, with a condition restricting them to working only in the business.

Applications to extend stay

In addition to the nationality requirements, applicants must show that they have actually established themselves in business, that their profits are sufficient to maintain themselves and their dependants, and that they will not take work outside the business. When applying, applicants must produce audited accounts to show the present financial position of the business. Applicants also need to show:

- in the case of companies, that they are actively involved in promoting and managing the company, that they have a controlling interest in it, that the company is registered in the UK and is trading or providing services in the UK, and that it owns the assets of the business;

- in the case of those who are in self-employment or partnership, that they are actively involved in trading or in providing services either, themselves or through the partnership, that they (alone or with their partners) own the assets of the business and, in the case of partnerships, that the applicant is not being employed 'in disguise'.

Extensions are granted for periods of up to three years.

Entry clearance and switching to stay under the Association Agreements

The decisions of the ECJ in September 2001 in *Gloszczuk*, *Kondova* and *Barkoci & Malik* made it clear that, although the rights under the Association Agreements are 'directly effective', member states are still entitled to have rules in place to control rights of entry and residence for those wanting to benefit from the Agreements. As part of this, it was confirmed that the host country is entitled to require that those wishing to establish themselves first obtain entry clearance. *However*, this requirement was not to be applied rigidly and inflexibly: there must be some ability to exercise discretion for those lawfully present in the host country. Such applicants who 'clearly and manifestly' meet the main requirements in order to exercise rights under the Agreements, should be able to make an application without an entry clearance.

Immigration rules and the entry clearance requirement

The immigration rules do require that all those wishing to enter in order to establish themselves under the Agreements must first apply for and obtain entry clearance in that capacity.

Until 9 August 2004, it was possible for people who had already been admitted to the UK in another capacity to 'switch' into these categories. However, from that date the Home Office implemented a 'no-switching' provision. The rules now require applicants applying in-country for an extension of stay to have entered the UK with a valid UK entry clearance as a person intending to establish themselves under an Association Agreement (see para. 217(i) HC 395 inserted by CM 6297).

Policy on waiving the entry clearance requirement

As in all cases, there is a discretion to waive entry clearance requirements. In Association Agreement cases, the immigration authorities use this discretion in order to comply with the EU law requirement (see above) that the state cannot, in all cases, rigidly insist on an entry clearance. Accordingly, Home Office policy states that a person seeking to switch into the Association Agreement category should 'normally' be refused but that 'it is necessary to consider the proportionality of the decision as a whole before it can be refused'. Home Office policy is contained in the IDI at Chapter 6, section 2 (Aug 2004 'substitute'). The guidance referred to here was valid as of 10 August 2005.

Whether the requirement for entry clearance will be waived depends largely on the applicant's immigration status when applying, as follows.

Applicants lawfully in the UK Applicants lawfully in the UK in another category will be permitted to switch if they can show that they 'clearly and manifestly' meet the main requirements of the rules. If they pass this test, they will only be refused on public policy grounds (▶see 552–4 for these grounds).

Applicants will pass the 'clear and manifest' test if:

'(i) from a brief perusal only
(ii) of the documents provided, together with any other information submitted,
(iii) it is readily apparent that there is
(iv) an established or potential viable business that meets the immigration criteria.'

The Home Office states that the test will not be met easily. There must be no room for doubt whether applicants meet the rules. Although the test implies that an interview is unlikely to be necessary, the Home Office accepts that 'it may be helpful to carry out checks on information submitted (such as alleged customers) if it can be done readily and easily'. Checks will only be concerned with 'straightforward facts'. If there is a need for any other checks, this will probably mean that there is too much doubt, and the

6

application will be refused. The Home Office stresses that the origin of any funds provided by another party must be credibly explained. However, a failure to pass the 'clear and manifest' test does *not* mean that it will be refused when submitted to the ECO overseas.

Applicants who are not lawfully in the UK Applicants in the UK unlawfully (illegal entrants, overstayers, those in breach of their conditions of entry) will only be permitted to remain if it would be 'disproportionate' to require them to return to apply for an entry clearance. This applies in these cases *even if* the 'clear and manifest' test is passed. Indeed, the Home Office will not necessarily even consider the merits of the application under the rules. The seriousness of the breach of immigration laws will be taken into account, as will whether the applicant has a 'realistic claim under the ECHR' (such as private and family life or property rights, under Article 8 and Article 1 of the First Protocol). Depending on the existing length of processing times at the relevant post overseas, applicants might also argue that delay in returning to make an entry clearance application is a relevant factor. Applicants in this category are only likely to succeed in switching in exceptional cases.

Applicants applying at port The guidance does not directly refer to those applying at port, or those who have temporary admission having made a different application for entry at port that is still being considered by the immigration authorities. A person arriving intending to claim asylum is very unlikely to be able to meet the 'clear and manifest' test, because they simply will not have the necessary plans and documents. A person who arrives intending to make an Association Agreement application who does have all the necessary documents might pass the test, and may be admitted if it would be disproportionate to require them to return and apply at the embassy. Immigration officers at ports, however, are not best placed to assess such applications. By far the safest route for such applicants is to obtain entry clearance before setting out. If a person's application would be strong enough to pass the 'clear and manifest' test on arrival, they should not have difficulty getting entry clearance.

Application procedures and showing that the requirements of the rules are met

Applications for entry clearance are made on Form VAF 6. In-country applications for limited leave to remain, or for indefinite leave to remain, should be made on Form ECAA Main. Unlike other in-country prescribed application forms, it is not compulsory to use Form ECAA Main, but the Home Office states that using it will both help applicants to ensure that they provide all the required information and enable the application to be dealt with speedily.

Before April 2003, officials at the UK embassies in Bulgaria and Romania held interviews with applicants, and then made decisions on the applications. However, this was a lengthy process, and the procedure therefore changed as embassies began to send the applications on to London. In March 2004 a new system was set up under which applicants could send their applications directly to London to be dealt with by the Business Cases Unit (BCU) in the UK. If approval was given, the applicant would then apply to the embassy for entry clearance. Following a political storm over allegations that improper applications were being approved by the BCU in Sheffield, and a report into the affair by Ken Sutton, procedures were changed again in August 2004. From this time, applications are again made to the embassies, interviews have been reinstated, and applications have been subjected to detailed scrutiny. On a practical level, it has become harder to qualify since the latest change in procedures.

What will the ECO look for?

These applications are essentially business applications, and so *some* of the information at ▶478–80 is also relevant. Applicants should generally produce a business plan containing a statement of the applicant's aim for their activities in the UK, including any qualifications he or she may have in connection with those activities, and any market research they have done.

The most recent guidance to ECOs is contained in the Diplomatic Service Procedure, Vol 1, General Instructions (DSPs), Chapter 18, part 18.17 (last issued on 21 July 2005; see also IDI, Ch 6, s2). Following the controversy (see above) over these applications, the guidance focuses on the 'credibility' of applications:

'The ECO should not grant entry clearance if he is not satisfied that the application is a credible one and that the applicant really will be able to comply with the requirements in practice.'

The 'Guidance Notes' attached to entry clearance Form VAF 6 also provide some assistance to applicants.

The DSP guidance accepts that applications will be very different for different businesses. It also accepts that it is not therefore possible to provide a strict checklist of documents required. Accordingly, the guidance does not set out absolute requirements. It is important that an applicant fully understands and is able to explain in interview any evidence submitted on their behalf. Important aspects of the guidance are as follows.

Establishment The application should include all of the following information:

- a detailed breakdown of the set-up costs for the business;
- details of any practical or financial requirements for setting up that kind of business in the UK;
- a timetable for establishment;
- projections for the performance of the business over the first 12 months, taking into account all potential expenses (such as overheads, administra-

tion and marketing), and which 'convincingly demonstrates' a reasonable chance that the profits will be enough to maintain the applicant and their dependants – the cost of living in the UK must be born in mind.

Pro-forma business plans The ECO will not completely discount a business plan which has been prepared with the help of 'another party', such as a representative, and which is similar to other plans. *However*, if it is clear that the applicant 'does not match up to the profile suggested by a *pro-forma* business plan', their application will be discounted. Also, if in interview the applicant cannot show an understanding of the plan, this will indicate that they will not be able to put the plan into action.

Funding To demonstrate the applicant's general financial worthiness and ability to fund the project, and that they have savings to rely upon until the business makes enough profit to maintain and accommodate themselves and their dependants, the following may be produced:

- six months' bank statements;
- a letter from the bank confirming the status of the applicant's account and their work history;
- financial records of any companies presently owned;
- a 'credible explanation' of any extraordinary payments into a bank account which cannot readily be accounted for by the work/business of the applicant;
- if the applicant is taking over or joining an existing company or business, a written statement of the terms on which the applicant is joining it or taking it over, and the business' previous audited accounts.

Business or worker? An important part of the assessment is whether the applicant is genuinely entering into business, or is really going to be an employee in disguise. Included in the factors that the ECO will have regard to as showing that the applicant is entering into business are:

- a lack of control or supervision of the work by another party;
- the applicant providing their own equipment;
- no obligation to accept work offered;
- ability to provide services to other companies at the same time;
- flexible work routines without fixed hours;
- payment of fees on the basis of work done;
- lack of benefits (such as sick pay, pension contributions, etc.);
- the applicant having responsibility for management and investment decisions;
- the applicant having responsibility for liabilities and taking out the appropriate insurance;
- the applicant putting capital into the business;
- being able to sub-contract;

- personal business address, business stationery, etc.;
- agreement with the Inland Revenue to tax on 'Schedule D' basis;
- being VAT registered.

Ability in English The applicant's language ability will be considered in the light of the nature of the business. For some businesses it will obviously be important for the applicant to speak English in order to negotiate, deal with customers, and so on. In others it may be less important.

Experience/qualifications For some businesses, experience and qualifications may be essential. Where qualifications are necessary, they should be recognised in the UK.

Forgeries ECOs may well take expert advice, locally in Bulgaria or Romania, or elsewhere, where they suspect documents to be forgeries.

Immigration history The ECO may take this into account in assessing the applicant's intentions to establish the business. However, the guidance states that a negative history 'including previous unlawful presence in the UK cannot, in itself, be conclusive in refusing an application'.

Settlement and family members

As indicated above, applicants are normally admitted at first for 12 months, and may extend their stay under the Association Agreements for a further three years. After a person has spent a continuous period of four years in the UK under the Association Agreements, they become eligible to apply for indefinite leave. They must show that they have met the above requirements throughout the four years and that they are still in business, and they must produce audited accounts for their first three years of trading, and management accounts for the fourth year.

The spouse, unmarried partner and minor children of people who are granted leave under the above rules may also be admitted and allowed to stay in line with Association Agreement country nationals. Under the rules, the dependants must have obtained entry clearance to come to the UK as a dependant in this capacity, whether they are applying to enter or to stay after they have already been admitted. Dependants are normally permitted to work.

TURKEY ASSOCIATION AGREEMENT

The EC–Turkey Association Agreement (the 'Ankara Agreement') did not give Turkish workers rights to *come* to the European Community, and that remains the case. It does, however, provide rights of continued residence to Turkish workers who have already been admitted and permitted to work (see below). It also provides additional rights to enter and remain for self-employed Turkish nationals (▶see 588–9). Further, the recent decision of the ECJ in *Gurol* was that Article 9 of Council decision 1/80 has 'direct effect'. This gives a right of equal treatment to Turkish children residing lawfully in a European country in relation to general education and vocational training. Such children may have a right of residence as well. Unfortunately, rights under the Turkey Association Agreement are not set out either in the EEA Regulations or the immigration rules. However, following the decisions of the High Court in *Ozturk & Akyuz* and *Payir* the Home Office may now make rules covering Turkish nationals in this category. Applications can be made on Form Turkish ECAA (Main).

Turkish workers

Turkish nationals who have been admitted to the UK and are permitted to work here obtain important rights under the Association Agreement. The 'Council of Association' has powers to adopt 'decisions' which are intended to further the aims of the Agreement. Article 6(1) of Decision 1/80 adopted by the Council of Association is to the following effect:

- after completing a period of one year in lawful employment, a Turkish national has a right to renew their permit to continue to work for the same employer;
- after completing a period of three years in lawful employment, a Turkish national has a right to renew their permit to continue to work in the same occupation (without the need to continue to work for the same employer);
- on completion of the fourth year in lawful employment, the Turkish national has a right to renew their permit to take up any employment for any employer.

The above three points are known as the first to third 'indents' of Article 6(1). If an applicant qualifies as permitted to take further work, this means that their residence permit (or, in the UK, 'leave') in order to continue employment should be extended. In practice, if an applicant qualifies, they are granted leave for 12 months at a time (see IDI, Ch 5, s10). Where the applicant is seeking to change employment, the Home Office view is that the new employer must show that the 'resident labour' test is passed – i.e. that the employer cannot recruit for the post within the EEA (see IDI, Ch 5, s10, para. 4.3).

Requirement to be lawfully working in a 'stable and secure' position

The above 'indents' only apply to those who have been working lawfully. Also, their access to the employment market, for any of the three time periods set out above, must be 'stable and secure'. So, those working while they do not have leave, or while in breach of their conditions of leave, will not qualify. In addition, time in employment while an asylum-seeker with temporary admission waiting for a decision on an asylum or other application, or while appealing against a negative decision, will not count. This is the case even if the applicant has been granted permission to work while on temporary admission. Working during a period of limited leave which permits the applicant to do the relevant work, and which is not an automatic extension of leave while a decision is made or while appealing, should generally qualify.

In *Birden*, the ECJ ruled that a Turkish national engaged in Germany on a one-year employment contract provided under a state-sponsored work opportunity scheme, who had been offered an extension of his contract on a part-time basis, was entitled to benefit from the provisions of the Agreement. This suggests that a Turkish national engaged on a work experience scheme with prospects of extension beyond one year should also qualify to stay. The Home Office view has been that Article 6(1) applies to Turkish students, trainees or *au pairs* (IDI, Ch 5, s10, para. 4.2). In *K v SSHD*, the IAT upheld this view, accepting that an *au pair* is not part of the labour-force, as their purpose of entry is mainly for study – i.e. learning English. *However*, in the decisions of *Ozturk & Akyuz*, the applicants had leave as students which permitted them to work part-time which they did. Newman J decided that they qualified as 'workers' for the purposes of the Association Agreement – they had leave which permitted them to work lawfully and the precise basis of the leave was not relevant. The High Court came to the same view in *Payir* in relation to *au pairs*. The judge held that the reason for the economic activity (which the Home Office argued was cultural exchange) was not relevant. Of course, the applicant would have to have been granted leave permitting them to work in order to qualify. Both cases were decided in July 2005 and both judges had no doubts about their decisions and therefore refused to refer the cases to the ECJ.

Applicants must also have been 'registered' as part of the workforce. This means that applicants must have complied with requirements such as payments of income tax and national insurance contributions.

As with other EU-law based rights, applicants can of course be disqualified from obtaining the benefit of the Association Agreement on public policy grounds (for which ▶see 552–4). Rights gained under the Association Agreement are not automatically lost by time spent in prison either on remand or serving a custodial sentence: *Nazli*, *Dogan* (ECJ).

Examples of Turkish nationals who may benefit

So, for those who have already obtained lawful, stable access to work in the UK, the Agreement provides further immigration rights. A good example of this is the case of *Kus*, decided by the ECJ. In that case, a Turkish man had been allowed to work and stay in Germany on the basis of his marriage to a German national. The Court confirmed that he was allowed to stay in Germany in order to continue his employment, even after his marriage broke down and the couple divorced. The German authorities were obliged to issue a residence permit so that he could continue this employment. The case also confirmed the 'direct effect' of Decision 1/80 in EU law.

In the UK context, the Association Agreement could therefore be useful, for example, to a Turkish national admitted as a spouse for a 24-month period who worked during this time for over a year, but whose marriage then broke down. Such an applicant would not qualify for settlement on the basis of a marriage which had broken down. However, if their employer confirmed that they wished to continue the applicant's employment, the applicant would be entitled to be granted leave to remain as a result of the Association Agreement. Similarly, a Turkish national who has completed at least one year of leave as a work permit holder should not lose the right to remain even if Work Permits (UK) refuses to grant further authorisation by extending the work permit. Provided the employer wishes to continue the employment, the Home Office is required to grant further leave to remain as a result of the Agreement.

In the case of *Sevince*, the ECJ confirmed that Turkish nationals who have worked legally in a job for three years are entitled to change employment in the same field and that, after four years, they may remain and work in any job.

Continuity of employment

Annual holidays, maternity absences, and absences due to accidents at work and short periods of sickness, will be treated as periods of legal employment for the above time periods (Article 6(2) of Decision 1/80). Periods of involuntary unemployment or long absences as a result of sickness are not counted.

Turkey Association Agreement 'stand-still' provision

The Association Agreement contains an 'Additional Protocol', which contains what has become known as the 'stand-still' clause. This clause states:

'(1) The Contracting parties shall refrain from introducing between themselves any new restrictions on the freedom of establishment and the freedom to provide services.' (Article 41)

This gives no right of entry to self-employed Turkish nationals, *but* it prevents signatory states from introducing more restrictive immigration regulations for self-employed persons than were in place when the Agreement became effective in that member state (see *Savas*, ECJ). In the case of the UK, this means that the rights of self-employed Turkish nationals to entry and residence must be no less generous than they were at the date the UK was bound by the Agreement, on 1 January 1973. On this date, the relevant immigration rules were HC 509 and HC 510. These rules were more favourable to applicants than the business rules now in force, because:

- there was no requirement that the applicant made a minimum level of investment of £200,000;
- there was no requirement that the business must employ a particular number of persons; and
- there was no absolute requirement for entry clearance.

Savas confirmed that applicants are entitled to be treated in accordance with the benefits of the stand-still provision even if they are overstayers.

Following this decision, in 2003 the Home Office made clear its view that, although the stand-still clause applied to overstayers, it did not apply to: those applying on entry, port applicants with temporary admission, those overseas applying for entry clearance, or illegal entrants. In a decision of May 2004, the Court of Appeal disagreed with the Home Office. It held that the stand-still clause did apply to all Turkish nationals, whether inside or outside the UK, including those with temporary admission. (It therefore applies to asylum-seekers granted temporary admission at port.) All such applicants were entitled to have their applications considered under the 1973 rules. The exception to this was those applicants who had committed fraud (see *R (Veli Tum & Dari) v SSHD*). In October 2004, the House of Lords made a reference in the case to the ECJ. This means that all similar outstanding cases are likely to be delayed. The ECJ will probably make a decision sometime in 2006.

The present position

Turkey Association Agreement applications to switch from those who have leave in the UK, or who are overstayers, can continue to be processed under the immigration rules in force on 1 January 1973. This is because those categories are covered by *Savas*.

Home Office guidance indicates that port applicants who arrive without entry clearance, and who wish to be admitted under the Association Agreement, will be considered under both the present rules and the 1973 rules. If they do not meet the present rules but seem likely to meet the 1973 rules, they will be granted temporary admission with a condition prohibiting employment but allowing them to take up their self-employment. After the ECJ has determined the position in *Tum*, their cases will be looked at again, and a decision made whether to grant or refuse leave to enter.

Home Office guidance further indicates that, while a decision in *Tum* is awaited, entry clearance cases will continue to be considered under the old rules. This is contrary to the decision of the Court of Appeal in *Tum*, and should be challenged. As for illegal entrants, the Home Office will probably only consider applications by them under the present rules, and not delay the removal of an applicant who is refused. The decision of the Court of Appeal indicated that those responsible for fraud would not benefit, and so those in this position will probably have to leave and re-submit their applications from abroad.

OTHER ASSOCIATION AND COOPERATION AGREEMENTS

In addition to the agreements referred to above, the EU has made, or is in the process of making, a number of agreements with other countries. However, these agreements generally provide for non-discrimination in working and social security rights between different nationals, rather than immigration rights.

Stabilisation and Association Agreements with Albania, Croatia, Bosnia and Herzegovina, Macedonia and the Federal Republic of Yugoslavia

The purpose of these 'Stabilisation and Association' agreements, which are largely still being developed, is to pave the way for the accession of these countries to the EU. The first agreement to come into force was that with Macedonia (1 April 2004). That Agreement contains non-discrimination provisions for workers lawfully employed in the EU, and also rights of establishment of companies, but it does not provide for rights of free movement of persons.

Agreements with other Eastern European and Asian countries

There are 'Partnership and Cooperation' Agreements with 13 other Eastern European and Asian countries, following the fall of the Soviet Union. The most prominent is, of course, Russia. However, these agreements do not provide for any free-movement rights.

Cooperation Agreements with Algeria, Morocco and Tunisia

The Cooperation agreements with Algeria, Morocco and Tunisia were originally made in 1987, and were known as the 'Maghreb' Agreements. They are now being added to by the 'Euro-Mediterranean Association Agreements', which are intended to create a free trade area between the EU and the Mediterranean countries (including countries additional to the Maghreb countries) by 2010. The Euro-Mediterranean Agreements do not provide for additional free-movement rights. The Maghreb Agreements themselves do not confer any rights to enter EU member states for the purpose of employment. However, they do outlaw discrimination against nationals of the signatory countries in relation to other EU nationals 'as regards working conditions or remuneration', and in the field of social security. This applies provided that the national of the 'Maghreb' country has been working with permission. In a ruling in the case of *Amimim Mohammed*, the Gibraltar Supreme Court decided that, having been in lawful employment, a Moroccan national could rely on the non-discrimination provisions with regard to working conditions to ensure a right to remain to pursue new employment. *However*, in the case of *El Yassini*, the ECJ rejected the argument that the right to non-discrimination concerning 'working conditions' covered rights of residence. In its view, it was too narrow to provide for rights of entry or stay in the member state.

Trade and development agreements with African, Caribbean and Pacific states

The trading and development agreements with the 'ACP' countries were renewed in June 2000 under the 'Cotonou' Agreement, signed in Benin. It covers very many countries of sub-Saharan Africa, the Caribbean and the Pacific. However, there are no specific rights of free movement of persons provided for.

Association Agreement with Chile

The European Parliament endorsed the agreement with Chile in February 2003. The agreement contains provisions about the right to establishment of persons (as well as legal entities) that appear similar to the Bulgarian and Romanian Agreements. However, the agreement is not intended as a precursor to accession to the EU, and may, therefore, be read much more restrictively.

6

Section 7 **Asylum**

Chapter 21
Refugee status 595

The relationship between refugees, human rights
and exceptional leave 597

Legal basis for asylum 598

Qualifying for refugee status under the
1951 Convention 601

Exclusion from protection under the
Refugee Convention 624

The Terrorism Act 2000 627

Ceasing to be a refugee and revocation of
indefinite leave 627

Refugees wishing to travel 631

Temporary protection 633

Chapter 22
Asylum procedures 637

Guidance from UNHCR and approach of UK courts 640

The New Asylum Model 641

General asylum procedures 644

The 'ordinary' SEF process 669

Detained fast track processes 673

Accelerated non-detained procedures including
the North West Project and Dover pilot schemes 681

Prosecution for non-possession of travel document 683

Unaccompanied minor asylum-seekers 686

Dependants of asylum-seekers 691

Permission to work 694

Special applications including those accepted
while still abroad 696

7

Preventing asylum-seekers coming to the UK   701

Chapter 23
Home Office decisions on asylum   705

Home Office country information   706
Credibility and the effect of the 2004 Act   708
'Non-compliance' refusals and 'group' decisions   715
Delays in making decisions and issuing documents   717
The Home Office decision and reviews   719
Fresh claims for asylum   730

Chapter 24
Third country cases   737

Third country cases under the 2004 Act   739
Challenging third country removals under the
2004 Act   743
The immigration rules   747
The Dublin Agreements   748
Discretion and third country removals   750
Unusual third country cases   751
Previous third country regimes:
July 1993–September 2004   752

Chapter 25
Refugee family reunion   757

Pre-existing spouses and minor children of
refugees under the immigration rules   758
Refugee family reunion outside the
immigration rules   762
Using the general immigration rules for
family members of settled sponsors   768
Family reunion and Article 8 ECHR   769

21 Refugee status

At the time that the Immigration Act 1971 was introduced, Home Office figures indicate that there were only 200 or so people who claimed asylum every year. There were over 110,000 applications in 2002, and 63,000 in 2003. The National Audit Office report 'Returning failed asylum applicants' (July 2005) suggested that there may have been some 283,000 failed asylum-seekers in the UK in May 2004.

Refugee flows depend upon political and human rights conditions abroad. The main nation-states of applicants for asylum at present are: Afghanistan, Angola, Bangladesh, China, the Democratic Republic of Congo, Eritrea, Liberia, India, Iran, Iraq, Jamaica, Nigeria, Pakistan, Serbia and Montenegro, Somalia, Sudan, Turkey, Uganda, Vietnam and Zimbabwe.

The asylum and human rights sections

The five chapters in this section deal with asylum under the Refugee Convention. Of course, the incorporation into UK law of most of the protections and guarantees of the 1950 European Convention of Human Rights (ECHR) has had a significant impact on the asylum system. Human rights has become a huge topic in its own right, and is now covered in a separate section of the *Handbook* (▶see Section 8). The provision of asylum support is covered in Chapters 41–42.

This chapter

In this chapter, we discuss the legal basis for asylum (▶598–601), and who qualifies for asylum as a refugee within the definition of the 1951 Refugee Convention (▶601–10). We also address a range of common refugee issues that may arise under the Convention: 'sufficiency of protection'; civil war situations; persecution and prosecution; the relevance of persecution in the past; refugees *sur place*; 'unreasonable' activities by asylum-seekers; claims based on sexuality; the position of female asylum-seekers; military service; those wrongly suspected of terrorism; and undertakings given by the Home Office (▶see the long table at 610–21). The chapter then deals with the 'internal flight' alternative, and the relevant standard of proof in asylum cases (▶621–3).

We then look at the circumstances in which people may be excluded from protection under the Refugee Convention even though they may be refugees, and we briefly examine the effect of the Terrorism Act 2000 (▶624–7).

The chapter then discusses the situations in which people may cease to be refugees under the Refugee Convention, and in which the Home Office may 'revoke' indefinite leave that has been granted to a refugee. We then deal with travel for refugees (▶627–33) and, finally, we discuss 'temporary protection', which is a new category under the immigration rules introduced in order to comply with EU Directive 2001/55/EC (▶633–5). We begin the chapter, however, by looking at the relationship between asylum under the Refugee Convention, human rights (including humanitarian protection and discretionary leave) and exceptional leave (▶597–8).

Chapter 22 deals with the procedures people have to go through in order to claim asylum. Details are given about: screening; finger-printing; the various fast-track detention and other processes for asylum determination (Oakington, Harmondsworth, Yarl's Wood and so on); interviews; the proposed 'new model' for asylum procedures; one-stop procedures; dependants; prosecutions for presenting without travel documents; 'special applications' made from abroad, including the 'quota re-settlement programme'; how unaccompanied minor asylum-seekers are dealt with; and permission to work for asylum-seekers.

Chapter 23 examines how the Home Office reaches decisions on asylum applications, and what it takes into account. It covers the provisions under the 2004 Act about what must be considered in determining the credibility of applications. It also deals with delays in making decisions, and fresh claims for asylum. Many of these topics overlap with human rights. Certification of claims as 'clearly unfounded' is looked at in Section 10, dealing with appeals (see ▶1073–8).

Chapter 24 deals with 'third country' cases,

Chapter 25 deals with the rights of refugees to family reunion with relatives. It covers the immigration rules, but also looks in detail at the policy framework outside the rules and at the 'principle of family' developed by the UNHCR.

The asylum debate

Over recent years, asylum has become the single most important and controversial issue in immigration and nationality. It has also become an issue of substantial political importance and the subject of intense public debate both during and between national elections. It is unfortunate that the debate has become so coloured by misunderstandings, misinformation, political expediency and, often, blatant prejudice. JCWI believes that the overwhelming majority of people fleeing to these shores are in genuine need of international protection, as a result of widespread oppression around the world. It is a matter of regret that the central objectives of British asylum policy continue to be to prevent potential applicants from reaching the UK, and to deter them from making the attempt (for the various measures used, ▶see the table at 703–4). JCWI will continue to lobby for a system that delivers fairness and justice to asylum-seekers, and in which their personal dignity is respected.

THE RELATIONSHIP BETWEEN REFUGEES, HUMAN RIGHTS AND EXCEPTIONAL LEAVE

'Refugees' are people who come within the definition set out in Article 1A(2) of the 1951 Refugee Convention as being people who the Convention is designed to protect (see definition on ▶599). Aside from the details given at the end of this chapter about 'temporary protection', this section is concerned with them. The immigration rules state that these people are to be granted 'asylum' and limited leave (paras 330, 335 HC 395). From July 1998, the Home Office practice has been to grant successful asylum applicants indefinite leave. However, the government's 'five-year strategy' stated that it intended to return to a system of granting limited leave initially. That is precisely what the government has done – positive decisions on or after 30 August 2005 result in a grant of leave of five years with the ability to apply to settle after that time (▶see 720–7).

Humanitarian protection, discretionary leave and exceptional leave

As well as granting asylum under the Refugee Convention, for many years the Home Office has recognised that there are those who, although they do not fit the definition of 'refugee', are in need of protection. In deciding whether to grant protection short of refugee status, the Home Office took into account the UK's international obligations other than under the Refugee Convention – for example, under the ECHR and the UN Convention Against Torture and Other Cruel, Inhuman or Degrading Treatment or Punishment 1984. As a result, the Home Office developed a discretionary practice of granting 'exceptional leave' (ELR) to those with deserving cases who were not 'refugees'. Of course, now that the ECHR has been incorporated, allowing people to stay on the basis of human rights has become a requirement under the law. From 1 April 2003, the Home Office introduced a complex system to replace ELR. Where refusal would be in breach of the UK's obligations under the ECHR, the Home Office will now grant either 'humanitarian protection' (HP) or 'discretionary leave' (DL). These changes are fully described in ▶Section 8 at 859–62. For an explanation of precisely who is entitled to HP and DL, the policy on granting limited leave to unaccompanied minors who do not qualify as refugees, and all matters connected to these forms of leave, ▶see 862–73 with reference to ▶720 onwards. (There are transitional arrangements for those granted ELR before 1 April 2003 – ▶see 873–5.)

Refugee status is the most favourable

In many cases, the reasons why a person wishes to remain in the UK are relevant both to a claim for asylum under the Refugee Convention and to rights under the ECHR. Claims and appeals under both conventions are often made together. Article 3 ECHR (prohibition against torture or inhuman or degrading treatment or punishment) provides protection in a greater number of cases than the Refugee Convention and so, in some cases, a refugee claim may fail but the applicant will still succeed under Article 3. For specific examples of circumstances in which this is likely to be the case, ▶see 796–9. The Home Office will always go on to consider the question of an applicant's human rights if it decides that the applicant does not qualify as a refugee (for this decision-making process, ▶see 719, 728). For example, if an applicant is excluded from the protection of the Refugee Convention because of their conduct (▶see 624–6), they may at least be entitled to a grant of discretionary leave (▶see 863–4, 865).

It is convenient for applicants who might qualify under the Refugee Convention and/or the ECHR to make an asylum claim and a human rights claim at the same time. As the courts have noted, refugee status is the most favourable because of the superior rights attached to it – for example, better family reunion rights and access to a Refugee Convention travel document (see *Saad, Diriye and Osario*, CA). Those granted HP or DL may obtain access to the brown 'certificate of identity' travel documents.

Non-ECHR-related leave

Discretionary Leave (DL) may also be granted in humanitarian or compassionate circumstances that do *not* come within the ECHR (▶see 865 and ▶see also 851–2).

Of course, there are many other circumstances, unrelated to asylum, human rights or 'protection', in which people can be granted leave 'exceptionally', where this simply means treating them more generously than the immigration rules strictly allow. Where the Home Office has a policy to treat people in different circumstances exceptionally, this is dealt with in the relevant part of the *Handbook*. For a list of the most important concessions under which leave may be granted outside the rules, ▶see 148–9. Although this may still be described as 'exceptional leave', the Home Office has introduced a yet further new term: 'Leave Outside the Rules' (LOTR).

LEGAL BASIS FOR ASYLUM

The basis of the law on refugees is the 1951 UN Convention Relating to the Status of Refugees and its 1967 Protocol. The Refugee Convention is one of a group of international instruments which are basic to international human rights law, and which were constructed following the

Universal Declaration of Human Rights of 1948 (UDHR). Article 14(1) of the UDHR guarantees the right of all individuals to seek asylum from persecution in other countries.

The Refugee Convention was prepared and debated in the aftermath of the Second World War to address the problem of mass displacement of people in Europe. In 1967 a Protocol was added to the Convention extending the definition of 'refugees' to include people forced to seek refuge because of events that took place after 1950.

The most important right guaranteed by the Refugee Convention is the right of a person who is a 'refugee' within the meaning of the Convention not to be returned to a country or territory where they are at risk of persecution.

Article 1A(2) of the Convention, as amended by the 1967 Protocol, defines a 'refugee' as any person who:

'…owing to a well-founded fear of being persecuted for reasons of race, religion, nationality, membership of a particular social group or political opinion, is outside the country of his nationality and is unable or, owing to such fear, is unwilling to avail himself of the protection of that country; or who, not having a nationality and being outside the country of his former habitual residence is unable or, owing to such fear, is unwilling to return to it.'

This obligation not to return a refugee, also known as the right of 'non-refoulement', is contained in **Article 33(1)** of the Convention, which states:

'No Contracting State shall expel or return ('refouler') a refugee in any manner whatsoever to the frontiers of territories where his life or freedom would be threatened on account of his race, religion, nationality, membership of a particular social group or political opinion.'

The definition of refugee in Article 1A(2) and the prohibition on return in Article 33 are repeated in the immigration rules (para. 334 HC 395 – 'grant of asylum'). On reading those two Articles, it might at first appear that a person who is a 'refugee' (has a 'well-founded fear' of persecution for a Convention reason) has to jump a second hurdle by showing that their 'life or freedom' would be threatened if they were returned before they were entitled to be granted asylum. However, the courts have decided that there is only one hurdle: if a person has a fear of 'persecution' within the meaning of Article 1A(2) in the country to which they are to be sent, then that is sufficient to show that their 'life or freedom' will be threatened there as well (see *Sivakumaran* in the House of Lords and *Adan v SSHD* in the Court of Appeal).

The UK is one of some 145 states bound by the Refugee Convention.

The 1951 Convention and UK law

Before 1993 the UK had no specific asylum law. Asylum was mentioned almost as an afterthought in the immigration rules, after all other ways in which people might qualify to come to the UK had been listed.

Asylum legislation Since 1993 several major Acts have been passed dealing with asylum: the Asylum and Immigration Appeals Act 1993, the Asylum and Immigration Act 1996, the Immigration and Asylum Act 1999, the Nationality, Immigration and Asylum Act 2002, and the Asylum and Immigration (Treatment of Claimants etc) Act 2004. More legislation is proposed.

Immigration rules and the API The Acts are supplemented by the immigration rules (part XI HC 395), which explain the procedures and list the factors which the Home Office will take into account when considering asylum applications. The Home Office also publishes its Asylum Policy Instructions (API), which give further guidance on asylum procedures and how decisions are taken. Unfortunately the API no longer appear in a systematic way – i.e. with sections and chapters. Instead, the website lists different instructions in alphabetical order, depending on the subject matter. This makes the API less easy to use, and it is also harder to tell when they have changed. Therefore, when we refer to the API we give a reference to the particular instruction by its title.

UK provisions which give effect to the Convention

The fact that the UK is a signatory to the 1951 Convention does not automatically make the Convention a part of the UK's own law. Signing a treaty only creates obligations between states in international law, not in domestic law. However, the 'non-refoulement' obligation (see above) is effectively part of UK law, as follows.

- Section 2 of the 1993 Act states that the immigration rules must not be interpreted as allowing the immigration authorities to do anything that would be contrary to the Refugee Convention.

- The immigration rules confirm that an asylum claim will be determined in accordance with the UK's obligations under the Convention, and that asylum will be granted if the applicant has arrived in the UK and satisfies the definition of refugee, and if their removal would be contrary to the Convention. In all other cases, asylum will be refused (paras 327–335 HC 395).

- Those who have claimed asylum must not be removed from or required to leave the UK while their claims are outstanding (s77 2002 Act, para. 329 HC 395).

- If the AIT finds that the decision of the immigration authorities to refuse asylum and to require that the appellant go back to the country of return would be in breach of the Refugee Convention, the appeal should be allowed (s84(1)(g) 2002 Act).

Although they are not specifically incorporated into UK law, the UK observes other obligations under the Convention – for example, the provision of Convention travel documents to refugees (Article 28), and giving refugees equal rights with UK citizens in the provision of welfare support such as social security and housing (Articles 21–24).

Although advice is given in the *UNHCR Handbook* about the procedures to be operated in determining who is a refugee, these are only advisory. The Home Office is not prevented, therefore, from making far-reaching administrative changes in how it deals with applications. It has set up radical programmes for the swift determination of claims that have been the subject of challenge. It has also, for example, frequently tightened the time-limits within which asylum-seekers must lodge their evidence (for all details about asylum procedures (▶see Chapter 22).

QUALIFYING FOR REFUGEE STATUS UNDER THE 1951 CONVENTION

The definition of 'refugee' in Article 1A(2) of the Convention can be broken down into a number of elements. The applicant must meet all of the following criteria:

- be outside their own country (▶602);
- have a 'well-founded fear' (▶602);
- of 'persecution' (▶602–5);
- for one or more of the reasons in the Convention (race, religion, nationality, membership of a particular social group or political opinion) (▶605–9);
- be unable (or unwilling) to obtain the protection of their country (▶610).

Below, we look at these separate elements in turn, and at some of the case-law interpreting them. We then examine some issues that regularly arise in applying the definition in particular circumstances (▶see the table at 610–21).

In the case of ***Adan & Aitseguer***, the House of Lords decided that there was only one true legal definition of a refugee within the meaning of the Convention. In theory, therefore, the definition of refugee is an international one applying to all the signatory states. In practice, signatory states have their own systems of law, and have interpreted the Convention in different ways, which has been an issue of particular concern where the Home Office has wanted to remove people to safe 'third' countries.

The *UNHCR Handbook* Help in the proper interpretation of the Convention is provided by the United Nations High Commissioner for Refugees (UNHCR), which is the UN agency set up and given responsibility for overseeing the concerns of refugees internationally. The *UNHCR Handbook*, on procedures and criteria for determining refugee status, was prepared as a guide to the interpretation of the Convention. It is helpful in preparing an asylum case, as its principles are generally accepted by the Home Office. It has been approved as a useful tool of interpretation many times by the courts – most enthusiastically by the Court of Appeal in the case of *Robinson*.

Outside country of nationality or former habitual residence

A person cannot be a refugee while they are still in their country of nationality (or, where they are stateless, their country of former habitual residence). The aim of the Convention is to help people who have sought protection abroad. This is one of the reasons why it is not possible, under the immigration rules, to apply for asylum from the country of origin. Also, because the central obligation under the Convention is not to return a refugee to face persecution, applications must generally be made by persons in the UK, and not to a post in a third country. There are, however, certain 'special procedures' under which the Home Office will exceptionally consider applications made from abroad (▶see 696–701).

Well-founded fear

The *UNHCR Handbook* suggests that fear of persecution can be seen in both subjective and objective terms. Whether there is a subjective fear depends upon the person's state of mind as to whether they actually believe they will suffer harm if returned to their country. It is usually this real mental fear of the claimant that triggers their flight from the country. Psychological trauma and post-traumatic stress experienced by the claimant constitute important evidence to be advanced in support of the claim.

However, in the landmark case of *Sivakumaran*, the House of Lords established that, in order to qualify as a refugee, it is necessary to establish not only a subjectively held fear, but *also* that there is an objective fear of persecution. This means that the applicant not only fears a certain outcome, but that there is an actual risk of that outcome occurring if they were to be returned. So, if a person, for whatever reason, genuinely fears a particular event but there is no risk of that event actually occurring, they will not be a refugee. In other words, the objective element of the test can override the subjective. The Court decided that this interpretation was justified because the Convention refers to the fear as being 'well-founded'. In practice, asylum decision-making focuses on the objective aspect of the fear since, if there is in fact a risk, it can generally be assumed that a person who has claimed asylum on the basis of it does indeed hold a fear in their own mind.

Persecution

The *UNHCR Handbook* states that threats to life or freedom will always amount to persecution. It also states that other serious violations of human rights can also qualify. So, for example, long-term discrimination and harassment, particularly in the context of an atmosphere of general insecurity, might also be considered as persecution, in addition to overt physical threats (paras 51–53). This is accepted by the Home Office (API, *Deciding claims: assessing the asylum claim*, para. 8). In *Jin Tao He v SSHD*, the Court of Appeal dealt directly for the first time with the possibility that discrimination in employment might amount to persecution. The appellant was a Chinese national and a member of the Zhong Gong sect who claimed that he had as a result been excluded from employment in both the public and private sectors. The Court found that, at the very least, what had already occurred was an 'indication' that the appellant had indeed been persecuted for a Convention reason. It sent the case back to the Tribunal for it to reconsider the matter, and to determine whether, if the same discrimination were repeated, it would amount to persecution.

'Persecution' defined by reference to human rights

The *UNHCR Handbook* notes that the attempts to formulate a general definition of persecution have met with little success. One approach, however, has been given approval by the courts. In his book, *The Law of Refugee Status* (1991), Professor James Hathaway explained how the Refugee Convention was a part of a family of human rights laws that are interlinked and internationally accepted. (For Hathaway's further recent publication, ▶see 1534.) He therefore saw the failure of a state's responsibilities under these human rights laws as constituting the kind of serious harm that amounts to 'persecution'. As to 'persecution', he stated:

'In sum, persecution is most appropriately defined as the sustained or systemic failure of state protection in relation to one of the core entitlements which has been recognised by the international community.' (p.112)

Hathaway constructed a hierarchy of human rights and fundamental freedoms, and defines persecution by reference to them. This hierarchy is reflected in the following four categories.

First category At the top of the hierarchy are rights such as the freedom from arbitrary loss of life; protection against torture or cruel, inhuman or degrading punishment or treatment; freedom from slavery and freedom of thought, conscience and religion. These rights should always be observed and protected by the state, even in times of acute crisis or emergency. Failure to observe them amounts to persecution.

Second category In the second category are those rights which states may exceptionally not observe in times of crisis or emergency: freedom from arbitrary arrest and detention; rights to a fair trial, personal integrity and internal movement; freedom of speech and association; and other basic democratic rights. Persecution will arise where a state fails to observe these rights unless it can show that it was necessary, having regard to the circumstances of the emergency, for those rights to be overridden.

Third category Into the third category come social and economic rights: to work and to decent working conditions; housing; medical care; social welfare; education; cultural expression. If a state ignores these rights altogether, or upholds them only in a discriminatory way, then the result may be persecution.

Fourth category The final category of rights are those not seen as 'core' entitlements in human rights law: the right to own and be free from deprivation of property, and to be protected against unemployment. Failure to observe these rights will not generally amount to persecution.

Hathaway's approach to 'persecution' as the failure of state protection in relation to core human rights has been generally accepted by the House of Lords (see Lord Steyn in *Ullah*, at para. 32 referring also to *Horvath* and *Sepet*). His general principles had initially been approved in the IAT case of *Gashi*. Although the APIs break human rights abuses down into only two categories, the Home Office also appears to accept the above general approach (see API, *Deciding claims: assessing the asylum claim*, paras 8.1–8.3).

Other approaches to persecution

However, in contrast to the above analysis, the courts have also some-times adopted much more straightforward approaches to persecution. In *Kagema*, a case concerning the displacement of Kikuyus from the Rift Valley in Kenya, the Court of Appeal suggested that the correct approach was to view 'persecution' as an ordinary English word which had simply to be applied to the facts of each individual case. Technical or general defi-nitions would not help the decision- maker in that task. The problem with this approach, which operates without any real framework, is that assess-ing persecution becomes far more arbitrary, and inconsistent decisions are more likely. It may also produce surprising and unfavourable results. The appellants in *Kagema*, for example, were unsuccessful in their claims, even though they had repeatedly been displaced from their homeland.

Must the acts be repeated?

Another question that often arises is whether persecution needs to involve continued or repeated acts. The short judgment of Staughton LJ in *Ravi-chandran* is often quoted for the statement that persecution must be at least 'persistent and serious'. It would be clearly wrong for this to apply in the face of a risk of a very serious incident of persecution, such as torture (see *Demrikaya*, CA). In *Kacaj*, the IAT recognised that *Article 3 ECHR* could be violated by actions that did not have a 'sufficiently systematic character to amount to persecution'.

General approach set out in *Ravichandran*

The general approach to persecution set out in the main judgment in *Ravichandran* is often quoted. In that case, the Court of Appeal held that the arbitrary rounding-up and detention of young Tamils immediately following terrorist atrocities did not amount to persecution, but that persecution had to be viewed 'in the round', with all circumstances taken into account, including the reasons motivating the particular treatment. The round-ups had taken place in the context of terrorist attacks. The Court indicated that, had the detention been long-term, accompanied by physical ill-treatment, or motivated out of malice to Tamils on the part of the Sri Lankan authorities, it would probably have constituted persecution (▶see also the case of *Sivakumar* on the investigation of terrorist activity, 620).

Fear of persecution must be present

Finally, there must be a *present* fear of persecution in order for a person to be a refugee. In *Adan*, the House of Lords had to decide whether a Somali, who had left his country because of a well-founded fear of persecution and was now 'unable to avail' himself of the protection of the state because the state had collapsed, was a refugee. It held that the fact that the applicant left because of a fear that existed at that point, combined with there being no presently functioning state in Somalia, was not enough. It was necessary to have a continuing well-founded fear of persecution for a Convention reason.

'Convention reason' for fear of persecution

Refugees have to show that the persecution they face is 'for reasons of' one or more of the reasons listed in the definition in Article 1A(2): race, religion, nationality, political opinion, or membership of a particular social group. We look at these reasons separately below. It is generally up to the asylum-seeker to satisfy the Home Office about their situation and the danger they would be in if returned. However, refugees may well not be able to identify or analyse Convention reasons themselves, and the *UNHCR Handbook* confirms that there is no duty on them to do so. Difficult problems sometimes arise in determining whether a Convention reason is the cause of the persecution. Decision-makers must carefully assess the 'real reason' for the persecution, which involves objective judgment.

Imputed opinions The focus for deciding whether there is a Convention reason for the persecution is upon what is in the mind of the persecutor, rather than in the understanding of the victim (see *Sepet and Bulbul*, HL). So, for example, a mistaken belief on the part of the persecutor that a person holds a particular political opinion is enough to bring any resulting persecution within the Convention. In addition, the persecutor may interpret certain acts, which others might view as quite innocent and innocuous, as signifying a political stance, and react disproportionately. In both situations, it is common for lawyers to talk of a political opinion that is 'imputed'. This concept was accepted at an early stage by the IAT (see, for example, *Asante*), and has subsequently been accepted by the higher courts and applied by the Home Office.

Severity of ill-treatment In some cases the very severity of unlawful ill-treatment, where it is used against persons from a particular social group or race, or to whom certain political attitudes are often attributed, will be strong evidence that it is being used for that Convention reason (▶see the decision of the House of Lords in *Sivakumar*, below at 620). An alternative approach, taken by Lord Rodger in *Sivakumar*, is to understand that severe ill-treatment may be inflicted for a number of reasons. In his view, if *one* of those reasons was one of the Convention reasons, that would be enough to show persecution for a Convention reason.

Overlapping reasons Often, the various different Convention reasons overlap in relation to the same fear. For example, a person from a particular tribe or ethnic background may be persecuted as a result of their race, but the state may also associate them with a particular political stance. The two Convention reasons that have caused the most debate have been 'political opinion' and 'membership of a particular social group'.

Political opinion

Political rights, such as freedom of expression and association, are obviously fundamental values in democratic societies, and the term 'political opinion' has to be understood in this context. Although there has been a heavy emphasis by decision-makers on the applicant's own opinion and active involvement in political activity, political opinion includes both directly held and attributed opinions. Although most 'political' refugees will have given some outward expression of their views, a person may still fall within the Convention even if they have had no opportunities to express their political opinions.

As with all the criteria that define a refugee, 'political opinion' should be interpreted broadly. In his book, *The Refugee in International Law* (1996), Professor Guy Goodwin-Gill comments that the concept of a 'political refugee' is of a person

'…pursued by the government of a state or other entity on account of his or her opinions which are an actual or perceived threat to that government or its institutions, or to the political agenda and aspirations of the entity in question.'

As was made clear in the IAT case of *Gomez*, 'political opinion' cannot be limited to party politics. So, for example, trade union activists have often been found to be persecuted on grounds of political opinion. In assessing whether an attitude amounts to a political opinion, it is important to look to the context of the particular country and apply a flexible meaning. In some cases, Commonwealth courts have found that violations of the dress code in certain Muslim states, or the exercise of human rights, such as in a breach of China's one-child policy, can be sufficient to establish a political opinion (and ▶see the different ways in which women may be persecuted for political reasons, 616–9).

Membership of a particular social group

The Convention reason over which there is most debate, and which is often the most difficult to establish, is membership of a particular social group. The *UNHCR Handbook* defines such groups as being formed by 'persons of similar background, habits or social status', and states that fear of persecution on these grounds often overlaps with others.

The question of whether certain groups constitute a 'particular social group' within the Convention depends upon the social conditions existing in the relevant country. This is an area in which state practice in recognising refugees has also varied. Gender-based claims and claims based on sexuality are often brought within the 'social group' category. Canada has granted asylum to a Saudi Arabian woman on the grounds of her activities challenging sex discrimination; and to a woman from Trinidad who had suffered physical abuse from her husband, on the grounds that there was no network of support for women in her position in Trinidad. The United States has granted asylum to women facing genital mutilation, forced marriage, and domestic violence.

The decision of the House of Lords in *Shah & Islam* is now the leading case on 'particular social group'. It concerned the circumstances in which women may form a particular social group, but it also laid down general principles (▶see the table below).

7

MEMBERSHIP OF A PARTICULAR SOCIAL GROUP: *SHAH & ISLAM*

In *Shah & Islam*, the following principles were laid down by the House of Lords in order to identify members of a particular social group.

- Members of a social group must have in common an 'immutable characteristic' that it is either beyond their power to change, or is so fundamental to their identity or conscience that they cannot be required to change it.

- The social group must exist independently of, and not be defined by, the persecution. If it were otherwise, anyone who was persecuted would be a member of a social group. This was also the central finding of the Court of Appeal in *Savchenkov*, which concerned alleged persecution by the Russian mafia. It was decided that persecution of a group comprising law-abiding citizens for refusing to cooperate with the mafia was not a group which existed independently of the persecution.

- Counteracting discrimination is a fundamental purpose of the Convention. Therefore, if there is discrimination against members of a group, that is a relevant factor in identifying whether that group is a 'particular social group'.

- The cohesiveness of the group is another factor that is relevant in determining whether it is a group within the meaning of the Convention, but there is no requirement that the group be cohesive.

See also the later decision of the Court of Appeal in *Skenderaj* (▶see 609 below).

In the actual cases of **Shah & Islam**, women from Pakistan were held to be a particular social group because they were identifiable by gender, they were discriminated against, and the state did not protect them. Since then the IAT has upheld a number of gender-based claims – for example, the claim of a Ukrainian woman forced into prostitution (**Dzhygun**); of an Iranian woman who left her violent husband and feared prosecution for adultery (**Fatemeh**); and of an Indian woman who had entered into an adulterous relationship, which led to the birth of her son (**Balvir Kaur**). In **Liu v SSHD**, a Chinese woman claimed asylum on the grounds that she would be forcibly sterilised and imprisoned in inhuman and degrading conditions. The adjudicator allowed the appeal on refugee grounds, but the IAT dismissed it. The Court of Appeal agreed the general principle that the social group must exist independently of the persecution. However, while persecution could not define the group, the actions of the persecutors might identify or even cause the creation of the group in society. Treatment amounting to persecution was relevant in identifying a particular social group where it demonstrated the state's attitude towards a particular class.

However, in **Fornah v SSHD** the Court of Appeal held (by a 2:1 majority) that a young woman who was at risk under Article 3 ECHR as a result of enforced female genital mutilation (FGM) did not face persecution for reason of her membership of a particular social group. In that case, it was held that the group did not exist independently of the persecution. The case will be heard by the House of Lords in 2006.

Immutable characteristic The meaning of 'immutable characteristic' (▶see above) has caused considerable debate. In the Court of Appeal in **Ouanes**, an Algerian midwife, whose work involved giving contraceptive advice, was held not to be a member of a particular social group. This was because her work did not have sufficient impact upon her individual identity or conscience to make it 'immutable'. However, the Court did indicate that other types of employment might be sufficiently connected to a person's identity: for example, work as part of a religious order. Similarly, conscientiously fulfilling a civic duty by seeking legal redress against illegal actions of police officers has been held not to make someone a member of a social group (**Storozhenko**).

Sexuality As to claims based on sexuality, in an older case in the High Court concerning an asylum-seeker from the Turkish Republic of Northern Cyprus, it was assumed, in the applicant's favour, that homosexuals could constitute a particular social group (**Binbasi**). In **Shah & Islam** the court commented that homosexuals could constitute a particular social group if they suffered discrimination as that group. More recently still, it was agreed on all sides in the Court of Appeal in **Jain** that homosexuals in India are a social group because of the adverse impact of Indian law. In most cases, it is now readily accepted that homosexuals constitute a particular social group. For details about persecution on grounds of sexuality, ▶see below at 615–6. For the relevance of Article 8 to such claims, ▶see 804–6 (for the need to show a 'flagrant' breach, ▶see 790–2).

Families In *Skenderaj*, the Court of Appeal again looked at the general meaning of 'particular social group'. It held that whether such a group exists is a mixed question of fact, policy and judgment, which has to be considered in the context of the society in question. Generally, the group should be seen as having a shared or defining characteristic, so that it is 'particular'. However, although cohesiveness and discrimination are relevant, they are not necessary to show the existence of the group. *Skenderaj* itself concerned whether the applicant's family, which was involved in a blood feud with a neighbouring family in Albania, was a particular social group. In a previous case based on 'family', the Court of Appeal had held that, for such a claim to succeed, the family had to be persecuted because it is 'that family', and not because of something done by one of the members of the family (*Quijano*).

In *Skenderaj*, the claim failed because, although it was held that kinship or family membership may give rise to a particular social group, the applicant's family was not thought of by Albanian society as being a distinct group, any more than were other families in the country. The applicant could not point to the feelings of the other family towards his own family as marking the family out as a particular social group, because the threat of persecution from them was a private matter, and it was not possible to rely on persecution from the other family in order to create the social group. On the facts of the case, it was further held that, even if the applicant's family were a particular social group, his fear was not 'for reasons of' his membership of the group, but was rather a fear of reprisals for his uncle's act of killing a member of the other family. *Montoya* was another case that failed on the grounds that the applicant could not show that the risk arose 'for reasons of' his membership of a particular social group. The applicant, a member of a wealthy land-owning family, had fled Colombia following threats from a Marxist opposition group to kill him for refusing to make payments to them. The Court of Appeal upheld the IAT's decision that the applicant was being persecuted, not as the result of his membership of a particular social group, but to extort money from him.

Race, religion, nationality

Race, religion and nationality are reasonably straightforward grounds. Claims based on race have to take into account the UN Convention on the Elimination of All Forms of Racial Discrimination. 'Religion' can also mean freedom of 'thought, conscience, and religion', as stipulated in the International Covenant of Civil and Political Rights. Religious belief arguably covers the right not to hold a theistic religious belief. However, in the Court of Appeal in *Omoruyi* it was held that the Ogboni secret cult in Nigeria, which practised certain rites and rituals, was an intrinsically criminal organisation, rather than a religion. 'Nationality' does not refer only to citizenship; it includes both ethnic and linguistic groups, and any national minorities within a country (API, *Deciding claims: assessing the asylum claim*, para. 9.3).

Unable or… unwilling to obtain the protection of the country

In order to satisfy this part of the test, those who have a country of nationality (most asylum-seekers) must be unable or unwilling to obtain the protection of their country of nationality. Those who are stateless must be unable or unwilling *to return* to their country of 'former habitual residence'. The decision of the Court of Appeal in ***Vallaj & Canaj*** suggests that protection may come from agencies that are not, in fact, state authorities, such as international peace-keeping forces and a UN interim administration. The Court rejected the argument that an ethnic Albanian from the Serbian province of Kosovo could not be excluded from refugee status on the basis of protection available from those other agencies. However, in ***Azad Gardi*** the Court of Appeal indicated that protection had to come from an entity capable of granting nationality in a form recognised internationally, and accountable under international law. Protection could not therefore have been provided by the Kurdish Autonomous Region (KAR) of northern Iraq in the time before the Baathists were removed from Baghdad. This would still be consistent with ***Vallaj & Canaj*** since, in that case, the UNMIK regime in Kosovo had the authority of the UN and the consent of the Federal Republic of Yugoslavia. The KAR was not an entity under international law at all. However, in ***SM and Others (Kurds – Protection – Relocation) Iraq CG***, the IAT took the opposite view to that of the Court of Appeal in ***Gardi***. It held:

'In our view therefore, the weight of the authorities very much favours the pragmatic approach to the issue of protection rather than the more limited approach which suggests that protection has to be provided by an entity capable of granting nationality to a person in a form recognised internationally…' (para. 49)

However, the question of 'protection' is not limited to this part of the definition of a refugee. The courts have found that the absence of state protection from the threat facing an asylum-seeker is an essential part of the definition of 'persecution' itself (see under 'sufficiency of protection' in the table below).

REFUGEE STATUS: COMMON ISSUES

The definition of refugee has led to a great number of court decisions, both in the UK and in the legal systems of the other signatory states, which explain the meaning given to the definition. The interpretation of the basic elements of the definition is set out above (▶601–10). In this table we look at some frequently reoccurring situations in asylum cases, and at the way in which the courts have applied the Convention in those circumstances.

Sufficiency of protection and non-state agents

In most cases, the applicant fears harm directly from the state or its agents – for example, police or security officials. In some cases, however, the risk is from offensive acts carried out by individuals or groups not connected to the state, often called 'non-state agents'.

In *Horvath*, the House of Lords examined the meaning of 'persecution' where the source of harm was 'non-state agents'. The case involved a Roma from Slovakia who had suffered extreme racially motivated violence from skinheads, and who claimed that the national authorities were not protecting him. The majority of the court decided that the word 'persecution' in the refugee definition does not simply mean sufficiently serious ill-treatment, but must *also* involve a failure of the state to provide protection against the ill-treatment. If the state is not failing in its obligations, then a person will not be a refugee, even if their fears are 'well-founded'. In deciding whether the state can be said to be providing protection, the central consideration is whether there is a 'sufficiency of protection' – in other words, a clear system of criminal justice operated by the state and a reasonable willingness by the state to use that system to provide a disincentive to those who would commit acts of serious harm against others. If a state tolerates or condones acts of serious harm by others, then its role in failing to provide protection enables that harm to qualify as 'persecution'.

For the argument about whether the 'sufficiency of protection' test also applies in Article 3 ECHR cases and the recent decision of the House of Lords in *Bagdanavicius*, ▶see 799–800.

The (perhaps surprising) conclusion reached in *Horvath* can be traced to the principle that the obligation to grant refugee status only arises if the person's own state is 'unwilling or unable' to discharge its duty to protect its own nationals. The reason underlying the decision was the view that the general purpose of the Convention was to enable a person who no longer had the benefit of protection of their own state to turn to the international community for 'surrogate' protection.

In a further decision interpreting what was meant by a sufficiency of protection, the Court of Appeal held that it will not be shown by the availability of remedies *after* ill-treatment has taken place. There must be adequate protection *against* ill-treatment (see *Kinuthia v SSHD*).

In most cases concerning state agents, it will be simple to show a failure of state protection, since the state is doing the persecuting. However, in some cases the question of protection will be important even in cases involving state agents. *Rolandas Svazas* was a Lithuanian communist who was at risk of continued detention and ill-treatment at the hands of the police. There was evidence that the police systematically abused their power despite the will of the government to stop it. The Court of Appeal decided that in such cases, where the persecutors were in fact state agents, in order to defeat the claim to asylum, there would have to be 'convincing evidence' that the state possesses the mechanisms to control its officials, and that it operates them to real effect. The standard required was higher than in non-state agent cases, because the applicant would have clear reasons for, in the language of the Convention, being 'unwilling to avail himself of the protection of [his] country'.

Civil war and 'singling out'

In certain cases, it may be that state control in the country of origin has broken down completely, so that no one authority can be said to be in control of the relevant country or territory. Frequently, in these cases, there will be internal conflict between the different groups competing for power. This was the case in *Adan*, where the House of Lords decided that what the claimants actually feared was death, injury or loss of freedom as a consequence of the civil war in Somalia, which applied to all Somalis. The civil war was being waged between different clans, with non-combatants of one clan being at risk of attack as a result of their perceived association with the interests of an opposing clan. The House of Lords held that an applicant would have to show a risk 'over and above' the risks inherent in the civil war in order to be successful in an asylum claim.

This was another surprising result, given that earlier case-law had made it clear that there is no need for a person to show that they will be 'singled out' for ill-treatment in order to show that they are at risk of persecution, and that ill-treatment as part of a group is enough. In *Jeyakumaran*, Taylor J had held that it did not matter that a Tamil family had not been targeted individually, but were part of a wide class of Tamils being similarly treated. The judge commented:

'Whilst I am conscious of the administrative problem of numbers seeking asylum, it cannot be right to adopt artificial and inhuman criteria in an attempt to solve it.'

It appears that a major concern in *Adan* was the likely number of people who might benefit from a decision that suggested all Somalis were potential refugees. *Adan* will only apply in very extreme cases, where there is a general state of chaos such that no one authority can be said to be dominant, controlling territory, and providing a minimum level of organisation, so that it may be recognised as the state authority. It will not, therefore, apply to countries where, although there is extensive armed unrest, there is a clear, functioning state authority.

Persecution or prosecution?

Persecution is distinct from prosecution, though the two can be connected. People who fear returning to their country because they may face criminal charges, even when these are connected with political activity, are often not considered to be at risk of persecution. This was confirmed by the Court of Appeal in *O v IAT*. However, few if any regimes will admit to persecuting their political opponents, and prosecution is often simply a mask for what is in fact persecution. It is therefore important to look to the particular circumstances to see whether either the existence of a particular offence in the law of the relevant country, or indeed the way in which the law is being applied, means that the law is being used as an instrument of oppression. Good indicators of this may include any of the following:

- the criminal penalties for a certain action in a particular country are disproportionate to those in most other countries;

- the law is being used to prevent legitimate political opposition or expression;
- a fair trial against the charge is denied, or is unlikely;
- there is evidence to show that the law is being applied in a discriminatory way – for example, against persons of a particular faith, group or political persuasion;
- the circumstances suggest that there are ulterior reasons for pursuing a prosecution against the individual in question.

Relevance of past persecution

As we have seen, there must be a presently held fear of persecution (*Adan*, HL). This does not mean that evidence of past persecution is irrelevant. It is usually of central importance, and often constitutes the best evidence that a person is likely to be persecuted in the future. If it can be shown that a person has been persecuted in the past, then, unless there has been a dramatic change in circumstances in the country the effect of which is to remove that risk in the future (for example, a change of government, or a complete and effective overhaul of the internal system for protection against human rights abuses), a risk of continued persecution in the future can often be assumed (see para. 45 *UNHCR Handbook*). In *Adan*, the House of Lords referred to the 'importance' of evidence of past persecution in showing a future risk. In the more recent decision in *B and Hoxha*, Lord Brown underlined that, where the Secretary of State is contending that a country which was previously unsafe for the applicant has become safe:

'It seems to me only right...he should place before the appellate authority sufficient material to satisfy them of that critical fact.' (para. 66; see also para. 29).

Applicants who did not 'flee' from persecution: refugees '*sur place*'

Just as the existence of past persecution is not conclusive evidence that a person is a refugee, neither is it necessary to have suffered persecution in the past to establish that there is a risk in the future. It may be that the asylum claimant managed to escape the country before they were actually subjected to ill-treatment. In other cases, it may be that the asylum-seeker did not actually leave their country because of a fear of persecution but that the fear has arisen due to events taking place after the person has left. Such a person can still qualify as being 'outside' their country owing to a fear of persecution. This is because they are claiming asylum on the basis that they are remaining outside their country because of their fear of return. Persons in this position are known as refugees '*sur place*'. For refugees *sur place* and credibility under the 2004 Act ▶see 712.

It may also be that the fear arises not as a result of a change in country conditions since the applicant left, but rather as a result of the activities overseas of the asylum-seeker. This may be, for example, if they have taken part in demonstrations, or if they have written public material critical of their own state after arrival in the host state. Activities seen as unreasonable or 'self-serving' may, however, raise questions of credibility (▶see below).

'Unreasonable' activities

In some cases it is argued that an applicant might avoid 'persecutory' consequences by taking avoiding action – for example, keeping quiet and not taking part in political or other activity. This question is most stark in cases where the Home Office or the court thinks that the applicant is proposing to engage in 'unreasonable' activities, and where they could be expected to exercise a 'measure of discretion' or 'sensitivity' to the community into which they are to be returned.

In *Iftikhar Ahmed*, a Pakistani national of the Ahmadi faith was determined to continue to express his Ahmadi beliefs openly if returned, despite the fact that others found the beliefs to be objectionable and were offended by them. It was part of his faith that he gave open expression to it. The Court of Appeal held that if, as a matter of fact, on their return the asylum-seeker would act in a way which could result in their being persecuted, they would be entitled to asylum. This was the case, however unreasonable the applicant's refusal was to accept a restraint on their activities. A similar issue arose in *Thomas Danian v SSHD* (CA), in which the applicant was alleged to have carried out political activities *after his arrival* in the UK that were found to have been cynically carried out in order to try to generate an asylum claim. In both situations, the law is the same. In *Ahmed*, the Court stated:

'Essentially what *Danian* decides is that in all asylum cases there is ultimately but a single question to be asked: is there a serious risk that on return the applicant would be persecuted for a Convention reason? If there is, then he is entitled to asylum. It matters not whether the risk arises from his own conduct in this country, however unreasonable…When I say that none of this matters, what I mean is that none of it forfeits the applicant's right to refugee status, provided only and always that he establishes a well-founded fear of persecution abroad. Any such conduct is, of course, highly relevant when it comes to evaluating the claim on its merits, i.e. to determining whether in truth the applicant is at risk of persecution abroad. An applicant who has behaved in this way may not readily be believed as to his future fears.'

It is clear from the above passage that, where an applicant involves themselves, or says they will involve themselves, in what appear to be unreasonable activities, or activities inconsistent with their previous conduct, questions of credibility will arise as to whether in fact the applicant will do, or will continue to do, as they say they will. Decision-makers will also be alive to the question of whether the state authorities will take such applicants seriously, and therefore have any real interest in them.

The issue of taking avoiding action has also arisen in claims based on sexuality (►see below).

It is possible that the Home Office may ask the Court of Appeal to reconsider *Danian* in the light of comments recently made by the AIT in a Zimbabwean test case, *AA v SSHD*. In that case, the Tribunal questioned whether the benefits of refugee status should be given to those who engage in dishonest acts giving rise to a risk of persecution when such people are adequately protected by Article 3 ECHR (para. 173).

Persecution on grounds of sexuality

As indicated above (►at 608), homosexuals have generally been accepted as constituting a 'particular social group' under the Convention. In recent times, a growing number of cases have been accepted under the Convention where there is a risk of persecution on grounds of sexuality. In *Jain*, the Court of Appeal found as follows:

- There is a broad international consensus that everyone has a right to respect for their private life, which includes their sexual life, and that this is a 'core' right.

- There is a spectrum of state conditions regarding attitudes to homosexuality which ranges from countries that enforce a criminal law prohibiting consensual homosexual activity in private (such laws are not acceptable to the international community) to countries where people are as free to engage in homosexual activity 'as [they are] to breathe'.

- As well as the state, pressures also come from the community, which may also be hostile to homosexuality.

- The issue for the decision-maker is where along the above spectrum the point comes at which a person can be said to face 'persecution'.

The Court in *Jain* did not directly answer the last question above, but it gave an indication as to when persecution may arise by its findings on the instant facts and its further comments. On the facts of the case, there was a criminal law prohibiting consensual homosexual activity, *but* there was no real risk of it being used against the applicant. The only real problems the applicant faced were difficulties in finding a partner, and some expression of disapproval by sections of the community. This was not enough to amount to 'persecution', but the Court stated:

'It may be that in some not greatly dissimilar circumstances facts could be shown from which a Tribunal would be entitled to infer that a particular individual had a justified fear of persecution.'

Can the Home Office say that an applicant could avoid persecution by taking avoiding action, for example, by not living an openly gay lifestyle and by being 'discreet'? This was considered by the IAT in *MN (Kenya)*. In that case, the Tribunal agreed that homosexuality is not just a question of sexual activity, but is also a matter of sexual identity. It held that an applicant who can avoid persecution only by living a lie – in other words, by persistently and against their will organising their affairs so that they live furtively, and at constant worry of discovery, is being oppressed. The Tribunal further stated:

'...depending on the nature of the oppression and his response to it, such oppression could well be so severe that it is persecutory.' (para. 23)

The Tribunal in *MN (Kenya)* also gave some useful general guidelines as to how to approach questions of persecution and sexuality, as follows (paras 28–33):

- first decide whether there is a real risk of persecution of homosexuals in the applicant's country;

- then decide whether the particular applicant is at risk;

- in order to decide whether the particular applicant is at risk, determine whether the applicant is reasonably likely to do something that will expose them to a risk of persecution;

- if the applicant is not likely to do such a thing, then determine whether they would:

'…want to do something that would put [them] at risk. Some people will be happy to live discreetly. However, if the appellant wants to do something that he feels inhibited about doing then he must explain what and why, and the adjudicator must decide if the legal or societal pressures that restrain the asylum-seeker are so severe that they are described properly as persecutory.'

The matter was also considered in the recent case of *Z v SSHD*. As with *Jain*, the Court of Appeal dismissed the case on its facts, finding that not every interference, however minor, with core human rights will amount to persecution. In relation to avoiding action, the Court seems to have accepted that the UK law marches hand-in-hand with Australian case-law. This has rejected the idea that, in the same context concerning sexuality, persecution stops being persecution just because the persecuted person could take steps to avoid offending the persecutors (*Appellant S395 v Minister for Immigration*, High Court of Australia). The Court of Appeal described the situation in this way (see paras 14–16 of *Z*):

'…a person cannot be refused asylum on the basis that he could avoid otherwise persecutory conduct by modifying the behaviour that he would otherwise engage in, at least if that modification was sufficiently significant in itself to place him in a situation of persecution.'

In cases involving sexuality, it is also worth raising the right to respect for private life under Article 8 ECHR as an alternative ground. For full details about sexuality and Article 8 'protection' cases, see ▶804–6.

Women refugees

Shah & Islam (▶see above at 607–8) is clearly an extremely important development for women asylum-seekers. Research had estimated that, while more than 60 per cent of the world's refugees are women, only about 15 per cent reach Europe to seek asylum. The particular difficulties faced by women in claiming asylum led to the development of gender guidelines, published by the Refugee Women's Legal Group (RWLG) in July 1998, for use by both advisers and decision-makers. The principal argument that the guidelines put forward is that women's cases should be dealt with under the main framework of the Convention, as are men's, rather than demanding special treatment, which might not afford women asylum-seekers the full protection of refugee status. They further argue that the history of the application and interpretation of the Convention to date betrays a lack of understanding of how women participate in political, religious and other struggles. As a result, the Home Office has marginalised and undervalued women's experiences of persecution. This, in turn, has reinforced a prejudice that women's cases are, in general, less meritorious.

The RWLG guidelines set out to establish legal and procedural principles to avoid these pitfalls, so that both advisers and decision-makers can listen more effectively to women asylum-seekers. Advisers may also find useful the guidelines issued by the UNHCR, *Gender-Related Persecution within the context of Article 1A(2) of the 1951 Convention and/or its 1967 Protocol* (HCR/GIP/02/01), 7 May 2002. The API have recognised the need to provide case-workers with a full understanding of women's experience of oppression, and how it may fall within the Refugee Convention. The API, in *Gender issues in the asylum claim*, state that gender may be relevant when (para. 3):

- **the form of persecution experienced is gender-specific – for example, rape and other forms of sexual violence; and/or**

- **the basis of the asylum claim is gender-related – i.e. gender is the reason for the persecution.**

They go on to state that there are many forms of harm that are used more frequently, or exclusively, against women, and which may amount to persecution. They include: marriage-related harm; violence within the family or community; domestic slavery; forced abortion; trafficking; female genital mutilation (FGM); sexual violence, abuse and rape. Women may also be particularly susceptible to the following forms of discrimination, which, taken in the round with other factors, may amount to persecution: family and personal laws; dress codes; employment or education restrictions; restrictions on freedom of movement or activities (para. 4). It is also recognised that there may be particular considerations relating to gender that make it more difficult for women to relocate internally in order to avoid persecution:

'The caseworker may need to take into account the implications of gender in determining the reasonableness of an internal flight alternative. For example, in certain countries, financial, logistical, social, cultural and other factors may result in particular difficulties for women or particular women, e.g. widows or single parents. Women may have family ties, i.e. children, which may have a bearing on the reasonableness of internal flight.' (para. 6)

Although *Shah & Islam* concerns women as a particular social group (but see also the existing negative decision of the Court of Appeal in *Fornah v SSHD* ▶608), it is important to recognise the specific ways in which women may face persecution for the other Convention reasons. The API accept that 'in many societies a woman's political views, race, nationality, religion and social affiliations are often seen as aligned with relatives or associates or with those of her community'. It is therefore important to determine whether a woman is being persecuted on Convention grounds that are attributed to her (para. 7). In addition, political activity is usually understood to mean such things as membership of political parties, speaking at or arranging meetings, producing and distributing leaflets, recruiting new members, and openly expressing opinions against the state. However, these activities are more often carried out by male than female activists and therefore women's roles do not easily fit into common perceptions of political activity. The above API (para. 7(v)) state:

'Whilst women will be involved in such conventional political activities and raise similar claims this does not always correspond to the reality of the experiences of women in some societies. The gender roles in many countries mean that women will more often be involved in low-level political activities – for instance hiding people, passing messages, or providing community services, food, clothing or medical care. Caseworkers should beware of equating so-called low-level political activity with low risk. The response of the state to such activity may be disproportionately persecutory because of the involvement of a section of society, namely women, [of whom] because of their gender it is considered inappropriate for them to be involved at all.'

The API also accept that women may come within the Convention on *political* grounds where they face punishment or ill-treatment for refusing to conform to social 'norms', resulting in a backlash from the state, family or religious institutions:

'Non-conformist behaviour in certain cultures, such as refusing to wear a veil, pursuing an education or choosing a partner could also lead to a woman having a political opinion attributed to her.' (See the above API at para. 7(v))

'A woman who opposes institutionalised discrimination against women or expresses views of independence from the social or cultural norms of society may sustain or fear harm because of her actual political opinion or a political opinion that has been imputed to her. She is perceived within the established political/social structure as expressing politically antagonistic views through her actions or failure to act. If a woman resists gender oppression, her resistance is political.' (API, *Deciding claims: assessing the asylum claim*, para 9.5)

B & Hoxha A particular aspect of the persecution of women was highlighted in the case of ***B & Hoxha***. In *B*, the Serb police had raided a family house, beat and stabbed the father, slashed the eight-year old son across the stomach with a knife, and raped the mother in front of both the family and 20 or 30 ethnic Albanian neighbours. As a result, there was a risk that the family would be ostracised by their own community if returned to Kosovo. The House of Lords acknowledged the force of various academic and UNHCR materials relating to the treatment of women, which made the following points:

- women are particularly vulnerable to persecution by sexual violence as a weapon of war;

- during war, women's bodies take on a symbolic importance and become part of the territory for a wider political struggle.

it was accepted that, if sexual violence is used in this way, the consequences for the woman and her family may be long-lasting, and that there are many cultures in which a woman will suffer almost as much from the attitudes of those around her to the degradation suffered as she did from the original attack. Although in that particular case there was insufficient evidence about country conditions and protection by the authorities in order to find in favour of the appellant (this part of the case had not been fully explored), the House of Lords noted (see paras 36–38):

'To suffer the insult and indignity of being regarded by one's own community…as 'dirty like contaminated' because one has suffered the gross ill-treatment of a particularly brutal and dehumanising rape directed against that very community is the sort of cumulative denial of human dignity which to my mind is quite capable of amounting to persecution. Of course the treatment feared has to be sufficiently severe, but the severity of its impact upon the individual is increased by the effects of the past persecution. The victim is punished again and again for something which was not only not her fault but was deliberately persecutory of her, her family and her community.'

Conscientious objection to military service

Generally, unwillingness to perform military service or desertion from the armed forces is not a ground for refugee status. According to paragraph 168 of the *UNHCR Handbook*, dislike of military duty or fear of combat, on their own, are not enough to constitute a well-founded fear of persecution. However, the requirement to perform military service may engage Convention protection in certain limited circumstances, as was recognised by the decision of the IAT in *Foughali* and the Court of Appeal in *Zaitz*. In both cases, the right of an individual to object to military service on genuine grounds of conscience was given some recognition.

Sepet & Bulbul The law is now contained in the decision of the House of Lords in *Sepet & Bulbul*. In that case, two Alevi Kurds objected to performing military service in Turkey on the basis that they were opposed to the policy of the government, and supported the right of self-determination for Kurdish people. They did not have an absolute conscientious objection to military service. Those who refused to perform military service in Turkey were liable to imprisonment for between six months and three years, and afterwards they would have to perform the military service. There was no alternative civilian service available.

The House of Lords held that it was not a breach of human rights under international law for states not to recognise a right of conscientious objection to compulsory military service. This means that Jehovah's Witnesses and other secular pacifists cannot qualify as refugees just because they object to all forms of military service, but may be required to perform it. In the instant case, the courts also held that there was no risk of the applicants having to engage in military action contrary to the basic rules of human conduct. This meant that the requirement to perform military service, and reasonable punishment as a result of failing to perform it, could not amount to persecution in their cases. *Sepet & Bulbul* therefore narrows the range of people who might qualify for asylum on military service grounds.

Applicants who can qualify for refugee status Following *Sepet*, only applicants in any of the following categories may come within the Convention on the basis of a compulsory requirement to perform military service (see also *B v SSHD*, IAT):

1) those who refuse service and who are at risk of grossly excessive or dispropor- tionate punishment for a Convention reason as a result;

2 those who can show that the conditions of their military service will be so severe as to amount to persecution, and that those conditions will be dis- criminately applied to them for Convention reasons;

3) those who refuse service on the grounds that it would involve their committing atrocities or gross human rights abuses contrary to the basic rules of human conduct, or their participation in a conflict condemned by the international community.

In the third category above, it is not necessary for the applicant to show that the war to which they objected has been specifically condemned by the inter- national community or international bodies, although international condem- nation is a relevant indicator that the action contravenes basic human conduct. Applicants can qualify under this third category if all of the following conditions are met (see *Krotov v SSHD*, CA and see para. 171 *UNHCR Handbook*):

• the military action violates internationally accepted 'basic rules of human conduct' or 'humanitarian norms', and such violations are carried out on a sys- temic basis as a deliberate policy, or on the basis of official indifference;

• they may personally be required to take part in the relevant military action;

• they risk punishment for refusing to do their military service;

• their reasons for refusing to take part are based on a genuine disapproval of the particular military conduct (so that an implied political opinion is established).

Wrongly suspected terrorists

In the case of *R (Sivakumar) v SSHD*, the applicant had been wrongly detained and tortured by the authorities in Sri Lanka as a suspected Tamil Tiger. The Adjudicator had dismissed the appeal on the basis that the treatment was not because of the applicant's political opinions, but because he had been wrongly suspected of terrorism. Before the House of Lords, the Home Office argument was that investigation of suspected terrorist activity was outside the protection of the Refugee Convention. The House of Lords decided that:

• not all means of investigating suspected terrorist acts (whether the suspicions were well-founded or not) were outside the protection of the Convention;

• excessive and arbitrary punishment can amount to persecution;

• there is no presumption that, where severe mistreatment is inflicted on a per- son of a particular social group or race, or to whom political opinions may be attributed, it is being inflicted for that 'Convention reason'. *However*, the severity of the treatment that the applicant had faced was relevant to whether the applicant was being persecuted for a Convention reason; in deciding the case, due weight had to be given to the torture that had taken place;

• on the facts of the case, there was therefore a strong claim that there was a real risk of persecution on grounds of race, membership of a particular social group or imputed political opinion; the case was sent back for further consideration.

Undertakings not to return in a particular way

Before the fall of Saddam Hussein in Iraq, the Home Office was issuing undertakings not to remove Iraqi Kurds who were from the Kurdish Autonomous Area (KAR) via Baghdad, or any of the territory of the main part of Iraq over which the Iraqi government exercised power. It was clear that Iraqi Kurds would be at risk if returned to any part of government-controlled Iraq. Such applicants would not be returned to the KAR until a safe route could be found.

The Court of Appeal held that, where an applicant did not have a fear of persecution in his home area (in this case in the KAR), they could not show they had well-founded fear of persecution if returned in accordance with the Home Office's undertakings. They would not be removed anywhere, or in any way which would expose them to risk (see *Gardi*; note that the Court of Appeal's decision was later declared to be a nullity, because the case should have been heard by the Court of Session in Scotland, but it remains persuasive). This situation arose in the special case of a state that was effectively split in two. The case could, however, have relevance in other cases where the Home Office undertakes only to return applicants in a particular way, so as to avoid the alleged risk.

Internal relocation

It has been argued by receiving states that there is no obligation to grant refugee status to an applicant from a country where, for example, there is a localised civil conflict. In those cases, the question has arisen as to whether it is reasonable to expect the applicant to seek protection in a separate safe area of the country, rather than obtaining protection abroad. This has become known as internal relocation, or the 'internal flight' or 'internal protection' alternative. It is reflected in the immigration rules, which state that a person may be refused asylum if there is a part of the country from which they come in which they do not have a well-founded fear of persecution, and to which it would be 'reasonable' to expect them to relocate (see para. 343 HC 395). Internal safe areas the Home Office has relied on in individual cases have included Colombo for certain Tamils from Jaffna, and Islamabad for Ahmadis from Karachi.

Until recently, the main case on internal flight was *Robinson*. In that case, the Court of Appeal considered the circumstances in which it might be appropriate to require asylum-seekers to relocate internally. The Court held that all the relevant circumstances had to be considered, such as: whether the safe area was accessible, whether the applicant would have to undergo great danger or hardship in order to get there, whether a new life would be viable there, and whether the applicant would enjoy the 'basic norms of civil, political and socio-economic human rights' in the relocation area. The Court approved a test of whether it would be 'unduly harsh' to expect a person to relocate.

In the recent case of *Hysi v SSHD*, the Court of Appeal sent a case back to the IAT to be reconsidered when the Tribunal had not properly considered whether it would be 'unduly harsh' or unreasonable to expect the claimant to relocate to a place where he would have to reject or deny his real ethnicity in order to protect himself.

Internal relocation and the decision in *AE & FE v SSHD*

The decision in *AE & FE* has made it more difficult for applicants to show that internal flight is not an option. The Court of Appeal found that, in deciding whether it is reasonable to expect the potential refugee to relocate, it was not possible to compare conditions in the relocation area with those in the UK. It was only permissible to compare the conditions in the relocation area with those in the home area. Therefore, the fact that the applicant would not have access to the 'basic norms of civil, political and socio-economic human rights' in the relocation area will not usually be relevant to refugee status, because those hardships are likely to exist throughout the country. The Court acknowledged that this changed the position from *Robinson* (▶see above), but the justification for this was that *Robinson* was decided before the HRA and the ECHR may now be relevant in cases where an applicant's claim depends on comparing conditions in the relocation area with conditions in the UK.

The decision-maker will therefore compare the conditions in the home area with those in the safe area, to determine whether the comparison made it reasonable for the applicant to seek protection abroad rather than relocating internally. So, in *AE* itself, while it may have been harmful for the applicant's wife's psychiatric condition for the family to return to Colombo (the relocation area) as opposed to staying *in the UK*, this did *not* mean that Colombo was not a safe haven as compared with Jaffna (the area of persecution). The Court was at pains to point out that a family in this position might be protected under the ECHR, or on other exceptional grounds. The case is likely to be heard by the House of Lords.

Standard of proof

In principle, the burden (or onus) of showing that the criteria for coming within the definition of 'refugee' are established rests with the asylum-seeker. However, the 'standard' of proof is a different legal concept from the burden of proof. The burden of proof concerns whose job it is to prove the relevant facts; the standard of proof states the degree of certainty to which a matter has to be proved before it is taken into account for legal purposes.

In criminal cases, the burden lies on the prosecution to prove the case against an accused to the standard of 'no reasonable doubt'. In most civil cases, the burden lies upon whoever is asserting a relevant fact to prove it to the standard of 'balance of probabilities', which means anything above 50 per cent. In asylum cases, although the investigative process often centres largely on what has happened in the past to a particular person, the actual question to be answered is what will happen in the future if the person is required to return. Inevitably, this question involves a degree of speculation and prediction, and is not as amenable to traditional concepts of 'proof'.

The approach that has been laid down by the courts is as follows.

Sivakumaran In *Sivakumaran*, the House of Lords decided that the standard of proof that had to be reached in showing that a fear was 'well-founded' was that there had to be a 'serious possibility' or 'reasonable degree of likelihood' or 'real risk' of it occurring. The standard of proof is therefore at the lowest end of the scale, and is less onerous than the ordinary civil standard of balance of probabilities. One indication given in *Sivakumaran* was that the standard was similar to showing a 'one-in-ten' chance.

How is evidence about past facts assessed? Whether there is a 'real risk' of a person being persecuted if returned is a simple enough question. However, over recent years the courts have had to consider how to approach the question of what has happened in the past, as it is part of the process of deciding what may happen in the future. Although the ultimate question is always whether there is a risk on return, the question of whether the applicant is telling the truth about what has happened in the past is, in many cases, extremely important in determining the claim. The correct approach to the assessment of past events was confirmed by the Court of Appeal in *Karanakaran*. The Court directed decision-makers to weigh all the evidence in assessing the risk of persecution. The decision-maker must not exclude anything from consideration unless they are in no doubt that it did not occur. Asylum-seekers are therefore to be given the benefit of any doubts the decision-maker has about the history they have given.

Reasons for low standard of proof There are two reasons for the low standard of proof. First, it recognises that people should be protected from serious harm if there is a significant risk of it occurring, even if that risk is not over 50 per cent. Secondly, it recognises that most asylum-seekers will not be able to produce documentary evidence or witnesses in order to back up their claims, but that this alone should not mean that their claims do not succeed. The lower standard must be applied by the Home Office in making the decision in the first place, and the AIT on any appeal.

EXCLUSION FROM PROTECTION UNDER THE REFUGEE CONVENTION

A small number of people who are 'refugees' can be excluded from the protection of the Convention. Exclusion applies to the following three groups of people:

1) those who do not deserve international protection (▶625);

2) those who are a danger to the security of the host country (▶625);

3) those who do not need any further protection from the host country (▶626).

These groups are discussed in turn below. Viewed simply from the point of view of the Refugee Convention, the effect of denying protection to certain refugees is to expose them, potentially, to persecution. These exclusions do not apply, however, to the protection given by Article 3 ECHR (torture and inhuman or degrading treatment or punishment). The absolute nature of Article 3 protection was confirmed by the European Court of Human Rights in the case of *Chahal v UK* (▶see 796). However, the Home Office will not grant humanitarian protection to those who fall within the above exclusions; it will instead only grant short periods of discretionary leave, and settlement will be delayed for at least ten years, and possibly longer (for further details, ▶see 863–4, 865, 869).

Because it arises less frequently, there is less case-law interpreting the grounds for exclusion. Before the Anti-terrorism, Crime and Security Act 2001, it was possible to argue that the seriousness or extent of the persecution feared had to be considered in deciding whether a person should be excluded on the grounds that they are not deserving of protection, or that they are a danger to the security of the host country – in other words, that there was a 'proportionality' assessment that had to be carried out. However, section 34 of the 2001 Act aims to prevent any such considerations from being taken into account. For the general procedural approach to be taken to exclusion issues on appeals ▶see 1080–1.

In certain cases, the Secretary of State may certify that the negative decision was taken on grounds of national security, or other similar grounds relating to the UK's relationship with other countries (s97 2002 Act). Often such cases are asylum cases involving exclusion from the Refugee Convention. In such cases, the right of appeal is to the Special Immigration Appeals Commission (SIAC), rather than to the AIT (see s2(1) Special Immigration Appeals Commission Act 1997). For more details about SIAC and these procedures, ▶see 1081–3. For the detention aspects of national security cases, ▶see 901–2.

Exclusion from protection now needs to be considered alongside the Home Office's new APIs issued in August 2005, which apply in relation to exclusion, cessation and cancellation of refugee status (▶see 721–7 and ▶see 862–9). We now look at the three excluded groups in turn.

1) Refugees who do not deserve international protection

Those who are undeserving of international protection are people for whom there are 'serious reasons for considering that' they have committed any of the following (see Article 1F of the Convention):

- a crime against peace, a war crime, or a crime against humanity;
- a 'serious non-political' crime outside the country of refuge before recognition as a refugee;
- acts contrary to the purposes and principles of the United Nations.

These exclusions are to be interpreted narrowly, and the burden of proving that an exclusion clause applies rests on the state. The standard of proof for exclusion under Article 1F ('serious reasons for considering') is lower than both 'beyond reasonable doubt' and 'balance of probabilities' (*Gurung*, IAT).

Serious non-political crime

A 'serious non-political crime' is not closely defined, because of the differences between countries' criminal laws. It would have to be a crime for which a very serious penalty could be imposed. There is a growing trend for governments to use this category to exclude political activists who have a connection with armed groups. In the case of *T,* the House of Lords decided that an Algerian who claimed to be a member of the Front Islamique du Salut (FIS), and to have been involved in bomb attacks on civilian targets, was excluded, even though there was a 'political' motivation for the crime. The Court ruled that a crime is a political one for these purposes only if it is both committed for a political purpose (such as overthrowing the government or bringing about a change in state policy) *and* there is a sufficiently close link between the crime and the political purpose. Where the act is out of all proportion to the political aim, the crime is to be treated as a non-political one.

Acts contrary to the purposes and principles of the UN

There is little case-law on the 'purposes and principles' of the United Nations, but SIAC has held that terrorist acts fall within this definition (*Singh & Singh*). Also, according to the IAT, private individuals can be guilty of an act contrary to the purposes and principles of the UN – the exclusion does not apply only to state officials who were in a position of power in the state, as the *UNHCR Handbook* indicates (*KK (Article 1F(C) Turkey) v SSHD*, para. 163 of the *Handbook*).

2) Refugees who are a danger to the host country

Articles 32(1) and 33(2) of the Convention exclude from the protection of the Refugee Convention those who are a danger to the security or order of the host country. Article 33(2) also excludes those who have been convicted of a 'particularly serious crime', and are a danger to the community. The letter granting refugee status contains a warning against activities involving violence so as to endanger national security or public order. Section 72 of the 2002 Act provides that, where a person is convicted in the UK of an offence and sentenced to imprisonment for at least two years, they will be presumed to have been convicted of a particularly serious crime, and to be a danger to the community. The presumption can be rebutted. Provision is also made for other crimes, and for crimes committed outside the country. Further details about how the Home Office will apply section 72 are contained in APU Notice 6/2004, *Section 72 of the NIA 2002: Particularly Serious Crimes* and the Nationality, Immigration and Asylum Act 2002 (Specification of Particularly Serious Crimes) Order 2004 (▶see further 1080–1).

Despite the provisions of section 72, the 'five-year strategy' states that the government intends to introduce:

'...much tougher rules to deny asylum to those who have committed serious crimes, on top of excluding terrorists.' (para. 30)

3) Refugees who do not need the protection of the Convention

Article 1D of the Convention states that persons who are 'at present' receiving protection or assistance from organs or agencies of the UN other than the UNHCR will not be protected by the Convention *unless* the UN protection ceases. If UN protection ceases without the position of those protected having been settled, those persons become entitled to refugee status.

In *Amer Mohammed El-Ali & Daraz v SSHD*, the Court of Appeal held that 'at present', for those purposes, meant at the time when the Refugee Convention was adopted, which was on 28 July 1951. The only relevant agencies providing protection at that stage were the International Refugee Organisation and the United Nations Relief and Works Agency for Palestinian Refugees in the Near East (UNRWA). So, Article 1D only affects those protected by these agencies at that time. The facts of *El Ali & Daraz* were that the applicants were Palestinians who were registered with UNRWA. However, they were born in the 1970s, and therefore could not come within Article 1D. As a result, in order to be protected by the Convention they had to demonstrate an existing well-founded fear of persecution, which they could not do. Even if they had fallen within Article 1D because they had been protected before the operative date, they would have had to show that UNRWA had actually wound up its operations before they would be in a position to say that they were entitled to refugee status. They could not say that UNRWA had ceased to provide protection, simply because they had removed themselves from its protection by coming to the UK.

A second class of persons who do not need the protection of the Convention are those who, although they are not nationals of the host country, are recognised by the authorities of the host country as having all the same rights as persons who are nationals of that country (Article 1E of the Convention).

THE TERRORISM ACT 2000

Although the Home Office indicated that the purpose of the Terrorism Act 2000 is not to affect asylum-seekers, it does have potentially serious consequences for some asylum-seekers who are, or have been, supporters or members of 'proscribed' organisations. The Terrorism Act brought together previous terrorist legislation and placed it on a permanent footing. It widens the definition of 'terrorism' to actions or threats of action involving serious violence against persons or property, for the purpose of influencing the government or intimidating the public, and which are carried out for political, religious or ideological causes. The Home Secretary is given power to proscribe organisations by order (s3 2000 Act). The list of proscribed organisations has grown since the Act was passed; there are presently 39 organisations on the list (Sch 2 2000 Act).

Criminal offences A series of criminal offences has been created, including belonging to a proscribed organisation, or inviting support for it by, for example, arranging meetings. An offence is also committed where there is reasonable cause to suspect that funds raised may be used for terrorism. Finally, it is an offence to fail to disclose information that a person has been involved with fund-raising or money-laundering for terrorist purposes when such information is obtained in the course of a trade, profession, business or employment. This could impact on people advising asylum-seekers who are not protected by professional legal privilege.

Dilemma for asylum-seekers The Act creates a dilemma for some asylum-seekers fleeing persecution on account of a well-founded fear of persecution for reasons of political opinion who, by demonstrating membership or support for a proscribed organisation, may expose themselves to the risk of prosecution in the UK. The list of organisations includes, for example, the International Sikh Youth Federation, the Liberation Tigers of Tamil Eelam (LTTE), the Kurdistan Workers' Party (PKK) and the Revolutionary Peoples' Liberation Party-Front (DHKP-C).

CEASING TO BE A REFUGEE AND REVOCATION OF INDEFINITE LEAVE

For general details about reviewing refugee status and the leave which goes with it under policy in force from 30 August 2005 ▶see 721–4. Under Article 1C of the Refugee Convention, a person who is a refugee may cease to qualify if any of the following circumstances apply:

1) if the refugee voluntarily re-avails themselves of the protection of the country of nationality;

2) if, having lost their nationality, the refugee voluntarily reacquires it;

3) if the refugee voluntarily acquires a new nationality and has the protection of the country of their new nationality;

4) if the refugee voluntarily re-establishes him or herself in the country from which they claimed a fear of persecution;

5) if there is a change in the circumstances that gave rise to the person's recognition as a refugee, so that the person no longer satisfies the criteria for recognition.

Although, logically, the cessation clauses only have effect after an applicant has been granted refugee status, an analogy has been drawn with (5) above (change in circumstances), where conditions change before a person's application has been decided. In cases where it is accepted by the Home Office that an applicant was previously a refugee, although no formal decision was made, but ceases to be one by the time the decision comes to be made, the situation is very similar to the Home Office invoking cessation. In such cases, there is a burden on the Home Office to show that the applicant can now be returned safely (see the decisions of the Court of Appeal in *Arif* and *Demrikaya*, and the decision of the House of Lords in *B & Hoxha*, at para. 66).

Cessation has rarely featured in asylum cases, partly because of the Home Office practice of granting indefinite leave to those who succeed in their asylum claims. However, under the Home Office's five-year strategy it has returned to a system of granting limited leave, and to keeping the situation in a refugee's country under review (for the operation of the new system of 'active review', ▶see 720–7).This means that changes of circumstance may become more important in the long-term stability of status granted to refugees.

In addition, under changes introduced by the 2002 Act from 10 February 2003, the Home Office has been able to revoke a refugee's (and their dependants') *indefinite* leave in any of the situations in (1)–(4) above (see s76 2002 Act). Note that this does not include change of circumstance cases (which come under (5)). In relation to (1)–(4) above, provided that the action giving rise to the revocation occurs on or after 10 February 2003, even indefinite leave granted before that date can be revoked (s76(6) 2002 Act). If indefinite leave is revoked on these grounds, refugee status will be revoked at the same time. At the same time as this power to revoke leave came into force, the government also established a specific power to remove persons who have had their leave revoked as a result of ceasing to be a refugee. Such people can be subject to administrative removal (see s10(1)(ba) 1999 Act inserted by the 2002 Act). There is a right of appeal to the AIT against decisions to revoke an indefinite leave (see s82(2)(f) 2002 Act).

Practical use of 'cessation' and revocation of leave

The use of cessation and revocation now must be read alongside the government's APIs published in August 2005 as to when these powers will be used (▶see 721–7). As indicated above, the first four 'cessation' circumstances (see above) may lead to revocation of indefinite leave where the applicant has, by their own voluntary action, ceased to be a refugee. Typical circumstances leading to this form of cessation are the obtaining, renewal and/or use by the refugee of a passport from their country of nationality. This can be seen as a 'voluntary availment' of the protection of the country of nationality. The API (*Cessation, Cancellation and Revocation of Refugee Status*, para. 3.3) state as follows:

'Obtaining a national passport or an extension of its validity, and then using it for travel, should not automatically lead to termination of refugee status. A refugee might have to obtain a passport and travel to his country of origin/habitual residence for a valid reason, such as the need to apply for divorce papers. In such a case he may have no alternative but recourse to a measure of protection from that country and such action would not of itself be regarded as re-availment, although all the circumstances of the case would need to be assessed. Consideration should be given to any exceptional compassionate circumstances e.g. the need to visit a sick relative, whether the request to travel has been made prior to the visit, and whether the length of the visit is commensurate with the nature of that visit.'

As to voluntary re-establishment, the above API state (para. 2.2):

'Voluntary re-establishment' means a return to the country from which protection was sought, with a view to taking up permanent residence. A lengthy stay would normally be involved. A short visit to the former country is not likely to constitute 're-establishment'. If, for example, the visit is undertaken for exceptional reasons which have been approved (such as for a family funeral or to visit a sick relative) it will not result in re-establishment. Where approval has not been sought prior to travel the case should be considered on its own merits, taking into account factors such as the length and nature of the visit, and whether there have been any previous visits. The application of this clause will not be appropriate in certain cases e.g. in Kosovan cases re-establishment is currently permitted, though advice should be sought on a case by case basis.'

For general details about refugees and travel, ▶see further below. Plainly, any refugee who is considering travelling back to their own country, or obtaining a passport other than a travel document issued by the Home Office, should first obtain careful advice. Plainly an applicant cannot generally travel while waiting for an application or an appeal to be decided (▶see 119–21).

As for cessation cases based upon a change of circumstances, i.e. where the circumstances have changed to such an extent that the person can no longer refuse the protection of their country of origin (Article 1C(5)(6) of the Refugee Convention), the API state:

'"Circumstances" refer to the circumstances of the individual refugee having changed in the country from which asylum was sought. The changes must be of a significant and non-temporary nature for the refugee's fear of persecution to be no longer regarded as well-founded.'

Dependants of refugees whose leave is revoked

Section 76 also enables the Home Office to revoke the indefinite leave of a dependant of a refugee when the refugee's leave is revoked. However, this will not generally be done where the dependants are refugees in their own right unless they too cease to be refugees under the criteria set out. The Home Office will also consider whether there are compelling reasons for not revoking the leave of dependants. Account will be taken of the length of time spent in the UK, and established ties here. Where the dependant is living apart from the refugee, it should be argued that it is not appropriate to revoke leave.

Does a person lose the protection of the Refugee Convention if they are no longer at risk of persecution but there are 'compelling' reasons why they should not return?

In the recent case of *B & Hoxha*, the appellants tried to argue that, where the circumstances which led to the applicant becoming a refugee in the first place have changed, then they should still be protected by the Refugee Convention if there are still 'compelling reasons' arising from their previous persecution why they should not return. The argument was taken from the proviso (i.e. the exception) to Article 1C(5) of the Convention.

The facts of the cases were that the appellants were ethnic Albanians from Kosovo who had suffered appalling persecution by the Serbian authorities in the period before June 1999, when NATO drove Serb forces out of Kosovo. Their claims for asylum were refused by the Home Office in June 2000. Despite the fact that the persecutor had been removed, the appellants claimed that they should still be protected by the Convention because, the continuing effects of the past persecution on them would make it less easy for them to cope with the conditions in the country if returned. The appellants faced an uphill struggle in their argument, because they were relying upon an exception to the cessation clause when they had not even been recognised as refugees.

The House of Lords held that the 'compelling reasons' exception only applied to a particular class of refugees – those who have been found to be refugees under international agreements *before* the 1951 Convention because of fears that existed at that time. For practical purposes, therefore, they confirmed that it was necessary in all cases to show a present well-founded fear of persecution. There was no continuing risk of persecution for the appellants, and they were therefore not protected by the Convention. The case has important implications not just for cases where the circumstances change during the time it takes to determine claims to asylum, but also now that the Home Office has implemented its proposal to grant only limited leave to refugees and to review their cases. Such applicants will probably have to demonstrate a continuing fear of persecution.

There are, however, two further points to bear in mind arising from *B & Hoxha*:

1) The House of Lords acknowledged that there may be some cases where the nature of the previous persecution might be linked to what would happen if the applicant were to be returned so that a person may still be at risk of persecution at the present time. For the particular example given of ostracism of women who have been subjected to rape, ▶see 618–9.

2) In cases where a person is particularly vulnerable as a result of the continuing effects of persecution, but does not have a present fear of persecution, this might constitute grounds for granting leave on a humanitarian basis (see Lord Hope at para. 26 and Lord Brown at paras 87, 88). The Home Office had itself stated in the course of the case:

'The Secretary of State accepts that there will be cases where an individual may be particularly vulnerable by reason of the continuing physical or psychological effects of persecution he has suffered in the past. Such problems may render him less able to cope with difficult conditions in his country of origin. It is open to such an applicant to apply for discretionary leave to remain in the United Kingdom on compassionate grounds.'

REFUGEES WISHING TO TRAVEL

A person recognised as a refugee is entitled to a travel document known as a 'Convention travel document' or 'CTD'. They are blue in colour (▶see 206 for an example). A fee is payable with the application (for present fees, ▶see 1509). The documents are valid for all countries except the one from which the person needed asylum. Where the applicant has indefinite leave, they are likely to be issued as valid for ten years. Where the refugee has only limited leave, the CTD will be issued as valid in line with the leave. For general details about travel documents and the procedures for applying for them and also for the requirements for obtaining a travel document for a person with humanitarian protection, discretionary leave, exceptional leave or indefinite leave (without refugee status), ▶see 880–3.

Where a refugees is granted indefinite leave, their leave does not lapse when they travel abroad unless they remain outside the country for two years. However, a refugee should be readmitted to the UK at any time during the validity of the travel document, so that remaining outside the UK for more than two years will not disqualify the refugee as it will other returning residents (see *Shirreh*). The refugee should continue to use the CTD, even after obtaining settlement, until they naturalise as British citizens. The consequences for the immigration status of refugees who travel back to their country of origin, or the country from which they sought asylum, can be severe (▶see 627–30, 721–3). Refugees with limited leave can also travel abroad (although not usually to their country of origin) and return to the UK. For general details about travel to and from the UK ▶see Chapter 5.

Some countries that have not signed the Refugee Convention do not recognise CTDs. Under the Council of Europe Agreement on the Abolition of Visas for Refugees 1959, refugees travelling on a CTD can generally travel to EU countries, without obtaining a visa, provided that the trip is for less than three months. However, not all countries are now complying with this. From 11 February 2003, the UK suspended its compliance meaning that people travelling to the UK on a refugee travel document must have a visa (and ▶see 633). Once a refugee has naturalised as a British citizen, they are of course entitled to a British passport and can travel using that (for the requirements for naturalisation, see Chapter 45).

Travel to Tsunami-affected areas

The Home Office has adopted a special policy for those granted refugee status, HP, DL or ELR from areas affected by the Tsunami that hit South-East Asia in December 2004 (APU Notice *Tsunami Affected Areas: those with protection based leave who wish to return*). The policy recognises that there are those with protection-based leave who may wish to return to the area for a short period following the disaster. The areas affected are: the coastal areas of the north, east, south and south-west of Sri Lanka; the province of Aceh on the Island of Sumatra in Indonesia; affected islands of the Maldives; in India, the coastal areas of Tamil Nadu, Kerela, Pondicherry, Andhra Pradesh and the Andaman and Nicobar Islands; certain areas of Somalia.

People would normally jeopardise their status in the UK if they returned to the country from which they claimed protection. Where a person does return, policy is to consider on a case-by-case basis whether a person granted leave on a protection basis should have their leave curtailed (otherwise called 'revoked', ▶see 721–7 and ▶see also above at 628–30) if they visit the country. The same case-by-case assessment applies in Tsunami-affected cases, but 'due weight should be given to the compassionate reason for such a visit'. Requests for permission to travel should be made to the Home Office.

Refugees hold Convention Travel Documents that will prevent them travelling to their country of origin, and many of those with HP/DL/ELR will hold a Certificate of Identity, which also prevents their travelling to their country of origin. Those in this position who wish to return will have to contact the Travel Document Section of the Home Office, in Croydon, setting out their reasons for wishing to go back in the light of the Tsunami, and the Section will consider the request to travel and for a travel document. Note that even where permission to return and a document permitting it are granted, the Home Office states:

'We cannot guarantee that a return trip would not raise issues about [the applicant's] need for continuing protection in the UK.'

Where passengers with protection-based leave who have returned to a Tsunami-affected area without Home Office permission come to light at port, they will be granted temporary admission, and their cases will be referred to the Home Office to be assessed, and to determine whether their status should be withdrawn.

Those recognised as refugees elsewhere who wish to travel to the UK

Refugees seeking to travel to the UK who hold CTDs that were not issued in the UK must give a record of their fingerprints on arrival. From 27 February 2004, UK entry clearances endorsed on CTDs that are issued by other states do not operate as leave to enter, unlike other UK entry clearances which do. They are issued in the old way, namely, as valid for presentation at a port within six months. The holder must arrive at the port within that time, and will be examined on arrival by the immigration officer in order to determine whether leave to enter will be granted (see Immigration (Leave to Enter and Remain) (Amendment) Order 2004 and see DSP Ch 4, para. 4.10) (▶see also 82–3).

TEMPORARY PROTECTION

A new category of 'temporary protection' was introduced into the immigration rules from 1 January 2005 (paras 354–356B HC 395 inserted by HC 164). This category is the result of an EU Directive called the 'Temporary Protection Directive' (2001/55/EC), which was adopted by the Council of the EU in July 2001. It sets out minimum standards for giving temporary protection to a 'mass influx' of displaced people from outside the EU. So, if there is a humanitarian crisis similar to Kosovo in the future, there should be a coordinated response across the EU to deal with it. If and when this occurs, the Temporary Protection Directive can be invoked by a decision of the Council of the EU, which will then mean that the protection standards must apply to persons who qualify. The amendments to the rules are in order to set out how the UK will implement the Directive if and when a further 'mass influx' occurs.

Granting temporary protection

Applicants who have arrived in the UK will be granted temporary protection if they satisfy both of the following requirements:

- they are entitled to temporary protection as defined by the Temporary Protection Directive; and

- they have not already been granted temporary protection by another EU state.

Applicants may be excluded from temporary protection on the same grounds as people can be excluded from the Refugee Convention (▶see above at 624–6). However, exclusions from temporary protection must also be based on the principle of proportionality. Where temporary protection is granted, applicants will be given leave for up to 12 months in the first instance. Extensions may be applied for and, if granted, will be given for six months at a time. Those granted temporary protection will be permitted to work and/or to enter into self-employment. The protection is indeed intended to be temporary, and there is no provision in the rules enabling applicants to settle in the UK.

Importantly, if an applicant claims asylum but they are eligible for temporary protection, the Home Office may decide not to determine the asylum application until the applicant is no longer entitled to temporary protection (see para. 355G HC 395). By this time, of course, the applicant is likely no longer to qualify for asylum and the greater benefits which it brings.

Dependants of those applying for or granted temporary protection

Dependants may be granted leave in line with the main applicant provided they also do not fall to be excluded under the Refugee Convention exclusions. The rules indicate that dependants may be included as dependants in the main applicant's application for temporary protection, or may apply for reunion after the main applicant has been granted protection. All dependants must be 'pre-existing' family members. This means that they must have been living with the main applicant as part of the family unit in the country of origin immediately before the mass influx.

Dependants are divided into two categories: 'family members' and 'close relatives' (▶see below). It is more difficult for close relatives to be admitted than it is for family members. Whenever considering an application by a dependant minor, the Home Office will take into account the 'best interests' of that child.

Family members

'Family members' are the spouse, minor unmarried child or unmarried partner of the main applicant. Unmarried partners must have been living together in a relationship akin to marriage that has subsisted for two years or more. The rules state that a dependant family member 'will' be granted temporary protection in line with the main applicant.

Close relatives

'Close relatives' are the parent, grandparent or unmarried adult child of the main applicant. 'Close relatives' also include 'any other relative... whom the Secretary of State considers to have a particularly close relationship' with the main applicant. In all cases, the close relative must have been 'wholly or mainly dependent' on the main applicant in the country of origin. The rules state that a close relative dependant 'may' in 'exceptional circumstances' be granted leave in line with the main applicant. The Home Office will look at each case on an individual basis and assess the 'extreme hardship the dependant close relative would face if the reunification did not take place'.

Previous forms of temporary protection

The forerunners of the temporary protection category were as follows. In 1992 the government announced that up to 1,000 Bosnian ex-detainees and their families would be allowed to come to the UK. They were allowed in very gradually. Only a small proportion actually arrived, and they were not formally recognised as refugees. On arrival they were given an unusual status, called 'temporary refuge', usually for six-month periods, and were told not to expect to be allowed to stay longer. In fact, they have been granted extensions of exceptional leave and, subsequently, granted settlement. Those granted exceptional leave were told that they could return for short trips to Bosnia in order to 'test the water' and, crucially, could be readmitted within their period of leave if they decided not to resettle in Bosnia.

The UK also participated in the Humanitarian Evacuation Programme in response to the crisis in Kosovo in 1998/99. Over 4,000 people were permitted to come here and, after a period of temporary protection, were offered an assistance grant to return home to 'explore and prepare' – that is, to see whether they could return. The vast majority have not had their exceptional leave extended, but have been returned on the basis that it is now safe for them to do so.

7

22 Asylum procedures

The Refugee Convention does not itself lay down any procedures for the determination of refugee status and therefore the governments that have signed the Convention and Protocol choose the procedure which they will adopt to decide whether people qualify. This chapter looks at the practical procedures for claiming asylum in the UK. It also looks at related matters such as applications from minors, dependants of asylum-seekers and permission to work.

The procedures operated by the immigration authorities when people claim asylum continue to be the subject of constant change. Procedures can differ between ports and in-country claims made at Asylum Screening Units (ASUs). The asylum process has also been complicated by the different 'detained fast track' processes (which the government is keen to extend, ▶see the five-year strategy and commentary 33–50), the 'non-suspensive' appeal regime, and procedures connected with National Asylum Support Service (NASS) support. Often the Home Office introduces pilot projects to assess the benefits of a new procedure and so different procedures are adopted for different people. A recent example of this is the North West Project (▶643 and 682–3). People using this part of the *Handbook* therefore need to be aware that it is not always possible to predict how the Home Office will act in an individual case and that further changes are always likely.

General background and guide to the chapter

We begin by looking at the very general guidance provided by the UNHCR on asylum procedures and the importance, which the UK courts have attached to the use of fair procedures (▶640–1).

New Asylum Model

Present government policy is to roll out its 'New Asylum Model', which it hopes to have fully operational by September 2006. Central to this is what it calls 'segmentation'. This essentially means dividing the processes by which asylum claims are decided into different procedures depending on the type of case. Of course this has been the practice to a greater or lesser extent for a number of years but this 'dividing up' is likely to become more systematic and intensive. In addition, by the summer of 2005, several of the essential 'segments' (detained fast track, non-detained accelerated procedures etc) were already in place. At ▶641–4 we give a general overview of the 'New Asylum Model' at the stage it has presently reached. This is a useful starting point for those wanting an overview on asylum procedures.

General asylum procedures

We then go on to look at *general* asylum procedures. These are procedures which apply generally across asylum claims. Obviously, depending upon the particular process or 'segment' to which the claim has been allocated, this general description must be read with modifications. Not all the procedures will apply in the same way to every case. In this description of general procedures we look at:

- the obligation on the immigration authorities to identify those trying to make asylum claims (▶645);
- applying for asylum at port and in-country (▶645–9);
- the 'screening' process (▶649–50);
- issue of identity documents, Asylum Registration Cards (ARCs) and Standard Acknowledgement Letters (SALs) (▶651–2);
- reporting and other conditions of temporary admission – we look here also at the policy on how frequent reporting should be and at the conditions, including electronic monitoring, which may be imposed (▶652–4);
- initial access to NASS support (▶654–5) (asylum support is covered generally in Chapters 41–42);
- general induction processes (▶655–7);
- asylum interviews, preparing for and handling such interviews and the new procedure for tape-recording interviews (▶657–62);
- the 'one-stop' procedure for raising additional grounds for staying in the UK and the penalties for not raising grounds promptly (▶662–4);
- providing evidence in support of asylum applications including specific documents, expert, witness and country evidence (▶665–7);
- procedures for voluntary return (▶667–8);
- the 'ILR family exercise' concession (▶668–9).

Particular asylum procedures

We then look in turn at the various separately identified procedures for processing claims:

- the 'ordinary' SEF (Statement of Evidence Form) and SEF-less procedures i.e. where applicants have not been allocated to one of the specific 'segments' described under the 'New Asylum Model' – we look at completing the SEF form, obtaining extensions to the time-limit, and at SEF/NINO (National Insurance Number) interviews (▶669–73);

- the *detained* fast track procedures: we look at policy concerning which applicants are likely to be processed in this manner and separately at the timetables used at Oakington Reception Centre and at Harmondsworth and Yarls Wood Immigration Removal Centres (▶see 673–9). The legal challenges, which have been brought to these procedures and the flexibility with which the Home Office has agreed to operate these procedures following challenge, are discussed (▶677 and 679–81). Those who are entitled to appeal after refusal and are detained will be put through a 'fast track' appeal process. This special appeals process is dealt with in the appeals section (▶1129–32). Powers of detention, legality of detention and getting people out of detention generally are covered separately in Section 9 (Chapters 30 and 32);

- accelerated non-detained processes (▶681–3). Four separate procedures are covered:

  - an accelerated timetable for those making 'potentially NSA' ('non-suspensive appeal') claims in Croydon;

  - an accelerated timetable for those making 'late and opportunistic claims' in Croydon;

  - the North West Project for those who make their claims in Manchester or Liverpool;

  - the Dover Pilot Scheme for those who claim in Dover.

Although 'third country' asylum cases are referred to in this chapter, full details about them are given in Chapter 24.

Important connected matters

This chapter also deals with several separate but very important matters connected to claiming asylum and asylum processes as follows.

- **Prosecutions under section 2 of the 2004 Act**. Section 2 enables criminal charges to be brought against those who attend certain interviews without an 'immigration document' (a passport or similar document). There have been a substantial number of prosecutions since the offence was introduced in September 2004 (▶see 683–6).

- **Unaccompanied minor asylum-seekers (UASCs)**. We look at Home Office policy on best practice for UASCs and the policy relating to lack of reception facilities. An important recent aspect has been 'age disputes' and we look at Home Office policy and challenges to decisions in this area in detail (▶686–91).

- **Dependants of asylum-seekers.** We cover who is able to claim as a dependant and at the relevant procedures (▶691–4). 'Family reunion' with a person who has been accepted as a refugee is a different matter and this is dealt with in Chapter 25.

- **Permission to work**. There have been several changes in policy relating to permission to work over the last few years and transitional arrangements have been made at the time of change in policy. We trace the policy over recent times and look at the change in the immigration rules relating to permission to work, which was made as a result of the EC Reception Conditions Directive (▶694–6).

- **Special applications.** There are a number of special asylum procedures which may be used in the minority of cases and which, significantly, allow persons to be accepted while abroad. They include the 'Gateway Protection quota refugee resettlement programme', 'mandate' refugees, the 'ten or more plan' as well as applications made from abroad, which do not fit any of these schemes. We also look at applications to transfer refugee status (▶696–701).

- **Government attempts to prevent and deter asylum-seekers** (▶701– 4).

'Fresh' asylum applications, which are made after a previous asylum application, are covered in Chapter 23 (▶730–5), which also covers credibility, Home Office country information and decisions, policy on leave from August 2005 and delays in issuing status papers.

GUIDANCE FROM UNHCR AND APPROACH OF UK COURTS

The *UNHCR Handbook* provides some guidance on asylum procedures. For instance, it recommends a particularly sensitive approach to both mentally disturbed applicants and unaccompanied minors. It states that consideration of claims from those groups requires special care, often involving the obtaining of medical reports and seeking evidence, as far as possible, from objective sources. Also, in a letter from UNHCR's UK office, written in relation to a case in the Court of Appeal about the nature of asylum appeals (*Massaquoi*), the UNHCR indicated that it views appeals procedures to be 'integral' to refugee status determination. Such procedures must be 'fair and effective'. The *UNHCR Handbook* states that an application for asylum should

'...be examined within the framework of specially established procedures by qualified personnel having the necessary knowledge and experience, and an understanding of an applicant's particular difficulties and needs.' (para. 190)

A shared responsibility

Generally, the burden of demonstrating that a person comes within the definition of 'refugee' rests with the asylum-seeker. However, as the *Handbook* also points out, often an applicant will neither have specific evidence, nor all the means to demonstrate that they have a well-founded fear of persecution. Therefore, at least at the stage of initial examination of the claim, there is a shared responsibility on both the asylum-seeker and the Home Office to obtain the evidence necessary to investigate all of the circumstances (para. 196). In practice, the Home Office cannot be relied upon to conduct all the necessary investigations into a claim and it is very much left to the asylum-seeker and their representatives to search for and collect evidence. This is particularly the case where the asylum-seeker's history concerns matters about which little is generally known.

UK courts' general approach

The courts in the UK have recognised the importance of the operation of fair procedures in asylum cases. Perhaps the most important principle which the UK courts have declared in relation to asylum procedures is that cases must be considered with the most 'anxious scrutiny' to ensure that the decisions are 'in no way flawed' (*Musisi*, HL). This is because asylum determination procedures concern the life and liberty of the individual and therefore only the highest standards of consideration and fairness are acceptable in order for the process to be lawful (*Thirukumar*).

In the recent *Refugee Legal Centre* case (►see below at 679), the Court of Appeal underlined that fast track processes must be operated with sufficient flexibility as to the timetable used so that there is no room for unfairness in individual cases.

UNHCR's 'Quality Initiative'

Part of the remit of UNHCR's London office is to advise the government on its asylum determination procedures. Since March 2004, UNHCR has been monitoring these procedures in a project called the 'Quality Initiative'. The project's interim findings are that some of the procedures are defective: misinterpretation of country information, poor reasoning in decisions, misapplication of the law and failure to consider obvious ECHR issues. Recommendations made so far include the requirement for senior case-work staff to be accredited in a similar way to immigration practitioners by April 2006 (►see Chapter 3).

European Asylum Procedures Directive

The European Union has been developing the text of a Council Directive on 'Minimum standards on procedures for granting and withdrawing refugee status' in member states. The drafting has been subject to debate and contention. The draft texts contain provisions on, among other matters, minimum standards on appeals, unfounded claims and third country cases. The Directorate was finally adopted by the Council of the EU (Justice and Home Affairs) on 2 December 2005.

THE NEW ASYLUM MODEL

The government's 'five-year strategy' for asylum and immigration, published in February 2005, trailed the idea of a 'new asylum model'. The aims of this are: to process claims even faster with the intention of reducing the costs of asylum support; reduce the number of asylum claims (particularly unfounded ones); and increase the number and speed of removals.

As we explain immediately below, by the summer of 2005, some aspects of the new asylum model have already been brought in. The target date for complete implementation is September 2006. Key features of the new asylum model are as follows:

- **'Segmentation'** Asylum claims are to be 'segmented' into different categories that will, in turn, determine the 'route' or procedure that will apply to the applicant. Segmentation involves increased use of 'fast track-ing' of claims (▶see below). Not all fast tracked cases will involve deten-tion. Some of those who are not detained will still have their claims determined quickly through accelerated procedures. Such applicants may be given very frequent reporting conditions and be dispersed to accom-modation close to their reporting centre.

- **Integrated 'end-to-end routes'** There will be 'end-to-end routes' for handling asylum applications from the outset to removal if the claim ultimately fails.

- **One Home Office official to have responsibility** A single Home Office official will have responsibility for the application throughout the entire process, including during appeal stage and actual removal. This is des-cribed as 'end-to-end case ownership'.

- **'Face-to-face' contact** Officers will have more direct contact with applicants through: more frequent reporting which may include electronic monitoring; making asylum support conditional on complying with reporting conditions; and increased use of detention.

Of course, some features of this model have been in place for a number of years. In particular, the 'segmentation' of certain asylum cases by selection for detained fast track determination processes, began at Oakington Reception Centre in March 2000.

'Segmentation'

Once an asylum applicant has been screened (▶see below 649–50), their claim will be allocated to a particular 'segment', which will then deter-mine the asylum procedure or 'route' which will apply. The 'segment' to which a case is allocated will depend on the nature of the claim.

Existing segmentation

Cases that do not come within any of the following 'segments' are likely to be determined in accordance with the 'Statement of Evidence Form' (SEF) procedure. Such applicants are not detained but instead issued with a SEF and are likely to be interviewed and have their claims determined without being 'fast tracked'. However, not all such applicants will be given a SEF, some may be given a substantive interview without a SEF. This is known simply as a 'SEF-less' procedure. For 'SEF' and 'SEF-less' proced-ures, ▶see 669–73.

Similarly, those who do not fall into any of the following segments and who require NASS support may initially be referred to an 'induction' centre for about 14 days where they are given information about the asylum process. Applicants are not 'detained' at the induction centres. For more details about them, ▶see 655–7.

The different existing segments are as follows.

Detained fast track processes at Harmondsworth and Yarls Wood
Certain asylum applicants will have their claims determined in accordance with a fast track procedure while they are detained at one of these centres. Those whose cases are assessed as ones which can be decided 'quickly' (largely determined on the basis of their nationality) and who are entitled to have an in-country appeal will be detained at Harmondsworth (single men) and Yarls Wood (women). For the fast track procedures, which apply at these centres, ▶see 673–81. Their appeals are also dealt with in a fast track appeal procedure (▶see the section on appeals at 1129–32).

'Potential NSA' and the detained fast track process at Oakington
Applicants who are nationals of, or are entitled to reside in, a country which is designated under the 2002 Act a 'non-suspensive appeal' or 'NSA' country, (▶see 675 for the list) are likely to be allocated to the 'potential NSA' segment. Many applicants in this segment whose claims are refused will also have them certified as 'clearly unfounded'. This will allow them to only have a non-suspensive appeal (NSA) which means they cannot appeal in-country. Unless the certificate is quashed on judicial review, they are therefore removed from the UK without a right of appeal. For further details about this type of certification, ▶see 1073–8. 'Potential NSA' applicants may either:

- be detained at Oakington Reception Centre where their cases are fast tracked. For claims determined through the Oakington process, ▶see 675–6 and 677–8; or
- if they claim asylum at Croydon Asylum Screening Unit (ASU) and they are not transferred to Oakington, be dispersed to Liverpool and subjected to a special 'non-detained' process in which their claim is accelerated. This accelerated, non-detained procedure is explained at ▶682.

'Late and opportunistic' A claim made at Croydon Asylum Screening Unit (ASU) may be assessed by the Home Office to be 'late and opportunistic'. Some of these applicants may be detained at Harmondsworth or Yarls Wood on the basis that their claims may be determined 'quickly'. If the applicant is not suitable for detention, they will be put through an accelerated 'non-detained' process either in Liverpool or Croydon. For the definition of late and opportunistic claims and details of the accelerated process ▶see 681–2.

North West Project (NWP) Certain asylum applicants who claimed asylum in the Liverpool and Manchester areas (▶see 682) from December 2004 are put through an induction process organised by the North West Consortium Induction Service (NWCIS). If they are not detained and request NASS support, they may be accommodated through the NWCIS. Their asylum applications are decided under an accelerated procedure, which is intended to 'deliver high quality decisions whilst claimants are still in induction accommodation or very soon after they are dispersed' (Home Office note to the Asylum Processes Stakeholder Group sent on 27 January 2005). Between December 2004 and April 2005, 117 people were 'routed through' the NWP and 81 decisions had been made. This process is described at ▶682–3.

Dover Pilot This process was introduced in December 2004 and targets those who make their asylum applications at the port in Dover or at the Dover Enforcement Unit (DEU). They are put through an induction process at the South East Induction Centre and their applications are decided under an accelerated procedure. For further details, ▶see 683.

'Third country' cases Applicants in this category can expect to be taken to a removal centre immediately. Those who are not detained may be subject to a condition to report frequently. If they are not housed close to a reporting centre, they may be subjected to electronic monitoring (▶see 652 for more details) as a condition of their temporary admission. For general details about third country cases, ▶see Chapter 24

Unaccompanied asylum-seeking minors (UASCs) UASCs will not be detained, although in the future the Home Office may expect them to comply with reporting conditions.

Planned segments

The Home Office has indicated that it will also be setting up the following further segments to which asylum claims will be allocated:

'High priority' Applicants categorised as 'high priority' may be put through a detained fast track process. If they are not detained, they may be expected to report as often as daily. If there are thought to be 'high barriers' to their removal, they may be expected to report less frequently, possibly through electronic monitoring technology (▶see 652). It is not clear which asylum-seekers the Home Office may categorise as 'high priority'.

'Standard priority' It can be presumed that those whose applications do not fall into any of the above segments will be 'standard priority' cases. Applicants are unlikely to be put through a detained process and will be expected to fulfil monthly reporting conditions. Detention or more frequent (fortnightly) reporting is a possibility if there are judged to be 'low barriers' to their removal.

GENERAL ASYLUM PROCEDURES

The following procedures and information is general to claims for asylum. Obviously, they apply to a greater or lesser extent and with modifications depending on whether the claim is being put into a particular segment.

After we have dealt with all of the following general procedures, we look at the specific procedures, which apply in 'ordinary' cases, detained fast track and other accelerated procedures.

Identifying asylum applicants

It should first be noted that the Home Office recognises that asylum applicants may not necessarily be able to express clearly in English that they want to claim asylum. They may not know the words 'asylum' or 'refugee' when trying to make a claim for asylum. Expressions of fear of return made in any manner should be assumed to be claims to asylum. Immigration officers at a port and officers at the Home Office are instructed as follows (API, *Handling Claims*, para. 1.2):

'If a person expresses an unwillingness to return to their country of nationality or habitual residence because they believe they would be in danger, we should assume that they are making an asylum application.'

Applying on entry to the UK: 'port applicants'

Those arriving in the UK at an airport, sea port or international train terminal in order to seek asylum should make their claim known to an immigration officer on arrival. Immigration officers are trained to recognise asylum claims (▶see above). Often people are afraid to approach an immigration officer having previously been persecuted by officials. People also may not know the correct procedure for applying for asylum and think that it would be safer to gain entry to the UK in some other category, for example, as a visitor, and later apply for asylum. Failing to claim on arrival, particularly before a decision is made by an immigration officer to refuse or grant entry, can have a negative effect on the credibility of the claim (▶see 710–12).

A decision on the claim is not made immediately. The immigration rules state that all decisions on asylum have to be referred to the Home Office.

Once an asylum claim is identified, the immigration officer will arrange for a 'screening' interview to be conducted. This will either take place shortly after arrival or the applicant will be asked to return to attend for screening in the near future. It is possible that the applicant will be detained while awaiting screening. Further details about screening are given at (▶649–50).

Claiming at port after passing through controls

Some applicants are unaware that they can claim asylum at the control desk. If they pass through immigration controls and *then* attempt to claim asylum at the port, they will normally be directed by the immigration officers or police to make a claim at an Asylum Screening Unit (ASU). The immigration service's *Port Screening Best Practice Guide* states that this is the correct approach, despite the fact that port immigration officers have the power to bring the person back within their jurisdiction and to register the asylum claim. This can be done by cancelling the grant of leave to enter within 24 hours, and then examining the person again at the port as though they had just arrived (see para. 6(2), Sch 2 of the 1971 Act).

However, families with children under 18, unaccompanied asylum-seeking children (UASCs), visibly pregnant women, asylum-seekers who are disabled, and asylum-seekers whose individual needs appear to require special consideration should always have their claim recorded immediately at the port (*Port Screening Best Practice Guide*). This is so that the necessary referrals can be made to NASS or a local authority for emergency accommodation (▶see 654–5).

Segmentation at screening

At the screening stage, the applicant's claim will be checked to see if it fits into one of the 'segments' set out above (▶643–4). So, applicants who meet the conditions for fast track detention laid down in the detained fast track processes suitability lists (▶see the table at 675–6), will be detained and transferred to Oakington, Harmondsworth or Yarls Wood. Those claiming at Dover or at the airports in Manchester and Liverpool may be allocated into the Dover or the NWP pilot respectively (▶642–3; 682–3). Those considered to be returnable to a safe third country are likely to be detained and transferred to a removal centre. Their claims are likely to be refused without substantive consideration (for third-country cases, ▶see Chapter 24).

Applicants who do not fall into a particular segment are most likely to be granted temporary admission and have their applications determined in accordance with the ordinary SEF process, which is described at ▶669–72. Temporary admission will normally be given on conditions that they report to an immigration officer at a particular time, that they remain at a fixed address and that they are prohibited from working. For further details about temporary admission, ▶see below at 652–4. Quite separate from the Dover and NWP pilots, and depending on their port of entry, such applicants may be required to stay at an 'induction centre' for 14 days as a condition of temporary admission.

After screening, applicants and each of their dependants, except for those that are detained, will be issued with a form of identity called an 'Application Registration Card' (ARC). If an ARC cannot be issued immediately, they will be issued with a 'SAL1' Standard Acknowledgement Letter. These documents are not usually given to those who are detained. These are discussed in more detail at ▶651–2 below.

Note that those applicants who are not put into a particular segment and who are issued with a SEF are likely to be called back to the same port at which they made their claim when they are required to appear for a detailed interview.

Applying 'in-country'

Applications that are not made at the port of entry are known as 'in-country' claims. A claim is made in-country if it is made after a person has passed through immigration controls. The most obvious cases are where people enter clandestinely (for example in the back of a lorry), or having been granted leave to enter the UK in another capacity (e.g. as a visitor or a student). Those who claim after having been granted leave may be declared 'illegal entrants' even if they got a proper stamp in their own passport but the Home Office thinks that they intended to claim asylum all along. Some applicants claim as overstayers i.e. after their leave has run out.

As indicated above, those who pass through controls at the port and then try to claim are likely to be directed to one of the in-country screening units. They are also 'in-country' applicants.

How and where to apply

Applicants must apply in person to the Home Office at one of the Asylum Screening Units (ASUs). The application should be made with as little delay as possible. No prescribed application form is needed.

Presently, following the closure of the ASU in Solihull (near Birmingham), there are only two ASUs:

- Lunar House, 40 Wellesley Road, Croydon, CR9 2BY
- Reliance House, Water Street, Liverpool, L2 8XU

Certain applicants only make their claim after being apprehended by the police or the immigration service. Immigration officers are instructed on how to recognise pleas for protection as asylum claims (▶see 645). Such applications must be given full consideration just like other claims but their credibility is likely to be damaged (▶see 710–12). Such claims are apt to be assessed as 'late and opportunistic' with the result that the applicant is liable to be detained and fast tracked or put through the accelerated non-detained procedure for late and opportunistic claims (▶see 681–2).

Applying by post

Since 8 February 2003, the Home Office has not been accepting postal applications for asylum. Such applications will be returned to the sender along with any original documents sent and a standard letter explaining to the applicant how to apply in person. The claim will not be 'recorded' as having been made so NASS support will not be available until the claim is made at the ASU.

However, if the Home Office accepts that there is an 'exceptional reason' why the applicant is unable to attend an ASU in person, for example severe illness or disability, it will make alternative screening arrangements for the applicant. This may be a home visit by officers, or an appointment at a local Immigration Service enforcement unit (see 1495 for details of the various enforcement units).

Segmentation at in-country screening

Following screening at the ASU, an asylum claim may be allocated to a particular route in accordance with the segmentation policy (▶above at 642–4). As a result, applicants may be taken to Oakington, Harmonds-worth or Yarls Wood if their cases are assessed as suitable for the detained fast track processes operated at those centres (▶see 673–81).

Applicants who claim at Croydon ASU will be put through a non-detained accelerated procedure (▶see 681–2) if their claims are considered to fall into the 'potentially NSA' or 'late and opportunistic' segments following screening and they are not considered suitable for detention. Those who claim at Liverpool ASU may alternatively be put into the pilot 'North West Project' (NWP) (▶see 682–3).

Applicants who are assessed as third country cases where removal may take place within a very short period of time, are likely to be detained. Their claims will not be considered substantively (▶see Chapter 24).

In all other cases, the applicant is likely to have their application deter-mined in accordance with the ordinary SEF process (▶see 669–73). In most cases (but see below), such applicants will be granted temporary admission with conditions requiring them to report, to stay at a particular address and prohibiting them from employment. For details about temporary admission see below (▶652–4). Such applicants may also be referred to an induction centre for an initial 14 days. These transfers operate independently of the Dover and NWP pilots, which also involve induction processes.

Those granted temporary admission will be issued with an ARC or, if an ARC cannot be issued immediately, an after-entry 'SAL2' Standard Acknowledgement Letter (see below).

In-country cases and liability for detention

As with asylum-seekers at port, in-country applicants who are not being put through a detained fast track process can still be detained while their claims are being decided if they give particular cause for concern.

Except as set out below, applicants cannot be detained while they have leave to be in the UK but the leave of such applicants:
- is made void if they are declared to be illegal entrants;
- can be curtailed on the basis that the applicant no longer satisfies the requirements on which they were granted leave (for the powers of curtailment, ▶see 141–3).

If either of the above procedures is operated, then the applicant will no longer have leave and is liable to be detained.

However, even where an asylum applicant has leave and the above powers are not, or cannot be used, the Home Office has special powers to impose the same restrictions upon them and their dependants as could be imposed if they were granted temporary admission. If the applicant breaches *those* conditions then they may be detained (see s71 2002 Act). For detention powers ▶see 902–5.

Screening

The initial process after any asylum claim is made, whether at port or in-country, is that applicants are 'screened'. Screening interviews are carried out in order to establish the following about an applicant:

- basic details about their identity;

- their travel route to the UK, how long was spent in each country, and whether or not asylum applications were made there. Answers to these questions will alert officers to whether the application should be treated as a 'third country' case;

- details of any entry clearance used to travel to the UK and previous visa applications for the UK or any other country;

- details of their family, including those who may be considered as dependants (▶see 691–4) to the asylum claim;

- the type of documentation used to travel to the UK; whether it is false, or has been destroyed; and the role of any agents during the journey and their identities. This information may be used to assess the applicant's credibility (▶712–13). It may also be used to determine whether a criminal offence has been committed (▶see 683–6);

- details about the timing of the claim. This will be relevant to whether NASS support may be granted or refused (▶655);

- education and employment details.

A standard screening interview form is used (presently Form V010105). Historically, there have always been problems about applicants being asked about the details of the substance of their claims at the screening stage. The form clearly states that an applicant will *not* be asked to give details about the substance of the asylum claim itself.

Copies of the screening interview record should be issued to the applicant and applicants should not hesitate to ask for a copy at the conclusion of the interview. Once screening has taken place, contact is made with NASS and the local refugee agency for the provision of emergency accommodation if it is necessary (▶see 654–5).

Screening may also be used in order to determine whether an applicant ought to be interviewed in relation to an offence under section 2 2004 Act (attending an interview without an 'immigration document') (▶see below at 683–6).

Obtaining fingerprints and photographs

Screening also involves fingerprinting and photographing the applicant. Fingerprint data will be stored on a Home Office database called the Immigration Fingerprint Bureau and checks will be made against it for any matches with other identities. The 1999 Act gives Home Office officials, including immigration officers, the power to use reasonable force to obtain fingerprints from asylum-seekers and their dependants. There is no power to compel an applicant who is not detained to have their photograph taken. In addition, it is possible that a refusal to provide fingerprints or to have a photograph taken might be taken into account in assessing the applicant's credibility on the claim. This is because it could be considered a behaviour which is intended or likely to conceal information, mislead or to obstruct or delay the handling of the claim (see s8(2) 2004 Act).

Fingerprints will now usually be retained for a period of ten years but, under the Anti-Terrorism, Crime and Security Act 2001, can be held for longer if the Home Secretary wishes. When a child under 16 is fingerprinted, another adult, either the parent or guardian or another responsible person (but not a member of IND staff), must be present. Children under the age of five will not be fingerprinted.

Legal representatives

Although representatives are allowed into the ASU to attend screening interviews, their attendance will not be funded by the Legal Services Commission (LSC) unless they are specifically authorised to do so. The position is the same as for substantive interviews (▶see below 659).

Failure to attend for screening or to cooperate

If temporary admission is granted before full screening and then the applicant fails to attend for screening without good cause, the applicant is likely to be treated as an absconder and may be detained when apprehended. In addition, as with a failure to attend any interview, this may lead to adverse consequences for credibility. It may also lead to a refusal on 'non-compliance' grounds i.e. on the basis of failing 'to make a prompt and full disclosure of material facts' (para. 340, HC 395 and ▶see 715–16). The API concerning 'non-compliance' states:

'If the applicant fails to attend a pre-arranged screening interview without good reason the application should be considered on the material available to the caseworker and, if the claim is not established, asylum should be refused. The onus is on the applicant or their representative to provide a reasonable explanation for the non-attendance.'

Reasonable explanations may include illness of the applicant supported by acceptable medical evidence, or transport problems. Non-availability of a representative is not considered a reasonable explanation. A failure to cooperate with the questioning or to provide complete and accurate information can also lead to NASS support being refused.

Application Registration Cards and Standard Acknowledgement Letters

From early 2002, most applicants and their dependants have been issued with credit-card sized forms of identity called Application Registration Cards (ARCs). An ARC will be issued to an applicant following a screening interview if the port at which they claimed has the appropriate facilities to issue ARCs.

If an ARC cannot be provided at screening, an applicant will be issued with a Standard Acknowledgement Letter (SAL), which will be valid for up to two months. SALs are double-sided A4 documents acknowledging an asylum claim – they were the forms of identity issued to all asylum-seekers before the introduction of ARCs. If a SAL is issued, the applicant will be told to contact the Home Office's Central Event Booking Unit (►see 1493 for address) before the SAL expires, to book an appointment at a port, asylum screening unit or reporting centre, which has the facilities to issue an ARC.

From February 2005, the immigration rules were amended to reflect the government's obligations under the EC Reception Conditions Directive (Council Directive 2003/9/EC and see paras 359–359C, HC 395). This states that all asylum-seekers, except for those in detention, should be issued with a document within three working days of the application being lodged. The document should give details of their identity and confirm that a claim for asylum has been made.

ARCs contain the following information relating to the identity of the applicant:

- name and gender;
- date of birth (the card will indicate if there is an age dispute – for age-disputed cases, ►see 688–91);
- nationality;
- a digital image of the holder;
- fingerprint data.

The card also holds the following information about the claim itself:

- Home Office or port reference numbers;
- where the claim was made;
- whether or not the claim is for asylum under the Refugee Convention, or for human rights protection under Article 3 of the ECHR;
- the number of dependants on the claim;
- the next reporting date;
- the language spoken by the applicant;
- whether permission to work has been granted.

The 2002 Act also introduced a series of criminal offences relating to the use, alteration, or manufacture of a false card (►1034).

When an applicant reports, their ARC must be produced. From January 2005, a new ARC-based reporting pilot project (REPARC) was set up requiring all asylum-seekers receiving NASS support in the Liverpool area to report with their ARC in order to access NASS payments.

Reporting and other conditions of temporary admission for asylum-seekers

Asylum applicants who are not detained are given 'temporary admission'. The conditions, which there is a power to impose upon a grant of temporary admission are, that the applicant:

- resides at a particular place or address;
- is prohibited from entering into work or business;
- reports to immigration officers or the police at specified times;
- cooperates with electronic monitoring.

Full details about the technicalities of temporary admission and applying for temporary admission as an alternative to detention generally, are given in the section on detention (▶950–7).

Electronic monitoring (EM) EM as part of temporary admission requirements was introduced by section 36 2004 Act, which came into force on 1 October 2004. There are three forms which EM can take:

- reporting by voice recognition technology;
- tagging, which involves the subject wearing an electronic tag bracelet which emits a signal to a receiver at their home address; and
- tracking, which uses global satellite technology to pin-point a person's whereabouts on a continuous basis – data can be transmitted in real time ('active tracking') or the tracking can be passive with data transmitted at different intervals.

At the time of writing, EM was still being trialled on about 100 applicants at a time. For full details about initial Home Office guidance about when EM may be used and what is involved, ▶see the section on detention at 953–5.

What conditions of temporary admission are likely to be imposed?

Most applicants will be given conditions requiring them to reside at a particular address. They will also be given conditions prohibiting them from working. For details about policy on employment restrictions and when they may be lifted, ▶see below at 694–6.

From June 2005, applicants who are granted temporary admission are required to report in line with the 'intelligent reporting' guidance laid down by the Home Office which is set out in the table below.

HOME OFFICE POLICY ON REPORTING CONDITIONS FOR APPLICANTS GRANTED TEMPORARY ADMISSION

Home Office 'intelligent reporting' guidelines (*Intelligent Reporting Policy and Procedure*, June 2005) on the nature of the reporting conditions to be imposed on asylum applicants granted temporary admission are as follows. These guidelines do not apply to those in the special non-detained accelerated processes. For further details about temporary admission, ▶see above and ▶see also 950–7.

Weekly reporting

The following groups will be given conditions to report to a centre or a police station weekly:

- those whose asylum claims are 'non-suspensive appeal' (NSA) cases and who either have travel documentation in place, or are likely to obtain it within four months of a negative decision;
- third country cases;
- those whose appeal rights are exhausted and where removal is likely within four months;
- cases where a negative initial decision has been made and the applicant has travel documentation in place, or is likely to obtain it within four months of a negative decision. Aside from the appeal process, there should be no 'significant outstanding barriers to removal';
- those who have no fixed address as part of their conditions of temporary admission and where reporting is the only means of contact with the applicant, and who either have travel documentation in place, or are likely to obtain it within four months of a negative decision.

Monthly reporting

The following groups will be given conditions to report to a centre or a police station monthly:

- those whose asylum claims are 'non-suspensive appeal' (NSA) cases and who do not have travel documentation in place and the documentation is unlikely to be obtained within four months of a negative decision;
- applicants who have complied with stricter reporting conditions for six months and where removal is unlikely within the next four months;
- those whose appeal rights are exhausted but where removal is not thought possible within four months following the final decision;
- those who have no fixed address as part of their conditions of temporary admission, where reporting is the only means of contact and where the applicant does not have existing travel documentation and is unlikely to obtain it within four months of a negative decision.

Cases fit for 'low reporting frequency'

Those who fall into the following categories should argue for any reporting conditions imposed upon them to be lifted altogether or reduced to less than monthly:

7

- the case has been referred to the Medical Foundation;
- for applicants who are pregnant, reporting should be suspended for six weeks either side of the expected date of birth. Any request should be supported by a medical certificate;
- those over the age of 65 years;
- minors should not normally be required to report before they are 17 years of age;
- those who have medical problems, which make it difficult for them to report.

Reporting centres and travel costs

There are presently 11 reporting centres across the UK. Anyone who resides within 25 miles of one of these centres is expected to report to one of them. If not, applicants will be expected to report to a local police station. The Home Office has informed JCWI that it will provide travel expenses for those receiving NASS support who are required to travel more than three miles to where they must report. Those who live less than three miles from the centre or police station, or who do not receive NASS support, will also be provided with travel expenses 'in cases of special need such as those with young children or with mobility problems'. The Home Office will meet travel costs by issuing travel tickets for the next reporting time each time someone reports.

Asylum process and initial access to asylum support

Financial support and accommodation for most asylum-seekers is provided by the National Asylum Support Service (NASS). Entitlement to NASS support is dealt with more fully in Chapter 41. For more on the procedures below ▶see 1367–70.

Emergency accommodation

The ASU or the port that conducts the screening interview will normally make a referral to the local voluntary-sector refugee agency that is contracted to NASS to provide emergency accommodation. The agencies involved are (their contact details are at ▶1500–1):

- Migrant Helpline (East Sussex, London);
- North of England Refugee Service (North East);
- Northern Ireland Council for Ethnic Minorities (Northern Ireland);
- Refugee Action (North West, East Midlands, South West and South Central);
- Refugee Arrivals Project (Heathrow, Gatwick, Luton, Stansted, and City airports);
- Refugee Council (West Midlands, Yorkshire and Humberside, London, Eastern England);

- Scottish Refugee Council (Scotland);
- Welsh Refugee Council (Wales).

Those who apply for asylum immediately upon arrival at a port and who require support will be referred to one of the above agencies for emergency accommodation or 'EA'. The agency will normally provide such accommodation on production of an ARC or SAL together with an IS96 document granting temporary admission. If an ARC or a SAL has not been issued, emergency accommodation may be restricted to one night only.

Section 55 decisions

Section 55 of the 2002 Act prevents NASS providing support to asylum applicants who do not claim as soon as reasonably practicable after their arrival unless their human rights would be breached by denying support. The general procedure has been that applicants at ASUs and those who claim asylum at a port after they have been granted or refused entry will have details of their claim (which may include the notes of the screening interview) faxed to the NASS Eligibility and Assessment Team (NEAT) for a 'section 55 decision' after they have been screened. NEAT should then fax a letter back to the officers authorising emergency accommodation pending a section 55 decision. Emergency accommodation is full board. This means that an applicant's basic food and hygiene needs will be provided, but not cash (▶see further 1368–70). The procedures are likely to be clarified further following the decision of the House of Lords in *Limbuela & Others* on 3 November 2005. The outcome was favourable for asylum-seekers (▶1307–11).

Applying to NASS

An asylum-seeker must access NASS support by making a formal application to NASS on form NASS 1. The form is quite long and assistance in completing it is provided by over 25 'one-stop services' across the UK, which are run by the refugee agencies listed above (their details can be found in the *Refugee Council Information Service* publication).

Induction processes

As stated earlier, once an applicant has been screened, they may be allocated to a particular 'segment' for the determination of their claim (▶see above at 642–4). Those who are not put into any of the specific segments (i.e. detained fast track, and non-detained accelerated processes such as 'late and opportunistic'; NWP and the Dover pilot, which have their own induction processes; third country cases; and UASCs) but who require NASS support, may first be referred to an 'induction centre'.

The induction centres are not places of detention. They are run by NASS and those referred there are granted temporary admission. Induction 'centres' or 'services' have been set up in the south east, Yorkshire and Humberside, and the north west. New induction services are planned throughout the UK and another will be opening in Hounslow in September 2006. The South East Induction Centre (SEIC) (also known as the Dover Induction Centre) comprises blocks of accommodation in Dover, Ashford, and Margate. In Yorkshire and Humberside, it comprises two blocks of accommodation, one in Leeds, and one in Barnsley. In the north west, houses and flats spread across nine of the 11 local authorities in Greater Manchester are collectively called the North West Consortia Induction Service (NWCIS).

Those with urgent special needs should not be referred to an induction centre and should immediately be referred to the local social services department. The duties of a local authority to provide support and accommodation to those with special needs are discussed at ▶1318–22.

Those who fall into the North West Project or the Dover Pilot are put through a very specific induction service with a particular timetable. This is dealt with at ▶682–3.

At the induction centres, applicants are to be provided with:

- information on the procedures through which their asylum claim will be decided;
- information on their basic rights and responsibilities while they are in the UK;
- assistance with a NASS support claim;
- health screening which includes a health check and a TB test.

Compliance with EC Reception Conditions Directive

The above induction package is intended to comply with the EC reception conditions directive (Council Directive 2003/9/EC), which requires information to be provided to asylum-seekers on their rights and obligations within 15 days of making an application for asylum. Information is also provided about non-governmental organisations that assist asylum-seekers to access benefits and services including legal advice. Where possible, this information should be in writing, translated into a language that the applicant 'may reasonably be supposed to understand' (see also paras 357–358A, HC 395).

Because of the location or timing of their claims, many asylum-seekers may not pass through one of the induction services that have been set up so far. Nevertheless, the duty to comply with the EC Reception Conditions Directive and the immigration rules applies to all non-detained asylum-seekers regardless of whether they are put through induction. Ports, immigration offices and ASUs are therefore required to provide similar information. For further details about the Directive, ▶see 1379–81.

After induction

NASS aims to move applicants out of induction service accommodation within 14 days. Applicants who have been referred to induction centres may be put through a 'SEF-less' process (▶see 672–3) and their substantive asylum interview may be booked at the induction centre itself. For brief details concerning refugee integration, ▶see 32.

Asylum interviews

The API on 'Interviewing' states that substantive interviews will be conducted for 'most' asylum applications. An interview may not be conducted where an applicant 'obviously falls to be granted refugee status', but 'we should always seek to interview before refusing an asylum application substantively' unless applicants face a non-compliance refusal (▶see 715–6).

Many applicants will be given a date for their substantive interview when they are screened. This is certainly the case for applicants whose cases are processed through one of the accelerated procedures described at ▶681–3. Those who are issued with a SEF (▶see below at 670) will often have an interview date set when the SEF is issued to them.

Criticisms of interviews and interview protocol

Asylum interviews are regularly criticised by representatives and asylum-seekers. Interviewing officers can be aggressive, dismissive or ask questions, which indicate that they do not really understand the basis of the claim, or the basic country conditions which the asylum-seeker has fled. Additionally, interviews are often used as a means of obtaining material to discredit an applicant's account. Asylum interviews that take place at ports have been particularly criticised (see *Breaking down the barriers*, ILPA, April 2000).

In October 2002, the Home Office issued a protocol containing guidelines on the conduct of substantive asylum interviews, and the standards that interviewing officers, interpreters and representatives are expected to maintain during the interview. This protocol is set out in Annex A to the API on *Interviewing* and can be found on the Home Office IND website. It states that the interview is:

'…essentially a fact-finding exercise, an opportunity for the applicant to elaborate on the background to his or her application, introduce additional information, and for the interviewing officer to test the information provided, if required. This process will assist the decision-maker to make a well-reasoned and sustainable decision on the application.'

Often the way the interview is handled has a very important impact on the case. It is therefore critical that any difficulties at interview are addressed immediately or, if not, shortly afterwards by letter. Such criticisms should not be left until an appeal by which time the claim will have been refused and complaints may be seen as self-serving.

Role of representatives

The API on *Interviewing* states that the Home Office does

'...not consider that it is necessary for an asylum applicant to be legally represented at the asylum interview, as it is a non-adversarial fact-finding exercise. However, the presence of a representative should not be objected to without specific reason and prior reference to a senior caseworker... Where a representative is present in the interview, their role is to ensure that the applicant understands the interview and has the opportunity to provide all relevant information.'

At the outset of a substantive interview, representatives are asked not to interrupt during the course of the interview and to make any comments at the end. The protocol warns that if a representative seriously disrupts the course of an interview, they may be excluded. Although there is no absolute right to have a legal representative at an interview, any decision of the immigration authorities to exclude a representative has to be a decision taken on proper and relevant grounds. The same approach applies to interpreters attending on behalf of the asylum-seeker. Any representative or interpreter who is excluded from an interview should ask for a statement of reasons for the decision so that its legality can be judged.

Preparing for interview

The Home Office relies on the detailed information given by the asylum-seeker as the basis for the claim to asylum. In cases where no SEF or statement has already been provided, it is necessary for the applicant to explain in depth details such as: exactly what has happened to them, what activities they have engaged in which could result in persecution and what has happened to members of the family or the particular group to which the asylum-seeker belongs. Advisers should go through these details with the asylum-seeker in date order, before any interview. If a clear and detailed statement or representations have already been provided about the claim either with a SEF form or otherwise, then it is likely that the interview will proceed much more smoothly as the interviewer will be more likely to understand the basis of the claim. In addition, if the applicant has a copy of their own statement to read, then that will help them to prepare for the interview.

Home Office interpreters

Many asylum-seekers do not speak English and their interviews will therefore be carried out through an interpreter, normally employed by the Home Office or immigration service on a sessional basis. The standard of interpreting provided through the Home Office's interpreters is variable and, unless someone is there to check what is interpreted, misunderstandings can easily arise. These misunderstandings can be fatal to claims for asylum. The Home Office has agreed that it is permissible to have an independent interpreter present, and indeed for such a person to interrupt the interview if 'major difficulties arise over interpretation'. However the LSC will not provide costs for the attendance of an independent interpreter unless one of the exceptions set out immediately below applies.

Public funding for representatives at interview

Since 1 April 2004, the LSC no longer funds the attendance of representatives or clerks at asylum interviews as a matter of course. This is despite the important part in decision-making that interviews play and the fact that representatives can ensure that their clients are treated fairly and are given every opportunity to present their case.

Under Rule 12.3.2 of the LSC's Immigration Contract Specification, authority will only be granted for the costs of attending an interview in any of the following cases where:

- the client is a minor, or is reasonably claiming to be a minor (for age disputes, ▶see 688–91);
- the client suffers from a 'mental incapacity';
- the client is subject to a Home Office 'fast track process' as defined by the LSC (this presently includes the fast track processes at Harmondsworth, Oakington and Yarls Wood but not any of the non-detained accelerated processes);
- the client is to be interviewed by an immigration officer under 'PACE' i.e. in anticipation of a possible criminal charge (this will usually be in relation to section 2 2004 Act offences, or the possibility of illegal entry, ▶see 683–6 and 1033–5);
- where it is alleged that the applicant is a threat to national security.

Many asylum-seekers are traumatised by their previous experiences and some are diagnosed as suffering from PTSD (post-traumatic stress disorder). Regrettably, the LSC has said that it will not generally fund the costs of attending interviews with such clients unless they have a 'mental incapacity'. This is defined by the LSC as an impairment or disturbance in the functioning of the mind or brain. The LSC has indicated that demonstrating PTSD alone will not be sufficient to show this.

Tape-recording of interviews

In *Dirshe*, the Court of Appeal held that the presence of a representative or interpreter provided a real safeguard against faulty interpreting or inadequate or inaccurate record-keeping at substantive asylum interviews. It noted that, since most applicants rely upon LSC funding to pay for their representation, this safeguard was no longer in place following the changes to public funding on 1 April 2004. The Court recognised that the substantive interview played a critical part in assessing the credibility of the applicant and the final decision. It therefore held that if a tape recording were not permitted when no representative or interpreter was present on the applicant's behalf, there would be real procedural unfairness.

To comply with the judgment the Home Office has commenced installing dual tape recording equipment at its interviewing facilities. Only those applicants who are not entitled to an LSC-funded representative at the interview (above) will be given the opportunity of having their interview taped. A copy of the tape is handed to the applicant at the end of the interview.

Travel warrants

Applicants in receipt of NASS support should now be given travel expenses to cover the cost of travel to their substantive interview. This will usually be in the form of a ticket issued at the screening interview or accompanying the letter containing the interview date.

Gender sensitivity

Asylum-seekers who have suffered particular experiences, for example a sexual assault, or who have certain strongly held beliefs, may prefer an interviewing officer and interpreter of the same gender. The Home Office has stated that 'such requests will be complied with as far as is operationally possible' (Home Office letter to ILPA, 27 March 2000). Furthermore, the Home Office should make 'every effort' to provide an officer and interpreter of the same sex as the applicant where 'there are grounds for considering that the interview might be particularly sensitive' (API, Interviewing, Annex C). If the interview is to be conducted in English and there is no representative present, the Home Office has indicated that the interview should be conducted by an interviewing officer of the same gender as the claimant, and if this is not possible, a 'third party' should be allowed to observe the interview 'to ensure that no accusations of impropriety can be made' (Ch2 Operational Processes Instructions, Conducting Asylum Interviews, pt 6).

The Home Office has stated that it will try to comply with a request for a same-sex interpreter but that this may be more problematic due to limited numbers available in certain languages. The Home Office will postpone an interview if one is not available, on two conditions, that firstly it is reasonable to assume that one could be provided in the future, and secondly, that 'failure to provide such an interpreter would adversely affect the applicant's ability to advance a full and accurate account of their case' (API *Interviewing* para. 2.4).

For details about particular issues concerning qualifying as a refugee and women, ▶see 607–8, 616–19.

Scars

The Home Office has issued guidance to interviewing officers about viewing scars in interviews (see letter to ILPA dated 21 September 2000). These state that an asylum-seeker can show an interviewing officer scars during an interview and the interviewing officer must make no judgment or comment on the scars but will make a factual record in the interview notes of what has been shown. If the injury is alleged to have been caused by a recent incident but looks so old as to cast doubt upon the account, the interviewing officer may ask questions to try to verify the claim. If viewing scars would require the removal of significant clothing, the officer may decline and the asylum-seeker may be asked to attend the medical centre after the interview for a note to be taken. Unwillingness to show evidence of scars during the interview itself will not be used to discredit the applicant, and, under no circumstances, can an applicant be required to show their scars to an interviewing officer.

Interviewing alleged victims of torture

The Home Office has produced two sets of guidelines for interviewing torture survivors – one is headed 'Medical Foundation' and the other is Annex C of the 'Interviewing' API. They require particular care and sensitivity to be employed by an officer when an interviewee claims to be a victim of torture, pointing out that it may be difficult to recount such experiences before an official whom they may not trust, and that the claimant may not be prepared to go into much detail. The API state that an officer should probe the issue with a sympathetic ear, in an atmosphere of trust, and not in an adversarial manner. The applicant may get very distressed during the interview and a read-over should be offered at the end of the interview.

The officer should suggest that the interviewee approaches the Medical Foundation for assistance if a 'credible' account of torture is given during the interview. The Home Office should grant a time extension to allow for the submission of Medical Foundation or other medical reports (▶see 671).

Being 'fit and well' for the interview

Asylum-seekers should be warned that asylum interviews can be very stressful, particularly at ports. Although applicants are asked whether they are fit and well to be interviewed, many feel too intimidated to say if they are feeling tired or unwell. In *Clavijo-Hoyos*, the IAT criticised reliance on an interview record, which, although signed by the applicant as a correct and true statement, had been obtained when the applicant was clearly extremely tired after a long journey without sleep.

Concluding the interview

At the end of the asylum interview, the applicant is invited to sign a declaration that they have understood the questions put to them and that they were given an opportunity at the end of the interview to make further comments. Previously, there was a practice of reading over the entire interview to check its accuracy and the applicant would have had the opportunity to make any corrections and then sign each page. 'Read-overs' no longer routinely take place. A read-over should, however, be offered by the interviewing officer if the applicant claims to have suffered torture (see above), seems traumatised, or if they are illiterate (Operational Processes Instruction, Ch 2, Conducting Asylum Interviews, pt 18). Applicants will be provided with a photocopy of the interview record as a matter of course.

The absence of read-overs now means that the notes of interview are a less authoritative record and should be checked by representatives against a tape-recorded copy of the applicant's evidence, particularly if the matter goes on to appeal.

One-stop procedure

The 'one-stop' procedure was first introduced by the 1999 Act and began in October 2000. It was extremely complicated. The 2002 Act simplified the legislation (▶see also 1066–7). The purpose of the procedure is to ensure that *all* the reasons any individual might have for staying in the UK are considered together by the Home Office and, if refused, are considered together at the same appeal. This is done by giving applicants 'one-stop' notices, which require them to disclose any additional grounds, which they have not previously given for staying in the UK.

For details about one-stop notices in the human rights context, ▶see 856.

'One-stop' notices under section 120 2002 Act

Under section 120 of the 2002 Act, the Home Office can, at any time, issue a notice in writing to anyone:

- who has made an application to enter or remain in the UK; *or*
- in respect of whom the immigration authorities have made or will take an 'immigration decision' (i.e. a decision which is appealable).

So, in principle, this covers asylum, human rights and ordinary immigration cases. The applicant does not have to have made a formal application to receive a notice – a person who may be removed or deported can be given a notice. The notice will usually state:

'You must now make a formal statement about any reasons why you think you should be allowed to stay in this country. This includes why you wish to stay here, and any grounds why you should not be removed or required to leave.'

In practice, when is a one-stop notice likely to be given?

Although the power to issue one-stop notices is very wide (above), the circumstances in which a notice will be issued as a matter of policy are set out in the API under 'Appeals – One Stop Procedures Warnings and Certificates'. This states that a one-stop notice should be issued to:

- all asylum and human rights applicants;
- all other types of applicant where the Home Office considers that the application may not succeed and it would be helpful to establish any other matters the applicant may try to put forward at an appeal or in order to resist enforcement of the decision;
- all those who will receive a negative 'immigration decision' (▶see 1053–4 for the definition of immigration decisions) whether or not a one-stop notice has previously been issued. This will include those:
  - who have been refused leave to enter the UK, entry clearance, or a certificate of entitlement;
  - whose leave has been varied so that they have no leave to remain;
  - who have been refused leave to remain and as a result have no leave;
  - whose indefinite leave has been revoked;
  - who are illegal entrants and a decision has been made to remove them;
  - who are overstayers or have breached their conditions and a decision has been made to remove them;
  - who receive a decision to make a deportation order or whose application to revoke a deportation order has been refused;
- those who have not previously been issued with a one-stop notice under the 1999 or 2002 Acts and are being considered for removal or other enforcement action.

In asylum and human rights cases, a one-stop notice will be issued together with a SEF when the applicant is screened. They are also given at the beginning of substantive asylum interviews when applicants are told:

'If there are any reasons, in addition to the reasons why you are making an asylum/human rights claim, why you or your dependants should not be removed from the UK if your asylum/human rights claim is refused, you should mention them during the course of the interview.'

Applicants are also given notices at the same time as negative decisions and appeal forms are issued.

How should additional grounds be put forward?

Applicants can use the forms issued by the Home Office, which are normally headed 'statement of additional grounds' or they can submit additional grounds in their own way, perhaps in a letter format.

The API (above) state that:

'Grounds can be raised in any form, for example orally or by a letter, if the person wishes, even if a form has been provided. An address for response to the one-stop warning should of course be given.'

There is no statutory time-limit for submitting additional grounds, but the API state that a reasonable time-limit should be imposed 'to encourage early submission of the additional grounds'. When a one-stop notice is issued with an appealable decision, the time-limit imposed will normally be the same as the period for appealing. Additional grounds that are received after the time-limit has expired should still be considered.

The API make it clear that the Home Office sees the requirement given in the one-stop notice as an ongoing one. This means that as and when additional grounds come to light, representations should be made to the Home Office.

Procedure for dealing with additional grounds

Additional grounds should always be considered. The procedure for dealing with them, which is set out in the API, varies depending on when the grounds are raised. If the grounds are received:

- before the decision is taken, they will be addressed in any notice of refusal and the reasons for refusal letter;
- while an appeal against the initial decision is pending, they should be considered and, if the decision is maintained, addressed in a letter supplementing the notice of decision. This will be issued before the appeal is heard and the grounds will be considered at the appeal;
- after an appeal has been dismissed, the substance of the grounds must be considered to see if the immigration decision should be reversed. They should also be considered under paragraph 353 of the immigration rules in order to determine whether they amount to a 'fresh claim' for asylum which gives rise to a further right of appeal (for fresh claims, ▶see 730–5). However, even if they are treated as a fresh claim, the Home Office may still try to certify the claim under section 96 of the 2002 Act so as to deny a further appeal (▶see below).

Section 96 2002 Act and one-stop notices

Where an applicant has *previously* received a one-stop notice in connection with an earlier application and the Home Office considers that grounds, which are later raised by an applicant, should have been put forward in response to the earlier notice, it may issue a certificate under section 96 of the 2002 Act. In such cases, the Home Office must also be able to say that there is 'no satisfactory reason' for the matter not having been raised in the earlier notice. If such a certificate is issued, the applicant will not able to appeal against the immigration decision unless the certificate is successfully challenged on judicial review.

Section 96 certificates can also be issued to prevent further appeals where the Home Office thinks that the new grounds could have been raised at an earlier appeal. For further details about section 96 certificates, ▶see 1067–9.

Providing evidence in support of asylum applications

Because the events, which an asylum-seeker describes have happened in a different country and often some of the incidents occurred a long time ago, it is often very difficult or impossible to provide evidence of them. Most claims depend very much on the asylum-seeker's own evidence of their circumstances which is why credibility plays such an important role in the process. Even though there are difficulties, asylum-seekers should do their best to produce what evidence they can to support their claims. Often asylum-seekers are penalised for not producing evidence, which they could have been expected to obtain.

Evidence can be given to the Home Office by hand at interviews or when the claim is made or sent in by post. Just because an asylum-seeker has not actually brought the evidence with them does not mean that efforts should not be made to produce it. If the asylum-seeker claimed asylum at a time when they didn't have representation, advisers should always check with them what evidence they have already handed in, as such evidence could sometimes be buried in a Home Office file and never properly taken into account.

Examples of evidence, which an asylum-seeker might produce, are set out in the table below.

Are the documents genuine?

At one point, it seemed to be the case that if an asylum-seeker produced documents in support of their case, they should be accepted as genuine documents unless the Home Office could *prove* they were forged. That has been overridden by the decision of the IAT in *Tanveer Ahmed* to the effect that:

- it is for the applicant to demonstrate that any documents they produce can be relied upon;
- the decision-maker will consider the credibility of the whole of the evidence and the claim in general in order to decide whether reliance can be placed on the document;
- it will, therefore, often not be necessary to make an allegation of forgery, but where such an allegation *is* made by the Home Office, it will have to produce evidence to justify the allegation to a high civil standard. However, failure to show that it is a forgery does not necessarily mean that the document is reliable.

The decision of the Court of Appeal in *Mungu v SSHD* is to a similar effect, in that it is open to a decision-taker to consider the reliability of a document in the light of all of the evidence. Of course, if the documents are self-proving, or if they are demonstrated by independent evidence, including expert evidence, to be authentic, then it may be much more difficult for the Home Office to dispute an account which is based on those documents (see *Davila-Puga*, CA).

EVIDENCE USED IN SUPPORT OF ASYLUM APPLICATIONS

Examples of evidence in support of applications are as follows.

Medical reports

Medical reports are often submitted in order to support a claim by an asylum-seeker that they have been tortured. They are useful in demonstrating both the physical scars or conditions left after mistreatment and that the asylum-seeker suffers from psychological or psychiatric conditions resulting from torture. They are rarely conclusive and the extent to which they can help depends upon the level and experience of the medical expert and the care taken in the preparation of the report.

The most experienced provider of reports is the Medical Foundation for the Care of Victims of Torture, ▶see address on 1504. The Home Office states that their reports 'should not be dismissed unless any concerns have been raised with the Foundation first'; that specific reasons must be given in the refusal letter if the report is dismissed; and where a report is submitted after an application has been refused, 'the case should be reviewed before any appeal'. The Home Office will delay making a final decision in anticipation of a medical report in certain circumstances (▶see 671).

Expert reports

Advisers regularly commission expert reports, often from academics who are particularly knowledgeable about the situation in the country concerned, to support asylum claims. Expert reports are normally used at the appeal stage rather than at the stage of the application. The IAT had increasingly insisted that experts' credentials and the basis and the sources of their knowledge are made clear. Experts should also approach the case from an independent stand-point, not as the supporter of the asylum-seeker (*Slimani*, IAT).

Arrest warrants/court documents

Documents issued by the state authorities that the asylum-seeker claims to fear can often win cases. Great care should be taken, however, when advising clients about these documents as both the Home Office and adjudicators are frequently very sceptical of them. The Home Office is often able to make checks to verify the documents to see whether they are false. Care should be taken to see if the dates and place names on the documents fit with the applicant's account. Asylum-seekers must also be able to explain how they managed to obtain the documents in the first place. Often it is advisable to ask a country expert to comment on the documents. These documents will not necessarily be accepted as reliable just because the Home Office cannot prove that they are forgeries (▶see above at 665).

Statements and letters from witnesses

Often asylum-seekers are able to produce supporting statements from other people in the UK or letters from those overseas who themselves know some-thing about the applicant's circumstances. The Home Office does not usually take this kind of evidence seriously as it considers that it can be easily manufactured. Where such evidence is put forward, the witness should state how they know about the evidence they are giving, for example, did they see it themselves? Letters from abroad should be accompanied by a copy of the envelopes in which they arrived.

Evidence from political organisations

Where asylum-seekers have continued their political activity in the UK, it is often useful to obtain confirmation from the branch of the political organisation based here. It may be that a letter can be written or photographs produced of certain activities. It may be that the organisation is able to provide details of the aims, ideas, structure and operation of the organisation, which will also help the claim.

Country evidence

In addition to the above, it is also useful to refer the Home Office to evidence about the general conditions in the country in question, which supports the claims made by the asylum-seeker. Advisers often produce large amounts of country material for appeals but it can also be useful to refer to at least some limited country material at the application stage, especially if the material covers ground which is relevant to the case and which is not covered in the Home Office's Country Information Policy Unit (CIPU) report. For more details about CIPU reports and other Home Office country information, ▶see 706–8 and for more details about the availability of country evidence generally, ▶see 1108–10.

Protection against removal and voluntary departures

Asylum-seekers may not be removed from the United Kingdom while their applications are outstanding. This applies to third country cases as well, at least until the Home Office decides that it is not going to consider the claim substantively (i.e. as to whether they have a well-founded fear in the country of origin) but instead it issues a certificate under Schedule 3 of the 2004 Act that the applicant is to be returned to a third country (see s77 of 2002 Act; para. 329 HC 395). Asylum-seekers who have in-country rights of appeal are also protected against removal until they have exhausted the whole appeal process (see ss78 and 104 2002 Act and for in-country appeals ▶see 1069–71, 1181–2).

If an asylum-seeker voluntarily leaves the UK while their application for asylum is outstanding, the Home Office will treat their application as having lapsed. An asylum-seeker who leaves the UK at a time when they have an in-country appeal outstanding will be deemed to have abandoned their appeal (▶see 1045 and 1104).

Voluntary returns

Sometimes asylum-seekers decide not to continue their claims but to return home instead. This may be because the situation in their country has improved and they feel it is safe to go back. If this is the case, they may be able to ask for financial and practical help from the International Organisation for Migration (IOM) (▶see 1028–9 and see 1505 for address). The IOM helps to run the Voluntary Assisted Returns and Reintegration Programme (VARRP). This enables asylum-seekers at any stage to obtain help and support in returning home.

The 'ILR family exercise' concession for asylum-seeking families who claimed asylum before 2 October 2000

On 24 October 2003 the Home Secretary announced that he would be 'clearing the decks for tough new asylum measures' by granting indefinite leave to 'long-standing' families who had sought asylum in the UK. The announcement came before the publication of the 2004 Bill.

Who qualified?

The intention was to clear a backlog of family cases by granting indefinite leave to a family:

- where the principal applicant had applied for asylum before 2 October 2000: *and*
- where the family included at least one dependent child who was under the age of 18 in the UK on 2 October 2000 or 24 October 2003 (the latter date was provided in an amendment to the policy).

The dependent child had to form part of the family unit on one of the relevant dates above and had to be 'financially and emotionally dependent' on the principal applicant on that date (see APU *Notice on the 'One Off Exercise'* which was still present on the Home Office website as of August 2005). The principal applicant, their spouse and all their children would all be granted indefinite leave to remain as long as they formed part of the family unit and were living in the UK on 24 October 2003.

Families would be eligible even if their applications and any subsequent appeals had been refused but they had not yet been removed or made a voluntary departure. Families who had claims pending, or had already been granted some other form of leave also qualified.

Families who were excluded

According to the APU Notice referred to above, an entire family would be disqualified from the concession if any member of the family who would have qualified under the concession fell into any of the following groups:

- had a criminal conviction for a crime committed abroad or in the UK, which was not 'spent' as of 24 October 2003. Where criminal investigations or court proceedings were pending, the Home Office officials would await their outcome. Furthermore, offences such as speeding which resulted in the issue of a fixed penalty notice were not considered to be criminal convictions;

- had an anti-social behaviour order or sex offender order;
- had made (or attempted to make) an application for asylum in the UK under more than one identity;
- presented a risk to security;
- stood to be excluded within the scope of Article 1F of the Refugee Convention (▶see 625) or whose presence in the UK was otherwise not conducive to the public good.

Where *all* family members could be removed on third country grounds, the family would also be excluded. The family would not be excluded however, if the claim of one family member fell to be considered in the UK.

Procedure

The Home Office initially set up a special team to identify eligible cases and forms were sent out to those families. Those who thought they were eligible but whom the Home Office had overlooked could also apply to the Home Office under this concession on a special form.

The deadline for making an application under the concession was 31 December 2004. However, JCWI is aware that decisions have been made in favour of families after this date, and any family who feels that they meet the terms of the concession, should seek advice on notifying the Home Office.

The Home Office has stated that the concession does not formally apply to human rights cases including those whose claim was based on Article 3 alone and not the Refugee Convention (Home Office Asylum Policy Unit letter to the Terrence Higgins Trust dated 4 April 2005). However, the same letter indicates that discretion may still be exercised in human rights cases:

'It was never intended that the policy should apply to human rights cases. In considering these cases in the context of our obligations under the law, we will consider in each case whether the circumstances are so compelling as to warrant the exercise of discretion, but we are not prepared to extend the application of the ILR exercise for asylum-seeking families.'

THE 'ORDINARY' SEF PROCESS

At the time of writing, asylum-seekers who are not allocated into one of the specific segments referred to at ▶643–4, are likely to be processed after screening by granting them temporary admission and issuing them with a Statement of Evidence Form (SEF). Most of the specific segment procedures (▶below at 673 onwards) do not use SEFs. However, some 'non-segmented' asylum-seekers may also be processed without a SEF (▶see below).

Applicants given a SEF are required to complete the form in English and return it within ten working days of issue, usually to the Asylum Co-ordination Unit at the Home Office (for address, ▶see 1493). The time-limit is strictly applied. If it is not kept to, the asylum-seeker is likely to be refused on 'non-compliance' grounds for failing to provide information about the claim (▶see 715–6). As to granting extensions of time for submitting the SEF, the Home Office stated in a letter to ILPA dated 29 January 2001:

'A decision to grant an extension will only be made in exceptional cases where there is a reasonable explanation for an applicant's inability to make a prompt and full disclosure of material facts.'

The SEF Form

The SEF presently in use dates back to October 2003 and is divided into different sections as follows:

- sections A and B ask for details about the applicant and their family;

- section C1 asks the applicant to set out details of the persecution, harassment or harm that they have suffered, who carried out these acts and why the applicant was targeted. Applicants should provide as many details as possible, setting out exactly why they feel they cannot return to their country. The form also asks if the applicant attempted to move to another part of their country for safety, and if not, why not. It also asks for details about military service, and any harm that has been suffered by the applicant's family;

- sections C2 to C5 ask the applicant to identify the basis of their claim, namely whether it is based on race, religion, nationality, political opinion or membership of a particular social group, and specific questions are asked tailored to each of these 'Convention' reasons. In some cases, the applicant will fear persecution for more than one of these grounds and there should be no hesitation in completing more than one section.

Asylum-seekers and representatives often find it easier to give the details in their own way by stating 'see attached' under many of the sections and then appending to the form a full statement which sets out the basis of the claim including all the details which they would otherwise put in the different sections.

SEF/NINO interviews

After the SEF has been considered, asylum-seekers are normally asked to attend an interview with the Home Office in order to clarify and expand upon the details they have already given in the SEF. These interviews now commence with a series of questions relating to the potential issue of a National Insurance number (NINO) if the claim is successful. The reason for this is the problems and delays which have been caused when successful asylum-seekers need to transfer from asylum support to social security benefits and work and the need to have a NINO in order to do this.

For details about the 'NINO requirement' and claims to benefit, ▶see 1283–4.

The Home Office uses offices in Leeds, Liverpool and Croydon to conduct these interviews. In reality, the interviews are often used as an opportunity to obtain material in order to challenge the credibility of the applicant. At the outset of a SEF interview, the asylum-seeker is read a statement explaining that it is not necessary to repeat all of the details, which have already been set out in the SEF. However, very unfairly, asylum-seekers are often penalised in Home Office refusal letters for failing to repeat information, which they have already given and which they reasonably believed had been taken into account. In rare cases, applicants may be called back for further interviews, usually because of previous misunderstandings or in cases where new evidence has come to light.

For more details about asylum interviews generally, ▶see 657–62.

Submitting further evidence after the SEF interview

The Home Office intends to make decisions 'immediately' after SEF interviews and so, if there is any further information or evidence which needs to be put forward before the decision, the asylum-seeker or their representative needs to act extremely quickly. If it is clear at the interview stage that it is intended to provide further evidence, this should be made known to the interviewing officer and the asylum-seeker should try to provide any evidence of the steps made to obtain the further information and when it will be provided. In the case of reports from the Medical Foundation for the Care of Victims of Torture, the Home Office position is that (API *Medical Foundation*, para. 2.1):

'Special arrangements have been agreed to allow requests for an extension…for post-interview representations to be submitted where the applicant has obtained an appointment with the Medical Foundation. Such requests should be carefully considered and only refused in exceptional circumstances. In all cases, the representatives or applicant should provide written confirmation from the Medical Foundation that the Medical Foundation has offered an appointment.'

However, this appears to apply not just to Medical Foundation report cases. In a letter to ILPA on 10 October 2001, the Home Office stated simply:

'Where evidence has been provided that a medical statement is to follow, for example, we have received an appointment card or letter confirming consideration of the applicant's case, a decision will be delayed for a reasonable time until the report is available.'

Practical problems

SEFs and the tight time-limits that have accompanied them have eroded the fairness of the investigation procedure. The *UNHCR Handbook* reminds states of the particular difficulties faced by those fleeing persecution and the likely lack of documentary evidence to support a claim.

The imposition of a rigid and very optimistic timetable for the submission of evidence works unfairly against applicants. It is no coincidence that the measures introduced following the White Paper, *Fairer, faster and firmer*, in 1998 to speed up decision-making, coincided with an increase in initial refusals.

Ten days is rarely sufficient for a newly arrived asylum-seeker, who may not speak any English, to be able to complete the SEF form, which undeniably requires a degree of expertise, if it is to be completed adequately. There is no doubt that an experienced adviser can improve an applicant's chances of recognition enormously by assisting to complete the written application, preparing a written statement and suggesting supporting documentary evidence to accompany it. However, many applicants find it difficult to instruct a representative following a reduction in the number of quality immigration solicitors available to do publicly funded work as a result of the contracting regime brought in from January 2000 and further changes since that time including the public funding cuts in April 2004. The combination of a fall in the supply of legal advice and the telescoping of procedures has led to a crisis with many applicants simply unable to find representation.

Added to this have been the effects of the Home Office's dispersal policy. Many applicants have found it difficult to find suitable representation in areas of the country where there is a lack of expertise in refugee law. The system has also made it extremely difficult for many asylum-seekers to stay in contact with their advisers, particularly if they have been dispersed hundreds of miles away from them.

'SEF-less' procedure

As indicated, even where an applicant is not put into one of the specific 'segments', in some cases they may be dealt with without a SEF. In such cases an applicant will face a substantive asylum interview which is likely to be scheduled very soon after they have been screened, often within two weeks. In these cases, the asylum-seeker is given a standard period of five days after the substantive interview in which to make further representations or provide further evidence. The five-day deadline will be extended if an appointment has been made with the Medical Foundation (▶see 671). No five-day time period will be given however if the applicant has been through an induction centre process because, during induction, it is expected that an applicant will have been told to have any information in support of the claim available by the time of the substantive interview.

The Home Office has confirmed however, irrespective of whether a five-day deadline is imposed, that in all cases, if representations are made before a decision is made, they will be taken into account (IND letter to the Asylum Processes Stakeholder Group dated 28 May 2004).

Of course, applicants assessed as third country cases are not issued with SEFs and nor are they interviewed about why they say they are in danger in their country of origin. Such cases are referred to the Home Office's Third Country Unit (TCU) following screening and a swift decision may be made to certify the case as suitable for third country removal. For details about third country cases, ▶see Chapter 24.

DETAINED FAST TRACK PROCESSES

At present, three detention centres operate a 'fast track' determination procedure: Oakington Reception Centre, Harmondsworth Immigration Removal Centre and Yarls Wood Immigration Removal Centre. Applications are determined quickly on a strict timetable.

In order to be placed into any of the detained fast track procedures, the application must be one which can be determined quickly (see the policy as most recently set out in the 'Fast Track Process Suitability List', May 2005). If the claim broadly qualifies for the detained fast track, the centre to which it will be referred depends on the factors set out immediately below. We then look at the general policy set out in the suitability list at ▶675–6. We then look separately at the different procedures, timetables and the legality of the processes at Oakington (▶677–8) and at Harmondsworth and Yarls Wood (▶678–71).

Oakington Reception Centre Many of the cases which are dealt with at Oakington are those, which, if refused, are expected to be certified as 'clearly unfounded' so that applicants can only appeal from abroad. These cases are also referred to as 'non-suspensive appeal' or 'NSA' cases (▶see 1073–8 for the types of cases that are subject to NSA certification). If their claim is refused *and* is certified as 'clearly unfounded', the applicant will have no right of appeal in the UK and is subject to immediate removal. If their claims are refused without being certified, they will have a right of appeal and should be released from Oakington in order to appeal. However, Oakington also processes cases, which are not ultimately given an NSA certificate. The Home Office intends to close Oakington by November 2006. It has stated that the process will not be 'transferred as a package to another centre' but that elements of the process will be developed under the 'new asylum model'.

Harmondsworth and Yarls Wood Immigration Removal Centres Fast track applications that are dealt with at Harmondsworth (for single men) and Yarls Wood (for women) are cases in which there is likely to be a right of appeal if the decision is negative. Those who are detained in these two centres and who decide to appeal against a refusal of their application will have their appeals determined in accordance with a fast track procedure (see the Asylum and Immigration Tribunal (Fast Track Procedure) Rules 2005). These rules also apply to those detained at Colnbrook House (which is at Harmondsworth) and Campsfield House. Details about the fast track *appeals* process are given at ▶1129–32.

For details about powers of detention generally, the lawfulness of detention and getting people out of detention, ▶see Chapters 30–32.

Who is likely to be put into the detained fast track?

The policy of the Home Office to detain and fast track certain types of application for asylum is set out in its 'Fast Track Processes Suitability List'. The latest issue is dated May 2005. The policy set out in this Suitability List is summarised in the table below.

In essence, the overriding consideration for allocation to the detained fast track is whether the claim can be determined 'quickly'. The Suitability List document states:

'Any claim, whatever the nationality or country of origin of the claimant, may be fast tracked where it appears after screening to be one that may be decided quickly, i.e. within the indicative process timescale.'

Until April 2004, only nationals of certain countries were deemed suitable to be put through these procedures. Since then, nationals of any country may be detained and fast tracked. *However*, in practice (and as set out in the box below) the nationality of the applicant plays a large part in whether an applicant is put into the detained fast track process in the following ways.

- The Suitability List has a list of countries which 'may well give rise to claims which may be decided quickly'.
- The NSA regime has a number of countries which are designated under section 94 2002 Act. Although any asylum or human rights claims can be certified as 'clearly unfounded', nationals of those countries are more likely to have their claims certified and are more likely to be referred to Oakington.

Categories exempt from the fast track

There are also certain categories of applicants who, although they would otherwise be eligible for the detained fast track, have personal circumstances that mean they are unsuitable for those procedures (see the table below). An example is unaccompanied minor asylum-seekers (UASCs). There have been frequent disputes, leading to judicial review challenges, as to whether certain applicants who claim to be UASCs and whom the Home Office has detained for fast tracking, are actually under 18. For details about age disputes, ▶see 688–91. UASCs generally are dealt with from ▶686.

APPLICANTS WHO ARE LIKELY TO BE PUT THROUGH A DETAINED FAST TRACK PROCEDURE

The information in this table is taken from the Home Office 'Fast Track Processes Suitability List' issued in May 2005. It should be read together with the notes above (►674).

The main consideration is whether a claim can be determined 'quickly'. Nationals of *any* country, even those not listed below, may be allocated to the detained fast track if, at screening, officers decide that their cases may be decided 'quickly'.

Applicants who come from a country that is designated under s94 2002 Act (so-called 'non-suspensive appeal' or 'NSA' countries) are likely to have their claims determined at Oakington Reception Centre. However, nationals of any country can receive an NSA certificate and also, Oakington processes non-NSA claims, which can be 'quickly determined' as well.

Other applicants who are liable to be detained in accordance with the following criteria are likely to be taken to Harmondsworth if they are males and Yarls Wood if they are females. Concerns have been raised about the provision of female interviewing officers and interpreters, ►see 660 for the Home Office's own guidelines on gender sensitivity.

Nationals likely to be fast tracked

Nationals of the following countries are *likely* to be considered suitable for the detained fast track. Those of the following countries that are designated NSA countries, are indicated by '(NSA)'. Nationals of those NSA countries will be detained and have their claims processed at Oakington rather than at Harmondsworth/Yarls Wood. These countries are:

Afghanistan	Gambia	Romania (NSA)
Albania (NSA),	Ghana	St Lucia
Bangladesh	Guinea-Bissau	Serbia and Montenegro
Benin	India (NSA)	including Kosovo
Bolivia (NSA)	Ivory Coast	(NSA)
Botswana	Jamaica (NSA)	Senegal
Brazil (NSA)	Kenya	Somaliland (but not
Bulgaria (NSA)	Macedonia (NSA)	Somalia)
Burkina Faso	Malawi	South Africa (NSA)
Cameroon	Malaysia	Sri Lanka (NSA)
Canada	Mali	Swaziland
Central African	Mauritania	Tanzania
Republic	Mauritius	Togo
Chad	Moldova (NSA)	Trinidad and Tobago
China	Mongolia	Turkey
Congo (Brazzaville)	Mozambique	Uganda
Djibouti	Namibia	Ukraine (NSA)
Ecuador (NSA)	Niger	Vietnam
Equatorial Guinea	Nigeria	Zambia
Gabon	Pakistan	Zimbabwe.

The Suitability List points out that the above list is 'not exhaustive or exclusive'.

Categories of applicant who are exempt from the detained fast track

Asylum-seekers in any of the following categories are *not* to be put through the detained fast track:

- applicants whose cases do not appear to be ones in which a quick decision can be reached;
- unaccompanied minors;
- applicants who are disputed to be minors and their 'appearance does not strongly suggest that [they are] over 18' (for details about UASCS and age disputes, ▶see 688–91);
- disabled applicants, 'except the most easily manageable';
- any person with physical and/or learning disabilities requiring 24-hour nursing care;
- any person who has a medical condition that requires 24-hour nursing or medical intervention;
- pregnant women of 24 weeks or more;
- any person who is identified as having an infectious/contagious disease;
- any person who has acute psychosis, such as schizophrenia, and requires hospitalisation.

The OEM adds to this list: those with criminal convictions (except where specifically authorised) and 'violent or unco-operative' cases which are likely to be allocated for detention elsewhere and referred for 'remote' determination (Ch 38.4). Cases are kept under review as far as suitability is concerned. Cases which initially appeared to be suitable for the detained fast track may turn out not to be, for example because they prove too difficult or complex to be determined within the strict timetable, or because further time is needed to gather evidence, ▶see further below.

In addition, at the appeal stage, non-Oakington detainees can apply to an Immigration Judge of the AIT for their case to be transferred out of the fast track (▶see 1132).

Access to legal representation in the detained fast track

At Harmondsworth and Yarls Wood, there are duty representation schemes, funded by the Legal Services Commission (LSC), to ensure that fast track applicants have access to a legal representative the day after their arrival at the centre. Only those advisers who have a specific contract with the LSC to do this work can provide publicly funded representation under the duty representative schemes (JCWI has a contract to assist Harmondsworth detainees). Applicants are allocated to the representative who is on duty at the time. At Oakington, only the Refugee Legal Centre and Immigration Advisory Service are permitted by the LSC to provide publicly funded representation.

In certain circumstances however, a fast track detainee can choose to have a representative who has already been assisting the applicant or one of their close family members. A close family member is defined by the LSC as the applicant's spouse, unmarried partner, child, sibling, parent, grandparent or grandchild.

Oakington fast track

There are separate fast track timetables for Oakington on the one hand and Harmondsworth and Yarls Wood on the other. Both timetables are strict and set the days on which an applicant will be interviewed and when they can expect a decision.

The use of detention as a fast track process was first piloted at Oakington Reception Centre when it opened in March 2000. It represented a major shift in asylum and detention policy because the policy reason given for detention was not that the applicants were at risk of absconding (indeed an applicant who is at risk of absconding is unsuitable to be detained at Oakington). The main consideration was simply whether the claim was capable of being decided quickly through the fast track process operated.

The detailed criteria for detention at Oakington are set out above. In addition, applicants who are not suitable for the 'relaxed' regime at Oakington, for example those who are at risk of absconding, are not detained there (and see *Saadi* below).

Legality of Oakington

The legality of detaining applicants for the 'administrative convenience' of determining their asylum claims was challenged in the case of *Saadi & Others*. Ultimately, the House of Lords decided that detaining asylum-seekers who were not at risk of absconding was in accordance with Article 5(1)(f) ECHR which permits detention in order to prevent a person making an 'unauthorised entry' to a country. They also found that detaining for a short period in such circumstances was not disproportionate or unreasonable. The case is being taken to the European Court of Human Rights, which declared the complaint to be admissible on 27 September 2005 (*Saadi v UK*, ECHR).

The Home Office intends to close Oakington by November 2006.

Timetable

The intended timetable for processing claims through Oakington is as follows.

Day	Activity
0	Arrival
1–2	Consultation with legal representative
3	Asylum interview
4–5	Submission of further evidence and representations Further consultations with legal representative

6	If not certified as 'clearly unfounded', then service of decision
7–9	Senior caseworker to review a decision that it is proposed will be certified
10	Service of decision if it is certified and removal directions.

During the *Saadi* case, the very short period of detention while the claim was processed was emphasised. However, in practice applicants have been detained for periods in excess of these time-limits. In *R (Johnson) v SSHD*, an ailing 64-year-old Jamaican with extended family in the UK was kept in detention for five-and-a-half weeks before a decision on his claim was made. He was further detained at Oakington for some weeks after the decision. The High Court found that this was unlawful and in breach of Home Office policy of releasing detainees if it became clear that their claims could not be determined within the original seven-day timetable.

Shortly after *Johnson*, the Home Office Minister announced a change to this policy. He referred to the need for more flexibility in the time-limits and stated:

'The purpose of this announcement is to set out our revised fast track process detention policy…the period of detention for making a quick decision will not be allowed to continue for longer than is reasonable in all the circumstances. We will aim to make decisions within ten to 14 days, but there will be occasions where it is quicker… However, we will continue to detain for the purpose of deciding the claim quickly, even beyond the ten to 14 day time scale, unless the length of time before a decision can be made looks like it will be longer than is reasonable in all the circumstances.' ('Fast track asylum and detention policy', Parliamentary written answer of the Minister, Desmond Browne MP, 16 September 2004, Column 157WS)

The Home Office has now implemented a flexibility policy which sets out the circumstances when someone should be taken out of a fast track process altogether (▶see below) which applies to fast track detention at Oakington.

Harmondsworth and Yarls Wood fast track

Following the fast track process at Oakington, fast track processes were rolled out at Harmondsworth from April 2003 for single males without dependants and at Yarls Wood for females in May 2005.

Timetable

The timetable, faster than that at Oakington, is breathtaking.

Day	Harmondsworth and Yarls Wood
0	Arrival
1 (morning)	Consultation with legal representative
(afternoon)	Asylum interview
2	Service of decision
	Detention continued, or temporary admission
3–4	Appeal to be lodged (two working days).

The timetable continues at break-neck speed during the fast track appeal process, which applies to appeals in respect of detainees at Harmondsworth, Yarls Wood, Colnbrook House and Campsfield (it does not apply to Oakington). The appeals and onward appeals timetable for these cases is set out at ▶1130–2.

Legal challenge to Harmondsworth and flexibility policy

In the *Refugee Legal Centre* case a challenge was brought to the legality of the fast track process at Harmondsworth. In November 2004, the Court of Appeal held that the system was not inherently unfair. However, the Court stated that there was a risk of unfairness in a rigidly operated timetable and that this risk must be reduced to an acceptable minimum. The Court stated that:

'A written flexibility policy to which officials and representatives can work will afford a necessary assurance that the three-day timetable is in truth a guide and not a straitjacket.' (para. 23)

In April 2005, the Home Office introduced the 'Detained Fast Track Processes Operational Instruction' setting out in what circumstances flexibility should be introduced to the timetable. This instruction applies to all detained fast track processes, including Oakington. The instruction states that applicants should be removed from the detained fast track process altogether if the time allowed under the fast track timetable is not sufficient to decide the case 'with the requisite degree of fairness'. The operational instruction sets out a number of factors that should prompt the Home Office to take someone out of the fast track process altogether, or extend the timetable in an individual case. The relevant elements of this are as follows.

Complexity Representations for release should be made in any case which has complicating factors or which raises issues that are unlikely to be resolved during the short timetable. A person whose case at first appeared to be one which could be dealt with quickly but which is later identified as being more complex should be transferred out of the fast track system.

Illness If, before the asylum interview, an applicant indicates that they do not wish to proceed with it because they are unwell, the interview should be delayed to the next day and the applicant offered medical attention. Subsequent requests to defer the interview will only be granted in the light of medical information. Representations for release should be made if the applicant's medical condition is such that detention is not appropriate.

Non-attendance or late attendance of representative An asylum interview will be delayed by up to one day if a representative is late or cannot otherwise attend that day and the applicant indicates that they do not wish to proceed without a representative present.

No competent interpreter If the interviewing caseworker is satisfied that the interpreter booked for an asylum interview is not competent because, for example, there are difficulties with the language or dialect spoken, then the interview will be delayed by up to one day.

More time to prepare for interview The Home Office considers that the time allowed under both the fast track timetables is adequate for an applicant and representative to prepare for the substantive asylum interview and that, according to the operational instruction, 'in most circumstances, it will not be appropriate to delay the interview'. Representatives should not however hesitate to request that the interview be deferred if they feel that the applicant needs more time to prepare for the interview. In the *Refugee Legal Centre* case, the Court of Appeal indicated that the timetable should be extended 'so that, for example, distressed and exhausted applicants are not put through the whole double-interview process in a single day'.

The Harmondsworth/Yarls Wood timetable allows no more than a few hours between a representative taking instructions and the asylum interview. The operational instruction seems to indicate however that an interview should be deferred where a 'representative has been instructed on the same day as the scheduled interview'. This indicates that representatives should ask for a delay if they see an applicant for the first time on the day of the interview.

More time to submit information or evidence after interview The Harmondsworth/Yarls Wood timetable allows hardly any time for further representations or evidence to be submitted because the substantive decision is made and served the next day following the interview. In all cases where this is insufficient time to enable the representative to put forward further important information, the operational instruction states that it will not be appropriate to delay the decision unless it would be unfair not to do so. The Home Office will want to know 'how central or critical to the issues' raised in the claim any further material will be and the instruction states that a decision will only be delayed for more than five days exceptionally. Applicants should be *released* altogether, according to the operational instruction, if:

'…the (Home Office) caseworker is satisfied that the applicant is obtaining supporting evidence, that fairness requires that it be taken into account when making the initial decision on the asylum claim, and that it will not be available within a period consistent with Fast Track processing even if the timetable were to be enlarged.'

Of course, a detainee may at any time lodge an application for bail. Those detained in the fast track may also apply to the AIT for an order taking them out of the fast track, which should have the result that they are released.

ACCELERATED NON-DETAINED PROCEDURES INCLUDING THE NORTH WEST PROJECT AND DOVER PILOT SCHEMES

There are four *non-detained* accelerated procedures:

- one for those claiming at Croydon ASU and who fall into the 'late and opportunistic' category who are not detained. Some are dispersed to Liverpool;
- one operating for those claiming asylum at Croydon ASU and who fall into the 'potentially NSA' category;
- the 'North West Project' for those who claim asylum in Manchester or Liverpool;
- the Dover pilot scheme.

With the exception of the Dover pilot, in these procedures, one Home Office manager or team will be responsible for the case throughout its life. They will deal with NASS support, the substantive interview, the decision, integration into the community if the claim is successful, appeal and removal if appropriate.

Those applicants who are dispersed to Liverpool are given 'facilitated access' to legal advice. This means that applicants are allocated an adviser from a rota managed by the LSC. Those who are not dispersed are not given facilitated access; they will instead be provided with a list of local 'devolved suppliers' (i.e. advisers who have contracts with the LSC to give out publicly funded immigration advice).

'Late and opportunistic' and 'potentially NSA' claims

From 20 June 2005, Croydon Asylum Screening Unit (ASU) has started identifying claims for asylum which may fall into the new 'potentially NSA' and 'late and opportunistic' segments.

Late and opportunistic claims An application will be categorised as 'late and opportunistic' if it is made:

- more than a month after entering the UK without a good reason for the delay. The Home Office has stated that medical circumstances may amount to a good reason;
- towards the end, or after the expiry, of a period of leave;
- following refusal of an application for leave; or

- after being caught working in breach of a condition of leave or without permission, or after being apprehended for a 'non-immigration offence'.

Potentially NSA claims As explained previously, applicants who are nationals of, or are entitled to reside in, a country which is designated under the 2002 Act as a 'non-suspensive appeal' or 'NSA' country, (▶see 675 for the list) are likely to be allocated to this segment.

Many of those falling into both the above categories will be judged to be suitable for one of the detained fast track processes in accordance with the Home Office Fast Track Processes Suitability List (see above). Those who are not detained and who need NASS accommodation, are immediately dispersed to Liverpool where they will be housed in special blocks close to the reporting centre (Reliance House) and where they will be required to report frequently. Those not needing NASS accommodation will be required to report frequently to Croydon ASU. Whether they are dispersed or not, their claims will be decided in accordance with the accelerated procedure set out below:

Day	Stage of claim
0	Screening and recording claim; possible immediate dispersal to Liverpool
5	Substantive interview
11	Service of asylum decision
12–21	Appeal to be lodged ('late and opportunistic' claims only)
14+	Removal if negative decision in a 'potentially NSA' claim which has been refused and certified as 'clearly unfounded'.

The timetable is likely to change because these two categories are in the early stages of development. The above are working days.

North West Project (NWP)

Adult claimants who apply at Manchester Airport, Liverpool ASU and Liverpool John Lennon Airport on or after 6 December 2004 will be put through an induction process by the North West Consortium Induction Service (NWCIS). Those that are initially housed in NWCIS accommodation will have their cases decided in accordance with the following timetable:

Day	Stage of claim
1	Screening and recording claim
9–14	Substantive interview
	Applicants dispersed from their induction accommodation will receive a travel warrant for their return to decision interview
17–19	Decision made and served at a 'third interview' when the applicant is informed about the subsequent appeal process or arrangements for integration.

The above are working days and are approximate. Details about the NWP are also given at ▶643–4. Appeals following refusals are not accelerated.

Dover Pilot

Applicants who claim asylum at Dover port or Dover Enforcement Unit are taken to the induction centre at Dover Port. This is run by Migrant Helpline who will then place the applicant in induction accommodation in Dover, Ashford or Margate, collectively known as the South East Induction Centre (SEIC). Applicants will be provided with an induction package, which includes a comprehensive briefing about how their asylum claim will be decided and about access to NASS support. Applicants receive health screening and a medical record which can then be taken to the GP in the area to which they will be dispersed.

Applications are processed in accordance with the following timetable.

Day	Stage of claim
0	Screening and recording claim. Induction process commences (see above). Travel warrant for attending substantive interview provided
10	Substantive interview. Applicants are dispersed from their initial induction accommodation following the interview
11	Decision made
12	Decision served.

PROSECUTION FOR NON-POSSESSION OF TRAVEL DOCUMENT

Section 2 of the 2004 Act came into force on 22 September 2004. It contains a new offence of not possessing an 'immigration document' at a 'leave' or 'asylum' interview. An immigration document is defined as a passport but may also be another document, which serves the same purpose as a passport. The document must be valid and must 'satisfactorily establish [the applicant's] identity and nationality'. A 'leave or asylum interview' means an interview with an immigration officer or other Home Office official at which a person seeks leave to enter or remain in the UK, or claims asylum. The offence also applies to those travelling or living with a dependent child who similarly does not possess a travel document.

Defences Those prosecuted for this offence will have a defence if they can demonstrate any of the following:

- that they are an EEA national or the family member of an EEA national;
- that they can produce a false document which they used 'for all purposes in connection with the journey' (a document is 'false' if it is designed to look like an immigration document, has expired or is being used by someone other than the person for whom it was issued);

- that they had a 'reasonable excuse' (▶see further below) for not being able to produce a document;
- that they never had an immigration document during their journey to the UK. Suspects will of course be questioned on how they managed to travel without a document.

'Reasonable excuse'

The deliberate destruction or disposal of a document will not be considered a reasonable excuse unless it was for a 'reasonable cause' or for reasons beyond the control of the applicant. Acting this way in order to delay a claim or increase its chances of success will not be considered to be a reasonable cause. Complying with the instructions of another person such as an agent will only be accepted as an excuse if the applicant can show that it was unreasonable for them not to comply with the agent's demands. The Home Office has drawn up an Operational Instruction (OI) for members of its staff on the section 2 offence (not yet available on the Home Office website), which suggests that this might be the case if the applicant was forced to comply through threats or intimidation.

The OI also points out that, although unaccompanied minors are not beyond prosecution (unless they are below ten years of age in England and Wales, or eight in Scotland), it accepts that they may destroy or throw away a travel document *en route* without fully appreciating the consequences of their actions. It is further accepted that some minors cannot be expected to challenge instructions given to them by another party.

If a document has been lost or stolen, this is also considered to be a reasonable excuse, however evidence should be produced.

Article 31 Refugee Convention and section 2 offences

Concerns have been raised that the section 2 offence is contrary to Article 31 of the Refugee Convention. It states that, provided certain conditions are met, refugees should not be penalised on the basis of their illegal entry or presence in the host country. In *Adimi* a successful legal challenge was brought concerning the practice of prosecuting asylum-seekers who resorted to unlawful means in relation to their arrival in the UK. These prosecutions were brought on the basis of previous legislation and were undermined by a failure to have proper regard to the UK's obligations under Article 31. The government then brought in Section 31 of the 1999 Act which is supposed to reflect the UK's obligations under Article 31 and provides a statutory defence against certain offences relating to forgery, falsification of documents and deception. It does not, however, provide a defence against the section 2 offence. The *Adimi* case and Article 31/section 31 are looked at in more detail at ▶1235–8.

Applicants charged under section 2 should not hesitate to argue that prosecution may be contrary to Article 31, particularly when they cannot successfully rely on one of the defences listed above. This is a defence, which is being used and tested in the courts in relation to section 2. At the time of writing, it has been relied upon unsuccessfully in a number of cases before the Crown Court but permission to appeal to the Court of Appeal has been granted in a number of cases.

Procedures involving section 2 cases

An applicant cannot be considered to have committed an offence under section 2 until an interview commences in relation to a leave or asylum application. This is the case even though the applicant may be suspected in advance of not possessing appropriate travel documentation.

If an in-country applicant does not produce an immigration document at their initial Home Office interview, they will be given three days from that date to do so. The three-day deadline can be extended depending on the individual circumstances of the case. It may be extended, for example, if the applicant needs emergency medical care or there is a family emergency or transport problems.

It is clear from the nature of the questions raised in the standard screening interview that the answers given by an applicant may lead to prosecution under section 2. The OI referred to above states that questioning can continue to establish whether or not one of the statutory defences listed above applies. If it appears unlikely that the person has a defence, then any further questions relating to the offence can only continue after the applicant has been arrested and cautioned in accordance with the Codes of Practice laid out under the Police and Criminal Evidence Act 1984 (PACE). This means that the applicant should be offered the opportunity of getting legal representation before having to answer any more questions, which might implicate them further. The LSC will pay for a representative to attend an interview conducted by an immigration officer under PACE. The ultimate decision to pursue a prosecution can only be made by the Crown Prosecution Service. Anyone who is suspected of, or is being questioned in relation to, an offence should obtain advice from a representative with experience of *criminal* matters.

The asylum (or leave) application is supposed to continue quite separately from any criminal matter. If, during a substantive asylum interview, further information arises which is relevant to the criminal case, this information can be passed on to the immigration unit that initiated the prosecution. However, the interviewing officer *cannot* ask questions for the sole purpose of obtaining information that might lead to a prosecution or assist ongoing proceedings.

7

Sentences and number of cases

Up to the end of June 2005, there had been 372 arrests for section 2 offences and 281 convictions, at least one of them an undisputed minor. Bail has only been granted in a handful of cases. Defendants can be tried in a Magistrates or a Crown Court, and if convicted, they may receive a prison sentence of up to two years. In *Bei Bei Wang*, the Court of Appeal substituted a ten-month sentence with one of two months. In that case the Court also gave some general guidance. In the further cases of *R v Da Hua Weng & Guo Xing Wang*, two men entered the UK without passports. One returned his passport to an agent, the other destroyed it. Both claimed asylum and were prosecuted. In sentencing them, the Crown Court judge dealt with them as economic migrants and they were given a term of nine months' imprisonment. On appeal, the Court of Appeal reduced the sentence to three months. The Court of Appeal noted that it was not the purpose of the Crown Court to determine the genuineness or otherwise of the claim for asylum.

Practitioners in other cases have drawn attention to the usefulness of calling live country expert evidence in prosecutions under section 2 where the defence relates to the difficulty of obtaining travel documentation from the national authorities as a result of persecution (case note from a prosecution at Isleworth Crown Court provided to ILPA by Chris Williams, Counsel, 14 September 2005).

UNACCOMPANIED MINOR ASYLUM-SEEKERS

Unaccompanied asylum-seeking children are often referred to in short-hand as 'UASCs'. The immigration rules make specific provision for them, which recognises their particular vulnerability (see paras 350-352 HC 395). Particular priority and care is to be given to their applications.

Interviews

The rules suggest that more consideration should be given to the objective factors showing a risk to them in their country of origin, rather than the child's understanding of the danger. Until 18 September 2002, the rules stated that children would not be interviewed about their claims 'if it is possible to obtain by written enquiries or from other sources sufficient information to properly determine the claim'. However, from that date the rules have stated:

'An accompanied or unaccompanied child who has claimed asylum in his own right may be interviewed about the substance of his claim or to determine his age or identity.' (para. 352 HC 395 as amended by Cm 5597)

Where an interview is considered necessary, a 'parent, guardian, representative or another adult who for the time being takes responsibility for the child' must be present. The officers who conduct the interview should have received training in dealing with children. The rules require that the interviewer should have particular regard to the possibility that the child will feel inhibited or alarmed. Children should be allowed to express themselves in their own way and at their own speed. The interview should be stopped if the child appears tired or distressed. Children under the age of 12 will not be interviewed (Local Stakeholder Meeting between ACG(N) and ILPA, 17 May 2005).

From 7 January 2004, all non-disputed minors no longer had their screening interview conducted over a counter at the ASU in Croydon. Special screening rooms were provided and a commitment was given that the same officer would deal with the child's case throughout the process (Home Office letter to ILPA, 12 December 2003).

Home Office 'best practice' for dealing with minors

The Home Office has disclosed a 'Best Practice' for staff at ports and Asylum Screening Units for dealing with unaccompanied non-asylum and asylum-seeking children (version, 30 June 2003) when they present for screening. Important points from the Best Practice are:

- where staff become aware of the presence of an unaccompanied minor, they should give them immediate attention;
- if the child appears unwell or distressed, immediate medical assistance should be obtained and it may be necessary to contact the local social services department;
- a child should only be detained in exceptional circumstances, for example if social services have declined to intervene but the immigration service have concerns regarding the suitability of the sponsor i.e. detention may then be in the best interests of the child – in such cases consideration should be given to contacting the police i.e. the local Child Protection Officer (the policy to only detain unaccompanied asylum-seeking children in exceptional circumstances is confirmed in the Operational Enforcement Manual (►see 911 and ►see also at 916) and in the Home Office's response of 10 June 2005 to the Save the Children report *No Place for a Child*);
- unaccompanied children must 'only ever be detained in the most exceptional circumstances, and then only overnight, with appropriate care, whilst alternative arrangements for their safety are made'. An Assistant Director of the immigration service 'must review detention at the earliest opportunity';
- interviews should be conducted as indicated above;
- if the child produces any information relating to criminal activity (e.g. trafficking or abuse), the interview should be suspended and the police should be contacted urgently;
- screening of minors should be 'non-probing' in most cases, although interviewing officers may exercise their judgment in testing evidence;

- when an asylum applicant claims to be a child but their appearance 'strongly suggests' that they are over 18, they are to be treated as an adult until there is credible documentary evidence to demonstrate the age claimed (for further details about age disputes, see below);
- all unaccompanied asylum-seeking children must be referred to the children's panel of the Refugee Council (►below) within 24 hours of the application being made.

Refugee Council Panel of Advisers for Unaccompanied Refugee Children

The Refugee Council has set up a panel of advisers to provide unaccompanied children with an individual adviser. There are approximately 30 advisers who travel all over the country to support unaccompanied asylum-seeking children. The adviser helps vulnerable children to deal with authorities such as social services departments, schools and the immigration service. Their role is also to find interpreters and legal advisers and to offer support and other help. If a child already has a legal representative, the representative should ensure that the Refugee Council's panel of advisers are aware of their involvement and that the panel has full details of the child (►see 1501 for their contact details). The panel may also help in liaising between the Home Office and social services' departments in cases involving age disputes. The number for the panel of advisers duty helpline is (020) 7346 1134.

Policy on exceptional leave where no reception facilities are available

The Home Office policy is not to remove from the UK an unaccompanied asylum-seeking child under the age of 18 *unless* there are adequate reception and care arrangements for them in the country of return. If this is not the case, the child will be granted a period of limited leave. The Home Office is seeking new ways of tracing families in the country of origin and, alternatively, ways to ensure that there are acceptable reception arrangements available. When the Home Office grants limited leave on the basis of this policy, it is obviously not accepting that the child is a refugee or granting 'asylum'. For details of this policy, the leave that is granted and the changes that the Home Office is seeking to make, ►see 865, 870–1.

Age-dispute cases

The Home Office will generally accept as proof of age an original and genuine passport, travel document, national identity card or birth certificate (see *Asylum Process Manual*, 'APM', Ch 5, Special Types of Case – Disputed Age Cases, paras 3.1–3.2, January 2005). In some cases, where there is no clear evidence of the age of the applicant, a dispute arises between the Home Office and the applicant as to age. These are cases in which the applicant claims to be a minor but the Home Office disputes this. Home Office policy on age-dispute cases as set out in the APM and other documents is set out in the table below.

The Home Office is suspicious that some people claim to be minors in order to obtain better treatment: unaccompanied minors benefit from the policy on removal referred to above and they are provided with support and looked after by local authorities under the Children Act 1989 rather than being supported by NASS. Also, Home Office policy is not to detain unaccompanied minors other than 'in the most exceptional circumstances' (►see above at 687 and ►see also 911 and see Operational Enforcement Manual (OEM) at Ch 38.9.3).

Where the Home Office decides that a person is to be treated as an adult, despite the fact that they claim to be a child, the person will be issued with form IS97M. Application Registration Cards (ARCs) issued before December 2003 will store details of the age dispute in the card's microchip. ARCs issued after December 2003 will display the word 'disputed' on the visible part of the ARC. Where there is an age dispute, the Refugee Council's panel of advisers must still be informed of the case.

Where an applicant has been refused leave having been treated as an adult at the time of the decision and the applicant subsequently submits satisfactory evidence to show that they were in fact a child at that time, the decision will be reconsidered (see APM, Ch 5, para. 10).

Public funding in age-dispute cases

Legal representatives may apply for public funding to obtain medical evidence where the client's age is in dispute (LSC newsletter 20/6/05). The costs of attending an interview will also be provided where there is a dispute if the minor's representative assesses that their client's claims are based on reasonable grounds.

HOME OFFICE POLICY IN AGE-DISPUTE CASES

In summary, Home Office policy relating to age-dispute cases is as follows.

1) Applicants who claim to be under 18 must be given the benefit of the doubt in relation to their age *unless* their physical appearance 'strongly suggests' that they are aged 18 or over. In such circumstances, the case is 'flagged' as a 'disputed minor' case and the applicant is treated as an adult until there is 'credible documentary or medical evidence to demonstrate the age claimed'.

2) In 'borderline' cases, the Home Office treats applicants as minors. A borderline case is one in which, based on the applicant's appearance, the Home Office believes that they are more likely to be over 18 but that they *could* be under 18.

3) An applicant who has claimed to be an *adult* and who subsequently claims to be a minor will be accepted as a minor only if their appearance 'strongly supports' the claim to be a minor; or they are able to produce credible documentary or

other persuasive evidence of their age (for example travel or identity documents, a birth certificate, a local authority social service age assessment).

4) The decision to dispute an applicant's age must always be confirmed by a senior officer (i.e. at Home Office Higher Executive Officer grade or a Chief Immigration Officer).

5) The Home Office does not use medical assessments to determine age but medical reports, which are submitted by applicants, for example prepared by a paediatrician, must always be considered. Care must be taken because, according to guidelines issued by the Royal College of Paediatrics and Child Health in November 1999 'age determination is an inexact science and the margin of error can sometimes be as much as five years either side' (but see further below as to the proper approach to these guidelines).

6) The Home Office will accept the conclusion of a 'full Social Services age assessment' (which takes into account wider cultural and social factors). This will be the case unless there are grounds for suspecting that the person who presented for the assessment is not the same person as the applicant. The Home Office will reverse its own decision to dispute age if a social services department subsequently concludes that an applicant is under 18.

Note

The above summary is taken from the various Home Office documents which were put before the High Court in *R (I and O) v SSHD* (►see further below) as setting out the policy including:

- Asylum Process Manual, Ch 5, Special Types of Case – Disputed Age Cases, January 2005;

- 'Unaccompanied Asylum Seeking Children' (July 2002);

- a witness statement in the case itself from the Head of the Home Office's Asylum Policy Team (dated 15 March 2005).

Chapter 38 of the Operational Enforcement Manual, which re-appeared on the Home Office website in revised form in autumn 2005, closely reflects the policy set out above (see at Ch 38.9.3.1).

In addition, a draft 'Joint Working Protocol' on age assessment has been agreed *in principle* between the Home Office and the Association of Directors of Social Services. The aim of the Protocol is to establish agreed working procedures, communication channels and recording conventions.

Legal challenges in age-dispute cases

The proper application of Home Office policy in age-dispute cases was examined by the High Court in *R (I and O) v SSHD*. In that case, the Home Office had kept two applicants who claimed to be minors in detention at Oakington Reception Centre even after it had received assessments from a consultant paediatrician which found that it was more likely than not that the applicants were under 18. The paediatrician had carried out a dental examination which, according to the same 'Guidelines' issued by the Royal College of Paediatrics (see as referred to in the policy above), gives an estimate with a margin of error of plus or minus two years for 95 per cent of the population. The applicants were only released when Cambridgeshire Social Services Department assessed the applicants as being under 18. The High Court held that the decision to continue to dispute age and therefore to detain the applicants after receipt of the paediatrician's report was unlawful.

The following matters are apparent from the judgment of the High Court.

- The Royal College's Guidelines, including the reference to a margin of five years either side, are directed to *all* paediatricians. Particular weight must, however, be attached to an assessment prepared by a senior paediatrician (for example a consultant) and/or one who has particular experience of age assessment.

- It is also clear from the Royal College's Guidelines that determination of age from dental development is generally accurate to within plus or minus two years.

- Social workers carrying out assessments may be of limited expertise and experience and, depending on the circumstances, it may not be open to the Home Office to prefer their reports over and above the reports of a paediatrician with extensive expertise and experience. Regard will be had to the scope and quality of the respective reports.

Other court decisions

In an earlier case, *R (A) v SSHD*, the Home Office accepted, without the case going to a full hearing, that they were not entitled to detain an applicant who claimed to be a minor on the basis of only an informal, unreasoned, imprecise social services assessment which did not reach the strong conclusion that an applicant was over 18.

In the context of local authorities carrying out age assessments of asylum-seekers, it is clear from the case of *R (B) v Merton LBC*, that an assessment may also take into account the credibility of the applicant who claims to be under 18. Questions may be asked to probe that credibility but if there are reasons to doubt the applicant's account, they must be put to the applicant so that the applicant has an opportunity to explain. In *B* that had not been done and the age assessment was therefore set aside by the Court. The immigration rules indicate that claimed minors can be interviewed as part of a Home Office age assessment procedure (see para. 352 HC 395). *B* also establishes that an age assessment cannot be arrived at on the basis of appearance alone and that reasons for a negative decision should be given to an applicant. Further, local authorities carrying out assessments for their own purposes cannot just adopt a decision as to age made by the Home Office; they must make their own decision.

DEPENDANTS OF ASYLUM-SEEKERS

If the application for asylum is successful, the dependants of an asylum-seeker who have been included in the application will be granted leave in line with the main applicant (para. 349 HC 395). If the main applicant is granted HP or DL instead, then the dependants will normally be given that status in line as well (API *Dependants*, para. 1).

Applying as a dependant or for family reunion?

Dependants of asylum-seekers and those seeking to stay on human rights grounds (►see 875–6) are treated similarly. Being considered as a dependant in an asylum application and applications for *family reunion* are different. Family reunion applications are those that are made after the main applicant has succeeded in their application and been granted status. For family reunion with those granted refugee status, ►see Chapter 25. For details about *family reunion* with those granted HP, DL or ELR, ►see 876–9.

Applying as dependant or claiming in own right?

Those who could be dependants may, however, also have a fear of persecution in their own right. If so, they may claim in their own right. If there is an independent fear and the dependant wishes to claim, they should do so straightaway, rather than leaving it until a decision has been reached on the principal's claim or later. This is because the immigration rules state:

'If the spouse or minor child in question has a claim in his own right, that claim should be made at the earliest opportunity. Any failure to do so will be taken into account and may damage credibility if no reasonable explanation is given.' (para. 349 HC 395)

In addition, if a dependant has a valid claim in their own right which is not raised when they are issued with a 'one-stop' notice issued under s120 2002 Act (►see above 662–4), and/or not raised on any appeal which they were included in as part of the principal's claim, the Home Office may try to prevent the dependant from bringing an appeal against a later independent claim for asylum by issuing a certificate under section 96 of the 2002 Act (see s96 2002 Act as amended by s30 2004 Act and see API *Dependants* at para. 7, although the API still refer to the old legislation). For further details about certificates issued under section 96 generally, ►see 1067–9.

Caseworkers are told to always confirm with the principal applicant and the dependants at interview whether a spouse and minor child wish to be treated as dependants for the purposes of the asylum application (API above, para. 2).

Which family members can be dependants?

Spouses and minor children (i.e. aged under 18) may be treated as dependants of the main asylum applicant (para. 349 HC 395, API *Dependants* para. 2). Sometimes there may be no clear evidence about the age of a child. The rules and the API both state that a dependant will be treated as under 18 if there is no documentary evidence establishing their age but they 'appear' to be under 18. A dependent child who is under 18 years at the date of the application, but who turns 18 before the decision, will continue to be treated as a dependant for the purposes of the application (API *Dependants*, para. 3). Non-British citizen children born to asylum-seeker applicants in the UK may also be added to a claim as a dependant (API *Dependants*, para. 8.3). There is, of course, nothing to prevent an application being made on behalf of a UK-born child who is not British by birth, for asylum in their own right. Where no application has been made for a child born in the UK and the parents are subsequently granted asylum, the Home Office is likely to invite an application to regularise the child's status.

Family members other than spouse/minor child

The API further state that relatives other than spouses and minor children, for example aged dependent parents, may be considered dependants if there are 'exceptional compassionate circumstances' (API, para. 3). When considering applications to be considered as a dependant, caseworkers should have regard to the right to respect for private and family life under Article 8 ECHR (API *Dependants* para. 1). This suggests that, depending on the circumstances, it *may* be that officers will be prepared to accept as dependants others who are dependent on the main applicant and with whom the main applicant has a relationship which amounts to 'family life' (▶see 823–6 for the relationships which may amount to family life) or indeed 'private life' (▶see 827, 846–7).

In all cases, in assessing a claim to be a dependant, officers need to be satisfied that the person claiming to be a dependant meets all of the following conditions, namely that they (API *Dependants*, para. 3.1):

- are related as claimed to the main applicant;
- were wholly dependent on the main applicant 'immediately prior to arrival in the UK'; and
- had formed part of the main applicant's pre-existing family unit abroad.

Is it necessary for a dependant to have arrived with the main applicant and to apply as a dependant at the same time as their claim to asylum?

The immigration rules state that the dependants should be 'accompany-ing' the principal applicant (para. 349, HC 395). However, in practice, provided the family members arrive and apply to be treated as dependants *before* an initial decision is made on the asylum claim, they are normally accepted as dependants on the claim (see API *Dependants*, para. 4). If they apply after a decision on the claim, they will not usually be treated as dependants but they will not be removed from the UK while the principal is appealing against the decision (API above, para. 2). If refugee status, HP or DL is eventually granted to the principal, the family member's application is then considered as an application for family reunion, which the Home Office should agree to consider in-country (▶see Chapter 25 at 759).

Status granted to dependants

While dependants will be granted leave for the same duration and on the same conditions as the main applicant, dependants do not have to be recognised as refugees. Dependants often do not want to be recognised as refugees – possibly they may wish to travel back to the country of origin (see API *Dependants,* para. 5).

PERMISSION TO WORK

If an asylum-seeker is granted temporary admission rather than being detained, one of the conditions that is normally attached to the temporary admission is that the applicant is not permitted to work. Under section 8 of the 1996 Act, employers are liable to be prosecuted for employing persons who are unauthorised to work. However, the Home Office has a discretion to lift the working restrictions from the temporary admission. This process is often referred to as granting 'permission' to work. It is, however, completely different from the system for granting work permits (for which ▶see Chapter 14). Whether the asylum-seeker is permitted to work or not is indicated on their ARC. If a SAL is still held, permission to work will be endorsed on that and it may also be found endorsed on an IS96 form (grant of temporary admission). Employers should take a copy (or other record in the approved form) of the ARC so as to avoid any criminal liability (for full details about criminal liability for employers and the defences, ▶see 496–500).

In some circumstances, asylum-seekers may effectively be required to work by participating in 'community activities'. Such a condition can be imposed in order for an asylum-seeker to continue to be provided with accommodation under the Home Office's 'hard cases' fund (see s4 1999 Act as amended by s10 2004 Act and ▶see 1386).

Before 23 July 2002

Before 23 July 2002, Home Office policy was normally to grant an asylum-seeker permission to work if no decision had been made on the asylum application within six months of the claim being made. Permission might also be granted before the six months was up if the asylum-seeker found a job. Permission was not automatic, asylum-seekers had to ask for it and it could be withheld if an asylum-seeker had failed to complete a SEF. Once permission had been granted, it would not normally be withdrawn until any appeal against a negative asylum decision had been dealt with. If asylum were refused within six months of the date of the claim and the applicant appealed, permission to work would not usually be granted however long the appeal took.

From 23 July 2002 to 4 February 2005

In July 2002, Home Office policy hardened. From 23 July 2002, there was no longer a presumption that permission to work would be granted after six months without an asylum decision. Applications to lift working restrictions were looked at on an individual basis with permission to work only being granted in 'exceptional' cases. On 15 January 2004, in reply to a parliamentary question, the Minister stated that the discretion was exercised 'sparingly' but 'might be appropriate in cases where an asylum-seeker has, through no fault of their own, waited for longer than 12 months for an initial decision on their claim'.

Transitional arrangements were, however, put in place. Asylum-seekers who were granted permission to work before 23 July 2002 could continue to work until a 'final decision is made on their claim'. Those who applied for permission before 23 July 2002 and were still waiting for a decision on that date had their applications determined in accordance with the policy that applied before 23 July 2002 (see Ministerial written answer of Beverley Hughes MP, 23 July 2002, *Hansard* Col 1043W-1044W).

From 4 February 2005: new immigration rules

From February 2005, the UK has been required to comply with an EU Council Directive, which lays down minimum standards for the reception of asylum-seekers (2003/9/EC) (▶see further 1379–81). Article 11 of the Directive requires states to set conditions under which asylum-seekers may be permitted to work after there has been a delay of 12 months in deciding their applications. The Home Office has responded by introducing new immigration rules from 4 February 2005 that deal with reception conditions for asylum-seekers (see part 11B HC 395 inserted by HC 194).

The rules now state that an asylum applicant may apply to the Home Office for permission to take up employment if no first decision has been taken on the asylum application within 12 months of the date on which the claim was recorded as having been made (see para. 360 HC 395). The rule does not set out the criteria applied by the Home Office in actually deciding whether to grant permission to work, except that it states that the application will not be considered if any delay in reaching the decision is the responsibility of the applicant. This might be the case, for example, if the applicant did not attend for an interview or delayed in sending in evidence when requested. Permission to work will be granted until the asylum application has been 'finally determined' (see para. 360A HC 395).

Where permission is granted under the immigration rules from 4 February 2005, the permission that is granted does *not* include permission to become self-employed, set up in business or to pursue a professional activity (para. 360 HC 395).

In-time asylum applicants whose leave enables them to work

Of course, if the asylum-seeker has previously been in the UK in a capacity which entitled them to work and then they applied for asylum in-country and in-time, their entitlement to work continues under the previous conditions of leave while the application and any appeal is determined. This is because their leave is automatically extended by statute (see s3C 1971 Act). This does not apply if leave is curtailed or if the applicant is treated as an illegal entrant.

Asylum-seekers and voluntary work

On 12 February 2001, the Home Office announced that it was 'keen to see asylum-seekers and recognised refugees take an active interest in the welfare of their own communities and the local community by undertaking voluntary activity in the UK'. It was stressed that such activity should not lead asylum-seekers to believe that they can necessarily remain in the UK. On the same day, the Home Office issued guidance to organisations that are considering offering voluntary work to asylum-seekers to ensure that the activity does not in fact amount to employment or job substitution. The guidance indicates that organisations are able to reimburse asylum-seekers for their food and travel costs in the course of their volunteering.

On 13 February 2004, the Home Office again issued guidance. It states that reimbursement can be made for meals, travel or other costs *actually incurred*, but *not* as a flat-rate allowance. The guidance goes on:

'There is a difference between volunteering and employment, which in general remains forbidden to asylum-seekers even where the employment is unpaid. An example of unpaid employment would be an arrangement in which a person makes an arrangement to help out in a business, perhaps on behalf of a relative, in return for some non-monetary benefit. But where the work is unpaid and is carried out on behalf of a charity, voluntary organisation or body that raise funds for either then it will be accepted for immigration law purposes as volunteering.' ('Guidance on undertaking voluntary activity', Home Office, 13 February 2004)

The National Centre for Volunteering has on-line information for volunteers and those who take on volunteers (www.volunteering.org). It provides useful information on recruiting refugees and asylum-seekers.

SPECIAL APPLICATIONS INCLUDING THOSE ACCEPTED WHILE STILL ABROAD

Under the Refugee Convention, people cannot be 'refugees' while they are still in the country in which they fear persecution. The first part of the definition of refugee is that a person must be 'outside' their country of nationality (▶602). They must therefore normally leave that country before claiming asylum in a safe country. The UK will also generally not accept responsibility for a person who is no longer in their own country but is outside the UK. This is because the obligation under Article 33 of the Refugee Convention is not to *send* people to persecution. There is no general obligation to admit refugees from other parts of the world. The presumption is that the application for asylum should be made to the authorities of the country where the person is. Of course, certain family members of refugees may apply to come to the UK for the purpose of family reunion (▶see Chapter 25).

However, if a claim is made to a post abroad and it is clear that the host state where the claim is made intends to subject the applicant to immediate, very serious injury, the ECHR may require the officials at the post to do what is reasonably necessary to protect the person from such treatment. The Court of Appeal gave this indication in the course of dismissing the appeals of two minors who had escaped from the Woomera Detention Centre in Australia and made their way to the British Embassy in Melbourne where they had claimed asylum (*R(B and others) v Secretary of State*, CA; see also the *European Roma Rights* case concerning events at Prague airport, ▶892–3).

In some cases, however, people do succeed in being allowed to *come* to the UK for the purposes of receiving international protection. These cases are classed as 'special' cases and the procedures and criteria that apply are set outside the immigration rules in the API. We look at the various different categories of special case in turn below.

The Home Office now only grants limited leave to refugees for the first five years. However, this new policy from 30 August 2005 does *not apply* to refugees who arrive under the resettlement schemes. They will continue to be granted indefinite leave immediately (API, *Refugee Leave*, paras 1, 2.3).

For the grant of 'temporary protection' (now contained in the immigration rules), ▶see 633–5.

Quota refugee resettlement programme ('Gateway Protection')

The quota refugee resettlement programme is operated by the Home Office together with the IND (see API, *Quota refugee resettlement programme*). This is also known as the 'Gateway Protection Programme'. Participants are people who fled to a third country and have been accepted as refugees by UNHCR. UNHCR identifies certain refugees as qualifying for resettlement because their human rights are at risk in the third country, or because they have no secure future there. UNHCR will then refer possible participants to the Home Office – applications cannot be made directly either to the Home Office or to UK posts abroad. When the Home Office receives an application from UNHCR, it is not automatically granted. An IND Overseas Resettlement Officer will normally interview the applicants overseas. It is possible (but rare) that the Home Office may disagree that the person is a refugee. The Home Office will also consider for themselves whether the criteria set out in the UNHCR's *Resettlement Handbook* are satisfied. Participants will also be given health screening and resettlement will not be offered to applicants with HIV/AIDS, multi-drug-resistant-TB or established renal failure. However, even in cases that would otherwise be refused under the programme, caseworkers are entitled to exercise discretion if the compassionate circumstances are strong enough.

Those who are successful are granted indefinite leave and will be granted refugee status in the UK. Their dependent spouse and minor children, and in some cases other dependants, may also be admitted. There is no right of appeal if an application put through by UNHCR is refused although, if circumstances change, the application can be re-submitted. A quota of applicants is to be accepted each financial year by the Home Office. For the year 2003/4, the quota was 500. The first refugees to arrive under the programme were from Liberia (who had been living in squalid conditions in refugee camps in Guinea) and the Democratic Republic of Congo (who were living in Ghana). This first group was resettled in Sheffield.

Mandate refugees

'Mandate refugees' are those who are in a third country *or* who are still in their own country and who have been recognised as refugees by UNHCR (see API, *Special applications: mandate refugees*). In most cases where an application is made to the UK, the UNHCR will have nominated the applicants for resettlement and the administration of the referral is then carried out on behalf of the UNHCR by the British Red Cross (BRC). It is advisable therefore to obtain the involvement of these agencies if any approach to the Home Office is to be made. However, mandate refugees may also make direct applications for entry clearance to posts abroad, which are considered exceptionally. They should present evidence that the UNHCR has recognised them as refugees. Applications that appear to be sufficiently compassionate will be referred to the Home Office's Asylum Policy Unit, which will consider:

- the applicant's circumstances in their present country; and
- whether the UK is the most appropriate country of refuge.

In deciding whether the UK is the most appropriate country of refuge, the Home Office will consider whether the applicant has 'close ties' with the UK, for example, close family members who are settled in the UK (although they do not need to have refugee status), or who are in the UK for a purpose which may lead to settlement. This includes family members with humanitarian protection or discretionary leave (for an explanation of these statuses, ▶see 597–8, 862–5). 'Close family members' for these purposes are: spouses, minor children and parents or grandparents over the age of 65. The following family members may be treated as meeting the 'close ties' requirement only in exceptional circumstances: a parent or grandparent under 65; adult sons, daughters, sisters, brothers uncles or aunts. The applicant may also have 'close ties' with the UK if they have previously resided here.

If the referral is made through the BRC, then no formal notice of decision needs to be given and there is no right of appeal. If a formal entry clearance application has actually been lodged then there will be a right of appeal against the refusal of entry clearance. If a mandate refugee makes an application for resettlement after arriving in the UK, it is processed as an asylum application, although UNHCR will be contacted for confirmation that the applicant has been recognised and UNHCR's views on the application are taken into account.

'Ten or more' plan

The 'ten or more' plan is a further scheme, which was established by the UNHCR and is run by the BRC. The aim is to enable the host country to admit ten or more disabled people who have been accepted by the UNHCR as refugees, together with their families, to be resettled to the participating countries (including the UK) each year. Referrals must be made to the Home Office through the BRC. Applications are assessed both by the UNHCR and by the Home Office. Factors taken into account include the severity of the disability, the availability of treatment in the country of refuge, the applicant's other circumstances in the country of refuge, the applicant's ties with any other country and whether the UK is the 'most appropriate country of refuge'. Applicants must have close ties to the UK (API, *Special applications: the ten or more plan*).

Group refugees

There have been limited government programmes for refugees from specific countries; for example, Chileans in the 1970s and Vietnamese during the 1980s. These programmes are based on a government decision to accept a quota of people who are already recognised as refugees. Such groups have usually been given permission to enter for four years and granted settlement at the end of that time. People who have come in this way may be referred to as 'programme refugees'. For further details about the new category of 'temporary protection' under the immigration rules, ▶see 633–5.

Transfer of refugee status

There are certain circumstances in which the UK will accept responsibility for people who have been recognised as refugees by another country (see API, *Transfer of refugee status*, updated August 2005). In accordance with the European Agreement on the *Transfer of Responsibility for Refugees of the Council of Europe* dated October 1980 (EATRR), provided that a 'transfer of responsibility' is deemed to have occurred (below), the Home

Office will accept responsibility for the refugee and grant leave to applicants who:

- are lawfully resident in the UK; and
- have been recognised as a refugee under the Refugee Convention by one of the countries which has ratified the EATRR (Denmark, Finland, Germany, Italy, Netherlands, Norway, Portugal, Romania, Spain, Sweden, Switzerland). (Note that the following countries have signed but not ratified the EATRR: Belgium, Czech Republic, Greece, Luxembourg, Poland.)

Transfer of responsibility

A 'transfer of responsibility' will be deemed to have taken place if *any* of the following conditions is satisfied:

- the applicant has been allowed to stay in the UK for two continuous years (not including periods spent studying, training, receiving medical treatment, in prison or pending an immigration appeal which is dismissed);
- the applicant has been granted indefinite leave in the UK;
- the applicant has been allowed to stay in the UK beyond the period of validity of the travel document granted by the other country, provided that the reason for the extension beyond that period was not studying or training and provided that the applicant is not readmissible to the first state (the applicant will be readmissible under EATRR, for example, if the UK request that they are readmitted within six months of the expiry of the travel document).

Discretionary cases

If the application does not come within the EATRR (above), then the Home Office may still exceptionally grant the transfer. Such applications may be made at a post abroad or in-country. Applicants will not always be interviewed. Transfers are only granted in these cases where the UK is 'clearly the most appropriate place for [the applicant's] long term refuge'. Factors taken into account are: length of time in the first country of refuge, strength of ties in the first country compared to ties in the UK and any compelling compassionate circumstances.

Procedures and leave granted

The process for making applications to transfer refugee status has not always been clear. In November 2003, the Home Office indicated that applications are not to be made in person to the ASU but that the best way to make the application was by letter with supporting documentation to the Asylum Casework Group, CMU8, 11 Floor, Lunar House, Croydon CR9 2BY (see correspondence from the Home Office to Deighton Guedalla Solicitors, November 2003). No application form or fee is required.

If the application for transfer is successful, the applicant will be granted leave for five years. They will be eligible for settlement after that time. The applicant will be subject to the same policy on reviews and settlement as applies in ordinary refugee cases (see API, *Transfer of Refugee Status*, para. 5.1).

Applications for asylum made from abroad

The above categories all concern people who have already been accepted as qualifying for some sort of protection and who are, effectively, applying for resettlement to the UK. In rare cases, the Home Office (on referrals from entry clearance officers) will agree to the admission of people who have not yet been recognised where they have made an application for entry clearance to come to the UK on asylum grounds from a third country. The following conditions must all be met (API, *Special applications: applications from abroad*):

- the applicant is a refugee within the meaning of the Refugee Convention;
- the applicant has close ties with the UK; and
- the UK is the most appropriate country of refuge.

For the meaning of 'close ties' and 'most appropriate country of refuge', see above under 'Mandate refugees' – the same meanings apply. These applications are exceptional. In most cases, the post is likely to encourage the applicant to approach the authorities in the third country for asylum, or to consult the local UNHCR representative.

PREVENTING ASYLUM-SEEKERS COMING TO THE UK

In common with other European countries, the UK has developed policies with the aim of discouraging potential asylum-seekers. While paying lip service to their international commitments, successive governments have introduced a range of administrative measures, the aims of which have been to reduce the number of persons arriving in the UK and claiming asylum. Recent measures are set out in the table below. They include measures that actually stop people from arriving in the UK and which are intended to deter people from wanting to claim asylum here. As the political debate about asylum has become increasingly intense, these measures have been introduced against a backdrop of widespread stigmatising of asylum-seekers by sections of the press and media as well as some leading politicians. The most frequently presented negative image is of asylum-seekers being mainly economic migrants abusing the asylum system.

The view of the present government is that, since the later 1980s there has been abuse of the asylum system by economic migrants claiming to be persecuted. According to the government:

'The major factors in encouraging this have been a slow and bureaucratic system of decision-making and appeals, and practical problems in returning failed applicants to the countries from which they have come given lack of co-operation from overseas Governments. This has left people believing they will be able to stay even if they have no right to be here.' (*Controlling Our Borders, Making Migration Work for Britain*, February 2005, para. 26)

The government is proud of having reduced the numbers of those seeking asylum from a peak of nearly 9,000 per month in October 2002 to under 3,000 per month by the start of 2005.

Effect of measures to prevent asylum-seekers

The effect of increasingly stringent methods of control aimed at deterring and preventing asylum-seekers from reaching countries of refuge, such as the UK, is that genuine asylum-seekers are increasingly thwarted in their attempts to flee persecution. Asylum-seekers are forced to rely upon irregular means of travelling to countries of refuge because there are insufficient legal routes for them to flee their countries and seek asylum. This is despite the fact that the right to seek asylum is part of international human rights law (see Article 14 of the Universal Declaration of Human Rights). Asylum-seekers are, by definition, usually unable to approach the authorities of their own country in order to obtain passports or exit visas. Even to approach the embassy of another country to apply for a visa could place them in great danger. Also, except in the rarest cases, asylum-seekers are unable to obtain a visa in order to seek asylum. As a result, asylum-seekers are forced to resort to agents, forged documents or clandestine entry in order to seek asylum. The very restricted routes for asylum-seekers to make applications from abroad are set out earlier in this chapter (▶see 696–701).

Under Article 31 of the Refugee Convention, refugees should not however be prosecuted on account of their illegal entry if they have travelled directly from the country where they fear persecution and claim asylum within a short time of their arrival (▶see further 1235–6). The High Court has decided that the UK is bound to honour this obligation (*Adimi*). In the same case, the Court commented that states which have signed the Refugee Convention seem to be 'increasingly striving' to prevent the arrival of asylum-seekers and that the combined effect of visa requirements and carriers' liability made it 'well-nigh impossible' for refugees to travel to countries of refuge without the use of false documents.

Measures such as visa regimes and carrier sanctions do not result in fewer asylum-seekers but rather in the increased use of illegal and, very often, dangerous means of securing entry. As certain recent cases both in the UK and in the Republic of Ireland have shown, the need to resort to these illegal means can result in tragedy with asylum-seekers having been discovered dead in the containers in which they have hidden.

PREVENTING AND DETERRING ASYLUM-SEEKERS

Visa regimes

A national of any of the countries listed as 'visa national' countries cannot travel to the UK without first obtaining an entry clearance (or 'visa'). The immigration rules do not allow applicants to apply for entry clearance to come to the UK to seek asylum. As economic or political instability affects particular countries, they are often added to this list so that it is harder for asylum-seekers from those countries to reach the UK. Recent examples are Zimbabwe, which was added to the list in November 2002, and Jamaica, which became a visa national country in January 2003.

Carriers' liability legislation and civil penalties

People without entry clearances still manage to travel to the UK and claim asylum. For this reason the Home Office enlisted the airlines to assist in immigration control through the Immigration (Carriers' Liability) Act 1987. This provided that airlines could be fined for each passenger they bring to the UK who does not have the correct documentation. This means that the airlines check people's documents and refuse to let them board unless they have valid documentation. The 1987 Act was repealed and replaced by Part II of the Immigration and Asylum Act 1999, which extended liability to the carriage of clandestine entrants in any vehicle, ship or aircraft.

Preventing asylum-seekers as transit passengers

The 1993 Act extended carriers' liability to transit passengers. It also created powers for the Home Office to decide which transit passengers are required to have entry clearance. The intention was to put an obstacle in the way of those who would otherwise seek to claim asylum in the UK while in transit. Recently, in June and October 2003, the Home Office has sought to prevent asylum-seekers from claiming asylum while in transit by adding some 22 countries to the list of countries who require a Direct Airside Transit Visa (DATV). For further details about transit visas and DATVs, ►see 243–6.

Checks abroad

Increasingly, immigration officials are being stationed abroad to advise airlines whether passports and entry clearances are genuine. They are called 'Airline Liaison Officers' (ALOs). In 2003, over 33,000 people were prevented from boarding at airports where ALOs operated. The government plans to expand the network of ALOs year on year. This is dangerous for those who wish to flee but who are banned from travelling by their national authorities as those authorities may be alerted to their attempts to leave when they are stopped at the airport. From 2001, immigration officers were stationed at Prague Airport in order to screen passengers boarding flights to the UK to determine whether they were potential asylum-seekers or overstayers. In the *Roma Rights Centre* case, the House of Lords declared the system to be unlawful as it was being operated so as to discriminate against people of Roma background (►see 892–3).

For a period in 2000, the British Embassy in Khartoum began asking some entry clearance applicants to sign a declaration that they did not fear persecution in Sudan and would not claim asylum on arrival in the UK. The implication was that anyone who refused to sign would not be believed as to the true purpose of their entry clearance application, or their intention to leave the UK at the end of their visit. Of course, such a requirement can have no value in assessing the credibility of a subsequent asylum claim i.e. where someone has signed such a declaration in order to escape from persecution.

Controls in Northern France and Belgium

UK immigration officers operate controls at departure points in France and Belgium in order to prevent the access of asylum-seekers to the UK. New technology has been introduced for searching freight for asylum-seekers in Calais (January 2003) and in Vissingen, Ostend and Zeebrugge (December 2003).

Detention and fast tracking

Large numbers of asylum-seekers are detained during the course of their asylum applications and the numbers are set to increase. The various detained and fast track processes are described earlier in this chapter. The government intends to step-up this process so that, by the end of 2005, up to 30 per cent of new asylum applicants will be put through a detained, fast track process (see the government's five-year strategy).

Access to support

Since 1996, governments have introduced increasingly restrictive arrangements for support. In 1996, asylum-seekers who failed to claim on arrival were removed from the social security system. In 1999/2000, the 'interim' and full asylum support systems were introduced, together with dispersal and vouchers. In January 2003, those who did not claim asylum 'as soon as reasonably practicable' were denied access to asylum support under section 55 2002 Act. Section 9 of the 2004 Act enables the withdrawal of support from failed asylum-seekers with families in the UK (for further details about welfare, ▶see Section 12).

Criminal liability

The 2004 Act imposes criminal liability on persons (expected to be asylum-seekers) who present themselves without travel documentation or a reasonable excuse for not having such documents (▶see 683–6).

For details about further developments relating to border controls, ▶see 40–1 and 49.

23 Home Office decisions on asylum

This chapter is about the way in which the Home Office makes decisions on asylum and the nature of those decisions. The system has become more complicated since the Home Office reverted to a system of limited leave and reviews from 30 August 2005.

The legal conditions that need to be satisfied in order to qualify for asylum under the Refugee Convention are set out in Chapter 21. Obviously, in deciding who qualifies, the Home Office is bound by the interpretation of the Refugee Convention handed down by the courts, as set out in that chapter. Nevertheless, the Home Office has also issued guidance and check-lists to its case-workers in order to help them to decide whether the legal conditions for asylum are met. It is sometimes worth checking to see whether the approach in a refusal is in accordance with the Home Office's own interpretation of the law (see API *Deciding Claims – Assessing the Asylum Claim*). That instruction emphasises (para. 3):

'Caseworkers must assess objectively in each individual case whether there is a reasonable likelihood of the fear of persecution being realised should the applicant be returned to their country of origin. The aim is to identify the genuine refugee as quickly as possible. When applying the test of reasonable likelihood, if the considerations are finely balanced, the benefit of the doubt should always be given to the applicant.'

This chapter

First in this chapter, we look at the important question of the country information available to Home Office case workers when making asylum decisions (▶706–8).

Next we discuss a central question that arises in many cases – the 'credibility' of what the applicant has stated. The 2004 Act contains new provisions setting out factors that must be taken into account in determining credibility (▶708–15). We then deal briefly with 'non-compliance' refusals, and cases where the asylum-seeker is said to be part of a 'group' (▶715–7).

We then deal with delays in the asylum process, and delays in issuing status papers to successful appellants (▶717–9).

Next we come to the asylum decision itself, and look at both grants of asylum and negative asylum decisions (sometimes accompanied by a grant of humanitarian protection or discretionary leave), at the new policy on leave and reviews in refugee, HP and DL cases, and at appeal rights (▶719–30). Finally, we look at the possibility of making 'fresh' asylum or human rights claims (▶730–5). For decisions and reviews in refugee, HP and DL cases, ▶see in particular the table at 721–7.

For details of asylum procedures (including: screening; 'fast track' detention processes; the development of the 'new asylum model'; prosecutions under the 2004 Act; dependants; unaccompanied minors; permission to work; 'special' applications from abroad; and voluntary returns) ▶see Chapter 22.

For details about 'third country' asylum cases, ▶see Chapter 24.

There are certain aspects of this chapter that overlap with Section 10 of the *Handbook*, on appeals. That section also deals with the circumstances in which the Home Office may certify an asylum or human rights claim as being 'clearly unfounded', with the result that there is no right of appeal against the decision while the applicant remains in the UK (▶1073–8). Note that the old system, under the 1999 Act, of 'certifying' claims for asylum (and/or human rights) so as to prevent appeals beyond the first tier (at that time, the Adjudicator) has ceased. Section 10 also deals with certificates issued under section 96 of the 2002 Act in order to prevent a claim from attracting a right of appeal where there has been an earlier appeal, or at least the possibility of an earlier appeal (▶1067–9). Such certificates are touched on in this chapter at the point where we deal with fresh claims.

HOME OFFICE COUNTRY INFORMATION

The Home Office considers applications in the light of the detailed information it has about the situation in different countries, and of how the applicant's history fits in with this. It also takes into account policy information made available to caseworkers. The various sources that caseworkers refer to, which are posted on the IND website, are set out below. The first source, country reports, is prepared by the Home Office's 'Country and Information Policy Unit' (CIPU). Under the 2002 Act, an Advisory Panel on Country Information (APCI) (▶see 1505 for address) was set up, and comprises a number of academics and representatives from organisations working in the country information and refugee fields. Its brief is to provide advice on CIPU's country material and to review and provide advice on its sources, methods of research, and quality control. APCI first met on 2 September 2003. In carrying out its reviews, the Panel accepts, and indeed invites, written representations from individuals and organisations. The papers and minutes of the Panel's meetings are published on its website, at www.apci.org.uk.

Where a case raises questions about particular events, Home Office case-workers deciding a claim are also able to contact CIPU for specific advice. Sometimes CIPU, in turn, may contact the Foreign and Commonwealth Office for more information.

For sources of country evidence generally ▶see 1107–9. For general evidence in asylum claims ▶see 665–7.

Country Reports

These reports provide general background information about the country issues that are most commonly raised in asylum and human rights claims. They do not contain Home Office opinion or policy. Each country assessment gives a brief summary of the country's history, geography, and political and human rights situation, drawing together information from a wide range of sources. They are updated twice yearly, in April and October. However, the country reports are only summaries. In introducing them on its website, the Home Office states: 'They are not intended to be a detailed or comprehensive survey.'

Quality of country reports The Home Office has been criticised for producing summaries that do not always accurately reflect what is generally known about the conditions in each country. The sources for the country conditions described in the body of each assessment are contained in footnotes towards the end, and the source material of any particularly contentious statement should be checked. CIPU itself keeps a copy of all the original source material referred to in the assessments. Immigration lawyers also frequently find that Home Office reasons for refusing asylum are contradicted by parts of the country assessment. Because the assessment attempts to summarise lots of sources, which may themselves be conflicting, they are often themselves contradictory. Applicants and their advisers should therefore conduct their own research into the relevant country conditions.

Countries for which there are reports Country reports are produced on the 20 countries that generate the largest number of asylum applications in the UK, plus any countries for which a particular operational need to have a report has been identified. As of May 2005, there were reports for: Afghanistan, Angola, Bangladesh, China, Democratic Republic of Congo, Eritrea, Liberia, India, Iran, Iraq, Jamaica, Nigeria, Pakistan, Serbia and Montenegro, Somalia, Sudan, Turkey, Uganda, Vietnam and Zimbabwe.

The number of countries for which the Home Office produces reports has shrunk since the last edition of the *Handbook*, in May 2002. Between that time and the present, the following countries have fallen off the list of countries for which a report is routinely produced: Albania, Algeria, Burundi, Cameroon, Colombia, Czech Republic, Ecuador, Ethiopia, Ghana, Kenya, Lebanon, Lithuania, Poland, Romania, Russia, Rwanda, Sierra Leone, Sri Lanka, Ukraine and Federal Republic of Yugoslavia. During the same period, the following countries have been added to the list of those that have reports prepared for them: Liberia, Jamaica and Serbia and Montenegro.

Bulletins

'Bulletins' are issued throughout the year, and also give information on conditions in individual countries. The purpose of the bulletins is to up-date the country reports by looking at changes in country conditions between the publication of the reports. However, the website contains back-copies of bulletins for previous years, and it also contains bulletins on countries for which there is no present country report (for example, Chad, Georgia, Guinea, Lebanon and Yemen, among others). Therefore, even if there is no country report on the applicant's country , it is worth checking to see if there is a bulletin.

Operational Guidance Notes

Operational Guidance Notes (OGNs) are produced by the Asylum and Appeals Policy Directorate. They provide a summary of country conditions, together with policy guidance on the main types of claim from the country that are likely to result in an applicant qualifying for asylum, humanitarian protection or discretionary leave. Operational Guidance Notes generally cross-refer to the existing country report for evidence about country conditions.

Fact-finding missions

Occasionally, CIPU arranges fact-finding missions to countries that produce asylum-seekers, in order to obtain information relevant to the issues that arise in asylum applications. Members of the missions interview both governmental and non-governmental organisations. There are presently fact-finding mission reports for Cameroon, Eritrea, India, Iraq (several), Nigeria, Rwanda, Somalia and Sri Lanka.

Importance of country evidence

Because there is often no individual proof or evidence to substantiate a fear of persecution, a decision will depend on the Home Office's assessment of the person's truthfulness. Background country evidence is important to the question of credibility, because if an asylum-seeker gives an account that fits in with what is generally known about the country, this supports their credibility. The courts have consistently emphasised that a credibility assessment should be made in the light of the objective country conditions.

CREDIBILITY AND THE EFFECT OF THE 2004 ACT

The success of an asylum application often depends on whether the applicant's account is believed. Many feel that negative credibility findings in relation to asylum-seekers are far too easily reached. The higher courts have warned against decision-making in immigration cases which focuses on credibility as though deciding whether someone is 'credible' were an end in itself. In truth, what is required is that the decision-maker assesses all of the evidence in order to determine whether there is a real risk of persecution on return. In considering a case, decision-makers must not exclude evidence of past events from their global assessment, unless they are in no doubt that they did *not* in fact occur (see the decision of the Court of Appeal in **Karanakaran**). The courts have also consistently repeated that the plausibility of events must be carefully judged against the back-cloth of evidence of country conditions, which may throw light upon the situation (see above for the Home Office's use of country evidence).

Despite the dangers of an over-emphasis on credibility distorting asylum decision-making, decision-makers are faced with a raft of provisions which require them to have regard to a range of specific matters in determining 'credibility'. This approach appears to be contrary to that recommended by the UNHCR, which has stated that:

'It is not advisable to list the factors which should be given special consideration in assessing an asylum-seeker's credibility. Evaluation of credibility is a process which involves the consideration of many complex factors, both objective and subjective, which are impossible to enumerate. Since all these may be equally important, singling out any of these factors will, by necessity, be incomplete and arbitrary.'

The matters decision-makers are told to have regard to are not even matters relating directly to the substance of the claim; they focus instead on the subsequent behaviour of the asylum-seeker.

Credibility under the Asylum and Immigration Act 2004

Section 8 of the 2004 Act requires decision-makers to take into account certain specified matters as 'damaging [the applicant's] credibility' when the decision-maker considers whether to believe a statement made by, or on behalf of, the applicant. It is likely that this relates to statements of applicants, and of their representatives made on their behalf, *but not* to separate statements made by witnesses in support of the claim. It applies to both asylum and human rights claims, and it applies to both the immigration authorities deciding the claim and to the AIT and to SIAC. If an applicant engages in behaviour which is not specifically mentioned in section 8, but the decision-maker thinks that the behaviour still undermines the applicant's credibility, it may still take it into account (see s8(12) 2004 Act).

Most of the matters in section 8 were previously contained in the immigration rules as matters which the *Home Office* would refer to in assessing credibility. On the same date that section 8 came into force, 1 January 2005, the rules were amended to delete from them the matters transferred into the Act. However, the rules still contain additional matters that must be taken into account in determining credibility, and that are not contained in section 8 (▶see below 714–5).

Application to *all* decisions from 1 January 2005 Section 8 also applies to decisions of the old Adjudicators and IAT that were taken between 1 January 2005 and the commencement of the AIT, on 4 April 2005 (see s8(13) 2004 Act). There may be appeals against such decisions that are still in the system. In *MM (Section 8: Commencement) Iran*, the AIT confirmed that section 8 also applies to decisions made after 1 January 2005 even if the claim was made before that date. The AIT also found that section 8 did not have a retrospective effect that was unlawful.

Extent to which the relevant factors damage credibility Although the decision-maker must take account of the factors set out in section 8, the extent to which they will actually damage an applicant's credibility (if at all) will depend on the circumstances of the case. While the Act was being considered, the Minister stated:

'The deciding authority will have discretion to decide what weight to give to [relevant behaviour], taking into account all factors relevant to the claim. The requirement to take that behaviour into account is not determinative of credibility and does not displace the obligation to consider all the circumstances of the case.' (Letter of Beverley Hughes MP to the Parliamentary Joint Committee on Human Rights, 27 January 2004, published as an appendix to the Committee's report)

In *SM (Section 8: Judge's process)*, the AIT held that even where section 8 applies to a case, an immigration judge should look at the evidence as a whole and decide which parts are more important and which less. Section 8 does not require the behaviour to which it applies to be treated as the starting point of the assessment of credibility (paras 7–10).

The section 8 factors are set out in turn below. In a case where any of the factors applies, applicants and their advisers must try to explain the circumstances, and why the matter does not damage the applicant's credibility.

Failure to claim before being 'notified' of an 'immigration decision'

The Act requires account to be taken of a failure by an applicant to make an asylum or human rights claim before they have been 'notified' of an 'immigration decision'. For these purposes, an 'immigration decision' is any of the following:

- a refusal of leave to enter or remain in the UK;
- a *grant* of leave to enter or remain;
- a decision to remove an applicant;
- a decision to deport an applicant;
- a decision to 'take action' connected to the applicant's extradition from the UK.

There are specific provisions that deal with the meaning of 'notified' in this context. Under those provisions, a person is taken to have been notified if they or their representative are given notice of the decision in any of the following ways (see Immigration (Claimant's Credibility) Regulations 2004):

- orally (including over the telephone);
- in writing, given by hand;
- in writing sent by fax, email or post to an address given by the applicant or their representative.

The above regulations also contain provisions about presuming that the applicant has received the notice unless it is proved otherwise.

So, this general factor is aimed at people in a number of situations. Leaving aside extradition cases, it may be used against:

- those who try to enter in some other capacity (such as visitor or student) and are refused entry, and then make an asylum and/or human rights claim;
- those who do manage to obtain entry in some other capacity, and only later make a claim;
- those who have been in the UK for some period of time who are then refused leave to remain;
- those in the UK who the Home Office decides to remove, and who then make a claim.

Justified delays in claiming   Many applicants will be unable or unwilling to apply immediately on arrival in the UK. People who have been tortured or brutally treated by officials may be traumatised, and will not be able to tell their story to the first official they meet. Organisations dealing with torture victims know that it can take a long time to build sufficient trust to talk freely about such experiences. The requirement is contrary to the spirit of paragraph 198 of the *UNHCR Handbook*, which states that people may well be afraid to give full and accurate accounts of their cases because of their past experiences. The case of *Ejon* is helpful, as it confirms that victims of torture can be expected to be reluctant to talk about their experiences without this necessarily affecting their credibility.

In many cases, people may legitimately hesitate before making an asylum application once they have escaped from immediate danger. Applying for asylum is a drastic step, it means cutting off the possibility of returning to one's home country and they may fear that it will put relatives and friends in danger. People are often reluctant to do this, and need time to think through the consequences with advisers or with others from the same community. For others, a failure to claim asylum immediately may simply be a reflection of their lack of knowledge of asylum procedures; or they may have been instructed by an agent, keen to avoid detection and to retrieve false travel documents after passage through controls, not to claim at the port of entry.

Last minute claims Even those who make 'last-minute' claims may still have claims with merit. For example, it may be that the applicant had every expectation of being able to remain in the UK on other grounds, and had no need to rely on asylum. They may only have claimed when, due to unforeseen events, they were suddenly faced with the prospect of removal.

Certain refugees 'sur place' Section 8 makes clear that claiming late is not a factor that should count against credibility if the claim is made 'wholly' as a result of circumstances that have arisen *after* the notification of the immigration decision. An asylum applicant who bases their claim on post-arrival events cannot be criticised for not claiming on arrival, or indeed until the relevant circumstances changed. Refugees in this position are called, by the French, refugees *sur place* (▶see also 613). The decision to claim for a person already happily residing abroad is a big one. Delays by such applicants can often be explained by their not wanting to cut ties, hoping for improvements, or not having sufficient information about changes in country conditions and how they may affect them.

Concealing information, providing misleading information or causing delay

Under section 8, decision-makers must take account of *any* behaviour they think is 'designed or likely' to conceal information, to mislead, or to obstruct or delay a decision on the claim. Examples given in the Act of conduct that *must* be treated as having this effect are:

- a failure, without a reasonable explanation, to produce a passport on request to the immigration authorities;
- presenting a document as a valid passport when it is not;
- destroying, altering or getting rid of a passport without a reasonable explanation;
- destroying, altering or getting rid of a ticket 'or other document connected with travel' without a reasonable explanation;
- failure, without reasonable explanation, to answer a question asked by a decision-maker.

For these purposes, 'passports' includes travel documents. A 'valid' passport is one that relates to the person producing it, has not been wrongly altered, and was not obtained by deception. The Home Office's concern is that people may destroy documents or return them to agents who will use them again. It is also concerned that applicants may have travelled through another country to which they would be returnable but that they are attempting to hide this so that their application will be considered in the UK. In all cases of failure to produce, or of destruction/alteration of documents, section 8 acknowledges that there may be a 'reasonable explanation'. Very often applicants will have been following the instructions of the only person they have to assist and guide them – namely an agent –

when they destroyed documents or handed the documents back. In a case concerning section 55 2002 Act (access to support and claiming asylum as soon as reasonably practicable), but which has relevance here as well, the Court of Appeal (see *R (Q) v SSHD*) noted that:

'...[to] disregard the effect that [agents] may have on their charges would be both unrealistic and unjust...'

As to those who present documents as though valid when they are not, for all the reasons discussed above, asylum-seekers may not feel secure enough on arrival to reveal the details of their case. These may include details of the documents on which they are travelling. The applicant may think that, if they reveal that they are using false documents, they could face immediate refusal and return to the country of danger.

Failure to claim asylum in a safe country

Decision-makers must also take into account a failure by an applicant to 'take advantage of a reasonable opportunity' to make an asylum or human rights claim in a 'safe country'. For these purposes, a 'safe country' is a country that is on the 'first list' of safe countries contained in Schedule 3 to the 2004 Act for the purposes of the third country regime (▶see 740–1).

Section 8 requires there to have been a 'reasonable' opportunity. In the part of the immigration rules dealing with the separate question of whether an applicant can be returned to a third country, reference is made simply to 'an opportunity at the border or within the third country'. The case-law on this immigration rule has interpreted the question of 'opportunity' of claiming in an objective, restrictive sense (▶see 747). The word 'reasonably' in section 8 suggests that a greater range of factors may be taken into account before deciding that the matter should damage an applicant's credibility. In particular, the fact that an applicant is acting reasonably under the influence of an agent in not claiming elsewhere is surely of importance under section 8.

Failure to claim before arrest

Decision-makers must take into account the fact than an applicant has failed to make a claim before being arrested for any of the following reasons:

- because they are liable to be detained under the administrative powers of detention under the 1971 Act;
- in relation to certain immigration offences (see under ss28A, 28AA, s28B, s28C 1971 Act);
- in relation to certain non-immigration offences for which immigration officers have the power of arrest (chiefly offences of fraud, theft, deception, trafficking, marriage; see s14 2004 Act for a full list);
- in relation to extradition.

This factor is to be taken into account unless either:

- the applicant had no 'reasonable opportunity' to make the claim before the arrest; or
- the claim relies 'wholly' on circumstances which have arisen *after* the arrest.

The immigration rules and credibility

After 1 January 2005, the immigration rules only refer specifically to three matters that the Home Office will additionally take into account as possibly damaging credibility (see para. 341 HC 395, as amended from 1 January 2005 by HC 164). The rules give these matters only as 'examples' of matters that can be taken into account. There is also nothing to prevent the AIT too having regard to them. They are set out in turn below. For further details of the Home Office's approach to credibility, see the API *Deciding Claims – Assessing the Asylum Claim*, under 'Assessing the veracity of the claim' (para. 10) and under 'Credibility' (para. 11).

False evidence or claims

'The applicant has adduced manifestly false evidence in support of his application, or has otherwise made false representations, either orally or in writing.' (para. 341(i) HC 395)

Often, and not just in asylum cases, people who have a good case are tempted to make their claims more elaborate in order to try to strengthen them further, because they are afraid of refusal. Making sure that this does not happen depends on getting good, early advice. If a person has already embroidered their claim with additional information that is clearly not true, then careful advice should be obtained about how this can be explained.

Application for asylum made in another country

'The applicant has lodged concurrent applications for asylum in the UK or in another country.' (para. 341(ii) HC 395)

If applications are made in more than one country, the Home Office will wonder whether the asylum-seeker is 'shopping' to see which will accept the claim, or using asylum as a basis for foreign travel for reasons other than a need for protection. It is possible that the Home Office may request details of the previous application, and then compare them with those given in the application made in the UK. If a claim has been made in another country, rather than considering whether the person is a refugee or not, the Home Office may also seek to return the asylum-seeker to that country on 'third-country' grounds (▶see Chapter 24).

Actions of agents

The rules also state that the actions of anyone acting as an 'agent' of the asylum applicant may be taken into account in considering the above factors (para. 342 HC 395). No definition of 'agent' is given. An asylum application may therefore be adversely affected by the actions of corrupt agents in the country of origin, incompetent advisers, or any friends who try to assist or advise the applicant. If relevant, these actions should be carefully explained. It is essential for advisers to make sure that any information put forward in connection with a claim is complete and correct, and that it is first agreed with the applicant. Statements or the contents of letters of representation should always be translated back to the applicant, so that they can confirm information being provided to the Home Office.

Inconsistent activities

Until 1 January 2005, the rules also stated that the following matter may damage credibility:

'The applicant has undertaken any activities in the UK before or after lodging his application which are inconsistent with his previous beliefs and behaviour and calculated to create or substantially enhance his claim to refugee status.' (previously para. 341(vi) HC 395)

The fact that this factor has been deleted does not mean that it will not be taken into account. A person who has been in clandestine opposition in their home country may be able to act more openly once in the relative safety of the UK and, therefore, they may have difficulty in showing that their views expressed in the UK are a continuation of long-held beliefs. Equally, public involvement in the UK may make it more dangerous to return to the country from which asylum is sought.

In **Senga** the High Court agreed that, depending on the circumstances, the fact that an application for asylum had been made at all could put a person in danger from the authorities of his or her country. While recognising this point in principle, in **Mbanza** the Court of Appeal indicated that this was only likely to be true in very few cases. The Court noted that a fraudulent claim to asylum was itself likely to undermine the credibility of any claim that a person has any real fear as a result of making the claim. However, as the Court of Appeal made clear in **Danian**, the ultimate question is whether the claimant has a well-founded fear of being persecuted for a Convention reason, and not whether they are to blame for creating that fear (►see further at 614). It was also recognised in **Danian** that any applicant who was at risk would, in any case, be able to raise Article 3 ECHR (►see also 796).

'NON-COMPLIANCE' REFUSALS AND 'GROUP' DECISIONS

A controversial means of disposing of asylum applications is to refuse them on 'non-compliance' grounds. The immigration rules state the following:

'A failure, without reasonable explanation, to make a prompt and full disclosure of material factors, either orally or in writing, or otherwise to assist the Secretary of State in establishing the facts of the case may lead to the refusal of an asylum application. This includes failure to comply with a notice issued by the Secretary of State or an Immigration Officer requiring the applicant to report to a designated place to be finger-printed, or failure to complete an asylum questionnaire, or failure to comply with a request to attend an interview concerning the applica-tion, or failure to comply with a requirement to report to an immigra-tion officer for examination...' (para. 340 HC 395)

In *Ali Haddad*, the IAT ruled that, even if an asylum-seeker has not com-plied with requirements made by the Home Office, cases should not be decided either by the Home Office or on appeal on that basis alone. The decision-maker must always consider the *actual evidence* before them that attempts to show that the person is a refugee. If a non-compliance case does go to appeal, representatives should therefore ensure that they fully prepare the case with all of the evidence necessary to show that removing the appellant will be in breach of the Refugee Convention.

Previous chaos in non-compliance refusals

In 2000 the Home Office started refusing a large number of claims on the basis that the applicants had not submitted their asylum questionnaires (Statement of Evidence Forms – 'SEFs') within the ten-day time-limit set. It soon became apparent that there was a systematic failure at the Home Office to link the forms to applicants' files, and that, in the vast majority of cases, applicants had in fact lodged the SEF in time. This placed many asylum-seekers in considerable difficulties, as the negative decision affect-ed their entitlements to benefits, made them liable to be dispersed under the NASS scheme, and affected their ability to obtain permission to work. Even when the asylum-seeker demonstrated that the form had been sent in in time, the Home Office initially refused to withdraw the decision to refuse asylum.

The problem came to court in the cases of *Karoaglan, Hadavi & Bashiri*. At this point, in May 2001, the Home Office agreed to change its policy and to withdraw decisions where, within three months of the decision, evidence was produced to the Home Office that the asylum-seeker had complied with the ten-day limit, and a request was made that the erron-eous decision be withdrawn. Approximately 7,000 cases were affected.

Application as part of a 'group' of other asylum-seekers

The immigration rules specifically refer to asylum applications where the applicant is 'part of a group whose claims are clearly not related to the criteria for refugee status in the Convention' (see para. 344 HC 395). In such a case, the rules state that the claim may be refused without exam-ination of the applicant's individual claim. Under the rule, the Home Office is still, however, required to have regard to:

'…any evidence produced by the individual to show that his claim should be distinguished.'

This is a provision that allows for accelerated and unsafe decision-making, and is against the spirit of the Convention, which requires that each case be assessed individually. It begs the questions of what is a 'group', and what or who is 'clearly' outside the Convention. It allows for the kind of stereo-typed, cursory decision-making that in the past has allowed Tamils and Kurds, later granted full refugee status, to be labelled initially as 'bogus'.

DELAYS IN MAKING DECISIONS AND ISSUING DOCUMENTS

Delays in making decisions and issuing documents have been a historical problem in asylum cases. The backlog that built up was greatly exacer-bated by the operational reorganisation caused by the Home Office's physical relocations in 1998/99 and 2001. Outside the Home Office's fast-track processes (▶see 673–83), the aim of the Home Office has been to decide claims within two months, and for appeals to be resolved in the following four months.

The Home Office claims to have dramatically reduced processing times between 1997, when they took an average of 22 months, and 2005, when it claims to make decisions within two months in approximately 82 per cent of cases. It further claims that around 60 per cent of cases go through the whole process, including the appeal system, within six months of the claim being made (Annex 2 of the government's five-year strategy, *Controlling Our Borders*). The new asylum model (▶see at 641–4) aims to speed up processing times further.

Backlog clearance concessions

The Home Office recognises the problem of claims being outstanding for many years, and it has for many years had a general policy of granting some form of leave where a claim has been undecided for seven years without a decision from the Home Office. Over the years, the Home Office has also had specific policies that have benefited specific categories of people who have experienced delay in the system:

1998 concession The government White Paper, *Fairer, Faster, Firmer* (July 1998) announced a concession for particular categories of applicant whose claims had been delayed. This related to claims made before 1 July 1993 and to claims made between 1 July 1993 and 31 December 1995. It is very unlikely that there are any claims which still go back this far and, in any event, they will have been outstanding for more than seven years. For details of the 1998 policy, see p. 220 of the 2002 edition of the *Handbook*.

Concession for asylum-seeking families For details of the recent con-cession for asylum-seeking families, ▶see 668–9. Note that some families may also qualify under the general 'seven-year' concession relating to children who have long residence (▶see 388–9).

Delays in issuing documents

A further problem has been the delay in providing documents to those whose asylum or human rights claims are successful – in particular for those who are successful on appeal. There have been cases of successful asylum-seekers applying for judicial review on the basis that they were being caused real hardship as a result. In *Deniz Mersin*, the High Court considered an asylum-seeker who had won his appeal against refusal but who had not received a grant of refugee status after seven and a half months. The Court decided that the Home Office had a duty to accept the Adjudicator's decision, given that it did not appeal against it, and grant the applicant leave within a reasonable time, having regard to the prejudice caused to him. In another case involving post-appeal delay, *Mambakasa*, the High Court stated that, although the applicant had already obtained his status papers by the time of the full hearing in the High Court, it was likely that a court would have intervened if papers had not been issued after about four months (this decision was not disturbed on appeal to the Court of Appeal). That was a case in which the applicant was suffering psychologically and wanted to sponsor an application for family reunion by his family, who were stranded abroad in a third country.

Delay cases depend on individual facts Delay cases are, however, fact-sensitive. There is no set time after which the failure to issue documents to a successful refugee will become unlawful. All will depend on the circumstances – not least the level of detriment being suffered by the applicant. The detriment is often severe, in addition to the above matters: applicants usually cannot work; may still be subject to reporting restrictions, and cannot travel. In addition, they may have difficulty accessing welfare support. They cannot usually receive benefits because they are 'subject to immigration control', since they have no leave. Also, after a grace period following the disposal of the appeal, their asylum support will cease because they are no longer 'asylum-seekers' within the meaning of the asylum support legislation (▶see 1343–5). For the possibility of applying for 'hard cases' support (▶see 1381–7).

Mistakes in documents When status letters are issued, often there have been problems with letters concerning mistakes as to the person's name and date of birth. This can lead to delays in establishing entitlements, and needs to be remedied immediately by sending the document back to the Home Office for correction.

Alternatives to judicial review Depending on how urgently the applicant needs their status papers, the following remedies are alternatives to judicial review: making a complaint to the Home Office (▶see 1223–7); or asking an MP to refer the matter to the Parliamentary Ombudsman (▶1229–35). In some cases, by taking these steps, applicants may be able to secure some form of financial compensation where they have been badly affected. If the new refugee has a 'sunrise' caseworker or 'Time together' mentor working with them (▶see 727), they may be able to help with these problems. For problems with NINOs ▶see 1283–4.

THE HOME OFFICE DECISION AND REVIEWS

After the Home Office has made a decision on an asylum application under the Refugee Convention, it must be communicated to the asylum-seeker. In many cases, asylum claims overlap with human rights claims, and applicants either expressly or implicitly make a human rights claim at the same time as they make their asylum claim. If a human rights claim has been made as well as an asylum claim, the matter progresses through the system in exactly the same way as if only an asylum claim had been made. Also, even if asylum is refused, the Home Office will always consider whether the applicant should succeed on human rights grounds. This will therefore involve considering whether to grant 'Humanitarian Protection' (HP) or 'Discretionary Leave' (DL). From 1 April 2003, these forms of leave have replaced what was previously asylum-related 'exceptional leave'.

The labels the Home Office uses for the different forms of leave are unnecessarily confusing. For a full understanding of the recent history of the different forms of asylum-related leave, ▶see 859–62. For an understanding of who qualifies for HP and DL, ▶see the tables at 862–5 and the explanations that follow (▶866–73). For an understanding of the system of leave and reviews in the refugee, HP, DL and ELR categories ▶see the table below at 721–7.

Because the grant of 'exceptional leave' to certain failed asylum-seekers has been abolished, we do not describe it here. For details of the previous practice and the length of leave previously granted, see pp. 216–18 of the 2002 edition of the *Handbook*. *However*, until 2007 there will still be people who have been granted 'exceptional leave' under the arrangements in force until 31 March 2003. Therefore, for the transitional arrangements for those granted exceptional leave and for details about their eligibility for settlement, ▶see 873–5 of this edition.

Decisions to grant refugee status

Strictly speaking, the Home Office does not 'grant' refugee status, but recognises someone as a refugee. This is because, applying the Refugee Convention definition, the applicant has been a refugee since they met the criteria under the Convention even though they have not yet been declared to be one (see para. 28 *UNHCR Handbook*).

The Refugee Convention does not require that states grant permanent residence to refugees. The immigration rules state that those who are recognised will be given limited leave. In *Adan*, the Court of Appeal suggested that it was open to the Home Office to grant limited leave and then seek to return persons previously recognised as refugees if the risk of persecution was later removed. Until the government White Paper *Fairer, Faster, Firmer* was issued in July 1998, refugees were granted leave for four years and could apply for settlement after that time. However, from 27 July 1998 the policy was to grant *indefinite leave* when recognising someone as a refugee. Dependants of refugees were granted indefinite leave in line with the applicant. Indefinite leave cannot have any conditions attached to it, so refugees were permitted to work and there are no restrictions on claiming public funds. The Home Office did, however, state that it would occasionally only grant limited leave to a refugee:

'People accepted as refugees will normally be granted indefinite leave when first recognised or upon request. However, on rare occasions it might be appropriate to refuse indefinite leave if an applicant has been convicted of a serious offence. If indefinite leave is refused because a serious crime has been committed it may be decided to grant (further) leave to remain (e.g. 12 months) in order for further character checks to be made when the applicant next applies...' (API *Deciding Claims – Assessing the Asylum Claim*, para. 14).

Of course, there are some cases where a 'refugee' is excluded from the protection of the Refugee Convention altogether (▶see 624–6), but such applicants are still likely to be granted DL (▶see 863–4, 865, 869).

The government's 'five-year strategy' (February 2005) announced an intention to return to the practice of granting only limited leave. It stated:

'[We will] grant refugees temporary leave to begin with and keep the situation in their countries under review. If it has not improved within five years we would allow them to stay, if it does they will be expected to return.'

Limited leave for refugees has been introduced for those who receive decisions on or after 30 August 2005. If the Home Office wishes to terminate a person's refugee status, it will bear a significant burden to demonstrate that the person has indeed 'ceased' to be a refugee within the meaning of the Convention (for details about cessation, ▶see 627–31 and see below). Maintaining refugees in a state of uncertainty as to their long-term future seems to be directly contrary to the government's general wish to see refugees swiftly integrated into the community.

New Home Office policy on the grant of refugee leave, HP and DL

The revised policies on leave for refugees have led to a complete change in the grants of leave.

Where refugee status is granted on or after 30 August 2005, five years' limited leave will be given. If there has been a very long delay in granting status which has led to a decision being made after that date, applicants can argue that they should still be granted indefinite leave. Similar arguments could be made if the Home Office acknowledges that the reasons for not granting status before that time were completely wrong. The new policies also affect those granted HP and DL. The table below deals with refugees but it also looks at reviews of status for those with HP and/or DL. For further details about leave granted as HP and DL ▶see 862–75.

HOME OFFICE POLICY ON GRANTING LEAVE, REVIEWING STATUS AND CESSATION

The policy on granting leave to both refugees and those who succeed in human rights claims changed radically on Tuesday 30 August 2005.

This table covers the new regime for granting limited leave and indefinite leave for refugees and review of refugee status. It also covers:

- review of status and eventual grant of indefinite leave for those granted humanitarian protection (HP) on or after 30 August 2005;
- active review and review during the period of leave to those granted either HP before 30 August 2005, exceptional leave (ELR) before 1 April 2003 or discretionary leave (DL).

For details about who qualifies for HP and DL and the periods of leave granted, ▶see 862–75 in the section on human rights. For making in-country applications generally, ▶see 125–38.

Where is the present policy to be found?

The present policy is set out in the following Asylum Policy Instructions (APIs) either issued or revised on 30 August 2005: API *Refugee Leave*; API *Active Reviews*; API *Cessation, Cancellation, and Revocation of Refugee Status*; API *Humanitarian Protection* and API *Discretionary Leave*.

Leave granted to refugees and review of their leave

Those granted refugee status on or after 30 August 2005 are granted five years' limited leave. No working or public funds restrictions will be imposed on the leave (API *Refugee Leave*, paras 2.1–2.2; paras 330, 335 HC 395). From July 1998–30 August 2005, refugees were immediately granted indefinite leave, and this still applies to refugees who arrive via resettlement schemes (▶see 696–701; API, *Refugee Leave*, para. 2.3).

The refugee's position will be reviewed in the following three circumstances:

1) the actions of the refugee justify a review (▶722–3) ;
2) there has been a change in country conditions (▶723);
3) the applicant has completed the five-year period of limited leave (▶723–4).

These three situations are looked at in turn below.

Where the refugee has existing limited leave, it may be decided to curtail it under paragraph 323 HC 395. This would either be because they no longer satisfy the rules on which they were granted leave (the Refugee Convention criteria), or because false representations have been made (▶141–3). Alternatively, in the case of an application for further leave, the Home Office can refuse to extend leave. In either case, where the result is that the applicant no longer has leave, there is an appeal to the AIT (see s82(2)(d)(e) 2002 Act). In cases of deception, the Home Office could take 'illegal entry' action (in 'on entry' cases) (▶1013–4), or 'administrative removal' action (in-country cases) (▶1007–8). In cases of misconduct, the Home Office could take deportation proceedings on 'non-conducive' grounds. Either of these latter three courses will result in the invalidation of the existing leave (ss5(1), 33 1971 Act; s10(8) 1999 Act). They may also be used in indefinite leave cases. Indefinite leave can also be revoked if obtained by deception but the person cannot be removed (s76(2) 2002 Act) (▶see 1008). In addition, indefinite leave can be revoked where a person ceases to be a refugee under Article 1C(1)–(4) below (▶see 1008). No-one may be removed in breach of the ECHR. Therefore, in some cases, refugee status will be replaced by HP or DL.

API Cessation, Cancellation and Revocation of Refugee Status uses those three terms to refer to different reasons for withdrawing refugee status in different circumstances. Their use may be confusing. 'Revocation' for example can easily be confused with the 'revocation' of leave (▶see 627–30, 1008). Each of the three terms refers to the withdrawal of refugee status. To simplify matters, we have referred to 'withdrawal' of refugee status as covering all circumstances in which that status is 'taken away'. When describing any consequent immigration action affecting 'leave', we have used the appropriate immigration term (curtailment, variation, invalidation etc).

For details of the likely changes to appeal rights under the 2005 Bill (which will affect refugees who have their status withdrawn), ▶see 1041–6.

1) Actions of the refugee

Where any of the following applies during the time that a refugee has leave, refugee status may be reviewed and leave taken away (see above for the technicalities). These categories are set out in the API *Refugee Leave*, para. 5.

Actions of person suggest they have ceased to be a refugee This applies where an applicant shows that they have 'ceased' to be a refugee under Article 1C(1)-(4) Refugee Convention. This may occur if they have:

- voluntarily re-availed themselves of the protection of their country of nationality;
- voluntarily re-acquired a lost nationality;
- acquired a new nationality and the protection of the new country;
- voluntarily re-established themselves in the country which they left.

For further details of these categories, see API *Cessation, Cancellation and Revocation of Refugee Status* at paras 2.2, 3.3-3.8 and ▶see further 627–30 and 1008.

Actions of refugee suggest they should be excluded from protection under Article 1(F) If, after admission to the UK, there are 'serious reasons for considering' that an applicant has committed an offence which is a crime against peace, humanity or a war crime, or they are guilty of acts contrary to the purposes and principles of the UN, then status will be reviewed (API *Refugee Leave*, para. 5.3; API *Cessation, Cancellation and Revocation of Refugee Status*, paras 8-10). Article 1(F)(b) is not generally in play here because that exclusion concerns crimes committed outside the country of refuge. For further details about the Article 1F exclusions, ▶see 624–6.

Refugee obtained leave by deception Status may be reviewed if new evidence suggests that it should not have been granted at all. It may be that status was obtained by misrepresentation, that the applicant has a different nationality or that, in fact, the 1F exclusion clauses applied. In all cases, applicants will be allowed to deal with allegations of deception and often there will be an interview under caution. UNHCR's views will also be obtained. Note that the Home Office may check information given by a family reunion applicant to see if it tallies with that given by the refugee (API *Refugee Leave,* para. 5.2; API *Cessation, Cancellation and Revocation of Refugee Status*, paras 5–7).

Other reasons It appears that, if certain serious matters arise which cause the Home Office to want to remove the refugee, this will trigger a review of status to see whether both status and leave can be taken away ie on any of the above grounds, or on the basis of a change in country conditions, ▶see below. Only if one of these conditions is met can status and leave be taken away (API *Refugee Leave*, para. 5.4; API *Cessation, Cancellation and Revocation of Refugee Status*, para. 11). The 'trigger' events which may cause a review are: actions bringing the applicant within Article 33(2) Refugee Convention (▶below at 724); criminal conviction of two or more years or for an offence listed in an order made under section 72 2002 Act (▶see 1080–1); court recommendation for deportation; entry of the refugee on the sex offenders register; an extradition request; the refugee's presence is not 'conducive to the public good' (for example because they have engaged in one of the 'unacceptable behaviours' ▶see 1019–20).

2) *Change in country conditions*

This category is set out in API *Refugee Leave*, para. 6 (see also API *Cessation, Cancellation and Revocation of Refugee Status*, para. 3.1). This basis for review reflects cessation clauses 1C(5)(6) of the Refugee Convention (circumstances in connection with which the person was recognised as a refugee have ceased to exist). The policy points to changes of circumstances 'of such a significant and non-temporary nature' that persons from that country no longer have a well-founded fear of persecution. In such cases 'Ministers may decide to have reviewed all grants of refugee status' made to those potentially affected by the change and who have been granted limited leave. Sometimes, the improved circumstances will be limited to a specific group of refugees in a given country or part of the country.

These general country decisions will only be taken after consultation with UNHCR and status reviews will then proceed on a case by case basis. For general details on change of circumstances as a ground for withdrawal of status, ▶see 627–30.

3) *Five-year stage*

Policy on what happens when the refugee comes to the end of their limited leave is not yet fixed (the first cases will arise in 2008). It is possible that refugees will have to pass an English language and 'knowledge of British life' test which, by then, may have been introduced for all settlement applicants (see the 'five year' strategy). Present policy suggests that there will be no 'in-depth' review to see whether the person is still a refugee unless they fail to submit an in-time application. Further leave may also be denied if it is decided that status should have been withdrawn earlier for any of the reasons given above (API *Refugee Leave*, para. 7).

Where refugee status is withdrawn but the applicant cannot be removed

In certain cases, while it may be possible to withdraw a person's refugee status, they will still be protected from removal by the ECHR. In this case, they are likely to qualify for HP or DL (for which, ▶see 862–5). This could happen if the applicant is excluded from Refugee Convention protection on Article 1F grounds (▶above), or on Article 33(2) grounds i.e. because there are 'reasonable grounds' for thinking that they are a 'danger to the security' of the UK or who, because they have been convicted of a particularly serious crime, are a 'danger to the community' in the UK (see API *Refugee Leave*, paras 5.4, 8.2, and ▶see 625–6 and 1080–1). Time spent with leave as a refugee will then count towards the qualifying period for indefinite leave under HP or DL (see API *Refugee Leave*, para. 8.2).

Note that under the new HP and DL policy, it is possible that ministers will decide to refuse leave altogether to an applicant who falls into the 'exclusion' categories (▶see 863–4, 865). This is likely to be challenged.

Procedure for conducting reviews of refugee status

The procedure for conducting reviews in refugee cases is set out in API *Refugee Leave*, paras 4.2–4.3. The important points are as follows. The burden of showing that the person is no longer a refugee is on the Home Office. A person will be given an opportunity to state whey their status should not be withdrawn. Interviews may be conducted particularly in complex cases. Where a case is to be reviewed on the basis of the actions of the applicant, UNHCR will be usually consulted (but not in all Article 1F cases).

Review of Humanitarian Protection granted on or after 30 August 2005

Applicants granted HP on or after 30 August 2005, will normally be granted limited leave for five years. The arrangements for granting indefinite leave are essentially the same as for refugees (API *Refugee Leave* as described above) together with any further requirements 'that may be imposed by the settlement policy in force at the time' (see API *Humanitarian Protection*, para. 1, 8).

A review of HP status will only take place during the period of leave on grounds which are very similar to those for when refugee status can be reviewed during the period leave (▶above) (API *Humanitarian Protection*, para. 7).

Where HP is withdrawn, the applicant will be considered for DL instead. This will particularly be the case where the applicant is found to fall into the exclusions from HP (▶see 863–4 and 624–6).

Where a person has held both HP and Refugee leave, the qualifying period for settlement remains five years with both periods combined together. Where a person has held both HP and DL, six years is the qualifying period for settlement.

Where leave was granted on HP grounds before 30 August 2005, the review arrangements remain as they were before that date (▶see below) i.e. a full 'active review' is carried out when the applicant applies for indefinite leave.

'Active review' for those granted HP before 30 August 2005, ELR before 1 April 2003 or DL

In addition to reviews which may take place in refugee cases, a separate API on 'Active Review' applies to people granted: HP before 30 August 2005; ELR/E before 1 April 2003; or DL. General points made in the API *Active Review* are as follows (for a separate look at these categories of HP, ELR and DL, ▶see below).

- In cases where the applicant applies to extend their leave on the same basis as leave was granted, caseworkers will consider whether the applicant is still eligible for leave on that basis, or whether the circumstances have changed. If new grounds are put forward, case-workers will consider whether those grounds qualify the applicant for HP or DL. If the applicant re-asserts a claim to refugee status, that will be considered.

- Usually the review will be carried out on the papers but an interview may be necessary where new representations are made, or there are doubts about the case, or the applicant was not previously interviewed.

There is, at present, a right of appeal against any decision to refuse to extend leave (or to curtail leave) if the result of the decision is that the applicant will have no leave.

HP granted before 30 August 2005

These applicants were granted three years' leave after which they are eligible for indefinite leave (in contrast to the position for those granted HP on or after 30 August 2005, who have to wait five years). *However*, those granted HP before 30 August 2005 are subject to 'active review' at the indefinite leave stage. If an applicant was initially given HP of less than three years, an active review will also be carried out before any further leave is granted. In carrying out the active review, caseworkers will (API, *Active Review*, para. 4.5; API *Humanitarian Protection*, Annex A):

- have regard to the present situation in the country of origin to see if it has changed;

- consider an applicant's character and conduct during the time that they have been in the UK (this will be in order to determine whether the applicant may be 'excluded' from HP, ▶see 863–4 and 624–6).

If the applicant continues to qualify for HP, indefinite leave will be granted. If they no longer qualify for HP, they may qualify for DL. If so, leave will be granted in accordance with DL policy (▶see 864–5, 868–70).

HP may also be actively reviewed during the period of leave if any of the following conditions apply (if it is withdrawn, a grant of DL will be considered)(API Humanitarian Protection, Annex A, para. 2):

- the applicant's actions show that they no longer need protection (these grounds are similar to those under Article 1C(1)-(4) Refugee Convention relating to voluntarily re-availment of the protection of the country of origin, ▶see above at 627–30);

- the Home Office issues a specific instruction that a particular category of case should be reviewed;
- the applicant falls within one of the exclusions from HP (▶see 863–4 and 624–6);
- the applicant obtained HP by deception.

Those granted less than four years' ELR

Before 1 April 2003, applicants were granted 'exceptional leave' to enter/ remain (ELR) rather than HP or DL. Normally, such applicants were give four years' ELR and can then obtain indefinite leave without a full review (API *Humanitarian Protection*, para. 11 and Annex A, para. 6). Where, before 1 April 2003, an applicant was refused asylum but granted less than four years' ELR, their cases will be actively reviewed. They will only be granted further leave if they presently qualify for either HP or DL (API, *Active Reviews*, para. 4.8).

Discretionary leave

As with HP granted before 30 August 2005, in order to obtain an extension of leave or indefinite leave on the basis of DL, there will first be an active review. Case-workers will consider whether the applicant continues to qualify for DL (API, *Active Reviews*, para. 4.6; API *Discretionary Leave*, paras 7–8). The factors considered will depend on the basis on which DL was granted. Examples are as follows.

- If DL was granted on the basis of family life under Article 8, the present family situation will be considered.
- If the applicant was granted DL as an unaccompanied minor (and remains under–18), caseworkers will look to see whether there are still no adequate reception conditions overseas. Those over-18 will be considered in the same way as any other adult.

DL will may be reviewed during the period of leave in any of the following circumstances (API *Discretionary Leave*, para. 6):

- the person's actions demonstrate that the grounds on which they were granted DL no longer exist (e.g. they leave their marriage);
- a change in country conditions referred to in a specific instruction to review a particular category of case affects the applicant's case;
- evidence emerges to show that the applicant falls within the 'excluded' categories (▶see 863–4 and 624–6) – if they cannot be removed but they have more than six months' leave, the leave will either be varied to six months' leave, or, exceptionally, withdrawn altogether (▶see 865, 869);
- there are other circumstances which make it appropriate to curtail leave – for example a family member becomes able to provide care for a child who was granted DL on the basis of there being no reception facilities available.

Note on refugees with indefinite leave

For further technical details about the circumstances in which indefinite leave can be 'revoked' (including indefinite leave granted to refugees), ▶see 1008. For the power of the Secretary of State to take deportation action (on non-conducive grounds) against most non-British citizens (including those with indefinite leave), ▶see 1018–21. There are circumstances in which a refugee with indefinite leave may have their refugee status withdrawn if they have either ceased to be a refugee, or they should never have been recognised as a refugee, or they have engaged in conduct which is sufficiently serious as to justify withdrawal of status. This is likely to happen if there are particular reasons why the immigration authorities wish to deport or remove the person and/or exceptional circumstances such as extradition proceedings (for further details, see API *Cessation, Cancellation and Revocation of Refugee Status*, paras 3.2, 3.9, 12.1; see also the last sub-paragraphs of paras 5 and 8).

Note on dependants

It appears that it will normally be the case that, where the status of the main applicant is reviewed, the immigration status of their dependants will be affected in line. Where there are compelling reasons why this should not be the case, representations should be made (see API *Refugee Leave*, para. 8.4; API *Cessation, Cancellation and Revocation of Refugee Status*, para. 13).

The letter recognising refugee status

The standard letters granting refugee status reflect the Refugee Convention, which provides for refugees to have the same civil rights and duties as UK nationals. The letter explains that the refugee:

- can stay in the UK provided they do not engage in violence such as to endanger national security;
- can work freely without needing to obtain permission to work;
- is eligible to apply for welfare benefits or social housing;
- can access the NHS and social services, and obtain funding as a 'home student' for further or higher education;
- can travel abroad. The letter suggests that travel might affect refugee status. This is because a voluntary return to the home country may trigger the cessation clauses and lead to a loss of refugee status. For more details about this ▶see 627–33, and ▶see 721–3.

The letter also informs the refugee that any NASS support will cease. This is because the refugee is no longer an 'asylum-seeker' and, if in need, is entitled to apply for social security benefits instead. The letter may come with details about the Home Office 'Sunrise' project in which refugees have 'one-to-one' sessions with a caseworker to help them integrate. Help will be given on benefits, housing, health and child education needs. Support continues for up to a year and includes 'sign-posting' to education and training. Another pilot, 'Time Together', pairs volunteer mentors with refugees for support sessions of five hours per month.

How many people are granted refugee status, HP, DL?

Home Office figures for the year 2003 show the following. There were (excluding dependants and rounding the figures to the nearest thousand):

- 68,000 asylum decisions;
- 56,000 refusals of asylum, HP, DL and ELR;
- 4,000 initial grants of asylum;
- 8,000 initial grants of HP, DL and ELR;
- 82,000 appeals determined by the IAA, of which 20 per cent were allowed.

Obviously, not all of the appeals were against decisions taken in 2003.

Refusal of asylum

Those refused asylum will receive a 'reasons for refusal' letter. This will set out a summary of the claim, followed by the Home Office's reasons for refusing it. Where asylum, HP and DL are all refused, the reasons for refusal letter should give separate reasons why each has been refused. Where asylum is refused but the Home Office has decided to grant HP or DL, the letter should state why the applicant did not qualify for asylum, but should give the basis upon which HP or DL are granted. Both HP and DL are granted without conditions about access to public funds and without any restrictions on work.

Reasons for refusal generally relate to: (1) the conditions in the relevant country; (2) legal reasons why the claim cannot succeed; (3) the credibility of the applicant. Examples of reasons in the second category are: the treatment which the applicant fears does not amount to 'persecution'; there is a 'sufficiency of protection' from the authorities in the country of return; there is no 'Convention' reason for the alleged ill-treatment; there is an internal flight alternative available to the applicant.

Over the years, these letters have become longer and more detailed. This does not, however, mean that the quality of the reasons given has necessarily improved. Often, reasons for refusal contain serious legal mistakes, reliance on defective country information taken from the Home Office's own country assessments, and inadequate treatment of the medical evidence. The refusal letter is important as it puts the applicant on notice of the main issues they will have to deal with at the appeal. Advisers have become frustrated by apparently 'systematic' refusal letters, which contain standard paragraphs, sometimes bearing little or no particular relation to the claim itself. For the general 'standard' paragraphs that may be found in refusal letters, see the API *Reasons for Refusal Letter* and its Annex. Totally inadequate refusal letters should be challenged with representations, as it is sometimes possible to get the decision reversed after it has been assessed by a different officer.

If the claim is certified as 'clearly unfounded' (for details of this ▶see 1073–8), this will also be stated in the reasons for refusal letter.

Documents issued with reasons for refusal and the 'immigration decision'

In addition to the reasons for refusal letter, the applicant will usually receive the following:

1) a notice of refusal containing details of an 'immigration decision' made as the consequence of the asylum refusal;

2) a 'one-stop' notice (▶see 662–4, 1066–7);

3) provided that there is an in-country right of appeal, appeal forms together with explanatory notes.

'Immigration decision' It is the notice of the immigration decision that actually triggers the right of appeal to the AIT, under section 82 2002 Act. Section 82(2) defines 'immigration decision', which is not the refusal of asylum but the consequent decision to operate the machinery of immigration control leading to the applicant's removal from the UK (▶1053–4). *Most commonly* in cases of outright refusal, these are:

- a refusal of leave to enter;
- refusal to vary leave (i.e. to extend leave);
- variation of a person's leave so that, when the variation takes effect, the person will have no leave;
- a decision that a person is to be removed from the UK as an overstayer, a person who has breached conditions of leave, or obtained (or tried to obtain) leave to remain by deception;
- a decision to make a deportation order;
- refusal to revoke a deportation order.

Curtailments The third kind of immigration decision listed here relates to circumstances where a person who already has leave in the UK is refused asylum. In such cases, the Home Office may decide to 'curtail' (i.e. cut off) their leave when it refuses an asylum or human rights claim (see s3(3)(a) 1971 Act and para. 323 HC 395). In many cases, the basis for curtailment will be because making the asylum claim indicates that the person no longer satisfies the requirements of the rules under which their leave was granted. For example, a visitor who claims asylum plainly no longer satisfies the visitor requirement of having an intention to leave at the end of their visit. The Home Office will generally not curtail leave where the applicant is married to a British citizen (or an EEA national exercising treaty rights), nor where the applicant has leave in a category leading to settlement (see API, *Curtailment of limited leave in cases where an asylum or human rights application is refused*, para. 4.2). As indicated, these curtailments do give rise to a right of appeal because they are variations of leave which, when they take effect, will mean that the applicant will have no leave. They therefore constitute an 'immigration decision' (see s82(2)(e) 2002 Act and see API above, para. 1). Where leave is not curtailed but the applicant has leave for more than a year, there is a right of appeal on asylum grounds under section 83 2002 Act (for further details about the operation of s83, ▶see 1079).

Appealing An asylum-seeker cannot be removed while they are exercising an in-country right of appeal against the decision (▶667, 1059–61, 1181–2). For claims certified as 'clearly unfounded' so as to deny an in-country right of appeal, ▶see 1073–8. Different considerations also apply to 'third country' cases (▶see above).

Where there is no outright refusal: HP or DL granted

If asylum is refused but HP or DL is granted, then there is no 'immigration decision' within the meaning of section 82. This is because there has been no 'refusal' of leave to enter or remain, or decision to remove the asylum-seeker – indeed, quite the opposite. However, there may still be a right of appeal under section 83 2002 Act. This gives a right of appeal to applicants whose asylum claim has been refused *provided* they have been granted leave for over one year. This is an 'upgrade' appeal, in which the asylum-seeker may argue before the AIT that they ought to have been granted refugee status. For further details about section 83 rights of appeal, ▶see 871 and 1079.

The importance of allowing refused asylum-seekers to appeal against refusals of refugee status, even if they have been granted some other form of leave, is clear from the decision of the Court of Appeal in *Saad, Diriye & Osario*. That case recognised the important rights that attach to refugee status, such as family reunion and travel.

Invitations to withdraw asylum applications

Sometimes, where asylum-seekers have also made some other immigration application, such as a marriage application, they are invited by the Home Office to withdraw their asylum application. Asylum-seekers should take careful advice before doing this. Firstly, a person could be left without any permission to be in the UK at all if the other application is refused. Secondly, even if some other form of leave is granted, it is likely to be less beneficial than refugee status. For example, in marriage cases, leave is initially only granted for two years, and renewal depends on satisfying the immigration rules. At least at present, refugees are entitled to immediate settlement. Even after the Home Office moves to a system of granting limited leave to refugees with 'active review', refugee status will still have significant advantages over most other categories under the immigration rules. For example, those seeking to extend leave or apply for settlement as refugees will almost certainly not have to satisfy the public funds requirements

FRESH CLAIMS FOR ASYLUM

Where an asylum application has gone through the process of decision and appeal and has still been unsuccessful, it is always possible to make further representations to try to reverse the decision. The Home Office must consider all further representations that are made. In relation to some second applications, the Home Office is required to go further and to acknowledge that a 'fresh claim' has been made. If this is the case, then a further formal immigration decision must be issued, against which there is a further right of appeal. A 'fresh' claim therefore re-triggers the whole asylum decision-making process as though it was a first claim.

The principles concerning fresh claims were established by the Court of Appeal in *Onibiyo*. In that case, a young Nigerian asylum-seeker, whose father was one of the first asylum-seekers to be returned following the execution of Ken Saro-Wiwa, disappeared after his return. As a result, the applicant (the son) sought to claim asylum again. On the facts of the case, the Court found that there was no fresh claim, but it set out a test for determining when further representations amount to a fresh claim. This test subsequently became part of the immigration rules.

For 'fresh claims' in the context of asylum support, ▶see 1342–3. For further details about fresh claims in the context of human rights claims, ▶see 858.

The immigration rules

Before 25 October 2004, the test for a fresh claim as set out in the immigration rules repeated almost exactly the test set out in *Onibiyo* (above) The rules stated:

'Where an asylum applicant has previously been refused asylum during his stay in the UK, the Secretary of State will determine whether any further representations should be treated as a fresh application for asylum. The Secretary of State will treat representations as a fresh application for asylum if the claim advanced in the representations is sufficiently different from the earlier claim that there is a realistic prospect that [asylum will be granted]. In considering whether to treat the representations as a fresh claim, the Secretary of State will disregard any material which:

i)   is not significant; or
ii) is not credible; or
iii) was available to the applicant at the time when the previous application was refused or when any appeal was determined.' (Para. 346 HC 395)

From 25 October 2004, the test in the immigration rules reads (although at the time of writing, they are still not shown in the version of the rules on the IND website):

'When a human rights or asylum claim has been refused and any appeal relating to that claim is no longer pending, the decision maker will consider any further submissions and, if rejected, will then determine whether they amount to a fresh claim. The submissions will amount to a fresh claim if they are significantly different from the material that has previously been considered. The submissions will only be significantly different if the content:

i) had not already been considered; and
ii) taken together with the previously considered material, created a realistic prospect of success, notwithstanding its rejection.

This paragraph does not apply to claims made overseas.' (See para. 353 HC 395 as inserted by HC 1112)

Effect of new rules

The new rules recognise that it is possible to make fresh human rights claims as well as fresh asylum claims. The new rule does not expressly require the Home Office to leave out of account material it does not find apparently credible, nor material previously available to the applicant, but which they did not produce.

It is not altogether easy to see how the immigration rules can determine what is a 'fresh claim'. Although operating under previous legislation, the courts in *Onibiyo*, and in other cases which followed, laid down the concept of 'fresh claim' as part of an interpretation of the meaning of 'claim' in the statute. They had to determine when a 'second' set of representations after an original appeal and decision was indeed a 'claim', which gave rise to the need for a further formal decision and right of appeal.

To the extent that the new rule is less restrictive than the previous one, it is possible that it represents an exercise of Home Office discretion as to when it will issue a further underlying 'immigration decision' so as to enable a further appeal. If so, as it is written into the immigration rules, the Home Office is bound by it. It has previously been recognised that the Home Office has a discretion, in any case where it might be unfair to an applicant not to give them a further right of appeal, to issue a fresh notice of decision. It may do this *even when* the further submissions do not satisfy the criteria for a 'fresh claim' (see the Home Office letter of 22 July 1994 referred to in *R v SSHD ex parte Kazmi*). This discretion has usually been used where an applicant has, for reasons which are not their fault, missed the opportunity of an earlier appeal.

Use of section 96 2002 Act

However, although the rules are less restrictive, in cases where the applicant relies upon material that was previously available, the Home Office may still try to deny a further appeal by another route. Even where a claim satisfies the new 'fresh claim' rule, the Home Office may still try to issue a certificate under section 96 2002 Act (as amended by s30 2004 Act), on the basis that the matter should have been raised on an earlier appeal. A flow-chart issued by the Home Office (see below) also indicates as much. For further details about section 96 certificates, ►see 1067–9.

The 'fresh claim' test under the case-law

As the position is still somewhat unclear, we shall set out the test under the existing case-law as reflected in the old immigration rule. Of course, as is clear from comparing the two rules, core elements from that test are still contained in the new rule.

Significance of new circumstances For a fresh claim to be shown, the new evidence or change of circumstances must be sufficiently different so as to have a significant impact on the outcome of the case. It is not necessary that the new material shows persecution from a new source. Fresh evidence of a pre-existing fear may be enough (*ex parte Ravichandran (No 2)*). It must be possible, however, that the further claim will now be successful even though the earlier one was not. Inevitably, therefore, the two claims will be compared in order to see if this is the case. So, if an asylum-seeker's account of events has been comprehensively disbelieved, significant evidence that could make a difference to the claim will be required. For example, if an applicant initially claimed that they were at risk as a result of their membership of an opposition political party, but the Immigration Judge on appeal comprehensively rejected their account to have been a member of that political party at all, new evidence of recent intensive persecution of members of the party will not be significant to the applicant's case. This is because they have simply not been accepted as being a party member in the first place.

Credible evidence The new evidence that is relied upon should be 'credible' before the representations will amount to a fresh claim. This does not, however, mean that the Home Office must, at the end of the day, accept that the evidence is 'true' or genuine, but simply that it must be 'apparently credible' (see *ex parte Boybeyi*, CA).

Evidence that was previously unavailable In many cases, people try to rely upon material which could and should have been put forward at the time of the earlier application or appeal. Such material is excluded when deciding whether the representations are a fresh claim. However, it has been recognised that asylum-seekers who are traumatised through unspeakable experiences may only be able to relate those events at a later stage, in an environment in which they feel able to do so. Where this is the case, the evidence should not be discounted (see *Ejon*).

'Fresh claim' procedures

In mid-2004, it became clear from meetings with the Home Office that it had no proper procedures for dealing with representations which asserted to be fresh claims. It was doing little about such cases unless the applicant was threatened with removal, a judicial review looked likely or, in some cases, an MP became involved.

In August 2004 the Home Office stated that fresh claim applications should be submitted in writing to the usual IND Lunar House address, with 'fresh asylum claim' in bold at the top of the letter.

Following this, in October 2004, the Home Office issued a fairly complex flow-chart explaining the process by which it deals with fresh claim cases (letter to ILPA enclosing 'Process for the handling of secondary asylum applications', dated 6 October 2004). According to the flow-chart, the representations are attached to the relevant Home Office file and then allocated to an officer in the case work section in order for them to determine whether the application is indeed a 'fresh claim'.

If the caseworker decides that it is not a fresh claim, then the applicant is informed by post of the decision to treat the application merely as further representations, and enforcement action continues. If the caseworker decides the representations do amount to a fresh claim, the Home Office will consider whether to 'immediately refuse' the application and to issue a certificate under section 96 (▶see above), so that there is no right of appeal. If that is done, then the applicant and representative are issued with the decision letter, and enforcement action continues.

Only if the claim is accepted as being a fresh claim *and* no section 96 certificate is issued is the matter then passed to the Asylum Directorate for further consideration. The applicant is then also informed about contacting NASS in order to obtain further support.

The Home Office issued a further API on fresh claims in August 2005 (*Further representations and fresh claims*). The API confirms that the Home Office will only consider whether to issue a section 96 certificate after a decision has been made that there is a 'fresh claim'. It further confirms that a 'fresh claim' will not be certified under section 94 2002 Act as being 'clearly unfounded'.

Concerns about fresh claim process

The above process gives cause for concern. As a matter of principle, in all cases where further representations are made, their substance needs to be carefully considered. The mere fact that a further claim does not meet the technical requirements for 'fresh claim', or that certain matters or evidence should have been put forward earlier, does not mean that they do not raise serious issues. This seems to be accepted by the Home Office in its API *Further representations and fresh applications*:

'When further representations are submitted by an asylum seeker following the refusal of their application, the question of whether or not the applicant qualifies for asylum must be reconsidered on the basis of all the evidence available including those representations.

The determination of whether the representations constitute a fresh application does not affect the reconsideration of the asylum application, but does govern the way in which that reconsideration is communicated to the applicant and whether there is any further right of appeal.' (para. 1.1)

Accordingly, the most logical approach is to consider whether, taking all the information together, the further representations should result in a grant of leave. If not, one would then go on to consider whether, although the representations are ultimately being rejected, they pass the threshold for 'fresh claim', so that (unless s96 is invoked) there will be a further right of appeal.

The concern is that, because of the (understandable) desire on the part of the Home Office to make a swift decision on the 'fresh claim' question – because it affects access to support (▶see 1342–3), and applicants have used judicial review to challenge delays in determining whether there is a fresh claim – the process described above appears to have distorted the decision-making process. Where a decision is made that there is no fresh claim, or that a section 96 certificate should be issued, it seems that the substance of the representations may be given only very brief consideration. Such cases apparently do not find their way to the Asylum Directorate for full consideration.

There are likely to be further developments in the procedural aspects of fresh claims.

Refusals of asylum before 2 October 2000

In cases where the decision of the Home Office refusing asylum that gave rise to the first appeal was before 2 October 2000, asylum-seekers who cannot pass the fresh claim test may still obtain a human rights appeal after the dismissal of their asylum appeal. This is the result of the undertaking given by the Home Office before the IAT in the case of *Pardeepan*, to the effect that those unable to raise human rights during the course of their asylum appeals would be given time to raise them subsequently, and to appeal if necessary. The Home Office has confirmed that it will not deny a right of appeal where (API, *Further representations and fresh claims*):

- the appealable decision was made before 2 October 2000;
- no further appealable decision has been made since that time;
- the human rights issue had not in fact been considered and determined in the earlier appeal; and
- there have been no findings of fact, which undermine the human rights claim, and which were made on the earlier asylum appeal.

However, even in those cases, the IAT issued guidelines to the effect that, when the second appeal is heard, the AIT will generally take the earlier determination as the starting point in deciding the second appeal (see *Devaseelan*).

24 Third country cases

There are some cases in which, although a person makes a claim to asylum or a human rights claim that they are at risk of ill-treatment in their own country, the Home Office does not decide whether they actually are at risk there before requiring them to leave the UK. This applies in cases where the asylum-seeker may be returned to a 'safe third country' for that country to decide whether the applicant is at risk if they were to be returned. The 'third country' concept was initially based on the belief that asylum-seekers should claim asylum in the first safe country they arrived at. It is not set out in the Refugee Convention but it has increasingly been relied upon, particularly by agreement among European states.

Most recently those states have negotiated the 'Dublin II Regulation' (a replacement for the first Dublin Convention, see below at ▶748–9), which allocates responsibility between European states for dealing with asylum applicants.

The 2004 Act

So, in third country cases, rather than determine the *substance* of the claim as it relates to the country of origin, the Home Office will issue a certificate under section 33(1) and parts 2, 3, 4 or 5 of Schedule 3 to the 2004 Act enabling it to remove the applicant to a 'third' country (i.e. not the country of origin). From 1 October 2004, these 2004 Act provisions have completely replaced the third country regime previously contained in the 1999 and 2002 Acts. The immigration rules were amended in line with the 2004 Act, although they lagged behind the Act a little (the amendments to the rules were effective from 25 October 2004, see paras 329 and 345 HC 395 as substituted by HC 1112).

In what follows we mainly describe the system as it stands from 1 October 2004. We first set out the essential system under the 2004 Act, summarise the four categories of third country case created by it and the legal protections and procedures which enable applicants to challenge removals in each category (▶739–43, including the table summarising the categories). We then provide some further analysis about challenging third country removals under both the Refugee Convention and the ECHR (▶743–6).

Immigration rules and discretion

As well as determining whether removal can be challenged on these grounds, applicants should also check the following:

1) Whether the immigration rules permit the Home Office to remove the applicant to the third country (see ▶747–8). The rules require that the applicant has either had an opportunity to claim asylum in the third country or that they are clearly admissible to the third country.

   In some cases, whether there is 'clear evidence' of admissibility may bring into question whether the Dublin arrangements have been properly complied with. We look at the 'Dublin II Regulation' at ▶748–9.

2) Whether there are reasons why the Home Office should exercise discretion not to remove the applicant to a third country even if the legal conditions allowing removal are satisfied (▶750–1).

Unusual cases

Occasionally advisers may come across unusual-looking third country cases. At ▶751–2, we give some brief examples.

Pre 1 October 2004 transitional cases

Although the 2004 Act deals with third country cases from 1 October 2004, there are transitional arrangements where a 'third country' certificate was issued before 1 October 2004 (see Art. 3 Asylum and Immigration (Treatment of Claimants) Act 2004 (Commencement No 1) Order 2004). In such cases, the system under the 1999 and 2002 Acts still applies. We therefore describe this system at ▶753–5. In addition, for background, context and case-law decided under the previous third country regimes, we have briefly traced the development of the third country system from how it stood before the 1993 Act down to the 2002 Act (▶752–3).

Government stance

By operating the third country regime, the government is able say that it is not in breach of its own obligations (under Art. 33 Refugee Convention or the ECHR) because, even if the person is at risk in the original country, they are not being returned there. The government also states that such applicants are not being returned to a place where they face a risk of being sent on in a manner which would put them at risk of persecution or breach their human rights. Inevitably, much of the controversy surrounding third country cases has been about whether the third country is indeed 'safe' in these terms, and/or whether there are other human rights reasons why a particular applicant should not be removed from the UK.

Note that a refugee who is 'lawfully' in the UK (i.e. with leave) cannot be removed to any country unless certain conditions are satisfied (Art. 32 Refugee Convention, see ▶625–6).

THIRD COUNTRY CASES UNDER THE 2004 ACT

The new third country regime under the 2004 Act came into force on 1 October 2004. Under the 2004 Act, there are *four* categories of third country case. Whether a case falls into any of the first three categories depends on the particular third country that the applicant is to be sent to. Accordingly, there are three 'lists' of countries. In the fourth category, the Home Office may return an applicant to any third country (including countries not on any of the lists) but which it decides is safe for the individual applicant. Note that a curious provision for third country removals on the basis of a certificate issued in response to a human rights claim still exists under the 2002 Act (▶see 755).

The legal protections available against third country returns are different for each of the four categories. The difference in legal protection reflects how 'safe' the government considers those countries to be.

In the table below, each category (and, where known, the countries on the lists) is described. In addition, the degree of legal protection available to applicants, including whether an appeal or judicial review is possible, is summarised. In particular, the legislation 'deems' (i.e. assumes) certain returns to be safe. The aim of this is to prevent applicants challenging removal on safety grounds. The 'deeming provisions' are different for the different categories of removal. More details about the means of challenging third country removals on Refugee Convention and ECHR grounds are set out after the table (▶743 onwards).

Where the deeming provisions apply, they apply to any 'person', 'tribunal' or 'court'. This is intended to make it clear that they apply to decisions made by immigration officers and Home Office officials as well as to the High Court if an applicant tries to apply for judicial review. They would also apply if, in any case, a third country issue were to come before the AIT.

The third country regime under the 2004 Act only applies in relation to proposed removals to a country of which the applicant is not a national.

THE FOUR CATEGORIES OF THIRD COUNTRY CASES UNDER THE 2004 ACT

In each of the first three categories, in order to use the third country process, the Home Office must:

1) be proposing to return the applicant to a country of which they are not a national;

2) issue a certificate stating that, it is going to remove the applicant to a country which is on the list relating to the category in question *and* that, in the Secretary of State's opinion, the applicant is not a national of that third country.

In fact the wording on the certificate is likely to refer to a country to which either parts 2, 3 or 4 (i.e. for categories 1–3 respectively) of Schedule 3 to the 2004 Act applies.

In the fourth category, the certificate must state *all* of the following, namely that the Secretary of State:

- proposes to return the applicant to a particular (stated) third country;
- in the Secretary of State's opinion the applicant is not a national of that country; and
- in the Secretary of State's opinion, the stated third country is safe in that the applicant is not at risk of persecution in that third country *nor* will the third country send the applicant on to another country if such would expose them to a risk of persecution.

The four categories are as follows. For further legal analysis about challenging removals, ▶see 743–6 below.

First category

First list (part 2, Schedule 3, 2004 Act)

The countries on the *first list* are the countries that are part of the Dublin arrangements (see ▶748 onwards). They are the members of the EU (including the ten accession states) plus Norway and Iceland:

Austria	Greece	Netherlands
Belgium	Hungary	Norway
Republic of Cyprus	Iceland	Poland
Czech Republic	Ireland	Portugal
Denmark	Italy	Slovak Republic
Estonia	Latvia	Slovenia
Finland	Lithuania	Spain
France	Luxembourg	Sweden
Germany	Malta	

Legal protection

- The Home Office does not have to determine the substance of the claim as it relates to the country of origin.
- Deemed safe under the Refugee Convention in that the applicant will not be at risk of persecution in the third country.
- Deemed safe under the Refugee Convention in that the applicant will not be sent from the third country to another country if such would expose them to a risk of persecution.
- Deemed safe under the ECHR in that the applicant will not be sent from the third country to another country in breach of the applicant's ECHR rights.
- There is no in-country right of appeal against a removal on any of the above bases.

- There is also no out-of-country right of appeal on grounds trying to overturn any of the deemed safety provisions set out above.
- An in-country right of appeal exists against a refusal of any *other* ECHR claim; that is claims other than allegations that the third country will send the applicant on in breach of the ECHR. *However*, the Home Office will certify all human rights claims as 'clearly unfounded' unless satisfied that they are not clearly unfounded. If the human rights claim is certified, the applicant will have to successfully challenge the certificate by judicial review in order to keep an in-country right of appeal. Otherwise the applicant can appeal outside the UK on human rights grounds that do not challenge the applicant's onward removal.

Second category

Second list (part 3, Sch 3 2004 Act)

The countries on the *second list* are not set out in the Act but are those countries that are specified in an order made by the Secretary of State. At the time of writing no such order has been made. The Home Office is keeping the situation under review. In the meantime non-Dublin third country cases are being dealt with as 'fourth-category' cases (▶see below and see Note (2) below).

Legal protection

- The Home Office does not have to determine the substance of the claim as it relates to the country of origin.
- Deemed safe under the Refugee Convention in that the applicant will not be at risk of persecution in the third country.
- Deemed safe under the Refugee Convention in that the applicant will not be sent from the third country to another country if such would expose them to a risk of persecution.
- There is no in-country right of appeal against a removal on any of the above bases.
- There is also no right of appeal from outside the UK on grounds trying to overturn any of the deemed safety provisions set out above.
- There is *no* deemed safety in relation to *any* ECHR claim.
- An in-country right of appeal exists against refusal of *any* ECHR claim. *However*, the Home Office will certify all human rights claims as 'clearly unfounded' unless it is satisfied that they are not clearly unfounded. If the claim is certified, the applicant will have to successfully challenge the certificate by judicial review in order to keep an in-country right of appeal. Otherwise the applicant can appeal from outside the UK on human rights grounds.

Third category

Third list (part 4, Sch 3 2004 Act)

The countries on the *third list* are not set out in the Act but are those countries that are specified in an order made by the Secretary of State. At the time of writing no such order has been made. The Home Office is keeping the situation under review. In the meantime non-Dublin third country cases are being dealt with as 'fourth-category' cases (▶see below and see Note (2) below).

Legal protection

- The Home Office does not have to determine the substance of the claim as it relates to the country of origin.
- Deemed safe under the Refugee Convention in that the applicant will not be at risk of persecution in the third country.
- Deemed safe under the Refugee Convention in that the applicant will not be sent from the third country to another country if such would expose them to a risk of persecution.
- There is no in-country right of appeal against removals on any of the above bases.
- There is also no right of appeal from outside the UK on grounds trying to overturn any of the deemed safety set out above.
- There is *no* deemed safety in relation to *any* ECHR claim.
- An in-country right of appeal exists against refusal of *any* ECHR claim. *However*, the Home Office *may* certify any human rights claim as 'clearly unfounded' (note that there is no presumption that the human rights claim will be certified as there is for lists one and two; but in legal terms this probably makes little difference as to how the Home Office approaches certification, see *ZL & VL* (CA)).
- If the human rights claim is certified, the applicant will have to successfully challenge the certificate by judicial review in order to keep an in-country right of appeal on human rights grounds. Otherwise the applicant can appeal from outside the UK on human rights grounds.

Fourth category

Other countries certified as safe for individuals (part 5, Sch 3 2004 Act)

There is no list of countries for the fourth category of case. This category allows the Home Office to return an applicant to any country (i.e. including to countries not contained on the three lists above) if the Home Office is satisfied that the particular country is safe for Refugee Convention purposes for the particular applicant. At the time of writing no order had been made to put countries on the second and third lists. This means that the fourth category is the only means of dealing with non-Dublin Convention third country cases.

Legal protection

- The Home Office does not have to determine the substance of the claim as it relates to the country of origin.
- There is no deemed safety either under the Refugee Convention or under the ECHR.
- There is no in-country or out-of-country right of appeal on Refugee Convention grounds either on the basis that the applicant would be at risk of persecution in the third country, or on the ground that the third country may send the applicant on to another country such as to expose them to a risk of persecution.
- The applicant can, by judicial review, challenge the Secretary of State's certificate that the third country removal is safe on Refugee Convention grounds.
- An in-country right of appeal exists against refusal of *any* ECHR claim. *However*, the Home Office *may* certify any human rights claim as 'clearly unfounded'. If the claim is certified, the applicant will have to successfully challenge the certificate by judicial review in order to retain the human rights in-country right of appeal. Otherwise the applicant can appeal from out of country on human rights grounds.

Note

1) Without a further Act of Parliament, the Home Office is able to add (but not remove) countries to the first list. This is likely to happen if another country joins up to the Dublin arrangements. The Home Office may also either add or remove a state from the second or third lists (see Part 6, Sch 3 2004 Act).

2) The countries on the *first list* are set out in the 2004 Act. The countries on the *second* and *third lists* are supposed to be set out in an Order to be made by the Secretary of State. At the time of writing no order had been made. The Home Office has told JCWI that it has no timetable for when an Order will be made but that the situation is under review. Until then, those that are not Dublin (*first category*) cases will be treated as *fourth-category* cases.

CHALLENGING THIRD COUNTRY REMOVALS UNDER THE 2004 ACT

The different deeming provisions and legal protections that apply to the four categories of case are as set out in the table above. Below we provide further explanation of the challenges that may be made under the Refugee Convention and the ECHR. For details about how to bring judicial review claims generally, see ▶1213–22.

Challenging removals under the Refugee Convention

Under the first three categories, countries are deemed safe under the Refugee Convention both in relation to a risk of persecution in the third country and the risk of being exposed to persecution by being sent on by the third country. There is also no right of appeal either in-country or outside the UK on Refugee Convention grounds. In relation to previous deeming provisions in section 11 of the 2002 Act, the courts upheld the Home Office's argument that the deeming provision meant that the courts could not interfere with the Home Office's decision to remove an applicant on the basis that the third country was safe for the purposes of the Refugee Convention (see *R (Ibrahim) v SSHD* (CA); *R (Mohamed) v SSHD*) (HC). This must also apply to the 2004 Act.

Because of these deeming provisions, if an applicant believes that the removal is unsafe under the Refugee Convention, they are likely to try to put their argument under the ECHR as well. This is the case even if the applicant is relying on the same facts for the ECHR claim. It is almost certainly the case that removing an applicant in breach of the Refugee Convention will also be a breach of the ECHR (for full details about the ECHR and 'claims to protection', see ▶792–808). It is notable that in *Mohammed* (above), the Home Office dropped its initial argument that the Refugee Convention deeming provision automatically also applied to a human rights claim that was based on the same facts. Therefore, in some cases, the applicant can argue that making an ECHR claim frees them from the 'deemed safety' problem. If so, the applicant can seek to appeal in-country on human rights grounds and, if a 'clearly unfounded' certificate is issued, challenge the certificate by judicial review (see further below under 'ECHR challenges').

However, in some cases, applicants will not be able to free themselves from the deeming provision by making the claim under the ECHR as well as under the Refugee Convention. This is so, if:

• the case is a *first-category* case; *and*
• the applicant's complaint is that the third country will expose them to risk by sending them on to another country.

This is because, for *these ECHR purposes only* i.e. 'sending-on' cases, the third country is deemed safe in *first-category* cases (third countries are not deemed safe for ECHR purposes, even in *first-category* cases, if the applicant alleges harm *in* the third country). It is possible that this deeming provision will be challenged on the grounds that it is not compatible with the ECHR and the HRA. Commentators have noted that to simply assume that the third country is safe in relation to 'chain' removal cases because that country applies the Dublin Convention is contrary to the spirit of the decision of the Strasbourg Court in *TI v UK*. Therefore, even in cases in which both the Refugee Convention and the ECHR deeming provisions apply, but there is strong evidence that the third country may send the applicant on in breach of the ECHR, it is worth making full representations and taking careful legal advice.

In the *fourth-category*, although there is no right of appeal on Refugee Convention grounds (in-country or outside the UK), there is no deeming provision either. Therefore applicants can challenge removals by using judicial review. In the judicial review, the court is not bound to treat the third country as safe for Refugee Convention purposes. However, judicial review challenges can only be made on narrow grounds (for grounds of judicial review and judicial procedures generally, see ▶1213–22). Where there is a Refugee Convention challenge which can be made to the removal in a *fourth-category* case, it is likely that the applicant will also be able to make a human rights claim in the alternative and seek to appeal on human rights grounds provided the claim is not certified.

Challenging removals under the ECHR

The only 'deeming' provision relating to human rights in the third country system applies to *first-category* cases. The extent of the deeming provision is that the third country is deemed safe in that it will not send the applicant on to another state if to do so would expose the applicant to a breach of their ECHR rights. There is a possibility that this deeming provision will itself be challenged in judicial review proceedings (see above). The legislation also prevents an applicant bringing an appeal in *first-category* cases where the complaint is that the third country will send the applicant on in breach of the applicant's human rights.

ECHR grounds for challenge

Aside from the above exception, in all third country cases, applicants may challenge their removal to a third country on human rights grounds. The human rights challenges that may be made include the following:

- the applicant is at risk of a breach of their human rights *in* the third country;
- the applicant is at risk of being removed from the third country to another country such as to expose them to a breach of their human rights;
- the removal would breach the applicant's right to respect for private or family life (under Art. 8 ECHR) established in the UK (and ▶see under 'discretion' below at 750);
- the removal would breach the applicant's private life in its 'physical and moral integrity' aspect because of the adverse effects on the applicant's health (this has been established in a number of cases, the most significant of which was *Razgar*, ▶see 816–9 for full details).

Removals contrary to the ECHR are dealt with generally in Chapter 27.

'Clearly unfounded' certificates

In *all* the above cases, the Home Office will consider whether to certify the claim as 'clearly unfounded'. In *first-* and *second-category* cases there is a presumption that the Home Office will certify the claim. In *third-* and *fourth-category* cases there is no such presumption but the claim may still be certified.

If the claim is certified as clearly unfounded, then there will be no in-country right of appeal unless the applicant successfully challenges the certificate by judicial review. The purpose of these certificates is to prevent an applicant from appealing to the AIT because it is thought that allowing them to appeal would be a waste of time, since the appeal would inevitably be dismissed. Therefore, essentially, on judicial review, the court will be looking to see whether it is worth letting the matter go before the AIT. Accordingly the test for deciding whether or not a claim is 'clearly unfounded' is as follows:

'If on at least one legitimate view of the facts or the law the claim may succeed, the claim will not be clearly unfounded' (see *ZL & VL*, CA at paras 56–58).

In *R (Thangarasa) v SSHD*, the House of Lords described the test as follows (they were considering legislation which used the words 'manifestly unfounded' but 'clearly unfounded' has been held to mean the same thing):

- the Secretary of State must be 'reasonably and conscientiously satisfied that the allegation must clearly fail' (Lord Bingham, para. 14);
- the Secretary of State must determine whether the 'allegation is so clearly without substance that the appeal would be bound to fail' (Lord Hope, para. 34);
- it must be 'plain that there is nothing of substance in the allegation' (Lord Hutton, para. 72).

The test for these certificates is the same as the test for certifying *non-third country* asylum or human rights claims, which the Home Office thinks are so weak that they would also be bound to fail on an appeal. (For further details of the test, Home Office policy and strategy in response see the section on appeals at ▶1077–8). Many such cases are certified after going through a fast track detention process (▶see 673 onwards).

Because the Home Office is taking such a grave step in denying an in-country appeal right on grounds affecting human rights, the High Court will look very carefully at 'clearly unfounded' certificates and subject them to 'rigorous examination'. It is one of the few instances in which, on a judicial review, the Court will itself assess the evidence – for example medical reports – to determine whether the case may succeed before the AIT (see *Razgar*, paras 17–18, 35, 69–70; *ZL & VL*, paras 28–29, 56 and ▶see 1077–8).

THE IMMIGRATION RULES

Under the immigration rules, the Home Office may not proceed on a third country basis under the 2004 Act unless *either* (para. 345(2) HC 395):

- the asylum-seeker did not arrive in the UK directly from the country where they claim to fear persecution but arrived from another country in which they have had 'an opportunity at the border or within the third country or territory to make contact with the authorities of that third country or territory in order to seek their protection'; *or*
- there is other 'clear evidence' that the asylum-seeker will be admitted to the proposed safe third country.

As to the 'opportunity' of claiming asylum, in **Kandasamy**, the High Court held that this requires that *all* of the following are satisfied, namely the applicant:

- knew that they were outside their own country where they feared persecution;
- were physically able (either directly or indirectly) to contact the authorities there to make their claim;
- there was no reason for thinking that the authorities would not accept the claim.

The fact that an agent has planned and dictated the applicant's actions has been held not to prevent the applicant from making their application in a third country (see **Dursun v SSHD**, CA).

'Clear evidence' of admissibility requires that there is strong evidence that the applicant will be accepted in the third country. Admissibility for these purposes only means that the applicant will be admitted initially on a temporary basis while their asylum application is considered. In Dublin Regulation cases (▶see below), evidence that the return is within the terms of the Dublin arrangements should be enough. In other cases, the requirement might be met if the applicant has a valid visa or residence permit for the country in question, or if it can be shown that the return is in line with a separate re-admission agreement.

In cases where there is no right of appeal, third country removal which is not in accordance with the rules, or where there has been an unlawful exercise of discretion (below) can be challenged by judicial review.

Discretion

Where a case falls into any of the four categories under the 2004 Act, the immigration rules state that the Home Office will 'normally' refuse to examine the asylum application 'substantively' (i.e. to decide whether the applicant is a refugee in relation to their country of origin) and issue the appropriate certificate under Schedule 3 2004 Act (see para. 345(1) HC 395). Although there is a presumption that the Home Office will, in such cases, proceed on a third country basis, the use of the word 'normally' indicates that there is a discretion *within* the immigration rules (the rule does not say 'shall' or 'is to' issue a certificate). For the circumstances in which an applicant may have strong grounds to ask for that discretion to be exercised in their favour so that the asylum application is considered substantively in the UK ▶see below 750–1.

THE DUBLIN AGREEMENTS

The original Dublin Convention was signed by European governments in June 1990 and came into force on 1 September 1997. The purpose was to set criteria under which responsibility among the member states for dealing with asylum applicants could be allocated. From 2 September 2003, it has been replaced by the 'Dublin II Regulation', which is a European Commission regulation (EC No 343/2003 implemented by EC Regulation No 1560/2003). Dublin II is not vastly different from the original Convention although the time limits for transfers have been tightened.

Criteria for allocating responsibility

The criteria for allocating responsibility between states are summarised below in the order in which they apply (reference should be made to the Regulation itself for its precise terms, which are more detailed). So, for example, a state in which the asylum-seeker has a family member who has been recognised as a refugee is the responsible state even if there are other states that meet any of the later criteria.

'Family member' is defined in Article 2(i) of the Regulations as including the spouse, children (unmarried and dependent) of the applicant. It also includes an unmarried partner provided the host state generally treats unmarried couples in the same way as married couples. It also includes the parents or guardian of an unmarried minor asylum-seeker.

The criteria, in order of responsibility, are:

1) a state in which the applicant has a 'family member' resident who is recognised as a refugee or whose asylum application is being considered substantively by the state. If the applicant is a minor, it is a state where his family is lawfully present provided that it is in the applicant's best interests. In the absence of any family members, the state responsible shall be that where the application was lodged (Arts. 6-8);

2) a state that has issued a valid residence document or visa to the asylum-seeker (Art. 9);

3) a state into which the asylum-seeker illegally crossed initially (however, responsibility ceases 12 months after the date on which the irregular crossing took place; responsibility transfers to a state in which the applicant has lived for a continuous period of five months since the claim was made) (Art. 10);

4) a state that an asylum-seeker entered on the basis of a waiver of the need for a visa (Art. 11);

5) a state in which the asylum-seeker makes an application in a transit zone (Art. 12);

6) where family members make applications on the same date, or close together, in different states, the state in which the greatest number of applications is made. If responsibility cannot be decided under this criterion, then it is the state in which the eldest family member has made an application (Art. 14).

Timetable for requests and removals

Since September 1997, asylum-seekers have been given a 'screening' interview to establish which country is responsible. If the Home Office believes the person can be returned, it will try to obtain the agreement of the third country before removing the applicant. The Regulation sets out a timetable for the negotiations to take place between states as to which has responsibility, as follows (Arts, 16-20):

- a member state must, within three months, request another member state to take the applicant back;
- a response to a request must be given within two months;
- however, the requesting state can demand an urgent reply and give the other member state only one week to respond;
- where an urgent request is made, in a complex case a response must be given within one month at the latest;
- failing to respond to a request within the time-limits is tantamount to accepting the request;
- transfer of the asylum-seeker must take place within six months of the acceptance of the request (except where there is a criminal conviction or absconding).

The Dublin Implementing Regulation (EC No 1560/2003) also contains provisions about the way in which requests should be made and the documentation which member states should provide to each other.

Before Dublin

Prior to the Dublin arrangements, the practice for third country returns was different. Refused asylum-seekers were sent to the last safe EU country through which they travelled before coming to the UK, rather than being sent directly to the first safe country they arrived at in the EU or whichever other country was appropriate under the above criteria. The earlier procedure involved the receiving country sending the asylum-seeker on again if it believed there was another country that should accept responsibility.

DISCRETION AND THIRD COUNTRY REMOVALS

As indicated above, even if the formal requirements for return to a safe third country are met, the Home Office retains a discretion to consider the asylum application substantively. Strong representations may be made in cases involving family links to the UK and in certain other cases.

Family links policy

Although the Dublin II Regulation contains provisions concerning family members that apply in *first category* cases, the Home Office has a general, long-standing 'family links' policy in relation to third country cases. The policy was reiterated by Beverley Hughes MP on 22 July 2002 (Parliamentary Answer, Hansard, Column 860W). Under this policy, claims will normally be considered substantively where:

- an applicant's spouse is in the UK (provided the marriage took place before the applicant's arrival in the UK);
- the applicant is an unmarried minor who has a parent in the UK;
- the applicant has an unmarried minor child in the UK.

In all cases 'in the UK' means either with leave to enter or remain in the UK *or* with temporary admission as an asylum-seeker *prior* to an initial decision on the application. Discretion *may* also be exercised favourably in cases where the minor is married, or where the applicant is an elderly or otherwise dependent parent or where

'...the family link was not one which would normally be considered but there was clear evidence that the applicant was wholly or mainly dependent on the relative in the United Kingdom and that there was an absence of similar support elsewhere.'

Home Office approach to policy and use of Article 8 ECHR

The Home Office states that cases falling into the category immediately above are rare. They also state that, in all cases, the purpose of the policy is to reunite members of an existing family unit, which has become separated due to circumstances beyond its control. Therefore, where the relationship did not exist before the applicant's arrival in the UK, the policy would only be applied in the 'most exceptional compelling cases'. Although the Home Office states that the policy is in accordance with Article 8, that does not mean that every application of the policy will be. In most cases where the applicant is relying on the family links policy, it will also be appropriate to make a formal human rights claim under Article 8 which may result in an in-country appeal if refused (▶see above). For Article 8 claims generally, ▶see 820–50.

Applicants may also want to make reference to Article 15 of the Dublin II Regulation, which is a humanitarian clause (that includes family grounds)

that allows a state to consider asylum applications substantively even if the state is not formally the responsible state under the Dublin arrangements.

Other discretionary cases

Other cases in which representations may be made that the Home Office should exercise discretion in favour of considering an application substantively include cases in which:

- the UK is already considering, or has considered, very closely related claims and therefore the UK is in a better position than another state to fairly consider the claim – there may, for example, be important witnesses in the UK who could conveniently give statements or provide other information to assist in determining the claim;
- the applicant has strong ties to the UK which are not necessarily family related: significant past periods of residence, strong cultural connections, or, particularly in the case of traumatised or vulnerable applicants, the availability of a support network from a particular community which would not be available in the proposed third country.

UNUSUAL THIRD COUNTRY CASES

7

Most third country cases follow established patterns: they are 'Dublin Convention' returns or the applicant has passed through an identified safe country. Occasionally, however, a third country case arises which is out of the ordinary, for example, where the Home Office has actively tried to find an alternative destination for an asylum-seeker outside of any existing international agreements or arrangements. Under the 2004 Act regime above, most such cases will probably fall under category four, although they might also be within categories two or three. These cases are likely to raise safety and other human rights issues.

The following are examples of these unusual third country cases:

Dr Al Masari Dr Masari is a well-known Saudi dissident who claimed asylum in the UK and who the immigration authorities tried to send to the Dominican Republic. He succeeded in showing that he would not be safe from the Saudi authorities there.

Afghan 'hijacked' aircraft case In February 2000, an Ariana 'hijacked' airliner landed at Stansted having been diverted during an internal flight in Afghanistan. Many of the passengers claimed asylum and ministers announced that they were seeking alternative countries of reception for them. In particular, it was suggested that they might be returned to safe 'neighbouring' countries. In the event ,they were not.

Close connection with another country If an asylum-seeker has close connections with another country as well as the one from which they are claiming asylum, the Home Office may suggest that asylum is not necessary because there is another country to which they could go. People who are dual nationals are always expected to go to their safe country of nationality. This has also been used, for example, for people of Jewish origin, who have been told that they could go to Israel. The Court of Appeal agreed with this view in the case of *Miller*.

In the above cases, as with all other third country cases, it must be the case that the asylum-seeker has either passed through the third country and had an opportunity to claim *or* that there is 'clear evidence' that the asylum-seeker will be accepted into the third country (see under 'immigration rules' above). In these kinds of cases the Home Office will usually be relying on there being 'clear evidence' of admissibility after it has negotiated with the country in question.

PREVIOUS THIRD COUNTRY REGIMES: JULY 1993–SEPTEMBER 2004

Before the 1993 Act, removals on third country grounds operated as a matter of practice and were not regulated by legislation. In February 1987, the House of Lords established in *Re Musisi* that the Refugee Convention prohibited indirect *refoulement* (return to a country or territory where there is a risk of being sent on to another country where the applicant is at risk of persecution) as well as direct *refoulement*. In that case the Court quashed a decision to return a Ugandan national to Kenya in the light of evidence of Kenya's practice of returning Ugandans back to Uganda, which the Secretary of State had not adequately considered.

Under transitional arrangements, the system in place under the 1999 and 2002 Acts still applies where a 'third country' certificate was issued before 1 October 2004 (▶see 753–5).

The 1993 Act: third country appeals

The practice of third country returns was first made formal in UK law under the Asylum and Immigration Appeals Act 1993. That Act created the system under which the Home Office could certify applications as being 'without foundation' if the claim should be dealt with by another country. It also created a right of appeal against the certificate. To the government's embarrassment, there was then a period in which appeals against proposed third country returns to other European states were very often successful. Often it was shown that there had been breaches of procedures and other failings, which indicated that applicants would not have their claims properly considered and may be removed to their country of origin even though they were at risk of persecution there.

The 1996 Act: judicial review in third country cases

The government responded with the Asylum and Immigration Act 1996 which withdrew the in-country right of appeal in respect of cases where the third country was an EU state or a 'designated country', namely Canada, the USA, Norway or Switzerland. The Home Office immediately resumed third country removals to EU states and applicants had to resort to judicial review in order to challenge their removal.

In the cases which followed, the courts decided that the Home Office was required to take reasonable steps to make sure that it was aware of the circumstances and procedures in the third country and ensure that there was no risk that the applicant would be sent on by the third country in breach of the Convention. Applying these principles, a decision to remove two Albanian Kosovars to Germany was quashed (*Gashi*). In *Adan & Aitseguer*, the House of Lords held that, where the third country wrongly interpreted the criteria under the Convention for satisfying the definition of 'refugee', the UK could not remove applicants to those countries. The Lords decided that there was no margin for different interpretations of the Convention by the different signatory states because the Convention has only one international meaning. In those cases, Germany and France were found to be lacking by not recognising persecution by 'non-state' agents (for the circumstances in which a person can be a refugee on the basis of fears from 'non-state' agents ▶see 610–11).

However in *Yogathas*, the House of Lords was again faced with a complaint about Germany's approach to the Refugee Convention in non-state agent cases and in relation to the internal flight alternative. The Lords held that, even though the applicant might not be protected by the laws that Germany had specifically made in order to honour its obligations under the Refugee Convention and the ECHR, German practice under its 'Aliens Act' gave the applicant enough protection. As a result, the applicant would not in practice be removed by Germany in breach of those Conventions. Provided that this was the ultimate result, differences in procedure and insignificant differences in law and practice did not matter. The House of Lords also referred to the similar decision of the Strasbourg Court in *TI v UK*.

These judicial review cases in which applicants challenged the safety of certain third countries, particularly EU member states, prompted the government to take yet further restrictive measures under the 1999 Act (below). The system was then slightly amended from April 2003, by the 2002 Act. From this time, the system operated on the basis of provisions in both the 1999 and 2002 Acts.

Third country cases under the 1999 and 2002 Acts

From 2 October 2000, in order to make even judicial review challenges far more difficult, the government passed legislation to 'deem' certain countries as safe ones to which to return asylum-seekers on a third country basis (see ss11, 12 1999 Act). Also, the 1999 Act gave the Dublin Convention (see above for its successor, the Dublin II Regulation) a direct effect in UK law by referring to certain third country returns as being in accordance with 'standing arrangements with member States'.

The system was slightly amended from April 2003 (see ss80, 93 2002 Act and the Nationality, Immigration and Asylum Act 2002 (Consequential and Incidental Provisions) Order 2003). We describe the system as amended, as it applied between *April 2003 and 30 September 2004*. This system is still of some practical importance because, under transitional arrangements, it still applies where a third country certificate was issued before 1 October 2004 (see Art. 3 Asylum and Immigration (Treatment of Claimants) Act 2004 (Commencement No 1) Order 2004).

The regime can be split into 'Dublin Convention' and 'non-Dublin Convention' cases as follows.

'Dublin Convention' cases under the 1999 and 2002 Acts

In Dublin Convention cases, the Home Office would generally issue a certificate under section 11 1999 Act to the effect that:

- the relevant EU member state had accepted its responsibility for the claim under the Dublin Convention; and
- the asylum-seeker was not a national of the EU state to which they were to be sent.

Section 11 'deemed' the third country to be safe for the purposes of the Refugee Convention. This presumption effectively prevented applicants from challenging their removal to the third country on the grounds either that they would be at risk of Refugee Convention persecution in the third country, or that the third country would send them on to their own country if they were at risk of persecution there. In *Ibrahim* in the Court of Appeal, the Home Office successfully relied on this presumption in a case involving the return of a Sudanese national to France in a case where the applicant claimed to be at risk from non-state agents in Sudan. However, the presumption in section 11 did not refer to the ECHR, so under the old legislation applicants could possibly challenge removals on human rights grounds even where the claim was that there was a risk of the third country removing the applicant on again in breach of human rights.

Applicants could also bring a human rights challenge to their removal on the grounds of private or family life connections to the UK; the detrimental effect on their health of being returned to the third country or breaches of human rights which might occur in the third country.

Applicants had an in-country right of appeal if they raised human rights grounds to prevent their removal but the Home Office could prevent that appeal from being exercised in-country by issuing a certificate that the claim was 'manifestly unfounded' (s72(2)(b) 1999 Act, from 1 April 2003, this became a 'clearly unfounded' certificate under s93(2)(b) 2002 Act, but the meaning is the same, ▶see 745–6). The only way to challenge such a certificate was by judicial review. The Home Office would normally not remove the applicant while the judicial review was outstanding, alternatively the applicant would ask the High Court to stay their removal while the judicial review was taking place.

'Non-Dublin Convention' cases under the 1999 and 2002 Acts

Other third country removals were dealt with by section 12 of the 1999 Act. Section 12 dealt with the following three categories of case:

1) non-Dublin Convention removals to EU member states;

2) removals to 'designated' countries (Canada, Norway, Switzerland, USA – see Asylum (Designated Safe Third Countries) Order 2000);

3) removals to all other countries.

In these cases, the Home Office could seek to remove the person to the third country after it had certified that:

- the applicant was not a national or citizen of the third country;

- the applicant would not be at risk of Refugee Convention persecution in the third country; and

- the third country would not send the applicant on so as to expose them to a risk of Refugee Convention persecution.

In all three categories of case, there was no presumption that the third country was safe. The Home Office's decision to remove could be challenged in judicial review proceedings on grounds of safety. Also, *in all three cases*, human rights claims challenging the third country removal could be made and there was an in-country right of appeal on human rights grounds. However, as with the Dublin Convention removals under section 11, in the case of removals to EU states and designated states (but not in the case of removals to non-EU/non-designated states) the Home Office could certify the claim as 'clearly unfounded' to prevent an in-country appeal (s93 2002 Act). The certificate could only be challenged by judicial review.

Use of section 94(7)(8) 2002 Act

There was, and still remains, a further general curious provision for certifying human rights claims in third country cases (see s94(7)(8) 2002 Act). It appears to apply to *all* third country cases. However, it conflicts with other provisions that appear to prevent a human rights claim from being certified in the case of removals to non-EU/non-designated countries. This power appears not to have been used by the Home Office.

7

25 Refugee family reunion

This chapter deals with the rights of those recognised as refugees in the UK to bring their family members to join them. The family reunion rights for those granted humanitarian protection, discretionary leave and, prior to 1 April 2003, exceptional leave to remain are covered in the section dealing with human rights, ▶at 875–9.

'Family reunion' applications cover the situation where family members want to be reunited with a sponsor who has *already been granted leave* in the UK. For the position of family members who arrive with the asylum-seeker, or who arrive before a decision is made on the principal's asylum claim and who wish to be considered as 'dependants' of the asylum-seeker, ▶see 691–4.

In an application for transfer of refugee status or in an application for asylum from abroad, family members may in some cases be able to rely upon the presence of a sponsor and other family members in the UK. These cases are rare, but for more details on them, ▶see 696–701.

Family reunion – the different options

For many years, the Home Office maintained a policy of allowing the spouse and minor children of those recognised as refugees to join them in the UK without having to satisfy stringent rules. In October 2000, this long-standing policy was finally incorporated into the immigration rules (paras 352A–352F HC 395) (▶see below).

The rules relating to refugee family reunion only cover the *pre-existing* spouses and minor children of the sponsor – in other words, those who were part of the refugee's family before they fled to seek asylum. If the family members of a refugee *cannot* satisfy the refugee family reunion rules, the following options should be considered.

- There is always discretion to admit other family members of refugees who do not come within the rules. In asking for that discretion to be exercised, applicants and advisers should consider the impact of both Home Office policy and the 'principle of family unity' developed under the Refugee Convention (▶see below 762–7).

- It is possible that the other ordinary rules relating to family members of persons present and settled in the UK can be satisfied (▶see Section 4 and 768–9 below).
- In the case of non pre-existing marriages, the Home Office has indicated that it is prepared to operate some flexibility in the application of the immigration rules relating to spouses (▶see below 769).
- There may be a compelling Article 8 ECHR case to be made for family reunion (▶see 769, 820–50).

'PRE-EXISTING' SPOUSES AND MINOR CHILDREN OF REFUGEES UNDER THE IMMIGRATION RULES

WHAT THE RULES SAY

In order to be admitted as the spouse of a refugee, all of the following conditions must be met (paras 352A–352C HC 395):

- the applicant must be married to a person who has been granted leave in the UK as a refugee;
- the marriage must have taken place before the refugee left the country of their 'former habitual residence' in order to seek asylum (i.e. they are the pre-existing spouse);
- the parties must intend to live together permanently as spouses and the marriage must be subsisting;
- the applicant must not be a person who would be excluded from the protection of the Refugee Convention under Article 1F if they applied in their own right for asylum.

In order to be admitted as the child of a refugee, the applicant must satisfy all of the following conditions. The applicant must meet all of the following requirements (paras 352D–352F HC 395):

- be the child of a person who has been granted leave in the UK as a refugee;
- be under 18;
- not be leading an independent life, nor be married, nor have formed an independent family unit;
- have been part of the pre-existing family unit at the time the refugee left the country of their 'former habitual residence' in order to seek asylum; and
- not be a person who would be excluded under Article 1F of the Refugee Convention if they were to seek asylum in their own right.

We discuss the meaning of these rules below. Significantly, the rules for family reunion do *not* require the above family members to be maintained and accommodated in the UK without recourse to public funds. If the application is accepted, the rules provide for limited leave to enter or remain to be granted. Leave is likely to be given in line with that of the refugee (▶720 onwards).

Applicants who are in the UK

Applicants who were made dependants of the original asylum application before it was decided will be granted leave in line with the main applicant when the latter is recognised as a refugee. This is not viewed as 'family reunion' as such – the family members were part and parcel of the asylum application, and were dependants of that application (for more details about dependants of asylum seekers, ▶see 691–4).

If the spouse/child was not a dependant of the asylum application, the Home Office states that it will not add them as 'dependants' subsequently. If the main applicant's application has been refused, the Home Office will usually defer the removal of the applicants pending any appeal by the main applicant. If the application has been granted by the Home Office, or is then granted on appeal, the application of the family members is treated as a 'family reunion' application (see API *Dependants*, para. 2). But will the family members be refused because they do not have an entry clearance in this situation? If the spouse/minor children are 'in-country' cases – i.e. are applying to the Home Office for leave to *remain* – the rules do not require them to have an entry clearance (see paras 352A–B, 352D–E, HC 395). *However*, the rules do *not* exempt 'port' applicant family members who are applying for leave to enter from the need to obtain entry clearance. However, generally such applicants should also not be refused just because they do not have an entry clearance. This is because it would make no sense of the Home Office policy to defer removal of the family members pending an appeal and then, if the appeal is successful, refuse on the grounds of no entry clearance anyway.

There is, of course, nothing to prevent dependants from making asylum or human rights claims in their own right if they are themselves at risk if returned.

Applicants who are abroad: the need for entry clearance

If the spouse/minor child is abroad, they must obtain entry clearance to come to the UK for family reunion with their refugee sponsor. Often, family members applying from abroad do not have, and are unable to obtain, travel documents in order to come to the UK from their own national authorities. Part of the reason for this may be that the family members are afraid to approach those authorities because their sponsor is wanted by them, and therefore the authorities may make it difficult for the family members to leave. Some family members may have left the country of origin without travel documents and be living in difficult circumstances in a third country. They too will face difficulties in obtaining travel documents. Overseas entry clearance posts are able to issue a 'Uniformed Format Form' upon which the entry clearance can be endorsed. This is normally valid for one-way travel to the UK and used to be called a 'GV3'; although the DSP has continued to refer to 'GV3'(see DSP, Ch 4, para. 4.16).

Entry clearance fees

The entry clearance fee is waived for the 'pre-flight dependants' of refugees. However, it is possible that the post may try to charge a fee where the dependants are not the spouse or minor children of the refugee. If so, applicants can point out to the ECO that fees should be waived for 'destitute persons', and that there is also a discretion to waive fees. It is likely that there will be good grounds for fees to be waived on at least one of these bases in the case of dependants of refugees (see DSP Ch 7, paras 7.4(e)(f) and 7.5; DSP Ch 16, para. 16.3(i) under 'Fees' and 'Other dependent relatives'). For further guidance on showing 'destitution' for these purposes, ▶see 878–9. For the amounts of the fees ▶see 1510.

The status granted to family members

Where family reunion is granted, the Home Office will normally recognise the family members as refugees themselves. However, family members may not always want to be recognised as refugees. If they are not at risk themselves, they may want to keep open the option of using their own national passports, or travelling to their country of origin for visits. In such cases, the Home Office will normally simply grant the family members leave in line with the refugee, but without actually recognising them as refugees themselves. Applicants are advised to make their wishes known. The Home Office has in the past been amenable to changing family members' status where they have been recognised as refugees but had no wish to be (see generally API *Family Reunion*, para. 3.1).

WHAT THE RULES MEAN

Person granted leave as a refugee

The family reunion rules are for those who have sponsors who have actually been recognised as refugees. Entry clearance will not be granted under the rules in order for a family member to come to the UK to join an asylum-seeker.

Pre-existing family

The rules allow the admission of family members who were part of the pre-existing family. For spouses, the marriage must have taken place before the person granted asylum left the country of their 'former habitual residence' in order to seek asylum. Child applicants must also have formed part of the family unit of the refugee at the time the sponsor left the country of their 'former habitual residence' in order to seek asylum.

In *A (Somalia)*, the IAT held that the country of 'former habitual residence' did not have to mean the country of persecution. An understanding of the facts of this case will make the point clear. What had occurred was that a Somali sponsor had fled Somalia to Ethiopia (where she did not claim asylum) in 1997. In 1999, while in Ethiopia, she married a man who was also a Somali who had fled. In 2000, the sponsor came to the UK, where she was recognised as a refugee, and her husband applied for family reunion. The IAT found that the sponsor had been habitually resident in Ethiopia and that she married before she left that country. It held that that was sufficient to satisfy the rules. The IAT had regard to the Final Act of the Conference which established the Refugee Convention (▶see below at 765), and found that a narrow interpretation of the rule would not be appropriate, having regard to the fact that the Final Act had recommended that governments take the necessary measures for 'ensuring that the unity of the refugee's family is maintained'.

The Home Office does not accept the IAT's interpretation in *A*. In correspondence commenting on the decision, the Policy Section at UK Visas stated, 'despite the IAT's judgement in this case, [the Home Office's] interpretation of "former habitual residence" is still that this refers to the applicant's home country/country of origin' (UK Visas letter to South Manchester Law Centre, 16 November 2004). The letter further suggests that, depending on the circumstances of the case, ECOs might grant entry clearance on a discretionary basis (possibly under the family reunion policy, ▶see below) where the applicants do not meet the Home Office interpretation of the rules. This position of the Home Office is not acceptable – the law as found by the courts is to be applied.

Note that, before the family reunion policy was made part of the immigration rules, it was possible to succeed with family reunion applications where the marriage had taken place *after* the grant of refugee status – for example, where the couple had been engaged but were prevented from marrying because of the refugee's flight. The IAT had held in the case of *Gamelsid* that these circumstances came within the policy.

Intention to live together/marriage subsisting

The requirement for spouses that the applicant and sponsor intend to live together permanently and that the marriage is subsisting was added to the rules from 18 September 2002 (Cm 5597 amending para. 352A HC 395). The meaning of the requirement is the same as in other marriage cases (▶see 306–7).

Children leading an independent life

The additional rule that requires the children of a refugee to be unmarried, not leading an independent life and not to have formed an independent family unit, is the same as that applying under the general rules relating to the admission of children (▶see 363).

Exclusion under Article 1F Refugee Convention

It will be very rare for family members to be excluded from family reunion on the basis that they would have been excluded under Article 1F if they had applied for asylum. This will occur only if the family member falls into any of the following categories:

- they have committed a crime against peace, a war crime or a crime against humanity;
- they have committed a serious 'non-political' crime outside the UK;
- they are guilty of acts 'contrary to the purposes and principles of the United Nations'.

For more details about when these circumstances apply to refugees generally, ▶see 624–6.

REFUGEE FAMILY REUNION OUTSIDE THE IMMIGRATION RULES

As in cases within the rules, under Home Office concessions outside the rules concerning refugee family reunion, generally only 'pre-existing' family members will be considered. The idea is that the policy for family reunion is based upon reuniting the family separated by persecution, not simply giving refugees an advantage over others in all family immigration applications.

Below we look, in turn, at applications made by family members other than their spouses and minor children, applications where a minor has been granted refugee status in the UK and at the 'principle of family unity' under the Refugee Convention which the Home Office has always indicated that it has based its own policy around.

Applicants other than spouse/minor children

The Home Office has always accepted that a pre-existing spouse and minor children can be admitted (▶see above). If the family members are not the spouse or minor children, as a concession outside the rules, the Home Office states that it may 'exceptionally' allow other family members to come to the UK if there are 'compelling, compassionate circumstances'. As to which family members may benefit if the compassionate circumstances are strong enough, the API give the example of elderly parents (API *Family Reunion*, para. 2). We suggest that family members who may be considered under this policy may include an adult refugee's minor siblings, children over the age of 18 who are still dependent on the sponsor and have not formed independent families of their own, and other relatives who have been dependent or particularly close to the sponsor, especially if such relatives are living in difficult or distressing circumstances abroad.

The Home Office has elaborated on the above statement in the API. In the case of *Abdi Hussen Mahamed*, the IAT directed the Home Office to provide further details of its refugee family reunion policy. On 29 June 2004, the Home Office's representative forwarded a note from the Home Office's Policy Unit to the IAT. In response to a question concerning present policy, the Unit stated:

'We will exercise discretion if a refugee is able to show that a person who is not a spouse or minor child was a dependent member of their immediate family unit prior to the time they fled to seek asylum. The policy therefore may be extended to other members of the family (e.g. elderly parents) if there are compelling, compassionate circumstances. Each case is considered on its individual merits.'

Read as a whole, this seems to indicate that if the applicant was a dependent member of the immediate family unit before the time the refugee fled, this will go a long way to demonstrate that there are indeed 'compelling, compassionate circumstances'.

Plainly, much will depend on the individual circumstances of each case and whether the nature of the application is in line with the purpose underlying the policy. Given that the policy appears to be based on the 'principle of family unity' developed under the Refugee Convention, it is worth drawing upon the way that policy has developed (▶see 764 onwards). For the relevance of policy outside the rules in family reunion appeals, ▶see 1124–6.

Applications where a minor child is granted refugee status in the UK

The Home Office has recently taken a hardline approach to family reunion where a minor is granted refugee status in the UK and wishes to be joined by relatives. Advisers believed that the policy was contained in a letter written by the then immigration minister, Barbara Roche MP, to an assistant of Lord Archer of Sandwell on 30 June 2000. That letter appeared to state that the Home Office would admit to the UK both the parents of a child who has been granted refugee status and the other minor dependent children of those parents:

'Under the family reunion concession, a minor who has been recognised as a refugee can immediately apply for his parents and any of their other minor dependent children to join them in the United Kingdom.'

However, in a letter from the Asylum Policy Unit on 26 February 2003 to Winstanley-Burgess Solicitors, the Home Office stated that applicants seeking to join a minor recognised as a refugee would have to demonstrate that there are 'sufficiently compelling compassionate circumstances' justifying the grant of family reunion. The Home Office apologised for the fact that this had not been made clear in Mrs Roche's letter. This restrictive policy was confirmed again in a further Home Office letter that was generally circulated (Home Office letter, 30 December 2003). It is confirmed again in the present API:

'The parents and siblings of a minor who has been recognised as a refugee are not entitled to family reunion. Such applications are considered under the criteria above, i.e. there must be compelling compassionate circumstances in order for the family to be granted entry to the UK.' (API, *Family Reunion*, para. 2)

This appears to be contrary to the spirit of policy as developed by the UNHCR (▶see below) and also to one of the recommendations made by the Council of Europe Committee of Ministers concerning family reunion for refugees and others on 15 December 1999, which was as follows:

'Member states should pay particular attention to applications for family reunion concerning persons who are in a vulnerable position. In particular, with regard to unaccompanied minors, member states should, with a view to family reunion, co-operate with children or their representatives in order to trace the members of the family of the unaccompanied minor.'

The 'principle of family unity' under the Refugee Convention

In previous statements, the Home Office has always stated that its own policy on family reunion is based around the 'principle of family unity' which is contained in the Final Act of the Conference which established the Refugee Convention (see government statement on Policy on Family Reunion, Nicholas Baker, 17 March 1995; Somali Family Reunion Policy, 17 May 1990 ([1993] Imm AR 40) at para. 8.1.1 – although the details of those policies are no longer in force, the general principle that the UK follows the 1951 Convention's lead on family reunion policy has never been contradicted).

Who this may be useful to

In asking the immigration authorities to exercise discretion to admit family members of the refugee, the factors referred to under the principle of family unity may be relevant to:

- family members other than spouse or children;
- in particular, children/adolescents who are related to the sponsor but are not their natural children – for example, dependent minor siblings, nephews/nieces or other step-children;
- other relatives who were dependent on the refugee in the country of origin;
- relatives of unaccompanied minors who have been granted refugee status in the UK.

Using the principle of family unity

The development of the principle of family unity can be drawn from the Final Act of the Conference itself; the *UNHCR Handbook*; Conclusions of the UNHCR's Executive Committee (ExCom) and papers occasionally issued by UNHCR. The UNCHR states of the ExCom Conclusions:

'Although not formally binding, they are relevant to the interpretation of the international protection regime. ExCom Conclusions constitute expressions of opinion, which are broadly representative of the views of the international community. The specialist knowledge of ExCom and the fact that its Conclusions are taken by consensus add further weight...' (UNHCR website).

Further, the UK has been an active and influential member of the Executive Committee, which has played a key role in developing the principle of family unity (letter of UNHCR Deputy Representative to South Manchester Law Centre, 7 November 2002). It would be very odd, therefore, if the UK immigration authorities did not have regard to the Executive Committee's Conclusions. In *Mahamed* (▶see above), the appellants appealed to the IAT on the grounds that the ECO had failed to have regard to the principle of family unity developed under the Convention, which, it was asserted, the Home Office had effectively incorporated within its own policy. The respondent's representative, in writing, 'acknowledged the force' of that ground of appeal and agreed that the Home Office had not given proper consideration to the matter. The appeal was allowed to the extent that the application remained outstanding for further consideration.

Depending on the facts of their cases, applicants and advisers may therefore be able to draw on some of the factors set out in the UN/UNHCR materials in making their applications. Due to limitations of space, it is only possible to summarise a certain amount of the material in the table (▶see below), but the ExCom Conclusions and Standing Committee papers are available on the UNHCR website (www.unhcr.ch).

THE 'PRINCIPLE OF FAMILY UNITY' UNDER THE REFUGEE CONVENTION

The 'principle of family unity' as developed under the 1951 Convention may be useful to certain applicants applying for family reunion with refugees (see above for an explanation of its relevance).

Final Act of UN Conference adopting the 1951 Convention

- The conference considered that the unity of the family, the natural and fundamental group of society, is an 'essential right of the refugee' and that such unity is 'constantly threatened' (note that Article 16 of the Universal Declaration of Human Rights also provides that that this 'fundamental' unit of society is entitled to protection by society and the state). The Final Act further recommends that governments take measures for the protection of the unity of the refugee's family, especially with a view to:

  – ensuring that the unity of the family is maintained, particularly where the head of the family has been admitted to their country;

  – the protection of refugees who are minors.

The *UNHCR Handbook*

The *UNHCR Handbook* states that the 'minimum' requirement is that spouses and minor children of refugees are admitted:

'In practice other dependants, such as aged parents of refugees, are normally considered if they are living in the same household...the principle of family unity operates in favour of dependants not against them.' (para. 185)

UNHCR's Executive Committee (ExCom) Conclusions

'Family Reunion', ExCom Conclusion No. 9 XXVIII – 1977

- The principle of family reunion is of 'fundamental importance'.

'Family Reunification', ExCom Conclusion No. 24 XXXII – 1981

- Family reunion should take place 'with the least possible delay'.
- It is hoped that countries of asylum will apply 'liberal criteria' in determining those family members who can be admitted 'with a view to promoting a comprehensive reunification' of the family.
- The lack of formal proof of the validity of a marriage or the fatherhood of children should not on its own be a barrier to family reunion.

'Refugee Children and Adolescents', ExCom Conclusion No. 84 XLVIII – 1997

- Due to the specific needs and vulnerability of refugee children and adolescents, they should be the first to receive 'protection and assistance' in 'any refugee situation'.
- The principle of the 'best interests of the child' and the role of the family as the fundamental group of society concerned with protection and well-being of children should be observed.
- Children and adolescents have a right to education, adequate food, and the highest attainable standard of health.
- Children affected by armed conflict have a right to special protection and treatment, taking into account the vulnerability of refugee children to being exposed to risks of injury, exploitation and death in connection with armed conflict.

'Protection of the Refugee's Family', ExCom Conclusion No. 88 (L) – 1999

- Underlines the need for the unit of the refugee's family to be protected by 'liberal criteria' to identify those who can be admitted, with a view to promoting 'comprehensive' family reunion.

Family Protection Issues (UNHCR ExCom Standing Committee paper, 4 June 1999, EC/49/SC/CRP.14)

- The concept of 'family' differs from state to state, and regionally within a state.
- 'Family' clearly involves the 'nuclear family' of husband, wife and minor children. Besides legally married spouses, couples who are engaged, who have

entered into a customary marriage, or couples who have lived together for a substantial period are understood to be a 'family' by UNHCR for resettlement purposes.

- In a number of societies, 'family is understood in a wider sense to embrace also dependent, unmarried children, minor siblings and dependent elderly parents of the adult family members'.

- Regard must be had to the cultural roots of the family and the society in which the family was formed.

- Both 'pragmatism and flexibility', in addition to 'cultural sensitivity', should be brought to bear in identifying members of the refugee family.

- Although the nuclear family is at the 'core', weight should in any case be given to physical, financial, psychological and emotional dependency in determining who should count as members of the family.

- Regard should be had to the fact that, when family unity is broken, certain family members may become more vulnerable.

- Maintaining family unity is particularly important for refugee children. As is stated in UNHCR's *Guidelines on the Protection and Care of Refugee Children* (1994): 'the single best way to promote the psychological well-being of children is to support their families. A family that is split or under serious stress may not fully meet the physical and emotional needs of their children'.

Among the recommendations in the concluding remarks of the 1999 paper, the UNHCR states:

'Governments are encouraged to deal with applications for family reunification of refugees in an expeditious and humane manner. A flexible definition of the term family, which takes account of the element of dependency among family members, should be used.'

Other family reunion policies

In addition to the immigration rules and the general concessions made to the immigration rules in family reunion cases, the Home Office sometimes operates concessions that relate to families of a particular nationality. From 1988 until January 1994, the Home Office operated a concession for Somali family members in Somalia, or in refugee camps in Ethiopia or Djibouti, who were unable to travel to a British embassy to apply for entry clearance. Their sponsors in the UK were able to apply to the Home Office, with documents in support, for an indication of whether entry clearance would be granted. The Home Office would then carry out a 'preliminary assessment' of the case and give a strong indication of whether entry clearance would, or would not, be granted. The Court of Appeal confirmed that there was no right of appeal against these 'preliminary assessments'. The applicants would then only make the difficult and dangerous trip to the entry clearance post in order to make the formal application if, following the outcome of the preliminary assessment, it seemed worth their while doing so. This made the process easier for displaced families, but the concession was withdrawn when the Home Office believed it had become safe for people to travel again. A similar arrangement for the families of Vietnamese refugees was also withdrawn on 1 November 1999.

Between 1988 and 17 January 1996, the Home Office operated the Somali Family Reunion Policy. In addition to the procedural concession mentioned above, it provided for a more flexible approach to the family members who could qualify. It enabled family members who were dependent members of the refugee's immediate family unit to be admitted. This was largely in recognition of the extended and interdependent nature of Somali families. The most beneficial aspects of the policy only applied to refugee sponsors, not to those with ELR. This policy remains relevant for those who made applications before 17 January 1996.

Refusals and appeals

If entry clearance for family reunion is refused, then there is a right of appeal to the AIT. It may be that the appellants can argue that they have been refused under the immigration rules when they should not have been. However, in family reunion appeals where the rules cannot be met, appellants often argue that the decision is 'not in accordance with the law', which is one of the grounds under the 2002 Act on which an appeal may be allowed. The 'law' here means the general law (see *DS Abdi*, CA). An appeal may be allowed where the ECO has failed to have regard to published policy, misapprehended facts or failed to take into account matters which are relevant to the policy, or failed altogether to consider the application as one for refugee family reunion. For further details about raising these kinds of grounds in family reunion appeals, ▶see 1124–6. However, success on this basis alone is likely to lead to the matter being effectively remitted to the ECO for further decision. It will of course be important also to raise Article 8 at these appeals.

USING THE GENERAL IMMIGRATION RULES FOR FAMILY MEMBERS OF SETTLED SPONSORS

The refugee family reunion rules and policies only apply to a marriage that pre-existed the refugee's flight to the UK. If after their arrival, for example, the refugee marries a person who requires leave to be in the UK, then the ordinary marriage rules must be used (▶see Chapter 11). The same applies for other dependent relatives. Also, as seen above, family members who are not spouses or minor children will only exceptionally be admitted. If the family members are unlikely to qualify under the rules/policies set out above, it is worth seeing whether the refugee sponsor can make use of the ordinary immigration rules relating to family members of persons present and settled in the UK (for all the relevant rules, ▶see Section 4). Spouses, partners and children who have become family members *since* the applicant has arrived and sought asylum in the UK are covered in the ordinary rules. So too are some other relatives (▶see Chapter 13).

Of course, the ordinary requirements of the rules have to be satisfied, including the maintenance and accommodation requirements, which are not a condition of the family reunion rules. Also, many non-spouse and non-minor applicants have to show that they are 'living alone outside the UK in the most exceptional compassionate circumstances' and with 'no other close relatives to turn to'. This is a stringent requirement, but often it can be met for families of refugees – for example, those who are themselves refugees and are stranded in a refugee camp with poor facilities in a third country.

Note, however, that after 30 August 2005, those granted refugee status are no longer granted indefinite leave. The family members of refugee sponsors who are affected by this will, therefore, no longer have immediate access to the rules for dependants of settled sponsors.

Flexible application of rules for non 'pre-existing' spouse and minor children

In at least some respects, the Home Office has indicated that it is prepared to be flexible about the immigration rules in cases involving settled refugees. In relation to marriage applications, the Home Office has stated:

'If the sponsor is a recognised refugee in the United Kingdom, caseworkers should be flexible about the application of the maintenance and accommodation requirements. This is because it might be unreasonable to expect someone who has fled persecution to be able to be self-sufficient here immediately.' (API *Marriage applications*, para. 3)

Children who are born in the UK and who were not included in the asylum application are in a similar position. They cannot have formed part of the family unit overseas. They will almost certainly be granted leave in line with the refugee (or person with exceptional leave) if an application is made. The API indicates that officers should invite parents of children in this position to apply to regularise their status (see API *Dependants*, para. 8.4).

FAMILY REUNION AND ARTICLE 8 ECHR

In all cases, applicants and advisers should consider the impact of Article 8 ECHR. Officers are expressly instructed to have regard to Article 8 in considering applications in this category (see the separate APIs on *Dependants*, *Family Reunion* and *Marriage*, all at para. 1; DSP Ch 16, para. 16.1). Generally, for obvious reasons, refugees will not be able to relocate to establish family life in their country of origin. In addition, whereas in some Article 8 immigration cases account is taken of 'voluntary' decisions by family members to separate, the decision of a refugee to flee leaving behind family members cannot be viewed as a voluntary act. This was underlined in *H (Somalia)* in which the IAT commented:

'It cannot be right to approach the disruption to family life which is caused by someone having to flee persecution as a refugee as if it were of the same nature as someone who voluntarily leaves, or leaves in the normal course of the changes to family life which naturally occur as children grow up.' (para. 14)

So, many refugee family reunion cases will also be compelling Article 8 cases. For full details about how Article 8 works in family cases, ▶see 820–50.

Section 8 **Human rights and discrimination**

Chapter 26
The European Convention on Human Rights 773
The rights 775
How the rights work – limitations on ECHR rights 777
Taking a case to Europe 781

Chapter 27
Human rights in immigration and asylum cases 785
'Extra-territorial effect' and 'flagrant breaches' 787
Claims for protection 792
Cases where removal will have a detrimental effect 809
Family or other connections with the UK 820
Leave outside the rules where there is no breach of human rights 851

Chapter 28
Raising human rights, humanitarian protection, discretionary leave, family reunion and travel 853
Making human rights claims 854
Human rights appeals and fresh claims 857
What leave is granted if a human rights claim is successful? 859
Family members 875
Travel documents 880

Chapter 29
Discrimination 885
Article 14 ECHR 885
Race discrimination 887

8

26 The European Convention on Human Rights

This section deals with the human rights protected by the European Convention on Human Rights (ECHR) and how those rights can be used in immigration cases. On 2 October 2000, the Human Rights Act 1998 (HRA) came into force. The importance of this was that most of the rights contained in the ECHR were incorporated into UK law, which means that they can be enforced in the UK courts. Before the HRA, in order to enforce their ECHR rights, a person would have to apply directly to the European Court of Human Rights (ECtHR) in Strasbourg, which is a long and complex process. The immigration rules reflect the HRA by requiring entry clearance officers, immigration officers and all staff at the Home Office's Immigration and Nationality Directorate to make sure that they carry out their functions in compliance with human rights (para. 2, HC 395).

This chapter gives a brief overview of the human rights that have been incorporated, and at the limitations on those rights (▶775–81). It also looks, very briefly, at procedures for taking a case to the European Court of Human Rights if all attempts in the UK courts have failed (▶781–4).

Chapter 27, the main chapter in this section, deals with how the rights can be used in immigration cases. In particular, it looks at three specific areas in which the rights have a substantial impact:

1) claims for 'protection' from harm in the person's country of return (▶see 792–809);

2) cases where forcing someone to leave the UK will have a particular detrimental effect upon them – largely cases involving health (▶see 809–820);

3) cases where the applicant has family or other connections with the UK (▶see 820–50).

Chapter 28 deals with how human rights claims are made (▶854–9), and with the complex policy about what kind of leave is given to those whose claims succeed (humanitarian protection and discretionary leave) (▶862–75 and ▶see also 721–7). It also looks at family reunion and travel (▶875–83).

Chapter 29 looks at the question of discrimination in immigration cases. It covers both Article 14 ECHR, which prohibits discrimination in the area of human rights, and the UK's own anti-discrimination legislation.

8

Article 5 ECHR is important in protecting rights in immigration cases, because it sets limits on the powers of the state to detain people for the purposes of immigration control. It is therefore dealt with separately, in the section dealing with detention (▶922–4, 925, 930). Claims for damages for unlawful detention, including detention in breach of Article 5, are covered in the chapter on civil claims (▶1175–81, 1205–10). Of course, Article 5 may also sometimes be used in claims for protection from harm overseas, and that is covered here in this section (▶800–2).

The European institutions and incorporation

European Convention on Human Rights (ECHR)

The European Convention for the Protection of Human Rights and Fundamental Freedoms (ECHR) is an international treaty of the Council of Europe that the UK ratified in 1951. The Council of Europe is an intergovernmental organisation that was formed at the end of the Second World War. In the aftermath of the battle against fascism, the European countries were keen to encourage respect for the rule of law, and to protect fundamental freedoms, and social and economic development. The purpose of the ECHR was to ensure a 'fair balance' between the various fundamental rights of the individual, on the one hand, and the interests of the wider community on the other. The intention was to enable people to enforce their individual rights against the state where it acted in breach of those rights, and, in some cases, to allow them to obtain compensation.

European Court of Human Rights (ECtHR)

The European Court of Human Rights is based in Strasbourg, France. The Court has ultimate jurisdiction on all matters concerning the implementation and application of the ECHR, both in cases of disputes between two states and in cases of an individual taking an action against a state. Each member-state nominates one judge to the Court. Before November 1998, if a complaint about human rights was to be taken to Europe, it first had to be made to the European Commission (EComm HR), which would decide whether the complaint was 'admissible' or 'manifestly unfounded'. If it was declared admissible, then the complaint could proceed to the Court itself. However, there is now one single court that both makes initial decisions about whether a complaint is admissible and also makes the final ruling on the case.

Before people complain to the Court about an alleged violation of their human rights, they must first go through all the court procedures in the UK. In practice, this means that few cases will now have to go to Strasbourg.

The Human Rights Act 1998

The HRA is the mechanism for incorporating rights granted by the ECHR into UK law. There are a number of 'protocols' to the ECHR which also contain rights, some of which have also been incorporated.

THE HUMAN RIGHTS ACT 1998

The following points about the HRA should be borne in mind:

- it states which rights under the ECHR and protocols are made part of UK law (s1, Schedule 1; ▶see below);
- it makes it unlawful for a 'public authority' (including the immigration authorities and the Asylum and Immigration Appeal Tribunal (AIT)) to act in a way that is incompatible with an incorporated ECHR right (s6);
- it allows the 'victim' of the breach of human rights to bring claims in the appropriate court against the public authority for actions in breach of the ECHR. In immigration cases, this will usually be by bringing an appeal on human rights grounds (s7);
- it requires UK courts and tribunals (including the AIT) to take into account ECtHR decisions when they are interpreting ECHR rights (but ECtHR decisions are not binding in the UK);
- it requires that legislation made by parliament, and also regulations and rules made by the government (including the immigration rules), are interpreted in a way that 'so far as possible' complies with the ECHR rights (s3);
- it allows certain courts to make 'declarations of incompatibility', where the legislation passed by parliament is not compatible with the ECHR (s4);
- it allows people to claim compensation for breaches of their human rights (s8; ▶see also 1202–4).

THE RIGHTS

The following rights contained in the ECHR and its protocols have been incorporated into UK law by the HRA.

ECHR

- the right to life (Article 2);
- prohibition on torture and inhuman or degrading treatment or punishment (Article 3);
- prohibition on slavery and forced labour (Article 4);
- right to liberty and security (Article 5);
- right to a fair trial (Article 6);

- protection from punishment for acts which were not offences at the time when they were committed (Article 7);
- respect for private and family life, home and correspondence (Article 8);
- freedom of thought, conscience and religion (Article 9);
- freedom of expression (Article 10);
- freedom of assembly and association (Article 11);
- right to marry and found a family (Article 12);
- prohibition of discrimination (Article 14).

Protocol 1 to the ECHR

- right to property (Article 1);
- right to education (Article 2);
- free and fair elections (Article 3).

Protocol 13 to the ECHR

- abolition of the death penalty and prohibition on condemnation to death (Article 1).

The above incorporated rights must also be 'read with' the rights under Articles 16–18 ECHR (see s1 HRA) (▶see 777). The actual text of most of the rights is given when we deal with claims for protection, in the next chapter (▶792–809).

The HRA does not incorporate the following two obligations upon the state: to ensure that everyone within its jurisdiction has their rights safeguarded (Article 1); to ensure that there is a way of enforcing the rights in the state's own courts or institutions (Article 13). The government says that the reason for not specifically incorporating these rights is that they are already secured by bringing in the HRA itself.

The prohibition on discrimination, Article 14 ECHR

Article 14 is different from most of the other incorporated rights because it cannot be used on its own: there is no general right to be free from discrimination. Article 14 states that:

'The enjoyment of the rights and freedoms set forth in this Convention shall be secured without discrimination on any ground such as sex, race, colour, language, religion, political or other opinion, national or social origin, association with a national minority, property, birth or other status.'

Article 14 provides a right not to be discriminated against in 'enjoying' the other ECHR rights, and must therefore be used together with at least one of those other rights. However, it is not necessary to establish an actual *breach* of the other ECHR rights in order to show that Article 14 is breached. The applicant only needs to show that:

- they have suffered less favourable treatment on one of the grounds mentioned or an equivalent ground; and
- that less favourable treatment *affects* their other rights under the ECHR.

There will be no breach of Article 14 if the state can show that there is a legitimate purpose for the discrimination, and that the detriment to those discriminated against is outweighed by the interests of the community (for further details, ▶see 885–7).

Articles 16–18 ECHR

The rights which are incorporated by the ECHR are also to be 'read with' Articles 16–18 ECHR. They state:

- states may impose certain restrictions on the political activity of aliens (Article 16);
- no state or group of persons can do anything with the aim of destroying the rights or freedoms set out in the Convention, or to limit them to a greater extent than the Convention allows (Article 17);
- the restrictions on the rights under the Convention should not be applied for any purpose other than those for which those restrictions are allowed under the Convention (Article 18).

The purpose of Article 17 is to prevent extremists – for example, fascists – from taking advantage of the rights in the Convention in order to destroy others' ECHR rights. The point of Article 18 is to underline that, where the Convention provides rights that are qualified, then the restrictions on the exercise of those rights can only be made for the purposes which the Convention states, and no other purpose. The use of Article 18 was recently brought to bear in conjunction with Article 5 in a case involving the detention of a Russian national (▶see 802).

HOW THE RIGHTS WORK – LIMITATIONS ON ECHR RIGHTS

Although the incorporated rights listed above read very grandly, in most cases they are subject to certain restrictions. This is because the rights are intended to strike a balance between individual freedoms and collective interests. The restrictions are either set out alongside the right in question in the Convention, or they may be implicit in the words used. So, in many cases it may be that, although a decision 'interferes' with a particular right, the interference can be justified on the basis of the restriction so that there is no actual breach of the right taken as a whole. However, some rights are 'absolute' – i.e. they are so important that interference with them can never be justified. Article 3 falls into this category.

In the case of any right which has these in-built restrictions, the state can, in any individual case, argue that the interference is justified. It does not need to take any general action in order to be able to rely upon the restriction. The vast majority of cases in which rights are limited are in this category, and we have referred to this process simply as 'restricting' rights.

Reservations and derogations

Quite separate from the 'in-built' restrictions discussed above are certain further circumstances in which a state is entitled not to observe the rights in the ECHR and protocols. A state may enter 'reservations' when it signs up to rights. In some cases, it may also later 'derogate' from them.

Reservation

A state can enter 'reservations' about any Convention rights when it signs up to them. The UK has entered a reservation about the requirement in Article 2 of the First Protocol to respect the right of parents to ensure that education and teaching are in conformity with the parents' religious and philosophical beliefs. The UK intends to comply with this right under its national laws 'only insofar as it is compatible with the provision of efficient instruction ... and the avoidance of unreasonable public expenditure'.

Derogation

A state can 'derogate' from the ECHR in times of 'war or other public emergency threatening the life of the nation' (Article 15). The state can only do this to the extent that the situation it faces 'strictly requires' the suspension of the rights. Again, some rights cannot be derogated from under any circumstances (see below). Under the ECHR, as well as the HRA, the UK has to go through a specific process in order to derogate from a right and specify the public emergency that applies. Of particular relevance to UK immigration law was the derogation made by the UK in relation to suspected 'international terrorists' (for this and the decision of the House of Lords in *A & Others v SSHD*, ▶see 901–2).

Limitations on ECHR rights

In the table below, we classify the rights into four groups, depending upon the ways in which they can be limited.

1) Rights that are absolute and cannot be restricted, and in relation to which no derogation is permitted.

2) Rights that can be restricted, but only in specifically defined circumstances.

3) Rights that can be restricted in more generally stated circumstances in the interests of society.

4) Rights that appear to be absolute, but which contain implied restrictions.

THE LIMITATIONS ON ECHR RIGHTS

The rights can be classified into four groups, according to the different ways in which they are limited (▶see above at 778). The classifications are not precise, but are useful in understanding the way in which the rights under the ECHR work. Note that the actual text of the rights is set out at ▶792–809.

1) Absolute rights that cannot be derogated from

For the ability of a state to 'derogate' from a right, ▶see 778 above. Rights that are absolute and 'non-derogable' are:

The right to life (Article 2) This right cannot be derogated from except where the death is the result of 'lawful acts of war'. Even though we have listed this right as 'absolute' in requiring the state to protect a person's life and to prevent it from being intentionally taken away, there are certain circumstances where the taking of a life is not regarded as breaching the right (▶see 792–3, where the right is set out in full).

Prohibition on torture and inhuman and degrading treatment and punishment (Article 3) The fact that no derogation can be made from Article 3 is very important in immigration cases because it means that, whatever the emergency, a person cannot be sent to a country where they will be exposed to the prohibited treatment (▶see further below).

Prohibition of slavery (Article 4 paragraph 1) The prohibition against holding people in slavery or 'servitude' is an absolute, non-derogable right. However, the right not to be required to perform forced labour can be derogated from (▶see below).

Prohibition on punishment for an act which was not a crime when it was committed (Article 7) Freedom from punishment for an action that was not a crime when it was done is another absolute, non-derogable right. However, this does not prevent criminal offences and penalties being imposed for acts which, at the time when they were committed, were recognised by 'civilised nations' as being crimes.

2) Rights that can be restricted, but only in specifically defined circumstances

The following rights are all subject to certain specific restrictions, which are set out in the Convention itself. They can also be derogated from by the state in times of war or public emergency.

Right to liberty (Article 5) A person may be detained provided that domestic law authorises it for any of the following reasons: if they have been convicted of an offence; have failed to comply with an order of a court; if they are suspected of committing an offence (or to prevent them from committing one); if they are of unsound mind, an alcoholic, drug addict or vagrant. Detention is also lawful under Article 5 in order to prevent the spread of infectious diseases, or to prevent a person making an 'unauthorised entry' into the UK, or for the purpose of deporting or extraditing them.

8

Right to marry (Article 12) The right to marry and to found a family can be restricted only by the 'national laws governing the exercise of the right'. There is no specific restriction on what laws the state is permitted to have, but they must not undermine the essence of the right to marry.

Requirement to perform forced labour (Article 4) Requirements to perform labour are permitted where a person is lawfully detained under Article 5, or where the work is military service (or alternative civilian service), or there is an emergency threatening the well-being of the community, or if it is work which is part of 'normal civic obligations'.

3) Rights that can be restricted by more generally stated circumstances, in the interests of society

The following rights are subject to more generally defined restrictions, which can be applied by the state to individual cases. These rights can also be derogated from by the state in times of war or public emergency:

- respect for private and family life, home and correspondence (Article 8);
- freedom for a person to manifest their religion or beliefs (Article 9);
- freedom of expression (Article 10);
- freedom of assembly and association (Article 11).

In the case of these rights, the ECHR provides a right in the first paragraph of the relevant article, followed by the circumstances in which the right can legitimately be interfered with in the second paragraph. In each case, it is for the applicant to show that the protected right is being interfered with. If the applicant can show an interference, the state must then demonstrate that the interference meets *all* of the following criteria:

- it is 'in accordance with the law' or 'prescribed by law';
- it is carried out for one of the purposes referred to in the relevant article (the permitted reasons given in the different articles vary slightly, but the following are examples: the interests of public safety, the rights and freedoms of others, the prevention of disorder and crime, the economic well-being of the country, national security);
- it is 'necessary' in the interests of a democratic society. This is generally taken to mean that the interference in the person's human rights must be 'proportionate' to, or in a fair balance against, the interest of the community that the state is seeking to uphold.

These elements are examined more closely under Article 8 (▶see 821 onwards). It should be noted that the exercise of the freedoms of expression, assembly and association of 'aliens' can be interfered with by the state without regard to the above rights (Article 16 ECHR), but the meaning of this restriction has rarely been considered by the ECtHR.

4) Rights that appear to be absolute but which contain implied restrictions

The following rights may appear to be absolute, but have actually been interpreted with implied restrictions. Another way of looking at them is to say that the actual content of a particular right is itself more limited than it might at first appear. These rights can also be derogated from by the state in times of war or public emergency.

Right to a fair trial (Article 6) The ECHR states that there is a right to a fair trial in deciding a person's 'civil rights and obligations', and in deciding any charge against them. Article 6 then goes on to state some basic minimum rights in criminal cases – for example, that everyone shall be presumed innocent until proved guilty, and that those accused are entitled to time to prepare a defence and to interpretation facilities. However, Article 6 does not define the actual meaning of 'fair trial'. Because the words are open to interpretation, the ECtHR has held that there is room for implying limitations where necessary (*Golder*).

Right to possessions, education, free elections (rights under the First Protocol) These rights are also limited by implication. For example, a state does not 'deny' a person an education provided that it grants equal access to the educational facilities that exist, and allows people to benefit from their education. Within those limits, the state is not required to set up particular types or levels of education (see the *'Belgian Linguistics'* case, ECtHR). States may reasonably regulate access to education – for example, a person who has not passed their qualifying examinations may be denied access to a university or a further education place.

TAKING A CASE TO EUROPE

After the Human Rights Act, people can still make complaints to the ECtHR in Strasbourg. But they must first try to overturn the decision that they claim breaches their human rights by all available means in the UK. In immigration cases, this will normally involve bringing a human rights appeal and/or using the court system. Applicants should seek advice if they think they have a case to take to the ECtHR.

Applications to the ECtHR proceed in two stages. There is first a decision as to whether the complaint is 'admissible'. If the application passes this stage, it proceeds to a decision on the 'merits'. If an application is declared to be admissible, the court may try to get the parties to agree to a friendly settlement. Legal decision-making used to be divided between the European Commission and the European Court of Human Rights, but from November 1998 there has been a single Court. The Court does, however, sit in the following divisions:

- Plenary Court. This does not hear cases, but deals with administrative matters, including adopting rules of procedure;

- 'Committees' of three judges;
- 'Chambers' of seven judges;
- 'Grand chambers' of 17 judges.

If the committee is unanimous, it can decide that an application is inadmissible. Otherwise, the decision on both 'admissibility' and 'merits' is heard by a chamber. Cases involving very serious matters affecting the interpretation of the ECHR are heard by the grand chamber.

Procedure for making an application

Applications should be made using the application form provided by the Court. The application must be made within six months of the final decision of the domestic court (see Article 35 ECHR). The time limit is very strictly applied by the Court – even if, for example, the application is made only one day late. In urgent cases, the application can be made by letter, provided the form is later sent without undue delay to the secretary of the Court. If an application is made by letter, the Court registry will acknowledge receipt and will send a form warning the applicant to complete the form within a reasonable time.

The form sets out clearly what information is needed by the Court. The form or letter can be lodged by post or fax. Failure to include the relevant information can lead to the application not being registered. Legal representatives must provide a letter of authority signed by the applicant.

In the application, applicants are required to provide the following information:

- their name, age, address and occupation;
- the name, address and occupation of anyone acting as their representative;
- the respondent country;
- a statement of the facts;
- the relevant domestic law;
- the articles of the Convention the applicant is relying on, together with any relevant case law;
- the object of the application;
- the details of the orders the applicant wants the Court to make;
- judgments, decisions and any other relevant documents relating to the application.

Completing the application form is the most important part of the application procedure. Legal advisers must set out the complaint fully when returning the form. Failure to raise an issue properly at the initial stage of the procedure will mean that the court will not subsequently entertain arguments about that issue.

Procedure before the Court

The usual procedure followed before the ECtHR can be summarised as follows.

- The application should be lodged within six months of the last domestic decision. The time limit can only be waived if there is a continuing breach of the applicant's human rights.
- The application is registered.
- The Court may contact a party for more information about the complaint.
- The case is examined by a committee of three judges. The majority of cases are declared inadmissible at this stage. There is no appeal if a case is declared inadmissible. The admissibility criteria under Article 35 ECHR includes a 'manifestly ill-founded' test. This is why it is so important to substantiate the claim properly at the initial stages.
- If the case is likely to be admissible, the committee will communicate notice of the application to the government concerned.
- Observations on the application are filed by the parties.
- An admissibility decision is made by chambers of seven judges. There is the possibility of an oral hearing, although most admissibility decisions are made without a hearing.
- Negotiations may at this point lead to a friendly settlement and the case will then be then be closed.
- A judgment is made by the chamber on the merits.
- Exceptional cases are referred to a grand chamber of 17 judges, which may receive oral and written evidence.

Interim measures

If the state is acting, or is shortly going to act, in a way that is alleged to be in breach of a person's human rights, occasionally the chamber or its president may suggest to the state any 'interim measures' it considers appropriate (rule 39 of the Rules of the ECtHR). This can be done at the request of the parties or by the Court acting on its own. Requests by parties should be made in writing and, if urgent, faxed. Advance notice should be given to the Court that faxes and any supporting documentation are on their way.

Requests for interim remedies are most common in deportation and extradition cases, but may also be made in any case where there is an 'apparent real and imminent risk of irreparable harm'. Rule 39 indications are not often made, and they are not binding on the state. However, the Home Office states that it is its practice to comply with a Rule 39 indication and to defer removal if such an indication is obtained (Operational Enforcement Manual, Ch 44.7).

8

Legal funding

Financial assistance from the UK's Community Legal Service Fund is not available for proceedings before the ECtHR. An applicant can request financial assistance from the Court. The registry will send a declaration of means form for the applicant to complete; assistance may be granted from the time that observations in writing are received from the respondent. However, the financial assistance rates are extremely low.

27 Human rights in immigration and asylum cases

Chapter 26 explained the basic nature of the rights under the ECHR, incorporated into UK law by the Human Rights Act 1998. This chapter looks directly at how those rights can be used in immigration and asylum cases. For other aspects of human rights in immigration – the practicalities of making claims, the treatment of unaccompanied minors who cannot be returned, qualifying for humanitarian protection and discretionary leave (and the old exceptional leave), and rights to family reunion and travel documents for those granted these forms of leave – ▶see Chapter 28.

In this chapter, we have divided the impact of the rights under the ECHR into three categories of case, as follows.

1) **Claims for protection** These are cases in which people are claiming protection in the UK as a result of their fear of ill-treatment or harm in their country of return. Such applicants are also likely to claim asylum under the Refugee Convention (▶Section 7). However, in some cases where applicants cannot qualify as refugees, they can still succeed on human rights grounds. Article 3 is the most important right in protection claims, but a range of rights are potentially relevant (▶792–809).

2) **Health or other detrimental effects of return** In some cases, an applicant claims that they cannot return to their country of origin because of the physical, mental or other detrimental effect that it would have upon them. Most of these cases concern the effect on the applicant's health if they were required to return. If such a person alleges that they will be denied medical or other facilities for a Refugee Convention reason, they may also claim asylum. These cases will usually raise issues under Articles 3 and/or 8 ECHR (▶809–820).

3) **Family or other connections with the UK** These are claims in which people argue that removing them from, or refusing to admit them to, the UK is a breach of their rights under Article 8 ECHR. This is because of their ties to family members who are established here and/or as a result of other connections they have developed with the UK (▶see below at 820–50).

The requirements for succeeding in a human rights claim are stringent. However, *even if* a human rights claim fails, the Home Office may still grant leave as a matter of discretion. It is clear that policy on 'discretionary leave' includes some categories where there is no breach of human rights (▶see 865). The courts have also stressed that the Home Office has a wide discretion, which may be exercised in compelling cases even if those cases do not show a breach of human rights. At the end of the chapter, we set out some of the comments which have been made by the courts in particular cases, and which may be useful when asking the immigration authorities to exercise discretion, or asking the AIT to make recommendations to the Home Office (▶see 851–2).

Note that Article 5 ECHR can be relevant to claims for protection, and it is therefore discussed in this chapter (▶800–2). However, it is also relevant to immigration detention carried out by the authorities in the UK, and it is therefore covered from this separate angle in the chapter on detention powers (▶see 922–4, 925, 930). For claims for unlawful detention, including claims under Article 5, ▶see 1175–81, 1205–10.

Occasionally an applicant may be able to rely on Article 6 ECHR other than in a 'protection' (above) context. In *Quaquah*, removal, which would undermine the claimant's ability to maintain a civil action against the Home Office for malicious prosecution, was found to be contrary to the principle of equality of arms. For civil claims generally ▶see Chapter 37. The Home Office may well agree to defer removal in such cases.

First questions

The bulk of this chapter is divided in accordance with the three categories of case described above. However, we begin the chapter by looking at two important questions.

- First, a key issue over the last few years has been which ECHR rights an applicant can rely on when they claim that they will suffer harm *in* the country of return. In order to analyse the law, the courts have referred to these cases as 'foreign cases', because the actual harm occurs overseas. As a result of the cases already decided in the European Court of Human Rights in Strasbourg, the Home Office has always accepted that Article 3 can be relied on in these cases. Because it looks at the effect of the ECHR where harm may occur overseas, the issue is sometimes referred to as concerning the 'extra-territorial' effect of the Convention. This debate does not affect claims in the third category outlined above (family and other connections) because, in those cases, a negative immigration decision interferes with rights enjoyed in the UK – for example, with family life here (such cases are referred to by the courts as 'domestic' cases).

- The second – and connected – issue is whether a more stringent test is applied to determine whether there is a breach of the ECHR in returning someone who claims they will be exposed to harm overseas, than where the harm would occur in the UK. Again, Article 3 is not affected: the issue is always whether there is a real risk of the applicant being subject to any of the harms falling within the simple definition of that Article. But with other rights, is there a higher test, or 'threshold'? For example, does the applicant have to show a 'flagrant' breach of their rights?

Both of these questions were dealt with by the House of Lords in *Ullah & Do*, and also applied in relation, to Article 8, in *Razgar*. We discuss them immediately below. *Razgar* is discussed again at ▶817–8.

Although, in principle, Article 3 cases are not affected by these questions, the courts have imposed a very significant limitation on using that right in certain cases. Where the harm overseas is not the result of human ill-treatment, nor the fault or responsibility of the authorities there, Article 3 rights are very narrow. This is the effect of the recent decision of the House of Lords in *N*, which deals with Article 3 in cases involving very serious illness where medical facilities abroad are insufficient. It decides that Article 3 will only provide protection in very exceptional cases (▶see 810–12).

'EXTRA-TERRITORIAL EFFECT' AND 'FLAGRANT' BREACHES

'Extra-territorial effect' is a label that has been attached to the question of whether the ECHR can protect people who are at risk of harm that will occur overseas if they are returned. As was stated by the IAT in *Kacaj*, it is a slightly misleading label, because a person who is here and who is facing removal is 'within the jurisdiction' of the UK, and therefore protected by rights under the Convention (Article 1 ECHR). The act of expelling them is an action that occurs in the UK. It is easy to see, though, why this phrase has been used, because it describes the situation where the alleged harm will be suffered by an applicant not on UK territory, but somewhere else.

Early Home Office position

Until the decision of the House of Lords in *Ullah & Do* in June 2004 (see below), the Home Office position was that, where a claim was based on harm that would occur in the country of return, only Article 3 could provide protection. The government's argument was that normally the ECHR deals with breaches of human rights by the authorities in the state whose actions are being complained of. Because Article 3 provides such fundamental protection, a more flexible approach had to be taken. The state must neither directly inflict Article 3 harm nor indirectly expose a person to such harm by sending them somewhere where it may occur. The European Court of Human Rights (ECtHR) had itself established this (see for example *Soering* and *Chahal*).

The decision in *Kacaj*

In July 2001, the IAT considered the question in *Kacaj*. It held that:

- all the articles of the ECHR (with, for special reasons, the possible exception of Article 2) have what had been called 'extra-territorial' effect;

- where an applicant is making a claim as a result of harm feared overseas, it will be rare that a breach of one of the generally qualified rights, such as Article 8 (for a general analysis of the ECHR rights, ▶see 778–81), can be established if Article 3 is not also breached. This is because in such cases the state will usually be able to justify the return on the grounds that it is in the interests of immigration control.

The decision in *Ullah & Do*

In *Ullah & Do*, as well as claiming to be refugees, the appellants alleged that returning them would be in breach of their rights under Article 9 ECHR (freedom of thought, conscience and religion). Mr Ullah was an Ahmadi from Pakistan who wanted to spread his beliefs by preaching. Before the adjudicator, it had been accepted that the ability of Ahmadis to practice their religion was restricted by the law and by societal attitudes. However, the adjudicator found that the difficulties faced by Mr Ullah were not enough to violate his rights under Article 3. What interference there was with his rights under Article 9 could be justified as proportionate. Ms Do was Vietnamese, and it was accepted that her Catholicism, which had involved her in teaching the religion to children, had resulted in her being discriminated against and harassed. Nevertheless, the adjudicator and the IAT found that the treatment was not severe enough to amount to 'persecution' or treatment contrary to Article 3, and that her rights under Article 9 were also not violated.

The Court of Appeal found for the Home Office. It decided that, in cases where the claim was *solely* based on risk of harm in the country of return, rights under the ECHR could only be relied on if the harm was severe enough to breach Article 3. The House of Lords found in favour of the appellants on the point of legal principle. However, both cases failed on their facts (see the table below).

THE DECISION OF THE HOUSE OF LORDS IN *ULLAH & DO*

In *Ullah & Do*, the House of Lords considered human rights claims in 'foreign cases' – that is, cases where a claim is based on harm that will occur *in* the country of return. The effect of the decision is as follows.

1) Where return to a country overseas exposes an applicant to a risk of harm in that country, but the level of harm is not sufficient to amount to a breach of Article 3, it is still possible for the removal to violate the applicant's rights under other articles of the Convention.

2) The cases in which non-Article 3 rights are breached will be 'exceptional'. Generally, this will depend on showing a 'very strong case', a 'gross violation', a 'real risk of a flagrant violation', an 'extremely serious breach', or a 'fundamental' breach of the relevant rights (Lord Bingham para. 24, Lord Steyn para. 50, Lord Carswell paras 68–70). The reason for this is that 'foreign' cases are an exception to the general rule that a state is only responsible for what

happens on its own territory and within its control. It is only indirectly responsible for what happens overseas as a result of its immigration decision to return a person.

3) The following further comments were made in relation to the separate rights.

Article 2. This may be relied on in a case where the 'facts are strong enough'. An applicant *might* need to show that there is a 'high risk' amounting to a 'near certainty' that they will lose their life (Lord Bingham, paras 15, 24). Lord Steyn thought that it was not right to draw 'a bright-line' between Articles 2 and 3 (para. 40).

Article 4. A claim strong enough to succeed under Article 4 would normally qualify under Article 3, but it seemed wrong to exclude a claim based on Article 4 from succeeding on its own (Lord Bingham para. 16, Lord Steyn para. 41).

Articles 5, 6. Applicants will face 'great difficulties' in making out cases under these articles, and only 'exceptional' cases are likely to qualify (Lord Bingham, paras 21, 24). Applicants may qualify if there is a real risk of 'flagrant' denial of justice or the rule of law as to personal freedom (Lord Steyn, paras 43–4).

Article 7. It is possible that cases could arise under Article 7. Where they do, the same test as for Articles 5 and 6 applies: Is there a real risk of a flagrant denial of Article 7 rights? (Lord Steyn, para. 45)

Article 8. A claim under Article 8 may succeed in a foreign case where the applicant can show that removal will 'seriously interfere' with his rights, and that the interference cannot be justified. This also requires a 'flagrant' denial of rights (Lord Bingham paras 18, 24, Lord Steyn para. 47, and see also the decision of the House of Lords in *Razgar*). *For further details about foreign/domestic Article 8 cases,* ▶*see below at 790–2. For protection cases involving sexuality,* ▶see 608, 615–6, 804–6.

Article 9. A successful Article 9 case would normally mean that an applicant could succeed under Article 3, or under the Refugee Convention, on grounds of 'religion'. However, it is possible that a claim based on Article 9 alone might succeed (Lord Bingham para. 21, Lord Carswell para. 67).

Articles 8, 9, 10, 11 and 14. In all of these rights, which involve general qualifications, an applicant might show a violation in a foreign case. The difficulty applicants face is not only that of showing a 'serious interference', but also of resisting the defence that the interference (even though serious) is proportionate. The Home Office will always have strong grounds for justifying removal based on the 'great importance of operating firm and orderly immigration control' (Lord Bingham para. 24, Lord Steyn para. 48).

4) The House of Lords did not expressly deal with any other rights. They tended to think that an applicant would not be able to rely on the right to education in Article 2, First Protocol to the ECHR (▶see further 820), but it did not decide the point.

Both cases were rejected on the facts, which were found not to be strong enough. Lord Steyn stated that neither came within a 'measurable distance of establishing that Article 9 was engaged' (para. 26). This underlines how strong a non-Article 3 'foreign' claim needs to be in order to succeed.

For further details about the application of individual Articles in claims for protection, ▶see 792–809.

The 'flagrant breach' requirement

The 'flagrant breach' test (▶see table above) had been suggested before *Ullah*. In *Soering*, the European Court had stated that a 'flagrant' breach of the right to a fair trial under Article 6 in the country of return might amount to a breach of the sending state's obligations. In *Devaseelan*, the IAT had applied this approach to Articles 5 and 6, and explained:

'The reason why flagrant denial or gross violation is to be taken into account is that it is only in such a case – where the right will be completely denied or nullified in the destination country – that it can be said that removal will breach the treaty obligations of the signatory state, however those obligations might be interpreted or whatever might be said by or on behalf of the destination state.'

In *Ullah*, the House of Lords stated that this reasoning also applied to the generally qualified rights under Articles 8–11.

Following the decision in *Ullah*, the Home Office has obviously had to change its position. In an Asylum Policy Notice on the judgment (1/2004), it has advised caseworkers that:

'A flagrant breach will only occur where conditions in a country are such that it is impossible for a person to exercise any meaningful aspect of a non-Article 3 ECHR right…'

The same notice gives two examples of circumstances in which, in the Home Office's view, there will not be a flagrant breach of human rights:

- trials where the quality of legal representation is poor, or where the standard of proof is the balance of probabilities (rather than 'beyond reasonable doubt') (Articles 5 and 6);
- an applicant will have to travel a long distance in order to exercise their religion, and will have to do so in a discreet way (Article 9 ECHR).

When is a 'flagrant breach' required in Article 8 cases?

Applicants only need to show a flagrant breach in a 'foreign' case (*Ullah* above ▶789). In the context of Article 8, this will be where the only claim is, for example, based on the denial of the rights of gay men and lesbians in the country of return, or the lack of facilities to treat an applicant's medical condition. There is no need to show a flagrant breach in a 'domestic' case where the immigration decision interferes with the applicant's ability to enjoy their rights in the UK, either by removing them from the UK or refusing to admit them. Domestic cases are those where the applicant has family and/or private life connections to the UK. This includes claims based upon relationships with spouses, partners or other family members in the UK, and private life claims based on long residence, work or study in the UK, or a combination of such circumstances.

The uncertainty in *Ullah*

The above is the position as we see it. However, although in *Ullah*, Lord Bingham gave clear technical definitions for 'foreign' and 'domestic' cases (paras 7, 9), certain parts of his judgement (and that of Lord Steyn) are not completely clear as to which actual cases are foreign, which are domestic, and in which cases an applicant needs to show a flagrant breach. In particular:

- At one point Lord Bingham seems to distinguish between (1) domestic family separation cases, such as *Abdulaziz*, where the *applicants* were the settled wives who complained that their rights were interfered with because they could not be joined in the UK by their husbands; and (2) other 'hybrid' cases (i.e. in between domestic and foreign cases) where the removal of a person with family connections in the UK deprives them of those family connections both in the UK and abroad (para. 18).

- Lord Steyn talks generally about family and private life expulsion cases having to establish that there will be a 'flagrant violation' of Article 8 (paras 39, 47).

Clarifying the matter: *Razgar*

However, in the House of Lords in *Razgar* (which was heard by the same judicial committee directly after *Ullah*), the judgment of Baroness Hale clarified this issue. Although she was in the minority in *Razgar* as far as the facts of that case were concerned, Baroness Hale's analysis of foreign and domestic cases, and of Article 8 generally, is not questioned elsewhere, and we would suggest it is correct. She explained that:

- the cases Lord Bingham referred to as 'hybrid' cases – where the applicant complains that their removal from the UK means both that they cannot enjoy their family life in the UK and that they will continue to be deprived of their family life while they are in the country of return – were in fact 'domestic cases' (para. 43);

- Article 8 cases where the applicant is not being removed but is applying to be admitted to the UK to join family members here, were also 'domestic' cases (paras 51 and 53);

- private life cases concerning the expulsion of people who have been living in the UK for a long period of time and who have a sufficiently high degree of social integration were also 'domestic' cases (para. 49);

- in all of the above domestic cases, there was no need to show a 'flagrant' denial of Article 8 rights. In a domestic case, the state must always act in accordance with ECHR rights. There is 'no threshold' relating to the 'seriousness of the violation or the importance of the right involved', and no test of the 'enormity or humanitarian affront' caused by the interference (paras 42–3);

- the case of *Bensaid* (for further details ▶see 816–7) was a case with both 'foreign' and 'domestic' aspects. The foreign aspects, probably requiring the high threshold which could not be reached in that case, concerned the alleged lack of psychiatric treatment in the country of return (Algeria). The domestic aspects were the relationships and support established by the applicant while in the UK – if it amounted to private life, the interference was justified as proportionate in that case (paras 57–8).

The Court of Appeal has also subsequently confirmed that there is no test of 'flagrancy' in Article 8 'domestic' cases (see *Huang & Others v SSHD*, para. 65).

For further details about Article 8 'protection' cases, ▶see 803–7. For Article 8 and health ▶see 816–9. For domestic cases involving family and/or private life connections to the UK, ▶see 820–50. For cases involving sexuality under the Refugee Convention ▶see 608, 615–6

CLAIMS FOR PROTECTION

Claims for protection are made by applicants who fear some form of ill-treatment in their country of return. In these cases, human rights claims overlap with claims for asylum as a refugee. As the courts have noted, obtaining refugee status is preferable to succeeding on a human rights claim or being granted exceptional leave (see *Karanakaran*; and *Saad, Diriye & Osario*, both Court of Appeal). This is because refugee status provides additional benefits, including quicker access to settlement, more favourable family reunion rights, and access to a 1951 Convention travel document. Therefore, where on the facts of their case it is possible, applicants should try to obtain refugee status. Where asylum is claimed and an applicant is found not to qualify as a refugee, the Home Office will always consider whether leave should be granted on the basis of ECHR rights (▶see 719, 854). Advisers should therefore always be ready to point out the human rights aspects of an asylum claim. In what follows, we have emphasised the situations in which a protection claim may succeed on the basis of human rights, even if the applicant does not qualify as a refugee.

In general, the Home Office accepts that the standard of proof in cases concerning protection and removal is whether there are 'substantial grounds' for believing that there is a 'real risk' of the applicant being subjected to a breach of their Convention rights (see API *European Convention of Human Rights*, para. 5.3). This is the same standard of proof as applies in asylum claims.

The right to life (Article 2)

1) Everyone's right to life shall be protected by law. No one shall be deprived of his life intentionally save in the execution of a sentence of a court following his conviction of a crime for which this penalty is provided by law.

2) Deprivation of life shall not be regarded as inflicted in contravention of this article when it results from the use of force which is not more than absolutely necessary:

a) in defence of any person from unlawful violence;

b) in order to effect a lawful arrest or to prevent the escape of a person lawfully detained;

c) in action lawfully taken for the purpose of quelling a riot or insurrection.

In many cases involving risk to life, Article 3 (►see below) may be applicable. However, in the House of Lords, in *Ullah*, Lord Steyn commented that there may well be cases where Article 3 does not apply but Article 2 does.

Article 2 prohibits the state from taking life (except in the lawful situations described), and also requires it to act positively to protect life. Article 2 can be used in cases where there is a risk of extra-judicial killing by agents of the state, or where there is a risk of fatal violence from others against which the state cannot offer the required standard of protection (*Osman*, ECtHR). However, Article 2 has been held not to protect a serving soldier whose occupation is a hazardous one (*Fadli*). In *Cicek* and in *Tas*, the European Court found that the Turkish authorities were responsible for the disappearances and deaths of individuals following their detention by those authorities. Of particular concern to the Court was Turkey's failure to investigate, explain or justify the deaths in custody of these persons. In the Court's view, this was a breach of the state's procedural obligation to protect the right to life under Article 2. The unacknowledged detention was also found to be a grave violation of Article 5. In *Tas*, the Court also found that the family members of the deceased had suffered a violation of their Article 3 rights, because of the state's attitude and reaction to them when they attempted to obtain information about the circumstances of the death of their relative.

Note that it may be that applicants need to show that there is not just a risk but a 'high risk' amounting to a 'near certainty' that they will lose their life before Article 2 can be relied on in immigration cases (see *Dehawari v Netherlands*, EComHR).

Death penalty

Article 2(1) also deals directly with 'judicial killing' in the form of the death penalty. As a result of Article 2(1), in *Soering* the European Court could not rule that it was contrary to Article 2 for a young man to be extradited to the US, where he faced the possibility of execution. Instead, the Court found that it would be inhuman and degrading treatment under Article 3 for him to be kept agonising on death row for many years before finding out whether the death sentence would be carried out or commuted. Of course, the way in which a death sentence is carried out may also breach Article 3, if it involves severe suffering. This was the case in *Jabari* (ECtHR), in which the applicant was at risk of death by stoning if she were to be returned to Iran.

Soering was decided before the UK signed up to the optional 'sixth protocol' to the ECHR (now substituted in the HRA by the Thirteenth Protocol to the ECHR, which the UK has also ratified, see Human Rights Act 1998 (Amendment Order 2004)). This states that the death penalty is to be abolished and that 'no one shall be condemned' to the death penalty or 'executed'. This probably means that no one should be sent to a country where they face being sentenced to death, even if the sentence may be commuted. Whatever the precise interpretation of the ECHR, the Home Office accepts that those at risk of execution under the death penalty should be granted Humanitarian Protection (▶see also 862–3, and API *European Convention on Human Rights*, para. 6.3 and at annex B).

Prohibition on torture or inhuman or degrading treatment or punishment (Article 3)

No one shall be subjected to torture or to inhuman or degrading treatment or punishment.

Article 3 has the greatest impact for asylum-seekers. It is not restricted in the protection it provides by qualifications or exceptions, and it provides broader protection than the Refugee Convention. In *Kacaj*, the IAT considered the standard of proof in Article 3 cases. It concluded that there was nothing to suggest that the standard should be different from the Refugee Convention standard. The question is whether the applicant has established that there is a 'real risk' that, if returned, they will be exposed to the prohibited treatment.

The 'harm' in Article 3 can be divided into three separate kinds:

- torture;
- inhuman treatment or punishment;
- degrading treatment or punishment.

In order to succeed in the claim, the harm feared overseas must be severe enough to come within any one of these forms of harm. Torture is the most severe; inhuman and degrading treatment are less severe. In deciding whether the treatment is severe enough, account is taken of the likely duration of the treatment, and factors relating to the victim, such as their sex, age and health and the effect that the treatment will have upon them (*Ireland v UK*, ECtHR). Harm that is inhuman or degrading may be inflicted by way of 'treatment' or 'punishment', and there is a large area of overlap between the two.

The critical question is: What protection does Article 3 provide that is not already provided by the Refugee Convention? In the table below we set out the circumstances in which Article 3 either will or may potentially provide protection when the Refugee Convention does not.

Note that, in the wake of the London bombings on 7 July 2005, the government is extremely keen to remove those who it believes are connected to, or support acts of terrorism. It is concerned that Article 3 may prove a barrier to such removals on the basis that returnees may be subject to torture. The government has therefore begun to agree 'memoranda of understanding' with the states concerned, which it will then try to rely on to show that returnees will not be ill-treated because the relevant state has provided assurances. (See parliamentary statement of Home Secretary of 20 July 2005 set out at ▶1020). Of course most states have signed up to international obligations which bind them to respect human rights but this does not prevent torture. The question will be whether these assurances are worth the paper they are written on.

Torture

Torture is the most serious form of harm. It is deliberate, inhuman treatment which causes very serious suffering (*Selmouni*, ECtHR). Torture is not defined in the ECHR, but it is given a definition in other international human rights instruments such as the UN Convention Against Torture and Other Cruel Inhuman or Degrading Treatment or Punishment. In international law, torture is usually considered to:

- cause severe pain or suffering, either physical or mental;
- be intentionally inflicted to obtain a confession or information, or to intimidate or coerce; and
- be inflicted by a public official.

Although the above factors are all relevant, torture under Article 3 is not limited to this definition. In addition, a single incident causing sufficiently severe suffering will constitute torture. In *Aydin*, in which a woman had been stripped, beaten, sprayed with cold water and raped, the European Court appears to have considered that the sexual violation itself would have been sufficient to meet the definition, without the added feature of the ill-treatment being carried out in order to obtain information.

Inhuman treatment/punishment

'Inhuman treatment' is less severe than torture, and it does not need to be deliberately inflicted. The level of suffering required is less intense (*Ireland v UK*, ECtHR). In the *Ireland* case, the 'five techniques' of wall standing, hooding, subjection to noise, sleep deprivation, and food and drink deprivation amounted to inhuman treatment. The threat of torture may also amount to inhuman treatment (*Campbell*), as may poor conditions of detention, if they are sufficiently severe, such as overcrowding, deprivation of contact with the outside world, and the withholding of food and medical treatment.

Degrading treatment/punishment

'Degrading treatment' also causes less suffering than torture. The distinctive quality of degrading treatment is that it 'grossly humiliates' or 'debases' the victim. Conduct resulting in a person feeling afraid, in anguish, or inferior is capable of humiliating or debasing them and breaking their resistance, so that the minimum level of harm is caused. Depending on what is at stake and on the circumstances, race discrimination may amount to degrading treatment (*East African Asians* case, EComHR). Some forms of corporal punishment may also be 'degrading'.

THE CIRCUMSTANCES IN WHICH ARTICLE 3 ECHR MAY PROVIDE PROTECTION WHEN THE REFUGEE CONVENTION DOES NOT

1) **No exclusions from protection.** The right to be protected under Article 3 is absolute and unqualified. A person excluded from protection under the 1951 Convention because of their conduct, or because they are a threat to national security, may not be removed if this will expose them to a risk of treatment contrary to Article 3. In *Chahal*, the applicant had been involved in political activities in the UK in support of the struggle for freedom in Punjab. The Home Secretary made a decision to deport him on the grounds of national security. He was detained, and eventually lost his case for protection under the 1951 Convention. In answer to Mr Chahal's claim that a return to India would expose him to a risk of torture, the government argued that there was a balance to be struck between the right and the person's conduct. The European Court rejected the government's argument, and stated:

'... whenever substantial grounds have been shown for believing that an individual would face a real risk of being subjected to treatment contrary to Article 3 if removed to another State, the responsibility of the contracting state to safeguard him or her against such treatment is engaged in the event of expulsion. In these circumstances, the activities of the individual in question, however undesirable or dangerous, cannot be a material consideration. The protection afforded by Article 3 is thus wider than that provided by Articles 32 and 33 of the United Nations 1951 Convention on the status of refugees.'

In the light of the London bombings on 7 July 2005, the government has indicated that it may re-argue in Strasbourg the way in which Article 3 should be applied in cases involving terrorism (and see the government's proposals re 'memoranda of understanding' (▶1020)).

2) **No 'Convention reason' needed.** Under the Refugee Convention, asylum-seekers have to show that they are at risk as a result of one of the reasons listed (race, religion, nationality, political opinion, membership of a particular social group). No such 'reason' for the harm has to be shown under Article 3. The purpose of Article 3 is to protect individuals from serious ill-treatment regardless of the reason for it. So, for example, those whose fears of returning to their country result from family pressure, or danger from criminal attacks from mafia gangs, may be protected by Article 3. A good example is the case of *A v SSHD*, where the Court of Appeal accepted that the applicant was protected by Article 3 because of a risk from Jamaican gang members who wanted to take revenge on her for reporting them to the police for killing her son. However, she was found not to qualify as a refugee because, although the gang were from an area dominated by one political grouping, she would not be seen as having taken a political stand.

3) Protection in civil war situations. Exposure to the 'ordinary' effects of a civil war will not amount to persecution for a 1951 Convention reason, unless the risk to the particular individual is 'over and above' the risk to the general population as part of the 'ordinary' consequences of civil war (▶see *Adan* at 612). However, Article 3 can give protection in these circumstances even though the risk to the applicant is the same as the risk to others (see *Ahmed*, ECtHR, where the asylum-seekers feared being returned to Somalia).

4) No need to show 'persistence'. It has become increasingly accepted that breach of fundamental rights under the ECHR and other international instruments is relevant to determining what amounts to 'persecution' under the Refugee Convention. In *Ullah*, the House of Lords again endorsed the formulation:

'...persecution is most appropriately defined as the sustained or systemic failure of state protection in relation to one of the core entitlements [i.e. human rights] which has been recognised by the international community.' (para. 32)

However, this approach is not always accepted (see the Court of Appeal decision in *Kagema*, where persecution was held to be an uncomplicated question of fact, not necessarily to be determined by reference to other rights). Questions remain as to whether actions need to have a persistent or repeated character in order to be 'persecution'. The short judgment of Staughton LJ in *Ravichandran* is often quoted for the statement that persecution must at least be persistent and serious (of course, this cannot apply in the case of a very serious incident of persecution, such as torture: see *Demrikaya*, CA). In *Kacaj*, the IAT recognised that Article 3 could be violated by actions that did not have a 'sufficiently systematic character to amount to persecution', but doubted whether there would be many instances in which treatment that breached Article 3 would not also amount to 'persecution'. There may therefore be some cases in which Article 3 provides greater protection because it does not carry with it a requirement of continuation or persistence.

5) Lower level of harm. It has been repeated many times that persecution is a strong word, requiring very serious harm. Article 3 also sets a high standard for the nature of harm, and torture will almost certainly amount to persecution. However, it is possible that the lower-intensity forms of harm (inhuman and degrading treatment and punishment) may provide protection where the harm is not severe enough to amount to 'persecution'.

6) No need for 'malignancy' or 'ill-treatment'. One of the classic definitions of 'persecution' (taken from the dictionary) was given by Nolan J in *ex parte Jonah*: 'to pursue with malignancy or injurious action'. Article 3 does not require these elements.

A good example is the first decision of the Court of Appeal in the case of *Batayav*, in which the applicant faced a prison sentence if returned to Russia and complained about the general conditions in Russian prisons. Referring to the Strasbourg case-law (including a case about Russian prisons, *Kalashnikov*), the Court noted that the conditions in which a prisoner is detained can be so unsatisfactory as to constitute inhuman and degrading treatment, even though there is no *intention* on the part of the authorities to humiliate or debase the victim. There was no need for the applicant to show that he would be ill-treated in a particular prison; the only question was whether there was a 'consistent pattern' of violations of the Article 3 rights of those detained in Russia, so that there was a real risk of the applicant being subject to inhuman treatment if returned. When assessing prison conditions, account has to be taken of their cumulative effect. Article 3 requires that states detain people with respect for their human dignity, that they are not subjected to distress or hardship over and above the level of suffering inherent in detention, and that prisoners' health is properly safe-guarded.

Article 3 can also be engaged where the risk of harm is not the direct or indirect responsibility of the authorities of the country of return at all. This is the situation in the health cases we discuss under the separate heading: 'Detrimental effect of return' (▶see 809–816, 819–20).

7) **Internal relocation cases.** The decision in the Sri Lankan case, *AE and FE v SSHD*, has made it more difficult for applicants to qualify as refugees where the risk of persecution is limited to their home area. The Court of Appeal found that, in deciding whether it is reasonable to expect the potential refugee to relocate to a 'safe' area of their country, it was not possible to compare conditions in the relocation area with those in the UK. It was only permissible to compare the conditions in the relocation area with those in the home area. Therefore, the fact that the applicant would not be entitled to the 'basic norms of civil, political and socio-economic human rights' in the relocation area will not usually be relevant to refugee status, because these hardships are likely to exist throughout the country. So, in *AE* itself, while it may have been harmful for the applicant's wife's psychiatric condition for the family to return to Colombo (the relocation area) as opposed to staying *in the UK*, this did *not* mean that Colombo was not a safe haven as compared with Jaffna (the area of persecution).

However, the Court was at pains to point out that a family in this position might be protected under the ECHR, or on other exceptional grounds. The Court was not specific as to how this might work. It appears that applicants who are at risk of persecution in their home area, and whose return to their country of origin – even to live in the relocation area – will cause them significant detriment (as compared with their position in the UK) might succeed in a human rights claim. This is despite the fact that they cannot succeed in their refugee claim because the general conditions in the relocation area are no worse than in their home area.

It is understood that, having won on the refugee aspects of the case, the Home Office is still seeking to appeal the case of *AE* to the House of Lords, because they are unhappy that the Court indicated that some applicants might be protected under the ECHR.

8) **British citizen children.** Article 3 does not require that a person is outside their own country. The Refugee Convention requires that a person is outside their country of nationality, or habitual residence. Article 3 applies to anyone within the territory of a contracting state. This means that Article 3 could apply, for example, to cases where a British citizen child will effectively be forced to leave with a non-British parent who is being required to leave, where

the conditions they would face in the place to which they are removed amount to inhuman and degrading treatment.

Threats from 'non-state agents' and Article 3

Where the Article 3 threat in the country of return comes from non-state agents (i.e. not the authorities of the state), then account will be taken of what level of protection is available from the state. In the House of Lords, in *Horvath*, it was decided that an essential element of 'persecution' under the Refugee Convention is that there must be a failure on the part of the state authorities in the country of origin to provide a 'sufficiency of protection' against the harm. This interpretation was taken from the way in which that Convention is drafted (see Refugee Convention, Article 1A(2)). There will be a sufficiency of protection if the state is willing and able to provide a reasonable level of protection having regard to the nature of the threat. Following *Horvath*, it seems that if there is no 'fail-ure' on the part of the state to provide this level of protection, then the applicant cannot qualify as a refugee *even* if the protection does not actually reduce the risk of harm to below the 'real risk' standard (▶see the Section on Refugees at 610–11 for more details about the 'sufficiency of protection' test).

What is the position in non-state agent Article 3 cases? As with the Refugee Convention, the European Court has held that Article 3 can apply where the danger comes from people who are not public officials (see *HLR v France*). So a decision had to be taken as to whether the 'suffic-iency of protection' test applied when applicants claimed they were in danger from non-state agents, for example, mafia members or drugs gangs. Unlike the Refugee Convention, the wording of Article 3 does not indicate that there has to be some state involvement or responsibility for the risk of harm – it simply prohibits exposure to certain forms of harm.

The issue has now been dealt with by the House of Lords in *Bagdanav-icius*. The Court held that the question was not whether an applicant was at risk of harm, however serious that harm was, but, instead, whether they were at risk of 'proscribed ill-treatment' under Article 3 in the country of return. Harm inflicted at the hands of non-state bodies was not Article 3 ill-treatment unless the state failed to provide a reasonable level of protection. So the House of Lords held:

'Non-state agents do not subject people to torture or the other pro-scribed forms of ill-treatment, however violently they treat them: what, however, would transform such violent treatment into Article 3 ill-treatment would be the state's failure to provide reasonable protection against it.' (para. 24)

So, in essence, a very similar test will apply to determine whether threats from non-state agents will result in a successful claim under the Refugee Convention and Article 3 ECHR.

Prohibition against slavery and forced labour (Article 4)

1) No-one shall be held in slavery or servitude.

2) No-one shall be required to perform forced or compulsory labour; for the purposes of this article the term 'forced or compulsory labour' shall not include:

a) any work required to be done in the ordinary course of detention imposed according to the provisions of Article 5 of this Convention or during conditional release from such detention;

b) any service of a military character or, in the case of conscientious objectors in countries where they are recognised, service exacted instead of compulsory military service;

c) any service exacted in case of an emergency or calamity threatening the life or well being of the community;

d) any work or service which forms part of normal civic obligations.

This article absolutely prohibits slavery. It has been little used, but may be relevant where returning someone would expose them to gangs trafficking in women or children for prostitution. Article 4 also prohibits forced or compulsory labour, but allows exceptions such as work required in the ordinary course of detention or military service. However, militia abductions of forced recruits is likely to be in breach of Article 4.

The right to liberty and security (Article 5)

1) Everyone has the right to liberty and security of person. No one shall be deprived of his liberty save in the following cases and in accordance with a procedure prescribed by law:

a) the lawful detention of a person after conviction by a competent court;

b) the lawful arrest or detention of a person for non-compliance with the lawful order of a court or in order to secure fulfilment of any obligation prescribed by law;

c) the lawful arrest or detention of a person effected for the purpose of bringing him before the competent legal authority on reasonable suspicion of having committed an offence, or when it is reasonably considered necessary to prevent his committing an offence or fleeing after having done so;

d) the detention of a minor by lawful order for the purpose of educational supervision or his lawful detention for the purpose of bringing him before the competent legal authority;

e) the lawful detention of persons for the prevention of the spreading of infectious diseases, of persons of unsound mind, alcoholics or drug addicts or vagrants;

f) the lawful arrest or detention of a person to prevent his effecting an unauthorised entry into the country or of a person against whom action is being taken with a view to deportation or extradition.

2) Everyone who is arrested shall be informed promptly, in a language which he understands, of the reasons for the arrest and of any charge against him.

3) Everyone arrested or detained in accordance with the provisions of paragraph 1(c) of this article shall be brought promptly before a judge or other officer authorised by law to exercise judicial power and shall be entitled to trial within a reasonable time or to release pending trial. Release may be conditioned by guarantees to appear for trial.

4) Everyone who is deprived of liberty by arrest or detention shall be entitled to take proceedings by which the lawfulness of his detention shall be decided speedily by a court and his release ordered if the detention is not lawful.

5) Everyone who has been the victim of arrest or detention in contravention of the provisions of this article shall have an enforceable right to compensation.

Article 5 states that everyone shall have the right to liberty except in certain limited circumstances, which are set out in the article – for example, normal criminal or legal processes that are clearly provided for in the law of the country concerned. The main purpose of Article 5 is to protect people from arbitrary detention. Article 5 also provides certain procedural safeguards for people who are detained, such as the right to be informed of the reason for their arrest, the overseeing of detention by a court, trial within a reasonable time, and a right to compensation for unlawful detention. Where a person is to be returned to their country in circumstances where they face detention in flagrant breach of these conditions, there may be a breach of Article 5.

Article 5 may offer protection not otherwise available – for example, where the applicant faces detention contrary to Article 5 but without the risk of ill-treatment. In *Ullah* (▶788–90), Lord Steyn referred to Article 5 as being of great importance in underlying the rule of law, and referred to the circumstances in which Article 5 may be relevant as follows:

'Imagine a case of intended expulsion to a country in which the rule of law is flagrantly flouted, habeas corpus is unavailable and there is a real risk that the individual may face arbitrary detention for many years… Assuming that there is no evidence of the risk of torture or inhuman or degrading treatment, is the applicant for relief to be told that the ECHR offers in principle no possibility of protection in such extreme cases? I would doubt that such an impoverished view of the role of a human rights convention could be right.' (para. 43)

It may be that Article 5 would protect against the general and arbitrary 'round-ups' of young Tamils in Columbo which, in *Ravichandran* (CA), were found to have been carried out for legitimate motives – to counter a terrorist threat – and not to amount to 'persecution'.

It is possible also that a claim for protection might be made by taking Articles 5 and 6, (below), together with Article 18 which states that restrictions to a person's rights under the ECHR can only be imposed for the strict purpose for which the ECHR allows. In *Gusinsky v Russia*, one of the reasons why the applicant's six-day detention was found by the European Court to be contrary to Article 5 was because the detention was effected not only for the permitted purpose concerning a criminal offence, but also for 'alien reasons' contrary to Article 18 ECHR. The separate motive of the state was an attempt to intimidate Mr Gusinsky into signing a commercial agreement with the state to sell his media assets. Thus it may be that, where the effect of a short detention is not severe enough to amount to 'persecution' or to treatment contrary to Article 3, improper motives on the part of the state would enable an applicant to claim a 'flagrant' denial of liberty under Article 5 (taken together with Article 18).

The final exception to the right to liberty under Article 5 is detention for immigration purposes (Article 5(1)(f)). This restricts the circumstances in which the immigration authorities may detain a person in the UK. (▶see 922–4, 925, 930 and ▶see 1175–81 for civil claims and detention).

The right to a fair trial (Article 6)

1) In the determination of his civil rights and obligations or of any criminal charge against him, everyone is entitled to a fair and public hearing within a reasonable time by an independent and impartial tribunal established by law. Judgement shall be pronounced publicly but the press and public may be excluded from all or part of the trial in the interests of morals, public order or national security in a democratic society, where the interests of juveniles or the protection of the private life of the parties so require, or to the extent strictly necessary in the opinion of the court in special circumstances where publicity would prejudice the interests of justice.

2) Everyone charged with a criminal offence shall be presumed innocent until proved guilty according to law.

3) Everyone charged with a criminal offence has the following minimum rights:

a) to be informed promptly, in a language which he understands and in detail, of the nature and cause of the accusation against him;

b) to have adequate time and facilities for the preparation of his defence;

c) to defend himself in person or through legal assistance of his own choosing or, if he has not sufficient means to pay for legal assistance, to be given it free where the interests of justice so require;

d) to examine or have examined witnesses against him and to obtain the attendance and examination of witnesses on his behalf under the same conditions as witnesses against him;

e) to have the free assistance of an interpreter if he cannot understand or speak the language used in court.

This is the most commonly used of all the ECHR rights. The European Court has itself indicated that returning a person to a country where they will suffer a 'flagrant' breach of their rights under Article 6 could amount to a breach of the Convention (*Soering*), and this has been confirmed by *Ullah* (▶see 788–90).

Note that immigration rights themselves have been held not to constitute 'civil rights' within Article 6 (*Maaouia*, ECtHR). Citizenship rights are probably not 'civil rights' either (see *Harrison v SSHD*, CA). So disputes about applicants' rights to a particular immigration or national status in the UK do not have the formal protection of Article 6. However, the standards of fairness required of tribunals and courts when dealing with immigration rights are in any case similar to those required under Article 6. For cases where an applicant may have a civil claim outstanding against the Home Office ▶see 847.

Prohibition on punishment for an act which was not a crime when it was committed (Article 7)

1) No one shall be held guilty of any criminal offence on account of any act or omission which did not constitute a criminal offence under national or international law at the time when it was committed. Nor shall a heavier penalty be imposed than the one that was applicable at the time the criminal offence was committed.

2) This article shall not prejudice the trial and punishment of any person for any act or omission which, at the time when it was committed, was criminal according to the general principles of law recognised by civilised nations.

Article 7 ECHR can be raised if a person faces prosecution and trial on return for an offence which was not an offence when the person carried out the act in question. Where a person is at risk of unfair prosecution and trial proceedings, the circumstances may also come within the 1951 Convention if there is a 'Convention' reason for the prosecution.

Right to respect for private life, family, home, correspondence (Article 8)

1) Everyone has the right to respect for his private and family life, his home and correspondence.

2) There shall be no interference by a public authority with the exercise of this right except such as is in accordance with the law and is necessary in a democratic society in the interests of national security, public safety or the

economic well-being of the country, for the prevention of disorder or crime, for the protection of health or morals, or for the protection of the rights and freedoms of others.

The rights under Articles 8, 9, 10 and 11 ECHR are all set out similarly. They all provide rights that can be interfered with if the interests of the community in preventing, for example, disorder or the economic well-being of the country justify such interference (▶780). In order to see whether an interference can be justified in any case, the harm to the individual caused by the interference has to be balanced against the interest of the community. We address the various steps of an Article 8 claim in detail when we discuss 'domestic' Article 8 cases (i.e. family/private life connections to the UK) (▶see 820–50). Article 8 is also relevant in cases where removal will have an adverse effect on health (▶see 816–9).

In Article 8 (as well as 9–12, and 14) claims to protection, applicants have both to demonstrate a flagrant breach of their rights and to defend against the Home Office's claim that the interference is 'proportionate' to the needs of immigration control (▶see *Ullah* at 788–9 and ▶see 790–2). In *Kacaj*, the IAT had stated that the interests of legitimate immigration control would 'almost certainly' mean that the interference was proportionate in cases that were not severe enough to be protected by Article 3. In *Razgar*, Lord Bingham stated that this might be an overstatement of the position, but only a small overstatement, and that decisions taken in accordance with ordinary immigration control would be proportionate except in the small minority of 'exceptional' cases (para. 20). He further stated that such cases would be identifiable on a case-by-case basis, which at least indicates that there will indeed be some cases where Article 8 is of benefit to applicants in protection claims. In *Ullah*, it was also stated that the removing state would always have

'...what will usually be strong grounds for justifying its own conduct: the great importance of operating firm and orderly immigration control...' (Lord Bingham, para. 24).

In Article 8 cases, it is normally the right to respect for 'private life' that is relevant in claims for protection.

Article 8 'protection' claims based on sexuality

Sexuality is an aspect of private life under Article 8 ECHR, and therefore restrictions placed upon a person's right to sexual identity and ill-treatment because of it, by either the state or the community, are capable of amounting to an interference with their Article 8 rights. We can look at the development of the law in this area using four decisions of the Court of Appeal. Finally, the decision of the House of Lords in *Ullah* is of some help to applicants making these claims. For sexuality and refugee claims ▶see 608, 615–6

Jain

Jain was a case which concerned a claim for refugee status before the ECHR was incorporated. However, it is important because the Court of Appeal agreed that there was a broad international consensus that everyone has a right to respect for their private life, which includes their sexual life. It noted that criminalisation of homosexual activity between consenting adults in private was not regarded by the international community at large as being acceptable. The Court had regard to the decision of the European Court in *Modinos*, in which a breach of Article 8 was found in circumstances where, although the law criminalised homosexual activity, the Attorney General in Cyprus had a policy of not actually prosecuting people. The Court of Appeal appreciated that 'the very existence of a legal prohibition can continuously and directly affect a person's private life'.

Z, A, M v SSHD

In the cases *Z*, *A*, and *M*, the applicants claimed that, if returned to Zimbabwe, they would be subjected to social and statutory inhibitions on living their homosexual lifestyle which amounted to breaches of Articles 3 and 8 ECHR. The Court of Appeal accepted that there may be restrictions on sexual life which interfere with Article 8 rights, even though such restrictions were not severe enough to amount to a violation of Article 3 (note that the European Court had previously found that harm less severe than Article 3 ill-treatment may still interfere with a person's private life under Article 8 in the area of their 'physical and moral integrity'; see *Bensaid*). The Court did not, however, accept that any restriction on sexual life which amounted to an interference with the right to respect for private life could not be justified by immigration control. It was also accepted on all sides that the mere existence of a law against consensual homosexual activity would not necessarily amount to an interference with Article 8 rights. The Court of Appeal clarified that in *Modinos* the European Court had not said that such a law's existence would alone demonstrate an interference under Article 8. *Modinos* was a case that had to be considered in context. The Court of Appeal's view was that it would always be necessary to look beyond the law to see whether there was a risk of enforcement, investigation and prosecution, and at all the circumstances of a case, to see whether there was in fact an interference with private life.

Hadiova v SSHD

In *Hadiova*, considering a claim made by a lesbian from the Czech Republic, which focused mainly on harassment from members of the public, the Court of Appeal accepted that the right to respect for private life meant both that the state should not interfere with private life and that it must provide for effective respect for it. However, on the facts of the case, the applicant had not been able to identify those who had harassed her, so it was difficult for the police to investigate the matter. In addition, if the police themselves were failing in their responsibilities, then there were ways of complaining against them which the applicants had not used. So the Court refused to intervene with the decision that the Czech authorities had not failed to respect the private life of lesbian couples (paras 26–7).

Z v SSHD

In December 2004, one of the Zimbabwean cases in *Z, A, M* (►see above) returned again to the Court of Appeal. However, this time the focus was upon the Refugee Convention rather than Articles 3 or 8 ECHR. The Court dismissed Z's appeal because the facts of the case were poor. The Article 8 argument was not pressed. In a 'one-liner' in relation to Article 8, the Court simply stated that, if the appellant could not win under the Refugee Convention, then 'by the same token he cannot succeed under Article 8' (para. 23). This comment seems to contradict the above cases. The decision in *Z* came after the decisions of the House of Lords in *Ullah* (►788–9) and *Razgar* (►see 817–8), which imposed the stringent 'flagrancy' test, which applicants claiming an interference under Article 8 on grounds of sexuality would have to meet. *However*, it seems that the Court of Appeal was not right to say that such a claim, which could not succeed under the Refugee Convention, would automatically fail under Article 8 (►see *Ullah* immediately below).

Ullah

In *Ullah* Lord Steyn indicated that a homosexual might succeed under Article 8 even though they could not win under the Refugee Convention. He stated:

'Another possible field of application could be the expulsion of an alien homosexual to a country where, short of persecution, he might be subjected to a flagrant violation of his Article 8 rights. In [the first decision in *Z, A, M* (see above), the Court of Appeal] was not prepared to rule out such an argument. In my view [it] was right not to do so. Enough has already been said to demonstrate that on principles repeatedly affirmed by the European Court, Article 8 may be engaged in cases of real risk of a flagrant violation of an individual's Article 8 rights.' (para. 47)

So, there may still be cases that succeed under Article 8 although they cannot be brought within the Refugee Convention. Advisers should not, however, abandon the Refugee Convention or Article 3 in these kinds of case.

For further details about refugee status on the grounds of sexuality, and the overlapping question of whether lesbians and gay men can be required to be 'discreet' about their sexual identity, ►see 608, 615–6.

Other Article 8 'protection' claims

'Private life' has never been completely defined, and it includes a wide sphere of personal interest. Advisers should therefore be creative in considering whether an immigration decision interferes with private life in the many different circumstances that present themselves in immigration cases. An example is *Yilka Bushati*, in which the IAT found that the stigmatisation of a rape victim by the community to which she would be returned, combined with her psychological vulnerability, was a sufficient risk to the 'physical and moral integrity' aspect of her private life under Article 8.

For the role of Article 8 in 'health' cases, ▶see 816–9.

Freedom of thought, conscience and religion (Article 9)

1) Everyone has the right to freedom of thought, conscience and religion; this right includes freedom to change his religion or belief and freedom, either alone or in community with others and in public or private, to manifest his religion or belief in worship, teaching, practice and observance.

2) Freedom to manifest one's religion and beliefs shall be subject only to such limitations as are prescribed by law and are necessary in a democratic society in the interests of public safety, for the protection of public order, health or morals, or for the protection of the rights and freedoms of others.

Article 9 was the main right relied on in *Ullah & Do*, in which it was held that only a flagrant denial of the right in the country of return might protect an applicant (▶see 788–90). It should be noted that *freedom* of thought, conscience and religion are absolute rights. It is the 'manifestation' of religion or beliefs that may be restricted by the limitations in Article 9(2). So, if a person can show that their right actually to hold their belief will be infringed if they are returned, the Home Office may not be able to rely upon the requirements of immigration control to justify returning them, nor on any justification that the receiving state may have for interfering with that right. In some cases where applicants have tried to raise Article 9, the European Court has treated the claim as raising issues under Articles 10 and 11 (in which restrictions apply in all circumstances) rather than Article 9. For example, in *Young* a personal conviction against joining a trade union was dealt with under Article 11, rather than Article 9.

Freedom of expression (Article 10)

1) Everyone has the right to freedom of expression. This right shall include freedom to hold opinions and to receive and impart information and ideas without interference by public authority and regardless of frontiers. This article shall not prevent states from requiring the licensing of broadcasting, television or cinema enterprises.

2) The exercise of these freedoms, since it carries with it duties and responsibilities, may be subject to such formalities, conditions, restrictions or penalties as are prescribed by law and are necessary in a democratic society, in the

interests of national security, territorial integrity or public safety, for the prevention of disorder or crime, for the protection of health or morals, for the protection of the reputation or rights of others, for preventing the disclosure of information received in confidence or for maintaining the authority and impartiality of the judiciary.

Article 10 guarantees the right to hold opinions and to impart information and ideas without interference by a public authority. The Article goes on to set out that such limitations may be imposed as are prescribed by law, and as are necessary in a democratic society. Cases usually involve issues of press freedom, but could also involve forms of political or cultural expression. The European Court found in the case of *Ozgur Gundem* that the state had unjustifiably interfered with a newspaper's right to express views about what was happening in the south-east of Turkey. It had arrested journalists and forced the closure of the newspaper. The Court found that there was a violation of Article 10.

Although the case did not concern a claim for protection, it is worth noting that in the case of *Louis Farrakhan*, the Court of Appeal considered that where the state refuses entry to an applicant, or decides to expel an applicant *in order* to prevent them from expressing views within that state's territory, this will engage Article 10. The case concerned the American spiritual leader of the Nation of Islam, who had been excluded from the UK on the grounds of the objectionable nature of his views, which were regarded as a threat to public order. The Court of Appeal found that the interference with Mr Farrakhan's freedom of expression was proportionate.

Freedom of assembly and association (Article 11)

1) Everyone has the right to freedom of assembly and freedom of association with others, including the right to form and to join trade unions for the protection of his interests.

2) No restriction shall be placed on the exercise of these rights other than such as are prescribed by law and are necessary in a democratic society in the interests of national security or public safety, for the prevention of disorder or crime, for the protection of health or morals or for the protection of the rights and freedoms of others. This article shall not prevent the imposition of lawful restrictions on the exercise of these rights by members of the armed forces, of the police or of the administration of the state.

Article 11 specifically includes the right to form or join trade unions. Again, the right is not absolute, and it is qualified in certain circumstances, as prescribed by law. Those who have been or will be prevented from forming or joining a political party, organisation or trade union may rely on Article 11.

CASES WHERE REMOVAL WILL HAVE A DETRIMENTAL EFFECT ON THE INDIVIDUAL

There are some cases where the effect of a person's removal may have such a detrimental effect on them as to amount to inhuman and degrading treatment (Article 3), or an unjustifiable interference with their private life (Article 8). These cases are different from claims to protection (▶see above), because the applicants are not at risk of ill-treatment as such, and are not usually claiming that the harm that awaits them is the fault or responsibility of the authorities in the receiving country. Most of these cases are about the effect of removal on people who are ill, where there are no adequate facilities for treating them in the country of return. In some cases, applicants have additionally claimed that the effect on their mental health of the very act of removing them will cause a breach of their human rights (▶see *Razgar*, below at 817–8).

A person cannot stay in the UK in order to receive treatment from the NHS under the rules relating to visitors. Those rules allow for the admission of a person to obtain private medical treatment for a 'finite' period, and the applicant must intend to leave the UK after the completion of that treatment (▶see 230–2). They must also be able to maintain and accommodate themselves without recourse to public funds. In cases where these rules cannot be met, the applicant falls back on rights under the ECHR and/or the Home Office's general discretion outside the rules (for this discretion, ▶see 851–2).

Below, we examine in turn the following aspects of these cases:

- health cases and Article 3 ECHR, to include the decision of the House of Lords in *N* (▶809–814);
- Home Office policy in ill-health cases (▶814–6);
- health cases and Article 8 ECHR, to include the decision of the House of Lords in *Razgar* (▶816–8);
- threats of suicide and self-harm (Articles 3 and 8) (▶817–9);
- health cases involving children (▶819);
- detrimental effect cases involving destitution (▶819–20);
- detrimental effect cases concerning education (▶820).

Health and Article 3 ECHR

In the landmark case of *D v UK*, the applicant, who was suffering from AIDS, was to be removed to St Kitts in the Caribbean. The abrupt withdrawal of the medical and welfare facilities provided to him in the UK, which had assumed responsibility for his care, and the absence of proper facilities in St Kitts, would hasten his death and expose him to acute mental and physical suffering were he to be removed. The European Court held that removal would amount to inhuman treatment *even though* the conditions in St Kitts did not themselves breach Article 3, and D's suffering would not be the responsibility of the public authorities there. In *Ullah*, Lord Steyn stated that it was clear that if D had not won under Article 3, he would have won under Article 2 instead (para. 40). Cases concerning HIV/AIDS are not the only health cases in which Article 3 may be used. On the basis of the principles which follow, other serious illnesses may equally raise issues under Article 3. Similarly, cases involving mental ill-health may raise issues under Article 3. *Bensaid* (ECtHR) was just such a case, but it was also a very significant case under Article 8, and we therefore deal with it under that head (▶see 816–7).

Recent case-law has treated *D* as a very exceptional case. For example, in *Henao v Netherlands*, the European Court declared as manifestly unfounded the application of an HIV-positive Colombian man who was fighting deportation from the Netherlands, where he had been imprisoned for drug importation. The Court compared the 'very exceptional circumstances' in *D* and the 'critical stage which [D's] fatal illness had reached' with the situation in the case before it as follows:

'The court notes that [the applicant] stated that he felt well and had worked, although he did suffer from certain side-effects of his medication. The court further notes that, according to the most recent medical information available, the applicant's current condition is reasonable but may relapse if treatment is discontinued. The court finally notes that the required treatment is in principle available in Colombia, where the applicant's father and six siblings reside...unlike the situation in [the earlier cases of *D and BB v France*]...it does not appear that the applicant's illness has attained an advanced or terminal stage, or that he has no prospect of medical care or family support in his country of origin. The fact that the applicant's circumstances in Colombia would be less favourable than those he enjoys in the Netherlands cannot be regarded as decisive from the point of view of Article 3 of the Convention.'

The decision of the House of Lords in *N*

In a majority decision, the Court of Appeal in *N v SSHD* (16 October 2003) took a very restrictive view of when an Article 3 claim can succeed in 'health' cases where the main problem is lack of facilities for treatment in the country of return. N was a Ugandan woman who arrived in the UK in March 1998, and who was admitted to hospital and diagnosed as HIV-positive almost immediately. By the end of the year she had developed AIDS. The evidence was that her life was being sustained by triple-combination anti-retroviral therapy in the UK. In Uganda, it was unlikely that she would be able to access the advanced treatment she required, as a result of lack of access and affordability. Without that treatment, she would suffer an early, distressing death, within perhaps 12 months to two years. In the UK, her condition had been stabilised, and she could expect decades of life.

The Court took the view that *D* represented an 'extension of an extension', as far as normal ECHR protection was concerned. By this the Court meant that the UK was being asked to protect the applicant not only from what would happen to her in a foreign country (extension 1), but also against harm that was not being caused deliberately or because of any fault on the part of the authorities (extension 2). Because applicants in these cases are asking for a 'double extension' of ordinary human rights protection, the Court made it clear that Article 3 would only help applicants in cases that are 'not only exceptional, but extreme; extreme, that is, judged in the context of cases all or many of which (like this one) demand one's sympathy on pressing grounds' (para. 40). In other words, an applicant would only be successful in a 'very exceptional case, where there are compelling humanitarian considerations in play'.

The House of Lords rejected N's appeal (▶see table below).

THE DECISION OF THE HOUSE OF LORDS IN *N*

On 5 May 2005, the House of Lords dismissed the appeal of *N*, a Ugandan woman living with HIV/AIDS. The Lords found that there would be no breach of Article 3 ECHR in requiring her to return to Uganda. Their findings can be summarised as follows.

1) A human rights claim about the return of an applicant to face, not intentional harm from state agents or non-state agents, but the effect on them of a naturally occurring illness, was, as the Court of Appeal had stated, an 'extension to an extension' to the ECHR (see above). Such an extension has limits (Lord Hope, para. 23).

2) The limits in (1) are that only cases in the 'exceptional' or 'very exceptional' category, such as *D v UK*, could succeed (Lord Hope, para. 48; Baroness Hale, para. 63; Lord Brown, paras 81, 86, 94).

3) The real reason why *D v UK* was exceptional was:

- D's present medical condition was that he was in the advanced, critical stages of terminal illness (Lord Hope, paras 36, 43; Baroness Hale, para. 68; Lord Brown, paras 80(3), 93).

- D was not seeking to remain in the UK in order to benefit from medical and social assistance (which the Convention does not generally permit). D was dying and beyond the reach of medical treatment – the question for him was the circumstances in which he would die, not those in which he might live (Lord Nicholls, paras 15, 16; Lord Brown, paras 88, 93; Lord Hope, para. 50).

4) Accordingly, in order to show a breach of Article 3, an applicant would need to demonstrate that their *present* medical condition had:

'...reached such a critical stage that there were compelling humanitarian grounds for not removing him to a place which lacked the medical and social services which he would need to prevent acute suffering while he is dying' (Lord Hope, para. 50; Lord Brown, para. 94)

8

'...reached such a critical stage (i.e. he is dying) that it would be inhuman treatment to deprive him of the care which he is currently receiving and send him home to an early death unless there is care available there to enable him to meet that fate with dignity.' (Baroness Hale, para. 69)

5) There may be other exceptional cases with equally compelling humanitarian considerations, which the law must remain flexible enough to accommodate (Baroness Hale, para. 70).

6) The advances in medical treatment since cases such as *D* and *BB* (see below) were decided means that, in most cases, HIV can be controlled effectively and indefinitely with anti-retroviral drugs so that the patient is in good health. In applying the above test, it appears that the court will look at *that* state of health (normally good), not the state of health the applicant would be in but for the drugs (see Lord Hope, para. 50; Lord Brown, paras 92–3). With her treatment, the applicant herself was presently healthy and fit to travel. Therefore she, like many of the other cases decided in the European Court since *D*, could not meet the test set out in (4) above (see Lord Hope, para. 51; Baroness Hale, para. 67; Lord Brown, paras 95–6).

7) In cases where the applicant has not reached the terminal stage, even if the treatment generally available in the country of return may be beyond the reach of the particular applicant as a result of accessibility or cost, this won't be enough to make the case 'exceptional'. It *might*, however, be different if there is a complete absence of treatment in the country of return, so that the applicant has 'no prospect' of treatment or support, and there is therefore an inevitable risk to the applicant. However, Lord Hope stated that such a situation is increasingly unlikely given the medical aid now reaching third-world countries (Lord Hope, paras 50–1; and see Baroness Hale, para. 68; Lord Brown, paras 84–5).

8) The Lords noted that the only other clear case (after *D*) where the test might be met was *BB v France*, where the infection had already reached an advanced stage, which had necessitated repeated stays in hospital, and where the care facilities in the receiving country were very precarious. Although BB's case was not as extreme as D's, BB was 'very ill' (Lord Hope, paras 38, 48; Baroness Hale, para. 64).

Note

The background to *N* is set out above (▶809–11). It is likely that *N* will apply to the European Court. The House of Lords did not consider whether return would be contrary to Article 8 ECHR. The IAT in *N* had not considered Article 8, and the Court of Appeal heard only limited argument about it, and stated that the applicant had no Article 8 claim – but it gave no reasons. For Article 8 and health cases, ▶see 816–8 below. For the discretion to grant leave even where such a case does not meet the ECHR ▶see 851.

Cases decided after the Court of Appeal in *N*

Examples of cases decided in favour of the applicant since the decision of the Court of Appeal in *N* (but before the decision of the House of Lords) are as follows.

CA v SSHD This was the case of an HIV-positive Ghanaian woman who was pregnant. The risk of transmission of the virus to the infant would be reduced by caesarean section, and other care that could be provided in the UK. The adjudicator decided that return of the mother would not on its own be contrary to human rights, but that the impact on the mother of her child being exposed to HIV would be inhuman or degrading, and made the case an exceptional one. The Court of Appeal confirmed that the adjudicator had been correct to focus on the human rights of the mother, and that for her to see the collapse of her newborn child's health, and perhaps his or her death, may be a form of suffering greater than confronting the same circumstances for herself. The decision was not flawed in the light of the decision in *N*.

Muwanguzi v SSHD In a humane and carefully reasoned decision, the IAT found that it would be a breach of both Articles 3 and 8 to remove a Ugandan woman who had been diagnosed as HIV-positive and was suffering from AIDS. The applicant was admitted to the UK as a visitor, and subsequently discovered that she was HIV-positive. After making detailed findings on the facts and the expert evidence, Professor Jackson distinguished the case from *N* for reasons which included the following (see paras 50, 68–72):

- the applicant showed present instances of treatment failure and resistance to drugs regimes, which made her even more vulnerable to further treatment change than would otherwise be the case;
- there was specific evidence of the effect on the applicant of changes to her drug regime, and the likely side-effects of resistance to it;
- there was evidence about the immediate consequences for the applicant of lack of treatment.

We suggest that the above cases, and other 'exceptional' cases, may still succeed even following the decision of the House of Lords in *N*. Particular note should be taken of the fact that, directly after she had referred to the normal test as being dependent on whether the applicant is 'critical (i.e. dying)', Baroness Hale stated:

'There may, of course, be other exceptional cases, with other extreme facts, where the humanitarian considerations are equally compelling. The law must be sufficiently flexible to accommodate them.' (See paras 69–70).

The House of Lords made clear in *N* that, even though she had not succeeded in showing a breach of Article 3, the Secretary of State still had a wide discretion as to whether to allow her to remain (▶see 851).

Appeals in HIV/AIDS and other cases involving serious illness

In *N* there was some criticism of the Home Office for failing to provide a presenting officer at the original appeal in the case. APU Notice 3/2003 now instructs officers that medical cases that are refused outright, which involve serious medical conditions, and where the applicant would be unlikely to access treatment in their country of origin, should be identified under the Home Office's 'Assured Representation at Appeal Scheme'. This ensures that a presenting officer attends the appeal.

When preparing for appeals or making representations, advisers should note that the Terrence Higgins Trust maintains up-to-date 'country bundles' about treatment and support for those with HIV and AIDS in many of the countries of return from which claims are made. They are made available to applicants and their advisers at an administration cost of £15 per bundle (▶see 1504 for address).

Home Office policy in health cases concerning human rights

The Home Office's understanding of its obligations under the ECHR in cases involving serious illnesses, including those with HIV/AIDS, and the procedures it follows, is contained in the IDI at Chapter 1, section 8, on 'Medical Examination'. This part of the IDI also gives a range of information about how health issues are dealt with and how the immigration rules are applied (for further details about policy including in cases involving a risk of suicide/self harm, ▶see 995–8). Here, we are only concerned with the Home Office policy as it interprets the rights under the ECHR (Ch 1, s8, para. 3). The relevant IDIs were updated in March 2004 after the decision of the Court of Appeal in *N*. It is possible that it will now be updated again following the decision of the House of Lords.

The Home Office view cannot be decisive of its obligations under the ECHR – it is only its view. For example, the policy suggests that ECHR obligations can only be engaged in after-entry cases. However, port cases clearly involve people who are in the jurisdiction of the UK for the purposes of Article 1 ECHR, and are therefore able to rely on ECHR rights.

The policy refers to cases involving applicants who suffer from 'a serious illness or medical condition'. 'Serious illness' means:

'…any seriously debilitating, terminal or life-threatening medical conditions, including AIDS/HIV and serious medical conditions such as post-traumatic stress disorder.'

The policy states that being a person who has HIV/AIDS, or other serious illness, is not in itself a reason for refusal under the immigration rules where the applicant would otherwise qualify. However, neither is it a ground in itself to justify the granting of discretionary leave (DL). Where a person applies for leave to remain on human rights grounds relating to a serious illness, officers are instructed to ask the applicant to provide a certificate from their doctor confirming:

- the nature of the specific medical condition;
- the treatment that the applicant has been receiving, the duration of the treatment, and the consequences of the treatment being withdrawn;
- the applicant's life expectancy if they continue to receive their current treatment, and their life expectancy if they do not; and
- the applicant's fitness to travel.

The policy states that the threshold for demonstrating inhuman or degrading treatment in cases involving ill-health is extremely high, and will only be reached in 'truly exceptional cases involving extreme circumstances'. It continues that 'factors that might demonstrate the exceptional circumstances required for a successful Article 3 claim' include the following:

- whether the applicant is in the terminal stages of illness, and has a short life expectancy even with treatment;
- whether the removal of the applicant would both significantly shorten their life expectancy and result in acute mental or physical suffering (although this factor may not, on its own, always be enough to mean that the Article 3 threshold is met);
- whether the applicant has been receiving treatment for the relevant condition in the UK for a long time (i.e. more than 4 years) and has become dependent on the treatment they are receiving to sustain life, even for a short period (e.g. kidney dialysis patients).

The Home Office considers that, because a case needs to be exceptionally compelling, a grant of DL will not be appropriate where 'the claimant would be in no worse position than the majority of the people in his country of origin who suffer from the same condition'. Factors that the Home Office considers would not in themselves amount to an exceptional case are if the applicant:

- would be unlikely to receive treatment in the country of origin, or if the treatment would be less effective than that being received in the UK;
- would not be able to pay for treatment;
- has no family in the country of origin.

EEA nationals and family members

The above policy applies equally to EEA nationals and their family members. However, EEA nationals will generally be admitted to the UK under European rights of free movement (▶see Chapter 18), although EEA nationals can be excluded on grounds of public health (▶554).

Carers policy

Those who wish to care for a relative with HIV/AIDS, or other serious illness, may be admitted as visitors under the immigration rules. The maximum permitted period for visitors is six months, but the Home Office operates a policy whereby extensions for carers may be granted under certain circumstances. During the period of time they are providing care, the carer is expected to make long-term care arrangements for the patient. Enforcement action taken against carers who enable disabled or ill patients to live an independent and dignified life at home may violate the private life rights of the person cared for (see *Camenzind*, ECtHR). For full details about policy relating to carers and case-law, ▶see 232–5.

Health and Article 8 ECHR

Article 8 can also be used where the removal of an applicant will have adverse effects upon their health. In some cases, it may be possible for an Article 8 claim to succeed on health grounds even where an Article 3 claim fails. A landmark case concerning health and Article 8, despite the fact that it failed on its facts, was the decision of the European Court in *Bensaid*. The case was brought under both Articles 3 and 8. It concerned an Algerian national who developed schizophrenia and began receiving treatment from the NHS in the UK. He claimed that returning him to Algeria would be a breach of his human rights because he would be likely to suffer a relapse, because it was 75km to the nearest hospital from his family home (the family did not have a car), and because medication would not be provided for free. The Court accepted the following principles:

- the suffering associated with relapse into hallucinations and psychotic delusions that involved self-harm, harm to others and a lowered ability to function socially, is harm that could come within Article 3;

- mental health is a crucial part of 'private life' within Article 8, because it is a necessary part of a person's personal identity and is required in order for them to develop relationships with others.

Importantly, the Court held that it was possible to meet the Article 8 threshold in a health case, even though the suffering that might be caused was not sufficient to amount to a breach of Article 3. The Court stated:

'…the Court's case-law does not exclude that treatment which does not reach the severity of Article 3 treatment may nonetheless breach Article 8 in its private life aspect where there are sufficiently adverse effects on physical and moral integrity.'

On the facts, the Court found no sufficient real risk that the applicant would suffer the harm feared as a result of the removal. This was because the applicant could have suffered relapse even if he remained in the UK, because medical treatment was available in Algeria (although not free), and because there was no evidence that the applicant could not travel to obtain the medical treatment even without a family car. The Court therefore dismissed the risk of deterioration in health as a result of lack of treatment as too speculative and uncertain, and therefore not sufficient to meet the high threshold required. Any interference with the private life relied upon – Mr Bensaid's connections, relationships and support in the UK – was justified under Article 8(2). For the requirement to show a 'flagrant' breach in Article 8 cases ▶see 790–2 with reference to *Ullah* (▶788–9).

Threats of suicide

In the case of *R (Razgar) v SSHD*, the House of Lords considered an Article 8 claim in a case where an Kurdish Iraqi asylum-seeker was fighting a 'third-country' return to Germany. Evidence from a consultant psychiatrist stated that, if returned to Germany, the applicant might attempt suicide. There was also evidence that the applicant might not receive appropriate treatment for his psychiatric condition in Germany until he became a suicide risk. The applicant did not have long residence or deep social roots in the UK, and he could not show any disruption in family life if he was removed. (For subsequent Home Office policy ▶see 996–8.)

The points of principle the Lords established are set out in the table below. However, applicants and advisers might find it helpful to see how Mr Razgar succeeded on the facts of his case. Of course, the Lords were only considering the matter in the context of a certificate issued by the Home Office stating that Mr Razgar's human rights claim was 'manifestly unfounded'. So, they only needed to decide whether, on an ordinary appeal, he might win. By a majority, and having regard to the following factors, the Lords found that he might indeed succeed on his appeal (paras 22, 73–6):

- in the UK, with psychiatric help, the applicant enjoyed a measure of freedom, independence and autonomy;
- in Germany the applicant may not enjoy the above, because he knew no one there, might not receive medical help, and might be accommodated in a remote refugee centre;
- if returned, the applicant might take his own life (this was very plainly a consequence of sufficient gravity to engage Article 8);
- the effect on the applicant of being returned to Germany, given his phobia about being returned there and his previous experiences in Iraq (where he claimed to have been tortured), might outweigh the immigration interest in removing him and therefore be disproportionate.

HEALTH AND ARTICLE 8: THE DECISION IN *RAZGAR*

In *Razgar* the House of Lords held that:

- An applicant may rely on their right to respect for private life under Article 8 to resist a removal where the claim is mainly based on the foreseeable consequences for their health of being removed to the receiving country, and not on the disruption of their family or social ties established in the UK. The Lords confirmed the decision in *Bensaid* on this point (paras 9–10).

- Article 8 may be engaged in such cases, even though the removal does not reach the higher threshold required to cause a breach of Article 3 (para. 10).
- In order to engage Article 8, the facts still need to be very strong. The leading speech of Lord Bingham does not actually refer to 'flagrant' breach, but this is almost certainly required, since the decision in *Ullah* is incorporated into the judgment, and Lord Carswell does refer to the need for flagrancy (for 'flagrancy' and how *Razgar* clarified *Ullah*, ▶see 790–2) (paras 2, 9–10, 72–3).
- As with Article 3 health cases, Article 8 cannot be engaged just because the medical treatment or facilities are better or more accessible in the UK than in the country of return. Something 'very much more extreme than relative disadvantage' has to be shown (paras 4, 10).
- It does not matter that an applicant's fears are irrational (Mr Razgar's fear that Germany would return him to Iraq, which Germany would not do, since that would be in breach of their obligations under the Refugee Convention or the ECHR). The real question was whether the fears in fact existed, and were so extreme as to lead to sufficiently adverse consequences for the applicant's mental health were he removed (paras 75–6).

A similar case to *Razgar*, in which a 'clearly unfounded' certificate in relation to a third country return was also quashed, was *R (Kurtolli) v SSHD*. That case involved the risk that the applicant's wife, who had suffered traumatic experiences in Kosovo that included seeing various of her relatives being killed, might commit suicide and/or cause harm to her children. Despite the safeguards the Secretary of State proposed to put in place to deal with the risk of suicide when the family was removed, the Court found that there was a reasonable claim under Article 3.

In *J v SSHD*, the Court of Appeal laid down the following principles to be applied to cases where an applicant alleges that they are likely to commit suicide if removed (paras 26–31).

- First, there needs to be an assessment of the severity of the harm. It must 'necessarily be serious' such that 'it is an affront to fundamental humanitarian principles' for the person to be removed.
- Second, there must be a clear link between the act of removal and the inhuman treatment.
- Third, because the harm is as a result of a naturally occurring illness, the threshold of suffering is particularly high.
- Fourth, an Article 3 claim can, in principle, succeed in a suicide case.
- Fifth, an important question will be whether the applicant's fear of ill-treatment in the receiving state is objectively well-founded. If it is not and the risk of suicide is based on that fear, this will weigh against the removal being in breach of Article 3.

- Sixth, another important question will be whether the removing and/or receiving state have effective mechanisms to reduce the risk of suicide. If they do, that also will weigh heavily against the Article 3 claim.

Picking up on this sixth point, the Home Office now have a policy to deal with the procedural aspects of suicide cases which is plainly intended to show that the UK does have effective mechanisms to deal with suicide-risk cases and cases involving possible self-harm. It was introduced in May 2005 and, because it deals directly with removal procedures, we look at it in the section on Enforcement, ▶996–8 (▶see also 995–6).

Note that there are special procedures under the Mental Health Acts that are occasionally used in relation to the removal from the UK of those who are psychiatric in-patients. We discuss those procedures in Chapter 33, dealing with enforcement.

Children and health

The Home Office has acknowledged that, in health cases, the human rights thresholds (set out above) that need to be reached by children:

'...in both Article 3 and Article 8 cases will be lower than for adults given their increased vulnerability.' (IDI, Ch 1, s8, para. 4.4).

Presence of child: effect on adult's application based on health

If a principal adult applicant makes a human rights application based on ill-health under Articles 3 or 8, which would usually be refused under the above criteria, the presence of a dependent child may mean that it should succeed. The Home Office has indicated that a grant of DL to both adult and child may be appropriate in the following circumstances.

'When, as a result of the principal applicant's reduced life expectancy, the child is likely to be orphaned in the near future and there are no relatives in the country of origin who would care for the orphaned child, consideration should be given as to whether the child qualifies under any aspect of DL policy.' (IDI, Ch 1, s8, para. 3.5)

Of course, if the child has been living in the UK continuously for seven years or more, then both child and parents may benefit from the general policy relating to children with long residence (▶388–9).

Effects of destitution

Claims based on destitution will be very hard to win. In *Fadele*, a complaint where children were to be forced to live in Nigeria in deprived circumstances detrimental to their health and education, was considered admissible under Articles 3 and 8. There was then a friendly settlement between the applicant and the UK government without the case having to go to a full hearing before the court. This suggests that it may be possible to show a breach of human rights where a person will be exposed to abject destitution and intense suffering as a result. However, in relation to 'welfare' considerations, the House of Lords made clear in *Razgar* that an applicant could not be successful just by showing that they would be relatively better off in the sending state (para. 10). In *Henao*, the European Court had also confirmed that a person could not ordinarily remain in the host state on the basis of their human rights simply in order to benefit from medical, social or other forms of assistance provided there.

Right not to be denied an education

In a number of cases, the European Court and the Commission have declared inadmissible claims that expulsion which would result in an inferior education for young children breaches their right under Article 2(1) First Protocol ECHR not to be denied an education (see *Jaramillo*, *Sorabjee* and *Ajayi*).

In *Holub*, the Court of Appeal considered the case of a Polish girl who claimed she had missed too much of the Polish syllabus while in the UK. She claimed, in particular, that the Polish educational system was so inflexible as to the factual knowledge required to progress through the system that she would be unable to catch up and would not be able to advance into higher education. In essence, therefore, it was the dislocation in her education that would be detrimental to her were she required to leave education in the UK and try to re-integrate into the Polish system. The Court decided that, given her abilities and the fact that she had kept up her Polish, she would be able to manage, and that the extent of any educational prejudice with which she might be faced was not severe enough to breach the Convention. The Court of Appeal also stated their view that the right not to be denied an education could not have 'extra-territorial effect' (for the meaning of 'extra-territorial effect', ▶see 787–9). However, this latter view was stated not to be 'authoritative', and the IAT in *Kacaj* later refused to follow it.

In the House of Lords in *Ullah*, Lord Bingham stated that he would be 'inclined' to accept that the right to education could not be relied on in this context but, ultimately, he left the question open (para. 21). It may therefore still be possible to raise education cases under this right, but the case would no doubt have to be truly exceptional to stand any chance of succeeding. It may be easier to raise educational points as a cumulative aspect of private life in claims about connections to the UK under Article 8 (▶see below).

FAMILY OR OTHER CONNECTIONS WITH THE UK

The third general situation in which rights under the ECHR have a major impact in immigration cases is where a person has family or other substantial connections with the UK.

Article 8(1) protects individuals against state interference with their private or family life, home and correspondence. Article 12 (the right to marry and to found a family) is unlikely to arise as the result of an immigration decision, unless Article 8 is also breached; nearly all relevant cases have been argued and dealt with under Article 8. Article 12 might be relevant separately if an immigration decision actually prevents a person from marrying (for details about the requirement for approval for marriage, introduced in early 2005, ▶see 296–300).

Article 8 does not give an automatic right of residence wherever a person has strong private or family ties in the UK. It is a restricted right, and it recognises the general right of the state to use immigration laws to control the admission of non-nationals into its territory. In immigration cases, where the applicant does not qualify under the immigration rules, Article 8 is therefore generally about striking a balance between two conflicting interests: the private and family life of the applicant(s) and the immigration law of the state.

When an application is made to the immigration authorities and Article 8 is raised, the decision must take into account the interests of all parties. For the debate about the question of whose human rights are relevant when it comes to an appeal, ▶see 858–9.

Article 8 ECHR states:

Right to respect for private life, family, home, correspondence (Article 8)

1) Everyone has the right to respect for his private and family life, his home and correspondence.

2) There shall be no interference by a public authority with the exercise of this right except such as is in accordance with the law and is necessary in a democratic society in the interests of national security, public safety or the economic well-being of the country, for the prevention of disorder or crime, for the protection of health or morals, or for the protection of the rights and freedoms of others.

The elements of Article 8

The application of Article 8 can be broken down into stages. An immigration decision affecting family life will be in breach of Article 8 if:

1) the relationship is covered by the meaning of family life (▶823–7); *and*

2) the decision 'interferes' with the 'right to respect' for family life (▶827–31); *and*

3) the decision is:

- not 'in accordance with the law' (▶831–2); or

- the decision is not made in order to further one of the legitimate interests of the state (national security, public safety, economic well-being of the country, prevention of disorder and crime, protection of health, protection of the rights and freedoms of others) (▶832); or

- the *extent* of the interference in family life caused by the decision cannot be justified as 'necessary in the interests of a democratic society' in order to fulfil the legitimate interest – this is also referred to as whether the decision is 'proportionate' (▶832–44).

The burden of showing (1) and (2) is on the applicant. If the applicant shows that the decision interferes with their right to respect for family life, then the burden switches to the state to show that none of the conditions in either (3), (4) or (5) apply. If the state cannot do this, then there is a breach of Article 8. Below, we discuss each of the above steps in turn. However, a summary of the general effect of Article 8 in immigration cases is contained in the general conclusions of the Court of Appeal in *Mahmood*, which are set out in the table below (▶see further at 836, 840).

The approach under Article 8 is broadly the same whether the immigration decision is to expel someone or to refuse to admit them, and so the steps described below are relevant in all cases. Some additional details about admission cases are given at ▶844–6.

It is not only connections of family relationship that can be relied on in immigration cases. In some cases, social and other ties to the UK by 'private' life can be relied on, either alone or taken together with family connections. Again, the same step-by-step approach that is explained below applies, but we look specifically at 'private life' at ▶827, 846–7.

Finally, at ▶847–50, we examine some additional case examples not covered in the main explanation of Article 8.

THE ARTICLE 8 PRINCIPLES SET OUT BY THE COURT OF APPEAL IN *MAHMOOD*

1) A state has a right, under international law, to control the entry of non-nationals into its territory, subject always to its treaty obligations.

2) Article 8 does not impose on a state any general obligations to respect the choice of residence of a married couple.

3) Removal or exclusion of one family member from a state where other members of the family are lawfully resident will not necessarily infringe Article 8, provided that there are no insurmountable obstacles to the family living together in the country of origin of the family member excluded, even where this involves a degree of hardship for some or all members of the family.

4) Article 8 is likely to be violated by the expulsion of a member of a family that has been long-established in a state if the circumstances are such that it is not reasonable to expect the other members of the family to follow the member expelled.

5) Knowledge, on the part of the resident spouse at the time of marriage, that rights of residence of the other party to the marriage were precarious, leans against a finding that an order excluding the applicant spouse violates Article 8.

6) Whether interference with family rights is justified in the interests of controlling immigration will depend on:

i) the facts of the particular case; and

ii) the circumstances existing in the state whose action is impugned.

Note

The principles set out in *Mahmood* (para. 55) should not be read as set in stone. As set out above, the Strasbourg case-law points to Article 8 cases depending on their own facts, and the above principles are stated in *Mahmood* to be a summary of the Strasbourg case-law. In *Cafer Bakir*, the IAT noted that the summary conclusions in *Mahmood* were not requirements that always had to be met. *Mahmood* is also relevant to whether an applicant should be required to apply from abroad (▶835 onwards).

The existence of family life

Whether 'family life' exists between the different parties does not depend only upon formal ties – for example, whether a couple are married. It depends largely on the strength of the ties that exist between the family members. The central question is whether there is a 'real existence' in practice of the 'close personal ties' necessary to family life. In certain relationships fundamental to the meaning of 'family life' under Article 8, those ties are generally assumed to exist. In other cases, they can be demonstrated by the facts. Unlike the definition of, for example, 'family visitor' in visitor appeals (▶see 1072), there is no simple definition in the ECHR of when family life exists. For the principles which can be taken from the case-law, see the table below. For same-sex relationships, ▶see 827.

8

DOES THE RELATIONSHIP AMOUNT TO FAMILY LIFE?

Although there is no definition of 'family life', the following principles can be taken from the decisions of the courts relating to particular relationships. They must also be read with the general factors set out at the end of the table (▶826).

Partners

Husband and wife

The relationship between husband and wife is central to family life; a lawful, genuine marriage is assumed to give rise to family life (*Abdulaziz*, ECtHR). However, a 'sham' marriage will not amount to family life (*Moustaquim*, ECtHR). Family life is not excluded because the marriage that has taken place is not in fact valid (*Cabales*, ECtHR).

Polygamous marriages

Relationships between the parties of polygamous marriages, even if they are formally invalid, may amount to family life (*A v Netherlands*). However, a country like the UK, which does not permit polygamy, will generally be able to justify denying entry to more than one spouse as proportionate under Article 8 (2) (*Bibi*, EComHR).

Unmarried partners

A relationship between unmarried partners can amount to family life (*Keegan, Johnston*, both ECtHR), even if the parties do not live together (*Kroon*, ECtHR). The particular factors to be taken into account are the length and stability of the relationship, the future intentions of the parties, whether they live together, and whether they have had children. (For same-sex relationships, ▶see 827.)

Transsexuals

Relations between a transsexual and their opposite-sex partner can amount to family life. In *X, Y and Z v UK*, the European Court found that there was family life between the parties and their child by artificial insemination.

Minor children and parents

Children and parents who are in marital or stable relationships

The relationship between a child born of a lawful, genuine marriage and their natural parents is assumed to amount to family life (*Berrehab*, ECtHR). Children born to stable non-marital relationships, where their parents are living together, are also assumed to have family life with both parents (*Keegan, Lebbink*, both ECtHR).

Later developments will only break family life between these parents and their children in 'exceptional circumstances' (*Berrehab*, ECtHR). For example, in the case of *Gul* (ECtHR), a separation of seven years between the applicant and his son did not exclude family life, as the applicant had continued to ask the Swiss authorities to admit his son from Turkey, and he had also continued to visit him. In *Berrehab*, divorce between the parents did not break the ties between father and child, who had maintained regular contact visits – cohabitation is not essential to show the existence of family life between parents and minor children. In *Boughanemi* (ECtHR), the father–child relationship involved family life even though the father only recognised the child ten months after the birth, and had made no provision for the child.

Children and natural father where parents not in stable relationship

Where a child is born out of wedlock and the parents are not in a stable relationship, while the existence of family life between mother and child is normally clear, family life between the father and child will not be assumed. It can, however, be demonstrated to exist. Relevant factors will be the interest shown in and commitment to the child by the father, both before and after the birth. In such cases, the concept of family life extends to the relationship that may develop in future between natural father and child, even though it has not yet fully developed (see *Lebbink, Nylund*, both ECtHR).

Adoptive children and parents (adoption lawful under national law and in compliance with international instruments)

The relationship between adoptive parents and children – where the adoption is lawful under the national law where it took place, is not a 'sham', and took place according to the relevant international instruments relating to the protection of children – will normally be treated as family life. This will still be the case even if family life has not yet been 'fully established' by cohabitation (see *Pini v Romania*, ECtHR).

Adoptive children and parents (adoption not recognised in UK and not in accordance with international instruments)

The mere fact that an adoption does not comply with various international instruments for the protection of children and is not valid in UK law does not automatically mean that there is no family life. In *Pawandeep Singh v ECO*, New Delhi, the adoption was valid in Indian law, but it was not valid in UK law and it did not comply with international instruments, because it took place as a result of the adoptive parents' desire to have another child, and not because the natural parents were unable to care for the child. Having regard to the fact that the adoption was in the 'best interests' of the child, and that there were real emotional bonds between the child and the adoptive parents, the Court of Appeal held that family life could exist.

Foster children

The relationship between foster parents and children probably amounts to family life (*Gaskin*, ECtHR) but this has not been as clearly established as it has for adoptive children and their adoptive parents.

Adult children and their parents; adult siblings

The Strasbourg case-law has stressed the need for evidence of continuing, particularly close links – for example, financial dependency – in order to show family life between adult children and their parents. In many cases, relationships between adult children and their parents and between adult siblings will therefore not amount to family life (*Advic*, EComHR), and strong evidence will be needed to show otherwise. In *Boughanemi*, the European Court presumed that family life continued to exist between an adult son (of 33 years) who was to be deported and his parents and seven brothers and sisters, but this approach is not normally taken.

The Court of Appeal has adopted a fact-based approach, with attention on whether there are additional ties of dependency beyond the normal emotional ties between such adults (►see *Kuguthas* under 'general factors', below). In *Senthuran v SSHD*, the Court of Appeal had to consider whether there could be family life between an asylum-seeker who was 17 when he arrived, but who had been living in the UK together with his adult siblings (who were in their thirties) for four years before the Home Office made a decision on the case. The Court remitted the case for further determination, holding that the question of whether there is family life between adult siblings is a 'fact-sensitive' one that depends on the circumstances. 'Striking' features of that case were that the applicant had lived with his siblings continuously since his arrival, and that the Home Office had delayed in making a decision (see paras 15–20).

Other relatives

Grandparents and grandchildren

In *Marckx*, the European Court stated its view that family life included 'at least the ties between near relatives, for instance, those between grandparents and grandchildren'.

Aunts, uncles, nieces, nephews

A relationship between uncle and nephew was held by the Commission to amount to family life in *Boyle* where the uncle had played the part of father to his nephew. In *Nhundu & Chiwera*, the IAT found that family life continued to exist between a minor orphaned nephew and his aunt; the child had grown up regarding his aunt as his mother. However, in the same case, family life had ceased to exist between the aunt and an adult, non-dependent nephew who was in good health and had employment experience.

General factors to be taken into account

Except in those cases where family life is generally assumed to exist (see above), the following factors will be of great importance in determining whether there is the 'real existence' in practice of the 'close personal ties' necessary to family life:

- the frequency of contact between the family members;
- the length of the relationship;
- whether the family members live or have lived together;
- the level of the emotional dependency between the family members;
- the level of any financial dependency between the parties;
- the level of any practical dependency between the parties.

In *S v UK* (EComHR) it was stated that:

'...generally, the protection of family life under Article 8 involves cohabiting dependants such as parents and their dependent, minor children. Whether it extends to other relationships depends on the circumstances of the particular case. Relationships between adults...would not necessarily acquire the protection of Article 8 of the Convention without evidence of further elements of dependency, involving more than the normal emotional ties.'

S concerned a mother and her 33-year-old son. In *Kuguthas*, which also concerned an adult's relationship with his mother and adult siblings, the Court of Appeal thought that the above passage was still relevant, although the further element of dependency did not have to be economic. So, in the case of the 'other relationships' referred to, it will be necessary to show that ties of support, either emotional or economic, are in existence and go beyond the ordinary and natural ties of affection that would accompany a relationship of that sort.

Same-sex relationships

Same-sex relationships have not been held to come within 'family' life (*Kerkhoven*, EComHR, *Mata Estevez v Spain*, ECtHR). However, same-sex relationships can be protected as part of the parties' 'private life' under Article 8 (*X and Y v UK*). It is possible, therefore, to apply the same general approach to same-sex partners as heterosexual couples. The factors taken into account to judge the strength of the ties between same-sex partners will also be the same as those for unmarried, heterosexual partners (▶see table above at 824, 826).

Although the language of the ECHR does not change, its interpretation develops to keep pace with modern-day conditions. The time when same-sex relationships will be fully recognised as amounting to family life under the ECHR must be drawing close. The UK courts have increasingly rejected attempts to treat such relationships less favourably (see *Fitzpatrick*, *Ghaidan*, both House of Lords and see also *M v Secretary of State for Work and Pensions*, CA). In *Pawandeep Singh* (▶see above at 825), Munby J reviewed the 'infinite variety of forms' which the family may take in contemporary Britain. He noted that there had been a 'sea-change' in society's attitudes towards same-sex relationships over the past few decades, so that such relationships are now entitled to respect and equal protection under the law. He could see no reason why the whole range of modern relationships that he described could not be viewed as 'family life' (paras 60–5). The equality of treatment between marriages and civil partnerships now recognised by the Home Office under the immigration rules (▶300–1) also strengthens the case.

Interference with the right to respect for family life

If the relationship(s) involve 'family life', it next has to be shown that the immigration decision excluding a person from the UK or removing them will result in an 'interference with the right to respect' for that family life.

Striking a balance

The case-law in this area can be confusing. Certain factors are sometimes considered by the courts under this heading of 'interference with the right to respect for family life', and sometimes the same factors are considered as part of the question of whether the interference in family life is 'proportionate' (▶see 832 onwards). One of the reasons for this is that both of these questions involve a balance being struck between the competing interests of the individual and the state (see, concerning interference/ respect, *Ciliz v Netherlands*, para. 61, ECtHR). Where the focus lies often depends on whether the case concerns admission or expulsion; and if expulsion, whether the ties have been established during a lengthy period of lawful presence. Demonstrating that there has been an 'interference' is more straightforward in cases involving long-established ties over a period of lengthy lawful residence (▶see 830–1). We further examine cases concerning admission from abroad below (▶844–6).

Relevant questions: *Abdulaziz*

In cases where the immigration status of the applicant in the UK is precarious, and family life is not long-established, showing that there will be an 'interference' with family life can be more difficult. According to *Abdulaziz* (ECtHR) the relevant questions are:

1) Are there 'obstacles' or 'special reasons' why family life cannot be established elsewhere?

2) Did the parties to the relationship know that they would not necessarily be able to maintain their family life in the country in which they wished to live at the time family life was established (e.g. when they began the relationship, or when they married)?

Cases where no interference found

All cases depend on their own circumstances, but the following are examples of cases where the European Court has rejected the argument that there are obstacles to relocation:

- closeness of settled partner to family in the UK and sickness of settled partner's father in the UK (*Abdulaziz*);
- risk of social rejection in the non-settled partner's country of origin (*Balkandali*, ECtHR).

A particularly harsh decision was *Gul* (ECtHR). In that case, a Turkish couple of Kurdish origin who had been granted the equivalent of exceptional leave in Switzerland, where the woman was also receiving specialist health treatment, were not able to be reunited with their two sons, who remained in Turkey. This decision is best understood on the basis that the couple had been able to return to Turkey for visits.

Examples of cases where there may be an interference

The following are examples of circumstances that may lead to a finding that there are obstacles preventing family life being established elsewhere:

1) it is not possible to obtain legal rights of residence for both family members in another country (*Beldjoudi*, ECtHR);

2) the family will suffer an interference with other human rights if they try to establish family life in another country – this might particularly benefit those who have been granted refugee status, humanitarian protection, discretionary leave, or exceptional leave on the basis that they cannot be expected to return to their country of origin (►see further 769–70). Note, however, the decision of the IAT in *SS Sri Lanka*, in which the IAT held that a past grant of refugee status does not by itself mean that there are insurmountable obstacles to return. If there has been a change of circumstances in country conditions since the grant of protection, the applicant may have to explain why there would now be an obstacle to relocating.

However, the problems do not have to amount to harms contrary to the ECHR in order to amount to 'obstacles' for these purposes. In *Nhundu*, the IAT stated:

'We would accept that in principle an appellant whose private and family ties in the UK were not on their own strong enough to give rise to a violation of article 8, could nevertheless succeed under that article if removal would expose him or her to a real risk of significant harms or serious obstacles, *albeit harms falling below the Article 3 threshold.*' (emphasis added)

On the facts of *Nhundu*, the IAT still found that the low-level form of harassment that the appellants faced was not enough to mean that Article 8 would be breached.

3) the person who is expected to leave has a child by a relationship that has now broken down, so that their previous partner cannot be expected to relocate abroad with them (▶see *Berrehab* below at 831);

4) there are wider family relationships that will be ruptured if one family unit is required to go to live in the other country. For example, the settled spouse may have living with them a child from an earlier relationship who has frequent and regular access to their other natural parent in the UK, and who cannot reasonably be expected to relocate to another country. In *Iskio*, the Court of Appeal ruled that this will not automatically show that there has been a breach of Article 8;

5) there will be severe health difficulties for any of the family members if they are forced to live abroad (see *Fadele* (EComHR), in which the children had actually suffered severe health difficulties on going to live in Nigeria).

Cumulative factors

It may be that 'obstacles' can be shown from a number of factors that, taken together, make it unreasonable to expect the family to relocate. Further factors of relevance are:

• whether the settled family member has long residence in the UK or other ties to the UK (e.g. property or employment);

• whether the settled family member has links with the proposed country of relocation (e.g. past residence there);

• the adaptability of family members to living elsewhere (factors relating to language, culture, religion, social practices, health and the ages of any children are all relevant);

• the existence of other family ties in the alternative destination and the other social, educational and economic prospects for the family there.

Because the question of what is necessary to show 'respect' for family life is a balancing exercise (▶827), it can be argued that, in considering whether there are 'special reasons' or 'obstacles', it is not necessary that all cases are measured by the same absolute standard or threshold. After all, in setting out these tests in *Abdulaziz*, the Court also said that:

'...in the area now under consideration, the extent of a State's obligation to admit to its territory relatives of settled immigrants will vary according to the particular circumstances of the persons involved.' (para. 67)

This has been repeated in the case-law many times. The question of whether there are sufficient 'obstacles', like the question of the parties' knowledge of the immigration problems they might face, appears to be one of the factors that needs to be weighed in the balance in order to determine whether the negative decision constitutes an interference. This is underlined by the decision of the European Commission in *Poku* (which was one of the cases from which the statement of principles in *Mahmood* was taken):

'Whether removal or expulsion of a family member from a Contracting State is incompatible with the requirements of Article 8 will depend on a number of factors: the extent to which family life is effectively ruptured, whether there are insurmountable obstacles in the way of the family living in the country of origin of one or more of them, whether there are factors of immigration control (e.g. breaches of immigration law) or considerations of public order...weighing in favour of removal.'

Where the applicant has lawful residence/long-established family life in the UK

In some cases, the applicant will have been lawfully residing in the UK for some time, including the point at which the family relationship was established. It may also be that family life is long-established in the UK. In such cases, it will be easier to show that an expulsion decision interferes with the right to respect for family life. The longer the period of lawful residence, the more this will be so. For example, in *Moustaquim v Belgium*, the applicant came to Belgium when he was less than two years old, and he remained there for nearly 20 years with his family (parents and seven siblings) before he was deported, having been convicted of some 22 offences (although the government relied on many more). The Court very quickly found an interference with family life (para. 36), but focused in detail on the question of proportionality under Article 8(2). After detailed examination, the Court found in his favour (paras 41–7; see also *Mehemi*, ECtHR).

A case involving a much shorter period of residence is *Boultif*, decided by the European Court in August 2001. The background was as follows:

- the applicant, an Algerian national, entered Switzerland with a tourist visa in December 1992;
- in March 1993 he married a Swiss citizen, and they lived together for about four years;

- they had no children;
- the applicant was imprisoned for two years for a particularly 'ruthless and brutal' robbery, and damage to property. He was also convicted for unlawful possession of firearms;
- in May 1998 the Swiss authorities refused to renew the applicant's resident permit to remain in the country, and he left sometime in 2000;
- the applicant raised the fact that, in Algeria, people live in fear of fundamentalism, and he also pointed out that he had worked successfully both before and after serving his sentence;
- although the applicant had lived in Italy before going to Switzerland and had returned there, he was staying there irregularly, and it could not be shown that both he and his wife would be permitted to live lawfully in Italy.

Again, without any detailed examination of the facts and circumstances, the Court had no difficulty in holding that the refusal to renew a resident permit interfered with the applicant's right to respect for family life, given that he was married to a woman who was settled in Switzerland (paras 40–1). The real issue was whether the decision was proportionate (for details of the proportionality considerations in **Boultif**, ▶see 843).

Contact with children

The ability to maintain contact with natural children is central to the notion of respect for family life. In the important case of **Berrehab**, a Moroccan national complained that he would not be able to continue to exercise his rights of access to his four-year-old daughter, from whose mother he was separated, if required to live overseas. The European Court had regard to the distance between the Netherlands and Morocco, the financial difficulties the applicant would have if returned, the age of the child, and the frequency of the pre-existing contact between father and child (four times a week for several hours each day). It was held that the immigration decision did constitute an interference with the applicant's right to respect for his family life. The interference was also found to be disproportionate, given that the applicant had lived in the Netherlands for several years and had a home and a job there.

The Home Office introduced changes to the immigration rules specifically to allow contact with children from parents abroad (▶372–5).

In accordance with the law

If the applicant shows that the immigration decision does amount to an interference with their right to respect for family life, the state must demonstrate that the interference is 'in accordance with the law'. This means that the immigration decision must be based upon a clear law, so that the decision does not arbitrarily interfere with family life. A decision based on the immigration legislation and rules will generally satisfy this condition. If the Home Office operates on the basis of policies and instructions outside the rules, then the criteria must be published and accessible. For the relevance of the marriage/enforcement instructions to Article 8 (DP/3/96), and for other instructions relevant to families and children, ▶see 337–43, 386–9, 998–1000.

One thing that should be noted in future is the publication of policy relating to family reunion with refugees, and with those with humanitarian protection, discretionary leave and exceptional leave. Home Office policy in these areas over the years has been notably unclear and changeable (▶see Chapter 25 and ▶see 876–9).

In pursuance of a legitimate aim

The immigration decision must also be made in the interests of society generally, for one of the reasons set out in Article 8(2) (▶see 821 above for the text). Immigration control in accordance with immigration law, has consistently been held both by the European Court and the UK courts to qualify as one of these reasons. Decisions taken according to immigration law and policy may be justified in order to prevent disorder, for the protection of the rights and freedoms of others, and/or to preserve the economic well-being of the country. In particular cases, they may also be justified in order to prevent crime or for national security reasons. The state can therefore almost always satisfy this condition.

Proportionality: is the extent of the interference 'necessary' in the interests of the community?

The more difficult job for the state under Article 8(2) is to show that the immigration decision is 'necessary' in order to protect the interests of the community. In order to do this, the interest of the community in pursuing immigration control is balanced against the interest of the individual, which is the interference with their family life. Another way of describing this balance is to say that the immigration decision must be 'proportionate' to the interference with family life.

The essential questions

The essential questions in determining whether an interference is proportionate are:

- What is the strength of the family/private life ties?
- What level of disruption in them will be caused by the immigration decision?
- What are the economic, cultural and social conditions like in the country of return?
- What difficulties would there be in relocating the family there or elsewhere?

- Is it possible, given the nature of the ties, to maintain effective family life from overseas (for example by visits, letters and other contact)?
- What will be the effect of the decision on other, third-party, family members?
- What are the state's reasons for interfering with family/private life, and how strong are those reasons in the individual case?
- Does the applicant have an adverse immigration history, and if so what is the extent of the breaches of immigration control?
- Are there any other general factors that may weigh in favour of the applicant? For example, the applicant might have a good working record or be supporting dependants who would otherwise be reliant on public funds.

While these are the overall questions that Article 8 asks when considering proportionality, as the UK case-law has developed since the HRA certain principles have emerged. Discussed below are: the general approach where the immigration rules cannot be met (▶834–5); in what circumstances the Home Office can rely on the applicant's ability to return and apply for entry clearance (▶835–40); the approach where family life is established during periods of Home Office delays in decision-making (▶840–3).

In some cases the Home Office may be relying not just on the interests of immigration control (in order to protect the rights and freedoms of others, or the economic well-being of the country), but on other interests, such as the need to control and prevent crime (for proportionality in cases involving crime, ▶843–4). For Home Office policy (DP/3/96) and Article 8 ▶see 840.

A genuine balance?

Sometimes Home Office representatives point to the part of the decision in *Razgar* that states that the IAT in *Kacaj* had only slightly overstated the case when it had said that 'legitimate immigration control' will 'almost certainly' mean that interferences are proportionate (House of Lords decision, para. 20). However, these comments made in *Kacaj* related to 'foreign' cases – i.e. where the harm would occur overseas. *Kacaj* was just such a case, in which the facts put forward for the Article 8 case were the same as those relied on under Article 3: Ms Kacaj claimed to be at risk of being abducted, forced into prostitution or otherwise ill-treated in Albania in order to punish her father for his political activities. Similarly, in *Razgar* (as in *Ullah*) the House of Lords was essentially looking at those cases where rights other than Article 3 may be engaged by treatment the applicant faces in the country of return. They were *not* dealing with cases about private and family life connections to the UK.

The Strasbourg case-law indicates that the approach to proportionality in Article 8 'domestic' cases about connections to the host country is a much more open matter, with no presumption that the interests of immigration control will 'almost certainly' trump an interference with family life. This is borne out by the number of successful cases there have been, as the review of the case-law in *Razgar* makes clear (see paras 44–53). The same cannot, of course, be said for 'foreign' Article 8 cases. Where it has been established that there will be an interference with the right to respect for family life established by the applicant in the expelling state, the European Court has been: '…unsympathetic to actions which will have the effect of breaking up marriages or separating children from their parents' (*Razgar*, para. 50). However, as the decision in the recent case of *Huang* shows (▶see below), UK case-law is becoming restrictive.

Proportionality and the decision in *Huang*

As we have seen, in *Mahmood* the Court of Appeal gave guidelines for dealing generally with Article 8 cases (for a summary, ▶see 822–3). In the important decision of *Huang, Abu-Qulbain, Kashmiri v SSHD*, decided in March 2005, the Court of Appeal focused on the specific question of 'proportionality' under Article 8(2). (Note that *Huang* is due to be reconsidered in the House of Lords.) In so doing it reviewed the IAT decision in *M (Croatia)*, which had very narrowly interpreted the powers of the appellate authorities (now the AIT) to overturn Home Office decisions on proportionality. Part of *Huang* is useful for applicants: rather than considering whether the Home Office has struck a balance falling within a 'reasonable range of responses', the AIT must normally consider for itself whether the decision is proportionate, and not defer to the view of the Secretary of State (paras 56, 60).

A restrictive approach However, while the AIT's *powers to review* Home Office decisions on proportionality were kept broad under *Huang*, it took a restrictive view of the *circumstances* under which a decision that is in accordance with the immigration rules may be disproportionate. *Huang* says that, where an applicant cannot satisfy the immigration rules, it will only be in an 'exceptional' or 'truly exceptional' case where the requirements of proportionality will mean that the rule must be departed from, and the applicant granted leave (paras 56, 60, 64). So, applicants may find that what was given with one hand has been taken away with the other. Of course, by its nature, Article 8 usually comes into play only when the rules cannot be satisfied. The nub of the ruling is that an immigration decision will only be disproportionate where:

'…the case is so exceptional on its particular facts that the imperative of proportionality demands an outcome in the appellant's favour notwithstanding that he cannot succeed under the Rules.' (para. 59)

So, the Court turned away from giving leeway to the Home Office by narrowing the powers of review on appeal; but *Huang* instead gives the Home Office automatic leeway by giving very great respect to the immigration rules.

The 'exceptionality' test and the facts in *Huang* However, a test that is as non-specific as 'exceptional circumstances' means that no case is completely ruled out, and it is open to applicants and advisers to make out why their particular circumstances are exceptional. In Mrs Huang's own case, the Court felt that the unusual history of the matter might well mean that it was 'truly exceptional', and it was sent back to the IAT for re-determination (see paras 6–10, 64). The main facts were as follows. Mrs Huang was a Chinese woman of almost 60 years of age, who enjoyed family life in the UK with her daughter, son-in-law and grandchildren. She had spent time in the UK on previous occasions after her husband had arrived here, and he had obtained settlement. She returned to China, however, in order to look after her father, who was ill. Subsequently she and her settled husband separated. It was noted that, had she not had to return to China when she did, she probably would have been granted indefinite leave. An example of a case after *Huang*, in which the High Court accepted that the circumstances could be 'exceptional', is *Lekstaka* (▶see 850 for further details).

The other joined cases in *Huang* However, in the other cases that were heard jointly with *Huang*, the Court of Appeal decided that there were no exceptional features. In one, a Palestinian from Lebanon had been in the UK for a few years awaiting the outcome of his asylum application. During that time he had worked hard to obtain further educational qualifications at his own expense, and become engaged to be married (*Abu-Qulbain*). In the other, a young Iranian man had deliberately stayed behind when the rest of his family travelled to the UK to claim asylum. When he later came himself, his own asylum claim was refused, but he claimed family life with his family members in the UK (*Kashmiri*).

Where no immigration rules apply But where there are no immigration rules generally applicable to the case, the principle in *Huang* does not apply. This is because, in such a case, it will not be a matter of determining whether there should be a 'departure' from particular rules in the individual case. However it is likely that much greater deference will be given to the decision of the Secretary of State in such cases, when conducting the balancing exercise (see *Huang* at paras 56, 61–2, referring also to *Samaroo*).

Comparison with Strasbourg cases It is unfortunate that UK case-law has gone down the road of requiring people to show that their cases meet some threshold of 'exceptionality' before human rights in this context can be said to have been breached. The Strasbourg cases do not refer to such a test; they look to the facts of the individual cases and apply to them the criteria under Article 8 in order to determine whether there is a breach.

Can the immigration authorities say 'The applicant should return and apply for entry clearance'?

Frequently, the Home Office will argue that a decision to require an applicant to leave the UK is not in breach of Article 8, because the applicant has the option of returning to their country of origin and applying for entry clearance to return in accordance with the immigration rules – i.e. as a spouse, unmarried partner, fiancé(e) or other dependant relative. This is often a powerful argument for the Home Office (although it has limits, ▶see the table below at 837–9), and it is one that the Court of Appeal has attached importance to.

The first important case on the point in the Court of Appeal was *Mahmood*. In that case, the appellant was a national of Pakistan, who entered the country unlawfully and then claimed asylum. The asylum application was refused, but he married shortly before the decision. The Home Office decision was that it was reasonable to expect the applicant's wife to return to Pakistan. She was a British citizen, but she originated from Pakistan, where she had lived until she was about 13 years of age, and could therefore readjust to life there. However, there was also an argument about whether, if the applicant wished to settle in the UK with his wife, he should be required to obtain an entry clearance, as others had to. Weighed against the interests of the applicant was the interest of the community in maintaining immigration control where the immigration law had not been complied with. The applicant argued that, although he had not obtained an entry clearance, there was no 'legitimate purpose' in requiring him to return to Pakistan, as he in fact satisfied the requirements of the immigration rules, such as maintenance and accommodation and intention to live together as spouses. It was only a procedural requirement that he had not complied with. However, the Court held that

'Firm immigration control requires consistency of treatment between one aspiring immigrant and another. If the established rule is ... that a person seeking rights of residence here on grounds of marriage (not being someone who already enjoys a leave, albeit limited, to remain in the UK) must obtain an entry clearance in his country of origin, then a waiver of that requirement in the case of someone who has found his way here without an entry clearance and then seeks to remain on marriage grounds, having no other legitimate claim to enter, would in the absence of exceptional circumstances to justify the waiver, disrupt and undermine immigration control because it would be manifestly unfair to other would-be entrants who are content to take their place in the entry clearance queue in their country of origin.' (para. 23)

In the later case of *R (Ekinci) v SSHD*, the appellant argued that it was no answer to his Article 8 case to say that he could apply from abroad, because he could *not* satisfy the immigration rules about maintenance and accommodation. The decision to require him to leave would therefore inevitably cause separation. The Court of Appeal agreed with the Home Office's argument that whether an applicant could or could not qualify to return to the UK was not relevant at the point of expulsion. It was matter that would be considered when the applicant applied from abroad. The Court added:

'It would be a bizarre and unsatisfactory result if, the less able the applicant is to satisfy the full requirements for entry clearance, the more readily he should be excused the need to apply.' (para. 17)

Ekinci is a hard decision for applicants. Does it mean that in all cases – even in very meritorious ones, where an applicant simply won't be able to qualify under the rules – they are required to seek entry clearance? That would be a particularly harsh result, for example, in the case of unmarried partners for whom it is not possible to complete the qualifying two-year period of living together required under the rules, because practical difficulties make relocation impossible, even for a short period. Such couples may never be able to qualify. They might, as with other cases, try to use the visitor rules to notch up the required period (▶322–3), but an applicant who has fought removal on Article 8 grounds may find it very hard to obtain a visitors' entry clearance in the future. A number of points can be noted about *Ekinci*, however, that may make it distinguishable:

- the decision of the Home Office did not actually accept that the applicant in that case would not necessarily be able to return either within or outside the rules (see paras 16, 19);
- the applicant had an extremely poor immigration history that involved lies, evasion of control, and failures to comply with conditions of temporary admission; poor immigration history is relevant to proportionality (see paras 1, 3, 17).

Note that in *Ekinci* the Home Office acknowledged that removal of the applicant would amount to an interference with the right to respect for family life, but relied upon the requirement to return to obtain an entry clearance as relevant to *proportionality*. In *Mahmood*, it was not entirely clear whether the entry clearance factor was relevant to whether there was an 'interference with the right to respect for family life' or to the issue of 'proportionality'. We have dealt with the question here under proportionality, where it seems to have been raised most frequently. The limits to the Home Office argument are set out in the table below.

THE LIMITS OF THE 'ENTRY CLEARANCE' ARGUMENT

As described above, the Home Office frequently defends its decisions in Article 8 cases by stating that the applicant should apply for entry clearance abroad. This table sets out the possible limits to this argument.

Do the rules require an entry clearance for the category of case in question?

The argument can only support the Home Office's case that interference is proportionate 'in the interests of immigration control' where that control would actually require an entry clearance for that particular category of case. There is no requirement in the immigration rules that any of the following applicants who wish to switch in-country must have entered with an entry clearance valid as family member:

- spouse applications, where the applicant has been permitted to remain under the rules for more than six months, and has limited leave (para. 284(i)(iv) HC 395);
- unmarried partner applications, where the applicant has limited leave under the rules (para. 295D(i), (iv) HC 395);
- applications for leave to *remain* as a dependent relative (para. 317 HC 395).

Arguably there is little 'immigration interest' in using the entry clearance argument to refuse human rights applicants in these categories, simply because the applicant cannot meet one of the other requirements of the rules; for example, they cannot be maintained and accommodated without recourse to public funds. The passage in *Mahmood* (para. 23, ▶see 836 above) is directly relevant here.

Certain overstayers

As an extension to the above category, the Home Office entry clearance argument is at least weaker in the case of an applicant who has legitimately resided in the UK for some other purpose, and then cannot meet the rules because they have become an overstayer. They have not obtained entry by circumventing the rules (including the requirements for entry clearance) from the outset. The reason they cannot meet the rules is that they cannot satisfy the requirement to have existing leave, not that the 'in-country' rules require applicants to possess an entry clearance.

According to the cases, the purpose of requiring people to return to obtain entry clearance is in order to discourage others from 'circumventing the entry clearance system' *(Ekinci* para. 17) and to be fair to others standing in the queue abroad (*Mahmood*). The applicants in both *Ekinci* and *Mahmood* were illegal entrants who never secured any basis for being in the UK. Different considerations arise for those whose presence in the UK has been entirely lawful for some time, and who later establish family life.

Although the circumstances were different, the same general distinction between applicants who first came to the UK legitimately and those who did not is made in the case of *Shala* (for further details of *Shala*, which is usually referred to in relation to delays in decision-making, ▶see 840–1). This was a case in which the applicant had a legitimate claim for protection when he arrived which, as a result of delay, had disappeared by the time his asylum claim was decided. Part of the Home Office argument was that the interference would only be a matter of months, because the applicant could apply to return from Kosovo and there was 'no reason to suppose that the application would not swiftly be granted'. Schiemann LJ stated that it was necessary to have regard to the *reasons* underlying the policy concerning entry clearance:

'Where someone has, without excuse, smuggled himself into this country without obtaining a visa and without permission and then forms a relationship one can see strong policy arguments for making him go abroad and go through the normal procedures, notwithstanding that relationship: to do otherwise may well encourage other would-be immigrants to come first and apply for permission afterwards and this would subvert the whole system.

Equally, successive Home Secretaries have recognised that there can come a time when it is no longer appropriate to insist that a particular individual who has established a family relationship in this country leaves that family and returns home.

The present case however is distinguishable from the mass of cases because the applicant came here at a time and in circumstances where his failure to apply for a visa was accepted by the Home Office as wholly explicable and where he applied for permission on the day he arrived from Kosovo which was in the middle of a dreadful civil war. He could not have done more. In short he was a meritorious applicant for permission to remain here, at any rate for a while… Automatically to apply to a person in his position a policy designed to discourage both meritorious and unmeritorious applicants from jumping the queue is a wrong approach to the difficult problem of deciding whether the interference with a person's rights under Article 8 is necessary in a democratic society.' (See paras 21–4)

Problems in returning to the UK

There may be problems in obtaining facilities to leave the country of return. As an illustration only, the US State Department report on Human Rights for Sudan refers to certain people being arbitrarily denied an exit visa. Is it possible that those who may be denied exit facilities are those (for example asylum-seekers) who previously left Sudan unlawfully? It may be that the applicant will have difficulties in actually making an entry clearance application, and/or would have to leave the country of return in order to apply for an entry clearance in a third country. For further cases on points about problems in applying for entry clearance, ▶see *Soloot* (IAT) and the cases discussed with it, below at 848–9.

Time in processing entry clearance applications

The time taken to process entry clearance applications might cause the applicant and their family severe detriment. In *Ekinci*, the Court was told that applications from the relevant post took only a month, and it was therefore clear that only a short period of time abroad was contemplated if the application was successful (para. 17). In *Talha Ahmed*, the IAT indicated that applicants should not be permitted to jump queues abroad, and that, provided that it would not take too long for a genuine application to be determined, the interference caused by temporary hardships would not be disproportionate. It is therefore worth checking present processing periods with the relevant post abroad. It is also worth checking to see whether the application would meet the criteria that require certain applications to be referred back to the Home Office by the ECO, as this will obviously add to the delay (▶see 92–3 for details about waiting times and referrals).

Delays

Delays in decision-making may also make a case sufficiently exceptional to mean that it would be unreasonable to require an applicant to return and obtain an entry clearance. Delay in general is discussed below, ▶at 840–3.

Proportionality and DP/3/96: the decisions in *Isiko* and *Mahmood*

The marriage/enforcement policy, DP/3/96, was drawn up with regard to Article 8. Both *Mahmood* and the further Court of Appeal case of *Isiko* considered it. The facts of *Mahmood* are set out above (▶836). In *Isiko*, there were a number of family relationships that would be disrupted by the removal of the two applicants, who were both citizens of Uganda who had married and then divorced, after which other family ties had been established. However, the immigration history of both applicants was described as 'deplorable'. One of the applicants had then been convicted of rape, and had made a 'baseless' claim to asylum to try to prevent removal.

In both *Isiko* and *Mahmood*, the Home Office had applied DP/3/96. (For full details about this policy, ▶see 338–43.) While the Court considered the policy to be lawful (although badly drafted), it stated in *Isiko* that this did not mean that 'every act of implementation of the policy is inevitably lawful'. Cases could arise where 'deportation would be a disproportionate response to the breach of immigration control', even in cases that did not satisfy the policy. It is clear, therefore, that the circumstances of each case need to be taken individually in order to understand whether, in fact, the decision of the immigration authorities complies with Article 8, even if it complies with DP/3/96. This principle must apply equally in cases involving the other family enforcement policies (▶see 386–9).

Are delays in decision-making relevant to proportionality?

Delay or inefficiency in decision-making by the Home Office, or in commencing enforcement proceedings, during which time an applicant has established family or private life ties to the UK, will generally be a factor to be weighed in the proportionality of decisions. The less the urgency with which the Home Office has acted, the more difficult it becomes for it to argue that there is a pressing need to take action to enforce immigration controls against an applicant. It cannot be reasonable to require of applicants that their entire private and family life is put on hold during periods of unreasonable delay.

Shala The *Shala* case involved a delay which had the effect of undermining the applicant's future immigration status. In *Shala*, the applicant was an ethnic Albanian asylum-seeker from Kosovo who had arrived in the UK in June 1997. Until mid-1999, the Home Office had a policy of granting such applicants at least exceptional leave to remain. However, his application was not dealt with until July 2001, by which time he had begun a relationship with a woman who was herself granted refugee status, and indefinite leave in May 2000. They later married. It was argued that, had the applicant's asylum application been determined within a reasonable time, he would at least have been granted exceptional leave, which would have enabled him to make an in-country variation application to remain as a spouse. The adjudicator and IAT decided that requiring the applicant to return to Kosovo would be an interference with family life, but not a disproportionate one. The Court of Appeal overturned these decisions. It held that these circumstances made the case sufficiently exceptional so that he should not be required to return to apply for entry clearance (see paras 14–16).

Subsequent IAT decisions accepted that the approach in *Shala* could also apply in cases of close relationships beyond marriage, but they have narrowly read the circumstances in which the approach would be justified. They restricted it to cases where all of the following apply: (1) the policy in force at the time of the decision demonstrates that the applicant would have been granted leave if the application had been determined within a reasonable period; (2) family life has become established during that period; (3) had leave been granted when it should have been, the applicant's immigration status would have permitted them to apply to remain from within the UK (see *DM (Proportionality – Article 8) Croatia CG* (IAT), *J (Serbia and Montenegro)* (IAT), and see also *Sadri Alihajdaraj v SSHD*, CA).

In the later case of *Strbac & Another v SSHD*, the Court of Appeal rejected the suggestion that *Shala* laid down a principle that an applicant whose claim was decided after the expiry of a reasonable time and would probably have met with success, should be treated as if it had been successful if they had established a family life in the UK. It held that the key fact in *Shala* was the loss of the advantage of being able to apply in-country on a variation of leave basis for leave to remain as a spouse of a British citizen. On the facts in *Strbac*, the applicants had not lost such an advantage. The Court did, however, indicate that the reasonable time for deciding an asylum application was a year and that administrative delay may, if substantial, and if it caused prejudice to the applicant beyond simply the wait, be a factor which decision-makers must consider.

Other cases However, even if the circumstances are not similar to those in *Shala*, delays in decision-making will still be a factor relevant to the proportionality of a decision under Article 8. The IAT accepted in *J* (see above) that delay may be relevant even if a case does not fall within the narrow boundaries of *Shala*. The decisions of the higher courts have also seen delay as a relevant factor and, as with *Strbac*, have preferred not to see *Shala* as a rigid principle.

In *Senthuran v SSHD*, the Court of Appeal considered the case of a Sri Lankan national who was 17 when he arrived in the UK and applied for asylum. He then lived continuously with his adult siblings for over four years, before the Home Office refused the asylum claim. The adjudicator referred to the unreasonable delay in determining the case, which had given the appellant the expectation that he would, in due course, be allowed to remain. He had obtained employment and studied. The IAT overturned the decision. While reaching no conclusion on the facts, the

Court of Appeal remitted the case and commented that, in addition to the years the applicant had spent living with his siblings,

'…an equally striking feature of the case is that more than four years elapsed between the appellant's arrival in the United Kingdom and the Secretary of State's refusal letter. The adjudicator described the length of time taken by the Secretary of State…as 'unreasonable'. It is difficult to quarrel with that observation.' (para. 19)

The Court of Appeal held that the delay was one of the factors that was 'manifestly relevant' to the consideration of Article 8 – in relation to both the existence of family life and the proportionality of any interference with it (paras 20, 22–3). Again, in *Janjanin & Musanovic v SSHD*, the Court of Appeal found that the applicants did not come within *Shala*, and found against the applicants; but delay was nevertheless a relevant factor in determining proportionality.

In *SSHD v Akaeke*, the Home Office submitted that delay could not be a relevant factor and certainly not a determinative one. The Court of Appeal ruled that delay was relevant (in that case three and a quarter years in reaching the decision under appeal) and that it reduced the weight of the public interest on the Secretary of State's side of the proportionality balance. The IAT had ruled that delay was the only significant factor in the instant case and that this alone made the decision disproportionate. The Court of Appeal did not interfere with this decision.

The High Court case of *R (Mthokozisi) v SSHD* provides a good example of the general relevance of delay, even where family circumstances would not give rise to leave and the case concerned private rather than family life. In that case an unaccompanied Ugandan national who was a minor when he arrived, waited nearly four and a half years for his asylum claim to be decided by the Home Office. After his arrival in the UK, the applicant had been placed in a children's home, and then with foster families. The Court rejected the argument that the applicant now had family life with members of his former foster families – he was now an adult, and there were no ties of particular dependency. It was accepted, though, that the decision would interfere with private life, although this would weigh less heavily in the balance. It was accepted that, had it not been for the delay, the applicant would have obtained exceptional leave on the basis of the policy relating to unaccompanied minors, and that he would probably have been granted indefinite leave on the basis of the time spent on exceptional leave. However, the Court did not think that this weighed as heavily as having a 'legitimate' claim for entry on the basis of protection, as in *Shala* (see above). Nevertheless, the Court quashed the decision of the Home Office on the basis that the delay, resulting in unfairness whereby the applicant lost the likelihood of being granted leave, was relevant. Owen J stated:

'In my judgment the Secretary of State adopted too narrow an approach to the decision in *Shala*. *Shala* is authority for the wider proposition that when striking the balance between an applicant's rights under Article 8 and the legitimate objective of the proper maintenance of immigration control, the decision-maker must have regard to delay in determining an application for asylum and its consequences.' (para. 29)

Criminal convictions and proportionality

In *Boultif* the European Court gave some 'guiding principles' on whether an immigration decision excluding a person is 'necessary' in the interests of the community (for the facts of *Boultif*, ▶see 830–1). Although what the Court said was of most relevance to cases where an applicant who is lawfully established in the country then commits acts which give rise to deportation, the factors referred to may be important in other cases as well:

'The Court will consider the nature and seriousness of the offence committed by the applicant; the length of the applicant's stay in the country from which he is going to be expelled; the time elapsed since the offence was committed as well as the applicant's conduct in that period; the nationalities of the various persons concerned; the applicant's family situation, such as the length of the marriage, and other factors expressing the effectiveness of a couple's family life; whether the spouse knew about the offence at the time when he or she entered into a family relationship; and whether there are children in the marriage, and if so, their age. Not least, the Court will also consider the seriousness of the difficulties which the spouse is likely to encounter in the country of origin, though the mere fact that a person might face certain difficulties in accompanying her or his spouse cannot in itself exclude an expulsion.' (para. 48)

Having regard to those factors in *Boultif's* case, the Court found that removal would be disproportionate. It is notable that the European Court considered the question of family relocation in the course of deciding whether the immigration decision was proportionate. Although it considered whether relocation was 'practically impossible', in reality a fairly low threshold was applied. The Court stated:

'The court has considered, first, whether the applicant and his wife could live together in Algeria. The applicant's wife is a Swiss national. It is true that the applicant's wife can speak French and has had contacts with her mother-in-law in Algeria. However, the applicant's wife has never lived in Algeria, she has no other ties with that country and indeed she does not speak Arabic. In these circumstances she cannot, in the court's opinion, be expected to follow her husband, the applicant, to Algeria.' (para. 53)

In cases of very long residence, where there are deep-rooted ties to the UK as well as settled family members here, removal even in cases of very persistent criminal offending will be hard for the authorities to justify (see cases such as *Moustaquim*, referred to above, and *Beljoudi*, ECtHR). In

8

Boughanemi, the European Court found that the interference was justified, but the offences in that case were more serious. In *Samaroo v SSHD*, a Guyanese national entered the UK in 1988, and obtained indefinite leave to remain on the grounds of marriage to a British citizen in 1990. The couple had a child. The applicant was then convicted of being knowingly concerned in the importation of class-A drugs worth £450,000, and was recommended for deportation as part of his sentence. He relied on evidence to show that he had been a model prisoner and was unlikely to reoffend. The Court of Appeal held that, although deportation would break up the family, the Home Office was allowed to view class-A drug-trafficking as particularly harmful, and was entitled to rely on its general policy of deporting those involved, with the aim of *deterring* others from similar involvement.

Article 8 and people wishing to come to the UK

Where a case concerns people who wish to come to the UK, rather than people being expelled, the same 'underlying criteria' as set out above are applied, (see *Box* (IAT), *Kuguthas* (CA) and *Ciliz* (ECtHR) at para. 61). The following observations from the decision of the House of Lords in *Razgar*, made in the context of some of the Strasbourg cases concerning the admission of children from overseas, are important on this point:

'There is a technical difference from the expulsion cases, in that the people living in the contracting state are relying on the state's obligation to take positive steps to enable family life to develop… But, as Judge Martens observed [in a dissenting speech in another Strasbourg case] the difference is hardly more than one of semantics – it has no bearing on the burden of proof or the standards of assessing a fair balance, in this case between the right to control immigration and 'a fundamental element of an elementary human right, the right to care for your own children.' (para. 53)

It must of course be recognised that, in cases where people are seeking to come to the UK, the facts are likely to be very different, and this may make it more difficult to make out the claim. For example, in determining whether the refusal of entry clearance shows an unjustified lack of respect for the applicant's family life, delay by the sponsor in seeking to achieve family reunion may be a relevant consideration (see *ECO, Accra v Emmanuel Attafuah*). Furthermore, in admission cases there may be arguments about whether family life 'exists' in the first place. In *ECO Lagos v Imoh*, the IAT held that the case of a four-year-old orphaned niece could not succeed because, she had no family life actually in existence with her aunt and uncle in the UK. Their only real connection with her had been to visit her once, and that they had paid for her care. The IAT held that Article 8 could not be used to attempt to 'create family life' in the UK.

However, this does not mean that all intended family life is excluded. In *Abdulaziz*, the UK government had argued to the Court that there was no existing family life between the couples, because no such family life had been established with any legitimate expectation of it being enjoyed in the UK. The Court held that not all intended family life falls outside the definition of 'family life', and that the word 'family' must include the relationship between spouses 'even if a family life of the kind referred to by the Government has not yet been fully established'. The Court also noted that the couples had had certain periods of cohabitation. As is set out above (▶824) family life will also generally be assumed to exist from birth between a child and their marital parents. That bond must continue, even if parent and child are not living together. The bond will only be broken by subsequent events in 'exceptional circumstances'.

Note that the IAT has indicated that the ability of an applicant who is outside the UK to rely on Article 8 should be seen as an exception. Its view was that the exception should not be extended beyond Article 8 (*Moon (Human rights, entry clearance, proportionality) USA*, but ▶see 808 concerning the decision in *Farrakhan*).

Children applying to come to the UK

A good example of a case dealing with children seeking to come to the UK is *Sen v the Netherlands*, decided by the European Court in December 2001. The Court found that there was a violation of Article 8, in a case where the Dutch authorities had denied a residence permit to allow an eldest child to join her two parents, who were legally resident and settled in the Netherlands. The parents lived in the Netherlands with their two younger children, both of whom had been born in the Netherlands. The Court noted that, although technically the case concerned the state's 'positive obligation' regarding 'respect' for family life (i.e. to admit the applicant) rather than a negative obligation not to interfere with family life, the 'principles applicable to such obligations are similar'.

On the facts of the case, the Court took into account the age of the child, her situation in their country of origin, and her degree of dependence on her parents. The Court noted that the child had spent her whole life in Turkey, had strong links with the linguistic and cultural environment there, and that she had relatives there. Against this was the fact that there was a major obstacle to the rest of the family's return to Turkey, given that the two other younger children had been born in the Netherlands and were at school there; they had few or no ties to Turkey. The Court noted that the parents had voluntarily left the eldest child in Turkey, but had not abandoned her, or the idea of being reunited with her in the future. The Court determined that the 'best way' of developing a family life with the family as it existed, given in particular the child's age, was for the child to come to the Netherlands. Accordingly, the Court decided that the Netherlands had failed to strike a fair balance between the applicants' interest and the state's interest in controlling immigration.

The Court in *Sen* seems to have determined the whole case on the basis of the lack of respect caused by the refusal to admit the child, and looked at questions of balancing the state's interests and the individual interest at that stage. This suggests that, in 'admission' cases, courts looks harder at the question of respect, and possibly apply a different threshold, but once this threshold is passed, denial of entry becomes difficult to justify as proportionate under Article 8(2).

In the earlier, harsh decision of *Gul*, the European Court refused an application where Turkish parents, who had been permitted to remain in Switzerland on humanitarian grounds, tried to be reunited with their eight-year old son, who remained in Turkey. They had another daughter who had been born in Switzerland, but who had been taken into care. *Gul* is probably best understood in the light of the fact that the parents had not achieved settlement rights, and that the father's returns to Turkey indicated that his reasons for claiming asylum from that country were no longer current.

Where the decision affects family life that is centred outside the UK

It is possible to rely on Article 8 where the immigration decision interferes with family life that will not necessarily be centred or located in the UK. For example, in *Kugathas*, the applicant argued against his removal to Sri Lanka on the basis that the greater distance (and expense of telephone calls) would undermine the family life he had with relatives who were settled as refugees in Germany. Before coming to the UK, the applicant has lived in Germany as well. From the UK, he hoped to enjoy some family life by visits and telephone calls. Although the case failed on the facts, because the applicant could not demonstrate 'family life' within Article 8, the Court of Appeal thought that in principle a case could come within Article 8 even though it related to family life that would be centred outside the UK.

Private life connections in the UK

A person may have connections in the UK, other than family ties, that are relevant to a human rights claim. The right to respect for private life under Article 8 includes the right of a person to develop their own personality and their relationships with other people (*Botta*, ECtHR). It covers same-sex relationships (▶827). Particularly in cases involving long residence, there may be significant elements of private life that need to be taken into account in addition (see for example, *Mehemi*, ECtHR). This may be the result of close friendships, or may derive from school, study or working life. It is also possible to *add* these elements of private life to any family connections to determine whether, taken together, there is a breach of Article 8. In *Nhundhu and Chiwera*, the IAT, after considering certain decisions of the European Court, stated:

'In the context of immigration and asylum cases, the court has come to view the right to respect for private and family life as a composite right.

This approach requires the decision-maker to avoid restricting himself to looking at the circumstances of 'family life' and to take into account also significant elements of the much wider sphere of 'private life' … One consequence of this approach is that a person may be able to establish a protected right under Article 8 either by reference to significant elements of family life or significant elements of private life or a mixture of both.'

In the recent case of *Slivenko v Latvia* (ECtHR), the applicants were a mother and child who were both ethnic Russians who had lived in Latvia all their lives, and who wished to remain there. They claimed that their removal from Latvia was in breach of their rights under Article 8. The mother was the wife of a former Soviet army officer who had returned to Russia after the independence of Latvia in 1991, and a treaty which had provided for the return of such officers. There was no interference with 'family' life, because the whole family was being deported; but the disruption of long-term residence and substantial social integration could amount to an interference with private life. On the facts, the Court found that the decision interfered with the applicants' right to respect for their 'private life' and their 'home' and that the interference was disproportionate (paras 96, 128–129).

In certain circumstances, the failure to recognise a permanent right of residence might interfere with a person's private life. This was the case in *Sisojeva & Others v Latvia* (European Court of Human Rights) where, although the Latvian authorities had made no formal deportation order, the applicants had been kept in a state of uncertainty and a precarious legal position on Latvian territory. The case was very strong on its facts but it is possible to see how prolonged delay in issuing leave to a person who is entitled to it could result in an interference with private life.

Exceptionally, there may be other human rights at stake arising from a person's connections to the UK. For example, in *Quaquah*, the High Court held, in circumstances where deportation would seriously interfere with the applicant's ability to prepare his civil action against the Home Office for malicious prosecution, that the decision interfered with the 'equality of arms' principle in Article 6 (right to a fair trial).

Further Article 8 case examples

The case-law under Article 8 has developed quickly since the HRA. The different elements of Article 8 are examined above. Here we provide some additional favourable cases, not considered above, which applicants and their advisers may find useful as examples of the operation of Article 8. Of course, there is no substitute for looking up the full details of any case.

Adegbie v Austria **(1995, EComHR)** The applicant complained under both Article 3 and Article 8 about a proposed removal to Nigeria. The applicant's wife was settled in Austria as a civil servant, and the main complaint in respect of relocation to Nigeria with his wife was that she would have to change her social environment 'radically', and give up her employment and career. The Commission rejected the claim in relation to the risks about return under Article 3, but found that the Article 8 complaint was admissible. The matter was later the subject of a friendly settlement.

***Sukhjit Gill* (December 2001, IAT)** An Indian national claimed that his removal to India would violate his Article 8 rights, because he acted as a carer for his father, who was settled in the UK and was suffering from diabetes. The adjudicator accepted that there was a close relationship between father and son, that the son cared for his father in the UK, and that, consequently, his removal from the UK would be disproportionate. On the Home Office's appeal, the IAT agreed that the son's removal was disproportionate. Among the factors considered relevant in determining whether the decision was 'necessary' were the considerable delay on the part of the Home Office, leading to the development of close ties in the UK, and the fact that the father's health might deteriorate if the son was removed, with the possible need for increased public provision for him.

***Romuald Andela Mindoukna* (November 2001, IAT)** The appellant was a national of Cameroon, and a failed asylum-seeker, who stated that removing him to Cameroon would violate his Article 8 rights with his partner and child. The IAT accepted that there were serious grounds for thinking that the applicant would not succeed in an application for settlement from Cameroon, or indeed in an application to come to the UK in order to visit his family. During the course of the proceedings, the IAT stated that a welfare report concerning the child should be produced by the local authority in whose area the child was living, in order for the court to have a better understanding of the effect of removal of the father. The IAT encouraged representatives in similar cases to invite adjudicators to request such reports. The IAT indicated that permanent separation as the result of an applicant's immigration history preventing their readmission may violate Article 8. The case was sent back to the adjudicator for re-hearing.

***AHR Soloot* (August 2001, IAT)** The IAT found that there was a breach of Article 8 partly on the basis that, if the applicant was required to return to apply for entry clearance, he would be unable to do so in Iran, where he was to be sent, as there were no facilities for doing so there. In addition, the applicant might be unable to exit Iran to make an entry clearance application, as he had previously left that country in violation of the exit regulations. At the very least, his exit would be delayed.

This decision should be compared with *HI*, in which the IAT found that it would not be an exceptional circumstance for the applicant to have to apply for an entry clearance under limited facilities available at that time in Pakistan – i.e. by post, or having to apply in a third country. In a further IAT decision, *Kidane*, the IAT noted that the applicant – who was to be returned to Eritrea where at the time there were no entry clearance facilities – might be able to apply for entry clearance in Sudan. However, that would only be after a long delay, as the applicant would first have to complete his military service in Eritrea. This, combined with other factors, made the removal decision disproportionate.

A further example of difficulties in this area relates to Iraqi applicants who are married to those settled in the UK. A number of IAT decisions have indicated that they may travel to Jordan and apply for entry clearance there. However, in January 2005 the UK office of the UNHCR was reporting that the road to Amman (Jordan) from Baghdad (Iraq) is highly dangerous, and also that air travel on civilian flights to Baghdad is also dangerous. They also reported that the road from the international airport at Baghdad to the city itself was dangerous. This would seem to make it unreasonable to expect a person to obtain entry clearance in Jordan. The situation is fluid and will no doubt change – but this illustrates the need to obtain up-to-date country evidence concerning issues of this kind.

***Immigration Officer, Gatwick South v Naomi Danino* (October 2002, IAT)** The IAT found that it was disproportionate to refuse entry to the unmarried partner of a German national who returned to the UK after a trip to Israel. The applicant was returning in order to resume cohabitation with her partner, with whom she had lived in the UK for 16 years. There were no obstacles to relocating to Germany, and normally an applicant such as this would be required to obtain entry clearance. However, the length of her residence in the UK with an EEA national who was exercising rights of free movement, together with contradictory information given to the applicant by the Home Office about her rights, made the case 'exceptional'.

***Jobe v SSHD* (November 2002, IAT)** A Gambian applicant applied for asylum, but the appeal was dismissed without his knowing because his solicitors had been closed down by the Law Society. In the meantime, he married a British Citizen and had two children. The relationship had been continuing for over three years. There were obstacles to the family relocating to Gambia, including poor economic circumstances. An accumulation of factors – including length of residence, strength of ties, consequences of removal for family members, and the possibility of some ill-treatment in Gambia – made removal disproportionate.

***Jakupovic v Austria* (February 2003, ECtHR)** The applicant was Bosnian, and went to Austria to join his mother and siblings when aged only eleven. At the age of 16 a residence prohibition was imposed on him, because of criminal offences that included a string of burglaries. It also appeared that he had attacked several people with an electro-shock device. The Court found that the interference with his family life was disproportionate: very weighty reasons would be needed to justify sending such a young man on his own to a country that had recently been a war zone, with all the adverse consequences for living conditions that would have. He also had no close relatives in his country of return (his father was reported missing). The Court came to this conclusion despite the fact that the applicant had only been in Austria for four years at the time of the expulsion decision, and that he had attended school in the country of return and was therefore assumed to be well acquainted with its language and culture.

R (Lekstaka) v IAT **(April 2005, High Court)** This was a case that was decided in the light of *Huang* (▶see above at 834–5). The applicant was a young ethnic Albanian from Kosovo who had spent time in Macedonia. As a result of war and disappearances, he had lost all of his immediate family. He arrived in the UK aged sixteen, claimed asylum and established family life with his aunt, uncle and cousin, who had indefinite leave in the UK as refugees. His asylum claim was refused after he had become an adult. The Court noted that the applicant had come close to qualifying under both the immigration rules and Home Office policy. Had he been a son (not an orphaned nephew) and applied before he reached 18 years, he may have qualified under the rules as a dependant – at least under the family reunion provisions. Had the aunt and uncle not already succeeded in their claims, and had he been a son, he may have qualified under the backlog concession for families. The Court also noted that returning the applicant was likely effectively to end, not just interfere with, family life. It had been suggested that he could continue contact from abroad through visits, but the Court referred to the cost of this and questioned whether in fact he would succeed in getting entry clearance for a visit. The nature of his circumstances made his case different from any case of the return of a young man to a country emerging from war and, as in *Jakupovic* (▶see above), the Home Office would have to show weighty reasons for interfering with family life in these circumstances.

While the Court was keen to point out that all cases depend on their facts, and that this case was not a precedent, the indication is that cases falling within the 'spirit' of the rules or policies might be 'exceptional' in the sense of *Huang*:

'It seems to me that one is entitled to see whether, in all the circum-stances, this case falls within the spirit of the Rules or the policies, even if not within the letter. It does in my view quite plainly fall within the spirit because, albeit only a nephew, he has no other family – his father having been killed and his mother and sister having disappeared – and he has been treated by his uncle as if he were indeed the son of the family and that in my judgment is certainly capable of constituting an exceptional state of affairs.' (para. 38)

However, this is a decision which must be read alongside the decision of the Court of Appeal in *Delo Mongoto v SSHD* in which the Court of Appeal rejected out of hand the argument that an applicant could rely upon a policy by analogy. It was emphasised that the Home Office was entitled to have a limited policy intended for the benefit of a limited category of applicants. Applicants could not have expectations based upon policies which did not directly apply to them (paras 23–25).

LEAVE OUTSIDE THE RULES WHERE THERE IS NO BREACH OF HUMAN RIGHTS

The policy concerning discretionary leave (DL) indicates that there are cases in which the Home Office is prepared to grant leave even if a human rights claim is not successful (►see 865). It is therefore often worth also asking for discretion to be exercised. If such a request is to be made, it may be worth referring to the indications in recent cases that, even where the high thresholds for showing a breach of human rights cannot be met, there may still be very strong humanitarian reasons for allowing certain applicants to remain (see below).

In addition, the AIT can be asked to make recommendations to the Home Office to treat the case exceptionally (►see 1127–9 for further details about such recommendations). If the Home Office agrees to exercise this discretion, it will of course grant leave 'exceptionally'. The Home Office has also begun calling exceptional leave 'leave outside the rules' (LOTR), but the different label makes little practical difference.

The following indications from the courts are given as examples only.

HIV/AIDS and other serious illness

In the House of Lords, in *N*, which concerned an appellant with advanced HIV/AIDs, the Lords narrowly interpreted the UK's obligations under the ECHR (►see above 810–2). However, the very compassionate nature of the case and similar cases is underlined by all of the judgments. At the close of his judgment, Lord Brown stressed that, even though removal would not be contrary to the ECHR, the Home Office had a wide discretion over whether to require the appellant actually to leave. He stated:

'Whilst, for the reasons given, I would not regard the return of this appellant to Uganda as a violation of Article 3, it by no means follows that the Secretary of State is bound to deport her. Plainly he has the widest discretion in the matter. The likely impact upon immigration control (and, doubtless, National Health Service resources) of an adverse Article 3 ruling in the case would be one thing; the favourable exercise of an administrative discretion in this individual case quite another. I am not saying that the Secretary of State *should* now exercise his discretion in the appellant's favour, still less that a refusal to do so would be challengeable; only that the appellant's return would not inevitably follow from the failure of her appeal.' (para. 99)

Mental ill health

In *Bensaid* (►see 816–7 above for details), three of the Judges of the European Court issued a separate decision agreeing with the main decision. They agreed that, because what would actually happen to Mr Bensaid's mental condition if he were returned was less certain and more speculative than what would happen in *D*'s case (►see above, 809–10), the application did not show a breach of the ECHR. *However*, they went on:

'Nevertheless, on the evidence before the Court, there exist in my view powerful and compelling humanitarian considerations in the present case which would justify and merit reconsideration by the national authorities of the decision to remove the applicant to Algeria.' (para. 0–16)

Family life cases that fail under Article 8

In the case of a failed Article 8 claim in *Shillova*, an adjudicator had made a recommendation that the applicant be allowed to stay in the UK on the grounds that many of his family members were lawfully in the UK and that he had computer skills that made him an asset to the country. The High Court underlined that there were still cases, following the HRA, where it would be possible and proper to make a recommendation that exceptional leave should be granted.

Internal relocation cases that fail under the Refugee Convention and the ECHR

In *AE & FE*, the Court of Appeal emphasised that it was important to distinguish clearly between (1) the right to refugee status, (2) the right to remain by reason of rights under the ECHR, and (3) considerations that might be relevant to the granting of leave to remain for humanitarian reasons. The Court was addressing cases in which an applicant had established a well-founded fear of persecution in their home area, but not elsewhere in their country. The Court felt that the difficulties an applicant would have in returning from the UK to the relocation area – i.e. comparing their circumstances in the UK with the conditions in the area of relocation – might be very relevant 'when considering the impact of the Human Rights Convention, *or the requirements of humanity*' (emphasis added; ►see 622, 798 for more general details about *AE*).

28 Raising human rights, humanitarian protection, discretionary leave, family reunion and travel

This chapter looks at the practicality of making human rights claims and appeals, at the kind of leave that is granted if a claim succeeds, and at the rights which follow. We begin by looking at the various ways in which a human rights claim can be raised. There is obviously some overlap with the procedures for claiming asylum, because often a human rights claim will be made in conjunction with an asylum claim (▶see Chapter 22 on asylum procedures, and Chapter 23 on asylum decisions). We then examine certain aspects of human rights appeals, including making fresh claims and appeals (▶857–9). Note that certification of claims on the basis that they are 'clearly unfounded', and that there has been an earlier appeal, is dealt with in the Section 10 on appeals. 'Third country' cases are discussed together with asylum in ▶Chapter 24.

The chapter then looks in detail at the system of granting 'humanitarian protection' (HP) and 'discretionary leave' (DL), where a human rights claim is successful on or after 1 April 2003 and on or after 30 August 2005 (▶see 859 onwards). We also deal with the length of leave granted (which depends on the basis on which the claim has succeeded); exclusions from humanitarian protection; 'active review' of cases; extension applications; settlement; and actions leading to loss of status. We also look at the transitional arrangements for those granted exceptional leave prior to 1 April 2003. The section on leave granted needs to be read together with the table at ▶721 onwards.

Discretionary leave is largely granted on a human rights basis, but it can also be granted in cases where a human rights claim fails. It is granted, for example, to unaccompanied asylum-seeking children (UASCs) for whom there are no adequate facilities for reception in their country of return. The leave granted to these applicants is quite complex (▶see 870–1).

This chapter then looks at family reunion rights for those granted humanitarian protection, discretionary leave and exceptional leave (▶875–9; family reunion for refugees is covered in Chapter 25). Finally, we cover the rights of those granted these forms of leave, and indefinite leave, to obtain the travel documents known as Certificates of Identity (▶880–3).

For details about the requirements that need to be satisfied to succeed in a human rights claim, ▶see Chapter 27.

MAKING HUMAN RIGHTS CLAIMS

The general principle is that a human rights claim can be made at any time, and it must be properly considered, even if an applicant has already been through the asylum and appeals process without expressly raising a human rights case (see API *Humanitarian Protection*, para. 5; IDI, Ch 1, s10, para 5.2). If an applicant makes an application without mentioning human rights, but the facts which they put forward indicate that human rights are an issue, officers should still consider the question of human rights in making their decision (IDI, Ch 1, s10, paras 5–6).

Even if a human rights claim is made orally, which is sometimes the case in relation to applicants who are detained and have limited access to representation, the immigration authorities should take notice of it. In a letter to Bindman & Partners in response to a complaint, the Home Office confirmed that an immigration officer should have accepted an oral allegation, made at an interview at Heathrow Terminal 2, that the action being taken was contrary to the applicant's human rights, and should have dealt with it (Home Office letter, dated 16 August 2002). Although that letter considered the position under s65 1999 Act, which is no longer in force, we suggest that the same must be true under the 2002 and 2004 Acts.

With these principles firmly in mind, we look at the various formal ways in which a claim may be raised:

- as part of an asylum application (▶see below);
- as an independent application, or connected to a non-asylum application (▶855–6);
- by filling in a one-stop notice (▶856);
- at an appeal (▶856–7).

From 1 January 2005, in deciding questions of credibility in any human rights claim, both the immigration authorities and the AIT are required to have regard to certain matters set out in section 8 of the 2004 Act. Account must be taken of matters such as failing to produce a passport, or destroying a passport without reasonable excuse, or not claiming while in a 'safe' third country. Section 8 of the 2004 Act applies equally to asylum claims, and is covered in more detail at ▶708–14.

Claiming as part of an asylum application

In many cases, Refugee Convention claims overlap with human rights grounds, and applicants either expressly or implicitly make a human rights claim at the same time as they make their asylum claim. Such claims progress through the asylum system in the same way as other asylum claims (▶see Chapter 22). If an asylum claim is to be refused, the Home

Office should always consider whether the applicant should succeed on human rights grounds. This will involve considering whether to grant HP or DL. The Home Office will consider Article 3 in particular, but where the circumstances alleged by the applicant indicate that one of the other rights is directly relevant, those rights should also be considered. This is the case even if human rights are not expressly raised by the applicant.

Independent application

A human rights claim can also be made on a 'stand-alone' basis. The legislation indicating how human rights claims are to be made is identical to that for asylum claims. It states that they should be made 'to the Secretary of State at a place designated by the Secretary of State' (s113(1) 2002 Act). However, as a matter of practice there are some differences.

Claims for protection

The Home Office has stated that, in general, asylum claims and human rights claims are to be made in the same way:

'Applicants wishing to make a human rights claim must follow the same course as an asylum applicant. If an applicant is *genuinely* medically unfit (this will require medical evidence) to make an asylum/human rights claim in person at a public caller unit, IND staff will arrange for his claim to be recorded and dealt with in a more suitable manner.' (Home Office letter to Hammersmith and Fulham Community Law Centre, 8 August 2003)

So, for many seeking to make a 'stand-alone' protection claim under Article 3 – for example, because they acknowledge that there is no Refugee Convention reason for the risk they face – the procedure is the same as for asylum claims. No form is required – indeed, the guidance notes for making applications issued on the Home Office website indicate that no form is needed for an application made under Article 3 ECHR. Of course, any Article 3 claim is defined as a 'claim for asylum' for asylum support purposes, and will therefore enable a person to obtain asylum support if they satisfy the other conditions for eligibility and go through similar NASS processes (see s 94(1) 1999 Act, s18(3) 2002 Act).

Non-Article 3 claims and non-'protection'-based claims

However, the Home Office has operated different arrangements where the human rights claim is not an Article 3 claim, and/or when it is not a claim for 'protection'. In a letter to the Immigration Advisory Service on 8 April 2004, the Asylum Policy Unit stated:

'... a human rights claim (other than a claim under article 3 of the ECHR) must be made on an application form. This means, for example, that someone who wished to make a claim under article 8 alone would have to complete an application form and take it to one of our public caller units, where they could submit it in person.'

In addition, in a written memo to the Asylum Processes Stakeholder Group on 17 June 2004, the Home Office stated that Article 3 claims submitted on the basis of medical grounds could be submitted on form FLR(O) or SET(O). However, no fee may be charged for any application made on Article 3 grounds (see s5(3)(6) 1999 Act). The Home Office has also stated that it will not charge for Article 8 applications where the application is linked with an asylum or an Article 3 claim (letter of Home Office Managed Migration Directorate to Hackney Law Centre, 27 January 2005). Of course, no form can be required in a 'port' case where the applicant is seeking leave to enter, rather than leave to remain. Such applications can be made to the immigration service at the port, who are likely to refer it to the Home Office.

It is often the case that applicants who are applying in-country on family grounds will submit the relevant application form (▶see 127–32), together with representations as to why, even if the application cannot succeed under the rules, it should be granted either under Article 8 or outside the immigration rules. In other cases, form FLR(O) may be used.

Communications with the Home Office indicate that it has struggled to establish procedures for making non-Article 3 and non-protection human rights claims, and so applicants and advisers should be alert to the fact that procedures may change.

One-stop notices

One of the purposes of the 'one-stop' procedure was to allow human rights grounds to be considered by the Home Office together with any other claim. The one-stop procedure under the 1999 Act was incredibly complicated (▶see pp. 606–11 of the previous edition of the *Handbook*). It has now been simplified (see s120 2002 Act). Where the notice is completed before a decision, and a 'statement of additional' grounds is returned, the Home Office should consider those additional grounds in coming to its decision. Where the notice is given after a decision but there is to be an appeal, the immigration authorities should reconsider the decision before the appeal. One-stop procedures do not apply only in cases that may involve human rights claims. For further details about the one-stop procedure, ▶see 662–4, 1066–7.

Claiming as part of another appeal

Although it is much better to raise human rights issues before a decision, or at least in response to a section 120 notice (▶see above), it is possible to do so before the AIT during the course of an appeal that is brought on different grounds. Applicants may appeal to the AIT on the grounds that the decision, or removal of the applicant, is unlawful under s6 HRA (public authority not to act contrary to the ECHR) as being in breach of the appellant's human rights (see s84(1)(c)(g) 2002 Act). Human rights appeals are considered on the facts as of the date of the decision.

HUMAN RIGHTS APPEALS AND FRESH CLAIMS

Under the 1999 Act, an applicant was entitled to appeal on human rights grounds whenever they made an allegation that the immigration authorities had taken a decision 'relating to the [applicant's] entitlement to enter or remain' in the UK that was in breach of their human rights (s65 1999 Act). In *Kariharan & Others*, the Court of Appeal interpreted this very widely. It was held that removal directions – whether they were consequent on an earlier decision to refuse leave to enter or remain, or were simply the latest 'administrative' decision and not part of the 'substantive' immigration decision – still attracted a right of appeal if the applicant alleged that they were contrary to their human rights. The Court felt that abusive and repeat applications could be dealt with under the existing separate mechanisms (certificates) to deal with abusive appeals.

The government's response to *Kariharan* was to pass legislation to reverse it. Under the 2002 Act, human rights appeals, like most other appeals, can only be brought against 'immigration decisions' as defined in section 82(2) 2002 Act (▶1053–4). One of the purposes of introducing the concept of an 'immigration decision' under the 2002 Act was to ensure that appeal rights *only* exist underlying 'decisions' about immigration status – whether to refuse leave to enter/remain, to vary or revoke leave, to determine that someone should be removed, etc. Other administrative steps taken that are built on top of those decisions – for example, simply the setting of removal directions, which of course might be deferred and re-set – do not themselves amount to 'immigration decisions' which can be appealed against.

Certification to prevent appeals

Where the Home Office certifies a human rights claim as 'clearly unfounded', the applicant will be prevented from bringing an appeal while they are in the UK; they will only be able to appeal from abroad. Such appeals are called 'non-suspensive appeals', because there is no right of appeal that 'suspends' removal. The only means of challenging the certificate so as to restore an in-country right of appeal is by judicial review. From 1 October 2004, powers to issue these certificates have been widened by s27 2004 Act. The same provisions apply to asylum claims, and we have therefore considered issues relating to unfounded asylum and human rights claims together, at ▶1073–8.

8

Third country cases

Where an asylum or a human rights claim is made, the Home Office can attempt to return the applicant to a safe 'third country', instead of returning them to their country of origin or previous residence. The third country provisions have been amended many times. The regime in force from 1 October 2004 is set out in section 33 and Schedule 3 to the 2004 Act. The law is very similar, as it applies to asylum and human rights claims, and is covered in the asylum section (▶see Chapter 24).

Fresh claims

If a human rights application or appeal has already been determined negatively, it is always open to applicants to make further representations seeking to change the decision. Those representations must always be properly considered together with the existing material in the case. Where the further representations and the material put forward in the case make the claim 'significantly different' from the earlier claim, then even if the application is refused again, an applicant may be able to establish that they have made a 'fresh claim'. If there is indeed a fresh claim, then the Home Office is obliged to issue a new notice of 'immigration decision', which gives the applicant a fresh right of appeal. The criteria taken into account to determine whether a fresh claim has been made are the same as for asylum cases (for full details of the criteria and the procedure used, ▶see 730–5). This has always been accepted by the Home Office (see API *Further representations and fresh applications*, para. 13), although from 25 October 2004, 'fresh' human rights claims have been part of the immigration rules as well (see para. 353 HC 395 inserted by HC 1112).

An example of a fresh human rights claim might be where an applicant's spouse becomes pregnant and gives birth to the couple's child after the original decision and appeal. Another example would be where there is further important evidence or information that comes to light in relation to a claim for protection, and that puts the case in a new light. If the Home Office refuses to accept that a fresh claim has been made, and therefore denies a further right of appeal, then the only remedy is judicial review.

A separate mechanism the Home Office may use to deny further appeal rights is to certify the claim on one of the bases under section 96 2002 Act. Indeed, the Home Office has expressly stated that, when a fresh claim is made that gives rise to a right of appeal, that claim may still be certified under section 96 (see API *Appeals – The One Stop Procedure Warnings and Certificates*, para. 2.5). For details of the operation of s96, ▶see 1067–9.

Whose human rights are taken into account on an appeal?

A further problem has arisen about the scope of human rights appeals in Article 8 cases. This is because the wording of the legislation refers to the 'appellant's' human rights (previously s65 1999 Act, now s84(1)(c)(g)

2002 Act). So what happens where an immigration decision affects the human rights of someone who is not an appellant? Can the AIT consider the human rights of that person? Most commonly this occurs in Article 8 family cases where the appellant's settled family members in the UK are also affected by the decision. In *R (AC) v IAT*, the High Court took the view that, in family life cases, the impact on the family life as a whole should be taken into account, because the impact on the settled family member will generally impinge on the human rights of an appellant. The interests will usually be difficult to separate out. This is a common sense, practical approach, because it means that the AIT can deal with all relevant matters. If the AIT cannot do so, then the rights of other interested parties could only be brought before the court in separate judicial review proceedings.

Unfortunately, in the past, the IAT/AIT has taken a more restrictive view to the effect that the rights of those who are not appellants will have to be dealt with elsewhere, i.e. in judicial review proceedings (see *SS Malaysia*, *NS Sri Lanka*, both IAT).

WHAT LEAVE IS GRANTED IF A HUMAN RIGHTS CLAIM IS SUCCESSFUL?

The leave granted to those who are successful in human rights claims has seen significant recent change. We explain the changes, together with the present decision-making process, below. At ▶862–5, there are tables setting out which applicants obtain humanitarian protection (HP) and which applicants are granted discretionary leave (DL). The tables also deal with who is 'excluded' from HP. At ▶866–75, we deal with various issues concerning those with HP and DP, including the length of leave granted, 'active review', rights to apply for settlement, leave granted to unaccompanied minors, upgrading, and events which can lead to loss of status. We also look at the transitional arrangements in place for those granted exceptional leave before 1 April 2003. The policy on reviewing and extending leave and status in the HP, DL and ELR categories is also covered together with policy on refugee leave in the table at ▶721–7. For a general understanding of all forms of leave given outside the rules, ▶see 147–9

Before 2 October 2000

For a long time before the rights under the ECHR were incorporated into UK law, on 2 October 2000, the Home Office had recognised that there were many people who, although they did not fit the definition of 'refugee', were in need of protection. The Home Office based its policies on determining whether such people should be granted protection under the UK's international obligations aside from the Refugee Convention: the ECHR, the UN Convention Against Torture and Other Cruel, Inhuman or Degrading Treatment or Punishment 1984 (UNCAT), and the International Covenant on Civil and Political Rights 1996 (ICCPR). As a result, the Home Office developed a practice of granting 'exceptional leave' to people who would benefit from the protection given by those Conventions, or where there otherwise appeared to be strong humanitarian reasons for treating them favourably.

Formally, in-country applicants were granted 'exceptional leave to remain' (ELR) and port applicants were granted 'exceptional leave to enter' (ELE – although this was usually also referred to as 'ELR', and we will refer to them both as 'ELR'). Wherever an application was refused, the Home Office would automatically consider whether to grant exceptional leave. Those granted ELR following a failed asylum application were normally granted leave for a period of four years that was not subject to working or public funds conditions. After four years, they were eligible to apply for settlement.

2 October 2000 – 1 April 2003

After the rights under the ECHR became a part of UK law following the HRA, most of those who were previously granted ELR as a matter of discretion had a *right* under UK law to be permitted to remain, because to require them to leave would be in breach of their human rights. However, the Home Office continued to treat them in the same way as it had always treated those falling into the ELR category. It continued to grant them four years' ELR, after which they were eligible to apply to settle (see para. 4.90, *Secure Borders, Safe Haven*, 2002 White Paper; and the previous API Ch5, s4, para. 4.3).

1 April 2003 onwards

It was odd that, even after 2 October 2000, the leave given to people, most of whose rights to be in the UK were underpinned by the ECHR, was still described as being 'exceptional', and has not specifically been provided for in the immigration rules. On 1 April 2003, the government made changes applying to all cases decided on or after that date. For the transitional arrangements for those granted exceptional leave before this date, ▶see 873–5. It stopped calling the leave granted to these classes of people 'exceptional leave'. The minister stated:

'We will be introducing a further robust measure with the ending of ELR. I believe that our use of ELR has encouraged abuse and acted as a pull factor, encouraging economic migrants to apply for asylum in the UK in the belief that they will be given ELR when their asylum claim is rejected.' (Beverley Hughes MP, Home Office press release, 29 November 2002)

The Home Office divided what had previously been described as ELR into two categories, which it called 'humanitarian protection' (HP) and 'discretionary leave' (DL). At the same time, it resolved to end the system of 'country policies', whereby nationals of a particular country would routinely be granted exceptional leave. HP and DL were only to be granted on an individual basis, and only to those who 'really need it'. Therefore, when the Secretary of State refuses an asylum claim, consideration will be given to whether the applicant qualifies for HP. If they do not qualify for HP, consideration will be given to whether they qualify for DL instead. Provided they satisfy the relevant criteria, HP and DL may also be granted where people make a free-standing human rights claim (i.e. without a claim under the 1951 Convention), or where they make a claim together with another non-asylum application.

The Home Office went further. The 'exceptional' leave often granted after the refusal of an asylum claim provides only one sense in which that term is used. Read literally, 'exceptional' leave is that which is granted to anyone who is treated more favourably than the rules expressly permit. Therefore, when anyone is granted leave on the basis of a policy outside the rules, or by waiver of aspects of the rules, they can be described as having been granted leave 'exceptionally'. However, the Home Office also announced that it would no longer call even those grants of leave – i.e. those made outside the context of asylum – 'exceptional leave'. The new name for leave granted in these circumstances was to be 'Leave Outside the Rules' (LOTR). However, the Home Office indicated that this change would take time to implement, as it amended its various instructions. Until this change becomes properly established, it will remain common for people to talk about 'exceptional' leave as being any form of leave granted outside of the rules. For general details about all forms of leave granted outside the rules ▶see 147–9.

Both HP and DL are distinct from 'temporary protection', which is a separate category added to the immigration rules from 1 January 2005. Temporary protection relates to situations where there is a mass influx of displaced persons who require assistance and protection for the time being (HC 164; for further details, ▶see 633–5).

From 30 August 2005

From 30 August 2005, the Home Office has operated a revised policy on HP and DL. Where leave was granted before that date, the arrangements for review (see below) will stay as they were. For those granted leave on or after that date, a different regime applies insofar as the periods of leave granted and the way in which the status is reviewed.

The unsatisfactory nature of the present system

These changes to the system and to the labels it uses continue to cause unnecessary confusion to applicants. In particular:

- The Asylum Policy Unit (APU) Notice issued on 1 April 2003 stated that HP would be added to the immigration rules, but not DL. Over two and a half years on, HP has still not been brought within the rules. The only substantial provision in the rules is a general one requiring the immigration authorities to carry out their duties 'in compliance with the Human Rights Act 1998' (para. 2, HC 395).

- Even after HP is incorporated into the rules, many applicants who are *entitled* to remain in the UK on the basis of their human rights will still be granted 'discretionary leave' (DL), although their rights do not depend upon the exercise of discretion.

- There is no logical reason for changing the label for all non-HP and non-DL 'exceptional' leave to 'leave outside the rules'. For as long as grants of HP and DL also remain outside the rules, the new label is confusing, since it obviously does not describe all those granted leave outside the rules.

Who is granted Humanitarian Protection and Discretionary Leave?

The circumstances in which HP and DL are granted are set out in the tables below. Unless stated otherwise, the information we provide in the tables and in the details about HP, DL and ELR that follow, is largely taken from APU Notice 01/2003, API *Humanitarian Protection* and API *Discretionary Leave*. The APIs on HP and DL were reissued with effect from 30 August 2005. Note that a few grants of DL will not be based on human rights under the ECHR, but upon general humanitarian considerations. For the *periods* of leave granted, and other relevant considerations relating to those with HP, DL or ELR, ▶see 866 onwards. For an overall summary of status and reviews relating to refugee status, HP and DL, ▶see 721–7.

If an applicant qualifies under more than one heading set out in the tables, then the Home Office will grant the most beneficial status. An example would be the case of an unaccompanied 17-year-old who is found to face a risk of torture for a non-1951 Convention reason, and for whom there are no adequate reception facilities in the country of return. Such an applicant should be granted HP for three years, rather than DL for the months up until their eighteenth birthday.

QUALIFYING FOR HUMANITARIAN PROTECTION

Those entitled to HP

HP is granted to those who face a serious risk to their life or person from any of the following *provided they are not excluded* (▶see below). The protection derives from Articles 2 and 3 of, and the thirteenth protocol to, the ECHR.

Death penalty

A person who faces a risk of the death penalty being imposed and carried out upon them will qualify. This category contemplates the death penalty being imposed by the judicial authorities of the country of return.

Unlawful killing

Those at risk of being killed unlawfully will include people at risk of extra-judicial killing by agents of the state, as well as people who are at risk from non-state agents. It includes people who face a risk of death if returned to a war/conflict situation. However, those whose lives are threatened by the use of force that is *absolutely necessary* in any of the following situations, will not qualify. This is force used:

- in defence of any person from unlawful violence;
- in order to make a lawful arrest or prevent the escape of someone who is lawfully detained;
- in order to deal lawfully with a 'riot' or 'insurrection'.

The exceptions referred to are taken from Article 2(2) ECHR (for death penalty/unlawful killing cases, ►see 792–4).

Torture, or inhuman or degrading treatment

Generally, those at risk of torture, or inhuman or degrading treatment or punishment within the meaning of Article 3 ECHR, will qualify for HP (►see 794–800). However, those who face Article 3 risks as a result of their medical condition (►see 809–20), or as a result of general conditions in their country of origin – such as a complete lack of water, food, or basic shelter – will qualify not for HP, but for DL (►see below).

Exclusions from Humanitarian Protection

If a person qualifies for HP under the above criteria, they will still not be granted HP if any of the following five conditions apply to them – although those excluded from HP here may qualify for DL instead.

1) They fall within the exclusion clauses of the Refugee Convention. This will apply if there are 'serious reasons for considering' that they have committed any of the following (Article 1F Refugee Convention):

- a crime against peace, a war crime, a crime against humanity;
- a serious non-political crime outside the UK before their admission to the UK (but see (3), below, for the alternative exclusion in HP cases only);
- acts contrary to the purposes and principles of the UN.

It will also apply if (see Article 33(2) Refugee Convention):

- there are 'reasonable grounds' for considering the applicant to be a danger to the security of the UK; or
- the applicant has been convicted of a 'particularly serious crime' and 'constitutes a danger' to the community in the UK.

Note: the above exclusions apply both to those who would otherwise qualify for refugee status *and* to those who would otherwise qualify only for HP. Neither will qualify for HP (for further details about the Refugee Convention exclusion clauses, ►see 624–6, 1080–1).

2) They are persons whose character, conduct or associations mean that it is appropriate to exclude them from HP. This may be the case where deportation action on 'non-conducive' grounds, or following the recommendation of a court, was considered but could not be followed through as a result of the

human rights claim. This exclusion may deny HP to some people who cannot be excluded by (1) above.

3) They are people who have engaged in 'unacceptable behaviours' (whether in the UK or abroad i.e. people who glorify or foment terrorist violence). This category is really a sub-category of (2) above (▶1019–20).

4) They have committed a 'serious crime' either in the UK or overseas. Again, this exclusion may deny HP to those not already excluded by (1) above. This is because, for these purposes, 'serious' is defined as a crime for which a custodial sentence of at least 12 months has been given, even if it is not serious enough for the purposes of Articles 1F or 33(2) of the Refugee Convention. Also, in contrast to the Refugee Convention exclusions, applicants may apparently be excluded even if the crime is a 'political' one (for the meaning of 'political/non-political', ▶see 625).

5) They are included on the sex offenders register.

Note: the text of the API merges the exclusions which the policy has taken directly from the Refugee Convention with the additional exclusions which the Home Office has added to the policy. For clarity, in the above, we have separated them out: (1) contains the exclusions taken from the Convention; (2)–(5) contain cases which might not be excluded under the Refugee Convention.

QUALIFYING FOR DISCRETIONARY LEAVE

DL may only be granted to those who do not qualify for refugee status or HP. It will be granted in the following circumstances.

Family or other connections with the UK

Where a person establishes a right to be in the UK under Article 8 ECHR as a result of their private or family life connections *in* the UK (▶see 820–50), DL will be granted.

Article 3 ECHR cases that do not qualify for HP

Persons whose return would subject them to inhuman or degrading treatment as a result of their medical condition (▶see 809 onwards), or for other severe humanitarian reasons (complete lack of essentials and shelter) (▶819–20) will be granted not HP, but rather DL.

'Flagrant' breaches of other ECHR rights

Following the decision of the House of Lords in *Ullah*, those who may face a 'flagrant' breach of their human rights by ill-treatment *in* the country of return (for example, under Articles 5, 6, 8, 9 ECHR) are entitled to protection even if their circumstances do not meet the Article 3 threshold (▶see 787–92, 800–9). The APIs indicate that they should be given DL.

Article 8 ECHR cases involving detrimental effect overseas

The API do not directly address cases where there is a claim that the conditions in the country of return mean that refusing a claim will lead to a breach of a person's private life (physical and moral integrity), for example for medical reasons (▶*Bensaid* at 816–9). Logically, a successful claim should qualify a person for DL, as with Article 3 medical cases (above).

Applicants *excluded* from HP

Those who have established that to return them would contravene their human rights, but who are excluded from HP for the reasons given above (▶863–4), should normally be granted DL unless Ministers decide that it is inappropriate to grant it. In such cases, applicants will simply be kept on temporary admission. It is possible that this is not lawful. Exclusion will affect the *period* of DL granted. In cases of persons who would, in any event, only qualify for DL and not HP, the same exclusions will be considered because, again, the *period* of DL granted will be affected (▶see 869).

Unaccompanied asylum-seeking children (UASCs)

UASCs who do not qualify for refugee status or HP, but for whom there are no adequate reception arrangements available in the country of return, will qualify for DL (▶see 870–1 below).

Other cases

The above are the main categories of DL. However, the API state:

'There are likely to be very few other cases in which it would be appropriate to grant [DL] to an unsuccessful asylum seeker. However, it is not possible to anticipate every eventuality that may arise, so there remains scope to grant [DL] where individual circumstances, although not meeting the criteria of any of the other categories listed above, are so compelling that it is considered appropriate to grant some form of leave.' (API *Discretionary Leave*, para. 2.5)

This suggests that there may be certain cases where a breach of human rights cannot be made out, but where it is still appropriate to grant DL (this suggestion is supported by decisions of the courts, ▶see 851–2).

Deferred removal cases

Where the circumstances that qualify a person for DL are expected to be short-lived, so that removal will be possible within six months of the date of the decision, the Home Office may decide to refuse DL but to defer removal (API *Discretionary Leave*, para. 5.3). The API also state that DL will not be granted on the basis that there is, for the time being, no practical way of removing a person – for example, the absence of a route or travel document.

HP and DL: periods of leave granted and settlement

Where asylum, HP and DL are all refused, the reasons for refusal letter will state this, and give reasons. When, after an asylum claim, HP or DL are granted, the decision letter will normally state why the applicant did not qualify for refugee status and (if DL is being granted) why they did not qualify for HP. The letter should also state the basis on which HP or DL is being granted. Both HP and DL are granted without conditions about access to public funds and without any restrictions on work. Additional details about review of status are given at ▶721–7.

Applications for HP granted on or after 30 August 2005

Where HP is granted after 30 August 2005, it will normally be given for a period of five years. It will only be reviewed during that period if certain 'trigger' events take place during that period to cause a review. They are the same trigger events which cause a review of refugee leave and are therefore set out at ▶721–3, 724. After five years with HP granted after 30 August 2005 an applicant is eligible for indefinite leave. In depth reviews will not normally be carried out at that stage.

Applications and 'active review': the system till 30 August 2005 (for HP) and the system for DL

Until 30 August 2005, the system for making further applications for HP or DL was as follows below. Where HP was granted before 30 August 2005, the arrangements remain as they were before that date (para. 1, API, *Humanitarian Protection*). The new system for HP is dealt with immediately above. The system described below remains in place for DL even where the first grant of leave is after 30 August 2005.

Applications for extensions of HP or DL *and* applications for settlement after the different qualifying periods (▶see below) have been spent were all subject to a process the Home Office calls 'active review'. This means that the application is examined in the light of the present circumstances, to see whether or not the applicant *still* qualifies for HP or DL. If they do not, the application will be refused (▶see 725–6 and below at 872–3). Applications to extend HP or DL, or to apply for settlement when the appropriate qualifying time has been reached, should be made on Form HPDL, to which dependants can be added. It should be addressed to the 'Active Review Team' at the Home Office. There is no charge for such applications. It is not necessary to repeat information the Home Office already has. The Home Office will review the original material, together with information provided with Form HPDL and its own up-to-date country information.

Applicants need to be sure that their application demonstrates that they still qualify. Therefore, if there have been significant changes of circumstance – for example, relevant changes in their country of origin that affect the basis upon which the earlier decision was made – applicants may need to spell out why they still qualify. If there are new reasons why HP or DL should be granted, these should be given, and there is a specific space on the form to do so. It may be that the application needs to be accompanied by detailed covering representations and/or further documentary evidence and information.

Form HPDL also asks for details about whether a person has travelled back to the country from which they asked for protection, and about absences from the UK. The answers to these questions may also be relevant to whether the applicant still qualifies for HP or DL. For example, they may indicate that the applicant is no longer at risk in their country of origin. These are considerations which may affect not only the decision on active review, but might also prompt the Home Office to take action during the period of leave (▶see 'variation of HP or DL', at 872).

If an extension/settlement is likely to be problematic, consideration should be given to whether the applicant qualifies under any of the immigration rules. It may be the case that the applicant could qualify, for example, under one of the economic categories if it were not for the 'switching' requirements. In such a case, the applicant might consider making both a HP/DL application, and an application under one of the categories of the immigration rules. It is likely that the applicant would have to request a waiver of the no-switching requirement in the application which is under one of the categories of the rules (for full details about switching, ▶see Chapter 7 and for switching outside the rules ▶see 187–8).

If an extension/settlement application on the basis of HP or DL is refused and no further leave is granted, then there will be a right of appeal. However, if further leave is granted, although not of the type requested (for example, if a further period of limited DL is granted rather than settlement) then there will be no right of appeal, as no 'immigration decision' falling within s82(2)(d) or (e) will have been taken. Applicants seeking extensions will normally already have had an opportunity to appeal on refugee grounds (see s83 2002 Act, ▶1079).

Period of Humanitarian Protection granted before 30 August 2005

Until 30 August 2005, HP was normally granted for three years, following which the applicant will be able to apply for settlement. Active review would be carried out to ensure that the applicant still qualified under the criteria for HP before settlement would be given. Further, if at the time of the review the applicant would qualify for HP, but circumstances have since arisen to mean that they fall into the excluded category (▶see 863–4), indefinite leave and HP would be refused, but DL may be granted instead. These arrangements continue for those granted HP before 30 August 2005.

If for any reason less than three years was initially granted – for example, because conditions in the country in question are subject to rapid change, meaning that an earlier active review is justified – further HP may be given to bring the period up to three years. Time spent on DL, or with leave in other categories, will not count towards the three-year qualifying period.

Period of Discretionary Leave

The periods of DL generally granted are as follows.

- Article 8 cases will result in a grant of leave for three years (▶see further 869–70 for a note on marriage cases).

- Article 3 cases based on medical state or poor humanitarian conditions in the country of return will also result in a grant of leave for three years.

- Other successful applications under the ECHR will result in leave being granted for three years.

- Those who fall into the exclusions set out above at ▶863–4, and who have therefore been excluded from refugee status and/or HP, and those who would only qualify for DL in any event, will only be granted DL for six months unless ministers decide that the applicant should be kept on temporary admission (▶see below).

- UASCs for whom there are no adequate reception facilities available will normally be granted leave for three years *or* until their eighteenth birthday (whichever is shorter). For further details, including the application of this policy to children from certain 'non-suspensive' appeal countries, ▶see 870–1.

- Other applicants granted DL because their individual circumstances are particularly compelling will also be granted leave for three years.

Non-standard grants of DL *However,* if the circumstances of the case 'clearly point' to a shorter period of DL being appropriate, then DL may be granted for less than the standard periods set out above. An example given in the API is where a person is granted leave on the basis of their family life with a person in the UK, but where it is known that the family member will be leaving within, say, 12 months. Similarly, applicants who are successful on health grounds relating to a finite course of treatment, or who are waiting for surgery, may also be granted a shorter period (APU Notice 3/2003). Those falling into the 'other' category are particularly likely to be given less than the standard period. For example, a person granted leave in order to participate in a court case (see *Quaquah*, HC) might be granted leave up to the date when the proceedings are expected to end. If a non-standard period is granted, reasons should be given.

DL, settlement, active review Applications for extensions can be made until applicants have spent six years on DL, at which point they are eligible for settlement. The Home Office will carry out an 'active review' for both extension and settlement applications (▶see above 866, 725–6). So, for example, if the family life upon which an Article 8 claim was based is no longer subsisting – or possibly even if the 'obstacles' which prevented the establishment of family life elsewhere have been removed – an extension may be refused. If the application is granted, leave will be extended for the same period of time as indicated for the first grant of DL (▶see above). Therefore an applicant initially granted three years is likely to be granted a second period of three years, after which they can apply for settlement.

'Excluded' categories given DL However, those in the 'excluded' category (▶see 863–4, 865) are only able to obtain extensions of six months at a time. Such applicants should expect the active review of their cases to be particularly probing, as they are persons who the Home Office would very much like to remove from the UK if their human rights permitted it. Such applicants are not eligible for settlement until they have spent ten continuous years on DL. Even after ten years, they may be denied settlement on the basis of a personal decision by the Minister that allowing them to settle would not be conducive to the public good. In such cases, further DL will be given. For as long as such an applicant remains in the UK, the question of whether denial of settlement should be maintained must be reviewed at least every three years. It is possible that no leave at all will be granted in an 'exclusion' case.

Prison cases and cases where DL eligibility likely to end Any time spent in prison will not count for the purposes of either the six- or ten-year qualifying period for settlement. If the active review at the point of settlement reveals that there is a 'clear basis' for considering that, within 12 months, the applicant will no longer qualify for DL, settlement will not be granted. Instead a further short period of DL will be given. However, applicants can only be denied settlement on this basis for a maximum of 12 months.

DL in Article 8 cases based on marriage or partnership

There has been confusion about the leave granted to those who succeed in Article 8 applications based on marriage or long-term partnerships. Before 11 April 2005, the policy was to grant leave for a period of two years in these cases. It appeared to advisors that this was because such cases were being treated on a similar basis to marriage/partnership applications under the rules. It was also believed that such applicants would therefore be able to settle after two years, as with the probationary period under the rules. This was then confirmed by a letter from the Home Office to South Manchester Law Centre (2 September 2003).

However, in subsequent correspondence the Home Office said that this was not in fact the position, and that the September 2003 letter was a mistake (Home Office letters to Wilson & Co, dated 16 March 2004, and to ILPA, dated 24 August 2004). This correspondence stated that the two years' DL granted in these cases was *not* equivalent to probationary leave, and would not enable settlement after two years. It was stated that, as with other DL cases, these applicants would only be eligible for settlement after six years' DL. Nevertheless, the Home Office indicated that it was open to applicants in this position to leave the UK at any point during the six years and to apply for entry clearance from abroad which, if successful, would result in a grant of the two-year probationary period, after which they would be eligible to settle.

On 11 April 2005, the Home Office modified the policy (see Asylum Policy Unit Notice 3/2005). From that date, those who succeed in an Article 8 claim based on marriage will be granted leave for *three* years, as in other Article 8 cases. A second three years will be granted if the person continues to qualify for DL. After six years, applicants will be eligible for settlement. Applicants who were granted two years' leave prior to 11 April 2005 will continue to be treated as previously – i.e., provided they qualify, they will continue to be granted leave in steps of two years, until they are eligible for settlement after six years (APU Notice 3/2005, para. 8).

UASCs for whom there are no adequate reception facilities

As indicated above, unaccompanied asylum-seeking children (UASCs) who do not otherwise qualify for asylum, HP or DL, and for whom there are no adequate reception and accommodation facilities available in their country of return, will be granted leave for three years *or* until their eighteenth birthday (whichever is the shorter). For UASCs and the asylum process generally, ▶see the section on asylum at 686–91.

The policy is elaborated on in the document 'Immigration Rules and Compassionate Circumstances', instructions to officers, 25 April 2004 (circulated by ILPA in August 2005):

'8.3 Unaccompanied Children

Enforcement action against children under the age of 16 who are on their own in the United Kingdom must not be contemplated unless we are satisfied that the child will be met on arrival in his/her home country and that suitable care arrangements are in place thereafter. Where this has been established there is no bar to taking removal action. Where it is not clear that these requirements are satisfied case workers should contact the welfare section of the appropriate Embassy or High Commission as well as the local Social Services Department.

In asylum cases where the applicant is an unaccompanied minor (under age 18) where adequate reception cannot be established, removal should not be attempted. Asylum claimants who are being treated as unaccompanied minors should fall within the responsibility of the asylum directorate for consideration at all stages.

If there is any evidence that the care arrangements are seriously below the standard normally provided in the country concerned or that they are so inadequate that the child would face a serious risk of harm if returned, consideration should be given to abandoning enforcement action. Where deportation or removal remains the right course, consideration will need to be given to whether an escort is necessary on the journey.'

However, there is an exception that modifies the policy. Where the UASC policy applies, and the applicant is from one of the following countries – all of which are listed in section 94(4) 2002 Act as 'non-suspensive' appeal countries – then the applicant will only be granted DL for a period of *twelve* months, or up to their eighteenth birthday (whichever is shorter): Albania, Bangladesh, Bulgaria, Jamaica, Macedonia, Moldova, Romania, Serbia and Montenegro, and Sri Lanka (see APU Notice, *Application of Non-Suspensive Appeal (NSA) Process to Asylum Seeking Children*, 5/ 2004, 1 October 2004). The 'three-year' policy (▶see above) continues to apply to applicants from the remaining countries listed in section 94(4) (Brazil, Bolivia, Ecuador, South Africa, Ukraine), as well as to applicants from all other countries. Note that Bangladesh has been removed from 'NSA' list following a court challenge.

Rights of appeal Where an applicant is only granted 12 months' (or less) leave, they have no right of appeal because:

- no 'immigration decision' has been made within the definition in s82(2) of the 2002 Act – i.e. because the applicant has been granted leave; and
- there is no 'refugee status' appeal under section 83 of the 2002 Act, because only applicants granted more than 12 months' leave can appeal under section 83.

When the applicant is no longer a minor, a further application can be considered under the ordinary rules, including asylum or human rights grounds. If it is refused, there will, unless it is certified as 'clearly unfounded', be an in-country right of appeal.

Also, if an applicant is originally denied a refugee status appeal because they are granted leave for 12 months or less (because they are from a country to which the 'modified' policy above applies), and they are then granted a *further* period of 12 months or less, then they will have a refugee status appeal at that point. This is the case provided that, adding together the periods of leave they have been granted, they have been granted leave for more than 12 months altogether. This follows from the fact that the right of appeal under s83 is only excluded if an applicant has been granted less than 12 months' leave *in aggregate* (see s83(1)(b) 2002 Act and APU Notice 5/2004 above, para. 15).

Further UASC developments There are likely to be further developments in this area. The government's 'five-year strategy' proposes to find new ways of returning UASCs whose claims have failed, without having to wait until they are 18 (Section 5, para. 76). Even if it is not possible to remove such children to parents or close relatives, the Home Office hopes to be able to 'create other acceptable reception arrangements'. The Home Office hopes to ask social services departments to undertake assessments as to children's needs, and then to match those with whatever care arrangements can be put in place in the country of return. An initial pilot project is proposed for 16 to 18-year-old Albanian boys. One frequent problem recently has been that the Home Office has disputed the age of applicants. If the Home Office presses ahead with its new plans to seek new arrangements for removing children, age disputes are likely to become even more intense (for details about dealing with age dispute cases, ▶see 688–91).

Upgrading

It is of course possible to apply to 'upgrade' from DL to HP (see API 'Humanitarian Protection', para. 5.2). Any new evidence or information indicating that the applicant should be upgraded should be included with Form HPDL. If the upgrading is refused but further DL is granted, then there will be no right of appeal, as no 'immigration decision' within the meaning of s82 of the 2002 Act will have been made. Obviously, if no further leave is granted, there is a right of appeal. Note that in some cases upgrading to HP may not be of particular benefit – for example, where the applicant is about to qualify for settlement on the basis of DL.

If an applicant asserts a claim for refugee status at a time when they have existing HP or DL and this is refused, then even if further leave is granted there will be a 'refugee status' appeal under s83 of the 2002 Act. This is the case provided that the applicant has been granted leave for more than 12 months altogether (i.e. adding together the periods of leave they have been given) (▶see 1079).

Variation of HP or DL

Grants of HP or DL will normally only be actively reviewed when a further application is considered (see above). However, it is possible for the circumstances to be reviewed during the period of leave that has been granted. Under the system in place for HP which was granted on or after 30 August 2005, the procedure for 'variation' is the same as for refugee leave (▶see 721–3). For HP granted before that date and for DL, the procedures are as follows (▶see below 872–3 and ▶see 725–6). Leave may be varied so that there is no leave remaining (the Home Office calls this 'revocation', although it may also be called 'curtailment'). Such variations leave the applicant open to removal, and constitute an 'immigration decision' under s82(2)(e) of the 2002 Act, and so there is a right of appeal against them. Leave may also be varied to grant a lesser period of leave (i.e. a period of DL rather than HP), against which there is generally no right of appeal.

Voluntary actions The same voluntary actions that can result in the revocation of indefinite leave granted to a refugee *might* also result in a revocation of HP: voluntary re-availment of protection of country of nationality, reacquisition of a lost nationality, acquisition of a new nationality, voluntary re-establishment in country of origin (see s76 of the 2002 Act, and ▶see 627–30 for a description). Whether revocation of HL is in fact justified by these voluntary actions will depend on the circumstances. For example, the Home Office may treat return to the country of origin as grounds for revocation where the HP claim was based on fear of ill-treatment in that country. However, the reacquisition of a nationality will not necessarily exclude a person who claimed fear of ill-treatment from non-state actors.

Having regard to the reasons why DL is granted, these types of voluntary action are less likely to lead to a person no longer qualifying for DL. The APIs indicate that people on DL will normally be expected to keep their own national passport valid. Revocation may be appropriate for other reasons, however – for example, if a marriage upon which an Article 8 claim was successful breaks down, or if a UASC granted leave on the basis of lack of reception conditions is contacted by an adult who is in a position to care for them.

For policy concerning returns to areas affected by the South-East Asian Tsunami in December 2004, ▶see the section on asylum at 632–3.

Change in country conditions The APIs state that revocation of HP or DL on the basis of a change in country conditions will not be appropriate unless the Home Office issues general instructions about the particular country or category of case in question. Consideration would still need to be given to how the change in conditions affected the particular applicant.

Exclusion category applies If, after the grant of HP or DL, it becomes clear that the applicant is within the excluded category (for which ▶see 863–4) either because of circumstances unknown at the time of the original decision, or as a result of the applicant's conduct after the decision, action may be taken. In the case of an applicant with HP, provided that the Article 2 or 3 reasons why they cannot return to their country of origin still pertain, their leave is likely to be varied to six months' DL (if they have more than six months leave remaining). DL applicants granted leave on the basis of Article 8 are likely to be the most seriously affected by a subsequent finding of exclusion. This is because the 'exclusion' grounds could be used to determine that the interference in their rights is proportionate under Article 8(2). So such a review could change the determination of whether there will be a breach of Article 8 at all if they were required to leave. If there is no breach, then the Home Office may revoke their leave. Alternatively deportation action could be taken, either on 'non-conducive' grounds or following a court recommendation. A deportation order has the effect of cancelling existing leave.

Deception cases If it is discovered that HP or DL have been granted on the basis of deception, and removal will not in fact be in breach of the applicant's human rights, revocation could again follow. In such cases, the Home Office might alternatively treat people as illegal entrants (if they obtained leave to enter), or set directions for removal on the grounds that leave to remain was obtained by deception (s10 1999 Act).

Transitional arrangements for those granted exceptional leave

Until 2007 there will still be people who have been granted exceptional leave under the arrangements in force until 31 March 2003. Those applicants will normally have been granted four years' ELR in one block, and when that period of time is complete they are eligible to apply for settlement. Provided these applicants still have a continuing fear of returning, they should apply for settlement using Form ELR, for which there is no charge. If there is no continued fear, applicants for settlement should use Form SET(O), for which there is a charge (Home Office letter to Kingsley Napley, 30 October 2003; see also section 3.5 of prescribed Form ELR, version 04/2005). In confirming this approach, the minister stated:

'However, I do accept that a four year grant of exceptional leave would usually have led to a grant of settlement and we will continue to honour this, although there can be no question of granting settlement to those who would not have qualified under the exceptional leave rules. We will continue to refuse settlement where there are strong reasons to do so, for example, where a person's presence in the United Kingdom is undesirable for reasons of character, conduct or associations, or where they represent a threat to national security, or it is clear that a person has made false representations.' (Letter of Beverley Hughes MP, Home Office minister, to Fiona Mactaggart MP, 27 February 2003. See also, to similar effect, the Home Office letter to Hackney Community Law Centre dated 24 January 2005)

So, unless the circumstances set out in the above passage apply, applicants will be granted settlement at the end of four years' ELR. Paragraph 11 of API, *Discretionary leave*, confirms that such applicants should be granted indefinite leave 'without a full active review'.

Where less than four years' ELR was granted

In cases where a person has been granted *less* than four years' ELR, and in cases where applicants apply for further leave when they have spent less than four years on ELR, their cases will be reviewed to see whether they qualify for HP or DL. They will then be treated as follows.

- If they do not qualify for HP or DL (or for leave on any other basis) as set out in the table above (or under any of the requirements of the rules), they will be refused further leave.
- If they have spent more than 12 months on ELR and they qualify for HP, they should be granted leave to bring their total period on ELR plus HP up to four years. After this period of four years, they will be entitled to apply for settlement although, the settlement application will be subject to 'active review' (▶see above at 725–6, 872–3).
- If they have spent less than 12 months on ELR and they qualify for HP, they should be granted three years' HP. The Home Office instructions are not clear, but it is assumed that these applicants will also be entitled to apply for settlement after their three years on HP.
- If they qualify for DL (but not HP), then they should be granted DL in accordance with the ordinary periods of DL set out above. Periods spent

on exceptional leave will not count towards the qualifying period for settlement that applies to those with DL.

The government's stated logic for this approach is that if a person was granted less than four years' ELR, this will have been because there was an expectation that such cases would be reviewed (see letter of 27 February 2003 above). Applications for extensions of exceptional leave where less than four years were granted should be made on Form HPDL, and incur no charge.

FAMILY MEMBERS

Family members of those with HP and DL are treated as follows. In all cases, even if the criteria below are not satisfied, applicants and advisers should consider making an application under Article 8 ECHR (▶see 820–50). Family reunion for refugees is covered in Chapter 25.

Dependants

The dependants of principle applicants who are applying for asylum and who, as an alternative to refugee status, may therefore be granted HP or DL, are dealt with in the API under 'Dependants'. Dependants who are not seeking asylum in their own right may be included in the asylum application. If the main applicant is not granted asylum, but is granted HP or DL, the dependants will normally be granted leave in line with them (para. 1). Spouses and minor dependants may be treated as dependants of the main applicant (para. 2). Non-British citizen children born to applicants in the UK may also be added to a claim as dependants (para. 8.3). A dependant child who is under 18 years at the date of the application, but who turns 18 before the decision, will continue to be treated as a dependant for the purposes of the application (para. 3).

The API further states that other relatives – for example aged parents – may be considered dependants if there are 'exceptional compassionate circumstances' (para. 3). The API further indicates that, when considering applications to be considered as a dependant, case-workers should have regard to the right to respect for private and family life under Article 8 ECHR (para. 1). This suggests that, depending on the circumstances, it *may* be that officers will be prepared to accept as dependants others who are dependant on the main applicant, and with whom the main applicant has a relationship that amounts to 'family life' (▶see 823–6 for the relationships which may amount to family life) or 'private life' (▶see 827).

In all cases, in assessing a claim to be a dependant, officers need to be satisfied that the person claiming to be a dependant meets all of the following conditions (para 3.1):

- they are related as claimed to the main applicant;

- they were wholly dependent on the main applicant 'immediately prior to arrival in the UK';
- they had formed part of the pre-existing family abroad.

For further details about dependants, ▶see the asylum section at 691–4.

Timing of application as dependant

Family members cannot apply to be recognised as dependants after the decision on the applicant's claim. If the applicant has already been granted HP or DL, then an application of the family member will be treated as an application for family reunion (▶see below). If the application of the main applicant is refused, then removal of the 'would-be' dependants will generally be deferred pending the main applicant's appeal (para. 2). Those who might qualify as dependants, or for family reunion, may also of course make an asylum and/or human rights claim in their own right, if they have grounds to do so.

Family reunion for those with HP or DL

Where the sponsor has been granted HP or DL in the UK, the admission of family members is mainly covered by the API under 'Family Reunion'. Under that policy the following family members may be admitted (para. 2):

- spouse and minor children who formed part of the family unit before the sponsor came to the UK (▶see further 760–1 for this concept of 'pre-existing' families); and
- exceptionally, other members of the family (e.g. elderly parents), provided there are 'compelling compassionate circumstances'.

Applicants must apply for entry clearance in order to join their sponsor in the UK (para. 4). Entry clearance will not be granted until the sponsor has been granted indefinite leave in the UK. In line with the policies set out above, this means that sponsors with HP will not be able to bring their family members from abroad to join them in the UK until they have had leave for three years. Sponsors with DL will normally have to wait for six years. Applications may be considered before the sponsor has been granted indefinite leave, but only if there are 'compelling compassionate circumstances'. However, the Home Office appears to indicate that where the family members are already in the UK, they will normally be granted leave in line with the sponsor – i.e. even if the sponsor has not completed the relevant period of time. This appears to apply whether a family member is an 'in-country' or a 'port' case. In all cases, applicants are expected to satisfy the maintenance and accommodation requirements of the immigration rules (see paras 3.3–3.4).

Note that the Diplomatic Service Procedures (DSP) state that spouses who are granted entry clearance to join a sponsor who has ELR for family reunion (for which see further below) should have a condition of 'no recourse to public funds' endorsed. They also state that HP and DL family reunion applications are dealt with in the same way (DSP, Ch 16, para. 16.3 (iii)(iv)).

Spouse applications – intention to live together permanently

Note that, although applications by spouses will be refused if the spouse does not intend to live together permanently with the sponsor, it has been recognised that care should be taken to allow for the fact that the applicant and sponsor may have been separated for a long time. In particular, they will usually have had to wait for a long period before being able to make the family reunion application. Refusal should therefore only be considered on these grounds if there is 'strong evidence' to suggest that the intention to live together requirement may be in doubt (e.g. the known existence of another long-term partner of the sponsor) (see DSP, Ch 16, para 16.3 (ii), (iii), (iv)).

Non-'pre-existing' spouses

Some discretion may also be exercised for spouses of those with HP or DL who do not fall within the 'family reunion' policy above because they were not the 'pre-existing' spouse before the sponsor came to the UK. Under the immigration rules, such applicants would have to wait until their sponsor had obtained indefinite leave. However, as with the above policy, the separate API relating to 'marriage applications' indicates that discretion may be exercised favourably to grant entry clearance earlier if there are 'truly compelling compassionate circumstances'. The same API further states that, where such applicants are already in the UK, leave may be granted on a 'discretionary basis'. The Home Office will expect the maintenance and accommodation requirements to be satisfied (para. 3).

Successful applicants will be granted probationary leave in line with the ordinary marriage rules, and applicants will be eligible for extensions of leave and indefinite leave in line with their sponsor (para. 4).

Applying under the rules

It should be remembered that, once the sponsor has been granted indefinite leave, their family members are also entitled to apply under any of the immigration rules relating to family members of persons present and settled in the UK (▶see Section 4, and in particular Chapter 13, dealing with dependant relatives other than spouse/minor child). However, where applications are made under the rules, it will be necessary to satisfy all the relevant requirements, which are more stringent than just showing that the maintenance and accommodation requirements are met.

Family reunion for those with ELR granted before 1 April 2003

From 1 April 2003, the system of granting 'exceptional leave' on humanitarian grounds to certain applicants whose asylum applications have been refused was ended (▶see 860 onwards for full details). However, there are transitional arrangements for those who were granted exceptional leave before 1 April 2003, which still enable them to obtain settlement after four years without their cases undergoing 'active review' (for the transitional provisions, ▶see 873–5).

As their status letter informs them, those with exceptional leave granted following a refusal of asylum have no 'right' to be joined by any family members. There is nothing in the immigration rules about them, and they have to rely on Home Office policy. Under this policy, as with HP and DL family reunion, the 'pre-existing' spouse and minor children may be considered for admission. The Home Office may 'exceptionally' allow other members of the family (for example, elderly parents) to be admitted if there are 'compelling compassionate circumstances'. However, family reunion will not normally be considered until the sponsor with ELR has completed four years in this category, which is the point at which the sponsor is eligible for settlement. Applications may be considered before the four-year point, but only if there are 'compelling compassionate circumstances'. Applicants who are abroad must apply for entry clearance. However, the Home Office has stated that, where the family members are already in the UK, they will normally be granted leave in line with the sponsor, whether the family members are 'in-country' or 'port' cases. In all cases, applicants are expected to satisfy the maintenance and accommodation requirements of the immigration rules (API, *Family Reunion*, paras 1, 2, 3.2, 4).

Fees for entry clearance for family reunion

Although fees for dependants of refugees are generally waived (▶see 760), the ECO may charge the fee to dependants of those with HP, DL or ELR (see DSP Ch 16, para. 16.3(ii) under 'fees', and para. 16(iii)(iv), applying the same approach to HP/DL family reunion applications). However, the DSP also states that entry clearance fees will be waived in the case of 'destitute' persons, and that there is a discretion to waive the fee (DSP Ch 7, paras 7.4(e) and 7.5). Applicants considering asking the ECO to waive the fee on the basis of destitution must always bear in mind how this might affect their application for entry clearance generally. In most cases (see above) applicants will have been expected to satisfy the ECO that the applicants can be maintained and accommodated without recourse to public funds. In Article 8 cases, and other cases relying on discretion, applicants may also have produced evidence of funds being remitted to the family overseas in order to demonstrate dependency.

In the High Court case of *Jama*, a decision of the embassy in Addis Ababa to refuse to waive fees was challenged in circumstances where the sponsor had exceptional leave and was claiming income support. The applicants abroad were minors living in a refugee camp with no resources. Before the final hearing of the case, the embassy agreed to waive the fees. On 14 January 2002, the Joint Entry Clearance Unit (now 'UK Visas') issued guidance in draft to ECOs which stated as follows:

- Fees for entry clearances can be waived in the case of 'destitute persons'. This most commonly occurs in family reunion cases, and only rarely in other cases.

- The result in *Jama* does not 'bind future policy', but it indicates that a judge would find in favour of applicants in cases where the circumstances are similar.

- It is for the applicants to show that they are destitute.

- In deciding whether an applicant is destitute, the ECO is entitled to consider what support the applicant could reasonably expect to receive from the sponsor. The receipt of income support and other allowances by the sponsor is 'not conclusive proof of financial incapacity', although it 'may be taken as pointing to financial incapacity and should be given due weight'. ECOs should also seek details of the savings held by the sponsor; if the applicant's travel to the UK is being met by the sponsor, the ECO can assume that there is an ability to pay the entry clearance fee. If the cost is being met by a charity or non-governmental organisation, this strengthens the claim of destitution.

Where the family members do not possess travel documents

In some cases involving family members of those seeking protection in the UK, the applicant(s) may not have, and will be unable to obtain, travel documents from their national authorities enabling them to travel to the UK. If this is case, then the post is able to issue a 'Uniformed Format form', upon which the entry clearance can be endorsed. This is normally valid for one-way travel to the UK and used to be called a 'GV3' (see DSP, Ch 4, para. 4.16; for further details, ▶see 207).

Appeals

If an application for entry clearance for family reunion is refused, there is a right of appeal. If appellants can satisfy the immigration rules, then they can be relied on. If the decision is not in accordance with published policy as set out above, appeals may be allowed on the grounds that the decision is 'not in accordance with the law'. For further information about appealing in family reunion cases on this basis, ▶see 1124–6. Appellants are also likely to rely upon Article 8 ECHR.

TRAVEL DOCUMENTS

If a person is unable to get or use a passport from their own national authorities, they may, in some circumstances, be able to obtain a travel document from the Home Office. There are four different types of travel document as follows.

1) 1951 Refugee Convention Travel Documents (blue) (for details about these and refugee travel, ▶see 631–3, 627–30).

2) Certificate of Identity ('CID') (brown) (▶see below).

3) 1954 Stateless Persons Document (red). This is for those who are stateless under the 1954 Convention relating to stateless persons.

4) IS 137 (one-way document). This can be issued to any foreign national to allow one-way travel from the UK. The holder cannot use it to return.

For the fees which are charged for travel documents, ▶see 1509.

'Certificate of identity' travel documents

Policy on issuing certificates of identity (CIDs) changed on 30 August 2005 at the same time as the policy on leave for those with refugee status, HP and DL also changed (▶see 720–7 and 866 onwards). The main change is that applicants with limited leave do not have to show a 'need to travel'. The 'need to travel' test had been introduced in March 2003 and imposed a very stringent requirement that required applicants to demonstrate, for example, that they had to travel for essential business or employment related reasons, on compassionate grounds, for study or for religious reasons or other compelling reasons of conscience. The requirement of 'need to travel' did not apply to those with indefinite leave but the fact that it has now been dropped for other cases is a welcome development.

A further change from 30 August 2005 is in the length of the validity of the CID. Those with indefinite leave will normally be issued with documents valid for five years. Those with limited leave will now be issued with documents in line with their leave.

Finally, children must now apply for a separate document. Those aged 15 or under should apply for a child's travel document for which the fees are presently £115 for CIDs and £25 for all other documents. Applicants aged 16 or over must apply for an adult document.

Very unfortunately, even after the policy was changed, the travel document application form available on the Home Office website had not been amended (Form TD 112, Rev 11) to cater for all the changes in policy.

Who qualifies for a certificate of identity?

For applications submitted with a post mark on or after 30 August 2005, applicants will qualify for a CID if they meet all the following requirements.

- The applicant has indefinite leave (not as a refugee), humanitarian protection or either of the following forms of limited leave following the refusal of their asylum claim: discretionary leave, exceptional leave.
- The applicant has been formally and unreasonably refused a passport/ travel document by their own national authorities.
- The applicant has more than six months' outstanding leave to enter or remain.

Applicants are exempt from having to show the second requirement (formally and unreasonably refused a passport) if they have been granted humanitarian protection on the grounds of a fear from their national authorities. The letter granting HP should state whether this part of the claim was accepted or not. If it was, then this letter should be included with the travel document application. However, if the applicant has been allowed to stay in the UK for other reasons, then they will be expected to provide a letter from their national authorities showing that they have been refused a passport and explain why this refusal is unreasonable. It appears that the Home Office will consider any of the following as *not* unreasonable grounds for refusing to issue a passport:

- the applicant has not completed military service;
- the applicant did not provide evidence to confirm their identity;
- the applicant had a criminal record in their own country.

Those who are nationals of a country that does not have a post in the UK are also exempt from the requirement to show a formal and unreasonable refusal of a passport. However, if there is a post in a nearby European country, it is possible that the Home Office will offer to issue a travel document enabling the applicant to travel there to obtain a passport.

Countries that do not accept CIDs

Applicants should beware because some countries do not accept CIDs as valid travel documents. The following countries, which are parties to the 'Schengen' agreement, will not accept them: Austria, Belgium, Denmark, Finland, France, Germany, Greece, Iceland, Italy, Luxembourg, Netherlands, Norway, Portugal, Spain and Sweden. South Africa also does not accept these documents. Before applying, applicants are advised to check with the national authorities of the country they wish to visit that their travel document will be acceptable.

Countries for which the CID will be valid for travel

Unfortunately, it is not clear from the Home Office's revised statements of policy (above), whether policy about the countries for which the CID will be valid has also been changed. The pre-existing policy is as follows. CIDs issued to those with limited leave (whether HP, DL or ELR) will only be valid for the specific countries to which the applicant has stated that they wish to travel. Those issued to applicants with indefinite leave will be valid for travel to all countries except the country from which asylum was sought and (if different) the applicant's country of origin. The Home Office states that only in 'very exceptional circumstances' will a travel document be issued as valid for travel to an applicant's country of origin, or to the country from which they have sought asylum.

Applicants must obviously be very careful about travelling to their country of origin as it could lead to their status being reviewed on the basis of a change in circumstances. For present policy about reviewing humanitarian protection and discretionary leave (and refugee status), see 721–7. As is indicated in the table on those pages, the refugee concept of 're-availment' of the protection the applicant's national authorities, can equally apply to an applicant with HP (and ▶see also at 627–30, which sets out that the Home Office can be contacted in advance to see if it will agree to the applicant's plans to travel to their own country where there is a particularly compelling need to travel).

For the special arrangements concerning travel to areas affected by the South-East Asian Tsunami of December 2004, ▶see 632–3.

Procedures for applying for travel documents

Applications for all four of the travel documents (see above) must be submitted by post on Form TD 112 (which can be downloaded from the website) and the fee (see 1499) to:

Travel Documents Section
Immigration and Nationality Directorate
Home Office
Lunar House
40 Wellesley Road
Croydon
CR9 2BY

The form is accompanied by guidance notes as to what documents are required. Applicants who need to check on the progress of the application cannot do so by calling in person. Instead they should call the Immigration and Nationality Enquiry Bureau on (0870) 606 7766. That telephone number can also be used to ask for help in completing the form. Applications are dealt with in the order in which they are received and the Home Office states that it takes 5-8 weeks for it to deal with an application. The Home Office will consider giving priority to an application if there is a medical emergency or a family funeral. In this case, documentary evidence must be submitted (eg recent medical report) and can be sent by fax to (0208) 760 3385.

Applications to replace lost or stolen travel documents require a full police report.

Plainly, applicants should generally not attempt travel while waiting for an application or an appeal to be decided (▶see 119–21).

8

29   Discrimination

This chapter covers discrimination in immigration cases. We begin by looking at the impact of Article 14 ECHR, which prohibits discrimination in the enjoyment of rights under the ECHR (▶below). We then look at the question of race discrimination under the Race Relations Act 1976 as amended by the Race Relations (Amendment) Act 2000 (▶see 887–93).

For claims for compensation for discrimination ▶see 1187–90.

ARTICLE 14 ECHR

The prohibition on discrimination in the ECHR is contained in Article 14 which states:

'The enjoyment of the rights and freedoms set forth in this Convention shall be secured without discrimination on any ground such as sex, race, colour, language, religion, political or other opinion, national or social origin, association with a national minority, property, birth or other status.'

Because Article 14 provides a right not to be discriminated against in 'enjoying' other ECHR rights and freedoms, it cannot be used on its own. It can only be used together with those other rights. However, in order for there to be a breach of Article 14, there does not have to be an actual breach of the other right. In order to show a breach of Article 14, the applicant must demonstrate:

- that they have suffered less favourable treatment on one of the grounds specifically mentioned in Article 14 above or an equivalent ground; and
- that the unfavourable treatment *affects* their other rights under the ECHR.

There will be no breach of Article 14 if the state can show that there is a legitimate purpose for the discrimination, and that the detriment suffered by those discriminated against is outweighed by the interests of the community. In the many circumstances in which the immigration laws do discriminate against different groups, the government's response would be that the difference is justified in the interests of maintaining proper immigration control. Three examples of the use of Article 14 in immigra-tion cases are the following.

Arman Ali In this case, the High Court stated that if the maintenance and accommodation requirements in the immigration rules did not allow a couple to be supported by others (third party support), they would not be compatible with Article 14 taken with Article 8. This was because the rules would then discriminate against those less able to support themselves (such as the ill or the disabled) in the area of their right to enjoy family life with sponsors in the UK. There would be no real justification for the less favourable treatment because there would be no increased demand on public funds.

Abdulaziz In this case, the European Court found that there was a breach of Article 14 taken with Article 8 ECHR. It was held that the different ways in which the immigration rules then in force treated husbands and wives who wished to join their spouses in the UK were unjustifiably discriminatory. However, in the same case the Court accepted the government's justification for those immigration rules which excluded entry based on marriages entered into for immigration reasons. Even though this rule had a greater negative impact upon marriages between people from the Indian subcontinent, the rule was found to be justified, and the court rejected the claim based on race discrimination. The court also rejected the applicant's argument that there was a breach of Article 8 itself. This was because it took account of the fact that there were no 'obstacles' or 'special reasons' that prevented the couples from establishing family life elsewhere, and also the fact that the marriages had been entered into when both parties knew that the non-settled spouse would not necessarily be admitted to the UK. The Court therefore decided that refusing entry did not show an interference with the right to respect for family life (for further details about the Article 8 aspects of ***Abdulaziz***, see ▶823, 828).

Saadi v UK In this case, the applicant is partly arguing that he was selected for detention at Oakington Reception Centre because he was an Iraqi Kurd and therefore a member of a group which could be considered for 'fast tracking' at that centre. He argues that his detention was therefore in breach of Article 14 taken together with Article 5 ECHR. The complaint was declared admissible on 27 September 2005 (▶see further 923). This means that it has got past the first stage of the European Court of Human Rights process and will progress to the final stage (▶see 783).

Approval for marriage

It may be possible to argue that the new law requiring certain people to obtain approval from the Home Office for their marriage is discriminatory on grounds of religion or race. The new provisions came into effect on 1 February 2005. From that date, all those who are neither British Citizens nor EEA nationals, and who do not have indefinite leave in the UK nor entry clearance for the purpose of marrying in the UK, must apply to the Home Office for a 'Certificate of Approval' to marry (for fuller details of the new requirements made by s19-25 2004 Act, see ▶296–300). However, Church of England marriages are exempt from the new requirements. Of course, one way to get around the new requirements would be for couples to undergo a Church of England marriage, but that will simply not be an option for couples of a different faith, for whom the religious aspect of their marriage is central to their beliefs and culture. Accordingly, the new requirements may be contrary to Article 14 taken with Article 8 and/or Article 12 (the right to marry). JCWI is intervening in a legal challenge on these grounds. It will be heard in 2006.

During the debate in parliament about the new provisions, the government argued that the changes were necessary because marriage registrars were reporting their suspicions of sham marriages in increasing numbers. Recently reported Home Office estimates ran to 15,000 sham marriages every year, mostly in London. However, this does not seem to tally with the reality: from April 2004 until the end of January 2005, only 49 people in the London region were prosecuted for offences concerning alleged sham marriages.

RACE DISCRIMINATION

The law on race discrimination is contained in the Race Relations Act 1976 (RRA). The main principle of the RRA is that persons of different races should be treated equally. 'Race' is widely defined to include: colour, race, nationality, national group and ethnicity. 'Muslims' and 'Rastafarians' have not been accepted as forming distinct ethnic groups, and therefore do not fall within the definition of 'race'. Discrimination under the RRA can be of two kinds – direct and indirect. Both are prohibited under the Act. Indirect discrimination is where a measure impacts disproportionately on a particular group, although it may not have been intended to do so. The most significant difference between the two, for the purposes of the RRA, is that there is a 'general justification' defence against allegations of indirect discrimination. Direct discrimination can only be justified by specific provisions of the Act.

Following the recommendations made by the report into the death of Stephen Lawrence, the government brought in the Race Relations (Amendment) Act 2000 (see Stephen Lawrence Inquiry, Sir William Macpherson of Cluny, CM 4262, TSO, 1999). The 2000 Act amended the RRA by expanding it to prohibit discrimination by 'public authorities' in carrying out their functions (s19B(1) RRA). The main purpose of this was to bring police functions within the ambit of the RRA, but it also incorporated immigration functions. So, since the 2000 Act came into force on 2 April 2001, it has been unlawful for public authorities (including immigration authorities) to discriminate on racial grounds in carrying out their functions.

The immigration rules also contain a prohibition on discrimination covering immigration officers, ECOs and all Home Office officials, when carrying out their functions under the rules. They are required to carry out their duties without regard to the race, colour or religion of persons seeking to enter or remain in the UK (see para. 2 HC 395).

There are, however, exceptions and qualifications to the prohibition on discrimination in public functions (see s19B–19F, RRA). Discrimination in immigration and nationality functions is permitted on grounds of either nationality or ethnic/national origin, provided that the discrimination is either required by legislation or has been authorised by the Home Secretary. Section 19D RRA gives ministers the power to issue 'authorisations' in order to allow officers to discriminate on grounds of nationality or ethnic/national origin in certain specific situations. Officers are therefore able to discriminate if acting within a relevant ministerial authorisation (▶see the table at 889–90. *However*, it remains always unlawful to discriminate on grounds of race or colour.

Ministerial authorisations

The first authorisation, which allowed discrimination in the examination of passengers and in removals, was made in April 2001. The format of the authorisation was later revised, after it was challenged in the High Court (see *Tamil Information Centre v SSHD*). The Court held that the minister had to exercise control personally over the authorisation. Now the minister must personally review the intelligence, information, and the statistical evidence of adverse decisions, breaches of immigration laws and trends relating to particular nationalities. Another contentious authorisation, which was also made in April 2001, and which allowed discrimination against specified national and ethnic groups, was revoked in June 2002.

The government states that it is committed to conducting reviews of the authorisations made, and the minister personally approves the relevant lists of nationalities each month on the basis of risk assessments prepared by the Immigration Service. The assessment identifies the basis for including nationalities in the list. So, the lists and authorisations are subject to change depending on intelligence and statistical evidence of adverse decisions and breaches. Those advising in this area therefore need to check whether the authorisation is still in force, which nationalities or groups are covered, and whether there have been any new authorisations issued. Unfortunately, the authorisations are not particularly accessible. They are not posted on the Home Office website. They are, however, listed in the annual report (2004–2005) of the Independent Race Monitor, Mary Coussey (▶see the table below).

Independent Race Monitor

The RRA created the post of the 'Independent Race Monitor' in order to oversee the operation of the Act in relation to immigration functions, including the ministerial authorisations. The Monitor produces an annual report and makes recommendations. The present Monitor is Mary

MINISTERIAL AUTHORISATIONS FOR DISCRIMINATION

The ministerial authorisations permitting discrimination under the Race Relations Act 1976 are as follows (listed according to the date they were made).

27 March 2001

Asylum work-streaming Officers may prioritise asylum applications from persons of particular nationalities, or ethnic or national origins, where a significant number of claims from the group in question are unfounded, or raise similar issues under the Refugee Convention or the ECHR.

Permission to work This authorises the employment concession outside the immigration rules for participants in BUNAC (▶468) and the Japan Youth Mobility Scheme (▶469).

Translation of documents There is no requirement to translate material into every language in use by applicants.

25 October 2001 (amended in March 2003)

Language analysis Asylum applicants from Afghanistan, Somalia, Sri Lanka and Iraq may be required to undergo language analysis, where there are doubts about an applicant's nationality.

23 May 2003

These authorisations replace earlier authorisations dating back to March 2001.

Examination of passengers Where certain conditions are met, the examination of certain groups of passengers on arrival can be prioritised on the basis of nationality.

Persons wishing to travel to the UK Discrimination is authorised in the operation of the Immigration (Leave to Enter and Remain) Order 2000 as to the granting of leave to enter before arrival in the UK (▶see 94).

Removal Directions. Under certain conditions, there can be prioritisation in the setting of removal directions on grounds of nationality.

30 May 2003

Sectors-Based Scheme (SBS) Certain discrimination has been permitted in the allocation of immigration employment documents for certain nationals coming to the UK under the SBS (i.e. for work in the food preparation and hospitality sectors; ▶448–50).

24 February 2004 (authorisation extended to 21 May 2004)

Examination of documents The prioritisation of the examination of travel documents of Somali origin is permitted.

Third country cases Additional examination is permitted of certain nationals (from Iraq, Turkey, Somalia and Sudan) who are most likely to have immigration status in other EEA states.

8

> **27 October 2005**
>
> **Examination of Eritrean nationals** This enables those of Eritrean nationality or national origin to be subject to more rigorous investigation and questioning (largely to obtain details about their journey to the UK).

Coussey. Her first annual report highlights the difficulties in ensuring that a proper balance is struck in maintaining selective and proportionate checks on travellers without being racially discriminatory. It was reported to her that air-side surveillance had changed – that previously it had been carried out by reference to passengers' colour or ethnicity, but that the 2000 Act had altered that approach. Following the 2000 Act, if there is intelligence about possible abuse on specific routes, all passenger documents are checked, rather than only those of passengers from 'suspect' groups and certain ethnic groups.

In her report for 2003/2004, the Monitor made a number of recommendations about how the authorisations were being used. She advised that the nationality authorisation relating to the examination of passengers on arrival was necessary to avoid both delay and the wasteful use of resources. However, she said that there was a possibility that identifying 'suspect' nationalities may become a self-fulfilling process. The more officers focus closely on certain suspected nationalities, and then obtain and use information about whatever abuses are found, the more entrenched becomes the view that those particular nationals are indeed 'suspect'.

Appeals in race discrimination cases

The 2000 Act amended the Immigration and Asylum Act 1999 in order to create a right of appeal on the grounds of race discrimination where it was alleged that officers had made a decision relating to entitlement to enter or remain that was discriminatory. The 1999 Act provisions about appeals were later repealed, but the 2002 Act also allows an appellant to appeal against an 'immigration decision' on the grounds of race discrimination contrary to s19B RRA (see se84(1)(b) 2002 Act). This ground of appeal also remains unchanged by the 2004 Act and the changeover to the Asylum and Immigration Tribunal from 4 April 2005.

Where an appellant complains that an immigration decision is tainted as a result of racial discrimination, then the ground of appeal can be made out. So an appeal can be allowed on the basis of race discrimination even if the immigration decision is otherwise in accordance with the immigration rules and the law. For example, if an immigration officer was racially abusive during the course of an interview, this might impact on the decision in a number of ways. It may be that the applicant felt less able to give a proper account of themselves in the interview; or it might indicate that there was likely to be some bias in the decision to refuse the application, whether under the rules or in exercising discretion outside the rules. This could then lead to the appeal being allowed on discrimination grounds.

Unfortunately, in some cases discrimination points have not been dealt with, and appeals have been allowed or refused under the immigration rules, without findings having been made on discrimination issues even when they have been raised. It is important that findings are made, partly because they are relevant to a discrimination claim the applicant may wish to make in the County Court (▶see further below). Immigration judges are required to make a separate finding on discrimination if it is raised as a ground of appeal (see s86(2) 2002 Act). The importance of immigration judges making such findings has been acknowledged. In *VE (Racial discrimination) Nigeria*, the IAT commented (note that the case was later heard by the Court of Appeal):

'We emphasise the need for Adjudicators to reach explicit findings and conclusions on race relations issues whatever the conclusions that they reach on other merits.'

The same point is made in the Practice Directions of the AIT (at para. 20). In addition, in the recent case of *ex parte Bibi*, the High Court held that the RRA did not prevent a person who had alleged that discrimination had occurred in the course of an immigration decision from bringing a discrimination claim in the County Court, simply because the question of discrimination had not actually been ruled on in the immigration proceedings (see s57A RRA). Again, the Court emphasised the need for immigration judges in the AIT to deal with any discrimination complaint, even if they allow the applicant's appeal on other grounds. Similarly, if an appeal is deemed abandoned because it is allowed on other grounds and leave is granted without any consideration of the discrimination question, the applicant can still bring a discrimination claim in the County Court (*VE v SSHD*, CA) (and see now the proposed changes under the 2005 Bill, ▶1045).

Where an applicant's complaint is only about particular treatment which the applicant received, but which cannot be said to have affected or be related to the immigration decision under appeal, then there will not be a discrimination ground of appeal to the AIT. Such applicants will have to raise the matter by using the Home Office complaints procedure (see ▶1223–7) or, if their case is particularly serious, by making a civil claim (▶see 1187–90).

Following through with a damages claim

If an appeal is allowed on grounds of race discrimination, the findings can be used to take a claim to a designated County Court (or, in Scotland, the Sheriff Court) for compensation to be assessed (see s57A(3) RRA). Damages can always include an element to compensate for injury to a person's feelings as a result of being discriminated against, and there is no upper limit for awards. However, awards tend to be modest. The County Court can't re-open a discrimination question decided on the immigration appeal (see s57A(4) RRA). So if an appellant is unhappy with the ruling made by the immigration judge, they should apply for a review through the ordinary AIT procedures. However, if the immigration judge has allowed the discrimination claim, the County Court and the Home Office must accept that ruling – the role of the County Court is then to decide on what damages should be paid.

A claim for compensation must be lodged within six months of the date of the event being complained about. In immigration cases, this time limit is extended and runs from the date that the appeal process comes to an end. So, if a discrimination appeal is allowed, the six-month time limit begins to run from the time that the Home Office's right to appeal (or apply for a review) ends. In cases where appeals are deemed to be 'abandoned' because leave has been granted, it is unclear whether time runs from the grant of leave to enter or remain, or from the time the AIT determines the appeal to be abandoned. It is therefore best to work on the basis of time running from the date on which leave is granted. Further details about civil claims are provided in Chapter 37 and for discrimination claims specifically ▶see 1187–90.

The *Roma Rights Centre* case

The *Roma Rights Centre* case concerned an agreement between the UK and the Czech Republic to permit British immigration officers to grant or refuse leave to enter the UK to passengers at Prague airport before they boarded the plane to come to the UK. The operation began on 18 July 2001, with the aim of preventing people from the Czech Republic from travelling to the UK in order to seek asylum, or otherwise to overstay their leave. The vast majority of applicants who had travelled to the UK for these purposes in the recent past were Roma. Czech Roma suffer serious problems in the Czech Republic which, in certain cases, have led to the grant of refugee status. The operation targeted all potential asylum-seekers, whether or not they had a good claim. The UK immigration officers based at Prague airport checked all those travelling to the UK with this purpose in mind, and it was clear that there was a much higher refusal rate for Roma travellers. Evidence was gathered by the European Roma Rights Centre, who monitored the operation. They found that a Roma was 400 times more likely to be rejected than a non-Roma. The Roma could be readily identified by their appearance, including their darker skin and hair.

Six Roma individuals who were refused leave to enter the UK, together with the European Roma Rights Centre, applied for judicial review. The case was lost in the High Court and in the Court of Appeal. In the Court of Appeal, Simon Brown LJ found that, on the one hand, 'it is unacceptable for someone to be treated less favourably because of his race, whatever the motives underlying such treatment and whether or not it results from the discriminator making stereotyped assumptions'. However, he concluded that the higher rate of refused entry for Czech Roma was not the result of less favourable treatment. Instead it arose:

'...because [the Roma] are less well placed to persuade the immigration officer that they are not lying in order to seek asylum. That is not to say that they are being stereotyped.' (see paras 81–6)

The appellants appealed to the House of Lords, who reversed the decision of the Court of Appeal and held that the officers, operating under the authority of the Home Secretary, had indeed unlawfully discriminated against Roma who were seeking to travel from that airport. The Roma had been treated less favourably on racial grounds than others seeking to travel to the UK. The Lords stated that setting up an operation prompted by an influx of asylum-seekers who were overwhelmingly from an easily identifiable racial or ethnic group required enormous care if it was to be done without discrimination, and that such care had not been taken in this case. The officers had treated Roma applicants more sceptically than the non-Roma. The House of Lords held that the operation had been inherently and systematically discriminatory, and therefore contrary to section 1(1)(a) of the RRA. The appellants' other grounds of appeal – which were based on the Refugee Convention and the unfairness in preventing Roma from leaving the Czech Republic and travelling to the UK where they might claim asylum – were not successful.

8

Section 9 **Detention and enforcement**

Chapter 30
Detention: powers, policy and legality 897

Background to immigration detention 898

Who can be detained under the immigration
legislation? 899

Who is likely to be detained – Home Office policy 905

International guidelines 917

Is the detention lawful? 919

Chapter 31
Detention places, conditions and procedures 933

Expansion of detention 933

Places of detention 934

Reasons, reviews and detention centre rules 939

Conditions: inspection and other reports 942

Chapter 32
Getting people out of detention 949

Temporary admission, temporary release and
restriction orders 950

Bail from immigration authorities or police inspector 957

Bail from the Asylum and Immigration Tribunal 958

Applying for bail before the AIT 965

Unlawful detention: High Court procedures 985

Chapter 33
**Enforcement: port removal, illegal entry,
administrative removal, deportation and
criminal offences** 989

The four basic 'enforcement' procedures and
the terms used 990

9

Recent developments in enforcement   991

Taking a decision that a person must leave
and policy   993

Port removals   1000

Administrative removal   1002

Illegal entry   1010

Deportation   1015

The process of removal and the possible countries
of return   1026

Other forms of enforcement and departure   1028

How people are traced and detected   1030

Criminal offences   1031

30 Detention: powers, policy and legality

This section (four chapters) looks at the use of detention by the immigration authorities as part of immigration control. It also deals with 'enforcement', which is the name given to the procedures that can be used to force people to leave the UK.

This chapter deals with when people can be detained for immigration reasons. After setting out the background to immigration detention (▶see below), we look at the powers of detention given to the immigration authorities by the legislation (beginning at ▶899). At ▶900–2 is a description of the important changes made to these powers since the last edition of the *Handbook*, in 2002. The table that follows at ▶902–5 sets out all the categories of people who can now be detained, together with references to the relevant legislation.

The next question is: Of those who can be detained under the legislation, who is likely to be detained? The Home Office has made various statements of policy on detention, and this is covered at ▶905–17 – in particular in tables 1–3, beginning at 899. We then look at some international guidelines concerning immigration detention; in particular at relevant guidance given by the UNHCR (▶917–9).

Finally, this chapter covers the circumstances in which Home Office detention decisions may be challenged as being unlawful. This covers circumstances in which there is no power to detain and circumstances in which the immigration authorities have unlawfully used their powers of detention. We look both at ordinary UK law and at Article 5 ECHR (▶see 919–32). The procedures used actually to get people out of detention are covered in Chapter 32.

Chapter 31 looks at the places where people can be detained under immigration powers, at some of the procedures used when people are detained, including the duty to give reasons to detainees and to review their position regularly, and at the Detention Centre Rules. It also summarises some of the reports, including the reports of HM Inspectorate, about places of immigration detention.

Chapter 32 looks at the different ways of getting people out of detention: temporary admission; bail from the immigration authorities; bail from the Asylum and Immigration Appeal Tribunal (AIT); and High Court procedures. It also gives detailed information about how to prepare and present a bail application before the AIT.

Chapter 33 covers the different ways in which people can be forced to leave the UK: the removal of 'port' applicants and illegal entrants, administrative removal, and deportation. These powers of 'enforcement' are often, but not always, used together with the powers of detention. The chapter also examines enforcement policy, possible countries of destination on removal, how people who are liable to enforcement are detected, and criminal offences.

BACKGROUND TO IMMIGRATION DETENTION

The powers to detain people for immigration reasons are very wide. There are no clear time-limits for how long a person can be detained for immigration reasons. There is also no automatic, independent control of the use of detention powers by the courts. In criminal cases, there is a 'right' to be released on bail unless good reasons are shown for keeping a person detained while the criminal matter is decided. There is no such right set down in the immigration legislation.

Despite all of this, the general law has always viewed restrictions on individual liberty very seriously. Where possible, the courts have placed limits on the extent to which people can lose their liberty, and they have approached the powers of immigration detention in this way. However, as a result of the broad way in which the powers of detention are framed in the legislation, these general principles have not prevented the development of a system in which immigration detainees have been locked up for months, or even years, while awaiting the resolution of their cases.

Quite aside from the *power* to detain people, neither the legislation nor the immigration rules state what factors must be considered before the immigration authorities can decide to detain someone. It is therefore up to the Home Office to decide which factors to take into account, and it has operated various policies for deciding when to detain. The perception among many of those affected is that detention is used as a means of punishment, and a disincentive to those seeking to come to the UK. The increased use of detention, in particular for asylum-seekers, has deepened the suspicion that detention is used as a deterrent.

Until March 2000, the Home Office's published detention policy remained – at least on the face of it – in keeping with general principles of law concerning the liberty of the subject. The guiding principle was that detention was only used as a 'last resort', where it was necessary because a person was likely to abscond if not detained, or for similar very pressing reasons. Since that time, the Home Office has added to the circumstances in which it may detain by also using detention powers in order to help the process of deciding an asylum claim 'quickly' – i.e. it has used detention powers for purely administrative reasons.

Full details are given in Chapter 22, dealing with asylum procedures, of:

- policy on who may detained under a fast track asylum determination process (▶673–7);
- procedures at the fast track detention centre at Oakington (▶677–8);
- procedures at the fast track detention centres at Harmondsworth and Yarls Wood (▶678–81).

WHO CAN BE DETAINED UNDER THE IMMIGRATION LEGISLATION?

The powers of immigration detention are contained in:

- **paragraph 16 of Schedule 2 and paragraph 2 of Schedule 3 of the 1971 Act** – these are the main detention powers (port cases, illegal entrants, deportees);
- **section 10(7) of the 1999 Act**, which applies the 1971 Act powers to 'administrative removal' cases (overstayers etc.);
- **section 62 of the 2002 Act**, which gives the 'Secretary of State' powers to detain in certain cases where, previously only the immigration service could detain (though this only affects who can *authorise* the detention – it does not change who can be detained);
- **section 71(3) of the 2002 Act**, which gives a power to detain asylum-seekers who have existing leave in the UK.

The legislation has caused confusion, largely because both the powers of detention and the power to grant bail have frequently been amended. Notably, the powers were amended by the 1999 Act in order to fit detention powers to the then new system of 'administrative removal'. The 1999 Act also amended powers so as to allow officers to detain persons if there was a 'reasonable suspicion' that they might be removed administratively, either as an illegal entrant or having been refused entry at a port.

The categories of people who can now be detained under the legislation as amended are set out in the table at ▶902–5, together with the relevant statutory reference. Where the legislation has been significantly amended since the last edition of the *Handbook* (April 2002), we have also included references to those amendments. Immediately below, we examine the main recent changes to the statutory powers.

Recent changes to detention powers

Changes to the statutory powers of detention since the last edition of the *Handbook* (April 2002) are as follows.

Family members in 'port removal' and illegal entrant cases Family members of people who are refused entry ('port' refusals) and of illegal entrants may be detained. There were already powers to detain and remove family members of those being administratively removed or deported. This new power dovetails with the new powers to enforce the departure of family members of those refused entry, and of illegal entrants. (Section 73(5) 2002 Act inserting reference to para. 10A Sch 2 1971 Act from 10 February 2003).

More categories of administrative removal and detention The following two groups have been added to the groups of people who can be administratively removed from the UK:

1) those who use deception to try to obtain leave to remain, even though they do not get leave (previously there was only a power to administratively remove a person who obtained leave by deception);

2) those whose indefinite leave is revoked because they have ceased to be a refugee.

The powers of detention have been amended in line so that these two groups can also be detained, pending a decision whether to administratively remove them and during the removal process. (Sections 74 and 76(7) 2002 Act from 10 February 2003).

Asylum-seekers who have leave Those who claim asylum (including those who make Article 3 claims) at a time when they have leave in the UK and their dependants can now be given the same conditions as apply to temporary admission. So, they can be given residence, reporting and employment restrictions. *If* the asylum-seeker breaches any of those conditions, they can now be detained. Of course, in some cases where a person with leave claims asylum, the Home Office was already able to 'curtail' the leave or to declare the applicant an illegal entrant, and then detain them on that basis (▶see 141–3, 1010–5). (Section 71 2002 Act from 10 February 2003.)

Those in the deportation process seeking bail The 2004 Act has changed the powers relating to detention following a recommendation for deportation and after a notice of intention to deport has been issued. Many such people may already be detained as a result of the criminal law, in which case immigration detention is not needed. Previously the power to detain was limited so that these people could not be detained under immigration powers if they were 'for the time being released on bail by a court having power to so release [them]'. But these words have now been removed. The intention seems to be that bail that is granted by the higher courts in particular should not stop immigration authorities from detaining people in these categories. The Home Office is concerned that these courts may grant bail while they are unaware of and not involved in the deportation process. The intention is also that bail granted by the courts before the deportation process was begun should not prevent the immigration authorities from detaining after the process starts. It is still clear, however, that, if the criminal court that made the recommendation, or that is hearing the appeal against the conviction or recommendation, directs release, then the Home Office will not be able to continue to detain (para. 2(1)(1A), Sch 3 1971 Act). Also, detainees will still be able to obtain effective bail from the AIT. (Paras 2(1)(2) to Sch 3 1971 Act as amended by section 34 2004 Act from 1 October 2004 and see the explanation in the Explanatory Notes to the 2004 Act, paras 159–161.)

The Secretary of State's powers to detain overlap with those of immigration officers Until the 2002 Act, the legislation carefully distinguished between those persons whom the immigration service could detain and those who could be detained by 'the Secretary of State'. Section 62 of the 2002 Act allows the Secretary of State – in effect, officers at the Home Office – to detain people, where previously only immigration officers could detain. The main purpose of this is to allow the same officer at the Home Office who is dealing with the asylum claim, and who therefore understands the case in full, also to authorise detention. The Home Office is given parallel powers with immigration officers in most other cases as well. They are too complex to include here, but references to the legislation are given in the table on ▶902–5. Detention in relation to deportation powers remains under the control of the Secretary of State. (Section 62 2002 Act from 10 February 2003).

Suspected international terrorists, *A & Others*, and the Prevention of Terrorism Act 2005 Until 14 March 2005 there was a power to detain people who the Secretary of State had certified as being a risk to national security, and were suspected of having connections to international terrorism (Anti-terrorism, Crime and Security Act 2001). Such persons could be detained in any of the normal circumstances given under the 1971 Act. So, these were immigration powers of detention, grafted onto the 1971 Act, and could only therefore be used against foreign nationals. *However*, the main difference was that these powers allowed a person to be detained indefinitely *even though* they could not be removed from the UK. It might be impossible to remove them for practical reasons, or perhaps because they would be at risk of ill-treatment within the meaning of Article 3 ECHR, yet people in this category could still be detained. This meant that the powers were contrary to Article 5 ECHR (which allows detention that is with a 'view to deportation'). Therefore, in order to justify these powers, the government had to 'derogate' from (i.e. state that it was not applying) Article 5 ECHR. It did so on the grounds that, following the 11 September attacks, there was a 'public emergency', in the form of a terrorist threat to the life of the nation.

In *A & others v SSHD*, the House of Lords held that the powers under the 2001 Act were unlawful: they were not a rational or proportionate response to the threat faced. In particular, the Lords found that the powers were unjustifiably discriminatory. This was because they could only be used against non-nationals, when the terrorist threat came from both non-nationals and nationals. Following this decision, the relevant provisions of the 2001 Act were repealed. In their place, the Prevention of Terrorism Act 2005 brought in a whole range of powers called 'control orders', which are aimed at preventing people from taking part in terrorist-related activity. These powers include taking away people's liberty, but they apply to British citizens as well as foreign nationals. The powers are supervised by the courts. The 2005 Act is long and detailed, and we do not attempt to cover it in the *Handbook*. Anyone affected by control orders should seek specialist advice. For details about immigration decisions taken on the grounds of national security and appeals to SIAC, ▶see 1081–3. (Section 16 of the Prevention of Terrorism Act 2005 repealing sections 21(1)–(5), 23 of the Anti-terrorism, Crime and Security Act 2001).

PERSONS WHO MAY BE DETAINED

Notes

1) This table should be read together with the details at ▶900–2, which explain the changes to the statutory powers since the last edition of the *Handbook*.

2) For each of the powers of detention below, the up-to-date statutory reference is given. The powers under the 1971 Act have been amended frequently. We have additionally given references for the significant amendments made since the last edition of the *Handbook*.

3) In the previous edition of the *Handbook*, there were two separate tables for detention authorised by immigration officers and detention authorised by the Secretary of State. As a result of the Secretary of State obtaining some of the powers of detention which were previously only held by the immigration service (see s62 2002 Act from 10 February 2003), we have no longer attempted to divide the powers of detention between officers of the immigration service and officers of the Secretary of State.

4) For the application of immigration detention powers to EEA nationals and their family members, ▶see 554–6.

People who fall into any of the categories below may, in principle, be detained under immigration powers.

Port cases

- Persons arriving in the UK, pending their examination to establish whether they can be admitted, and pending a decision as to whether to admit them.
  Power to detain:
  Immigration Act 1971, Sch 2, para. 16(1)
  Nationality, Immigration and Asylum Act 2002, s62(2)(a)(b)

- Those who arrive in the UK with leave to enter given to them before they arrive, but whose leave is then suspended by an immigration officer, pending their examination by an immigration officer and pending a decision on whether to admit them or to cancel their leave.

Power to detain:

Immigration Act 1971, Sch 2, para. 16(1A)

- Those refused leave to enter, those reasonably suspected of having been refused leave to enter, and those reasonably suspected of being the family member of a person refused leave to enter, pending a decision on whether to give directions for their removal, and pending their removal after removal directions have been given.

Power to detain:

Immigration Act 1971, Sch 2, para. 16(2) as amended by s73(5) 2002 Act from 10 February 2003

Nationality, Immigration and Asylum Act 2002, s62(1)(a)(b), (2)(c)(d)

Illegal entrants

- Illegal entrants, those reasonably suspected of being illegal entrants, and those reasonably suspected of being the family members of an illegal entrant, pending a decision on whether to issue removal directions, and pending their removal after removal directions have been given.

Power to detain:

Immigration Act 1971, Sch 2, para. 16(2) as amended by s73(5) 2002 Act from 10 February 2003

Nationality, Immigration and Asylum Act 2002, s62(1)(a)(b),(2)(c)(d)

Administrative removal cases

- Those who overstay their leave in the UK; those who breach any of their other conditions of leave; those who used deception in trying to obtain leave to remain (whether they got leave or not); those whose indefinite leave is revoked as a result of their ceasing to be a refugee; those who are family members of a person who has been given directions for removal because they fall into any of the last four categories; and anyone who is 'reasonably suspected' of falling into any of the last five categories. All of these people may be detained pending a decision on whether to remove them, and pending their removal after removal directions have been given.

Power to detain:

Immigration and Asylum Act 1999 s10(1)(a)(b)(ba)(c),(7) as amended by section 74 and 76(7) 2002 Act from 10 February 2003

Immigration Act 1971, Sch 2, para. 16(2)

Nationality, Immigration and Asylum Act 2002, s62(1)(a)(b),(5)

9

Crews of ships and aircraft

- Members of the crews of ships or aircraft who remain beyond the leave granted to enable them to join their ship or aircraft, or who intend to remain beyond that leave, or those who abscond or intend to abscond having lawfully entered without leave, or anyone who is reasonably suspected of being in any of those categories. They may be detained pending a decision as to whether to remove them, and pending their removal after removal directions have been given.

Power to detain:

Immigration Act 1971, Sch 2, para. 16(2)

Nationality, Immigration and Asylum Act 2002, s62(1)(a)(b)

Asylum-seekers with leave

- Those who claim asylum (including an Article 3 ECHR claim) at a time when they have leave to enter or remain, and who breach a condition imposed on them as to residence, reporting or occupation. Dependants of asylum-seekers who fall into this category may also be detained.

Note: other asylum-seekers may of course be detained under the other powers referred to in this table.

Power to detain:

Nationality, Immigration and Asylum Act 2002, s71 read with Sch 2, para. 16 1971 Act

Notice of intention to make a deportation order

- Persons who have been given notice of intention to make a deportation order, pending the making of the deportation order.

The following people may be given a notice of intention to make a deportation order and detained under this power: those whose presence is not 'conducive to the public good', those who are recommended for deportation following conviction for an offence by a criminal court, and the family members of persons who are, or who have been, ordered to be deported.

Power to detain:

Immigration Act 1971, Sch 3, para. 2(2) as amended by:

a) s114(3) and Sch 7, para. 7 of the 2002 Act from 1 April 2003 (and note also s3(5)(6) 1971 Act and s82(2)(j) of the 2002 Act);

b) s34(2) 2004 Act from 1 October 2004.

Recommendation for deportation

- Persons who have been issued by a criminal court with a recommendation that they be deported following their conviction for a crime, unless the criminal court that made the recommendation (or the criminal court dealing with an appeal against the conviction or the recommendation) has directed that they be released. These people may be detained 'pending' the making of a deportation order.

Power to detain:

Immigration Act 1971, Sch 3, paras 2(1), (1A) as amended by s34(1) 2004 Act from 1 October 2004.

Deportation orders

Persons who have a deportation order in force against them, pending their removal or departure from the UK (note that family members can be issued with a deportation order after they have received notice of intention to deport – see above). If a person is already detained under the powers above for deportees when the deportation order is made, then they 'shall' continue to be detained unless the Secretary of State directs otherwise, or unless they are released on bail.

Power to detain:

Immigration Act 1971, Sch 3, para. 2(3)

Non-immigration reasons for detention

The table above sets out the powers to detain people for immigration reasons. There are circumstances in which there is a power to detain people both for immigration reasons and for other reasons. For example, an immigration detainee may also be held while suspected of or charged with a criminal offence, or as the result of a prison sentence given for an offence or, occasionally, under the Mental Health Act. It is of course possible for someone to be detained for criminal reasons on suspicion of having committed an offence relating to immigration. An example is the new offence, under section 2 of the 2004 Act, of attending an interview without a passport or travel document (▶see 683–6). Other examples are breaching conditions of leave and illegal entry. For details about immigration-related criminal offences, ▶see 1031–5.

WHO IS LIKELY TO BE DETAINED – HOME OFFICE POLICY

Where a person can be detained because they fall into any of the above categories, it doesn't mean that they automatically will be. Wherever a person can be detained, there is also a power to grant that person temporary admission so that they are not detained. A person who is detained may at any time be granted temporary admission, and a person granted temporary admission may later be detained. For more details about temporary admission, see ▶652–4, 950–7.

Within the limits of their powers, the immigration authorities have a wide discretion as to when to detain. In order to guide officers in making detention decisions, the Home Office has detailed policy dealing with when to detain. If the immigration authorities fail to follow their own guidelines properly as to when to detain, the detention will be unlawful (▶see 929–30). We have set out Home Office policy on detention in three tables below. They cover:

1) **The Operational Enforcement Manual (OEM) – Table 1 (▶909–12)**

2) **Form IS 91R –** *pro forma* **'reasons for detention' notice – Table 2** (▶913–4)

3) **Other sources of policy (Home Office letters, statements etc.) – Table 3** (▶914–7)

The three tables outline Home Office policy for most detention cases. However, there are some further aspects of detention policy that are looked at elsewhere in the *Handbook*. For policy on detention for fast track asylum determination purposes (Oakington, Harmondsworth, Yarls Wood), ▶see 673–81; for more on detention in age-dispute cases, ▶see 688–91; for immigration detention in prisons and police cells ▶see 936–8 (and ▶see also 912).

Many detainees are asylum-seekers. Sometimes asylum-seekers are detained at the time they attend in person to make their claim. All asylum applicants are put through an initial 'screening' process. Part of the purpose of screening is to decide whether the applicant should be detained. For details about asylum procedures generally see Chapter 22 and, for screening processes in particular, ▶see 645–50.

Development of detention policy

In what follows, we briefly trace the sources of detention policy from the early 1990s (when the numbers of asylum-seekers began to rise) to the present time.

Instructions to staff in 1991 and 1994

Policy instructions issued to immigration service staff, dated 3 December 1991 and 20 September 1994, stated that detention should be authorised 'only when there is no alternative', and that 'the overriding consideration is whether the person is likely to comply voluntarily with any restrictions imposed, including any arrangements for removal'.

White Papers: *Fairer, Faster, Firmer* (1998) and *Secure Borders, Safe Haven* (2002)

The 1998 White Paper (published in July 1998) confirmed that there is a presumption in favour of granting temporary admission. It stated that detention would be justified in the following circumstances:

- where there is a reasonable belief that the individual will fail to keep to the terms of temporary admission or release;
- initially, in order to clarify a person's identity and the basis of their asylum claim;
- where their removal is imminent.

It continued:

'In particular, where there is a systematic attempt to breach immigration control, detention is justified wherever one or more of those criteria is satisfied.'

The White Paper also stated that:

- evidence of torture should weigh strongly in favour of temporary admission while an asylum claim is being considered;
- the detention of families with young children should be planned so that it is operated as close as possible to removal, to ensure that families are not normally detained for more than a few days;
- unaccompanied minors should not be detained other than in the most exceptional circumstances, and then only overnight with appropriate care – for example, if they arrive unaccompanied at an airport.

Much the same policy was repeated in the 2002 White Paper, *Secure Borders, Safe Haven*.

Detention for the purpose of quick decision-making: 2000

In March 2000, the Home Office opened the Oakington Reception Centre. The policy for detention at Oakington was quite different from earlier detention policy. A person would be detained if they claimed asylum and that claim was capable of being decided quickly (i.e. within seven to ten days). The traditional policy concerns of preventing absconding and other breaches of conditions did not form part of the policy. Indeed, those at risk of absconding, or who presented similar problems, were decided *not* to be suitable for the 'relaxed' Oakington regime, and could not be detained there.

Since then, the government has opened other fast track facilities (Harmondsworth, Yarls Wood), where applicants are detained while their asylum applications are considered. For details about policy relating to detention at these fast track facilities and the relevant procedures, ▶see 673–81. For the fast track *appeals* regime, ▶see 1129–32.

Change in policy on detaining families: 2001

The policy set out in the 1998 White Paper on the detention of families (▶see above) meant that family detention was rare. In a letter circulated to immigration lawyers in October 2001, the immigration service announced that the new detention centres at Yarls Wood, Dungavel and Harmondsworth contain dedicated family accommodation, which ensures that family members are not separated. It was stated that the same general detention policy would therefore apply to families whose circumstances justified their detention as that applied to single applicants. It was nevertheless stated that:

'In every case, the detention of a family, especially those with children, will have to be considered necessary in all the circumstances of the case. There will remain a general presumption in favour of granting temporary admission and release. No family will be detained simply because suitable family accommodation is available.'

Operational Enforcement Manual

The 1991, 1994 and 1998 policy statements were consolidated in the OEM at Chapter 38. The policy lists the factors that should be taken into account in deciding whether to detain.

Applicants and the courts have all proceeded on the basis that Chapter 38 of the OEM represented government detention policy (see *Saadi*, paras 15–16; *Nadarajah*, paras 26, 30, 55; *ID & Others* , para. 35). However, in the High Court case of *R (I and O) v SSHD* (heard at the end of April 2005), the Home Office drew attention to the fact that that part of the OEM no longer appeared on the website, as much of the OEM was being updated. The Home Office stated to the Court that the version previously published no longer represented up-to-date or accurate guidance to Home Office staff. It had been 'withdrawn and is in the process of being re-drafted'. It was stated that after it had been revised, it would be put on the website together with other revised parts of the OEM. However, the Court noted that the Home Office had provided no evidence of when it had been withdrawn, and expressed its surprise that there should be any lack of clarity. The Court did not, on the facts of the case, have to resolve the problem as to whether it was still the policy. This confusion and lack of clarity in detention policy is a bad omen for lawful and consistent decision-making in this important area. However, the OEM policy has still continued to be published in very similar form in the European Directorates' Instructions (EDI), at Chapter 3, section 5.

In the autumn of 2005 (precise date unclear), Chapter 38 reappeared on the Home Office website. It again carries detailed criteria relating to decisions to detain. Although it has been revised from the previous version, much of the substance remains the same. **Table 1** (▶909–912) contains extracts from Chapter 38 OEM in the autumn 2005 revised version.

Form IS 91R

Form IS 91R is the form given to people when they are detained to explain why they are being detained. Its contents are also set out in Chapter 38 of the OEM, and it was referred to in *Nadarajah* as being 'an important part of the published policy' (see at paras 27, 55–6). Various different versions of the form have been published.

It is reproduced in **Table 2**. For other detention policy details, see **Table 3** below.

Five-year strategy

The government's five-year strategy pledges to expand the capacity for immigration detention to allow more detention for fast tracking asylum claims, and also so that 'over time...we will move to the point where it becomes the norm that those who fail can be detained' (▶see 39, 934).

TABLE 1: DETENTION POLICY: OPERATIONAL ENFORCEMENT MANUAL

Notes

1) Set out below are extracts from Chapter 38 of the OEM in the version which reappeared on the Home Office website in the autumn of 2005 (▶see 908 for background). The *Bail: Guidance Notes for Adjudicators* (third edition, May 2003) indicate that those hearing bail applications should have regard to the OEM policy (para. 1.3). The version of the OEM which is attached to the the the Bail Guidance Notes is the old one. It is understood that the Bail Guidance Notes are presently being revised.

2) The previoius version of the OEM was also relied on by the Court of Appeal in *Nadarajah* (set out at para. 26 of the Court's judgment).

3) Certain aspects of detention policy are not set out in Tables 1–3.

- For policy on detention for fast track asylum determination purposes (Oakington, Harmondsworth, Yarls Wood), ▶see 673–81.

- For policy on detention in age-dispute cases, ▶see 688–91 and ▶below.

- For policy on transfers from or to detention in prisons, ▶see 936–8 (some details on when immigration detainees will be kept in prisons are given in the OEM, below). For procedures when detaining a family ▶see 998–1000

'38.1 Policy

General

In the White Paper *'Fairer, Faster and Firmer – A Modern Approach to Immigration and Asylum'* published in July 1998, the Government made it clear the power to detain must be retained in the interests of maintaining effective immigration control. However, the White Paper confirmed that there was a presumption in favour of temporary admission or release and that, wherever possible, we would use alternatives to detention (see 38.20 and chapter 39). The White Paper went on to say that detention would most usually be appropriate:

- to effect removal;

- initially to establish a person's identity or basis of claim; or

- where there is reason to believe that the person will fail to comply with any conditions attached to the grant of temporary admission or release.

...

Use of detention

In all cases detention must be used sparingly, and for the shortest period necessary. It is not an effective use of detention space to detain people for lengthy periods if it would be practical to effect detention later in the process once any rights of appeal have been exhausted. A person who has an appeal pending or representations outstanding might have more incentive to comply with any restrictions imposed, if released, than one who is removable.

...

38.1.1.2 Article 8 of the ECHR

Article 8(1) of the ECHR provides: 'Everyone has the right to respect for private and family life...'

It may be necessary on occasion to detain the head of the household only, thus separating a family [reference to the elements of Article 8 ECHR concluding with a statement that it may be legally defensible under the HRA to interfere with family life by detention in order to enforce immigration control]...

But it would have to be shown to a court that a decision to detain (and thereby interfere with family life) was proportionate to the legitimate aim pursued... The conclusion reached will depend on the specific facts of each case and will therefore differ in every case.

...

38.3 Factors influencing a decision to detain

1) There is a presumption in favour of temporary admission or temporary release.

2) There must be strong grounds for believing that a person will not comply with conditions of temporary admission or temporary release for detention to be justified.

3) All reasonable alternatives to detention must be considered before detention is authorised.

4) Once detention has been authorised, it must be kept under close review to ensure that it continues to be justified.

5) Each case must be considered on its individual merits.

The following factors must be taken into account when considering the need for initial or continued detention.

For detention:

- what is the likelihood of the person being removed and, if so, after what timescale?
- is there any evidence of previous absconding?
- is there any evidence of a previous failure to comply with conditions of temporary release or bail?
- has the subject taken part in a determined attempt to breach the immigration laws? (e.g. entry in breach of a deportation order, attempted or actual clandestine entry);
- is there a previous history of complying with the requirements of immigration control? (e.g. by applying for a visa, further leave, etc.);
- what are the person's ties with the United Kingdom? Are there close relatives (including dependants) here? Does anyone rely on the person for support? Does the person have a settled address/employment?
- what are the individual's expectations about the outcome of the case? Are there factors such as an outstanding appeal, an application for judicial review or representations which afford incentive to keep in touch?

Against detention:

- is the subject under 18?
- has the subject a history of torture?
- has the subject a history of physical or mental ill health?

...

38.3.1 Oakington

[The OEM gives details about detention at Oakington – the most important condition is that the applicant has claimed asylum and that the claim is capable of being dealt with quickly. Details about policy on detention for the purposes of fast-tracking asylum claims are given at ▶673–81]

...

38.9.3 Young persons

Unaccompanied minors (i.e. persons under the age of 18) must only ever be detained in the most exceptional circumstances and then *only normally overnight*, with appropriate care, whilst alternative arrangements for their care and safety are made. This includes age-dispute cases where we are treating the person concerned as a minor. This exceptional measure is intended to deal with unexpected situations where it is necessary to detain unaccompanied minors very briefly for their care and safety.

In circumstances where responsible family or friends in the community cannot care for children, they should be placed in the care of the local authority as soon as practicable.

[For further details about detention of minors, ▶see 687, 916, 998–1000. For reports on the detention of minors ▶see 947–8]

...

38.9.3.1 Persons claiming to be under 18

[Under this head, the OEM gives details about policy in age-dispute cases, but this is discussed fully at ▶688–91]

...

38.9.4 Families

The decision to detain an entire family should always be taken with due regard to Article 8 of the ECHR (see 38.1.1.2). Families, including those with children, can be detained on the same footing as all other persons liable to detention. This means that families may be detained in line with the general detention criteria – see 38.3...

Detention of an entire family must be justified in all the circumstances and, as in any case, there will continue to be a presumption in favour of granting temporary release. Detention must be authorised by an Inspector at whatever stage of the process it is considered necessary and, although it should last only for as long as necessary, it is not subject to a particular time limit...

... As a matter of policy we should aim to keep the family as a single unit. However, it will be appropriate to separate a child from its parents if there is evidence that separation is in the best interests of the child. The local authority's social services department will make this decision. In such cases, prior arrangement and authority will be required from MODCU [the Management of Detained Cases Unit] and the child's parents should provide agreement in writing. As long as the child is taken into care in accordance with the law and following a decision of a competent authority Article 8 of the ECHR will not be breached (see 38.1.1.2).

[For further details about policy concerning detention of families with children, ▶see also the table below at 916 and 998–1000; for reports on the detention of families, ▶see 947–8]

...

38.10 Persons considered unsuitable for detention

Certain persons are normally considered suitable for detention in only very exceptional circumstances, whether in dedicated IS accommodation or elsewhere. Others are unsuitable for IS detention accommodation, because their detention requires particular security, care and control.

The following are normally considered suitable for detention in only very exceptional circumstances, whether in dedicated IS detention accommodation or elsewhere:

- unaccompanied children and persons under the age of 18 (but ▶see 38.9.3 above);
- the elderly, especially where supervision is required;
- pregnant women, unless there is the clear prospect of early removal and medical advice suggests no question of confinement prior to this [but the policy is modified for those in the early stages of pregnancy who are detained at Oakington or Yarls Wood];
- those suffering from serious medical conditions or the mentally ill;
- those where there is independent evidence that they have been tortured;
- people with serious disabilities.

38.10.1 Criteria for detention in prison

Immigration detainees should only be held in prison establishments when they present specific risk factors that indicate they are unsuitable for immigration removal centres, for reasons of security or control. [For details of these circumstances ▶see 937–8]...

All cases who have completed a prison sentence will be assessed by DEPMU [the Detention Escorting and Population Management Unit] on an individual basis as to whether they should remain in prison or be transferred to an IS removal centre...

[Chapter 38 of the OEM also provides policy on: detention of illegal immigrants and those subject to administrative removal who are facing or have been convicted of criminal offences (38.11.1); detention pending criminal proceedings (38.11.2); detention in deportation cases (38.11.3) and detention after an appeal has been allowed (38.12.2).]

TABLE 2: DETENTION POLICY: FORM IS 91R

Notes

1) The *pro forma* Form IS 91R is a 'check-list' of reasons to be given to detainees when detained. It contains a set number of reasons for detention and a number of factors relevant to whether certain reasons exist. For details about the procedures for giving reasons and review of detention, ▶see 916 and ▶see 939–40.

2) Because it is a *pro forma* list of possible reasons, Form IS 91R gives an insight into detention policy. In *Nadarajah*, the Court noted that IS 91R was referred to in Chapter 38 of the OEM, and stated that it was an 'important part of the published policy' (see paras 55–7).

3) The form has been amended several times. A version of the Form IS 91R was contained in the previous version of Chapter 38 of the OEM at Ch 38.5.2. At para. 27 of *Nadarajah*, a very slightly amended version was reproduced (with the addition of detention for the purposes of obtaining fingerprints where the applicant has not provided them voluntarily). Below, we reproduce a later version still, which includes detention for the purpose of fast-tracking an asylum claim (previously this reason appeared as an 'addendum' to the form). The version we reproduce below is also essentially the same as the version which appears in the latest version of Chapter 38 of the OEM (Ch 38.6.3, autumn 2005).

'IS 91 R

NOTICE TO DETAINEE

REASONS FOR DETENTION AND BAIL RIGHTS

1 To

_____

_____.

I am ordering your detention under powers contained in the Immigration Act 1971 or the Nationality, Immigration and Asylum Act 2002.

1) Detention is only used when there is no reasonable alternative available. It has been decided that you should remain in detention because (tick <u>all</u> boxes that apply):

a You are likely to abscond if given temporary admission or release.

b There is insufficient reliable information to decide on whether to grant you temporary admission or release.

c Your removal from the United Kingdom is imminent.

d You need to be detained whilst alternative arrangements are made for your care.

e Your release is not considered conducive to the public good.

f I am satisfied that your application may be decided quickly using the fast track procedures.

This decision has been reached on the basis of the following factors (tick <u>all</u> boxes that apply):

1) You do not have enough close ties (e.g. family or friends) to make it likely you will stay in one place.

2) You have previously failed to comply with conditions of your stay, temporary admission, or release.

3) You have previously absconded or escaped.

4) On initial consideration, it appears that your application may be one which can be decided quickly.

5) You have used or attempted to use deception in a way that leads us to consider you may continue to deceive.

6) You have failed to give satisfactory or reliable answers to an Immigration Officer's enquiries.

7) You have not produced satisfactory evidence of your identity, nationality or lawful basis to be in the UK.

8) You have previously failed or refused to leave the UK when required to do so.

9) You are a young person without the care of a parent or guardian.

10) Your health gives serious cause for concern on grounds of your own well-being and/or public health or safety.

11) You are excluded from the UK at the personal direction of the Secretary of State.

12) You are detained for reasons of national security, the reasons are/will be set out in another letter.

13) Your unacceptable character, conduct or associations.

14) I consider this reasonably necessary in order to take your fingerprints because you have failed to provide them voluntarily.'

TABLE 3: DETENTION POLICY: OTHER SOURCES OF POLICY

In addition to the comprehensive statements of detention policy set out in Tables 1 and 2, it is possible to glean further details about the interpretation and operation of the policy from various other sources, as follows.

Removal not 'imminent' if court challenge begun

As a working practice, the Home Office does not treat removal as 'imminent' for the purposes of the policy (see point 'c' of Form IS 91R above) if proceedings challenging the removal (which will normally be judicial review but could also be an appeal) have actually begun. *However*, in deciding whether to detain on this basis, the Home Office will not have regard to an indication that proceedings may be brought. In *Nadarajah*, the detentions were ruled to be unlawful because, at that time, this part of the policy had not been published, and applicants and their advisers were unaware of it (*Nadarajah* at paras 42, 58, 66–7) (see also OEM at Ch 38.14).

'Imminent' removal is not enough on its own

Even if removal is 'imminent', this is not enough on its own to justify detention. People subject to imminent removal will only be detained if there are additional reasons – for example, if they have previously failed or refused to leave the UK when required to do so (point 8 in Form IS 91R), or if there is a greater risk of absconding given that removal is very close (*Nadarajah*, paras 42–3, 56–7, 61) (see also OEM at Ch 38.14).

No presumption of detention after completion of a criminal sentence where a person is recommended for deportation

The legislation indicates a presumption of immigration detention for those recommended for deportation, and who have come to the end of their criminal sentence (para. 2(1), Sch 3, 1971 Act). However, the Home Office has agreed that it will not apply this presumption. It has agreed that, when a person who has been recommended for deportation finishes their criminal sentence and is liable to be detained under immigration powers, it will not automatically continue to detain them or operate a presumption to do so. Instead, it will consider, usually before or on the date of release from criminal detention, whether immigration detention is justified. If detention is to be continued, reasons should be given (see *Sedrati & Others*, a High Court case settled by agreement between the parties, on terms which confirmed this Home Office approach to these cases).

The following general statement about detention at the end of a prison sentence is contained in the European Directorate's Instructions (EDI):

'A decision on whether detention is necessary should be made shortly before any prison sentence is due to be completed. In all cases where no deportation order has been made a detention order must be signed

...

Where detention is not considered necessary the prison must be informed so that they release the person on completion of sentence. This is particularly important in those cases where the person has been recommended for deportation by the court as paragraph 2(1) of Schedule 3 to the Immigration Act 1971 provides that these people will be detained on completion of sentence unless the Secretary of State directs otherwise.' (Ch 3, s5, para. 5.2)

Third country cases

It seems that it is also Home Office policy to detain in 'third country' asylum cases, where 'there is clear evidence that another EU Member State has responsibility for determining an asylum application' (Letter of the Minister, Beverley Hughes MP, to Lord Avebury, August 2002). In early 2005, over 200 applicants a month were being returned to EU countries.

9

Detention of families with children – ministerial approval beyond 28 days

In addition to what is stated in Table 1 (▶911), cases involving the detention of children are 'subject to rigorous review against the published detention criteria'. Such cases are dealt with 'as expeditiously as possible to ensure that the period of detention is kept to a minimum'. Cases where families with children are to be detained for more than 28 days are very few, and a minister's approval must be obtained in order to do this. After 28 days' detention, ministerial authorisation is then obtained on a weekly basis (see letter of the Minister, Lord Bassam, to Lord Avebury, dated 5 July 2004). (Further details about review of detention in cases involving children and/or unaccompanied minors are contained in the OEM at Ch 38.8 and 38.9.3).

The response of the Home Office (dated 10 June 2005) to the Save the Children report on detention and children (*No Place for a Child*) states:

- families with children will not normally be detained at Dungavel or Tinsley House for longer than 72 hours (although they may be transferred back to Yarls Wood);

- the Home Office rejects the argument that there should be a seven-day statutory maximum time limit for detaining families with children but affirms that detention should be for the shortest possible time and subject to rigorous review – 'very few families are detained for more than just a few days';

- the Home Office accepts that welfare assessments should be carried out for all children who have been detained for 21 days (but not after seven days): 'Arrangements are now in place with the relevant social services departments to ensure that welfare assessments are undertaken in respect of all children at the 21 day point…outcomes of these assessments will be disclosed to Immigration staff who are responsible for reviewing detention and details of the assessment will be included in the submission to the Minister seeking authorisation for continued detention beyond 28 days. It will not necessarily be the case that where a child's welfare and well-being is found to be negatively affected by detention that the family will be released. Such concerns always need to be considered alongside the need for immigration enforcement action';

- the Home Office rejected the proposal for case-by-case assessments in order to determine whether it would be better for a child to be detained with their family or separated: 'It has very occasionally been the case that, once a child is detained with his/her parents, it has become clear that there are parenting or child protection issues that require intervention from local social services. These issues are never ignored and the safety and well-being of the child is paramount in such cases. It is difficult to see how pre-detention assessment would necessarily provide a better mechanism for identification of these issues…'.

The 'needs' and individual circumstances of the child and the family will be taken into account before a family is detained (letter of Detention Services Policy Unit of the Home Office to BID, 7 October 2004). For reports on children and family detention, ▶see 947–8. For detention of minors and age disputes, ▶see 688–91.

For details about procedures for detaining and removing families ▶see 998–1000.

Special exercises

From time to time, the immigration authorities have initiated 'special exercises'. The immigration service has stated that these take place 'when we perceive there to be a threat to the integrity of immigration control, as, for example, when people whose asylum applications have been refused and whose appeals have been dismissed by the [appeals authorities] simply return to the UK…and make a fresh application for asylum'. The Home Office exchanged correspondence with BID about these exercises between October 2000 and January 2001. It was acknowledged that special exercises existed, but not that they form the basis for decisions to detain.

Weber and Gelsthorpe's study, based largely on interviews with immigration officers and CIOs, also takes note of special exercises, stating that they take the form of temporary instructions requiring officers to detain persons of particular nationalities who are thought to be involved in 'systematic breaches of the control' ('*Deciding to Detain: How decisions to detain asylum-seekers are made at ports of entry*', University of Cambridge 2000; see also Tolley's *IANL*, Vol 15, No. 3, 2001, p. 151, at p. 152). Such practices may be unlawfully discriminatory unless authorised (▶see 888–9).

INTERNATIONAL GUIDELINES

Although they are not formally part of the law, and therefore not binding, further useful indications of when detention may be authorised can be taken from the United Nations High Commissioner for Refugees (UNHCR), the International Covenant on Civil and Political Rights (ICCPR), and the UN Convention on the Rights of the Child.

United Nations High Commissioner for Refugees

The UNHCR Geneva office issued revised guidelines on the detention of asylum-seekers in February 1999: *UNHCR Guidelines on the Detention of Asylum Seekers*. A copy of these guidelines is attached to *Bail: Guidance Notes for Adjudicators* (third edition, May 2003), at Appendix 2. That guidance is still valid, and it indicates that, in dealing with bail applications, regard should be had to UNHCR's Guidelines, particularly Guidelines 2 and 3 (at para. 1.3).

In their introduction, the UNHCR Guidelines state that the detention of asylum-seekers is 'inherently undesirable', and that this is particularly so in the case of vulnerable groups such as single women, children, unaccompanied minors and those with special medical or psychological needs. The UNHCR then list ten guidelines. As the Guidance Notes to the AIT indicate, UNHCR Guidelines 2 and 3 are the most important.

Guideline 2

Guideline 2 is headed 'General Principle'. It states:

'As a general principle asylum-seekers should not be detained.

According to Article 14 of the Universal Declaration of Human Rights, the right to seek and enjoy asylum is recognised as a basic human right. In exercising this right asylum-seekers are often forced to arrive at, or enter, a territory illegally. However the position of asylum-seekers differs fundamentally from that of ordinary immigrants in that they may not be in a position to comply with the legal formalities for entry. This element, as well as the fact that asylum-seekers have often had traumatic experiences, should be taken into account in determining any restrictions on freedom of movement based on illegal entry and presence.'

Guideline 3

Guideline 3 states that there is a presumption against detention, and that it should only 'exceptionally be resorted to' for the following reasons, after full consideration of all possible alternatives, or where other methods of control have been unsuccessful. It should only be carried out when it is 'proportional' to do so, and it should be for a 'minimal' period. The only permissible reasons for detention are:

- to verify identity;
- for the purposes of a preliminary interview to determine the 'elements on which the claim for asylum is based' (this is only in order to obtain the essential facts, not for the full determination procedure);
- where the applicant has destroyed or used fraudulent travel or identity documents in order to mislead the authorities of the state, or where they have refused to cooperate with the authorities;
- in order to protect national security and public order.

Remaining UNHCR Guidelines

Useful as they are, there is not enough space here to cover the other Guidelines. As a summary:

- Guideline 1 deals simply with the scope of the Guidelines;
- Guideline 4 looks at alternatives to detention (conditions of release and monitoring);
- Guideline 5 deals with procedural safeguards (reviews of detention and access to representatives);
- Guidelines 6–9 deal with the detention of minors, other vulnerable people, women and stateless persons;
- Guideline 10 looks at conditions of detention.

Note that, in discussing vulnerable people, Guideline 7 recommends that unaccompanied elderly people, torture or trauma victims, and those with a mental or physical disability, should only be detained if a qualified doctor certifies that detention will not adversely affect their health and well-being.

International Covenant on Civil and Political Rights

Further guidance may be obtained from the UN International Covenant on Civil and Political Rights (ICCPR). The ICCPR is ratified by the UK, but is not incorporated into UK law. It gives an indication of the approach to detention in international human rights law. Article 9 of the ICCPR provides protection to the individual against arbitrary detention. Applying the ICCPR in relation to the detention of boat people seeking asylum in *A v Australia*, the UN Human Rights Committee stated that the detention of an asylum-seeker could be considered arbitrary if it was:

'…not necessary in all the circumstances of the case, for example, to prevent flight or interference with evidence.'

UN Convention on the Rights of the Child

The UN Convention on the Rights of the Child states:

'37. Parties shall ensure that:

c) No child shall be deprived of his or her liberty unlawfully or arbitrarily. The arrest, detention or imprisonment of a child shall be in conformity with the law and shall be used only as a measure of last resort and for the shortest appropriate period of time.'

IS THE DETENTION LAWFUL?

On the face of it, the powers to detain people for immigration reasons, as they are written into the legislation, appear very wide. People can be detained 'pending' various forms of immigration action – pending examination, a decision on their case, or their removal or deportation. Despite this, there are strict legal limits to the powers. In the High Court case of *Hardial Singh*, Woolf J (as he was then) said:

'Whilst of course, Parliament is entitled to confer powers of administrative detention without trial, the courts will see to it that where such a power is conferred, the statute that confers it will be strictly and narrowly *construed* and its *operation* and effect will be supervised by the court to high standards.' (emphasis added)

So, the limits to the legal powers come from:

- the narrow interpretation of the powers of detention as applied by the courts (the above quote uses the lawyers' term 'construe' – this just means 'interpret');
- the ability of the courts to review very carefully decisions of the Home Office when it uses detention powers (the above quote uses the lawyers' term 'supervise', which means the same thing). In any case, this may

involve considering: the legality of detention policy; whether detention was in line with policy; whether the detention was reasonable and proportionate; whether the decision has been properly and carefully taken with all relevant matters considered; and whether fair procedures have been used;

- the right to liberty and security contained in Article 5 ECHR.

Applying the above limits, detention may be ruled to be unlawful for a range of reasons. The circumstances in which detention is unlawful are traditionally divided between:

1) cases in which there is no *power* to detain; and

2) cases in which, although there is a power to detain, the power has been *used* (or 'exercised') unlawfully.

In order to help explain the different circumstances, we have stuck to the above categorisation. In each of these two categories, we have set out further subcategories. Note, however, that dividing lines in this area are not at all easy to draw: the lines are blurred and overlapping, and cases may fall into more than one category. The traditional categorisations are also more uncertain since the decision of the House of Lords in *Khadir* (for the details of which, ▶see 956–7). So our categorisation and the examples we have given are for guidance and explanation purposes only – they should not be thought of as a straitjacket.

For the legality of detention in the case of age-disputed minors, ▶see Chapter 22, at 688–91.

Challenging detention in the courts If the lawfulness of the detention is going to be challenged in the courts, the above categorisation is an important consideration for which procedure should be used to challenge it. For details ▶see Chapter 32, at 985–7.

Civil claims Where a person is unlawfully detained under immigration powers, they will be able to claim compensation in the form of damages. This was recently confirmed by the Court of Appeal in *ID & others v The Home Office*, despite the Home Office's attempts to limit the circumstances in which damages can be claimed. For full details about unlawful detention and civil claims, ▶see 1175–81, 1205–10.

No power to detain

The following cases are examples of situations in which there may be no power to detain.

Non-statutory purpose

Under the 1971 Act, detention may only be used for the purpose of carrying out the particular immigration action that the legislation sets down. It cannot be used for any other purpose (see *Hardial Singh*). The purposes referred to in the legislation are generally 'pending' examination of the applicant, a decision being made on their case or their removal, deportation, or departure. Examples of circumstances in which a person is not held for a statutory purpose are as follows.

- If the real reason for detaining them is not the particular immigration action justifying detention – i.e. if an applicant is detained as a form of punishment, intimidation or coercion, for example to encourage them into making a 'voluntary' departure (however, this may be very difficult to prove).

- Although the immigration authorities initially intended to carry out the immigration action referred to, they no longer intend to do so (see *Khadir* at para. 32). This may happen, for example, if the applicant is detained pending removal to their particular country, and the immigration authorities then adopt a blanket policy of not returning anyone to that country for the foreseeable future but neglect to release the applicant.

- There is no prospect of actually carrying out the immigration action, or the prospect is so remote as to make it irrational to continue to detain. This occurred in the Privy Council case of *Tan Te Lam* (decided under very similar legislation relating to detention), in which the state effectively accepted that there was no possibility of removing the applicants because the Vietnamese government simply would not accept their return (see further *Khadir* at paras 4, 32–3. ▶see 957). A similar case was *Youseff v Home Office*, in which the claimant brought a claim for damages on the basis that his detention pending his removal to Egypt was unlawful. The High Court held that, although Mr Youseff's initial detention was lawful, it became unlawful and amounted to a false imprisonment when it became clear that negotiations with the Egyptian authorities would not be successful in providing sufficient guarantees that he would not be subjected to Article 3 treatment on his return.

Note that in *Saadi & Others*, the House of Lords held, in relation to the power to detain an asylum-seeker in order to examine their claim, that the Home Office did not have to show that it was *necessary* to detain in order to fulfil the statutory purpose. So the Home Office did not have to show that the immigration purpose could not be carried out without detention in the sense that the applicant would otherwise abscond. It was enough that the detention was required in order to reach a *speedy* decision (para. 24). For further details about this case, ▶see below 923.

Statutory conditions not satisfied

Another situation in which there may be no power to detain is where the detainee simply does not fall within the circumstances described in the legislation. This is where, on the facts of the case, there is no power for immigration authorities to take the immigration action against the person which is the purpose of the detention. For example, there is no immigration power to remove a British citizen, and so there can be no immigration detention power for the purposes of such a removal. That is a very clear example, but there may be other cases where the basic facts that give rise to a power of immigration enforcement (for example, a breach of conditions of leave), and therefore detention, simply do not exist.

Note, however, as set out in the table above (▶902–5), that many of the powers are triggered if the immigration authorities have 'reasonable grounds' for suspicion that the person who has been refused entry is, for example, an illegal entrant and that they are therefore liable for removal. So, where a person comes to the attention of the immigration authorities, and if they cannot immediately decide what the person's status is, detention is permissible provided that there are reasonable grounds to suspect them of falling into the relevant categories. *However*, In *O'Hara v Chief Constable of the RUC*, the House of Lords explained the meaning of 'reasonable suspicion' in the policing context. It decided that (1) there must be a genuine suspicion on the part of the individual officer, and (2) there must be objective, reasonable grounds for the suspicion. It is clear that a mere suspicion, or 'hunch', will not be enough. If detention is carried out on the basis of 'reasonable grounds' but these conditions are not satisfied, it is likely to be unlawful.

Detention 'unlawful' under Article 5(1) ECHR

The first requirement under Article 5 is that any deprivation of liberty must be 'in accordance with a procedure prescribed by law' and 'lawful'. These words include the law of the particular country. Therefore, any detention contrary to UK law will also be in breach of Article 5 (see *Winterwerp*, ECtHR; *Evans* No 2, HL).

However, in order to be 'lawful' under Article 5, there must also be a clear domestic law that underpins the detention in the first place. A good example is the case of *Amuur* (ECtHR), where a number of Somali asylum-seekers were detained in an airport transit zone in Paris. They could depart by aircraft, but they could not enter France. The French authorities argued that they were not actually being 'detained', because they were free to leave. The Court, however, held that holding the asylum-seekers in those circumstances was a 'deprivation of their liberty' under Article 5. The Court also held that the detention was arbitrary, and therefore unlawful, because French law did not make any proper allowance for it in those circumstances (probably because it did not consider it to be detention). In particular, the asylum-seekers had no proper access to legal and other assistance. Generally, the 1971 Act and other legislation provides the underpinning for immigration detention in the UK (▶see 899, 902–5).

In order to be 'lawful' under Article 5, detention must also not be 'arbitrary'. This consideration is more likely to arise in considering the *use* of the power to detain (▶see below).

Detention not for a purpose permitted by Article 5(1)(f) ECHR

Article 5(1)(f) ECHR states:

'5.1 Everyone has the right to liberty and security of person. No-one shall be deprived of his liberty save in the following cases and in accordance with a procedure prescribed by law:

...

f) the lawful arrest or detention of a person to prevent his effecting an unauthorised entry into the country or of a person against whom action is being taken with a view to deportation or extradition.'

Therefore, under Article 5, immigration detention can be carried out for one of two reasons only:

1) to 'prevent [the person] effecting an unauthorised entry into the country' (the first part of Article 5(1)(f));

2) where 'action is being taken with a view to [the person's] deportation or extradition' (the second part of Article 5(1)(f)).

We look at each in turn.

The first part of Article 5(1)(f) The first part covers those who wish to be admitted to a country. In *Saadi & Others*, the House of Lords ruled that detention simply for the purposes of examining an asylum claim (i.e. for the purposes of deciding whether to grant leave on the basis of asylum), even where there was no risk of the applicant absconding, fell within the first part. It was therefore not contrary to Article 5 (paras 35–6). As with the second part, the Lords also ruled that detention could be justified under the first part even if it was not 'necessary' to prevent an unauthorised entry (paras 37–8). Effectively, this meant that it was permissible to detain for the purpose of administrative convenience. This case was a challenge to the whole basis of detention at Oakington Reception Centre. Dr Saadi's case was unanimously declared admissable by the European Court of Human Rights on 27 September 2005 (▶see further 677–8, 886, 931). The applicant's argument is that he was detained contrary to his human rights because:

- detention for the sole purpose of examining a claim to asylum is not carried out in order to prevent a person from effecting an unauthorised entry;

- the detention was arbitrary and disproportionate;

- he was discriminatorily selected for detention contrary to Article 14 taken with Article 5 ECHR;

- insufficient and inadequate reasons were given for his detention contrary to Article 5(2) ECHR (*Saadi v UK*, ECHR).

The second part of Article 5(1)(f) The second part ('against whom action is being taken with a view to deportation or extradition') covers those who have been in the UK, probably for some time, and whom the host state wants to remove. 'Deportation' in Article 5(1)(f) means any form of enforced departure. In the UK, it therefore includes deportation and any other form of removal (▶see 990–1). 'Extradition' is, of course, a criminal procedure, used for returning those who are charged with criminal offences in another country.

In *Chahal*, the Secretary of State made a decision to deport an Indian national, who had lived in the UK for many years, on the grounds of national security. He was detained. Following the decision to deport, Mr Chahal made a claim for asylum. His detention had to be justified under the second part of Article 5(1)(f) because he was clearly an after-entry case, and his departure was going to be enforced. The ECtHR commented that the second part of Article 5(1)(f) did not mean that the state had to show that it was 'reasonably necessary' to detain Mr Chahal – for example, to prevent him absconding or committing offences – in order to deport him. The state only had to show that action was being taken to enforce the departure of the person. The Court of Appeal has also confirmed that this is the law as far as the second part of Article 5(1)(f) is concerned (*Sezek*).

Under the second part, deportation must also be 'possible', because deportation proceedings must be in progress. They cannot be progressed if deportation cannot be achieved (*Ali*, EComHR). The second part of Article 5 could not, therefore, be used to justify detaining a person who cannot be removed – for example, because they are permanently unfit to travel, or because the country to which they could legally be removed simply will not accept them despite any negotiations.

Unlawful derogation from Article 5

Under the Anti-terrorism Crime and Security Act 2001, the government attempted to set aside ('derogate' from) its obligations under Article 5 in order to detain foreign nationals suspected of international terrorism. In *A & others v SSHD*, the House of Lords held that this was unlawful (for further details, ▶see 901–2).

Unlawful *use* of the power to detain

Even if there is a power to detain, in order for the detention to be lawful the power must be exercised lawfully. Examples of unlawful use of the power to detain are given below. Again, the categories may overlap and, on the facts of some cases, there may be an overlap with the 'no power' cases outlined above.

Unreasonable length of time

In *Hardial Singh*, Woolf J set out important limitations on detention powers relating to the *length of time* a person could be detained for. The points he set out were later confirmed by the House of Lords in *Saadi* (paras 22, 25–6) and the Privy Council in *Tan Te Lam*, which concerned the detention by the authorities in Hong Kong of certain Vietnamese boat-people who were claiming asylum.

Hardial Singh principles relating to time The principles set out were:

1) A person may only be detained for as long as it is reasonably necessary to carry out the immigration action for which the power is given.

2) The immigration authorities must act with speed to ensure that the immigration action is carried out within a 'reasonable time'.

3) If it appears that the purpose cannot be carried out within a reasonable time, then detention will no longer be lawful, and the person must be released (this is a separate requirement and sometimes means that the applicant should be released even though the period in (1) above has not yet passed, ▶see 929, *R(I) v SSHD*).

For many years, it has been thought that these restrictions limit the actual power to detain a person. However, the House of Lords has recently clarified that, in fact, they are restrictions on the use of the power to detain (see *Khadir* at paras 32–3). The result is the same: if the principles are breached, the detention will be unlawful.

Article 5 and prolonged detention Similarly to the *Hardial Singh* principles, detention for an excessive period, where the immigration authorities are not taking prompt action, will also be unlawful under Article 5. In *Chahal* (see above), the European Court stated that the deportation or removal proceedings must be 'in progress', and must be being carried out with 'due diligence' by the state. If they are not, then the detention will be unlawful. *Chahal* itself was an exceptional case, because the applicant was a Sikh separatist leader whom the Home Office wanted to deport on the grounds that he was a threat to national security. The Court held that, even though the deportation proceedings were being conducted with due diligence, and even given the national security considerations, five years was still an excessively long period of time for him to be detained. Clearly, in other cases, periods of much less than five years will be considered to be excessive.

Facts of *Hardial Singh* and *Mahmod* In *Hardial Singh* itself, following a two-year prison sentence for burglary, the applicant was served with a deportation order and detained for five months under immigration powers, pending his removal. During this time, the Home Office was trying to secure a travel document for him from the Indian High Commission, so that he could be returned to India. He had no documents to prove his identity, and the Indian authorities would not give him a travel document. The Court adjourned the hearing for a few days, stating that the applicant should be released unless it was possible to remove him within a very short period of time.

In *Mahmod* (*Wasfi Suleman*) (HC), the applicant had to be released because the Home Office had been unable to obtain the agreement of the German authorities to accept him back. The applicant had refugee status in Germany, but had been convicted of drugs offences in the UK and had been detained for ten months after he was eligible for parole. The Court found that the reasonable period had 'certainly' been 'exceeded'. It stated that it was

'...entirely unacceptable that this man should have been detained for the length of time he has while nothing but fruitless negotiations have been carried on.'

What factors are taken into account in deciding what is a 'reasonable period'? What counts as a 'reasonable period' will depend on the circumstances of the case. In *Hardial Singh*, the Court took into account the following matters:

- the applicant was prepared to return to India;
- the Home Office had dragged their feet in taking the necessary action;
- the applicant was distressed and had attempted suicide.

As indicated in *Hardial Singh*, an applicant who is not cooperating with the authorities or the removal process may be detained for longer while arrangements continue to be made (see also *Tan Te Lam*, PC; *Chahal*, ECtHR). When assessing the actions of the Home Office and the likely period of future detention, the court will, however, be very careful not to second-guess what the government says about diplomatic negotiations (see *Youssef v the Home Office*).

A good recent example of the application of the *Hardial Singh* time principles and the factors taken into account is the case of *R (I) v SSHD* (▶see table below at 927–9).

Obtaining travel documents and agreements with other states The inability of the government to obtain a travel document or the agreement of the country of origin to accept the return of the detainee, which cause prolonged detention, has been a common issue. In a letter to Lord Avebury dated 9 August 2004, the minister explained the problem as follows:

'The vast majority of countries worldwide recognise and accept the use by the United Kingdom of either a document issued under the terms of the Chicago Convention, (or) the European Union Standard Format Letter/Laissez-Passer (commonly known as the EU Letter). However, a number of countries do not do so and insist instead upon official applications being made for their own nationality specific Emergency Travel Documents. Such countries will usually only issue documents to those in respect of whom they are satisfied as to nationality and identity, and their processes, criteria, and evidential requirements vary considerably. In many cases, receiving countries insist upon carrying out detailed and lengthy verification enquiries in the receiving country and the Home Office has no direct control over the time taken for such checks to be carried out. In order to address these difficulties, the Immigration Service Documentation Unit was created in 1998 in order to coordinate document applications and to liaise directly with Embassies and High Commissions in order to seek and secure adequate documentation in order to effect returns. Officials negotiate workable arrangements for securing documentation, manage the submission of applications, and liaise with Consular Representatives in individual cases with considerable success, and continue to work hard to prosecute successfully the document applications that are presented to receiving countries.'

In *Amirthanathan*, the Court of Appeal seemed to suggest that the need to document a detainee might itself be a good reason for detention (see at paras 71–2, and para. 18(3), Sch 2 1971 Act).

From 22 September 2004, under the 2004 Act, a new criminal offence was created of failing to cooperate with instructions from the Home Office which will help in the obtaining of a travel document in order for removal to take place (s35 2004 Act). For example, people may be required to: provide information or documents to the Home Office; to obtain documents; to cooperate with an application made to another government; to complete forms accurately and completely; and to attend interviews and answer questions. Failure to comply is an offence punishable by up to two years' imprisonment.

The Home Office often says that it is in the process of obtaining agreement, but it is worth trying to pin officers down as to exactly what steps have been taken, what the response of the other government is, and when removal can be expected. Disclosure of this information may make it clear that removal of the applicant will not be possible within a reasonable period. As will be clear from *R(I) v SSHD* (▶see table below), that would mean that the detainee should be released immediately, even if they had not yet been detained for what would otherwise be a 'reasonable' period.

The worst delays in obtaining travel documentation have occurred in cases of detainees from China, Algeria, Pakistan and India, but they have occurred in relation to other countries as well. By March 2003, the Home Office reported that the Algerian Embassy had agreed to prioritise documentation for detained nationals but, depending on the amount of information available, cases could still take weeks or months to resolve.

In relation to Chinese nationals, a recent programme in 2005 called 'Operation Elucidate' has been operated. This programme was agreed between the Home Office and the Chinese Embassy to deal with documentation issues preventing the removal of Chinese nationals. Detained Chinese nationals are interviewed by Chinese Embassy staff at Tinsley House, and then moved to other centres while the process is completed.

APPLICATION OF THE *HARDIAL SINGH* PRINCIPLES: THE CASE OF *R(I) V SSHD*

R (I) v SSHD (CA) is a good example of the application of the principles in *Hardial Singh*. It is also useful in analysing the factors that should be taken into account when the Home Office decides to detain.

Facts of the case

The case concerned an Afghani asylum-seeker who had been refused asylum but granted exceptional leave to remain, and who was then convicted of indecent assault. He was sentenced to custody and ordered to be deported on the recommendation of the criminal court. At the end of his criminal sentence, he was detained under immigration powers. During this time, he claimed asylum again, but this was refused and an appeal was dismissed. However, there were no direct flights to Afghanistan, and the UK was in continued negotiations to secure forced returns. A means of making voluntary returns was established just before the hearing in the Court of Appeal.

An application for *habeas corpus* (▶see 987) and judicial review was brought for his release, which was finally ordered by a majority decision of the Court of Appeal after he had spent approximately 16 months in custody.

It must be remembered that this was a case involving criminal conduct.

Decision of the Court of Appeal

In assessing the lawfulness of the continued detention, the Court of Appeal stated the following:

- in deciding whether removal was going to be possible within a 'reasonable' further period, the length of time the appellant had *already* been detained was of central relevance (paras 20, 26, 48);

- the risk of the appellant re-offending was a generally relevant circumstance – if it was highly likely that the appellant would commit serious offences, that would justify detention for a substantially longer period of time (paras 29, 48–9)

- the risk of the appellant absconding was also a generally relevant consideration (paras 29, 48–9). However, the Court stated

  'The relevance of the likelihood of absconding, if proved, should not be overstated. Carried to its logical conclusion, it could become a trump card that carried the day for the Secretary of State in every case where such a risk was made out regardless of all other considerations, not least the length of the period of detention. That would be a wholly unacceptable outcome where human liberty is at stake.' (para. 53)

- the conditions in which the detainee is being kept and the effect of the detention on them and their family were relevant circumstances (para. 48). In the present case, the appellant was in his cell for over 19 hours per day, there were no places available on work or educational programmes within the prison for him, and he was depressed and needed medication to sleep (paras 18, 56);

- the nature of the obstacles preventing removal was relevant (para. 48);

- the speed and effectiveness of the steps taken by the Home Office to deal with the obstacles were relevant (para. 48);

- on the facts of the case, given that the appellant had been detained for 16 months and that the Home Office could only show a 'hope' of forcibly returning him in the near future, it needed substantially more evidence of a risk of re-offending (and not just absconding – of which there was a risk but not a probability) to justify continued detention (paras 37, 56);

- whether the appellant would accept voluntary repatriation could be relevant, but only because it was *evidence* of whether the appellant would abscond if released – refusal of voluntary repatriation could not alone make a period of detention reasonable (paras 50–2, 54). It was of limited relevance in this case because: (1) the possibility of voluntary departure had only just come to light, and (2) the appellant was claiming asylum, and it was therefore not surprising that he should refuse voluntary repatriation – the appellant had not yet exhausted the asylum appeal process: he still had a right to seek leave to appeal to the IAT, and so this factor did not necessarily mean that he would abscond (paras 5, 31-32, 37, 50, 54);

- an appellant will generally not be able to rely on delays caused by their own asylum application (see also *Chahal*, ECtHR); but because the applicant could not be returned for political and practical reasons during the whole period of the asylum claim, the claim was not to be treated as the *cause* of the delay in removal for the purposes of assessing whether detention had become unlawful (paras 35–6, 55);

- the burden is on the Secretary of State to show, on the balance of probabilities, that a person is being properly detained 'pending' removal (para. 37);

- there may be circumstances in which, although a 'reasonable' period has not yet passed, it becomes clear that the detained person cannot be removed within a 'reasonable' period; if that is the case, the Home Office must release the detainee (paras 47, 57).

Detention in breach of published policy

Where the Home Office detains someone in breach of its own published policy criteria, the detention will be unlawful (see *Nadarajah* CA, paras 35–6, 54 and ▶see above 909–17). In *Konan*, the High Court held that removal could no longer be 'imminent' after a judicial review application had been lodged. It was therefore in breach of Home Office policy and unlawful. Of course, this does not mean that no-one who has made a claim for judicial review to challenge removal can be detained. They cannot be detained on the grounds that their removal is 'imminent' *but* there could be other reasons for their detention.

In *R (Johnson) v SSHD*, an ailing 64 year old Jamaican detainee was kept at Oakington for five-and-a-half weeks before a decision was made on his asylum and human rights application (after which he was detained for a few more weeks). This was despite clear Home Office statements to the effect that detention at this fast track centre would be kept under review and that, if the claim could not be decided within the period of one week timetabled, the detainee would be released. The Home Office argued that the statements made did not amount to a policy but only a 'target' time. The High Court held the Home Office to the timetable it had set, and found that the detention became unlawful after the sixth day. Subsequently, the Home Office changed its policy (▶see 678).

In other cases, the courts have been similarly strict in ensuring that detention is rational and justified in the light of Home Office policy. In *B*, by reference to similar policy criteria as those outlined in Tables 1 and 2 above at ▶909–14, the High Court held that the continuing detention of an asylum-seeker for two months after his identity had been established and sureties offered, was unlawful. In *AKB*, McCullough J indicated that the possession of false documents alone was not a good reason to detain an asylum-seeker, and that all the factors needed to be balanced. In *Ferko*, the High Court dealt with the practice of detaining heads of households in order to deter other family members from absconding. That approach was held to be lawful only so long as there was a reasonable apprehension that the person being detained is otherwise likely to abscond. The Home Office OEM had itself stated that:

'Detention for purposes such as deterrence to others where detention is not necessary for the purposes of removal of the individual is not compatible with Article 5 ECHR.'

For detention policy in the case of age-disputed minors, and challenges to the lawfulness of detention in those cases (including *R (I and O) v SSHD*), ▶see 688–91.

Unlawful policy

Detention based on a policy that is itself unlawful will also be unlawful. In order to determine whether detention policy was lawful in *Nadarajah*, the Court of Appeal considered whether it allowed treatment that was 'arbitrary' or 'irrational' (para. 60).

Unreasonable and/or disproportionate detention

Under Article 5 ECHR, detention must be 'lawful'. Although this means that it must, firstly, be in accordance with domestic (i.e. UK) law (▶see above at 922), this also protects people from detention that is 'arbitrary'. Detentions that are 'arbitrary' under Article 5 ECHR would probably also be declared unlawful by the High Court, applying ordinary UK principles of common and public law as being 'unreasonable'. Examples of detention that may be unlawful on this basis are as follows.

Disproportionate detention 'Proportionality' is a legal term used in many contexts. It sounds complex, but in fact, in essence, it is straightforward. It really means that public authorities should not take a sledgehammer to crack open a nut. If there are less drastic ways of achieving the objective, then they should be used instead. There must be a balance between the measures taken towards the objective being pursued and the consequences that the measures will have for those affected. Detention is a drastic step. In each case, when the two are balanced against each other, there must be a reasonable relationship of 'proportionality' between the serious step of using detention (with the effect that has on the detainee) and the aim of that detention in the interests of immigration control (and see *Evans* (No 2) HL, pp. 38C–E; *Amirthanathan* in the High Court, paras 50–1, 56, 60; *Saadi* HL, paras 27, 44–7; *Nadarajah & Amirthanathan* CA, paras 50–3; *ID & Others* CA, paras 100, 123, 130).

In *Saadi*, the House of Lords decided that, in principle, the detention did not have to be *necessary* in the sense of preventing the applicants from absconding (in which case immigration control over them would be prevented). So, in carrying out this balancing exercise, what is it that is balanced? The answer seems to be that there must be proportionality between the *reason given* by the immigration authorities for using detention, on the one hand, and the detention and its effects, on the other. In *Saadi* the *reason* given for the detention was not the risk of the detainee absconding, but the speed of decision-making – i.e. decisions on the applicants' cases could be reached much more quickly if they were detained (see also the way in which the House of Lords describes the question relating to proportionality at the end of para. 27 and para. 44).

Factors relevant to this balancing exercise will include the length and physical conditions of the detention, as well as the strength of the reason put forward by the Home Office (as in *Saadi*). We suggest the following factors will also be relevant:

- the effect of the detention on the individual and their family;
- the age of the person, and their other personal circumstances;
- whether the person is responsible for the situation that may have led to their detention;
- whether other conditions of temporary admission could be used that would be enough to satisfy the requirements for which detention has been used. For the conditions of temporary admission, including the new forms of electronic surveillance, ▶see 952–5.

Arbitrary and unpredictable detention Detention must not be carried out in an unpredictable way, on the basis of unknown and unpublished criteria. In *Nadarajah & Amirthanathan*, the detention of the applicants was ruled unlawful because the Home Office relied on unpublished criteria that it would not have regard to an indication from representatives that an appeal or judicial review proceedings were about to be brought (paras 64–72). The recent uncertainty over Home Office detention policy may raise questions here (▶see 908).

No proper assessment A detention carried out on the basis of a flawed assessment of the circumstances of the applicant may also be unlawful. A good example is the case of *R (Mohamed) v SSHD.* In that case, the Court severely criticised a bail summary prepared by the Home Office containing reasons for opposing bail before an adjudicator. The summary had given the wrong date for when asylum had been claimed, which made it look as though the claim was late and opportunistic. Also, the summary made the 'utterly erroneous' claim that the applicant, who had been convicted of a serious offence, had committed a *further* offence. There was also a failure properly to consider the fact that the applicant's asylum appeal had been allowed (although the Home Office wished to appeal). The Court found that all of this showed that the Home Office had failed in its ongoing duty to assess and review the claimant's circumstances so as to come to a proper decision to maintain detention:

'There is no evidence of careful reappraisal at [the time of the bail summary] or of any attempt to weigh the long period of immigration detention against the perceived prospects of success [of the Home Office] appeal, and the duration of the appeal process. The Secretary of State was entitled to consider his position, but it was incumbent upon him to address the continued detention of the claimant with the utmost care...' (para. 20)

Unfortunately, such failings are not unusual. In *Johnson* (▶see above), the Court found that the continued detention of the applicant might have been influenced by completely incorrect information apparently held on file (and also used in a bail summary) that the applicant had been arrested for motoring offences. In *Konan*, too, the Court referred to the information put forward in the bail summary as 'misleading'.

Filing errors Overlapping with cases in the above category are cases where the Home Office gets its files mixed up, or where there is some other incompetence or error that results in detention. Such cases will also result in unlawful detention. Indeed, in *ID*, the Court confirmed that compensation could be claimed in these cases as in other cases (para. 121).

Failure to take into account relevant considerations

In *ID & Others v Home Office*, the Court of Appeal noted that the failure to take into account relevant considerations – for example, in the case of the detention of a minor, having no regard to the requirement in the UN Convention on the Rights of the Child that detention should be a matter of last resort (▶see 919 above) – can mean that the decision to detain is unlawful. However, in line with the findings in *Saadi* that the short period of detention in Oakington was lawful, the Court did not think that a challenge on these grounds in the present case could succeed (paras 111, 122).

Failure to take into account a change of circumstances

Detention that may be lawful at the outset may become unlawful due to a change in the circumstances. So, in *R v (1) Special Adjudicator (2) Secretary of State ex p. B*, the Administrative Court granted a declaration that detention following a significant change in the strength of the asylum claim prior to eventual release was unlawful.

31 Detention places, conditions and procedures

While Chapter 30 deals with the powers of detention, the policy for detaining people, and when detention is lawful, this chapter discusses the conditions of detention, and some of the procedures that apply when people are detained, and during their detention.

We begin by looking at current government policy for the expansion of immigration detention (▶below). We then discuss the different places in which detainees can be kept, Home Office policy on immigration detention in prisons, and transfers of detainees within the immigration detention estate (▶934–9). The main places of immigration detention are 'removal centres'. Since the time of the 2002 White Paper, this has been the name given to what were previously known simply as 'immigration detention centres' (see also s66 2002 Act). The purpose of this name change was to underline that detention is primarily part of the process of removing failed asylum-seekers and others. In reality, many asylum-seekers are detained for the purpose of fast tracking their asylum claims. Very approximately, 85 per cent of detainees are asylum-seekers.

We then address some procedural aspects of immigration detention: the need to give reasons for detention, to provide updates on those reasons, and to review the need for detention frequently (▶939–40). Detention in removal centres is regulated by the 'Detention Centre Rules', and we summarise these at ▶940–1. For the requirement for ministerial approval for the prolonged detention of children ▶see 916; and for procedures for detaining families, ▶see 998–1000.

Finally, we discuss some of the reports of HM Chief Inspector of Prisons, which cover places of immigration detention. We also look at some other reports that cover various aspects of immigration detention (▶942–8).

EXPANSION OF DETENTION

The five-year strategy is clear that detention is to play an increased role. It projects that, by the end of 2005, up to 30 per cent of new asylum claims will be fast tracked. It further states:

'We will expand the detention capacity we have for those whose claims are considered under our current fast track processes, for those suitable for a quick decision. We will open a new detention facility for single females linked to the fast track process.' (*Controlling Our Borders: Making Migration Work for Britain. Five-year strategy for asylum and immigration*, para. 68)

As to those who fail in their claims, the Prime Minister's foreword states:

'And over time, we will move towards the point where it becomes the norm that those who fail can be detained ...'

Detention instead of 'accommodation centre' Partly in line with these plans, on 14 June 2005 the minister announced that, although the government was not going to proceed with the planned construction of an 'accommodation centre' outside Bicester in Oxfordshire, or any other accommodation centres, it was considering instead building a secure removal centre at the Bicester site, 'as part of an ongoing review and expansion of the removals estate'. This was part of the need to fast track asylum claims and closely control the whole process. The statement also notes the fall in numbers of asylum-seekers since the project for accommodation centres began in 2001 (Written Statement, Column 9WS, 'Accommodation Centres').

Contradiction in policy Previously, of course – and notably in *Saadi* – the government has made the point that the detained fast track processes were needed because of the *high* level of asylum-seekers, and the difficulty of processing them all. On government figures, at the time that case was decided in the House of Lords, in October 2002, asylum applications were running at 9,000 per month. By February 2005, they were running at under 3,000 per month. Indeed, the five-year strategy, also published in February 2005, points to a drop from the previous 'peak' of 67 per cent (Five-year strategy, Executive Summary at para. 1, report at para. 27, and see Annex 2). Official figures released in the summer of 2005 note further falls in the numbers claiming asylum. To follow the logic through, given the fall in numbers, it might be expected that the government would reduce the extent to which it has to resort to the drastic step of detention. However, the government's plans are quite the opposite. Now that numbers are falling, it seems that yet more detained fast track processes are necessary. The new detained fast track asylum process for women detained at Yarls Wood began in May 2005.

PLACES OF DETENTION

Detainees can be held in immigration removal centres, prisons and police stations. They may also be held in short-term holding facilities at ports, screening units, and appeal hearing centres. The recent reports of HM Inspectorate of Prisons was very critical of the conditions found in several short-term holding facilities (▶944–5).

Immigration removal centres

As was noted in the introduction, immigration detention centres are now called 'removal centres'. The centres are as follows (▶see 1496–7 for contact details and visiting arrangements):

- **Campsfield House** in Kidlington, near Oxford. Subject to some planning problems it is to be expanded, but in the meantime is being refurbished.

- **Colnbrook** at Harmondsworth. Opened in August 2004. The main intention was to provide a removal centre for the London area, and a facility for detaining those picked up in the London and Thames Valley areas, and for use as a short-term facility, to relieve police cells in London, and also to detain those with behaviour problems. It is more secure than other centres.

- **Dover**

- **Dungavel** in Scotland. A former country estate mansion house, previously used by the Scottish Prison Service as a prison, before being refurbished and used as a detention centre. It has been controversial because children have been detained there, sometimes for long periods.

- **Harmondsworth**, near Heathrow Airport. For the detained fast track asylum process for men that operates here, ▶see 673–4, 678–81.

- **Haslar**

- **Lindholme**

- **Oakington** in Cambridgeshire. Opened in March 2000 in order to process asylum claims that could be determined 'quickly', it includes family accommodation, but it will close in September 2006 when the site will be handed back to the Ministry of Defence for housing redevelopment. For the fast track procedure operated here, ▶see 673, 677–8.

- **Tinsley House**, near Gatwick Airport. Opened in May 1996 as the first purpose-built detention centre, it includes facilities to hold families briefly – either just after arrival, or just prior to removal.

- **Yarls Wood** in Bedford. Now operates a fast track asylum determination procedure for women, and has a small hearing centre nearby, ▶see 673–4, 678–81.

The Detention Centre Rules 2001 state that the purpose of immigration removal centres is to provide for the:

'…secure but humane accommodation of detained persons in a relaxed regime with as much freedom of movement and association as possible, consistent with maintaining a safe and secure environment, and to encourage and assist detained persons to make the most productive use of their time whilst respecting, in particular, their dignity and the right to individual expression.' (Rule 3)

Immigration service detention centres are intended to have a less structured regime than prisons, with easier access for visitors and longer hours of association, when detainees are able to mix with each other, rather than being locked in cells.

The Detention Centre Rules also establish a visitors' committee for each detention centre, which makes reports to the Secretary of State and can hear complaints from detainees. Complaints relating to a person's detention can also be made to the detention centre manager, or to the Home Office.

For further details about the Detention Centre Rules, ▶see the table at 940–1.

Detention in prisons

Prisons are not appropriate places for immigration detention. The ethos of the prison service is geared towards punishment and addressing offending. Prisons were not designed for immigration detention. Because remand prisoners are intended to be held only for a short period, prison conditions for them are often poor. The regimes emphasise the need for security and control rather than the therapeutic needs of detained asylum-seekers, who may have suffered detention and torture before. It is also more difficult to maintain contact with legal representatives from within prison detention – i.e. to receive phone calls and faxes, apply for bail, and so on.

As long ago as 1998, the government's White Paper, *Fairer, Faster, Firmer*, gave a commitment to reduce the use of prisons as places of detention. The UNHCR has previously commented that no other country in Europe uses prisons in this way. The 2002 White Paper stated that the withdrawal of the use of local prisons as places of immigration detention had been completed in mid-January 2002. The Home Office stopped using the dedicated immigration accommodation section at HMP Rochester, and similar facilities at HMP Haslar and HMP Lindholme were re-designated as 'removal centres' and operate under the Detention Centre Rules. HMYOI Dover was also re-designated as a removal centre.

The Home Office has not, however, completely stopped using prisons for immigration detention. The 2002 White Paper states (para. 4.79):

'It will always remain necessary to hold small numbers of immigration detainees, including asylum seekers, in prison for reasons of safety. This would include suspected international terrorists detained under the Anti-terrorism, Crime and Security Act 2001. Any asylum seeker who is held on suspicion of having committed a criminal offence or is serving a custodial sentence will also be held in prison.'

In a further parliamentary answer, given on 2 July 2002, the minister stated that those facing criminal charges will 'not normally be held in an immigration removal centre'.

Further details of Home Office policy on when a detainee may be transferred to a prison were circulated to the Home Office's 'Detention User Group' in June 2002, and are set out in the table below (▶937).

Disturbances in detention centres and use of prisons

After a fire and disturbance at Yarls Wood in February 2002, the Secretary of State stated that 'detainees with a history of violent or criminal behaviour and those considered a danger to safety have been transferred to prison'. In July 2004, there were further disturbances caused by an apparent death by self-harm of a detainee facing imminent removal. There were also incidents at Dungavel Removal Centre. Some 196 detainees were moved to prisons all around the country as a result (others were removed to other detention centres). Other than the 17 or 18 persons who were charged by the police, the others were ultimately moved back to immigration detention. In 2005, there were hunger-strikes by detainees, at Campsfield and elsewhere, protesting against removal to Zimbabwe.

HOME OFFICE POLICY ON DETENTION IN PRISON

In June 2002, the Deputy Director of Detention Services circulated to the Home Office's 'Detention User Group' written policy setting out when a transfer from an immigration removal centre to a prison may take place. It stated that detainees may 'exceptionally' be moved to prisons on security or control grounds but that, first, all options for transfer within immigration detention facilities must be considered. In making a decision to transfer to prison, the following factors will be taken into account:

- **national security** – for example, whether there is information that a person is a member of a terrorist group, or has been engaged in terrorist offences (and see the Operational Enforcement Manual (OEM), Ch 38.15);

- **criminality** – for example, whether the detainee has convictions in the UK or abroad, in particular for violent, sexual or arson offences;

- **security** – for example, whether the detainee has escaped or attempted to escape from the police, from prison or from immigration custody, or planned or assisted others to do so;

- **control** – for example, whether the detainee has been involved in disorder, arson, violence or damage, or in planning such activities or assisting others to be involved in them.

The policy continues:

'In some cases decisions will be based on hard information such as convictions. In other cases judgements have to be made about the quality of criminal or other intelligence. The overriding concern is to protect society and the safety of detainees and staff, but with a presumption that detainees should remain in Immigration Service detention if at all possible.'

Decisions to transfer a detainee to prison are made at immigration inspector level and will be based on advice and information received from immigration service staff and contractors.

The cases of those detained in prisons are reviewed at deputy director level.

The above policy is set out in almost the same terms in Chapter 38 of the OEM as it reappeared on the website in autumn 2005 (see at Ch 38.10.1).

9

Detention in police cells

People can be detained under immigration powers in police cells, but they should only be kept there for very short periods of time. The Operational Enforcement Manual (OEM) states:

'Detainees should preferably only spend one night in police cells, with a normal maximum of two nights. In exceptional cases, a detainee may spend up to 5 nights continuously in a police cell (7 nights if removal directions have been set for within 48 hours) if, for instance, he is awaiting transfer to more suitable IS [Immigration Service] or Prison Service accommodation *and* the police are content to maintain detention. Such detention must be authorised by an Inspector, who must take into account the IS duty of care for detainees and the likelihood that police cells do not provide adequate facilities for this purpose in the long term.' (Ch 38.13.2)

Transfers between places of detention

Often 'operational reasons' mean that detainees are transferred between different places of immigration detention. This often causes distress and anxiety, and representatives have complained that they lose contact. Certain safeguards to the process were outlined in the letter of the minister, Lord Filkin, to John McDonnell MP, dated 21 March 2003. The letter states that:

- notice to the detainee should normally be given of a transfer of a person from one place of detention to another;
- in 'no instance' should the new location of the detainee be a secret;
- the detainee should be permitted to tell his representative and family of the proposed move.

In addition, the letter states:

'...a detainee who, for example, has a hospital appointment or an interview booked with their representative, would not normally be moved.'

In June 2002, the Deputy Director of Detention Services circulated to the Home Office's 'Detention User Group' written details concerning transfers within the immigration removal centre estate. Among the points set out were:

- transfers, for whatever reason, are kept to a minimum;
- removal centres have different facilities – some have better facilities for detainees who need to be temporarily removed from association (rule 40, Detention Centre Rules) or who are 'refractory' (resist control or discipline) (rule 42);
- in some cases, it will be sensible to move someone with a conviction for a sexual offence to an all-male centre;

- healthcare factors may influence a transfer on the basis of the healthcare facilities available;
- transfers may be arranged for domestic or compassionate reasons;
- transfers may be arranged in order to enable a detainee to be visited more easily by a representative;
- there may be operational reasons for transfers – for example, 'as a stage towards removal from the UK' or in order to 'create vacancies in a particular centre'.

REASONS, REVIEWS AND DETENTION CENTRE RULES

If detention has to take place, the first essential procedural requirement is that detainees are given clear reasons why their liberty is being taken from them. There is then an ongoing duty to review the case to see whether continued detention is really necessary. Detention in removal centres is regulated by the Detention Centre Rules 2001, which give detainees certain rights and protections.

Reasons for detention

Firstly it should be noted that detainees have an immediate right to be given reasons under the ECHR. Article 5(2) states:

'Everyone who is arrested shall be informed promptly, in a language which he understands, of the reasons for his arrest and of any charge against him.'

In April 1998, Lord Williams of Mostyn, speaking for the government in the House of Lords, accepted that the giving of written reasons improves decision-making (i.e. on whether to detain), and stated that detainees

'...will know and have at least a degree of moral consolation that their detention is not an unthinking exercise of administrative power.'

The question of adequacy of reasons for detention is one of the complaints made in the *Saadi* case which is to be heard by the European Court of Human Rights (▶see 923).

How and when are reasons given?

The Detention Centre Rules require that detainees be given initial reasons for detention, and then further reasons every month (rule 9). The Operational Enforcement Manual also states that when a person is detained, written reasons should be given at the time of the detention and at monthly intervals thereafter (Ch 38.6, 38.6.3, 38.7.1).

Since October 1999, immigration officers have served the initial written reasons for the decision to detain in the form of a checklist (Form IS 91R). The form allows officers to tick boxes to indicate the reasons for detention that apply in the particular case. For the reasons to be given on Form IS

91R (which are also a reflection of government policy), ▶see 913–4. A version of the form can also be found in the OEM, at Ch 38.6.3. The monthly reasons for continued detention are notified on Form IS 151F.

Information about bail Detainees are also told the power under which they are being detained, and they should be told of their rights to apply for bail (OEM Ch 38.6.3. This is normally done by providing detainees with Forms IS 98, IS 98A, and B1, so that detainees can apply for bail to the immigration authorities and/or to the AIT. The information given on all of these forms should, if necessary, be translated for detainees when they are detained.

Reviews of detention

Although the OEM and the Detention Centre Rules refer to *reasons* being given monthly (above), it seems that *reviews* of detention should be more frequent. It states that reviews of detention should take place 'after 24 hours by an Inspector and thereafter, as directed, usually weekly by an Inspector'. Detention should also be reviewed at the point of any change of circumstances. Detention is reviewed by a CIO or Inspector at 28 days and at higher levels up to Director level after 12 months (OEM Ch 38.8). For reviews of the detention of children (▶see 916).

Consular protection

As well as having access to legal advice, those detained should be asked whether they wish to contact their High Commission or Consulate in the UK. Those who do are to be given the appropriate telephone number. Consular representatives should, if the person agrees, be permitted to visit the detainee and consult privately with them (OEM at Ch 38.18).

Rules covering treatment in detention

The Detention Centre Rules 2001 provide a comprehensive set of rules and procedures covering the treatment of those in detention (▶see the table below). Although they are called the 'Detention Centre' Rules, they apply to centres of detention which are now called 'removal centres' (see s66 2002 Act).

DETENTION CENTRE RULES

The Detention Centre Rules 2001 state as follows.

- Detainees may keep their personal property while in detention, apart from cash or where allowing them to keep it would be contrary to the 'interests of safety or security' of the centre.

- Personal searches are to be carried out on a person's reception at the centre, and may also be carried out at other times if the detention centre manager thinks that it is necessary to do so.

- Written reasons for detention must be given to a person at the time of their detention and every month thereafter while they are detained.

- If a detainee asks for an update on the progress of their case, the Home Office must provide the relevant information to them within 'a reasonable time'. This includes a progress report on an asylum claim, any other application to enter or stay in the UK, a nationality application, a claim to stay under EU law, removal or deportation from the UK, an appeal or judicial review involving their immigration case, and bail applications.

- Men and women are to be provided with separate sleeping accommodation.

- Detainees may wear their own clothes and must be provided with additional clothing where it is necessary. On release, detainees must be given suitable clothing.

- Food and drink is to be wholesome and nutritious, and it must meet all religious, dietary, cultural and medical needs. Alcohol is not allowed, except where required for particular medical or religious reasons.

- Detainees must be able to have a bath or shower and a shave every day, and must be able to have their hair cut regularly.

- Detainees must have access to: physical education and recreation (at least one hour in the open air every day); a library in the centre that has books relevant to different cultures and in a range of languages, and includes religious books; any paid activity provided by the centre.

- Ministers of the different religions are to carry out services for those detained, and visits are to be arranged to individual detainees if they so wish.

- Detainees are able to write and receive letters and faxes and use the available public telephones. Where a detainee does not have the necessary funds, the Home Office should pay for a reasonable number of letters to be sent and calls to be made.

- Detainees can receive 'as many visits' as they like within 'reasonable limits'. Visits must generally take place in the view of an officer, but generally not in the hearing of an officer. Legal visits are also to be in confidence, but may be in the sight of an officer. However, the Home Office may prohibit visits to a detained person 'for such periods of time as [it] considers necessary' in order to ensure safety and security and to prevent crime.

- Provided that they consent to it, detainees are medically examined within 24 hours of admission to the centre. The doctor must report to the detention centre manager any case where the detainee may have been the victim of torture, or is potentially suicidal.

- A detainee can be prevented from associating with other detainees where necessary 'in the interests of security or safety'. The authority of the Home Office must be obtained in order to remove rights of association for more than a day. In similar circumstances, detainees can be put in 'special accommodation' or under 'special control or restraint'.

Note: This table sets out some of the most important but not *all* of the Detention Centre Rules.

CONDITIONS: INSPECTION AND OTHER REPORTS

Not only are the powers of immigration detention extremely wide – very serious concerns have been raised in recent years about conditions of detention. A recent example is the BBC undercover documentary, shown on 2 March 2005, 'Detention Undercover – the Real Story'. This showed a very disturbing picture of life at Oakington Reception Centre, previously held up by the Home Office as a centre with a 'relaxed' environment providing for the quick determination of asylum claims – an aim that was justified as being as beneficial to genuine asylum-seekers as to good administration. The documentary appeared to show that some asylum-seekers there were being assaulted, racially abused and sexually humiliated by some of the private security personnel contracted by the government to guard the centre. Furthermore, and unknown until this point, the documentary appeared to show the arbitrary use of 'prison cell' type solitary detention as punishment and deterrence for certain inmates of the centre. The Home Office commissioned its own report into the matter.

We now turn to some of the reports of HM Chief Inspector of Prisons, and some further reports covering various aspects of immigration detention.

Inspection

HM Chief Inspector of Prisons, presently Anne Owers CBE, has a duty under the 1999 Act to investigate immigration removal centres. The remit of the role has been extended to cover short-term holding facilities and escort arrangements. The extended remit will be put on a statutory basis by the Immigration, Asylum and Nationality Bill 2005.

The visiting committees set up under the Detention Centre Rules (▶see above) also have a duty to provide annual reports to the Home Office concerning the state of immigration detention centres.

Criteria for inspection used by the Inspectorate

HM Inspectorate applies four tests in order to determine whether there is a 'healthy custodial environment', as follows:

1) Whether detainees are held in safety – i.e. protected from physical and psychological harm, and with an ability to access timely information about the progress of their cases so as not to increase their anxiety and insecurity.

2) Whether detainees are treated with respect as individuals. This includes a range of matters: staff attitudes; reception; the availability of interpreters; the availability of translated information; race relations; welfare; quality of accommodation; food; healthcare; the ability to practice their faith; an effective complaints system.

3) Whether detainees are engaged in constructive activity to enable them to be active, fit and healthy during their detention.

4) Whether detainees are able to maintain contact with the outside world and prepare for their release, transfer or removal.

The detailed criteria used by the Inspectorate to assess whether the above tests are met have recently been published by the Inspectorate in *'Immigration Removal Centre Expectations'* (May 2005). *'Expectations'* draws on both domestic and international legal standards, and includes detailed criteria from the moment of arrival until release, with the aim of improving the conditions and treatment of detainees.

We summarise *some* of the Inspectorate's reports below.

First reports following statutory responsibility – April 2003

In April 2003, the Inspectorate published five inspection reports – the first since it had been given formal responsibility under the legislation for inspecting immigration removal centres.

Applying the above four tests, the April 2003 reports found as follows.

Campsfield The Inspectorate could not conclude that the centre was a place of safety, largely due to poor levels of supervision. Detainees were treated with respect but there was inadequate attention to their welfare needs outside, and a lack of information about their cases and access to competent advice.

Haslar The centre did not do enough to help detainees settle and to provide them with a safe environment. The quality of accommodation was poor, and there were inappropriate incentive and anti-bullying schemes, which were based on prison practice. There was a lack of information about cases, visiting times were restricted, and detainees were not properly occupied. There was inadequate provision for contact with the outside world and preparation for release.

Lindholme The centre was not a healthy establishment for detainees, and far-reaching changes were needed to bring it up to expected standards. Only 15 per cent of detainees reported that they felt safe, and feelings of safety decreased with the length of time spent at the centre. There was no proper ongoing information about the progress of cases, and detainees did not have information about how to obtain legal advice. Staff did not show a sufficient understanding of the distinction between immigration detainees and prisoners.

Oakington The centre offered a high standard of care where, apart from splitting families during and after detention, the needs and dignity of detainees were met. There was also access to information and advice. Arrangements for those leaving the centre needed improvement. Those who were being further detained after the decision-making process were

9

not informed until the day of their departure, and seemed unable to contact family and representatives at this stage.

Tinsley House Detainees experienced a good standard of care, and were treated with respect. However, their security was undermined by the fact that they were not easily able to find out about the progress of their cases, receive help with outside welfare needs, or access specialist legal advice. They were also not properly prepared for their release, transfer or removal.

Reports issued on Tinsley House and Dungavel House in 2005

In early 2005 the Inspectorate issued reports on Tinsley House and Dungavel House Removal Centres following visits in November and December 2004.

Tinsely House The Inspectorate found that, although the centre remained generally safe, there was still no joint working with local social services on child protection, and documentation on the use of force needed to be improved (medical assessments were missing from some files). Staff–detainee relations were good, but race relations and complaints procedures needed improvement. Not enough was being done to prepare detainees for transfer, removal or release.

Dungavel House The first full inspection of Dungavel was in 2002. The report had highlighted the risk to the welfare and development of children detained there, and called for independent assessments of the welfare of detained children. Referring to its earlier report, the Inspectorate found that there was still no independent assessment or review of the welfare, educational and developmental needs of children, and that agreed procedures for their detention were not being followed. Learning provision for children was deficient, and required urgent attention. Access to primary and secondary healthcare remained good, but further work was required. Communications from and to families and friends remained difficult, and the Inspectorate was concerned about the isolation and vulnerability of detainees who had little understanding of English. Among other recommendations, the Inspectorate stated:

'The detention of children should be exceptional and for the shortest possible period. Within a matter of days, there should be an independent assessment of the welfare, educational and developmental needs of each child held in detention to inform decisions about the necessity of continued detention. This should be repeated at regular intervals to advise on the compatibility of detention with the welfare of the child and to inform reviews of detention.'

Detention at short-term holding facilities – August 2005 reports

On 16 August 2005, the Chief Inspector published reports of unannounced visits to four short-term immigration detention holding facilities, which took place between November 2004 and January 2005 at Gatwick

Airport North Terminal, Gatwick Airport South Terminal, London City Airport and Dover Asylum Screening Centre.

It found that the facilities at Gatwick Airport, London City Airport and Dover Asylum Screening Centre were not suitable for overnight stays, and that they had inadequate facilities. The Inspectorate also found that, although all the facilities could be used to hold men, women and children, there was no proper separation of these groups. The facilities did not have sufficient child protection arrangements. The Inspectorate also found that:

- no centres had regular visits from healthcare staff;
- suicide and self-harm procedures and training were lacking in three of the centres;
- complaints procedures were non-existent, and record-keeping was irregular;
- detainees were sleeping in inadequate conditions, without adequate bedding or heating.

In an interim response, the Home Office emphasised that the facilities were only intended to hold people briefly, usually for a few hours, and that, since the inspections had taken place, steps had been taken to improve conditions in a number of areas raised in the reports.

Earlier reports

Earlier reports concerning immigration detention also make disturbing reading. The former HM Chief Inspector of Prisons, Sir David Ramsbotham, following a short unannounced visit to HMP Rochester in 1999, stated:

'Most of all I must express my concern at the poor treatment and conditions of the numbers of asylum seekers, immigration detainees and other foreign nationals who form almost half the prison population.

Detainees were treated as if they were unconvicted prisoners. This approach seemed to be based on guidelines from the Immigration and Nationality Directorate and was adopted by prison staff in their dealings with them.'

One incident witnessed by Sir David illustrated the lack of care and sensitivity with which immigration detainees may be faced:

'A detainee who had never been in custody before, was placed in a double cell with another who was from Poland and who spoke no English. The officer escorting him addressed the Pole and said in a clear loud slow voice, 'You tell him what goes on' and closed the cell door on the two people. The new arrival was from Albania and spoke no English. The Pole and the Albanian did not share a common language. We asked on what basis he had been allocated to that particular cell and found it was because of available space and the fact that both names ended with an 'I'. The member of staff concerned made no effort to discover whether either person had understood what he had just said, could communicate with each other or knew what was going to happen to them next. When we challenged this approach, the member of staff concerned assured us that this was common practice and invariably resulted in the detainees communicating at some level.'

Other reports on aspects of detention

In addition to the official reports of HM Inspectorate, there are a range of other reports on various aspects of the immigration detention process that applicants and advisers will find of interest. They may also be useful in preparing bail applications. Again, we can provide only short summaries. Advisers may also find Amnesty International's recent report useful: *Seeking asylum is not a crime: Detention of people who have sought asylum* (2005).

Attitudes of immigration officers to detention

In *Deciding to Detain: How decisions to detain asylum seekers are made at ports of entry* (University of Cambridge, 2000), Leanne Weber and Loraine Gelsthorpe, with the cooperation of the immigration service, interviewed 35 immigration officers and 25 chief immigration officers. Each official was asked what they thought was the main purpose of detaining persons on their arrival. The response form enabled each officer to give two answers. Although 51 per cent of those interviewed thought preventing asylum-seekers absconding was a main reason for detention, 15 per cent felt that encouraging someone to withdraw their asylum application was a main purpose, and 13 per cent gave deterring other people from seeking asylum as a main purpose.

Weber and Gelsthorpe's report also identified very wide disparities in the detention rates between the different ports, with the probability that certain officers were responsible for a disproportionate amount of detention. They also found serious problems in procedures for informing asylum-seekers about their detention and enabling them to challenge it.

The main findings of *Deciding to Detain* are set out in three articles published in Tolley's *Immigration, Asylum and Nationality Law* (Vol 15, No. 3, 2001, p. 151; Vol 15, No. 4, p. 200; Vol 16, No. 1, 2002; p. 7).

Risk of absconding

The report *Maintaining Contact: What happens after detained asylum seekers get bail* (Irene Bruegel and Eva Natamba, June 2002, published by South Bank University) examines the extent to which asylum-seekers who obtain bail, in the face of opposition to bail by the Home Office, do actually comply with bail conditions. The report indicates that the decision whether to detain often depends on arbitrary factors, such as the availability of detention space. They also find that, at most, eight to nine per cent of those who obtained bail subsequently attempted to evade the system, meaning that over 90 per cent are unnecessarily detained. The report also draws attention to worrying examples of the Home Office opposing bail where it is accepted that the detainee has mental health problems. The huge costs of unnecessary detention are highlighted.

Families in detention and risk of absconding by families

In *A few families too many: the detention of asylum-seeking families in the UK* (published by Bail for Immigration Detainees ('BID'), April 2003), Emma K. H. Cole details the findings of a small study based on interviews with some nine families about their experiences of immigration detention. The research was prompted by the change in government policy in October 2001 (described at ▶907, above), when it decided that it would detain families on the same general detention criteria as in other cases. The report investigates the likelihood of absconding in family cases, and the incentives that families have for staying in touch with the immigration authorities. Among the key findings of the report are that:

'Families are unlikely to abscond, for a variety of reasons, including their need to access services such as healthcare and education for their children, and their desire to be granted leave to remain.'

And that:

'Children suffer emotional, physical, mental and social harm as a direct result of being detained by the Immigration Service. Responses to detention recorded in the sample included: loss of appetite, serious mouth infection, weight loss (which took 6 months to regain on release), listlessness, boredom, incontinence, difficulty sleeping, continuing fear (even after release), loneliness.'

The report recommends that children should not be placed in immigration detention. The report provides useful information for those seeking to obtain the release of families from detention.

A further report by Save The Children, *No Place for a Child*, made detailed recommendations to the Home Office about the detention of families with children. For Home Office policy following the response to it, ▶see 916.

Pregnant asylum-seekers, those with babies and those with health needs

Detention policy states that pregnant women should not be detained unless there is a clear prospect of early removal, and medical advice suggests that that there is no question of confinement before the time for removal. Such women should only be detained in 'very exceptional circumstances'. The same applies to other particularly vulnerable groups of people: unaccompanied children, the elderly, those with serious medical conditions or disabilities, those who are mentally ill, and those who have been tortured (▶see policy at 912).

However, the study *A Crying Shame* (September 2002, published by Maternity Alliance, BID and the London Detainee Support Group), found that pregnant asylum-seekers and those with babies were among those detained for many months, even where there was no prospect of early removal. The research found that the use of prolonged detention for pregnant women and mothers with young children 'inflicts physical and psychological harm disproportionate to the policy aim of immigration control'. While the report considered the impact of detention on pregnant women and mothers with young babies, it is also relevant to the detention of the other vulnerable groups. BID has also published *Fit to be Detained? Challenging the detention of asylum-seekers and migrants with health needs* (2005).

32 Getting people out of detention

This chapter deals with the various methods of getting people out of detention. Where the immigration authorities have a power to detain, they always have an alternative power to grant 'temporary admission' on conditions if necessary. The first means, therefore, of helping a person who is detained or may be detained is to persuade the immigration authorities to grant temporary admission.

We begin by looking at the power to grant temporary admission and two similar forms of limited licence to be in the UK (▶950–7). Note that, throughout the *Handbook* and in this chapter specifically, we have used the term 'temporary admission' to include all three forms of this very limited status. They are granted in technically different circumstances, but they are essentially the same. We also look at the different conditions that can be attached to temporary admission, including 'electronic monitoring' under the 2004 Act. We deal also with the question of when an applicant can argue that they should be granted 'leave', rather than temporary admission.

The immigration authorities (Chief Immigration Officers and Home Office officials) also have a power to grant 'bail'. This is similar to temporary admission, but it allows the immigration authorities to accept sureties for a person's release which they cannot otherwise do (▶see 957–8).

Next (beginning at ▶958) we look at the powers of the AIT to grant bail. The powers themselves, together with references to the relevant legislation, are set out in the table at ▶960–2. In certain cases, bail applications are instead made to the Special Immigration Appeals Commission (SIAC, ▶see 965).

At ▶965–85 we deal with making bail applications to the AIT. This includes: submitting the original application; fully preparing the bail application; dealing with sureties and presenting the bail application itself before the immigration judge. We also look at what happens if the applicant is granted bail but then fails to comply with their conditions.

Finally, if it is alleged that detention is *unlawful*, it may be appropriate to apply to the High Court to obtain the release of an immigration detainee in judicial review or *habeas corpus* proceedings. The circumstances in which a detention may be unlawful are set out in Chapter 30, at

▶919–932. We look briefly at these High Court procedures in relation to detention at ▶985–7. For *general* details about judicial review procedures, ▶see 1213–22.

TEMPORARY ADMISSION, TEMPORARY RELEASE AND RESTRICTION ORDERS

'Temporary admission', 'temporary release' and admission under a 'restriction order' are all ways of allowing people who could be detained to be lawfully 'at large' in the UK. They are a sort of limited licence to be in the UK, to which conditions can be attached. *These three forms of status are very similar, and both lawyers and officials often use the term 'temporary admission' to cover all three. We have done likewise in the Handbook.*

Technically, however, the three powers are as follows.

1) **'Temporary admission'** can be granted to a person who is:

- awaiting examination concerning their right to enter the UK;
- awaiting a decision about whether they should be granted entry (including re-entry);
- awaiting a decision as to whether they should be removed as an illegal entrant, an overstayer, or a person who has breached conditions of entry, tried to obtain leave to remain by deception, or had their indefinite leave as a refugee revoked; or
- in any of the categories in the last point above who is refused entry, or if a decision is made to remove them and they are awaiting removal.

(para. 21, Sch 2, 1971 Act and s10(7) 1999 Act)

2) **'Temporary release'** can be granted to a person in any of the groups in (1) above who is actually detained. Note that, confusingly, those who are released on bail by the immigration authorities (▶see 957–8) are sometimes also referred to as being 'temporarily released'. We have used 'bail' to refer to release under these circumstances.

(para. 21, Sch 2, 1971 Act and s10(7) 1999 Act)

3) **Restriction orders** The following people can be free in the UK under 'restriction orders' granted by the Secretary of State: those who have been served with a notice of intention to deport, pending the making of a deportation order; those who have a deportation order against them, and are awaiting removal; and those who have been recommended for deportation.

(para. 2(5)(6), Sch 2, 1971 Act)

Note that the powers under (1) and (2) above used to be operated only by immigration officers. However, under the 2002 Act, in many of those cases the Secretary of State (i.e. officers at the Home Office) has been given powers to detain equal to those of the immigration service. In such cases, officers at the Home Office *also* have powers to grant temporary admission. Both immigration officers and officers at the Home Office can vary the conditions of temporary admission imposed by each other (see s62(3)(4) 2002 Act). These changes under the 2002 Act simply extend the same powers to different officers – there is no change in the powers themselves. The purpose of the change was to give greater flexibility to the authorities, and also, in asylum cases in particular, to allow the official at the Home Office who has 'ownership' of the case file and knows most about the case also to make decisions about detention.

In principle, where a person has been granted temporary admission, they may at any time be detained. Similarly, a person who has been detained can be granted temporary admission (or similar status). However, there are legal limits to when detention can be used instead of temporary admission. In some cases, even though at first glance it looks as though a person falls into one of the categories of persons who may be detained under the legislation, detaining them may still be unlawful (▶see 919–932 for details about when decisions to detain will be unlawful). Where detention is or would be unlawful, the applicant must at least be granted temporary admission.

In the case of **Khadir**, it was argued that, in certain cases where it would be unlawful to detain, the Home Office must actually grant the applicant *leave* to enter or remain in the UK. The House of Lords rejected that suggestion, finding, that there remains a power to keep someone on temporary admission even where it would not be lawful to detain (▶956–7).

For further details about temporary admission in the asylum context ▶see 652–4.

The Home Office has the power, aside from the National Asylum Support Service (NASS) system of support, to provide accommodation and board to those granted temporary admission or bail (see s4 1999 Act). For further details, ▶see 1381–7.

Applying for temporary admission

An attempt should be made in the first place to speak on the telephone to the official dealing with the case, requesting the reasons for detention. Representatives should try to address the policy setting out the criteria for detention listed (▶see 909–914), and explain why detention is not appropriate in the particular case (▶see 1495–7 for contact details of ports and immigration offices). It is more likely that an individual will be released if suitable accommodation is offered. If the matter cannot be solved by a telephone call, it is important to follow up in writing the request for temporary admission.

Detention is supposed to be regularly reviewed (▶see 940). So, even if the first request is refused, repeated requests can be made and should be carefully considered. New factors, like the distress caused to the detainee and their family, medical evidence of the effect of the detention, or a new address becoming available, should all be notified to officers.

Conditions of temporary admission

If temporary admission is granted, it will normally be subject to conditions. The possible conditions are: requirement to reside at a particular address; requirement to report; and a prohibition on employment or business. In addition, a requirement to cooperate with electronic monitoring can be made a part of residence or reporting conditions. Following release, an application can be made to the same authority to change these conditions.

Residence

Temporary admission will normally be given requiring the applicant to reside at a particular address. It is difficult to obtain temporary admission without an accommodation address. Where the person is an asylum-seeker and cannot provide an address through their own contacts in the UK, they may be entitled to support from NASS (▶see Chapter 41). That support can include the provision of accommodation. For details about detainees and the provision of a NASS address for the purposes of bail, ▶see 971. Residence conditions can also be imposed requiring applicants to reside at a particular induction centre for 14 days while they are introduced into the asylum process (s70 2002 Act; for further details about induction centres, ▶see 655–7).

Employment restrictions

In most cases, a person granted temporary admission will not be permitted to work or enter into business. In asylum cases, in particular, a restriction will routinely be imposed at least for the first 12 months. (Policy on asylum-seekers and employment restrictions has changed frequently: ▶see 694–6 for details.) In non-asylum cases, there may be more flexibility. For example, the EDIs state the following in relation to deportation cases:

'The power to impose a restriction as to employment or occupation is discretionary. The employment restriction will be appropriate in the majority of straightforward cases where the person is single and there is a reasonable expectation of early removal. However, the employment restriction may be omitted if it is clear from the outset that considera-tion of the case will be protracted and where, for example, the potential deportee is giving continuing support to his family by employment.'
(EDI, Ch 3, s5, para. 5.7)

Reporting

Conditions of temporary admission can require persons to report at a reporting centre, a port or a police station (and see the OEM at Ch 38.20).

Asylum-seekers whose claims are put into a 'segment' for quick determination will usually have specific reporting conditions imposed on them, in accordance with the timetable that applies to that segment (►see Chapter 22). From June 2005, all other applicants who are not detained will be required to report in line with the 'intelligent reporting' guidance laid down by the Home Office (for details of this guidance and the likely frequency of reporting conditions, ►see 652–3). The Home Office can make payments to persons to enable them to travel to report when they are on temporary admission or bail (s69 2002 Act; ►see 654).

Electronic monitoring

Electronic monitoring (EM) was introduced as part of the possible temporary admission conditions by section 36 of the 2004 Act. It came into force on 1 October 2004. EM may be made a part of either residence or reporting conditions (s36(2)(3)). JCWI has voiced its concerns both during the passage of the Bill and during the implementation of EM. It tends to criminalise people who have committed no crime, and certain forms of EM are arguably disproportionate to the alleged scale of absconding.

There are three forms electronic monitoring can take:

- reporting by voice recognition technology;
- tagging, which involves the subject wearing an electronic tag bracelet that sends a signal to a receiver at their home address;
- tracking, which uses global satellite technology to pinpoint a person's whereabouts on a continuous basis – data can either be transmitted in real time ('active tracking') or the tracking can be passive, with data transmitted at various intervals.

Each of these forms of EM is described in more detail below. At the time of writing, EM is being trialled on about 100 people at any one time, the majority having to report via voice recognition. Its use is being evaluated by the government before it is rolled out on a wider scale. In principle, EM can be imposed by the immigration authorities when they grant temporary admission or bail, or by an immigration judge of the AIT when they grant bail.

The Home Office has subsequently issued assessment criteria to determine who can have EM conditions imposed. With the exception of voice recognition, it is apparent from the limited guidance published so far that the Home Office views EM as an alternative to detention – i.e. to be used when a person would otherwise be detained. It has stated that an individual risk assessment should be conducted in every case. Assessment criteria have been drawn up on Form EM1, which lists the following factors in favour of using EM:

- the person is not removable as a result of their country of origin;
- no travel document is presently available;

- the lack of any compassionate circumstances (e.g. pregnancy, old age, illness, disability);
- there has been a breach of previous temporary admission or bail conditions;
- there is no suitable surety available;
- the person has criminal convictions;
- there is a previous history of 'non-compliance with the requirements of immigration law';
- lack of personal ties to the UK (no fixed address, no family, unemployed);
- there are no outstanding applications that 'may afford an incentive to remain in touch with the department'.

The Home Office has also stressed that a decision to impose EM must comply with Article 8 ECHR by demonstrating that

'...tagging or tracking is a reasonable and proportionate measure in mitigating against *the risk of the individual absconding*. In deciding whether these measures are appropriate, we should consider the number of factors within the assessment criteria that apply in an individual case, and the extent to which they apply (i.e. degree of previous non-compliance). The consideration process is the same as that for (temporary admission/temporary release), bail or detention, and EM should be viewed as an *additional* option within this range of measures' [emphasis added]. (Home Office guidance on selecting individuals for the EM pilot).

The three forms of EM presently available, depending on the level of risk of absconding, are as follows.

Voice recognition Biometric voice recognition technology is used to enable someone to report over the telephone via a fixed landline from a fixed address at a notified time, instead of reporting in person to a reporting centre. It may be imposed as a condition upon those who are assessed as posing a low risk of absconding. The Home Office has stated that it regards voice recognition 'as a benefit to the subject, as it is more convenient than reporting in person to the reporting centre'. Likely candidates for this method of reporting include those who are:

- at the beginning of the asylum process;
- not currently removable by virtue of their country of origin;
- 'difficult to document';
- not living within a reasonable distance of an immigration reporting centre.

Tagging This involves wearing a bracelet similar to a wristwatch, which emits a signal to a receiver at the subject's home address. The Home Office can require the wearer to be at home for specific periods during the week, to confirm that they are complying with a residence restriction. It has stated that tagging may well be used in detained cases where an individual is being considered for bail, but is unable to provide suitable sureties.

Tracking Tracking uses global positioning satellite technology to pinpoint someone's whereabouts on a continuous basis. The Home Office has accepted that this form of monitoring is the most intrusive, and is therefore likely to be appropriate only for those with an adverse immigration history who are apprehended by enforcement officers, but are not imminently removable. There are three types of tracking:

- 'active tracking', which allows for data to be transmitted in 'real time';
- 'hybrid tracking', which retrospectively transmits data at specific intervals during the day, with a real-time alert if the tag is removed or tampered with;
- 'passive tracking', which transmits data retrospectively at the end of the day.

'Temporary admission' conditions imposed on asylum-seekers with leave

As set out above, temporary admission is a status given, while the immigration process is taking its course, to those who do not have leave to enter or remain in the UK. However, the 2002 Act allows asylum-seekers and their dependants who have *existing leave* when they make their asylum application to be made subject to the same conditions as those with temporary admission. Although such an asylum-seeker cannot generally be detained, the Act gives a new power for them to be detained *if* they fail to comply with their conditions (s71). The government has done this in order to

'...ensure that all asylum-seekers, whatever their circumstances prior to making a claim, can be subject to the same basic process including, for example, the requirement to keep in touch through regular reporting.' (Explanatory Notes to 2002 Act, para. 197).

End of period of temporary admission

Temporary admission is often given for a set period of time, at the end of which the person has to report to the immigration authorities (they may well have had to report at intervals in between). If there has been no change of circumstances in the case, but it has not been resolved by that time and the conditions have been complied with, temporary admission will normally be renewed for a further period. Often this can be done in writing, without the person actually having to report.

If, however, the case appears to be moving towards the stage where the immigration authorities will soon be enforcing the individual's departure, then the person may be detained when they report. Sometimes the initial period of temporary admission is cut short for this purpose. For obvious reasons, it is very unlikely that the immigration service will confirm in advance that they will detain someone when they report.

If an applicant can't be removed, should they be granted leave rather than temporary admission: the case of *Khadir*

The idea behind temporary admission is that it can be granted while an applicant is waiting for some immigration action, decision or procedure to be completed. The powers to grant it are given to officers when a person is 'liable' to be detained. On the face of it, therefore, temporary admission is simply an alternative to detention, and can be granted whenever there is a power to detain – i.e. 'pending' examination, a decision, removal, and so on (▶see 899, 902–5 for the statutory powers of detention). Logically, this seems to mean that whenever there is no power to detain, there is no power to grant temporary admission either. As discussed at ▶924–7, it is unlawful to detain 'pending removal' – for example, when removal cannot be carried out in a reasonable time. Should a person in this position therefore be granted leave instead of temporary admission? The scheme of immigration control doesn't seem intended to keep people in indefinite limbo.

This argument came before the House of Lords in *Khadir*. In that case, the appellant was a Kurd from the autonomous area of northern Iraq ('KAA' or 'KAR') whose asylum claims had failed. However, over a prolonged period of time the Home Office could not find a safe way of returning him. It would be unreasonable to detain such a person (see *Hardial Singh* at ▶924–5), but did that mean that he could also no longer be granted temporary admission? The House of Lords held that (paras 31–5):

1) the power to detain 'pending' removal meant simply 'until' removal – there was still a *power* to detain a person who was awaiting removal on a long-term basis;

2) prolonged detention for an unreasonable period was indeed *unlawful* (as in *Hardial Singh*), but that is because it was an unlawful *exercise* of the power to detain, not because there was no power to detain;

3) because there continued to be a *power* to detain, even though removal arrangements were taking a very long time, there was still a power to grant temporary admission and, therefore, the appellant did not have to be given leave instead.

The Home Office had been so concerned about this case that it passed legislation to be absolutely sure that it did not have to grant leave to persons in this position. The further legislation stated that any of the following persons could continue to be granted temporary admission (s67 of the 2002 Act):

• those who cannot for the time being be removed from the UK because of a 'legal impediment' connected with the UK's international obligations (this ensures that those waiting for a final determination of their asylum or human rights claims can be granted temporary admission);

- those who cannot be removed because there are practical difficulties preventing or delaying their removal;
- those who cannot be removed because there are practical difficulties or insufficient resources preventing or delaying a decision being made on their cases.

The decision of the House of Lords made it clear that, at least in relation to cases about practical problems with removal, section 67 was unnecessary. The Lords found that the law had all along permitted temporary admission to continue to be given in such situations.

Nevertheless, the Home Affairs Committee of the House of Commons has been very critical of the practice of granting only temporary admission with strict conditions in these situations. In their report on asylum removals, issued on 8 May 2003, they stated their view that it is 'absurd' to refuse leave to people who, for whatever reason, cannot be removed. They recommended that such people be granted a temporary status that would allow them to support themselves.

Will there ever come a point when the applicant has to be granted leave?

Despite the above findings, the House of Lords in *Khadir* did indicate that there may come a time when an applicant might have to be given leave:

'There may come a time when the prospects of the person ever being able safely to return, whether voluntarily or compulsorily, are so remote that it would be irrational to deny him the status which would enable him to make a proper contribution to the community here...' (Baroness Hale, para. 4)

This might also be the case where, although detention has not continued for as long as is implied by the quote above, it is clear that there is simply no prospect of achieving removal (see *Khadir* at para. 32). In such cases, it remains open to applicants to argue that leave, rather than temporary admission, should be granted.

BAIL FROM IMMIGRATION AUTHORITIES OR POLICE INSPECTOR

In addition to the powers to grant temporary admission (see above), the immigration authorities, and in some cases the police, have the power to grant bail as well. These powers are contained in: paras 22, 29(1)(2), Sch 2 1971 Act; paragraphs 2 (4A), 3, Sch 3 1971 Act; section 10(7) 1999 Act.

It used to be the case that only the immigration service, acting through a Chief Immigration Officer (CIO), could operate these powers. However, from 1 April 2003, officers of the Secretary of State at the Home Office can also grant bail if the application is made after the applicant has been detained for over eight days (see s68(1)(2) 2002 Act). Detainees do not have to apply to the immigration authorities for bail before they apply to the AIT.

The difference between bail and temporary admission is that, with bail, the CIO and the Home Office can accept sureties. In some cases they may be prepared to grant bail on sureties even though they would not trust the applicant with a simple grant of temporary admission. Normally, therefore, the immigration authorities will want to see sureties before granting bail. Bail is not often granted by the immigration authorities, partly because they tend to ask for very substantial amounts from sureties. This has led to advisers not requesting bail from them but going directly to the AIT for bail instead. Sometimes the immigration authorities may suggest bail if sureties can be found. The OEM gives an idea of the level of surety the immigration authorities might ask for:

'The amount of bail should be viewed in relation to the means of the applicant and his sureties, and should give a substantial incentive to appear at the time and place required. Each case should be assessed on its individual merits but a figure of between £2,000 and £5,000 per surety will normally be appropriate. Where there is a strong financial incentive to remain here, it is justifiable to fix bail (or suggest to the adjudicator [now AIT] that it be fixed) at a larger sum. Property such as houses or businesses, or cars, may be offered but they are difficult to seize and should be rejected unless there are wholly exceptional circumstances in view of the potential hardship this could cause to others who have no part in the bail application.' (Ch 39.6.1)

If there are sureties available, it is often worth trying to get bail from the immigration authorities, if the application for temporary admission fails. Although there is no requirement in the legislation to back it up, officers may often require that the sureties have at least settled status. The OEM directs officers to this effect, and states that persons on temporary admission or with limited leave will rarely be acceptable as sureties because their own status may be cut short, and is in any case limited (OEM, Ch 39.6.2). The immigration authorities may also impose EM conditions to bail (s36(1)(d)(4) 2002 Act).

Where the immigration authorities refuse bail, reasons should be given (OEM, Ch 39.7.1.3).

BAIL FROM THE ASYLUM AND IMMIGRATION TRIBUNAL

The powers of the AIT to grant bail have often been confusing, and have changed over the years. In many cases, there are overlapping powers to grant bail. For instance, a person may be entitled to apply for bail on the grounds that they are to be removed having been refused entry, but also because they have an appeal outstanding before the AIT against the decision to refuse entry. When a person is detained and is eligible to apply for bail, they should be given a form by the immigration authorities (forms

IS98, IS98A, B1) informing them of their right to apply for bail, and how to apply.

At the outset of a bail hearing, the AIT may wish to satisfy itself that it has the power to grant bail. This has become less important now, because there is a power to grant bail in almost any situation. The relevant powers of the AIT to grant bail, together with the statutory references, following amendments made by the 2002 and 2004 Acts since the last edition of the *Handbook*, are set out in the table below, at ▶960–2. The amendments made accommodate the new appeals regime introduced under the 2002 Act and, secondly, the abolition of the two-tier appeal system by the 2004 Act.

For the powers to grant bail in national security cases, ▶see 965.

Who cannot get bail?

The powers to grant bail set out in the legislation are not easy to ascertain, and it may still be possible to find one or two examples of circumstances where people may be detained under the powers described at ▶902–5 where there may be a question-mark over the power to grant bail. However, just as powers to detain are to be interpreted narrowly, powers to grant bail should be read generously. The only clear gap in the powers is new arrival cases (▶below).

New arrival cases

The only situation in which the legislation clearly shows an intention to continue to deny the right to apply for bail is the case of new arrivals to the UK who do not arrive with existing leave, who are not illegal entrants, and who are detained while they are examined by the immigration officer before a decision regarding their entry is made. They cannot apply for bail during the first seven days following the date of their arrival. After the seven-day period, they can be granted bail (see para. 22(1B), Sch 2, 1971 Act).

'Bail gap' concerning deportees now closed

In the last edition of the *Handbook* (pp. 513, 515–16) we identified a further gap where, in several circumstances connected with deportation, there was no power to grant bail unless there was an in-country appeal outstanding. The government has been true to its word (see para. 4.83, 2002 White Paper) and has closed that gap (see s54 1999 Act inserting para. 2(4A) into Sch 3 of the 1971 Act from 10 February 2003). Bail may now be obtained in deportation cases, even where there is no appeal pending.

PERSONS WHO MAY BE GRANTED BAIL BY THE AIT

The AIT has the power to grant bail to people who fall into any of the following categories. The statutory powers referred to should be read together with the notes at the end of the table.

Port cases

- New arrivals to the UK who are detained while being examined by the immigration officer – *but they cannot be given bail until seven days after the date of their arrival in the UK* (for further details, ▶see 959).

Power

Immigration Act 1971, Sch 2, para. 22(1)(a), (1A), (1B)

Nationality, Immigration and Asylum Act 2002, s62(3)(a)(c)

- Those who already have leave to enter when they arrive in the UK which is suspended by an immigration officer, and who are detained while they are examined further, or while a decision is being made as to whether to cancel the leave, or after removal directions have been set after the cancellation of leave.

Power

Immigration Act 1971, Sch 2, paras 22(1)(aa), (1A), 34

Nationality, Immigration and Asylum Act 2002, s62(3)(a)(c)

- Those who arrive in the UK and are refused leave to enter (or are suspected of being such persons), and those who are reasonably suspected of being the family members of such persons, who are detained pending the giving of directions to remove them or after removal directions have been given.

Power

Immigration Act 1971, Sch 2, paras 22(1)(b), (1A), 34

Nationality, Immigration and Asylum Act 2002, s62(3)(a)(c)

Illegal entrants

- Those detained as illegal entrants (or suspected of being illegal entrants), and those who are reasonably suspected of being the family members of such persons, who are detained pending the giving of directions to remove them or after removal directions have been given.

Power

Immigration Act 1971, Sch 2, paras 22(1)(b), (1A), 34

Nationality, Immigration and Asylum Act 2002, s62(3)(a)(c)

Overstayers and others subject to administrative removal powers

- People in any of the following six categories who are detained pending the giving of directions to remove them, or after removal directions have been given:
  1) overstayers; 2) persons who have breached conditions of leave; 3) persons

who used deception in trying to obtain leave to remain; 4) persons whose indefinite leave is revoked as a result of their ceasing to be a refugee; 5) those who are family members of a person who has been given directions for removal because they fall into any of these categories; 6) anyone who is reasonably suspected of falling into any of the categories 1–5.

Power

Immigration Act 1971 Sch 2, paras 22(1)(b), (1A), 34

Immigration and Asylum Act 1999, s10 (7)

Nationality, Immigration and Asylum Act 2002, s62(3)(a)(c)

Crews of ships and aircrafts

- People in any of the following four categories, who are the members of the crews of ships or aircraft and who are detained pending the giving of directions to remove them, or after removal directions have been given: 1) those who remain beyond the leave granted to enable them to join their ship or aircraft; 2) those who intend to remain beyond that leave; 3) those who abscond (or intend to abscond) having lawfully entered without leave; 4) anyone who is reasonably suspected of falling into any of the categories 1–3.

Power

Immigration Act 1971, Sch 2, paras 22(1)(b), (1A), 34

Asylum-seekers with leave

- Those who are detained having claimed asylum or made an Article 3 ECHR claim (and their dependants) at a time when they had leave to enter or remain, who breach a condition imposed on them as to residence, reporting or occupation.

Power

Immigration Act 1971, Sch 2, paras 22(1), (1A), 34

Nationality, Immigration and Asylum Act 2002, s71(3)(b)

Notice of intention to make a deportation order

- Those detained following service of a notice of intention to make a deportation order pending the making of the deportation order.

Power

Immigration Act 1971, Sch 2, paras 22(1), (1A), 34; Sch 3 para. 2(4A)

Recommendation for deportation

- Those detained after a criminal court has issued a recommendation that they be deported following their conviction for an offence, pending the making of the deportation order.

Power

Immigration Act 1971, Sch 2, paras 22(1), (1A), 34; Sch 3 para. 2(4A)

Deportation orders

- Those detained who have a deportation order in force against them, pending their removal or departure from the UK.

Power

Immigration Act 1971, Sch 2, paras 22(1), (1A), 34; Sch 3 para. 2(4A)

Those who have 'appeals pending'

- Those who are detained under any of the powers above (as port cases; illegal entrants; overstayers and others subject to administrative removal powers; crews of ships or aircrafts; asylum-seekers with leave who have breached conditions; those given a notice of intention to deport; those recommended for deportation; those made the subject of a deportation order), who have an appeal 'pending'.

For the meaning of appeal 'pending', and more information about the power to grant bail and the appeal system, ▶see below at 962–4.

Power

Immigration Act 1971, Sch 2, para. 29(1)(3),

Immigration Act 1971, Sch 3, para. 3,

Immigration and Asylum Act 1999, s10(7)

Nationality, Immigration and Asylum Act 2002, s62(3)(a)(c), s71(3)(b)

Notes

The references above to paragraphs 22 and 29 of Sch 2 and paragraph 3 of Sch 3 to the 1971 Act are straightforward – they are the basic powers to grant bail in the above situations. The other references need some further explanation as follows.

1) The references to s62(3)(a)(c) of the 2002 Act in the above bail powers are necessary because, in many cases, the powers to grant bail refer to people detained under paragraph 16, Sch 2 1971 Act – detention by immigration officers. Section 62 allows the 'Secretary of State' (i.e. Home Office officers) to detain in similar circumstances. Section 62(3)(a)(c) makes clear that, even where the power to detain has been exercised by the Home Office, there are similar rights to apply for bail.

2) The reference to section 10(7) of the 1999 Act in the above is necessary because, again, in many cases, the powers to grant bail refer to people detained under paragraph 16, Sch 2 1971 Act. Section 10(7) expressly applies powers to grant bail in relation to detention in administrative removal cases. It also generally applies the power of detention in paragraph 16 of Sch 2 1971 Act to administrative removal cases.

3) The reference to section 71(3)(b) of the 2002 Act is necessary because it applies paragraph 16, Sch 2 1971 Act to allow the detention of certain asylum-seekers who have leave. Such detention is therefore apparently subject to the same powers to grant bail as in other paragraph 16 detention cases.

Bail where 'appeal pending'

As indicated in the table, applicants may apply to the AIT for bail where they have an 'appeal pending' under part 5 of the 2002 Act (which deals with appeals). So, a person who has an appeal outstanding before the AIT against an 'immigration decision' (s82), or an asylum status appeal (s83), may be granted bail by the AIT. It also *appears* that a person with an appeal outstanding to the Court of Appeal against a decision of the AIT (ss103B, 103E 2002 Act) may be granted bail by the AIT.

This is further clarified by section 104 2002 Act, which spells out what counts as a pending appeal under section 82 2002 Act. Obviously, there will be a pending appeal where notice of appeal has been given and the appeal is awaiting determination at first instance by the AIT. However, this section states that the appeal will continue to be pending, during any of the following periods. It therefore *appears* to be the case that there is a power for the AIT to grant bail during the following periods:

- while the applicant is still within time to apply for a review of the original decision of the AIT (under s103A 2002 Act);
- while an application has been made within time for a review of the original decision of the AIT and the application is still outstanding;
- after there has been a decision to order a reconsideration of the appeal, but the reconsideration has not been completed (this includes all further hearings of the appeal that has been ordered to be reconsidered);
- after an appeal has been remitted to the AIT by the Court of Appeal and is still waiting to be determined;
- while an applicant is still in time to make an application for permission to appeal to the Court of Appeal after the AIT has completed a reconsideration of an appeal (s103B 2002 Act);
- while an application has been made within time for an application for permission to appeal to the Court of Appeal, after the AIT has completed a reconsideration of an appeal (s103B 2002 Act);
- while an applicant is still in time to make an application for permission to appeal to the Court of Appeal, after the AIT has determined an appeal sitting as a panel (s103E 2002 Act);
- while an application has been made within time for an application for permission to appeal to the Court of Appeal, after the AIT has determined an appeal sitting as a panel (s103E 2002 Act);
- while an appeal to the Court of Appeal under the above powers is outstanding;
- while a reference of application for a review of the AIT's determination is outstanding before the Court of Appeal, having been referred to it by the High Court (s103C 2002 Act).

Essentially, therefore, the AIT has a power to grant bail throughout the appeal process, including where appeals are made to the Court of Appeal. If an appeal is withdrawn or abandoned, it will no longer be pending, and there will be no right to apply for bail on the basis of an appeal alone. The same is true if the Home Office makes a deportation order while an appeal is pending (s104(5) 2002 Act). However, the Home Office may not do that while an appeal against a decision to make a deportation order may be brought or is pending (s79 2002 Act).

Even if there is no power to grant bail on the basis that there is an appeal pending, there is *still* likely to be a power to grant bail on the basis of the applicant's immigration status (▶see the table above).

Note that legislation seems to give the Home Office the power to prevent bail from being granted where it is being applied for on the basis that there is an appeal pending by not 'consenting' to bail being granted. In practice this power is not used – almost certainly because it would undermine the decision of the AIT to grant bail (see para. 30(1), Sch 2 1971 Act).

EEA cases

Although the circumstances in which people can be refused admission or residence rights to the UK in EEA cases are very different, the powers of detention in EEA cases for those who are refused or are to be removed cross-refer to the ordinary immigration powers (▶see 554–6).

In such cases, the powers to grant bail are essentially the same as those set out above. This includes the fact that an appeal against an 'EEA decision' under the EEA 2000 Regulations gives rise to the same rights to apply for bail as an appeal under the 2002 Act (see reg. 24(2), 25(3), 26(2)(3), 32(6) EEA 2000 Regulations).

Orders for release from the criminal court

Deportation cases often involve criminal offences where the criminal court has powers to order detention and release. The 2004 Act has tilted the balance towards the powers of the Home Office to detain, so as to override a decision of a criminal court to release where the criminal court may not have been involved in (and is unaware of) the deportation procedure taking place. This is more fully explained at ▶900–1. However, the criminal court involved in recommending deportation, or hearing an appeal against recommendation for deportation, still has clear powers to direct the release of the applicant where they are detained (see para. 2(1)(1A), Sch 3, 1971 Act).

Repeal of automatic bail hearing provisions

Important safeguards on the wide powers of detention contained in the 1999 Act were repealed on 10 February 2003 (see s68(6) 2002 Act). In particular, the repealed provisions provided for automatic bail hearings before the statutory appeal authorities or the Magistrates Court after eight days and 36 days in detention, respectively. They also gave a 'general right' to be released on bail. These provisions were, alas, never brought into force and, since repeal, there is now no prospect of them being implemented.

The reason given in the 2002 White Paper for not bringing them in was that they were:

'...inconsistent with the need to ensure that we can streamline the removals process in particular and immigration and asylum processes more generally. The significant and continuing expansion in the detention estate since the proposals were first put forward would make the system unworkable in practice.'

The House of Commons Home Affairs Committee, in its report of 8 May 2003 on asylum removals, stated its view that there may be a case for automatic bail hearings after three months, and recommended that there be a further automatic hearing after 12 months of detention. They believed also that there should be a presumption of release unless there are compelling reasons why continued detention is in the public interest, or unless the detainee was being uncooperative.

Even though there is no statutory presumption that detainees should be granted bail, a presumption should still be applied (▶see 978).

SIAC cases

Those in any of the following categories must apply to the Special Immigration Appeals Commission (SIAC) for bail instead of the AIT (see s3 and Sch 3 Special Immigration Appeals Commission Act 1997):

- those whose detention has been certified by the Home Office as necessary in the interests of national security;
- those who are detained following a decision to refuse them leave to enter on the ground that their exclusion is in the interests of national security;
- those detained following a decision to make a deportation order against them on the ground that their deportation is in the interests of national security.

It is essential that anyone who falls into any of the above categories is referred for specialist advice. For appeals in SIAC cases, ▶see 1081–3.

APPLYING FOR BAIL BEFORE THE AIT

The procedure for bail applications to the AIT is set out in the Asylum and Immigration Tribunal (Procedure) Rules 2005, rules 3(1)(e), 37–42. We have referred to them simply as the 'Procedure Rules'. Where an appeal is subject to the 'fast track' Procedure Rules, an application for the applicant to be removed from the fast track may have the same effect as a bail application – namely, of the person being released. However, bail applications can also be made in those cases.

Further guidance about bail applications can be found in *Bail: Guidance Notes for Adjudicators* (third edition, May 2003). Although this was issued by the Chief Adjudicator and addressed to 'adjudicators', it remains a valid document. This is because it is one of the guidance notes referred to in the introduction and Annex C of the Practice Directions issued by the President of the AIT on 4 April 2005, as still valid unless and until the AIT issues its own guidance. JCWI understands that the *Notes* are in the course of being updated and so advisers should look out for a new edition. Below, we have referred to these as '*Guidance Notes*'. Attached to them are 11 appendices, which are also useful in applying for bail. The first appendix is the detention policy from Chapter 38 of the OEM (▶see the extracts from the revised, autumn 2005, edition of this at 909–12); the second are the UNHCR's *Guidelines on the Detention of Asylum Seekers* (▶see summary at 917–8); the fourth is a notice to applicants, representatives and sureties, and Appendix 6 is a 'surety checklist' (▶set out at 981–2).

There is a further relevant *Guidance Note* issued by the appellate authority, which is still valid: *Guidance Note* No. 6 (June 2003): *Guidance for adjudicators on deposit of recognisances.*

Applications for bail should be heard within three working days of the application being submitted (▶see 977).

Public funding (legal aid) is available for representation at bail hearings, as it is for appeals. The form of public funding is 'Controlled Legal Representation' and is discussed in more detail at ▶69–71. However, some applicants are unrepresented in bail hearings. Bail for Immigration Detainees (BID) has produced a *Notebook on Bail* (January 2004). The *Notebook* is in two parts: part one is aimed at helping applicants to obtain bail through legal representatives, and part two is a guide for people who are representing themselves at bail hearings. It is available from BID (▶see 1502 for contact details).

Submitting the application

An application for bail should be started by completing the prescribed bail application form – form 'B1'. It is attached in a schedule to the Procedure Rules. It can also be obtained from the AIT (▶see 1498 for addresses and website). As well as personal details, the questions asked on the form relate to:

- details of the applicant's representative;
- the date the applicant arrived in the UK;
- whether they have an appeal pending, and if so its reference number;
- the address they plan to live at if bail is granted (▶see further 971);
- the amount of the applicant's 'recognisance' ('deposit' in Scotland) – this is the amount of money that the applicant is prepared to put down;
- details of any sureties (name, address, occupation, nationality, passport details and amount of recognisance) – there is space on the form for two sureties (▶see 974–7, 980–2 below);
- whether an interpreter is required at the hearing, either for the applicant or sureties; and, if so, in which language;

- whether the applicant would like to be considered for electronic monitoring.

The form also leaves space for the applicant to give details of the grounds of the application for bail (it states that continuation pages can be used). The issues which the applicant should consider in setting out grounds are dealt with below, under 'preparing the application'. Of course, there is nothing to prevent applicants from raising additional matters at the bail hearing itself. However, if particular facts are to be relied on that challenge the Home Office's reasons for detaining, it may be a good idea to state them clearly in the grounds. This will prevent the Home Office stating at the hearing that they have not had any chance to check them. In addition, if there are factual details that are challenged, it is a good idea to state this in the grounds as well, so the Home Office has no excuse for not producing evidence to back up its case.

The intention is for electronic monitoring (EM) to be rolled out and used more extensively as a condition of temporary admission or bail. At the time of writing, EM was still in the process of being trialled by the Home Office. (For details of the different forms of EM, ▶see 953–5.) The form does not quite allow for the necessary information to be given in relation to EM – it asks only whether the applicant would like to be considered for EM. In fact, the Procedure Rules specify, where the applicant is over 18, that they should be asked:

'38(2)(e) ... whether he will, if required, agree as a condition of bail to co-operate with electronic monitoring under section 36 of the 2004 Act.'

If it appears that EM is a possibility and the applicant agrees, then the application should make clear that the applicant agrees to cooperate as stated. The specific power to grant bail subject to EM conditions is contained in section 36(1)(d)(4) of the 2004 Act.

The bail application form should be sent to the AIT hearing centre closest to where the applicant is detained. If the applicant wishes the application to be heard at a different centre – for example, because the sureties are closer to that centre – then the applicant will have to write to that different centre giving reasons why they wish the application to be heard there (*Guidance Notes*, paras 2.13-2.14; Notice to Applicants at Appendix 4 to *Guidance Notes*, para. 2).

Preparing the application for bail and grounds for bail

As with appeals, bail applications are likely to be won or lost in the preparation. In what follows, we look at preparation for bail hearings. When it comes to the bail hearing itself (▶978 onwards), what we cover here are obviously the same points that will be put to the immigration judge in submissions. No amount of rhetoric, or tear-jerking speeches about detention, will obtain the applicant's release unless the groundwork is done. Initial questions for advisers to ask themselves are:

- What are the reasons for detention, and how are they to be countered?

- What instructions about the circumstances and events are needed from the applicant themselves?
- What evidence is needed?
- Is there a ready address?
- What sureties are available, and how can it be proved that their decision to risk their money will be effective in exercising control over the applicant? (▶see 974–7, 980–2)
- What effects will continued detention have on the applicant and their family?
- What parts of Home Office policy and other guidelines suggest that the applicant should not be detained?
- Is detention undermining the applicant's ability to prepare for their case – i.e. their ability to obtain evidence, contact potential witnesses and consult with representatives?

Address the reasons for detention

The essential point of the grounds for bail is to deal with the reasons the Home Office has given for detention. The applicant should have been given reasons for their initial detention on Form IS 91R, and should have been provided with monthly updates (▶see 939–40). For the contents of the *pro forma* Form IS 91R, ▶see 913–4.

Common issues arising include:

- Why did the applicant enter with false documentation?
- Were officers told that the documents weren't genuine straightaway?
- Why didn't they approach an immigration officer immediately on arrival?
- Why did they not inform the immigration officer immediately, when questioned, that they wished to make an application for asylum?
- Why did they 'choose' to enter the UK clandestinely?
- What reasons are there for having previously failed to comply with conditions of temporary admission?
- Why did they fail to claim asylum in a third country they had passed through?
- Does the applicant have contacts in the UK?
- Does the applicant have an address?
- What prospects does the applicant have of remaining in the UK? Is there an appeal outstanding that provides an incentive to comply with conditions?
- Has the Home Office disputed the applicant's identity or nationality?

Common responses are: the inability to leave the country of nationality with a valid passport; distrust of officials following experiences in the applicant's own country; the detainee having followed the instructions of an agent; and inability to enter the UK through legitimate means as an asylum-seeker. However, in order to convey these reasons to the AIT, the detainee's own response will have to be obtained prior to the hearing.

In the Divisional Court in **Adimi & Sorani**, Simon Brown LJ acknowledged that failure to claim asylum at the border could be due to 'the effects of trauma, language problems, lack of information, previous experiences with authority, and feelings of insecurity'.

In **Bugdaycay**, Lord Bridge made the following comments about the circumstances of the case under consideration before the House of Lords:

'... the appellant has always put forward the explanation that he had been advised to try to gain entry as a visitor and then to seek asylum through the "refugee office" in London, which seems not to be wholly implausible.'

Often there is a dispute about the applicant's identity and/or nationality, and the applicant has no documents that clearly prove who they are or where they have come from. If so, it will be important to find out if there are any witnesses in the UK who can confirm the applicant's identity. It may well be that further evidence is required in order to back up the above points. If no independent evidence can be obtained, then often it is best to take a statement from the applicant, so at least their full explanation can be put before the AIT. A statement might explain the applicant's background and where they come from and give particular details about their place of former residence in their country of origin.

Other reasons Other issues that often arise are:

- The applicant has no further appeals – but it may be that the applicant has made or is making further representations, has obtained fresh evidence, or is making a judicial review challenge to their removal. If the case is a third-country case, it will be essential to decide whether removal to the third country will be challenged.

- The applicant will be removed when travel documents become available – but the travel document may take some time to obtain. It is worth probing the Home Office to confirm what steps have been taken, and when and how long travel documents from the applicant's particular country of nationality generally take to be issued.

- The applicant refused to cooperate with a voluntary departure, or with attempts to get their own authorities to issue them with a travel document. If this is the case, the applicant may have done so because they were afraid of their country's authorities and still had (or wanted to make) asylum or human rights representations with the Home Office about their situation in their own country (for general details about attempts to obtain travel documents for the purpose of removal and the new criminal offence, ▶see 925–7; ▶see also the case of *I* at 927–9).

- The applicant is a long-term overstayer. It will be relevant here to determine what is now going to happen to their case – i.e. is the applicant going to make, or have they made, any other applications? How long will they take to determine? Why were they not made before? What advice did the applicant previously have available when they overstayed?

- The applicant has breached their other conditions of leave, failed to attend an interview, or failed to report. A full explanation should be obtained as to why the applicant did this, and whether they were aware of doing so.

Further reasons given in bail summary Of course, in the course of preparing for the bail hearing, applicants should receive the 'bail summary' from the Home Office (▶see 977–8). The purpose of this document is to give full explanation of the reasons for detention. In a letter of January 2001 to Bail for Immigration Detainees, the Home Office described bail summaries as follows:

'Detainees now receive the reasons for detention form IS91R giving them details of why they have been detained. Unless circumstances have changed significantly between detention and the hearing, the bail summary is basically an amplification of those reasons.'

Applicants should be careful to see whether the bail summary really is an 'amplification' (i.e. further explanation) of the reasons originally given (or given during the monthly updates as the situation changed). If it looks as though the summary contains new reasons not previously notified when they should have been, then this may weaken the Home Office case for detention. If the reasons given in the bail summary were the real reasons and were important reasons, why were they not mentioned before? Detention for immigration purposes is an exception to the fundamental right to liberty contained in Article 5 ECHR; it is not something that can be justified by reasons made up on the hoof.

Consider what points are in support of the applicant

It is important to bring out at the bail hearing the strongest points in support of bail. Representatives will have to take detailed instructions from their clients. Some important areas are:

- Does the applicant have a family and a stable address where they have been living for some time?
- Does the applicant have outstanding applications and appeals with reasonable prospects of success?
- Has the applicant got a good record of complying with immigration control and conditions of temporary admission or leave?
- Will the family members of people who are dependent on the applicant, or who they care for, suffer if the applicant is detained?
- What links does the applicant have to the community in which they live that would make it less likely that they would 'go to ground'? (clubs, organisations, community groups, churches, studies – evidence from any such organisations might be useful).

Address

Providing an address where the applicant will stay is obviously important. It enables the authorities to know where the applicant will be, and it makes it less likely that the applicant will 'disappear'. This is particularly true if the applicant will be staying with one of the sureties, who will therefore be in a position to keep an eye on them and exercise control over them. The conditions of bail will almost certainly require the applicant to live at the address given. If the applicant is staying with relatives or friends, some evidence of the accommodation and their willingness to accommodate the applicant should be available.

The Procedure Rules state that if the applicant is unable to give an address, the reason why an address cannot be given should be stated on the application form (rule 38(2)(d)). This allows applicants who will seek accommodation from NASS to explain why they do not yet have an address. Where this is the case, written evidence will have to be produced that NASS will support the applicant and provide accommodation (see *Guidance Notes*, para. 2.4.3 and also NASS Policy Bulletin 64). If bail is granted in such cases, the bail condition given will read:

'To reside at such accommodation as is directed by NASS in accordance with the terms and conditions of support given, and to notify the [AIT], the Chief Immigration Officer and the Secretary of State for the Home Department of the address of such accommodation within 24 hours of being provided with it.'

The above wording was approved by NASS. NASS Policy Bulletin 64 states that an application for support for a person detained under immigration powers should be processed in the ordinary way. Applicants should inform NASS that they are applying for bail. The Bulletin states that, if support is to be provided, it is vital that NASS caseworkers notify the permanent address without delay so that the bail hearing can be held (para. 2.47).

Use of Home Office policy

Breach of Home Office policy can be grounds for challenging the *legality* of the detention, which is not the purpose of the bail hearing. However, there is no reason why the factors set out by the Home Office as influencing decisions to detain should not also be taken into account in deciding whether to grant bail. The *Guidance Notes* themselves indicate that the AIT should have regard to Chapter 38 of the OEM (see para. 1.3). If the applicant is being detained when, on consideration of the factors set out by the Home Office, it would seem inappropriate to do so, this should be brought to the attention of the immigration judge. This will be particularly important in cases of the detention of minors, those with a history of torture, of physical or mental ill-health, those with serious disabilities, the elderly, and pregnant women.

To see what Home Office policy says about detention in these and other cases, ▶see Tables 1–3 at 909–917. In addition to the policy set out there, Home Office policy may also be relevant in bail applications in the following two situations.

Detention in prisons or police stations Policy restricts circumstances in which applicants should be detained in prisons (▶936–7), including after serving a sentence (▶915), and police stations (▶938).

Detention in age-dispute cases As the general policy sets out, un-accompanied minors should only be detained in 'very exceptional circumstances'. For further details about detention and age-dispute cases, ▶see 688–91.

Use of other guidance and studies

Applicants may also make use of the UNHCR's *Guidelines on the Detention of Asylum Seekers* (February 1999). These are attached to the *Guidance Notes* as Appendix 2, and the *Guidance Notes* (para. 1.3) indicate that the AIT should have regard to them, particularly Guidelines 2 and 3 (for a summary of them, ▶see 917–8). In the case of the detention of families, children and pregnant women (or those with young children) and other vulnerable groups, advisers may find it useful to obtain and refer to the research studies that we have only been able to summarise briefly at ▶946–8.

Case-law on legality of detention

In order for 'bail' to be granted, it is assumed that the detention is itself lawful. If it were not, then there would be no need for bail. So, strictly, the *legality* of detention is challenged in other ways (▶see below 985–7). However, some of the case-law dealing with the lawfulness of detention is useful, because it also refers to the factors that are relevant in assessing whether detention is justified. The lawfulness of detention is dealt with at ▶919–32. Of particular relevance is the decision of the Court of Appeal in *R(I) v SSHD* and the factors it sets out as relevant: length of the existing detention; obstacles in the way of removal; the speed of steps being taken by the Home Office in order to remove; the conditions of detention; the effect of detention on the applicant; the risk of absconding; and the risk of committing offences.

The case of *I* also examines the relevance of the refusal by an applicant to make a voluntary departure. In particular, in that case, the Court noted that the relevance of absconding should not be overstated – it should not be a trump card in every case, and must be viewed together with all the other factors in the case (the *I* case is set out in the table at ▶927–9). The *Guidance Notes* also draw attention to the relevance of this case (para. 2.6.2).

Conditions in place of detention and effect on applicant

The conditions of detention and any particular effect that detention is having on the applicant are also relevant. Details about places and conditions of detention are given in Chapter 31. If the applicant has not been treated properly in accordance with the Detention Centre Rules (summarised at ▶940–1), this should be brought to attention. Do the conditions in which the applicant is being kept comply with standards set by HM Inspectorate, as it has applied them to immigration removal centres, to determine whether there is a 'healthy custodial environment'? The four tests the Inspectorate uses are set out at ▶942–3, and the detailed criteria it uses to assess whether those conditions are met are set out in its publication *Immigration Removal Centre Expectations* (May 2005).

As in any other case, if there are particular problems, it may be worth taking a statement from the applicant covering them. Advisers might also want to examine the most recent report of the Inspectorate concerning the detention centre where the applicant is detained to see whether it offers any corroboration of the problems that the applicant says they are experiencing. We have provided brief summaries only of some of the recent reports at ▶943–6.

If the applicant is suffering ill-health in detention, or if the effect of the detention on them is particularly severe because they are vulnerable, medical evidence will be useful. Applicants should, in the first instance, have made the difficulties clear to officers and medical services available at the detention centre, and advisers should try to obtain any medical reports or other records relating to the applicant that have been kept by those services.

Human rights

Human rights may be relevant in the context of the conditions in which the applicant is detained (Article 3), or in terms of family separation (Article 8). It may be worth providing statements from the applicant and their family members on this issue. Whether or not the family separation actually amounts to a violation of Article 8, the degree of difficulty that separation is causing, or the difficulties experienced by a whole family that is detained, are still relevant factors in considering bail. Article 5 is relevant to whether detention is lawful, and is considered in detail at ▶922–4, 925, 930–1.

What conditions of bail should be offered

Release on bail will almost always be subject to conditions, and the detainee must agree to those conditions before being released. It is therefore advisable for representatives to describe to the applicant the likely conditions, and ensure that they understand and are willing to comply with them. Common conditions include reporting at a reporting centre or a police station at specified times, and residing at a particular address. A detainee (and their sureties) should also be advised that a failure to comply with the conditions is likely to lead to re-detention, with little prospect of further release on bail, as well as the possible loss of the sureties' money. Breach of conditions could also have negative consequences for the resolution of the person's case. Electronic monitoring is still being trialled in this area, but is likely to become an important part of the conditions that can be attached to bail (▶see above at 953–5).

Second and further applications for bail

If it is not the applicant's first bail application, then the grounds of the application should give full details of any change in circumstances since the refusal (Procedure Rules, rule 38(2)(h)). The next immigration judge is not bound by the previous decision, but the AIT will generally be looking for new grounds, new evidence or some change in circumstances. The passage of time can in itself amount to a change of circumstances. If at least 28 days have passed since the first application, the AIT should be willing to reconsider the original arguments for bail (see *Guidance Notes*, paras 3.1–3.3).

Sureties and personal recognisance

The requirement for the applicant to offer a recognisance is generally seen as a formality and, if they have no resources, a nominal sum of, say, £10 can be put forward, which they do not actually have to produce.

Although the form on which to apply for bail gives the impression that two sureties must also be provided, in reality there is no such legal requirement. This is confirmed in the *Guidance Notes*, which remind immigration judges that asylum-seekers rarely have friends or relatives in the UK to act as sureties, that they may have to rely on assistance from voluntary associations, and that 'sureties are only required where you cannot otherwise be satisfied that the applicant will observe the conditions you may wish to impose'. In cases where there is no prospect of the applicant getting sureties, but where there is a case for granting bail in principle, the immigration judge should consider whether 'more stringent conditions might meet the particular needs or concerns of the case' (para. 2.2).

In the case of *Brezinski & Glowacka*, Kay J stated:

'Clearly it would be wrong to require sureties if there were no need for sureties, but where one reaches a situation where one cannot otherwise be sure that the obligation will be observed, Parliament has rightly provided that that extra ammunition is available to a Special Adjudicator dealing with these matters if, in fact, that will have the consequence that a person who might not otherwise be granted his liberty will be granted it'.

In *Lamin Minteh*, the Court of Appeal decided that it was unlawful for an adjudicator not to grant bail simply because there were no sureties, regardless of whether there was evidence that the applicant was likely to abscond.

There is always the potential for a conflict of interest for a representative when dealing with a detainee and their sureties. For these reasons, representatives often advise sureties that they should get independent advice if they are unsure or uncertain of the commitment that they are entering into.

Ability of surety to exercise control

Apart from the size of the amounts offered, the most important quality of the surety is the extent to which their involvement will exercise control over the actions of the applicant. Will the applicant be deterred from absconding from bail for fear of the surety losing their money? It is therefore always useful to take details from sureties about how well they know the detainee, and how long they have known each other for.

The AIT will usually prefer a surety who will be living with or near to the bail applicant. Where the applicant is not going to live with the surety, there may be concern about how the surety will supervise the applicant and ensure that they are complying with conditions of bail. Details should be taken as to whether the surety could arrange a certain time to meet the applicant, or make regular visits to the address where the applicant will be staying, or whether they would agree to telephone the applicant on a regular basis in order that contact be maintained. Sureties may wish to assure the court that, should the applicant abscond or fail to comply with conditions of bail, then they would immediately notify the immigration service and the applicant's solicitors of this fact.

Consideration should also be given to whether the surety can provide any evidence to counter the reasons given for detention. For example, where the immigration authorities are questioning the identity of an applicant, a surety may be able to give evidence about this, and produce documentary evidence in support, such as photographs.

Amount and evidence of surety

Sureties should provide evidence of the money they are putting forward as the amount they are prepared to stand. Bank or building society savings statements of account are often produced for this purpose. Evidence of statements and passbooks should cover the past three months, with evidence of current balances. If the money is in a savings account, then the account should be in the sole name of the surety. If the account is in joint names, then a letter should be obtained from the other account holder confirming that they consent to the funds being used in this way. Where a large amount of money has recently been placed in an account, the AIT may be suspicious as to whether the money really does belong to the surety, or has simply been placed there for the purposes of the bail application, and may shortly afterwards be transferred back. Details should therefore be taken of any significant recent transactions contained in the statements. Sureties should also produce wage-slips or, if self-employed, a copy of their latest set of accounts. If other assets (e.g. property) are being relied on, documentary evidence of their value and equity should be produced.

As to the amount of money offered by the sureties, a relatively small sum would still amount to a significant loss to a person who is on a low income with a family. Therefore, it is often important to convey to the immigration judge what the consequences would be for the surety if they were to lose the money being offered. This has been acknowledged in the *Guidance Notes*, which state that the amount of the surety should be fixed with regard to the surety's means. It should be within those means, and not 'so high as to be prohibitive' (para. 2.3.3). In very few cases, however, will a 'nominal' amount be acceptable:

'The only exception may be where the surety is the applicant's spouse or partner, or someone at whose home the applicant is to live, and they are on a low income with no savings. However, even then you may require another surety in a more substantial amount if you find the risk of non-compliance too great.' (para. 2.3.4)

The means of the surety, therefore, can sometimes cut both ways. Where a surety is relatively comfortable, there is the danger of the AIT entering into a bidding war with sureties – i.e. requiring larger amounts, having regard to the surety's apparent means. The immigration judge will want to ensure that sum is not fixed at an amount that, frankly, the surety would not miss if it were forfeited. It is therefore necessary to be able to antici-pate any suggestion that the failure to put forward all monies available in support of the bail application indicates either any lack of real commit-ment by them, or lack of trust between the surety and the applicant. This can be achieved by evidence that there are good reasons why any additional savings are not being offered in support – for example the surety's children's welfare, emergencies, or other pressing financial com-mitments.

Fortunately, the amounts seen as reasonable are less now then they once were. There was a time when it seemed almost mandatory to produce sureties willing to stand thousands, rather than hundreds of pounds. It is now fairly common, where the sureties are of limited means, for bail to be granted on the basis of a few hundred pounds per surety, and sometimes less.

Other evidence required from sureties

There is no absolute requirement that a surety be a British citizen or settled in the UK. The Home Office presenting officer may raise objections to sureties who are not settled, since the OEM states that acceptable sureties should be 'aged 18 or over and settled in the UK' (para. 39.6.2). Despite this, in some cases asylum-seekers have themselves successfully acted as sureties. Those with an unlawful immigration position in the UK will, however, clearly be unsuitable.

Sureties should therefore usually bring to court evidence of their identity, nationality (usually their passport) and, if they are not British, their immigration status. In addition to the above evidence, the 'Notice to

Applicants' at Appendix 4 to the *Guidance Notes* states that sureties should also bring their rent book or mortgage statements, together with other documentation showing their address, such as a driving licence or NHS medical card (para. 5). This evidence will obviously be important if the applicant is to live with the surety. If the property is rented, some immigration judges may require evidence that the landlord has no objection to the applicant living there.

For further details about what may be required of sureties, see the 'surety checklist' addressed to immigration judges (▶981–2).

Deposit of sureties

At one stage a practice developed of representatives indicating that the surety had deposited monies with them, and undertaking to hold those monies 'to the order of the court' – i.e. not to return them to the surety until the appellate authority allowed them to do so. It has been decided that there is no lawful power for the AIT to require this in England, Wales and Northern Ireland, and that the practice should not be followed. It can still be done in Scotland (*Guidance Notes*, para. 2.3.2).

Those who do not have sureties who know them

For those without sureties, the Bail Circle, set up by the Churches Commission for Racial Justice, has a register of people who are prepared to act as sureties for detainees. The number of people they have available is limited. If no surety can be found, applicants and advisers should not be deterred from making bail applications.

Procedure after the application has been submitted

After the AIT has received the application, it must send a copy to the Home Office straightaway and fix a hearing.

How long before a bail application is heard?

Applications for bail are – 'if practicable' – listed to be heard within *three* working days of receipt of the Form B1. For these purposes, if a notice is received by the AIT after 3.30pm on a particular day, it is treated as if it had been received on the next business day (see para. 19, Practice Directions, 4 April 2005).

Checking sureties

The Home Office will arrange for the police to check the status of any sureties named on the form before the application is heard. People with criminal convictions, or who have come to adverse attention in other immigration matters, are unlikely to be acceptable as sureties.

Bail summary

If the Home Office is going to oppose the application for bail, it must send to the AIT and the applicant a 'written statement' of the reasons for opposing bail. This document is known as the 'bail summary'. Bail summaries have often been of poor quality, and sometimes contain serious factual inaccuracies (▶see for example in **Mohamed** and **Johnson**, at 931–2). Applicants should read them carefully and decide whether they need evidence to deal with any factual points that are wrong. In **AKB**, McCullough J stated of the bail summary prepared by the Home Office in that case:

'I am not happy that this document is an adequate statement of reasons for continuing [detention]. There is no balance in the document. It simply sets out arguments for continued detention. It does not acknowledge that there were other arguments raised against continued detention and that the two had to be considered together and balanced before a decision was reached.'

The bail summary must be filed no later than 2.00pm on the business day before the bail hearing. The exception to this is if the Home Office is given notice of the hearing less than 24 hours before that 2.00pm deadline, in which case the summary should simply be provided 'as soon as reasonably practicable' (Procedure Rules, rule 39(2)).

This requirement in the Procedure Rules is intended to give applicants and representatives some notice of the Home Office's detailed reasons before the bail hearing, so that they can address them. It is intended to rectify the previous situation, in which the bail summary was often only produced or read out at the hearing itself.

The bail hearing before the AIT

Although not stated in the legislation, it is generally accepted that there is a presumption in favour of granting bail similar to the 'right to bail' that applies in criminal law. It is important to remember, therefore, that the hearing should not be approached as if the applicant has to 'prove' that they should be released. Instead, it is for the Home Office to show strong grounds why detention should be maintained (*Guidance Notes*, paras 1.4, 2.5, 8). The *Guidance Notes* also state that this presumption will not apply in favour of the applicant if any of the following apply (para. 1.4 and see para. 30(2), Sch 2, 1971 Act):

- the applicant has previously breached conditions of bail;
- the applicant is likely to commit an offence or cause a danger to public health if released;
- the applicant is suffering from a mental disorder that makes detention necessary in the person's own interests, or for the protection of others;
- the applicant is under the age of 17, and no satisfactory arrangements for their care have been made.

Three stages

The *Guidance Notes* indicate that the AIT should approach the bail application in three stages:

'First, is this a case where bail is right in principle, subject to suitable conditions if necessary? Second, are sureties necessary? Third, are the sureties and recognisances offered satisfactory?' (para. 2.7.4)

Note that the *Guidance Notes* are being revised and it is possible that this 'three stage' approach may be changed. JCWI's view is that it would be very unfortunate if an applicant got past Stage 1 (perhaps even had factual findings in their favour) and then had to start all over again if the application did not proceed because of lack of adequacy of sureties etc.

Stage 1: Bail in principle

If the Home Office is opposing bail, it will have prepared a statement giving its reasons for doing so – the bail summary. Often the presenting officer will simply rely on the summary. The applicant's representative will be asked to respond to the reasons given for continued detention. In considering what submissions to present, all the points set out above under 'preparing the application' are relevant.

Factual disputes Although, in bail hearings, representatives are generally given latitude to make submissions 'on instructions' – i.e. on the basis of what they have been told by their clients – where there are important factual disputes between what the applicant states and the Home Office position, it may be that evidence will need to be heard. If there is evidence to be heard, this will normally take place before the submissions mentioned above. Evidence heard may relate to: the circumstances in which the applicant was detained; whether they cooperated; whether a false identity was maintained; whether an applicant tried to rely on a false travel document or passport; whether previous conditions of temporary admission or bail were complied with, and so on. Even though there are unlikely to have been formal directions, it is best to have a statement from the applicant (or other witnesses) in such cases. Remember, the general burden of proof is on the Home Office. The *Guidance Notes* state:

'If allegations in the bail summary are contested in evidence then the Secretary of State should adduce evidence, including any documents relevant to the decision to detain, to support such allegations.' (para. 2.5.3).

So, if there are such disputes, it is a good idea to ensure that the Home Office is fully on notice of the applicant's version of events before the hearing. This can be done by presenting to them that account in previous representations for temporary admission or grounds set out in the B1 bail application form. That way there will be no excuse for the Home Office if it fails to produce evidence on the day.

Applicant's overall chances of success The bail hearing is obviously not a dress rehearsal of the applicant's main case for remaining in the UK if they have an appeal outstanding. The immigration judge dealing with the bail hearing will not be able to come to any conclusions about the general case. However, the apparent strength of the case is relevant because, if the applicant thinks that they have very good chances of winning, they are unlikely to give up that chance by going to ground, rather than pushing ahead with their appeal and attending the appeal hearing. In *some* cases, where the applicant has particularly good evidence in support of their case and/or the reasons given by the Home Office for refusing the application are particularly bad, it may be worth referring to the strength of the general case.

No bail summary The Procedure Rules state that, if the Home Office wants to object to bail being granted, it 'must' file a bail summary with the AIT and the applicant (rule 39(2)). If no summary is produced, the AIT should still go ahead with the application and, as the *Guidance Notes* indicate in commenting on this rule, this 'implies that bail would have to be granted'. If the summary is produced late, it can still be considered, but if it contains allegations that the applicant disputes, this will affect the weight given by the AIT to those allegations (para. 2.7.2).

Stage 2: Are sureties or other conditions necessary?

If the AIT agrees to grant bail in principle, the next question will be whether sureties (and other conditions) are necessary. It may be that the AIT feels able to grant bail without sureties, on the basis of any of the other conditions set out below. This is really for the immigration judge to decide, and there will then be an examination of whether the conditions will in fact be sufficient. The conditions that can be imposed are all considered above. They are:

- the participation of sureties;
- residence at a particular address;
- reporting – this will normally be to an immigration officer at a reporting centre or to a police station (the immigration judge will usually ask the presenting officer for guidance as to the best place to report). The likely frequency of initial reporting is once per week, but this may be reduced later (*Guidance Notes*, para. 2.4.5);
- electronic monitoring (▶see 953–5).

There is no power to impose conditions concerning employment, as conditions can only be imposed that will make it likely that the applicant answers to their bail (*Guidance Notes*, para. 2.4.6). However, in most cases it will still be an offence for an employer to employ a person whose only immigration status is that they have been granted immigration bail (▶see 1030 and 496–500).

Stage 3: Are the sureties adequate?

Plainly, the sureties should attend the bail hearing. (For considerations relating to sureties, ▶see 974–7.) Attached as Appendix 6 to the *Guidance Notes* is a 'Surety checklist', which is for the attention of the immigration judge (below ▶981–2). It sets out the nature of the examination of the sureties. Applicants, advisers and sureties should take note of this, as it makes clear what will be required of them at hearing. We have summarised the checklist in the table below.

Additional sureties If a surety has not come forward until the day of the hearing, the problem that arises is that there will have been no opportunity for the Home Office to check their credentials before the hearing. The AIT will often be willing to allow a short adjournment for the presenting officer to telephone through the details of a surety, so that they can be immediately checked. At the end of the day, however, it is for the immigration judge to form their own view of the suitability of the sureties (*Guidance Notes*, para. 2.7.1).

Taking the surety elsewhere If a surety is unable to appear in person, it is possible for the AIT to fix the conditions of bail and the amounts to be provided by the surety, with a view to the bail actually being taken before another responsible person, such as an immigration officer, police officer or solicitor. If this course is taken, the applicant will not be released until the bail is taken. This approach is unusual, however, and should only be used as a last resort (see paras 22(3), 29 (6), Sch 2, 1971 Act; *Guidance Notes*, para. 2.7.9).

9

SURETY CHECKLIST

The following is taken from the checklist addressed to those deciding the bail application, attached as Appendix 6 to the *Guidance Notes*.

If the immigration judge decides that bail can be granted subject to suitable sureties, evidence should be taken from them. The immigration judge is likely to question the applicant on the following matters, and whether they have the following relevant evidence.

1) Identification:

The surety should present:

- their passport or other ID;
- if the surety has a limited right of residence in the UK, evidence of when it expires;
- proof of address;
- a telephone number for future reference.

2) Relationship to the applicant:

- Is the surety a relative of the applicant?

- How long has the surety known the applicant?
- How much contact has there been between the surety and the applicant in the UK?
- What obligation will the applicant feel towards the surety?
- Will the applicant live with the surety?

3) Occupation and income:

- What is the nature of the surety's employment or occupation?
- What evidence is there of the surety's income (pay-slips; bank or building society accounts; accounts submitted to the Inland Revenue)?

4) Assets and liabilities:

- What assets does the surety have which add weight to their financial standing?
- What liabilities does the surety have?
- What evidence is there of assets and liabilities?
- If the value of equity in a property is to be taken into account in taking the surety, can the money be easily obtained – for example, by an affordable re-mortgage?

5) Documentary evidence

Documentary evidence about financial circumstances (see above) is generally required to support oral evidence. Absence of documentary evidence is not fatal to the application, but will affect the weight given to oral evidence.

6) Criminal convictions

The presenting officer should be able to give details of any convictions if they have checked the sureties. However, the immigration judge may also ask about criminal convictions.

7) Stability

The immigration judge will check that the surety leads a stable lifestyle. This will relate to factors such as: marital status, details of family, nature of employment, and standing in the community.

8) Awareness of obligations

The immigration judge is likely to ask the sureties to explain their own understanding of their obligations, and what the consequences are for them of the applicant failing to answer to their bail.

Withdrawal of bail application

Since bail applications can be made quite quickly, there may be some cases where it is tactically better to withdraw the application rather than proceed with it to the bitter end, and have a refusal of bail on record. For example, in some cases the immigration judge is prepared to grant bail in principle, but it is clear that the sureties are not acceptable because the proper evidence is not yet available, or because they have not turned up. If the judge is not prepared to adjourn the remainder of the application, it may be better to withdraw it and make a fresh application in a few days' time. If, however, an application is dismissed on grounds such as these, representatives should try and ensure that the reasons given in the notice of refusal reflect this. This will make it easier to persuade the next immigration judge to grant bail when the gap in the necessary evidence has been closed.

The decision of the AIT on bail

The approach to bail varies considerably from one immigration judge to another. Some continue to approach applications in the belief that two sureties, each offering a substantial sum of money, are required for an application to succeed. However, the approach of the majority of them (previously adjudicators) has changed enormously over the years.

In *Brezinski & Glowacka*, it was stated by the High Court that 'one only restricts a person's liberty if it is essential to do so and one judges that by having regard to all the factors that are properly to be considered'.

In *AKB*, McCullough J indicated that an adjudicator should justify his or her decision to refuse bail. It was not enough to say that there was a chance that the applicant would abscond; there had to be a 'significant risk'. The same obviously applies to immigration judges of the AIT.

The immigration judge will give the parties notice of the decision granting or refusing bail. Where bail is refused, the notice should give reasons for refusing bail (Procedure Rules, rule 39(5)).

If bail is granted

If bail is granted, the main condition will be that the applicant appears before the AIT or an immigration officer at a specified time. In the *Guidance Notes*, this is called the 'primary condition' (with reporting, residence etc. all 'secondary conditions'). The period for which bail is granted will depend on the circumstances. The immigration judge will take into account the date of any appeal hearing, and bail will often be granted to that date. If the applicant is to be removed, the immigration judge will take into account any details given by the presenting officer about when removal is to be expected. The maximum period for which bail is likely to be granted at any one time is three months (*Guidance Notes*, para. 2.7.8).

Following the grant of bail, the applicant will be released. The Procedure

Rules state that the person 'having custody of the applicant' must release them when given a copy of the decision to grant bail (rule 41). Forms are completed showing the conditions of the bail (i.e. the 'primary condition' as well as conditions relating to residence, reporting and sureties). Copies of the forms are given to the applicant, representative and the sureties.

If bail is refused

If bail is refused, further applications for bail may still be made. A different immigration judge may make a different decision. However, the applicant is required to state on the application form what change of circumstances there has been since the last application. As stated above, the passage of time can count as a change of circumstance, even if there have been no other changes (▶see 973–4).

Applicants should do all they can to address the reasons given by the previous immigration judge for refusing bail. Was there some important matter held against them upon which it would be possible to produce evidence? If it is felt that the decision to refuse bail is legally flawed, or so completely unreasonable that it is unlawful, then the way to challenge a decision of the AIT refusing bail is judicial review (for judicial review procedures generally, ▶see 1213–22). Remember, however, that judicial review is a complex and involved process. If the decision seems completely unreasonable, it may be easier and quicker to try persuading another AIT judge to grant bail.

Bail continuation or variation

If the case has not been resolved by the time the bail expires, an application to 'renew' (or 'continue') bail is usually made on that date, if the applicant's bail conditions are for them to return to the AIT. If the applicant's bail conditions are for them to appear before an immigration officer, then in most cases, provided that conditions have been complied with, the applicant will be granted temporary admission. If the applicant is subject to removal at that stage, they may be particularly vulnerable to re-detention. If there is a legal challenge or representations outstanding, the applicant or their advisers should make that clear before the applicant attends, and it is useful for the applicant to have some evidence of the position with them when they do attend.

Provided that the person has stuck to the conditions of bail and there have been no changes of circumstance, bail renewal applications are normally a formality. The bail applicant should appear before the AIT on each application to extend bail. Sureties should normally attend, unless they were previously given permission not to attend, and at the very least should confirm in writing that they are happy to continue to act as sureties.

Varying bail conditions

Bail renewal hearings can also be used as an opportunity to 'vary' the bail conditions – for example, to reduce the times at which the person must report. If a change of circumstances occurs while a person is on bail – for example, if a person needs to change their address – an application to vary the conditions of bail must be made.

Failure to answer to bail

If bail is granted and the applicant fails to reappear at the time and place fixed on the return date, both they and their sureties risk losing part or all of the money they have offered. The proportion that is lost is as much as the AIT sees fit. The proceeding before the AIT in which this is done is known as 'forfeiture' (paras 23 and 31, Sch 2 and paras 2(4A) and 3, Sch 3, 1971 Act).

In deciding whether to forfeit all or part of the sum, the AIT may question sureties on whether their trust in the applicant was well founded, whether they were vigilant in monitoring compliance with the bail conditions, and whether they could have reasonably suspected a failure to comply with bail conditions (in which case they would be expected to have alerted the authorities). The AIT will take into account (*Guidance Notes*, para. 6.4):

- the level of the surety's responsibility for the applicant's failure to attend;
- the steps the surety took to ensure that the applicant complied with their conditions;
- whether the surety reported any concerns to the immigration authorities;
- any explanations provided by the surety.

Forfeiture proceedings are rare.

Arrest and detention of those on bail

An immigration officer or a police officer may arrest and detain any person who they reasonably believe to be in breach, or likely to breach, their conditions of bail. A person arrested under this power is to be brought before the AIT (or a JP or Sheriff, depending on which part of the UK they are arrested in), who will decide whether to continue the bail or direct that the person be detained.

UNLAWFUL DETENTION: HIGH COURT PROCEDURES

In order to obtain temporary admission or bail (set out above), applicants do not need to show that their detention is unlawful. The focus of the above procedures is simply on persuading the Home Office or the AIT that the use of detention powers is not justified in the individual case, and that the applicant can be trusted to comply with any conditions.

Chapter 30 explains in detail the general powers of detention. In particular, it describes the circumstances in which detention may be unlawful (▶919–32). Where detention is unlawful, an application to the High Court may be made to obtain release. Article 5(4) ECHR requires that detainees have a 'speedy' route by which to challenge the lawfulness of their detention.

Two High Court procedures

There are two High Court procedures that may be used: judicial review and *habeas corpus*. The courts have indicated that lawyers should try to use these procedures together where there is an overlap, rather than using them separately. In time, the two will probably merge together. Very often they raise identical issues which will stand or fall together (see the decision of the Court of Appeal in *R (I) v SSHD* at para. 6).

Traditionally, *habeas corpus* is used where there is no *lawful power* to detain a person. Judicial review is appropriate where, although there is a legal power, it is being exercised unlawfully. The distinction is not always easy to make. In any case, specialist advice should be obtained before using either of these procedures. If an applicant is already challenging a decision of the immigration authorities in judicial review proceedings, they may also apply to the High Court or the Court of Appeal for bail (▶see below).

Of course, even if an applicant thinks that their detention is unlawful (and the Home Office maintains that it is lawful), this does not prevent the applicant making an ordinary bail application to the AIT, instead of applying to the High Court. Although the AIT does not have the power to consider the lawfulness of the detention, it may still be the quickest and easiest route to obtain release.

Judicial review in detention cases

Judicial review has been used to challenge detention that is alleged to be without proper regard to (or not compliant with) the Home Office's policy; or where the detention policy itself is alleged to be unlawful; or where there has been a disproportionate or unreasonable use of the power to detain. It is also probably the right procedure to use now where the length of time for which a person has been detained is unreasonable in all circumstances (▶see *Khadir* below at 987).

General procedures for applying for judicial review are covered in Chapter 38, at ▶1213–22. Damages claims as part of judicial review claims against detention are covered in Chapter 37, at ▶1193–4 and ▶see 1175–80.

Bail in the course of judicial review proceedings

It is also possible to obtain bail from immigration detention in the High Court or the Court of Appeal, as an additional application in the course of judicial review proceedings. For example, if a person is making a claim for judicial review against a 'clearly unfounded' certificate issued by the Secretary of State, and is also detained, the High Court has the power to release the person on bail during the proceedings relating to the lawfulness of the certificate. It has the power to do this both at the 'permission' stage of judicial review proceedings and at the main stage (see *Turkoglu*, CA).

However, since there is a statutory right to apply for bail to the AIT, bail should generally be sought from the AIT. In the case of *Kelso*, Collins J was prepared to deal with a bail application in judicial review proceedings in circumstances where a bail application to the appeal authorities could result in a further application for judicial review if bail was refused, or if they imposed unsatisfactory conditions.

Habeas corpus

Habeas corpus is a very old procedure under which those whose freedom is taken away are entitled to apply to the court in order to obtain their liberty. It goes back at least to the time of Edward I. The person detaining has to show the court why the detention is lawful. In *Khawaja*, the House of Lords confirmed that, although this protection is often referred to as being for the benefit of 'British subjects', it can equally be claimed by non-nationals.

Applications for *habeas corpus* have procedural advantages for detainees, in that the court gives a very high priority to getting the application dealt with quickly. It is less usual for immigration detainees to be able to apply for *habeas corpus* because the powers of detention are so wide. *Habeas corpus* may be the appropriate procedure where the statutory pre-conditions for detention are simply not met. This may be the case, for example, where a person is being detained under a power allowing them to be detained 'pending removal', but where the Home Office has no real intention of removing them, or where there is no prospect of the person being removed at all. Until recently, *habeas corpus* proceedings were appropriate where people had been detained for an unreasonable period awaiting the relevant immigration action (which is usually removal). However, the decision of the House of Lords in *Khadir* has clarified that this type of case is really a challenge to the *exercise* of the power to detain, rather than to whether there is a power at all. Such cases will probably, therefore, now be brought as judicial review applications (see *Khadir* at paras 32–3) (▶see 956–7, 924–7).

9

33 Enforcement: port removal, illegal entry, administrative removal, deportation and criminal offences

Those who are in the UK but who do not have a right to remain under the immigration rules, or otherwise, and who cannot persuade the immigration authorities to exercise discretion to allow them to stay, can be required to leave. If they do not leave, they can be arrested and detained until their departure from the UK is enforced. Detention, covered in Chapters 30–32, is one of the main weapons the immigration authorities have in enforcing immigration control.

This chapter covers the different ways in which a person's departure can be enforced. We begin by summarising the four basic 'enforcement' procedures (▶990–1). We then look at recent developments in enforcement procedures and at proposals for further changes, both in terms of policy and under the 2005 Bill (▶991–3). Just because there is a power to enforce someone's departure does not mean that that power should automatically be used. In the next part of the chapter, we cross-refer to related government policy and relevant immigration rules and we look at some further, specific policy developments significant to decisions to enforce (▶993–1000) – for most cases the factors which are relevant are contained in the immigration rules (▶see 1009–1010, ▶see also 387–8).

Beginning at ▶1000, we then deal in turn with the four main enforcement procedures themselves: 'port' removal, administrative removal, illegal entry and deportation. We look at the procedures relevant to each and at the particular factors which influence decisions to enforce departure under each procedure. We then look at the actual process of removal itself (the final stage of all enforcement procedures) and at the countries of destination to which people can be sent (▶1026–8).

There are a few other forms of enforcement and departure not covered by the basic four procedures; they include voluntary departure and removals under the Mental Health Act. We look at them briefly at ▶1028–9.

Finally, we look at how those who are liable to enforcement may be discovered by the immigration authorities (▶1030–1) and at criminal offences (▶1031–5).

Appeals Where removal is being challenged by an in-country appeal, the appellant will be protected from enforcement while the appeal is proceeding (ss78–79, 92, 104 2002 Act, ▶1069–71, 1181–2 and ▶see 1059–61 for which appeals are in-country). *Although in this chapter we refer in passing to appeal rights against enforcement decisions, full details about rights of appeal against enforcement (and other) decisions are given in Chapter 34.*

Judicial review Where the challenge is by judicial review, the situation is not so straightforward and it *may* be that the applicant will need to obtain an injunction from the High Court in order to prevent removal before the challenge can be heard. For details about judicial review procedures, ▶see 1213–22. For details about 'deferring' (i.e. postponing removal) where a claim for judicial review will be brought, ▶see 1220.

THE FOUR BASIC 'ENFORCEMENT' PROCEDURES AND THE TERMS USED

The particular procedure used for enforcing the departure of any person who has no right to be in the UK, depends on their immigration status. The different ways in which people can be required to leave are:

1) **Port removal** (▶1000–2). This applies to people who arrive in the UK and who are denied entry. It is easy to get these people confused with some of the categories below because, by the time they are being required to leave, they may have been in the UK for a long time on temporary admission, for example, as asylum-seekers.

2) **Administrative removal** (▶1002–10). People can be removed from the UK under Home Office powers of administrative removal if they have overstayed their leave, breached their conditions of leave, obtained (or tried to obtain) leave to remain by deception or if their indefinite leave has been revoked because they have ceased to be refugees. Until 2 October 2000, the procedure for requiring some of these categories of people to leave was 'deportation'.

3) **Illegal entry** (▶1010–5). Illegal entrants are those people who enter the UK in breach of the immigration laws. This can be done in a number of ways including by deception.

4) **Deportation** (▶1015–26). The categories of people who are 'deported' has been very much reduced as a result of 'administrative removal' (above). The remaining categories of people who are deported are:

- those who are recommended for deportation by a criminal court after being convicted of an offence;

- those whose presence in the UK is not 'conducive to the public good';

- family members of those in the above two categories.

We look at these four procedures in more detail in turn below. When a person may have immigration control enforced against them in one of these four ways, they have often (although not always) committed a criminal offence. Usually, the authorities are happy to simply enforce immigration control but, in some cases, there may be prosecutions.

Only deportation completely prevents a person's return to the UK (until the deportation order is revoked), although enforcement under the other procedures will usually affect future immigration decisions made, concerning the same applicant.

Terms used

The terms that are used to describe the above procedures can be confusing. Most confusing of all is that the last stage of all the procedures is 'removal'. People in all four groups are finally issued with 'removal directions', which are the directions given to the carrier to convey the person away from the UK. So, those who are being deported after a deportation order has been signed are, at that stage, 'removed'.

Another general term, often used by immigration officials and lawyers, is 'enforcement'. Sometimes when this term is used, it is intended to describe only deportation and illegal entry (and possibly also administrative removal). In ordinary language, the removal of people who have applied and been refused at port is just as much an 'enforcement' of their departure. In addition, the 1999 Act introduced language which defines 'enforcement action' as covering all the above kinds of removal (see the amended s24A(2) 1971 Act). We have therefore used the term 'enforcement' to cover all four procedures.

Exemptions from enforcement

There are certain people who are exempt from enforcement. They include certain Commonwealth and Irish nationals who were resident in the UK on 1 January 1973 and have long residence in the UK, who are exempt from being deported or administratively removed. Those with diplomatic privilege also enjoy exemption from being removed from the UK in certain cases. Persons in these categories should seek more detailed advice if the immigration authorities are seeking to enforce their departure (see ss7–8 1971 Act, s10(10) 1999 Act).

RECENT DEVELOPMENTS IN ENFORCEMENT

The five most significant changes in legislation affecting enforcement since the last edition of the *Handbook* are:

- family members of those being removed from the UK as 'port removals' or illegal entrants can also be removed (s73(1) 2002 Act amending Sch 2 to the 1971 Act). Similar provision already existed for those subject to administrative removal and for deportees;

- those who *try* to obtain leave to remain by deception can be subject to administrative removal even if they are not successful (see s74 2002);

- if a person is liable to deportation, or has obtained their leave by deception, their *indefinite leave* may be revoked *even if* they cannot be removed from the UK (s76(1)(2) 2002 Act, ▶see below 1008, 1025–6);

- if a person 'ceases' to be a refugee, their *indefinite leave* may be revoked and they are then liable to administrative removal from the UK (s76(3)(7) 2002 Act, ▶see below 1008);

- the 2004 Act has created a criminal offence of failing to cooperate with the obtaining of a travel document for deportation or removal – this is looked at in an earlier chapter at ▶927.

Present policy developments and further proposed changes under the 2005 Bill are set out in the table below.

ENFORCEMENT PROPOSALS: POLICY AND THE 2005 BILL

Under political and media pressure, the Home Office is determined to step up the pace of enforced departure from the UK. The National Audit Office report, 'Returning failed asylum seekers' published on 19 July 2005, suggests that there may have been 283,500 failed asylum-seekers in the UK in May 2004.

The 'five-year strategy'

In its 'five-year strategy' (February 2005), the government states that it will:

- by the end of 2005, aim to ensure that the monthly rate of removals is greater than the number of unfounded asylum applications;

- fast track the cases of more asylum-seekers;

- detain more failed asylum-seekers;

- negotiate more return agreements with other countries and also work with those countries to ensure that they re-document and accept back failed asylum-seekers. It has been made clear that if countries fail to cooperate, this will have implications for the wider relationship between the UK and those countries, including access of their nationals to some migration schemes (for the difficulties in documenting failed asylum-seekers ▶see 926–7 and for the ability to exclude countries from the working holidaymaker scheme ▶see 237; returns agreements are also to be linked with the low-skill work schemes, which the government is in the course of developing);

- the government says that it has successfully negotiated return agreements with Afghanistan, Bulgaria, China, India, Romania, Sri Lanka, the Somaliland authorities, Turkey, and Vietnam (note also that, in a separate development, the government is seeking to conclude 'memoranda of understanding' with countries to which it wishes to return those connected with terrorism where the applicant may have a claim under Article 3 ECHR ▶see 1020);

- prosecute those who arrive without documents, in order to prevent applicants 'concealing their identity to frustrate removal' (▶see 683–6);

- find further ways to return unaccompanied asylum-seeking children (▶see 870–1).

'Tackling terrorism' – unacceptable behaviours

After a short consultation period beginning on 5 August 2005, the Home Office set out new guidelines on 24 August 2005, for the deportation or exclusion of 'extremists' on the grounds that their presence in the UK is 'not conducive to the public good'. The guidelines take the form of a list of behaviours that the government believes foment and provoke acts of terrorism. For further details, ►see 1019–20 below.

Immigration, Asylum and Nationality Bill 2005

The 2005 Bill makes the following proposals.

- If a decision is made to administratively remove a person, any existing leave they have will be invalid from the time they are notified of that decision and not, as is presently the case, when removal directions are issued (see s10(8) 1999 Act). Removal directions may of course be issued much later, perhaps after an appeal. So, if a person is subject to administrative removal on the basis of breach of conditions or deception, the purpose of this proposal is to *immediately* prevent any access to benefits they may have, which is based on their leave.

- An applicant who has their indefinite leave revoked because they have 'ceased' to be a refugee and who therefore becomes liable for administrative removal (see s10(1)(ba) 1999 Act and s76(3) 2002 Act), will have two rights of appeal: firstly, against the decision to revoke (a right which they have already); and secondly, against administrative removal.

- Applicants who apply in time will become overstayers after a negative decision on their application – they will no longer have automatic leave during any appeal.

9

TAKING A DECISION THAT A PERSON MUST LEAVE AND POLICY

Just because the conditions exist which give a *power* to enforce a person's departure, does not mean that the immigration authorities must always automatically use it. In all cases, a decision must be made as to whether it is right, in the circumstances of the case, to carry out enforcement. The factors that are to be taken into account in making this decision, in administrative removal and deportation cases, are set out in the immigration rules (►see 1009–10, ►see also 387–8). In other cases, although there are no factors set out in the rules, advisers can still make representations on their client's behalf, often relying on similar factors. In illegal entry cases, the Home Office has stated it will apply the same factors (►see 1010).

As we look at the four different forms of enforcement (►below), we also look at some of the factors, which arise in those cases that are relevant in reaching the decision to actually enforce.

In addition, in many cases, there may be human rights reasons why a person should be able to stay in the UK, in particular, because they have family life here, or removing them would expose them to torture or inhuman and degrading treatment or punishment (►see Section 8 for details about human rights).

In addition, there may be a policy outside the immigration rules that applies to the case, which may allow a person to remain, although they have no rights under the immigration rules. Some of these policies used to be outside the rules but are now contained within them. These rules and policies are covered in the appropriate part of the *Handbook* as follows:

- enforcement against people with a spouse settled in the UK (►see 337–41 on DP/2/93 and DP/3/96);
- enforcement against people with an unmarried partner settled in the UK (►see 342–3);
- enforcement against families with children who have long residence in the UK (►see 386–9, 998–1000 on DP/069/99, DP/4/95, DP/4/96); and for enforcement against unaccompanied children ►see 390–3, 688, 865, 870–2;
- long-residence rules (►151–7);
- those who are caring for a friend or relative in the UK (►232–5);
- those with serious health conditions where enforcement may raise human rights issues (►see 814–6);
- those who have been the victim of domestic violence (►see 345–51).

Before dealing with the four main forms of enforcement, we now look briefly at some recent further policy developments in enforcement procedures relating to those over 65 (►below), medical issues (►995–6), self-harm/suicide (►996–8) and enforcement against families (►998–1000).

Enforcement against those aged over 65

For many years, Home Office policy was, as a general rule, not to remove those who are 65 years or over and who otherwise have no basis of stay in the UK. In September 2004, the Home Office appears to have modified this policy. An IND Policy document (EPU 10/04), disclosed to Elder Rahimi & Co Solicitors stated as follows (the same policy is reproduced in the OEM at Ch 36.8):

'Previous policy was that as a general rule, we did not enforce the departure of those aged 65 or over. Whilst this position is reflected in the [OEM] and [IDI], the policy has been interpreted by many as a blanket "age concession". There is now no specified age limit.

Ministers have agreed that a person's age is not, by itself, a realistic or reliable indicator of a person's health, mobility or ability to care for themselves. Many older people are able to enjoy active and independent lives. Cases must be assessed on their individual merits.

Age is just one of several factors to taken into account when considering a person's enforced removal from the United Kingdom. Other factors include the length of residence in the UK, strength of connections, domestic and other compassionate circumstances.

The onus is on the applicant to show that there are extenuating circumstances, such as particularly poor health, close dependency on family members in the UK coupled with a lack of family and care facilities in the country of origin, which might warrant a grant of leave.'

Nevertheless, under 'factors to be taken into account when deciding whether deportation or administrative removal is appropriate', the OEM and the IDI still state:

'Age – A person will normally be considered for deportation if he is aged between 16 and 65 but the younger or older a person is, the more weight might be attached to age as a compassionate factor.' (OEM, Ch 36.1.2)

Enforcement in cases where there are medical problems

In cases concerning the ill health of the applicant, there will very often be human rights reasons why the person cannot be removed (Articles 3 and 8 ECHR). For details about using human rights in cases of ill health, ▶see 809–19. For Home Office policy in health cases concerning human rights, ▶see 814–6.

For cases involving self-harm and suicide, which are directly linked to the removal process, see below.

However, health can play a part in deciding whether it is right to remove a person *even if* the health problem is not enough to mean that it would be a breach of the person's human rights for them to be removed. In enforcement cases, the Home Office is required to take into account the compassionate circumstances of any case (▶see 1009). For indications from the courts that ill health falling short of a human rights case should still be carefully considered in taking immigration decisions, ▶see 851–2.

Depending on the nature of the case, ill health or disability can certainly qualify as a compassionate circumstance. In deciding how to approach representations where the case involves health problems, applicants and advisers should note that, where medical problems are put forward as a reason for not removing, officers will want (see OEM at Ch 36.9):

- to know full details of the condition, so they may try to obtain a consent form from the applicant allowing them to check medical records where this becomes necessary;
- to see a doctor's letter, or a letter from a hospital giving details of the condition;
- to know from a doctor whether the person is fit to travel and when (or if) the person will be fit;

- to know if the person has anyone in their home country who could provide care;
- to know if the person's life expectancy may be reduced as a result of removal;
- to check with the relevant country officer in the Home Office's Country Information and Policy Unit (CIPU) to see if there is a chance of treatment being available in the person's country of origin (CIPU may make enquiries of the Foreign and Commonwealth Office).

The same information will be sought if it is a family member of the principal person who is to be removed, who has the medical problems.

Where there is a risk of suicide or self-harm on removal

In some cases, the applicant alleges that the effect of removal itself will have such an impact on their mental health as to amount to a breach of Articles 3 or 8 ECHR. Such cases are normally those where the applicant has an existing mental health condition, sometimes as a result of past ill treatment. The potential effect on their health of enforcement may be the result of their own subjective reaction to what they may face abroad (even in a third country). The effects of this may still be very real. They may be so real, that the applicant is at risk of suicide or self-harm, which again raises human rights issues. These human rights issues have notably been considered by the courts in the cases of *Razgar*, *Kurtolli*, *J v SSHD* and *Bensaid*, which we deal with at ▶816–9.

In May 2005, the Home Office introduced a new policy for dealing with removal where a claim is made that removal should not be carried out because there is a risk of suicide or self-harm (IDI, Ch 1, s10, para. 8). This policy is summarised in the table below.

HOME OFFICE POLICY ON SUICIDE AND SELF-HARM

The following is a summary of Home Office policy on risk of suicide and self-harm, which was introduced in May 2005 (IDI, Ch 1, s10, para. 8). For the human rights issues that arise in cases concerning these risks, ▶see 817–9.

The policy deals with:

- the approach to decision-making in such cases; and
- the procedural steps to be taken in order to reduce the risk so that removal is possible.

The policy applies to claims of suicide or self-harm at any stage i.e. while in the UK, while awaiting removal, during removal and in the receiving state after removal. Where it is accepted that there are 'substantial grounds' for believing that removal would mean that a person would be at risk of serious harm or loss of life through suicide or self-harm so as to breach the UK's obligations under Article 3, or a flagrant denial of Article 8 rights, the person will be eligible for a grant of discretionary leave.

Approach to decision-making

The policy states that:

'It is not necessary for the steps to eliminate the risk entirely but all reasonable steps must be taken. Removal will not be precluded, notwithstanding evidence of the risk of suicide or self-harm, where the risk does not meet the threshold for the relevant ECHR-protected right.'

When considering a risk under Articles 3 and 8 ECHR, applicants and advisers should bear in mind that caseworkers are told to:

- expect medical evidence to be provided in support;
- take into account any 'acceptable medical evidence';
- take account of whether the evidence provided is from a qualified psychiatrist;
- take into account whether, and for how long, the medical expert has been treating the applicant;
- consider any ongoing psychiatric treatment the claimant may be receiving and/or any suicide assessment that has been carried out;
- take into account whether the applicant has a previous history of self-harm and/or suicide attempts;
- take account of the length of time the applicant spent in the UK before the self-harm issue arose and whether the applicant has ever been an in-patient (or has been sectioned) for similar reasons;
- consider whether any risk of self-harm/suicide existed before the person was subject to removal and, if so, consider whether the risk is affected by the decision to remove:

'This is a question of causation. The test to be applied is whether there are substantial grounds for believing that there is a real risk of a significantly increased risk of serious harm or loss of life through suicide or self-harm. If the risk is unaffected by the prospect of removal, the risk will not result from IND's actions' (Ch 1, s10, para. 8.4);

- see whether there is any adverse credibility finding which undermines the claimant's version of events (for example negative credibility findings from the AIT in relation to ill-treatment which the applicant claims is connected to their mental ill-health).

Steps to reduce the risk so that removal is possible

The steps that the policy says should be taken are as follows:

- those detained in removal centres should be assessed by a nurse for risk of self-harm or suicidal behaviour on arrival;
- IND staff and detention contractors must comply with the Home Office's 'operating standard' on suicide and self-harm prevention, all staff are to be trained to recognise suicide risks;
- care plans should be developed for those thought to be at risk;

9

- for those in detention, a member of the 'health care team' should be advised about any decision to remove and should be present at the time the decision is notified to the applicant;

- for those at risk who are not detained, caseworkers should arrange personal service of the negative decision and tell legal representatives in advance so that they can accompany the applicant when the decision is given and arrange any treatment or referral;

- where the applicant will not be accompanied by family members or representatives, the Home Office will arrange for a medically qualified person to be present when the notification is given;

- where an applicant is known to be receiving treatment for self-harm, the Home Office should report any further threats of self-harm or suicide made, to the medical professionals who are treating the applicant;

- those removed who may be at risk of self-harm or suicide shall be accompanied by a suitable escort, including a medical escort if necessary;

- appropriate persons in the country to which the applicant is to be removed should be made aware of the person's arrival and of the risk of suicide and self-harm. They should have agreed to have adequate reception arrangements in place to receive the person:

'If caseworkers are unable to ensure proper reception arrangements, they will have to consider if conditions in that country as they understand them would create a breach of Article 3 or Article 8...' (Ch 1, s10, para. 8.28).

Enforcement against families

For the references to the main policies in enforcement cases involving families and children, ▶see 994 above. Here we note a certain further procedural requirement about how detention and enforcement in family cases is to be carried out.

On 13 November 2003, the Home Office's Asylum and Appeals Policy Directorate issued a statement concerning removals in family cases. It stated that the government 'agreed that the separation of a child of an asylum-seeker from both parents should happen only in the most exceptional of circumstances' but it also stated:

'In instances whereby one parent had deliberately chosen to leave the family home in an attempt to frustrate the removal of a full family unit, the Government does not consider it acceptable that the whole family should remain in the United Kingdom while one parent remains in hiding.'

The statement further states that if an older child becomes deliberately separated from the family unit just before removal, the removal of the remaining family members would only take place if authorised by an

Assistant Director at the IND. In such cases, social services would be notified and every effort made to ensure the safety of the child.

Concern has been raised about detaining children from schools separately from their families. The Immigration Service has stated that visits to families in order to detain and remove them take place at a time when it is hoped that all the family members will be at home together. Research is apparently done to determine a time when the family is likely to be at home together. If it is necessary to pick a child up at school, or elsewhere, the immigration service will 'attempt to ensure that a parent accompanies staff to collect the child' (letter of the Immigration Service's Enforcement Policy Unit to the Asylum Policy Stakeholders Group dated 4 March 2004).

In July 2005, the Enforcement Policy Unit issued a 'Family Removals Policy' notice (EPU 07/05) which expands on the above. This notice should eventually be incorporated within the OEM. It notes that, before removal, a 'pastoral visit' will usually be paid to the family by the Immigration Service to gather information about the circumstances of the family so that important issues concerning medical or social needs can be taken into account in deciding on arrest, detention, transportation and removal. However, the notice goes on:

'...where there is good reason to suggest that a pastoral visit would adversely affect our attempts at removal (e.g. if there is evidence to suspect that the family may abscond following a pastoral visit), a written report or file minute detailing the reasons for the suspicion, must be submitted to an Immigration Inspector (HMI). The HMI will then decide whether or not the pastoral visit should be undertaken.' (para 2.2)

If the immigration authorities arrive in order to arrest a family and one or more family members is not present at the address, consideration will be given to whether it is appropriate to continue with the operation. If it is decided to proceed then, in the case of absent children, officers should consider the following options (EPU 07/05, para. 8):

- detaining the other family members and collecting the child on the way to the place of detention;
- taking the family members to the place of detention and then asking a parent to accompany officers to collect the separated child;
- if neither of the above options are possible, visit the address where the child is and ask a responsible adult to accompany the child until they are reunited with their family.

Where an adult is absent, officers should consider the following options (EPU 07/05):

- arrest and detain the family members who are present and leave a written message for the absent adult stating the place where their family have been taken to and inviting them to join the family in detention prior to removal;

9

- if the whereabouts of the adult are known, visit that location in order to arrest them;
- if the whereabouts of the adult are not known and cannot be discovered, the procedure for considering removal of incomplete families may be triggered (below).

Where only part of the family had been taken into detention, proceeding with removal directions which would result in only part of the family being removed must be authorised at the level of Assistant Director of the Immigration Service or above. Officers must make the reference to the Assistant Director in writing (EPU 07/05, para. 5.1).

For further details about the actual process of removal, ▶see below at 1026–7.

PORT REMOVALS

Those who arrive at a port in the UK, apply for leave to enter and are refused, can be removed through an uncomplicated procedure (paras 8, 10-10A Sch 2 1971 Act). We have called this 'port removal'. This is not an official term but there is no other general phrase which is used to describe removal in this category. Immigration officers often talk about 'port' cases however. Beyond the decision that they do not qualify for entry, there is no need for the immigration officer to make any decision or declaration about the applicant or their intentions (as there is with illegal entrants). Also, the immigration officer does not have to decide whether the applicant falls into a category that would make them liable to 'administrative removal'. Nor is there a complex two-stage process as with deportation (▶see below for all these other forms of enforcement).

A person who is refused leave to enter in one category, can ask for entry in a different category and each such application must be considered. It is unusual for the second application to be accepted if the first is refused because the two applications are likely to be incompatible. The immigration authorities are unlikely to accept that the second stated purpose is a genuine one. For example, the fact that a person has asked for entry in a category leading to settlement would itself demonstrate that they did not intend to leave the UK and would therefore undermine a second application as a visitor or a non-degree course student.

Sometimes asylum-seekers, who do not fully understand the procedures for claiming asylum, arrive and present a passport seeking entry in one capacity and, when refused, state their true reasons for coming to the UK and claim asylum. While a person is waiting for a decision on granting leave to enter, they may either be detained or given temporary admission. So, in an asylum case, a decision will not be made on arrival but will be referred to the Home Office to decide. This means that the applicant may be on temporary admission for many months, or even years, but still be a 'port' case. If their application is eventually refused, even after appeals, the means of enforcement against them is still 'port removal'.

From 10 February 2003, members of the family of a person who is being removed in this category can also be removed (s73 2002 Act amending Sch 2 to the 1971 Act). The Home Office's particular concern in making this change (and a similar change for family members of illegal entrants – see below) is to ensure that all non-British citizen children born in the UK to those being removed in this way can also be removed. The powers of administrative removal and deportation already enable family members to be removed with the principal person being removed.

Although the concessions which apply in 'enforcement' cases including spouses/partners (▶337–43) and children (▶386–9) formally apply only in cases of illegal entry, administrative removal and deportation, the Home Office has stated:

'Although the concessions that may apply to enforcement cases do not automatically apply to port cases, the Immigration Service will have regard to them in the context of the case under the Rules and whether it is appropriate in the circumstances of an individual case to waive any Entry Clearance or visa requirement' (see para. 5, *Immigration Rules and Compassionate Circumstances*, instructions to officers, 25 April 2004 and see para. 8.5.3 to the effect that the immigration service will have regard to the 'underlying principles' of the concession relating to families with child/ren who have resided in the UK for seven years or more).

Those arriving with leave/entry clearances

People who return to the UK when they already have leave, for example because it did not lapse when they left, and that leave is cancelled on their arrival, are also liable to be removed as port removals. So too are people who arrive in the UK with an entry clearance (which now operates as leave to enter) and are refused entry, because the immigration officer cancels the leave and grants no other leave. When leave is cancelled to people who arrive in these circumstances, they are treated in the same way as if they had been refused leave to enter (see para. 2A(8)(9) Sch 2 1971 Act and also para. 321 HC 395). They may then be removed as port removal cases.

On-entry procedures can be complex. For full details about them, ▶see 95–101. For details about which leave does not lapse when a person departs, ▶see 107–9.

Appeals

When people are refused leave to enter, they are issued with a notice to this effect informing them of their liability to removal and of any appeal rights. 'Refusal of leave to enter' is an 'immigration decision' which, in general, gives an in-country right of appeal if the applicant makes an asylum or human rights claim, or arrives with an entry clearance. However, the rules about appeals 'on entry' to the UK are complex. For full details, ▶see 1053–60.

ADMINISTRATIVE REMOVAL

'Administrative removal' is a procedure, introduced from 2 October 2000 (see s10, 1999 Act; part 13, para. 395A–395F HC 395). Since section 10 was amended by the 2002 Act from 10 February 2003, it allows the following categories of people to be removed from the UK:

- those who have overstayed their leave;
- those who have breached a condition of their leave;
- those who have obtained, or have tried to obtain, leave to remain by deception;
- those whose indefinite leave has been revoked on the grounds that they have 'ceased' to be a refugee;
- family members of a person in any of the above four groups who is being administratively removed.

These groups are looked at further below. Before 2 October 2000, most of the above groups would have been 'deported' from the UK. The two most important consequences of the replacement of deportation by administrative removal for these people are as follows.

1) Rights of appeal There is no effective in-country right of appeal against administrative removal except on asylum or human rights grounds. For the special considerations about appeals, which apply in 'refugee revocation' cases, ▶see 1008. Before 2 October 2000, an overstayer would be given a notice of intention to deport and could appeal against it. If the person had last entered the UK seven years or more before the time that the notice was given, they could rely upon all the compassionate and other features of their case in the appeal and argue that, on balance, the decision to deport should not have been made. If they had not been in the UK for seven years, they could only appeal on the grounds that there was no legal power to deport them (an appeal which could hardly ever succeed). In these cases, the practice was for appellants to ask for a recommendation on compassionate grounds.

2) Speed The process is a much shorter one. There is only one real stage: the decision that the person will be removed. The removal directions themselves, which follow later, are simply administrative steps after the main decision has been made. This makes administrative removal like port removal and illegal entry and very different from the two-stage process in deportation cases.

Those who are being administratively removed will be given a notice informing them of the decision to remove them. They may also be detained or alternatively granted temporary admission. If a person has overstayed, breached their conditions, or used deception in applying for leave to remain, this can count against them in future applications that they make to enter or remain in the UK. This is because all of these circumstances are covered in the general grounds upon which leave can be refused under the immigration rules (▶see 97–9, 140–1).

Regularisation of Overstayers Scheme: still dealt with by deportation

The administrative removal procedure does *not* apply to people who the Home Office decided to deport before 2 October 2000. It also does not apply to those people who applied to the Home Office before the 2 October 2000 deadline under the 'Regularisation of Overstayers Scheme', which allowed people who were overstayers, or in breach of conditions, to apply to the Home Office to regularise their stay. In such cases, if the decision of the Home Office is still negative, then even if the decision was made after 2 October 2000, the applicant is still treated under the deportation procedure and maintains their rights of appeal under that procedure. Many people were successful in their regularisation applications.

The Home Office believed that it had completed cases under the scheme by August 2003 but in fact there were still cases outstanding at that time. It is possible that there are still some cases in the system.

Overstaying

Overstaying is the most common of the reasons for the Home Office to try to remove someone administratively. All limited leave has a date of expiry and a person is expected to either leave the UK or make a further application to remain within the time of their leave. If they do not, they become overstayers and can be removed. As with liability for administrative removal on the grounds of breach of conditions or being a family member of someone who is being removed, there is no need for the person to know that they are overstaying in order for them to be liable to be removed. A person can also become an overstayer if their leave is curtailed by the immigration authorities. For details of the grounds upon which leave can be curtailed ▶see 141–3. If a further grant of leave is given after a person has overstayed, then they are no longer liable to be removed as an overstayer, unless they overstay the fresh leave.

Automatic extensions of leave and overstaying

If the person applies to the Home Office for an extension of leave before their existing leave expires, and the Home Office does not make a decision on the application before the leave expires, the applicant is treated as having been given an extension of leave until ten days (i.e. the time for appealing) after the Home Office makes a decision on the application. The legal provision that has this effect is section 3C of the 1971 Act which was inserted by the 1999 Act (and then replaced again by the 2002 Act) and replaces the previous provisions of the Variation of Leave Order 1976. Applicants do not become overstayers during this period. Only valid applications for extensions completed on the appropriate forms with all the required original evidence will count for these purposes.

If the decision on the extension is positive then, obviously, the applicant will have further leave. If it is negative, the applicant becomes an over-stayer and liable to administrative removal *unless* they appeal. People who have applied for an extension of leave and are waiting for their appeal to be dealt with are treated as still having the same leave until the end of the whole appeals process (including challenges beyond the first decision of the AIT provided applications/appeals are made in time). However, under the 2005 Bill, the position will change: applicants will only be treated as not overstaying their leave while they are waiting for the Home Office decision. There will be no automatic extension of leave during the appeal process. For more details about automatic extensions of leave (▶see 143–6).

It should be noted that, during these periods of automatic extension, it is the old leave that is treated as continuing to have effect and so the old conditions continue. Therefore, if a person has a prohibition on claiming public funds or on working on their existing leave, this continues until they get a positive decision, even if the leave they have applied for (e.g., indefinite leave) would not contain these conditions.

Other consequences of overstaying

If an applicant's conditions of leave, before it ran out, were generous, for example, they did not prohibit recourse to public funds or working, then a person loses these rights when they overstay. For example, a person given exceptional leave to remain for four years who fails to apply for indefinite leave in time, becomes a person 'subject to immigration control' as an overstayer and unable to obtain most social security benefits until the application for an extension is decided in their favour.

In addition to making someone liable for administrative removal, the other effects of overstaying are that it breaks a period of continuous law-ful leave. This may have an impact on a later application for indefinite leave where there is a requirement for a continuous period of leave. It also may affect an application under the ten-year lawful residence concession.

Breach of conditions

As well as overstaying, a person is liable to administrative removal if they breach one of the other conditions of their leave. Which conditions will be imposed on the leave depends upon the category in which a person is admitted. Immigration officials refer to the various different combinations of these conditions as 'codes' and the table at ▶190–1 sets out the different conditions, which are normally given under the different cate-gories of leave. Indefinite leave cannot have any conditions attached to it.

A person will not be in breach of their conditions of leave just because they no longer meet the requirements of the immigration rules upon which they were given leave. There is an important difference between the 'requirements' in order to get leave in the first place and the *conditions* that are attached to the leave. So, in the Court of Appeal case of *R (Zhou) v SSHD*, a student who had stopped regularly attending their course but continued to work in accordance with their conditions of leave and the general approval given to students to work, could not be detained and removed as in breach of their conditions. There was no 'condition' attached to the leave that the student attended the course. The conditions will be clear from looking at the document (usually in the passport), which grants leave.

However, where a person no longer meets the *requirements* of the category they have been given leave in, the Home Office does have alternative powers as follows.

1) It may 'curtail' leave if a person no longer fulfils the requirements upon which leave granted (see para. 323(ii) HC 395). The person would then have no leave and could be removed as an overstayer.

2) If the failure to satisfy the rules is not a result of a change of circumstances, but deception was used to obtain leave to remain the first place (in the above example, the person never truly intended to study), then administrative removal action could be taken on that basis (▶see below at 1007–8). If the leave is indefinite leave, but the person cannot be removed for legal and practical reasons, the indefinite leave can still be 'revoked' (▶see 1008).

3) If the situation is the same as in (2) above but the applicant obtained leave to *enter* rather than leave to remain, the Home Office could declare the applicant an illegal entrant (▶see under 'illegal entry' below).

We look at the different *conditions* which can be attached to leave immediately below. Note that, in addition to those conditions, immigration officers can also require that someone entering the UK reports to a medical officer for examination or treatment (para. 7 sch 2, 1971 Act). This is infrequent and although breach of it does not seem to lead directly to 'enforcement', refusal to undergo a medical examination can lead to refusal of leave under the immigration rules. In addition to administrative removal, breach of conditions can also lead to criminal charges.

The different conditions which can be attached to leave

The conditions that may be attached to a person's leave are as follows. For a table of the likely conditions in each category, ▶see 190–1.

'Prohibition' on employment or occupation This prevents the person from doing any kind of work or business in the UK, paid or unpaid. Even helping out at a friend's shop could mean that a person is in breach of their conditions. Visitors, for example, are all given a prohibition on working although the rules are interpreted flexibly for 'business' visitors and certain others (see Ch 9 at ▶220–1). However, the OEM states that breach of working conditions will have to be 'of sufficient gravity' in order to justify administrative removal action. It states that there 'must be firm and recent evidence (within six months) of working in breach' and that the evidence should be in one of the following forms (OEM, Ch 10.6.4):

- an admission under caution by the offender;
- a statement by the employer;
- documentary evidence such as pay slips, pay-roll, national insurance or tax records, P45;
- witness evidence from an immigration officer or police officer – this evidence should generally be backed up by other evidence.

'Restriction' on employment or occupation Working restrictions are generally intended to prevent people from working other than in the job that they have been admitted in order to do, except in specified circumstances. They are usually expressed as restrictions preventing work other than work that they have been given permission to do. For example, a work-permit holder will be able to work in the employment approved by their work permit.

Previously, students could not work without first obtaining specific permission. However, there is now a general approval for most of them to do some work without getting individual permission (▶see 263–6).

Registration with the police Those aged 16 or over who are nationals of any of the countries that are listed at ▶1527 (Appendix 2, HC 395), or who are stateless, or who hold a non-national travel document, may be required to register with the police. None of the countries listed are Commonwealth countries. People will usually be required to register if they are in any of the following three categories, namely (see paras 325–326 HC 395 as amended from 4 February 2005 by HC 194):

- they have been given leave to enter for more than six months;
- they have been given leave to remain which allows them to stay in the UK for longer than six months counting from the date of arrival (i.e. not from the date the leave to remain is given) – such people may be given a registration condition even if they did not have one when they arrived;
- exceptionally, in their particular case, the immigration officer thinks it is necessary to ensure that they comply with the terms of their leave.

However, those given leave in any of the following categories should *not* normally be given a requirement to register:

- seasonal agricultural worker;
- private servant in a diplomatic household;
- minister of religion, missionary or member of a religious order;
- spouse or unmarried partner of a person settled in the UK;

- a person exercising rights of access to a child;
- the parent of a child at school;
- those granted asylum.

In order to register, a person must go to their local police station within a week of the condition being imposed and provide: their name; address; details of employment; marital status; their photograph; and payment for the registration fee. Any changes in these details must be registered within a similar period of time. The police will provide the person with a 'certificate of registration'.

Maintain and accommodate themselves and any dependants without recourse to public funds Since 1 November 1996, the immigration authorities have been able to impose a requirement that people maintain and accommodate themselves and any dependants without recourse to public funds. We suggest that this must be interpreted, in line with the immigration rules, as meaning additional recourse to public funds. People in many of the categories under the rules have this condition imposed on their leave. The main effect of this condition is to prevent people from getting public funds in the first place. For full details about what counts as having recourse to public funds and important recent amendments to the immigration rules on this point, ▶see 308–18.

Obtaining leave to remain by deception

A person who obtains leave to remain in the UK from the Home Office by deception can also be administratively removed. This is similar to illegal entry by deception (▶see 1013–4). Importantly, this power can be used to deal with people who have obtained indefinite leave to remain when they were not entitled to it. Overstaying and breaches of conditions (above) can only apply to people granted limited leave.

Following amendments by the 2002 Act, the Home Office is now able to administratively remove someone who *tries* to obtain leave to remain by deception, even if they are not successful in getting leave (s74 2002 Act).

The classic situation for administrative removal on the basis of deception would be where the immigration authorities later discover that a spouse or unmarried partner obtained indefinite leave to remain when the relationship had, in fact, broken down by the time they got it. Before this power was introduced, the only way in which the Home Office could enforce the removal of such a person was by deporting them on the ground that their presence was not conducive to the public good. The deportee would then have full appeal rights against the decision.

Home Office policy about when administrative removal action will be appropriate in deception cases states:

'The evidence of deception should be clear and unambiguous in order to initiate action under section 10. Where possible, original documentary evidence, admissions under caution or statements from two or more witnesses should be obtained which substantiate that an offence has been committed before authority is given to initiate action... The deception must be material – in other words, had the officer known the truth, the leave would not have been given. The evidence must always prove to a high degree of probability that deception had been used to gain the leave, whether or not an admission of deception is made. The onus – as always in such situations – is on the officer making the assertion to prove his case.' (OEM, Ch 10.7)

Revocation of indefinite leave obtained by deception

Even if a person cannot be administratively removed for practical or legal reasons but the Home Office still judges that they have obtained indefinite leave by deception, that indefinite leave can now be revoked (see s76(2) 2002 Act). This is to deal with the situation where there are practical problems in establishing the person's nationality or the lack of a safe route for return. Unless the person is granted limited leave instead, this will leave them in a *limbo* situation: unable to work or access benefits. Although this power was introduced on 10 February 2003, this action can still be taken where leave was granted before that time. There is an in-country right of appeal against the revocation and the revocation will not take effect while the appeal is outstanding.

Indefinite leave revoked because person has ceased to be a refugee

Until recently, all those granted asylum as refugees were given indefinite leave to enter or remain. Under section 76(3) of the 2002 Act, the Home Office may 'revoke' the indefinite leave to enter or remain of a person who has 'ceased' to be a refugee as result of their own voluntary conduct. Their dependants' leave can also be revoked. The powers to do this are based on Article 1C of the Refugee Convention. For details about what conduct can lead to a person ceasing to be a refugee, ▶see 627–30 and for the general operation of policy on reviewing refugee status/leave since August 2005 ▶see 721–4. For revocation of indefinite leave in deportation cases ▶see 1025–6.

After leave has been revoked in this way, the person may then be administratively removed from the UK under section 10 of the 1999 Act (as amended by section 76(7) of the 2002 Act). There is an existing in-country right of appeal against revocation of indefinite leave and the revocation won't take effect while an appeal is outstanding against it (s82(2)(f),(3) 2002 Act). At the moment there is no separate right of appeal against the next stage i.e. the decision to administratively *remove* a person whose leave has been revoked because they are no longer a refugee. The 2005 Bill proposes that those whose indefinite leave is revoked for these reasons will have a right of appeal against the revocation *and* then a separate right of appeal when a decision is taken to remove them (▶1042–3).

Family members of those being administratively removed

Family members (spouses and minor children) of those who have been given directions that they are being removed administratively for the reasons stated above can also be removed (▶see also 387–8). However, the family members must be notified that they are being administratively removed no more than eight weeks after the departure of their principal. If a family member ceases to be a family member before removal is carried out, for example, there is a divorce, removal directions against the family member are no longer valid.

Deciding whether a person should be administratively removed

Even though there is a power to remove a person administratively, the Home Office has to make a decision that it is appropriate to remove them given the circumstances of their individual case. In making this decision, the factors set out in the immigration rules must be considered (paras 364–368 as applied by 395C HC 395). The considerations set out in the rules are exactly the same as for deportation cases. So, although people who are being administratively removed have lost important appeal rights compared to when they used to be 'deported', the *Home Office itself* must still apply the same factors when making its decision as to whether to force them to leave.

Under the rules, the Home Office has to consider whether removal is the right course, balancing the public interest in maintaining immigration control against the compassionate circumstances of the case. Although each case must be considered on its own merits, the Home Office must aim to come to decisions which are consistent between one case and another. Where it is a case of overstaying or of breaching conditions, removal will 'normally' be the correct decision but the Home Office has to take into account all known relevant factors including:

- the person's age;
- their length of residence in the UK;
- their strength of connections with the UK;
- their personal history, including character, conduct and employment record;
- their domestic circumstances;
- the nature of any offence of which the person has been convicted;
- the person's previous criminal record;
- any compassionate circumstances;
- any representations received on the person's behalf.

Guidance to caseworkers on the application of the above criteria are set out in the document, *Immigration Rules and Compassionate Circumstances* disclosed to Wilson & Co Solicitors by the Home Office on 1 August 2005 and circulated by ILPA in the same month.

The above factors are not the only relevant ones – the rules refer to all 'relevant factors' made known to the Home Office. For example, in *Bakhtaur Singh*, the House of Lords ruled that the interests of a particular community were, in principle, relevant in keeping a person who was a particularly talented performance artist, in the UK. Removal of each family member must be considered separately and where a spouse or child is liable to be removed, further factors still, must be taken into account to determine their cases (▶see 387–8). For the special policy considerations that apply in cases of marriage and children ▶see 337–43, 386–9, 998–1000. For enforcement against unaccompanied minors ▶see 390–3, 688, 865, 870–2.

ILLEGAL ENTRY

Illegal entry means entering, or seeking to enter, the UK unlawfully in breach of the immigration laws. Like port removals and administrative removal cases (above), illegal entrants can be removed from the UK in an uncomplicated process by the setting of directions for removal (s33(1) and paras 9-10A, Sch 2 1971 Act). Illegal entrants can be detained pending their removal. The 2002 Act now gives a power for the members of the family of an illegal entrant to be removed as with port cases (above and see s73 2002 Act). There is only an in-country right of appeal on asylum or human rights grounds.

Challenges to decisions that a person is *in fact* an illegal entrant (which are also challenges to detention if a person is detained on that basis) have traditionally been brought by judicial review. In these cases, it is for the Home Office to demonstrate that the person has entered unlawfully. In many cases, the Home Office is alleging fraud on the part of the applicant, and this must be proved to a high degree of probability (▶see *Khawaja*, below).

As with other cases where there is a power to remove, representations can be made to the Home Office concerning any compassionate or other features of the case which suggest that removal should not be carried out. The Home Office should consider the same factors as are set out in the immigration rules in administrative removal cases before taking illegal entry enforcement action (see OEM, Ch 36.1.1) (▶see 1009 above).

Following the introduction of administrative removal, the importance of 'illegal entry' has diminished. This is because, previously, the effect of an illegal entry decision was to make the person liable to summary removal without the protections of the deportation system. The procedure for administrative removal is, however, just as quick as the illegal entry route.

Illegal entry decisions do, however, remain important in those cases where a person still has a substantial period of leave remaining and is not in breach of their conditions, and is therefore not liable to administrative removal. When the immigration authorities declare someone to be an illegal entrant, any leave that they have is automatically invalid from that time. Therefore, an in-country application from someone who has been declared to be an illegal entrant, to remain as a spouse or unmarried partner cannot meet the immigration rules because the applicant does not have any leave and is in breach of the immigration laws. The refusal of such an application would not carry a right of appeal.

A person who enters the UK in any of the following ways can be declared to be an illegal entrant:

- without seeing an immigration officer at all;
- without obtaining leave to enter when this was required;
- while there is a deportation order signed against them, which is still in force;
- by deceiving an immigration officer, for example, as to their identity, nationality, or some other matter relevant to their right to enter.

Although the above four categories are the most common, there are some other, less obvious examples of illegal entry. A person who asks for leave to enter at port and who is detained or temporarily admitted and later absconds or breaches their conditions of temporary admission could be treated as an illegal entrant. In addition, an illegal entrant can be someone who has tried to enter unlawfully. It is possible, therefore that someone who tries and fails to enter using false documents or having lied to an entry clearance officer to obtain entry clearance (and see OEM Ch 3.10), could be treated as an illegal entrant. Such a person is, however, more likely to be dealt with as a port removal.

We look at these four categories in turn below. The concept of illegal entry was originally designed to cover people in the first three categories but the definition was then greatly expanded by the Home Office and the courts.

Entry without seeing an immigration officer

The category of people who enter without seeing an immigration officer covers those who, for example, arrive in a small boat on a deserted beach at midnight. This is not common. Far more common among these 'clandestine' entrants, are those who arrive concealed in the back of lorries or containers who are not discovered until after they have passed through the immigration control area and who have therefore entered the UK without going through controls. Many asylum-seekers arrive in this way and, under the 1999 Act, carriers' liability sanctions were extended so that those carrying people arriving in this manner would be charged fines for each clandestine entrant. There have been court decisions about the legality of these sanctions.

If a person confesses to having entered by avoiding examination by an immigration officer, there is no way of arguing that he or she is not an illegal entrant.

Entry without obtaining leave from an immigration officer

Immigration officers are required by the Immigration Act 1971 to examine people when they arrive to decide whether they need leave to enter the UK and whether or not to give them leave. If they fail to examine someone who needs leave and instead pass them through into the UK without stamping their passports, those people can be treated as illegal entrants because they have not obtained leave. This was confirmed by the Court of Appeal in the case of *Rehal*. Mr Rehal was a British Overseas citizen whose passport was not stamped on entry because the immigration officer mistakenly assumed that he was a British citizen, who therefore did not need leave. The Court accepted that he had not deceived an immigration officer, but decided nevertheless that he was an illegal entrant.

In cases of 'unwitting' illegal entry, officers may decide not to treat the applicant as an illegal entrant (OEM, Ch 2.4.1). In such cases, strong representations should be made to show that the entrant was not responsible for their illegal entry and to show how they would have been admitted to the UK had they been properly examined.

Entry through Ireland

It is also possible for people who enter through Ireland to be treated as illegal entrants by not obtaining leave from an immigration officer. There is no passport control between the two countries. Normally people do not require leave to travel within the 'Common Travel Area' (the UK, Republic of Ireland, Channel Islands and Isle of Man) so they do not have to see an immigration officer. However, some people do require leave, and if they enter without it, they have entered illegally. For the categories of entrant from Ireland who are illegal entrants if they enter without leave, ▶see 105–6.

Records are not generally kept of people entering through Ireland, so such people are only likely to be treated as illegal entrants if they apply to the Home Office for an extension or a change of status, or if they happen to come to the attention of the authorities in some other way and the Home Office then makes checks on their entry.

Entry in breach of a deportation order

If someone enters the UK while still the subject of a deportation order that has not been revoked, the entry is illegal. It would be rare for a person travelling in his or her true identity to be readmitted, so people who enter in breach of a deportation order will usually have entered with a false passport, which is illegal entry in itself. If there is a current deportation order, then the Home Office has a choice: it could remove the person under the deportation order, which automatically cancels any leave that the person managed to get when they arrived anyway, or it can declare the person to be an illegal entrant and remove them as such.

Deception of an immigration officer

Many of those dealt with as illegal entrants are so treated because the immigration authorities find that they entered by deception. The deception may be by the use of false passports, or a passport which is not false but which did not truly belong to the passenger who used it.

However, a person may also enter by deception without misusing documents. They may appear to have been lawfully allowed into the country and have stamps on their own genuine passports granting leave to enter. The immigration authorities may allege, however, that they told lies or deliberately hid information when applying for entry clearance or leave to enter, or they may claim that the person did not give information, which, if the immigration officer had known it, would have affected the decision to grant entry.

A person may also be an illegal entrant if the deception is carried out by a third party in order to gain entry for the passenger although the passenger themselves did not play a part in the deception. This could be the case, for example, if a relative makes false representations at an entry clearance interview or in writing and entry is granted on that same basis, or if a person accompanying the passenger makes false representations about them to the immigration officer at the port.

Entry by deception has been the subject of many court cases. The most important decision came in the joined cases of **Khawaja & Khera**. In these cases, the House of Lords decided that it is for the Home Office to prove, on the balance of probabilities but to a high standard, that false representations were made to the immigration authorities and that leave to enter was granted on the basis of that false information. Mr Khera was found not to be an illegal entrant. He had applied as a child to come with his mother to join his father but had married in India while the application was still under consideration. He did not know that this made any difference and was not asked whether he was married, so it was accepted that he had not deceived the immigration authorities. Mr Khawaja, on the other hand, was held to be an illegal entrant. He had entered as a visitor saying that he would spend a week with his cousin but applied to the Home Office shortly afterwards to remain as a husband, having married his wife in Belgium before travelling to the UK and married her again in the UK during his visit. He was held to have deceived the immigration officers on arrival and therefore to be an illegal entrant.

Since then, court decisions have further widened the interpretation of illegal entry. The Court of Appeal held in the cases of **Durojaiye** and **Akinde** that merely showing a passport with a previous immigration stamp of leave to remain to an immigration officer can count as deception if the reason for which the previous leave was given is no longer present. For example, a student who decides to give up their course but has several months' leave remaining, travels out of the UK with leave that does not lapse and returns to the UK within this time. If the person enters by presenting their passport with evidence of their unlapsed student leave and represents themselves to be a student, they could be considered to have deceived the immigration officers on return because they are no longer in fact entitled to entry as a student.

Establishing illegal entry by deception

Where an illegal entry decision is based on misrepresentations as opposed to false documents, there is often no evidence to support the Home Office's view and the only way that the allegation can be proved is through the 'confession' of the person concerned.

For example, if a woman who was given entry as a visitor on the basis that she was visiting her sister for a two-week holiday, is subsequently found working, she is likely to be questioned by immigration officers about her intentions when she first came to the UK. Had she really intended just a visit? Had she always wanted to work here? Did she know before she came that she would work? Had she always intended to stay longer than she said? If the answer to any of the questions is 'yes', immigration officers may allege that she had concealed her true intention of coming to the UK to work. If this had been revealed on entry, it would have resulted in refusal of leave to enter. Therefore, entry was gained by deception, as she was never really a genuine visitor.

Many suspected illegal entrants are questioned by immigration officers after arrest, perhaps after being detained in a police station for some hours, and without advice. If they have any advice it will usually be because the police have contacted a duty solicitor on their behalf, but these lawyers will nearly always be experienced in criminal law with little or no special knowledge of immigration procedures. The arrested person is unlikely to fully understand the reasoning behind the questions or what the officer is getting at. They are likely to be unaware of the difference between remaining in the UK unlawfully after any leave has run out and being an 'illegal entrant'. They may make admissions in response to questions about their original intentions, believing they are talking about their present situation.

It is always important to ask the immigration office or police station concerned for a copy of its record or the tape of the person's interview, which may clarify what the person has said and whether the responses have been misunderstood. Interviews carried out at police stations will generally be tape-recorded, as with any criminal investigation, and other immigration interviews may also be recorded.

Decision to treat a person as an illegal entrant

As with other cases concerning enforcement, even if a person is in fact an illegal entrant, officers do not have to *treat* them as such. The courts have made it clear, and the immigration authorities have accepted, that there are two separate stages (OEM, Ch 7):

1) Is the person an illegal entrant?

2) Should they be treated as an illegal entrant?

In considering (2), we suggest that factors which officers may be asked to take into account are: the nature of the illegal entry; whether the applicant in fact does satisfy the requirements of the immigration rules; their present circumstances; and any compassionate features. Even after illegal entry papers have been served, it is possible to make representations to try to reverse the decision.

Removal and return of illegal entrants

As with others who may be required to leave, illegal entrants who are not detained may leave the country voluntarily by obtaining a ticket and leaving. Those who do not wish to challenge removal may explain this to immigration officers. They may be asked to sign a disclaimer, indicating that they are leaving voluntarily, particularly if other issues, such as marriage, have been raised before they go. The disclaimer forms are IS 101 (voluntary departure – illegal entrant) and IS 101 (asylum).

There are no formal procedures laid down to restrict people removed as illegal entrants from applying to return. They may apply immediately, but will have to show that they satisfy the requirements of the immigration law and rules for the category in which they are seeking to return. However, applicants should bear carefully in mind the fact that entering the UK by deception on a previous occasion is a ground for refusing an application to return under the general grounds for refusal in the immigration rules (▶see 98–99). This is the case *even if* the applicant satisfies all the other requirements for entry under the rules, for example as a spouse or an unmarried partner. An applicant with a poor immigration history will, therefore, often have significant problems in returning – this is a factor to consider carefully and many applicants will want to make strong representations as to why they ought to be able to stay in the UK without having to return to apply for entry clearance.

If the person does leave and wishes to return for a purpose for which they do not need entry clearance, it may be advisable to get one anyway. This will avoid being refused at port having spent the money on a ticket and having travelled.

DEPORTATION

Deportation powers can be used against people whether they have no leave, limited leave or indefinite leave. Deportation powers are also used in EEA cases (for details about enforcement in EEA cases, ▶see 554–6). The remaining cases where the Home Office uses deportation powers are as follows.

Recommendations for deportation Those who are convicted of either immigration or non-immigration criminal offences can be recommended for deportation by the criminal court as part of their sentence for the offence.

Deportation conducive to the public good People can be deported on the grounds that their presence is not 'conducive to the public good'. They may or may not have committed criminal offences in order to be liable for deportation on these grounds.

Family members of people being deported Family members of people in the above two categories can also be deported.

Deportation can also be used against those who applied under the Regularisation of Overstayers Scheme and are refused (▶above at 1003). There are unlikely to be many (if any) such cases still outstanding.

People who have indefinite leave and who are liable to deportation but cannot be removed for 'legal reasons' can still have that indefinite leave revoked (▶see 1025–6).

The effect of a deportation order when it is made and while it continues in force, is that it invalidates any existing leave and it prevents any further leave from being given. Therefore, when a deportation order is made, the person cannot return to the UK unless the deportation order has first been 'revoked' (▶see below). Deportation can be used even if the person could be removed in another way, for example, as an overstayer.

Recommendations for deportation

In criminal cases for which the maximum sentence is a prison term, the court has the power to recommend deportation as part of the criminal sentence for people aged 17 or over.

When the criminal court may make a recommendation

In 1980, in *Nazari*, the Court of Appeal gave the following guidelines for criminal courts in deciding whether to make recommendations for deportation:

- the court should consider the potential detriment to the country by the person's presence – this depends on the seriousness of the offence, the harm caused to the community by it and the risk of the person committing further offences;
- the court should also bear in mind the effect on innocent third parties of the person being deported, for example, family members who are settled in the UK and who would be separated from the deportee. Article 8 ECHR will now be an important consideration in looking at the effect on these people;
- the court should not consider the political system in the country to which the person will be sent and their future life there, as this is the job of the Home Office in considering whether to act on the recommendation.

Those who are convicted must be given at least seven days' notice that the criminal court is considering making a recommendation for deportation and be permitted to make representations to the court about it. This notice is sometimes known as 'Form IM3'. This may mean that the court has to adjourn before sentencing the person who has been convicted (see s6 1971 Act).

After a recommendation for deportation has been made

The only formal appeal against the recommendation itself is through the criminal appeals system against conviction or sentence. The appeal may therefore be to either a Crown Court or the Court of Appeal. Often criminal solicitors, with little understanding of immigration law, are unaware of the possibility of a recommendation being made or of the right of appeal against it. An appeal may be brought against the recommendation, even if no other part of the sentence or the conviction itself is being appealed. Appeals have frequently been successful for procedural reasons, for example, because the criminal court failed to give the appellant the required seven days' notice that it is considering a recommendation so that the person can make representations, or because the court has failed to give sufficient reasons that deal with the relevant factors referred to in *Nazari* above.

The final decision as to whether to proceed with deportation rests with the Home Office, which has to consider any representations made as to why it should not carry out the court's recommendation. If representations are made to the Home Office, it is important to explain any special or compassionate circumstances, human rights grounds or reasons why deportation should be delayed, for example, to enable a person to complete a course of studies.

Where a recommendation has been made, the person may be detained under immigration powers while awaiting deportation proceedings. Alternatively, the person may be released by the immigration authorities and given temporary admission.

Notices of intention to deport and appeals in recommendation cases

In most deportation cases, it is clear that the Home Office must first issue a 'decision' to deport (▶see 1021–2). For many years, that was not necessary in 'recommendation' cases; the Home Office could proceed directly to signing the order. However section 82(2)(j) 2002 Act gives a right of appeal against a 'decision to make a deportation order under section 5(1)' of the 1971 Act. Section 5 covers deportation in 'recommendation' as well as the other cases (previously the right of appeal had referred only to decisions taken under section 3(5) 1971 Act which do not include 'recommendation' cases, see s63(1) 1999 Act). This is a strong indication that the Home Office must issue a 'decision' to deport (otherwise called a 'notice of intention' to deport) in recommendation cases if it is going to take up the recommendation. The applicant will then have an *in-country* right of appeal against it, ▶see 1054, 1059.

Despite the change in legislation, Home Office practice has not been made clear. It is clear that it will issue an initial 'decision' to deport in all 'non-conducive' cases (▶below). It is also clear that it will issue a 'decision' to deport in the case of EEA nationals who are recommended for deportation (although, confusingly, it will do so on 'non-conducive' rather than 'recommendation' grounds; see European Directorate Instructions, Ch3 s1, OEM Ch 13–14, para. 381 HC 395). JCWI's view is that a 'decision' to deport is the correct decision to make if the Home Office wishes to proceed in recommendation cases as well.

However, even if no 'decision' to deport is issued, the applicant still has a right of appeal *after* the deportation order has been signed. This is because an applicant can make representations asking the Home Office to revoke the order and there is a right of appeal against a decision to 'refuse to revoke' a deportation order (s82(2)(k) 2002 Act). *However*, this right of appeal can only be brought in-country if the applicant claims asylum or makes a human rights claim (s92 2002 Act).

Conducive to the public good

The Home Office may deport a person on the ground that their presence in the UK is not 'conducive to the public good'. It can do this on the basis of criminal offences even if the court made no recommendation for deportation (see above). In deciding whether to deport on conducive grounds, the Home Office has to consider a wider range of factors than the criminal court considers in deciding whether to recommend deportation. *However*, in a case where the criminal court has taken a positive decision not to recommend deportation, or the criminal division of the Court of Appeal has set aside a recommendation, the judgment of the criminal court is a relevant matter for the Home Office to take into account in deciding whether to press ahead on 'non-conducive' grounds. The Home Office is permitted to take a different view to the criminal court even if there are no new facts or evidence, but where it does so, it must give reasons for taking that different view (*M v SSHD*, CA).

In many cases, where the Home Office takes deportation action against those settled in the UK, there will be important Article 8 issues to consider. Long-term residents are likely to have strong family roots and other ties to the UK. The family members themselves, who have not been involved in any criminal activity, are likely to suffer. In such cases, the Home Office will have to consider whether deportation will have a disproportionate effect on the interests of those who will be affected (see *Allan Samaroo & Mehmed Sezek v SSHD*). In *Samaroo*, the Court of Appeal found that the Home Office had been entitled to view Class A drug-trafficking offences as particularly serious and harmful to society. The Home Office could validly attach importance to its general policy of deporting those convicted of importation of such drugs in order to protect UK residents from their harmful effects and to deter others. Although the deportation would break up the family in that case, it was fair and reasonable to do so.

For full details about Article 8 in family life cases, ▶see 820–50.

There is a full in-country right of appeal against a notice of intention to deport made on these grounds, regardless of the length of time the person has lived in the UK. No order can be signed while such an appeal is outstanding (s79 2002 Act).

Provoking terrorism

After a short consultation period beginning on 5 August 2005, the Home Office set out new guidelines on 24 August 2005, for the deportation or exclusion of 'extremists' on the grounds that their presence in the UK is 'not conducive to the public good' (see 'Tackling terrorism: behaviours unacceptable in the UK', Home Office press release, 24 August 2005). The guidelines are aimed against those who the government believe, foment or provoke others to commit acts of terrorism.

'Non-conducive' action will be taken against those who 'foment, justify or glorify terrorist violence in furtherance of particular beliefs' by doing any of the following:

- writing, producing, publishing or distributing material;
- public speaking including preaching;
- running a website; or
- using a position of responsibility such as being a teacher, community or youth leader to express such views.

Action will also be taken against those who:

- seek to provoke others to commit terrorist acts;
- foment other serious criminal activity or seek to provoke others to serious criminal acts;
- foster hatred which might lead to inter-community violence in the UK.

It was stressed by the Home Office that the above list is 'indicative', but did not reflect all the circumstances in which non-conducive action may be taken to deal with 'extremists'. The Home Secretary further stated:

'Individuals who seek to create fear, distrust and division in order to stir up terrorist activity will not be tolerated by the Government or by our communities. By publishing the list today I make it absolutely clear that these are unacceptable behaviours, and will be grounds for deporting and excluding such individuals from the UK.'

The Home Office states that the policy is not intended to stifle free speech or legitimate debate about religious or other issues. There are, however, obvious concerns that the general way in which the policy is expressed could lead to breaches of the right to freedom of expression under Article 10 ECHR.

Memoranda of understanding There are also concerns that, in implementing the above policy, the government will seek to return to countries with appalling human rights records those who it has decided are not welcome in the UK. In the original parliamentary statement of the Home Secretary which announced that the government was to take the above measures after a period of consultation, it was also stated:

'In the past, there have been some successful challenges to proposed deportations under article 3 of the European Convention on Human Rights. For that reason, we have actively been seeking memorandums of understanding with a number of governments to address those legal concerns. I am pleased to announce today that the Governments of the United Kingdom and the Hashemite Kingdom of Jordan have reached agreement in principle on the provisions of such a memorandum of understanding, regulating the arrangements by which assurances regarding the treatment of particular individuals can be sought prior to their deportation.' (Parliamentary Statement of Home Secretary, 20 July 2005)

Concluding 'memoranda of understanding' with countries that routinely torture political opponents is surely no adequate safeguard unless there is positive evidence that the country is safe for the individual concerned. JCWI's view is that the proper way to deal with the kinds of concerns that the policy is aimed at is the criminal rather than the immigration law (for example under the Terrorism Act 2000, ▶see 627). This would, of course, deal with the threat from both British citizens and foreign nationals and would not discriminate against those who are subject to immigration control.

Criminal convictions and risk of re-offending

As far as criminal convictions are concerned, the decisions of the courts have varied as to whether it is necessary to show that there is a risk of re-offending or whether deportation on these grounds can proceed if the offence in itself was sufficiently serious to justify deportation. In *Santillo*, the Court of Appeal suggested that the fact of a conviction alone would not be enough. In any case, the criminal conviction must be sufficiently serious to justify the decision and the kinds of conduct that have resulted in deportation are serious violent or sexual offences, robberies and the importation or supply of controlled drugs.

A fuller consideration of this topic and Home Office policy in this area is given in the chapter concerning EEA nationals (▶see 552–4).

In all cases, the public interest in deportation must be weighed against the compassionate circumstances of the case, applying the same rules as for administrative removal (▶above).

Other non-conducive grounds

The power can also potentially be used where a person has committed offences overseas, has criminal connections which are likely to result in adverse consequences for the community in the UK, or where the person has obtained leave by fraud (see the interesting case of *R (Saribal) v SSHD* in which it was alleged that the applicant had used fraud in order to win his asylum appeal). Where deception is used and leave has been granted, however, it is more likely that the Home Office will use illegal entry powers or administrative removal powers (▶see 1007–8, 1013–4).

Family members

The spouse and minor children of people being deported can also be deported. However, a deportation order cannot be signed against a spouse or minor child more than eight weeks (excluding any time during which the family member is appealing against the decision to make the deportation order) after the principal has been deported. A deportation order is no longer effective against a family member who ceases to be a member of the family of the principal who is deported. Family members must be given independent consideration and the factors in the rules set out above (▶see 1009–10), as well as those particular to spouses and minor children (▶387–8), must be applied.

The deportation process

As noted above, the first step for the Home Office to take in the deportation process is to issue a notice of intention to deport (or a 'decision to deport'). In those cases, it will only move to actually make the deportation order after any appeal rights have been exhausted.

In all deportation cases, the Home Office decision as to whether to issue a notice of intention to deport and to make a deportation order is taken with regard to the same factors as for cases of administrative removal (▶see above at 1009–10).

Notice of intention or 'decision' to deport and appeal

Before issuing a decision to make a deportation order, the Home Office will normally write to the person stating that it is considering deportation proceedings and asking for any representations to be made within a certain time. If a decision to deport is made, this will be sent or given to the person. Before 2 October 2000, the form used was 'Form APP 104' but this has now been replaced with forms ICD.1070 to ICD.1076 and ICD.1914 (the precise form used will depend on the circumstances), which provide the reasons for deportation. The notice of decision should include details about how to appeal, as it carries a full right of appeal. The notice of decision to deport also gives the immigration authorities the power to detain a person pending deportation. A recommendation for deportation has the same effect with regard to detention.

In the appeal against the decision to deport, the deportee can argue that:

- the decision should not have been made, applying the factors to be considered under the immigration rules (or any relevant Home Office policy) to the circumstances of the case;
- there are human rights reasons why they should not be deported; or
- if they have claimed asylum, their removal would be in breach of the Refugee Convention.

Deportation order

If no appeal is brought to the AIT against a notice of decision to deport, or to the criminal court against a recommendation given by the criminal court, or if such appeals are dismissed, the Home Secretary can then make a deportation order. It is possible to make written representations to the Home Office again at this stage if there is relevant information which has not yet been considered or if circumstances have changed, for example, a child may have been born to the family or indeed, if there has been a further substantial passage of time during which the person has become yet more established in the UK. Deportation orders are signed by a minister on the basis of a written submission prepared by caseworkers. Particularly contentious cases may be submitted to the Secretary of State for their personal consideration.

Although the practice of serving deportation notices 'on the file' (at the Home Office) where the Home Office has no knowledge of the whereabouts of a particular person is no longer used, notices may still have been served at a person's last known address, even when the person had a representative. People therefore still sometimes find, after living unlawfully in the UK for many years, that a notice has been given which stops the clock for the purpose of the long-residence rules (▶see 155).

The same factors under the immigration rules are considered at the stage of signing the order (▶see 1009–10, 387–8).

If a person is serving a criminal sentence, the Home Office will usually wait until near to the end of the period of the sentence before considering deportation. As soon as the order is signed and before it is given to the deportee, a deportation order is effective. A deportee can ask the Home Office to revoke the order and appeal in-country on asylum and human rights grounds against a refusal to revoke it (otherwise the appeal will be from outside the UK). Of course if the person has already had a right of appeal or appealed on such grounds, for example against the notice of intention to deport, the Home Office can prevent an appeal by certifying it (s96 2002 Act).

Once the deportation order is made, it means that any existing leave is invalid and no further leave can be granted (even if the applicant leaves the UK and applies to return) until it has been revoked. For 'revocation', ▶see below.

Removal

After the order has been signed then, as in other enforcement cases, the immigration authorities have the power to set removal directions (for removal generally, ▶see below).

Alternatives to deportation: voluntary and supervised departures

In many cases, where a person has lost their appeal against the decision to deport or against a recommendation and there are no other grounds for staying in the UK, it is in the person's interests to leave before an order is made. This is because, if the order is not signed, the person is at least eligible to return to the UK. If the order is signed, they cannot return until it is revoked.

It may take some time for an order to be signed, which gives time for the person to make a voluntary departure. At any time, a person may make a voluntary departure from the UK by buying their own ticket and leaving. It is worth informing the immigration service of travel plans, so that it is less likely that a deportation order will be signed before they leave.

In addition, it is also possible for anyone who is liable to be deported and who is going to live permanently abroad, to make a 'supervised departure' from the UK (see s5(6), 1971 Act). This is where the immigration authorities pay the travel expenses of the person and any members of their family or household who wish to leave with them.

If a voluntary or supervised departure is made after a person has been given a notice of intention to deport, then the person's passport will usually be endorsed that they were served with the notice of intention to deport to show that a deportation decision has been made.

However, even if a person leaves before the decision to deport is given, future applications can still be affected. Firstly, the Home Office has stated that information about people removed under the supervised departure process is available to immigration officers and to ECOs overseas. Secondly, if people apply for entry clearance, they are required to declare their circumstances on the application form where they have had previous immigration difficulties and it is likely that the application will be referred to the Home Office to be checked against their Home Office file. The general considerations under the immigration rules allow applications to be refused, among other cases, when a person has convictions, or on the grounds of their character or conduct, or because their exclusion is conducive to the public good, or because they have previously obtained leave by deception.

Those convicted of criminal offences who have completed their prison sentences and who cannot obtain bail, may wish to leave the UK rather than spend further time in immigration detention awaiting the deportation process. However, people in detention are very vulnerable to suggestions and it has been alleged that sometimes immigration officers may try to persuade them to make voluntary departures and request that they sign disclaimer forms stating that they do not want to appeal. Even when this has been done, people can change their minds and lodge an appeal, or if the time-limit has passed, submit the notice of appeal out of time and explain the reasons for the delay.

Revocation of deportation orders

After an order is signed, it must be revoked before a person can return. If a person does gain entry while there is still a valid deportation order against them, they have entered illegally and can be arrested and removed as an illegal entrant. A deportation order will not be signed after a person has left. If it can be shown that the person had already left by the date an order was signed, the order will be invalid and should be revoked.

It is possible to urge the Home Office to revoke a deportation order while the person is in the UK, but this is unlikely. Such an application is only likely to be considered if the deportation order was signed a long time ago and there have been changes in circumstances since the order was signed and the person has only recently been traced. All the changes in the person's circumstances and any compassionate or family reasons should be put forward.

If a person claims asylum or makes a human rights claim while in the UK, then this is treated as an application for the order to be revoked and there is an in-country right of appeal against the refusal to revoke the order on these grounds.

Immigration rules and revocation

The immigration rules state that an order will not normally be revoked until the person has been out of the UK for at least three years after the order was signed, except in the most 'exceptional circumstances' (see paras 390–392 HC395). If an application is made sooner, it should contain full details of the exceptional circumstances justifying revocation earlier than normal. The rules state that relevant factors will include:

- the grounds on which the deportation order was made;
- any representations made in support of revocation;
- the interests of the community, including the maintenance of an effective immigration control;
- the interests of the applicant, including any compassionate circumstances.

Having a spouse and children settled in the UK, who have reasons for being unable to join the deportee abroad, for example, may be strong compassionate circumstances for earlier revocation. This may be the case even if those grounds were not considered strong enough to avoid removal under the policy guidelines on enforcement in cases involving marriage and children. It may be possible to argue that the prolonged separation of the family is contrary to Article 8 ECHR.

However, the Home Office approach to revocation concerning the category of case still dealt with by the deportation procedure, is unlikely to be generous. The rules themselves state that a person may be required to be absent for a 'long term' of years where serious criminal offences were committed. This means considerably more than three years. In some cases, the Home Office may be expected to keep the order in force for perhaps ten years. The Home Office also has powers to exclude persons from the UK on the grounds that their presence is not conducive to the public good.

If revocation is refused, there is a right of appeal from abroad against the refusal. The full merits of the case can be raised as well as any human rights grounds.

If the deportation order is revoked

If a deportation order is revoked, this does not give the person an automatic right to return to the UK. It simply means that there is no longer a legal obstacle to them applying to return. The person will still have to fit into all the requirements of the immigration rules in the category in which he or she is seeking to return. The Home Office is likely to consider the application in great detail. Therefore, even if the person is not a visa national and is not seeking to return in a category for which entry clearance is always required, it is advisable to apply for entry clearance so as to minimise the risk of refusal at the port.

Revocation of indefinite leave in deportation cases

9

In cases where a person is liable to deportation *but* they cannot be deported for 'legal' reasons, the Home Office may instead revoke their indefinite leave to remain (s76(1)(4)(5) 2002 Act). This power may be used:

- whether the person is liable to deportation either on the basis of a recommendation of the criminal court *or* on 'non-conducive' grounds;
- whether the leave was granted before or after this new power came into force (10 February 2003);
- whether the applicant's conduct which has made them liable to deportation took place before or after the new power came into force.

The power may also be used in relation to family members. The kind of situation in which it may be used is explained in the Explanatory Notes to the 2002 Act:

'An example of how this power might be used would be where a person has committed a serious criminal offence such that their deportation would be conducive to the public good but where they cannot be deported to their country of origin because removal would be contrary to Article 3 of the European Convention on Human Rights' (para. 208).

There is an in-country right of appeal against revocation of indefinite leave and revocation won't take effect while an appeal is outstanding against it (s82(3) 2002 Act). As with the similar power referred to above (►1008), unless the person is granted limited leave instead, revocation will leave them in a *limbo* situation: unable to work or access benefits.

THE PROCESS OF REMOVAL AND THE POSSIBLE COUNTRIES OF RETURN

'Removal' is the final practical means of enforcing the departure under any of the four main procedures described above. This can be confusing because when the word 'removal' alone is used, it could mean that any of the above procedures have been used. The 'directions for removal' themselves are given to the captain of a ship or aircraft or to a train operator to remove the person. The directions are also notified to the person who is to be removed. Often the person will be detained. Where the person is not detained, they will normally be given a notice that they must attend at a port at a particular time in order to be removed as a condition of their existing temporary admission.

Following the death of Joy Gardner, Home Officer ministers made a public commitment that, other than in the 'most exceptional circumstances', people detained by the immigration service would not be removed on the day of detention. This policy remains in force. Where same-day removal is proposed, it must be authorised by an officer at Assistant Director level within the immigration service or above and the reference to that officer should have been made in writing (EPU Notice 07/05 at para. 4).

The removal itself may be carried out by force if necessary. The immigration service has been very severely criticised in the past for the inappropriate use of force. In some cases, the immigration authorities make arrangements for escorts to accompany the returnee on the journey back. The Operational Enforcement Manual (OEM) states that where:

'…an offender shows violent tendencies or a determination not to be removed, a discipline escort may be required and where an offender has a medical condition and requires medical supervision on the flight, a medical escort may be required…

Where more than two escorts are felt to be necessary, and in particularly disruptive cases, a prior planning meeting between all those agencies likely to be involved should be arranged to discuss the case e.g. the escorts, IS representatives, perhaps police officers, social services and/or community liaison officers and the carrier…' (OEM, Ch 40.1)

In some cases, mechanical restraints may be authorised. These may be handcuffs and/or, in wholly exceptional cases, leg restraints. No other form of restraint may be used (OEM, Ch 40.2–40.2.2). As far as the control and restraint of minors is concerned, the Enforcement Policy Unit has stated that:

'The control and restraint of minors is limited to where the situation is such that it becomes necessary for an officer to use physical intervention to prevent harm to the child or any individual present. It is *not* to be used simply to enforce the removal of children where there is no threat of violence. In the vast majority of cases there will not be a need for officers to exercise physical control or restraint of minors.' (EPU 07/05, para. 12.1)

For details about Home Office policy on procedures where there are threats of self-harm or suicide on removal, ▶see 996–8 above. For details about civil claims for unlawful removals, ▶see 1181–2 and for assaults during the process of removal, ▶see 1182–3.

Where can people be removed to?

When people are removed from the UK, the list of countries to which they can be sent depends upon which procedure is being used to enforce their departure. In cases of port removal and illegal entry, the person can be sent to a country (paras 8–10A, Sch 2 1971 Act):

- of which they are a national; or
- which has provided them with a passport or another travel or identity document; or
- from which they embarked for the UK; or
- to which there is 'reason to believe [they] will be admitted'.

In cases of deportation or administrative removal, people can be sent to a country (para. 1(1), Sch 3 1971 Act; Immigration (Removal Directions) Regulations 2000; OEM Ch 11.4):

- of which they are a national; or
- to which there is 'reason to believe [they] will be admitted'.

There are special considerations in cases where asylum-seekers are being removed on 'third-country' grounds (▶see Chapter 24) but they are additional to the above rules, which apply to all cases.

If the immigration authorities are seeking to return someone to a country where there is 'reason to believe they will be admitted', it is not enough for them to show that the person ought to be admitted there. There must be clear evidence that they are in fact likely to be accepted.

Travel documents

Countries are bound to accept the return of their own nationals but sometimes removal to a country of which a person claims to be a national becomes impractical and is delayed because that country refuses to accept their return. In many cases of, for example, asylum-seekers who do not possess travel documents, the Home Office may seek to return them using its own one-way identity documents. However, the immigration authorities may also need to obtain travel documentation for them from their own national authorities.

Some countries, for example Algeria, have been known to be very slow to document and accept the return of their own nationals and returns can be very much delayed as a result. If a person is detained while awaiting travel documentation, then the delay may make that detention unlawful (►for this and for procedures and difficulties in obtaining travel documents, ►see 925–7).

OTHER FORMS OF ENFORCEMENT AND DEPARTURE

In addition to the above procedures, there are some additional procedures for enforcement and departure, which are sometimes used.

Removal of those detained under the Mental Health Act

Certain patients who have been detained under the Mental Health Act can be removed from the UK in order for their medical care to be continued in their own country. The initiative for triggering the procedure is with the hospital where the patient is receiving care rather than with the Home Office. Where a person who has leave to be in the UK is suffering from a very severe mental illness such that they are detained as an inpatient under the Mental Health Act 1983, there is a specific procedure for their removal from the UK (see s86 1983 Act). The patient cannot be removed under this procedure unless (see, in addition to the 1983 Act, IDI Ch1, s8, para. 4):

- specific arrangements have been made for the person's care and treatment in their own country;
- the doctor in charge of the case considers that it is in the interests of the patient to be removed;
- the patient is fit to travel;
- a medical escort is provided to accompany the person to their destination; and
- the patient has a valid passport and any necessary transit visas.

The Home Office must obtain the approval of the Mental Health Review Tribunal before proceeding.

Repatriation/voluntary departure

In setting out the forms of enforcement above, we have mentioned the possibility of voluntary departure. Applicants can opt to leave voluntarily and, in deportation cases, there is a scheme for 'supervised departure' before the deportation order is signed (►1023–4). However, other than in supervised departures, applicants who leave voluntarily will probably have to pay for their travel unless they can take advantage of a Home Office-backed scheme.

The old scheme for paying for people, together with their family or households, to leave the UK to live abroad permanently was set up under section 29 of the 1971 Act. That scheme was intended for the benefit of non-British nationals most of whom were settled in the UK, and who had decided to repatriate. It had to be shown that it was in the interests of the applicant to do so. The majority of people who used the scheme were Jamaican nationals. The scheme itself was operated by the International Social Service of Great Britain. Section 29 has now been repealed.

In place of section 29, there is a further scheme for funding voluntary departures from the UK (s58 2002 Act). This scheme allows the Home Office to help 'voluntary leavers' if they are leaving the UK for a place where they hope to take up permanent residence. The Home Office must be shown that it is in their interests to leave the UK. The kind of help that can be provided is broader than under the previous scheme. In addition to meeting travel expenses for voluntary leavers and their families, the Home Office can now meet costs connected with their immediate arrival and reception and also longer-term support to allow them to re-integrate. 'Explore and prepare' visits by people who want to return to see what the prospects are for returning permanently, can also be funded. Schemes are run for the Home Office by the International Organisation for Migration in partnership with Refugee Action (▶see also at 667–8 and, for addresses, ▶see 1501, 1505).

The section 58 scheme cannot be used by British citizens or EEA nationals. *However*, there is a separate power for local authorities to make arrangements for travel for EEA nationals and those who have been granted refugee status by an EEA state. They can be funded to travel back to the EEA state concerned (see the Withholding and Withdrawal of Support (Travel Assistance and Temporary Accommodation) Regulations 2002 (▶see 1314)).

Removal of EEA Nationals and their family members

For details of the circumstances in which EEA nationals and their family members can be required to leave and the appeal rights that they have, ▶see 551–9.

Extradition

People who have been charged with criminal offences overseas may be extradited in order to stand trial in the foreign country. The main piece of legislation is the Extradition Act 2003. The *Handbook* does not cover extradition, which is a very complex area. For suggestions about where to find further information, ▶see 1535.

HOW PEOPLE ARE TRACED AND DETECTED

The immigration authorities may come to know of people who are in breach of the immigration laws in many ways. The applicant may have been in contact with the Home Office, for example, by applying for an extension of leave which was refused, or they may have lost an appeal and remained in the UK after this trying to persuade the Home Office to allow them to stay.

If the person has not been in contact with the Home Office, but has simply stayed beyond the leave granted or worked without permission, they may be traced through various sources. Many authorities, such as the Benefits Agency, local authority housing departments, marriage registrars, health authorities, employers and colleges may now check on immigration status and make enquiries. In addition, the police or the immigration authorities may have received information anonymously. Following the 2002 White Paper, the Home Office set up a 'hotline' for people to report suspected immigration offenders.

Police

The police frequently ask for evidence of identification and immigration status from those who are black or 'foreign-looking', or those who do not have English as their first language. People may come into contact with the police for entirely separate reasons: they may have been stopped on suspicion of a traffic offence, at a demonstration, or they may be wanted as a witness to an accident or crime. People may call the police because of a burglary or an assault and then be asked to prove their status. If it is then suspected that the person may be in breach of the immigration laws, the police can check with the immigration service or their own records. They are then likely to hold the person 'on suspicion' of committing an immigration offence and call immigration officers to interview them and they may then be detained under immigration powers.

Duty to report 'suspicious' marriages or civil partnerships

Under the 1999 Act, there is a duty on marriage registrars to report suspicious or 'sham' marriages to the Home Office. The same will apply to 'suspicious civil partnerships' (see s24A 1999 Act as inserted by the Civil Partnership Act 2004). These are marriages and partnerships which are entered into for the purpose of avoiding the effect of immigration law. Even before these developments, the courts had said that there may be a duty on housing authorities to report to the Home Office people they believe to be in the UK unlawfully (see *R v Secretary of State for the Environment ex p Tower Hamlets LBC*).

Employers

The government states that, in 2004, it carried out 1,600 enforcement operations against illegal work, a 360 per cent increase on the previous year. It picked up 3,330 people who were working unlawfully.

It is a criminal offence for employers to employ a person who is not permitted to work in the UK although employers have a defence to prosecution if they have carried out certain checks and kept certain documents (▶see 496–500). Information may be relayed back to the immigration authorities by employers. In addition, sometimes the immigration authorities conduct raids on particular premises when they have information that people who have an irregular immigration status are working there.

Some employers are prepared to collaborate with the immigration authorities but the Home Office has indicated that, in some cases, it will not try to obtain assistance in advance from the employer because:

'...efforts to enlist the cooperation of the employer would undermine the effectiveness of a planned operation. Visits will be authorised where there is apparently reliable information that immigration offenders will be found. Particular account will be taken of whether there is a history of the premises being used by offenders.'

Further detection powers under the 2002 Act: employers, local authorities, tax authorities, search of business premises

The 2002 Act made further changes to assist in detection. Under its provisions, local authorities in whose area the immigration authorities believe a person to have been living can be required to provide information about that person. Employers may also be required to produce information about their employees if they are suspected of being illegal entrants, overstayers or in breach of their conditions. The inland revenue (tax) authorities are also allowed to disclose information to the immigration authorities in order to establish the whereabouts of a person who has worked in breach of conditions of leave or temporary admission (see ss129–138 2002 Act).

The 2002 Act also expands powers to enter premises to search for immigration offenders. It gives powers to police and immigration officers to enter business premises, in some cases without a warrant, to search for illegal entrants, overstayers and those in breach of conditions of leave or temporary admission (now contained in ss28CA, 28FA–28FB 1971 Act).

CRIMINAL OFFENCES

Immigration law creates many criminal offences. Because some of the offences can lead to enforced departure, in most cases the authorities are content that immigration control is enforced and people are not actually charged with the criminal offence. Some of the most important offences created by immigration law (although not all of them) are noted in the table below.

This Handbook does not cover the full range of criminal offences, defences, the procedures that apply and the possible penalties. Anyone being questioned by police or prosecuted in relation to an immigration-related offence should seek legal advice from a lawyer experienced in both criminal and immigration matters.

For more details about:

- *criminal sanctions against employers* for unlawfully employing a person not entitled to work and the defences to any such prosecution, ►see 496–500;
- prosecutions under the 2004 Act for entering the UK and attending an interview without a valid passport, ►see 683–6;
- failing to cooperate with obtaining a travel document for deportation or removal (s35 2004 Act), ►see 927.

The use of criminal sanctions against asylum-seekers for illegal entry may, in some cases, be unlawful following the decision of the High Court in *Adimi*. In that case, the Court found that to impose penalties by prosecuting certain asylum-seekers was unlawful and contrary to Article 31 of the Refugee Convention, which states that refugees should not have penalties imposed on them if they enter directly from the place where they fear persecution and claim asylum without delay. For details about when *Adimi* applies and compensation for wrongful prosecution, ►see 1235–8.

Powers of arrest and search

The 1999 Act specifically extended the powers of arrest held by immigration officers and gave them police-like powers in relation to search, entry and seizure in dealing with the immigration offences of illegal entry, overstaying, obtaining leave to enter or remain by deception and breaking conditions of leave. Officers are permitted to use 'reasonable force' in carrying out these functions. The aim of the powers is to decrease the dependency of the immigration service on the police by enabling them to carry out such functions without police presence, as was previously required. As stated above, the 2002 Act expands these powers in relation to business premises.

Section 14 of the 2004 Act gives immigration officers acting 'in the course of exercising' functions under the immigration legislation, the power to arrest, without warrant, people whom they reasonably suspect of committing a whole range of general offences: theft and other dishonesty offences, forgery, false statements under the Perjury Act, trafficking etc. Powers of entry and search are given to them in relation to these offences as well.

The Immigration, Asylum and Nationality Bill 2005 proposes to give new powers to allow the search of ships, aircrafts and vehicles in order to detect illegal entrants and to allow these powers to be exercised by 'authorised persons' as well as by police and customs officials.

Again, this *Handbook* does not attempt to cover the range of powers of arrest and search and the procedures which apply.

CRIMINAL OFFENCES UNDER THE IMMIGRATION ACTS

This table briefly sets out some of the many criminal offences connected to immigration law.

Entry without leave or in breach of a deportation order

Persons who 'knowingly' enter the UK either in breach of a deportation order or without obtaining leave (which they need) are liable for prosecution (s24, 1971 Act). These forms of entry are illegal but do not necessarily involve deception.

Deception in obtaining leave or preventing enforcement

A person who obtains, or tries to obtain, leave to enter or leave to remain by deception and people, who by deception avoid any form of action to require them to leave the UK, can be prosecuted (s24A, 1971 Act).

It is important to distinguish between the criminal offences relating to illegal entry and the immigration status of an illegal entrant. It will be seen from the categories of illegal entrant set out above that, for a person to be declared an illegal entrant by the immigration authorities, it is not necessary for them to have any intention to act unlawfully or any knowledge of the unlawful act. The criminal offence requires knowledge.

Overstaying and breach of conditions

When a time-limit is placed on a person's leave in the UK, it is an offence to stay beyond it. It is also an offence to breach any of the conditions that are attached to the leave, for example, by working when forbidden to do so. People can also be prosecuted for breaching the terms of their temporary admission or bail. The criminal offence is committed by 'knowingly' over-staying or breaching conditions of leave (s24 1971 Act). For the purposes of administrative removal, however, someone can be in breach of their con-ditions, or overstaying their leave, without knowing that they are doing so, although they may not be committing the criminal offence.

Overstaying is a continuing offence, running from the day after the expiry of leave until the person either leaves the UK or is given fresh leave to remain by the Home Office. Anyone who applies even a day late to the Home Office for an extension and is aware that their application has not been submitted in time may be committing this offence, despite the fact that their application remains under consideration. This is because, even though the delay may have been a mistake, they may still be overstaying 'knowingly'. The authorities may not, in practice, want to prosecute if they consider the overstaying was inadvertent.

Assisting asylum-seekers to enter the UK

It is an offence for a person to help another person, whom they have reason-able cause to believe is an asylum-seeker or will make a human rights claim, to

9

arrive in the UK. Note that the offence is committed by persons who help the asylum-seekers 'for gain' and does not apply to a person acting for an organisation which aims to help asylum-seekers and does not charge for its services (see s25A, 1971 Act).

This offence was introduced because of the decision of the House of Lords in *Naillie*. In that case, the House of Lords held that, where those travelling to the UK claimed asylum on arrival, there was no illegal entry and so anyone helping them to come here could not commit the offence of assisting illegal entry. The offence is aimed at racketeers who charge to help secure entry of asylum-seekers clandestinely or with false documents.

Assisting unlawful immigration to a member state

It is an offence to knowingly do anything, which helps a non-EU national breach the immigration law of any EU state (s25 1971 Act).

General offences under the 1971 Act

Included among the general offences under the 1971 Act are refusing to be examined by an immigration officer or to produce information or documents, which are required for the examination; making false representations; using false or altered documents which are required for immigration control or obstructing an immigration officer in carrying out their duty (s26, 1971 Act).

Application Registration Cards

There are various offences connected to misuse of the Application Registration Cards (ARCs), which are given to asylum-seekers (s26A 1971 Act). Included in these offences are making a false card, altering a card, possessing a false or altered card and using a false card.

Immigration stamp

It is an offence to be in possession of an immigration stamp (the stamp used by immigration officials for issuing leave) or a replica stamping device (s26B 1971 Act).

Provision of advice

Those who provide immigration advice in contravention of the rules set out in Chapter 3 may be prosecuted for an offence (s91, 1999 Act).

Offences connected with the support of asylum-seekers

In relation to asylum support, it is an offence to make false representations; to fail to notify a change of circumstances; to obstruct an officer in operating the support scheme; or, as a sponsor, to fail to maintain a person whom they have signed an undertaking to support and who later claims asylum support (see s105–108, 1999 Act).

Trafficking

There is an offence of trafficking in prostitution. This offence is committed when a person arranges for, or assists, a person to enter, travel within or leave the UK in circumstances where they will be 'controlled' in prostitution in the

UK or elsewhere (s145 2002 Act).

Under the 2004 Act there is also an offence of trafficking people for the purposes of 'exploitation'. This offence is committed by arranging or assisting a person to enter, travel within or leave the UK where the person will be exploited in the UK or elsewhere (s4 2004 Act). 'Exploitation' can be:

- slavery or forced labour within the meaning of Article 4 ECHR;
- encouraging or expecting a person to do something which would be a criminal offence under the Human Organ Transplants Act 1989;
- subjecting a person to threats, force or deception to get them to provide services of any kind;
- taking advantage of a person's illness, disability, youth or family relationship, to get them to do things which they would not otherwise do.

Entering the UK without a passport

Section 2 of the 2004 Act creates the offence of entering the UK without a valid passport or similar document, which demonstrates the person's identity and nationality. The offence is committed when a person is first interviewed by an immigration officer after arriving in the UK. There have been a substantial number of prosecutions under this section which is discussed more fully at ▶683–6.

Failing to cooperate with obtaining a travel document

The 2004 Act has created a criminal offence of failing to cooperate with obtaining a travel document for deportation or removal (s35). For further details, ▶see 927.

Employer sanctions

From 27 January 1997, it has been an offence for an employer to employ a person who requires, but who either does not have leave, or whose leave prevents them from working in the job in question (s8 1996 Act). For full details about this offence and the means by which employers can ensure that they are not prosecuted for it ▶see 496–500.

The Immigration, Asylum and Nationality Bill 2005

The Immigration, Asylum and Nationality Bill 2005 proposes yet further offences including:

- knowingly employing an adult who has not been granted leave to enter or remain, whose leave is invalid or expired, or whose conditions of leave prevent them taking employment (there will also be a civil penalty scheme for employers who employ those not entitled to work);
- obstructing or assaulting a person authorised by the Secretary of State to search a ship, aircraft, vehicle etc. for illegal entrants.

9

Section 10 **Appeals**

Chapter 34
Rights of appeal 1039
Proposed changes under the 2005 Bill 1041
Appeal system – an overview 1046
When can people appeal? 1052
Notice of decision 1061
Giving notice of appeal 1062
The 'one-stop' system 1066
Certificates under section 96 2002 Act 1067
Appeal pending: protection from removal and immigration status 1069
Family visitor entry clearance appeals 1071
Cases certified as 'clearly unfounded' 1073
Asylum 'status' appeals under section 83 2002 Act 1079
Appeals involving 'exclusion' from refugee status 1080
Special Immigration Appeals Commission 1081

Chapter 35
Conducting first instance appeals before the AIT 1085
Procedure rules and practice directions 1086
Timetable and basic procedure for appeals 1088
Parties to the appeal, representation and funding 1090
Preliminary decisions on notices of appeal and late appeals 1091
Respondent's reasons and explanatory statements 1094
Standard appeal directions 1095
Case management review hearings and further directions 1095

10

Additional matters that may be raised before
hearing, including at a CMR   1097

Adjournments   1100

Determining appeals in the absence of a party,
without a hearing or without deciding the
substance   1102

Preparing for the full hearing   1105

Using case-law   1110

Conducting the full hearing before the
immigration judge   1112

Deciding appeals and the powers of the AIT   1118

Fast track appeals   1129

Chapter 36
Challenging decisions of the AIT   1133

Applying to the AIT for an order for reconsideration 1134

Applying to the High Court for an order for a
review of the AIT decision   1140

Reconsideration hearings before the AIT   1143

Appealing to the Court of Appeal following
reconsideration determinations   1147

Other routes to the Court of Appeal   1149

When can judicial review still be used?   1150

Transitional appeal arrangements   1151

Public funding (legal aid) considerations   1153

Showing an error of law   1155

Mistakes of fact and fresh evidence   1159

Time-limits   1162

34 Rights of appeal

This section is about appealing against negative decisions of the immigration authorities. The right of appeal, at first instance, is to the new Asylum and Immigration Tribunal (AIT).

This chapter looks at who has the right of appeal, and at various connected matters. In particular, it deals with:

- the proposed changes to rights of appeal under the 2005 Bill (▶see the table at 1042–6);
- the structure of the appeals system in force from 4 April 2005, and of the rights of review and further appeal (▶see the table at 1047–9; full details about challenging decisions of the AIT are given in Chapter 36);
- the development of appeal rights under recent legislation (▶1050–2)and the personnel of the AIT (▶1049–50);
- when people have a right of appeal, when the right of appeal is excluded, and whether the right of appeal is in-country – this is the most important part of the chapter and these three questions are dealt with in Tables 1–3, at ▶1052–61;
- notices of appealable decisions issued by the immigration authorities (▶1061–2);
- giving notice of appeal on the prescribed forms, and complying with the requirements of the forms (▶1062–6);
- the 'one-stop' appeal system (▶1066–7), and when appeals can be excluded by the Secretary of State issuing a 'section 96' certificate stating that the matter should have been raised before (▶1067–9);
- protection from removal while an appeal is 'pending', and other issues concerning the immigration status which an appellant has while the appeal is pending (▶1069–71);
- family visitor appeals against refusals of entry clearance (▶1071–3);
- the ability of the Home Office to exclude in-country rights of appeal where an asylum or human rights claim is made, and where that claim is certified as 'clearly unfounded', and challenging such certificates (▶1073–8);
- appeals against refusal of asylum where the applicant is granted leave in

10

another capacity (also known as 'status' appeals) under section 83 2002 Act (▶1079);

- appeals in cases where the Home Office decision is to exclude the applicant from the Protection of the 1951 Refugee Convention under either Article 1F or 33 (▶1080–1);
- cases heard by the Special Immigration Appeals Commission (SIAC) – we discuss this only briefly; those with SIAC appeals should take specialist advice (▶1081–3).

Chapter 35 gives guidance on conducting appeals at first instance before an immigration judge of the AIT. It looks at all aspects of the Procedure Rules and Practice Directions, including the overall timetable for appeals; case-management review hearings (CMRs); appeal directions; adjournments; and the actual appeal hearing itself. It also examines the powers the AIT has in deciding appeals.

Chapter 36 deals with challenging decisions of the AIT. The system for further reviews and appeals changed radically when the new appeal system was introduced on 4 April 2005. The chapter addresses: applying to both the AIT and the High Court for a review of a first decision of the AIT; reconsideration hearings before the AIT and appeals to the Court of Appeal. It also gives some guidance on identifying errors of law, in order to prepare grounds of challenge to decisions of the AIT.

Time-limits

In all cases involving appeals, it is important to make sure that the time-limits under the appeals system are complied with, and that time is counted correctly. The different time-limits are set out in the three chapters as and when necessary. However, a table dealing with all the relevant time-limits and how time is counted is given at the end of the section, at ▶1162–7.

Other appeals, decisions and challenges

The three chapters in this section deal with cases where there is an appeal against a negative immigration decision to the AIT. However, some specialised aspects of appeals to the AIT are covered elsewhere in the *Handbook*, as follows.

- For appeals and challenges in **'third country' cases**, ▶see 739–46. See in particular the table dealing with legal protection, the presumptions of safety which apply, and whether there is an effective in- or out-of-country right of appeal (▶739–43).
- For cases involving **EEA nationals** and their family members who can appeal against 'EEA decisions', ▶see 556–9, 562.
- For further details about appeals involving **discrimination**, ▶see 890–1.

- For further details about **Article 8 ECHR** cases where it is not just the human rights of the appellant that are at stake, ▶see 858–9.

  In addition, included in the immigration system as a whole, there are certain other kinds of 'appeals' and challenges that can be brought, which are covered elsewhere in the *Handbook* as follows.

- **Bail applications** and hearings are not strictly 'appeals', but they can be heard by the AIT (▶see 958–85).

- It is possible to appeal to the **Asylum Support Adjudicator** about decisions concerning asylum support (▶see Chapter 42).

- For appeals against a refusal to issue an **Immigration Employment Document** (IED), ▶see 439–40.

- For details about the kinds of decision that can be challenged by **judicial review,** ▶see 1216; and for details about the judicial review procedure, ▶see 1213–22.

- In addition to dealing with judicial review, Chapter 38 also discusses **complaints** to the Home Office; the Home Office scheme for consolatory payments; involving an **MP**; and complaining to the **Parliamentary Ombudsman**.

PROPOSED CHANGES UNDER THE 2005 BILL

The Immigration, Asylum and Nationality Bill 2005 proposes to make certain important changes to rights of appeal. Very significant appeal rights are excluded in relation to entry clearance appeals, and appeals against decisions to refuse leave to enter, to refuse to extend leave, and to vary leave. The appeal system is also modified in line with the change to the leave granted to refugees. This is to allow them to appeal against decisions to refuse to extend leave, or to refuse to continue to recognise them as refugees.

All of the changes are described in detail in the table below.

The 2005 Bill is likely to complete its passage through parliament in 2005. It entered the committee stage in the House of Commons on 18 October 2005. No date is yet known for when the appeal provisions will come into force; nor is it known what transitional arrangements there may be. For JCWI's views on changes to appeals ▶see 48 and 1072–3.

10

PROPOSED CHANGES TO APPEALS: THE IMMIGRATION, ASYLUM AND NATIONALITY BILL 2005

References to 'sections' in this table are to sections of the 2002 Act, unless otherwise stated.

1) In general, no right of appeal against decisions to curtail, or refuse to extend, leave

At present, there is a right of appeal against decisions to refuse to extend ('vary') leave, and to curtail leave so that there is no leave left at all. The Bill withdraws both of these as 'immigration decisions' in section 82 2002 Act. There may, therefore, no longer be a right of appeal against them *except* in the situations under (2) and (3) below. This potentially removes rights of appeal in all sorts of cases where people are seeking to extend their leave in the UK in economic categories, or as students or family members, and so on.

Of course, in all cases of decisions to curtail or refuse to extend leave, an applicant cannot be removed unless and until *another* immigration decision is made – normally a decision to administratively remove them as an overstayer. This right of appeal will remain – but remember, in contrast to the variation/ curtailment rights of appeal, which will disappear, it is not an in-country appeal unless brought on asylum or human rights grounds.

As a further consequence to this proposed change, the legislation about 'grounds of appeal' will be amended. This is in order that, when the applicant does have a right of appeal (against removal), on that appeal they can *also* argue that the earlier decision to vary or curtail leave was wrong on any of the normal grounds (not in accordance with the rules, law etc).

2) Right of appeal for refugees refused further leave or whose leave is curtailed

As an exception to (1) above, there will be a right of appeal against a decision to curtail or refusal to extend leave where the applicant's existing leave is as a refugee and, as a result of the decision, the applicant has no leave. Such decisions will be included in the definition of 'immigration decision' in section 82. This appeal right is intended to cater for the new system of granting only limited leave to refugees. If a refugee's application to extend leave on active review is refused, or their leave is curtailed, they will be able to appeal even though other decisions on extension and other curtailments do not give a right of appeal.

3) Right of appeal for certain other categories where further leave is refused or leave is curtailed

As a further exception to (1) above, there will be a right of appeal in the same circumstances as in (2) above in non-refugee cases in circumstances that the Secretary of State may set out in secondary legislation. It is not yet clear what other cases the government has in mind. Again, such decisions are added to the definition of 'immigration decision' in section 82.

4) 'Status' appeal for those no longer recognised as refugees but who are allowed to stay on other grounds

There will be a new right of appeal on asylum grounds where an applicant, who was previously granted leave as a refugee, is determined no longer to qualify as a refugee, but is still permitted to remain in another capacity. Again, this caters for the new system of granting limited leave to refugees, and it is another kind of refugee 'status' appeal. The existing refugee status appeal under s83 allows those granted leave for over 12 months to appeal, whether or not they were previously recognised as a refugee. This new right of appeal will probably be added to section 83 as 'section 83A'.

5) New appeal right where a decision is made to *remove* a person whose indefinite leave as a refugee is revoked

The rights of appeal against an immigration decision to remove a person administratively in section 82 (as an overstayer etc.) will be amended to include a right of appeal against a decision to remove a person whose indefinite leave as a refugee has been revoked. When, in February 2003, the power to administratively remove a person on these grounds was added to the 1999 Act by the 2002 Act, no right of appeal was given against *removal* on these grounds. This was odd, because a decision to administratively remove a person on all other grounds gave a right of appeal. So, an appeal right will now be given when a decision to remove on these grounds is taken. This means that there will now be two appeal rights in these cases:

- an appeal against the revocation decision itself, which is an 'immigration decision' under the existing legislation; *and*
- a new appeal against removal of a person whose indefinite leave as a refugee has been revoked.

The government believes that, because of the importance of refugee status, both appeal rights are necessary. For more details about revocation and this change, ▶see 1008.

10

6) Exclusion of all entry clearance appeals in non-family-visit and non-dependant cases unless appeal is on human rights or race discrimination grounds

There are existing restrictions on the right of appeal against refusal of entry clearance decisions (and in other cases) where a person: does not satisfy a requirement of the rules as to age or nationality; does not have an immigration document of a certain kind; seeks to enter for longer than permitted by the Rules, or for a purpose not covered by the Rules (s88). There is also a general power to make secondary legislation to prevent appeals in other entry clearance cases (s88A) (▶see Table 2 below). Under the 2005 Bill, all these exclusions and powers will stay in place.

There are also existing exclusions that prevent non-family visitors, short-course students, prospective students, and dependants of students from appealing against refusal of entry clearance (ss90–91). The Bill seeks to replace these provisions about visitors and students with a new set of provisions that remove non-human rights/discrimination rights of appeal against *all* refusals of entry clearance *unless* the application was made *either*:

- in order to visit a class of persons which will be set out in regulations; *or*
- to enter as the dependant of a person in situations that will also be set out in regulations.

This will severely limit the circumstances in which people can appeal against entry clearance refusals. It seems that refusals of entry clearance as a student, or in any of the worker and business categories, will be excluded. As for the two categories, discussed above, in which there still will be rights of appeal, the Bill and its Explanatory Notes (para. 20) indicate that 'visit' appeal rights are likely to be restricted to family visitors (as at present), and that regulations will define 'family member' for these purposes, as well as defining 'dependant'. It is assumed that 'dependant' appeals will include appeals in spouse and partner cases – the regulations will no doubt make this clear. However, even in these two categories, the Bill and Explanatory Notes indicate that the regulations may narrow the right of appeal to cases in which:

- the sponsor is settled in the UK; and/or
- the applicant and sponsor have lived together for a specified period of time.

In addition, the 'five-year strategy' indicates that the definition of 'family member' may be made narrower than it is at the present time, and that the right to oral hearings may be removed:

'We will retain appeals for family visits because we recognise the importance of family life. But we will remove the possibility of an oral hearing and deal with all appeals on paper only; and we will limit the right of appeal to cases where the proposed visit is to a close family member. This will discourage speculative appeals. We will subsequently review whether to charge for these appeals.' (Five-year strategy, para. 34)

In summary, under the Bill, entry clearance appeals may be restricted so that applicants can only appeal in certain family visitor or dependant cases. They will *also* be unable to appeal if the refusal is based on any of the existing grounds that exclude the right to appeal in section 88 (age, nationality etc.). *However* – as with the present exclusions on the right to appeal against entry clearance decisions – even when the right to appeal is, in principle, excluded in any of these ways, there will still be a right of appeal on human rights and/or race discrimination grounds.

For details about the existing exclusions on entry clearance appeals, ►see 1055–8, and for details about existing family visit appeals, ►see 1071–3.

7) No appeal against refusal of leave to enter in all non-asylum, human rights or discrimination cases unless entry clearance is held

At present, visitors and certain students who are refused leave to enter cannot appeal if they do not have an entry clearance (s89, and ►see Table 2 below). This exclusion is intended to catch those who do not necessarily *need* an entry clearance under the Rules (non-visa nationals and non-specified nationals), but who are refused entry on other grounds (those who need entry clearance and are refused leave to enter because they don't have it are excluded from the right of appeal under section 88 on the grounds that they do not have a required 'immigration document'; this is the case whether they are seeking entry as a visitor or student, or in any case that does not involve an asylum, human rights or discrimination claim).

The new provision under the Bill replaces section 89 with a new section that extends the need to have an entry clearance in order to have a right of appeal against refusal of leave to enter to *all* categories. So, in all cases, whether an applicant needs an entry clearance or not under the Immigration Rules, where an applicant in the UK is refused leave to enter they will not have a right of appeal against the decision unless:

- they have an entry clearance on their arrival in the UK *and* they are seeking entry for the same purpose as stated in that entry clearance; *or*
- they wish to appeal on asylum, human rights or race discrimination grounds.

8) Abandonment of appeals

At present, all appeals against 'immigration decisions' are abandoned if a person leaves the UK, or is granted leave to enter or remain in the UK (s104(4)). This section will be amended so that it only applies to appeals brought while a person is in the UK. So, if a person is appealing against an entry clearance refusal (for example, for settlement as a dependant), but is later granted leave to enter as a visitor and enters and/or leaves the UK using the visitor entry clearance, they will still be able to continue with the appeal against the settlement refusal.

In addition, the section will be amended to prevent appeals brought on race discrimination grounds from being treated as abandoned if leave to enter or remain is granted.

10

9) Continuation of leave

At present, when a person appeals against a refusal of an in-time application to extend their leave and no decision is made until after their existing leave runs out, they have an automatic grant of leave under section 3C 1971 Act. If the applicant appeals, the automatic leave continues throughout the appeals process, including during review, reconsideration and further appeal to the Court of Appeal (▶see further 145–6). The Bill amends section 3C so that the automatic extension of leave ends when the immigration decision is made – there will therefore be no leave during the period when the applicant is appealing. This proposal may well be amended at the committee stage.

This will prevent access to benefits during the appeals process for those whose existing grant of leave allowed them access to public funds. This will apply, for example, to those with humanitarian leave or discretionary leave, and may also affect those seeking to extend leave as refugees under the new provisions for granting refugees only limited leave. For further details on this benefits issue, ▶see 1254–5 with reference to 1250.

Regulations are likely to be made stating the circumstances when notice of the immigration decision will be treated as having been received by the applicant (and therefore when, precisely, the leave comes to an end).

10) Legal aid

The provision for funding in section 103D of the 2002 Act will be amended so that representatives can be granted Community Legal Service (CLS) funding for work done in preparation for a reconsideration hearing, even if that hearing does not proceed because the Home Office concedes the appeal, the appeal has to be treated as abandoned, or the appellant withdraws the appeal. The existing wording of the legislation does not allow funding to be granted for such work which takes place after reconsideration has been ordered but before the hearing takes place.

Note

- The Bill also contains other small amendments that are necessary as consequences of the main changes outlined above. This is in order that the legislation does not refer to appeal rights that have been withdrawn, and that it accommodates the general systems of grounds of appeal, rights to appeal in-country, rights to apply for a review or reconsideration, and so on, for the amended rights of appeal.

- For further details of certain amendments concerning alleged terror suspects as the Bill entered Committee, ▶see 52–3.

APPEAL SYSTEM – AN OVERVIEW

The immigration appeals system allows decisions made by the Home Office, the immigration service and British posts abroad (ECOs) to be reviewed by an independent judicial body.

The table below gives a ten-point overview of the appeals system in force since 4 April 2005. Full details about challenges to the decisions of the AIT are given in Chapter 36.

From 4 April 2005, the Asylum and Immigration (Treatment of Claimants, etc.) Act 2004 introduced a new appeal structure. Most importantly, it abolished the 'two-tier' system of adjudicators and the Immigration Appeal Tribunal, and replaced them with the single Asylum and Immigration Tribunal (AIT). From this date, all asylum and immigration appeals are heard by the AIT. This is except for national security-related cases, which are heard by the Special Immigration Appeals Commission (▶see 1081–3). For the transitional arrangements for cases that were already in the appeal system on 4 April 2005, ▶see 1151–3.

The original draft of the 2004 Act very drastically reduced rights to appeal beyond the first-instance decision of the AIT, and this led to an outcry among both lawyers and judges. The government was forced to compromise. The outcome was a 'one-tier' system, but with a right to ask both the AIT and, if it refuses, the High Court for an order that the AIT reconsider its original decision. So, in effect there is still a 'two-stage' process in appeals before the statutory body but, in a clumsy way, it is now contained within one single tier. The High Court can still be involved at the stage of getting the AIT to reconsider its original decision, and there remains a route for appealing to the Court of Appeal.

THE APPEALS STRUCTURE FROM 4 APRIL 2005: A TEN-POINT OVERVIEW

The following points summarise the new appeals system as a whole. For full details of all the procedures referred to below concerning reviews, reconsiderations and appeals to the Court of Appeal, ▶see Chapter 36.

1) Notice of appealable decision given to potential appellant

After an immigration decision that can be appealed is made (▶table 1 below), proper notice of it must generally be given to the potential appellant (▶1061–2).

For an overview of the timetable for what happens as an appeal goes through its first-instance hearing, see the tables at ▶1088–9 (ordinary appeals) and 1130–2 (fast-track appeals).

2) First-instance decision of AIT

After notice of appeal is given, the AIT will hear the appeal and issue its decision allowing or dismissing the appeal.

3) Review of AIT first-instance decision by AIT

If the appeal in (2) is dismissed by a single immigration judge (or by two AIT members) it will be open to either party to apply to the AIT for a *review* of that decision. The AIT will decide that application on the papers only, and will *either*:

- make an 'order for reconsideration'; *or*
- issue a decision stating that it 'proposes' to make no such order.

4) Appeal to Court of Appeal from first-instance AIT decision

If the appeal in (2) is dismissed by a panel of three or more legally qualified members, it is possible to appeal directly (with permission) to the Court of Appeal. This will only be the correct means of challenge in a very small number of cases, where the AIT thought the case raised such important issues that it should sit as such a panel to hear an appeal at first instance. In most cases, the means of challenge to the AIT's decision is as in (3), and, if that fails, to apply to the High Court as in (5).

10

5) Review of first-instance AIT decision by High Court

If the decision in (3) is to 'propose' to make no order for reconsideration, the application for a review of the original decision of the AIT can be renewed to the 'appropriate' higher court (in England and Wales, this is the Administrative Court division of the High Court). The High Court will consider the application on the papers and make one of three decisions:

- order the AIT to 'reconsider' the decision on the original appeal;
- dismiss the application;
- refer the appeal to the Court of Appeal (this will be done in cases raising very important points of law, and so will only occur rarely).

6) Reconsiderations of decisions of the AIT by the AIT

If the decision in either (3) or (5) above is to order that the AIT reconsider its decision, then the AIT will hold a 'reconsideration' hearing. An order for reconsideration will have been made if the AIT or High Court decided that the original AIT 'may' have made an error of law. So, at the reconsideration hearing, the first job of the AIT will be to decide whether there was in fact a material error of law. If there was no such error, then the AIT will uphold the original decision. If there was such an error, the AIT will consider the merits of the appeal again.

The AIT will hold at least one hearing to decide an appeal on reconsideration. If, after deciding that there was a material error, further evidence is necessary, it is likely to 'transfer' the hearing to another AIT for a further hearing. This is very similar to the old 'remittals' from the IAT back to the adjudicator for rehearing. In all cases, a written decision will be issued by the AIT.

7) Appeal to the Court of Appeal following reconsideration by the AIT

Following a decision of the AIT on a reconsideration as in (6) above, either party can appeal (with permission) to the Court of Appeal.

8) Decisions of the Court of Appeal

If permission to appeal to the Court of Appeal is granted either by the AIT or by the Court of Appeal, as in either (4) or (7) above, or if the appeal is referred to the Court of Appeal by the High Court, as in (5) above, the Court of Appeal may make any of the following decisions:

- allow the appeal;
- dismiss the appeal;
- remit the appeal to the AIT;
- *if* the appeal was referred to the Court of Appeal by the High Court as in (5) above, as well as doing any of the above, it may send the matter back to the High Court for that court to consider.

9) Decision of AIT after remittal from the Court of Appeal

If a case that reached the Court of Appeal in any of the ways referred to in (8) above (i.e. on appeal after a panel of three or more of the AIT has heard the appeal, by referral from the High Court, or on appeal after a reconsideration hearing) is then remitted back to the AIT by the Court of Appeal as in (8) above, the AIT will reconsider the appeal at an oral hearing or hearings, and issue a decision. Either party may appeal (with permission) to the Court of Appeal against this further decision.

10) Appeal to the House of Lords

From the Court of Appeal, there is a right of appeal on a point of law of general public importance, with permission, to the House of Lords.

Notes

- Whenever the decision of the AIT is being challenged it is necessary to show one or more legal errors in the determination (otherwise known as 'errors of law'). The meaning of this is explained in the decision of the Court of Appeal in *R (Iran) & Others v SSHD*. For further details about what amounts to an error of law, and identifying grounds of challenge, ▶see 1155–8.

- In (8) above, the Court of Appeal also has the power to affirm, vary or give different directions to those given by the AIT when it decided the appeal (for details about directions, ▶see 1126–7).

The members of the AIT and their functions

The members of the AIT are divided into (paras 1–2, Sch 4 2002 Act):

- 'legally qualified' members (qualified lawyers of at least seven years' standing *or* with sufficient legal experience); and

- 'non-legally qualified' members (those with non-legal experience that makes them suitable for appointment).

The 'legally qualified' members are divided into (Asylum and Immigration Tribunal (Judicial Titles) Order 2005):

- immigration judges;

- designated immigration judges (each designated immigration judge has ten full-time immigration judges in their 'team' to whom they provide a supervisory/mentoring role); and

- senior immigration judges (they can be either a 'resident' senior immigration judge, in which case they are the face of the hearing centre – like the old Regional Adjudicators *or* they may be a 'legal' senior immigration judge in which case they are like the old 'Vice Presidents' of the IAT – they work out of Field House dealing with reconsideration hearings but will also go 'on circuit' and may hear complex cases at first instance).

At the top of the tree is the President of the AIT, who must be a serving or former High Court Judge. The existing President is Mr Justice Hodge.

10

There can also be Deputy Presidents. The President and the Deputy President are also senior immigration judges.

On 4 April 2005, those who were previously adjudicators or members of the Immigration Appeal Tribunal became 'members' of the new AIT. Those who were legally qualified members of the IAT became 'legally qualified' members of the AIT. Those who were previously adjudicators did not automatically become 'legally qualified' members of the AIT, but could be appointed as such (paras 26–27, Sch 2 2004 Act). Of course, further members of the AIT may be appointed by the Lord Chancellor.

Among the President's powers are the authority to:

- allocate cases to specific classes of AIT members;
- require or permit certain cases (or parts of the proceedings) to be transferred from one class of AIT members to another;
- issue practice directions (▶see 1087–8).

Although the AIT is formally a one-tier structure, the hierarchy of its membership and the above powers effectively allow a 'two-tier' functioning within the one tier. This is also supplemented by the Asylum and Immigration Tribunal (Procedure) Rules 2005 (referred to as 'the Procedure Rules') and the Asylum and Immigration Tribunal Practice Directions (referred to as the 'Practice Directions'; see details of who may do what in the Practice Directions at para. 2.2). So, for example:

- unless the case is particularly complex, first-instance hearings are to be heard by a 'legally qualified' member, who is likely, therefore, to be an ordinary 'immigration judge'. However, it is possible that the hearing will be before a panel of two with an immigration judge sitting with a designated immigration judge or senior immigration judge who will sit with them in order to give advice and support – this may occur even though the case is not complex;
- reconsideration hearings are heard by a 'legally qualified' member, or two or more members one of whom is legally qualified. If a material error of law is found, so that the case has to be heard from scratch, it is possible that it will be transferred to be heard by a less senior member of the AIT – i.e. an 'immigration judge' who is not a designated or senior immigration judge (similar to old-style remittals to the old Adjudicators);
- only legally qualified members ('immigration judges') who are *authorised by the President* may decide applications for a review of first instance decisions of the AIT (Procedure Rules, rule 26(1));
- applications for permission to appeal to the Court of Appeal can only be determined by a senior immigration judge (Procedure Rules, rule 36(1)).

Development of the appeals system and legislation

The appeals system was originally set up by the Immigration Appeals Act 1969, but it has undergone many changes since that time. In particular, how it works has become more complex. In what follows, we do not trace the development of appeals in third country cases. Third country decisions and challenges to them are covered in Chapter 24.

Appeals under the 1971 and 1993 Acts

Before October 2000, rights of appeal were contained in part 2 of the Immigration Act 1971 and section 8 of the Asylum and Immigration Appeals Act 1993. One of the major changes in the 1993 Act was to give rights of appeal before removal to all asylum-seekers.

Changes under the 1999 Act and the HRA 1998

The appeals system under the Immigration and Asylum Act 1999 came into force on 2 October 2000, the same day the Human Rights Act 1998 took effect. Rights of appeal and limitations on appeal rights were set out in part 4 of that Act. The 1999 Act introduced an in-country, free-standing right of appeal on human rights grounds. The 1999 Act also introduced a one-stop appeal to try and ensure that all relevant issues were dealt with in one appeal.

Appeals against 'immigration decisions': the 2002 Act

Part 5 of the Nationality, Immigration and Asylum Act 2002 tried to make appeal rights simpler by defining, in one section, the 'immigration decisions' against which an appeal could be brought (see s82 2002 Act – which is still in force; section 83 was introduced to deal with asylum 'status' appeals). In addition to making the system simpler, a main intention of this was to prevent people appealing on human rights grounds every time removal directions were set. An 'immigration decision' is the underlying decision of the immigration authorities as to the applicant's rights in the UK. Removal directions can be set and re-set based on that same immigration decision – they are simply the administrative mechanism for carrying through the main immigration decision.

The 2002 Act removed 'suspensive' (i.e. in-country) rights of appeal from anyone whose asylum or human rights claim was certified as 'clearly unfounded', and created a list of countries whose nationals were likely to have their cases declared as such. The consequence of certification is serious, because it means that a person can be returned to the country where they fear persecution before being able to appeal against the removal. The individual involved could appeal from abroad, but there are obvious difficulties with preparing and presenting such appeals. There is a further potential problem: What responsibility, if any, does the Home Office have for helping to return a successful appellant to the UK in such cases?

The 2002 Act also changed the powers of the IAT so that it could only allow appeals from decisions of Adjudicators on a point of law. Judicial Review was replaced by High Court 'statutory review' in cases where an

10

appellant wished to challenge a decision of the IAT refusing permission to appeal to the IAT.

The Asylum and Immigration Tribunal: 2004 Act

The 2004 Act establishes the AIT and the system for reviews, considerations and further appeals summarised in the table at ▶1047–9. Accompanying the introduction of the AIT, there have been new Procedure Rules for both ordinary and 'fast track' appeals, and also a new set of 'Practice Directions' issued by the President of the AIT (▶see 1086–8).

However, although the nature of the appeal body and the structure for challenging decisions has changed, the basic provisions about who has the right of appeal are still as originally set out in the 2002 Act. Certain changes to rights of appeal were made by the 2004 Act, and further changes are proposed by the 2005 Bill (▶see the table at 1042–6). We now look directly at who has the right of appeal.

WHEN CAN PEOPLE APPEAL?

When the immigration authorities make a decision about any person and, as a result, that person has a right of appeal, *generally* the notice of decision must inform them of that right (▶see 1061–2). In what follows, we deal with three questions: When is there a right of appeal? When are rights of appeal excluded? Is the appeal in-country or out-of-country? These questions are answered in three tables.

Where a relevant change is proposed by the 2005 Bill, this is mentioned in the tables. For more details of the changes to the rights of appeal proposed by the 2005 Bill, ▶see 1041–6 above.

Table 1 This sets out the decisions against which, *in general*, there is a right of appeal (▶1053–5).

Table 2 If it has been established from Table 1 that there is a right of appeal in principle, this table states the circumstances in which the right of appeal is *excluded* (▶1055–8). If the right of appeal is excluded in the individual case, then the only way to challenge the decision will be by judicial review .

Table 3 If there is a right of appeal (Table 1) and the right of appeal is not excluded for the particular appellant (Table 2), Table 3 states whether the appeal can be brought while the appellant is in the UK – i.e. whether it is an 'in-country' appeal (▶1059–61). For details about protection from removal while an appeal is outstanding, ▶see 1070–1 (and ▶see 1181–2). If there is a right of appeal (which is not excluded) but it cannot be brought in-country, it can still be brought out-of-country. In some cases, a decision is made while a person is in the UK against which they can only appeal after they have left the UK.

While this chapter looks at rights of appeal, it does not cover the powers of the AIT in deciding them. This is dealt with at ▶1118–1129. Neither does this chapter cover EEA appeals (for which ▶see 556–9, 562), nor appeals against and challenges to 'third country' decisions (▶see Chapter 24).

Objecting to destination

Under the 1999 Act and preceding legislation, there was a specific right of appeal against removal on the grounds that the applicant objected to the destination to which they were to be sent. That specific right of appeal no longer exists. *However*, in giving notice of decision in a removal case, the immigration authorities have to state the country of proposed removal. The countries to which an applicant can lawfully be removed under the different enforcement processes are set out at ▶1026–8. If the applicant has a case that they cannot, under those powers, lawfully be removed to the country stated by the immigration authorities, then they may be able to argue that the decision is 'not in accordance with the law', which is a general ground of appeal under sections 84(1)(e), 86(3)(a) 2002 Act (▶see 1124–6).

TABLE 1: DECISIONS AGAINST WHICH THERE IS A RIGHT OF APPEAL

This table sets out the decisions against which, in general, there is a right of appeal under sections 82–83 2002 Act and section 40A British Nationality Act 1981. However, even where there is a right of appeal in general set out in this table, there may still not be a right of appeal in a particular case. In some cases, the right of appeal is excluded, ▶see Table 2 below.

There is a right of appeal against:

1) 'immigration decisions';

2) certain refusals of asylum where leave is granted;

3) decisions to deprive a person of their citizenship.

For the right of appeal against 'EEA decisions', ▶see 556–9, 562.

1) 'Immigration decisions' (s82 2002 Act)

There is a right of appeal against the following, which are defined as 'immigration decisions':

- refusal of leave to enter the UK (as well as those who arrive without any leave who are then refused entry) this includes applicants who arrive in the UK with leave that was granted to them before they arrived, and whose leave is then 'cancelled'; this could include any of the following: people who return to the UK having left the UK with leave which did not lapse when they left; those given leave to enter while they were outside the UK before their arrival; those who arrive with an entry clearance. See para. 2A(8)(9), Sch 2, 1971 Act and ▶see 100–101;

- refusal of entry clearance;

10

- refusal of a certificate of entitlement to the right of abode under section 10 2002 Act (►see 1418–21 for further details of these certificates);

- refusal to vary a person's leave to enter or remain (i.e. refusal to extend leave) in the UK if the result of the refusal is that the person has no leave to enter or remain (the 2005 Bill proposes to remove this right of appeal except in certain cases, such as where the applicant was previously granted leave as a refugee – ►see 1042–3);

- variation of a person's leave to enter or remain in the UK if, when the variation takes effect, the person has no leave to enter or remain – i.e. 'curtailment' of leave (the 2005 Bill proposes to remove this right of appeal except in certain cases, such as where the applicant was previously granted leave as a refugee – ►see 1042–3);

- revocation of indefinite leave to enter or remain under section 76 2002 Act (for further details about these revocations, ►see 1008, 1025–6);

- a decision that a person is to be removed from UK as: an overstayer; someone who has breached a condition of leave to enter or remain; a person who has obtained (or tried to obtain) leave to enter or remain by deception; or as the family member of someone being removed on any of these grounds (the 2005 Bill will add to this decisions to remove a person whose indefinite leave was revoked because they ceased to be a refugee, ►see 1043);

- a decision that a person who is an illegal entrant will be removed from the UK;

- a decision that a person is to be removed from the UK as the family member of a person who is being removed having been either refused leave to enter or determined to be an illegal entrant;

- a decision to remove a crew member of a ship or aircraft who remains beyond their leave, or who is reasonably suspected of intending to do so (there are some exclusions from the right of appeal in such cases that we do not set out here – those seeking to appeal in such cases should obtain advice on this point);

- a decision to make a deportation order which may be: on the grounds that a person's presence in the UK is not conducive to the public good; following a recommendation made by a criminal court; in relation to the family member of a person who is being deported (for a note on 'recommendation cases', ►see 1017–8);

- refusal to revoke a deportation order.

  Only the above are 'immigration decisions' for appeal purposes. The following are examples of decisions that are not defined as immigration decisions, and thus do not give a right of appeal: variations of leave where a person still has leave; imposing additional conditions on leave; decisions to grant leave when the leave given is not for the purpose, length or on the terms applied for.

2) Refusals of asylum where leave is granted (s83 2002 Act)

In most asylum cases, a refusal of asylum will be accompanied by an 'immigration decision' within the meaning of section 82 (see above). In such cases, the applicant will then be able to appeal. However, if the asylum-seeker is granted leave (for example, humanitarian or discretionary leave), then there is no 'immigration decision' under section 82, and therefore no right of appeal.

However, in these circumstances, parliament has given a specific right of appeal on asylum grounds, under section 83 2002 Act (and see s84(3) 2002 Act). This right of appeal exists provided that the applicant has been granted leave to enter or remain in the UK for over 12 months. These appeals are sometimes called 'status' appeals. For further details about them, ►see below at 1079.

The 2005 Bill will create a new right of appeal where an applicant was previously granted leave as a refugee, who is no longer accepted to be a refugee but who is permitted to remain in a different capacity.

3) Appeals against deprivation of citizenship (ss40-40A BNA 1981)

Where the Home Office makes a decision to deprive a person of their citizenship (i.e. as a British citizen; a British overseas territories citizen; a British overseas citizen; a British national (overseas); a British protected person, or a British subject), the person has a right of appeal against that decision. The appeal is brought before the Home Office makes the actual order for deprivation of citizenship.

As with other appeals, the right of appeal is to the AIT, and the same system of onward reviews and appeals applies (see s40A BNA 1981 as amended by para. 4, Sch 2, 2004 Act).

Note

- For full details of the proposed changes under the 2005 Bill noted above, ►see 1042–6.

TABLE 2: EXCLUSIONS FROM RIGHTS OF APPEAL

In all of the circumstances listed below, applicants are excluded from the right of appeal *even though* a right of appeal in principle exists as set out in Table 1 above (see ss82(4), 88–99 2002 Act). Therefore, anyone falling into any of the following categories *cannot* appeal.

1) Appeals against certain refusals of entry clearance, refusals to grant leave to enter, refusals to extend leave and variations (i.e. curtailment) of leave (s88 2002 Act)

People refused entry clearance, leave to enter or an extension of leave, or whose leave is curtailed, cannot appeal if the decision of the immigration authorities was taken on any of the following grounds:

- they do not satisfy a requirement of the immigration rules as to age, nationality or citizenship (for example, only nationals of certain countries can come to the UK as *au pairs*, and 'retired persons of independent means' must be at least 60);

10

- they do not have an 'immigration document' of a particular kind. For these purposes, 'immigration documents' are: entry clearance, a passport (or similar document), a work permit or other immigration employment document (for details about immigration employment documents or 'IEDs', ▶see 418–20). Those who attempt to 'switch' in-country, where this is prohibited by Immigration Rules which state that the applicant must have entered with the required entry clearance, are excluded from the right to appeal by this provision;
- they ask for leave for longer than is permitted by the immigration rules (visitors, for example, can only be admitted for up to six months);
- they are seeking to enter or remain in the UK for a purpose other than one permitted by the immigration rules;
- they are the dependant of an applicant who has received a negative decision based on any of the above reasons;

However, a person excluded from appealing on any of the above grounds can still bring an appeal on asylum, race discrimination or human rights grounds.

The 2005 Bill proposes to remove rights of appeal in all non-family visit, non-dependant entry clearance cases, unless the appeal is on human rights or race discrimination grounds.

2) Refusal of entry clearance (s88A 2002 Act)

A person may not appeal against a refusal of entry clearance if the decision is taken on grounds that both:

- relate to the immigration rules; *and*
- are specified for that purpose by the Home Office in secondary legislation.

This exclusion was inserted by the 2004 Act from 1 October 2004. No secondary legislation has yet been made specifying the grounds of refusal that will lead to exclusion under this provision.

However, a person excluded from appealing under this provision can still bring an appeal on race discrimination or human rights grounds (they cannot appeal on asylum grounds – this is because the appeal is against an entry clearance decision).

3) Visitors and certain students who are refused leave to enter and who do not have entry clearance (s89 2002 Act)

Those who applied for leave to enter in any of the following categories cannot appeal against a refusal of leave to enter if, at the time they are refused, they do not have an entry clearance:

- visitor;
- short-course student (i.e. students accepted onto courses that will last six months or less);
- prospective student (i.e. those who wish to study but have not yet been accepted onto a course);
- the dependant of a person in any of the above three categories.

Of course, those who *need* entry clearance under the immigration rules (visa nationals and specified nationals) and who are refused because they don't have it are excluded from the right of appeal under (1) above. This exclusion from the right of appeal catches those who do not need entry clearance but are nevertheless refused entry on other grounds.

However, a person excluded from appealing on any of the above grounds can still bring an appeal on asylum, race discrimination or human rights grounds.

The 2005 Bill proposes to extend to all cases the need to have an entry clearance in order to appeal against a refusal of leave to enter. It also provides that there will be no right of appeal if the applicant is not in fact seeking entry for the same purpose as is stated in their entry clearance.

4) Non-family visitors refused entry clearance (s90 2002 Act)

Those refused entry clearance as a visitor may only appeal if they applied for entry clearance in order to visit a member of their 'family'. *However*, a person excluded from appealing under this provision can still bring an appeal on race discrimination or human rights grounds.

For further details about family visit appeals against entry clearance decisions, ▶see 225–7, 1072–3.

The 2005 Bill proposes to remove rights of appeal in all non-family visit, non-dependant entry clearance cases unless the appeal is on human rights or race discrimination grounds.

5) Certain students who are refused entry clearance (s91 2002 Act)

Those who are refused entry clearance to come to the UK having applied for it for any of the following reasons cannot appeal against the decision:

- short-course students (i.e. students accepted onto courses that will last six months or less);
- prospective student (i.e. those who wish to study but have not yet been accepted on to a course);
- the dependant of a person in either of the above two categories.

However, a person excluded from appealing under this provision can still bring an appeal on race discrimination or human rights grounds.

The 2005 Bill proposes to remove rights of appeal in all non-family visit, non-dependant entry clearance cases unless the appeal is on human rights or race discrimination grounds.

6) Certificate issued stating that the matter should have been raised earlier (s96 2002 Act)

There is no right of appeal if the Secretary of State certifies that the matters the applicant has raised, about which they now wish to appeal, should have been raised in an earlier appeal or in response to an earlier 'one-stop' notice. For further details about section 96 certificates, ▶see 1067–9. The right of appeal can be restored if the applicant successfully challenges the certificate by judicial review.

10

However, the Home Office cannot, by issuing a section 96 notice, stop an appeal in its tracks after notice of appeal has been given (see s96(7)).

7) National security cases (s97 2002 Act)

If the case involves national security issues and the Secretary of State issues a certificate under section 97 2002 Act, then the applicant will be not be able to appeal to the AIT either against an 'immigration decision' under section 82, or on a 'status' appeal under section 83. However, the applicant will instead have a right of appeal to the Special Immigration Appeals Commission (SIAC); (for details, ▶see 1081–3).

If a section 97 certificate is issued while an appeal is pending, the appeal lapses (s99 2002 Act; Procedure Rules, rule 16). Again, in this situation the applicant can appeal to SIAC instead.

Appeals against deprivation of citizenship involving national security matters may also be certified in this way, in which case there is also a right of appeal to SIAC (s40A(2) BNA 1981).

8) Public good grounds (s98 2002 Act)

If the Secretary of State was personally involved in a decision and the decision was taken wholly or partly on the grounds that that the exclusion or removal from the UK of a person is 'conducive to the public good', there is no right of appeal against *either*:

- a refusal of leave to enter; *or*
- a refusal of entry clearance.

However, a person excluded from appealing under this provision can still bring an appeal on race discrimination or human rights grounds (or, additionally, on asylum grounds if the decision was to refuse leave to enter).

If a section 98 certificate is issued while an appeal is pending, the appeal lapses (s99 2002 Act; Procedure rules, rule 16).

Notes

- For restrictions and exclusions of rights of appeal in third country cases, see Chapter 24 and, in particular, the table at ▶739–43.
- For more details of the proposed changes under the 2005 Bill that are noted above, ▶see 1042–6.

TABLE 3: IS THE APPEAL IN-COUNTRY?

This table states which appeals are 'in-country'. This means that the appeal can be brought while the applicant remains in the UK. For the provisions preventing people from being removed while an in-country appeal is pending, ▶see 1069–71.

All of the following appeals are in-country appeals. If the appeal is not listed in this table, then it can only be brought from outside the UK. In the case of out-of-country appeals, the applicant may already be outside the UK at the time of the decision, or they may be in the UK at the time of the decision and have to leave the UK in order to appeal.

1) Appeals against certain 'immigration decisions' (s92(2) 2002 Act)

Appeals against the following immigration decisions are in-country:

- refusal of a certificate of entitlement to the right of abode under section 10 2002 Act;
- refusal to vary a person's leave to enter or remain (i.e. refusals to extend leave);
- variation of a person's leave to enter or remain in the UK where, when the variation takes effect, the person has no leave to enter or remain (i.e. 'curtailment' decisions);
- revocation of indefinite leave to enter or remain under section 76 2002 Act;
- a decision to make a deportation order.

However, where the applicant has made an asylum or human rights claim, or both, *and* the Secretary of State certifies the claim(s) as 'clearly unfounded', the right of appeal against the first three of the above decisions is *not* in-country – i.e. an appeal against: refusal of certificate to the right of abode; refusal to vary leave; a curtailment decision (s94(1A) 2002 Act).

The right of appeal against the last two decisions above (a revocation of indefinite leave under section 76 2002 Act, or a decision to make a deportation order) remains an in-country right of appeal *even if* the appellant has made an asylum and/or human rights claim that has been certified as clearly unfounded.

2) Appeals against refusals of leave to enter where applicant has entry clearance (s92(3)-(3C) 2002 Act)

An appeal against a refusal of leave to enter to someone who has arrived in the UK is in-country if, on their arrival, the applicant has an entry clearance. Until 1 October 2004, possession of a work permit would also qualify a person to an in-country right of appeal, but, for most people, this protection has now been withdrawn (see further under (3) below).

Note that applicants who arrive in the UK with leave that was granted to them before they arrived, and whose leave is then 'cancelled', are treated as falling into this category of people who are refused leave to enter at a time they had entry clearance. This could include: those who return to the UK having left the UK with leave which did not lapse when they left; those given leave to enter

10

while they were outside the UK before their arrival; those who arrive with an entry clearance (see para. 2A(8)(9), Sch 2, 1971 Act and ▶see 100–102).

However, there will still *not* be an in-country right of appeal if the refusal of leave to enter (or the cancellation of leave under para. 2A(9), Sch 2, 1971 Act above) is on the grounds that the applicant has in fact come to the UK for reasons other than that for which they were granted entry clearance. Guidance has been issued to officers to enable them to distinguish between cases where the applicant seeks entry for different reasons to those stated on the entry clearance and cases where there is a change of circumstance (Immigration Service Interim Operational Instruction, No. 3/2005 ▶see further 102–103).

3) Appeals against refusals of leave to enter to British nationals with work permits (s92(3D) 2002 Act)

Anyone falling into one of the following categories who is refused leave to enter after they arrive in the UK, and who has a work permit, may appeal in-country against the refusal:

- British Overseas Territories citizen;
- British Overseas citizen;
- British National (Overseas);
- British Protected Person;
- British Subject.

4) Asylum-seekers and those who have made human rights claims (92(4)(a) 2002 Act)

Those who make asylum or human rights claims while in the UK have an in-country right of appeal against any 'immigration decision' made against them following refusal of their claim(s) (see Table 1 above for the definition of 'immigration decision' under s82 2002 Act).

However, an applicant will *not* have an in-country right of appeal against an immigration decision if the Secretary of State certifies the claim(s) as being 'clearly unfounded' (s94(2) 2002 Act). In such cases, appellants can only appeal from abroad. For further details about 'clearly unfounded' certificates, ▶see 1073–8. An in-country right of appeal can be restored if the applicant wins on a judicial review challenge to the certificate.

Those who are making 'status appeals' under section 83 will have been granted leave, and so their appeals are also in-country (▶see 1079 for further details about section 83 appeals).

5) EEA nationals/family members who make EU claims (s92(4)(b) 2002 Act)

If an 'immigration decision' (i.e. a decision listed at ▶1053–4) is made against an EEA national, or the family member of an EEA national, and that person claims that the decision breaches their rights under the Community Treaties either to entry to or residence in the UK, they may appeal in-country. However, in most EEA cases, the appeal will be against an 'EEA decision' (for which ▶see 556–9, 562).

Note

- For restrictions and exclusions of rights of appeal in third country cases, ▶see Chapter 24 and, in particular, the table at ▶739–43.

NOTICE OF DECISION

When the immigration authorities make a decision against which there is a right of appeal, there is an obligation on them to give a notice of the decision which:

- includes, or is accompanied by, a statement of the reasons for the decision;
- if the decision is a refusal of leave to enter, a decision to make a deportation order or a decision that a person is to be removed, states the country to which the person is to be removed;
- explains the right of appeal and the time-limit for appealing;
- states whether the appeal is an in-country one;
- explains the grounds on which such an appeal can be brought and any limitations to the right of appeal;
- explains the availability of advice and assistance in connection with the appeal;
- states where and how the appeal can be lodged (by post, hand or fax);
- includes a copy of the notice of appeal that may be used.

These requirements are set out in the Immigration (Notices) Regulations 2003 (the 'Notices Regulations').

10

Cases in which information about appeal rights is not required

However, in certain cases the Notices Regulations do *not* require that the notice of decision gives any information about appeal rights or encloses a notice of appeal (regs 5(5)–(8)). These are cases in which the applicant is generally excluded from the right of appeal *but*, as an exception to that exclusion, they are in fact allowed to appeal on asylum, human rights or discrimination grounds only. These cases are those listed at points (1), (3), (4), (5) and (8) of Table 2 above, at ▶1055–8.

However, as soon as the applicant in any of these cases, after receiving the decision, makes a claim that the decision is contrary to their human rights or their rights under the Refugee Convention, or is racially discriminatory, then the immigration authorities must re-serve the notice of decision, and the notice must this time comply with all the requirements above about information concerning appeals. A copy of a notice of appeal must also be sent to the applicant. In these cases, time for appealing runs from the re-service of the notice of appeal.

Invalid notices

Notices of decision that do not comply with the above requirements may be invalid, in which case time will not begin running. Whether the notice is invalid or not depends on how serious is the failure to comply with the requirements. For example, a notice that fails to notify a right of appeal when there is a right of appeal is likely to be invalid. In *R v IAT ex parte Jeyeanthan*, the Court of Appeal held that, in each case, in order to determine whether the notice is valid, it will be necessary to consider whether the rules have been 'substantially' complied with even if they have not been strictly complied with. It will also be necessary to consider whether the non-compliance should be waived.

Service of notice

Notices of decision can be delivered by hand, by fax or by post to the applicant or their representative. Where no address has been provided, there is no last-known address or business address, or the address is no longer in use and there is no representative acting, the notice of decision may be served 'on the file' at the Home Office. Notice will then be deemed to have been given. However, when the person comes to light, they are to be given the notice as soon as practicable (see reg. 7(1)–(3)). It does not appear that time for appealing starts running again in this situation. This is obviously of much concern, as it may lead to applicants losing their rights of appeal.

Unless it can be proved that they have not been received, or were received at a different time, notices sent by post are deemed to have been served on the second working day after posting, or 28 calendar days after posting if sent to an address outside the UK. In both cases, the day on which the notice is posted is not counted (see reg. 7(4)-(5)).

In cases in which it cannot be argued that the original notice of decision was not in fact received at the time it should have been and that the appeal is in time on the basis of when it was in fact received (and it cannot be argued that the notice was not a valid one and needs to be served again), appellants can alternatively ask for time to be extended. In all cases in which there is uncertainty about whether the appeal is in time or not, or where it may be ruled out of time, a request for an extension should be made at least in the alternative (▶see below).

GIVING NOTICE OF APPEAL

Following the introduction of the AIT on 4 April 2005, there have been certain changes in the rules about giving notice of appeal.

Appealing in time

Applicants must first, of course, ensure that they get their notice of appeal in within time. Details about when the notice of decision is treated as having been served are given above. The time-limits for appealing and details about calculating time are given in the table at ▶1162–7. For details about extending time when the original notice of appeal is out of time, ▶see 1092–4.

The appeal forms

There are now a number of different first-instance appeal forms, and their format has changed from 4 April 2005. The forms are attached in a schedule to the Procedure Rules, and are also available on the AIT website. They are accompanied by guidance notes. The different forms are:

- AIT-1, for in-country appeals;
- AIT-1-FT, for fast track appeals;
- AIT-2, for out-of-country appeals against refusal of entry clearance;
- AIT-3, for appeals where the applicant must leave the UK in order exercise their right of appeal and certain other cases – it is not to be used for entry clearance appeals.

The AIT-3 will be completed, for example, by an applicant who has made an asylum or human rights claim in the UK that was certified as 'clearly unfounded', and where the certificate has not been quashed on judicial review (▶see 1073–8). Other examples of those who have out-of-country appeals against decisions made in the UK and must leave before they can appeal are those removed as illegal entrants or as 'administrative removal' cases where no asylum or human rights claim was made while they were in the UK.

Completing the appeal form

The relevant prescribed form should be fully completed. In particular, it should include the name and address of the appellant, state whether they have an authorised representative to act for them in the appeal (if so, give the representative's name and address), set out the grounds for the appeal, give reasons for the grounds of appeal, and 'so far as reasonably practicable' list any documents which the appellant intends to rely on as evidence at the appeal. The notice of decision appealed against should also be sent back with the notice of appeal, and the notice should be signed and dated by the appellant or their representative (if signed by the representative, they are required to certify that they have completed it in accordance with instructions from the appellant – Procedure Rules, rule 8).

The appeal forms also asks if people want an oral hearing and an interpreter at the appeal. If the appellant has any concerns about understanding or speaking English, an interpreter should be requested. An interpreter may also be needed for witnesses. If special dialects are required, then these should be asked for. It is the responsibility of the AIT to book an independent interpreter in the correct language, and only their approved interpreters will be used at the hearing.

Applicants have to be careful to ensure that the procedural requirements concerning notices of appeal are complied with – otherwise there is a risk that the application will be treated as invalid, which will prevent an appeal being made. In particular, the definition of 'appellant' in the 2005 Procedure Rules (rule 2) is someone who has given 'notice of appeal to Tribunal against a relevant decision in accordance with these Rules'. This is new since the last Rules, and in theory it might give the AIT power to rule that someone is not an 'appellant', and therefore has no appeal, if the notice is not filled out correctly. Although this is not expressly provided for in the Procedure Rules (as compared, for example, with the ability to reject a notice of appeal as 'invalid' if there is no appealable decision – see rule 9), the possibility can't be completely excluded. In addition, the Practice Directions state that appeal notices will be 'scrutinised' by the AIT soon after receipt.

'Grounds' and 'reasons' for appeal

Each form is particularly detailed in the questions it asks about the grounds and reasons for the appeal. For example, if it is an asylum or human rights case, AIT-1 and AIT-3 ask for details about grounds of appeal in relation to: the situation in the country of origin; internal flight; credibility; Convention reasons; the application of articles of the ECHR to the case, and so on. Form AIT-1 also asks for details any 'statement of additional grounds' made in response to a one-stop notice (for the 'one-stop' procedure, ▶see below).

In addition to the forms themselves, the Department of Constitutional Affairs' 'Guides' to completing the forms tell appellants that they must state all their grounds, otherwise they may not be able to mention them later. The only apparent backing in the Procedure Rules for this is the power to give directions in rule 45. Directions can be given to limit the issues that are to be addressed at the hearing (rule 45(4)(f)(iv)). It is unlikely that the AIT would prevent people from raising legitimate grounds at a hearing because they had not been mentioned in the notice of appeal, but caution should be exercised. If an important 'ground' is not raised in the notice of appeal, it should at least be brought to attention at the CMR hearing, where there is an opportunity to amend grounds, or at least before the hearing of the appeal itself. Failure to raise an available ground of appeal before the AIT can result in a *later* right of appeal being denied if the Home Office issues a certificate under section 96 2002 Act (▶see below at 1067–9).

Applicants and advisers must comply with the requirements of the appeal form, but, at the same time, not give grounds and reasons upon which they have not taken full instructions, and which may conflict with what they will finally wish to say at the hearing. Remember, the appeal concerns all of the facts of the case – not just law – and it is always difficult to give details about facts at short notice and under pressure of time.

'Grounds' of appeal for the purpose of the notice of appeal is probably a reference to the statutory definition of grounds of appeal in section 84 2002 Act – namely, where:

- the decision was not in accordance with the immigration rules;
- the decision was unlawful as in breach of section 19B of the Race Relations Act 1976 (race discrimination);
- the decision was unlawful under section 6 HRA (decision contrary to appellant's ECHR rights);
- the appellant is an EEA national (or the family member of an EEA national) and the decision is in breach of the appellant's rights under the Community Treaties;
- the decision was not in accordance with the law;
- a discretion under the immigration rules should have been exercised differently;
- removal of the appellant would be in breach of the UK's obligations under the Refugee Convention;
- removal of the appellant would be in breach of the HRA as in breach of their ECHR rights.

Note that in the course of the consultation about the new appeal forms it was stated that appellants will not be penalised for filling in the form incorrectly, and that filling in a section incorrectly would not mean that a notice of appeal would be treated as invalid. It was stated that the form is intended to encourage appellants to express in more detail why they disagree with the Home Office decision, not to punish them for failing to do so.

Serving notice of appeal

Notice of appeal has to be returned in accordance with the details stated on the notice of the decision, which should give an address to which the notice of appeal can be sent or taken by hand. The notice of decision should also give a fax number for service by fax. In a change from the previous Procedure Rules, under which notice of appeal was given to the immigration authorities, notice of appeal is now generally given to the AIT directly (see Procedure Rules, rule 6). This change is probably the result of the lengthy delays that had built up at the Home Office in forwarding notices of appeal and documents so that appeals could proceed.

However, in the following cases there is a choice as to where to file the notice of appeal:

10

- a person who is detained under immigration powers may either give notice of appeal to the AIT, or to the person who 'has custody of him';
- a person who is outside the UK and who wishes to appeal against a decision of an ECO may give notice of appeal either to the AIT or to the ECO.

For what happens after the notice of appeal is received, filing late notice of appeal and the rest of the first-instance appeals process, see Chapter 35, beginning at page 1081.

THE 'ONE-STOP' SYSTEM

Under section 120 2002 Act, the immigration authorities can, at any time, issue a notice in writing to anyone who:

- has made an application to enter or remain in the UK; or
- in respect of whom the immigration authorities have made an 'immigration decision' (▶see 1053–4 for the definition of 'immigration decision').

This has simplified the previously complex provisions dealing with one-stop notices that existed under the 1999 Act (see pp. 187–9, 606–11 of the 2002 edition of the *Handbook*). The notice requires the person to state additional grounds and reasons they have for wishing to enter or remain in the UK, or for why they should not be required to leave the UK. The power to issue such notices is very wide, and notices can be issued in asylum, human rights and ordinary immigration cases. Home Office policy about when a notice will be issued is set out in the API under 'Appeals – One Stop Procedures, Warnings and Certificates'. The cases in which they are normally issued include: all asylum and human rights cases; cases in which the Home Office thinks the application may not succeed; and cases in which a negative immigration decision is to be issued. For further details of this policy, one-stop notices generally and completing the 'statement of additional grounds', ▶see 662–4.

Certain of the prescribed appeal forms used for some notices of appeal to the AIT have a special box for applicants to fill in their statement of additional grounds, in cases where the notice of decision included a one-stop notice (section 5 of the in-country appeal form AIT-1, and section 4 of the fast track appeal form, AIT-1-FT). The API indicate that if additional grounds are put forward while an appeal against the initial decision is pending (presumably including where additional grounds are given in the appeal form), they will be considered and, if the decision is maintained, addressed in a letter supplementing the notice of decision. This supplementary statement of reasons should also be before the AIT when it comes to consider the appeal.

Unfortunately, when additional grounds are put forward they are not always considered and responded to before the appeal. It may be thought that where the Home Office does not, for example, consider additional grounds raising Article 8 ECHR because the appellant has married, it would be very difficult for the Home Office to justify a decision to remove the person from the UK as 'proportionate' under Article 8(2). The Home Office, of course, has the burden of demonstrating that a decision is proportionate. If no decision has in fact been taken, how can the decision be shown to have been taken as 'necessary' in the interests of one of the reasons set out in Article 8(2)? Unfortunately, immigration judges, led by decisions of the IAT and higher courts, have been willing to take notice of the public interest in maintaining immigration control in any case even where no apparent consideration has been given to the question by the Home Office.

The AIT has the power to consider any additional grounds raised in response to a one-stop notice, whether they are put forward before or after notice of appeal is given (s85(2)(3) 2002 Act). Unless there is a good explanation, if grounds which arise at the time are not put forward in the appeal in response to the one-stop notice, then the Home Office can prevent a later appeal based on those grounds (▶see s96 2002 Act below).

Completing the statement of additional grounds

It is very important that applicants obtain advice before completing one-stop notices so that they do not miss out on the opportunity to have important matters considered by the immigration authorities and/or the AIT. Often there are immigration policies operated outside the rules which the appellant is not aware of. The Home Office and an immigration judge will not necessarily consider everything that may benefit the appellant or their dependants if it is not pointed out. Indeed, it may be that the immigration authorities are unaware of certain facts that could benefit the appellant, but have not been put forward because the appellant did not realise that they were important.

Continuing duty to state additional grounds

The API make it clear that the Home Office sees the requirement given in the one-stop notice as an ongoing one. This means that, as and when additional grounds come to light, representations should be made to the Home Office.

CERTIFICATES UNDER SECTION 96 2002 ACT

The purpose of certificates issued under section 96 2002 Act is to prevent people from appealing when they could have raised the same matter they want to appeal about either in an earlier right of appeal or in response to an earlier 'one-stop' notice. From 1 October 2004, section 30 2004 Act has substituted a new, simplified section 96 in place of the old one.

10

When can section 96 certificates be issued?

Since 1 October 2004, section 96 certificates can be issued in either of the two following situations.

1) Where the applicant had a right of appeal under section 82 against a previous immigration decision (whether they used that right of appeal or not) and the matter raised in the present claim or application about which a decision has been made should have been raised in an appeal against the previous decision.

2) Where the applicant received a 'one-stop' notice in relation to a previous application or decision and the matter raised in the present application or claim about which a decision has been made should have been raised in the earlier one-stop notice (for details of the 'one-stop' procedure ▶see above at 1066–7).

There will be no right of appeal if the immigration authorities certify that facts set out in either (1) or (2) above exist *and* certify that, in their opinion, there is 'no satisfactory reason' for that matter not having been raised previously. So, for example, an asylum-seeker who previously appealed against an immigration decision on asylum grounds but failed to raise any relevant human rights grounds may be prevented from later raising human rights grounds in order to bring a further appeal.

In order to obtain the right of appeal, section 96 certificates can be challenged by judicial review. Section 96 certificates issued after notice of appeal has been given cannot prevent the appeal from continuing (s96(7)).

Home Office policy on issuing section 96 certificates

The API (Appeals – One Stop Procedures, Warnings and Certificates) indicate that the following circumstances might provide satisfactory reasons for failing to raise a matter earlier:

- where there has been a significant change of circumstances in the country of origin;
- where, since the previous appeal or one-stop notice, the applicant has begun a relationship which falls within the protection of Article 8 ECHR;
- where there has been a serious failure by a representative to put forward a very important issue.

When will the Home Office actually need to use section 96?

Of course, the immigration authorities will only need to issue section 96 certificates if there would otherwise be an appeal. If there has already been a previous 'immigration decision' (and a right of appeal against it), the Home Office may be able simply to remove the applicant on the basis of the existing 'immigration decision'. There is no right of appeal simply against removal directions, because they are not an 'immigration decision'. Take, for example, the situation where the applicant applied for leave to enter on asylum grounds and was refused, and an appeal against refusal of leave to enter was dismissed. When further representations are refused, the immigration authorities may simply set directions for removal on the basis of the power to remove that exists as the result of the earlier refusal of leave to enter that has been upheld. However, in the same example, if the applicant has made what amounts to a 'fresh claim' for asylum, the Home Office will be required to make a new 'immigration decision' on it. That new refusal of leave to enter gives a new right of appeal. In order to prevent that right of appeal from arising, the immigration authorities would have to issue a section 96 certificate. For more on 'fresh claims', see below.

In the following example, however, the immigration authorities *will* need to issue a certificate to prevent an appeal. If the applicant previously appealed against a curtailment of their leave, having entered as a student, and then claimed asylum, and that appeal was dismissed, a further 'immigration decision' will have to be made before they can be removed. That will normally be a decision to remove them as an overstayer. Unless it is certified as clearly unfounded, there will then be an in-country asylum or human rights appeal against that decision. If the appellant tries to raise matters that they could have raised in the earlier appeal (and the conditions set out below are satisfied), then the immigration authorities can prevent that right of appeal by issuing a section 96 certificate. Note that the 2005 Bill proposes to prevent most curtailment decisions from being immigration decisions carrying the right of appeal (▶1042).

Of course, if the appeal goes ahead and the appellant relies on the same matters as were raised (or should have been raised) in the earlier appeal, the AIT may simply decide it in line with the earlier appeal decision (see the decision of the IAT in *Devaseelan*, covered at ▶1123–4).

'Fresh claims'

If the applicant has tried to generate a further right of appeal by a 'fresh claim' to asylum, the Home Office will first consider whether their representations amount to a fresh claim in response to which a new 'immigration decision' is required. If there is no fresh claim, then in most cases there will be no need to make a further immigration decision. In such cases, there will be no need to issue a certificate. However, if there is a fresh claim, then the immigration authorities may still decide to certify it under section 96. For further details about fresh claims, and also the relationship between fresh claim decisions and decisions under section 96, ▶730–5.

APPEAL PENDING: PROTECTION FROM REMOVAL AND IMMIGRATION STATUS

Those with an in-country right of appeal against an immigration decision cannot be removed or required to leave the UK while the appeal is 'pending' (s78 2002 Act). However, this does not prevent the setting of removal directions or other action that prepares for removal, provided removal does not actually take place. In addition, no deportation order can be made against a person while an appeal against a decision to make it is pending (s79 2002 Act).

The period during which an appeal is 'pending' is defined in section 104 2002 Act. It begins when it is 'instituted' – i.e. when notice of appeal is given (see above). The appeal then remains 'pending' while it is waiting to be heard by the AIT *and* while any of the following are outstanding:

- an application for a review of the decision of the AIT;
- a reconsideration of the appeal by the AIT;
- a further decision on the appeal after it has been remitted to the AIT by the Court of Appeal;
- an application for permission to appeal to the Court of Appeal;
- an appeal to the Court of Appeal;
- a reference to the Court of Appeal by the High Court.

An appeal will also still be 'pending' if the applicant is still within time to apply for a review of the decision of the AIT, or for permission to appeal to the Court of Appeal. 'Court of Appeal' for all these purposes also means the Court of Session in Scotland. So the immigration authorities cannot remove someone who is still within time to ask for a review or permission to appeal. However, applicants have no protection from removal if, after that time runs out, they have not submitted their application. If they submit the application late together with an application to extend time, they will have no protection unless and until the application for a review or permission is decided in their favour – once such a decision is made, the appeal will remain outstanding before the AIT for reconsideration, or it will be outstanding before the Court of Appeal.

An appeal will also no longer be 'pending' if it is withdrawn, abandoned by the applicant leaving the UK, or if it lapses because the Home Office issues a 'national security' or a 'conducive to the public good' certificate under sections 97–98 2002 Act (▶see Table 2). However, even where these certificates are issued, in national security cases the right of appeal transfers to SIAC, and people cannot be removed while an appeal to SIAC is outstanding (s2(2)(b)(c)(j) Special Immigration Appeals Commission Act 1997). In some situations where a 'public good' certificate is issued, an applicant can still appeal (see Table 2).

It is unlawful for an applicant to be removed while they have an in-country appeal pending, and if such an applicant is removed, they may bring a claim for damages (▶see 1181–2, 1205–10).

Continued status while appeal 'pending'

As is well known, if a person applies to extend their leave to remain 'in time' – i.e. while they have existing leave – their leave is automatically extended if the application is not decided before the existing leave runs out (s3C 1971 Act) (▶see further 143–6). If this is the case, the leave *also* continues during the following periods:

- after a negative immigration decision is made on the application but the applicant is still in time to appeal to the AIT;
- when an appeal against the decision is 'pending' ('pending' here has the same meaning as above in relation to protection from removal).

However, the Immigration, Asylum and Nationality Bill 2005 proposes to change this so that the automatic extension of leave ends when the immigration decision is made, so that there is no leave during the time when the appeal is pending (▶see 1045–6).

If the 'immigration decision' taken is either:

- a curtailment of the applicant's leave (i.e. cutting the leave short so that the applicant no longer has leave); or
- a revocation of indefinite leave under section 76 2002 Act,

then the curtailment or revocation does not actually take effect while the applicant is still in time to appeal to the AIT, nor while the applicant is appealing against that decision and the appeal is 'pending' (s82(3) 2002 Act). Again, 'pending' has the same meaning as above.

Appeals which end without being determined

An appeal against an immigration decision is treated as abandoned if the appellant (s104(4) 2002 Act) is either:

- granted leave to enter or remain in the UK; or
- leaves the UK.

Appeals are also treated as finally determined if they are withdrawn. As stated above, appeals can also be brought to an end if the Secretary of State issues a 'national security' or a 'public good' certificate but, in such cases there may still be an appeal to SIAC or to the AIT on human rights, discrimination or asylum grounds (see Table 2). Once notice of appeal has been filed, an appeal can no longer be brought to an end by the Home Office issuing a certificate under section 96 2002 Act (i.e. stating that the matter relied on should have been raised earlier – see s96(7) 2002 Act).

The 2005 Bill will make certain changes to when an appeal is treated as abandoned (▶see 1045).

FAMILY VISITOR ENTRY CLEARANCE APPEALS

The only people entitled to appeal against refusal of entry clearance as visitors are those who wish to visit a 'family member' (see s90 2002 Act). The entry clearance application form asks a person to state whether they are applying for a family visit or not by ticking one of two boxes.

10

For these purposes, the Immigration Appeals (Family Visitor) Regulations 2003 define 'family member' as the applicant's:

- spouse;
- parent;
- son;
- daughter;
- sibling;
- grandparent;
- grandchild;

- uncle;
- aunt;
- nephew;
- niece;
- first cousin;
- stepfather;
- stepmother;

- stepson;
- stepdaughter;
- stepbrother;
- stepsister;
- spouse's parent;
- spouse's sibling
- spouse's son or daughter.

'Family member' also includes a person who the applicant has lived with as a member of an unmarried couple (heterosexual or same-sex) for a least two of the three years before the date of the application.

In the 2005 Bill, the government proposes to change the law about the ability to bring entry clearance appeals generally, and this includes certain proposals about visit entry clearance appeals. These proposals are set out at ►1043–4.

A further proposal relevant to these appeals, which is mentioned in the government's five-year strategy (February 2005), is to 'remove the possibility of an oral hearing and deal with all appeals on paper only'. Part of the intention is to 'discourage speculative appeals'. The five-year strategy also proposes to review whether to charge again for family visit appeals. It is not clear whether these proposals will be implemented. The research referred to below finds that this change would be an incredibly unfair one, and it would be viewed as an attempt to prevent such appeals both from being pursued and from succeeding.

Charging and oral appeals: some context

Family visit appeals against entry clearance refusals were reintroduced in October 2000. Appellants initially had to pay £500 for an oral appeal and £150 for a paper appeal. In January 2001, these fees were reduced to £125 (oral) and £50 (paper). The fees were abolished in May 2002.

The proposal to limit such appeals to paper-only hearings is particularly unfair. Research has shown that appellants stand a far greater chance of success in oral appeals than in paper ones. In 2001, a research study was undertaken by the Immigration Research and Statistics Service of the Home Office to assess the reasons why rejected visa applicants decided whether or not to appeal, and to identify the reasons why there was such a disparity in outcomes between oral and paper appeals (see Gelsthorpe, Thomas and Crawley, *Family Visitor Appeals: An Evaluation of the Decision to Appeal and Disparities in Success Rates by Appeal Type*, Home Office Online Report, 26/03). The results of the research can also be found in *Family visitor appeals* (Tolley's *IANL*, Vol 18, No 3, 2004 pp. 167–85).

There was an overall difference of 35 per cent in the success rates between oral and paper appeals (and 21 per cent in the sample case-files examined to assess the reasons for the disparity). In summary, the reasons found for the differences in success rates were:

- evidence given by the sponsor at the oral hearing;
- the role of legal advice and representation;
- the attendance of a Home Office Presenting Officer (HOPO) (strangely, a higher number of appeals were *allowed* when a HOPO attended);
- the provision of additional documentary evidence;
- concerns expressed by the IAT that adjudicators did not provide adequate scrutiny of paper appeals.

The imposition of further restrictions on rights of appeal in visitor entry clearance cases is even more worrying given recent indications of the upward rate of refusals in family visitor cases. In his article *Family visitor visas: ECO decision-making 2000–2003* (Tolley's *IANL*, Vol 18, No 2, 2004 pp. 100–5), Richard Dunstan, Immigration Policy Officer for Citizens Advice, found that the global rate of refusal of family visit applications had risen steadily since 2000. He also found that there had been substantial increases in the rate of refusals at some of the largest entry clearance posts. He found that the family visitor rates of refusal were considerably higher than the rate for non-settlement visas generally.

CASES CERTIFIED AS 'CLEARLY UNFOUNDED'

The 2002 Act allows the Home Office to exclude in-country appeal rights for those who have claimed asylum or made a human rights claim if it thinks that the claim is 'clearly unfounded'. These appeals are also known as 'non-suspensive appeals' (NSA) because they are appeals which do not 'suspend' removal, as other asylum and human rights appeals do (see above).

In order to make the appeal a 'non-suspensive' one, the Secretary of State issues a certificate under section 94 2002 Act to the effect that the asylum claim or human rights claim (or both) is 'clearly unfounded'. The only way to challenge the certificate is by judicial review. Normally, the applicant will be able to remain in the UK while the judicial review claim takes place. If the judicial review challenge is successful then, in most cases, the Home Office will withdraw the certificate, and there is an in-country appeal against the original decision. If the judicial review claim fails, the certificate stands and the applicant has to leave the UK in order to appeal. The applicant is not permitted to bring their appeal while in the UK, and the time-limit for appealing is 28 days from when the applicant leaves the UK (▶see 1162–3 and ▶see 1063).

10

If a person has to appeal from abroad, then the appeal is considered as though that person had not been removed from the UK (s94(9) 2002 Act). So the applicant can still complain that their removal is in breach of the Refugee Convention, or in breach of their human rights. The main problem with this, of course, is that people may be subjected to the serious harm they fear before they can actually bring and succeed in their appeals. Conducting appeals from abroad is very difficult. Appellants may find it hard to keep in touch with their representatives, and will not usually be able to attend to give live evidence. However, in the third country case of *R (Ahmadi) v SSHD*, evidence was given by video-link.

Many of those who are likely to have their claims certified as clearly unfounded are put through the asylum fast track detained processes (►see 673–81).

Will a 'clearly unfounded' certificate exclude all in-country appeal rights?

If the applicant would otherwise have an in-country appeal only because they have an asylum or human rights claim, then the certificate will remove that in-country right of appeal (s94(2)). However, as set out in Table 3 above, if the applicant has an in-country right of appeal against revocation of indefinite leave or against a decision to make a deportation order, those in-country rights of appeal will not be removed if an asylum or human rights claim is made that is then certified. However, in-country appeals against refusals of certificates of entitlement to the right of abode, refusals to extend leave, and curtailment of leave so that the applicant no longer has any leave, will be excluded by a 'clearly unfounded' certificate (s92(2), 94(1A) 2002 Act).

It is also likely that, where an applicant would have had a right of appeal against refusal of leave to enter because they have an entry clearance (or arrived in the UK with leave), a certificate will also remove their in-country rights of appeal. This is because, if such applicants make an asylum or human rights claim, the Home Office will probably be able to say that they are seeking entry for a purpose other than that stated in their entry clearance. In this case, they do not have an in-country right of appeal based on their entry clearance (see Table 3 above).

'Clearly unfounded' certificates do not affect in-country 'status' appeals under section 83 of the Act (see s94(1)).

Which nationals are likely to receive 'clearly unfounded' certificates?

Nationals of any country can receive a 'clearly unfounded' certificate. However, if the applicant is 'entitled to reside' in one of the countries listed in section 94(4) 2002 Act, the Secretary of State 'shall' certify the claim as 'clearly unfounded' unless 'satisfied that it is not clearly unfounded'. Although the Home Office in issuing (and the High Court in reviewing) a certificate should go through much the same mental process whether the applicant is from a country that is listed or not, in practice a person from one of the listed countries is more likely to have their claim certified (see *ZL v VL*, CA, paras 56–8).

Before 1 May 2004, the list of countries included all the EU accession countries, but they have now been removed from the list. The present list of countries is:

Albania	India	Serbia and Montenegro
Bolivia	Jamaica	South Africa
Bulgaria	Macedonia	Sri Lanka
Brazil	Moldova	Ukraine
Ecuador	Romania	

India was added to the list from 15 February 2005. Bangladesh was on the list, but this was successfully challenged in *R (Husan) v SSHD*, and Bangladesh was removed on 22 April 2005.

The Secretary of State can, by order, add or remove a country (or part of a country) from the list. In order to add a country, the Secretary if State has to be satisfied that in that country (or part of the country) there is, in general, no serious risk of persecution, and that removal there will not, in general, breach the UK's obligations under the ECHR. In addition, the Secretary of State has the power to add to the list, countries that are safe in respect of particular categories of person defined by gender, language, race, religion, nationality, membership of particular social group, political opinion or other personal characteristics.

Home Office policy on when to certify a case

The guidance given to caseworkers is set out in detail in the API, available on the Home Office website under 'Certification'. Important points from the guidance include the following.

- Each case, even if the applicant comes from one of the countries listed above, should be considered on its individual merits, and only if the application is to be refused does the question of certification arise.
- It is crucial that Home Office caseworkers consider objective country information when considering whether a claim is clearly unfounded.
- Asylum and human rights claims should be considered for certification separately.
- Decisions to certify will pass before more than one pair of eyes.
- It will be rare for a case to be certified on the basis of credibility alone – in the majority of cases, caseworkers will need to be able to certify on the basis that, even accepting a person's account as credible and taking that account 'at its highest', the claim is bound to fail.

10

In addition the Home Office sets out the following categories of potentially 'clearly unfounded' claims.

1) Where there is no fear of mistreatment expressed – for example, where an applicant is fleeing poverty or unemployment.

2) Where an applicant does express a fear of mistreatment, but it is not objectively based.

3) Where evidence of the feared mistreatment, for example discrimination, is accepted, but it does not amount to persecution. Past persecution does not prevent certification if the future ill-treatment feared does not meet the threshold for protection under the Refugee Convention or the ECHR.

4) Where there is a 'sufficiency of protection' available – for example, where there is clear evidence that the state is able and willing to provide the necessary protection.

5) Where a person's claim is not clearly unfounded when assessed in relation to their home area, but where internal relocation is obviously available and it would not be unduly harsh to require the person to relocate.

6) In an asylum claim where the fear expressed is unconnected to a Refugee Convention reason – for example, where someone has fears from a neighbour dispute. This reasoning could not apply to a human rights claim, because human rights protection does not require that there is a Refugee Convention reason.

7) Normally, Article 8 ECHR claims where:

- the applicant claims close family ties in the UK but those ties clearly do not exist (for example, there is no evidence of the existence of the claimed family members, or no evidence that there is a long-standing bond between them and the claimant);

- there are no strong reasons why the applicant could not return to their country of origin and seek entry clearance under the Immigration Rules to return to the UK; or

- there are no insurmountable obstacles to the family member(s) in question living with the applicant outside the UK.

The above represents Home Office policy. The criteria set out may, in many cases, lead to claims being certified where it is obvious that there is room for more than one view. If this is the case, then the claim should not be certified – the test for 'clearly unfounded' is a very stringent one, as is explained immediately below.

Full details about asylum and human rights claims are given in Sections 7 and 8. Article 8 'connections' claims are discussed in detail at ▶820–50.

Legal test for deciding whether a claim is 'clearly unfounded'

If a 'clearly unfounded' certificate is issued, the applicant will need to consider whether to challenge it by judicial review. Because certification on these grounds is such an important decision, the court will look very carefully and closely at cases which come before it. The approach the court will take is as follows. For judicial review procedures generally, ▶see 1213–22.

The test for certifying an asylum and human rights claim as 'clearly unfounded' under the 2002 Act is the same as the test for certifying claims as 'manifestly unfounded' under the old section 72(2)(a) 1999 Act. In **Yogathas and Thangarasa**, a case under the old legislation, the judgements of the different Lords contain the following comments about when the Home Office will able to certify a case (see also **Razgar**, HL, at para. 16):

- the Secretary of State must be 'reasonably and conscientiously satisfied that the allegation must clearly fail' (para. 14);
- the Secretary of State must determine whether the 'allegation is so clearly without substance that the appeal must be bound to fail' (para. 34);
- it must be 'plain that there is nothing of substance in the allegation' (para. 72).

Also in relation to the 'clearly unfounded' test, in **ZL & VL**, the Court of Appeal held that:

'If on at least one legitimate view of the facts or the law the claim may succeed, the claim will clearly not be unfounded.'

As to credibility, the Court in **ZL & VL** said:

'When an applicant's case does turn on an issue of credibility, the fact that the interviewer does not believe the applicant will not, of itself, justify a finding that the claim is clearly unfounded. In many immigration cases findings of credibility have been reversed on appeal. Only where the interviewing officer is satisfied that nobody could believe the applicant's story will it be appropriate to certify the claim as clearly unfounded on the ground of credibility alone...'

Normally, in judicial review, the court will not get involved in considering the facts and evidence of a case. However, in considering 'clearly unfounded' certificates, the Court has made it clear that it will itself look at the evidence and decide for itself whether the case is 'clearly unfounded' or not, and that it is in as good a position as the Home Office to do this (see **ZL & VL**; **Razgar** both in the CA and HL). If a person produces medical evidence, then the question of whether the claim is clearly unfounded must generally be decided on the basis that the medical evidence is correct unless the Home Office produces any medical evidence to the contrary, or the applicant's evidence is completely unreliable.

10

Where evidence is produced from both sides and the evidence conflicts, if a reasonable person could find in favour of one or the other side, then, again, the 'clearly unfounded' decision must be made on the basis of the evidence most favourable to the applicant. Fresh evidence that comes after the date of the decision to certify may also be taken into account by the court.

Steps for dealing with a 'clearly unfounded' certificate

The following steps may be taken in order to protect a person from removal on the basis of a 'clearly unfounded' certificate.

- First, identify whether the claim has been certified as 'clearly unfounded'. If it has been, the reasons for refusal letter will say so. The immigration authorities may try to remove such people very quickly. Applicants should obtain specialist advice urgently.

- Next, identify what is the basis of the asylum or human rights claim. Who and what is the applicant afraid of? Is the person afraid of persecution for a Refugee Convention reason and/or are they afraid of human rights abuses? Is there a sufficiency of protection in the country of origin? Would it be unduly harsh for the person to relocate?

- Next, identify the basis for the certificate. On what basis is the Home Office stating that the case is 'bound' to fail if it were allowed to go before the AIT? Has the application been refused on credibility grounds alone, in which case the APIs should be attended to (see above), since they state that it will be rare that such cases will be certified for that reason alone.

- Is there any objective evidence for the applicant's fears? Are there any examples of persecution or of human rights abuses for the category of persons within which the applicant falls? Are the objective sources accurate, and is the case-law on country guidance accurate? Has the Home Office taken into account country evidence that has been provided in support of the application?

- Check all the documents that have at some stage been put before the Home Office – does the decision indicate that regard has been given to them?

- Is there any chance of getting fresh or further evidence – for example, medical or country evidence, or evidence authenticating specific documents? Such evidence could then be used to challenge the 'clearly unfounded' certificate. If such material exists, further representations, together with that further evidence, should be made.

If it is felt that the certificate can be challenged, specialist advice is needed in order to bring a claim for judicial review. For judicial review procedures generally, ▶see 1213–22. The Home Office is likely to give only limited time for bringing judicial review proceedings before it proceeds to remove the applicant (▶see 1220–2).

ASYLUM 'STATUS' APPEALS UNDER SECTION 83 2002 ACT

In most cases where an applicant is refused asylum, an 'immigration decision' will be made. This is, effectively, a decision that the applicant has no rights to be in the UK. In such cases, there is an appeal under section 82. However, as was made clear by the Court of Appeal in the case of *Saad, Diriye & Osario*, refugee status brings very important additional benefits above and beyond protection from removal. For example, it gives rights to family reunion and a refugee travel document. Therefore, denial of refugee status, even if the applicant is not to be removed, is seen as such an important decision in itself that a right of appeal has been given.

So, there is a right of appeal if (s83 2002 Act):

- the Home Office rejects the claim for asylum; *and*
- the applicant has been granted leave to enter or remain for more than 12 months (or for periods of more than 12 months 'in aggregate').

So, in cases where an asylum-seeker is refused asylum but granted humanitarian protection or discretionary leave for more than 12 months, there is no 'immigration decision' under section 82, but there is a 'status' appeal on asylum grounds under section 83. The legislation is not clear, but it is probably the case that, in counting up the period of (over) 12 months, the applicant can add together leave granted before and after the refusal of asylum. On an appeal under section 83, only asylum grounds can be raised. Human rights grounds cannot be relied on (*LA, Eritrea*, AIT).

Note that an asylum-seeker will also have no right of appeal against a rejection of asylum where they are granted no leave, but where no 'immigration decision' is taken either – i.e. they are just given a 'reasons for refusal' letter explaining why the claim for asylum is refused, but where this is not accompanied by a notice of refusal of leave to enter, decision to remove an illegal entrant, etc. Of course, where no such notice has been given, the person is not (yet) being removed from the UK. When the immigration authorities do take steps to enforce their removal, a proper notice will have to be given against which there will be a right of appeal.

For 'status' appeals in EEA cases, ▶see 557.

The 2005 Bill

The new system of granting only limited leave to refugees means that there are likely to be more status appeals. The 2005 Bill will give a new status right of appeal in cases where the applicant is no longer recognised as a refugee but is granted leave on other grounds. In addition, the 2005 Bill preserves rights of appeal against curtailment and refusals to extend leave (which are to be abolished in other cases) for cases in which a refugee's leave is curtailed, or where they are refused an extension of leave. For details of these proposed changes, ▶see above at 1042–3.

APPEALS INVOLVING 'EXCLUSION' FROM REFUGEE STATUS

Where the Home Office is trying to exclude a person from the Refugee Convention under Articles 1(F) or 33, there are special considerations that apply to appeals *both* to the AIT and to SIAC (for general details about exclusions on these grounds, ▶see 624–6). Of course, even if an applicant is excluded from the Refugee Convention, they can still succeed in their appeals under Article 3 ECHR, or on other human rights grounds.

For further guidelines on procedural matters, particularly where exclusion is raised late or raised by the AIT itself, see the decision of the IAT in *Gurung*.

No special consideration of gravity of harm

In considering whether the person should be excluded under either Article 1(F) or 33(2), the AIT/SIAC cannot consider the *gravity* of the persecution that the appellant is at risk of (see s34 Anti-terrorism, Crime and Security Act 2001). This provision has been made because, in some non-UK cases, there had been a suggestion that, in considering whether the exclusion clauses should bite, the seriousness of the harm feared had to be weighed in the balance. The 2001 Act makes it clear that the seriousness of the harm is not a relevant consideration.

Presumption that the appellant has been convicted of a particularly serious crime and is a danger to the community of the UK

One of the grounds for excluding people from the protection of Article 33 of the Refugee Convention is that '[having] been convicted by a final judgment of a particularly serious crime [they constitute] a danger to the community of [the host country – i.e. the UK]' (Article 33(2)).

In any of the following circumstances, the above definition is *presumed* to apply (s72 2002 Act).

1) Where the appellant has been convicted in the UK of an offence and sentenced to prison for two years or more.

2) Where the appellant has been convicted outside the UK of an offence, sentenced to prison for two years or more, and could have been sentenced to at least two years if they had been convicted of a similar offence in the UK.

3) Where the appellant is convicted in the UK of an offence contained in the Nationality, Immigration and Asylum Act 2002 (Specification of Particularly

Serious Crimes) Order 2004 (there is a very long list of offences, including offences concerning: explosives; class A and B drugs; immigration matters; biological and chemical weapons; hostage-taking; hijacking and related matters; nuclear materials; terrorism; money-laundering; dishonesty (theft, robbery etc.); criminal damage; public order; sexual matters; false imprisonment; crimes of violence; offences against children).

4) Where the appellant is convicted outside the UK of an offence the Home Office certifies is similar to an offence in (3) above.

The Order in (3) above came into force on 12 August 2004, and the purpose of the additional categories in (3) and (4) was explained in a Home Office letter to the Asylum Processes Stakeholder Group dated 23 July 2004:

'The purpose of the Order is to enable the Secretary of State to specify offences which, by their very nature, whatever the length of sentence imposed, connote such a degree of seriousness that it would be appropriate to make the presumption that the offender is a danger to the community. For such serious crimes the normal expectation will be that the courts would impose a sentence well in excess of two years, but there may be rare situations where a shorter sentence is imposed.'

The appellant is allowed to try to 'rebut' (i.e. challenge) the presumption that Article 33(2) applies to them. They may argue that they have not been convicted of an offence as alleged or that, even if they have, they are not in fact a danger to the community.

Where the Home Office issues a certificate alleging (1)–(4) above, the AIT or SIAC must first consider and make a decision on whether they agree with the certificate, or whether the appellant has managed to overturn the presumption. If it agrees with the Home Office, it must then dismiss the part of the appeal that deals with the Refugee Convention.

10

SPECIAL IMMIGRATION APPEALS COMMISSION

A very small number of people are excluded from the normal system of appeals, and must use a separate appeal system. This is the case where the Secretary of State is personally involved in the decision, and where the decision was taken:

- in the interests of national security or of the relationship between the UK and another country; or
- on the basis of information that should not be made public in the interests of national security, the interests of the relationship between the UK and another country or otherwise in the public interest.

Where the Secretary of State certifies that the decision was made in accordance with the above conditions under section 97 of the 2002 Act, there is no right of appeal to the AIT, either against an 'immigration decision' under section 82 or against a rejection of asylum in a 'status' appeal under section 83. Instead, the applicant will have a right of appeal to SIAC (see s2(1) Special Immigration Appeals Commission Act 1997). If a section 97 certificate is issued after an appeal has already begun before the AIT, then the appeal automatically lapses and, again, there is a right of appeal to SIAC instead (s99 2002 Act; Procedure Rules, rule 16; s2(1)(b) 1997 Act).

Appeals against deprivation of citizenship involving national security matters may also be certified in this way, in which case there is a right of appeal to SIAC (s40A(2) BNA 1981).

The SIAC panel is usually made up of three people: a High Court judge, an immigration judge and another person who is not necessarily a lawyer but who has experience of security matters.

The *Handbook* only looks in broad outline at SIAC procedures (below). It is essential that anyone who is subject to a decision giving rise to an appeal to SIAC is referred for advice from an immigration solicitor experienced in such matters.

Why was SIAC set up?

Until 1998 there was no right of appeal against decisions to exclude people based on reasons of national security or the interests of the UK's political relations with another state. All that existed was a chance to put a case to a panel of three 'advisers' (the 'three wise men'), but with no right to be given the Home Office's reasons, or to be represented at the hearing. Even if the advisers accepted the person's case, the Home Secretary was not bound by their decision.

In November 1996, the European Court of Human Rights held, in the case of *Chahal*, that this procedure was inadequate, and a decision was made to set up a special commission that would give a right of appeal, but with safeguards to protect national security.

SIAC also heard appeals and reviews against certificates issued by the Secretary of State stating that a person was a 'suspected international terrorist', and could therefore be detained indefinitely. In *A & Others*, the House of Lords held that the provisions for indefinite detention were unlawful (▶see 901–2).

SIAC procedures

SIAC has its own special rules of procedure: the Special Immigration Appeals Commission (Procedure) Rules 2003.

The main differences between proceedings before SIAC and those before the AIT are as follows. Appellants are entitled to two sets of legal representatives. They have a 'special advocate' appointed by the government, who represents their interests in the part of the hearing concerning national security issues. The special advocate is able to see the 'sensitive' national security material that the Home Office is relying on and to make representations about it, and to cross-examine Home Office witnesses. That part of the hearing is in closed session, and the appellant and the public are excluded from it and are unable to see the sensitive material. After the special advocate has seen the sensitive material, they are no longer able to have direct contact with the appellant.

The appellant also has another legal representative who remains in contact with them throughout the hearing, and who represents their interests in the open part of the hearings, but who – like the appellant – is not allowed to see the sensitive material. This representative is not appointed (or on a panel appointed) by the government.

There are preliminary hearings in which the special advocate may argue for greater disclosure than the Home Office has made. In those hearings the special advocate may try to argue that certain material being treated as 'closed' should be made 'open', and shown to the appellant so that they can deal with it.

For applying to SIAC for bail, ▶see 965.

10

35 Conducting first instance appeals before the AIT

This chapter looks at the procedures that operate when an appeal comes before the Asylum and Immigration Tribunal (AIT – formerly the Immigration Appellate Authority or IAA) for hearing at 'first instance' (the first level of appeal). The appeal is likely to be heard by a single 'immigration judge' who is a member of the AIT. Although this sounds very grand, hearings are very similar to hearings before the old 'adjudicators', and the immigration judge may have previously been an adjudicator.

This chapter deals with first instance appeals to the AIT only. Details about applying for reviews of decisions of the AIT, identifying errors of law, conducting reconsideration hearings, appeals to the Court of Appeal, and retrospective funding orders are given in Chapter 36. Time-limits are an essential part of the appeal system. While relevant time-limits are given in this chapter as they crop up, there is a detailed table setting out all the relevant time-limits (and how time is calculated) in Chapter 36 at ▶1162–7.

For details about rights of appeal, notices of decision, serving notices of appeal, and the 'one-stop' appeal procedure, see Chapter 34. That chapter also deals with *particular kinds of appeal* and the procedures that apply to them: 'upgrade' appeals where leave has been granted, family visitor appeals, SIAC cases and certified appeals such as 'non-suspensive' appeals.

10

This chapter

We begin by noting which procedure rules and practice directions regulate appeals, and we then provide a basic timetable and overview of the appeal procedures (▶1086–9). Representation at appeals is critical, and we look at who may act as representatives, and at their duties (▶1090–1). The first decisions the AIT may have to make are whether there is a right of appeal at all, and whether a late appeal should be allowed to proceed (▶see 1091–4).

The respondent is under a duty to file with the AIT the basic papers allowing the appeal to go ahead (▶see 1094–5), and the AIT will also issue standard appeal directions to both appellants and the Home Office relating to further documents that should be produced (▶1095). In in-country, non-fast track asylum appeals there will be a case-management review (CMR) hearing. CMRs may also be arranged in other cases. At these hearings, the parties are expected to deal with various standard matters (▶1095–7), but they are also a good opportunity for appellants to raise other issues they may seek directions on (▶1097–1100).

The powers to adjourn hearings are very carefully limited. Appellants who need an adjournment should prepare the application carefully, and follow the procedures set down (▶1100–2). Although appeals proceed in most cases by way of an oral hearing at which both sides are present, the AIT has certain powers to proceed in the absence of a party, or to proceed without a hearing. In some cases, where for example the appeal is withdrawn or abandoned, the AIT will not issue a decision on the merits of the appeal at all. All these matters are dealt with at ▶1102–5.

After discussing all of the above preliminary matters, we go on to cover the further steps which appellants must take to prepare for the full hearing – in particular the obtaining and presenting of evidence in a trial bundle (▶1105–10). Using case-law before the AIT is straightforward when it comes to producing decisions of the higher courts, but appellants need to understand the AIT's approach to its own decisions and those of the previous IAT (▶1110–12). We then go on to look at conducting the full hearing before the immigration judge – in particular at giving evidence and making submissions (▶1112–8).

The chapter then discusses the powers of the AIT in deciding appeals. We deal with: the date on which the immigration judge will focus in deciding the appeal; the evidence they can consider; the burden and standard of proof; the grounds on which an appeal can be allowed; the directions which can then be given to the respondent; and the ability to make recommendations in dismissed appeals (▶1118–29).

Finally, we look at the fast track appeal process and at the timetable and basic procedures that apply. In particular, the chapter discusses the ability to make applications to remove applicants from the fast track appeal system (▶1129–32).

PROCEDURE RULES AND PRACTICE DIRECTIONS

The rules setting out the procedure for appeals, whether they are immigration, asylum or human rights appeals, are the Asylum and Immigration Tribunal (Procedure) Rules 2005. In this chapter, we refer to them as the 'Procedure Rules' or simply the 'Rules'. The 'overriding objective' of the Procedure Rules is to ensure that appeals are handled as 'fairly, quickly and efficiently as possible' (Rule 4).

Separate procedure rules apply to 'fast track' appeal case, which cover those detained at the following 'Immigration Removal Centres':

• Campsfield House

- Colnbrook House
- Harmondsworth
- Yarls Wood

The rules setting out the procedure for fast track appeals are the Asylum and Immigration Tribunal (Fast Track Procedure) Rules 2005 (the 'Fast Track Rules'). While the Fast Track Rules apply many of the procedures contained in the ordinary rules to fast track cases, they also short-circuit many of the normal procedures, and they lay down a quick timetable for the appeal process. We deal specifically with fast track appeals at ▶1129–32.

Details of the procedures for the immigration authorities to give notice of immigration decisions that can be appealed against are set out in the Immigration (Notices) Regulations 2003.

Transitional arrangements for procedure rules

The 2005 Procedure Rules apply to appeals from 4 April 2005. They also apply to appeals pending before the adjudicator or the IAT before that date, which were fed into the new system by the transitional arrangements made under the 2004 Act. (For transitional arrangements about rights of appeal, ▶see 1151–3.)

The Procedure Rules contain their own transitional arrangements – most importantly (Rule 62):

- where the immigration decision is served before 4 April 2005 and notice of appeal is given on or after that date, the old Procedure Rules on time-limits for appealing to the adjudicator apply;
- the speeded-up timetable by which the *AIT* must act under the 2005 Procedure Rules does not apply to appeals that were pending before 4 April 2005.

10

Practice Directions

In addition to rules of procedure contained in legislation, the AIT can itself issue 'practice directions' to set out the practice to be followed in appeals (see s107 and para. 7 of Sch. 4 2002 Act). Following the replacement of the IAA by the AIT, all practice directions made by the Chief Adjudicator and the President of the IAT are no longer effective. After a period of consultation, on 4 April 2005 the President of the AIT issued a consolidated set of 'Practice Directions' (paras 1–21 with annexes). We have referred to them simply as the 'Practice Directions'. Both the Practice Directions and the 'Guidance Notes' (below) can be downloaded from the AIT website, www.ait.gov.uk.

The 'Guidance Notes' issued by the Chief Adjudicator and the Deputy Chief Adjudicator between 2001 and 2004 are still effective as guidance, unless and until the AIT issues its own guidance dealing with the same issues. Obviously, the Guidance Notes have to be read in the light of the general changes to the system. These notes give separate guidance on:

- the sitting of part-time adjudicators (now immigration judges);
- transfers of proceedings;
- pre-hearings;
- delayed promulgations of determinations;
- unrepresented appellants;
- unrepresented appellants who do not understand English;
- bail (for applications for bail, ▶see 965–85) (it is understood that the bail guidance notes are in the process of being revised);
- deposits of recognizances for bail;
- withdrawals of appeals;
- unaccompanied children.

TIMETABLE AND BASIC PROCEDURE FOR APPEALS

The time appeals take to go through the process has varied historically. Often it depends upon the numbers of appellants and available resources as much as on the requirements of the Procedure Rules. The government's efforts over recent years have focused on deciding appeals ever more quickly.

The system in place from 4 April 2005 again tries to speed the process up. In order to shorten procedures, appellants now generally serve their notice of appeal on the AIT, rather than on the immigration authorities who made the decision (for more details about giving notice of appeal, ▶see 1062–6). For the time-limits for appealing to the AIT, ▶see 1162 onwards.

The broad timetable for first instance appeals to the AIT in non-fast track appeals is set out in the table below.

TIMETABLE FOR FIRST INSTANCE APPEALS TO AIT

After notice of appeal has been given, the general timetable for first instance appeals to the AIT in non-fast track cases is as follows.

1) The AIT must serve a copy of the notice of appeal on the immigration authorities 'as soon as reasonably practicable' (Rule 12(1)).

2) Having received the notice of appeal, the immigration authorities must file with the AIT and the appellant the essential documents relevant to the appeal (▶see 1094–5). The AIT may direct that this is done within a particular time. If there are no such directions, it must be done 'as soon as reasonably practicable', and no later than 2pm on the business day before 'the earliest day appointed for any hearing'. This includes the Case Management Review (CMR) hearing (Rule 13).

3) For all in-country, non-fast track, non-'upgrade' asylum appeals (including appeals that are partly asylum appeals, even if other grounds are raised), the following further rules apply:

- A CMR hearing will be held unless the AIT specifically directs that there will be no CMR hearing (Practice Directions, paras 6.1, 6.10). Given the date to be fixed for the main hearing (see below), the CMR hearing is likely to be within a week or two of the AIT receiving the notice of appeal.

- The *main* hearing of the appeal must be fixed for not later than 28 days after the date on which the AIT received notice of appeal (or 28 days after service of the preliminary decision on a late notice of appeal, if notice of appeal was given late). Where an appeal is to be determined without a hearing (▶see 1103–4), the AIT *must* determine it within 28 days of these dates. These time-limits apply *provided* that the immigration authorities have filed the documents referred to in (2) above. If they have not, the hearing is likely to be put back (Procedure Rules, Rule 23(1)–(3)(7)). Of course, just because the hearing is 'fixed' does not mean that the hearing cannot be adjourned to another date (▶see 1101–2).

- The AIT is to send its determination of the appeal to the immigration authorities within ten business days of the hearing finishing (or within ten days of determining the appeal if there was no appeal hearing, Rule 23(4)).

- The immigration authorities must serve the determination of the AIT on the appellant within 28 days of receiving the determination from the AIT. If the decision is negative, the appellant will then consider whether to apply for a review (▶see Chapter 36). If the immigration authorities decide to apply for a review (or to apply for permission to appeal to the Court of Appeal, if that is appropriate), then they must serve the decision on the appellant at the same time that they make that application (Rule 23(5)(a)).

- The immigration authorities must inform the AIT that they have served the determination on the appellant. If the AIT does not receive this notification after 29 days from the date when the determination was sent to the immigration authorities, the AIT must send its determination directly to the appellant 'as soon as reasonably practicable' (Rule 23(5)(b)).

  It remains to be seen whether this very tight timetable for in-country, non-fast track asylum appeals can be maintained.

4) Where the case does not fall within (3) above because it is a non-asylum case, an upgrade appeal (under s83 2002 Act) or an out-of-country appeal, the timetable for hearing the appeal is more relaxed. However, after the hearing of the appeal finishes, the AIT must promulgate its determination within ten business days. If the appeal is determined without a hearing, the determination is to be promulgated within ten business days after the immigration judge has made their decision on the appeal. In all of these cases, the AIT serves the determination directly on both the appellant and the immigration authorities (Rule 22).

Note

Fast track appeal cases are dealt with even more quickly than any of the above appeals (for details, ▶see 1130–1).

In this table, 'Rules' refers to the Asylum and Immigration Tribunal (Procedure) Rules 2005.

10

PARTIES TO THE APPEAL, REPRESENTATION AND FUNDING

The person appealing is known as the 'appellant'. The Secretary of State (the Home Office), the immigration officer or entry clearance officer who made the decision being appealed is the 'respondent'. The appellant and the respondent are the 'parties' to the appeal. In asylum appeals, the United Kingdom Representative of the UNHCR is entitled to give notice to the AIT that they wish to take part in the proceedings. In such cases, the AIT must allow the UK Representative to make submissions in the case, and documents served in the case must also be served on them (Procedure Rules, Rule 49). In practice, the UNHCR will only become involved where there are important standard-setting principles at issue that will have a wide effect.

Representation

People intending to appeal should always try to obtain representation. The law and procedures can be very complex, particularly in asylum appeals. A much higher proportion of represented appeals are successful than those that are unrepresented. Specialist representatives have not only substantial experience and knowledge of the law and procedures, but also access to evidence and reports.

As in other areas of immigration advice, appellants may only be represented by persons permitted to provide immigration services under the 1999 Act. Further details of the regulatory system can be found in Chapter 3. Non-lawyers not acting under the supervision of lawyers must be exempted or registered under Part 5 of the 1999 Act if they are to represent people at appeals (▶see 63). For those registered or exempted by the Office of the Immigration Services Commissioner (OISC), only those practising at Level 3 (the highest level) are allowed to do appeals work, including lodging the appeal. This means that any voluntary sector adviser or paid consultant practising at a lower level needs to pass the case to a solicitors' practice or a Level 3 (OISC) practitioner when a refusal is received (see ss84–6 1999 Act and Procedure Rules, Rule 48(1)).

Those who have legal representation should discuss with their representative who will represent them at the hearing, and whether or not legal aid funding will be available towards the costs of representation (▶see below and ▶see 67–73). The AIT will be reluctant to postpone appeal hearings because an appellant has not obtained representation, or where there has been a last-minute change of representative because of problems with funds.

Duty to notify AIT about representation

When a representative begins acting, they must notify the AIT and the immigration authorities in writing that they are instructed. A postal address at which documents can be served must be given. Copies of documents sent out by the AIT should be sent to both the appellant and their notified representative. If an address changes, the new address should be notified straight away. Until a party notifies a change of address, documents will continue to be served at the old address, and will be 'deemed' to have been properly served.

It is of fundamental importance that these basic practice points should be handled correctly. There are frequent problems of appellants losing appeal rights and missing appeal hearings as a result of not receiving correspondence. Once an appellant has got, or been put, into a mess, and an appeal is decided in their absence, it can be very difficult to put matters right. If a representative ceases acting, both they and the appellant should notify the AIT and the immigration authorities of this, and of the name and address of any new representative (see Procedure Rules 48(4)(6)(7)(9), 55(3), 56).

Legal aid

Since 1 January 2000, Controlled Legal Representation (CLR), a form of legal aid, has been available to enable immigration advice providers to represent, or arrange for representation, at appeals in England and Wales. The provider must have a Specialist Help Quality Mark and hold a contract with the Legal Services Commission (LSC). Access to funding depends on the appellant passing both a means and a merits test and these are discussed in more detail in Chapter 3 at ▶71–73. The organisations that typically hold the Specialist Help Quality Mark and who are allowed to provide CLR-funded representation are discussed at ▶60 and 62. Legal aid funding is also available in Scotland under the 'Assistance By Way of Representation' (ABWOR) Scheme (▶see 61–62). Legally aided representation is also available in Northern Ireland (▶see 61–63).

Accreditation of representatives in England and Wales

By August 2005 it became a contractual requirement that all legally aided representatives in England and Wales must be 'accredited' under the Immigration and Asylum Accreditation Scheme administered by the LSC and Law Society. The Scheme has three levels, and those providing representation at immigration and asylum appeals must be accredited up to Level 2 (Senior Caseworker). The Accreditation Scheme is set out in more detail at ▶73–4.

PRELIMINARY DECISIONS ON NOTICES OF APPEAL AND LATE APPEALS

In most cases, notices of appeal are now to be lodged with the AIT rather than the immigration authorities. Those who are detained may alternatively give the notice of appeal to the officers who have custody of them. Those outside the UK who wish to appeal against a decision of the ECO may file the notice of appeal with the ECO (Procedure Rules, Rule 6).

General details about notices of immigration decision and lodging the notice of appeal are given in Chapter 34 at ▶1061–6.

In some cases, after a notice of appeal has been lodged, there is a question as to whether there is right of appeal or not. For example, is the appeal excluded because:

- there has been no 'immigration decision' made within the meaning of section 82(2)?
- the decision has been taken on the ground that the person does not satisfy a requirement of the immigration rules as to age, nationality or citizenship? (see s88(2) 2002 Act) (▶see 1055)
- the appellant can only exercise an appeal from outside the UK?

In such cases, the AIT has to make a decision as to whether there is a valid appeal. If it decides that there is not, then the AIT will not accept the notice of appeal. The AIT must then notify the person who has given the notice of appeal and the respondent of the decision (Procedure Rules, Rule 9; Practice Directions, para. 3). It appears that the way to challenge such a decision is by judicial review.

Late notice of appeal

Where a notice of appeal is given to the AIT out of time, the appellant should, in the notice of appeal, apply to extend time (Procedure Rules, Rule 10; Practice Directions, para. 4. For details about time-limits, ▶see 1162–7). The appellant should:

- state the reasons why the time-limit has not been met; and
- provide 'written evidence' to back up those reasons.

The written evidence might be a written statement from the appellant and/or their representative explaining what has happened. It may also include documentary evidence – for example, if the appellant was hospitalised at the time that the decision was received, evidence from the hospital demonstrating this should be submitted.

Where the AIT receives a notice of appeal which *appears* to be out of time but does not include an application to extend time, the AIT may either:

- extend time on its own initiative (the Practice Directions stress that appellants must *not* assume that the time-limits can be ignored, and that this power is intended to be used when, for example, the postal service is disrupted); or
- give the appellant notice that it may treat the notice of appeal as out of time.

If the appellant is given notice by the AIT that the appeal may be treated as out of time, the appellant must, within three business days of receiving that notice (ten business days where the appellant is outside the UK), file representations with the AIT. The representations can argue that:

- the notice of appeal was given in time; and/or
- if the notice was out of time, there were 'special circumstances for failing to give the notice of appeal in time, which could not reasonably have been stated in the notice of appeal'.

Written evidence in support of the above representations should be filed with the AIT at the same time.

AIT decision on timeliness

In any case where a question arises as to whether the appeal was in time, the AIT will make a decision on whether the notice of appeal was in fact given out of time. In all cases, where the appeal was given *out of time*, the AIT will then decide whether to extend time. It may extend time if it is 'satisfied that by reason of special circumstances it would be unjust not to do so'.

In making its decision, the AIT may only take account of:

- the matters stated in the notice of appeal;
- evidence filed by the appellant as indicated above;
- 'any other relevant matters of fact within the knowledge' of the AIT.

The decision is made without a hearing. If the decision is negative, it appears that the means to challenge this is by judicial review. Before the new Procedure Rules, the immigration authorities could make an initial decision as to whether an appeal should be accepted as being in time.

Notice of decision on timeliness

In in-country asylum cases, where the AIT refuses to extend time, the AIT will serve the notice of its decision on the immigration authorities only. The immigration authorities must serve it on the appellant within 28 days. Failing this, the AIT will serve the decision directly on the appellant. As with the rules relating to service of appeal determinations in asylum cases, this allows the immigration authorities to detain an applicant and to set directions for their removal at the same time as they give them notice of the negative decision. In other cases, the AIT will serve its decision about timeliness on all parties.

Late notice of appeal in 'imminent removal' cases

The 'late notice' of appeal procedures are modified in 'imminent removal' cases (Procedure Rules, Rule 11). These are defined as cases in which the Home Office notifies the AIT that removal directions have been issued against the appellant under which they are to be removed within five days from the date the notice of appeal was given. In such a case, the AIT:

- must make a decision about the timeliness of an appeal, and about extending time before the date and time of the proposed removal, if it is 'reasonably practicable' to do so;

- may give notice orally (including over the telephone) that the appeal may be treated as out of time. The appellant then has the opportunity to respond; and

- may shorten the time-limits (see above) for giving evidence about the timeliness of the appeal and/or direct that such evidence be given orally (including over the telephone).

Decisions in such cases will normally be dealt with by 'senior immigration judges' on a rota basis. The judge will decide whether to exercise the above powers depending on the circumstances of the case. The judge will take into account whether the appellant is able to give evidence by telephone (language considerations will be relevant; see Practice Directions, para. 5.3).

RESPONDENT'S REASONS AND EXPLANATORY STATEMENTS

Except where the appellant filed the notice of appeal with the ECO, after receiving notice of appeal the AIT will send it to the respondent immigration authorities (Procedure Rules, Rule 12). After the immigration authorities have received it, they must, as soon as reasonably practicable, file with the AIT and the appellant copies of *all* of the following documents (Procedure Rules, Rule 13):

- the notice of decision and any reasons given for the decision. These are the formal notice of the immigration decision – for example, a refusal of leave to enter or directions for removal as an overstayer, and any reasons for refusal letter;

- any unpublished document referred to in the notice of decision/reasons for refusal letter (for details about reasons for refusal letters see ▶728);

- any SEF completed by the appellant;

- any record of interview with the appellant.

Where notice of appeal was given to the ECO, the ECO is required to forward the same documents to the AIT within ten working days, if that is possible (Procedure Rules, Rule 6(6)(c)). There is no obligation on the respondent in the Procedure Rules (as there once was) to file a separate 'explanatory statement' setting out the reasons for a negative decision in more detail. In non-asylum/human rights cases where there is no detailed reasons for refusal letter, often the respondent will file a statement further explaining the reasons for the decision. However, detailed reasons for refusal letters are becoming more common in 'ordinary' immigration cases, which lessens the need for a further explanatory statement at the appeal stage. Historically, there were very long delays in filing such papers, particularly in entry clearance cases.

It is not uncommon for important documents to be left out of the bundle of papers the respondent prepares and sends to the AIT. The Procedure

Rules only direct that the above documents be filed with the AIT. Therefore, appellants should check to see whether the respondent has included documents and evidence that were produced to the decision-maker, and which the appellant wants to rely on. If they are not, such documents should be produced by the appellant themselves in their own bundle.

STANDARD APPEAL DIRECTIONS

In most cases, including those where no CMR hearing will be held, the AIT will normally give the parties 'standard' directions for the conduct of the appeal (see table below). These directions will normally be given with the notice of hearing. Where there is to be a CMR, the standard directions will usually have to be sent out before the CMR.

STANDARD DIRECTIONS

The standard directions given by the AIT for first instance appeals before the AIT are as follows (Practice Directions, para. 6.5).

1) Not later than five working days before the full hearing, the appellant shall serve on the AIT and the respondent:

- witness statements of the evidence to be called at the hearing (such statements are then to stand as evidence in chief at the hearing);
- a paginated and indexed bundle of all the documents to be relied on at the hearing, together with a schedule identifying the essential passages;
- a 'skeleton argument' setting out all the relevant issues and citing any authorities relied on;
- a chronology of events.

2) Not later than five working days before the full hearing, the respondent shall serve on the AIT and the appellant a paginated and indexed bundle of the documents to be relied on at the hearing, with a schedule identifying the relevant passages together with a list of any authorities to be relied on.

10

CASE MANAGEMENT REVIEW HEARINGS AND FURTHER DIRECTIONS

As indicated above, a case management review (CMR) hearing will normally be held in every in-country asylum appeal (other than fast track appeals and reconsideration appeals; Practice Directions, para. 6.1).

This will be the first court hearing that the appellant has in preparation for their full appeal. The main purpose of the CMR is to ensure that the appeal is ready to go ahead and to make any necessary further arrangements for the conduct of the case. Further directions beyond the normal directions (see above) may be given. CMRs are usually listed before a single immigration judge, and may take place at any hearing centre.

Both parties should attend or be represented at the CMR. The dangers of not attending a CMR are emphasised in the Practice Directions (para. 6.2): the appeal may be determined without a hearing or in the absence of the appellant.

The CMR is a good opportunity to address various matters concerning the appeal. Appellants should not treat it is as a mere formality, but should think carefully about what they can achieve at the CMR that may maximise their chances of winning the case. The immigration judge will require the parties to deal with various standard matters at the CMR (▶see below), but appellants should consider whether there are any other particular matters, which they can raise or have dealt with (▶see below at 1097–1100, including the table). Both parties are expected to provide the immigration judge with a written draft of any further directions they are requesting (Practice Directions, para. 6.3(d), 6.4(b)).

General matters to be dealt with at CMR

The general matters the immigration judge will expect the parties to be able to deal with at the CMR are as follows (Practice Directions, paras 6.3–6.4 and note that a further Guidance Note on 'Case Management Review Hearings' was issued in July 2005).

Appellant

With the original notice of appeal, appellants should already have provided grounds of appeal and 'reasons in support' of those grounds. They should also have indicated what documents may be relied on at the appeal (▶see Chapter 34 at 1062–6). The judge may ask for clarification of the grounds of appeal, and if the grounds are to be amended this should also be done at the CMR (Procedure Rules, Rule 14). Appellants are also expected to provide details of witnesses who are to be called, and of any witness statements or reports that will be relied on. Appellants may also be asked to clarify whether an interpreter is required and has been booked in the correct language and dialect. A time estimate for the hearing may also be required. While representatives should try to provide as much information as possible, it is important not to commit to certain witnesses or evidence unless they have full instructions and are in a position to do so.

Respondent

The immigration authorities should already have served on the AIT and the appellant the documents referred to at ▶1094–5. If they have not, this should be raised at the CMR. The rules do not directly state that all documents produced by the applicant in the application should be forwarded to the AIT. It may be that original documents lodged with the embassy that are important for the judge to consider at the full hearing have not been produced. If they are important, a direction may be sought at the CMR that the original documents be produced. The respondent should also give details of any amendment to the reasons for the decision.

Narrowing the issues

Another standard purpose of the CMR is to determine whether the issues that will be fought over at the main hearing can be narrowed. This is important because it then allows appellants to focus their preparation on the real issues.

The CMR is therefore a good opportunity to extract concessions from the Home Office. For example:

- Which parts of the appellant's account are accepted?
- In an asylum/human rights case, is it accepted that, if the appellant's account is accepted, they will be at risk if returned?
- In a case in which various elements of the immigration rules have been raised, are any of the elements now conceded (perhaps in the light of further evidence), such as financial dependency, maintenance and accommodation, or intention to live together?
- In an Article 8 case in which a 'staged' approach is adopted, which, if any, of the stages are accepted?

At the end of the CMR hearing, the immigration judge should give to the parties a written note (Practice Directions, paras 6.6, 6.9) confirming:

- any further appeal directions that have been given;
- any issues that have been agreed between the parties at the CMR hearing;
- any concessions which have been made by either party.

ADDITIONAL MATTERS THAT MAY BE RAISED BEFORE HEARING, INCLUDING AT A CMR

As well as the standard directions to the parties and the general matters dealt with at the CMR (see above), the AIT has a general power to make directions. Appellants should consider whether any particular directions or arrangements should be made. The table below (▶1098–1100) provides details of other specific matters appellants may wish to raise, and of the procedural rules which apply to them.

These matters are most conveniently raised at a CMR, but can be raised in writing at any time. In a case in which there is to be no CMR, and in which the direction sought cannot be dealt with in writing alone, parties can ask for a direction that a CMR be held, which will enable them to deal with the particular matter they wish to raise (Procedure Rules, Rule 45(4)(d)(ii)). The specific powers to give directions (Rule 45), additional to the directions set out above, are that directions may:

- 'relate to any matter concerning the preparation for the hearing' (see further the table below);

- state the time period in which a particular action or step is to be taken;
- vary time limits given in the Procedure Rules or in directions previously given;
- require a matter to be dealt with as a preliminary issue;
- require a party to provide further details of their case, or any other information which 'appears to be necessary for the determination of the appeal';
- limit either the number of documents which may be relied on, the time for oral submissions, the time for examining witnesses, or the issues to be dealt with at the hearing;
- require steps to be taken to allow appeals to be heard together;
- provide for a hearing to be conducted or evidence given by video link;
- make provision for the anonymity of a party or a witness.

Note that where an appellant is not represented, the AIT is not allowed to give them directions unless it is sure that the appellant will be able to comply with them.

WHAT FURTHER DIRECTIONS MAY BE REQUESTED OR APPLICATIONS MADE?

Adjournment

(For fuller details about adjournments ▶see 1100–2 below.)

In an in-country asylum appeal, by the time of the CMR it is likely that a date will have been given for the main hearing. The timetable for dealing with these appeals in particular is extremely fast (▶see 1088–9). It may be that, in these cases in particular, the appellant will simply not be able to prepare the case properly in the time permitted. If this is the case, then a properly worked out application for an adjournment should be made. There will need to be good reasons for asking that the date be put back – for example, it may be that a medical or other crucial expert is instructed but that the report will not be ready within the strict timetable set for determining the appeal, or that a key witness lives abroad and cannot attend within the time allowed.

Appellants will be expected to show that they have done everything they can to be ready as early as possible, to provide evidence of their attempts, and to state when they will be ready. For further details about adjournments, ▶see 1100–2 (Rule 21).

Combined hearings

The AIT can join together appeals where similar questions arise, where the appeals concern members of the same family, or where for 'some other reason it is desirable for the appeals to be heard together' (Rule 20). Often in cases involving members of the same family, or appellants who know each other, the relevant facts of the cases overlap, and appellants are relevant witnesses in each others' cases. Because of the large number of appeals, the Home Office and the AIT will often not have linked the cases.

Sometimes it will be in the interests of appellants to have the cases heard together – the evidence may be mutually beneficial, and it may save appellants time and money. Great care should, however, be taken before applying for cases to be linked. Representatives should be sure they have seen everything that has already been said in the other case, and be aware of what further evidence will be produced in that case before advising their clients to have the cases joined.

Further details of the respondent's case

It may be that the reasons for refusal letter or explanatory statement is unclear about what the Home Office's case is on certain issues, and/or that the appellant does not know whether a particular requirement of the rules or some other matter is in dispute. Before spending time and effort dealing with the point, and if the Home Office will not respond directly, in some cases it may be appropriate to ask for a direction for 'further particulars' of the Home Office position.

If the Home Office has made factual assertions about certain matters – for example country conditions – that appear to be unsupportable, it may be worth asking for the specific evidence relied upon. Care should be taken: if there is no good material, or if it is out of date or not produced, this will expose a weakness in the Home Office case. However, it is possible that asking for such disclosure may prompt the Home Office to strengthen its case.

Summoning witnesses

The AIT may be asked to issue a witness summons to require any person who is in the UK to attend the appeal as a witness, and to produce any documents that are under their control and that relate to a matter in the appeal (Rule 50). This is another way of obtaining disclosure of specific documents. A summons might be requested in relation to a Home Office official to require them to attend a hearing *and* produce documents that are critical to the appeal, and that the respondent clearly has but has not produced. Persons who can give critical oral evidence in an appeal may also be made the subject of a summons. Note that the AIT cannot require that a party or witness give evidence or produce evidence that they could not be required to give or produce in an ordinary civil claim.

Witness summonses are, however, rarely made, and appellants should always consider whether, tactically, it is best to ask for further evidence or particulars when they do not know exactly what may be produced. If a witness summons is issued at the request of a party, they must be prepared to pay the expenses of the witness in attending the appeal.

Exclusion of the public from the hearing

Appeal hearings are open to the public unless the AIT directs otherwise (Rule 54). The public generally, or particular members of the public, can be excluded from a hearing (or part of a hearing) if the AIT agrees that this is necessary for any of the following reasons:

- in the interests of 'public order or national security';
- to protect an appellant's private life;

10

- to protect the interests of a minor.

Sometimes, in cases of minors or victims of particularly serious abuse such as rape, where the appellant would find it difficult or distressing to have to give evidence in public, advisers ask for private hearings. Similarly, if the issues in the appeal affect very sensitive areas of the person's private life, the public can be excluded. This has happened, for instance, in some cases involving HIV/AIDS infection.

The AIT may also exclude the public:

'…in exceptional circumstances…to ensure that publicity does not prejudice the interests of justice, but only if and to the extent that it is strictly necessary to do so.' (Rule 54(4))

This may be the case if, for example, an appellant would not wish to pursue an appeal, or would not be able to be as open in the evidence they gave if it was likely to be given publicity. In certain asylum and human rights cases, it may also be that publicity is likely, and that it may increase the risk to the appellant in their country of origin.

If the AIT is being asked to determine whether a document is a forgery, the public will be excluded (and appellants and their representatives may be excluded) while the forgery allegation is being investigated. This is in order to prevent the methods of forgery detection becoming public (see s108 2002 Act).

Anonymity

The anonymity of parties or witnesses is often maintained by identifying them only by initials or other letters in the determination. However, the AIT may issue directions generally to 'secure the anonymity' of parties and witnesses. Therefore other means could possibly also be used to secure anonymity as well (see Rule 45(4)(i)).

Constitution of AIT

In particularly complex or detailed cases, it may be appropriate for more than one member and/or senior members of the AIT to hear the appeal. The AIT is not required to consider any representations by the parties about the constitution of the AIT in any appeal. This does not prevent appellants making representations if they wish to do so (Rule 44).

Note

References to 'Rules' in this table are to the Asylum and Immigration Tribunal (Procedure) Rules 2005.

ADJOURNMENTS

Getting an adjournment of a hearing is always difficult. Immigration judges are under pressure not to adjourn, and the Procedure Rules tightly control the circumstances in which they can be granted (Procedure Rules, Rules 21, 47; Practice Directions, para. 9). In particular:

- the AIT must not adjourn unless the appeal cannot be determined 'justly' without an adjournment;

- the AIT should not adjourn for further evidence to be produced *unless* the evidence relates to a matter in dispute in the appeal *and* it would be unjust to determine the appeal without giving a further opportunity to produce the evidence. Where the party has failed to comply with directions for the production of the evidence, they must have provided a satisfactory explanation for the failure.

Procedures on adjournment applications

The party applying for an adjournment should notify the other side as soon as possible of the application, show 'good reason' why an adjournment is necessary, and produce evidence of any fact relied on in support of the application (Procedure Rules, Rule 21(1)). So, if, for example, the reason is a vital medical or other important appointment that cannot be changed, evidence of this should be produced. Similarly, if the appellant is waiting for vital evidence, evidence should be produced of the attempts that have been made so far to get it, and of when the evidence will be available.

The Practice Directions set out further procedures about adjournments (para. 9). They originally stated that applications should be made not later than 4pm, one clear working day before the date of the hearing. This was an error, the President has clarified that this should read '12 noon' (AIT Stakeholder Group, 22 April 2005). This means that if a case is listed for hearing on Friday, the written application for an adjournment must be made by 12 noon on Wednesday. The application and supporting documents should be copied to the Home Office presenting officer. It is a good idea to get the presenting officer to support the application. If they agree to support it, there is more chance that it will be granted.

If it is not possible to make the application within this time, it is almost certain that the appellant and their representative will have to attend the hearing to make the application to adjourn. Of course, if the application to adjourn is refused in writing before the hearing, there is no reason why the application cannot be made again orally, perhaps with more evidence, on the day of the hearing. It should never be assumed that an appeal will be adjourned. Until the point when an appeal is adjourned, appellants and their representatives must continue to prepare as though the hearing will proceed. If an adjournment is not granted and a party fails to attend the hearing, the AIT will proceed with the hearing if it is satisfied that valid notice of the hearing has been given and that there has been no satisfactory explanation for absence on the day of the hearing (▶see below at 1102–4).

10

Re-fixing the hearing

If an appeal is adjourned, the AIT will fix a new hearing date, which is to be no more than 28 days after the original hearing date unless there are exceptional circumstances that justify a longer adjournment. In all cases, the adjournment should be for no longer than is 'strictly required by the circumstances necessitating the adjournment' (Procedure Rules, Rule 21(4)).

DETERMINING APPEALS IN THE ABSENCE OF A PARTY, WITHOUT A HEARING OR WITHOUT DECIDING THE SUBSTANCE

Generally, all appeals are to be considered at oral hearings with both parties in attendance. Some time after the oral hearing, and after reviewing all the evidence, the immigration judge will issue a determination containing their findings and stating whether the appeal is allowed or dismissed. There are exceptions to this basic procedure, as follows:

1) the fact that a party does not attend at the hearing does not alone mean that the appeal hearing will not go ahead. The AIT may proceed to hear an appeal in the absence of a party;

2) there are some circumstances in which appeals may be determined on the papers without a full hearing;

3) in some cases, appeals do not proceed to a determination of the appeal on its merits, but are disposed of without a decision to allow or dismiss the appeal.

We discuss each of these three situations in turn below.

1) Appeals where a party does not attend the hearing

Where there is a hearing, appellants will very severely lessen their chances of winning if they do not attend. The appeal may well go ahead without them (see Procedure Rules, Rule 19).

If an appellant does not attend at an oral hearing, the AIT *must* hear the appeal in the absence of the appellant or their representative if the AIT is satisfied *both* that the appellant or their representative:

- has been given notice of the date, time and place of the hearing (▶see 1090–1 for details about notifying the AIT of representatives, addresses etc); *and*

- has no satisfactory explanation for their absence.

Even if the AIT is not required to proceed in the absence of an appellant for the above reasons, the AIT *may* still proceed in the absence of an appellant in *any* of the following situations:

- the appellant's representative is present at the hearing;

- the appellant is outside the UK;

- the appellant is suffering from a communicable disease or there is a risk of them behaving in a violent or disorderly manner;

- the appellant is unable to attend the hearing because of illness, accident or for some other good reason;

- the appellant is unrepresented and it is impracticable to give them notice of the hearing;
- the appellant has notified the AIT that they do not wish to attend the hearing.

If an appellant is not going to make it to the hearing, it is usually essential that there is an application for an adjournment. Preferably this should be made before the day of the hearing (see above). Adjournments are *not* easy to obtain.

Where the respondent does not attend an appeal hearing

The above rules apply to the immigration authorities as a party to the appeal, just as they apply to appellants. In some cases the Home Office fails to send a representative to the hearing and, rather than asking for an adjournment, is happy for the appeal to go ahead in its absence. In *MNM*, the IAT gave guidelines on the approach adjudicators should take in these cases. The same points can now be applied to the AIT as follows.

- The immigration judge is not to treat the decision as withdrawn or automatically to allow the appeal just because the Home Office does not attend.
- The judge should take care to read all the evidence in the papers before the hearing, even if this means adjourning for a short time.
- Where the appellant's credibility is raised in the refusal letter, the judge should ask the appellant's representative to deal with those issues in the evidence they take from the appellant or in submissions.
- Where there are matters that are of concern to the judge relating to credibility or other issues that have not been raised by the Home Office in the refusal letter, the judge should ask the representative to deal with those matters in the evidence called or in submissions.
- The judge should not take over the role of the Home Office in the appeal by acting as the appellant's opponent, or by conducting a detailed investigation into the appellant's circumstances beyond the evidence which has been put before them.
- Where the judge wishes to refer to country material that is in the public domain – such as US State Department reports, Amnesty International reports or Home Office country reports – they should state this to the representative and ask for their comments.
- A judge should only adjourn an appeal in these cases in exceptional circumstances, where they feel that the issues cannot be properly dealt with in the absence of the Home Office.

2) Determining an appeal without a hearing

The immigration judge may proceed to determine an appeal without holding an oral hearing in the following circumstances (Procedure Rules, Rule 15(2)(3)):

- all the parties to the appeal agree that the appeal should be decided in this way;
- the appellant is unrepresented, and it is either not practical to give them notice of hearing, or they are outside the UK;
- a party has failed to comply with a provision of the Rules or a direction of the AIT (this power can only be exercised if the AIT is satisfied that 'in all the circumstances, including the extent of the failure and any reasons for it, it is appropriate to determine the appeal without a hearing');
- the AIT is satisfied, on the basis of the information it has, that the appeal can be justly determined without a hearing – the AIT can only do this after it has first given the parties a chance to make written representations about whether there should be a hearing.

In the above cases, as with cases where the hearing goes ahead in the absence of the parties, the judge will consider the relevant material before it and make a decision on the appeal. The parties may apply for a review of the determination under section 103A of the 2002 Act in the ordinary way.

3) Where the AIT makes no decision on the substance of the appeal

In the following cases, there is no oral hearing of the appeal *and* the AIT does not need to make a decision on the substance of the appeal (Procedure Rules, Rules 15(1), 16, 17, 18).

- the appeal 'lapses' under section 99 of the 2002 Act; (this occurs if, while an appeal is pending, the Home Office issues a certificate to the effect that the decision was made on national security or similar grounds – in which case there may be an appeal to SIAC, ▶see 1081–3; see also Rule 16 – note that the Home Office can no longer issue a certificate under section 96 of the 2002 Act to prevent an appeal after notice of appeal has been given (see s96(7) 2002 Act). The purpose of section 96 is to prevent a right of appeal on the basis that the appellant had an earlier right of appeal or should have raised a matter at an earlier stage (▶see 1067–9));
- the appeal before the AIT is treated as abandoned because the appellant is either granted leave to enter or remain in the UK, or leaves the UK (this does not apply to asylum 'upgrade' appeals);
- certain appeals may be treated as finally determined because a deportation order has been made against the appellant;
- the appeal is withdrawn by the appellant – an appeal may be withdrawn orally at a hearing, or at any time by written notice;
- the appeal is treated as withdrawn because the respondent notifies the AIT that the decision appealed against has been withdrawn.

In the above cases, the AIT will simply issue a notice that the appeal has lapsed, has been treated as abandoned, finally determined or withdrawn. It *appears* that such notices are not 'decisions on the appeal' (see s103A 2002 Act), but are preliminary or ancillary decisions for which the only means of challenge is by judicial review. However, this is a point which is likely to need clarification by case-law.

PREPARING FOR THE FULL HEARING

Most appeals are won or lost at the preparation stage. Preparation should be careful and comprehensive. By the time of the hearing, not only should all the documentation have been served in accordance with the directions, but the appellant's representative needs to have a thorough knowledge of the case and the evidence. Hearings dash by, and it is easy to miss points. Representatives need to be able to point the immigration judge quickly to evidence dealing with particular points that may arise during the hearing. They should be able to answer all the points raised in the letter of refusal, and anticipate additional points that may arise at the hearing and the questions that they may be asked by the immigration judge.

Evidence generally

The kind of evidence required for an appeal depends on the nature of the case, and is similar to the evidence referred to throughout the *Handbook* for the various different categories of applicant. For evidence that is often produced in asylum applications – specific documents, expert evidence, country evidence, witnesses, and so on, ▶see 665–7, 706–8 and ▶see also below at 1106–10. If the evidence was not produced for the application, it can still be produced at the hearing.

Obviously, on appeal, appellants will focus on producing evidence to deal with the particular grounds of refusal. For example, in a marriage case in which the 'intention to live together' requirement of the rules is disputed, and in which the appellant has, since the refusal, amassed a great deal of correspondence showing the continued affection between the couple, this will be important evidence of their commitment and intentions. If the Home Office disputes an applicant's account of torture in the reasons for refusal letter, medical evidence of scarring will be relevant. Some of the most respected medical reports are provided by the Medical Foundation for the Care of Victims of Torture (▶see 1504 for address).

The question of whether evidence of events that have occurred after the date of decision is relevant on appeal, is not always a straightforward one (▶see 1119–1121).

No strict rules of evidence

There are no strict rules of evidence in appeals before the AIT. Any relevant oral or documentary evidence can be produced, even if it is 'hearsay', and would not be admitted as evidence in an ordinary court of law (Procedure Rules, Rule 51(1)). 'Hearsay' evidence is indirect evidence – evidence from people who have not directly witnessed the events which they are referring to. While evidence that is not ideal because it is indirect, vague or incomplete can be taken into account, its indirect nature will affect the *weight* the AIT will give to it in making their assessment.

The AIT must be particularly flexible in its consideration of imperfect evidence in asylum and human rights cases, where the consequences of getting the decision wrong are severe, and it is notoriously difficult to produce clear, corroborating evidence. If objections are raised, it is worth reminding the AIT of comments made about evidence by the Court of Appeal in *Karanakaran v SSHD*. In that case, the Court stressed that the statutory appeal authorities are not restricted by the rules of evidence that apply in civil litigation, and that they must take into account all material considerations when making their assessment about the future. In particular, Sedley LJ directly referred to the role of the appeal authorities as being an extension of the decision-making process that required them to 'take everything material into account'. He continued:

'Their sources of information will frequently go well beyond the testimony of the applicant and include in-country reports, expert testimony and – sometimes – specialised knowledge of their own... No probabilistic cut-off operates here: everything capable of having a bearing has to be given the weight, great or little, due to it. What the decision-makers ultimately make of the material is a matter for their own conscientious judgment, so long as the procedure by which they approach and entertain it is lawful and fair...' (para. 18)

Translations and originals

Documentary evidence should be in English, or it should be accompanied by a certified translation. In appeals held in Wales, documents may be filed in Welsh (Procedure Rules, Rule 52). But it is always worth taking the original of any documentary evidence to the appeal hearing. Copies are sometimes unclear, and the original may often give more 'life' to the case. The AIT may also require that the original be produced (Procedure Rules, Rule 51(5)).

Witnesses and witness statements

In most appeals, the evidence given by the appellant is of critical importance. Often it is the only direct evidence of the facts in dispute, and the credibility of the appellant is central. It is not so important, however, in cases where the issue depends largely on documentary evidence. For example, the ability to maintain and accommodate without recourse to public funds can usually be dealt with by evidence such as bank statements, letters from employers, or pay-slips.

Although, in most cases, much of the preparation for the appeal will involve preparing the statements of the appellant and any witnesses, the appellant's side should not automatically think they have to call oral evidence. If, for example, the essential facts upon which the claim or application is based are accepted by the immigration authorities but the application has been refused for legal reasons, there may be no point in calling witnesses. The points in dispute can be clarified at CMRs. In addition, in asylum and human rights cases, the appellant is occasionally so traumatised that they are not able to give a proper account of themselves. In these cases, it is important to obtain clear and detailed medical evidence from an appropriate expert to demonstrate this.

The witness statement, particularly in the case of the appellant, will generally need to be more detailed than any interview notes that have been produced by the Home Office, and will need to address points made about the appellant's credibility in the reasons for refusal letter. Witness statements, if well prepared, are very helpful to appellants. They enable them to present instantly to the AIT a comprehensive account of what is often a complex set of events, which might otherwise be difficult for them to recount step-by-step.

Other witnesses in an asylum appeal may be family members, friends of the asylum-seeker who may be aware of what the appellant has experienced in the past, political party colleagues, or experts on the country in question. In family cases, the sponsor or relative being joined or visited is usually called to give evidence.

Witnesses can be useful in backing up the evidence of the appellant, but care must be taken. For example, in asylum cases in particular, witnesses can be asked about matters spanning a great number of years, and there is a good deal of scope for witnesses to contradict each other. Inconsistencies arise, not necessarily because witnesses are not telling the truth, but because memories fade and perceptions differ. Even so, presenting officers and immigration judges may take this to show that the witness, or the appellant, or both, are not being truthful.

The appellant and their witnesses should be well prepared. Before the hearing, they should be thoroughly familiar with their own witness statements, and can also read each others' statements as well as the other important papers in the case. They should also have explained to them what the issues in the case are, as this will help them to understand the purpose of the questions they are asked in the hearing, and to give more effective evidence. Often, appellants and witnesses are bewildered when they give evidence, because they do not really understand why certain questions are being asked or where the questions are leading.

The appellant should meet with the person who is going to represent them before the hearing in order to discuss the case and to enable the representative to explain the procedure at the hearing. Some appellants even like to visit a hearing centre before their own hearing, and observe some other hearings so that they know what to expect, and will be less nervous on the day.

Country and expert evidence

An important part of the evidence in many asylum and human rights cases relates to the conditions in the appellant's country of origin. The Home

10

Office Country Information and Policy Unit (CIPU) prepares country reports as background information for use in asylum appeals involving those countries that produce the most asylum seekers. Often, despite the directions, the Home Office does not actually produce its assessment until the day of the hearing. It is therefore important that the appellant or their representative is aware of the contents of the report beforehand. Country reports are available on the Home Office website. For further details about CIPU country reports and other country evidence that may be produced by the Home Office, ▶see 706–8.

CIPU reports have been criticised for painting a rosy picture of the countries of feared persecution, of quoting selectively from their primary sources, and of concentrating on the past history or political constitution of the country to the exclusion of the most common issues arising in asylum appeals. The Immigration Advisory Service (IAS) website carries detailed reports evaluating CIPU assessments. Where the Home Office is likely to rely on particular passages from a CIPU or similar report, it is worth checking the primary source to see what it actually says about the situation. Sometimes the sources are out of date, or they have been incompletely summarised in the CIPU report.

It is obviously important that advisers obtain information from independent sources about country conditions. Sources of material to which appellants can turn are set out in the table below (▶see further 665–7). Note that appellants cannot assume that the AIT will have regard to any background reports, or will take 'judicial notice' of (in other words, have regard to what is commonly known about) country conditions. The country reports relied on will have to be produced (Practice Directions, para. 8.6).

Expert evidence

Appellants may also use expert evidence in support of their cases. Usually the expert does not come to the hearing, but will provide a written report. However, if the expert is prepared to give oral evidence, that is all the better. The expert should be provided with at least the appellant's statement and the reasons for refusal. Their reports must be prepared from an independent perspective: experts are not there to act as 'cheerleaders' for appellants, but to give a truly professional assessment that helps the immigration judge come to their decision.

Experts can often give an explanation of why, given a certain set of facts, a person is at risk in a particular country. Where credibility is challenged, experts can also sometimes help by painting the background to a person's claim, which can then be used to explain why what they are saying is plausible in the light of the conditions in that country. What they should not do is give a direct view on whether or not they consider the appellant to be a truthful witness, because that is for the immigration judge to decide.

COUNTRY MATERIAL

It is often useful to refer to the country material at the time of the application, so that it can be taken into account by the Home Office in its decision. The Legal Services Commission rules require firms with immigration contracts to keep country information for the main nationalities they represent. A lot of up-to-date information can now be downloaded from the internet.

The following sources can be investigated:

- **Amnesty International** has detailed information about most countries of the world, and its researchers may be able to provide references or information to support what the asylum-seeker has said. It publishes a yearly review, with brief details about each country and many detailed briefings and bulletins that are invaluable.

- The **United States State Department** country human rights reports are published on the internet annually. These are very detailed, and great weight is attached to them by the Home Office and the AIT. Much of the detail in the Home Office country assessments is taken from them. However, they may reflect US political bias towards some countries.

- The **Minority Rights Group** publishes in-depth studies of particular groups, which are very helpful.

- The **Refugee Legal Centre** has considerable up-to-date country information, but most of it is only available to other organisations or individuals if they subscribe through the RLC's external information service.

- **Human Rights Watch** produces reports on the human rights situation in particular countries – mainly in Africa, Asia and the Middle East.

- The **Immigration Law Practitioners' Association** has published a directory that identifies academic and other experts on different countries who may be able to provide background and corroborative evidence. Expert evidence is particularly useful in cases where the particular circumstances described by the appellant are not covered in the other general country reports.

- The **United Nations High Commissioner for Refugees** may offer support in particular cases, or its views on the situation in particular countries. It produces a regularly updated CD-ROM of collated material relevant to asylum claims, called Refworld.

- **HJT Country database** (previously the ICCID) offers up-to-date country material covering over 90 countries. It is available through the EIN website on a subscription basis.

10

Preparing trial bundles

The AIT has give detailed guidance about how to prepare trial bundles (Practice Direction, para. 8). Appellants should read that guidance carefully. The most important points are:

- bundles should be paginated;

- all documents in the bundle should be relevant to the issues in the appeal, legible, and presented in a logical order;
- where the document is not in English, a certified translation should be produced;
- where a long document is produced, the important parts should be highlighted or drawn attention to in the index or skeleton argument by page cross-reference;
- there should be a comprehensive index showing the page(s) at which each document appears in the bundle.

USING CASE-LAW

Where a party wishes to rely upon a particular decided case or other legal authority, copies should be produced (Practice Directions, para. 8.2(f)). With decisions of the higher courts, producing case-law is straightforward. However, where a party wants to rely on a decision of the AIT itself (or the previous IAT), the process is more complicated, and the AIT has given specific guidance, outlined below (see Practice Directions, paras 17–18).

How are determinations of the AIT and IAT classified?

Generally, a determination of the single immigration judge of the AIT hearing an appeal at first instance will not be given any 'neutral citation number' (►see below), and nor are they published. They are simply sent to the parties.

Where an appeal is heard by a senior immigration judge (sitting alone or with one or more others), or where it is heard by the President or Deputy President of the AIT, the determination will either be 'reported' or 'unreported'. 'Reported' decisions are anonymised and given a neutral citation number (in the format, '[2005] UKAIT 000'). They are generally available, and can be found on the AIT and EIN websites (the case-law database can only be accessed by members and so it is necessary to subscribe). Decisions can also be accessed through the 'bailii' website (www.bailii.org). 'Unreported' decisions are not so widely available, although a copy of such decisions will be lodged in the Supreme Court Library, which is in the Royal Courts of Justice on the Strand, in London.

Which AIT and IAT decisions are authoritative?

Certain reported determinations of the AIT and IAT are 'starred'. This means that they are treated as binding in relation to the particular matter(s) they are starred for.

Certain reported decisions of the AIT or IAT are 'country guidance' determinations. They are easily identifiable, as they have the letters 'CG' in their title. These decisions are to be followed in relation to the country guidance issue dealt with in the determination, unless and until they are superseded by a later such decision. However, as we explain below, CG cases have their limitations. A list of CG cases in relation to the different countries is maintained on the AIT website.

Neither a starred nor a country guidance determination will be followed if it is inconsistent with another higher authority that is binding on the AIT.

Which AIT and IAT decisions can be relied on before the AIT?

Reported decisions (including starred determinations and CG cases) can be relied on before the AIT. Unreported decisions of the AIT or the IAT, determinations following first-instance hearings before a single immigration judge, and determinations of adjudicators, may not be cited *unless* either:

- they are determinations concerning the same appellant in a previous appeal, or a member of the appellant's family; or
- the AIT gives permission.

The Practice Directions state that permission will only be given 'exceptionally' and that an application for permission to cite such a determination must do each of the following:

- include a full transcript of the decision;
- state the point for which the determination is to be cited;
- certify that the point is not dealt with in any reported determination of the AIT, IAT or higher authority;
- include a summary of all decisions of the AIT and higher authority that relate to the same point, and were promulgated during the period beginning six months before the unreported decision that the party wants to cite (and ending two weeks before the date of hearing).

If a party wants to cite a determination of the IAT that has a neutral citation number before [2003], they must be able to state that the point being relied on has not been dealt with in more recent, reported determinations of the AIT or IAT.

Country guidance cases

Country guidance (CG) cases are different to starred decisions. Starred decisions are binding on points of law. Country guidance cases give authoritative guidance on particular country conditions – the objective of which is to prevent the AIT coming to different conclusions about the risk to applicants of a similar profile from the same country.

The list of CG cases on the AIT website gives the countries in alphabetical order, and indicates what country guidance cases there are and what issues they cover. The list is updated regularly. Representatives are expected to know and to be able to deal with current CG determinations. So, for example, if the case is about whether female draft evaders are at risk of harm on return to Eritrea, it will be important to check the website for any CG determinations on that issue. There are at present a number of

CG determinations on that question. Representatives can rely on CG cases without having to serve all of the evidence referred to in them.

If a CG case is negative to the appellant's case, then it is likely that this will be stressed by the Home Office. In such cases, appellants should consider whether:

- there is any country evidence dating from after the CG case, and showing that the situation has changed in the appellant's favour;
- there is any relevant evidence – available at the time but not put before the AIT – which decided the CG case and which would alter the position;
- the facts of the appellant's case are, in truth, completely covered by the CG case, or whether there are features of their case which mean that the risk to them is different to that considered by the CG case; or
- on close consideration, the CG case does not deal adequately with the relevant country evidence or material which was before the AIT.

It may be worth sending negative CG cases to a country expert to comment on. If none of the above can be done or shown, it will be very difficult to win the case. The AIT will have to have a valid reason for not following a CG case. The Practice Directions (para. 18.4) state:

'Because of the principle that like cases should be treated in like manner, any failure to follow a clear, apparently applicable country guidance case or to show why it does not apply to the case in question is likely to be regarded as grounds for review or appeal on a point of law.'

Where a representative is given notice that their case is likely to be heard as a CG case, representatives must bear in mind that the outcome will be important not just for the appellant, but for many other cases as well. In such cases it will be even more important for the country material submitted to be comprehensive.

CONDUCTING THE FULL HEARING BEFORE THE IMMIGRATION JUDGE

Immigration and asylum appeals are supposed to be informal, but many of those attending will find them a formal and even intimidating experience. The immigration judge controls the conduct of the proceedings, and usually sits at a slightly raised desk. Normally at first instance hearings, there is only one judge. However, it is possible to have a 'panel' of two or three members of the AIT sitting to hear the case. This may happen if the case is particularly complex. Even in a non-complex case, a 'designated immigration judge' or a 'senior immigration judge' may sit with an immigration judge in order to provide support and advice (see the description of the roles of the different judges at ▶1049–50). The appellant's representative normally sits at one side of the room, and the Home Office presenting officer, representing the official who made the decision, sits at the other. The appellant (and witnesses in their turn) usually sit in the middle, directly opposite the immigration judge. If there is an interpreter, they will usually sit next to the appellant or witness. The practice of most immigration judges is to ask witnesses to wait outside until it is their turn to give evidence. After they have given evidence, they can remain to watch the rest of the hearing.

Appeals are usually listed to start at 10am, and the appellants and representatives for every case on the list should be at the hearing room ready to begin at that time. Although there will be an order in which the cases are listed, immigration judges will not always begin with the first case and finish with the last; it is up to the judge what order to take the cases in. Often the judge will run through the list to check who has arrived and who is ready to start, and to deal with any initial problems or applications for adjournments.

Dealing with the presenting officer and Home Office conceding appeals

It is always a good idea to speak to the Home Office presenting officer before the hearing in order to check that each side has received all the evidence that has been put in by the other. Sometimes, if it has not already been done in a CMR hearing, it is possible to narrow the issues in the appeal so that both sides know what they have got to deal with. In some cases there is the possibility of negotiation – it may be that the presenting officer is prepared to concede certain issues – for example, that a person has been truthful about their history of detention and torture.

In a letter to South Manchester Law Centre dated 22 April 2005, the Appeals Directorate of IND set out the circumstances in which it *may* be appropriate for a presenting officer to concede an appeal. In every case, presenting officers will have to obtain approval from a senior caseworker or team manager. The circumstances in which appeals may be conceded are:

- where there has been a change in the law since the decision which fundamentally affects the appeal in the appellant's favour, or it is clear that the decision-maker did not consider the law correctly and correct application of the law would 'have led to a grant';
- where the Country and Information Policy Unit has advised that there have been significant developments in a particular country which mean that a particular applicant would be persecuted for a Convention reason if returned;
- where further credible evidence is produced before or at the hearing which shows that the applicant clearly meets the requirement of the rules (at the date of the decision in a non-asylum appeal);
- where at the time of the decision there was further and compelling evidence from the appellant's side in an entry clearance appeal.

Preliminary matters

At the outset of the hearing it is a good idea to ensure that the immigration judge has all the material that has been filed. Documents sometimes go missing at the AIT, and it is important that the judge has an appreciation of the important documents before the hearing starts. Any preliminary issues that have not already been dealt with – for example, as to whether the AIT has the power to hear the appeal – will be dealt with first.

Dealing with a failure to comply with directions

If, at the hearing, it is clear that either party has failed to comply with the directions setting the time-limits for filing evidence, then the consequences can be severe. The AIT (Procedure Rules, Rule 51(4)):

'...must not consider any written evidence which is not filed or served in accordance with those directions unless satisfied that there are good reasons to do so.'

If this is the position, appellants or their representatives at the hearing should be ready to explain all failures and delays fully, and to address the extent to which the Home Office has been prejudiced (often the presenting officer will only have picked up the file very late in the day, and there will be little or no prejudice). If there is any evidence being produced on the day, it should be handed up at the beginning of the hearing, not during or after it. Again, the judge will expect an explanation as to why it was not sent in accordance with directions.

Evidence given by the appellant and witnesses

Both sides have the right to call witnesses, although it is almost always only the appellant's side that does so. The immigration judge *may* require oral evidence to be given on oath or affirmation (Procedure Rules, Rule 51(3)). This practice is unusual nowadays, although a witness can ask to give sworn evidence if they wish. The appellant and any other witnesses need to be confident about what they are saying, and to have organised their thoughts in advance. In asylum appeals in particular, the 'credibility' of the appellant's account of past events is of central importance. When an interpreter is used, it is important that the witness and interpreter first confirm that they understand one another. Sometimes appellants have their own interpreters sitting in the hearing room who are able to pass a note to the representative if they feel that important matters are being misinterpreted.

The sequence in which evidence is taken from the appellant and any witnesses is as follows.

Evidence-in-chief

In most cases, a witness statement will have been prepared in advance and, under the standard directions, the witness statement 'stands' as evidence-in-chief: that is, as the evidence that the appellant's representative wishes to call from that witness. At the outset of their evidence, appellants and witnesses should 'adopt' their witness statement and confirm that its contents are correct. However, most judges are sympathetic to allowing a representative to ask some supplementary questions of the appellant and other witnesses. The Practice Directions state (para. 6.7):

'Although in normal circumstances a witness statement should stand as evidence-in-chief, there may be cases where it will be appropriate for appellants or witnesses to have the opportunity of adding to or supplementing their witness statements.'

The Practice Directions refer parties to the guidance given by the Court of Appeal in *R v SSHD ex parte Singh* on this point. In *Singh*, although the Court of Appeal upheld the Adjudicator's direction which stated that the appellant's statements were to stand as evidence-in-chief at hearing, the Court indicated that, where appropriate, it may be necessary to allow some oral elaboration to be given in-chief where the interests of justice require. Sir Patrick Russell stated:

'That does not mean that at the hearing the applicant or his representative should not have the opportunity of adding to the witness statement anything that is necessarily supplementary to it. It may well be – indeed the papers in this case demonstrate it to be the case – that in the future conduct of this particular inquiry the adjudicator will permit some supplementary answers to be given in order to bring to life the witness statement which as a whole should stand as the evidence-in-chief. Everything depends upon the way in which the adjudicator exercises his discretion to conduct the inquiry before him.'

It can be unnerving for an appellant to begin their evidence by being questioned by the Home Office representative, and supplementary questions from their own representative may steady appellants at the outset. Provided that the witness statement is reasonably detailed and full, representatives will usually focus on anything that needs to be clarified from the witness statement, and any changes of circumstance that have occurred since the witness statement was made. This may include commenting on documents produced by either side since the statement was prepared.

Cross-examination

The purpose of cross-examination is to test the truth of what the appellant is saying on the important issues. Often, however, it takes the form of questioning about matters not directly concerned with the important issues in the appeal. Asylum appellants are often questioned about their route to the UK and the circumstances in which they claimed asylum. Section 8 of the 2004 Act now requires a deciding authority to take into account such matters in assessing credibility (for details about section 8 ►see 708–14).

Cross-examination of the appellant, in particular, is likely to be the most time-consuming part of the appeal. Judges tend to give presenting officers some leeway and to allow them to ask about matters not directly raised in the refusal letter. However, cross-examination is not intended to give the Home Office an opportunity to conduct a 'fishing expedition' into the appellant's background, covering all sorts of issues not raised in the appeal so far, in the hope that something damaging to the appellant's case will be revealed. Nor is cross-examination an opportunity for the Home Office to ask the appellant to recount all of their evidence again, as in an interview, in the hope that they make some mistake that produces an inconsistency relevant to credibility. If the presenting officer begins to ask questions of this nature, then it is open to appellant's representative to object. They can also object to questions which are so vague or complex that the witness (especially through an interpreter) cannot understand them. They may also object to questions that the witness cannot be expected to know the answer to. For example, witnesses are often asked to explain why the authorities in their country of origin have behaved in a particular way, or to explain the motivations of other people which, in most contexts, they cannot know.

Questions from the immigration judge

The judge can intervene to ask questions at any time. Usually the judge will ask some questions to clear up various issues of particular concern to them after the presenting officer has finished asking questions. The judge is not supposed to 'enter the ring' and cross-examine the witness.

Re-examination

Following the questions of the presenting officer and the judge, the appellant's representative is invited to ask any further questions in 're-examination' of the appellant. The purpose of this is to clarify matters arising out of the questions that have been asked in cross-examination, or by the judge. It is *not* an opportunity to raise new issues, but a chance for the appellant's representative to repair any damage that has been caused by cross-examination, if they think that the witness has more to say about some of the matters they have been asked about.

Other witnesses

The same process as described above is used for all of the witnesses called. Normally the appellant gives their evidence first, which is then followed by their other witnesses, but there are no hard-and-fast rules. The appellant and their representative can choose the order in which to call their evidence.

Submissions

After all the witnesses have given their evidence, first the presenting officer and then the appellant's representative have the chance to make oral submissions to the judge. The 'submissions' consist of a speech to the immigration judge summing up the appellant's and the respondent's case, and trying to persuade the immigration judge to allow or dismiss the appeal.

The appellant's representative should have prepared a detailed chronology and skeleton argument in accordance with the directions. When it comes to submissions, this document should be of great help, because it sets out the groundwork for the appellant's case. If the judge has read it, they will know in advance the main points the appellant wants to make.

It is always useful for representatives to have planned at least the basic structure of their submissions beforehand. In cases where the appellant's submissions have been set out fully in the skeleton argument and no real new issues have arisen, the oral submissions will be shortened. The structure of submissions for any case depends on the style the representative has developed and on the particular issues in the case. Representatives must be prepared to accommodate any new issues that have arisen in the appeal, and to deal with the way the oral evidence has come out. If the evidence has been somewhat different to what was expected, the representative must be prepared to think quickly and to modify their submissions to meet the circumstances.

Checklist for submissions

The following is a suggested list of the matters that should be covered.

- Set out what the appeal(s) or grounds for appealing are, and identify the essential immigration rules or legislation with which the appeal is concerned.
- Identify the other basic issues between the parties in the appeal.
- Set out any legal issues in the appeal, including submissions about the Home Office's approach to the law.
- Set out the essential facts that the adjudicator is being asked by the appellant to find.
- Remind the immigration judge of the evidence supporting the facts, namely:
  - the appellant's evidence;
  - the particular evidence that supports the appellant – for example, from other witnesses or from specific documents.
- Deal with any matters relied on by the Home Office for doubting the appellant's or other witnesses' credibility both those raised in the refusal letter and any further matters raised on the day.
- For asylum and human rights cases, if the basic facts are accepted, explain what the risk is to the person if they are returned to their country of origin.
- Deal with any country guidance determinations (both for and against).
- Present any background country material in support of the case and identify the parts that are most essential for the judge to consider. These may well already have been highlighted in the schedule prepared in

10

accordance with the standard appeal directions (see above).

- Ask for the appeal to be allowed with any appropriate directions (►see 1126–7).

During submissions the judge may ask questions on certain aspects of the evidence, or may indicate their thinking on particular issues, and ask to be addressed on others.

Keeping a record of proceedings

The judge is required to keep a proper record of proceedings of any hearing (Practice Directions, para. 11). Sometimes, where there is a dispute about what happened at the hearing and the matter is not clear from the determination itself, appellants will need to ask later on for the record of proceedings to be produced.

After the hearing and appeal determinations

In most cases the judge will 'reserve' their decision. This means that they do not give their decision on the appeal at the end of the hearing. Instead, the judge will normally take the papers away with them, together with their record of proceedings, with a record of the further evidence taken and the submissions made. The judge will then consider their decision and prepare a written determination. Sometimes, in a case where the issues are straightforward, they may state their decision on the appeal on the day, and state that the full reasons for the decision will be set out in the written determination to follow.

If there is evidence that was unavailable at the time of the hearing and the judge was not prepared to adjourn to await it, it may still be worth asking them to allow the applicant to submit the evidence (together with any written submissions on it) after the appeal hearing. If the judge agrees, the immigration authorities will be given an opportunity to respond. If essential and unforeseen evidence or case-law arises after the hearing, but before the decision is promulgated, appellants should consider submitting it to the AIT with a covering letter making any necessary representations. A copy should always be sent to the respondent.

For details about the time allowed for service of the determination and how it is served, ►see 1088–9. Determinations of the AIT are all issued in the same format: they have the same front sheet, each paragraph must be numbered, and the final 'decision' must be set out at the end in standard form (Practice Directions, para. 16 and Annexes A–B). If the decision is negative, appellants will obviously need to consider whether to challenge it. This is dealt with in Chapter 36.

DECIDING APPEALS AND THE POWERS OF THE AIT

The kind of evidence that can be submitted to the AIT and considered by it is discussed above (►1105 onwards). Here we look at the 'jurisdiction' –

the powers – of the AIT when it has to decide an appeal: What date should it be looking at when it assesses the facts? What standard of proof does it apply to different cases? When must it allow/dismiss an appeal? What else can it do when it allows or dismisses an appeal?

What date does the AIT focus on, can it look at 'after-decision' evidence?

Single immigration judges considering first-instance appeals are not restricted to considering whether the Home Office has made some technical legal mistake (lawyers often call these 'errors of law' or 'misdirections of law'). They can consider all of the facts of the case again and assess whether a different decision should be arrived at.

Can evidence that was not before the decision-maker at the time the decision was made be produced before the AIT? The answer is yes. Such evidence can always be considered if it relates to circumstances as at the date of the decision. In many cases (but not all – see below) it will also be relevant to the appeal even if it concerns matters that arise after the date of the decision (see s85(4)(5) of the 2002 Act). However, on this last point, when considered alongside the case-law, the legislation unfortunately does not make the position completely clear.

In considering these issues, cases can be divided into three categories as follows.

1) Asylum and human rights cases concerning removal

Since the decision of the Court of Appeal in **Ravichandran**, it has been possible in asylum appeals to submit evidence to show the position as of the date of the hearing. That case made the common-sense point that it is not sensible to look at what the position was in the country a year previously if circumstances had since changed. Asylum appeals should be concerned with practicalities and the realities of removal at the present time. The 1999 Act made the same provision for Article 3 cases, and case-law has extended this approach to all human rights cases concerning removal (see **S&K**, IAT; **Razgar**, HL).

Even if an asylum application has been refused on grounds of non-compliance, the AIT must consider the merits of the appeal on the basis of whatever evidence is available at the appeal itself (**Haddad**, IAT).

2) Non-asylum and non-human rights immigration cases

The 2002 Act states that the AIT may consider evidence about 'any matter relevant to the substance of the decision', including 'evidence which concerns a matter arising after the date of the decision' (s85(4) 2002 Act). This means that the AIT may consider evidence about new *facts* (i.e. 'matters arising') after the date of the original decision. But this new wording to the legislation (which also formally applies to asylum and human rights cases as in (1) above) does not make it completely clear whether the same approach should be applied to these cases as in asylum and human rights cases. The position before the 2002 Act was always that evidence about events that took place after the decision could be considered, provided that it was relevant to the circumstances as of the date of the decision. The legislation may simply be confirming this position rather than changing it.

This question can be illustrated with the example of a case of the rejection of a spouse application because the decision-maker does not accept that a couple have the intention to live together permanently. If there is 'after-decision' evidence of the couple's continued devotion – living together for a prolonged period between decision and appeal, sharing of finances, or pregnancy – this evidence may 'throw light' on what the true circumstances have been all along. There is a long line of case-law to show that this kind of evidence was always admissible to throw light on the intentions of the couple at the date of the decision. Because the Act continues to refer to the 'substance of the decision', it is possible that it is simply confirming the position as stated in the case-law for these cases. If so, then evidence about major changes of circumstance after the date of the decision may not be considered.

3) Entry clearance/certificate of entitlement cases

Section 85(4) 2002 Act (see above) does not apply in appeals against refusals to grant entry clearance or a certificate of entitlement (see s85(5)). Again, this does not mean that evidence that was not before the ECO cannot be produced at the appeal: it can. What it does mean is that only evidence that relates to the circumstances existing at the date of the decision will be considered. So, if at the time of the decision the ECO did not accept that a tenancy agreement relating to accommodation for the appellant in the UK demonstrated that the accommodation was 'adequate' for the purposes of the rules, evidence later produced about the number and size of the rooms in that same accommodation will be relevant to show that the accommodation that existed at the date of the decision was adequate.

It is clear from the decision of the AIT in *DR (Morocco)* that post-decision evidence going to show the intentions of sponsor and appellant as regards living together as *of the date of the decision* will be admitted:

'There was an issue about whether at the time of the decision, the couple intended to live together as man and wife. In the language of the statute, did the circumstances appertaining to the date of the decision include that intention? Evidence that those were then the circumstances can be provided by subsequent actions which cast light upon what the position then was. This is not the same as evidence which shows that the position has subsequently changed and that there now is an intention which previously was lacking. Evidence about a subsequent change in intention is clearly excluded.' (para. 25)

So, if the appellants tried to rely on evidence of 'intervening devotion' to show that they formed an intention to live together permanently *subsequent* to the decision, this evidence would not be admitted in an entry clearance case. Similarly, the AIT stated that evidence about an event which takes place after the decision, the likelihood of which is disputed at the date of hearing, would also not be admitted in an entry clearance case (para. 27).

What approach to the date of assessment will ultimately be taken to an entry clearance appeal brought on human rights grounds – for example on the basis of Article 8 – remains to be seen.

Burden and standard of proof

The 'burden of proof' describes who must prove the facts. The 'standard of proof' describes the level of certainty to which the facts must be proved for the purposes of the case. So, 'beyond all reasonable doubt', 'balance of probabilities' and 'reasonable degree of likelihood' are examples of different *standards* of proof.

The general approach of the law to the burden of proof is that a person who makes an assertion carries the burden of proving it. Broadly, this approach is followed in immigration appeals (see Procedure Rules, Rule 53).

Asylum cases

In asylum cases, the burden of proof is on the appellant – the person trying to show that they are a refugee in need of protection. However, the *standard* of proof is a very low one. Appellants must show that there is 'a reasonable degree of likelihood' or 'real risk' of persecution. This reflects the wording of the Refugee Convention, which defines a refugee as a person with 'a well-founded fear of being persecuted'. The definition allows applicants to qualify for refugee status even when their fate is far from certain (for further details ▶see 622–3). This was decided by the House of Lords in the case of *Sivakumaran*, which concerned six Tamils who had been refused asylum and returned to Sri Lanka. Evidence of past persecution of the appellant will go a long way to show a risk of persecution in the future (▶see further at 613).

The application of the standard of proof to the assessment of past facts (for example, what has happened to an appellant previously) was developed in the case of *Kaja*. In that case, the IAT, despite the dissent of one of its members, stressed that the lower standard applies to all aspects of the decision-making process. The IAT stated that it was important in any determination to make clear all of the following:

- that the assessment of whether a claim to asylum is well-founded is based on the evidence as a whole (relevant to the past, present and future), and is according to the criterion of 'reasonable degree of likelihood';
- the evidence grounding the decision;

- how the person deciding the appeal has moved from the evidence to the conclusion.

Although the decision of the Court of Appeal in *Karanakaran* was a subtle one, it approved the essential approach in *Kaja* and developed it (▶see 623). This put to rest the attempts of some to argue that a higher standard (balance of probabilities) applied to the assessment of historical facts in asylum cases.

If, on an asylum appeal, it has previously been decided – or the Home Office accepts – that the applicant previously qualified for refugee status, but that circumstances have changed by the time of the hearing, there will be a burden on the Home Office to show that this is the case (for further details about this ▶see 628). This may become more important as the Home Office has implemented a system of active review of refugee cases, with successful refugees being granted only limited leave initially. Of course, where the Home Office revokes an indefinite leave granted to a refugee (▶see 1008), it will carry the burden of justifying the revocation.

Human rights cases

In *Kacaj*, the IAT held that the standard of proof in appeals under Article 3 of the ECHR is the same as that in asylum appeals. This was in spite of efforts by the Home Office to argue that the standard of proof in such cases was a very high one. The IAT concluded, understandably, that it would be strange, given the similarity of the issues arising in asylum and Article 3 cases, if the same evidence had to be considered on the basis of a different standard.

The burden of proof in human rights cases is also normally on the appellant. However, where the appellant shows that there would be an interference with a restricted right, (for example, an interference with the right to respect for family life under Article 8 ECHR), the burden switches to the Home Office to show that the extent of the interference is justified (for the elements of Article 8, ▶see 821–2).

Immigration cases

Usually the burden is on appellants to make their case – for example, that they satisfy the relevant requirements of the immigration rules – and to establish the truth of what they say. But there are cases where the burden rests with the immigration authorities – for example:

- where the Home Office is alleging that documentary evidence is forged (see *Shen*). However, a document is not necessarily to be accepted as reliable evidence just because it is not shown to be a forgery – documents will be considered in the light of the case and evidence as a whole (this applies equally in asylum and human rights cases; ▶see 665);
- where the Home Office is seeking to show grounds for deportation, or is alleging a breach of conditions giving rise to enforcement action;

- where the Home Office has made particular allegations against an appellant that justify their being refused under the general grounds of refusal in the immigration rules (for which, ▶see 98–9, 140–1).

The standard of proof the immigration judge must apply in non-asylum, non-human rights cases is generally the balance of probabilities. This is the standard that applies in most civil cases. It means that the evidence must prove that the facts alleged are more likely to have happened than not – i.e. that there is a more than 50 per cent chance that they did occur. Where the Home Office case involves making serious allegations against an appellant – for example, that they have used deception to gain entry in the past – although this 'civil' standard still applies, the firmness and clarity of the evidence required to show that this is the case is of a much higher order.

Previous appeals concerning the appellant

Where the AIT (or an Adjudicator/IAT) has, in an earlier appeal, made factual findings about the appellant, those findings will be the starting point for the factual findings to be made on the current appeal. Guidelines were laid down by the IAT in *Devaseelan* (see paras 39–42) which were upheld by the Court of Appeal in *Djebbar*. Important points contained in these guidelines (as they now apply to the AIT) are as follows:

- the first determination should be the starting point – it is to be treated as an authoritative assessment at the time it was made;
- events occurring since the earlier determination can be taken into account – if those events lead to a different conclusion on the appeal, then the two determinations are not inconsistent;
- events occurring before the first determination that were not relevant to the issues in the first appeal, but that are relevant to the issues in the second appeal, can be taken into account; the first appeal is not authoritative as to those facts;
- alleged facts which could have been (but were not) brought to light in the first appeal will be treated very cautiously at the second appeal unless those facts are beyond dispute;
- where the facts put forward in the second appeal are essentially the same as those relied on in the first appeal, and the evidence is the same as that *available to the appellant* (even if that evidence was not used – for example, where an appellant did not give oral evidence) in first appeal, the AIT should regard the issues as settled by the earlier appeal – it should make findings in line with those made in the first determination;
- however, if there is some 'very good reason' why the appellant did not put forward the relevant evidence at the earlier appeal, this will not be held against the appellant.

10

When an appeal must be allowed

The AIT must decide whether to allow or dismiss the appeal. In so doing, it must decide all the matters which are raised as grounds of appeal, including matters raised in a one-stop notice. The broad grounds which may be raised are that the decision is: not in accordance with the immigration rules; discriminatory under the 1976 Act; contrary to the appellant's human rights; contrary to EU rights of free movement; otherwise 'not in accordance with the law' – or that a discretion within the immigration rules should have been exercised differently (s84 2002 Act).

The immigration judge must therefore allow the appeal if they find that (s86 2002 Act):

- the decision was not in accordance with the immigration rules;
- the decision was not in accordance with the law; or
- a discretion exercised within the immigration rules should have been exercised differently.

We discuss each of these circumstances below.

If the immigration judge finds that none of the above apply, then they must dismiss the appeal. If the appeal is allowed, they may give directions (▶see 1126–7). Note that, in asylum 'upgrade' appeals under section 83 of the 2002 Act, the grounds of appeal are restricted to asylum matters, preventing appellants from arguing human rights grounds (▶see 1079).

Not in accordance with the immigration rules

If the immigration authorities have decided that an appellant does not satisfy the rules when, in fact, they are satisfied, then the appeal is to be allowed. The immigration authorities may have misunderstood the relevant rules, or they may have made an incorrect decision about the facts of the case when applying the facts to the rules. In either case, the AIT can overrule the decision and allow the appeal. As well as all of the other categories of entry, the immigration rules deal with asylum, and appeals against incorrect asylum decisions can be allowed under the rules.

Not in accordance with the law

Obviously the 'law' here incorporates statutes such as the HRA as relevant to an appellant's human rights (and see s84(1)(c)(g) 2002 Act) and EU law relating to free movement. The previous provisions of the 1999 Act referred expressly to the '*appellant's* rights' in relation to human rights. Regrettably, this has meant that in family cases under Article 8, where family life has involved the interests of the *family members of the appellant* as well as the appellant themselves, the IAT has interpreted its jurisdiction narrowly (▶see 858–9). This seems out of step with the interpretation given to the 'law' by the higher courts as set out below. In addition, there may be more scope under the 2002 Act to argue that the

AIT must look broadly at the whole family's interests, so advisers should look out for further developments in this area.

Relevant considerations In addition to human rights and EU law, 'not in accordance with the law' must also refer to the 'immigration laws' as defined by the 1971 Act (see s33(1)). However, the higher courts have accepted that the 'law' for these purposes is wider than just the immigration rules and legislation. The highest authority for this is *Bakhtaur Singh*. That was a case decided under the deportation immigration rules, in which the House of Lords accepted that the Home Office and the statutory appeal authorities were bound to have regard, as a relevant consideration, to the effect on the community of the appellant's deportation, where it was alleged that there would be a significant impact. They held that this followed not just from the immigration rules, *but also* from the general principles of public law that require all relevant matters to be taken into account. The decision in that case was reached for both of these reasons.

Policy In a case involving the Somali family reunion policy, the Home Office accepted – with the Court of Appeal proceeding on the same basis – that 'not in accordance with the law' included all 'established principles of common or administrative law' (*DS Abdi*). The most important use of this power is in relation to cases where it is found that the immigration rules are not met but yet an established Home Office policy has not been properly applied. It may have been improperly applied because the decision-maker has simply not had regard to the policy, has misapplied the terms of the policy, or (as in *DS Abdi*) has incorrectly assessed the individual facts of the case that are relevant to applying the policy. However, success in such arguments is likely to mean that, although the appeal is 'allowed', the respondent is not necessarily obliged to reverse the decision, but only to give it genuine reconsideration on the correct legal and factual footing as found by the AIT.

Other 'public law' grounds Beyond this, and despite the decision in *Bakhtaur Singh*, the precise extent of the 'not in accordance with the law' jurisdiction is sometimes contentious. In the '*Mumin*' case, the High Court suggested that public law matters were best left to the High Court. It is nevertheless open to appellants to argue that decisions taken in breach of the rules of procedural fairness, inconsistently with other cases, or in breach of a person's legitimate expectations of how the immigration authorities will act (see for example *Odozi*, IAT) are 'not in accordance with the law'. A further application of these principles by the IAT was in their ruling in another case involving family reunion – *Onen* – which held that an appeal may be allowed on these grounds if relevant matters were not taken into account in determining whether there were 'exceptional compassionate circumstances' for the purposes of exercising discretion under a Home Office policy.

Under the 2002 Act, in most cases there is of course no right of appeal where an application is made for a 'purpose' which is outside the immi-

10

gration rules (see s88(2)(d) 2002 Act and ▶see 1056). However, this does not mean that applicants do not get the chance to run 'not in accordance with the law' arguments. For example, the fact that a family reunion case does not fully meet the requirements of the immigration rules does not mean that the application is for a 'purpose' which is not known to the rules.

Discretion should have been exercised differently

The immigration judge can only 're-exercise' the discretion of the immigration authorities if it is a discretion exercised *within* the immigration rules. This is because the legislation states that, for these purposes, where the immigration authorities refuse to exercise their discretion to depart from the rules (i.e. to grant some form of exceptional leave), this is not treated as an exercise of discretion (see s86(6)).

So, for example, most categories of the immigration rules state that leave 'may' be granted if a particular set of requirements is satisfied (not in asylum cases, however, where the rules state that the immigration authorities 'will' grant leave – see paras 334–5 HC 395). The word 'may' involves a discretion which could be exercised against the appellant if, for example, any of the general grounds of refusal applied. Application of the general grounds themselves usually involves an exercise of discretion, because they also state that, where certain conditions are satisfied, leave will 'normally' be refused. 'Normally' restricts the scope of the discretion as to what should happen in most cases, but it still leaves room for the exercise of discretion. Further, the rules about curtailing leave state that it 'may' be curtailed if the relevant conditions are satisfied. All of these exercises of discretion can be reviewed by the AIT.

Where, however, the appellant is asking the immigration authorities to exercise their general discretion to waive the rules and to grant leave outside them, the judge cannot re-exercise the discretion.

Discrimination cases

As indicated above, the AIT must determine *all* the grounds upon which an appeal is brought. This is particularly important in discrimination cases. This is because, in cases where there is a finding of discrimination, the appellant can bring a claim in the County Court. On that claim, the court is bound by the findings of the AIT (see s57A of the Race Relations Act 1976). In such cases it is therefore particularly important that the AIT determines the discrimination issue even if it is not relevant to the ultimate determination of the immigration appeal (and see Practice Directions, para. 20). For discrimination and discrimination appeals generally, see Chapter 29.

Directions where appeal is allowed

When an appeal is allowed, the AIT may give directions 'for the purpose of giving effect to its decision' (see s87 2002 Act). The immigration authorities are required to comply with the directions given. The directions do not have effect, however, while the appeal determination is under challenge.

Commonly, directions will be given that the immigration authorities grant leave, an entry clearance or a certificate of entitlement. Normally the immigration authorities will take this action when an appeal is allowed, without the need for a specific direction. Old case-law indicates that appellants could apply to the AIT after the decision for directions, having seen the findings in the determination and, for example, if the respondent does not implement the decision in the way the appellant wishes.

In certain cases where an appeal is allowed – particularly where entry is sought for limited purposes only – the time that has passed since the original decision may mean that circumstances have changed, and that the purpose of the proposed trip to the UK has passed. This may justify the AIT in not giving directions to an ECO to grant entry clearance. Instead, the ECO may be required to reconsider the present position and circumstances. However, insofar as they are relevant, the positive findings of the AIT as of the previous date of decision will generally bind the ECO.

In addition, it may be that, even though the appeal is allowed, there are still outstanding matters that require consideration by the respondent that make it inappropriate for a direction to be issued that leave or entry clearance be granted. This may occur where the immigration authorities have simply not considered the application under the correct immigration rules, and where the AIT does not feel it appropriate to make a first-instance decision on the merits of the case. It may also be the case where the immigration authorities failed to consider an applicable concessionary policy, and the policy itself gives the immigration authorities a discretion as to whether to treat the applicant favourably.

Recommendations where an appeal is dismissed

If an appeal seems to have a limited chance of success, but there are strong compassionate or other circumstances suggesting that the Home Office should exercise discretion in favour of the appellant, a judge may be persuaded to make a 'recommendation' to the Home Office. Another situation in which recommendations have traditionally been considered is where the court can only consider the circumstances as of the date of the decision (i.e. in entry clearance appeals), at which point the rules were not met, but where there has, since that time, been a change of circumstances such that the rules are met by the time of hearing. Recommendations in such cases may help prevent costly and time-consuming reapplications.

The ability to make such recommendations is not contained in the legislation – it is a completely discretionary course of action. Because the ability to make a recommendation is not part of the immigration judge's official functions, recommendations do not form part of the 'determination' of the appeal itself, and a failure to give one cannot usually be challenged on review (see *Chavrimootoo*, High Court). However, where a recommendation is based on factual findings reached after hearing oral evidence, the immigration authorities cannot, without good reason, refuse to accept those factual findings in making their further decision (see for example *Danaie* (CA)).

Is the power to make recommendations still relevant?

Recommendations grew out of the restriction of rights of appeal in deportation cases imposed by the Immigration Act 1988. That Act restricted many deportation appeals to the question of whether there was a 'power in law' to deport people, and so adjudicators were prevented from considering all of the other factors in the rules relating to whether it was right to deport the appellant. In passing that legislation, the government relied on the ability of appellants to request recommendations in deserving cases. These appeals may still arise in a very few cases where a person is refused under the 'regularisation of overstayers' scheme, and where that person last entered the UK less than seven years before the date of the notice of intention to deport.

Since the HRA and the resulting immigration legislation, which allows appeals to succeed on human rights grounds, the IAT has suggested that the scope for giving recommendations has diminished. However, both the Strasbourg Court and the House of Lords, when hearing human rights cases, have drawn attention to the ability of the government to exercise discretion in compassionate and deserving cases that do not meet the exacting thresholds set under the ECHR (for details ►see 851–2). In this context, the discretion to make a recommendation surely remains an important one.

Also, in *Shillova* (decided in June 2002), the High Court indicated that recommendations continued to serve a useful purpose. In that case, the appellant's asylum and human rights claims were dismissed, but a recommendation was made that he be allowed to stay in the UK on the basis that his computer skills made him an asset to the country, and because many of his family members had leave to remain in the UK. The High Court held that, after the coming into force of the Human Rights Act, there remained circumstances in which it was possible and proper for a recommendation to be made in dismissed appeals.

Policy on following recommendations

At the time of the 1988 Act (►see above), the Home Office policy on when it would accept a recommendation was generous: it stated that the Home Office would 'invariably' follow recommendations. Since then, and as appeal rights have become ever more restricted, there has also been a long march away from the practice of routinely accepting recommendations. Home Office policy now states as follows:

'16.3 Recommendations in a dismissed appeal

When dismissing an appeal or when an appeal is withdrawn, the

Appellate Authorities can make a non-statutory recommendation that the Secretary of State should exercise his discretion in favour of the appellant by reconsidering the application or granting exceptional leave to remain. However, recommendations made in dismissed appeals have no force in law and the Secretary of State is not bound to accept them. Such recommendations should be acted upon only where the determination and/or recommendation discloses clear exceptional compassionate circumstances which have not previously been considered and which would warrant the exercise of the Secretary of State's discretion outside the Immigration Rules...

16.4 Consideration of Recommendations

A decision to accept a recommendation must be referred to a SCW [senior case-worker] for authorisation and in asylum cases result in a grant of Humanitarian Protection or Discretionary Leave... Determinations which contain a form of words suggesting that the Secretary of State reconsider a case but which are not strictly recommendations should be considered as if they were recommendations in accordance with the advice above.' (*Immigration Rules and Compassionate Circumstances*, instructions to officers, 25 April 2004)

FAST TRACK APPEALS

An appeal will be a 'fast track' appeal where the appellant is detained in a specified removal centre, when they are served with the immigration decision they are appealing against and have continued to be detained in that centre or one of the other specified centres (Rules 3, 5, 15 and Sch 2 to the Asylum and Immigration Tribunal (Fast Track Procedure) Rules 2005 ('the Fast Track Rules')). The specified removal centres are:

- Campsfield House in Oxfordshire;
- Colnbrook House in Harmondsworth;
- Harmondsworth;
- Yarls Wood.

There are detailed fast track asylum determination procedures for those detained at Harmondsworth and Yarls Wood. These procedures and the strict timetable that applies are described in detail in Chapter 22 (►673–81, for Harmondsworth/Yarls Wood ►see 678–81)). Here we look solely at the procedures applying at the *appeal* stage of the fast track process, not leading up to the initial decision. The procedures are set out in the Fast Track Rules, although many of the general Procedure Rules also apply. The AIT's Practice Directions, issued on 4 April 2005, also have specific provisions dealing with the fast track.

Although there is a detained fast track process at Oakington Reception Centre, those detained there are not put through the detained fast track *appeal* system. Most cases dealt with at Oakington that are refused are

10

likely to be certified as 'clearly unfounded', so that there is no in-country right of appeal at all, and they are likely to be removed shortly after refusal. These cases are also referred to as 'non-suspensive appeal' or 'NSA' cases. Details about the fast track determination process at Oakington are given at ▶677–8. For details about NSA cases generally, ▶see 1073–8.

The time-limits for appealing to the AIT and challenging its decisions, as *well* as the timetable according to which appeals are determined, are much stricter in fast track cases. The pace is bewildering, and there is plenty of scope for unfairness and loss of important rights. The basic procedure and timetable is set out in the table below.

For full details about time-limits for appealing in all cases, including fast track appeals, and about calculating time, see the table at ▶1162–7. Note that the method of calculating time for fast track cases is slightly different to that for ordinary cases.

In fast track cases, both the appellant and respondent are permitted to serve the material referred to in the standard appeal directions either at the hearing itself or, if practicable, on the business day before the hearing (Practice Directions, para. 7).

FAST TRACK APPEALS BASIC PROCEDURE AND TIMETABLE

Unless otherwise stated, all references to the 'Rules' in this table are to the Asylum and Immigration Tribunal (Fast Track Procedure) Rules 2005

1) Appellants must appeal to the AIT within two days of being served with the decision. This time-limit can only be extended if the AIT is satisfied that, because of circumstances outside the control of the appellant or their representative, it was not practicable for the notice of appeal to have been given in time. This is a more stringent test than that applying under the general rules (Rule 8).

   Issues about timeliness are not decided under the procedure described at ▶1092–4. Instead they are determined as a preliminary issue at the hearing of the appeal (Rule 12). However, if a notice of appeal is late, the appellant must still ask for an extension of time in the notice of appeal. Reasons should be stated why the appeal is late, and written evidence in support of the reasons should be given (see Rule 6(c)).

2) If notice of appeal is given to officers at the detention centre (▶see 1065–6), those officers must forward it to the AIT 'immediately' (Rule 7). If notice of appeal is given directly to the AIT, it must 'immediately' serve a copy of it on the respondent (Rule 9).

3) The respondent must file the documents relevant to the appeal (notice and reasons for decision, interview notes, and so on) no later than two days after receiving the notice of appeal (Rule 10).

4) The AIT will fix a hearing date within two days (or as soon as is reasonably

practicable after two days) of receiving the above documents filed by the respondent. The AIT must serve notice of the hearing as soon as is reasonably practicable, and always at least by midday on the business day before the hearing (Rule 11). This refers to the main hearing of the appeal. There are no routine CMR hearings in fast track cases (see Practice Directions, para. 6.1). For applying for adjournments and orders removing the appellant from the fast track appeals system, see ▶1132 below.

5) The AIT must serve its determination on all parties to the appeal no later than two days after the date of the hearing (or two days after determining the appeal, if there was no hearing) (Rule 14).

6) The time-limit for applications to the AIT for a review of the determination of the AIT is two days (Rule 3, Asylum and Immigration Tribunal (Fast Track Time Limits) Order 2005).

7) The AIT must serve copies of the review application on the other party 'as soon as practicable' (Rule 17(a)).

8) The party that is not applying for the review may file submissions in response to the application no later than one day after the day on which they are served with the application (Rule 17(b)).

9) The AIT must serve its decision on the application for a review not later than one day after receiving the written submissions in response (or one day after the time for filing those submissions ran out, if no submissions were received) (Rule 19).

10) The time-limit for applying to the High Court to review the AIT decision is two days (Rule 4, Asylum and Immigration Tribunal (Fast Track Time Limits) Order 2005).

11) Where an order for reconsideration is made, the AIT must fix a hearing for the reconsideration to take place no later than two days after the date on which the order for reconsideration is served on the parties. If the AIT is unable to arrange a hearing in that time, it must be fixed 'as soon as reasonably practicable' afterwards (Rule 21).

12) Applications to the AIT for permission to appeal to the Court of Appeal must be made within two days (Rule 25).

13) The AIT must determine the application for permission to appeal, and serve the determination on the parties, not later than one day after the AIT receives the application (Rule 26).

Note

- For further details about the procedure for applications for reviews and reconsideration hearings, including the modifications made for reconsideration hearings in fast track cases, ▶see Chapter 36.

- For full details about time-limits, including those in fast track appeals, and about calculating time, ▶see 1162–7.

10

Getting an appellant out of the fast track appeal process

Given the speed of the proceedings, advisers dealing with fast track cases will often apply for adjournments or for an order to transfer their clients out of the fast track, in order to enable time for preparation of the appeal (see Rules 13(b)(c), 28, 30, Fast Track Rules).

Adjournments

A fast track appeal may only be adjourned if one of the following circumstances apply (Rule 28, Fast Track Rules):

- there isn't sufficient time to hear it;
- a party has not been properly served with the notice of hearing;
- the AIT is satisfied by evidence given by an appellant that the appeal cannot be justly determined on the date on which it is listed and there is a date not more than ten days after the original date of hearing by which it can be justly determined.

Transfers

Alternatively, appellants can apply for an order under Rule 30 of the Fast Track Rules that the case be transferred out of the fast track, in which case it may also be adjourned. Rule 30 applications can be made both at the stage of the first appeal and in reconsideration proceedings. The AIT must transfer a case out of the fast track if any of the following apply:

- all the parties – namely the appellant's representative (or appellant if unrepresented) and the Home Office – give their consent;
- the AIT is satisfied that there are exceptional circumstances meaning that the appeal cannot be justly determined while in the fast track;
- the Home Office has failed to comply with a provision of the Fast Track Rules or a direction of the AIT, and the appellant would be prejudiced by that failure if the appeal remained in the fast track.

Therefore, on Rule 30 applications it is important for advisers to be able to identify to the immigration judge why the case is complex and unsuitable for the fast track, and also, if further evidence is needed in preparation for the appeal, to explain persuasively why the appeal cannot go ahead in the fast track procedure.

If a case is taken out of fast track, it is likely also to be adjourned, and the judge may give directions for the future conduct of the appeal. A new hearing date will be set, within 28 days, at the same time as the adjournment. The ordinary Procedure Rules will also start to apply to the appeal (see Rules 30(2) and 31, Fast Track Rules).

Release and bail

Note that if an appellant is removed from the fast track appeal system, they are also likely to be released from the fast track detention centre. However, aside from this, it appears to be the case that appellants within the fast track are also entitled to apply for bail.

36 Challenging decisions of the Asylum and Immigration Tribunal

This chapter deals with the system for challenging decisions of the Asylum and Immigration Appeal Tribunal (AIT) which has been in force since 4 April 2005 following the Asylum and Immigration (Treatment of Claimants, etc) Act 2004. Since that time, there is no longer a formal 'appeal' within the statutory appeal system itself. The two-tier system of adjudicators and the Immigration Appeal Tribunal (IAT) has been abolished and replaced with the single-tier AIT. The new personnel of the AIT, including 'immigration judges' and 'senior immigration judges', is explained at the beginning of the Section (▶1049–50).

However, the system of review and reconsideration by the AIT of its own decisions still contains features of the old system. In addition, although the government had wanted largely to exclude the jurisdiction of the higher courts, there are still opportunities to apply to those courts. For an overview of the appeal system under the 2004 Act, ▶see 1046–52 and, in particular, the table at ▶1047–9 for an overview of the structure of the system for challenging decisions of the AIT.

We deal with the relevant procedures in the following six parts:

- applying to the AIT for a review of the first determination of the AIT (▶1134–40);
- applying to the High Court for a review of the first determination of the AIT (▶1140–3);
- reconsideration hearings before the AIT (▶1143–7);
- appealing to the Court of Appeal following reconsideration decisions of the AIT (▶1147–9);
- other routes to the Court of Appeal (▶1149–50);
- circumstances in which judicial review can still be used (▶1150–1).

The chapter then goes on to deal with the following matters:

- **Transitional arrangements** There were no hearings before adjudicators or the IAT after 3 April 2005. Therefore, if the case was already in the system by that time, applicants need to know how their case is brought within the new structure. This is covered by detailed 'transitional' arrangements, which we deal with at ▶1151–3.

10

- **Public funding** The 2004 Act contains important provisions about legal aid public funding of challenges to the AIT. These are covered at ▶1153–5.
- **Errors of law** Throughout the appeal system there is reference to having to show an 'error of law' and a 'material error of law' (the latter just means an error of law which may have made a difference to the outcome). We look at errors of law and provide a general checklist of what may amount to an error of law at ▶1155–8.
- **Mistakes of fact and new evidence** In some cases it may be possible to show an error of law when the AIT has made a mistake about facts even when the mistake about the facts can only be demonstrated by evidence that was not before the AIT when it made the decision. The rules are not straightforward. They are described at ▶1159–61.
- **Time-limits** For all procedures to challenge the AIT, strict time-limits apply (especially in 'fast track' cases). In dealing with each procedure we set out the time-limit that applies. The table at the end of the chapter sets out all the time-limits for appeals and reviews generally and gives guidance as to how time is calculated in the different cases (▶1162–7).

Because the system and procedures from April 2005 may be unfamiliar to applicants and advisers, in this chapter we have given fairly detailed references to the relevant legislation, rules and Practice Directions.

APPLYING TO THE AIT FOR AN ORDER FOR RECONSIDERATION

After the AIT has considered an appeal and issued its determination for the first time, either party can apply to the AIT for a 'review' of that determination. The purpose of the review is to ask for an order that the AIT 'reconsider' its decision on the appeal (s103A 2002 Act and part 54.28-54.35 Civil Procedure Rules as inserted by the Civil Procedure (Amendment) Rules 2005).

The general intention is for these applications to be decided by the High Court. *However*, in order to relieve that Court of the pressure caused by a large number of applications, for the present time the application will first be considered by a single immigration judge of the AIT itself (see para. 30, Sch 2 2004 Act). This procedure, which has been referred to as the 'filter' system, is stated to be 'transitional' and it is unclear how long it will continue for. The form for making the application will be sent out with the appeal determination but it can also be downloaded from the AIT website at www.ait.gov.uk. It is to be served on the AIT at: Asylum and Immigration Tribunal, Arnhem Support Centre, PO Box 6987, Leicester, UK, LE1 6ZX (or the hearing centre which heard the appeal in fast track cases). In all cases, check the address given on the documentation sent out with the determination.

The immigration judge will make an order for reconsideration only if s/he thinks (rule 26(6) of the Asylum and Immigration Tribunal (Procedure) Rules 2005, 'the Procedure Rules'):

- the AIT may have made an error of law; *and*
- there is a 'real possibility' that the AIT would decide the appeal differently on reconsideration.

So, an order for reconsideration will be made provided that, arguably at least, the AIT made an error of law in its original determination *and* the outcome of the appeal might have been different had the error not been made.

Cases in which it is not possible to apply for a review

In the following cases, a party cannot apply for a reconsideration of an AIT decision.

- If the AIT sat as a panel of three or more legally qualified members to hear an appeal, then the only right of appeal is to the Court of Appeal (▶see 1149–50 below). In such cases, neither party can apply for a reconsideration order (s103A(8) 2002 Act). It is expected that these cases will be very rare.

- Where a reconsideration order has previously been made in relation to the appeal (s103A(2)(b) 2002 Act), no further reconsideration can be applied for. If a party has already had a reconsideration hearing, which has been dismissed, the only right of appeal is to the Court of Appeal.

- Where the AIT has made a 'procedural, ancillary or preliminary' decision (s103A(7)(a) 2002 Act) a reconsideration cannot be requested. The only way to challenge such decisions is by judicial review (▶see below 1150–1).

- Where the AIT has reached a decision following a remittal from the Court of Appeal (i.e. where the Court of Appeal has sent it back to the AIT for further consideration) (s103A(7)(b) 2002 Act), the way to challenge the decision is to appeal to the Court of Appeal again.

Time-limits for applying for a review and calculating time

Despite much protest from those working in the field, the time-limits are very strict and have led to real difficulties for those seeking representation at this stage. The time-limits are (s103A(3) 2002 Act):

- five days if the applicant is in the UK or if it is the immigration authorities who are seeking to appeal;
- 28 days if the applicant is outside the UK.

If the applicant is within the detained 'fast track' appeal system, then the time limit for either party to apply for a review is only two days (rule 3, Asylum and Immigration (Fast Track Time Limits) Order 2005). For further details about the fast track process generally, the unfairness to which it can lead as identified by the Court of Appeal in *R (Refugee Legal Centre) v*

SSHD and the need to transfer some cases out of the fast track, ▶see 679–81, 1132.

When does time begin? Time begins from the date on which the person applying is treated as receiving the AIT decision (s103A(3)). *Unless the contrary is proved*, a person is treated as receiving the decision (rule 55, Procedure Rules):

- on the second day after it was sent, if the decision is sent by post or DX from and to a place in the UK;
- on the 28th day after it was sent, if the decision is sent by post or DX from or to a place outside the UK;
- in any other case (for example, fax, email or personal service) on the day on which it was sent, delivered to, or left with the person.

So, unless the appellant can prove that the decision was not received, if a determination was posted from within the UK to the applicant in the UK on Monday 20 June, it will be treated as having been received on Wednesday 22 June 2005. Note that in asylum appeals against immigration decisions, the Procedure Rules make provision for the Home Office to receive the determination and subsequently serve it on the appellant (see rule 23, Procedure Rules).

Counting time Although the rules about when the decision is treated as having been received are contained in the AIT Procedure Rules, the rules about counting time for the purposes of the above time-limits are contained in the general Civil Procedure Rules (CPR) which apply to the High Court (see s103A(4)(a) 2002 Act; para. 30(3)(b) Sch 2 2004 Act; CPR part 54.28(4)). This means the relevant provision for counting time is CPR part 2.8 ('Time'). The AIT has itself confirmed that it is these provisions of the CPR which apply (see letter from the Office of the President of the AIT to the Refugee Legal Centre, 29 September 2005. The CPR state that:

- the day on which the time period 'begins' is not counted;
- where the time-limit is five days or less, the following days are not counted: Saturdays, Sundays, Bank Holidays, Christmas Day and Good Friday.

Our interpretation is as follows. Take the same example as above in the case of a five-day time-limit with the decision treated as being received on Wednesday 22 June. The time period 'begins' on the 'date on which [the party] is treated [in accordance with the Procedure rules] as receiving notice of the [AIT's] decision' (s103(A)(3)(a) 2002 Act). However, because of the effect of CPR part 2.8, the day on which the period 'begins' i.e. 22 June, is not counted. Therefore, the first day of the five-day time period is Thursday 23 June. The last day for submitting the application for reconsideration is Wednesday 29 June. This is because 25 and 26 June are not counted as they are a Saturday and Sunday.

Where the applicant is outside the UK Where the applicant is outside the UK, for example in an entry clearance case, the time-limit is 28 days and so weekends and holidays are all counted as days. Note also that the decision is not treated as being received by the appellant until 28 days after it has been sent because it is being sent to them outside the UK (▶see above). However, in cases where the decision is also sent to representatives in the UK, it may be dangerous to assume that the time-limit does not begin running until 28 days has passed because of this 'deemed receipt' rule. This is because the Procedure Rules state that documents served on a person who has notified the AIT that they are 'acting as the representative of a party' (▶1090–1) are 'deemed' to have been served on that party (see rule 55(3)(4) Procedure Rules). In such a case, it may therefore be that the 28-day time-limit begins running when the representative in the UK is treated as receiving the decision sent to them from in the UK i.e. on the second day after it was sent. In such cases, in order to be safe, it is therefore better to start counting time from that point.

Out of time applications for review

Applications for a reconsideration outside the above time-limits may be considered if the immigration judge thinks that the application could not 'reasonably practicably have been made within that period' (see s103A(4)(b) 2002 Act; rule 26(5)(a), Procedure Rules). On the face of it, this is a stringent test. It is stricter than that under the previous rules for extending time to apply for permission to appeal to the IAT which could be done if 'by reason of special circumstances it would be unjust not to do so' (see previous rule 16(2), Immigration and Asylum Appeals (Procedure) Rules 2003). This more flexible extension rule still applies for initial notices of appeal to the AIT.

If the application is being made out of time, an application to extend time must be made in the application for review. Full reasons should be given for the delay in making the application as well as why a reconsideration should be ordered. The reasons why the application could not reasonably have been made in time should be presented in a statement setting out the relevant facts, which must be 'verified by a statement of truth' (CPR part 54.30). This means that the statement must confirm that its contents are true. Depending on the reasons being put forward, it will normally be appropriate for a statement to be submitted by the applicant and/or their representative.

Procedures and guidance in applying to the AIT for a review

Further details of the procedure for applying for a review are set out in CPR 54.28-54.31 and rules 25-26 Procedure Rules. The CPRs can be downloaded from www.dca.gov.uk. Important points are as follows:

- the application should be sent to the AIT (▶see above at 1134);
- if the applicant is detained under immigration powers, the application can be served on the immigration authorities who have custody of them at the detention centre;

10

- in order to make the application, the applicant should send to the AIT: the application notice; the notice of the immigration decision originally appealed; the 'reasons for refusal' letter (if any) accompanying the original immigration decision; the grounds of appeal against the initial decision; the AIT's determination on the appeal and any other documents 'material to the application' which were before the AIT;
- the application notice is Form AIT/103A (Application for Reconsideration); there are separate forms for in-country and out-of-country cases – available on the AIT website (www.ait.gov.uk);
- the applicant should also include with the application written submissions containing both the grounds for the review and reasons in support of those grounds;
- the application will be considered on the papers and without a hearing. The immigration judge will consider the applicant's written submissions and any other documents filed together with the application notice.

Preparing the grounds

It is essential that all grounds be fully argued on each point of law, which the applicant relies on to show that the AIT determination is not sustainable. The rules require both the 'grounds' and the 'reasons' for those grounds to be given.

When preparing the grounds, it is often best to begin by explaining, as briefly as possible, what the appeal is about and the essential reasons why the AIT dismissed the appeal. Determinations can be very long but they are now set out in numbered paragraphs, as the Practice Directions require. This has become a general judicial trend to make it easier to refer to particular parts of the determination. Therefore, where appropriate, the grounds should cross-refer to the paragraphs in the determination to make it easier for the immigration judge to identify the points that are being made.

It is then necessary to identify clearly what legal errors were made by the immigration judge. It is often useful to identify separate broad errors and give each error its own heading so that the AIT can understand the flow of the written submissions. A checklist of legal errors is set out in the table at ▶1156–8. If there is any question that the original AIT may have come to the same decision *even if* they had not made the legal errors alleged, reasons should be given as to why the errors would or could have made a difference to the outcome.

The person preparing the grounds should read the determination through very thoroughly and know exactly what documentation was before the AIT when the appeal was considered. If there are any documents referred to in the written submissions in support of the application and which are particularly relevant to the grounds for review, they should be included in the documents sent to the AIT and carefully cross-referred to.

AIT decision on application for reconsideration

The application will be decided by an immigration judge of the AIT who is authorised by the President of the AIT to deal with such applications (rule 26(1), Procedure Rules; Practice Direction, para. 2.2(9)). It should be decided not later than ten days after the AIT receives the application notice (rule 26(4), Procedure Rules). If the application is successful, the immigration judge will make an 'order for reconsideration'. If not, the judge will state that they propose to make no such order. The decision will usually only be a page containing details of the applicant's name, the decision and summary reasons for the decision. As stated above, the immigration judge will only make an order for reconsideration if they think that the original AIT may have made an error of law and the appeal may be decided differently on reconsideration.

At the same time as ordering a reconsideration, the immigration judge should (rule 27(2), Procedure Rules; Practice Directions, para. 13.9):

- state the grounds on which the AIT is ordered to reconsider the decision;
- give any directions for the reconsideration (which may include directing a case management review hearing (CMR) before the reconsideration hearing and may state the nature of the panel which should hear the reconsideration).

Points not raised in the grounds

The immigration judge is not required to consider grounds for making a reconsideration order which are not included in the application notice (rule 26(3), Procedure Rules). However, we suggest that the AIT should still order reconsideration if an obvious point has not been raised in the grounds. This principle comes from the case of *Robinson* in which the Court of Appeal held that the IAT had an obligation to consider obvious points of Convention law that had not been made by the applicant in the application. This was in order to fulfil the IAT's obligations under the Refugee Convention. In a further more recent case, *Miftari*, the Court of Appeal confirmed that the IAT could consider obvious Convention points which had not been put forward in the grounds of appeal. However, the Court also suggested that this appeared to be a 'one way street' for appellants and that the Home Office may not be able to rely on the *Robinson* principle. *Miftari* confirmed that, aside from the *Robinson*-type cases, the IAT had no jurisdiction to consider errors of law which were not raised in the grounds of appeal.

10

If the application has been rejected, the applicant is entitled to renew the application again to a High Court (▶see below).

Service of the decision of the AIT on an application for reconsideration

The decision of the AIT on the application for reconsideration must be sent to all parties. Where the application is not successful, the High Court should also be notified (see 30(4)(b) Sch 2 2004 Act). In asylum cases, the Procedure Rules make special provision for decisions to be sent to the Home Office and for it to send them on to the appellant (see rule 27). The Home Office must serve the documents on the appellant within 28 days and tell the AIT it has done so. If it does not, the AIT is to proceed to serve the appellant with the decision.

Accelerated procedure in fast track cases

In fast track cases, the immigration judge must, as soon as practicable, serve the other party with a copy of the application notice. That party has one day to make submissions in response and, just a day after that, the immigration judge must make and serve its decision on the application (rules 17–19, Fast Track Rules). The Home Office is to serve the decision on the appellant straight away.

APPLYING TO THE HIGH COURT FOR AN ORDER FOR A REVIEW OF THE AIT DECISION

If the AIT rejects the application for a review under section 103A 2002 Act, the applicant can renew the application to the 'appropriate' higher court. These applications have also been referred to as 'opt-in' applications. The 'appropriate court':

- for appeals decided in England and Wales is the High Court (in practice the 'Administrative Court' which is the same part of the High Court that deals with claims for judicial review);
- for appeals decided in Scotland, is the Outer House of the Court of Session;
- for appeals decided in Northern Ireland, is the High Court in Northern Ireland.

It *appears* that the court can re-consider both whether to make an order that the AIT reconsider the decision on the appeal *and* whether to extend time where the application to the AIT for a review (above) was made outside the relevant limit (s103(A) 2002 Act; para. 30(5), Sch 2 2004 Act). In order to renew the application to the higher court, the applicant must file a notice at the Administrative Court Office.

Dealing with the AIT refusal

This application for a review is a further chance to challenge the original decision of the AIT dismissing the appeal. It is not an application made against the AIT's latest decision to refuse the review. Nevertheless, the AIT will have given reasons for refusing the application for a review. By renewing the application, the applicant will obviously not agree with the reasons given by the AIT and it is a good idea for applicants to respond to those reasons so as to try to persuade the higher court not to refuse the application for similar reasons. Therefore, in addition to their first written submissions, applicants should aim to make further written submissions dealing with the AIT's reasons for refusing the first application for the review. The CPR anticipates that applicants will provide these additional submissions (see CPR 54.31(5)).

Again, this procedure can only be used on one occasion in relation to the same appeal (see s103A(2) 2002 Act).

Time-limit for renewing the application to the High Court

The time-limit for submitting the application for a review to the higher court is five days in all cases, except for fast track cases, in which the time-limit is two days. Time runs from the date of deemed receipt of the decision of the AIT refusing the application for a review (see para. 30(5)(b), Sch 2 2004 Act; article 4, Asylum and Immigration (Fast Track Time Limits) Order 2005). Time is calculated in the same way as for the initial application for a review to the AIT (▶see above at 1136–7).

Note that the application form for renewing the application (PF244), the DCA's guide to completing the forms and the Administrative Court Office's (ACO's) newsletter of July 2005 all suggest that the time-limit for submitting the 'opt-in' renewal application to the High Court in out-of-country cases is 28 days from the deemed date of receipt of the decision of the AIT. The time-limit for the initial application to the AIT for a review in such cases is clearly 28 days (▶see above 1135–7 and see s103A(3)(b) 2002 Act as applied to the initial application by paras. 30(1)–(3), Sch2 2004 Act). It appears, therefore, to be the practice to accept out-of-country applications as in-time if made within this time-limit in renewed applications as well. In stating that the time-limit is five days in all cases (above), we have erred on the side of caution in sticking to what seems to be the formal position in the legislation (para. 30(5)(b) Sch2 2004 Act).

Extending time If the application which is made to the higher court is made outside this time-limit i.e. for renewing the application, the higher court can also extend this time-limit if it decides that the application could not 'reasonably practicably have been given' within the time-limit (para. 30(5)(c)(ii), Sch 2 2004 Act). Again, the applicant should explain in the notice of application why the time-limit could not be met and a statement of truth should be provided in support (CPR part 54.31(4)).

Procedures for applying to the High Court

The procedures for applying to the Administrative Court Office of the High Court ('ACO') for a statutory review under section 103A 2002 Act are set out in CPR 54.28–54.35 which are the provisions added to the Civil Procedure Rules by the Civil Procedure (Amendment) Rules 2005. Guidance on these procedures was also given in some detail in the Administrative Court Office's Newsletter for July 2005. That newsletter noted that, since the introduction of the new system, there had been a 100 per cent increase in applications which had caused a backlog. Applications are made on Form

10

PF244 RCJ (Application for Reconsideration). Separate forms are available on the HMCS (Her Majesty's Court Service) website for in-country and out-of-country applications (www.hmcourtservice.gov.uk).

Documents required In addition to the application form and submissions, the documents which are required by the Court are (CPR54.29, ACO July 2005 newsletter):

- the notice of the original decision against which the applicant appealed to the AIT and the notice/grounds of appeal to the AIT;
- the reasons for refusal letter which accompanied the above decision;
- the Form AIT/103A (Application for Reconsideration) which was submitted to the AIT together with the grounds of review;
- the determination of the AIT on the appeal;
- the decision of the AIT on the initial application for a review and any reasons given for it;
- any written evidence in support of an application for an extension of time in which to file the application;
- a fee of £400 for the application or an application for fee exemption or remission on Form Ex160;
- any other documents material to the application which were before the AIT.

Form PF244 (Application for Reconsideration) The form is split up into a number of parts. Note that Part 'C' invites applicants to respond to the reasons given by the AIT for its decision to propose not to make an order for reconsideration. Part 'D' asks applicants who are represented by solicitors, a charity or a 'not-for-profit' organisation to state whether they are seeking an order for costs under section 103D 2002 Act.

Costs As indicated above applicants who are being represented may apply for their costs to be paid out of the Community Legal Service Fund (see s103D 2002 Act). The High Court will only make such an order if the applicant has applied for one and if the application is refused or if it is referred to the Court of Appeal. If the application is granted, the Tribunal may order that the applicant's costs are met out of the Fund after it has heard the reconsideration (see s103D(2)(3) 2002 Act).

Lodging applications Applicants should always check up-to-date practice. At present it seems that applications can be submitted in person, by DX, or post, or by fax provided that the applicant is fees exempt and the fees exemption form is completed at the same time. In cases where the applicant is not fees exempt but it is the last day for lodging, the Court may treat the fax application as in time provided that the applicant's solicitor also undertakes to lodge the fee the next day and does indeed do so.

Decision of the High Court on application for review

The application is decided by a single judge of the High Court on the papers without a hearing. Applications will be referred to a judge for consideration within five working days of receipt during formal Court 'term-time'. Unless the Court orders otherwise, it will not receive evidence that was not submitted to the AIT (CPR part 54.33(3)). The High Court can do one of three things (CPR part 54.33(4)(5)):

1) if the High Court judge thinks that the AIT 'may have made an error of law' and there is a 'real possibility' that the AIT may come to a different decision if it reconsiders the appeal, the Court will order the AIT to reconsider the decision on the original appeal;

2) dismiss the application;

3) refer the appeal to the Court of Appeal under s103C 2002 Act – this is only likely to occur in rare cases that raise very important points of law (▶see 1149 below).

The CPR states that the Court's decision on this application is 'final'. This means that there is no means of appealing against the decision or renewing the application to another court (part 54.33(7)). This means that, by contrast with judicial review, under this final form of High Court challenge, applicants have no right to an oral hearing of their application to review the AIT's original decision and no right to apply to the Court of Appeal. As a result, a legal challenge has been brought to attempt to restore applicants' rights to apply for judicial review (▶see below at 1151).

Where the application for review relates to an asylum claim, the Court will send the decision to the Home Office which is then responsible for serving it on the applicant. The Home Office should serve the decision within 28 days. In non-asylum cases, the Court serves the order. The Court may also serve the order in an asylum case where the Home Office fails to do so within 28 days (CPR 54.34).

10

RECONSIDERATION HEARINGS BEFORE THE AIT

As stated above, the AIT or the High Court will give an order for reconsideration if the AIT *may* have made an error of law and there is a real possibility that a different outcome may be reached. So, the first task for the AIT in carrying out the reconsideration is to decide whether the original AIT did in fact make a 'material error of law'. This is defined as an error that 'affected the Tribunal's decision upon the appeal'. Take the example of an immigration judge who disbelieved an appellant's account of events for a whole range of reasons and therefore made factual findings that meant the appeal had to be dismissed. If the judge made an error of law in relation to one of those reasons, but it is very clear that the judge would have made the same factual findings for a whole host of other reasons which they gave and that no reasonable AIT would believe the appellant, the AIT is unlikely to make an order for reconsideration.

If there was no material error of law, then the Tribunal must order that the original determination of the appeal stands. If the AIT finds that there was a material error of law, then it must go on to make a fresh decision on the merits of the appeal (see rule 31, Procedure Rules and see, for the same approach under the previous system, as set out by the Court of Appeal in *CA v SSHD* at para. 15 – at least in asylum and human rights cases, this will involve considering the facts at the time of the reconsideration hearing).

Procedure in preparation for a reconsideration hearing

Both parties will be sent the order for reconsideration, which has been made by the AIT or the High Court. Reconsideration hearings must take place 'as soon as reasonably practicable' after the order for reconsideration has been served (no later than two days after the order has been served, or as soon as practicable after two days in fast track cases). Details of the procedures to be followed before the AIT on reconsideration are set out in some detail in the Practice Directions issued by the President of the AIT in April 2005 (see paras 14.1–14.14). Most of the general rules that apply to AIT hearings, which are set out in Chapter 35, for example about hearing in the absence of a party, adjournments etc, also apply to reconsideration hearings. Also of relevance, in particular to reconsideration hearings where issues of law arise, is the part of the Practice Directions that deals with citation of determinations, starred determinations and Country Guidance Determinations (▶see 1110–12)

Reply

If the party which did not apply for review wants to argue that the original determination of the AIT should be upheld for reasons which are different, or additional to those given in the determination, it must file with the AIT and the other side a 'reply' setting out their argument (rule 30, Procedure Rules).

Further evidence

If a party wants to ask the AIT to consider evidence not submitted at the time of the original appeal, it must send to the AIT and to the other side, a notice stating the nature of the evidence and the reasons why it was not previously submitted. This should be done as soon as possible after the order for reconsideration has been made. The AIT will then decide whether to admit the further evidence and may give directions about it (rule 32, Procedure Rules). Where this evidence is being relied on to show that the previous AIT made a *material error of law*, the tests set out at ▶1159–61 will have to be satisfied. If the reconsideration reaches the second stage, where the AIT is making a further decision on the appeal, there should clearly be no difficulty relying on, for example, updated country evidence or evidence showing changes of circumstances.

Bundles

The AIT has given general guidance about preparation of trial bundles which it is assumed applies to bundles to be prepared for reconsideration hearings as well (▶see 1109–10). Of course, the AIT will have the documents that have been submitted in support of the application for a review. However, appellants may need to supplement this material in view of the fact that, at the hearing, the AIT may proceed to make their own decision on the appeal if that can be done without hearing oral evidence again (▶see below).

Reconsideration hearings and decisions

The hearing is likely to be before two or more members of the AIT, at least one of whom will be a 'legally qualified' member (Practice Directions, para. 2.2(3)). The others may be non-legally qualified members. Where a case raises particularly important legal or procedural issues, two or three members may be legally qualified, and the decision may be 'starred' or 'reported' (▶see further 1110–12).

In non-fast track cases, the parties can assume that the issue at the first reconsideration hearing is restricted to whether the original AIT made a material error of law and, if so, whether on the basis of the original AIT's findings of fact, the appeal should be allowed or dismissed. If there is no material error of law, then the AIT will not consider the merits of the case further and will determine the appeal on that basis (Practice Directions, para. 14.1 and similar directions at 14.6–14.9 for transitional cases in which the IAT granted permission to appeal against a decision of an adjudicator and which were pending on 3 April 2005).

Therefore, if the AIT is satisfied that the earlier AIT did make a material error of law, then the original decision is, in effect, set aside and the AIT is obliged to make a further decision to either allow or dismiss the appeal. In practice, once a material error of law has been found, the AIT is likely to adopt one of the *three following courses of action* (but note that in fast track cases and in transitional cases where it has already been determined that there is a material error of law, the procedure is different – see further below).

10

1) The same AIT may proceed to consider the appeal itself. It will probably do this if it feels that it is able to determine the matter on the basis of the submissions of the parties. These are likely to be cases in which the AIT can adopt the existing findings of fact, or make further findings of fact without hearing oral evidence. Therefore, in non-fast track cases, at the first reconsideration hearing, representatives should be ready to deal with: (a) whether there is a material error of law; (b) the merits of the appeal on the basis of the original findings of fact i.e. without preparing to call live evidence again (Practice Direction, para. 14.1).

2) The AIT may decide that it cannot proceed straight away to make a further decision to allow or dismiss the appeal. The AIT may take this approach if

further detailed factual findings are needed which will probably require the evidence to be heard again. In such a case, the AIT will adjourn the hearing to a later time when the evidence can be taken. The AIT will prepare a statement of reasons for finding that the original AIT made a material error of law (Practice Direction, paras 14.2–14.3).

3) The AIT may come to the same conclusion as in (2) but decide to transfer the proceedings to be heard by a differently constituted AIT. Again the proceedings are effectively adjourned to a later date. The AIT will prepare reasons for finding that the original AIT made a material error of law and those reasons will be attached to the determination of the AIT which later makes a fresh decision on the appeal (Practice Direction, paras 12, 14.2–14.3). This course enables the AIT to 'transfer' the hearing to a less senior AIT. It is obviously similar to the previous procedure where the IAT would 'remit' a case to be heard afresh by an adjudicator.

Reconsideration hearings in cases remitted by the IAT or a court

In transitional cases in which the IAT or a court has remitted an appeal to the adjudicator and which were pending on 3 April 2005, it will already have been decided that the original determination cannot stand. The AIT will therefore proceed directly to hear the matter afresh and the parties should come ready to deal with the whole appeal including calling witnesses. It is possible that there will be a case management hearing before the main hearing but appellants and their advisers must be careful to check the notice of hearing to determine whether this is the case (see para. 14.11 Practice Direction and see Memorandum issued by the Resident Senior Immigration Judge for Taylor House on 7 April 2005).

Reconsideration hearings in fast track cases

In fast track cases, the AIT is generally required to fix a hearing date for reconsideration only two days after the order for reconsideration (or as soon as practicable thereafter) and to reconsider its decision at that time (rules 21, 23 Fast Track Rules). Therefore, at the first reconsideration hearing, the parties are:

'...expected to attend with all necessary witnesses and evidence that may be required if the Tribunal should decide that it is necessary to re-hear the appeal.' (Practice Directions, para. 14.13)

It is unlikely that the hearing will be adjourned. It will only be adjourned if: there is insufficient time to hear it; a party has not been served with a notice of hearing; the AIT is satisfied by evidence given that the appeal cannot be justly determined on that date but can be so determined within ten days; or the AIT decides to transfer the case out of the fast track (▶see 1132) (rules 28 and 30, Fast Track Rules).

Following the reconsideration decision

If, following reconsideration, the appeal is dismissed either because there is no material error of law in the original decision, or after the merits of the appeal have been fully reconsidered, the applicant cannot apply again for a reconsideration order. The remedy for the losing party is to apply to appeal to the Court of Appeal (▶below).

APPEALING TO THE COURT OF APPEAL FOLLOWING RECONSIDERATION DETERMINATIONS

If the determination following the reconsideration hearing/s is negative, either party may appeal (with permission) to the Court of Appeal (s103B 2002 Act). For appeals decided in Scotland, the appeal is to the Inner House of the Court of Session. If the appeal was decided in Northern Ireland, the right of appeal is to the Court of Appeal in Northern Ireland. A section 103B appeal to the Court of Appeal may be brought against decisions of the AIT following:

- a 'reconsideration' of the original appeal (▶see above);
- a remittal of an appeal back to the AIT from the Court of Appeal after an earlier appeal under this same provision (i.e. s103B); or
- a remittal of an appeal back to the AIT from the Court of Appeal after it has reached the Court of Appeal in either of the ways referred to below at ▶1149–50.

Applications for permission to appeal must be made first to the AIT by filling out the form which will be sent with the determination (Form AIT 4) and providing written grounds for appealing (s103B(3) 2002 Act; rule 34 Procedure Rules). The application will be considered on the papers by a senior immigration judge of the AIT. The other side in the appeal will be notified by the Tribunal that an application for permission to appeal has been made. An appeal may only be brought on a 'point of law' and therefore permission is only likely to be granted if the decision of the AIT involves an arguable error of law important to the decision.

Normally the AIT will either grant or refuse permission to appeal. However, where the senior immigration judge intends to grant permission to appeal, but they think that the AIT has made an 'administrative error' in relation to the proceedings, they can instead 'set aside' the AIT's earlier decision. In such a case the senior immigration judge will direct that the appeal be re-heard by the AIT (rule 36(3), Procedure Rules).

The decision of the senior immigration judge will be issued in writing with summary reasons.

Renewing application to the Court of Appeal

If the senior immigration judge refuses permission to appeal, the application for permission to appeal can be renewed to the Court of Appeal itself (s103B(3)(b) 2002 Act and see CPR part 52). In order to apply to the Court of Appeal for permission to appeal, the applicant has to file a notice of appeal and apply for permission to appeal in that notice. The forms are available from the Court Service website. The Court of Appeal requires grounds of appeal and also a skeleton argument in support of the reasons. It is important that applicants are helped by experienced advisers if the matter is taken to the Court of Appeal.

The Court of Appeal also considers applications for permission to appeal on the papers and will issue a decision granting or refusing permission to appeal in writing. If permission is refused, the applicant may ask for an oral hearing of the application for permission to appeal. Occasionally, the Court will not make a final decision on the application for permission to appeal but will direct that the application for permission should be heard at an oral hearing often with the other side able to attend and make submissions. If, after an oral hearing, the Court of Appeal refuses permission to appeal, there is no further appeal.

Time-limits

The time-limit for submitting an application for permission to appeal to the AIT is ten days (five days if the applicant is detained under immigration powers and two days in fast track cases). The AIT has no power to extend this time-limit (rule 35, Procedure Rules; Rule 25, Fast Track Rules). Time runs from 'after [the applicant] is served with the Tribunal's decision'. For these purposes, the same deeming provisions as to when the applicant is treated as having received the decision apply as above at ▶1136 (see rule 55). The day that the determination is treated as having been received is not counted as a day for the purposes of the time-limit and nor are 'business days' (i.e. Saturdays, Sundays, Bank holidays, 25–31 December and Good Friday) (rules 2, 57).

The time-limit for filing the notice following the decision of the AIT to refuse permission to appeal is 14 days (CPR part 52.4(2)(b)). The Court of Appeal can extend time for this application and, if an extension is needed, it should be applied for in the notice. Within seven days of it being lodged with the Court, the party appealing should also serve the other side with a copy of the notice.

Before the Court of Appeal

If permission to appeal is granted either by the AIT or the Court of Appeal, then there will be a hearing of the appeal before the Court of Appeal. Once permission has been granted to an appellant, it is possible that the Home Office may agree what the outcome should be and the parties are able 'by consent' to agree an order which the Court of Appeal should make. Often this will be limited to remitting the appeal back to the AIT for reconsideration. The Court of Appeal has the following powers, it can: uphold the decision of the AIT; set aside the decision of the AIT and make any decision that the AIT could have made on the appeal; or remit the appeal to the AIT (see s103B(4) 2002 Act).

When the AIT determines an appeal, it has the power to give 'directions' for the purpose giving effect to its decision (see s87 2002 Act). For example, if it allows an appeal against a refusal of entry clearance to an appellant, it may 'direct' the ECO to grant entry clearance in a particular capacity. The Court of Appeal also has the power to affirm or vary any directions that have been given by the AIT; it may give any other direction that the AIT could have given.

The House of Lords

If the decision of the Court of Appeal on the full appeal is negative, either party to the appeal can ask the Court of Appeal for permission to appeal to the House of Lords and they may petition the House of Lords themselves for permission to appeal. Permission will only be granted if the case raises a point of law of 'general public importance'. Few cases reach the House of Lords.

OTHER ROUTES TO THE COURT OF APPEAL

In addition to the above, there are two further routes by which an appeal might reach the Court of Appeal under the appeal system in force from 4 April 2005.

Reference by the High Court

Where the High Court (or other appropriate court in Scotland and Northern Ireland) is considering an application for a review of a first decision of the AIT under section 103A, instead of dismissing the application or making an order for reconsideration, it may 'refer' the appeal to the Court of Appeal. The High Court will only do this if it thinks that the appeal raises a 'question of law of such importance that it should be decided' by the Court of Appeal (see s103C 2002 Act; CPR part 54.33(4)). The High Court can do this on its own initiative but there is nothing to prevent an applicant suggesting this course to the High Court in a case where it is warranted.

Where a reference is made, the Court of Appeal has exactly the same powers as above to affirm the AIT's decision, make its own decision or to remit the case to the AIT. Alternatively, the Court of Appeal can also send the matter back to the High Court for it to continue to consider the application for a review. If the appeal is sent back to the High Court, that Court cannot again refer it to the Court of Appeal (CPR part 54.33(6)).

AIT sitting as a legal panel

Where the AIT, which considered the appeal, sat as a panel of three or more legally qualified members, applicants have no right to apply to the

AIT or the High Court for a review of their decision (s103A(8) 2002 Act). In order to challenge the decision of such a panel, applicants must appeal on a point of law to the Court of Appeal (or appropriate appellate court where the appeal was decided in Scotland or Northern Ireland) (see s103E 2002 Act).

The reason behind this is that a legal panel is only likely to have been appointed to deal with the case if it raised complex or important issues of law. Parliament has presumably therefore felt that it is not appropriate for immigration judges of the same tier to be reviewing the initial decision on appeal and that very important points should go directly up to the Court of Appeal. An appeal can still only be brought with the permission of the AIT or, if the AIT refuses permission, the Court of Appeal (as described above). On the appeal, the Court of Appeal has exactly the same powers as above to affirm the AIT's decision, make its own decision, or to remit the case to the AIT as set out above.

WHEN CAN JUDICIAL REVIEW STILL BE USED?

The procedures for 'statutory review' of the old IAT decisions refusing permission to appeal (under the 2002 Act) and the present system of applying to the High Court for a review of the AIT's decision have largely replaced judicial review. However judicial review remains relevant in the context of the appeal system, in circumstances set out below.

For details of judicial review procedures, ▶see 1213–22.

Decisions of the Home Office concerning appeals

Judicial review remains open:

- in cases certified by the Home Office as 'clearly unfounded' so that there is no in-country right of appeal (▶1073–8);
- in cases in which the Home Office refuses to accept that a fresh claim giving rise to an appeal has been made (▶730–5);
- in cases where the Home Office issues a certificate under section 96 of the 2002 Act to deny an appeal on the grounds that there has been an earlier right of appeal (▶1067–9).

For the use of appeal and judicial review in 'third country' cases, ▶see 739–46. Of course, the Home Office may take a range of other decisions against which there is no right of appeal and against which judicial review will lie in immigration cases (▶see 1216–7).

Decisions of the AIT that are 'procedural, ancillary or preliminary'

Procedural, ancillary or preliminary decisions cannot be challenged by asking the AIT or the High Court for a section 103A review (see s103A(7)(a) 2002 Act). Unfortunately, the legislation does not give a definition of what is meant by these decisions and where the line is to be drawn between judicial review and a section 103A review. It seems clear that a refusal of an application for bail could only be challenged by judicial review. Other decisions which may fall into this definition and only be challengeable on judicial review might be: refusal to exercise discretion to extend time, where a notice of appeal against the decision of the immigration authorities has been submitted late; a decision that an appellant has abandoned an appeal; delay of the AIT in decision-making and other rulings of the AIT declining jurisdiction.

Statutory application to the High Court not a good enough remedy

As discussed above, from 4 April 2005, if the AIT refuses an application to review the decision made on the original appeal by the AIT, the applicant can then ask the High Court to review the decision (s103A 2002 Act). This procedure is similar to the procedure of statutory review introduced under the 2002 Act to replace the system of judicial review of IAT decisions to refuse permission to appeal. The difficulty with both of these procedures is that the decision of the High Court is said to be 'final'. Applicants have no right to an oral hearing and neither can they go to the Court of Appeal.

In *R (G) v IAT* and *R (M) v IAT* (CA), as well as applying for statutory review of the IAT's decision, the applicants also brought applications for judicial review. The Court of Appeal held that, while the High Court still has a jurisdiction to hear applications for judicial review, because there is an adequate alternative remedy, which balances the need to protect rights against the need to determine asylum applications quickly, the High Court can properly use its discretion to refuse to hear a judicial review claim of issues that are the same as those which arise on the statutory review. In those two cases, the grounds relied on were the same in the judicial review claims as in the statutory review applications (see at paras 5, 6). The Court of Appeal also found that the general inability to claim judicial review was not unlawful as being discriminatory. *G & M* are being appealed to the House of Lords. The outcome will be relevant to the ability to use judicial review in cases generally governed by the old statutory review regime (in transitional cases) and under the 'section 103A' review procedure under the 2004 Act.

Note that the Court in *G & M* accepted that judicial review would remain open in cases where the alleged errors could not be brought on statutory review (para. 27). However, the decision of the Court of Appeal in *E & R* indicates that possible grounds of appeal under 'error of law' are probably just as wide as grounds for judicial review (para. 40) and so it is not clear what additional space for judicial review was intended by this.

TRANSITIONAL APPEAL ARRANGEMENTS

From 4 April 2005, adjudicators and the Immigration Appeal Tribunal no longer exist. Therefore, from that date, no appeals have been heard by those bodies. What has happened to those cases that were in the system on 3 April 2005 and had not been finally resolved by that date? This includes appeals which were pending before adjudicators and the IAT, applications for statutory review pending before the Administrative Court and appeals to the Court of Appeal. It also includes cases in which a decision within the appeal system had been made by 4 April 2005, but there was still an opportunity to challenge it on or after that date.

In order to accommodate outstanding cases into the new system, transitional arrangements had to be made. These are contained in Articles 3-9 of the Asylum and Immigration (Treatment of Claimants, etc) Act 2004 (Commencement No 5 and Transitional Provisions) Order 2005. They explain how appeals or applications in the two-tier system are transported into the new system. The effect of those provisions is as follows.

1) Where an adjudicator or the IAT had completed the hearing of an appeal before 4 April but had not produced their determination or the determination had not been served on the parties, that adjudicator or IAT are treated as continuing to exist until the determination is completed and served.

2) An appeal or application that was pending before an adjudicator before 4 April, continues as an appeal or application to the AIT. If dismissed, in most cases, it may be challenged by applying to the AIT for a review (s103A 2002 Act).

3) An appeal pending before an adjudicator before 4 April having been remitted to an adjudicator by the IAT or a higher court continues as an appeal to the AIT as a reconsideration hearing (▶see 1143–7). When the appeal is determined, it can be challenged by an appeal (with permission) to the Court of Appeal.

4) An appeal pending before the IAT before 4 April, continues as an appeal to the AIT as a reconsideration hearing (▶see 1143–7). When the appeal is determined, it can be challenged by an appeal (with permission) to the Court of Appeal.

5) An application for permission to appeal to the IAT, which was made before 4 April but which was still outstanding at that date, continues as an application for a review under s103A 2002 Act. The new public funding provisions, which enable the High Court or AIT to decide whether funding should be given for the application do not apply to such cases.

6) Where an adjudicator has determined an appeal before 4 April, but no application for permission to appeal to the IAT was lodged before that date, the applicant can apply for a review of the determination and an order for reconsideration under s103A 2002 Act. If the time-limit for permission to appeal to the IAT began to run before 4 April, then the more generous time-limits under the old Procedure Rules will apply, instead of the normal time-limits for a review under section 103A.

7) An application for statutory review of a decision of the IAT to refuse permission to appeal, which was pending on 3 April continues in the same way as if the relevant provision allowing statutory review had not been

repealed. Similarly, an applicant who, on 3 April, would be able to apply for a statutory review of the IAT's decision, would still be entitled to make that application after 3 April. In deciding the application, the High Court judge can either affirm the refusal of permission by the IAT, reverse the decision of the IAT to grant permission to appeal *or* make an order for reconsideration by the AIT.

8) An appeal, or application for permission to appeal, to the Court of Appeal under section 103 of the 2002 Act, which was pending on 3 April, continues after that time as if that section had not been repealed. Where an application for permission to appeal to the Court of Appeal was pending before the IAT on 3 April, the application would be determined by the AIT.

9) Anyone who, on 3 April, was entitled to apply to the IAT, or to the Court of Appeal, for permission to appeal to the Court of Appeal, could still apply for permission to appeal as if section 103 2002 Act had not been repealed. In cases where the applicant was entitled to apply to the IAT for permission to appeal, the application would be considered by the AIT.

Note that, obviously, the transitional arrangements do not relieve applicants from having to comply with the applicable time-limits. As to general procedures, with some limited transitional arrangements (►see 1087), the Asylum and Immigration Tribunal (Procedure) Rules 2005 apply to those appeals or applications to the adjudicator or IAT which were pending on 3 April 2005 (see rule 62 Procedure Rules).

PUBLIC FUNDING (LEGAL AID) CONSIDERATIONS

The 2004 Act introduces new public funding provisions which act to restrict funding in applications for a review of the AIT's original decision on the appeal (see further s103D 2002 Act; Community Legal Service (Asylum and Immigration Appeals) Regulations 2005; rules 28A, 33 Procedure Rules; Practice Directions, paras 2.2(11) and 15.1–15.9).

10

The provisions apply to applications to the AIT and the High Court for a review of a decision of the AIT on an appeal and to the reconsideration hearing if reconsideration is ordered. They only apply in relation to appeals that were decided in England and Wales, and not to those decided in Scotland. The provisions do not apply to fast track cases, or where an application for review has been made by the Home Office, or applications pending before the IAT prior to 4 April 2005.

The effect of the new provisions is that practitioners need to apply to the High Court and the AIT for an order that public funding is granted. They should do so as part of the review application. The AIT will normally hear oral submissions on funding at the end of the reconsideration proceedings (Practice Directions, para. 15.5).

When will funding be granted/refused?

Funding is not automatically granted. The following points should be noted.

- If the section 103A review application is refused, funding will only be granted where there has been a change in circumstances, or the law, since the application was made and if, at the time when the application was made, the appeal had 'significant prospects of success' (see below) upon reconsideration.

- If the High Court refers the case to the Court of Appeal, it should grant funding.

- If the AIT allows an appeal after reconsideration, it will order funding.

- If the AIT dismisses an appeal after reconsideration, it should only order funding if, when the application was made, there was a 'significant prospect' (►see below) that it would succeed on reconsideration.

- A funding order can be made where there has been an order for reconsideration but no reconsideration hearing takes place, for example because the immigration decision appealed against is withdrawn. Funding can be granted for the review but it will not necessarily be granted for the preparation for reconsideration.

- Where funding is granted, advisers may be able to obtain an increase (an uplift) on the ordinary funding rates. If funding is refused, the reasonable costs of interpreters and experts are still claimable.

Decisions on orders for funding made by the AIT after reconsideration hearings must be set out in a separate written determination. Representatives may ask for a review of such determinations by application in writing. Such reviews are determined by a senior immigration judge who was not involved in the decision that is being reviewed.

The Legal Services Commission (LSC) has given advisers who hold contracts to provide publicly funded representation under the Controlled Legal Representation (CLR) scheme, devolved powers to grant themselves CLR if the appropriate means and merits tests are satisfied (set out in Chapter 3 at 71–3). However, payment under the CLR scheme is subject to the grant of a funding order by the High Court or AIT. 'Significant prospects of success' is not defined in legislation or by the LSC. However, in a letter to the President of the Bar Council on 23 February 2005, the Lord Chancellor stated:

'It will be for the judiciary to interpret what is meant by significant prospects of success but the intention is that if a supplier acts in good faith and pursues a case through to the reconsideration stage they can expect to be paid for their work. It is important, however, that every case is decided on an individual basis and that success at the review stage is not in itself sufficient to secure funding...

Please be assured that the scheme has not been designed to deny representation to appellants with good, albeit not certain, prospects of success. Funding will be awarded based on merit not success…taking on a case will involve financial risk only if its prospects of success are poor. Representatives that act conscientiously and pursue meritorious cases can expect to be paid.'

In the case of *Seidi* the AIT has made a finding on the meaning of 'significant prospects of success' which equates it to that of 'a real possibility'.

Impact on access to justice

The effect of the above is that, in order to pursue cases, legal representatives will have to undertake work without knowing whether that work will be funded. If, ultimately, funding is not granted, this means that practitioners will not be paid for the work that they have done.

The upshot is that representatives work on a basis which is similar to a 'no win, no fee' arrangement. This is likely to mean that applicants will find it hard to obtain good quality representation to pursue challenges against the AIT. Many representatives may be deterred by the risk that they may receive no funding for the substantial work involved in making the review application and representing at the reconsideration hearing. Additionally, it may be that they take on such cases only in a limited number or type of case. Inevitably, there will be applicants who are denied justice as a result.

SHOWING AN ERROR OF LAW

As set out above, showing that there is an error of law is central to challenging decisions of the AIT. This can be summarised as follows.

- An order for reconsideration will only be made if either the AIT or the High Court thinks that the AIT 'may have made an error of law' and there is a 'real possibility' that the AIT would make a different decision on reconsidering the appeal (s103A(2)(a) 2002 Act; CPR part 54.33(5); rule 26(6) Procedure Rules).

- If an order for reconsideration is made, the AIT will only reconsider the merits of the case afresh and make a fresh decision on the appeal if it is satisfied that the original AIT 'made a material error of law' (rule 31(2)(3), Procedure Rules).

- Appeals to the Court of Appeal may only be brought on a 'point of law' (s103B(1), 103E(1) 2002 Act).

In *CA v SSHD*, the Court of Appeal underlined the importance of having to show an error of law. It distinguished between a system where challenges may only be made on the basis of error of law and the system in place before the 2002 Act when appeals from the adjudicator to the IAT could be on fact as well as law (see paras 14–16, 30 and the rejection by the Court that anything approaching an error of law had occurred in that case, paras 24–28).

For a checklist of typical errors of law, see the table below. For further details about the developing area of mistakes of fact which can amount to errors of law and fresh evidence, ▶see 1159–61.

IDENTIFYING ERRORS OF LAW

When considering whether there are any legal errors in the decision of the AIT, the person preparing the grounds of challenge should ask themselves the following questions. Note that this checklist does not cover all possible errors of law. It should also be borne in mind that the same error is often capable of being described in different ways.

- Has the AIT considered and dealt with all the relevant appeals and grounds of appeal that were brought?
- Has the AIT applied the correct burden and standard of proof? (▶see 1121–3) (and see how the standard of proof is set out in particular in *Karanakaran*).
- Has the AIT used the correct date for making findings of fact? (*Ravichandran, Kotecha* and see s85(4)(5) 2002 Act and ▶see 1119–21)
- Has the AIT made an error in understanding, or failing to apply, or properly considering the law set out in the:
  - immigration rules;
  - legislation;
  - Refugee Convention;
  - ECHR; or
  - case law interpreting any of the above?
- Has the AIT properly considered any Home Office policy upon which the appellant relied in order to say that the decision of the respondent was 'not in accordance with the law'? (*DS Abdi* and see s84(1)(e), 86(3)(a) 2002 Act).
- Did the applicant, the immigration authorities and the AIT proceed on an understanding of the relevant law subsequently discovered to be wrong? (*Ivanauskiene*)
- If the AIT has found against the appellant on grounds of credibility, was the determination prepared in a reasonable time after hearing the evidence? The traditional rule of thumb has been that if the determination is prepared over three months after the hearing and credibility is in issue, the evidence will have gone stale in the AIT's mind and the findings may be unsafe (*Subaskaran; Mario v SSHD*).
- Did the AIT conduct the proceedings unfairly? It may be that decisions made in the course of the appeal have led to unfairness: should the AIT have transferred a fast tracked case to the ordinary track? If an adjournment request was refused, were adequate reasons given for the refusal? (*Sesay, Cabrera*).
- Does the determination make proper findings of fact and give sufficient reasons for the decision? In the case of *Amin*, Schiemann J stated, in relation to a non-asylum appeal, that it must be stated with clarity what evidence is accepted, what evidence is rejected and what evidence, if any, the decision-maker cannot make their mind up about. In an asylum or human rights case,

the findings and reasons must be particularly well set out and, if there is evidence that the AIT is uncertain about, they must bear in mind the low standard of proof and the positive role which, the courts have decided, must be given to any uncertainty. In *R (Iran) v SSHD* it was said that a decision may be set aside for inadequacy of reasons if the decision-maker has failed to identify and record the matters which were critical to the decision on material issues in such a way that they are understandable (▶see below).

- As an example of a failure to give proper reasons, in an Article 8 case, has the AIT considered and given reasons for the decision adopting the 'step by step' approach to the different aspects of Article 8? (▶see 821–2)

- Were there any matters on which the AIT drew negative inferences as to an appellant or their witnesses' credibility but which were: (1) not in the Home Office's grounds of refusal; (2) not put to the appellant or their representative in order for them to be addressed; (3) could not reasonably have been anticipated, and (4) in all the circumstances of the case, unfairly not put to the appellant? (*SSHD v Balasingham Maheshwaran, Bahar, Gaima, Mayiso-kele, Sahota v IAT*).

- Has the AIT taken into account all relevant evidence, which was put before it? (*S v SSHD*) The determination may be flawed if, for instance, the AIT has failed to have regard to:
  - evidence of witnesses *(AK (Turkey))*;
  - statements in support of the case even if the witnesses were not called;
  - background evidence of country conditions (*Horvath, Danleu*);
  - expert reports;
  - medical evidence – careful and specific consideration should be given to medical reports (*Swaleh Mohammed; R (Beqaraj) v Special Adjudicator*);
  - specific documentary evidence relating to a particular case, for example direct evidence of charges, arrest warrants or membership of a political party or other organisation.

- Has the AIT failed to apply a country guidance case without good reason? (Practice Directions, para. 18.4; *R(Iran) v SSHD*):

- Has the AIT rejected an appellant's credibility:
  - just because it has not been supported by other sources? (*Kasolo*)
  - because the account given is implausible in the view of the AIT but that implausibility, in reality, reflects assumptions made by the AIT based on its own perspective, rather than on what may be the case in the very different conditions of the appellant's country of origin? (*Mendes, Adebizi*)
  - solely because the appellant has not given live evidence? (*Coskuner*)

- Has the AIT rejected a witness's credibility solely because they are related to the appellant or have some other interest in the appeal? (*Ahmed (Kalem)*)

- Has the AIT rejected facts or an appellant's credibility even though the Home Office agreed to concede the relevant facts? (*R (Ganidagli) v SSHD*)

- Has the AIT simply 'rubber stamped' the decision of the immigration

10

authorities without properly independently considering the issue for itself? (see *A (Nigeria) v ECO*).

- Has the AIT misunderstood the basis of the claim, the appeal or important evidence in the case?

- Is the decision based on an error of subsequently established facts such that the decision is unfair? (*E v SSHD*, ▶see below at 1159–61).

- Has the AIT inaccurately recorded evidence given at the appeal leading to incorrect findings?

- Are the factual findings of the AIT so against the weight of evidence that they can be described as 'perverse' or 'irrational' i.e. so unreasonable that no decision-maker with all of the evidence in mind could properly have made those findings?

- In asylum/human rights cases, where the AIT has accepted part, although not all, of an appellant's account, has the AIT properly considered whether the applicant is at risk in their country of origin on the basis of the facts that were accepted by the AIT?

- In a case where the Home Office presenting officer did not attend the hearing, has the AIT followed the guidelines set down for such cases in *MNM*? (▶see 1103–4)

Summary of errors of law set out in *R (Iran) & Others v SSHD*

In *R(Iran) & Others v SSHD*, the Court of Appeal provided the following summary of the most commonly occurring errors of law (paras 9–10):

- making perverse or irrational findings on a matter or matters that were material to the outcome ('material matters');

- failing to give reasons or any adequate reasons for findings on material matters;

- failing to take into account and/or resolve conflicts of fact or opinion on material matters;

- giving weight to immaterial matters;

- making a material misdirection of law on any material matter;

- committing or permitting a procedural or other irregularity capable of making a material difference to the outcome or the fairness of the proceedings;

- making a mistake as to a material fact which could be established by objective and uncontentious evidence, where the appellant and/or their advisers were not responsible for the mistake, and where unfairness resulted from the fact that a mistake was made.

Note that the Court underlined that each of the descriptions of errors of law above contained the word 'material' (or 'immaterial'). Errors of law which make no difference to the outcome of the appeal have no relevance.

MISTAKES OF FACT AND FRESH EVIDENCE

Lawyers are always careful to distinguish between 'fact' and 'law'. Challenges to the AIT depend on showing an error of law (above). In any cases where judicial review can be used, this is also normally the case (▶see 1150–1 above and ▶see 1214–6). So, it seems strange to suggest that the AIT might commit an error of law by misunderstanding the facts.

If the AIT has simply made a complete mistake about certain matters, or misread relevant important evidence that was before it, then it is fairly straightforward to see that such amounts to an error in law. In such a case, the AIT will have simply misunderstood the case and therefore the appeal will not have been properly considered and the reasons for dismissing it will be flawed. However, in *E & R v SSHD*, the Court of Appeal had to consider the question of whether there can be an error of law if the mistake of fact is only apparent from evidence which was *not* before the decision-making body at the time it heard the appeal and before it promulgated its decision. In those cases, the appellants submitted new country evidence (which had not been before the IAT) to the IAT at the point at which they applied for permission to appeal to the Court of Appeal.

E & R concerned an appeal to the Court of Appeal under the *1999 Act*. It also occurred at a time when the Procedure Rules gave the IAT a broad power to set aside the IAT's own decision and direct that an appeal be re-heard by the IAT instead of granting or refusing permission to appeal to the Court of Appeal. The power of the present AIT to set aside its own decisions when faced with an application for permission to appeal to the Court of Appeal is narrower. It is restricted to where the AIT has made an 'administrative error' (rule 36(3) Procedure Rules). However, in its starred decision, *MA (Fresh Evidence) Sri Lanka v SSHD*, the IAT held that the principles set down in *E & R* are relevant more generally. Those principles are set out below – a summary of the present position for practical purposes comes at the end of our description of the principles (▶see 1161).

The test under *E & R v SSHD*

The new evidence in *E & R* was intended to show that the decision of the IAT was mistaken regarding the objective risk to the appellants. Could that evidence show that there had been error of law? The Court of Appeal held (see paras 63-67, 91(ii)):

'In our view, the time has now come to accept that a mistake of fact giving rise to unfairness is a separate head of challenge in an appeal on a point of law, at least in those statutory contexts where the parties share an interest in co-operating to achieve the correct result. Asylum law is undoubtedly such an area.'

The Court indicated that, in order to show such an error, the appellant will normally need to show that:

- there has been a mistake as to an existing fact, including a mistake about the availability of evidence on a particular matter;
- the fact or evidence has now been 'established' i.e. the evidence must be clear, not contentious, and the established fact must be objectively verifiable;
- the appellant, (or their adviser) who is seeking to rely on the evidence, is not responsible for the mistake; and
- the mistake influenced the decision on the appeal.

MA Sri Lanka illustrates the application of the above test. The IAT applied the tests strictly and the only part of the test to be passed was the fourth point above. In that case, a *Sunday Times* journalist gave evidence that the appellant had led her escort to the leader of the LTTE for an interview on a major change in LTTE policy and that the appellant was a middle-ranking LTTE officer. The evidence did not meet the second test above and it was said to be rare that disputed oral evidence could be non-contentious and objectively verifiable. To be genuinely non-contentious, the evidence had to be the sort of evidence that would lead anyone to say that 'of course' a mistake had been made and it was a mistake about an identifiable fact. The appellant was also found to be to blame for the mistake (see *MA* at paras 48–55).

But the above test only deals with the requirements for showing an error of law in principle. In new evidence cases, the Court of Appeal also held that appellants face a separate hurdle: should the evidence be admitted for consideration in the first place? (Para. 36 and ▶see below.)

But will the new evidence be admitted?

The Court in *E &R* held that before the new evidence could show an error of law, a further question has to be asked of whether it should be admitted at all. The normal test that the courts use to decide whether evidence not put before the original decision-maker should be admitted on appeal is set out in a well-known case, *Ladd v Marshall*. That case decided that new evidence is not admissible unless it meets *all* of the following requirements, namely it:

- could not, with 'due diligence' have previously been obtained;
- would probably have had an important influence on the outcome of the case;
- is 'apparently credible' (this means 'believable on the face of it', although not conclusive).

The Court in *E & R* confirmed that the test in *Ladd v Marshall* is the starting point for deciding whether the new evidence should be considered. *However*, it also confirmed that there is a discretion to admit the new evidence in exceptional cases where the interests of justice require it even if the above requirements are not satisfied (see paras 81-82, 91(iii)). Often, there will be a need for flexibility in operating this discretion in asylum and human rights cases where obtaining reliable evidence is difficult and because of what is at stake if mistakes of fact are made. From previous decided cases on this topic, it seems that the requirements of fairness in the context of the individual case will have a large part to play in deciding whether the evidence should be admitted.

Present practical impact of the above rules about fresh evidence

The IAT in *MA (Fresh Evidence) Sri Lanka* demonstrated that the principles in *E & R* have wide relevance. For the purposes of the appeal system in place since 4 April 2005, we suggest the practical upshot is as follows.

If the determination of the AIT can be shown to be mistaken as a matter of fact by evidence which was not before the AIT, then that evidence can be relied on where the applicant needs to show an error of law, or that there may have been an error of law, namely in:

- applications for review (to the AIT or High Court);
- reconsideration hearings at the first stage where the AIT is deciding whether the earlier AIT has made a material error of law; and
- applications for permission to appeal (to the Court of Appeal) (and see the Practice Directions at para. 13.8).

Using the criteria laid out above, the grounds of the application should set out how the two tests described above are met, i.e. that:

1) there has been a mistake of fact leading to unfairness; and

2) the further evidence is admissible to show (1) above either applying the *Ladd & Marshall* principles or, at the very least, on the basis of an exercise of discretion in the interests of justice.

If, however, important further evidence comes to the applicant's attention after a hearing but before the determination of the AIT is promulgated, it should be submitted to the AIT and the other side before the decision is issued (see *E & R* at paras 27, 92(i)). It is a good idea to explain the importance of the evidence in written submissions. It is possible that the AIT will reconvene to hear oral submissions.

For the procedure which must be followed in relation to further evidence in reconsideration hearings generally, and the approach at reconsideration to further evidence after a material error of law has been found, ▶see 1144–6 above.

If the new evidence is rejected by the AIT or the Court as not satisfying the above tests, applicants can still put the material to the Home Office either as part of a 'fresh claim', or simply in order for the case to be reviewed again whether or not the 'fresh claim' conditions (▶for which see 730–5) are satisfied.

10

TIME-LIMITS

In all cases it is extremely important to ensure that appeals and applications are made within the strict time-limits that are set down. Immigration and asylum appeals probably involve tighter time-limits than any other area of law. This is because the government puts a premium on deciding cases quickly and believes that some applicants attempt to 'string out' appeals. This is despite the fact that, as anyone with experience of the system will be aware, a great deal of time lost is due to Home Office inefficiency and maladministration. The time-limits in fast track cases are almost impossibly tight.

The relevant time-limits are set out in the table below.

TIME-LIMITS FOR APPEALING

For further details about bringing the particular appeals/applications referred to, follow the cross-references, which are given in the table.

Unless otherwise stated, references to:

- 'Procedure Rules' are to the Asylum and Immigration Tribunal (Procedure) Rules 2005;
- 'Fast Track Rules' are to the Asylum and Immigration Tribunal (Fast Track Procedure) Rules 2005;
- 'Fast Track Order' are to the Asylum and Immigration (Fast Track Time Limits) Order 2005;
- CPRs are to the Civil Procedure Rules as amended by the Civil Procedure (Amendment) Rules 2005.

For the rules about calculating time, see the notes at the end of the table.

APPEAL/APPLICATION	TIME-LIMIT
Appeals to the AIT	
Appeal to AIT where appellant is appealing while *in* the UK (▶1061–6, 1091–4). **(rule 7(1), Procedure Rules)**	Ten days after being served with notice decision.
	Five days after being served with notice of decision if appellant is detained under immigration powers (non-fast track) when served with the decision.
Appeal to AIT where appellant is appealing while *outside* the UK (▶and see further 1061–6, 1091–4). **(rule 7(2), Procedure Rules)**	28 days after being served with the notice of the decision.
	28 days after they left the UK in a case where the appellant was in the UK when the decision was made but is not permitted to appeal while in the UK.

The above time-limits may all be extended if the AIT is satisfied that there are 'special circumstances' which make it 'unjust' not to extend time (rule 10(5), Procedure Rules). For further details, ▶see 1092–4.

APPEAL/APPLICATION	TIME-LIMIT
Appeals to AIT where appellant was detained at one of the following 'fast track' centres on the day the notice was served, and continues to be detained there: Campsfield House, Colnbrook House Harmondsworth, Yarls Wood (▶1063–6, 1130). **(rules 5, 8 and Sch 2, Fast Track Rules)**	Two days after being served with notice of the decision.

This time-limit can be extended but only if the AIT is satisfied that 'because of circumstances outside the control of the person giving notice of appeal or his representative, it was not practicable for the notice of appeal to be given' in time (rule 8(2), Fast Track Rules).

APPEAL/APPLICATION	TIME-LIMIT

Application to the AIT for a review of determination of the AIT

APPEAL/APPLICATION	TIME-LIMIT
Application to the AIT for a review of determination of the AIT under section 103A 2002 Act (▶1134–40). **(s103A(3) 2002 Act)**	Five days from the date when the applicant is treated as receiving the decision of the AIT in cases where they are *in* the UK when they make the application.
	Five days from the date when they are treated as receiving the decision of the AIT in cases where it is the immigration authorities that are asking for a review.
	28 days from the date when the applicant is treated as receiving the decision of the AIT in cases where the applicant is *outside* the UK when they make the application (but ▶see further 1136–7).
Application to the AIT (by either party) for a review of determination of the AIT under section 103A 2002 Act where appellant was detained at one of the following 'fast track' centres on the day the original notice of decision of the immigration	Two days from the date when the applicant is treated as receiving the decision of the AIT.

10

APPEAL/APPLICATION	TIME-LIMIT

authorities was served, and
continues to be detained there:
Campsfield House, Colnbrook
House, Harmondsworth, Yarls Wood.
(Article 3, Fast Track Order)

Time-limits for applications to the AIT for a review of decisions of the AIT can be extended but only if the AIT thinks that the application 'could not reasonably, practicably have been made within' the time-limit (s103A(4)(b) 2002 Act; paras 30(1), (4) Sch 2 2004 Act, rule 26(5)(a) Procedure Rules)(▶see 1137).

APPEAL/APPLICATION	TIME-LIMIT

Application to the High Court for a review of a decision of the AIT

Application to the High Court for a review of a determination of the AIT under section 103A 2002 Act – this is a renewed application after the AIT has refused the application (▶1139–40) (see further 1140–43 and in particular note the position in relation to out-of-country cases). **(para. 30(5)(b), Sch 2 2004 Act)**	Five days from the date when the applicant is treated as having received the decision of the AIT proposing to refuse to make an order for reconsideration.
Application to the High Court for a review of a determination of the AIT under section103A 2002 Act where the appellant was detained at one of the following 'fast track' centres on the day the original notice of decision of the immigration authorities was served, and continues to be detained there: Campsfield House, Colnbrook House, Harmondsworth, Yarls Wood. **(Article 4, Fast Track Order)**	Two days from the date when the applicant is treated as having received the decision of the AIT proposing to refuse to make an order for reconsideration.

Time-limits for applications to the High Court for a review of decisions of the AIT can be extended but only if the High Court thinks that the application 'could not reasonably practicably have been made within' the time-limit (para. 30(5)(c)(ii), Sch 2 2004 Act; CPR part 54.31(4))(see ▶1141).

APPEAL/APPLICATION	TIME-LIMIT
Application to AIT for permission to appeal to the Court of Appeal	
Application for permission to appeal to the Court of Appeal from decision of the AIT (▶1147–8, 1149–50). **(rule 35, Procedure Rules)**	Ten days after being served with notice of decision. Five days after being served with notice of decision if appellant is detained under immigration powers (non-fast track) when served with the decision of the AIT.
Application for permission to appeal to the Court of Appeal where the appellant was detained at one of the following 'fast track' centres on the day the notice was served, and continues to be detained there: Campsfield House, Colnbrook House, Harmondsworth, Yarls Wood (▶1131). **(rule 25, Fast Track Rules)**	Two days after being served with notice of the decision of the AIT.

The AIT cannot extend the time-limits for applications for permission to the AIT to appeal against the decision of the AIT (rule 35(2), Procedure Rules; rule 25(2) Fast Track Rules) (▶1148).

For renewed applications for permission to appeal to the Court of Appeal, ▶see 1147–8.

NOTES ON CALCULATING TIME

'Being served'/'treated as having received'

The above time-limits are all triggered by the applicant either 'being served' or being 'treated as having received' the decision. So, in order to determine when time starts running, it is necessary to know when these events occur. In all cases, the rules about this are contained in rule 55 of the Procedure Rules (applied to fast track cases by rules 3(3) and 27 of the Fast Track Rules; applied to 'section 103A' review cases by s103A(3) 2002 Act and para. 30(5)(b), Sch 2 2004 Act).

Unless the contrary is proved, a person is treated as being served with or receiving the decision:

- if the decision is sent by post or DX from and to a place in the UK, on the second day after it was sent (▶see 1136 for an example and explanation);
- if the decision is sent by post or DX from or to a place outside the UK, on the 28th day after it was sent (but ▶see 1136–7 and 1141 for cases where a determination on the appeal is sent from the UK to a representative in the UK);

10

- in any other case (for example, fax, email or personal service) on the day on which it was sent, delivered to, or left with the person.

The Rules have been drafted in accordance with the decision of the Court of Appeal in *Saleem*. That case declared as unlawful earlier rules, which had had the effect of 'deeming' notices and determinations as having been received even when in fact they had not been. So, if an apparent time-limit is missed because the applicant had not received the notice of decision, it is up to the applicant to show they did not, in fact, receive it. Note that the Procedure Rules state that documents served on notified representatives, or the applicant's last notified address, will be deemed to have been served on the applicant (rules 55(3), 56).

Counting time: appeals to the AIT and applications to the AIT for permission to appeal to the Court of Appeal

For these appeals/applications (rules 2, 57, Procedure Rules):

- the day on which the period begins is ignored – so if the decision is treated as having been served on Monday 18 July, the first day of the specified time-limit is Tuesday 19 July;
- where the time-limit is ten days or less, only 'business days' are counted. The following days are not 'business days' and are therefore ignored: Saturdays; Sundays; Bank Holidays; 25-31 December; and Good Friday. So, these days will not be ignored in the 28-day time-limit cases i.e. where the appellant is appealing from outside the UK (▶see 1062–3, 1148).

Counting time: appeals to the AIT and applications to the AIT for permission to appeal to the Court of Appeal in fast track cases

For these appeals/applications (rule 57 Procedure Rules applied to fast track cases by rules 3(3) and 27 Fast Track Rules but modified by rule 2(3) Fast Track Rules):

- the day on which the period begins is ignored (as above);
- where the time-limit is ten days or less, only 'business days' are counted. The following days are *not* 'business days' for these purposes and are therefore ignored: Saturdays; Sundays; Bank Holidays; 25–31 December; Maundy Thursday; Good Friday; and the Tuesday after the last Monday in May (note that the definition of non-business days is slightly different to the definition in non-fast track cases above). The time-limits for fast track cases are less than ten days (▶see above) and so these days will be excluded.

Counting time: applications to AIT or High Court for review of decision of AIT

For these applications (CPR parts 2.8 and 54.28(4); s103A(4)(a) 2002 Act; para. 30(3)(b) Sch 2 2004 Act)(and ▶see 1136–7, 1141):

- the day on which the time period 'begins' is not counted;
- where the time-limit is five days or less, the following days do not count: Saturdays; Sundays; Bank Holidays; Christmas Day; Good Friday (note the days which do not count are slightly different from appeals to the AIT and

applications for permission to appeal to the Court of Appeal in both non-fast track and fast track cases above). The time-limit for most of these cases is five days (two days in fast track cases) and so these days will therefore be excluded in those cases. They will not, however, be excluded in cases where the applicant is *outside* the UK *and* is making the initial application to the *AIT* to review the determination – the time-limit in such cases is 28 days.

Counting time for serving notice of appeal

Notices of appeal against decisions of the immigration authorities which are served directly on an officer detaining an appellant, or (by a person appealing from outside the UK) on an entry clearance officer under rules 6(3)(b) and 6(4)(b) Procedure Rules, are treated as being served on the day on which they are in fact received by that person (rule 55(6), Procedure Rules).

Other than the above, the Procedure Rules do not directly state when the AIT is treated as having received documents or notices of appeal/application. Under the old Procedure Rules, in all cases, they were treated as being received on the date on which they were in fact received: see rule 54(7) of the 2003 Procedure Rules. In principle it seems that appeals may be lodged by post, DX, fax or email to any address specified by the AIT for that purpose (rule 55(1) Procedure Rules). It is safest to ensure that the appeal or application has, before the expiry of the time-limit, actually reached the AIT in a method and at an address specified by the AIT for that particular purpose in the documentation sent out by the AIT. Evidence (of recorded delivery, fax transmission etc) should be kept as proof of delivery.

10

Section 11 Civil claims, judicial review and other remedies

Chapter 37
Civil claims   1171

When can a civil claim be made   1172

Unlawful detention   1175

Places of detention and conditions of detention   1177

Unlawful removal   1181

Unlawful family separation   1182

Assault   1182

Unlawful searches of premises   1183

Maladministration and delay in making decisions
and issuing documents   1184

Discrimination   1187

Dispersal and denial of adequate support   1190

Malicious prosecution   1191

Making a civil claim   1192

General procedures in ordinary civil claims   1210

Chapter 38
**Judicial review, complaints, Ombudsman
and *Adimi* claims**   1213

Judicial review   1213

Complaints to and compensation from
the Home Office   1223

Contacting a Member of Parliament   1227

Parliamentary Ombudsman   1229

Compensation for unlawful conviction of
asylum-seekers under the *Adimi* principle   1235

11

37 Civil claims

This section deals with the various remedies that are available when people affected by immigration control are treated unlawfully, unfairly, or where their cases are subject to administrative failures. This chapter deals with the civil claims (also called 'civil actions') that can be made to the courts to obtain financial compensation when immigration powers are used unlawfully so as to cause people harm. First, the chapter lists the common immigration situations in which the question of making a civil claim might arise – for example, unlawful detention or unlawful removal (▶1172). We then summarise briefly the different aspects of the law that can be used to bring a civil claim in immigration cases (▶1172–4). Next, the chapter looks at each of the different immigration situations in turn in detail, and analyses the different legal claims that can be made (▶1175 onwards). Then the chapter moves on to consider the important procedural aspects of making a claim (▶1192 onwards). Included in that part of the chapter is a guide to which court the claim should be brought in (▶1193–4), time-limits (▶1196–7), and the criteria for obtaining public funding (▶1199–1201); and there is a table of comparators to help assess the level of damages in certain kinds of case (▶1205–10). Finally, we look at the stages of a civil claim in the County Court or High Court (▶see 1210–12).

There is no doubt that people who are considering bringing any of the claims referred to in this chapter should obtain legal advice from a professional experienced in the field of both immigration and civil litigation (for obtaining immigration advice generally, ▶see Chapter 3).

Chapter 38 looks at other remedies and, inevitably, it describes a number of different processes and procedures. It refers to the immigration situations in which judicial review is still the right remedy, and it describes, in outline, the procedures for applying for judicial review and obtaining injunctions (▶see 1213–22). Chapter 38 also covers the procedure for making complaints to the Home Office, and at the Home Office schemes for paying compensation for financial loss caused by its own administrative errors and making consolatory payments (▶1223–7). Should a complaint not have the desired outcome, a person may consider involving an MP, although MPs can also be asked to intervene in general immigration decisions (▶1227–8). A further remedy for those affected by administrative failures is to complain to the Parliamentary Ombudsman (▶1229–35). Finally, **Chapter 38** deals with obtaining compensation for the wrongful prosecution of asylum-seekers after the decision of the court in *Adimi*, and the criminal defence based on Article 31 of the Refugee Convention that followed that case (▶see 1235–38).

The section does not deal with appeals against immigration decisions about entry to and remaining in the UK. These appeals are dealt with in Section 10. Certain special kinds of appeal – for example, reviews of decisions to refuse an Immigration Employment Document, or applications for bail – are covered in the most appropriate part of the *Handbook* (for a list of other appeals/reviews and where to find them in the *Handbook*, ▶see 1040–1).

WHEN CAN A CIVIL CLAIM BE MADE?

In the context of the immigration system, a civil claim for damages could arise in any of the following potential 'immigration situations':

- unlawful detention by the immigration authorities or the police (▶1175–7);
- unacceptable places and conditions of immigration detention (▶1177–81);
- unlawful removal from the UK (▶1181–2);
- unlawful actions causing family separation (▶1182);
- assaults and unreasonable force used while carrying out immigration control (▶1182–3);
- misuse of immigration powers in carrying out searches of premises (▶1183–4);
- failures and delays in making immigration decisions and issuing documents (▶1184–7);
- treating certain groups of people less favourably than others (discrimination) (▶1187–90);
- inadequate support and dispersal (▶1190–1);
- malicious prosecution (▶1191–2).

The above list describes general immigration situations in which a civil claim *might* arise. Just because an act is unlawful under the immigration law does not necessarily mean that a civil claim can be made.

Where a civil claim is outstanding, the Home Office may agree to defer any removal of the claimant (▶see 847).

The law that can be used to bring a civil claim

In order to see whether a claim can be made, it is necessary to look to the wider law. Included in this chapter is reference to four aspects of the wider law that may enable a civil claim to be made in immigration cases (as of course they can be brought in other cases). They are as follows.

1) The law of torts

'Tort' is the French for 'wrong' (although the British pronounce the second 't'!), and refers simply to the law of wrongful acts. There are lots of different 'torts', which have mostly been developed out of case law rather than legislation.

Matching the tort to the immigration situation In some cases, it is easy to match the relevant tort to the above immigration situations. For example, a claim in the tort of false imprisonment can be made in cases of unlawful immigration detention; and where a person is assaulted, by the immigration officers or the police, it may be possible to bring a claim in the torts of 'assault' or 'battery'. In the event that a search is carried out without power this may amount to the tort of 'trespass'.

Where the match is not straightforward In other cases, the match is not so straightforward. 'Negligence' is a tort that is committed where a person who owes a 'duty of care' to another breaches that duty and causes them damage as a result. It can arise in all sorts of situations. It may apply, for example, if the authorities fail to take proper care of someone in detention who is at risk of self-harm, and who then injures themselves. There is a general tort of 'breach of statutory duty' which, in certain circumstances, allows a claim to be made where a person does something that a piece of legislation forbids them from doing. This *may* apply, for example, where a person is prematurely removed from the UK in circumstances where the legislation prohibits their removal until they have had a chance to appeal against an immigration decision. 'Misfeasance in public office' is a tort providing a remedy against acts of a public officer, such as an immigration officer, where they either know, or are reckless as to whether, their act is unlawful, and damage will result. An example of this could be if immigration officers remove a person from the UK in the knowledge that they have no power to do so. The tort of 'malicious prosecution' is the malicious wrongful setting of the law in motion against a person, without reasonable cause. The prosecution must eventually be determined in the claimant's (the person wrongly accused's) favour. This could occur, for example, where a person is arrested by the police having been wrongly accused by a police officer of assault, and on the basis of this evidence is charged before proceedings are determined in their favour.

Rules and requirements of torts All the torts have their own rules and requirements that need to be satisfied before the liability of the defendant to pay damages is established. Usually claimants will have to show that they have suffered specific forms of damage (loss of liberty, physical, emotional or financial), and that they would not have suffered those losses if the defendant had not behaved as they did. Because the rules are derived from case law they are quite general, and in some cases it is difficult to know in advance whether a court will uphold the claim.

11

2) Human rights

Where the actions of a public authority have breached a person's human rights as incorporated by the Human Rights Act (HRA), it may be possible to bring a claim for damages. Generally, damages can be granted if the court is satisfied that an award is necessary in order to provide the applicant with 'just satisfaction' for the violation of their rights (s8 HRA; ►see further 1202–4). Immigration cases may, in particular, give rise to claims under Articles 3, 5, 8 and 14 ECHR. The level of damages may, however, be modest, ►see commentary on *Greenfield* (HL) at 1203–4.

3) Discrimination

Where the actions of the immigration authorities, or their agents, discriminate against a person on the grounds of sex or race, there may be a claim for damages either under the Race Relations Act 1976 (as amended), the Sex Discrimination Act 1975, or the HRA, Article 14 in combination with Articles 3, 5 and 8 ECHR.

4) Data Protection Act

Where the immigration authorities or their agents have kept inaccurate personal data and an individual has suffered damage, there may be claim for damages under this Act.

Essential approach to civil claims

In *some* cases, the above aspects of the wider law overlap, so that it is possible to use more than one of them in order to bring a claim in any particular immigration situation. Therefore the easiest way to approach questions about civil claims is:

1) decide whether any of the above immigration situations broadly apply;
2) see whether any aspects of the wider law can be used to bring a claim and, if so, which one(s);
3) determine how the case is to be funded;
4) determine what is the appropriate procedure for bringing a claim, and what other practical considerations there may be.

As far as possible, this chapter approaches civil claims in the same way. First we look first at each potential 'immigration situation' in turn. Within each situation, drawing on the wider law, we consider the different bases upon which a claim might be made, and the matters that need to be shown in order to make out the claim. We then turn to look at the appropriate procedures for bringing claims, and deal with the practical aspects of bringing a claim.

UNLAWFUL DETENTION

The powers of detention for the purposes of immigration control are contained in Schedules 2 and 3 of the 1971 Act (as amended). On the face of the legislation, the powers are very wide-ranging indeed, but they are subject to limitations as a result of the interpretation of the legislation by the courts, and they are also restricted by Article 5 ECHR (right to liberty and security). Even if there is a power to detain, the immigration authorities must exercise that power lawfully. If, on careful examination of the detention powers and their limitations, there is no power to detain in the individual case, or there was a power but it was exercised unlawfully, then the detention itself will be unlawful, and a civil claim may be made. In a recent case, the Court of Appeal confirmed that, even where there is a formal power to detain, if the power is not exercised lawfully this will give rise to a claim for damages for false imprisonment (see *ID & others v Home Office* (CA)).

Claims may be brought as an action in tort for false imprisonment and/or under Article 5 ECHR. In extreme cases, where the immigration authorities appear to have knowingly acted contrary to their powers, there may also be a claim in tort for misfeasance in a public office (for the general principles concerning misfeasance, see ▶1181–2).

Whether a person is being detained lawfully under immigration powers or should be released is part and parcel of immigration advice, quite aside from whether a civil claim can be brought. The lawfulness of immigration detention is therefore fully explained in Chapter 30 (▶see 919–32). The information given here should therefore be read together with that part of the section on detention. For powers of detention ▶see 899–905 and for Home Office policy and detention ▶see 905–17.

Detention as the result of errors and incorrect information

Unfortunately, it is not uncommon for the immigration authorities to detain someone as the result of their acting on the basis of incorrect or out-of-date information that they have recorded about a detainee and their case. These situations are discussed in the chapter on detention powers at ▶931–2. An example is the detention of a person thought by the immigration authorities to have exhausted all in-country appeal rights, so that they can be removed, whereas in fact it has not been recorded that they have lodged an appeal that has not yet been determined. In such cases, it is likely that there will be a claim for false imprisonment. For example, in cases of a mistake on the facts of the case, there may simply be no power to detain on the true facts of the case (e.g. *I v Home Office*), and/or the Home Office's failures to assess the case properly may mean that the detention is in breach of its own policy, or arbitrary.

Although, in ordinary language, detentions in this category might be described as 'negligent', they are probably not covered by the tort of negligence. It was decided by the Court of Appeal in *W v Home Office* that it would be inconsistent with the proper performance of an immigration officer's responsibilities for them to owe a 'duty of care' to a person in taking decisions to detain. It was therefore held that a person who was wrongfully detained for nine days because of a filing error had no cause of action in negligence. However, in *ID* the Court of Appeal made it clear that a person wrongfully detained because of a filing error, or some other incompetence, should be entitled to claim in the tort of false imprisonment.

Data Protection Act

There is, however, another basis of claim that people detained in these circumstances may look to. They might make a claim under the Data Protection Act 1998 (DPA). Particular consideration should be given to bringing a DPA claim *in addition* to a claim in false imprisonment/Article 5 in cases where the Home Office might try to point to the reasonableness of the initial decision to detain. For example, it may be that the individual officer(s) who authorised the detention had reasonable grounds to detain on the basis of the information available to them. However, it may be that, had the immigration authorities properly recorded and updated their files with the relevant information, the decision to detain would not have been made. A claim for compensation under the DPA can be brought by any person who has suffered loss as a result of a failure to keep accurate and up-to-date personal data (section 13 DPA). It is a defence to prove that reasonable care was taken to keep the information accurate.

There have been no reported cases of claims against the immigration authorities under the DPA. However, in the police context, in *Ogle v CC Thames Valley Police*, an individual was arrested by a police officer on the basis of erroneous information entered into the Police National Computer (PNC). The Court of Appeal held that he had no claim for wrongful arrest and false imprisonment because the officer had 'reasonable suspicion' as a result of the PNC entry. However, the Court indicated that he would have a claim under the Data Protection Act 1984 (which was in force at the time). In principle, therefore, there is no reason why a claim under the DPA should not be brought if the Home Office has failed to exercise reasonable care to record accurate immigration data, resulting in a person losing their liberty when they would not otherwise have been detained.

Detention by the police

The police have no inherent power to arrest and detain a person who needs leave to be in the UK. However, the 1971 Act also provides powers of arrest for both police and immigration officers where persons are liable to be detained under the general administrative powers of detention used as part of immigration control (▶899 onwards and ▶see the table at 902–5; see also para. 17, Schedule 2; para. 2(4) Schedule 3). Where a police officer arrests a person for these reasons, it is probable that the same principles as those outlined at ▶929–42 apply in order to determine the lawfulness of detention. In practice what normally happens in the case of police involvement is that the police arrest and interview the person under PACE. The applicant may then later be detained under the authority of an immigration officer under the 1971 Act.

The immigration legislation creates many offences. For some of these, the legislation also provides a power of arrest, which may be exercised either by the police or immigration officers. The most important are: illegal entry (in various forms); overstaying; breaches of conditions; frustrating enforcement action (sections, 24–24A 1971 Act) and entering the UK and attending an interview without a valid passport or travel document (section 2 2004 Act). Police and immigration officers may arrest in relation to these offences if they have 'reasonable grounds' for suspecting that they have been committed (section 28A(1) 1971 Act, s2(10) 2004 Act). The burden of proving the lawfulness of an arrest is on the police and, unless they can do so, any detention will constitute a false imprisonment (see for example, *Okot v Commissioner of Police for the Metropolis*, CCt). Generally, three conditions all need to be satisfied for the police to demonstrate the lawfulness of an arrest:

1) there was a power to arrest;
2) the decision to exercise the power to arrest was carried out lawfully;
3) in the criminal context, reasons are given to the person being arrested as soon as practical after the arrest; this is so even if the reasons are obvious (see section 28 of Police and Criminal Evidence Act 1984).

If the above criteria are not satisfied, there may be a civil claim for damages for false imprisonment.

PLACES OF DETENTION AND CONDITIONS OF DETENTION

Those held under the administrative powers for immigration detention may be detained in such places as the Home Office directs (see para. 18(1) of Sch 2, para. 2(4) of Sch 3 1971 Act). This has resulted in people being detained, for example, at ports, removal centres, prisons, police stations and hospitals (see the Immigration (Places of Detention) Direction 2004). For practical details about places, conditions and procedures relating to immigration detention, ▶see Chapter 31.

11

Places and conditions of detention: false imprisonment

Home Office policy gives some guidance on where people should be detained under immigration powers – for example, who may be detained at a prison, where women and children may be detained, who may be detained in the 'relaxed' regime at Oakington (▶see 673–81, 899–917). It is unlikely that a claim for false imprisonment could be brought on the basis that there was no power to detain a person who was liable to be detained, because they were detained in one place rather than another. It is also difficult to argue that conditions of detention undermine a power to detain. Conditions of detention were considered in the prison law context by the House of Lords in *Hague v Deputy Governor of Parkhurst Prison and others, Weldon v Home Office*. The case was brought by prisoners claiming that their removal from association amounted to a false imprisonment. The claims were dismissed on the basis that, as they were lawfully detained, they had no liberty capable of being deprived by the prison regime. Following the HRA, the Court of Appeal considered similar issues in *Munjaz v Mersey Care National Health Service Trust & S v Airedale National Health Service Trust*, concerning the seclusion of a mental health patient. It was held that the seclusion did not give rise to a claim for false imprisonment or a breach of Article 5, because a person who is detained under a lawful power cannot complain about the conditions in which they are held by making a false imprisonment or Article 5 claim. The House of Lords in *Munjaz* agreed with this approach (see at paras 30, 84–86, 111; but see also the different view expressed by Lord Steyn at paras 42–43).

Despite these decisions, it may still be possible to argue in an immigration case that the exercise of a power to detain is unlawful and allows a claim for damages where, having regard to the conditions or places of detention available, the *use* of the power was disproportionate in a particular case (Article 5 ECHR). It will be disproportionate where the Home Office has failed to strike a fair balance between the needs of immigration control and the particular effect on the individual of losing their liberty. So, for example, if the immigration authorities decide to detain someone knowing that there are only presently places available in a prison when detention in prison would not be suitable for the particular person (as it isn't for most immigration detainees), then the exercise of the power in such circumstances might be disproportionate. Similar issues might arise in relation to the detention of people with particular needs, or those with children.

Places and conditions of detention: 'negligence' and other claims

Even if there is no claim for false imprisonment, a person detained in poor conditions may have other claims they could make. Generally, in order to bring a claim for negligence, it is necessary to show all of the following:

- the defendant owed a 'duty of care' to the person damaged;
- the defendant breached that duty;
- the breach of duty caused the damage.

Negligence and the duty of care

It is the first issue – the question of whether the situation gives rise to a duty of care – that is often the most contentious. In *Caparo Industries plc v Dickman*, the House of Lords held that the court must decide three questions before a duty of care would be held to exist. These are: (1) that the damage caused could have been foreseen; (2) that there is a sufficiently proximate (i.e. 'close') relationship between the person causing the harm and the victim; and (3) that it is just and reasonable to impose a duty of care (often called the 'policy' consideration).

We suggest that the immigration authorities owe a duty of care to those who they detain to take reasonable care for their safety, health, welfare and security. Support for this can be found in *Kirkham v Chief Constable of the Greater Manchester Police*, where it was held that the police had a duty to inform the prison authorities of the deceased's suicidal tendencies. Also, in *Commissioner of Police for the Metropolitan v Reeves*, the House of Lords held that the police had a duty to take reasonable steps to prevent the deceased committing suicide. In *Orange v Chief Constable of West Yorkshire Police*, it was held that the duty to take reasonable care for the health and safety of a person in custody – again in the context of a death by suicide – only arose where the custodian knew or ought to have known that the individual prisoner presented a suicide risk. The same principles would probably be applied to health and safety generally.

Negligence and the Detention Centre Rules

Rule 35 of the Detention Centre Rules 2001, which apply to immigration detention centres, requires that the detention centre doctor informs the detention centre manager, and that the manager informs the Secretary of State, if a detained person's health 'is likely to be injuriously affected by continued detention or any conditions of detention', or if there is concern that the detained person 'may have been the victim of torture'. It is possible that there will be a claim for negligence against the detention centre health care supplier and/or the manager of the detention centre where there is a failure to comply with these requirements. In order to bring an action, it would be necessary to establish that the failure had caused the damage. This may be the case if, for example, the failure leads to a worsening of the medical condition. It may also be the case if the failure leads to further detention, i.e. cases in which it can be said that, had the duty been complied with, it would have lead to release. For a summary of some of the Detention Centre Rules, ▶see 940–1.

Unacceptable conditions and removal from association

Unacceptable conditions could also give rise to a human rights claim, in particular under Article 3. In the Scottish case of *Napier v The Scottish Ministers*, it was held that the conditions in which a prisoner was placed – which were overcrowded and necessitated slopping out – breached Article 3 ECHR. It is possible that poor conditions might also give rise to a claim of interference with private life under Article 8 (▶see *Bernard* 1190–1 below, although that was not a detention case).

The Detention Centre Rules also contain provisions enabling officers to manage detainees to ensure control. In certain circumstances, detainees can be removed 'from association' for a period of up to 14 days (rule 40), and can be subjected to 'temporary confinement' for a period of up to three days (rule 42). In *O v Home Office*, a claim was brought in the County Court alleging that a removal from association for 14 days, carried out on the incorrect basis that the claimant was a sex offender, was a breach of the Data Protection Act, Article 8, and was a misfeasance. After proceedings were brought, the Home Office settled the claim for £3,000. In other cases, claims have been made for the unacceptable conditions in which those removed from association have been held.

Places and conditions of detention: transfers

Transfers should be kept to a minimum. It is recognised that detention in prisons of immigration detainees who have committed no criminal offence should be avoided if at all possible. Home Office policy is that detainees may exceptionally be moved to prisons on security or control grounds. Options for transfers within the detention centre estate should be exhausted before consideration is given to transfer to a prison. A number of factors, such as national security, criminality, security and control, should be taken into account and balanced in reaching decisions. In some cases, decisions will be based on hard evidence, such as convictions; in other cases judgements will be made about the quality of criminal or other intelligence. The overriding concern is to protect security and safety of detainees and staff, but with the presumption that detainees should remain in immigration-service-provided detention if at all possible. Decisions on transfer to prisons are made at Immigration Inspector level by the Detainee Escorting and Population Management Unit (DEPMU).

For more details about Home Office policy on detention in prisons and transfers, ▶see 936–9.

The Immigration Service has indicated that, in every case of a transfer, a detainee will be told about the reasons for the move and about any allegations made against them. If a detainee disagrees with the decision, it should be open to them to make representations. Judicial review claims may arise if individuals are wrongly removed to prisons.

Situations in which a claim concerning a transfer may arise

Civil claims may arise in the following situations:

- false evidence from officers leading to removal from association and/or transfer from an immigration detention centre to prison may give rise to a claim in misfeasance;

- inaccurate personal data leading to a removal from association or transfer may give rise to a claim under the DPA or the HRA (see *O v Home Office*, above);

- a claim may also arise under the HRA for a wrongful transfer, in breach of policy, of a detainee from a removal centre to a prison.

In order to make out a claim, it will normally need to be shown that damage has been caused and, in a HRA claim, that there is a need for an award of damages in order for there to be 'just satisfaction'.

UNLAWFUL REMOVAL

The law only permits the removal of persons from the UK for immigration reasons in particular circumstances (▶see Chapter 33). For example, an individual cannot lawfully be removed from the United Kingdom pending a claim for asylum (section 77 2002 Act) (▶1070–1 and for which appeals are in country ▶1058–60), nor while an in-country appeal is pending (sections 78, 92 2002 Act). Any attempt to remove such an individual will be unlawful, and can be challenged by way of judicial review in order to prevent the removal taking place – or, if the removal has taken place, to try and provide for the person's return, if that is possible (for judicial review procedures, ▶see 1213–22).

Unlawful removal: claims which may be brought

Damages claims may also arise from an unlawful removal, and can be brought within both judicial review and private law proceedings (for correct procedure ▶see below at 1193–4). An unlawful removal, or proposed unlawful removal, may give rise to a number of potential claims, which may be brought individually or together in the same proceedings. There may have been detention prior to the proposed removal taking place, and this may be unlawful (see above), and may therefore be a false imprisonment, a breach of Article 5 and/or a breach of the DPA. If an unlawful removal does take place, any force used will amount to an assault and battery, and any confinement during the course of the removal will be an unlawful detention.

Another potential alternative basis of claim, in the event that a person is removed, is for breach of statutory duty – i.e. breach of the legislation which prevents the removal. In order to be successful, though, it would have to be shown that parliament intended to create a civil remedy in damages for a person removed in breach of the statute (see, for example, the decision of the House of Lords in *Hague*). This has not yet been established in immigration cases.

Another alternative, if the facts allowed, might be a claim for a breach of the procedural rights under Articles 3 and 8. There may also be a substantive claim if the removal causes the individual to be subjected to treatment that breaches these Articles, or if it causes a severe rupture in family life.

Unlawful removal: misfeasance in public office

Unlawful removals (and the associated detention) might, in very serious cases, also permit a claim in the tort of 'misfeasance in public office'. The three general requirements for a claim on this basis are that the defendant:

- is a public officer (officers of the various immigration authorities count as public officers);
- was exercising power as a public officer when they committed the acts complained of; and

- *either* acted with malice (exercise of a power for an improper or ulterior motive) in order to cause disadvantage to the person, *or* acted without malice but yet knowing, *or* being reckless to, the fact that they had no power to act as they did, and being aware that the act would probably injure the victim.

(See *Three Rivers DC v Bank of England* (No 2) (HL))

The difficulty in bringing a claim for misfeasance is in proving that the public officer acted maliciously, or knew or was reckless as to whether the act was lawful, as opposed to merely acting inadvertently. Misfeasance may therefore arise where the officer(s) knew that the individual could not lawfully be removed, or simply did not care whether the removal was lawful or unlawful.

UNLAWFUL FAMILY SEPARATION

Unlawful acts that cause family separation may give rise to claims under Article 8 ECHR. In the European Court of Human Rights case of *Berrehab v The Netherlands*, it was a breach of Article 8 to deport the applicant, a Moroccan citizen, from the Netherlands, where he had contact with his daughter. In another case, determined in Strasbourg, *Ciliz v The Netherlands*, the expulsion of a Turkish national from the Netherlands while he was involved in formal access proceedings relating to his child was held to have violated Article 8. In both cases, damages were awarded in order to afford 'just satisfaction'.

Not every separation, though, will amount to a violation of Article 8. In *M*, heard together with *Anufrijeva* (▶see below), it was held that administrative delays in facilitating family reunion for a refugee whose family remained stranded abroad did not breach Article 8. The Court of Appeal was particularly influenced by the fact that, although there were shortcomings in the process, there was no evidence of a deliberate obstruction of the family's attempt at reunion so as to demonstrate that there had been a lack of 'respect' for the family life (see also *Askar*, EComm HR). Cases may still be able to be brought if there is evidence of obstructive behaviour by the immigration authorities, or if it is as a direct result of their actions that a family has been separated, for example, in an expulsion case such as *Berrehab* or *Ciliz*, referred to above.

ASSAULT

Claims brought for assault by those affected by the immigration system have generally related to events at the point at which they are detained, during detention, or while removal is being enforced against them (see, for example, *Harm on Removal: Excessive Force against Failed Asylum Seekers*, Medical Foundation, 2004). There have also recently been disturbing reports of alleged assaults when people have attended to sign on in accordance with their conditions of temporary admission. In addition, the BBC documentary on Oakington in March 2005 implied that violence had been used by staff at the point of removal in order to discourage disruptive behaviour by detainees. The Home Office has indicated that 'monitoring staff' have since been appointed to observe removals at certain points (information given to the Detention User Group on 25 April 2005).

Although 'assault' is an ordinary word which everyone understands, there are in fact two torts that can be used to make a claim in the circumstances described here:

Battery This can be defined as the 'the least touching of another in anger' (*Cole v Turner*). Not all intentional touching with force will be a battery. The inevitable physical contact that is generally acceptable in everyday life will not count. There must also be no lawful excuse for the use of force (see *F v West Berkshire Health Authority*, HL).

Assault Technically, this is a direct act indicating an intention to commit a battery when the person doing the act is physically able to do so (see for example *Stephens v Myers*). So raising of the fists in a threatening way while close to the victim can be an assault. An assault can thus be carried out without there being contact, and without there being a battery.

Any force, including handcuffing, used during the course of an unlawful detention or an unlawful removal will also generally be a battery and an assault. However, where the immigration authorities are acting lawfully within their powers in detaining or effecting a removal, then there will only be the possibility of a battery or an assault if the force used is unnecessary or unreasonable (*F v West Berkshire Health Authority*). The assessment of whether force is unnecessary or unreasonable will depend on all the circumstances of the case – so, for example, firm restraint used to control an individual violently resisting a lawful removal may be reasonable, but kicking someone who is in handcuffs or on the ground, and who is not resisting, would certainly not.

11

UNLAWFUL SEARCHES OF PREMISES

Any entry and search of a person's premises or property must be justified under the law; otherwise it will amount to a trespass. These acts will be justified if permission is granted from the person entitled to grant entry to the premises, or if there is a statutory power to enter and search. The immigration legislation provides for powers of search. For example, section 28D of the 1971 Act gives a justice of the peace power to grant a warrant for the search of property for immigration purposes in certain circumstances. There are also certain powers of search that may be exercised without a warrant. These powers permit searches of the premises in which a person was found when arrested, premises where the person was immediately before they were arrested (section 28E 1971 Act), or premises occupied or controlled by a person who has been arrested (section 28F 1971 Act).

Was there a warrant and did it cover the search?

Care will need to be taken to determine whether a person has a claim for trespass. If the search was by warrant, a copy of the warrant must be requested before an action is brought (s6 Constable Protection Act 1750). If a warrant was obtained and on its face it appears to authorise the search, there is unlikely to be a claim. If it does not appear to authorise the search that in fact took place – for example, if the warrant names a different address, or if the search was more extensive than was permitted – then there may be a claim in trespass (see *Hoye v Bush*).

If the warrant does cover the search but it is alleged that the warrant was improperly obtained, then although there may be no claim in trespass, there may be a claim for 'malicious procurement' of the warrant, or even under Article 8 ECHR (the elements of right to respect for 'private life' and 'home'). To make out a case of 'malicious procurement', it will need to be established that the warrant was sought and obtained maliciously and without reasonable cause. Malice can be inferred from the absence of a reasonable cause.

Loss

A claim can be brought and damages recovered for trespass even where the claimant has suffered no actual loss (*Stoke on Trent Council v W&J Wass Ltd*). However, it is unlikely to be appropriate to bring a claim, particularly with the benefit of public funding, unless actual damage can be shown. This might be damage to property, or psychiatric or physical damage as a result of the search, or of the way in which it was carried out. It is possible that other claims may arise following an unlawful search. There may be assault or battery claims in the event that unlawful force or threats of force are used. Where the unlawful search has followed an unlawful arrest, there may also be a claim for false imprisonment.

MALADMINISTRATION AND DELAY IN MAKING DECISIONS AND ISSUING DOCUMENTS

A recurring problem in recent years has been maladministration and delays in the immigration system that have operated to the very severe disadvantage of those affected. This has included:

- failures to issue and delays in issuing status papers to those entitled to a particular status, with the result that people are unable to work, travel, access various forms of welfare, and sponsor applications for family reunion;
- mistakes made on immigration documents with similar consequences.

Where such delays have caused great disadvantage, applicants have successfully challenged Home Office inaction by judicial review in order to ensure the issue of their papers. In *R v SSHD ex parte Mersin* (HC), a seven-

and-a-half-month delay in issuing status papers to an asylum applicant who had succeeded at his appeal was found to be unlawful. In **R (Mambakasa) v SSHD**, the judge in the High Court indicated that, in the circumstances of the case, the failure to issue status papers after about four months would have been declared unlawful (paras 65–66). However, these were cases in which applicants were *entitled* to be issued with certain papers – i.e. they had succeeded at their appeals. Moreover, the period of time that is reasonable will depend on the circumstances of the case. In particular, the extent of the detriment caused to the applicant by the delay will be relevant. In most cases, the bringing of proceedings has achieved the desired result without the case having to go all the way through the judicial review process.

Claims which may be brought

However, we are concerned here with actions for damages. The courts have been very resistant to the idea that statutes concerning the provision of social welfare may allow claims for damages in the tort of 'breach of statutory duty' when the duty is not fulfilled. They have found that this kind of legislation was not intended to give rise to claims for loss (see **O'Rourke v Camden LBC**, concerning homelessness duties under the Housing Act 1985). In some cases, it may still be possible to make a claim for civil negligence, or under the HRA for a breach of Articles 3 or 8 ECHR (►see below).

In the next chapter, we look at some alternative ways of obtaining financial redress for errors and maladministration: the Home Office scheme for compensating monetary loss and its system for 'consolatory payments' (►see 1223–7), and the effect of complaining to the Parliamentary Ombudsman (►1229–35). Following the decision of the Court of Appeal in *Anufrijeva*, these options need to be carefully explored (►see 1195, setting out the Court's guidance on procedures).

Maladministration: negligence

In *R(A & Kanidagli) v SSHD*, the High Court held that the immigration authorities owed a duty of care in negligence to the claimants in the administrative implementation of the immigration decisions that had been made in their cases. In the case of *A*, this was to ensure that she was not given an inappropriate condition on her entry clearance, which became a condition of leave, with the result that she could not claim benefit that she was rightfully entitled to, leading to financial loss. In *Kanidagli*, it was to ensure that the claimant received a status letter that he could then use to access benefit. In each case, it was held that the duty of care had been breached, and that the claimants were entitled to compensation for the financial losses that they had suffered.

The Home Office appealed to the Court of Appeal and the appeal was due to be heard in late February 2005. However, it was realised that the Home

Office had a scheme for compensating financial loss; on the basis that the Home Office agreed to pay the full extent of the financial losses under the scheme, together with the legal costs, the case did not proceed. Before any claim for negligence is made in order to recover financial loss as a result of maladministration, a complaint should be made to the Home Office with a request for compensation (▶see 1223–7).

Maladministration: human rights

In *Anufrijeva v Southwark LBC, N, M v SSHD*, the claimants (all asylum seekers) alleged that official maladministration had resulted in a breach of legal duties under which the claimants were entitled to receive various benefits or advantages. They also alleged that these breaches amounted to a violation of their rights under Article 8 ECHR, and that they were entitled to recover damages under the HRA. In each case, the claimants did not complain about action that was taken, but about *failures* to act. In *Anufrijeva*, a family complained that the local authority had failed, under s21 National Assistance Act 1948, to provide them with accommodation that met their special needs, with the result that their quality of family life was significantly reduced. In *N*, the claimant alleged that maladministration in handling his asylum application caused delay that resulted in inadequate financial support and psychiatric injury brought on by stress. He therefore complained that his private life ('physical and moral integrity') had been infringed. In *M*, the claimant alleged that the administrative failures and delays in issuing him with his asylum status, after he had succeeded in his asylum appeal, caused a delay in his being able to bring his dependants to the UK under the family reunion provisions in the immigration rules.

In each case, the claims were dismissed by the Court of Appeal because they all fell foul of one or other of the following principles established by the Court:

1) If a public body, in breach of its duties, fails to provide an individual with a benefit or advantage they are entitled to, this may breach Article 8 *provided* there is 'culpability' (i.e. blame) on the part of the public body. Isolated acts of even significant carelessness are unlikely to be enough. (In *Anufrijeva*, the Court found that, overall, the local authority had been careful to try to accommodate the family's special needs. In *M*, although there were several administrative failings and delays, the officers were found to be trying, although often inadequately, to move the process along.)

2) The effect on private or family life must be sufficiently severe before failures to take action can amount to a breach of Article 8.

3) At the very least, the public body must *know* that, if it does not carry out its duty properly, the particular person's private or family life are at risk in the serious way required for a breach of Article 8. (In *N*, while the Home Office may generally have been aware that the failures complained of would lead to stress, it was held that it could not have foreseen that *N*, because of his particular vulnerability, would suffer psychiatric harm.)

4) The failure to provide welfare support may amount to a breach of Article 8 ECHR, but the Court thought that, in almost every such case, the effect would have to be so serious as to amount to a breach of Article 3. Article 8 will more readily be breached where a family unit is involved, as was the case in **Bernard** (▶see 1190–1).

Maladministration will therefore only give rise to a claim for damages under Article 8 where severe harm is caused to an applicant's Article 8 interests, officers are seriously at fault, and the officers could have foreseen the particular serious consequences of their actions. Even in such cases, before bringing an action for damages for maladministration under the HRA, applicants will need to have careful regard to the guidance given by the Court of Appeal in **Anufrijeva**, as to appropriate procedures in cases of this kind (▶1195), and to the question of whether the level of damages that may be obtained justify the cost. Note that comments made about the *level* of damages in **Anufrijeva** and **Bernard** have been overruled by the House of Lords (▶see also 1202–4 on damages in human rights cases).

DISCRIMINATION

There are three possible ways in which the actions of the immigration authorities could lead to a claim for damages on the grounds of discrimination:

1) Treatment that unjustifiably discriminates against a person *in the context of one of their human rights*, because they belong to a particular group, will be contrary to Article 14 ECHR, taken together with the relevant right under the ECHR.

2) Section 20 of the Race Relations Act 1976 (RRA) prohibits acts of racial discrimination. There has, however, been controversy as to the extent to which this covers public bodies like the police and the immigration authorities. Following one of the recommendations contained in the Stephen Lawrence Inquiry Report, the Race Relations (Amendment) Act 2000, amended the 1976 Act in order to provide explicitly that 'public authorities' (such as the Immigration and Nationality Directorate and Foreign and Commonwealth Office, but not for example the security services) must not, in carrying out their functions, discriminate on 'racial grounds' (see s19B RRA). These grounds are defined as colour, race, nationality, or national, ethnic or racial origin (section 3 RRA). *However*, the legislation also allows the Secretary of State to issue 'authorisations' to make exceptions to section 19B in order to permit discrimination on grounds of nationality, or on the grounds of ethnic or national origin, in specific circumstances. However, no authorisation may be made to permit discrimination on grounds of race or colour.

3) Section 29 of the Sex Discrimination Act 1975 (SDA) prohibits discrimination on the grounds of sex. The SDA applies to acts committed by, or for the purposes of, a Minister of the Crown, or a government department,

11

and to an act carried out on behalf of the Crown by a statutory body, or a person holding a statutory office 'as it applies to a private person' (section 85 SDA). Whether section 29 of the SDA (or section 20 RRA) applies to immigration authorities carrying out immigration functions is also controversial (see below).

We do not deal here with the question of what *constitutes* unlawful discrimination on the above three grounds. If there is unlawful discrimination in making an immigration decision, then, quite aside from the question of making a civil claim, this needs to be addressed as part of ordinary immigration advice in order to challenge the decision. Details about what constitutes discrimination under the ECHR, the requirements of the RRA (as amended), and the many authorisations which have been made, are covered in Chapter 29.

Using the AIT Where the action complained of is an 'immigration decision' as defined by section 82(2) 2002 Act, it should be appealed to the Asylum and Immigration Tribunal (see s84(1)(b) 2002 Act). Of course, the AIT cannot award damages, and not all actions taken by the immigration authorities that are discriminatory will be appealable in this way. Immigration detention, for example, cannot be appealed against. Therefore a civil claim concerning discrimination will be needed in order to recover damages following either a finding of discrimination in the immigration appeal jurisdiction; or following a successful appeal of an 'immigration decision', when an allegation of discrimination is made but there is no express finding; or in cases where the discrimination complained of does not relate to an 'immigration decision' (and ▶see 890–2).

Overlapping claims The bases for a claim in discrimination overlap, and we examine each in turn below. Claims for race and sex discrimination could also be made under Article 14, *provided* the person is being discriminated against in the context of one of their human rights, which would be the case in relation to a detention. Best practice may be to argue claims in the alternative. So, for example, in *ID & others v The Home Office*, the claim that the families' detention was discriminatory was brought under both section 19B and section 20 RRA (the section 20 claim was struck out in the County Court), *as well as* for a breach of Article 14 in combination with Article 5. Of course, Article 14 covers discrimination not just on grounds of race or gender, but would include, for example, sexual orientation.

Discrimination claims may be included in other, wider civil claims. It may be, for example, that there are grounds to add such a claim to a civil action against the police for an unlawful arrest/detention where there were no objective grounds to suspect an immigration offence (see *Okot v Commissioner of Police for the Metropolis*). They may also arise if there is evidence that the immigration service is unlawfully targeting particular nationalities for detention. *ID* is also an example of a claim for sex discrimination because the Home Office was targeting the adult male member of the family, the 'head of the household', for detention.

Discrimination: human rights claims

An example of a human rights discrimination case taken to the Strasbourg Court is *Abdulaziz & Others v UK*. The case was successful in showing that the then immigration rules discriminated between men and women, in relation to the ability of each to bring their spouses to settle and enjoy their family life in the UK. The discrimination was based on sex, and the relevant human right in relation to which discrimination was found was family life under Article 8. So, a violation of Article 8 taken together with Article 14 was found.

However, *Abdulaziz* is a reminder that damages will not always be awarded for breaches of the ECHR. The Court also found that there had been no interference with the right to respect for family life under Article 8 *taken alone*. This was because the couples had not shown that there were either 'obstacles' or 'special reasons' preventing them from establishing family life elsewhere (in either their or their husbands' countries of origin), and that each knew at the time of their marriage that the husband would not be admitted to the UK. Therefore the Court accepted that the family had not been prevented from living together, and that family ties and long-term plans had not been adversely affected. In those circumstances, the Court decided that its declaration that there had indeed been a violation of Articles 8 and 14 taken together was enough to constitute 'just satisfaction'.

Discrimination: claims under the Race Relations Act and Sex Discrimination Act

Most cases of discrimination will involve human rights, often taking Article 8 together with Article 14. In addition, in some cases, it will be possible to bring a claim under the RRA or SDA. In any case under the RRA or SDA, it is necessary to compare the treatment of the complainant's group that is alleged to be discriminatory, with the treatment of another group in the same, or not materially different, circumstances (see section 4 RRA, section 5(3) SDA).

As indicated above, the extent to which the SDA and RRA (section 20) cover acts by public authorities in the exercise of their public functions, particularly in the area of immigration, is controversial. So, for example, in *R v Immigration Appeal Tribunal Ex parte Kassam*, the Court of Appeal concluded that Section 29 SDA did not apply to the Secretary of State when giving leave to enter or remain in the UK. In *R v Entry Clearance Officer Ex parte Amin*, the House of Lords took a similar approach. However, the courts have not been consistent in their approach to what amounts to public authority functions and the application of these provisions of the SDA and RRA (e.g. *Savjani v Inland Revenue Commissioners*; *Farah v MP*). Also, the legislation must now be interpreted in the light of the obligations under the HRA and the Convention rights that it incorporates. It may therefore be possible to persuade a court that some immigration functions fall within the scope of these provisions.

However, under the RRA, immigration-related claims may be brought on the basis of section 19B. In this case, it is possible that the Home Office will try to defend the action on the basis of one of the authorisations (▶888–9) which permit discrimination. As indicated above, an authorisation cannot permit discrimination on the grounds of race or colour. Advisers will need to consider: (1) whether the authorisation does in fact apply; and (2) whether any challenge can be made to the legality of the authorisation. Careful advice should be taken as to whether proceedings should be brought under section 20 RRA, in addition to a claim under section 19(B). The court may find that the claim more properly falls under section 20, which would then exclude the possibility of a claim under section 19(B).

In relation to claims against the police, section 76A RRA, as inserted by Section 4 of the Race Relations (Amendment) Act 2000, makes the Chief Officer of Police vicariously liable (i.e. responsible) for the actions of their police constable for the purposes of a claim in race discrimination. Care should be taken, though, to ensure that the defence under section 32(3) RRA will not be relied on. This states that it is a defence if the Chief Officer 'took such steps as were reasonably practicable to prevent the employee from doing that act, or from doing in the course of his employment, acts of that description'. If this defence is likely to be raised, the officers may need to be named personally as defendants.

DISPERSAL AND DENIAL OF ADEQUATE SUPPORT

Although by far the most important priority for those denied access to proper support is actually to get that support, it is possible that a claim for damages could arise in extreme cases where the lack of support (or the nature of the support provided) has been unlawful, and has resulted in severe suffering. As stated above, the courts have generally not responded well to claims of breach of statutory duty in this area, but that does not shut out human rights claims, or possibly negligence claims. This might arise in any of the following circumstances:

Conditions of support

It is possible that unacceptable conditions of support might lead to a claim. In *Bernard v London Borough of Enfield*, a local authority failed to provide suitably adapted accommodation for a disabled woman, in breach of its duties under s21 National Assistance Act 1948. As a result, she suffered very severe discomfort and distress, and was denied the existence of any meaningful private or family life. The High Court found that the conditions breached Article 8, and awarded damages of £10,000; £8,000 to be apportioned to the disabled woman and £2,000 to her husband.

Dispersal and separation

It is possible that damages for Article 8 breaches might result from separation between family members caused by dispersal of an asylum seeker away from family members resulting in severe distress and emotional harm. In a case in which NASS's policy concerning dispersal and family separation (▶see 1361–3) was not followed, then if the resulting separation had a sufficiently severe effect to amount to an interference with the right to respect for family life, the question of whether it was 'proportionate' or not would not arise, because the interference would not be 'in accordance with the law' under Article 8(2) (for the elements of Article 8, ▶see 821–2).

Dispersal and conditions

It is possible that damages would be available for dispersal if this led to the claimant being placed in conditions that breached Article 3 or Article 8. The question was considered by the Court of Appeal in *Gezer v SSHD*. The claimant was an asylum seeker who had been housed in an estate in Glasgow where he and his family suffered racial abuse. The Court of Appeal rejected the claim on the basis that NASS had no knowledge of specific problems regarding the suitability of the accommodation, and that Article 3 did not impose any general duty of enquiry on NASS. Also, when NASS became aware of the problems they withdrew the requirement that the claimant and his family return to the estate. In order to bring such a claim in Article 3, it will therefore be necessary to show that the public authority was or should have been aware of the risk that their action would breach Article 3, and took the decision to disperse regardless of this.

Denial of support

In a string of cases, the courts have held that denial of support to asylum seekers who had not claimed asylum 'as soon as reasonably practicable' was in breach of Article 3 ECHR (▶see 1307–11, 1350–2). Extreme cases might result in a claim for damages.

MALICIOUS PROSECUTION

Classic circumstances in which a claim in the tort of 'malicious prosecution' might arise are where a person is arrested and detained unlawfully, subjected to some unlawful violence during the course of the arrest, and where the security firm or police then allege that the person arrested assaulted the arresting officer, and a charge is brought.

In order for a claim to be made out, all of the following five elements need to be shown:

1) There must have been a prosecution. This does not mean that there must have been a trial, but there must been have a criminal charge rather than simply an arrest for a suspected offence.

2) The person or body against whom the civil action is being brought (the defendant) must have initiated the prosecution. This is straightforward if the prosecution is based on evidence from the police, but it can be complicated where a prosecution is brought by the police but on information provided, for example, by an immigration officer or a detainee custody officer. In these cases, it may be the informant who is the appropriate defendant. In *Martin v Watson*, the House of Lords held that the informant may be the 'prosecutor' where they falsely and maliciously give a police officer information indicating that an individual is guilty of an offence, and state that they are prepared to give evidence in court. In such cases, it will have to be shown that the informant caused the prosecution and that the police were unable to exercise any independent discretion as to whether charges should be brought. An immigration or other officer may be the 'prosecutor' (and therefore be the defendant in the civil action) if a prosecution is brought solely on the basis of his/her false allegation that a detainee assaulted him or her. The position is more complicated when the evidence of the officer is simply one part of the reason why a prosecution is brought.

3) The outcome of the prosecution must have ended favourably for the person prosecuted (the claimant in the civil claim) whether on appeal or otherwise.

4) There must have been no 'reasonable or probable' cause for the initiation of the prosecution, *and* the defendant must have acted with malice. There will be no reasonable or probable cause if the defendant did not honestly believe that the person being prosecuted was guilty. Malice is often described as 'improper motive', which is a motive other than the desire to bring the guilty to justice. Often the presence of malice can be inferred from the absence of reasonable and probable cause.

5) The claimant in the civil claim must have suffered as a result of the defendant's actions – but it is difficult to think of a malicious prosecution which would not result in some damage to the person prosecuted even if it is only damage to feelings.

MAKING A CIVIL CLAIM

The initial questions to ask in deciding whether to bring a civil claim, and in taking steps to begin one, are as follows:

- Which procedure should be used? County Court or High Court in an ordinary civil claim, or the Administrative Court (part of the High Court) in a claim for judicial review? (▶1193–4).
- Should compensation be sought in a way other than by bringing a civil claim? (▶1195).
- Who is the correct person to claim the damages against? (▶1195–6)
- What are the relevant time-limits for bringing the claim? (▶1196–7).
- What further information might be useful in deciding whether there is a

claim or not? Should a request be made under the Data Protection Act or Freedom of Information Act? (▶1198–9)

- Does the case meet the criteria in order to be granted public funding? (▶1199–1201). Public funding is an essential consideration, as it is relevant to the costs that a claimant may have to pay.

- How would damages in the case be assessed, and what level of damages might be awarded? (▶1201–4). This question is obviously relevant to whether public funding will be available. In relation to immigration detention and removal cases, a table of awards/settlements is provided that may be used for comparisons (▶1205–10).

We look at each question in turn below.

Which procedure?

The correct procedure for bringing a civil claim will depend on the circumstances of the case. This is a developing area, and advisers will need to keep abreast of developments. Claims might be brought in the ways set out below.

Claims made by ordinary civil action

If the claim is mainly about damages, in most cases it can be brought in the County Court or the High Court (reference should be made to the High Court and County Courts Jurisdiction Order 1991). Whether it should be brought in the County Court or the High Court will depend on the nature and complexity of the claim and its value. The usual rule is that proceedings should only be issued in the High Court if the financial value is more than £15,000. If the case involves personal injury, i.e. physical or psychiatric injury, the claim should be above £50,000 before it is brought in the High Court (save for cases involving medical negligence). However, it was recently recognised by the Court of Appeal, in *ID & others v Home Office*, that civil claims against the immigration service and the Home Office are a developing area of law that may give rise to novel or complex issues, so that they should be heard by a High Court judge with Administrative Court (judicial review) experience. Therefore, depending on the nature of the claim, it may be advisable to issue proceedings in the High Court in some immigration-related cases.

The basic procedures for making an ordinary civil claim are described below, at ▶1210–2.

Claims made as part of a judicial review

Where a claimant is not just seeking damages in relation to the alleged unlawful act, but also needs to challenge and reverse that act, the Administrative Court (part of the High Court), using its powers on a claim for judicial review, can make the necessary orders against the Home Office (see CPR Part 54(2)(3)). In such cases, a claim for damages may be

11

included in the claim for judicial review. If damages are claimed as part of a judicial review, they must arise from 'any matter to which the application [for judicial review] relates' and it must be the case that the claimant would have been awarded damages had they made a claim in the ordinary civil courts, as above (see s31(4) Supreme Court Act 1981). So if, for example, the claimant is trying to quash a decision to detain and remove them in judicial review proceedings, it is possible to make a claim for damages as part of the judicial review claim.

It is not possible to claim damages in judicial review proceedings where that is the only remedy sought (see CPR 54.3(2)). If the only remedy sought in the judicial review proceedings is a 'declaration' that the detention is unlawful, and there is likely to be a significant dispute on the facts, then any claim for damages may best be brought by an ordinary civil claim. This may apply in a detention case where the detainee has already been released before proceedings are begun, and therefore judicial review is not necessary to actually 'quash' the detention. However, if proceedings have already begun and then the claimant is released, depending on the circumstances, it may be more convenient to continue with the judicial review claim. Alternatively, it is possible for the claim to be transferred to be proceeded with as an ordinary civil claim (see CPR 54.20). If the claim for judicial review is successful, the assessment of damages will normally be dealt with separately at a later date. Again, it may at that stage be transferred out of the Administrative Court part of the High Court, to the Queen's Bench Division.

For a description of the procedures for making claims for judicial review and injunctions, ▶see Chapter 38 at 1213–22.

Data Protection Act claims

Claims under the DPA can be brought in either the County Court or High Court (section 15 DPA). They can be brought either as free-standing claims, or more usually as an addition to a claim in tort and/or under the HRA. On the question of which court such a claim should be brought in, see above.

Race/sex discrimination claims

Where a claim is for sex or race discrimination, it must be brought as an ordinary civil claim in an appropriate County Court (section 66 SDA, section 57 RRA). An allegation that an 'immigration decision' – i.e. one that can be appealed to the AIT – is discriminatory on grounds of race, has to be brought first within an immigration appeal. Once there has been a finding on the appeal, a claim for damages can be brought in the County Court (for further details, ▶see Chapter 29 at 890–2 and ▶see 1187–9).

Alternatives to bringing a claim

In all cases attempts should be made to settle claims without the necessity of issuing proceedings, by following pre-action protocols (►see 1210 below). In particular, in cases concerning damages for 'maladministration' under the HRA, applicants need to consider whether there is an alternative means of obtaining compensation which should be used, rather than bringing a civil claim of any sort. In these specific cases, the Court of Appeal in *Anufrijeva* (►see also 1186–7, above and 1203–4) gave the following guidance:

- The courts will generally expect HRA claims for damages as a result of maladministration to be made by judicial review (of course, a claim cannot be made by judicial review for damages alone, and so the claim must at least include a request for a declaration, CPR Part 54.3 (1), (2)).

- Before a claim is commenced, consideration should be given to using any internal complaints procedure (►see 1223–7 for complaints to the Home Office and its compensation schemes), complaining to the Parliamentary Commissioner for Administration (otherwise known as the Parliamentary Ombudsman, ►see 1229–35 for Ombudsman complaints in immigration cases), or to the Local Government Ombudsman. Before permission to apply for judicial review will be granted, claimants will be asked to explain to the Administrative Court judge why these procedures are not more appropriate remedies.

- If the claim for judicial review involves a legitimate claim for an order other than damages for maladministration, the court may allow that other claim to proceed while adjourning the damages matter until use has been made of alternative dispute resolution, internal complaint or ombudsman, as appropriate.

Who should the claim be made against?

Civil claims against immigration officers, and against the officers of the Secretary of State in the IND, for acts committed in the course of the officers' employment, are brought against their 'employer'. This is known as 'vicarious liability' – the employer is responsible for the actions of its employees carried out in the course of their employment. The Home Office is regarded as the employer, being the authorised government department (see s17(3) Crown Proceedings Act 1947 and List of Authorised Government Departments 2004). If the claim is brought in ordinary 'private law' proceedings, i.e. in the County Court or the Queen's Bench Division of the High Court, the 'Home Office' should be named as defendant.

If the claim is brought by judicial review ('public law') proceedings in the Administrative Court division of the High Court, the defendant in these cases is the 'Secretary of State for the Home Department'. The solicitor and address for service in both cases is: The Treasury Solicitor, Queen Anne's Chambers, 28 Broadway, Westminster, London SW1H 9JS (see s18 Crown Proceedings Act 1947 and List of Authorised Government Departments 2004).

If the claim is against another public servant and none of the authorised government departments are appropriate, or there is reasonable doubt about who the proceedings should be against, then the 'Attorney General' can be named as defendant (s17(3) Crown Proceedings Act 1947).

In many cases of detention, the claimant may have been detained at a privately managed removal centre. The Home Office will still be the defendant in an ordinary civil claim for false imprisonment and/or breach of Article 5, because the detention was *caused* by an immigration officer or an officer of the Secretary of State who authorised it (see *ID & others v Home Office*). If the claim involves an assault and battery by employees of a private contractor, it will probably be against the private company which is the employer. In a claim of negligence concerning medical care while in detention, the claim may often be made against the body contracted to provide the care.

Technically, a police officer is neither an employee of the Crown nor of the police authority, and this has caused problems about who to sue. The position has now been rectified by section 88 of the Police Act 1996, which provides that the Chief Officer of police for any police area is made liable:

'...in respect of torts committed by constables under his direction and control in the performance or purported performance of their functions in like manner as a master is liable in respect of torts committed by his servant in the course of their employment.'

In any case, an issue may arise as to whether an officer's or a constable's acts were outside the course of their employment, and therefore whether the employer is indeed vicariously liable. This defence will only be available in extreme cases. An example from a different context is the Court of Appeal decision in *T v North Yorkshire*, where it was held that a teacher who sexually abused a schoolboy with learning difficulties during a school trip was not acting in the course of employment. If this kind of defence is likely to be raised, consideration should be given to joining the actual individual employee as a defendant to the proceedings. It must be considered whether the individual will have sufficient funds, if the claim is successful, to pay both damages and the legal costs payable. There are also other cases in which there may be more than one defendant. For example, a person may have been unlawfully arrested and detained under the authority of the police, with the detention then continued under the authority of an immigration officer. In such a case, the claim may be against both the Chief Officer of police and the Home Office.

Time-limits

Claims must be brought within certain time-limits. In the context of civil claims, these time-limits are often referred to as 'limitation periods'. The relevant time-limits, and the possibilities for extending them, are set out in the table below. In an action for tort, if a person is under a disability – i.e. is either a child or a person of unsound mind – the limitation period does not start to run until they cease to be under a disability or die (s28 Limitation Act 1980). Claims should always be brought promptly. If there is any doubt as to whether a claim is outside the limitation period, specialist advice should be sought.

TIME-LIMITS FOR BRINGING CIVIL CLAIMS

Basis of claim	Time-Limit
• **Discrimination case under the Race Relations Act/Sex Discrimination Act**	Within six months of the discriminatory act complained of. There is provision for an extension of time where the court considers it 'just and equitable'. In race claims, it is possible for claimants to seek the assistance of the Commission for Racial Equality, and where an application is made for this, the period of time is extended by two months.
• **Claim to European Court of Human Rights**	Within six months of the claimant exhausting all their domestic remedies.
• **Claim under Human Rights Act against a public authority**	Within one year of the breach of human rights (subject to any rule imposing a stricter time-limit in relation to the procedure in question); the court can allow a longer period if it is considered 'equitable having regard to all the circumstances'.
• **Negligence, nuisance or breach of duty which involves a claim including personal injury or death**	Within three years of the date of knowledge of the damage. The court has a discretion to extend the time-limit in certain circumstances.
• **Other tort claims, including false imprisonment; assault; misfeasance in public office; malicious prosecution; breaches of statutory duty (unless a claim for personal injury is involved) or the limitation period is defined in the Act.**	Within six years. There is no discretion to extend the time-limit.
• **Defamation or malicious falsehood**	Within one year.

Note

Legal advice should be taken about time-limits so as to be sure not to miss the deadline.

11

Obtaining further information

In order to investigate whether to bring a claim, in some cases it might be useful to seek further information. Two specific pieces of legislation give rights of access to information: the Data Protection Act 1998 (DPA) and the Freedom of Information Act 2000 (FOIA). This legislation is useful for gathering information in immigration cases generally, not just in the context of civil claims. The discrimination legislation enables information to be gathered through a questionnaire procedure.

Data Protection Act

As set out above (▶1176), the DPA can give rise to a claim for damages. However, the DPA also gives a right of access to all personal information recorded by a government department about a particular person. This may enable a person to obtain useful information recorded about them concerning the dates when applications were made and determined, and records from Home Office case-files.

A request for personal information under the DPA is called a 'subject access request'. These requests can be made by writing to the IND's 'Subject Access Bureau' ('SAB'; ▶see 1505). An *original* signed authorisation from the 'subject' is required. A £10 fee is charged, and the IND is required to provide the information within 40 days of receipt of the fee. Where the request is indeed for personal information, it must be made as a subject access request and *not* under the FOIA (▶below).

Freedom of Information Act

The FOIA came into force on 1 January 2005. It allows people to write to government departments to ask them to disclose specific information held by them about how they work. So, it is possible to ask the Home Office for information, for example, about a policy or criterion that is normally used where a particular kind of decision is to be made. Requests should be made in writing and they should:

- be as specific as possible – otherwise the authority may write back and ask for more details of the information requested;
- not be for information which is already available – it is necessary to check that the information requested has not already been published, for example, in the IDIs.

Requests should be carefully directed to the particular department or section likely to hold the information requested. For example, Work Permits (UK) has set up a specific team to deal with FOIA requests. The 'WP(UK) FOI' team can be contacted with requests for information about: the HSMP, work permits, the sectors-based scheme, the seasonal agricultural workers' scheme, and the worker registration scheme (▶see 1505 for address). Requests should be responded to within 20 working days. Normally, FOIA requests will be responded to without a charge, but charges may be made for administration (postage, photocopying etc). Where the request involves significant work, a charge of £20 per hour may be made for any time spent dealing with the request beyond the first hour.

Not all requests will be satisfied. There are some 23 'exemptions' from rights of access under the FOIA. For example, information that would prejudice the operation of immigration controls may be withheld. If information is withheld, reasons should be given. If a person is dissatisfied with the response to a request, they may write to request a review to the IND's 'Briefing & Complaints Section (BCS)' (▶see 1493 for the address) and/or to the Home Office's 'Information Access Manager' (▶see 1505 for address). If the review is unsuccessful, it is possible to complain to the Information Commissioner (▶see 1505 for address).

Discrimination questionnaires

Both the SDA and the RRA have a questionnaire procedure to enable a proposed claimant to serve questionnaires on a proposed defendant seeking information in order to clarify whether a claim should be brought. Although there is no absolute requirement for the defendant to answer the questionnaire, an adverse inference can be drawn if there is no response.

Public funding (legal aid)

Most if not all private law civil claims against the immigration authorities and their contractors will be dealt with under the 'action against police etc.' Legal Service Commission (LSC) category. This allows a contracted provider to give initial 'Legal Help'. Among other actions, these contractors are also licensed to apply to carry out LSC 'certificated' work in cases against any body or person with the power to detain, imprison or prosecute in any of the following kinds of claims: assault; trespass; false imprisonment; malicious prosecution; personal injury or death in custody; misfeasance in public office; or other abuse of authority or neglect of duty. If the adviser does not have an 'action against the police etc' contract, guidance should be sought from the LSC as to how the case can be funded. In determining whether a case should be granted a certificate of public funding, the LSC applies the 'Funding Code' introduced under the Access to Justice Act 1999.

Those who are considering bringing a claim with the use of public funding should be given advice about the 'statutory charge', under which the LSC may claim back parts of any damages awarded.

Investigative Help

If the prospects of success for the claim are uncertain and substantial investigative work is required before those prospects can be determined, an application should be made for 'Investigative Help' (Funding Code, section 5.6.2). The criteria for Investigative Help are that:

- It will only be granted if there are reasonable grounds for believing that, when the investigative work has been carried out, the claim will be strong enough to satisfy the relevant criteria for 'Full Representation' (▶see below) (section 5.6.4);

- If the claim is primarily a claim for damages and has no significant wider public interest, Investigative Help will be refused unless the damages are likely to exceed £5,000 (section 5.6.3).

Full Representation

An application for a certificate for 'Full Representation' will be refused if the prospects of success are unclear or borderline, unless there is a 'significant wider public interest' in the case, or it is of 'overwhelming importance to the client' (see further below). Funding will be refused if the prospects of success are poor (section 5.7.2). For a claim to have 'significant wider public interest' it must have the potential to produce real benefits for people other than the individual client. These must go beyond the benefits to the public at large that normally flow from court proceedings of the type in question (section 2.4). Examples of claims that have a wider public interest would be those involving a challenge to a policy concerning detention under which many people are being detained (e.g. *Saadi*), or establishing a right to bring an action in the tort of false imprisonment for unlawful detention (*ID & others v Home Office*). The term 'overwhelming importance to the client' means a case that has exceptional importance to the client, beyond the monetary value (if any), because the case concerns the life, liberty or physical safety of the client or his or her family, or the roof over their head (section 2.4). This is more likely to apply to a judicial review than to a private damages claim.

In determining whether an application for Full Representation should be granted, the LSC also applies cost–benefit tests.

Cost-benefit test in straightforward claims The tests for straightforward damages claims are:

1) if the prospects of success are very good (80 per cent or more), likely damages must exceed likely costs;
2) if the prospects of success are good (60 to 80 per cent), likely damages must exceed likely costs by a ratio of 2:1;
3) if the prospects of success are moderate (50 to 60 per cent), likely damages must exceed likely costs by a ratio of 4:1 (section 5.7.3).

The level of damages an applicant might expect in an immigration civil claim is discussed below.

Cost-benefit test where claim has significant wider public interest If the claim has significant wider public interest, the cost–benefit criterion is more flexible: it requires that the likely benefits of the proceedings to the applicant and others justify the likely costs, having regard to the prospects of success and all the other circumstances (section 5.7.5).

'Serious wrong-doing' cases Some claims against the immigration authorities will fall into section 8 of the Funding Code, which covers claims against public authorities concerning serious wrongdoing, abuse of position or power, or significant breach of human rights. In these cases, Full Representation will be refused (section 8.3.2) if *either*:

- the prospects of success are poor; *or*
- the prospects of success are unclear or borderline *and* the case does not appear to be of overwhelming importance to the client or to raise significant human rights issues.

Again, there is a cost–benefit criterion which is more flexible in section 8 cases. It requires that the likely benefits of the proceedings to the applicant and others justify the likely costs, having regard to the prospects of success and all other circumstances (section 8.3.3).

Appeals against funding decisions If public funding is refused, an application can be made for the decision to be reviewed. If the refusal is confirmed, there is a right of appeal to a Committee convened by the LSC. If the Committee refuses the funding application, the only recourse is judicial review.

Damages

It is important to consider the likely level of damages at the outset of the case, both in order to decide whether to proceed and to assess whether public funding may be provided. 'Damages' means the financial award which the claimant is entitled to obtain from the defendant for the wrongs done to him or her. The different types of damages are set out in the table below. For an alternative means of obtaining compensation in some cases, ▶see 1223–7 and 1229–35. Note that, following the decision in *Greenfield*, damages in human rights claims may be lower than they might be thought to be by using other UK comparisons.

Lawyers often talk of 'recovering' damages, because they are essentially intended to provide compensation to claimants for the losses they have suffered as a result of the unlawful action of the defendant(s). The traditional principle in cases of tort is that the damages payable are intended to put the 'party who has been injured, or who has suffered, in the same position as he would have been in if he had not sustained the wrong for which he is now getting his compensation. In practice, this principle is easy to apply where the losses are 'financial' – for example, loss of earnings. In such cases, the losses can be assessed by a process of calculation. Where the losses are more 'general' – for example, the effect of being detained for a particular period of time, or the trauma of separation for family members – they are more difficult to assess. In such cases, the courts often award what appears to be a 'fair' amount having regard to the nature of the loss or injury.

11

THE DIFFERENT FORMS OF DAMAGES

- **Basic damages**

  These are damages intended to provide compensation for the loss or injury suffered. For example, in a case involving an assault, battery and false imprisonment, damages will need to be assessed for any physical or psychiatric injury suffered, as well as for the fact of the imprisonment. Guidance on awards for physical and mental injuries can be obtained from the Judicial Studies Board (JSB) Guidelines for the Assessment of General damages in Personal Injury Cases. These damages are also often referred to as 'general damages'.

- **Special damages**

  This covers quantifiable losses, such as the loss of potential earnings and out-of-pocket expenses. The loss that they are intended to compensate is sometimes referred to as 'financial loss' or 'purely financial loss'.

- **Aggravated damages**

  An additional sum of compensation intended to reflect the way in which the sense of injury or loss may have been made worse by the manner in which, or the motive with which, the injury or loss was caused.

- **Exemplary damages**

  This is a further sum intended to reflect public disapproval of arbitrary, oppressive or unconstitutional conduct on the part of servants of the government or where the defendant's conduct has been calculated to make a profit. It may be awarded if it is considered that the sum allowed in basic, special and aggravated damages is not sufficient for this purpose.

Damages in human rights cases

In deciding whether to award damages for a breach of human rights – and, if so, on the level of damages – the courts are required to taken into account the 'principles applied by the European Court of Human Rights' in relation to awards of compensation under Article 41 ECHR (see s8(4) HRA). In *Anufrijeva*, the Court of Appeal observed that the Strasbourg 'principles' upon which damages are awarded, are far from clear. What is apparent is that not every breach of human rights will result in an award of damages. Damages may only be awarded when it is 'just and appropriate' to do so, and when it is 'necessary' in order to afford 'just satisfaction' (s8(3) HRA). The exception to this is that, in relation to breaches of Article 5, the Convention requires that claimants should have an enforceable right to compensation (Article 5(5)). A further point, made by the House of Lords, in the context of a claim for a breach of Article 6 in the recent case of *R v SSHD ex parte Greenfield*, is that, in order to award damages, the European Court has generally required that the loss complained of was actually caused by the breach of the human rights in question. The House of Lords in *Greenfield* also underlined that, in deciding whether to award damages, and if so, how much, the Court is not strictly bound by the principles applied by the European Court but it must take them into account (para. 6).

Factors taken into consideration In deciding whether to make an award of damages, factors such as the seriousness and the manner of the violation of human rights, and the severity of the damage which it leads to, will be taken into account. The court will also consider whether the effect of any other order it makes to remedy the breach, or simply to declare that there has been a breach, will be enough to provide 'just satisfaction'. *Abdulaziz*, in which the couples were not actually prevented from living together, although they had been the victims of discrimination, is an example of a case in which the European Court decided that no damages were necessary in order to afford just satisfaction (▶see also 828, 886). By contrast, in another successful Article 8 case before the European Court, *Berrehab v Netherlands*, following his deportation from the Netherlands to Morocco, the applicant was separated from his young child, with whom he had had frequent and regular access. The court awarded 20,000 guilders (approximately £6,190) for his non-financial losses (an unspecified amount was awarded for travel expenses). Also, in *Ciliz v Netherlands*, an award of damages was made for a breach of Article 8 where the father's deportation during the course of contact proceedings had denied him any further involvement in those proceedings, and had prevented him from developing family ties with his child.

Assessment of human rights damages As to the basis upon which damages under the HRA are to be assessed if a decision is made to award, the principle (see above) of returning a person to the position they would have been in had the breach of human rights not occurred may be applied if the breach of human rights has clearly caused specific financial loss. Indeed, in such cases the court will usually find it just to make an award of damages. This was the case in the Strasbourg case of *Lustig-Prean and Beckett v UK* (awards of compensation to homosexuals discharged from the army for loss of earnings and pension rights). However, where the losses are not purely financial, the approach to assessment of damages is more flexible and less clear cut. In *Greenfield*, the House of Lords recognised, in the context of a breach of Article 6 (the right to a fair trial), that the European Court has been cautious in making awards for stress and anxiety falling short of psychiatric injury. In the instant case in *Greenfield*, the House of Lords thought that the finding of violation alone was enough afford just satisfaction and there was no justification for an award of damages. *Greenfield* also overruled the earlier UK decisions which had held that human rights damages awarded under section 8 HRA should take account of and apply domestic scales of damages. In *Anufrijeva*, *Bernard* and *KB*, the courts had referred to scales of damages for comparable torts and Local Government Ombudsmen awards. The House of Lords held that this was wrong. Damages did not *generally* need to be awarded in order to encourage compliance with the ECHR because countries were bound by international law to act within the ECHR. The purpose of the HRA was not to give victims better remedies than in the European Court but simply to allow them to access their rights and remedies more quickly and easily. The House of Lords continued:

'The [European Court] routinely describes its awards as equitable, which I take to mean that they are not precisely calculated but are judged by the Court to be fair in the individual case. Judges in England and Wales must also make a similar judgment in the case before them. They are not inflexibly bound by Strasbourg awards in what may be different cases. But they should not aim to be significantly more or less generous than the court might be expected to be, in a case where it was willing to make an award at all.' (para. 19)

Examples of damages

Examples of awards made for damages in immigration cases, mainly in cases of unlawful detention and removal, are set out in the table below (▶1205–10). We have also included some non-immigration cases that are of general use and importance as guidelines. Where the case is an immigration case, this will be clear from the very basic details given. The cases are listed in order of the length of detention. Many of the cases referred to are in fact 'settlements', in which the case did not proceed to full hearing before the court because the parties were able to agree an amount of damages to be paid. For this reason, many of the cases are not 'reported' in any series of law reports, and nor are they available on the electronic databases of unreported cases. For what references do exist, ▶see the full case index at 1551.

A number of other points also need to be kept in mind in considering these awards/settlements:

- Cases depend on their individual facts, and individuals suffer differently depending on their circumstances; there will never be an exact comparator for any one case.

- Cases do not necessarily represent the full value of the relevant claim, because settlements usually involve claimants compromising what they think is the full monetary value of their claim to reflect the 'litigation risk', i.e. the risk that they may go to court and lose overall, and therefore not recover any damages. Obviously, the extent of this risk (and therefore the extent to which the claimant is prepared to compromise) will vary according to the strength of the case.

- In the older cases, in order to make a proper comparison, it will be necessary to use an inflation table to update the award to today's value. In each case, we have given the approximate date of the award or settlement, and the court.

LEVELS OF DAMAGES: DETENTION AND/OR REMOVAL CASES

Length of Detention	Case	Award of basic compensation and notes
40 mins	*Goswell v Commissioner of Police for the Metropolis* (CA) (1998)	£100 Note that the detention was lawful after 40 mins
1 hr	*Thompson and Hsu v Commissioner of Police for the Metropolis* (CA) (1997) This case gives general guidelines for basic damages in all cases of unlawful detention, and is often referred to.It also throws light on the circumstances in which 'exemplary' and 'aggravated damages' may be awarded and levels of these awards.	£500
2 hrs 30 mins	*Roberts v Chief Constable of Cheshire* (CA) (1999) A technical false imprisonment after a failure to hold a review.	£500
2 hrs 45mins	*Commissioner of Police for the Metropolis v Gerald* (CA) (1998) *Hill v Commissioner for the Metropolis* (CA) (1998)	£1,500
3 hrs 45 mins	*C v Commissioner of Police for the Metropolis* (CC) (Feb 2003) Settlement following claim by an asylum-seeker for false imprisonment and for racial discrimination following arrest for immigration offences.	£8,000 Note that the claim included a claim for race discrimination.
12 hrs	*Barnett & Wilkinson v Chief Constable of West Yorkshire* (CA) (1998) It was held that they had been reasonably detained for six hours prior to the unlawful detention.	£600 The initial shock of detention was not a factor here.
1 day	*Thompson and Hsu* (CA) (1997) (see also above)	£3,000

11

LEVELS OF DAMAGES: DETENTION AND/OR REMOVAL CASES *cont.*

1 day	*EZ v Home Office* (HC) (January 2004) £15,000 Settlement where a mother was detained under immigration powers with her child. A separate settlement was made for the child, the terms of which are confidential.	Note that there was an element of psychiatric damage.
30 hrs	*Dudy v Home Office* (CC) Claimant held in police custody on the instructions of the Home Office for just under 30 hours. On the facts, it was alleged that there was no reasonable suspicion that an immigration offence had been committed. It appeared that the Home Office/police had acted on wrong information. The case was settled after proceedings were begun.	£3, 000
40 hrs	*A v Home Office* (HC) (January 2004) £7,500 Settlement for 40 hours' unlawful detention including an unlawful removal.	This includes damages for unlawful removal.
36–48 hrs	*Zafiu v Home Office* (CC) (c1999) Settlement for a Roma man unlawfully detained and removed over a weekend while he had an application for permission to appeal outstanding before the IAT. His dependants remained in the UK.	£12,000 This includes damages for unlawful removal.
5 days	*S v Home Office* (HC) (November 2003)Settlement for failed asylum seeker in a claim for unlawful detention and an unlawful removal when they had an outstanding human rights claim.	£13,000 This includes damages for unlawful removal.
6 days	*Perks v UK* (ECtHR) (1999) Compensation for violation of Article 6 (no legal aid where facing possible term of imprisonment).	£5,500
6 days	*I v Home Office* (HC) (June 2004) Settlement for a claim for false	£10,000

LEVELS OF DAMAGES: DETENTION AND/OR REMOVAL CASES *cont.*

	imprisonment and breach of Article 5 for unlawful detention (which, following issue of proceedings, was admitted). The detention was on the basis that removal was imminent, as it was contended that she had exhausted all appeal rights. In fact her case had been remitted by the IAT.	
6-7 days	*Nela v Home Office* (CC)(2001) Case settled at the door of the court. The claimant had reported in accordance with his conditions and was detained and removal directions were set. The claimant sought to raise his human rights and claimed that he was removed without a proper opportunity to appeal.	£17,000 (includes damages for unlawful removal)
8 days	*R (Q) v SSHD* (HC)(28 January 2005) Settlement where the Secretary of State accepted that he had unlawfully removed a family from the UK. The family were detained both before and after their unlawful removal – i.e. they were detained again when they were returned to the UK. The awards for two members of the family reflected exacerbation of psychiatric injury.	£40,000 apportioned between four members of a family. The claims also included damages for unlawful removal.
9 days	*D v Home Office* (HC) (February 2003) Settlement for failed asylum-seeker in claim for false imprisonment and breach of Article 5 for unlawful detention prior to an unlawful removal, when he had an outstanding human rights claim	£13,000 Includes damages for unlawful removal.
16 days	*O v Home Office* (CC)(February 2004) Claimant was lawfully detained, but was removed from association for 16 days under the Detention Centre Rules on the basis of false information that he was a sex offender. A claim was made for breaches of Article 8, misfeasance in public office and under the DPA. The claim was settled.	£3,000 This is a lawful detention case where the complaint related to the conditions of detention

11

LEVELS OF DAMAGES: DETENTION AND/OR REMOVAL CASES *cont.*

1 month	*R (on the application of M) v SSHD* *(HC)*(2004) This case involved a national from DRC who challenged his detention by judicial review, on the grounds that there was no prospect of removal within a reasonable timescale. Following his release the judicial review was continued until a compromise was reached with the payment of damages for the detention.	£11,300
42 days	*Lunt v Liverpool City Justices* (CA) (1991) The entirety of detention was unlawful.	£25,000
46 days	*Assessment of damages, I (Lord Brennan QC)*(CCU, 02 2/5/28) This is an *ex parte Adimi* case (wrongful prosecution of asylum-seekers for method of entry – ▶see 1225–8). The claimant served 46 days following his conviction for possession of a false document and attempting to obtain services by deception in June 1996. His conviction was set aside in March 2002.	£30,000
53 days	*R (Johnson) v SSHD* (HC) (November 2004) A judicial review claim was brought to challenge a five-and-a-half-week detention in the Oakington 'fast track'. It was held that the applicant should have been released after 6 days when it was clear that his claim could not be dealt with 'speedily'. The claimant was also unlawfully detained following the decision on the claim. The damages claim was settled.	£15,000
59 days	*Ex parte Evans (No. 2)* (HL) (c2001 Detention following miscalculation of release date. No aggravated or exemplary damages *but* also the case was distinguished from *Lunt*, because in that case the court was concerned with someone of good reputation.	£5,000 This is a case of detention following lawful imprisonment.

LEVELS OF DAMAGES: DETENTION AND/OR REMOVAL CASES *cont.*

63 days	*R v (1) Special Adjudicator, (2) Secretary of State ex p. AKB* (HC) (1998) This was a case involving the irrational use of detention powers, which were challenged in judicial review proceedings. A declaration was granted and the matter was then transferred to a Master for the assessment of damages. Note that £10,000 was awarded for basic damages for 63 days' false imprisonment. A further £8,000 was awarded for the exacerbation of the psychiatric condition. No aggravated damages were awarded, as there was no bad faith or deliberate attempt to humiliate or injure.	£18,000 The award included an element of damages for psychiatric condition. Note that the unlawful detention came at the end of a long period of lawful detention.
69 days	*N v Home Office* (2004) A settlement was agreed following a mediation hearing and before issuing proceedings. The detention had been unlawful from the outset. There had been two attempted unlawful removals and a degree of psychiatric injury.	£30,000
87 days	*Huzzey v Brent, Kensington and Chelsea NHS Trust* (HC) (2001) False imprisonment in a psychiatric hospital. This was a jury verdict.	£26,000
3 months	*DS v Home Office* (HC) (October 2001) Settlement for three months' immigration detention after lengthy period of lawful detention.	£15,000
220 days	*P v Home Office & Parole Board* (HC) (March 2001) Settlement following admission of liability by the Home Office and the Parole Board in relation to a delay in arranging a Parole Board. Claim was brought as a breach of Article 5(4) ECHR.	£11,250 An issue arose in this case as to whether the entirety of the delay caused excessive detention.

11

LEVELS OF DAMAGES: DETENTION AND/OR REMOVAL CASES *cont.*

6 months	*K* (HC) (2004) This concerned a mother and baby detained unlawfully under 1971 Act powers. The baby was ill in detention and continued to show adverse behavioural symptoms after the detention.	£32,500 for mother, £27,500 for baby
15 months	*I* (HC) (2004) This was a 15-month detention under 1971 Act powers. The damages settlement followed a successful application for *habeas corpus*. An issue arose as to exactly how much of the 15 month detention was unlawful.	£40,000

GENERAL PROCEDURES IN ORDINARY CIVIL CLAIMS

To bring an ordinary civil claim in the County Court or the High Court against the immigration authorities or others, potential claimants should obtain specialist advice. What follows gives an overview of the stages an action takes, and an explanation of the terminology used. Common terms used in civil claims are as follows.

Pre-action protocol Parties are encouraged by the Civil Procedure Rules to exchange information and explore whether a claim can be settled without the need to issue proceedings. The steps required by the pre-action protocol should be carried out before a claim is progressed. The various pre-action protocols are contained in Volume II of the 'White Book' and are available on the Courts Service Website (www.hmcourts-service.gov.uk).

Letter before claim This is usually the first formal step in the pre-action protocol. The claimant writes to the potential defendant to put them on notice of the claim, and to allow them an early opportunity to settle the matter before proceedings are begun.

Proceedings The process by which the claim will be pursued through the courts against the defendant in the absence of an early settlement of the matter. The following terms are also used:

- *Claim Form* The document lodged with and issued out of the court in order to commence proceedings.
- *Particulars of Claim* The formal document setting out the details of the claim, which will be served upon the defendant in due course with the Claim Form.
- *Defence* The formal document served by the defendant setting out the details of their case in response to the Particulars of Claim.

- *Statements of Case* This is the general term for the formal legal documents setting out the case on behalf of each party – i.e. the Particulars of Claim, the Defence, and any later clarification or elaboration provided by either or both parties.
- *Settlement* This is the process by which the claim may be concluded by the agreement of the parties at any stage before the end of the trial. It is difficult to predict which cases will be settled. Both the claimant and defendant may make offers to settle the claim under CPR Part 36. If not accepted, these offers can have costs consequences for either party.
- *Trial* In the event that the case is not settled, matters will proceed to trial, where each party may present evidence and legal argument in support of their case, and the judge and/or jury (in certain cases) will determine the facts, and whether the defendant is liable to the claimant.

The stages of a claim

The table below contains a case plan for a civil claim. It is not designed to cover all possible events, but is intended as a guide to the progression of a civil claim in both the High Court and the County Court.

THE STAGES OF A CIVIL CLAIM

Step	Explanation
1) **Assessment of case**	An early assessment will need to be made as to whether there is a potential civil case, or what further information is required for a proper assessment to be carried out. In the event that there is a potential civil claim, it will need to be determined whether it satisfies the LSC's criteria and cost–benefit analysis (▶see 1199–1201).
2) **Obtaining of Legal Services Commission funding**	The claimant will need to persuade the LSC that the case meets the relevant criteria, including the cost–benefit considerations, so as to justify public funding.
3) **Gathering of further information if necessary**	▶See 1198–1209 above.
4) **Notification to the Defendant**	Let the other side know that a claim is being considered, so that the defendant can ensure that they preserve all relevant paperwork.
5) **Letter before claim**	It is important to give the defendant a proper opportunity to respond to the claim, and to explore the question of settlement. Claimants should not issue and serve their proceedings until they have given the defendant in the region of four months to consider the claim.

11

6) **Issuing & service of proceedings**	In the event that a personal injury is alleged, an expert report will need to be served with the Claim Form and the Particulars of Claim.
7) **Defence**	See above.
8) **Allocation and directions**	The court will decide how the case should be conducted up to and including the trial. The court will usually also arrange a case management conference to discuss and agree a timetable for the further preparation of the trial. It is a good idea for all parties to attend the conference.
9) **Clarification of statements of case**	It may be necessary to ask for, or to respond to, a request for further information about each party's statement of case (Part 18 CPR).
10) **Fixing trial date**	The court will fix the date for trial having regard to the parties' dates to avoid. The precise time in the process when the court will fix the trial date will depend on the circumstances of the case.
11) **Disclosure**	This is the process by which the parties disclose documents as required by Part CPR 31. It may be that a specific request will need to be made and, if disclosure needs to be enforced, an application to the court will be necessary.
12) **Witness statements**	At the same time, the parties exchange their witness statements, which cover the factual evidence that they will rely on in support of their case.
13) **Expert reports**	The defendant serves any expert reports upon which they intend to rely. The claimant will also have to serve any further expert evidence. The parties can then ask for clarification of the reports (Part 35 CPR), and there may be a meeting of experts in order to try to agree the evidence.
14) **Listing Questionnaire**	At about this stage, the court will request information about the proposed trial date and try to ensure that the trial takes place on the date planned. There may be a hearing to discuss this.
15) **Trial preparation**	There will be extensive preparation before the trial, and there may be some formal requirements such as to exchange skeleton arguments before the trial date.
16) **Trial**	The hearing of the case in court.

38 Judicial review, complaints, Ombudsman and *Adimi* claims

This chapter looks at various remedies which might be used in order to deal with specific problems faced by those affected by immigration control. 'Judicial review' is a procedure that the government has gradually tried to remove as a remedy in immigration matters. Recent legislation has largely cancelled its role in challenging decisions made by Adjudicators and the Immigration Appeal Tribunal (IAT), and now by the Asylum and Immigration Tribunal (AIT), and replaced it with more limited forms of statutory review (▶see 1046–9 and Chapter 36). Judicial review can still, however, be used as a remedy in a variety of situations, which are flagged up at the appropriate parts of the *Handbook* (and see the situations mentioned at ▶1216–7). This chapter gives a general description of judicial review procedures (▶1213–22).

The chapter also covers the following remedies:

- complaining to the Home Office, and the Home Office schemes for compensating financial losses and making 'consolatory' payments in cases of errors and administrative failures (▶1223–7);
- seeking the intervention of a Member of Parliament (▶1227–8);
- the redress which can be obtained by complaining to the Parliamentary Ombudsman about maladministration by the Home Office and entry clearance posts, and the effect that such complaints have had in other cases (▶1229–35);
- obtaining compensation for the wrongful prosecution and detention of asylum-seekers following the decision of the court in *Adimi, Sorani & Kaziu* (▶see 1235–8).

JUDICIAL REVIEW

Judicial review is a High Court procedure that can be used to challenge decisions made by public authorities, including the immigration authorities. Judicial review can only be used where both of the following conditions are met:

- there is no other available way of challenging the decision (for example, where there is no right of appeal); and

- there are grounds for challenging the decision as being *unlawful* in a sense recognised by judicial review principles (▶see below).

General considerations The branch of the High Court that deals with judicial review cases is called the 'Administrative Court' (formerly the 'Crown Office'). What we provide here is a basic outline only of the procedures. Anyone who thinks that they may need to use judicial review should obtain proper legal advice from a solicitor from the outset. If the claim is to proceed, the solicitor will almost certainly instruct a barrister to help bring the claim. Public funding for advice and representation is available for those who do not have the means to pay, and whose cases have a good enough chance of succeeding (▶see 59–63 for general details about advice and funding). Claimants who lose in judicial review proceedings – particularly those who are not fully publicly funded – may face a bill for the legal costs of the other side as well as their own.

Rules for judicial review The basis for judicial review is contained in section 31 of the Supreme court Act 1981. The rules dealing with procedure are mostly set out in Part 54 of the Civil Procedure Rules (CPR), which have been in force since 2 October 2000. Other important documents for understanding judicial review procedures are the CPR Part 54 Practice Direction (both the Practice Direction and the CPR are available at www.dca.gov.uk), and the 'Administrative Court Office Notes for Guidance on Applying for Judicial Review' (available at www.courtservice. gov.uk). The Notes for Guidance indicate that it is possible to telephone the Court Office with questions about procedural matters (tel: 020 7947 6205), although the staff are unable to give legal advice.

Grounds for judicial review

In a judicial review case, the court may intervene in a decision if it is:

- **'illegal'** – for example, if it is contrary to the legislation, the immigration rules or a person's human rights;
- **'irrational'** – i.e., if the decision-maker failed to take into account relevant matters, or had regard to irrelevant matters, or if the decision was one which no reasonable person could possibly have reached; or
- **procedurally unfair** – for example, if the decision-maker failed to give the applicant a chance to make representations, or failed to take into account a relevant policy or concession which would normally be applied to the type of case in question.

These grounds are not set in stone; they are really just one way of classifying the principles of 'public' or 'administrative' law that are followed by the court. The claimant's grounds may fall into more than one of the above categories. For example, a failure to provide reasons for a decision may be contrary to a requirement of legislation that reasons for a particular decision be given. Depending on the nature of the decision, the same failure might also be in breach of the requirements of procedural fairness, which require, in many cases, that the person affected be told why a particular conclusion has been reached.

Does the court reconsider the facts for itself?

The purpose of judicial review is to enable the courts to supervise decisions made by public bodies, to ensure that they are not arrived at unlawfully in any of the senses described above. So judicial review cannot be used in the same way as an immigration appeal, where appellants ask the AIT to revise the factual findings that have been made by the immigration authorities.

The exceptions to the rule that the court will not assess the facts and evidence for itself are as follows:

- Decisions that a person may be detained and removed as an 'illegal entrant' (▶see 1010–5). If a determination of illegal entry is challenged by judicial review, the Home Office must prove the facts relied upon to show the illegal entry, so that the court is satisfied by considering the evidence that the person is indeed an illegal entrant (*Khawaja & Khera*, HL);

- Where the Home Office limits appeal rights by issuing a certificate stating that a person's asylum or human rights claim is 'clearly unfounded', the court is entitled to review the evidence for itself to determine whether the claim is indeed unfounded (see the decisions of the Court of Appeal in *ZL & VL v SSHD, R (Razgar & Others) v SSHD* ▶see 1077–8).

Powers of the court in judicial review

Even if a claim for judicial review is successful, the court will not re-take the decision that the public authority has made. In most cases, the most the court can do is to 'quash' the existing decision or 'declare' it to be unlawful, with the result that the public body has to reconsider the matter. Of course, when the public body reconsiders it must do so lawfully and in accordance with the legal findings made by the Administrative Court. In many cases, this will lead to a favourable outcome for the applicant (who is called a 'claimant' in judicial review proceedings), but this will not inevitably be the case. The court also has a discretion as to what action to take, even if the claim is successful. In rare cases, the court may decide not to take any action against the decision at all, even if it upholds the claim.

As is explained at ▶1193–4, claimants may add a claim for damages to their judicial review claim. They may only do this if there is a legal basis for making a civil claim for damages, as set out in Chapter 37. Judicial review does not provide any independent right to claim damages.

Judicial review proceedings may take months, and the Administrative Court also has the power to issue injunctions. Injunctions may be asked for in order to prevent effect being given to the decision under challenge while the claim is being dealt with by the court. For example, an injunction may be obtained to prevent a person from being removed from the UK while a decision concerning their removal is subject to challenge. Injunctions may be requested on an urgent basis (►1221–2), but the court may also grant non-urgent injunctions at any stage during the proceedings. Where claimants are detained, bail can be requested in the course of judicial review proceedings (►986).

Common circumstances in which judicial review is used

Judicial review is commonly used in immigration cases in order to challenge:

- certificates issued by the Home Office that an asylum, human rights or other claim is 'clearly unfounded', so that the claimant has no in-country right of appeal (s94 2002 Act (►1073–8));

- refusal by the Home Office to accept that a 'fresh claim' has been made entitling the claimant to a further right of appeal, or a refusal to take an 'immigration decision', which also enables a right of appeal (►730–5; see also para. 353 HC 395, see s82 2002 Act);

- certificates issued by the Home Office denying a person a right of appeal on the grounds that: they had an earlier right of appeal and are now seeking simply to delay their removal; or that they could have raised the grounds in an earlier appeal/'one stop' notice and failed to do so; or the grounds being raised were dealt with in an earlier appeal (s96 2002 Act; ►1067–9);

- decisions about removals to 'safe' third countries (►739–46);

- unlawful decisions to detain a person under immigration powers (►986, and for the related High Court procedure of *habeas corpus*, see 987);

- Home Office nationality decisions concerning naturalisation or registration (►see Chapter 45);

- decisions of NASS where there is no right of appeal to the asylum support adjudicator (►1389–91);

- decisions of asylum support adjudicators (►Chapter 42);

- decisions of local authorities concerning community care or 'interim' asylum support (►see 1299–1328);

- unreasonable delays in taking administrative steps, such as issuing status papers, causing severe detriment to those affected (►718–9);

- decisions of the AIT which are not decisions to allow or dismiss an appeal but are 'procedural, ancillary or preliminary' decisions (see rule 2, Asylum and Immigration Tribunal (Procedure) Rules 2005) (►1150–1).

As indicated above, the main reduction in judicial review in immigration cases is a result of the recent changes made to the immigration appeals system (►see 1051–2, 1046–9). Previously, many judicial reviews concerned challenges to the IAT's refusal to grant leave to appeal. However, if the government's latest proposals relating to appeals are implemented, the scope for the use of judicial review may widen further. The 'five-year strategy' announced in February 2005 and the 2005 Bill propose to end appeals relating to entry concerning work and study (▶1041–6). It may be that the only means of challenging negative decisions in these categories will be by judicial review.

Before the claim: pre-action protocol

Before commencing a claim, claimants should make sure that they have complied within the terms laid out in the 'Judicial Review Pre-Action Protocol', which has applied since March 2002. The main requirement is that claimants should send the defendant a 'letter before claim', setting out the date and details of the decision or act which is challenged, summarising the facts, identifying the issues in dispute, stating what action the defendant is expected to take, and asking for any further information which the claimant requires. The letter should normally give defendants 14 days to reply, and within that time the claimant should not begin the proceedings. The purpose of the letter is to see whether the dispute might be resolved, for example by the defendant changing the decision, or taking the required action.

Where the proposed claim concerns an immigration, asylum or nationality case, the letter before claim should be sent to 'The Judicial Review Management Unit' at the IND (▶see 1497 for the address). Depending on the nature of the case, the letter should also contain the Home Office reference number, the port reference, the Immigration Appellate Authority or AIT reference number, and/or the NASS reference number. It should also contain the full name, nationality and date of birth of the claimant. Annex A to the Protocol contains a skeleton standard format for these letters.

Urgent cases and cases where the defendant can't change the decision

A letter before claim does not have to be sent in urgent cases – 'for example, when directions have been set, or are in force, for the claimant's removal from the UK' (see the Protocol). Nevertheless, even in urgent cases it is good practice to warn the defendant of the proceedings, although obviously without giving the defendant anything like 14 days to respond. In such cases, the letter might simply set out the issue and state that the relevant paperwork is in the course of being prepared and will be issued at court if the defendant does not contact the claimant with a revised position. For urgent cases and injunctions, ▶see below, 1221–2. Another situation in which a letter before action will not be appropriate is where the defendant does not have the legal power to change the decision being challenged.

Time-limits

The time-limit for bringing judicial review claims is that they should be filed 'promptly' and 'in any event not later than three months after the grounds to make the claim first arose' (CPR Part 54.5). This does not mean that a claimant can delay for up to three months – they must act 'promptly'. Time is not suspended while the Pre-Action Protocol is being complied with, which underlines the importance of not delaying the letter before claim. If there is unnecessary delay, the claim may be refused. The court has the power to extend time-limits, but will only do so where there are very good reasons for the delay, and the delay hasn't caused detriment to others.

Making a claim

Claim form Judicial review is initiated by completing the claim form, Form 'N461', which must be filed together with the issue fee of £50 (cheques are made payable to HM Paymaster General and must be supported by a cheque guarantee card presented at the time the application is lodged). All the court forms, such as N461, are available on the Court Service website (www.hmcourts-service.gov.uk). Certain claimants on low incomes can gain an exemption from the fee (see Civil Procedure Fees Order 2004). Among the details required by the form are: full details of the claimant, the defendant and any 'interested parties' (i.e. anyone else who is likely to be directly affected by the proceedings); details of the decision or action challenged, and a statement of what action the claimant would like the court to take if the claim is successful.

Filing the bundle The claim form must include, or have attached to it, a statement of the relevant facts of the case and a statement of the legal grounds on which the claim is being brought. The claim form should be placed at the start of a bundle including other documents in support of the claim. These documents will include the decision being challenged, evidence relevant to the decision, other documents relied upon, and relevant legislation. The bundle should be very carefully prepared: it should not contain irrelevant documents and it should be properly paginated and indexed, with a list near the front of documents that are essential reading for the judge. Two copies of the bundle must be filed with the court. Extra copies of the claim form are required, which should be presented to the court office in order to obtain the court's seal before they are served on the defendant and interested parties. It is then the job of the claimant to serve the bundle with the claim form on the defendants and other interested parties within seven days of the date of the court seal. A certificate of service must then be lodged with the court by the claimant (form N215).

Defendant's acknowledgement of service After the claim has been issued with the court and served on the defendant, the defendant has 21 days to lodge with the court an 'acknowledgement of service' (form

N462). This states whether the defendant is going to oppose any part of the claim; and, if so, the defendant must give a summary of their grounds of opposition. The papers will then normally be submitted to a High Court judge, together with a briefing note prepared by a lawyer in the court office. The judge will consider whether to grant 'permission' to apply for judicial review (▶see below).

The two stages of judicial review

There are two stages to judicial review. The first is the 'permission' stage. The second is the 'substantive' or 'full hearing' stage.

Permission stage

In order to be granted permission to apply for judicial review, it is necessary to show the judge that it is 'arguable' that the decision was unlawful. Initially, a judge will consider the papers prepared by the claimant's lawyers without a hearing. The judge's decision is then communicated to the parties in writing, using form JRJ, and the reasons given are usually very brief. If the judge rejects the claim after looking at the case papers, the claimant has another opportunity to get past the first stage at a court hearing. In order to do this, the claimant must, within seven days of the date of the order refusing permission, lodge a notice (which will be sent out with the decision on permission) with the court asking for an oral hearing. Oral permission hearings are generally allocated 30 minutes of court time. If permission is refused orally, the claimant can immediately ask the judge for permission to appeal to the Court of Appeal. If refused, the claimant can also, within seven days, ask the Court of Appeal for permission to appeal. It should be noted that the Court of Appeal has recently expressed grave concerns about judicial review cases which follow this route when there is no real legal case to put.

'Substantive' stage

If the first stage is successful and permission is granted, the matter may proceed to the second stage, which will culminate in what is often called the 'full' or 'substantive' hearing of the judicial review. The claimant must pay a further fee if they wish to continue with the claim after permission has been granted. In many cases, the defendant decides to concede after permission has been granted. If the defendant decides to fight on, they are required to lodge detailed grounds for their opposition to the claim, and any written evidence or further documents they wish the court to see. When these are received, the claimant will decide whether they need to respond to the defendant's evidence by putting in further evidence of their own. At the full hearing the court will hear the legal arguments of the parties in full – the advocates for each side will have provided in advance 'skeleton arguments' of what they are going to say. The court will then decide finally whether the decision was unlawful and what, if any, orders it will make.

11

Appeals

In some cases it may be possible to appeal to the Court of Appeal against the decision made in the Administrative Court after the full hearing. If an appeal is to be brought, it is first necessary to get permission to appeal either from the judge in the Administrative Court or in the Court of Appeal. Again, very careful advice should be obtained before trying to appeal.

Imminent removals and Home Office practice where claim issued

For some time, the Home Office has operated an arrangement with the Administrative Court in cases where removal directions have been issued and the claimant wishes to bring judicial review proceedings. Provided that an application for judicial review is lodged, and an Administrative Court Office number for the case obtained, within five working days of the relevant decision (or three working days where the claimant is detained), removal directions will not generally be enforced at least until the decision of the judge on the papers concerning permission. Plainly, if permission is granted, removal should not be enforced while the pro-ceedings are continuing, and there are no changes of circumstance. If permission is refused on the papers and the claimant seeks an oral hearing, the Home Office will normally not remove while the claim is out-standing. This 'Concordat' was referred to by the Court of Appeal in the recent case of *Ben Pharis v SSHD* (see paras 15–20). The policy is set out in similar terms in the Operational Enforcement Manual (Chapter 44.2). However, the Home Office has been reviewing its policy on these issues (letter to ILPA, 9 February 2005). We would therefore suggest that claim-ants should always check the position on their individual case with the Home Office and, if possible, obtain confirmation in writing that removal will not be enforced while the claim is outstanding. If an assurance is not given, consideration should be given to asking the court for an injunction (▶see below).

Imminent removals and the Court of Appeal

In *Pharis* (above), the Court of Appeal noted that no such arrangement had ever been made with the Court of Appeal in relation to appeals from judicial review decisions made by the Administrative Court (note that different considerations apply in the case of appeals from the Immigration Appellate Authority/AIT). The court commented that, although it appeared that the Home Office operated a similar practice before the Court of Appeal as it did before the Administrative Court, it was not obliged to. The Court drew attention to what it saw as the continuing abuse of the procedure for appealing to the Court of Appeal and declared that, in future, notice of appeal to the Court of Appeal in judicial review cases should not be regarded as automatically stopping the removal process. In order to stay the removal, applicants must now make a specific application to the Court of Appeal.

Urgent cases and injunctions

In most cases, claimants' lawyers are able to persuade the Home Office that whatever action it is threatening to take should be delayed while a claim is brought (this is often in accordance with the general practices referred to above). However, if this fails the Administrative Court also has the power to deal with urgent cases and to give orders to the defendant to maintain the status quo until the claim has been fully dealt with.

Any orders given by the court before the final hearing are generally known as 'interim orders'. For example, the court can order that the immigration authorities do not remove the claimant from the UK while the claim is outstanding, or that a destitute asylum-seeker is not denied support. In deciding whether to make an order, the court will look to see whether the claimant has a reasonable case to argue, and will also balance the harm caused to the claimant if the decision is left to stand while the claim is being considered against the harm to the defendant and the public interest if the decision is not allowed to stand while it is being challenged.

Although the rules mainly talk about 'injunctions', the same interim orders may also be referred to as a 'stay', which may be the more appropriate term, because the body is a public authority being challenged in judicial review proceedings, rather than a private party in an ordinary civil court (see *R v Secretary of State for Education and Science ex parte Avon County Council* [1991] 1 QB 558). We will continue to refer to such orders as 'injunctions'.

Procedures for urgent cases and for urgent injunctions

If a claimant needs to have their application for permission to claim judicial review considered urgently, or requires an urgent injunction, they must complete form N463, the 'Request for Urgent Consideration'. On the form the claimant must explain the reason why the matter is urgent, and the timescale within which it must be dealt with. Form N463 should be provided to the court, together with grounds for making the interim order, a draft of the order asked for, and ideally a witness statement setting out the relevant facts, from which the urgency should also be clear. These documents should be copied to the defendant and interested parties by both fax and post, so that they can make any written representations to the court.

In order to get a decision on the same day, the papers should be provided to the court by 2.00 pm. The judge will look at the papers without a hearing and consider what order to make. It is often best in these urgent applications simply to ask for an injunction, rather than also for permission to apply for urgent judicial review. This is because the claimant may be unable to present the application in the best possible way if it is prepared urgently, and may wish to supplement the written argument or documents later. Also, the judge may be less prepared to grant permission to apply for judicial review without the defendant having had a proper chance to provide their summary grounds of defence, than to grant an injunction. After all, an injunction can be set aside far more easily than a grant of permission.

The details of the urgent procedure are set out in a 'Practice Statement' issued by the court, which is published in the *All England Law Reports* ([2002] 1 All ER 633). There are, however, penalties for abuse of the system. The court can make a 'wasted costs' order, according to which claimants may have to pay the public expenses wasted by making inappropriate applications.

Urgent NASS 'section 55' cases

Following the denial of asylum support to asylum-seekers who did not claim 'as soon as reasonably practicable' after their arrival in the UK, unless support was required to avoid a breach of their human rights (see s55(1), (5) 2002 Act), the court was deluged with urgent judicial review applications for injunctions (for further details about s55, ▶see 1350–2, 1368–9). In *R (Q & Others) v SSHD*, the Administrative Court gave some procedural recommendations to try to reduce the need for so many injunctions in such cases:

- NASS should have an efficient system for making swift decisions and reconsidering decisions where further information comes to light or representations are made;
- representations made by applicants' advisors to NASS should be full and detailed;
- if a judicial review claim is going to be brought, NASS should quickly (within a day) consider providing (and should usually provide) support until the permission decision is made. If NASS refuses, the asylum-seeker can proceed to ask for an injunction.

Out-of-hours cases

In the minority of very extreme cases, where an order is needed out-of-hours, it is possible to apply to the duty judge on the telephone for an injunction. The point of initial contact is the security personnel at the main gate to the Royal Courts of Justice in London (▶see 1498 for address and telephone number). In the asylum support cases, the Court has stated that it will only respond positively to out-of-hours telephone applications in very exceptional circumstances. An example might be the case of an asylum-seeker with a severe medical condition who would be extremely badly affected unless an injunction is immediately obtained. Again, it is vital that people seek specialist advice from an experienced solicitor before attempting any of these procedures.

COMPLAINTS TO AND COMPENSATION FROM THE HOME OFFICE

Complaints made about the IND should be made *in writing* and in English to the IND Complaints Unit (▶see 1493 for address). The Home Office divides the complaints it receives into two categories:

- operational complaints, which relate to the way the IND works – for example, complaints about delays, or inadequate information;
- formal complaints, which are about the conduct of particular members of staff – for example, if they have been inefficient, unprofessional or rude.

The Home Office recommends that people who are unhappy with the service they have received should first try to resolve it with the person in question, and then, if this cannot be done, take the matter up with their supervisor. If this does not resolve the situation, a complaint can be made by writing to the Complaints Unit within three months of the incident or problem. When writing in, complainants should obviously give full details of themselves as well as a full description of the problem (including any request for compensation or a consolatory payment, ▶see below) and the names of the officer(s) involved. Copies of papers relating to the matter should also be sent in. Complaints about NASS can be directed to NASS Complaints, PO Box 1384, Croydon, CR9 3YT (fax: 020 8760 8485).

The Home Office aims to provide an answer to operational complaints within four weeks, and to formal complaints within eight weeks (in the case of formal complaints it is necessary for the staff involved to be interviewed). The investigating officer may also contact the complainant to clarify details. If the complaint is successful, the Home Office will normally apologise and try to improve its service, and it may also pay compensation. However, the complainant may have other specific action they wish to be taken. If the complainant is not happy with the outcome of the complaint, they may write back to the Complaints Unit, who will see that the complaint is reviewed. If the result is still negative, the next step that a determined complainant might make is to complain to the Ombudsman (▶see below, 1229 onwards).

It should be noted that an independent 'Complaints Audit Committee' monitors IND's handling of complaints.

Complaints about Work Permits (UK) or entry clearance posts While much of the above applies equally to Work Permits (UK), complaints about their service should be made in writing to the Customer Relations section at Work Permits (UK) (▶see 1494 for address). Operational complaints are dealt with within 15 working days, and formal complaints within 12 weeks. Complaints about service at an entry clearance post are probably best made to the post itself, which is likely to refer the matter to the Policy Section of UK Visas (see DSP, Ch 28, para. 28.2).

11

Home Office compensation schemes

A complaint to the Home Office may result in the payment of compensation. There are two possible bases for compensation. First, the Home Office may offer to compensate a victim for their direct financial losses caused by the Home Office's errors. Secondly, in 'exceptional circumstances', the Home Office may consider making a 'consolatory payment' in respect of non-financial losses such as distress. We look below at each of these in turn. As with complaints in general, if the applicant cannot get satisfaction from the Home Office, they can take the matter up with the Ombudsman.

Compensation for financial loss

Information on the IND website under 'Complaints' and 'Am I entitled to compensation?' explains compensation for financial loss as follows:

'Where you can show, usually by producing receipts, that you have suffered financial loss as a direct result of an error of IND's, we will consider whether compensation should be paid. When considering claims, we will establish whether the costs incurred are reasonable and have been actually and necessarily incurred.

When deciding whether a payment of compensation should be made, reference is made to the Government Accounting Manual, which exists to ensure the proper handling of public funds. The general principle is that redress will be provided, which is fair and reasonable, in light of all the facts and circumstances of the case.'

It seems that, provided that the complainant can prove the extent of the loss caused by the Home Office, they will be reimbursed in full. The Framework Document referred to below, although it deals with *non*-financial loss, says the following about *financial* losses:

'We pay compensation for financial loss for reasonable costs that have been necessarily incurred, with the aim of restoring the complainant to the position he or she would have enjoyed had the maladministration not occurred.'

In *R (A & Kanidagli) v SSHD*, at the time of the Home Office's appeal to the Court of Appeal in February 2005, the Home Office agreed to pay the full amount of the financial loss caused by the loss of income from social security benefit which had been caused by the Home Office's error (for further details ▶see 1185–6).

Claims for compensation in complaints about posts abroad apparently arise for a number of reasons, but the most common is where a visa national is informed by the post that they do not need an entry clearance for the UK. If, acting on this advice, the person travels to the UK (if they manage to board the aircraft, etc.) and are then refused entry – or even if the person is prevented from boarding – they may submit a claim for the cost of the wasted fare and/or having to change their arrangements, and any distress caused. The post will refer the matter to UK Visas, who will then take legal advice about the claim (see DSP, Ch 28, para. 28.21-28.2).

So, where specific financial loss has been caused by errors by the immigration authorities, it is worth making a complaint and asking for a compensatory payment, setting out all the details and providing evidence to demonstrate the amount of the loss.

Consolatory payments

The Home Office scheme for providing 'consolatory payments' for non-financial losses, such as distress, embarrassment, inconvenience and damage to health, came to general attention in the course of a High Court judicial review hearing in December 2002. The claimant was seeking damages under Article 8 ECHR for delays and errors which in turn caused a delay in a sponsor being able to bring his family to the UK under the family reunion provisions for refugees (*R (Mambakasa) v SSHD*). The Home Office produced a witness statement from the Head of the Complaints Section, that attached the IND's *Framework Document for Consolatory Payments for Non-Financial Loss*, drawn up in late 1999.

The Framework was drawn upon at the request of, and in consultation with, the Parliamentary Ombudsman (►see below). The Ombudsman may well have encouraged the Home Office to operate such a scheme, having regard to the extent of the difficulties caused by Home Office failures of administration. Although the Framework was clearly drawn up in consultation with the Ombudsman, it is not clear that the Ombudsman actually agreed the document and tariffs set out. It seems unlikely that the document was agreed, because the general view expressed by the Ombudsman is that anyone who has suffered injustice as the result of maladministration should, as far as possible, be put back in the position they would have been in had the maladministration not occurred. By contrast, the principle under the Consolatory Scheme is not to fully compensate the victim for the harm suffered, or to restore them to their position before the mistakes. As its title suggests, the scheme provides only 'consolation' for the error, and payments will only be paid where there are 'sufficiently compelling circumstances'. The witness statement in *Mambakasa* stated:

11

'The level of payments made pursuant to the Framework Document was not intended to be on a par with damages that might be awarded by the courts (say, in a claim for personal injury) ...'

Further, the Framework Document itself states:

'While account will be taken of the level of distress, the payments are consolation payments only and are not intended to be based on a comprehensive assessment of the distress actually suffered ...'

This accounts for why the levels of consolatory payments are low. The table below provides further details of the consolatory payments scheme and of the level of awards. Note that the tariff amounts are those contained in the document as issued in late 1999. It was stated in 2002 that the amounts were then due to be reviewed, and indeed the Framework Document states that the level of awards should be reviewed 'annually'. There has, however, been no published update to the figures.

The Framework Document does not expressly mention many of the forms of maladministration that commonly arise – for example, delayed or incorrect issue of immigration documents, delays in returns of passports, delays in dealing with applications causing losses or failures, and errors made by NASS. However, these forms of loss are clearly within the reach of the scheme when regard is had to the examples given. As will also be seen from the table, even if no request for a consolatory payment is made, the Home Office should still consider whether it is appropriate to make such a payment if it receives any complaint, and a request for compensation.

CONSOLATORY PAYMENTS FOR NON-FINANCIAL LOSS

The Home Office scheme to provide consolatory payments for non-financial loss, as disclosed in December 2002 in *Mambakasa*, is to the following effect.

General

- All payments of compensation in cases of maladministration are *ex gratia*.
- Compensation is paid for *financial loss* for reasonable costs that have been necessarily incurred, with the aim of restoring the complainant to the position he or she would have enjoyed had the maladministration not occurred.
- Compensation for *non-financial loss* will only be paid in exceptional circumstances and only where there are sufficiently compelling circumstances to justify such a payment ('consolatory payment'). Such payments must also take account of the normal requirements for the proper care and use of public funds.
- The Home Office needs to be reasonably satisfied that their maladministration led to the distress as claimed.
- Where there is no explicit request for a consolatory payment, it should nevertheless be considered whether it would be appropriate to make such a payment.
- The same considerations apply whether the claim is made by the complainant directly or through representatives or the Ombudsman.

Quantum (i.e. level of payments) (to be reviewed annually)

- Consolatory payments are a recognition of the exceptional distress, embarrassment, inconvenience, damage to health, etc caused.
- While account will be taken of the level of distress, the payments are consolation payments and are not intended to be based on a comprehensive assessment of the distress actually suffered.

- Payments in many cases will be between £50 and £250. More serious cases will merit higher payments, which may be up to £1,000.
- Payments are likely to be higher where there is more than one element of distress.

When consolatory payments may be made

- When serious or persistent errors have been made.
- When the claimant has clearly suffered significant distress as a result of Home Office maladministration.

Circumstances potentially meriting payment

The following list is illustrative only, and is not intended to be either prescriptive or exhaustive. All cases will need to be considered on their merits, in respect of both whether a payment should be made and how much compensation should be offered. The illustrative amounts are per person, and will need to be increased if more than one person suffers distress, etc.

- Passport lost resulting in worry and inconvenience only: no payment.
- Passport lost resulting in missed holiday: £50–£100.
- Passport lost resulting in:
  - missed family wedding or other family celebration: £100–£250,
  - inability to attend a dying relative or family funeral: £500–£750.

  The closeness of the relationship is likely to affect the sum awarded.
- Interviews/appointments cancelled without notice: no payment.
- Immigration Officers visit an address where illegal entrants are (wrongly) thought to be staying and cause unnecessary worry for the occupier: £50–£200.
- Passengers denied boarding by airline because passports incorrectly endorsed: £100.
- Breach of confidentiality by passing on information to a third party: £100–£250 (▶see also Data Protection Act claims, 1176).
- Complaints/compensation claims badly mishandled/delayed: £50.

11

CONTACTING A MEMBER OF PARLIAMENT

If a person has already been through the formal processes of dealing with the immigration authorities without success – making an application, appealing against a refusal, losing the appeal – it may be worth contacting the local Member of Parliament and asking them to make representations to the Secretary of State. MPs can be involved in cases of maladministration (▶see above), or in cases where the problem is the actual immigration decision itself. If, however, MPs try to intervene while an appeal is still pending, they are usually told that their representations will not be considered until after the appeal has been decided.

Making contact

If the applicant is in the UK, their own constituency MP can be contacted. If the applicant is abroad, it is possible to contact the constituency MP of one of the friends or relatives the person is coming to be with. Some MPs refuse to make representations in cases, and some are highly unsympathetic or may take a good deal of persuading. MPs have regular surgeries in their constituencies, and so a good way to get them involved is to visit them at their surgery so that the problem can be explained in person. Occasionally – particularly if the case has wider implications or is well known – it may be possible to involve sympathetic MPs even if they do not have constituents with a direct interest in the case. The House of Commons Information Section (020 7219 4272) should be able to give details of who a local MP is if they are provided with the details of the applicant's or sponsor's address. They may also be able to give the number of the MP's secretary or constituency office. In order to find the contact details of a particular local MP, it is also possible to send an email to hcinfo@parliament.uk.

How MPs can intervene and their effect

The way in which MPs will often make representations is by passing on, together with a brief covering letter, a letter that the applicant or their representative has themselves written. It is therefore important to be able to give the MP a full written account of the case and the relating problems, together with any important evidence in support. If the MP is willing to help, they may either write to the Member of Parliament Correspondence Section (MPCS) at the Immigration and Nationality Directorate, or contact the Home Office Minister's office directly. The intervention of an MP can also sometimes help to get an imminent removal deferred, particularly if matters are raised through an MP which have not been considered before.

For questions concerning entry clearance applications, UK visas encourage MPs to use its Visa Correspondence Section (VCS) quoting the full name, date of birth, application number and the name of the post where the application was made and providing as much other detail as possible. There is also an MP's hotline in operation (see *Visa News*, a newsletter for MPs and their constituents issued by the Foreign and Commonwealth Office and the Home Office, Summer 2005).

For further details about the way in which the immigration authorities handle representations from MPs about enforcement see Chapter 43 of the Operational Enforcement Manual. Where the MP contacts the Minister's private office directly, a decision on removal will have to be taken by the private office after consulting caseworkers. It seems that removal is most likely to be deferred if the information provided by the MP is 'new and compelling'.

PARLIAMENTARY OMBUDSMAN

The formal title of the Parliamentary Ombudsman is the 'Parliamentary Commissioner for Administration', as it is set up under the Parliamentary Commissioner Act 1967. The Parliamentary Ombudsman has the power to investigate complaints of administrative failures, or 'maladministration', across a wide range of government departments and other public bodies. Both the Home Office and the Foreign and Commonwealth Office are government departments subject to investigation by the Ombudsman (see s4 and Sch 2 1967 Act). Complaints may therefore be made to the Ombudsman about the activities of the IND, NASS and Work Permits (UK). Complaints may also be made about entry clearance officers and posts overseas, but in such cases, if the complainant does not usually live in the UK, it may be best for a sponsor to take the matter up (see ss5(3), 6(4)(5) and para. 2 to Sch 3 1967 Act).

Typical cases

As the activity of the Ombudsman in immigration cases is not well known among immigration advisers, in the table below (▶1231–5) we have provided details of other immigration cases dealt with by the Ombudsman over the last few years. Complaints have been made about matters such as: delays in determining applications and issuing travel documents; delays in implementing decisions made after appeal; failures to transfer status; incorrect endorsements of leave; delays in forwarding appeal papers to the court for appeals to be heard; loss of files or documents; non-compliance refusals where self-completion forms have clearly been returned but not linked to the file; failures to reply to correspondence sent by representatives; and the giving of incorrect advice. These failures have caused all sorts of losses – for example, inability to travel (for business, holiday or family purposes); family separation; inability to obtain, or loss of, employment; denial of access to benefits; unnecessary travel; and, of course, accompanying distress and inconvenience. Although the Ombudsman has no power to enforce the recommendations it makes, they are usually accepted. The range of measures that complainants have obtained as an outcome of their complaint to the Ombudsman is clear from the example cases given.

Complaints in 2003–2004

Some 99 cases involving the IND were brought to a conclusion by the Ombudsman in the year 2003/04, most without the need for a full investigation. In the same year, the Ombudsman received some 17 complaints against the Foreign and Commonwealth Office, most of which related to the actions of foreign posts. Referring to complaints made about the IND, the Ombudsman's report for 2003/04 comments: 'Some of the complaints we have dealt with have had a profound and adverse effect on people's lives'. The report refers in particular to a recent case involving a Mr T, in which the immigration authorities had not endorsed his passport with leave when he originally arrived in the UK in 1999, as a minor, to settle with his parents (Case 841/03). As a result, in 2000 Mr T was detained in Turkey while travelling back from a holiday in China, and was in fact returned to China. His file then passed between different parts of the IND for nearly 18 months, with no action being taken on it. During that period Mr T could not return to the UK, and was separated from his family. The Ombudsman upheld Mr T's complaint and, as a result, the Home Office apologised, arranged for his immigration position to be regularised, offered a consolatory payment of £1,000, and agreed to consider a further claim for financial loss.

Making a complaint to the Ombudsman

The Ombudsman expects the complaint to have been put to the relevant body, and that any internal complaints procedure has been used before the Ombudsman is approached. It is not possible for individuals to raise a complaint directly with the Ombudsman; complainants must instead ask an MP to refer their complaint to the Ombudsman (▶see above for contacting MPs). The recommended way to put the complaint to the MP is to use the form posted on the Ombudsman's website (for address and website of Ombudsman, ▶see 1505). The form can also be obtained by contacting the Ombudsman's helpline on 0845 015 4033, or 020 7217 4163. The form itself contains notes about how to complete it, and full details of the matter should be set out. As well as the form, it will also be necessary to provide supporting evidence and correspondence.

Procedure after the complaint is made

The Ombudsman does not proceed with all complaints referred to it. Its first task is to decide whether the complaint is one it has the power to investigate – i.e. that it is a complaint about maladministration, and that it concerns a body overseen by the Ombudsman. If the complaint falls within the Ombudsman's powers, the Ombudsman will then consider whether, on the face of it, there is evidence of administrative failure that has caused personal injustice that the Ombudsman's intervention may help to put right. The Ombudsman may also consider whether its intervention would be of benefit to others. Depending on the answer to these questions, the matter may be taken further. If so, the Ombudsman will usually begin making enquires of the public body concerned. In many cases, the complaint can be satisfactorily settled at this stage – namely, after the Ombudsman has intervened but without it having to start a full 'statutory' investigation. Many complaints against the IND and about ECOs appear to be satisfactorily resolved at this initial stage.

Full investigations If a full investigation is required, complaints may take months, because the Ombudsman may wish to examine the public authority's papers and interview their staff, and it may also interview the complainant. At the end of the investigation, a report is drawn up. Even in cases where a full investigation is begun, it is possible that a satisfactory settlement will be reached during the course of the investigation, in which case the investigation may be discontinued. Decisions made by the Ombudsman throughout the process are generally communicated to the MP who referred the complaint, and the MP is expected to pass the information on to the complainant.

Previous investigations in immigration cases

Every year the Ombudsman submits a report to parliament about its work. The annual reports summarise some of the cases dealt with during the course of the year, including immigration-related cases. Additionally, for some cases, the Ombudsman publishes the full report on its website (www.ombudsman.org.uk). Separately again, the Ombudsman some-times publishes summaries of reports into particular areas. For instance, in 2002 a document was issued with specific IND case-studies.

The table below gives details of the outcomes of some complaints made to the Ombudsman about immigration cases over the past five years, taken from the above sources. Of course, some complaints are not taken up at all, and some do not result in any action being taken by either the Ombudsman or the public body concerned. The examples given in the table are those of cases in which the effect of the Ombudsman, either in making initial enquiries or in making findings following an investigation, has resulted in a positive outcome for the complainant.

OUTCOME OF COMPLAINTS TO OMBUDSMAN IN IMMIGRATION CASES AND COMPENSATION OFFERED

Note The case numbers given are the references assigned to the case by the Ombudsman.

C = Complainant

PO = Parliamentary Ombudsman

Failure to record information given – travel costs

C614/99 C complained that, on her visits to the High Commission in Islama-bad, she had been informed that she could not succeed in having her child endorsed on her British passport unless she provided certain documentation (which she did not have), or unless she returned to the UK. After the PO investigated the matter, it was agreed that instructions would be issued to staff at posts to keep records of unusual visits and to reimburse C for travel expenses incurred.

Delays in processing family reunion entry clearance applications

C/867/99, C12/00, C13/00 In these three cases, the PO upheld complaints about excessive delays in processing family reunion entry clearance applications, which appear to have been referred back to the IND. The IND apologised, gave information about procedures put in hand to remedy the situation and, in the first case, offered £100 for expense, trouble and worry. In

11

the second case, an undertaking was given to process the application without any further unnecessary delay.

Delay in determining application for leave, inadequate arrangements to enable applications to be chased, loss of earnings in visiting IND

C290/00 A delay in processing an application for a residence permit meant that C and his wife were unable to travel at certain important times. They were poorly served in their attempts to chase the application by inadequate arrangements at IND's telephone enquiry line. Following the PO's investigation, an apology was received, an explanation given as to the steps taken to improve the service, and an *ex gratia* payment made in relation to an unpaid day off work which C and his wife took in order to visit IND to sort out their application, and in relation to their inability to travel.

Failure to determine application – inability to visit dying relative and attend funeral, distress

C378/00 The PO found that a delay by the IND in resolving an immigration application prevented C from visiting his father before he died and attending his funeral. An *ex gratia* payment of £750 was made by IND in recognition of the severe distress caused.

Delay in authorising entry clearance following successful appeal – distress/anxiety and cost of continued remittances to relatives abroad

C1304/00 C's family's appeal against entry clearance refusals in a Somali family reunion application was successful (it concerned a husband, two children and mother). There then followed a nine-month delay by IND in authorising the issue of entry clearances. The IND/FCO argued that they should be permitted between a month and three months at the beginning of the period in order to process the matter. Even allowing for a three-month maximum period for processing the case, the PO found the IND to be at fault. The delay had been caused by the IND mishandling correspondence. An *ex gratia* offer of £800 was made in relation to C's costs of continued remittances to her relatives during the period of delay. £100 was offered for anxiety and distress. The package also included an apology and an improvement in procedures.

Failure to determine urgent but straightforward application for indefinite leave and to issue travel documents, causing inability to travel, distress and costs of attempts to expedite

C1441/00 A straightforward application to issue indefinite leave to remain and travel documents to refugees became urgent, as C's mother was dying and the couple needed to travel. The original indefinite leave application had been made in October 1998, and had been 'chased' by letters in February, March and April 1999. On 6 July 1999, C notified that the matter had become urgent. Travel documents were finally issued in October 1999 (three months after the mother's death). The PO upheld the complaint, criticised the delays and welcomed £750 offered by IND for distress. IND also offered to consider making payments for C's costs of visiting the IND and in making telephone calls to them. IND also agreed to reimburse C for the costs of obtaining medical reports from Bosnia in relation to the mother's illness. Had the application been treated with the priority it deserved, it would not have led to C seeking further evidence in order to try to persuade IND to expedite the application.

Delay and failure to decide application and act on appeal, benefit losses

C1472/00 The PO upheld C's complaint about a three-year-and-eight-month delay in deciding an asylum application, and acting on a successful appeal. The IND offered an *ex gratia* payment of £1,000 in respect of benefit losses (full-level income support). The IND did not accept in principle that an *ex gratia* payment should be linked to any particular level of benefit, but stated that they would be prepared to consider cases individually.

Delay in transferring stamps, inability to travel to see relatives, distress and anxiety, business loss

C1500/00 C complained that there was a five-month delay in transferring C's stepson's conditions of leave in the UK from C's wife's passport to C's stepson's new Russian passport. The result was that they had been unable to visit relatives in Russia over the holiday period (one of whom was dangerously ill). Also, C's wife had not been able to accompany him abroad, which caused business losses (she was his interpreter). The PO noted that the application for transference of conditions was 'such a minor, straightforward task that one would have expected IND to be able to complete it in a matter of minutes'. The PO upheld the complaint. Compensation was recommended by the PO in respect of distress and anxiety, and the PO welcomed the offer of £1,000 in recognition of the distress and anxiety caused to C and his family. The IND also agreed to consider providing compensation for business losses if they could be proved. An apology was also given.

Loss of documents leads to processing application without passport and assistance to obtain new passport

C250/01 C complained that the IND had lost or failed to return his family's passports and his driving licence following his wife's application for leave to remain. Following the PO's intervention, the IND stated that it could not determine whether the documents had been lost or somehow misplaced in the external post. The IND nevertheless apologised, agreed to process C's wife's application without her passport, and wrote to C's wife's embassy to assist her in obtaining a new passport. The IND also offered to make a consolatory payment of £50, and to pay for the processing of the new passport.

Failure to issue travel document, inability to travel, distress

C1208/01 There was a delay in obtaining a travel document for one year. Following the PO's enquiries, C was provided with an *ex gratia* award of £250 in recognition of the distress caused by this, and by his inability to visit his wife's family abroad after her death.

Delay in dealing with employment application, loss of earnings

C1232/01 The PO upheld a complaint that a delay in dealing with an application for leave to remain in the UK for employment resulted in C being unable to take up the employment she had been offered. The IND apologised for mishandling the application and offered an *ex gratia* payment of £4,725 for 18 days' loss of earnings. The Permanent Secretary at the Home Office assured the PO that the IND had taken steps to improve their service.

Delay in issuing leave after successful appeal, inability to travel

C612/02 C was successful in her immigration appeal, and there was then a delay in issuing her leave. The consequence was that C lost a job offer, and was unable to travel to visit her mother during her last illness or to attend her sister's wedding. The PO found that the IND had no effective procedure for monitoring the outcome of asylum appeal hearings. The IND offered £400 in respect of the losses.

Delay and failure to return passport, inability to travel, distress

C1430/02 C complained that a delay by the IND in processing an indefinite leave to remain application, and failure to return a passport, prevented C from visiting a sick relative and taking up an offer of work overseas. Following PO's enquiries, IND offered £250 in view of the distress caused by C's being unable to visit the relative and, later, to attend the funeral.

Failure to endorse leave and endorsement with later date corrected so as not to cause future disadvantage

C1919/02 C complained that the IND failed to issue him with a status letter to confirm his grant of exceptional leave, and that the public enquiry office had refused to endorse his passport with the exceptional leave. When the letter was finally issued, it showed a grant of leave from a later date (February 2002 instead of September 2000). This put back the time at which C would be eligible to apply for indefinite leave. After the PO's enquiries, the IND agreed to endorse C's passport immediately with the correct stamp, and stated that he would be eligible to apply for indefinite leave in line with the correct endorsement.

Delay leads to grant of leave to remain

C111/03 The PO upheld a complaint concerning the IND's delay for over a year in deciding whether to grant leave to remain following a recommendation by Work Permits (UK) that C be allowed to take up an offer of employment. The IND subsequently granted C leave to remain, primarily as a result of the delay – she would not have qualified under the immigration rules. An *ex gratia* payment of £50 was also made.

Earlier failure to endorse leave results in person stranded outside UK, distress and family separation

C841/03 An initial failure to endorse stamps resulted in C being unable to return to the UK. The PO upheld the complaint and the IND offered a consolatory payment of £1,000, plus financial loss (►see above at 1224–5).

Incorrect issue of passport, financial and other losses

C356/04 The PO found that the High Commission had incorrectly issued C with a British passport. C believed it to be correctly issued, and went about arranging her financial and other affairs accordingly. C was offered a consolatory payment of £750, and the Foreign Office agreed to consider a claim for C's financial losses.

Delay in preparing appeal submissions – legal costs, contribution to travel costs, family separation

C968/04 C complained about a delay of over five years by the IND in preparing appeal submissions in her son's appeal against refusal of entry clearance to join her in the UK. C incurred expenses in travelling to see her sons. After the PO's intervention, the IND accepted that they had unreasonably delayed, and offered a £200 consolatory payment, agreed to consider paying additional legal costs caused by the maladministration, and to make a contribution to C's travel costs if the appeal was successful. The IND also agreed to review its procedures.

COMPENSATION FOR UNLAWFUL CONVICTION OF ASYLUM-SEEKERS UNDER THE *ADIMI* PRINCIPLE

Asylum-seekers who are convicted of certain offences concerning their entry to the UK *before* the statutory defence to such charges came into force on 11 November 1999, may seek compensation for their conviction and detention. The statutory defence was introduced by the 1999 Act, and is modelled on the 1951 Refugee Convention.

The background is that in July 1999, the Divisional Court considered the UK's practice of prosecuting certain asylum-seekers for deception and use of forged documents concerning their travel and entry to the UK (see *R v SSHD & CPS ex parte Adimi, Sorani & Kaziu*). The court found that the practice of prosecuting asylum-seekers travelling on false documents to gain entry to a country to make a claim was unlawful, on the basis that 'no arm of state, neither the Secretary of State, the DPP, nor any one else, had apparently given the least thought to the UK's obligations arising under article 31 [of the 1951 Convention relating to Status of Refugees]'.

Article 31(1) of the 1951 Refugee Convention states:

'The Contracting States shall not impose penalties, on account of their illegal entry or presence, on refugees who, coming directly from a territory where their life or freedom was threatened in the sense of Article 1, enter or are present in their territory without authorisation, provided they present themselves without delay to the authorities and show good cause for their illegal entry or presence.'

Article 31 recognises that, because of the immigration controls imposed by countries of potential refuge, those fleeing persecution may well have to resort to 'unlawful' means in order to escape harm. Following the judgment in *Adimi*, the government enacted a statutory defence based on Article 31 (see s31 Immigration and Asylum 1999 Act). The defence actually provides less protection than Article 31 envisages. For example, the defence is only available to an asylum-seeker who stopped in another country if they are able to show that they could not reasonably have been expected to be given protection under the Convention in that other country. But Article 31 provides protection if there is a short-term stopover en route to the country of refuge without the asylum-seeker having to demonstrate that there was no protection available in that other country. Also, the defence under the 1999 Act only covers three specific offences, and not all offences that might be contrary to Article 31. In *R (Pepushi) v CPS*, the Divisional Court considered the question of this lower standard of protection under the 1999 Act. The Court observed that parliament had now considered the whole matter in the light of Article 31, and had chosen to use clear words that offered less protection than the Convention. The narrower protection intended by parliament had to be applied. The Court in *Pepushi* also held that any challenge to the appropriateness of any prosecution should be brought in the criminal proceedings themselves, rather than by an application for judicial review.

Compensation for those wrongly convicted

Asylum-seekers who, before 11 November 1999, were wrongly convicted of an offence as referred to above, and who did not argue a defence based on Article 31 during their original trial, may be able to obtain compensation. It must first be considered whether the defence could have been applicable. For instance, the asylum-seeker should have presented themselves to the authorities 'without delay'. There are then two steps that must be taken in order to obtain compensation. First the conviction itself must be quashed, and then the person concerned must apply for compensation.

Getting the conviction quashed

Most of the convictions occurred in the Magistrates Court, and the simple procedure that lawyers have used is to request that the Magistrates Court where the particular asylum-seeker was convicted re-open and re-list the case before different justices. This can be done under section 142(2) of the Magistrates Court Act 1980, which allows this where 'it appears to the court that it would be in the interests of justice to do so'. When this is done, the Crown Prosecution Service (CPS) has generally withdrawn the prosecution, provided it is satisfied that Article 31 ought to have been considered and that, if it had been, no prosecution would have been brought. This will then result in the original conviction being quashed.

The 1999 Act also makes provision for an application to be made to the Criminal Cases Review Commission for a referral of a wrongful conviction to the Court of Appeal, and it is probable that this procedure should be followed if the conviction was in the Crown Court (s31(8) 1999 Act).

Claiming compensation

Once the conviction is quashed, the next step is to make a claim for compensation. There is no automatic entitlement to compensation for a wrongful conviction or charge, and the process is dealt with in a number of stages. Initially, an application needs to be made under the statutory and *ex gratia* (i.e. discretionary) compensation schemes to the Office for Criminal Justice Reform, Claims Assessment Team, Trial Policy & Procedure Unit of the Home Office. The Home Office provides leaflets about these schemes. The statutory compensation scheme is established under section 133 Criminal Justices Act 1988, but this type of claim does not fall very naturally within its scope. For this reason, it is believed that the Home Office has been dealing with claims under the *ex gratia* scheme.

The *ex gratia* scheme was established following a statement made in parliament by the then Home Secretary on 29 November 1985. It was stated that compensation would be paid to applicants where the conviction (or period of detention without charge or conviction) 'resulted from serious default on the part of a member of the police force or some other public authority'. In these cases it can be argued that there has been serious default by many public bodies in failing to have regard to and uphold the obligations of the UK government under Article 31.

Claims do not need to be made within a particular period after the conviction is quashed, but it is good practice to make claims as soon as possible. The letter of application should provide an explanation of why the Home Office should pay compensation under the scheme. This should be a brief description of how the applicant was unlawfully prosecuted and imprisoned in breach of Article 31, and should set out that this was in the context of serious default on the part of the authorities (the police, CPS and Home Office) in relation to the UK's obligations under Article 31. (It is worth highlighting that the Home Office had been on notice from Amnesty International as early as 1996 that their practice was in breach of Article 31.) A decision on whether the claim is eligible for compensation will then be made. Decisions may take up to nine months to be dealt with. There is no right of appeal against a refusal, which can only be challenged by judicial review if there are grounds for bringing such a claim (for a description of judicial review and the general grounds that can be argued in judicial review, ▶see 1213–22).

The level of compensation

If a decision is made to make a payment under either the statutory or *ex gratia* scheme, the assessment of compensation is made by an independent assessor appointed by the Home Office. The assessment is made based on written representations setting out the relevant facts. Therefore, in addition to providing the asylum-seeker's date of birth and that of any children, together with any previous convictions, it is important to set out the full facts of the case, which should include the following information/evidence:

- The way in which the particular applicant has suffered from the point of arrest to the end of sentence. Psychiatric and other medical evidence may be needed to prove claims about trauma, and to show that the cause of any trauma was the conviction. Asylum-seekers may be particularly vulnerable to trauma resulting from imprisonment (psychological trauma caused by the imprisonment may significantly increase the amount of compensation).

- Details of any particularly regrettable circumstances and conditions in which the asylum-seeker was imprisoned. It may be helpful to quote from the prison inspectors' reports. Those relating to the conditions in HMP Wormwood Scrubs, where a lot of asylum-seekers were detained, are particularly critical.

- Any 'special' damages – i.e. particular identified financial costs. Examples are items lost or destroyed by the police or prison, and loss of earnings due to inability to gain employment by virtue of having a criminal conviction.

- The cost of instructing a lawyer to deal with the compensation matter.

A memorandum will be prepared by the Home Office for submission to the independent assessor. This will be sent to the applicant's lawyer and, once agreed, to the assessor, who will provide an assessment that includes an offer of settlement. The time taken for an offer to be made will depend on the complexity of the case, but should be in the region of six to nine months. The sum offered will take account of both financial and non-financial factors, and will obviously depend on all the facts of the case, as well as times spent in prison. Examples of offers known to JCWI are as follows:

- £40,000 for three months served
- £40,000 for six weeks served (in a case involving a single mother with two children)
- £32,000 for two months served
- £32,000 for six weeks and three days served
- £30,000 for six weeks served

The assessor will not enter into correspondence or discussion about the award, and the Home Office will not consider approaching him/her on the applicant's behalf, unless there are good grounds for believing that the assessor has failed to take a material point into account, or has taken into account erroneous or irrelevant material. There is thus no appeal mechanism, and if an applicant is not satisfied with the award the only available remedy is judicial review.

Section 12 **Welfare**

Chapter 39
Welfare benefits   1241

Summary of welfare benefits system   1244

Access to welfare benefits and immigration
status: a 'ten-point' outline   1247

'Subject to immigration control' test   1249

Exceptions to the 'subject to immigration
control' test   1255

The 'habitual residence' test   1259

The 'right to reside' test   1264

'Accession 8' nationals and the right to reside   1268

Additional tests for certain benefits   1273

Contributory benefits   1276

Claiming for dependants   1276

Additional benefit rights for EEA nationals and
reciprocal agreements   1281

Transferring to benefits   1282

Refugees and backdating claims for benefit   1284

Refugee integration loans   1286

General matters: going abroad, links between
departments   1287

Chapter 40
**Housing, social services, Children Act and
health care**   1289

Housing   1289

Social services   1299

Children Act 1989   1322

Health care   1328

Education   1335

12

Chapter 41
Asylum support and 'hard cases' support   1337

  Who qualifies for asylum support?   1341

  Exclusions from asylum support   1350

  What support is provided under the NASS
  scheme?   1360

  NASS procedures and temporary support   1367

  'Interim' asylum support   1371

  EU minimum standards for the reception of
  asylum-seekers   1379

  'Hard cases' support   1381

Chapter 42
Asylum support appeals   1389

  When can a person appeal to the Asylum
  Support Adjudicators?   1389

  Appeal procedures   1391

39 Welfare benefits

This section deals with the effect of immigration status on access to various forms of welfare provision. Access to welfare entitlements has been progressively eroded since the mid1990s and the present 'five-year strategy' states that the government intends to review eligibility for 'benefits and public services' and how they are enforced to see if 'any tightening is necessary'.

This chapter covers access to welfare benefits. In this chapter we do *not* cover the requirements in the immigration rules under which applicants must show that they can maintain and accommodate themselves 'without recourse to public funds'. Only at the outset do we look at the relationship between the immigration rules and access to benefit entitlement. For full details about public funds and the immigration rules, ▶see 308–318.

The *Handbook* cannot give guidance on the general conditions of eligibility for all the welfare benefits, which is a huge topic (for further sources of information ▶see 1534–5). However, at ▶1244–7 there is a table giving a general summary of the welfare benefits system to show which benefits are available in which general circumstances. Aside from that summary, we focus on the special rules that affect access to welfare benefits *based on immigration status* (▶see beginning at 1247).

The rules about benefit entitlement and immigration status are complex. *After our overview of the benefits system, we provide a 'ten-point' outline of how immigration status impacts on access to benefit (▶see 1247–9). For those seeking an answer to a problem, it may be easiest to look at that outline first and then follow the page reference given by the outline to the part of the chapter that deals with the particular issue in more detail.*

Chapter 40 looks in turn at access to local authority housing; support from a local authority social services department ('community care' services); support under the Children Act 1989; health care under the National Health Service; and education.

Chapter 41 deals with asylum support provided by NASS, together with 'interim' asylum support provided by a local authority. That chapter also covers 'hard cases' support under section 4 Immigration and Asylum Act 1999.

Chapter 42 covers appeals to the Asylum Support Adjudicator.

Abbreviations

In many places, we have used initials to refer to the different benefits. The benefit abbreviations used are set out in the table below. The regulations relating to benefit entitlement are many and detailed. We have also, in this chapter, shortened our references to the different regulations. The full titles of the different regulations referred to are also set out in the table.

ABBREVIATIONS USED IN THIS CHAPTER

Benefit abbreviations

- attendance allowance (AA)
- bereavement benefits: widow's payment (WP); widow's parent's allowance (WPA); bereavement allowance (BA)
- carer's allowance (CA)
- child benefit (CB)
- child tax credit (CTC)
- cold weather payment (CWP)
- contribution-based incapacity benefit (IB)
- contribution-based jobseeker's allowance (JSA)
- council tax benefit (CTB)
- disability living allowance (DLA)
- guardian's allowance (GA)
- housing benefit (HB)

- income-based jobseeker's allowance ((IB) JSA)
- income support (IS)
- industrial injuries benefit (IIB)
- non-contributory incapacity benefit (IB based on youth incapacity)
- maternity allowance (MA)
- severe disablement allowance (SDA)
- state pension credit (SPC)
- statutory adoption pay (SAP)
- statutory paternity pay (SPP)
- statutory maternity pay (SMP)
- statutory sick pay (SSP)
- social fund payments (SFP)
- state retirement pension (RP)
- winter fuel payment (WFP)
- working tax credit (WTC)

Abbreviations of regulations

- 'Accession Regulations' – Accession (Immigration and Worker Registration) Regulations 2004, SI No. 1219
- 'Accession Amendment Regulations' – Immigration (European Economic Area) and Accession (Amendment) Regulations 2004, SI No. 1236

- 'Child Benefit Regulations' – Child Benefit (General) Regulations 1976, SI No. 965
- 'Child Benefit Amendment Regulations' – Child Benefit (General) (Amendment) Regulations 2004, SI No. 1244

- 'Council Tax Regulations' – Council Tax Benefit (General) Regulations 1992, SI No. 1814
- 'EEA 2000 Regulations' – Immigration (European Economic Area) Regulations 2000, SI No. 2326
- 'Habitual Residence Amendment Regulations' – Social Security (Habitual Residence) Amendment Regulations 2004, SI No. 1232
- 'Housing Benefit Regulations' – Housing Benefit (General) Regulations 1987, SI No. 1971
- 'Income Support Regulations' – Income Support (General) Regulations 1987, SI No. 1967
- 'Jobseeker's Allowance Regulations' – Jobseeker's Allowance Regulations 1996, SI No. 207
- 'Persons from Abroad Regulations' – Social Security (Persons from Abroad) Miscellaneous Amendments Regulations 1996, SI No. 30

- 'Social Security Immigration Regulations' – Social Security (Immigration and Asylum) Consequential Amendments Regulations 2000, SI No. 636
- 'Pension Credit Regulations' – State Pension Credit Regulations 2002, SI No. 1792
- 'Tax Credits Residence Regulations' – Tax Credits (Residence) Regulations 2003, SI No. 654
- 'Tax Credits Immigration Regulations' – Tax Credits (Immigration) Regulations 2003, SI No. 653
- 'Tax Credits Residence Amendment Regulations' – Tax Credits (Residence) (Amendment) Regulations 2004, SI No. 1243

Note

There is a general list of legislation abbreviations used in the *Handbook* at ▶1530–3.

Relationship to 'no recourse to public funds' under the immigration rules

This chapter is about *access* to welfare provision and not about the effect which claiming, trying to claim, or needing to claim public funds has on immigration status. Full details about the meaning of 'public funds' and satisfying the maintenance and accommodation requirements are contained in the section dealing with family and dependants at ▶308–318. That section also covers the recent changes to the immigration rules, which allow certain applicants who are exempted from the exclusions from benefits that apply to those who are 'subject to immigration control', to claim benefits without damaging their immigration status. To understand which claimants are covered by this, it is necessary to read ▶309–311 together with the table on ▶1255–8.

Public funds themselves are defined in paragraph 6 of the Immigration Rules (HC 395) as (▶see 1242 for the abbreviations used):

- AA;
- CA;
- CB;
- CTC;
- CTB;
- DLA;
- HB;
- (IB) JSA;
- IS;
- SPC;
- SFP;
- WTC.

12

The tax credits, CTC and WTC, were added to the list of public funds from 15 March 2005 (see HC 346).

In most cases, where an immigration applicant has to satisfy the 'maintenance and accommodation' requirements of the immigration rules, if the application is successful, a formal condition requiring them not to have recourse to public funds will be attached to the leave (▶see 190–1 for a table of conditions generally imposed for the different categories of entry under the rules). The endorsement in the passport containing the leave, or the document issued by the Home Office granting leave, will state what, if any, conditions have been attached to the leave. Breach of any condition can lead to serious consequences: it is both a criminal offence and can lead to the person being administratively removed from the UK (▶see 1004–7).

In cases where claiming may have an impact on a person's immigration status or applications they may make in the future, advice should be obtained.

SUMMARY OF WELFARE BENEFITS SYSTEM

The social security system contains an array of welfare benefits payable to claimants who satisfy strict criteria, which are set out in the regulations. Some benefits are 'means tested' which means that they are only available to claimants who have low levels of income and capital. Others are based upon 'contributions', which means they can only be obtained if the claimant has paid a sufficient amount of national insurance contributions.

The main pieces of legislation providing for social security benefits are: the Social Security Contributions and Benefits Act 1992, the Jobseekers Act 1995, the State Pension Credit Act 2002 and the Tax Credits Act 2002. Most of the detail concerning welfare benefits is set out in regulations made under this legislation.

The very general circumstances in which the various benefits are available to different categories of people are set out in the table below.

GENERAL SUMMARY OF WELFARE BENEFITS SYSTEM: WHAT BENEFITS ARE THERE AND WHO IS ELIGIBLE FOR THEM?

Means-tested ('income-related') benefits

These are the benefits of last resort where entitlement is based upon lack of financial resources or savings below a prescribed limit.

- **Income-based jobseeker's allowance ((IB) JSA)** This pays basic living expenses for those not in work. Claimants must be capable of working, available for work and actively seeking work. When JSA came into being, many claimants became entitled to JSA instead of income support. The amount paid contains:

an element for the adult, an element for dependent children (but this is gradually being replaced by CTC, see below) and various additional payments called 'premiums'. (IB) JSA has a twin, contribution-based JSA (below), which is payable for a maximum of six months if the claimant has made sufficient national insurance contributions.

- **Income support (IS)** This is payable at the same rates as (IB) JSA above. A range of people can claim IS including:

  – people with child-care responsibilities and carers;

  – sick and disabled people.

  Where a person claims IS based on incapacity, they have to pass the same tests for incapacity as someone claiming incapacity benefit (see below).

- **State pension credit (SPC)** This is a means-tested benefit paid to pensioners in place of IS. It has more generous rules in relation to savings.

- **Housing benefit (HB)** This is paid by local authorities to help pay for rent. There may be shortfalls due to ineligible charges, and restrictions on the amount of benefit paid where the tenancy is in the private sector.

- **Council tax benefit (CTB)** This is paid by local authorities to help pay council tax. Note that both HB and CTB may be paid to a claimant who is in work but on a low income.

- **Social fund payments (SFPs)** This scheme provides for one-off payments. Maternity grants, funeral expenses and cold-weather payments are based on *entitlement*. Community care grants and budgeting loans are *discretionary* payments. Eligibility generally depends on being in receipt of a 'qualifying benefit' i.e. IS, (IB) JSA, SPC, HB, CTB, CTC and WTC. This rule does not apply to crisis loans although the claimant may need to show that they have sufficient funds to repay the loan in the future.

Non-means-tested benefits

The following benefits are paid generally regardless of the level of the claimant's income or savings and regardless of the level of any national insurance contributions made.

- **Disability living allowance (DLA)** Entitlement is based on the extent to which the claimant's disability creates care needs (the care component), or affects their mobility (the mobility component). DLA is paid at several different rates. There are two rates for the mobility component and three rates for the care component.

- **Attendance allowance (AA)** This can be claimed by people over 65 who have care needs. There is no mobility component.

- **Carer's allowance (CA)** This benefit is linked to receipt of AA, or DLA when they are paid at least at the middle rate of the care component. CA is the replacement for invalid carer's allowance. For CA there are some restrictions on how much the claimant can earn. Claimants may also qualify for the carer's premium which may result in extra IS, (IB) JSA, SPC or HB/CTB.

- **Child benefit (CB)** This is a universal benefit, which is paid in respect of every child.

12

- **Incapacity benefit (IB)** for incapacity in youth. This can be claimed by those who became incapable of work in youth and have therefore not made enough national insurance contributions to qualify for contribution-based IB. A claimant will normally qualify if their incapacity began between the ages of 16 and 20 years (or, in certain circumstances, before they were 25). Those who were under 20 on 6 April 2001 and were getting a benefit called 'Severe Disablement Allowance' (SDA), automatically qualify for long-term IB on the basis of incapacity for work in youth.

Other non-means-tested benefits include: industrial injuries benefit (IIB); guardian's allowance (GA), category D retirement pension (payable to those over 80) and severe disablement allowance (SDA). SDA was abolished for new claimants from April 2001.

Contributory benefits

In order to be entitled to these benefits, the claimant must have paid sufficient national insurance contributions. These payments are normally linked to past employment.

These benefits include the following.

- **Contribution-based JSA** This is payable for a maximum of six months. It is paid to those who used to be paid 'unemployment benefit'.

- **Contribution-based incapacity benefit (IB)** This is payable at three rates: a lower short-term rate, a higher short-term rate and a long-term rate. Claimants must be assessed or treated as incapable of work. The tests used are the 'own occupation' test or the 'personal capability assessment'.

- **Maternity allowance (MA)**

- **Retirement pension categories A and B (RP)**

- **Statutory maternity pay (SMP), statutory paternity pay (SPP) and statutory adoption pay (SAP)**

- **Statutory sick pay (SSP)**

- **Bereavement benefits** These include bereavement payment (BP), a lump-sum payment; widow's parent's allowance (WPA) paid to those who have qualifying children; and bereavement allowance (BA), a weekly benefit paid for up to 52 weeks to widows or widowers who were 45 or over when their spouse died.

Note, that in February 2005, the government announced that it would be reforming incapacity benefit as part of its five-year plan for welfare reform. IB will be replaced by two new benefits: 'rehabilitation support allowance' and 'disability and sickness allowance'. The purpose of this is to distinguish between those with severe conditions and those with more manageable conditions.

The schemes for statutory sick pay and maternity pay are operated by employers.

Tax Credits

The tax credits are a further form of means-tested, non-contributory benefit. They were introduced on 6 April 2003 and are administered by the Inland

Revenue. They are assessed on an annual basis in line with the tax year from April to April. For further details regarding the immigration rules about no recourse to public funds and the tax credits, see ▶310–11.

There are two kinds of tax credit as follows.

- **Working tax credit (WTC)** This is an income-based credit for working adults on a low income (but savings are ignored). It is a minimum condition that the claimant works for 16 hours or more a week. Additional money can be paid for childcare, disabilities or where the claimant is 50 or over. If the claimant is over 25, not responsible for a child and not disabled, then they must work for a minimum of 30 hours per week.

- **Child tax credit (CTC)** This is an income-based credit for low-income families where the claimant/s are in or out of work and have responsibility for a child. CTC is gradually replacing the dependants' allowance within all claims for (IB) JSA or IS where the claimant is responsible for a child.

ACCESS TO WELFARE BENEFITS AND IMMIGRATION STATUS: A 'TEN-POINT' OUTLINE

The following is a ten-point outline on the effect of immigration status on access to welfare benefits.

The rest of this chapter gives more detail on each point at the page references given.

1) Those who are 'subject to immigration control' are generally excluded from non-contributory benefits, both means-tested and non-means- tested (s115 Immigration and Asylum Act 1999). The 1999 Act has a special definition of 'subject to immigration control' for these purposes. The same definition is used to restrict access to other welfare provision (▶see Ch 40 and 1315–6). Although section 115 of the 1999 Act does not refer directly to them, the same 'subject to immigration control' general exclusion also applies to CTC and WTC (see regs 2, 3(1) Tax Credits (Immigration) Regulations 2003). In order to decide whether a person is 'subject to immigration control' and for the precise benefits that they are excluded from in that case, ▶see 1249–55. EEA nationals cannot be 'subject to immigration control' for these purposes.

2) *However*, there are exceptions to the 'subject to immigration control' general exclusion. If a claimant comes within one of the exceptions, then they are able to access benefit *even though* they are 'subject to immigration control'. Different exceptions apply to different benefits. Some of the exceptions apply as transitional arrangements from earlier, less restrictive, benefit rules. To see whether a claimant is within one of the exceptions, ▶see 1255–9. These exceptions are set out in regulations 2, 12 and the Schedule to the Social Security (Immigration and Asylum) Consequential Amendments Regulations 2000 and regulation 3 of the Tax Credits (Immi-

gration) Regulations 2003. If an exemption applies, the applicant can generally claim without undermining their immigration status (▶309–11).

3) For certain benefits, an additional 'habitual residence' test has to be passed before claimants can be entitled to benefit. These benefits are: IS; (IB) JSA; SPC; HB; and CTB. This test was originally introduced by the Social Security (Persons from Abroad) (Miscellaneous Amendments) Regulations 1996 and it is contained as part of the separate regulations, which deal with each of these benefits. Some people are, however, exempt from having to pass the habitual residence test. For details about habitual residence and the exemptions ▶see 1259–64.

4) From 1 May 2004, a further gloss has been painted on over the top of the habitual residence test. From that date, claimants who do not have a 'right to reside' cannot be 'habitually resident'. These claimants are therefore also excluded from the benefits to which the habitual residence test applies (IS; income-based JSA; SPC; HB; and CTB). This change was introduced by the Social Security (Habitual Residence) (Amendment) Regulations 2004. However, the right to reside test has *also* been imposed on two additional benefits to which the habitual residence test does not apply: CB and CTC. At present, this test is only in force until 1 May 2006 (see regs 1–3 of the Tax Credits (Residence)(Amendment) Regulations 2004; regs 1–4 of the Child Benefit (General) (Amendment) Regulations 2004).

British citizens, those with the right of abode and those with leave to enter or remain in the UK, have the right to reside. Therefore, the purpose of the right to reside test is to exclude from benefit entitlement those EEA nationals, particularly A8 nationals, who are in the UK but who are not exercising legal rights of free movement.

For details about the 'right to reside' test ▶see 1264–8 and for the impact on A8 nationals in particular see point (5) below.

5) The 'right to reside' test has a particular effect upon 'Accession 8' or 'A8' nationals i.e. nationals of eight of those countries which acceded to the EU on 1 May 2004. This is because they have no initial free-movement rights to reside in the UK in order to seek work (see regs 4–5 of the Accession (Immigration and Worker Registration) Regulations 2004) and also many of them must register to work in the UK. Those who are working in the UK in accordance with the Accession Regulations have the right to reside and can obtain 'in-work' benefits. The rules relating to A8 nationals are complex and there are significant exceptions to the restriction on their access to benefit entitlement, which apply, for example, for those who have worked lawfully in the UK for 12 months. For full details about A8 nationals and the effect of the 'right to reside' test, ▶see 1268–73.

6) A number of benefits have residence tests additional to those referred to above (▶see 1273–5):

- claimants of the following benefits must be 'ordinarily resident' in GB: AA, CA, CB, CTC, DLA, WTC;
- claimants of the following disability benefits must have been present in GB for at least 26 of the past 52 weeks: AA, CA, DLA, non-contributory IB;
- special rules about presence in GB over the past 52 weeks apply to CBD;
- for most claims made on the social fund, the claimant will generally indirectly have had to pass the 'habitual residence' and 'right to reside' tests because access usually depends on access to benefits to which those tests apply.

7) Access to contributory benefits does not depend upon any of the particular 'immigration tests' above, but applicants will have had to have paid sufficient contributions and satisfy a presence and/or ordinary residence test (►1276).

8) EEA nationals are entitled to the additional protection of EU law in relation to benefit entitlement. Further, some countries have a reciprocal arrangement with the UK relating to benefit rights. For these aspects, ►see 1281–2. We do not cover these matters in detail; those who think a point arises in relation to these protections should seek advice.

9) Asylum-seekers who succeed in their asylum claim (or who are granted HP or DL) will, after a grace period, cease to be entitled to asylum support and will transfer to welfare benefits. Various problems have arisen in making this transfer including delays and access to a national insurance number. Those found to be refugees are at present able to claim backdated benefit for IS, HB, CTB, CB, GA, CTC and WTC. However, the government intends to replace the system of backdating benefits with a system of 'integration loans' for refugees (see s12–13 2004 Act). At the time of writing, these changes have not come into force. For further details of all of these matters, ►see 1282–7.

10) Advisers may have to deal with a number of further general matters as follows. Can claimants obtain benefits to cover their dependants who are 'subject to immigration control'? In some cases, in particular if the claimant is able to claim benefit because they are within one of the exceptions to the 'subject to immigration control' test, this is possible. In other cases it is not (►1276–81). What is the effect on benefit entitlement if the claimant goes abroad? There are limited circumstances in which benefit may continue to be paid while a claimant is absent abroad. Finally, advisers should be aware of the links between the benefit authorities and the immigration authorities (►1287–8).

12

'SUBJECT TO IMMIGRATION CONTROL' TEST

The general rule is that anyone who is 'subject to immigration control' (see the table below and the text which follows it) within the meaning of section 115(9) Immigration and Asylum Act 1999, is excluded from access to any of the following benefits (for the abbreviations used ►see 1242):

- AA;
- CA;
- CB;
- CTC;
- CTB;

- DLA;
- HB;
- (IB) JSA;
- IS;
- SFP;

- SDA;
- SPC;
- WTC.

Section 115 1999 Act does not directly refer to the tax credits but the 'subject to immigration control' test is also applied to these benefits by separate regulations (see reg 3(1) Tax Credits Immigration Regulations).

For the exceptions to the 'subject to immigration control' test, ▶see 1255–9.

THE 'SUBJECT TO IMMIGRATION CONTROL' TEST: SECTION 115 1999 ACT

A person is only 'subject to immigration control' for welfare purposes if they fall into any of the following categories:

- those who need leave to be in the UK but who do not have it (▶1251–2);

- people who have leave but the leave has a condition attached to it that they will not have recourse to public funds (▶1252–3);

- people given leave as the result of a 'maintenance undertaking' (otherwise known as a 'sponsorship' agreement) (▶1253–4);

- people who have leave 'only as a result of paragraph 17 of Schedule 4 [to the 1999 Act]' (▶1254–5).

'EEA nationals' (this includes A8 nationals) are not 'subject to immigration control' even if they are not exercising rights of free movement (see s115(9) 1999 Act).

Therefore the following groups are not 'subject to immigration control' for welfare purposes:

- those with the right of abode in the UK (mainly British citizens);

- EEA nationals;

- non-EEA nationals who qualify for free-movement rights as the family members of EEA nationals (because then the family member will also not need leave to be in the UK);

- those exempt from the requirement to obtain leave (e.g., diplomats);

- those who have leave which does *not* fall into any of the following categories:

    – leave subject to a condition that the applicant will not have recourse to public funds (note that indefinite leave *cannot* be subject to conditions);

    – leave granted as a result of a maintenance undertaking;

    – leave which exists only as a result of paragraph 17 of Sch 4 of the 1999 Act.

See immediately below for further details about the above groups of people.

'Subject to immigration control': people without leave

Aside from British citizens and EEA nationals exercising rights of free movement, those who do not need leave are: (1) a small number of Commonwealth nationals who have the right of abode in the UK (►see 1417–20); (2) certain categories of people who are exempt from having to obtain leave, including diplomats and members of some visiting armed forces (►see 472–6); (3) family members of EEA nationals who are exercising rights of free movement – such family members also do not need leave to be in the UK (for details of who counts as a family member for these purposes, ►see 526 onwards). Of those who need leave, those who do not have it should be easy to identify. They include:

- overstayers;
- those declared to be illegal entrants;
- those with temporary admission;
- those who have had a deportation order signed against them;
- those who have had their leave 'curtailed' while they are in the UK or 'cancelled' on their arrival;
- those who never obtained leave in the first place.

Evidence of leave

In order to determine whether a person has leave, the first place to check is the person's passport. Examples of the various stamps indicating leave, its length and conditions are set out in Chapter 8 which also gives examples of documents such as notices of temporary admission, illegal entry and deportation orders. Many people have become confused about how long leave lasts when it is granted as the result of an entry clearance ('visa') operating as leave to enter, and have become overstayers as a result. To check how long leave lasts when granted as a result of an entry clearance ►see 87–8.

Passport stamps are not always conclusive. For example, a person still has leave if they make an 'in-time' application to extend their leave (i.e. they apply to extend their leave at a point when they still have leave) even though their original grant of leave runs out while they are waiting for a Home Office decision on the application. Such applicants get an *automatic extension* of leave until they are notified of a decision on the application. If the decision is negative but there is a right of appeal, the applicant continues to have leave until time for appealing runs out. If the applicant does appeal, they continue to have leave while the appeal is still pending (see s3C 1971 Act as substituted by s118 2002 Act from 1 April 2003 and for further details of automatically extended leave ►see 143–6; but note that there are proposals under the 2005 Bill to change this, ►see 1045–6).

Because this leave is automatically extended i.e. without any express grant of leave from the immigration authorities, there is no direct evidence of it.

12

The only evidence will usually be: evidence of the date on which the last grant of leave expired; evidence of the application to extend leave which was made; evidence of the date of the application (for example recorded delivery confirmation or Home Office acknowledgement of the application) or evidence of an outstanding appeal against a decision to refuse to extend leave.

If the applicant needs leave and does not have it, they are 'subject to immigration control'. If they *do* have leave, they may still be subject to control depending on the nature of the leave (see below).

'Subject to immigration control': Condition prohibiting 'recourse to public funds'

Those who have a condition attached to their leave that they should not have recourse to public funds are also 'subject to immigration control'. In order to be granted leave under most categories under the immigration rules, applicants have to show that they will be able to maintain and accommodate themselves without recourse to public funds (▶see 307–18 for a full understanding of these requirements). In order to exclude someone from benefits, however, it is not enough that they had to satisfy these requirements; they must also have *actually had* a public funds condition attached to their leave. In most cases where the rules have public funds requirements, a public funds condition will have been attached to the leave. However, it is always worth checking the actual grant of leave endorsed on the passport (▶see 193 for an example and for a full list of conditions which the Home Office generally attaches to leave in different categories, ▶see 190–1).

The power to impose conditions, including public funds conditions, comes from the 1971 Act (see s3(1)(c)). This only gives power to impose conditions on a limited leave and, therefore, indefinite leave cannot have conditions attached. Therefore no one with indefinite leave can be 'subject to immigration control'. This will generally include refugees (at present); relatives granted family reunion with sponsors settled in the UK; spouses/partners after the probationary period; and those granted indefinite leave after spending four continuous years in a particular capacity. *However*, some of those granted indefinite leave might have been given it on the basis of a maintenance undertaking (see below), which is another way of making them 'subject to immigration control'.

Categories of limited leave where no 'public funds condition' should be imposed

The categories under the rules in which a person may be granted *limited* leave *without* having to satisfy any requirements about maintenance and accommodation and therefore in which it is very unlikely that a public funds condition has been attached are:

- refugees and their dependants (despite the present practice of granting indefinite leave, *the rules* state that limited leave only has to be granted and the Home Office had said it intends to move to a system of granting limited leave);
- those admitted for family reunion with refugees (see as above for refugees);
- those granted 'temporary protection', and their dependants;
- non-British citizen children born in the UK who are seeking to stay with their parent(s);
- transit visitors.

Where a condition has been attached to leave in any of the above cases, it is the Home Office that should be challenged. This is because the Home Office's decision to attach a condition is conclusive as far as the benefit authorities are concerned (Commissioner's decision, *R (SB) 2/85*). Those granted leave outside the rules for compassionate reasons will generally not have conditions attached, but again it is necessary to check. For example, those granted humanitarian protection and discretionary leave, do not have to satisfy the public funds requirements and will not have public funds conditions attached to their leave.

'Subject to immigration control': people given leave as a result of a maintenance undertaking

Those given leave to enter or remain in the UK as the result of a maintenance undertaking are 'subject to immigration control'. These are undertakings given by a sponsor in the UK that they will maintain and accommodate the applicant so that they will not have to have recourse to public funds. They can be used in cases where either limited or indefinite leave has been granted. They are most often used in cases of dependent family members who, on their first application, are granted indefinite leave in order to join settled relatives (for example applicants who are elderly dependent relatives). Undertakings are used in such cases precisely because a public funds condition cannot be attached to the indefinite leave (▶403–4).

In order to be effective the undertaking must be 'in writing' and given 'in pursuance of the immigration rules' (see s115(10) 1999 Act). An informal arrangement will not normally be enough. However, in *Begum* the High Court held that the completion of a prescribed Home Office form (RON 112 or SET(F)) was not essential for there to have been an effective undertaking. It was a question of fact in each case. Where the 'agreement' is not contained in the prescribed form, it is necessary to look at the language actually used. In a Court of Appeal case, *Ahmed*, the claimant had gained entry on the basis of a maintenance undertaking given by his nephew as his sponsor. The agreement used the following words:

12

'I declare that I am able and willing to maintain and accommodate the applicant without recourse to public funds.'

The Court held that this was not effective as an undertaking because the declaration referred to the nephew's current ability and intention and did not amount to a promise for the future. The Court noted that an undertaking could be used both as the basis to recover benefit paid as well for criminal prosecutions. In those circumstances a decision-maker 'should not be too ready to assume that an undertaking has been given in the absence of reasonably plain language expressive of a promise.'

In a further recent case, *CIS/1697/2004*, the Commissioner summarised the relevant case law as follows.

1) The fact that the appropriate official form in use at the time is not used does not necessarily mean that an effective undertaking has not been given (*Begum*).

2) The statement in question must be 'sufficiently formal and definite to constitute an undertaking' (*Begum*, para. 31). In *Begum* itself there was a formal declaration, drawn up by solicitors and witnessed, that included an express undertaking that the claimant would be maintained and accommodated without recourse to public funds.

3) An undertaking involves:

'…something in the nature of a promise or agreement, prima facie contractual in form, albeit this arises in a public law context, which obliges a sponsor to maintain and accommodate the dependent relative' (*Ahmed*, para. 28).

4) Ultimately, it is a question of fact whether a document amounts to an effective undertaking (*Begum* approving Commissioners' decisions *CIS/2474/1999*, *CIS/47/2002* and *CIS/2816/2002*).

In the *CIS/1697/2004* case itself, the Deputy Commissioner held that regard could be had to surrounding documents (e.g. a solicitor's covering letter) in deciding whether there was an effective undertaking.

'Subject to immigration control': people who have leave 'only as a result of paragraph 17 of Schedule 4' of the 1999 Act

Those who only have leave 'as a result of paragraph 17 of Schedule 4' of the 1999 Act are also 'subject to immigration control'. This provision of the 1999 Act had the effect of automatically extending a person's leave *during the period of their appeal* against a decision to refuse to extend leave where the applicant made an in-time application for further leave. So, if an applicant had been granted limited leave *without* public funds conditions and not on the basis of a maintenance undertaking (for example, 'exceptional leave', HP or DL) and was then refused an extension of leave, they would be 'subject to immigration control' during the period they were appealing. This group would not be 'subject to immigration control' while they appealed if it were not for this specific exclusion in section 115. This is because they would have an automatic extension of leave with no public funds condition attached. The exclusion does not, however, apply to the initial period of automatic extension while the applicant is waiting for a decision by the Home Office.

However, paragraph 17 of the 1999 Act was repealed from 1 April 2003 (see Sch 9 2002 Act). The provision which now automatically grants applicants leave while they are appealing against a refusal of an in-time application for further leave is section 3C 1971 Act (as inserted by s118 2002 Act). But section 115 1999 Act has not been changed in line to say that people with leave under section 3C 1971 Act are 'subject to immigration control'. Therefore, after 1 April 2003, those who have automatic extensions of leave after making an in-time application, both while they are waiting for a Home Office decision *and* while they are appealing, do not appear to be 'subject to immigration control'. They are not, therefore, excluded from benefits during these periods. This is *provided* of course that their original leave was not subject to a public funds condition, or granted on the basis of a maintenance undertaking. If it was, then they will be subject to immigration control for these reasons – it has always been assumed that the conditions on which leave was originally granted, continue to apply during the automatic extension of leave.

Note that the 2005 Bill proposes to change the arrangements about automatic extensions of leave. Under the new Bill, there will only be an automatic extension until the immigration authorities make a decision on the application and not during the appeals process. For further details about automatic extensions of leave, ▶see 143–6.

EXCEPTIONS TO THE 'SUBJECT TO IMMIGRATION CONTROL' TEST

If a person is 'subject to immigration control' the next step in determining whether they can access the benefits excluded by this test is to check whether they come within any of the exceptions. The limited classes of claimants who can still obtain benefits even though they are 'subject to immigration control' are set out in the table below. Different groups of claimants are exempted from the 'subject to immigration control' test for the different benefits. Most of the exceptions are self-explanatory.

12

EXCEPTIONS TO THE 'SUBJECT TO IMMIGRATION CONTROL' TEST

The general rule is that those who are 'subject to immigration control' are excluded from the means-tested and non-means-tested non-contributory benefits (▶see 1249–50 for list of benefits affected). The exceptions to this rule are set out below for the different benefits. They are contained in the following regulations:

- regs 2, 12 and the Schedule to the Social Security Immigration Regulations;
- reg. 3(1), Tax Credits Immigration Regulations;
- reg. 16, Social Security (Incapacity Benefit) Regulations 1994.

Income-based JSA, income support (including non-contributory youth incapacity benefit), state pension credit, social fund payments, housing benefit, and council tax benefit

Those in the following groups are able to claim the above benefits even if they are subject to immigration control.

1) People who had to satisfy the immigration authorities, under the immigration rules, that they can maintain and accommodate themselves without recourse to public funds *and* who are 'temporarily' without funds because there has been a disruption in funds received from abroad. There must be a 'reasonable expectation' that the supply of funds will begin again. Inevitably, because of the nature of this exemption, benefit will only continue to be paid for a temporary period. It can only be paid for a maximum of 42 days in any one period of leave (see reg. 2(8) Social Security Immigration Regulations; reg. 71(2) Income Support Regulations).

2) People who were granted leave on the basis of a maintenance undertaking *either* where the sponsor who gave the undertaking has died, *or* where the claimant has been living in the UK for five years. The five-year period begins running from the date of the person's entry into the UK or the date on which the maintenance undertaking was made, whichever is the later. Only time spent in the UK counts towards the five-year period.

3) People who are nationals of states which have ratified either the European Convention on Social and Medical Assistance (ECSMA) or the Council of Europe Social Charter (CESC) *and* who are 'lawfully present' in the UK (for further details, ▶see below 1259).

4) Asylum-seekers who claimed asylum on or before 2 April 2000 either 'on arrival' in the UK or within three months of a 'declaration of upheaval'. These declarations were made in relation to Zaire – now the Democratic Republic of Congo – on 16 May 1997 and Sierra Leone on 1 July 1997. In either case, benefit entitlement ends as soon as the claim to asylum is recorded as determined *and this is notified* to the applicant (see *Anufrijeva*, HL), or the applicant abandons the claim to asylum. If the asylum decision is negative and the applicant appeals, the asylum-seeker becomes eligible for asylum support instead. There will be very few claimants left who still benefit from this exception.

5) Asylum-seekers who claimed asylum (on arrival or otherwise) before 5 February 1996, whose claims had not been finally decided by that date and who were entitled to these benefits immediately before 5 February 1996. They will only be entitled if they have not received a decision on their claim, from either the Home Office or appellate authorities, after 5 February 1996. Those who benefit from this exception will continue to benefit from it even if there is a break in their entitlement, for example if they begin work and then lose employment again (see *Yildiz*, Court of Appeal).

6) People who were granted leave on the basis of a maintenance undertaking made before 5 February 1996 and who were also entitled to these benefits before that time.

Note that (4), (5) and (6) above and (4) below are exemptions which provide what is called 'transitional' protection. In other words, they allow people who had an entitlement to benefit as the law previously stood, to continue claiming even though changes have been introduced which would otherwise exclude them. Note also that (5) and (6) above do not apply to income-based JSA, which had not come into being by February 1996.

Further note that those who are exempt from the 'subject to immigration control' test because their funds have temporarily dried up, because they are transitionally protected, or because they entered on the basis of a maintenance undertaking and their sponsor has died, are all only entitled to IS or (IB) JSA at the 'urgent cases' rate (90 per cent of the normal personal allowance plus full amounts for any premiums and housing costs).

For access to benefit for dependants of those re-included to benefit entitlement on the basis of the exceptions above, ▶see below at 1276 onwards.

Attendance allowance, carer's allowance, disability living allowance, social fund payments, child benefit

Those in the following groups are able to claim the above benefits even if they are subject to immigration control.

1) Non-EEA national family members of EEA nationals. 'Family members' is not defined for these purposes but probably includes all those who are defined as family members for the purposes of EU rights of free movement (▶see 527). Of course, non-EEA national family members who are actually benefiting from EU rights of free movement should not be 'subject to control' in the first place as they do not require leave. This would apply, for example, to a non-EEA national whose EEA-national spouse is working in the UK. Such people do not need to rely on any exemption.

2) Nationals of the following countries, which have made an agreement with the EU, that provides for the 'equal treatment of workers...in the area of social security': Algeria, Morocco, Slovenia, Tunisia, and Turkey. However, such claimants must be 'lawfully working' in Great Britain and their family members who are living with them are also exempted from the 'subject to control' test for the purpose of these benefits.

3) People given leave to enter or remain on the basis of a maintenance undertaking. This is an important exception, which re-entitles those people who would otherwise be 'subject to control' and excluded from benefit as a result of the undertaking.

4) People who were entitled to attendance allowance, invalid care allowance (now carer's allowance) and disability living allowance before 5 February 1996 and to child benefit before 7 October 1996. Entitlement to these benefits continues until the person's claim to asylum (if they have made one) is determined by the Home Office, or until the social security authorities revise the award of benefit, or until a time-limited award of benefit expires. A break in

12

entitlement to the claim of these benefits brings this transitional protection to an end (see *M*).

A further exemption from the 'subject to immigration control' test for the purposes of CB, AA and DLA, applies in the case of nationals of certain countries with whom the UK has a reciprocal agreement (►see 1282 below).

Child tax credit and working tax credit

Those in any of the following five groups are able to claim CTC and WTC even if they are 'subject to immigration control'. Regulation 3(3) Tax Credits Regulations refers to them as five 'cases'. Note that the exemptions apply differently to CTC and WTC as indicated.

1) People given leave to enter or remain on the basis of a maintenance undertaking who have been 'resident' in the UK for at least five years beginning with the date of their entry to the UK, or the date on which the undertaking was given (whichever is the later date) (applies to WTC/CTC).

2) Where the person giving the undertaking has died (applies to WTC/CTC).

3) People who have leave to enter or remain in the UK which is subject to a condition that they do not have recourse to public funds and who are 'temporarily' without funds because there has been a disruption in funds received from abroad. There must be a 'reasonable expectation' that the supply of funds will begin again. This exemption can only apply for a period of 42 days during any one period of leave (applies to WTC/CTC).

4) Nationals of countries that have ratified the European Convention on Social and Medical Assistance (ECSMA) or the Council of Europe Social Charter (CESC), and are lawfully present in the UK (applies to WTC). This exemption will also apply to CTC where the person was entitled to IS or (IB) JSA in relation to a child immediately before this award of CTC.

5) Where the claim is for CTC, nationals of those countries that have made an agreement with the EU, which provides for the 'equal treatment of workers…in the area of social security': Algeria, Morocco, Slovenia, Tunisia, and Turkey. However, such claimants must be 'lawfully working' in Great Britain.

A married or unmarried couple can claim and be entitled to the relevant tax credit(s) calculated as though both of them were not subject to immigration control, provided that *one* of them is either (see reg. 3(2)(3) of the Tax Credits Regulations):

- not 'subject to immigration control'; *or*

- is within one of the exempt cases in 1–5 above.

For further details about the immigration implications of claiming tax credits, ►see 310–11.

ECSMA or CESC nationals who are lawfully present

Nationals of a country which has ratified the European Convention on Social and Medical Assistance (ECSMA) and/or the Council of Europe Social Charter (CESC) who are 'lawfully present in the United Kingdom' are not excluded from benefits even if they are 'subject to immigration control' (see exception (3) in the first list of exceptions above, ▶1256) .

Of course, many of the countries which have ratified ECSMA or the CESC are EEA countries and EEA nationals cannot be 'subject to immigration control' for welfare purposes in the first place. Before 1 May 2004, the non-EEA countries that had ratified either ECSMA or CESC were: Croatia, Cyprus, Czech Republic, Hungary, Latvia, Malta, Poland, Slovakia and Turkey. Following the accession to the EU of the ten further states from 1 May, Croatia, Macedonia and Turkey are the three remaining non-EEA countries that have ratified either ECSMA or CESC (note Estonia also ratified the ECSMA on 20 July 2004, but it had also acceded to the EU on 1 May). However, ratification of these treaties is an ongoing process and more non-EEA countries may ratify them in due course.

In order to benefit from the exception, the ECSMA or CESC national must be 'lawfully present'. They will be lawfully present if they are here with leave. Until recently, the law was that a person with temporary admission who had applied for asylum at port could not qualify as being lawfully present (see *Kaya*, CA). However, the House of Lords has now decided that such applicants are 'lawfully present' (see the decision in *Szoma*, explained more fully at ▶1298). Croatian, Macedonian and Turkish benefit claimants may gain from this. However, it would appear that such applicants (unless they have a benefit claim from before 1 May 2004 in which case they may be transitionally protected, see Habitual Residence Amendment Regulations 2004, and ▶see 1266) must still show that they have a 'right to reside' (▶see 1264). As yet, the DWP has not issued official guidance on the entitlement of these claimants.

THE 'HABITUAL RESIDENCE' TEST

For certain important benefits, even if a person satisfies (or is exempted from) the 'subject to immigration control' test (above), claimants must also satisfy the 'habitual residence' test. This is that they must be 'habitually resident' in the Common Travel Area ('CTA' i.e. the UK, Channel Islands, Isle of Man, or Republic of Ireland). The test affects those who have recently come to the UK and it applies to British nationals as well as overseas nationals.

From 1 May 2004, an additional aspect was added to the habitual residence test so that in order to be 'habitually resident', claimants must also have a 'right to reside' in the CTA. We deal with this further aspect separately at ▶1264–8.

12

The benefits to which the habitual residence test applies are as follows:

- IS;
- (IB) JSA;
- SPC;
- HB;
- CTB.

The habitual residence test also applies, indirectly, to those claims on the social fund that require the claimant to be entitled to the above benefits (►see 1275).

Certain categories of claimant are exempt from having to pass the habitual residence test.

The table below summarises the meaning of the habitual residence test and states which claimants are exempt from it.

THE HABITUAL RESIDENCE TEST AND EXEMPTIONS FROM THE TEST

The habitual residence test and the exemptions from it for the various benefits are set out in the following regulations (all as amended by the Habitual Residence Amendment Regulations):

- reg. 21(3), Income Support Regulations;
- reg. 85(4), Jobseeker's Allowance Regulations;
- reg. 4A, Council Tax Regulations;
- reg. 7A, Housing Benefit Regulations;
- reg. 2, Pension Credit Regulations.

Habitual residence

The general habitual residence test can be summarised as follows:

- whether a person is habitually resident is a question of fact to be decided by looking at all the circumstances of each case;
- to become habitually resident the claimant must have a settled intention to remain in the CTA and must have been here for an 'appreciable period' (*Nessa*, HL);
- in the majority of cases, the length of the appreciable period before a person is habitually resident will be between one and three months (Commissioner's decision, *CIS/4474/2003*).

For further explanation, ►see at below at 1262–3.

Habitual residence and the *Swaddling* case

In certain cases (►see below at 1263–4), the EU meaning of habitual residence is applied. This is a result of the decision in the ECJ in *Swaddling*. This test can be summarised as follows:

- the following factors are taken into account in determining whether the claimant is habitually resident: the place of the claimant's main centre of interest;

the length and continuity of their residence here; the length and purpose of their absence from their previous country of residence; the nature of any employment in the previous country; their intentions (*Di Paolo*, ECJ);

- length of residence is less important if there has been a permanent change in the claimant's centre of interest; no minimum period of residence is required (*Swaddling*, ECJ);

Exemptions

Many of those who are exempt from the habitual residence test would pass it were they not exempt. Also note that those who are actually working will generally not be eligible for IS or (IB) JSA. However, those in work, but on low incomes, may be entitled to HB and CTB.

Claimants in any of the following groups are exempt from the habitual residence test. This means that they are treated as passing the habitual residence test without their personal circumstances being taken into account. Note that the exemptions in 1–4 apply to EEA nationals (including British citizens) who are exercising the stated EU free-movement rights. Exemption (5) applies to certain A8 nationals.

1) 'Workers' for the purposes of Council Regulation (EEC) No. 1612/68. This covers those who are in paid work, which is 'genuine and effective', and which is not on such a small scale as to be 'marginal and ancillary' (*Levin*, *Kempf*, ECJ). Those who have worked in the UK and who leave work voluntarily or involuntarily but who remain in the labour market by looking for further work may continue to be workers for these purposes (see *R (IS) 12/98*, *R (IS) 9/99*). A claimant who has not worked in the UK and who has come to the UK in order to look for work (i.e. who is simply a work-seeker) is not exempt (see *CJSA/4065/1999* – the decision of the Commissioner in *Collins* after the ruling in the ECJ; R(IS) 3/97).

2) 'Workers' for the purposes of Council Regulation (EEC) No. 1251/70. This regulation gives a right to reside to certain retired or incapacitated workers. It covers the following two groups:

- those who gave up work because of a permanent incapacity and who *either* had resided in the UK continuously for at least two years when they gave up work, *or* the incapacity resulted from an industrial injury or disease entitling them to a disability benefit or incapacity benefit, *or* their spouse is a British citizen;

- those who retired on or after pension age who had *either* resided continuously in the UK for at least three years and were employed in the UK for at least 12 months just before retiring, *or* their spouse is a British citizen.

3) Those with a 'right to reside' in the UK under Council Directive No. 68/360/EEC. This Directive implements the above Council Regulations to give rights to reside to the above workers and members of their family. Family members for these purposes covers spouses, children under 21, grandparents and other dependent relatives.

4) Those with a 'right to reside in the UK' under Council Directive No. 73/148/EEC. This covers the self-employed and those who are providing or receiving

12

services on a commercial basis in the UK. It also covers their family members as in (3) above.

5) 'Accession state workers' who require registration but who are treated as 'workers' and therefore as 'qualified' persons under reg. 5 of the EEA 2000 Regulations read together with regs 5 and 7 of the Accession Regulations. This applies during the 'accession period' i.e. from 1 May 2004 to 30 April 2009. Note that A8 nationals who do not require registration (▶see 1270–2) may be exempt under the above two categories.

This definition, which exempts certain A8 nationals, is fairly complex. In simple terms, the claimants who are exempted from the habitual residence test under it are A8 nationals who are *actually working* in the UK *and* who are either:

- registered to work under the Accession Registration Scheme;

- within one of the exceptions to being registered set out in exception (8) in the table dealing with A8 nationals and benefit entitlement at ▶1272–3; or

- temporarily out of work in the circumstances described for A8 nationals at ▶1273, but this only appears to apply for up to a month.

6) 'Refugees' within the meaning of the 1951 Refugee Convention.

7) Those who have been granted 'exceptional leave' (this must include the new forms of leave outside the immigration rules – humanitarian protection and discretionary leave; for the meaning of these terms ▶see 860–1).

8) Those who are in the UK as a result of their having been deported or otherwise compulsorily removed from another country to the UK *and* who are not 'subject to immigration control' (▶see 1250) for the purposes of section 115 1999 Act.

9) People who have left Montserrat since November 1995 because of volcanic activity.

Note: A claimant who is actually in receipt of IS, (IB) JSA, SPC should not be refused HB or CTB on the basis of habitual residence (see regs 7A(4)(5) Housing Benefit Regulations, 4A(4)(5) Council Tax Regulations).

Habitual residence: the general test

The general habitual residence test in social security requires the claimant to show that they have genuinely adopted the UK as their place of normal residence. Whether a particular claimant meets the test is a question of fact and will depend on all the circumstances of their case. However, a person must have a settled intention to live in the UK.

The House of Lords in *Nessa* decided that, in addition to this settled intention, the test required a past period of residence. The Lords decided that an 'appreciable period' was necessary before a person could become habitually resident. However, the appreciable period is not a fixed period. The House of Lords accepted that it might be as short as a month, depending on the circumstances of the case. In *CIS/3280/2003*, a Commissioner accepted that, in the general run of cases, the 'appreciable period' would normally be between one and three months. Cogent reasons would be needed to justify requiring a significantly longer period. However, the Commissioners have stressed that any guidelines or rules of thumb should not be treated as rigid. In an exceptional case, a claimant might be accepted as habitually resident after less than a month.

If a claim for benefit is refused, the claimant can appeal to an appeal tribunal. Generally, tribunals are to decide cases on the basis of the circumstances at the date of the decision under appeal. But this leads to obvious problems in habitual residence cases where the claimant may have become habitually resident in the meantime. In *CIS/3280/2003*, the Commissioner attempted to ease the problem. He reasoned that, as the DWP has the power to make an award of benefit 13 weeks in advance, the tribunal has the same power. This was provided that, as of the date of the decision under appeal, the claimant had formed a settled intention to remain in the UK. This means that the appeal tribunal can make an award of benefit from the date on which habitual residence is established if this is within 13 weeks of the date of the decision under appeal. In the case of *Bhakta*, the Court of Appeal will consider whether this approach is correct.

Special considerations apply to people who have been habitually resident in the UK and who leave and then return after a temporary absence. They may have never lost their habitual residence in the UK when they went abroad and so may be treated as habitually resident as soon as they return (*Nessa*, HL).

The above general test in *Nessa* applies in most cases. In *Gingi*, the Court of Appeal rejected an argument that the EU test for habitual residence set out in *Swaddling* (▶below) applies generally.

Habitual residence: the *Swaddling* case

The meaning given to habitual residence in EU law under Council Regulation (EEC) 1408/71 is broader than that in domestic law. The test focuses on a change in the claimant's 'base' or 'centre of interest', rather than on their length of residence in the new country. In *Swaddling*, the ECJ held that no particular period of residence is required before a person is habitually resident. A Commissioner has explained this to mean that, although the length of residence remains a relevant factor, it is not an essential one (*R(IS) 3/00*).

This test for habitual residence referred to in *Swaddling* will apply where the facts of the case are similar to those in *Swaddling*. Swaddling was a British national who had worked in France until he was made redundant. He then returned to the UK and claimed income support. The ECJ ruled that, in the case of a person who has exercised rights of free movement in order to establish themselves in another member state in which they have worked and set up their habitual residence, and who have returned to their member state of origin in order to seek work, the EU meaning of habitual residence applies. This may also apply to other EEA nationals who have strong ties to the UK.

The decision in *Collins*

In *Collins* the ECJ held that an EU state may restrict access to benefits to cases in which it can be shown that 'a genuine link exists between the person seeking work and the employment market' in that state. Part of showing that link may include a residence test. The case was then referred back from the ECJ to the Commissioner (*CJSA/4065/1999*) who held as follows:

- The residence requirement for (IB) JSA was justified by objective consider-ations independent of the nationality of the claimant. It was necessary in order for the national authorities to be clear that the claimant was genuin-ely seeking work. Further, the criteria for the habitual residence test meet the requirement of being clear and being issues that can be known in advance.

- On the facts, Mr Collins was not habitually resident at the time he made his claim as he had been actively seeking work for less than one month and had been away from the UK for more than 17 years.

Mr Collins has obtained permission to appeal to the Court of Appeal against the decision. Meanwhile the same Commissioner has decided that the use of the domestic habitual residence test for the purposes of income support is also not prevented by EU law concerning discrimination (*CIS/2680/2004*).

THE 'RIGHT TO RESIDE' TEST

From 1 May 2004, a new requirement was introduced that no claimant is to be treated as 'habitually resident' unless they have a 'right to reside' in the Common Travel Area (UK, Channel Islands, Isle of Man, or Republic of Ireland). So, from that date, in order to be 'habitually resident', claimants need to both:

- satisfy, (or be exempted from) the test for habitual residence as it is set out above; *and*

- have a right to reside.

Although the 'right to reside' test is set up as part of the habitual resi-dence test, in fact it is easier to see it as a further test which needs to be satisfied in order to qualify for the benefits covered by the habitual residence test (▶see 1242 for abbreviations):

- IS;
- (IB) JSA;
- SPC;
- HB;
- CTB.

It is inserted into all of the separate regulations dealing with all of those benefits by the Habitual Residence Amendment Regulations.

However, for claims made on or after 1 May 2004, the right to reside test has also been added to two additional benefits:

- CB; and
- CTC.

At present the addition of this test to CB and CTC is a temporary measure – it remains in force only until 1 May 2006 (see regs 1–3 of the Tax Credits Residence Amendment Regulations amending the Tax Credits Residence Regulations; and regs 1–4 of the Child Benefit Amendment Regulations amending the Child Benefit Regulations). After that date, claimants and advisers will have to check to see what the position is.

The DWP intends to review the 'right to reside' test again in the light of the 'Rights of Residence Directive' on the rights of citizens of the EU and their family members to move and reside freely. This Directive has been under consideration in the European institutions and is unlikely to be implemented before 2006.

Main effects of 'right to reside' test

The table below (▶1266–8) contains a summary of who has the 'right to reside'.

The main effects of the new test are to exclude from benefit the following groups:

- A8 nationals who are only work-seekers and who have not worked in the UK lawfully for 12 months (for a much fuller explanation of the effect on A8 nationals, ▶see below at 1268–73);
- all EEA nationals who are not exercising EU rights of free movement.

So, the main effect of the change is to exclude *certain* EEA/A8 nationals from *certain* benefits.

Many EEA (including A8) nationals who are working will still wish to show that they have the right to reside so that they can claim the following benefits: HB, CTB, CB and CTC (WTC is not affected by the right to reside test).

The rights of most other foreign nationals are not changed by the right to reside test because their rights are *already* so restricted by the 'subject to immigration control' test under section 115 1999 Act which does not itself exclude any EEA nationals. At the same time as reducing the rights of EEA and A8 nationals, the government has preserved the rights of British citizens and those with leave – the right to reside test will not make it more difficult for those groups to show that they are habitually resident.

12

Transitional arrangements

There are transitional arrangements, which protect claims for benefit from the right to reside test. These arrangements apply for IS, (IB) JSA, SPC, HB and CTB where someone was entitled to benefit on or before the right to reside test came into force on 1 May 2004. It may be possible for claimants to retain this protection even if there is a break in one benefit, so long as entitlement continues for one of the other specified benefits. There are no transitional arrangements for CB or CTC.

Possible challenges

If an A8 national is refused access to benefits solely on the basis that they have not completed 12 months of registered employment, there may be an argument that this is incompatible with EU law on the following grounds:

- First, it is arguable that the scope of the derogation under the Treaty of Accession is confined to workers' access to the labour market under Articles 1–6 of Council Regulation No. 1612/68. The Accession Regulations 2004 are therefore unlawful in so far as they claim to exclude A8 nationals who have been working in the UK from equal access to social advantages as workers.

- Secondly, where an A8 national has worked in the UK and becomes involuntarily unemployed or temporarily incapacitated, it is arguable that to deny them access to social assistance is discriminatory following the ruling in *Trojani* (ECJ). This held that where someone cannot rely directly on EC legislation for a right to reside in the member state, they may still be able to rely on the non-discriminatory provision in Article 12 of the EC Treaty as a Citizen of the Union under Article 17.

There may well, therefore, be legal challenges to the new test.

WHO HAS THE RIGHT TO RESIDE?

The term 'right to reside' is not fully defined in the Regulations, but the position may change in the light of case-law (►see Note below 1268).

Those with the 'right to reside'

The following are examples of those who have a 'right to reside':

- British citizens and citizens of the Republic of Ireland;
- those with indefinite leave;
- those with limited leave (although many will have leave subject to a condition not to have recourse to public funds and will therefore be excluded because they are 'subject to immigration control' for welfare purposes);
- EEA nationals exercising EU rights of free movement including workers, the self-employed while they are providing services, self-sufficient persons, retired persons, and students. It also includes work-seekers from non-A8 EEA states

normally for up to six months and for longer if they are still genuinely seeking work with a realistic chance of getting it. For the self-employed, self-sufficient, retired persons and students, see also below;

- A8 nationals who are working in the UK *and* who are registered for work under the Accession Regulations or who are in an exception to the need to be registered;
- family members of those in the last two categories who benefit from free-movement rights as dependants.

Those who do not have the 'right to reside'

Those in the following groups will not normally have a 'right to reside':

- A8 nationals who *are seeking work* and who will need to register for work if they begin working and who are not self-sufficient. Such persons are expressly stated not to have a right to reside (see reg. 4(2) Accession Regulations).
- A8 nationals who are working but who are not registered and are not within the exceptions to the need to be registered (see regs. 2, 4(4), 5, 7 Accession Regulations).
- EEA nationals who are not exercising EU free movement rights. For example, work-seekers who are not (or who are no longer) genuinely seeking work with a realistic opportunity of getting it. A work-seeker who has not found work after six months may well fall into this category.

The 'right to reside' for A8 nationals is complex. It is looked at in more detail below (▶1268–73).

People who should generally have 'sufficient resources'

For certain EEA nationals, their free movement rights which give them a 'right to reside' are subject to the requirement that they have sufficient resources to prevent them from becoming a 'burden on the social assistance system of the United Kingdom'. This applies to: self-sufficient persons, retired persons and students (see reg. 3 EEA 2000 Regulations). Such people may therefore find it difficult to demonstrate that they still have a 'right to reside' if they claim benefits. *However*, the self-employed, for example, do not cease to have a right to reside simply because they are temporarily incapable of work due to illness or accident. The question may depend on 'proportionality' considerations to determine whether the claimant has become an 'unreasonable' burden on the state. Relevant factors might be (see DWP Explanatory Memorandum, March 2004 at paras 17-18) (▶see also 563):

- how much assistance will be required;
- over how long a period the assistance is likely to be required for;
- how long the claimant has already been in the UK while being self-sufficient.

The official guidance for HB/CTB states in relation to the retired and lone parents (A22/2004 at para. 86):

'86. The fact that a person has no prospect of finding work or becoming self-sufficient may be considered an unreasonable burden on the state. Each case will be considered on its merits and considerations will include the length of time they are likely to be dependent on public funds. If a claim for benefits is made by an EEA inactive they would need to demonstrate that their private funds would resume before long and that they would not be an unreasonable burden on public funds.'

Of course, most students are ineligible for housing benefit but there are exceptions for lone parents; single people who are looking after foster children; people who are temporarily looking after another person and people with other caring responsibilities.

Note: In early 2006, a tribunal of commissioners will consider various issues concerning the lawfulness and application of the 'right to reside' test (*CIS/3573/05*).

Official guidance

Official guidance is available in the following forms:

- Explanatory Memorandum of the DWP concerning the new regulations issued to the Social Security Advisory Committee in March 2004.

- Decision-maker's Guide ('DMG').

- The DMG above is mainly superseded by DMG Vol. 2, Ch 7, Part 3, 'Habitual Residence and the Right to Reside' (updated June 2005) at http://www.dwp. gov.uk/publications/dwp/dmg/.

- Official Guidance on change of habitual residence test for HB/CTB. Circular HB/CTB A22/2004, 'EU enlargement and changes to the Habitual Residence Test' at http://www.hbinfo.org/menu3/circs2004/word/a22-2004.doc.

'ACCESSION 8' NATIONALS AND THE RIGHT TO RESIDE

As indicated above, one of the main purposes of the new 'right to reside' test was to restrict entitlement to certain nationals of the 'Accession 8' countries i.e. eight of the countries which joined the EU on 1 May 2004: the Czech Republic, Estonia, Hungary, Latvia, Lithuania, Poland, Slovakia and Slovenia.

Summary of the effect on A8 nationals

In general terms, when A8 nationals arrive in the UK to seek work they do not have the 'right to reside' and therefore cannot access mainstream benefits. When they obtain work, they are required to register with the Home Office under the registration scheme within one month of starting employment. If they do this, they have the right to reside. They will then be eligible for the following benefits, which can be claimed while in work: CB, HB, CTB and CTC. A8 nationals who establish themselves as self-employed and have a right to reside as a result have the same benefit rights as other EEA nationals (▶see above at 1261–2, 1266).

A8 nationals may also be eligible for WTC, which is not affected by the right to reside test. In order to qualify for WTC, the claimant (or their partner) must be:

- in work; and
- have a sufficiently low income.

The number of hours which must be worked in order to qualify varies. For example if they:

- have a disability which puts them at a disadvantage in getting a job they must work at least 16 hours a week;
- are aged 25 years or over they must work at least 30 hours a week;
- themselves or their partner are aged at least 50 they must work at least 16 hours a week and qualify for a 50-plus element of WTC.

Claimants must also be present and 'ordinarily resident' in the UK (►see 1273–4). Where the claimant is a member of a married or unmarried couple, they must make a joint claim (see s3(3)(a), (5), (6) of the Tax Credits Act 2002).

An A8 national who becomes unemployed within the first 12 months of employment loses the right to reside and benefit entitlement will cease. It is only after an A8 national has been registered as employed for a continuous period of 12 months that they have the same rights to benefits as other EEA nationals.

This is only a summary of the position and there are exceptions to the general rules. The system is somewhat complex and it is set out more fully in the table below.

A8 nationals may also access disability benefits (disability living allowance, attendance allowance and carer's allowance, as these are also not affected by the right to reside test, but they must satisfy the residence rules referred to below) (►1273–4).

For further details about free movement immigration rights for A8 nationals after accession, the process of registration and the restrictions on their obtaining residence permits while they are required to register for work, ►see Chapter 19.

'ACCESSION 8' NATIONALS AND BENEFIT ENTITLEMENT

This table sets out the effect on A8 nationals of the 'right to reside' test introduced by the Habitual Residence Amendment Regulations. The benefits affected are: IS, (IB) JSA, SPC, HB, CTB, CB, and CTC. For a more general look at the right to reside, ►see the table at 1266–8.

In order to cross-reference to the law which is set out in this table, advisers should look at: regs 1, 2, 4, 5 and 7 of the Accession Regulations as amended by the Accession Amendment Regulations; and reg. 5 of the EEA 2000 Regulations (for abbreviations ►see 1242–3). Unfortunately, the information is not set out in the regulations in a straightforward way.

12

Those exercising EU free-movement rights can generally be described as having the 'right to reside'. However, for the period from 1 May 2004–30 April 2009, the Accession Regulations restrict the normal free-movement rights as they apply to A8 nationals. Under the regulations, an A8 national 'work-seeker' (who is not self-sufficient) does *not* have the 'right to reside'. In addition, most A8 nationals who obtain work must register for work under the Accession Registration Scheme in order to have the right to reside and therefore be eligible for benefit. From this, we can draw up 'general rules' to show which A8 nationals are excluded from benefit. The Accession Regulations also provide a number of exceptions to the general rules. We set these out in turn.

Note that what is set out below are rules applying specifically to A8 nationals. It must, however, be remembered that any EEA (including an A8) national will not have the right to reside through free-movement rights if they are not, or are no longer, exercising such rights. So, a work-seeker who has not found work after six months may have lost the right to reside in any event i.e. even if they are within the exceptions to the general rules below.

General rules

The general rules are that non-self-sufficient A8 nationals in any of the following three groups do not have the right to reside (although ▶see Note at 1268). They therefore cannot pass the habitual residence test and are therefore excluded from the above benefits.

1) A8 nationals who are seeking work (this is even though they may be genuinely seeking work with a realistic genuine chance of getting it and six months has not passed while they are looking for work).

2) A8 nationals who cease working in the UK and who are again seeking work in the UK.

3) A8 nationals who are working in the UK but who do not hold a valid registration certificate having registered under the Accession Registration Scheme.

Work-seekers (groups (1) and (2)) will be affected by being excluded from all the above benefits. Those in group (3) will be particularly affected by being excluded from the benefits that can be claimed while in work: CB, CTC, HB, and CTB.

Those in group (3), i.e. those who obtain work can obtain the right to reside by registering for work. If they do, then provided they are otherwise 'habitually resident' and satisfy the general requirements for the particular benefit, they will be able to obtain the above 'in work' benefits.

Exceptions to the general rules

A8 nationals in any of the following categories are not excluded from the right to reside because they fall into any of the three excluded groups above. They are, therefore, still eligible for benefits as exceptions to the general rules.

1) Those who, on 30 April 2004, had leave to be in the UK and that leave had no

restrictions on working at all. This will not apply to those who have been granted leave allowing them to work only in a particular employment or to students. This is because, although such claimants may have been legally working, their rights to work were still restricted. Examples of those with no working restrictions at all are: people with indefinite leave, humanitarian protection or discretionary leave; spouses/partners of those settled in the UK who are granted the 'probationary' period of leave; and certain dependants of those granted leave in an economic category (claimants should always check the conditions actually given; for full details of the conditions of leave which are normally attached, ►see 190–1).

2) Those who, on 30 April 2004, had leave to be in the UK and that leave allowed them to do the work that they were then doing. For example, a work-permit holder who was working in accordance with leave which allowed them to do the work stated in the work permit. Those in this category must *also* have been legally working in the UK on 1 May 2003 and have continued to legally work until 30 April 2004 with breaks of not more than 30 days in total.

3) Those who, on 30 April 2004, were entitled to reside because they were exercising EU rights of free movement and were, therefore, allowed to do the work that they were then doing. This would apply, for example, to an A8 national who, before 1 May 2004, was working in the UK as the family member of an EEA national. Those in this category must also have been legally working in the UK on 1 May 2003 and have continued to legally work to 30 April 2004 with breaks of not more than 30 days in total.

4) Those who work in the UK for a 12-month period, which can *either* begin before 1 May 2004 and end after that time, *or* it can begin and end at any time after 30 April 2004. So, for example, a claimant who worked between 5 February 2004 and 4 February 2005 is within this group. A claimant who worked between 10 July 2004 and 9 July 2005 is also within this group. However, the claimant must *also* have been legally working during the 12-month period. For these purposes, this means that:

- for any of the 12-month period that was *before* 1 May 2004, the claimant must *either* have had leave to be in the UK under conditions which allowed them to do the work, *or* they were entitled to reside and work in accordance with free-movement rights (►see as described for exceptions 1–3 immediately above);

- for any of the 12-month period, which falls *on or after* 1 May 2004, the claimant must *either* be registered under the Accession Scheme, *or* any of the exceptions at (5)-(8) below applies to them for the period in which they were not registered.

In both cases, the claimant must have been legally working both at the beginning and at the end of the 12-month period, and continue to work legally throughout the 12-month period with any breaks being not more than 30 days in total. Changes in employment during the 12 months are permitted provided any breaks are kept down to this level. Claimants only benefit from this exception to the general rules after they have completed the 12-month period. Official guidance states as follows:

'A person is to be treated as having worked for an uninterrupted period of 12 months if he is not legally working for less than 30 days in total, provided that he was legally working at the beginning and end of that period.' (DMG, Vol. 2, 02/04 at para. 37).

Example This is an important exception. An example of a claimant in this category is an A8 national who, after 1 May 2004, comes to the UK and registers under the Accession Scheme. The A8 national then works while registered for 12 months. During that time the worker is entitled to 'in-work' benefits as they had a right to reside as an A8 national because they are registered. If, after 12 months, the same A8 national then loses their employment, they will have the 'right to reside' while they are genuinely seeking further employment. This is because they have spent a 12-month period registered under the Accession Scheme and they are no longer required to register if they obtain further employment. Such persons have a right to reside while they are genuinely seeking work with a realistic chance of getting it just as do non-A8 EEA nationals. Because, they have a right to reside in order to seek work, they may now claim benefits during this period as well, most importantly income-based JSA. When they obtain work again, they will remain eligible for the in-work benefits.

5) A8 nationals who are *also* nationals of the UK, a non-accession EEA state or Switzerland.

6) Those who are 'posted workers'. This covers those who have been posted to the UK in order to provide services on behalf of an employer who is established abroad. This exception only applies while the worker actually is a posted worker and so if they lost their employment and became a work-seeker in the UK, the general rules (above) would probably apply at that point.

7) Those who are 'family members' of a Swiss or EEA national who is in the UK as a worker (other than as an A8 worker who needs to register); a self-sufficient person; a retired person; a self-employed person or a student. For these purposes, family members of workers are their spouse and children who are under 21 or dependent on them. Family members of all others are their spouse and their dependent children.

8) In any of the following further cases, A8 nationals who are working in the UK after 30 April 2004, have the right to reside even though they do not have a valid registration certificate authorising them to work for a particular employer. Note that the exceptions below only apply until a certain event takes place at which point the exception ceases to apply:

- if the claimant was legally working on 30 April 2004 in that they *either* had leave to be in the UK and that leave allowed them to do the work which they were then doing, *or* they were entitled to reside on that day because they were exercising EU rights of free movement *and in either case*, the claimant has not ceased working for that employer;

- if the claimant made a valid application to register within a month of starting work but has not received a decision either granting the registration certificate, or a notice refusing registration and the claimant has not ceased working for that employer since the application to register was made;

- where the claimant began working for an employer on or after 1 May 2004, the claimant has a grace period of *one month* from the date on which the work began during which they have a right to reside – effectively (and together with the exception immediately above), this means that claimants will not be prejudiced in terms of benefit rights provided they apply to register within a month of starting work;

- where, before 1 May 2004, the claimant was granted leave to enter the UK as a seasonal worker at an agricultural camp and, on or after 1 May 2004, they begin working as a seasonal worker at such a camp, they have a right to reside from the date they start work until they cease working for that employer, or 31 December 2004 (whichever of these two dates comes earlier)(for general details about seasonal workers, ▶see 450–2).

Note on those temporarily unable to work and involuntarily unemployed

EEA nationals who are temporarily unable to work as a result of illness or accident, or who have involuntarily been made unemployed (and this is recorded by the relevant employment office), do not, for these reasons alone, lose the right to reside (see reg. 5(2) EEA 2000 Regulations). This saving does not, however, apply to A8 nationals who generally lose their right to reside in these circumstances. *However*, there is a very limited protection for A8 nationals in this position. The limited protection applies to A8 nationals who began in registered employment on or after 1 May 2004 and who, within a month stop working for the above reasons. Such claimants will continue to have a right to reside (and are, therefore, still eligible for benefits) for a short grace period, which appears to run to the end of that same month (see reg. 5(2)(3) Accession Regulations).

Note also the possible challenges under EU law, ▶see 1266.

ADDITIONAL TESTS FOR CERTAIN BENEFITS

In addition to the 'habitual residence' and 'right to reside' tests, there are further residential requirements for certain benefits. These are set out below.

12

Ordinarily resident: tax credits, child benefit, disability benefit, and retirement pension (category D)

A number of welfare benefits require the claimant to be 'ordinarily resident' in Great Britain. They are:

- CTC;
- WTC;
- CB;
- DLA;
- AA;
- CA;

- IB for incapacity in youth; and
- RP (Category D).

'Ordinarily resident' is not defined but there is case law which explains its meaning. In *Shah*, the House of Lords decided that a person's ordinary residence is their

'...abode in a particular place or country which he has adopted voluntarily and for settled purposes as part of the regular order of his life for the time being, whether of short or long duration.'

Ordinary residence may, depending on a person's circumstances, begin on their arrival in the country and it can also continue during periods of temporary absence. A person here for a temporary purpose, for example, to study, is still here for the time being for a settled purpose and can, therefore, be 'ordinarily resident'. It is also possible to be ordinarily resident in more than one country at the same time. It should also be noted that most benefits also require that the claimant is present in the country in order to claim.

Presence over the previous twelve months: disability benefits

As explained above, those claiming the disability benefits listed below must be 'ordinarily resident' in Great Britain. However, in order to be entitled to the following benefits, claimants must also have been present in GB for at least 26 of the last 52 weeks:

- DLA;
- AA;
- CA; and
- IB for incapacity in youth.

There are exemptions for serving members of the armed forces, mariners and offshore workers. In certain circumstances, people may be treated as present for the purposes of the 26-week qualifying period when they are temporarily absent during that time. If claims are made for babies who are less than six months old, they only have to have been present for 13 out of the previous 26 weeks.

Presence over the previous twelve months: child benefit, guardian's allowance

In order to be entitled to CB, it is necessary that:

- the person claiming benefit for the child has been in GB for more than 182 days in the last 52 weeks (six months of the previous year); and
- either the child or one of the parents of the child has been in GB for more than 182 days in the last 52 weeks.

The above is the general rule for CB although there are some, quite complex, exceptions to the above rules and there are special rules for people who are working overseas, including civil servants and serving members of the armed forces. There is a further related benefit, guardian's allowance. Entitlement to GA depends on entitlement to CB. In addition, at least one of the child's parents must have been born in the UK or, at some time after reaching the age of 16, spent a total of 52 weeks in any two-year period in Great Britain.

Social fund

Although there are no independent additional hurdles for those who wish to make claims from the social fund, many of the possible claims on the social fund are linked to entitlement to other benefits. Therefore, the 'habitual residence' and 'right to reside' tests apply indirectly before a claimant is able to access certain parts of the social fund. The relevant links to other benefits are as follows:

- maternity expenses payments can be claimed only by those entitled to income support, income-based JSA or one of the tax credits;
- funeral expenses payments can only be claimed by those entitled to income support, income-based JSA, housing benefit, council tax benefit (including the second adult rebate) or one of the tax credits;
- cold weather payments are available only to those entitled to income support or income-based JSA;
- eligibility for community care grants or budgeting loans is restricted to those entitled to income support or income-based JSA; there is however some flexibility for crisis loans.

Winter fuel payments (for those aged 60 or over) are available regardless of entitlements to other benefits.

'Category D' pension

Although category A and B retirement pensions are contributory (below), category D pensions are non-contributory. For category D, entitlement depends on whether the claimant was 'ordinarily resident' in the UK on the day they reached 80, or the later date that the pension was claimed. The claimant must also have been resident for at least ten years in any continuous period of 20 years before they reached 80.

Industrial injuries benefits

Access to the industrial injuries benefits (disablement benefit, reduced earnings allowance, constant attendance allowance, exceptionally severe disablement allowance) also does not depend on immigration status. However, the claimant must have been working in GB when the accident or illness arising from the work occurred.

12

CONTRIBUTORY BENEFITS

Access to the contributory benefits, for which national insurance contributions are required, does not depend on immigration status as such. However, a person's immigration status may indirectly mean that they are unable to obtain these benefits simply because they have not been in the UK long enough to have made sufficient contributions, or they have not been permitted to work so as to enable them to pay contributions. These benefits are:

- contribution-based JSA;
- contribution-based incapacity benefit (IB);
- maternity allowance (MA);
- retirement pension categories A and B (RP);
- statutory maternity pay (SMP), statutory paternity pay (SPP) and statutory adoption pay (SAP);
- statutory sick pay (SSP); and
- bereavement benefits, which include bereavement payment (BP), widow's parent's allowance (WPA) and bereavement allowance (BA).

So, for example, a claimant from overseas who has worked in the UK and who has made sufficient contributions before they lost their employment would be able to obtain contribution-based benefits. To meet the contributory conditions for JSA, for example, contributions will need to have been paid (or credited to the claimant) in each of the last two complete tax years before the calendar year in which the claim is made.

The contributory benefits are not listed as public funds for the purposes of the immigration rules. *However*, claimants should beware. If their employment has ceased and they were granted leave under a category under the immigration rules in order for them to do that work, they are no longer likely to be in the UK in accordance with the rules under which they were granted leave. This will leave them vulnerable to having their leave curtailed.

The schemes for statutory sick pay and maternity pay are practically operated by employers. Statutory sick pay is paid to people for up to 28 weeks if they are unable to work through sickness. Statutory maternity pay is a minimum payment to employees who take time off as a result of pregnancy or childbirth. There are no special rules about immigration status, although the rules for these benefits do focus on whether the person has been employed here (or in another EU country).

CLAIMING FOR DEPENDANTS

In some cases, members of the same family have different immigration status. This can raise wider questions about other forms of support. However, asylum support and support from social services will not normally be available if benefit can be paid to cover all members of the family. Below, we look at the effect of 'mixed status' on benefit entitlement for claimants and their dependants for the various benefits. Note that the regulations are complex and open to interpretation. Our interpretation is as follows (given the circumstances, we have given fuller than normal references to the legislation).

Income support/income-based JSA

Where a claimant, their partner and their children are all not 'subject to immigration control' for the purposes of section 115(9) 1999 Act (i.e. each is a British citizen, settled in the UK with indefinite leave or has other leave not subject to a public funds condition e.g. HP, DL or some other form of exceptional leave), the claim for IS or (IB) JSA can include these family members. Additional amounts are paid as part of the award for these dependants.

A claimant who is subject to immigration control (and not exempt from that test) cannot receive IS and (IB) JSA for themselves or their dependants. For general details about the 'subject to immigration control' test and who is 'exempt', ▶see 1249–59.

What if the household is a 'mixed' one? If the claimant is able to get IS and (IB) JSA for themselves (either because they are not subject to immigration control or because they are exempt from that test), can they *also* claim for dependants who are subject to immigration control? The general rule is that claimants cannot claim for dependants in this situation (see para. 16A, Sch 7 to the Income Support Regulations; para. 14, Sch 5 to the Jobseeker's Allowance Regulations). If this is the case, dependants may have to look to other forms of support (▶see Chapters 40–41). *However*, there are two sets of exceptions to this general rule:

1) Where the main claimant is entitled to IS or (IB) JSA at the 'urgent cases' rate, they can claim for dependants. Urgent cases payments are often called simply 'UCPs'. UCPs are claimed by *some* (but not all) main claimants who are entitled to IS/(IB) JSA because they fall into one of the categories that are exempt from the 'subject to immigration control' test (▶see immediately below 1277–8).

2) Benefit can sometimes be paid to dependants under the 'special cases' rules. This mainly involves cases in which there are children in the household (▶see 1279).

Urgent cases payments UCPs of IS and (IB) JSA are paid at 90 per cent of the ordinary rate. In addition, dependants of the those claiming UCPs can be included in the claim and benefit is paid to cover their needs as well as the needs of the main claimant (reg. 71(1)(d) and para. 16A of Sch 7 to the Income Support Regulations; reg. 85(4) and para. 13A of Sch 5 and 5A to the Jobseeker's Allowance Regulations). The following categories of claimant who are entitled to and are claiming benefit are entitled to UCPs

12

of IS and IB (JSA) rather than benefit paid at the ordinary rate (see reg. 70(2A) Income Support Regulations; reg. 147(2A) Jobseeker's Allowance Regulations; reg. 2 Social Security Immigration Regulations):

- asylum-seekers who are still entitled to benefit because they are transitionally protected from the changes to the benefit rules made *either* in 1996 *or* 2000 under the 1996 rules (reg. 2(4)(a) Social Security Immigration Regulations applying 12(1) Persons from Abroad Regulations; reg. 2(5) and 12(3)-(5) Social Security Immigration Regulations);

- those temporarily without funds because remittances from abroad have been disrupted (reg. 2(1), para. 1 of Part 1 of the Schedule to Social Security Immigration Regulations);

- those granted leave on the basis of a maintenance undertaking who have not been resident in the UK for five years but whose sponsor has died (reg. 2(1) and para. 2 of Part 1 of the Schedule to the Social Security Immigration Regulations); and

- people who were granted leave on the basis of a maintenance undertaking made before 5 February 1996 and who were also entitled to IS at that time – this is another transitionally protected group (reg. 2(4)(a) Social Security Immigration Regulations applying 12(2) Persons from Abroad Regulations).

Note that the categories of persons eligible to claim UCPs listed below are made up of *some* of those who are entitled to claim benefit because they are *exempted* from the subject to control test. These categories themselves are more fully described above at ▶1255–8. In many cases where one partner is entitled to benefit paid at the ordinary rates and the other partner is entitled to UCPs, it will be better for the UCP partner to claim rather than the other partner. This is because, although the rates are lower, the UCP partner can claim for both whereas the other partner can only claim for themselves.

Claimants who are *not* subject to immigration control in the first place *and* the following categories (who are the remaining categories of claimants exempted from the subject to immigration control test) claim IS or (IB) JSA at the ordinary (non-UCP) rate. They cannot therefore claim for their dependants (unless the situation falls within any of the 'special cases' below):

- those granted leave on the basis of a maintenance undertaking and who have been resident in the UK for five years beginning on the date of entry or the date of the undertaking (whichever date is the later) (regs 2(1) and 12, para. 3 of Part 1 of the Schedule to Social Security Immigration Regulations); and

- nationals of countries which have ratified the European Convention on Social and Medical Assistance or the Council of Europe Social Charter and who are 'lawfully present' in the UK. (reg. 2(1) and para. 4 of Part 1 of the Schedule to the Social Security Immigration Regulations).

'Special cases': claiming IS and (IB) JSA for children

In addition to the rules relating to UCPs, there are special rules for claiming IS and (IB) JSA where there are children involved. Those rules are as follows.

- If the claimant is not subject to immigration control, or is exempt from that test, but their partner is subject to control, the claim can include an amount of benefit for the claimant and for any child who is not subject to control who is a member of the family. The claim can include a claim for any premiums. No amount will, however, be paid for the partner (para. 16A(a) of Schedule 7 to the Income Support Regulations; para. 13A(a) of Schedule 5 to Jobseeker's Allowance Regulations).

- If the couple are both not subject to immigration control (or both exempt) but the child is subject to control, then an amount can still be paid in respect of the child (reg. 17(1)(b)(c) Income Support Regulations; reg. 83 (b) and (d) Jobseeker's Allowance Regulations).

- If the claimant is a lone parent who is not subject to control (or is exempt from that test) but their child is subject to immigration control, then the benefit paid will still include an amount for the child (reg. 17(1)(b)(c) Income Support Regulations; reg. 83(b), (d) Jobseeker's Allowance Regulations).

- Where the lone parent is subject to immigration control they will not be entitled to any amount of benefit, even though their child is not subject to immigration control.

The position of children who are born in the UK but are not born British (because their parents are not British citizens or settled) has often caused problems. Although such children are not overstayers, illegal entrants etc, they have no right of abode, and still need permission (leave) to be in the UK (see s1(2), 3(1)(b) 1971 Act). They are therefore probably 'subject to immigration control' for benefits purposes under the 1999 Act. For details about regularising the position of such children so that they are given leave, ▶see 393–5.

Note, however, that dependent children cannot be included in a new claim for IS or (IB) JSA made after 6 April 2004. Claimants with dependent children have to claim CTC for them instead of having them included in a claim for IS or (IB)JSA.

State Pension Credit

For SPC, a partner who is 'subject to immigration control' will not count as part of the claimant's household (see reg. 5(1)(h) Pension Credit Regulations). In this situation, SPC will therefore only be paid at the single person's rate.

Housing benefit/council tax benefit

There is no such thing as a joint claim for HB or CTB. A couple can agree which one of them should make the claim (reg. 71 Housing Benefit

Regulations; reg. 61 Council Tax Regulations). It is obviously best for the partner who is not subject to control (or who is exempt) to make the claim. While the other member is, because they are subject to immigration control, not eligible to claim HB/CTB, the regulations still allow the claimant to obtain HB/CTB calculated for a couple. Because HB/CTB is calculated taking into account the needs of dependants, this may be more than if the claim was for a single person. This could have implications for those given leave with a condition of no recourse to public funds, or those making immigration applications where they have to meet the 'no public funds' requirements. However, there will be no recourse to public funds for the purposes of the immigration rules, if the partner claiming benefit would anyway have received *full* HB/CTB as a single person because their income is so low.

Tax credits

Where one partner of a couple is either not subject to immigration control, or is within one of the classes which are exempted from that test for the purposes of the tax credit in question (▶see 1258), then the couple is entitled to that tax credit as though both of them were not subject to immigration control (see reg. 3(2)(3) Tax Credits Immigration Regulations).

Child benefit

Only one person can be awarded CB for a particular child (see ss141-143 of the Social Security Contributions and Benefits Act 1992). Where more than one person is eligible, they can decide which of them receives the award (see reg. 14, Child Benefit (General) Regulations 2003). The amount of CB paid for each child remains the same whether the person responsible for the child is single or a member of a couple.

'Accession 8' nationals

Where A8 workers are living together as a couple and both are in registered employment during the first 12 months of employment (▶see 569, 563 onwards) then either member can be the principal claimant and benefits will be assessed in the ordinary way. The rules about individual eligibility for benefit for A8 nationals are set out at ▶1268–73. Where two A8 nationals are married and one is unemployed but the other is still in registered employment, then benefits should be assessed for the couple in the ordinary way because the unemployed spouse has free-movement rights as the family member of the worker.

Where both A8 nationals have become unemployed within the first 12 months of registered employment, they will lose entitlement to welfare benefits under the present domestic regulations, as they will not have a 'right to reside'.

When the A8 national is the spouse of an EEA national exercising free-movement rights in the UK, then the A8 national will share the same benefit rights as their spouse. This is because the family member does not require leave to be in the UK and is therefore not 'subject to immigration control' within the meaning of the 1999 Act. Nor are they required to register under the registration scheme if they begin working.

After both members of an A8 couple have spent more than 12 months as a registered worker, then they have the same rights to benefits as an EEA national exercising free-movement rights in the UK and either member of the couple may be the principal claimant for benefits.

ADDITIONAL BENEFIT RIGHTS FOR EEA NATIONALS AND RECIPROCAL AGREEMENTS

EEA nationals and their family members are entitled to the additional legal protections of EU law in relation to access to benefits. The ways in which EU law can give additional rights are listed below. Both EEA nationals and their family members who are not EEA nationals can benefit from these rights. This is a complex area and claimants who think that an important EU legal issue arises should take advice and/or consult one of the further sources of information listed at ▶1534–5.

Co-ordination of benefits within the EEA

EC Regulation 1408/71 provides for the co-ordination of benefits. It protects those people who pay, or who have paid, national insurance contributions. It also protects non-EEA nationals who are refugees or stateless persons. The Regulation:

- prohibits discrimination on grounds of nationality in social security;
- allows people to count periods of employment, residence and contributions in one EEA state towards entitlement in another; and
- allows people to take certain benefits abroad to another EEA state.

This means that an EEA national may straight away satisfy the additional residence or contributions requirements for some benefits. Most benefits are covered by the Regulation except for housing benefit and council tax benefit.

Free movement

The non-discrimination provisions in EU law mean that those who are exercising EU rights of free movement are entitled to the same tax, housing and social 'advantages' as nationals of the member state. It has been settled by the courts that social security benefits are part of these advantages.

EU citizenship and residence

The European Court of Justice has also considered the link between citizenship of the EU under Article 17 of the EC Treaty, benefit entitlement

12

and the prohibition of discrimination on grounds of nationality under Article 12 of the EC Treaty. The Court has held that an EEA national who is not economically active may, as a citizen of the EU, still rely on the prohibition of discrimination on grounds of nationality (see *Sala*, ECJ), especially where that person has been 'lawfully resident' in the host member state (*Trojani*, ECJ).

This was the approach taken in *Grzelczyk* (ECJ), which concerned the entitlement of a student to benefits. The student had been self-funding for the first three years of his degree but got into financial difficulties in the last year and claimed social assistance. Of course, students' free-movement rights depend on their not making claims for social assistance. Nonetheless, the Court concluded that, it would be disproportionate to deny him a right to reside in the circumstances of the case and he was entitled to be treated equally with Belgian nationals in relation to access to social assistance.

Reciprocal agreements

The UK has certain 'reciprocal' agreements with other countries relating to social security (see s179 Social Security Contributions and Benefits Act). The effect of these reciprocal agreements is limited – they generally help claimants to qualify for certain benefits by allowing periods of residence and contributions that are paid in one state to count in the other. Although there are agreements between the UK and other EEA countries, the protection given by EU law (▶above) is generally just as wide and so it is not necessary to rely upon them.

It is, therefore, only really necessary to consider the agreements with non-EEA states, for example, Australia, Barbados, Canada, Israel, Mauritius, New Zealand, Turkey, or the USA. All the agreements are different in their terms and their benefits. The reciprocal agreements deal in particular with: CB, AA and DLA. Regulation 2(3) of the Social Security Immigration Regulations states that, for the purposes of these benefits, the 'subject to immigration control' test does not apply to a person covered by the reciprocal agreements. Further details of the reciprocal agreements can be obtained from the following part of the DWP website: http://www.dwp. gov.uk/lifeevent/benefits/social_security_agreements.asp.

TRANSFERRING TO BENEFITS

If an asylum-seeker's claim or appeal is successful, they will become eligible for mainstream benefits when they are granted leave as refugees or they are granted humanitarian protection or discretionary leave. Entitlement to asylum support from NASS or a local authority will cease 28 days after the notification of the decision (▶see further 1344–5).

At least two problems have arisen in applicants transferring to benefits: delays in receiving status documents granting leave and access to national insurance numbers. Those accepted as refugees may apply to backdate their benefit entitlement but this system is being replaced by the availability of 'integration loans' under the 2004 Act.

Delays in receiving status documents

Problems can arise where an asylum-seeker receives notification of a successful decision on appeal but does not receive their status documents from the Home Office due to delays in administration. Until the claimant has actually been granted *leave* (as a refugee, or HP or DL), they are still 'subject to immigration control' and excluded from benefits by the 1999 Act. In cases of significant delay causing significant detriment, advisers should consider judicial review proceedings and writing a letter before claim requiring the documents to be provided (▶718–9). The 'Sunrise' project may help to overcome these problems (▶727–8).

In the High Court in *A and Kanidagli*, the Home Office was found liable in negligence where its delay in providing the necessary status documents resulted in the applicant losing entitlement to benefits. When the case reached the Court of Appeal, however, it emerged that the Home Office had a compensation scheme and the issue was resolved by the making of an *ex gratia* payment. The compensation scheme was first made public in the High Court case of *Mambakasa*. For full details of the scheme, ▶see 1224–7.

National insurance number requirement

In order to claim benefits, a claimant is required to provide the DWP with details and documents so that it can assess entitlement. There is also a statutory 'national insurance number (NINO) requirement', which benefit claimants must meet (see ss1(1A) and (1B) Social Security Administration Act 1992). However, a Commissioner has ruled that where a claimant's partner is not allowed by law to have recourse to public funds, the NINO requirements do not have to be satisfied in relation to the partner (*CH/3801/2004*).

A claim for benefit is treated as an application for a NINO; alternatively a NINO can be applied for on a separate form available from the DWP. In order to satisfy the NINO requirement, a claimant must *either* provide their NINO together with evidence that it has been issued to them, *or* provide information or evidence allowing the benefit authority to determine the NINO that has been allocated to them or provide evidence or information allowing a NINO to be allocated to them.

The evidence that is required in order to be allocated a NINO is evidence of identity: birth/marriage certificates, passports, travel documents, identity cards. Often asylum-seekers and refugees have difficulties satisfying the NINO requirement because the DWP will not accept their evidence of identity, in particular if original documentation is not produced. For the kind of evidence that should be accepted, reference can be made to the DWP's own leaflet – 'How to prove your identify for social security' (GL25).

12

Where the only bar to entitlement is delay in allocating a NINO, a formal complaint or a letter before claim may be necessary. For details about the authorities obtaining information for NINO purposes early on in the asylum process ▶see 670–1.

Another possible solution is to ask the DWP to make an 'interim' benefit payment. Such payments are available on a discretionary basis where a benefit claim cannot be processed immediately (see reg. 2 Social Security (Payments on Account, Overpayments and Recovery) Regulations 1988). The interim payment provision was amended from 18 March 2005 to make it clear that such payments could be made where it was:

'...impracticable to satisfy immediately the national insurance number requirements in section 1(1A) and (1B) of the Administration Act.' (amendments made by regs 3(a)(ii) and 10(1) of the Social Security, Child Support and Tax Credits (Miscellaneous Amendments) Regulations 2005).

Where there has been a refusal to allocate a NINO and this has resulted in a decision to refuse benefit, then both issues can be raised in any benefit appeal to the tribunal (see *CIS/0345/2003*).

For official guidance on NINOs regarding housing benefit and council tax benefit, see http://www.hbinfo.org/menu3/circs2004/word/a34-2004.doc and see circular HB/CTB A10/2004 at http://www.hbinfo.org/menu3/circs2004/pdf/a10-2004.pdf.

REFUGEES AND BACKDATING CLAIMS FOR BENEFIT

For many people who are eventually accepted as being refugees, the system of backdating benefits for refugees, has given them a 'start up' amount of cash, which they have been able to use to buy essential clothes and other household items, which they had been missing. The backdating scheme was first introduced by the Asylum and Immigration Act 1996 and is presently contained in section 123 of the 1999 Act and in regulations.

The following benefits can be backdated: IS, SPC, HB, CTB, CB, GA, CTC and WTC (see below for brief details relating to the separate benefits). Those who become entitled to income-based JSA, cannot backdate it but should make a claim for backdated IS instead. Obviously backdating depends on whether the claimant would, but for their immigration status, have been entitled during the period of the asylum claim. For example, most asylum-seekers will not have had rent liability (having been accommodated by NASS) and will therefore not be entitled to housing benefit.

Section 12 2004 Act abolishes the main provisions for backdating benefit and Section 13 replaces them with a system for providing 'integration' loans instead, which the refugee must repay (it is the government's intention to also end the backdating arrangements which are not specifically referred to in section 12). These changes are intended to come into force together. As of the end of July 2005, they had still not been brought into force, the backdating system was still in existence and there were no integration loans. The government intends that no one who is recognised as a refugee after section 12 2004 Act is brought into force will be eligible for a backdated payment. There are unlikely to be any transitional arrangements.

Income support

Most backdating claims are for IS. The rules for backdating for IS, HB and CTB are similar. The position is different depending on whether the claim to asylum was made before or after 2 April 2000 (see regs 21ZA–21ZB Income Support Regulations; reg. 7B and Sch A1 to the Housing Benefit Regulations and reg. 4A and Sch A1 to the Council Tax Regulations). Evidence of means during the period since the asylum claim, should be provided to the benefit authority in the form of form NASS 35 which is issued to asylum-seekers at the point their NASS support ceases.

Asylum claim made on or before 2 April 2000 In these cases, refugees are entitled to backdated benefit paid at the urgent cases rate (90 per cent) from the date the claim to asylum was originally *refused*, if the claim was made on arrival. If the claim was made in-country, benefit is paid from the date of the claim, or from 5 February 1996 if that was later. The refugee must claim income support and backdating within 28 days of being notified that the Home Office has recognised them as a refugee.

Asylum claim made on or after 3 April 2000 These refugees must also claim benefit and backdating within 28 days of being notified that the Home Office has recognised them but they are entitled to backdate benefit at the full rate from the date of their claim to asylum. However, for these claimants, the award of benefit is *deducted* by the value of any asylum support received during the period of the backdating. This may cancel out much of their backdated entitlement. The refugee will there-fore get the 30 per cent difference between income support and asylum support.

The 28-day time limit for backdating is a strict one. There is no provision to extend the 28-day deadline for 'good cause' which is the test normally used in social security for backdating benefits. Time starts to run from the date the claimant is notified of their refugee status. The 28-day time limit can also start from the date the solicitor is notified of the decision (*CIS/3797/2003*). Where a request for backdating is received outside the 28-day time limit, entitlement cannot be backdated. However, even in such cases, the decision-maker should still consider whether any back-dating at all is possible under the ordinary 'good cause' criteria (*CJSA/4383/2003*). For IS, CB, WTC and CTC this will be up to three months, but for HB/CTB and SPC it can be up to 52 weeks.

12

Tax credits and pension credit

In relation to the tax credits, the claim and the request for backdating must be made within three months of the decision granting refugee status being notified. In terms of the amounts recoverable, the claimant will be treated as having claimed tax credits on the date of their asylum claim and in the following years. They will therefore be paid tax credits from whichever is the later date: either the date of their asylum claim, or the date on which the tax credits came into being (6 April 2003). Again, there are deductions for asylum support received (see regs 3(5)–(9) and 4 Tax Credits Immigration Regulations).

Child benefit/guardian's allowance

CB and GA may also be backdated (see Child Benefit and Guardian's Allowance (Miscellaneous Amendments) Regulations 2004). Note that GA may be paid to people looking after children whose parents have died. It may also be paid where one of the parents has died and the whereabouts of the other parent are either unknown, or the parent has been sentenced to a term of imprisonment of two years or more, or they have been detained in hospital by an order of a court.

REFUGEE INTEGRATION LOANS

The scheme for providing 'integration loans' for refugees will be implemented at the same time as the backdating scheme is abolished (see s13 2004 Act). The purpose of the loan is to help refugees integrate into the community. It is to be noted that the definition of 'refugee' for the purposes of these loans only refers to those who have been recognised as refugees *and* who have been granted *indefinite* leave in the UK. The government is moving to a system of granting limited leave to refugees initially and not granting indefinite leave until up to five years have passed. On the basis of the existing legislation, this would mean that applicants would have to wait years before they are eligible for an integration loan. This may change. Only those aged 18 or above may receive loans and only one loan can be made.

The government plans to make regulations, which will set out the system for loans in more detail. The regulations are expected to set out:

- how refugees can apply for a loan;
- the factors which the Home Office will take into account in deciding whether or not to make a loan, including the refugee's income and assets and their likely ability to repay the loan;
- the minimum and maximum levels of the loan;
- the conditions that may be attached to a loan – these conditions may include conditions about the use of the loan; and
- how the loans are to be repaid.

Although the government has a power to charge interest on integration loans, it is likely that the loans will be interest-free. One way of loans being repaid is likely to be through the DWP by deductions from benefit.

The Immigration, Asylum and Nationality Bill 2005 proposes to amend the power to grant loans to refugees to enable those granted limited leave as refugees to obtain a loan as well as those with indefinite leave.

GENERAL MATTERS: GOING ABROAD, LINKS BETWEEN DEPARTMENTS

Finally we look at some further general matters concerning immigration status benefits: what happens to benefit entitlement if a claimant goes abroad for a temporary period and the links which exist between benefit departments and the Home Office.

Effect on benefits of going abroad

A claimant who is in receipt of benefit and intends to go abroad should notify the DWP and/or the local authority. Where claimants go abroad for temporary purposes, they can continue to be entitled for short periods. In ordinary cases, entitlement continues for four weeks for IS and (IB) JSA. This can be extended up to eight weeks in certain circumstances. HB can be paid for temporary absences of 13 weeks and for a period not in excess of 52 weeks in certain circumstances. The rules for CTB are similar. Where a claimant has not informed the relevant body, their benefit can be terminated from the date they went abroad. In those circumstances a new claim will have to be made upon the claimant's return. A request to backdate the claim can be made but this may still result in some loss of benefit.

If someone intends to move abroad on a permanent or long term-basis, the rules for which benefits can be exported and to what countries and under what conditions are complex and may depend on EU law or a reciprocal arrangement. Claimants should obtain specialist advice *in advance of* any move. For details of further sources of information, ▶see 1534–5.

12

Links between departments

Claimants should note that there are established links between benefit and immigration authorities. The most important benefit authority is the Department of Work and Pensions (DWP) but note that the Inland Revenue now administers both CB and the tax credits. Sometimes when a claim is made, enquiries about a person's immigration status are made by telephone or letter to the Home Office. The claim form for income support and income-based JSA asks whether the claimant or any member of their family has come to the UK in the last two years. If the answer is 'yes', further questions are asked.

Checks with the Home Office have been known to be triggered by other factors: a 'foreign sounding' name, lack of fluency in English or not having a national insurance number.

Examples of the effect that checks with the Home Office can have are as follows:

- the benefit authority may obtain information about the claimant's immigration status, which indicates that they should be excluded from benefit (for example because they are 'subject to immigration control' because they have a condition attached to their leave prohibiting access to public funds);
- the Home Office is alerted to the benefits claim, which may then be used to refuse a future immigration application on the grounds that the applicant is not able to meet the immigration requirement that they can support themselves without recourse to public funds;
- the Home Office may be able to identify the whereabouts of persons of whom it had lost track but who have no legal basis for remaining in the UK. This could lead to Home Office enforcement action against the claimant.

There are also links between the Home Office and local authorities and this should be kept in mind when applications are made to the local authority for benefits (HB and CTB), housing and social services support.

40 Housing, social services, Children Act and health care

This chapter looks at how access to the following forms of welfare provision is affected by immigration status:

- housing (▶1289–98);
- social services ('community care services') including support under the 'withholding and withdrawal of support' Regulations (▶1299–1322);
- support under the Children Act (▶1322–8);
- access to health care (▶1328–35);
- access to education (▶1335).

Chapter 39 deals with access to welfare benefits.

Chapters 41–42 cover asylum support, appeals to the Asylum Support Adjudicator and 'hard cases' support.

HOUSING

The housing duties of local authorities can be split into two:

Housing for the homeless When a local authority is approached by someone who is apparently homeless (or threatened with homelessness), the local authority should carry out investigations into their circumstances. The authority must determine whether the person is 'eligible' for housing assistance, is homeless, is in 'priority need', is intentionally homeless and whether they have a 'local connection' (▶see 1296–7) with the area of the authority. Depending on the result of these investigations, the authority may be required to provide housing for them. Whether a person is 'eligible' for this assistance can be affected by their immigration status.

Allocation of housing accommodation All local authorities have allocation schemes governing how they allocate secure and assured tenancies to those waiting for accommodation. Local housing authorities can only allocate accommodation to 'qualifying persons'. This is done in accordance with the authority's 'allocation scheme', which may be based on a points system. Whether a person can qualify to be on an allocation scheme can be affected by their immigration status. An existing secure or (in certain cases) assured tenant remains eligible for an allocation whatever their immigration status.

Access to housing: three tables

As indicated, immigration status affects access to both of the above forms of housing. The three tables below explain how access is affected by immigration status as follows. Note that the Scottish and Welsh regulations and codes have slight differences. We have focussed on the English regulations.

Table 1: General exclusion This sets out who *in principle* is excluded from *both* forms of housing provision. People may be excluded if they fall into *any* of the four following groups, namely they:

- are 'subject to immigration control' within the meaning of the Immigration and Asylum Act 1996;
- are not 'habitually resident' in the CTA;
- do not have a 'right to reside' in the UK;
- have a right to reside but only under Council Directives 90/364/EEC or 90/365/EEC (economically inactive persons).

If an applicant does not fall into any of the above groups, then they are not excluded by their immigration status. Of course, they must satisfy the other conditions for the form of housing in question, for example the requirement to be in 'priority need' for assistance as a homeless person. We do not, in the *Handbook*, describe the non-immigration related parts of the housing duties. For further details of those matters, one of the further sources referred to at ▶1534–5 should be consulted.

However, even if a person is excluded in principle because they do fall into any of the above groups, they can still be 're-included' for both homelessness assistance (Table 2), or eligibility for the allocation of housing accommodation (Table 3). It is not completely settled whether if an applicant falls into any of the 're-included' classes in Tables 2–3, they will always be eligible i.e even if they do not have the 'right to reside' in the UK. This issue is likely to be looked at by the Court of Appeal in the *Barnet* case (▶1295–6).

Table 2: Eligibility for homelessness assistance This sets out classes of people who are 'subject to immigration control' and may be re-included for eligibility for homelessness assistance *even though* they are excluded in principle because they fall within any of the groups set out in Table 1. For brief details about the 'local connection' requirements under the homelessness legislation and the effect on an application of the immigration status of other members of the family, ▶see below at 1296–8.

Table 3: Qualification for inclusion on to an allocation scheme This sets out classes of people who are 'subject to immigration control' and are re-included for eligibility for entry onto a local authority allocation scheme so that they can be allocated accommodation *even though* they fall into any of the groups set out in Table 1.

TABLE 1

GENERAL EXCLUSION FOR HOMELESSNESS ASSISTANCE AND ALLOCATION SCHEMES

Applicants are *in principle* excluded from *both* forms of housing provision (homelessness assistance and access to an allocation scheme) if they fall into *any* of the following four groups. For the 're-inclusions', see Tables 2–3.

It should be noted that the first group consists of those 'subject to immigration control' whereas the remaining exclusions (groups 2–4) are aimed at those not subject to immigration control.

First group: 'subject to immigration control'

(ss160A, 185(2) Housing Act 1996; s13 Asylum and Immigration Act 1996)

Applicants are excluded if they are 'subject to immigration control' within the meaning of the Asylum and Immigration Act 1996. Under this Act, a person is 'subject to immigration control' if they need leave to enter or remain in the UK. The test therefore excludes everyone other than:

- those with the 'right of abode' in the UK (mostly British citizens and some Commonwealth citizens, ▶1418–20);
- EEA nationals and their family members who are exercising rights of free movement (see s7 Immigration Act 1988; those who are not exercising EU free movement rights need leave to be in the UK instead);
- Irish nationals;
- those exempt from having to obtain leave (▶472–6).

This test is stricter than the 'subject to immigration control' test under section 115 Immigration and Asylum Act 1999 (▶1250). In particular, this test excludes people who require leave to be in the UK even if they presently have leave.

Second group: not 'habitually resident'

(reg. 4(1)(a) Homelessness (England) Regulations 2000; reg. 5(1)(a) Allocation of Housing (England) Regulations 2002 both as amended by the Allocation of Housing and Homelessness (Amendment) (England) Regulations 2004).

Subject to certain exemptions (below) applicants are excluded if they are not 'habitually resident'. Whether a person is 'habitually resident' is a question of fact to be decided by looking at all the circumstances of the case. For further general details about the habitual residence test, see the chapter on welfare benefits at ▶1259–64.

The English Code of Guidance (Homelessness Code of Guidance for Local Authorities – note that a new code is expected at the end of 2005) at Annex 22 suggests the following factors should be taken into account where the applicant has come to the UK for the first time:

- any work arrangements;
- any pattern of work;

12

- whether the applicant is joining friends and family;
- the person's plans;
- length of residence in another country;
- the applicant's centre of interest.

    However, the following persons are exempt from the habitual residence test for housing purposes and cannot therefore be excluded on the basis of this test (reg. 4(2) Homelessness (England) Regulations 2000; reg. 5(2) Allocation of Housing (England) Regulations 2002 as amended):

- persons who are 'workers' for the purposes of Council Regulations (EEC) No 1612/68 or (EEC) No 1251/70 (▶1261, categories (1), (2));
- 'accession state workers' who are treated as 'workers' and therefore as qualified persons under regulation 5 EEA 2000 Regulations read together with regulations 5 and 7 of the Accession Regulations (▶see 1262, category (5));
- persons with a right to reside under the EEA 2000 Regulations which is derived from Council Directive No 68/360/EEC or 73/148/EEC (▶1261–2, categories (3), (4));
- persons with a right to reside under the EEA 2000 Regulations which is derived from Council Directive No 75/34/EEC – this concerns the rights to remain in an EEA state for EEA nationals who have been in a self-employed activity;
- people who left Montserrat after 1 November 1995 because of the volcanic eruptions there.

Third group: no 'right to reside'

(reg. 4(3) Homelessness (England) Regulations 2000; reg. 5(3) Allocation of Housing (England) Regulations 2002 as amended)

From 1 May 2004, an applicant who does not have the 'right to reside' in the UK is also excluded. The basis upon which this group is excluded is that they are deemed not to be habitually resident in the CTA (see above). This exclusion does not, therefore, appear to apply to the groups referred to above who are exempt from the habitual residence test for housing purposes.

Fourth group: 'economically inactive'

(reg. 4(1)(b) Homelessness (England) Regulations 2000; reg. 5(1)(b) Allocation of Housing (England) Regulations 2002 as amended)

Those who have rights of residence derived only from Council Directive No 90/364/EEC or 90/365/EEC (those who are self-sufficient persons including retired persons) are also excluded.

TABLE 2

ELIGIBILITY FOR HOMELESSNESS ASSISTANCE

This table sets out those groups of people who are subject to immigration control within the meaning of the 1996 Act (i.e. they need leave ►see 1291) and are re-included for eligibility for homelessness assistance *even though* they are in principle excluded under Table 1. The regulations actually call the groups 'Class A, B' etc as indicated. So, if an applicant is within any of the following groups, they are eligible for homelessness assistance and cannot be excluded on the basis of their immigration status.

These re-inclusions are contained in regulation 3 Homelessness (England) Regulations 2000.

The re-included groups who are eligible are:

1) People 'recorded' by the Home Office as refugees (**Class A**).

2) People who have been granted exceptional leave which is not subject to a condition that they maintain and accommodate themselves without recourse to public funds (exceptional leave is not generally given with this condition) (**Class B**). Although the legislation refers to 'exceptional leave', the Office of the Deputy Prime Minister has advised local authorities that 'humanitarian protection; and 'discretionary leave' also fall within this class (for explanations of 'exceptional leave' ►see 147–9, 597–8, 859–62).

3) People who have indefinite leave and who are 'habitually resident' in the Common Travel Area (►see 1539) except people who were given leave on a written maintenance undertaking in pursuance of the immigration rules who have not been in the UK for five years (beginning on the date of entry, or the date when the undertaking was made, whichever is the later) and whose sponsor is still alive (**Class C**).

4) People who left Montserrat after 1 November 1995 because of the volcanic eruptions there (**Class D**).

5) A person who is habitually resident within the Common Travel Area and is either:

• a national of a state which has *ratified* ECSMA or the Social Charter and is 'lawfully present' in the UK (the non-EEA states which have ratified one of these treaties are Turkey, Macedonia and Croatia; for the meaning of 'lawful presence' ►see below 1298) (**Class Ei**); or

• a person who was owed a duty by the local authority under the homelessness provisions before 3 April 2000, is still owed a duty and is a national of a state which has *signed* ECSMA or the Social Charter. (Note that while many states have signed and ratified one of these treaties – see the above limb – there are some states that have signed but not yet ratified one of them. So the list of countries which have signed one of the treaties is longer than the list of countries which have ratified one of them. The non-EEA states which have *signed* one of the treaties are: Croatia, Macedonia, Liechtenstein, Romania, Switzerland, Turkey and Ukraine) (**Class Eii**).

12

6) A person who claimed asylum before 3 April 2000 on their arrival in the UK and whose asylum application has neither been decided by the Home Office nor abandoned (**Class F**).

7) A person who claimed asylum before 3 April 2000 who was in Great Britain at the time when the Home Office made an 'upheaval' declaration (see 000) in relation to their country of origin, who claimed asylum within three months of the date of the declaration, and whose claim has neither been decided by the Home Office nor been abandoned (**Class G**).

8) A person who claimed asylum on or before 4 February 1996, who was entitled to housing benefit on 4 February 1996 and who has either not received a further negative decision from the Home Office on their asylum claim since 4 February 1996, or who has had an appeal outstanding against the asylum refusal since 5 February 1996 or before (**Class H**).

9) A person who is entitled to and is receiving income support or income-based Jobseekers' Allowance *other than* on either of the following two bases:

- they are exempt from the 'subject to immigration control test' for those benefits because they are temporarily without funds as the supply from abroad has been disrupted (►see the table at 1256) (**Class I**); or

- they are deemed to have been granted leave to enter or remain in the UK exceptionally under regulation 3 Displaced Persons (Temporary Protection) Regulations 2005 (**Class I**).

TABLE 3

QUALIFICATION FOR ALLOCATIONS SCHEME

This table sets out the groups of applicant who are subject to immigration control within the meaning of the 1996 Act (►see 1291) and are re-included for eligibility for entry onto a local authority's allocation scheme so that they can be allocated accommodation *even though* in principle they are excluded by Table 1.

These re-inclusions are contained in regulation 4 Allocation of Housing (England) Regulations 2002.

Those who are re-included are:

1) People 'recorded' by the Home Office as refugees (**Class A**).

2) People who have been granted exceptional leave which is not subject to a condition that they maintain and accommodate themselves without recourse to public funds (exceptional leave is not generally given with this condition) (**Class B**). Although the legislation refers to 'exceptional leave', the Office of the Deputy Prime Minister has advised local authorities that 'humanitarian protection' and 'discretionary leave' also fall within this class (for explanations of 'exceptional leave', ►see 147–9, 597–8, 859–62).

3) People who have indefinite leave and who are habitually resident in the Common Travel Area *except* people who were given leave on a written maintenance undertaking in pursuance of the immigration rules, who have *not* been in the UK for five years (beginning on the date of entry or the date when the undertaking was made – whichever is the later) and whose sponsor is still alive (**Class C**).

4) A person who is habitually resident within the Common Travel Area and is either:

- a national of a state which has *ratified* ECSMA or the Social Charter and is 'lawfully present' in the UK (the non-EEA states which have ratified one of these treaties are Croatia, Macedonia and Turkey; for the meaning of 'lawful presence' ▶see 1298 below) (**Class Di**); or

- a person who was owed a duty by the local authority under the homelessness provisions before 3 April 2000, is still owed a duty and is a national of a state which has *signed* ECSMA or the Social Charter. (Note that while many states have *signed and ratified* one of these treaties (see the above limb) there are some states that have *signed* but not yet ratified one of them. So, the list of of countries which have signed one of them is longer than the list of countries which have ratified one of them. The non-EEA countries which have signed one of the treaties are: Croatia, Liechtenstein, Macedonia, Romania, Switzerland, Turkey and Ukraine) (**Class Dii**).

A8 nationals and EEA nationals and eligibility for housing assistance

The 'right to reside' test was introduced mainly to exclude most Accession 8 nationals from housing and social security 'out of work benefits' for at least the first 12-month period while they are in the UK. The right to reside test is also intended to exclude all EEA nationals (including A8 nationals) who are not exercising free movement rights in the UK. For a full explanation of the 'right to reside' test, ▶see 1264–8. For how it applies to A8 nationals, ▶see 1268–73.

However, it should be noted that there may be some applicants who are, for whatever reasons, receiving income support or income-based jobseekers allowance and therefore fall within re-included Class I for homelessness purposes (see Table 2 above at ▶1294; note that this is provided that benefit is *not* being received for the reasons there set out). This may particularly be the case in relation to an EEA national who is still receiving these benefits because they are transitionally protected from the 'right to reside' test for benefit purposes which began to apply on 1 May 2004 (▶see 1266). If such an applicant is in fact receiving these benefits, then they may be re-included and access homelessness assistance. This argument was successful in an appeal in the County Court (***Habiba Sheich v Bristol CC***). The counter argument for local authorities is that whenever an applicant is re-included by the regulations in Tables 2 and 3 above, they can *still* be excluded if they fail to satisfy the right to reside test set out in

12

Table 1 above. This matter is due to be looked at by the Court of Appeal in *Abdi & Ismail v Barnet LBC*. The same argument may arise in other cases, e.g. those claiming to be re-included on grounds of 'lawful presence' (►see Class E at 1293 and D at 1295 and ►see 1298).

Homelessness: local connection

An applicant will not be able to get assistance from a particular authority under the homelessness provisions if they make an application to that authority but they have a 'local connection' to the area of another authority (ss198-199, Housing Act 1996). A person can have a local connection with an area for one of four reasons:

- past residence of choice;
- employment;
- family connections; or
- special circumstances.

Where the applicant has a local connection to another area and no local connection to the area of the authority to which they have applied, the authority can refer the duty under the homelessness legislation to the local authority to which the applicant has a local connection. Official guidance suggests that an applicant will have a local connection by residence in an area if they have been living there for at least six months during the previous 12 months, or for not less than three years during the previous five years (see *Guidelines for Local Authorities on Procedures for Referral*, 2001, issued by the Local Government Association and available on its website, www.lga.gov.uk).

Al-Ameri

In the House of Lords in *Al-Ameri*, it was held that, because an asylum-seeker could not be said to have exercised any real choice about where they lived when they are dispersed under the NASS scheme, they do not acquire a local connection with the dispersal area by residence of choice. Therefore, successful asylum-seekers could apply to other local authorities for homelessness assistance.

Section 11 2004 Act

The government did not accept the ruling in *Al-Ameri* and enacted section 11 Asylum and Immigration Act 2004 to reverse it. Section 11 came into force on 4 January 2005. This amends the local connection rules so as to give asylum-seekers who have been granted leave, a local connection to the area in which they were last provided with asylum support by NASS. The position now, therefore, is as follows.

Dispersal to England or Wales If an asylum-seeker is dispersed by NASS to an area of England or Wales, then later obtains leave to enter or remain and applies as homeless to, for example, a London authority, that authority is entitled to refer the application back to the authority for the dispersal area on grounds of local connection (see also the *Homelessness Code of Guidance for Local Authorities*, Office of the Deputy Prime Minister, July 2002, as revised by further guidance, *Local Connection and Referral* effective from 4 January 2005; the guidance is available on the Office of the Deputy Prime Minister's website, www.odpm.gov.uk). *However*, if the applicant is able to show a local connection with the authority they are applying to, for example on the grounds of family associations or previous residence there, then the authority will not be able to make the referral.

Dispersal to Scotland The rules are different for those dispersed to NASS accommodation in *Scotland*. The homelessness provisions in Scotland do not treat section 95 1999 Act (NASS support) as creating a local connection. Even if an applicant, who has been provided with section 95 support in Scotland, has no local connection with the area that they have been dispersed to, they will still be entitled to assistance from the Scottish housing authority provided that they have no local connection with the area of any other local authority. However, they can also apply to a different authority in Scotland on the basis that they have no local connection to the area in Scotland to which they were dispersed. However, if an applicant who has been dispersed to Scotland subsequently applies for housing to an authority in England or Wales to which they have no local connection, the housing authority will not be under a full duty to provide accommodation under the 1996 Act. The authority should still provide temporary accommodation and advice and assistance in order to give the applicant a reasonable opportunity of securing accommodation for themselves (s11(2)(3) 2004 Act).

Homelessness: ineligible members of the household

In order to be provided with accommodation as a homeless person, one of the requirements of the legislation is that the applicant is in 'priority need'. If there is a child in the household, this would normally bring the family into the 'priority need' category. This will not be the case, however, if the child is 'subject to immigration control' (section 185(4) of the Housing Act 1996).

In October 2005, the Court of Appeal decided the case of *Morris* which involved a British citizen with a dependent non-British child. The Court confirmed the above interpretation of the legislation but also declared it to be incompatible with Article 8 ECHR. The Court also held that the local authority was permitted, though not obliged, to consider using its alternative powers to secure accommodation for the family under section 192(3) of the Housing Act 1996 (this is the residual power in the Housing Act which allows a local authority to provide accommodation to homeless persons *even though* they do not have priority need), section 17 Children Act 1989 (▶1322 onwards) or section 2 Local Government Act 2000 (▶1321–2). It is possible that the case will be appealed to the House of Lords.

12

For the purposes of assessing 'priority' under the allocation scheme (not the homelessness provisions), the applicant's needs will be assessed on the basis that their household includes their children, regardless of the status of those children (see the decision of the High Court in *Kimvono*).

Homelessness and allocation schemes: 'lawful presence' under ECSMA and the Social Charter and the decision in *Szoma*

For the purposes of both the homelessness provisions and allocation schemes, there are 're-inclusions' to entitlement for those who are nationals of states which have 'ratified' (or, in some very limited circumstances, simply 'signed') either the European Convention on Social and Medical Assistance (ECSMA) or the Council of Europe Social Charter (CESC). They must also be 'lawfully present' in the UK.

In *Kaya*, the Court of Appeal rejected the applicants' case that, because they had temporary admission to the UK, they were 'lawfully present'. In late 2005, this decision was overruled by the House of Lords in *Szoma v Secretary of State for the Department of Work and Pensions.* The decision in *Szoma* concerned income support but the reasoning applies equally to the housing legislation. Mr Szoma was a Polish national who arrived in the UK and claimed asylum on arrival. During the period of his claim for benefit, he was granted temporary admission under the authority of an immigration officer (para. 21, Sch 2 1971 Act). The House of Lords held that, for the purposes of the regulations, he was 'lawfully present' in the UK. Poland has since become part of the EU but the judgment in *Szoma* is important for social security and housing applicants who are nationals of Croatia, Macedonia or Turkey (all of which have ratified at least one of these treaties). In housing cases, it may assist EEA nationals also (►below). For welfare benefits ►see 1256, 1259. For housing applicants, see Class Ei in Table 2 above (►1293) and Class Di in Table 3 above (►1295).

As distinct from the position regarding welfare benefit claimants (►see 1259), applicants for homelessness assistance and allocations should be re-included under Classes Ei and Di above if they are lawfully present, regardless of whether they have the 'right to reside' in the UK. This appears to be the case because the 're-including' regulations referred to, seem to make applicants eligible without having to satisfy the 'right to reside' test. The matter is not settled, however, and is due to be considered by the Court of Appeal (►see 1295–6). Note that the 're-inclusions' only apply to those 'subject to immigration control' within the 1996 Act (►see 1291). All EEA nationals (including A8 nationals) other than Lithuanians are nationals of countries that have ratified CESC or ECSMA. Any such nationals who are 'subject to control' because they are not exercising EU rights of free movement (and therefore need leave) *may* be lawfully present. For example, if they have temporary admission as asylum-seekers (as well as Croats, Macedonians and Turks with TA) they will be lawfully present and therefore re-included.

For further general details about 'temporary admission', ▶see 950–7.

SOCIAL SERVICES

In this part, we look at who can obtain support from the social services departments of local authorities. These services are also sometimes referred to as 'community care services', which is an umbrella term for services provided under the National Assistance Act 1948 together with the Chronically Sick and Disabled Persons Act 1970, the Health Services and Public Health Act 1968, the National Health Services Act 1977 and the Mental Health Act 1983. The legislation is supplemented by government circulars and directions.

Although in what follows we are describing support available from social services departments, we also cover here the exclusions from support under Schedule 3 2002 Act in general. These exclusions do not just apply to the services looked at here, they also apply to asylum support (provided by NASS or a local authority), temporary asylum support, 'hard cases' support and some forms of interim housing.

The circumstances in which people may be considered eligible for assistance and the support that they can receive are described in outline below.

The best 'way in' to this part is to look first at the overview in the table below below at ▶1300–1 and then follow the cross-references.

Turning to social services: how it arose in 1996

In February 1996, the government introduced severe restrictions on benefit entitlement for those coming to the UK from abroad. Those claiming asylum were denied benefit unless they claimed 'on arrival' or within three months of a declaration of upheaval being made in relation to their country of origin. JCWI brought court proceedings against the government which resulted in the regulations being struck down as, by reducing asylum-seekers to destitution, they prevented them from properly pursuing their claims for asylum in the UK. The government responded by passing the Asylum and Immigration Act 1996 which gave firm grounding for the same regulations.

As a result, and in these 'pre-NASS' days, many asylum-seekers in particular were left without access to any alternative form of support at all. As a result, many turned to the social services departments of local authorities. They mainly applied to be supported under section 21 of the National Assistance Act 1948, part of the local authorities' 'community care' responsibilities. They also made use, however, of section 17 Children Act. In *MPAX* (also known as the *'Westminster'* case), the Court of Appeal held that local authorities had a duty, in most cases, to support destitute asylum-seekers under the 1948 Act.

12

SOCIAL SERVICES SUPPORT: AN OVERVIEW

The support that can be provided

The support that can be provided by social services derives from various pieces of legislation. The best known is the National Assistance Act 1948. We look individually at the different provisions and the support available at ▶1318–22.

Support can also be provided under the Children Act 1989. We look at the Children Act separately at ▶1322–8.

The restrictions imposed by legislation

Over the years since 1996 and the decision in *MPAX* (see above), the following key legislative changes have been made which have had the result of restricting access to social services support (as well as other support).

1) *Introduction of asylum support*

From April 2000, the asylum support scheme was introduced under the 1999 Act (from 6 December 1999 in the case of 'interim' asylum support provided by local authorities). The effect of this was that the vast majority of asylum-seekers who needed support would be provided with asylum support either by NASS or through local authorities. Asylum support is covered in Chapter 41. That chapter also looks at 'hard cases' support (also introduced under the 1999 Act, ▶see 1381–7) which was brought in as a means of providing a 'safety net' for asylum-seekers who had come to the end of the process and others who had no means of support but, for a number of reasons, did not deserve to be left destitute.

A small number of asylum-seekers are entitled to social services support rather than asylum support. This group contains those who have needs which arise not solely as a result of their lack of funds – this group can still get access to social services support *despite* the exclusion under (2) below (for them, ▶see 1316–8).

2) *'Subject to immigration control' restriction under the 1999 Act*

Some of the duties of local authorities under the social services legislation were amended by the 1999 Act at the same time as the interim asylum support scheme came into force (6 December 1999). The legislation had the effect of excluding access to some forms of social services support where the applicant is 'subject to immigration control' within the meaning of the 1999 Act (s115(9)). This is the same test which applies to exclude claimants from mainstream non-contributory welfare benefits. However, even those who are 'subject to control' but who are in need of assistance not 'solely' on the grounds of destitution, can still access support from social services. For the 'subject to immigration control test', the services to which it applies and the exception to it, ▶see 1315–8 below.

In order to determine whether a person can get social services support, advisers need to consider *both* the restrictions under the 1999 Act *and* the exclusions under the 2002 Act ((3) below).

3) *Exclusions from support: schedule 3 2002 Act*

From 8 January 2003, Schedule 3 of the Nationality, Immigration and Asylum Act 2002 has excluded certain 'classes' of persons from most social services support, certain Children Act support and some interim housing provision. The exclusions in Schedule 3 also apply to asylum support and hard cases support. For the 'classes' of people who are excluded, ▶see below at 1302–6. However, the Schedule 3 exclusions came with two safeguards as follows.

- There is a 'human rights' exception to the exclusions i.e. excluded support must still be provided *if* it is necessary to do so in order to avoid a breach of the applicant's human rights. The human rights exception may apply differently, however, in three separate kinds of case: cases in which it is clear that the applicant must remain in the UK for the time being (▶see 1307–11 including the explanation of the *Adam & Limbuela* decision); cases in which the authorities say that the applicant can return freely to their country of origin (▶see 1311–4); and cases in which local authorities have a dilemma as to whether and how to provide support when an asylum-seeking family has been excluded from support under Schedule 3 (▶see 1325–8, 1354–7). Note that the human rights exception is written in the same terms as that under section 55 2002 Act (▶see 1350–1).

- The 2002 Act made way for the 'Withholding and Withdrawal Regulations' which, quite aside from human rights obligations, give local authorities a power to provide support in the case of *certain* of the excluded classes in *certain* circumstances (▶see 1314–5).

4) *Families who fail to leave the UK voluntarily: new excluded class*

From 1 December 2004, the Asylum and Immigration (Treatment of Claimants etc) Act 2004 added a further 'class' to the list of excluded classes under Schedule 3 ((3) above). The newly excluded class is failed asylum-seekers with dependent children who fail to take reasonable steps to leave the UK voluntarily. This class is outlined, together with the other excluded classes at ▶1303 and ▶see 1305–6. For NASS policy on the procedure used to exclude them, ▶see 1354–7. For the human rights considerations in deciding how/whether they should be supported, ▶see 1325–8.

Exclusions under Schedule 3 of the 2002 Act

12

From 8 January 2003, various 'classes' of people are excluded from social services support and other forms of support. The forms of support which are excluded under section 54 and Schedule 3 2002 Act are listed immediately below. The excluded classes are set out in the table at ▶1303 and further explanation of them is at ▶1302–6. The 'human rights' exception under which these excluded classes can be re-included is summarised at ▶1306. For the 'Withholding and Withdrawal' Regulations, which allow local authorities to provide some support for certain excluded people, ▶see 1314–5.

Which forms of support are excluded under Schedule 3?

The following forms of support are excluded by paragraph 1 of Schedule 3 2002 Act:

- section 21 and 29 National Assistance Act 1948 (accommodation and welfare, ▶1318–20);
- section 45 Health services and Public Health Act 1968 (welfare for the elderly, ▶1321);
- section 21 and Sch 8 to the National Health Service Act 1977 (services for prevention of illness and after care, ▶1321);
- section 17, 23C, 24A or 24B Children Act 1989 (welfare and other services which can be provided in relation to adults, ▶1322 onwards);
- section 188(3) or 204(4) Housing Act 1996 (accommodation pending review or appeal);
- section 2 Local Government Act 2000 (promotion of well-being, ▶1321–2);
- asylum support, interim asylum support or temporary asylum support provided under the 1999 Act or the 2002 Act (Chapter 41);
- 'hard cases' support provided under section 4 1999 Act (▶see 1381–7).

Equivalent or similar social services and Children Act support and interim housing provision which is provided for under legislation specific to Scotland and Northern Ireland is also excluded. This is support under the following provisions: section 12 or 13A Social Work (Scotland) Act 1968 (social welfare services); Article 7 and 15 Health and Personal Social Services (Northern Ireland) Order 1972 (prevention of illness and social welfare); section 29(1)(b) Housing (Scotland) Act 1987 (interim duty to accommodate in case of apparent priority need where review of a local authority decision has been requested); Articles 18 and 35-36 Children (Northern Ireland) Order 1995 (welfare and other services which can be provided in relation to adults); ss22, 29, 30 Children (Scotland) Act 1995 (welfare and other services which can be provided in relation to adults).

Note that support under the Mental Health Act and the Chronically Sick and Disabled Persons Act (▶1320) is not excluded by Schedule 3.

Which classes of person are excluded under Schedule 3?

The excluded classes are set out at paragraphs 4-7A, Schedule 3 2002 Act (▶see table on 1303).

Third and fourth excluded classes under the 2002 Act

At first glance the third excluded class (former asylum-seekers who have failed to cooperate with removal) and the fourth class (non-asylum-seekers unlawfully in the UK) look very similar. 'Asylum-seeker' for these purposes is defined as a person who is 18 or over and who has made either a

CLASSES OF PEOPLE EXCLUDED BY SCHEDULE 3 2002 ACT

Paragraphs 1, 4–7A, Schedule 3 2002 Act

The excluded classes are:

- those who have been granted refugee status by the government of another EEA state (or who are the dependants of persons in the UK who have been granted refugee status by another EEA state) (**first class**);

- those who are nationals of another EEA state (or who are the dependants of a person who is a national of another EEA state) (**second class**);

- former asylum-seekers who have failed to co-operate with removal directions and their dependants (**third class** ▶see 1302–5);

- persons who are in the UK 'in breach of the immigration laws' and who are not asylum-seekers (**fourth class** ▶see 1302–5);

- asylum-seekers with dependant children whose claims have failed, who have exhausted appeal rights and in respect of whom the Secretary of State has issued a certificate stating that they have failed, without reasonable excuse, to leave the UK voluntarily or to put themselves in a position to do so (**fifth class** ▶1305–6).

The fifth class was added from 1 December 2004 by section 9 2004 Act.

However, the exclusions under Schedule 3 do not prevent the provision of any support or assistance to either a British citizen or a child (para. 2, Sch 3 2002 Act).

The third, fourth and fifth classes require a little more explanation, see the text ▶1302–6.

claim to refugee status, or a claim under Article 3 ECHR which is either awaiting determination or in respect of which there is an appeal pending (or an appeal could be brought in time) (see para. 17(1)(2)(3), Schedule 3).

On the face of it, therefore, it appears that, even if a person did not fall within the third class as a failed asylum-seeker who has not cooperated with removal directions, they would still be in the fourth class. This is because the fourth class appears to include anyone who is 'not' an asylum-seeker (i.e. including both those who have never been asylum-seekers *and* those who are no longer asylum-seekers because their appeals have been exhausted). But if the fourth class sweeps up everyone in the third class as well as others, this would mean that there is no point in having the third class at all. This is an unlikely result as it is always assumed that words in legislation were intended to have some effect.

Two possible explanations of the inter-relation between classes three and four are as follows (these issues are likely to be have to be decided by the courts). It is emphasised that the following are only suggested approaches.

12

1) **Both classes apply to former asylum-seekers in principle but 'on arrival' former asylum-seekers are given greater protection** The fourth class only includes applicants who are 'in the United Kingdom in breach of the immigration laws within the meaning of section 11 [2002 Act]'. In order to come within this definition, as well as not having the right of abode or leave and not being exempt from control and not having an EU right to reside in the UK, the applicant must actually be 'in' in the UK (see s11(1) 2002 Act). For these purposes, an applicant who has properly presented themselves on arrival and is granted temporary admission on arrival (rather than entering unlawfully, or entering and then overstaying etc) appears to be treated as not 'in' the UK (see s11(1) 1971 Act as applied by s11(3) 2002 Act).

So, arguably, former asylum-seekers who originally claimed asylum on arrival and who are temporarily admitted so that they do not enter the UK are not treated as 'in' the UK unlawfully and cannot be excluded under the fourth class. Such an asylum-seeker could only be excluded from the relevant forms of support if and when they actually *fail to cooperate with removal directions* and, therefore, come within the third class. It would be understandable that a failed asylum-seeker who had done everything expected of them from the moment they arrived, would be given more protection than an overstayer or an illegal entrant.

Note, of course, that failed asylum-seekers with no children who have exhausted their appeals will not be entitled to asylum support in any event. This is because they are no longer asylum-seekers for asylum support purposes. The real effect of these exclusions for such asylum-seekers is to exclude social services and other support.

Note also that, on the above reading, those who have not claimed asylum, but who have simply been temporarily admitted at port having made another application which could not be determined immediately, could not be excluded from support under Schedule 3. This is because they do not fall into either the third class (because they are not former asylum-seekers, see para. 6(1)(a), Sch 3), or the fourth class (because they are not 'in' the UK).

2) **Only the third class applies to former asylum-seekers** A further possible means of making sense of the third and fourth classes is to view only the third class as applying to former asylum-seekers. The wording of the third class refers to those who were, but who are no longer, asylum-seekers whereas the wording of the fourth class refers simply to those who are 'not' asylum-seekers. While, strictly, both forms of words catch those who claimed asylum and whose appeals have been exhausted (see the definition of asylum-seeker in para. 17, Sch 3), it is perhaps odd that different wording should have been used. It possibly means that the fourth class was not intended to apply to those who have claimed asylum at all, whether they are former asylum-seekers or otherwise. Against this, however, it is possible that the fourth class is intended to catch any applicant

who is unlawfully in the UK, whether they have claimed asylum or not, whereas the third class *only* applies to former asylum-seekers. The other difficulty with this approach is that it might mean that asylum-seekers who are not port applicants could not be excluded at all (because the third class does not apparently apply to those who are not 'in' i.e. who have not 'entered' the UK).

Fifth excluded class: asylum-seeking families who do not leave

The fifth excluded class, introduced by the 2004 Act, has been the subject of intense controversy because of the effect it can have of separating parents from minor children. Cases excluded as falling into the fifth class are often referred to as 'section 9 cases' because this class was inserted into the 2002 Act by section 9 2004 Act. Section 9 came into force on 1 December 2004 and has initially been piloted in Manchester, Leeds, Bradford and parts of London.

People who come within the fifth class Applicants fall into the fifth excluded class if all of the following conditions apply, namely (para. 7A 2002 Act):

- they are still an asylum-seeker for support purposes only because their household includes a dependent child who is under 18 (▶1345);
- the Secretary of State has *certified* that, in his or her opinion, the person has failed, without reasonable excuse, to take reasonable steps to either:
  - leave the UK voluntarily; or
  - place themselves in a position in which they will be able to leave the UK voluntarily; and
- the applicant has received a copy of the Secretary of State's certificate.

The applicant (and their dependants) are excluded from support after a period of 14 days following their receipt of the Secretary of State's certificate.

Purpose of the fifth class The purpose of this class is to exclude from asylum support, social services support and hard cases support, asylum-seekers who have dependent children and who would otherwise be entitled to support as a result. It is designed to encourage families to leave the UK voluntarily and/or to comply with travel documentation procedures which are intended to enable them to return. The measure is part of a concerted assault on asylum-seekers who fail to comply with re-documentation procedures. Section 35 2004 Act provides for the prosecution of those who fail to comply with steps designed to help re-document them (▶see 927).

NASS has drawn up detailed policy for determining when a family has failed to take 'reasonable steps' to leave and to state what constitutes a 'reasonable excuse'. The policy sets out a detailed procedure which should be applied in the lead up to certification. As the policy is drawn up in the context of exclusion from asylum support, it is looked at in Chapter 41 (▶see the table at 1354–7). In the typical case, it appears from the policy that an asylum-seeking family will have their NASS support withdrawn and the local authority is left to carry the can as to what will happen to the family. For the options open to local authorities in exercising their Children Act powers, ▶see below at 1325–8.

The 'human rights' exception to exclusion under Schedule 3

Even if an applicant falls within any of the excluded classes 1–5 above, Schedule 3 does not exclude them from support if it is necessary to provide support to them in order to avoid a breach of (para. 3, Sch 3 2002 Act):

- a person's human rights under the ECHR; or
- a person's rights under the Community Treaties.

It is the 'human rights' exception which is of importance. Section 55(5)(a) 2002 Act makes the same 'human rights' exception in relation to asylum support for people who would otherwise be excluded from asylum support (including temporary asylum support) and hard cases support if they fail to claim asylum 'as soon as reasonably practicable' after their arrival. For details about the 'reasonably practicable' test, ▶see 1350–2 (note the 'reasonably practicable' test also applies to support under section 2 2000 Act, and some interim housing support).

Three different types of case The human rights exception may be approached differently depending on the circumstances of the case. We can divide the different cases into three:

1) cases in which the applicant cannot be expected to return to their country of origin at least for the time being and denial of support will lead to the applicant being destitute in the UK (see immediately below and the decision of the House of Lords, on 3 November 2005, in *R v SSHD ex parte Adam, Limbuela & Tesema* set out in the table which follows ▶1307– 1311);

2) cases in which the applicant can freely return to their country of origin and, if they are without the necessary means, have been offered the funding to do so (▶see 1311–4);

3) cases in which an asylum-seeking family has been excluded from support and an authority needs to consider whether it should provide support for the child or the child and the family together in order to avoid a breach of their human rights (▶see 1325–8).

Aside from the human rights exception, advisers should also consider whether it is worth asking an authority to provide support under the 'Withholding and Withdrawal from Support' Regulations (▶1314–5). Note, however, that these regulations only impose a power (not a duty) to provide support and can only be used where the applicant (1) has a dependent child with them; and (2) is in excluded classes one, two or four.

Human rights exception: cases in which the applicant cannot return

Where an applicant has an undetermined claim that they will persecuted or subject to a breach of their human rights in their own country (or an appeal against a negative decision on such a claim), the issue will generally be: should support be provided in order to prevent a breach of the applicant's human rights by their being in the UK, on the streets, without any form of support?

This will almost always be the question in section 55 cases (at least while the application or appeal is still outstanding). It will also be the question in other cases where it is clear that the applicant will be remaining in the UK at least for the time being perhaps because they have no means of leaving the UK (for example because they have no resources to do so), or because there are practical reasons why they cannot do so (for example lack of travel documentation, no safe route to their country of origin, or personal reasons particular to the applicant). In some cases, applicants may be making further representations to the Home Office as to why they cannot return and should be permitted to stay, or they are awaiting a further Home Office decision on such an application.

In these cases, the Home Office/local authority will generally apply the guidance given in the *Adam* case (see the table immediately below).

THE HUMAN RIGHTS EXCEPTION: DECISION OF THE HOUSE OF LORDS IN *ADAM, LIMBUELA & TESEMA*

References to paragraphs are to the paragraphs of the House of Lords judgment.

Relevance of the decision

All three cases concerned asylum-seekers who were found not to have claimed asylum 'as soon as reasonably practicable' after their arrival in the UK (s55(1) 2002 Act). The issue, therefore, was whether it was necessary to provide support for them:

'...for the purpose of avoiding a breach of [their ECHR] rights' (s55(5)(a) 2002 Act)

This 'human rights exception' in section 55 (for the purposes of asylum support and hard cases support) is in the same terms as the exception contained in paragraph 3, Schedule 3 2002 Act for the purpose of allowing support to be provided when it would otherwise be denied because the applicant falls within one of the excluded classes in Schedule 3.

In principle, the decision of the House of Lords applies to both 'section 55' and 'Schedule 3' exclusion cases, but ▶see 1311–3, for how its relevance may be side-lined in cases in which it cannot be taken for granted that the applicant must stay in the UK for the time being.

12

The decision itself

For practical purposes, the important points and guidance to come from the decision are as follows.

1) The regime which is imposed on late-claiming asylum-seekers under which they are excluded from asylum support under section 55 2002 Act (as well as from other support) and under which they are not permitted to work for at least 12 months while their claims are being considered (▶694–6), can amount to 'treatment' within the meaning of Article 3 ECHR. In principle, therefore, applicants can complain that denying them support may amount to inhuman or degrading treatment within Article 3 (Lord Bingham, para. 6; Lord Scott at paras 67-68 and see Lord Hope at para. 56)

2) The threshold for showing a human rights case is a high one. It is more stringent than the ordinary test for asylum support which is whether a person is likely to become 'destitute' within 14-days, Lord Hope paras 43, 58. The threshold is particularly high because these are not cases which involve the deliberate infliction of pain or suffering. Nevertheless:

'...that threshold may be crossed if a late applicant with no means and no alternative sources of support, unable to support himself, is, by the deliberate action of the state, denied shelter, food or the most basic necessities of life.' (Lord Bingham, para. 7; Baroness Hale, para. 79)

The question is:

'...whether the treatment to which the asylum-seeker is being subjected by the entire package of restrictions and deprivations that surround him is so severe that it can properly be described as inhuman or degrading treatment within the meaning of the article.

...

It is possible to derive from the cases which are before us some idea of the various factors that will come into play in this assessment: whether the asylum-seeker is male or female, for example, or is elderly or in poor health, the extent to which he or she has explored all avenues of assistance that might be expected to be available and the length of time that has been spent and is likely to be spent without the required means of support. The exposure to the elements that results from rough-sleeping, the risks to health and safety that it gives rise to, the effects of lack of access to toilet and washing facilities and the humiliation and sense of despair that attaches to those who suffer from deprivations of that kind are all relevant.' (Lord Hope, paras 58-59)

3) It appears that, if there is evidence that the applicant will be required to sleep rough on an ongoing basis, that may well be enough to show that the threshold under Article 3 is crossed:

'It is not...possible to formulate any simple test applicable in all cases. But if there were persuasive evidence that a late applicant was obliged to sleep in the street, save perhaps for a short and foreseeably finite period, or was seriously hungry, or unable to satisfy the most basic requirements of hygiene, the threshold would, in the ordinary way, be crossed.' (Lord Bingham, para. 9; see also Lord Hope at para. 60)

'For my part, information that a particular asylum seeker was having to sleep out of doors would be a very strong indication that the threshold had been reached.' (Lord Scott, para. 72 and see also para. 71 and the comments of Baroness Hale at para. 78)

'Generally speaking I would suggest that imminent street homelessness would of itself trigger the Secretary of State's requirement under section 6 of the Human Rights Act 1998 to provide support (if only by way of night shelters and basic sustenance...)' (Lord Brown, para. 102)

4) The applicant does not need to show that they are actually or have actually suffered within the meaning of Article 3 in order for the human rights exception to mean that the authorities should step in to provide support to prevent a breach of human rights:

'[the duty under s55(5)(a) arises]...when it appears on a fair and objective assessment of all relevant facts and circumstances that an individual applicant faces an imminent prospect of serious suffering caused or materially aggravated by denial of shelter, food or the most basic necessities of life. Many factors may affect that judgment, including age, gender, mental or physical health and condition, any facilities or sources of support available to the applicant, the weather and time of year and the period for which the applicant has already suffered or is likely to continue to suffer privation.' (Lord Bingham, para. 8, emphasis added; see also Lord Scott at para. 72)

'The key to a proper understanding of section 55(5)(a)...lies in its use of the word "avoid" in the phrase "avoid a breach"...
...
The purpose of section 55(5)(a)...in this context is to enable the Secretary of State to exercise his powers to provide support...before the ultimate state of inhuman or degrading treatment is reached. Once that stage is reached the Secretary of State will be at risk of being held to have acted in a way that is incompatible with the asylum-seeker's Convention rights, contrary to section 6(1) of the 1998 Act...' (Lord Hope, paras 43-44)

'...the wording of section 55(5)(a) shows that its purpose is to prevent a breach from taking place, not to wait until there is a breach and then address its consequences.
...
It may be, of course, that the degree of severity which amounts to a breach of article 3 has already been reached by the time the condition of the asylum-seeker has been drawn to his attention. But it is not necessary for the condition to have reached that stage before the power in section 55(5)(a) is capable of being exercised. It is not just a question of "wait and see"...as soon as the asylum-seeker makes it clear that there is an imminent prospect that a breach of the article will occur because the conditions which he or she is having to endure are on the verge of reaching the necessary degree of severity the Secretary of State has the power...and the duty...to act to avoid it.' (Lord Hope, paras 61-62)

12

5) Attention was also drawn to the particular considerations which may attach to women asylum-seekers:

'If a woman of Mr Adam's age had been expected to live indefinitely in a London car park, without access to the basic sanitary products which any woman of that age needs and exposed to the risks which any defenceless woman faces on the streets at night, would we have been in any doubt that her suffering would very soon reach the minimum degree of severity required under article 3? I think not.' (Baroness Hale, para. 78)

Conceptual part of the decision

The judgments also contain some complex analysis of human rights concepts concerning the positive and negative obligations of the state. This is omitted from the practical points set out above. Essentially, the House of Lords took a more straightforward approach to that taken by the Court of Appeal. It held that, although it is necessary to judge cases on their individual facts, the Article 3 test was not more stringent because the alleged ill-treatment resulted from what was put forward as 'legitimate government policy' to address the problem of late-claiming asylum-seekers. 'Proportionality' considerations could not be introduced by the back-door. The essential issue was whether the treatment resulted from conduct of the state for which it was directly responsible and whether the resulting suffering reached the minimum level of severity required under Article 3 (see Lord Hope at paras 53-55; Baroness Hale at paras 77-78; Lord Brown, paras 89-90, 92-93).

Decision on the facts of the individual cases

All cases have to be judged on their own facts in light of the guidance given by the House of Lords set out above. For illustrative purposes, however, advisers may find it useful to know the brief facts of the three cases before the House of Lords. In all three cases, the first instance judges in the High Court had found in favour of the asylum-seekers i.e. that support was necessary in order to avoid a breach of their human rights. The majority of the Court of Appeal upheld the decision of each judge. The House of Lords unanimously agreed that the Court of Appeal was correct to uphold the first instance decisions (paras 10, 63, 74, 79, 103).

Adam

Mr Adam claimed asylum at the Asylum Screening Unit in Croydon and, on the same day, was excluded from NASS support because he had not claimed as soon as reasonably practicable. For approximately a month, until an injunction was obtained, he was forced to sleep in a sleeping bag in a car park outside the Refugee Council in Brixton. During the day, he would wash himself and his clothes at the Refugee Council and have tea/coffee and hot meals. There was no shelter in the car park so Mr Adam was cold and wet at night and could not sleep. Abuse had been shouted at him and he had been moved on by the police. He had lost weight and was developing a cough and felt that his mental and physical health had worsened. He felt totally humiliated (see paras 30-32).

Limbuela

Mr Limbuela was evicted from NASS accommodation and then spent two nights sleeping rough. During that time he had no money, access to food or washing facilities. He asked the police for a blanket but was not provided with one. He begged for food but was not given anything. He then obtained accommodation for four nights through Migrant Helpline but was then required to leave. At that point and injunction was made granting him support. Had the injunction not been granted, he would have had no choice but to sleep rough and beg for food. Mr Limbuela also had health problems: stomach pains, constipation, problems with his testicles, dizziness, heartburn. He was also afraid to sleep outside because of his experience in Angola of being beaten by the police (see paras 19–21).

Tesema

Mr Tesema obtained an injunction requiring that he be supported when he was on the point of being evicted from his emergency NASS accommodation. He had never slept rough but that would have been the position he would have been in had the injunction not been obtained. He would have also had to beg for money and/or food. Mr Tesema also had medical complaints: earache, backache, pain in his knee all as a result of beatings in Ethiopia. A consultant psychiatrist had reported that Mr Tesema presented with ongoing psychological difficulties of lowering of mood and anxiety. Mr Tesema had stated that, when he was about to be evicted, he had felt traumatised and felt that he may become suicidal. Details were given of the regular attempts made by Mr Tesema to obtain support from the Oromo Community in London as well as from Ethiopian and Eritrean community centres. None had been able to provide him with support (see paras 25–27).

Human rights exception: cases in which it is said that the applicant may return to the country of origin

Where the applicant is able, in principle, to return to their country of origin, local authorities may be able to avoid a breach of the applicant's human rights other than through providing ongoing support. In some cases, the courts have upheld decisions to provide support in order to help the applicant return to their country of nationality. The following three decisions of the Court of Appeal are relevant

1) **London Borough of Lambeth v Grant** In this case the applicant for support was a Jamaican national who had care of three children. She had no leave to be in the UK and was seeking to remain on compassionate grounds outside the immigration rules. She was excluded from support under Schedule 3 because she was in the fourth class (above) of excluded persons. The local authority agreed to provide temporary support but determined that it would be in the best interests of the claimant and her family for them to return to Jamaica. It offered to fund the cost of travel under section 2 Local Government Act 2000 (▶see 1321–2 below). On a short term basis, pending the return of the applicant under that offer (and

pending the Court proceedings), the authority exercised its discretion to provide support under the 'Withholding and Withdrawal of Support' Regulations (▶see below 1314–5). The Court of Appeal held:

- although the applicant was generally excluded from support, the authority was able to use the human rights exception to provide support (under s2 2000 Act) to pay for her return to Jamaica (see paras 24, 31, 47, 50);

- it could use the powers contained in the 'Withholding' Regulations in conjunction with the 2000 Act to achieve that end:

'To my mind there is no reason why, in considering how best to avoid a breach of the Convention rights of Mrs Grant and her children in the *circumstances of this case*, the Council should not decide to use the powers conferred by section 2 of the 2000 Act and the power conferred by Regulation 3(3) of the Withholding Regulations in conjunction with each other, to the extent that it considers necessary to achieve that object.

That is what the Council seeks to do in this case. It takes the view that, in order to avoid a breach of Convention rights, it is necessary to use the power to accommodate only for as long as Mrs Grant is unable (through lack of resources) to return to Jamaica and to use the power to fund travel arrangements so as to enable her to do that.' (paras 50-51)

In the *Grant* case, the Court held that the authority could act in this way *even though* the applicant had not yet received formal notice of the decision from the Home Office refusing to allow her to remain on the grounds of long residence and even though she might try to appeal (paras 4, 25-27, 30-31).

2) ***R (Kimani) v Lambeth LBC*** In an earlier similar case, *Kimani*, the Court of Appeal rejected a challenge to the withdrawal of support under Schedule 3. The challenge was brought on the basis that the applicant ought to be supported in order to remain in the UK until the outcome of an immigration appeal which was being brought on the grounds of Article 8 (family connections to the UK):

'She has been permitted to remain here to pursue an appeal in which she advances *inter alia*, an Article 8 claim, which we consider to be clearly specious. Even if it were not, no infringement of Article 8 would result from requiring her to return to her own country pending the determination of her appeal. There is no impediment to her returning to her own country. A state owes no duty under the Convention to provide support to foreign nationals who are permitted to enter their territory but who are in a position freely to return home.' (*Kimani*, para. 49).

3) ***M v Islington LBC*** The above two cases have to be balanced against the decision in *M*. The most important point made in *M* relates to the ability of local authorities to provide support under the 'Withholding' Regulations (for which see further below). Those powers are available to local authorities, in certain cases, where an applicant falls into one of the excluded classes. They are therefore additional to and separate from the requirement

of the authority to provide support under social services legislation in order to avoid a breach of the applicant's human rights. The decision is nevertheless relevant to the issue addressed in the above two cases.

The facts of *M*, were that the applicant was an overstayer from Guyana who was seeking to remain in the UK on Article 8 grounds. She had care of a daughter (who was a British citizen) and the daughter had contact with her father who had indefinite leave in the UK. The applicant herself was separated from her daughter's father. In relation to her immigration status, the applicant had been granted leave to appeal to the IAT. The local authority maintained an offer of one-way plane tickets (paid for under Children Act powers) to allow the applicant and her daughter to return to Guyana. Islington believed this to be in the child's best interests.

The Court of Appeal in *M* held that the local authority had misunderstood its powers under the Withholding Regulations: under those powers it could continue to provide accommodation to the applicant unless and until she failed to comply with any removal directions. On this basis, the authority was required to reconsider its whole decision (for this aspect, ▶see further below at 1315). *However*, in the course of coming to its conclusions, it seems that the Court's view was that, in order to act consistently with the human rights of all concerned, the authority may be required to continue to provide accommodation at least for the time being. The following parts of the judgments are important.

- The majority of the Court (Waller and Maurice Kay LJJ) noted that there was only a power to provide support under the 'Withholding Regulations'. However, Maurice Kay LJ noted that the appeal was not an obviously hopeless or abusive one (para. 57) and Waller LJ, after stating that the Court would declare that the authority had the power to provide accommodation, said:

  'That does not impose a duty, simply reflecting the ambit of Islington's powers. However, it is right to add that in exercising those powers Islington will have to be aware of their Convention obligations. That, in real terms, may leave them little choice but to offer accommodation.' (para. 81, and see also para. 79)

- Buxton LJ disagreed with the majority of the Court. He held that the 'Withholding' Regulations only allowed the applicant to be provided with support for a very short period of time (the Guidance had indicated ten days). In his view, the authority would have to consider what it should do under the Children Act in order to avoid a breach of the applicant's human rights under Article 8 ECHR. But what is important about his judgment is not the particular power that he thought the authority could act under, but his approach to whether the authority's offer of flight tickets was enough to comply with its duty to respect human rights. He drew attention to the fact that there was an outstanding appeal to the IAT and that the applicant's, the child's and the child's father's human rights were all in issue. He remarked that it would be (see paras 38, 45–49, 52):

12

'...difficult not to see an offer of tickets with an alternative of no accommodation (made not for social reasons but in an attempt to enforce immigration control other than by the issuing of removal directions) as an unjustifiable interference with the article 8 rights of [the applicant] and of the child.'

Withholding and withdrawal of Support Regulations

In addition to the 'human rights' exception to the exclusion from support under Schedule 3 2002 Act (above), the 2002 Act makes way for Regulations to allow local authorities to provide support to certain of the excluded classes (paras 2(1)(c), 8-12, Sch 3 2002 Act). Those Regulations are the Withholding and Withdrawal of Support (Travel Assistance and Temporary Accommodation) Regulations 2002 (the 'Withholding Regulations'). They came into force on 8 January 2003.

Support for those in the first and second excluded classes

The first excluded class under Schedule 3 is those with refugee status in another EEA state. The second excluded class is EEA nationals (▶see above at 1303). The Withholding Regulations allow local authorities themselves to make 'travel arrangements' to allow people in these two classes to return to the relevant EEA state. So, local authorities can pay for them to return. Although the Withholding Regulations do not give local authorities the power to pay for those in the other excluded classes to return, the courts have held that authorities can do this under separate powers (see above).

Where the local authority makes travel arrangements (or is going to make those arrangements) for those who fall into classes one or two, it may provide accommodation to the applicant/s for the period before they travel. Accommodation may only be provided if the person 'has with him' a dependent child. The child can also be accommodated (Regulation 3(1)(2)(4), Withholding Regulations). So, the authority cannot provide accommodation to those in these classes unless travel arrangements are also being made. Note that no cash payments can be made under these powers (Regulation 4(3), Withholding Regulations).

Support for those in the fourth excluded class

The Withholding Regulations give local authorities the power to provide accommodation for people in the fourth excluded class under Schedule 3 2002 Act (Regulation 3(3), Withholding Regulations). The fourth class is people in the UK unlawfully who are not asylum-seekers (▶see 1303 above and see 1302–5). Accommodation can only be provided for those who have a dependent child with them and no cash can be provided (Regulations 3(4), 4(3)). Those in this group are likely to be illegal entrants or overstayers who have no formal right to remain in the UK.

Unlike the power to provide accommodation for those in the first and second excluded classes (above), the power is not restricted to the time during which arrangements are being made for them to leave. However, Regulation 3(3) only allows the authority to make arrangements for the applicant's accommodation provided that the applicant has not 'failed to co-operate with removal directions'.

In *M v Islington LBC*, the Court of Appeal had to decide whether a local authority could provide ongoing accommodation to an applicant within the fourth class given that the Guidance issued by the Secretary of State stated as follows:

'31 Accommodation is purely a temporary measure to allow a person with dependent children to be accommodated pending departure from the UK...

...

32 For those persons returning to EEA Member States, it is preferable if accommodation does not continue for a period of more than a further 5 days from the date the family first presented for support or assistance to the local authority. For those returning to other countries, it is preferable if accommodation does not continue for a period of more than a further 10 days from the date the family first presented for support or assistance to the local authority'.

The Court decided that, despite the Guidance and although the Regulations refer to 'temporary' accommodation in their title, the Regulations gave the authority a power to provide support during the whole period that the applicant was waiting for the immigration authorities to set removal directions (including the period taken for appeals). It was noted by the Court that 'it is common knowledge...that there are many circumstances in which [the wait for removal directions] may last for months or even years' (para. 57). For further details of the circumstances in *M*, ▶see above at 1312–4.

Of course, the Withholding Regulations only provide a power to provide support, there is no absolute duty to do so.

Restrictions under the 1999 Act

As a result of the Immigration and Asylum Act 1999, those who are 'subject to immigration control' are excluded from the most important support which may be provided by social services if they are in need of the services 'solely' as a result of destitution (ss116–117 1999 Act). The test for being 'subject to immigration control' is the same as that which excludes many people from non-contributory welfare benefits.

The following people are 'subject to immigration control' (s115(9) 1999 Act):

- those who need leave to enter or remain in the UK but who do not have it;
- people who have leave which has a condition attached to it that they will not have recourse to public funds;

12

- people given leave as the result of a 'maintenance undertaking' (otherwise known as a 'sponsorship' agreement); and
- people who have leave but only because they are appealing against a refusal to extend leave.

For full details of these four categories, ▶see 1250–5.

The services which are restricted under the 1999 Act are set out in the table below.

SERVICES RESTRICTED BY THE IMMIGRATION AND ASYLUM ACT 1999

(Sections 116–117 1999 Act amended the relevant social services legislation)

The services restricted by the 1999 Act are:

- 'residential accommodation' and the board and services which go with it under section 21 National Assistance Act 1948 (but see the note below);
- arrangements for the 'promotion of the welfare of old people' under section 45 Health Services and Public Health Act 1968;
- 'arrangements by local authorities for the prevention of illness and for care and after-care' under paragraph 2, schedule 8 National Health Service Act 1977;
- 'residential accommodation' (or cash to access such accommodation) and the board and services which go with it under s2 Local Government Act 2000 (this restriction is also the result of s3(1) 2000 Act, ▶see below at 1321–2).

Note

Section 21 National Assistance Act requires local authorities to provide residential accommodation for two classes of people:

1) people who are aged 18 or over and who are in need of care and attention by reason of age, illness, disability, or 'any other circumstance';

2) expectant and nursing mothers who are in need of care and attention.

The restriction under the 1999 Act applies only to the first class. Nursing or expectant mothers who are subject to control may, therefore, still obtain accommodation and support.

'Solely' as a result of destitution

Even though they are both based on the 'subject to immigration control' test, there are two important differences between the welfare benefit exclusions and the exclusion from social services support:

1) under the social services exclusion, applicants are not 're-included' if they fall into certain categories set out in regulations (▶see the table at 1255–8 for those re-included for welfare benefits purposes);

2) *however*, under the social services exclusion, there is a further requirement which needs to be satisfied before people are excluded: an applicant is only excluded from assistance if they are claiming to need it *solely*:

- because they are destitute; or
- because of the physical effects, or anticipated physical effects, of their being destitute.

'Destitute' for these purposes has the same meaning as for asylum support, namely, a person who is without adequate accommodation or the means to obtain it, or who is unable to meet their essential living needs. The government's intention was to reverse the effect of the *'Westminster'* case (above at ▶1299). It is intended that most asylum-seekers and others who are subject to immigration control will not be entitled to social services support unless they are able to show that their needs do not arise solely because of their lack of resources or the effect of their lack of resources (for the meaning of this test, see immediately below).

Meaning of 'solely' as a result of destitution

The first main case to consider the meaning of 'solely because [he or she] is destitute' was *O & Bhika*, which was a case concerning section 21 1948 Act support. The two applicants in that case were not asylum-seekers and would have been on the streets if they were not assisted. They also had fairly pronounced illnesses and so, they argued, their needs for care and attention were not caused 'solely' by their destitution. They said that they should be able to add the fact that they had no resources to the fact of their illnesses which, in combination, resulted in the authority being required to provide support for them.

The Court of Appeal agreed with the applicants. It stated that, in order to satisfy the test, it is not necessary that the person's needs arise completely independently of their destitution. Therefore, they do not have to show that, even if they were not destitute, they would still qualify for assistance. It was accepted that it was enough if the applicant could show that their needs were made 'materially more acute' by reasons other than lack of resources (or the ability to provide for themselves through not having permission to work). Needs could be made more acute by, for example, age, illness or disability. A person who is significantly disabled will be likely to have a more 'acute' experience of homelessness and be less well able to fend for themselves than an able-bodied person.

The next question the courts had to consider was whether the above reasoning also enabled asylum-seekers to obtain social services support, even though they might otherwise get support from NASS (see immediately below).

Asylum-seekers eligible for social services support

Having decided (above) the essential test for obtaining social services support for those subject to immigration control, the courts had to consider whether some asylum-seekers may also get social services support instead of asylum support. In *NASS v Westminster*, the House of Lords confirmed that social service departments are responsible for providing

12

support under section 21 1948 Act to certain adult asylum-seekers with care needs. This has been particularly important for certain asylum-seekers with care needs who have wished to avoid dispersal.

So, a local authority will be required to provide services to a person who is subject to immigration control (whether they are an asylum-seeker or not) if their needs are, to any material extent, made worse by illness or some other factor beyond destitution. A local authority (rather than NASS) will have to provide accommodation for a destitute asylum-seeker with a disability *even though* that disability would not normally mean that an authority would have to provide residential accommodation for them (see the decision of the Court of Appeal in *Mani*). In *Mani*, the test of being in need of care and attention not solely due to destitution was satisfied in relation to a man whose right leg was half the length of his left leg because of a congenital disability. Other examples of circumstances in which the test may be satisfied are where applicant is HIV positive (*R (J) v Enfield LBC*) and, in principle at least, in relation to a victim of domestic violence (see *R (Khan) v Oxfordshire CC* (CA)).

Where a disabled adult asylum-seeker had two children, the Court of Appeal ruled that the local authority had a duty to the adult but this duty did not extend to supporting the children. NASS had to help with support for the children and, therefore, a joint approach was needed (*R (O) v Haringey LBC*, CA).

What social services support can be obtained?

The support which can be obtained from social services is spread out over various pieces of legislation which we now look at. We have already looked at the 'withholding and withdrawal of support' regulations (above). The most important is the National Assistance Act 1948. Much of the legislation needs to be read together with guidance issued by the Department of Health called either 'directions' or 'approvals' (the most important is Local Authority Circular, 'LAC', (93) 10 together with its appendices). For applying and being assessed for services, ▶see below at 1322. Children Act support is dealt with separately at ▶1322–8.

Section 21 National Assistance Act 1948

Local authorities have a duty to provide residential accommodation under section 21 1948 as part of their overall 'community care' responsibilities. The basic conditions for qualifying for support are that the applicant is:

- in 'need of care and attention' which is 'not otherwise available';
- *either* 18 years or over and in 'need of care and attention' by reason of age, illness, disability *or* 'any other circumstance', or is an 'expectant' or 'nursing' mother; and
- 'ordinarily resident' in the area of the local authority approached for assistance, or of no settled residence, or not ordinarily resident in the area of that local authority but in 'urgent need' of accommodation.

The requirement that the care and attention is 'not otherwise available' indicates that the service is one of last resort. Aside from the case of expectant or nursing mothers, the 'need for care and attention' must arise for one of the given reasons. The reason of 'age' is applied to the elderly. There is no definition of 'illness' or 'disability' for these purposes. However, there is policy guidance that services should be made available to those whose need for them arises by reason of alcohol or drug misuse (see LAC (92)12 and LAC (93) 2). The 1948 Act does not define 'ordinarily resident' but official guidance on the term can be found in LAC (93) 7. For the general meaning which has been given to 'ordinarily resident' by the courts, ▶see 1274.

The main purpose of section 21 is the provision of residential accommodation, although other support such as food, board, laundry and personal hygiene facilities may be provided as part of a package together with the accommodation. The courts have decided that an authority has no power to provide other services and support, for example, food or vouchers without also providing accommodation. A person does not have to be imminently homeless in order to become eligible for accommodation and the support connected to it under section 21. Where a person who has no resources, continues have a roof over their head, but not the means to continue to pay their rent or otherwise provide for themselves, an authority is bound to consider whether, looking at the person's overall position, it should take responsibility for them by providing alternative accommodation and services (see *Gorenkin*).

Residential accommodation and the services provided in connection with it under this section are restricted for those who are 'subject to immigration control' (see above). In order to obtain support, such applicants must, therefore, not be in need of care and attention *solely* because they are destitute (above at ▶1316–8).

Section 29 National Assistance Act 1948

In order to qualify for services under this provision, a person needs to satisfy all of the following requirements. They must be:

- over 18;
- ordinarily resident (▶1274) in the area of the authority approached for help;
- blind or deaf or dumb or suffering from a mental disorder of any description; or substantially and permanently handicapped by 'illness, injury, congenital deformity'; and
- in need of services to 'promote' their 'welfare'.

The services which may be provided include:

- advice and social support;
- facilities for social rehabilitation and adjustment to disability;

- occupational, social, cultural and recreational facilities, and, where appropriate, payments for work undertaken by the service users;
- holiday homes;
- free or subsidised travel;
- assistance in finding accommodation;
- hostel accommodation and board and other amenities for those undertaking occupational activities in a workshop provided as part of occupational facilities.

Services are *not* restricted for those who are 'subject to immigration control' (see above).

Section 2 Chronically Sick and Disabled Persons Act 1970

In order to qualify for services under this provision, the person needs to be:

- ordinarily resident (▶1274) in the area of the authority approached for services;
- blind or deaf or dumb or suffering from mental disorder of any description; or substantially and permanently handicapped by 'illness, injury, congenital deformity'; and
- in need of any of the services listed below.

The services which may be provided include the following: practical assistance in the home (cleaning, cooking etc); provision of or assistance with getting TV, radio, library facilities, hi-fi, or computers; recreational/educational facilities; assistance with travel; adaptation of the home to make it more safe and comfortable for the person's needs; assistance in taking holidays (including funding the cost of the holiday in appropriate cases); provision of meals at home or elsewhere; provision of or assistance with obtaining a telephone and any special equipment needed to operate it (loud bell, flashing signal etc). People may qualify for support under this provision regardless of their age.

Services are *not* restricted for those who are 'subject to immigration control' (see above). Note that support under this provision is also not excluded by Schedule 3 2002 Act.

Section 117 Mental Health Act 1983

In order to qualify for support under these provisions, the person may be of any age but must have been compulsorily detained under the Mental Health Act. The services which may be provided are unlimited but are directed towards after-care until the local health authority or social services authority decides that the person is no longer in need of services.

Services are *not* restricted for those who are 'subject to immigration control' (see above). Note that support under this provision is also not excluded by Schedule 3 2002 Act.

Section 45 Health Services and Public Health Act 1968

The purpose of this provision is to make services available to promote 'the welfare of old people'. 'Old people' is not defined but typically provided for are the housebound, those living alone, the bereaved, those about to be discharged from hospital, and other persons over 75 who are living in the community. The services which may be provided include meals and recreational facilities, assistance in finding accommodation, social work support and advice, home help and adaptation of property. Other services may be provided with the individual approval of the Secretary of State.

Services are restricted for those who are 'subject to immigration control' (see above). However, those who qualify for services are likely to pass the test that they are not in need of assistance 'solely' because they are destitute.

Schedule 8 National Health Service Act 1977

Services may be provided for people in order to prevent illness, to care for people suffering from an illness and to look after them after they have been suffering from illness. Services include day centres, social services support and recreational facilities. Services are restricted for those who are 'subject to immigration control' (see above). However, those who qualify for services are likely to pass the test that they are not in need of assistance 'solely' because they are destitute.

Section 2 Local Government Act 2000

This provides a power for local authorities to do anything which they consider is likely to promote the 'improvement of the social well-being of their area'. This includes the power to give financial assistance to any person and to 'provide staff, goods, services or accommodation' to any person (s2(4)(a)(f) 2000 Act).

Although the 1999 Act did not expressly cover section 2 2000 Act, section 2 has its own in-built restriction in section 3(1) of the Act. Section 3(1) states that the section 2 powers do not allow a local authority to do anything which they are not permitted to do as a result of a prohibition contained in other legislation. Therefore, in *R (Khan) v Oxfordshire County Council*, the Court of Appeal held that, although section 2 had a 'broad purpose' which should not be narrowly interpreted and that although an authority had a 'wide discretion to exercise its powers to promote well-being', the 1999 Act restrictions imposed on section 21 National Assistance Act also restricted the powers under section 2. The Court confirmed that this meant that the power in section 2 could not be used to provide accommodation to people who could not be provided with accommodation under section 21 because of the restriction on providing accommodation to those subject to immigration control whose needs arise 'solely' as a result of destitution (▶see 1316–8). Similarly, section 2 could not be used to provide cash in order for the applicant to obtain that accommodation for themselves, or to

12

provide other services in connection with the accommodation (see paras 43 and 50 of the decision of the Court).

However, the Court of Appeal confirmed that there were still some services which could be provided under section 2 2000 Act which were not subject to the 1999 Act restriction. These were services which were not provided in connection with accommodation, for example support in order to buy clothes (see paras 57–58).

Note that asylum-seekers are also excluded from section 2 support if they fail to claim asylum 'as soon as reasonably practicable' (s55(3)(4)(c), ▶see 1350–2 for this test). This exclusion is also subject to the general human rights exception (s55(5)(a) 2002 Act).

Community care assessments

Where a person who may be in need of any of the community care services comes to the attention of a local authority, the authority is under a duty to carry out an assessment of the needs of that person for those services and decide whether the needs 'call for' the provision of services.

In deciding on what provision should be made, the authority must have regard to the nature and extent of the need identified and may also have regard to the priorities of the community more generally. To a more limited extent, an authority may also have regard to its own resources (*Barry*). There are some situations where the consequences of not making provision to meet the need is so severe for the person concerned that an authority could not reasonably fail to provide the service.

Once the process of assessment has been completed and it has been decided what services should be provided, the arrangements for making those services available are set out in a 'care plan'. It should be noted that, if the need for services is urgent, as may well be the case for those who are affected by immigration control, then it is possible for those services to be provided on an emergency basis before the process of assessment and the drawing up of a care-plan has been completed (see s47(5), 1990 Act).

CHILDREN ACT 1989

Both unaccompanied minors and families with children who do not have access to welfare benefits or asylum support, may be provided with support from a local authority under the Children Act 1989. Most asylum-seeking families will be entitled to asylum support and will not need to rely on the Children Act. Below we look at the support which may be provided. *However*, there are important circumstances in which a local authority can deny support. These restrictions are derived both from legislation and case law (▶see below at 1325, 1328).

Note that, in some cases, the courts have indicated that, where a local authority assesses that it is in the best interests of the child, part of the support it provides may be to fund the child/family to return to their country of origin. As the case of *M* demonstrates, however, the authority will have to carefully consider the human rights implications of taking this course (▶see above 1312–4).

Unaccompanied children Unaccompanied child asylum-seekers and other unaccompanied children may be supported under section 20 Children Act.

Children and families The main power which allows local authorities to provide support for the family of the child as well as the child is section 17. This is because section 17 places local authorities under a duty to promote the upbringing of children in need by their families where that is consistent with promoting the child's welfare. Section 17 states that any service which is provided under it may be provided for family members of the child as well as the child.

Applying to the authority There is no set way in which an application must be made to the local authority. A local authority to which representations are made about a child, should make an assessment to see whether they are 'in need' and, if so, what support should be provided in order to meet those needs. Assessments are referred to in section 17 and Schedule 2 of the Act and are subject to guidance.

The provision of support

Section 17 Children Act requires local authorities to 'safeguard and promote' the welfare of children within their area who are 'in need' (see below) by providing a range and level of services which are appropriate to the child's needs.

Section 20 Children Act allows a local authority to provide accommodation for a child who is 'in need' as a result of there being no person with parental responsibility to care for them, their being lost or abandoned or the person who was caring for them being prevented from providing the child with suitable accommodation.

Meaning of 'in need'

A child is 'in need' if they are disabled , or if unless services are provided:

- the child is unlikely to achieve or to maintain, or to have the opportunity of achieving or maintaining, a reasonable standard of physical or mental health or development; or

- the physical or mental health or development of the child is likely to be significantly impaired or further impaired.

The 'development' of the child can mean the child's physical, intellectual, emotional, social or behavioural development. Clearly, a child whose parents are destitute and who is without other means of support, is likely to satisfy the above conditions unless support is provided by the local author-

12

ity. A child is 'disabled' for these purposes if they are 'blind, deaf or dumb or suffers from a mental disorder…or is substantially and permanently handicapped by illness, injury or congenital deformity'.

The support, which may be provided under the Children Act to the child in need and to the family of the child includes both accommodation and support to meet living needs. The support may be by giving assistance in kind or the authority may provide cash.

Age disputes

Unaccompanied child asylum-seekers continue to be supported under the Children Act. In some cases, an issue may arise over the applicant's age i.e. as to whether they are actually under-18. In conducting age assessments, authorities will take into account the following guidelines given by the High Court in *R (B) v Merton LBC* (see also NASS Policy Bulletin, 33):

- in obvious cases, there will be no need for prolonged enquiry – except in a clear case authorities should not make a decision based solely on the person's appearance;
- in less clear cases, a personal history should be taken from the applicant;
- the applicant's appearance, behaviour and credibility of their account will all reflect upon each other and be relevant;
- where credibility is in doubt, questions designed to test the applicant's credibility will have to be asked;
- concepts of onus of proof are best avoided;
- the applicant should have a reasonable opportunity of responding to the concerns of the authority;
- the authority must make its own decision, it cannot just rubber-stamp a decision made by the Home Office as to age;
- if the authority decides that a person claiming to be a child is not under 18, reasons should be given.

Further guidance on age assessments was given by the High Court in the case of *R (T) v Enfield*. For details about lawful age assessment processes in the context of the child's immigration application and possible detention, ▶see 688–91.

When the child reaches the age of 18

When a local authority has provided support for a child, it may continue to Ohave duties to them even after they reach the age of 18. The most important duties are in relation to children who have been 'looked after' by the local authority. Unfortunately the situation has been complicated because the definition of 'looked after' changed on 7 November 2002 (see s116(2) Adoption and Children Act 2002 amending s22(1) Children Act). Before 7 November 2002, children were 'looked after' by a local authority if they were provided with *any services*. Therefore children were 'looked after' whether they were supported under section 17 or section 20 Children Act. From 7 November 2002, children accommodated under section 17 are not 'looked after'.

The upshot is that if the authority has looked after the child before 7 November 2002 under section 17, or section 20, then when the young person reaches 18, the authority may owe them a duty to provide them with any necessary accommodation and support to ensure that they can continue with their education or begin work. This may include paying for educational equipment (books etc) and travel expenses (see ss24-24B Children Act as amended by Children (Leaving Care) Act 2000).

Even if the authority claims to have only been looking after an unaccompanied minor under section 17 after 7 November 2002, it is arguable that such support should have been provided under section 20 and so the authority is under the same duty as above (and see *R (Behre) v Hillingdon LBC*).

Following the Children (Leaving Care) Act 2000, authorities are also required to carry out assessments of those leaving their care with a view to determining what advice, assistance and support is required when the young person is no longer being looked after. The authority should develop a 'pathway plan' for them, keep in touch with them and appoint a personal adviser to help keep the young person's situation under review.

Where an applicant is still an asylum-seeker when they become 18, NASS will normally pay the local authority the costs of supporting the young person so that they can remain living in the same accommodation and in the area of the authority.

Section 9 2004 Act 'exclusion' cases and the Children Act

Asylum-seeking families will not generally need to turn to the Children Act because they will normally be provided with asylum support. They continue to be treated as 'asylum-seekers' for asylum support purposes even after the conclusion of the asylum appeals process (▶see 1345). However, following the introduction of section 9 2004 Act (new class of applicant excluded from support under Schedule 3 2002 Act), NASS have been withdrawing support from 'end-of-immigration-process' asylum-seeking families if they fail to take reasonable steps to leave the UK *(for details of NASS policy and procedure on this, ▶see 1354–7)*. The Children Act support *which may be available to adults* is also excluded under Schedule 3 when an applicant falls into one of the excluded classes. Authorities are therefore left in a difficult position and have to think carefully about what support they can provide in order to avoid a breach of the applicants' human rights (below).

The British Association of Social Workers made its views known in a press statement issued on 5 August 2005:

12

'The [Association] deplores the implementation of Section 9 of the Asylum and Immigration Act 2004. Whilst we appreciate that difficult decisions sometimes need to be made about immigration and deportation, as long as individuals remain in the UK they must have their human rights respected. It is inhumane to withdraw all means of basic support from children and their families rendering them destitute.'

What are the authority's options in section 9 cases?

In a typical case, the family will be excluded from NASS support after the Home Office has certified the case so that the family falls into the fifth excluded class under Schedule 3 (▶see 1305–6 above). The local authority should be kept informed during the whole period of the 'section 9' process and copies of the various letters at stages 1-5 of the procedure (▶see 1354–7) should be copied to the local Director of Social Services. Once the family has been excluded (and any appeal to the Asylum Support Adjudicator has failed), the difficulties for the authority and the options available are as follows.

- The authority may consider providing support for the child alone under either section 20 or section 31 Children Act. These powers are not excluded under Schedule 3 and so the authority could consider trying to use them. However, section 20 requires that, generally, the child's wishes are taken into account. It also enables a parent to remove their child from local authority accommodation after they have been taken into care.

- The authority might opt to take the child into care under section 31 but before it can do that it would need to show that the child is suffering or is likely to suffer significant harm as a result of the care (or lack of it) being provided by the parent. The authority also needs to obtain a court order in order to take this step.

- If the authority provides no support to the child, then the child, although with their family, will be without accommodation and food which is very likely to be contrary to Article 3 ECHR.

- Any decision to provide support for the child alone will mean separation of parents and child, not because the parents are a danger to the child or because they do not wish to care for them, but because they lack the means to do so. Such decisions are likely amount to an interference with the right to respect for family life under Article 8 ECHR as well as to raise serious issues under the general 'welfare principle' in section 1(1) Children Act.

- If the authority concludes that taking the child into care will amount to an unjustifiable interference with human rights, then the authority will be able to provide (otherwise excluded) support in order to avoid the human rights breach. This would re-open the door to allow the authority to use the powers under section 17 to provide support for the family.

The human rights considerations in these cases are more likely to arise under Article 8 (in the sense of family separation as above), than Article 3 (as a result of the parents being left destitute on the streets as in *Adam &*

Limbuela). This is because, in order to be excluded under the fifth class in Schedule 3, the family will have already failed to take steps to leave the UK when it has been judged that they are able to do. If the family subsequently take the steps required of them, Article 3 issues will more readily arise.

In relation to the Article 8 issue, guidance issued by NASS to its case-workers, to help them to determine whether it is necessary to continue to provide support in order to avoid a breach of Article 8 in section 9 cases, is set out in the table below.

WITHDRAWAL OF SUPPORT TO ASYLUM-SEEKING FAMILIES: HOME OFFICE GUIDANCE ON ARTICLE 8 ISSUES

The following guidance is contained in instructions for caseworkers issued by NASS on 15 November 2004. It sets out the factors which NASS officers should take into account in deciding whether it would be contrary to Article 8 ECHR to withdraw support from an asylum-seeking family which has failed to take reasonable steps to leave the UK (para. 7A, Schedule 3 2003 Act inserted by section 9 2004 Act).

It may be that local authority social workers will have regard to similar factors although they will be far less well-placed to judge any weight to be attached to the prejudice to immigration control by the family's failure to take steps to leave.

'Will the withdrawal of support constitute an interference and, if so, can that be justified (the Article 8 balance)

8.16 In all cases, even in those when you do not believe that Article 8 rights are engaged, you should carry out an Article 8 balance. The following may be relevant (under both heads depending on the facts) as to whether there is an interference (but all cases must be considered on their own facts):

i) whether the family can return home…;

ii) the number and ages of any children;

iii) any physical or mental impairment of any member of the family;

iv) whether there are any elderly members of the family;

v) whether there are one or two parents;

vi) the length of time it will take for a travel document to be issued (if one has been applied for) or other arrangements to be made for return.

8.17 If there is an interference caseworkers need to decide whether it is both necessary and proportionate to the legitimate aim. Relevant factors to consider here are:

i) the need to maintain the integrity of the immigration and asylum system;

ii) the consequences of the parents' refusal to take steps (this could either be steps to return home, or steps to acquire documents)(i.e. removal may be postponed indefinitely);

12

> (iii) the social consequences for those concerned, and for the wider community, of having a group of people with no settled status;
>
> (iv) the impact on social cohesion of families with no right to remain staying in the country at public expense and not taking reasonable steps to leave;
>
> (v) the fact that the family have been told in detail the likely consequences of a refusal to return/to cooperate with documentation.'

Limitations on support under the Children Act

As well as contesting that the child is really 'in need' etc, local authorities may also refuse support under the Children Act on any of the following bases.

Extent of the duty under section 17 of the Children Act

In *A, W & G*, the House of Lords had to consider the nature of the duty to provide assistance under section 17. By a majority, the Court ruled that section 17 creates a general or 'target' duty in relation to promoting the welfare of children in need in the community. It does not create a specific, enforceable duty to provide services to a particular person. This means that section 17 does not impose an absolute duty on authorities to provide accommodation and services in accordance with the needs of the family which have been assessed. This has given local authorities a latitude in how they perform their duties.

Asylum-seeking families with disabled children

In *R (A) v NASS*, the Court of Appeal held that the duty to provide accommodation and support to meet the needs of a destitute asylum-seeking family with disabled children rested with NASS and not the local authority under section 17 Children Act. While NASS has a duty to provide support to the family, the local authority should carry out an assessment in order to determine whether the child needs any additional care or support under the Children Act.

HEALTH CARE

Access to national health service (NHS) care needs to be looked at in two parts. First, we look at access to hospital treatment (▶immediately below). Then we look at access to services provided by GP practices and help with paying certain fixed medical fees such as for prescription charges and dental fees (▶see 1333–5).

For the rules about coming to the UK as a medical visitor who is paying privately for medical care, ▶see 230–2.

In certain, very limited, cases, the Home Office may grant leave to people to stay in the UK in order to obtain treatment because to return them would be contrary to their human rights (▶see 809–19). For policy and procedures where a person indicates that they may commit self-harm or suicide if removed, ▶996–8 (▶see also 995–6).

For Home Office policy about the grant of leave outside the rules for those caring for relatives or friends in the UK, ▶see 232–5.

Hospital and connected treatment

The basic principle set out in the National Health Service (Charges to Overseas Visitors) Regulations 1989 (as amended) is that the NHS will charge and recover payment for treatment provided to 'overseas' visitors (reg. 2). An 'overseas visitor' is someone who is not 'ordinarily resident' in the UK (reg. 1(2)).

In *Reffell*, the Court of Appeal indicated that the meaning of 'ordinarily resident' for these purposes had to be looked at in the context of the regulations relating to charges and that the meaning given to it in *Shah* (▶see 1274) could not be applied in the same way. *Shah* refers to 'ordinary residence' as living lawfully in the UK voluntarily and for a settled purpose as part of the regular order of the person's life. *Reffell* involved a young Nigerian who had come to the UK as a medical visitor for a kidney transplant and further dialysis in the meantime. The private funds dried up. The court rejected his argument that, because he was living in the UK for the settled purpose of obtaining medical treatment, he was 'ordinarily resident'.

Accordingly, it seems that non-British citizens and those who do not have indefinite leave in the UK are vulnerable to charges for hospital treatment as 'overseas visitors' unless they fall within the exemptions (see the table below). The exemptions were tightened up from 1 April 2004 and the government plans to bring primary care (GPs) more into line with restrictions on access to hospital treatment (▶see 1333).

Note, however, that even where there is no exemption from charges, the court in *Reffell* did accept that a health authority always has a discretion whether or not to withhold treatment if payment, or an undertaking to pay, is not made in advance. In a case where lack of treatment will inevitably lead to the need for more expensive emergency treatment (which the health authority must provide, see the table below) then a failure to provide the initial treatment may be challengeable by judicial review. It is notable that, in this context, a 2003 consultation paper issued by the Department of Health states:

'2.8 The Regulations place the responsibility of establishing whether a person is ordinarily resident on the hospital providing treatment...

...

12

2.9 Ideally this process should take place before any treatment begins. But it is important to note that treatment that a health professional considers to be immediately necessary to save life or avoid a pre-existing condition from worsening should not be delayed just because there are doubts about whether the patient may be chargeable...' (*Proposed Amendments to the National Health Service (Charges to Overseas Visitors) Regulations 1989: A Consultation*, Department of Health, 28 July 2003)

Exemption

Under the above Regulations, treatment can still be provided to 'overseas visitors' for free in the following four broad situations :

1) certain kinds of *treatment* are exempt from charges;

2) there are a number of *groups of people* who are specifically exempted from charges under the regulations;

3) a number of groups of people are allowed free treatment *for medical conditions which arise* during their time in the UK;

4) there are 'exceptional humanitarian reasons' which justify granting an exemption.

These categories are set out in more detail in the table below.

ACCESS TO FREE HOSPITAL TREATMENT

Access to free hospital treatment is taken for granted by most people. For those from abroad, it cannot be taken for granted. Detailed regulations set out when charges can be made: National Health Service (Charges to Overseas Visitors) Regulations 1989 (as amended by Regulations in 1991, 1994, 2004 and 2005).

This table summarises those regulations and sets out the circumstances in which people are *exempt* from charges even though they are an 'overseas visitor'.

Particular forms of treatment which are exempt from charges

The following services are exempt from charges (regulation 3 and Sch 1):

- treatment provided at a hospital accident and emergency department or a casualty department (up until the applicant is accepted as an in-patient);

- treatment provided at a 'walk-in' centre which is similar to treatment given at an accident and emergency department;

- family planning services;

- treatment for any of the following diseases: cholera, food poisoning, plague, relapsing fever, smallpox, typhus, acute encephalitis, acute poliomyelitis, amoebic dysentery, anthrax, bacillary dysentery, diphtheria, leprosy, leptospirosis, malaria, measles, meningitis, meningococcal septicaemia, mumps, ophthalmianeonatorum, paratyphoid fever, rabies, rubella, scarlet fever, tetanus, tuberculosis, typhoid fever, viral haemorrhagic fever, viral hepatitis, whooping cough, yellow fever, salmonella infections, staphyloccal infections likely to cause food poisoning and severe acute respiratory syndrome (see Sch 1 to the Regulations);

- treatment for sexually transmitted diseases (either at a special clinic or by a referral from such a clinic) *but*, in the case of HIV infection, the only services exempt from charge are diagnosis and the counselling associated with the result;

- services provided to those detained under the Mental Health Act 1983; and

- psychiatric treatment required by a court as part of a probation order.

Groups of people who are exempted from charges

The following are the main groups of people who are exempt from charges (regulations 4, 4A, 6, Sch 2):

- those present in the UK for the purpose of employment (with a UK based employer) or self-employment;

- those present in the UK for the purpose of taking a full-time course of study which is either substantially funded by the UK government or lasts for at least six months;

- those present in the UK for the purpose of taking up permanent residence here;

- those who have lived lawfully in the UK for a period of at least a year immediately before the time when they receive the relevant treatment *unless* they were previously granted leave as a private medical visitor (note: (1) people are exempt from the time they qualify under this exemption even if they have previously been charged for the same continuing course of treatment; (2) people are also exempt for the remainder of a course of treatment that began to be provided on the basis that no charge would be made; see regulation 4(2)(3));

- those accepted as refugees, or who have applied for refugee status and their application has not yet been decided;

- those who have, at any time, had ten years' continuous lawful residence in the UK and who are now in employment overseas which has lasted for less than five years;

- those who work in another EEA state and who pay national insurance contributions in the UK;

- EEA nationals (or those accepted as refugees or stateless persons in other EEA states) who have been referred to the UK for treatment (they should have documentation that demonstrates that they are insured for healthcare);

- those who are in prison or who are detained under the 1971 Act;

- those who can obtain particular services because the UK has a reciprocal agreement with any of the following countries/territories which allows referral to the UK for specific treatment: Anguilla, Austria, Barbados, British Virgin Islands, Bulgaria, Czech Republic, Falkland Islands, Gibraltar, Guernsey and its

12

Bailiwick, Hungary, Iceland, Isle of Man, Israel, Jersey, Malta, Montserrat, New Zealand, Poland, Romania, Russian Federation, St Helena, Slovak Republic, Sweden, Turks and Caicos Islands, USSR (excluding Estonia, Latvia, Lithuania and the Russian Federation) and Yugoslavia (see Sch 2 to the Regulations);

- those receiving a UK state retirement pension who live at least six months per year in the UK and who are not registered as resident in any other EEA state;

- those who are part of NATO armed forces where the treatment required cannot easily be provided by the person's own armed forces' medical services; and

- the spouse, civil partner or child of a person in any of the above groups.

Also exempt are: certain health volunteers; those employed on ships/vessels registered in the UK; those receiving benefits or pensions under a personal injuries scheme or a service pension; diplomats; members of HM forces; certain crown servants; British Council or Commonwealth War Graves Commission employees and certain people who are working in UK government funded employment.

People who are exempt from charges for treatment for medical conditions which arise during their time in the UK

There will be no charge for services provided to treat medical conditions which arise during the course of the person's stay in the UK if the patient falls into any of the following groups (regulation 5 and Sch 2):

- EEA nationals, refugees or stateless persons who are resident in an EEA state and the member or the family of any one of them;

- those who have, at any time, had not less than ten years' continuous lawful residence in the UK (or who have given ten years' continuous service as a Crown servant and who are receiving a state pension) and who are in receipt of a UK state pension, and the spouse, civil partner or child of such a person;

- those who have, at any time, had not less then ten years' continuous lawful residence in the UK and who are resident in another EEA state, or a country or territory (excluding Israel) that is listed in Schedule 2 to the Regulations (these countries/territories, which have reciprocal arrangements with the UK, are listed above under 'Groups of people who are exempted from charges') and the spouse, civil partner or child of such a person;

- those who are resident in a country or territory (excluding Israel), that is listed in Schedule 2 to the Regulations (these countries/territories, which have reciprocal arrangements with the UK, are listed above under 'Groups of people who are exempted from charges');

- those who do not have enough resources to pay the charge and who are nationals of countries which are contracting parties to the European Convention on Social and Medical Assistance 1954 (the only non-EEA contracting party is Turkey).

Exemption from charges for exceptional humanitarian reasons

Where *all* of the following conditions are met, the Secretary of State may, on the application of the patient, decide to grant an exemption in relation to a particular course of treatment (regulation 6A):

- the overseas visitor has been granted leave to enter the UK for a course of treatment (for the rules concerning private medical visitors to the UK, ▶see 230–2);
- the treatment is not available in the applicant's home country;
- arrangements have been made for the applicant's and their family's accommodation;
- arrangements have been made for the return of the applicant and their family to their home country when the course of treatment ends; and
- the Secretary of State considers that there are 'exceptional humanitarian reasons' which justify granting an exemption.

Family members of people in this category are also exempt from charges for any services provided to them in order to treat a condition arising during their stay in the UK (regulation 5(f)).

Note

The Department of Health website contains information on treatment for overseas visitors (see www.publications.doh.gov.uk/overseasvisitors). The Department has also issued Guidance to NHS Trust Hospitals on 'Implementing the Overseas Visitors Hospital Charging Regulations' which can be downloaded from the same website.

Primary health care – GPs and others

The above services provided through hospitals are known as 'secondary' health care, provision. Treatment provided by GPs, dentists etc is known as 'primary' care. GPs are not presently subject to the above rules about charging for treatment. However, the government has made it clear that it intends to change that. It proposes to bring free primary services more in line with free secondary services. In the foreword to the consultation paper, *Proposals to Exclude Overseas Visitors from Eligibility to Free NHS Primary Medical Services*, May 2004, the Minister states:

'We want to make it clear to overseas visitors that whilst they will continue to be entitled to receive emergency or immediately necessary treatment, free of charge, under these proposals they would not be eligible for other free NHS primary medical services. We would like to be similarly clear that failed asylum seekers will not be eligible for free routine NHS primary medical services.'

So, under the proposals, failed asylum-seekers and many 'overseas visitors' who do not fall within exemptions similar to those set out in the table above, may be excluded from most primary (i.e. GP etc) care as well as general hospital treatment.

Access to GP services

People get access to primary care either by approaching a practice directly in order to register or by contacting their local 'Primary Care Trust' which

12

can then allocate them to a practice. GPs practices have a discretion to accept or register people as patients although, if they reject them, they must have 'reasonable grounds' for doing so which do not relate to their race, gender, social class, age, religion, sexual orientation, appearance, disability or medical condition. People can be registered as either permanent patients or, if they have lived in the area for less than three months, temporary patients.

So, at present, practices may offer treatment to all UK residents and to 'overseas visitors' from any country but they may also reject them. *However*, a practice must offer free treatment to anyone who asks for it if, in the professional opinion of the doctor, that treatment is 'immediately necessary'. This is treatment which is essential and which the doctor believes cannot be delayed or avoided. Asylum-seekers are able to register with a GP practice. However, after they have lost their claim and any appeal, they may be charged for routine (but not emergency or 'immediately necessary') services.

A person who is not entitled to free secondary treatment provided through a hospital (above) does not become entitled to that treatment for free just because they are referred for it by a GP practice at which they have registered. So, a person who is able to register with a GP but who needs hospital treatment for a serious illness, will not be able to access that treatment free of charge unless and until their condition becomes so serious that they have to present to an accident and emergency department.

Although a person who is registered at a practice is entitled to free treatment, they may still, unless they obtain an exemption (see below) be charged for certain fixed costs such as prescription or dental charges.

Help with health costs

The NHS has fixed charges for some of its services: prescriptions, dental treatment, eye-tests, wigs etc. Some people are completely exempt from paying these charges and can also obtain help with travel costs to hospital and the cost of glasses. Others are entitled to a partial exemption because they are on a low income. We look at each separately.

Exempt If the applicant is exempt, they will be provided with an 'HC2' certificate issued by the Department of Health and valid for six months. Those exempt from health charges include:

- asylum-seekers, or the dependants of an asylum-seeker, who are receiving support from NASS or a local authority (these asylum-seekers should be provided with the HC2 certificate by NASS on behalf of the Department of Health);
- claimants (and members of their family) who are in receipt of income support, income-based job-seekers' allowance or tax credits (where the award comes with a Tax Credits Exemption Certificate) (people in this

category will generally be able to demonstrate that they are entitled to exemption by proof of receipt of benefit rather than having to actually produce the certificate);

- hospital in-patients;
- those aged under 16, or aged 16-18 who are in full-time education;
- those with specific medical conditions (see the list on HC2).

Partially exempt If someone is not exempt from charges, they may be eligible for a partial exemption under the low income scheme. A person will qualify for help if their income and savings are within prescribed limits (the limits are similar to those for income support). An HC1 claim form needs to be completed. These forms are available from JobCentrePlus offices, the DWP, post offices, NHS hospitals or by calling 08701 555 455. If the applicant is eligible, they will be sent an HC3 certificate which gives details of how much they will be expected to contribute.

EDUCATION

Access to grants and loans for both fees and support in order to study at colleges and universities in the UK is dealt with in the chapter on students at ▶284–8.

Immigration status does not presently affect the duties of local education authorities to provide education for children of school age. Under the Education Act 1996, local authorities are required to provide schooling to children who are living in their area either temporarily or permanently. They must provide education regardless of the child's, or their parents', immigration status.

There are proposals to relieve local authorities of these duties for the children of asylum-seekers who are placed in 'accommodation centres' (see s36 2002 Act). If the Home Office ever sets up these accommodation centres, children will receive separate education which will be provided in the accommodation centre itself. However, if the child has special educational needs which cannot be properly addressed in the accommodation centre, the centre will contact the local authority and ask it to arrange education for the child.

12

41 Asylum support and 'hard cases' support

The first part of this chapter deals with asylum support provided by the National Asylum Support Service ('NASS'). The following aspects are covered:

- qualifying for asylum support: the definition of 'asylum-seeker' for support purposes; the definition of 'dependant' of an asylum-seeker; when a person stops being an asylum-seeker; and the definition of 'destitution' (▶1341–50);

- exclusions for asylum support based on: section 55 2002 Act, Schedule 3 2002 Act, the Asylum Support Regulations 2000 and providing false/incomplete information (▶1350–60);

- the support that is actually provided by NASS including 'dispersed' accommodation and the general rates paid in order to meet a person's essential living needs (▶1360–6);

- NASS procedures and obtaining temporary support (▶1367–71).

The chapter then goes on to deal with the following:

- the 'interim' scheme of asylum support operated by local authorities (▶1371–9);

- the European Directive on minimum standards of reception for asylum-seekers (▶1379–81);

- 'hard cases' support provided under section 4 1999 Act (▶1381–7).

Appeals to the Asylum Support Adjudicator against decisions made by NASS are covered in Chapter 42.

First though, we look briefly at four initial matters: (1) the other support that is available to some asylum-seekers; (2) the basic relationship between NASS asylum support and 'interim' asylum support; (3) the outcome of the plan to introduce 'accommodation centres' to support asylum-seekers; (4) where the basic legal materials on asylum support are to be found.

1) What other forms of support may be available to asylum-seekers?

1337   Asylum support is intended as a replacement for welfare benefits (see Chapter 39), and support through local authority provided housing, social services and the Children Act support (see Chapter 40). However, a very limited number of asylum-seekers, may be able to obtain welfare benefits (▶see 1255–9 for the categories of people who are exempted from the 'subject to immigration control' test). In addition, the following asylum-seekers are still the responsibility of local authorities under their social services or Children Act powers, or powers under the 'Withholding and Withdrawal of Support' Regulations:

- unaccompanied minor asylum-seekers (▶see 1322–5);

- a small group of asylum-seekers who have needs for 'care and attention' which arise not 'solely' as a result of their destitution but because they are disabled, ill, elderly etc (▶see 1317–8);

- certain failed asylum-seekers, who have exhausted their claims and appeals and who have been denied further asylum support who turn to local authorities as a last resort (▶see in particular at 1314–5 and ▶see 1301–4; although, depending on their circumstances, such applicants may also turn to hard cases support, ▶see 1381–7).

2) What is the basic relationship between asylum support provided by NASS and 'interim' asylum support provided by local authorities?

Local authorities *also* have responsibility for some 'ordinary' adult, able-bodied asylum-seekers and for asylum-seeking families although not through their social services functions. For some asylum-seekers, local authorities have powers to provide 'interim' asylum support. The first form of asylum support to be introduced under the 1999 Act, on 6 December 1999, was indeed 'interim' asylum support. Essentially, asylum-seekers who were, at that time, being supported by local authorities under social services powers were switched over to be provided with interim asylum support instead. The NASS scheme for asylum support was introduced in April 2000 and, since that time, the two schemes have run in parallel, each providing for separate categories of asylum-seeker.

However, the interim asylum support scheme was originally only intended to continue in existence until 1 April 2002. By that time, it was hoped that NASS would be able to provide for all asylum-seekers. NASS does indeed presently provide for the vast majority of asylum-seekers and, since September 2000, all new asylum-seekers have been the responsibility of NASS. However, for those asylum-seekers who were already being supported under the interim scheme, the scheme has been continually extended. Most recently it was extended until 3 April 2006. Under the 'Interim Scheme Project', between June 2005 and 31 March 2006 the government is moving all outstanding interim support cases over to NASS asylum support so that, by that date, NASS will be directly responsible for all asylum-seekers who are eligible for asylum support.

Note that, even where it is NASS that is responsible for making decisions about and providing support, NASS is able to arrange for the support to be delivered by other bodies such as local authorities. This is still NASS asylum support although it may *appear* otherwise. These arrangements should not be confused with support provided by local authorities under the interim scheme.

Although the interim scheme is dying out, we look in more detail at it and at which groups of asylum-seekers are still supported under it at ▶1371–9.

3) What has happened to the plan to introduce 'accommodation centres'?

In the last edition of the *Handbook* (pp. 719–720) we explained the government's intention to set up a system of 'accommodation centres' and what they would involve. The idea was to house certain asylum-seekers who are need of support in these centres, which might be miles from ordinary residential areas, where the asylum-seeker would be required to reside and where they would be provided with all their other essentials. The children of asylum-seekers would be provided with education at the centre (▶see further at 1335). As of February 2002, the Home Office had identified eight potential sites for accommodation centres. Part two of the 2002 Act lays the statutory basis for the project and re-structures the system of asylum support with accommodation centres as a central feature.

However, the process of setting the centres up has been beset by controversy and planning disputes. None have been brought into being and the legislation to use them to provide support has not, therefore, been used. It now seems that the government will not be pressing ahead with accommodation centres at all. On 14 June 2005, the minister stated:

'After detailed consideration, I am announcing today that we will not proceed with the construction of an accommodation centre for asylum-seekers at the former MOD site outside Bicester in Oxfordshire. Neither will we proceed with accommodation centres at any other potential site.' (Tony McNulty MP, written statement)

It is possible that the Bicester site will become a 'removal' (i.e. detention) centre instead.

12

4) What are the basic materials containing the law and policy on asylum support?

Important basic provisions about asylum support (NASS support and under the interim scheme) are contained in part six of the Immigration and Asylum Act 1999 and parts two and three of the Nationality, Immigration and Asylum Act 2002 Acts. We have noted the most important provisions in the text. However, much of the detail of the NASS scheme is set out in the Asylum Support Regulations 2000 (in this chapter we refer to these as the 'Asylum Support Regulations' or simply just 'Regulations' or 'Regs'). The details of the interim scheme are contained in the Asylum Support (Interim Provisions) Regulations (we refer to these as the 'Interim Provisions Regulations', although in the past dealing with interim support they are also referred to simply as the 'Regulations' or 'Regs').

The underpinning for 'hard cases' support is contained in section 4 1999 Act but the details are now set out in the Immigration and Asylum (Provision of Accommodation to failed Asylum-seekers) Regulations 2005.

Asylum support appeals are provided for in section 103-104 1999 Act. The procedure for asylum support appeals is governed by the Asylum Support Appeals (Procedure) Rules 2000 (which we have called the Asylum Support Appeals Rules).

NASS Policy

Practical and policy details about asylum support (and hard cases support) are contained in NASS Policy Bulletins. They can be downloaded from the IND website and they are often revised. Important examples, are the Policy Bulletins dealing with:

- 'mixed households', this is where some members of the family are entitled to other forms of support such as welfare benefits or housing (Bulletin 11);
- failure to travel (Bulletin 17);
- the Medical Foundation for the Victims of Torture (Bulletin 19);
- the asylum support appeal process (Bulletin 23);
- transition at the age of 18 years (Bulletin 29);
- 'dispersal guidelines' (i.e. policy on dispersal) (Bulletin 31);
- age disputes (Bulletin 33);
- maternity payments (Bulletin 37);
- HC2 (health) certificates (Bulletin 43);
- arrangements for 'dis-benefitted' cases i.e. those in which the asylum-seeker ceased to be entitled to welfare benefits (Bulletins 52–53);
- applications for support from those who are detained under the 1971 Act, or who are granted bail (Bulletin 64);
- domestic violence (Bulletin 70);
- hard cases support under section 4 1999 Act (Bulletin 71);
- employment and voluntary activity (Bulletin 72);
- provision of emergency accommodation (Bulletin 73);
- late claims (Bulletin 75);
- failure to comply with removal directions (Bulletin 77);
- false or incomplete information (Bulletin 79);
- racist incidents (Bulletin 81);
- the duty to offer support, family unity, vulnerable persons and the withdrawal of support (Bulletin 83).

WHO QUALIFIES FOR ASYLUM SUPPORT?

This part looks at who is entitled to asylum support provided under the NASS scheme. The essentials about the requirements for qualifying for support are the same for 'interim' asylum support provided by local authorities. There are, however, some differences (interim asylum support is covered at ▶1371 onwards).

In order to qualify for asylum support, an applicant must satisfy all three of the following conditions.

1) The applicant must be *either* (s95(1) 1999 Act):
- an 'asylum-seeker' (▶1341–5) or
- the 'dependant of an asylum-seeker' (▶1345–7).

    For when a person who was an 'asylum-seeker' reaches the end of the asylum process and stops being an 'asylum-seeker' for these purposes, ▶see 1343–5.

2) The applicant must appear to the Secretary of State to be 'destitute', or to be 'likely to become destitute', within a 'prescribed period'. These periods are: 14 days for new applicants and 56 days for people who are already being supported (s95(1) 1999 Act, reg. 7 Asylum Support Regulations). For details about determining destitution, ▶see 1347–50.

3) The applicant must not be excluded from support. An applicant may be excluded from support for a range of reasons:
- exclusions under section 55 2002 Act (requirement to claim asylum 'as soon as reasonably practicable' but there is an exception where it is necessary to provide support in order to prevent a breach of the person's human rights) (▶1350–2);
- exclusion for providing false or incomplete information (▶1352–3);
- the applicant is excluded because they fall into one of the 'excluded classes' in Schedule 3 2002 Act (this includes the exclusion for asylum-seeking families who fail to take reasonable steps to leave the UK) (▶1353–7);
- exclusions under the Asylum Support Regulations; this could be for a number of reasons including cases where the applicant is entitled to another form of support such as welfare benefits, or the asylum-seeker might be excluded because of their conduct (▶1357–60).

Who is an 'asylum-seeker' for asylum support purposes?

In order to count as an 'asylum-seeker' for support purposes, a person must satisfy *all* of the following conditions (ss94(1), 95 1999 Act):

1) be 18 years of age or over (unaccompanied children under 18 are entitled to support under s17 Children Act 1989, ▶see 1322–5; families with such children, however, are eligible for asylum support);

12

2) have made a 'claim for asylum';

3) the claim to asylum has been 'recorded' by the Secretary of State; and

4) the claim to asylum has not been 'determined'.

Except for the age requirement, we look at each of these conditions in turn below. Note that section 44 2002 Act (which is not yet in force) will make it a further requirement that the applicant claims at a place 'designated by the Secretary of State'.

Claim for asylum

A 'claim for asylum' means a claim that it would be a breach of the UK's obligations under either the Refugee Convention *or* Article 3 ECHR for the person to be removed from, or required to leave, the UK. For procedures about claiming asylum, ▶see Chapter 22. For qualifying for refugee status, ▶see Chapter 21 and for qualifying to stay under Article 3, ▶see 794–800.

If a potential applicant expresses an unwillingness to return to their country of nationality (or habitual residence) because of some perceived danger, an asylum application must be deemed to have been made. If the reason for the fear does not appear to be covered by the Refugee Convention, this may be a reason for refusing the refugee application in due course but the claim must be considered substantively.

As to how the claim must be made, the case law of the Social Security Commissioners as to what amounts to a 'claim for asylum' for welfare benefit purposes indicates that it is not necessary to go through any formal process, or to complete any particular forms (*CIS/4341/98*). The Commissioners have also held that 'an indication of a desire to claim asylum is itself a claim for asylum' (*CIS/4439/98*, *CIS/3867/98*). For other purposes, immigration law has also recognised that what is necessary to amount to a claim for asylum is to be seen very broadly.

From February 2003, the Home Office stopped accepting postal asylum applications. However, if the applicant is vulnerable (pregnant women, the disabled, families with children etc), the Home Office may agree to record a claim made at a local office rather than requiring the applicant to attend at one of the screening units.

Fresh claims Where a 'fresh claim' is accepted to have been made, an applicant who had ceased to be an asylum-seeker i.e. after their first claim to asylum has been determined (▶see 1343–5 below for when an asylum-seeker stops being eligible for support on this basis), becomes an 'asylum-seeker' again. Such a person is again entitled to asylum support.

In order to make a 'fresh claim' it is not enough just to make further representations to the Home Office. The 'test' for fresh claims was first developed in the context of failed asylum-seekers who were trying to re-trigger the asylum appeal process. The courts set down a stringent test for what amounted to a fresh claim, which was then put into the immigration rules (see *Onibiyo*, CA and for further details ▶see 730–5). The courts have since held that the same test applies when an applicant is trying to re-trigger the asylum support process and that, before support is re-triggered, the Home Office must have accepted that the claim is a 'fresh' one and 'recorded' (see below) the further claim (*R (Nigatu) v SSHD*, HC). However, before a decision is made as to whether the representations are a fresh claim or not, the applicant may be able to obtain 'hard cases' support (▶see 1381 onwards).

Claim for asylum has been 'recorded by the Secretary of State'

It is necessary that the claim to asylum has been 'recorded by the Secretary of State'. An early indication of the lack of technicality to this procedure is provided in an open IND letter of 15 September 2000 to the effect that a claim will be 'recorded' when it is notified to the Home Office in person at one of the screening units. There are no rules which define when a claim to asylum has been 'recorded'. There is some case law under the old social security benefit regulations concerning the slightly different question of when a claim to asylum is 'recorded by the Secretary of State as having been determined'. The effect of those cases is that, in order for such a 'record' to exist, there needs to be a reliable document (*Karoui & Abbad*, HC) constituting a clear decision that the claim has been determined, regardless of whether the applicant had been notified or not (*Salem*).

The case law of the Social Security Commissioners relating to the 'record' of a claim to asylum for benefit purposes, can also be applied to the recording of claims for asylum support purposes. In one case, a Commissioner held that there was 'no specified way in which a [claim for asylum] should be recorded'. The Commissioner used a letter from the Home Office in response to a complaint as to how a person had been treated on entry to the UK as either sufficient itself as a record of the claim or, alternatively, as secondary evidence of a Home Office record (*CIS/4439/98*). In another case, the Commissioner accepted that a record of the claim to asylum had been made during the course of a telephone conversation between the asylum applicant and an immigration officer before the applicant was subsequently issued with a Standard Acknowledgment Letter (SAL) (*CIS/3867/98*, and see *CIS/259/99*).

12

Usually the question of whether the claim has been recorded will not be controversial. It will become an issue, however, where the applicant makes a second claim to asylum, which they state is a 'fresh claim' (above) but the Home Office either refuses or has not yet determined whether to record the claim.

Claim for asylum has not been 'determined'

A person remains an 'asylum-seeker' for support purposes until the claim has been 'determined'. Unless there is a child dependant in the household (see below), the claim for asylum is treated as having been determined (and asylum support ceases) *following a grace period* after either (see s94(1)(3)(4)(5) 1999 Act and the Regulations below):

1) the Home Office notifies the applicant of the decision on the claim to asylum by notice in writing; *or if the applicant appeals*

2) the expiry of the time-limit for applying to appeal further.

So, a person continues to be an asylum-seeker for support purposes during the whole appeals process. A person is therefore an 'asylum-seeker' during any time (s94(4) 1999 Act, s104 2002 Act):

- they may appeal to the AIT;
- the appeal to the AIT is outstanding;
- an application for a reconsideration (in-time) could be made or has been made and is awaiting determination;
- a reconsideration has been ordered but not completed;
- an appellant may apply (in-time) for permission to appeal to the Court of Appeal;
- an appellant has appealed to the Court of Appeal and the appeal is awaiting determination;
- an appeal has been remitted to the AIT and is awaiting determination;
- a reference by the High Court to the Court of Appeal is awaiting determination.

However, if the applicant submits an application for reconsideration, or for permission to appeal out of time, then that application will be enough to mean that they are still an asylum-seeker (and see *R (Erdogan) v SSHD*, CA). If the application is successful, they will be an asylum-seeker again at that point.

Grace periods With effect from, 8 April 2002, the grace periods referred to above, during which applicants continue to be entitled to support after the trigger to end support has occurred are (see reg. 2(2)(2A) Asylum Support Regulations 2002, reg. 2(6)(7) Interim Provisions Regulations 1999):

1) 28 days following either:
    - notice of decision to grant refugee status (under the 1951 Convention); or
    - notice of decision to grant any form of limited leave (normally humanitarian protection or discretionary leave); or
    - notice of decision of the AIT/court allowing the appeal against the Home Office decision;

2) 21 days in all other (i.e. unsuccessful) cases.

Transition to benefits and delays At the point that status is granted, the (former) asylum-seeker becomes eligible for welfare benefits. This is because they have leave that is not subject to a public funds condition and they are, therefore, not 'subject to immigration control' for welfare benefits purposes (see s115 1999 Act). There have, however, been significant delays between an *appeal* being allowed and the Home Office actually issuing the applicant with the grant of leave. This leaves the applicant in limbo since they cease to be an 'asylum-seeker' for asylum support purposes after the fixed grace period of 28 days but, until they are actually granted leave, they are still 'subject to immigration control' for benefits purposes. During the limbo period they therefore have no formal entitlement to either benefits or asylum support.

One option in these delay cases is to ask NASS to continue the existing support as 'hard cases' support. If that fails or if the delay becomes prolonged to the great prejudice of the applicant, it is possible to ask the High Court to force the Home Office to grant leave without further delay (see *Mersin*, *Arbab*, both High Court ▶see 718–9).

For further details about the problems involved with making the transition from asylum support to benefits, ▶see 1282–4. For back-dating benefits for successful applicants, ▶see 1284–6.

Households including a child

If the asylum-seeker has within their household a child who is under the age of 18 and who is their dependant, then entitlement to asylum support continues even after the asylum application and any appeal has been determined. It can continue while the family remains in the UK and the child either becomes 18 or leaves the household (s94(5) 2002 Act). *However*, asylum support can be still be excluded to failed asylum-seeking families under Schedule 3 2002 Act. Most importantly, from 1 December 2004, Schedule 3 excludes failed asylum-seeking families who fail to take reasonable steps to leave the UK unless to deny support would result in a breach of their human rights (▶see below at 1354–7).

Who counts as the 'dependant' of an asylum-seeker?

In addition to 'asylum-seekers', the 'dependants' of asylum-seekers are also eligible for asylum support. The table below sets out who qualifies for asylum support as a dependant.

12

A person qualifies for asylum support as the 'dependant' of an asylum-seeker if they are related or connected to the asylum-seeker in one of the ways listed below. Note that the following persons qualify as dependants for the purposes of either the NASS or 'interim' asylum support schemes. However, for NASS asylum support, the following categories must be read with the slight modifications set out immediately after the list.

The regulations setting out the following definitions are regulation 2(4) Asylum Support Regulations and regulation 2(1) Asylum Support (Interim Provisions) Regulations 1999. Note that the references to 'civil partner' and 'same-sex couple', are added to the definitions from 5 December 2005 as a result of amendments made by Articles 1, 2 and Schedule 13 to the Civil Partnership Act 2004 (Amendments to Subordinate Legislation) Order 2005.

Dependants under the asylum support and 'interim' support schemes

A person is the dependant of an asylum-seeker if they are:

1) the spouse or civil partner of the asylum-seeker;

2) the child of the asylum-seeker, or a child of the spouse or civil partner of the asylum-seeker, who is both under 18 and dependent on the asylum-seeker;

3) a person who is under 18 and a member of the asylum-seeker's or their spouse's or civil partner's 'close family' (there is no definition provided for the meaning of 'close family');

4) a person who is under 18 and who has been living as part of the asylum-seeker's household *either* for at least six of the 12 months before the claim for support was made *or* since birth;

5) a person who is in need of care and attention from the asylum-seeker or a member of their household by reason of a disability and either:

- they are a member of the asylum-seeker's or their spouse's close family; or

- they have been living as part of the asylum-seeker's household for either six of the 12 months before the claim to support was made or since birth;

6) a person who has been living with the asylum-seeker as a member of an unmarried couple (a couple who are living together as if married) for at least two of the three years before the claim to support was made;

7) a person who has been living with the asylum-seeker as a member of a same-sex couple (i.e. a same-sex couple who are not civil partners but who are living together as if they were) for at least two of the three years before the claim to support was made;

8) a person who is living with the asylum-seeker as part of their household and who was receiving assistance from a local authority under section 17 Children Act immediately before 6 December 1999;

9) a person who is being treated by the Home Office as the dependant of an asylum-seeker for the purposes of the asylum claim. Under the immigration rules, only the spouse and minor children of asylum-seekers are considered as

dependants on the asylum claim but the immigration authorities have a discretion to treat other family members as dependants (►see 691–4);

10) an asylum-seeker if their dependant is the person who has claimed support.

If a person falls into any of the above categories, they qualify as a dependant. They do not need to satisfy any additional tests showing, for example, that they are emotionally or financially dependent on the asylum-seeker (*Dirrshe*, HC).

Modifications to definition of dependant for the purpose of NASS asylum support

A person is a dependant of an asylum-seeker under the NASS scheme if they fall into any of the above categories with the following minor differences.

- In categories 2, 3 and 4 above, a person counts as a dependant if they are under 18 or they were under 18 either:
  - at the time the application for support for them was made; or
  - *if* they joined the supported asylum-seeker in the UK, at the time when they joined them.

These dependants therefore continue to be entitled to receive support even after they reach 18.

- In categories 6 and 7, a person qualifies if they were living with the asylum-seeker as an unmarried couple or same-sex couple for at least two of the three years before the time when the application for support was made *or* the date that they joined the asylum-seeker in the UK.

- In addition to the categories referred to above, a person qualifies as a dependant under the NASS scheme if they are living as part of the asylum-seeker's household and, immediately before 3 April 2000, they were receiving support from a local authority in Scotland or Ireland under the equivalent provisions of the Children Act. This is because the interim scheme did not apply in Scotland and Ireland and so this is intended to ensure that dependants in Scotland and Ireland are provided for by NASS rather than by social services.

'Destitute' or likely shortly to become 'destitute'

12

In order to qualify for support, asylum-seekers and their dependants have to be either 'destitute' or 'likely shortly to become destitute' within a particular period of time (s95(1), Sch 9 para. 1(2) 1999 Act). 'Destitution' itself is given a special definition (see below).

When must a person be destitute/likely to become destitute?

The periods within which an applicant must be destitute, or likely to become destitute, are (reg. 7 Asylum Support Regulations):

- 14 days for new applicants; and
- 56 days for people who are already being supported.

Destitution

A person is destitute if either (s95(3), Sch 9 para. 3 1999 Act):

- they do not have 'adequate accommodation' or any means of getting adequate accommodation; or
- they have adequate accommodation or the means of getting it but cannot meet their other 'essential living needs'.

Determining destitution

The matters which are taken into account in determining destitution for asylum support under the NASS scheme and the interim scheme are slightly different. The relevant factors under the NASS scheme are as follows (for the interim scheme, ▶see 1375).

Adequate accommodation and essential living needs In considering whether an applicant does have adequate accommodation and whether they can meet their essential living needs, NASS takes into account (reg. 6, Asylum Support Regulations):

- any income, which the applicant or their dependants have or may reasonably be expected to have;
- any other support which is available, or which may reasonably be expected to be available, to the applicant or their dependants; and
- any of the following assets which are available to them or which they might reasonably be expected to have available: cash, savings, investments, land, vehicles and goods for trade or business.

The government intends that support from friends and relatives in the UK or from voluntary sector organisations can be taken into account. NASS must, however, not count any assets, which are not in the list above. The notes that accompany Form NASS 1 (the application form for support) state that NASS will ignore items of jewellery, personal clothing, bedding and medical or optical items (e.g., wheelchairs). However, NASS does require that applicants state any items of jewellery or watches belonging to them or their dependants, which are worth over £1,000 at the present market value, and to inform NASS immediately if any of those items are subsequently sold and how much they were sold for. The intention is that NASS may then take into account the money received as a result of the sale.

Whether existing accommodation is 'adequate' Where an applicant already has some form of accommodation, NASS must decide whether the existing accommodation is 'adequate'. NASS must take into account whether (reg. 8, Asylum Support Regulations):

- it is 'reasonable' for the applicant to continue to occupy the accommodation;
- the accommodation is affordable;

- the applicant can gain entry to the accommodation;
- if the accommodation is a house-boat, a caravan or some other moveable structure, which may be lived in, the applicant has a place where they can lawfully place it;
- the applicant will be able to live in the accommodation together with their dependants; and
- the applicant is likely to suffer domestic violence if they continue to live in the accommodation.

Accommodation for a disabled child will not be 'adequate' if it is of a lower standard than that which would be provided for a disabled person if an authority provided residential accommodation under section 21 National Assistance Act 1948 (*R (A) v NASS*, CA). NASS Policy Bulletin 70 deals with when accommodation will not be adequate as a result of the risk of domestic violence. NASS will pay the reasonable expenses of alternative accommodation that is found by an asylum-seeker who is forced to flee NASS accommodation due to domestic violence. Accommodation where the asylum-seeker is not safe because of racial harassment or violence will also not be adequate (see NASS Policy Bulletin 81).

There are also certain matters, which cannot be taken into account in determining whether a person has adequate accommodation. These are (s95(6) 1999 Act):

- that the applicant does not have a legal right to stay in the accommodation, (although NASS will not consider that the accommodation is adequate if the applicant has actually been required to leave the accommodation, for example, by the owner or as a result of a court order for possession);
- that the accommodation (or part of it) is shared with others;
- that the accommodation is temporary; and
- the location of the accommodation.

Essential living needs Whether a person has the means to obtain items such as food, toiletries, and clothing, is relevant in determining whether they can meet their essential needs for living. However, in deciding whether a person's essential living needs are met regarding clothing, NASS cannot take into account 'personal preferences' regarding clothing although it can take into account a person's 'individual circumstances' regarding clothing.

In addition, none of the following are treated as essential living needs: the cost of faxes, computers and computer facilities, the cost of photocopying, travel expenses (except the cost of the initial travel to dispersed NASS-provided accommodation or another address where the applicant has notified the Home Office that they will live), toys and other recreational items and entertainment expenses (reg. 9, Asylum Support Regulations).

12

Note, however, that costs for some of these items may be met when NASS decides what support to provide (▶see 1366).

EXCLUSIONS FROM ASYLUM SUPPORT

Below we look at the exclusions from NASS asylum support in four stages:

1) exclusions under section 55 2002 Act (requirement to claim asylum 'as soon as reasonably practicable' after arrival in the UK) (▶below);

2) exclusion for providing false or incomplete information (▶1352–3);

3) exclusions under Schedule 3 2002 Act (this includes the exclusion for asylum-seeking families who fail to take reasonable steps to leave the UK) (▶1353–7);

4) other exclusions under the Asylum Support Regulations (▶1357–60).

There are important exceptions to the exclusions under (1) and (3) in particular. One of those exceptions is that applicants cannot be excluded under those provisions if to do so would result in a breach of their human rights (s55(5)(a) and para. 3 Sch 3 2002 Act). This 'human rights' exception and the case law that interprets it (most importantly *Adam & Limbuela*) is the same as applies to exclusions from all forms of support under Schedule 3 2002 Act. It is therefore covered in the previous chapter at ▶1306–1314.

Exclusion under section 55 2002 Act

From 8 January 2003, section 55(1) 2002 Act, excludes asylum-seekers from asylum support if:

'...the Secretary of State is not satisfied that the claim [for asylum i.e. on refugee or Article 3 ECHR grounds] was made as soon as reasonably practicable after the person's arrival in the United Kingdom'.

For the meaning of 'as soon as reasonably practicable' ▶see 1351–2 below. NASS decisions that an applicant has not claimed asylum as soon as reasonably practicable cannot be appealed to the Asylum Support Adjudicator (s55(10)). Challenges to section 55 decisions therefore have to be made by judicial review. After section 55 was introduced, this resulted in a great number of judicial review applications combined with applications for urgent injunctions for accommodation (for judicial review procedure, ▶see 1213–22 and for injunctions against NASS in particular, ▶see 1221–2).

Many of these claims challenged not only the decision about whether the asylum-seeker claimed in-time but also whether the asylum-seeker fell within the human rights exception i.e. whether support was necessary in order to protect the asylum-seeker's human rights. After the decision of the Court of Appeal in *Limbuela* and pending a decision in the House of

Lords, NASS acknowledged that, as a result of the human rights exception, it could not refuse support under section 55 unless it was positively satisfied that the individual had other support available. Following the decision of the House of Lords, which was favourable to the asylum-seekers (for full details of it, ▶see 1307–11), it remains to be seen whether and how the government will continue to make section 55 exclusion decisions.

For details about NASS procedures and section 55 decisions, ▶see 1367–9.

In addition to asylum support, the following forms of support are excluded to these 'late-claiming' asylum-seekers:

- temporary asylum support (▶1368–9);
- hard cases support under section 4 1999 Act (▶see 1381–7);
- support in an accommodation centre (but the 'accommodation centre' project is not being progressed);
- interim provision of housing under section 188(3) or 204(4) Housing Act 1996 (and equivalent Scottish legislation) i.e. housing from a local authority pending a review or an appeal against its refusal;
- support under section 2 Local Government Act 2000 (promotion of well-being, ▶see 1321–2).

The exceptions

Even if an applicant is judged to have failed to have claimed asylum 'as soon as reasonably practicable', the following support may still be provided (s55(5)):

- any support if such is necessary in order to avoid a breach of the applicant's human rights (the meaning of this exception is fully explained at ▶1306–14);
- asylum support for the dependent child (under 18) of an asylum-seeker under section 122 1999 Act;
- the provision of temporary asylum support to a child (under 18) and the household of which that child is a part.

Section 55 has not generally been used, therefore, to exclude asylum-seeking families or unaccompanied minors.

Claiming asylum 'as soon as reasonably practicable'

Although the decision of the House of Lords in *Adam, Limbuela & Tesema* did not consider the test for claiming asylum 'as soon as reasonably practicable', the following side comments were made by Lord Hope:

'In practice a claim which is made to an immigration officer at the port of arrival will always satisfy this test...A claim made after a person has passed the point of immigration control is likely to be regarded as

12

having been made too late, unless there are special circumstances.' (para. 39)

Main test In *R (Q) v SSHD*, the Court of Appeal held that the test is as follows:

'On the premise that the purpose of coming to this country was to claim asylum and having regard to the practical opportunity for claiming asylum and to the asylum seeker's personal circumstances, could the asylum seeker reasonably have been expected to claim earlier than he or she did?' (paras 37, 119)

Further factors The Court of Appeal in *Q* further held that Collins J (in the High Court) had been correct to state that regard should be had to the effect of anything that the asylum-seeker may have been told by their agent (para. 43). In the further decision of *R (S, D and T) v SSHD*, the High Court referred to various factors, which may be useful to asylum-seekers faced with possible exclusion on these grounds. In particular, the court noted that many asylum-seekers know very little about airport procedures and claiming asylum, that many depend completely on agents and that it is common that immigration officers will not ask questions at port or may only speak to the accompanying agent.

NASS 'three-day' test Following the above and other decisions of the courts, in December 2003 the government decided that it would not exclude asylum-seekers under section 55 provided that they could provide a 'credible explanation' that they have claimed asylum within three days of their arrival. Note also that asylum-seekers who claim in-country as the result of a major change of circumstances in their country (known as refugees *sur place*, ▶613), will also not be excluded (see NASS Policy Bulletin 75).

Procedures Procedures for making section 55 decisions had to be amended after *Q* because the Court of Appeal also found that NASS were not operating a fair system of decision-making. For example, interviews were conducted to a 'standard form' and were not sufficiently flexible. Also asylum-seekers were not being given a fair opportunity to respond to officers' concerns. In addition, caseworkers did not have the correct legal test properly in mind and the purpose of the section 55 interview was not being clearly explained to the asylum-seekers. For further details on procedures, ▶see 1367–71.

As indicated above, decisions excluding applicants under section 55 were largely suspended awaiting the decision of the House of Lords in *Adam, Limbuela & Tesema* (▶see now at 1307–11).

Exclusion for providing false or incomplete information

NASS may refuse to consider an application for support where it believes that the information given in the application is not complete or accurate, or if the applicant is not cooperating with further enquires which NASS makes (see reg. 3(4)(5) Asylum Support Regulations introduced following s57 2002 Act). This exclusion is also covered in NASS Policy Bulletin 79, 'Application for support: false or incomplete information 2002 Act guidance'.

An example of where NASS has refused support under this provision is where the asylum-seeker does not give complete information as requested on the form about their route of arrival to the UK. The means of challenge to decisions to exclude asylum-seekers on this ground is judicial review. There is no express 'human rights' exception that lets applicants back into the provision of support if refused on this basis.

Exclusions under Schedule 3 2002 Act (as added to by section 9 2004 Act)

The following 'classes' of people are excluded from support under Schedule 3 2002 Act (paras 1, 4-7A, Schedule 3):

- those who have been granted refugee status by the government of another EEA state (or who are the dependants of persons in the UK who have been granted refugee status by another EEA state) (**first class**);

- those who nationals of another EEA state (or who are the dependants of a person who is a national of another EEA state) (**second class**);

- former asylum-seekers who have failed to cooperate with removal directions and their dependants (**third class**);

- persons who are in the UK 'in breach of the immigration laws' and who are not asylum-seekers (**fourth class**);

- asylum-seekers with dependent children whose claims have failed, who have exhausted appeal rights and in respect of whom the Secretary of State has issued a certificate stating that they have failed, without reasonable excuse, to leave the UK voluntarily or to put themselves in a position to do so (**fifth class**) (►see further below, including the table at 1354–7).

The same excluded classes are also excluded from a range of social services support, interim housing provision and 'hard cases' support. For a more detailed description of the **third, fourth** and **fifth** classes, ►see 1302–6. For NASS policy relating to the fifth class, see immediately below.

Exceptions

The exclusions under Schedule 3 do not prevent the provision of support (paras 2-3, Sch 3 2002 Act):

- to either a British citizen or a child;

- where to deny support would result in a breach of the applicant's rights under the ECHR (►see 1306–1314, 1325–8) or under EU law.

12

Fifth excluded class: asylum-seeking families who do not leave

Cases excluded as falling into the fifth class are often referred to as 'section 9 cases'. This is because the fifth class was inserted into the 2002 Act by section 9 2004 Act. It came into force on 1 December 2004. Applicants are excluded if *all* of the following conditions apply, namely (para. 7A 2002 Act):

- the main applicant is still an asylum-seeker for support purposes but only because their household includes a dependent child who is under 18;
- the Secretary of State has 'certified' that, in his opinion, the applicant has failed, without reasonable excuse, to take reasonable steps to either:
  - leave the UK voluntarily; or
  - place themselves in a position in which they will be able to leave the UK voluntarily; and
- the applicant has received a copy of the Secretary of State's certificate.

The applicant (and their dependants) are excluded from support after a period of 14 days following their receipt of the Secretary of State's certificate. The table below sets out NASS policy on the procedure that is operated, what counts as failing to take 'reasonable steps' and what may count as a 'reasonable excuse'.

Where NASS decide to exclude a person from their support, the local authority will have to decide what, if any, support can be provided to the family or to the child/ren. *For details about what support may be available from the local authority and the options open to the authority,* ▶*see 1325–8.*

EXCLUSION OF ASYLUM-SEEKING FAMILIES UNDER SECTION 9 2004 ACT: HOME OFFICE POLICY AND PROCEDURE

The policy/procedures set out in this table are taken from a detailed instruction issued by NASS to its caseworkers on 15 November 2004 (i.e. shortly before section 9 came into force).

Cases in which the section 9 procedure does not need to be used

After the main applicant's asylum claim has been fully determined, and all appeal rights have been exhausted, if the family can be removed, enforcement action should take place promptly. Where removal cannot take place promptly because, for example, the family does not have appropriate valid travel documentation and the family is receiving NASS or local authority support, the section 9 procedure may be appropriate.

Reasonable steps

The following will generally be considered by the Home Office to be 'reasonable steps' taken either for the family to leave the UK voluntarily, or to place themselves in a position to do so (as with the 'reasonable excuse' list below, the list is not exhaustive):

- asking the Home Office to approach the authorities of their country to obtain travel documents on their behalf;
- providing correct and complete information to the Home Office and/or the relevant Embassy/High Commission to enable travel documents to be issued;
- attending interviews with the Home Office and/or the relevant Embassy/High Commission in order to obtain travel documents;
- approaching their own national authorities in order to obtain travel documentation (i.e. without the assistance of the Home Office);
- applying to the International Organisation for Migration (IOM) (or other group) for help in arranging a voluntary return;
- purchasing one-way tickets or asking the Home Office to obtain tickets for them.

The Home Office stresses that taking reasonable steps is an ongoing process. It is not enough, for example, to make an application to the IOM but to then fail to respond to IOM requests for information.

'Reasonable excuse' for failing to take reasonable steps

The following will generally be considered by the Home Office to be 'reasonable excuses' for failing to take steps to leave voluntarily, or to place themselves in a position to do so:

- where the applicant is in need of emergency medical care so that they are unable to attend an interview and/or are unable to provide information - a medical certificate must be produced;
- inability to travel to an interview due to problems with transport (e.g. a rail strike).

Procedure

Stage 1

The immigration authorities send a letter to the family (or give it to the family at weekly reporting), which tells them that they must now leave the UK and explain how they can leave voluntarily. The letter encloses the IOM leaflet 'Offering asylum-seekers help and advice to return home'. The letter will set out that support may be withdrawn if the family fails, without reasonable excuse, to take reasonable steps to leave or to place themselves in a position where they may do so. If they have not been already, the adult family members will be placed on weekly reporting restrictions.

Stage 2

Three weeks after the 'stage 1 letter' above, if it appears that the family are not taking reasonable steps, a 'stage 2' letter will be sent inviting them for interview.

Stage 3

Stage 3 is the interview at which an immigration officer will:

- remind the family that they are not permitted to remain in the UK and must leave;
- warn the family that support may be withdrawn;

12

- ask the family what steps they have taken to leave following notification of the failure of the asylum claim;
- determine the reason for any delay in taking steps to leave;
- where appropriate, warn the family that they may be liable for prosecution under section 35 2004 Act (▶see 927);
- tell the family that if they make their own arrangements via their Embassy, confirmation of the approach to their national authorities would have to be provided within a two-week period;
- obtain details from the family of any personal circumstances which might affect a decision to withdraw support;
- obtain details of what other support networks the family has (e.g. extended family members or friends);
- take down the details of any reasons given why the family should be permitted to remain in the UK (two weeks is given for providing further evidence in support of any claims made).

If the immigration officer believes that the family has failed to take reasonable steps to leave the UK or to place themselves in a position to do so, a 'stage 3' letter is sent to the family (copied to legal representatives and to the director of the local social services authority) telling the family of the officer's views and warning them that failure to take these steps, without reasonable excuse, may lead to withdrawal of support. The family are given seven days to submit evidence that they are now taking steps.

If no satisfactory response is received to the 'stage 3' letter, the immigration officer should proceed to record that the case is to be certified. The policy describes the nature of the suggested certificate as follows:

'Generally speaking, if the family has travel documents but has not left the UK (and has no reasonable excuse) certification will be on the basis that they have failed to take reasonable steps to leave the UK voluntarily. If the family is not in possession of travel documents (and has no reasonable excuse for failing to obtain them or assisting with steps to obtain them on their behalf) certification will be on the basis that they have failed to place themselves in a position in which they can leave the UK voluntarily.'

However, the suggested certificate is not yet sent to the family. All of the papers are passed to NASS for the purposes of Stage 4.

Stage 4

On receipt of the papers, NASS officers will consider whether support is necessary to avoid a breach of an applicant's rights under the ECHR. This consideration will be based on the information about the family's circumstances taken at interview. NASS may need to make further enquiries. If NASS decides that support is not necessary to avoid a breach of a family's rights, the papers are passed back to the immigration service for a letter, including the certificate, to be prepared and sent.

> Support will end 14 days after the applicant has received the certificate. If the asylum support withdrawn is NASS support, there will be a right of appeal to the Asylum Support Adjudicator (▶see 1389–90).
>
> *Stage 5*
>
> Stage 5 is the actual withdrawal of support itself.

Exclusions under the Asylum Support Regulations

People who must be excluded

The following three categories of people cannot obtain asylum support from NASS where they make an application for themselves alone. The regulations referred to are the Asylum Support Regulations 2000.

1) **People entitled to benefits** People who are not excluded from getting welfare benefits (income support, income-based job-seeker's allowance, housing benefit and council tax benefit) by their immigration status are excluded from asylum support (reg. 4(1)–(4)(6)). The principle is that those who are entitled to benefits should claim those instead of being able to get asylum support (for details of those who can get these benefits even though they are 'subject to immigration control', ▶see 1255–8).

2) **Interim support available** People who are able to obtain interim asylum support from a local authority are excluded from NASS asylum support (reg. 4(2)(3)(4)(a)(5)) (▶see 1371–9). Interim support is due to be phased out by 31 March 2006.

3) **People not treated as asylum-seekers/dependants** People who are not being treated by the Home Office as if they have made claims for leave as an asylum-seeker or the dependant of an asylum-seeker for immigration purposes (reg. 4(2)(4)(c)). Note that the definition of 'dependant' for asylum support purposes is very wide (▶above 1345–7). This exclusion may cause problems for a dependant who comes within the asylum support definition but where the Home Office is not prepared to exercise discretion (i.e. beyond the normal spouse/minor child categories) to accept the person as a dependant for immigration purposes (▶see 691–4).

Family applications/mixed household cases

Where more than one person applies for asylum support as part of a group (i.e. normally as a family), the family is not excluded from asylum support unless *all* members are excluded because they fall into one of the three categories above (reg. 4(3)(4)). The purpose of this rule seems to be to ensure that a family can be supported by NASS if one of its members is not excluded. Applicants should, of course, access all other means of support before asylum support is available. The other support which is provided to the family (through benefits etc) will be taken into account by

12

NASS in deciding what level of asylum support to provide (further details about mixed households are given in NASS Policy Bulletin 11). For details about claiming benefit for dependants, ▶see 1276–81.

People already receiving support whose support may be suspended or discontinued

The following exclusions all apply to asylum-seekers (and their dependants) who are already being supported. NASS 'may' (i.e. it has a discretion) exclude from support anyone falling into any of the following categories.

1) **Breach of rules of accommodation** People can be excluded if support is being provided for them and NASS has reasonable grounds to believe that they or their dependant have committed a 'serious breach of the rules' of the accommodation (reg. 20(1)(a)).

2) **Serious violence** A supported person may be excluded if NASS has reasonable grounds to believe that they (or their dependant) have committed an act of 'seriously violent behaviour' whether the act occurs in accommodation provided by NASS or elsewhere (reg. 20(1)(b)).

3) **Asylum support offences** Where a supported person (or their dependant) commits an offence relating to asylum support (one under part VI 1999 Act, for example dishonest representations made in order to obtain asylum support), they may be excluded (reg. 20(1)(c)).

4) **Abandoned address** Where NASS has reasonable grounds to believe that a supported person (or their dependant) has abandoned the accommodation where support is provided to them (or another address notified by the applicant as to where they will live), without informing NASS and without permission, they may be excluded from support (reg. 20(1)(d)(6)(d)).

5) **Failure to comply with requests for information** Where a supported person has not complied with a request from NASS for information relating to asylum support within a reasonable period (the reasonable period will not be set at less than five working days), they may be excluded from support (reg. 20(1)(e)).

6) **Failure to attend interview** A supported person who fails, without reasonable excuse, to attend an interview about asylum support may be excluded (reg. 20(1)(f)). Applicants will be given at least five working days' notice of such interviews.

7) **Failure to comply with request for information relating to asylum claim** Where a supported person (or their dependant) fails to comply, within a reasonable period, with a request for information made by the Secretary of State which relates to their claim for asylum, support may be excluded. The reasonable period shall be no less than ten working days (reg. 20(1)(g)).

8) **Hidden resources** Where the Secretary of State reasonably believes that a supported person (or their dependant) has hidden their financial resources, they may be excluded (reg. 20(1)(h)).

9) **Failure to comply with reporting requirements** Where a supported person (or their dependant) fails to comply with a reporting condition of temporary admission (for the different kinds of temporary admission, ▶see 950–1) or bail, they may be excluded from support (reg. 20(1)(i), (6)(d)).

10) **Further asylum claim** Where NASS has reasonable grounds to believe that a supported person (or their dependant) makes, or tries to make, a further claim for asylum before the first claim has been determined and that the further claim is not put forward as part of the first claim, they may be excluded from support (reg. 20(1)(j)). An applicant can be excluded on this basis whether the further claim is made in their own name or a different name. This exclusion is not completely clear. It appears to be intended to prevent multiple claims being made in an abusive way without connection to the first. It surely does not penalise further representations being made about an existing claim which, of course, are advisable if circumstances change or if there is further important evidence to be submitted.

11) **Breach of 'relevant' condition** Where a supported person (or their dependant) fails, without reasonable excuse, to comply with a condition of residence attached to the provision of asylum support (reg. 20(1)(k) with reference to regs 19(2), 20(6)(c)), they may be excluded. NASS may try to use this (or (1) or (4) above) as a basis for excluding applicants from asylum support when they fail to travel from their temporary accommodation or they leave their accommodation (▶see further below at 1363–4).

Note that changes were made to the exclusions under the Asylum Support Regulations from 5 February 2005 so as to comply with the EU Minimum Standards of Reception Directive (▶see below at 1379–81). The above list incorporates those changes. So, for example, a person can no longer be excluded on the basis of 'intentional destitution'. In addition, the Regulations now echo the words of the Directive that decisions must be taken individually, objectively and impartially (see reg. 20(3)).

If a decision is taken to exclude a person under categories (1)–(11) above, NASS may *either* 'suspend' *or* 'discontinue' the support. For example, NASS could decide to suspend the provision of support on the basis of 'reasonable grounds' to believe that an applicant comes within (1) but then, on full enquiry, decide that support should not be discontinued after all.

Where support is suspended or discontinued under (4) or (9) above and the asylum-seeker is later traced or reports voluntarily, NASS will consider whether to re-instate support based on the reasons for the person's absence (reg. 20(5)).

12

Further applications after suspension or discontinuation

Where an asylum-seeker has had their support suspended or discontinued as described above, NASS can refuse to consider a further application for support by that person unless (reg. 21):

- there has been a 'material change of circumstances' (▶see 1370) since the decision to withdraw support; or
- NASS considers that there are 'exceptional circumstances' which justify reconsidering the application for support.

However, this does not affect the position as stated above in cases where support is suspended or discontinued under (4) or (9) above (applicants who abandon their address or fail to comply with reporting requirements). If such applicants later come to light, NASS will carefully consider whether to re-instate support even if there is no material change of circumstances (regs 20(5), 21(1)).

WHAT SUPPORT IS PROVIDED UNDER THE NASS SCHEME?

NASS can provide asylum support in any of the following ways (s96(1)(2) 1999 Act):

- accommodation, which is adequate for the asylum-seeker and their dependants;
- support to meet the essential living needs of the asylum-seeker and their dependants;
- support to meet the expenses (other than 'legal expenses'), which the asylum-seeker has in connection with their asylum claim;
- expenses that the asylum-seeker has, or their dependants have, in attending bail hearings in connection with the asylum-seeker's or their dependants' immigration detention; or
- if the circumstances of the particular case are 'exceptional', NASS may provide any other form of support, which it thinks is necessary to support the asylum-seeker and their dependants.

NASS may also provide services in the form of education, English language lessons, sporting and other developmental activities (reg. 14, Asylum Support Regulations).

Support may be provided in any of the above ways. So, an applicant who is destitute because they have nothing for their essential living expenses but who does have accommodation provided for them (for example through friends) can simply obtain support for their essential living needs. If the government had gone ahead and set up accommodation centres, it had intended to introduce regulations, which would prevent subsistence-only support being provided to an applicant who had been offered support in an accommodation centre (see s43 2002 Act).

General matters NASS will have regard to

Although there is a table setting out the 'rule of thumb' amounts to be provided for essential living needs (see below), in deciding the nature and level of support to be provided, NASS may take into account similar factors as when it is deciding whether the person is destitute (above). NASS must take into account (reg. 12(3)):

- any income which the asylum-seeker has or may be expected to have;
- any support which can reasonably be expected to be available to them; and
- any assets (cash, savings, investments, land, cars/vehicles/goods used for trade or business held in the UK or elsewhere), which are or may reasonably be expected to be available to the asylum-seeker.

As an alternative to paying the asylum-seeker less as a result of their income/assets, NASS could pay asylum support as normal but require that the supported person make contributions by way of payments to NASS (reg. 16). In addition, if assets which were not liquid at the time support began to be provided, later become realised (or able to become realised), NASS may recover monies paid over to the asylum-seeker (reg. 17).

As it continues to provide support to a particular asylum-seeker, NASS can also have regard, in deciding what support to continue to provide, to the extent to which the supported person/s are complying with residence conditions attached to the support (reg. 19).

Providing accommodation and 'dispersal'

The ability of NASS to make arrangements with other agencies for the provision of support rather than providing support directly is a crucial part of the dispersal scheme. It enables NASS to arrange for local authorities and others up and down the country to provide support in different areas. Policy is to provide accommodation on a 'no choice' basis for destitute asylum-seekers in dispersal areas around the country.

Legislation on dispersal Formally, the legislation which underlies the dispersal arrangements is as follows. When providing accommodation (i.e. the nature and location of accommodation) NASS must have regard to (s97(1) 1999 Act):

12

- the fact that accommodation is only being provided temporarily during the period of the asylum claim; and
- the desirability of providing accommodation for asylum-seekers in those areas where there is a good supply of accommodation, for example, areas outside London. It is the government's view that there is an acute shortage of accommodation in the London area.

In making the decision about the accommodation to be provided, NASS is not entitled to take into account the asylum-seeker's preferences about any of the following matters:

- the area in which the asylum-seeker wishes to be accommodated (s97(2)(a) 1999 Act);
- the nature of the accommodation which is to be provided (reg. 13(2)(a)); and
- the nature and standard of the fixtures and fittings in the accommodation (reg. 13(2)(b)).

However, despite this, in deciding where and what kind of accommodation will be provided, NASS can still take into account the asylum-seeker's 'individual circumstances' as they relate to their accommodation needs (see reg. 13(2)(b)). For example, in a case decided under the similar provisions of the interim scheme, *Mahdia*, the High Court held that location close to a mosque was not just a matter of choice or preference but was connected to the applicant's religious and emotional needs and was therefore relevant to their 'welfare'.

Policy on dispersal According to the guidance notes which accompany the NASS 1 form on which applications for NASS support are made, NASS take into account the following matters as relevant to the place in which accommodation will be provided and the nature of the accommodation:

- the applicant's ethnic group and/or religion so that accommodation can be found in an area where there is an existing community of people of a similar culture, together with support organisations which are sensitive to the asylum-seeker's cultural background and needs;
- the applicant's medical or psychological conditions or any disabilities which they have and any treatment they are receiving for those conditions;
- any special dietary needs of the asylum-seeker and their dependants;
- any ongoing medical or psychological conditions, which the asylum-seeker or their dependants have, together with the treatment, which is presently being provided for them.

NASS policy generally is to disperse asylum-seekers to accommodation outside London and the South East. However, according to NASS Policy Bulletin 31 ('dispersal guidelines'), NASS may be persuaded not to disperse a person if:

- they have family connections, which make dispersal inappropriate, but dispersal will normally be appropriate unless there are 'exceptional circumstances' relating to this factor (however, ▶see the provisions concerning family connections under the EU Reception Condition Directive and the UK Reception Conditions Regulations which followed it, 1380–1);
- they have children who are in their school or college year leading up to GCSE, AS or A-level exams provided that they have been at the educational establishment for a 'significant part of the previous' year (nominally at least a term) (in such cases, dispersal may be deferred); or
- the area where the asylum-seeker is residing is the only area in which they can properly worship.

The above examples are all stated by NASS to be circumstances in which the asylum-seeker's human rights would be infringed by dispersal; in particular the right to respect for family life and home, the right not to be denied an education and the right to freedom of religion (see Articles 8, 9 and Article 2 to the First Protocol ECHR). NASS will generally not disperse young people who reach 18 without a final decision having been made on their claim if they have been accommodated under section 20 Children Act (for details see Policy Bulletin 31, paras 4.1, 6.8 and Bulletin 29). NASS has also indicated that it will be sympathetic to deferring dispersal where an applicant has been referred to the Medical Foundation for the Care of Victims of Torture for assessment and it will provide non-dispersed accommodation where the Medical Foundation decides to accept the referral and to provide treatment (see NASS Policy Bulletin 19). Note that on 1 December 2005 NASS issued Policy Bulletin 95 containing new guidelines on 'dispersing asylum-seekers with health care needs'.

In *Wanjugu*, the applicant was suffering from complex post-traumatic stress syndrome as a result of being the witness to members of her family being killed. She was being treated at a specialist traumatic stress clinic in London and she challenged her dispersal. The High Court rejected her challenge that it was unlawful to restrict the non-dispersal aspect of the policy to cases where the asylum-seeker was receiving treatment from the Medical Foundation but not other institutions (paras 28–30). However, it is clear from the judgment that, where any detailed case is being made that appropriate treatment will not be available in the dispersal area, NASS will have to give careful consideration to whether dispersal is appropriate. The case was referred back to NASS for further consideration (see paras 34, 38, 42, 71-72).

However, where an asylum-seeker asks to be accommodated in a particular *dispersal* area, that request will normally be met if there is accommodation available in that area.

Failing to travel and leaving accommodation After a decision has been made to provide NASS accommodation in a dispersal area, for example after a period of temporary or 'emergency' NASS accommodation, it is likely that a condition of the support will be that the asylum-seeker travels to and resides at the new accommodation. People may find their support withdrawn if they do not travel and they may also be excluded from support if they fail to reside there (▶see above 1358–9 and see NASS Policy Bulletin 17). There have, however, been serious and well-documented cases of people who have left dispersed accommodation because they have been the victims of racial harassment and domestic violence. Exclusion on the basis of abandoning accommodation or breaching conditions about residing at a particular place is not automatic (▶see above 1358). NASS will have to consider the circumstances (and ▶see the procedure for when a person is traced or voluntarily reports, 1359, reg. 20(5)).

In cases of failure to travel, however, NASS may well withdraw the temporary support in London but leave open the offer of accommodation in the dispersal area. This has the effect of making the dispute between NASS and asylum-seeker really about the *location* of the accommodation

12

not its refusal, with the result that there is no right of appeal *at present* (►see 1390–1).

In harassment cases, the Asylum Support Adjudicators have stated that the degree, frequency, persistence and organisation of any harassment and its effect on the asylum-seeker are all relevant. They have also indicated that the effectiveness of the local police in dealing with harassment is relevant. In **Gezer**, the High Court (upheld in the Court of Appeal) held that it was not a breach of Article 3 to disperse an asylum-seeker to an area where there was hostility. The Secretary of State was however, required to provide protection when they come to know of the racial abuse and harassment. The protection does not, however, have to amount to a guarantee against the danger.

Providing for essential living needs

When the scheme originally came into force, under the 1999 Act, NASS had to provide the majority of an asylum-seeker's support other than by providing them with cash. Following the government's internal review of the support system, and in particular the effectiveness of voucher support, that provision of the 1999 Act was repealed from 8 April 2002 (see Asylum Support (Repeal) Order 2002).

In addition, the Asylum Support Regulations 2000 (reg. 10(6)) initially laid down that, as a general rule, NASS support would involve a person getting vouchers exchangeable for cash only to the extent of £10 per week per person. That rule was also abolished. Asylum-seekers are now provided with cash payments, which replaced cash vouchers on 4 June 2004. As 'a general rule' the weekly amounts that will be provided are those set out in the table (reg. 10(2) as amended by Asylum Support (Amendment) (No.2) Regulations 2004). Of course it is possible that more or less could be paid depending upon the particular circumstances of the applicant/s. In particular, the amounts shown in the table may be reduced if NASS is providing accommodation as part of the support package and included with the accommodation is some provision for essential living needs; for example, if bed and breakfast is provided (reg. 10(5)).

NASS ASYLUM SUPPORT RATES

The rates set out below are those as updated in April 2005. They are likely to continue to be updated each April. References to 'regs' are to the Asylum Support Regulations 2000 unless stated otherwise

Person/s	Amount
A married couple, an unmarried couple, a civil partnership couple or a same-sex couple at least one of whom is 18 or over but where neither is under 16	£61.71
Lone parent aged 18 or over	£39.34

Single person aged 25 or over	£39.34
Single person aged at least 18 but under 25	£31.35
Person aged at least 16 but under 18 (except a member of a couple as referred to above)	£33.85
Person aged under 16	£43.88

The rates were originally calculated to be about 70 per cent of income support levels which the Home Office justified on the grounds that asylum-seekers will have the costs of their utility bills, council tax and certain other expenses already met through the provision of accommodation.

The references above to 'civil partnership couple' and 'same-sex' couple are added to the definitions from 5 December 2005 as a result of amendments made to the Asylum Support Regulations by Schedule 13 to the Civil Partnership Act 2004 (Amendments to Subordinate Legislation) Order 2005.

In the above list of rates:

- to count as a 'married couple', the couple must be a man and a woman who are married to each other and who are members of the same household (regs 2(1), 10(4)(a));

- to count as an 'unmarried couple', the couple must be a man and a woman who, although not married, are living together as though they are married (regs 2(1), 10(4)(a));

- to count as 'civil partnership couple', the couple must be same-sex civil partners who are members of the same household (regs 2(1), 10(4)(a));

- to count as a same-sex couple, the couple must be same-sex and, although not civil partners, living together as if they were (regs 2(1), 10(4)(a));

- a 'lone parent' is a person who is not a part of a married, unmarried, civil partnership or same-sex couple who is the parent of a child who is under 18 and support is being provided for that child (reg. 10(4)(b)(d));

- a 'single person' is a person who is not part of a couple or the parent of a child under 18 for whom support is being provided (reg. 10(4)(c).

Additional support for pregnant women and children under three

From 3 March 2003, the Regulations were amended to provide a supplement to the weekly cash payments of NASS support for pregnant women and children aged under three (reg. 10A). In addition to the amounts set out above, a further amount of £3 per week will be paid to a pregnant woman, a further £5 per week will be paid for each child aged under one and a further £3 per week for each child aged between one and two. A woman must provide evidence of her pregnancy to NASS in order to claim this supplement.

In addition, one-off 'maternity' payments of £300 may be made to asylum-seekers in order to help them meet the special costs of their new baby. Either parent can apply to NASS for the payment close to the date of the birth (see NASS Policy Bulletin 37).

Additional Single Payments

NASS used to make an additional single payment of £50 to asylum-seekers after every period of six months during which asylum support had been

12

provided. This was provided in recognition of delays in the process, which meant that applicants might be kept on very low incomes for substantial periods of time. This was abolished on 4 June 2004 (revocation of reg. 11 by Asylum Support (Amendment) (No. 2) Regulations 2004).

Expenses in connection with asylum claims

NASS can meet expenses which are connected with an asylum claim (s96(1)(c) 1999 Act). These expenses do not include 'legal' expenses so NASS would not, for example, meet the costs of paying a lawyer to prepare the immigration case and represent the applicant. These can be met through the Community Legal Service (▶see Chapter 3). However, NASS can meet travel expenses for attending appeals or medical or other examinations in connection with a claim or attending immigration interviews. It may also cover expenses such as preparing and copying documents and sending letters and faxes in order to obtain further evidence. It will be noted that there is a clash between items that appear to be covered under this heading and certain items that are expressly excluded (▶see 1349–50).

Travel costs to attend bail hearings are expressly covered (s96(1)(d)(e)). It should also be noted that, under a quite separate power, the Home Office can pay travel expenses to enable a person to travel to comply with reporting restrictions imposed by any of the forms of temporary admission (▶see 950–1 and ▶see 652–4 for the different kinds of temporary admission) or immigration bail (s69 2002 Act). For travel to asylum support appeals, ▶see 1395.

Services

In terms of services, NASS is able to provide both education (including English language lessons) and sporting or other development activities. These services are not necessarily provided automatically to those receiving NASS support but can be provided in order to 'maintain good order' among supported asylum-seekers (reg. 14).

Exceptional support

There is a general 'sweep up' power for NASS to provide support in 'such other ways as [NASS] considers necessary' for the support of the asylum-seeker and their dependants (if any) (s96(2) 1999 Act). There is no indication of what further support can be provided under this power but no apparent limitation either. The only additional criterion for support to be provided under this power is that the circumstances must be 'exceptional'.

For access to health care, including free NHS prescriptions, dental treatment and other fixed expenses, ▶see 1328–35.

NASS PROCEDURES AND TEMPORARY SUPPORT

The NASS scheme incorporates the services of various voluntary sector agencies, for example the Refugee Arrivals Project, Migrant Helpline, Refugee Action, the Refugee Council and the Scottish and Welsh Refugee Councils, in order to help identify applicants for support and to assist them in making their applications and producing relevant information to NASS. NASS funds these voluntary organisations to provide 'reception assistance' which involves both providing temporary (or 'emergency') support (▶see below 1368) and helping applicants to apply for full NASS support by completing the application form (see immediately below).

The address for NASS is:

National Asylum Support Service
30 Wellesley Road
Croydon
Surrey
CRO 2AD

NASS can be telephoned on 0845 602 1739.

The application

NASS support must be applied for using the Form 'NASS 1' which is attached as a 'Schedule' to the Asylum Support Regulations. It should also be available from the above assistants who can help the asylum-seeker to complete it. It can be downloaded from the IND website. Only one form needs to be used for an applicant and their dependants. If a person wishes to obtain support as the dependant of a person who is already being supported by NASS, it is not necessary to complete the application form again; NASS will consider providing additional support for the dependant person if it is notified of their existence.

The NASS 1 form is accompanied by detailed 'Guidance Notes', which help to explain how the form should be completed and some of the procedures that will be followed. The form asks for details of the asylum-seeker and their dependants. If a person is applying as the dependant of an asylum-seeker, the form asks for details of the asylum-seeker themselves and their other dependants. The form also asks for details of the stage which the asylum claim has reached, the kind of support needed, details of current accommodation, any other kinds of support which the applicant has (including support from friends or relatives, cash, savings, investments or other property, employment, state benefits), and also about any disabilities or special needs that the applicant has.

In relation to many of the details asked, NASS requires documents to confirm what has been stated. It also requires four passport-size photographs of the person applying for support. In order to save time and for the application to be considered as soon as possible, the form can be

12

sent to NASS by fax, otherwise it can be sent by post. If the form is sent by fax, the original is also to be sent by post (▶see 1494 for the NASS fax number). After the application is made, NASS may make further enquiries of the applicant.

Awaiting the decision from NASS

There are no time-limits in the Regulations, which state when NASS must make a decision. However, NASS's target time is two working days of receiving the application (see Guidance Notes). If no decision has been made within seven days of making the application, NASS should write to the applicant explaining the delay.

Access to temporary (or 'emergency') NASS support immediately after claim

Before the above process of making and getting a decision on an application for NASS support is made, NASS can provide 'temporary' asylum support. This is normally provided directly by one of the assistants referred to above, although it is formally NASS's responsibility and is paid for by NASS (see s98 1999 Act). The legislation states that temporary support may be provided to an asylum-seeker or the dependant of an asylum-seeker who 'it appears' may be destitute. As with full NASS support, temporary support can be provided subject to conditions given in writing.

Practical processes involving section 55 and temporary support

Like full asylum support, section 98 'temporary' support is not available to applicants who do not claim 'as soon as reasonably practicable' unless it is necessary in order to avoid a breach of their human rights (see s55 2002 Act). However, it is not always possible to make a section 55 decision on the day that the applicant arrives and applicants may be granted temporary accommodation while decisions are being made. For details about the operation of section 55 and the decision of the House of Lords in *Adam, Limbuela & Tesema*, ▶see 1350–2 and ▶see 1307–11 (table).

So how do asylum-seekers get immediate access to at least temporary support? All people who claim asylum are subject to an initial 'screening' process (asylum procedures are set out in full in Chapter 42 and the screening process for both port asylum-seekers and those who claim in-country is set out more fully at ▶645–50).

Port cases An asylum-seeker who arrives at port and who appears to be destitute should have little problem in accessing temporary asylum support. Even if first-level formal screening cannot be carried out on the day and they cannot immediately be provided with an Application Registration Card (ARC), it should be clear from the notice of temporary admission given, that the applicant has claimed on arrival. This should allow reception assistants to provide temporary accommodation.

In-country cases When an applicant claims in-country at one of the screening units, the procedure used from 28 June 2004 onwards has been as follows:

1) The applicant is given an initial screening interview in the ordinary way (for details about screening, ▶see 649).

2) A new team was set up called the NASS Eligibility and Assessment Team ('NEAT') which links making the 'section 55' decision with the assessment of the NASS application.

3) If a decision cannot be made immediately, NEAT issues a letter of authorisation for access to temporary support.

4) The asylum-seeker then accesses temporary accommodation and can be assisted to complete the 'NASS 1' application for asylum support (above).

5) When the NASS 1 is received, it is linked by NEAT to the level 1 screening form. NASS then obtains whatever further information is required either from the applicant or their representative.

6) A decision on support, including a decision on the section 55 questions, can then be made. If it is decided that the applicant did not claim as soon as reasonably practicable (for the test about this, ▶see 1351–2), or if there is insufficient information to decide this issue, then NASS will consider whether it is necessary to provide support in order to avoid a breach of the applicant's human rights (▶see 1306 onwards).

7) Under s55(5)(human rights), NASS will not refuse unless positively satisfied that the person has some alternative form of support (this has been the position following the decision of the Court of Appeal in *Limbuela* but is unlikely to change given the applicants' success in that case, ▶see 1307–11).

8) If it is not possible to make a decision, then the applicant will be invited for a further (level 2) interview before a 'section 55 decision' is made.

These procedures are fluid and are likely to change. In particular, NASS may change its procedures now that the House of Lords have decided *Limbuela*. For a list of the relevant 'agents' for different areas ▶see 654–5.

12

NASS decision

If the decision on the application for support is negative, then the asylum-seeker will be asked to leave the temporary accommodation. Any negative decision taken on section 55 grounds cannot be appealed to the Asylum Support Adjudicator (s55(10) 2002 Act). The only means of challenging such decisions is by judicial review. An asylum-seeker whose application for full (i.e. not temporary) asylum support is refused can appeal to the Asylum Support Adjudicator (▶see 1389–91). NASS normally gives a brief explanation of the reasons for refusal.

If NASS decides to provide support, it will write to tell the applicant that the application has been accepted and to inform them of the package of support which will be provided.

Changes of circumstances

Those who are provided with support must notify NASS of relevant changes of circumstance. Relevant changes are if either the asylum-seeker or their dependants (reg. 15, Asylum Support Regulations):

- are joined in the UK by a dependant;
- receive or get access to any money or savings, investments, land, cars or other vehicles, goods for the purposes of trade or other business, which have not previously been declared to NASS;
- become employed;
- become unemployed;
- change their name;
- get married;
- form a civil partnership;
- begin living with another person as their spouse;
- start living with another person as if a civil partner of that person;
- get divorced;
- become a former civil partner after the dissolution of their civil partnership;
- separate from a spouse or from a person with whom they have been living as if married to that person;
- separate from their civil partner or from a person they have been living with as if they were civil partners;
- become pregnant;
- have a child;
- leave school;
- begin to share their accommodation with another person;
- move to a different address or otherwise leave the accommodation;
- are admitted into hospital;
- are sent to prison or some other form of custody;
- leave the UK;
- die.

After NASS has obtained all the necessary information about any change of circumstances, it may make a decision changing the nature or level of the existing support or withdrawing support.

The references to civil partnerships in the above definition of change of circumstance are inserted from 5 December 2005 as a result of amendments made to the Asylum Support Regulations by Schedule 13 to the Civil Partnership Act 2004 (Amendments to Subordinate Legislation) Order 2005.

Further applications for support and appeals

If an applicant is refused support, in most cases there is nothing to prevent them from making another application at any time and NASS must consider any application that is made. The circumstances in which the rules allow NASS not to 'entertain' an application for support are where (regs 3(4), 21(1); s103(6) 1999 Act):

- the application is not made by properly completing the application form;
- the information provided is not complete/accurate;
- the applicant is not cooperating with enquiries made by NASS;
- a person has previously had their support suspended or discontinued;
- a further application for support is made after an appeal to the Asylum Support Adjudicator is dismissed.

In the last two cases, NASS must still consider a further application for support if there has been a material change in circumstances (reg. 21(1)(c)(2), s103(6) 1999 Act and ▶see 1359 above for where support is withdrawn after an applicant leaves their accommodation).

'INTERIM' ASYLUM SUPPORT

The 'interim' scheme for the support of asylum-seekers by local authorities came into effect on 6 December 1999. It was intended as a temporary measure until the NASS scheme could be applied to all asylum-seekers. Originally, the scheme was intended to end in April 2002. It has in fact been repeatedly extended. It is due to end on 3 April 2006 (see Asylum Support (Interim Provisions) (Amendment) Regulations 2005).

Interim asylum support from local authorities and asylum support from NASS are alternatives. The idea is that if a person generally qualifies for asylum support, then some asylum-seekers are entitled to support from NASS and others will get it from an authority under the interim scheme. However, the vast majority of asylum-seekers (and all new asylum-seekers) are now the responsibility of NASS. For those asylum-seekers still supported under the interim scheme, see the table below.

12

Much of the scheme for interim support is the same, or very similar to that for asylum support (above). However, there are certain differences. The regulations that set out the scheme, the Asylum Support (Interim Provisions) Regulations 1999 (we have referred to them as the 'Interim Provisions Regulations' or simply the 'Regulations' or 'Regs'), are much less detailed than the Asylum Support Regulations. This is probably because it was felt that the interim scheme would last for a short period only and did not, therefore, need to be over-elaborate.

Appeals?

Unlike under the NASS scheme, there is no right of appeal against refusals to provide interim support or withdrawals of support. The only legal means of challenging decisions of local authorities on decisions concerning support is judicial review.

Which asylum-seekers get NASS support and which get interim support?

There has been much confusion over who is eligible for interim support and who is eligible for NASS asylum support. The main reason for this confusion is that the 1999 Act itself does not say who is entitled to which and neither do the Regulations.

The division of responsibility between NASS and the local authorities is set out in a series of 'directions' made by the Secretary of State under paragraph 14, Schedule 15 1999 Act (▶summarised in the table below). The effect of the directions is to treat the 'interim period' as having come to an end for certain classes of asylum-seeker. Although the situation is set out in detail in the table, it can be shortly summarised as follows:

1) Since 30 August 2000, no *new* asylum-seeker, wherever they make their application for asylum, has been able to get interim asylum support. If they are able to get asylum support, it must be claimed from NASS.

2) The 'interim period' during which local authorities are able to provide interim support is set to end on 3 April 2006 (reg. 2(6) Interim Provisions Regulations as amended). If it is not extended, local authorities will not be able to provide interim support beyond that point and all applicants will be eligible for NASS asylum support.

3) From June 2005, the Home Office has been issuing directions to move (in seven phases) all existing asylum-seekers supported by local authorities under the interim scheme, into the NASS regime by directing that the 'interim period' has come to an end for the various particular asylum-seekers supported by different local authorities.

NASS SUPPORT OR INTERIM SUPPORT AND THE 'INTERIM SCHEME PROJECT' TO MOVE ALL ASYLUM-SEEKERS TO NASS SUPPORT

The 'interim period' is set to end on 3 April 2006. At that point, NASS is expected to take responsibility for all asylum-seekers.

Between June 2005 and April 2006, the Secretary of State is issuing 'directions' to move all those classes of asylum-seeker who are still eligible for interim asylum support, over to asylum support provided by NASS. NASS is also taking direct responsibility for 'dis-benefitted' asylum-seekers, many of whom have formally been NASS responsibility from 25 September 2000 but for whom NASS has been providing funding to local authorities in order for them to arrange support. The process of transferring all asylum-seekers to NASS is called the 'Interim Scheme Project'. Altogether between 5,000 and 6,000 interim cases and about 350 'dis-benefitted' cases were expected to transfer.

It is *also* intended to transfer to NASS asylum-seekers in Scotland and Northern Ireland, where the interim scheme does not apply but where asylum-seekers have been provided with support under separate legislation. This has required amendments to legislation.

So, it is necessary to look at the three following questions (and see below):

1) which residual classes of asylum-seeker were still being supported under the interim scheme as the 'Interim Scheme Project' to move them to NASS support began in June 2005?

2) when are people being moved over to NASS support?

3) what are the practical implications of being moved over to NASS support – is an asylum-seeker likely to be dispersed at that point?

1) Which asylum-seekers were still eligible for interim support as at May 2005?

At the point that the Interim Scheme Project' began to move *existing* supported asylum-seekers from the interim scheme over to support provided by NASS (June 2005), *all new* asylum-seekers had, for a long time (i.e. since 30 August 2000) been eligible for NASS rather than interim support. The division of responsibility was set down in Directions 1-4 made by the Secretary of State under paragraph 14, Schedule 15 1999 Act. For a detailed look at how those directions operated, see the table at pp 695–696 of the 2002 Edition of the *Handbook*. Here we simply state the classes who were still being provided with interim support from local authorities. They were:

- Asylum-seekers who claimed asylum before 3 April 2000 at port, or within three months of a declaration of upheaval and who were recorded as having their claim to asylum determined by the Secretary of State before 25 September 2000, *except* those who were living in Kent or Medway and who received their decisions on or after 17 April 2000. This class of asylum-seeker was entitled to welfare benefits until a decision was made on their asylum claim (▶see 1256). They are therefore often referred to as 'dis-benefitted' asylum-seekers.

- Asylum-seekers who claimed asylum in-country at any time *before* the 'relevant date' for the region in which they were living (the 'relevant dates' were: Kent and Medway, 17 April 2000; London, 24 July 2000; North East/Yorkshire/Humberside/Wales, 31 July 2000; North West/East Midlands/Eastern/South-West/ South-Central, 14 August 2000; West Midlands/Sussex, 29 August 2000).

- Asylum-seekers with dependent children who have previously been provided with or who were eligible for interim asylum support and who make a further asylum application. These asylum-seeking families also remained the responsibility of local authorities.

2) When are people being moved over to NASS support under the Interim Scheme Project?

It is the intention of the government to move all the asylum-seekers listed in (1) above over to NASS support by 31 March 2006 in time for the ending of the

12

interim period on 3 April 2006. There are also a number of cases for which NASS is formally responsible as 'dis-benefitted' asylum-seekers who were refused after 25 September 2000, for whom NASS has funded local authorities to provide support. They too should all be directly provided for by NASS by 31 March 2006 (see Interim Scheme Project, Information Sheet No 1, 4 July 2005). Applicants are being moved over to NASS support in seven phases with the final phase due to begin on 6 March 2006. Asylum-seekers are being transferred by area. It is not possible to list the transfers by region (North East, West Midlands etc) because asylum-seekers from the same region are being moved in different phases depending on the particular area they live in within that region. The transfer of asylum-seekers supported in London is taking place on a borough-by-borough basis with a number of London boroughs making up the final phase (for Southwark, the situation was more complicated still with asylum-seekers being transferred according to their surname, see the direction issued on 9 May 2005).

So, for up-to-date details of the transfer process and the various phases, applicants and advisers should look at the 'Interim Scheme Project' section of the IND website which contains the directions given so far, as well as information briefings and explanatory letters to the Chief Executives and Directors of Social Services of the local authorities.

3) What are the practical implications of being moved over to NASS support under the 'Interim Scheme Project'?

Asylum-seekers who are transferred from the interim scheme to NASS asylum support are dispersed in line with normal NASS dispersal policy. This means that those living in London and the South East are likely to be offered accommodation in a dispersal area outside London. However, NASS will apply its ordinary policy on when it is not appropriate to disperse such persons (▶see 1361–3). For those who are living outside London and the South East, NASS will consider whether they can support them in their existing accommodation. If not, NASS will offer other accommodation locally or in one of the nearest 'cluster' areas.

NASS will also re-assess the circumstances of all applicants as they transfer to check that they are indeed entitled to asylum support.

Much of the above information is taken from the letter of NASS Operations to all local authority Chief Executive Officers dated 23 March 2005 and the NASS Interim Scheme Project 'Questions and Answers' issued in May 2005 and in August 2005.

Deciding whether a person qualifies for interim support

The basic conditions which need to be satisfied, in order to qualify for interim asylum support are the same as for asylum support. An applicant must be (para. 1(2) Sch 9 1999 Act, reg. 2(1)(2) Interim Provisions Regulations):

- an asylum-seeker or the dependant of an asylum-seeker;
- likely to become destitute within 14 days.

The applicant must also, of course, be eligible for support under the interim scheme instead of the NASS asylum support scheme (see the table above). For details of who is an 'asylum-seeker' and when a person ceases to be an asylum-seeker, ▶see 1341–5. For the definition of 'dependant' of an asylum-seeker, ▶see the table at 1346–7.

In addition, a person is 'destitute' for the purposes of the interim scheme if they (s95(3) 1999 Act applied by para. 3, Sch 9 1999 Act):

- do not have adequate accommodation or any means of obtaining it; or
- they have adequate accommodation but cannot meet their essential living needs.

For details of this general definition of destitution, ▶see above at 1347–8.

There are no special or additional rules contained in the Interim Provisions Regulations about what should be taken into account in deciding whether a person can meet their essential living needs. In determining whether a person has adequate accommodation, no account can be taken of (s95(6) 1999 Act as applied by para. 3, Sch 9 1999 Act):

- the fact that they do not have a legal right to stay in that accommodation;
- the fact that they share the accommodation, or part of it, with other persons;
- the fact that the accommodation is temporary; or
- the location of the accommodation.

Providing interim support

If an applicant is entitled to interim support, the local authority is required to provide (reg. 5(1)(3), Interim Provisions Regulations):

- accommodation, which is adequate for the asylum-seeker and their dependants (if any);
- support to meet the essential living needs of the asylum-seeker and any dependants; and
- support to meet the applicant's reasonable travel expenses in attending the hearing of their asylum appeal and any interview concerning their claim to asylum that has been requested by the immigration authorities.

Providing both accommodation and support for essential living needs

Under the Regulations, the local authority must provide both accommodation and support to meet an asylum-seeker's essential living needs. Only if the circumstances of a particular case are 'exceptional', can support be provided in terms of either accommodation or support to meet essential living needs (reg. 5(4) Interim Provisions Regulations). In addition, where the circumstances are 'exceptional', the authority is not restricted to the forms of support set out above but is to provide support in any way 'necessary' in order for a person and their dependants to be supported.

Where however a person is eligible for interim support and their household includes a child who is under 18 and is their dependant, the local authority is not restricted in the same way and can provide either accommodation or support for essential living needs or both (reg. 5(2)).

Deciding on the level of support and where it is provided

In deciding what should be provided in terms of accommodation and essential living needs, the local authority must have regard to (reg. 6):

- the income that the asylum-seeker has or may reasonably be expected to have;
- support or assets that the asylum-seeker has or which might reasonably be expected to be available to them;
- the welfare of the asylum-seeker; and
- the cost of providing support.

Accommodation In providing accommodation, the authority cannot take into account a person's expressed preferences as to (reg. 6(2)), Interim Provision Regulations:

- the location of the accommodation;
- the nature of the accommodation; or
- the fixtures and fittings contained in the accommodation.

As with the NASS scheme, however, this does not mean that the local authority can ignore the asylum-seeker's interests and circumstances in deciding what accommodation to provide to them. This is because the authority, in providing any form of support, is bound to have regard to the 'welfare' of the supported person and their dependants (see reg. 6(1)(c)). It may well be that the welfare of the individual claimant can only be properly safeguarded if they are located near to appropriate medical facilities, certain other family members or the school where the children of the household have been admitted and have already settled. In addition, the accommodation that is provided must also be 'adequate' for the 'needs' of the supported person and any dependants they have (reg. 5(1)(a)). This also indicates that the authority must address any individual or particular need, which the asylum-seeker has.

Essential living needs Under the scheme as it was originally introduced, the Regulations stated that asylum-seekers could only receive support for their essential living needs in cash of up to £10 per person each week. The rest was to be provided by vouchers or in kind. These restrictions were removed on 8 April 2002 and so authorities may now provide all such support in cash.

Unlike under the NASS scheme, however, there are no set rates for the levels of support that should be provided to asylum-seekers. Comparison can of course be made with NASS rates in order to see what levels of support can be expected (▶see the table at 1364–6). It should be remembered that the table of rates assumes that NASS is paying household bills. However, in *R (Satu) v Hackney LBC*, the Court of Appeal confirmed that the Asylum Support Regulations (under the NASS scheme) do not apply to interim asylum support and that there was nothing which required the local authority to apply the NASS rates.

Exclusions from interim asylum support

Even if they meet the basic conditions, asylum-seekers and their dependants may be excluded from interim asylum support if they come within any of the following categories. It should be noted that, unlike the Asylum Support Regulations, the Interim Provisions Regulations were not amended following the EC Receptions Conditions Directive (for details of the Directive, ▶see 1379–81). Where an applicant is excluded contrary to the Directive, the exclusion will be unlawful.

1) **Intentional destitution** An applicant who has 'intentionally made himself and his dependants (if any)' destitute is excluded. This is the case if they are destitute as a result of a deliberate act or failure to do something without any reasonable excuse (reg. 7(1)(a)(2) Interim Provisions Regulations). Following the EC Reception Conditions Directive, this basis of exclusion has been removed from the asylum support scheme but the Interim Provisions Regulations have not been amended in line. Exclusions on this basis may, therefore, be contrary to EU law.

2) **Claim to another local authority** An applicant who has made a claim for support to another local authority is excluded (unless the claim for support is 'transferred' from the first authority to the second one, see below at 1379) (reg. 7(1)(b)).

3) **Claim to authority other than one to which previous application made** An applicant is excluded if they are claiming support from a local authority which is different from a local authority to which they have, in the previous year, made a claim for assistance under section 21 National Assistance Act 1948 or section 17 Children Act 1989 (reg. 7(1)(c)).

4) **Able to claim welfare benefits** Certain applicants who are not prevented from getting income support as a result of their immigration status are excluded (reg. 7(1)(d)). Note that anyone who is able to get welfare benefits is likely to be excluded on the grounds that they are not destitute and/or there is income which they may reasonably be expected to have (see s95(3) 1999 Act, reg. 6(1) Interim Provisions Regulations). For details of those who are able to get welfare benefits even though they are 'subject to immigration control', ▶see 1255–9.

5) **Not an asylum-seeker/being treated as the dependant of an asylum-seeker** Plainly those who are not 'asylum-seekers' are not eligible for support unless they are the dependants of an asylum-seeker. A person

12

who claims to be a dependant of an asylum-seeker will be also be excluded, however, if they are not being treated by the Home Office as the dependant of an asylum-seeker for immigration purposes (reg. 7(1)(e)).

6) **Excluded under Schedule 3 2002 Act** An applicant is excluded from support if they come within any of the excluded classes under Schedule 3 2002 Act. This does not, however, exclude support being provided to a child, or support being provided in order to avoid a breach of a person's ECHR or EU rights (see paras 1(1)(l)-7A Sch 3 2002 Act). For details of the excluded categories and the exemptions, ▶see 1301–14.

7) **Failure to comply with conditions** An applicant may be excluded if they (or their dependant) fails, without reasonable excuse, to comply with a condition on which support has been provided (regs 5(6)-(8), 8(2)(a)).

8) **Leaving the accommodation provided** An applicant may be excluded if they (or their dependant), without reasonable excuse, leaves accommodation in which support is provided for more than seven days (reg. 8(2)(b)).

Note that, under categories, (7) and (8), even if all of the conditions for excluding a person from support are satisfied (including there being no 'reasonable excuse' for the breach of condition or leaving the accommodation), the authority still has a *discretion* in the Regulations as to whether to exclude them from support. In addition, for these two categories, it is not automatic that support is ended indefinitely as the local authority may either 'discontinue' or 'suspend' the support (reg. 8(2)). For example, an authority might suspend the provision of support until the asylum-seeker has put the breach of conditions right or returned to the accommodation.

If a person falls into categories (1)-(5), the Regulations do not provide a discretion; they state that interim asylum support 'must' be refused. As indicated, the 'human rights exception' (▶1306) directly applies to any exclusion under category (6).

Procedures for getting interim support and temporary interim support

The interim support regulations themselves do not provide any particular procedures for applying for and getting support. Many asylum-seekers were referred to the authority by an adviser or representative. The asylum support teams within local authorities have largely been connected to social services departments. The Interim Provisions Regulations do refer to 'claims' for support (see, for example, reg. 3(3) and see para. 2(2) Sch 9 1999 Act). It is debatable whether a claim needs to be made, or whether an authority has a duty to assess those who come to its attention and who may qualify for support in order to determine whether they are eligible.

While an authority is making a decision on support, it should provide adequate temporary support (reg. 4, Interim Provisions Regulations).

Unlike in the NASS scheme, there are no rights of appeal to an independent body against decisions refusing to grant or terminating interim support. It is, therefore, essential that local authorities proceed with care, fairness and thoroughness in making these decisions. There are no regulations dealing with how the support provided may be reviewed owing to a change in a person's circumstances after they have been awarded support. However, it is implicit that an authority may review a person's situation if there is a change in circumstances, for example, if the asylum-seeker obtains employment.

Transferring claims for support

In certain circumstances, the local authority to which the claim for support is made may transfer the claim to another local authority. The local authority to which the claim is transferred then has the responsibility for determining whether the asylum-seeker is eligible for support and for providing support if they are eligible.

The circumstances in which local authorities are able to transfer claims for support are not set out in the Regulations themselves but instead the local authorities are able to make their own agreed arrangements for the circumstances in which they may transfer claims (see reg. 9, Interim Provisions Regulations). The agreement, which was reached by local authorities complemented the general NASS policy of dispersing asylum-seekers away from London and the South East wherever possible. Because no new asylum-seekers are now the responsibility of local authorities under the interim scheme, these transfers will now generally have already taken place.

EU MINIMUM STANDARDS FOR THE RECEPTION OF ASYLUM-SEEKERS

An EU Council Directive of 27 January 2003 lays down minimum standards for the reception of asylum-seekers (2003/9/EC). The Directive arose out of a special meeting in Tampere on 15 and 16 October 1999, where the European Council agreed to work towards establishing a common European asylum system based on the full application of the 1951 Refugee Convention. This common system was to include common minimum conditions for the reception of asylum-seekers.

As with other EU legislation, where the requirements of the Directive are sufficiently clear and precise, it has direct effect in UK law and can be relied on over and above UK legislation.

The Directive required member states to bring laws into force to comply with the Directive by 6 February 2005 (article 26). Some of it has been implemented by the Asylum Seekers (Reception Conditions) Regulations 2005. In addition, both the Asylum Support Regulations 2000 and the Immigration Rules have been amended in order to comply with the Directive.

12

The important provisions of the Directive together with the Reception Conditions Regulations and other changes are summarised in the table below.

EU MINIMUM STANDARDS FOR THE RECEPTION OF ASYLUM-SEEKERS AND CHANGES TO UK REGULATIONS

The Directive

The EU Council Directive of 27 January 2003 lays down minimum standards for the reception of asylum-seekers (2003/9/EC).

The Directive is detailed and covers the following areas: information to be provided to asylum-seekers (article 5); documentation to be issued to asylum-seekers (article 6); residence and freedom of movement (article 7); schooling (article 10); employment (article 11); vocational training; material reception conditions (articles 13-14); reduction and withdrawal of reception conditions (article 16); persons with special needs (Chapter IV); Appeals (Chapter V).

Particularly important aspects are:

- member states are to inform asylum-seekers within a reasonable time (not more than 15 days after they have lodged their application for asylum) of any established benefits and of the state's obligations about providing support (the information must be in writing in a language which the asylum-seeker understands) (art. 5);

- within three days of an asylum claim being made, the state must issue the applicant with a document certifying their status as an asylum-seeker (art. 6) (for ARCs, ▶see 651–2);

- states must determine a time, starting from the date when an asylum claim was made during which time an applicant shall not be entitled to obtain employment and states must decide on conditions for granting the right to work if a decision has not been taken within a year (art. 11) (for access to employment for asylum-seekers, ▶see 694–6);

- the material conditions of reception are to be 'such as to ensure a standard of living adequate for the health of applicants and capable of ensuring their subsistence' (art. 13);

- housing must be provided which assures the protection of the asylum-seeker's family life and the possibility of communicating with relatives, legal advisers, representatives of the UNHCR and other NGOs (art. 14);

- decisions on reduction, withdrawal or refusal of support must be proportionate and they must be taken individually, objectively, and impartially and reasons must be given (art. 16.4);

- negative decisions 'relating to' the granting of support shall carry with them a right of appeal (art. 21).

Reception Conditions Regulations

In order to respond to the Directive, the government introduced the Asylum Seekers (Reception Conditions) Regulations (in force from 5 February 2005).

Under these regulations:

- when accommodating asylum-seekers, either temporarily or under the full asylum support duty, NASS must have regard to the need for family unity and, insofar as it is reasonably practicable to do so, ensure that family members are accommodated together ('family' member means spouse, unmarried partner or minor child) (reg. 3(1));

- in providing support, NASS must take into account the special needs of vulnerable persons whether they are asylum-seekers or members of their family: minors, disabled persons, elderly persons, pregnant women, lone parents with minor children, persons who have been subject to torture, rape or other serious forms of violence (reg. 4);

- in order to protect an unaccompanied minor's best interests, the Secretary of State must try to trace the members of the minor's family as soon as possible after they claim asylum (reg. 6).

Changes to Asylum Support Regulations

From 5 February 2005, the Asylum Support Regulations 2000 have been amended in line with the Reception Conditions Directive (see Asylum Support (Amendment) Regulations 2005). Most importantly, the amendments modify the circumstances in which the Regulations permit a person to be excluded from support or have their support suspended or discontinued (these changes are incorporated into the text at ▶1358–60 but ▶see also 1377–8). An applicant can no longer, for example, be denied support because they are 'intentionally' destitute.

Changes to Immigration Rules

The immigration rules were amended from 4 February 2005 so as to comply with the Reception Conditions Directive. Changes include (see part 11B HC 395 inserted by HC 194):

- within at most, 15 days of the claim, the Home Office must provide information concerning support and legal assistance;

- the information must be provided in writing and in a language which the asylum-seeker understands;

- asylum-seekers must notify the Home Office of their present address and of any changes of address;

- in non-detained cases, a status document (i.e. an ARC) must be provided within three working days of the asylum claim (and see 651);

- asylum-seekers must be permitted to apply for permission to work if their applications are still outstanding after a year (for full details, ▶see 695–6).

12

'HARD CASES' SUPPORT

At the same time as the 1999 Act introduced a system of asylum support, it also created a power to provide support as a 'safety net' for when people do not qualify for support under the legislation but do not deserve to be left unsupported (s4 1999 Act). This became known as 'hard cases' support and, in practice, it is presently provided by NASS. Under changes made by the 2004 Act, the Home Office has made regulations setting out the conditions on which hard cases support may be provided to failed asylum-seekers and allowing NASS to attach conditions to the provision of support. In particular, NASS may make it a condition that the applicant participates in 'community activities'.

Hard cases support continues to be a safety-net, in particular for asylum-seekers whose claims and appeals have been determined against them but who cannot at present be expected to leave. The Immigration, Asylum and Nationality Bill 2005 proposes to give local authorities the power to provide hard cases support as well as NASS.

Who can get hard cases support?

There are two powers to provide support under section 4 1999 Act. The Secretary of State can provide support to:

1) those who have been 'temporarily admitted' to the UK or released from detention under para. 21, Sch 2, 1971 Act, or released on bail from any immigration detention (s4(1));

2) those who are no longer asylum-seekers because their claims for asylum have been rejected (support may also be provided to their dependants) (s4(2)).

Anyone who falls within (1) may be provided with support; applicants do not have to be, or have been, asylum-seekers. In (2) above, the applicant must be a failed asylum-seeker. The meaning of claiming asylum for these purposes is that they must have made a claim for either refugee status, or protection under Article 3 ECHR or both. They must also no longer be an 'asylum-seeker' for the purposes of asylum support (s4(4)); the idea being that they are no longer able to get asylum support.

The regulations which have been made under section 4 to set out criteria for deciding whether an applicant should be granted support are the Immigration and Asylum (Provision of Accommodation to Failed Asylum-Seekers) Regulations 2005. They came into force on 31 March 2005. The Regulations only appear to apply to the power to provide support in (2) above. They don't appear to regulate the power in (1) above.

The conditions for obtaining support as set out in these regulations and NASS policy on hard cases support are set out in the table below.

Exclusions from hard cases support

Although hard cases support is intended to be a 'safety net' form of support, as with other forms of support it is subject to the following two exclusions.

- Those who claim asylum on or after 8 January 2003 are excluded from hard cases support if the requirements of section 55 2002 Act are not met (see s55(2)(a) 2002 Act). Such applicants should therefore have claimed asylum 'as soon as reasonably practicable' after their arrival in the UK (▶see above at 1350–2).

- Applicants who fall into any of the excluded classes in Schedule 3 2002 Act (▶see 1302–3) are also excluded (para. 1(1)(l), Sch 3, 2002 Act).

However, in relation to both of these exclusions, applicants can still be provided with hard cases support if it is necessary to provide it in order to avoid a breach of their human rights (s55(5), para. 3, Sch 3, 2002 Act) (▶see 1306–14, 1325–8, 1354–7).

'HARD CASES' SUPPORT: REGULATIONS AND POLICY

The legislation from which the information in this table is taken is section 4 1999 Act and the Immigration and Asylum (Provision of Accommodation to Failed Asylum-Seekers) Regulations 2005.

Information about practice is taken from NASS Policy Bulletin 71 (31 March 2005 issue). The Bulletin gives details about the evidence required to satisfy the various conditions.

Requirements to be met by the failed asylum-seeker

The first condition is that the failed asylum-seeker must appear to be destitute. 'Destitute' here has the same meaning as for asylum support: the applicant is destitute if they do not have adequate accommodation and food and other essential items (regs 2, 3(1)).

In addition to being destitute, the applicant must satisfy *one* of the five conditions set out below (regs 3(1)(b), (2)).

In order to *continue* receiving support, applicants must continue to satisfy the above conditions. NASS has said that it will periodically review the position to ensure that those provided with hard cases support remain eligible (NASS Policy Bulletin 71, para. 3.2).

1) *Reasonable steps taken to leave*

The first alternative condition is that the applicant is taking all reasonable steps to leave the UK, or to place themselves in a position in which they are able to leave the UK. This may include cooperating with attempts to obtain a travel document to be able to leave (this condition is similar to the basis upon which asylum-seeking families can be excluded from asylum support and other support under Schedule 3, 2002 Act, for NASS policy concerning those exclusions, ▶see 1354–7).

Evidence required: the applicant should provide confirmation from the immigration service that an application for a travel document has been made. Alternatively, confirmation could be provided from the International Organisation for Migration that an application for assistance in returning has been made.

12

2) *Unable to leave*

The second possible condition is that the applicant is unable to leave the UK because of 'some physical impediment to travel', or for some other medical reason.

Evidence required: a letter from the applicant's doctor stating 'in clear terms' that the applicant is not fit to travel and the date when they are expected to able to travel. Women in the late stages of pregnancy should provide recent medical evidence stating the expected date of delivery. Those with new-born children (under six weeks) should provide the long birth certificate or other medical documents showing the birth date.

3) *No viable route available*

The third possible condition is that the applicant is unable to leave the UK because, in the opinion of the Secretary of State, there is presently no viable route of return available.

Evidence required: a statement of policy that the Home Office considers that there is no viable route of voluntary return to the applicant's country of origin.

4) *Application for judicial review made*

The fourth possible condition is that the applicant has made an application for judicial review of a decision relating to their asylum claim (and if the judicial review claim has been made in England, Wales or Northern Ireland, 'permission' or 'leave' to apply for judicial review must have been granted).

Evidence required: a copy of the order of the court granting permission, or confirmation of this from either the Treasury Solicitor or the applicant's legal representative. In Scotland, there is no 'permission' stage and so, in Scottish cases, all that is required is evidence that a judicial review application has been made.

5) *Human rights exception*

The fifth possible condition is that the applicant needs to be provided with accommodation in order to avoid a breach of their human rights under the ECHR.

This is the same 'human rights exception' as applies to section 55 2002 Act and Schedule 3 2002 Act exclusions. NASS will consider whether it is reasonable to expect the applicant to leave the UK and, if not, whether it is necessary to provide support in order to avoid a breach of the applicant's human rights by their being destitute in the UK. For details about the factors relevant to a consideration of these issues, ▶see 1306–14, 1325–8, 1354–7.

In relation to hard cases in particular, NASS has stated that the circumstances in which it would accept that it would *not* be reasonable to expect the applicant to leave the UK *include* the following:

- the applicant has made further representations to the Home Office which are put forward as a 'fresh claim' for asylum (▶see 730–5) and these have not yet been considered; hard cases support will be provided in these cases *unless* 'it is clear to the NASS caseworker that the further representations simply rehearse previously considered material or contain no detail whatsoever';

- the applicant has submitted a late appeal against a decision of the Home Office to refuse asylum and the AIT is still considering whether to allow the appeal to proceed out of time.

Cases

The circumstances in relation to different countries on the above issues are ever-changing. The following details, concerning Zimbabwe and Iraq, give an illustration only. Advisers will need to identify the up-to-date position in relation to the case at hand, including further developments in relation to the country in question.

Zimbabwe

In *R (Guveya) v NASS*, an asylum-seeker argued that, since the Home Office's policy at the time was not to return failed asylum-seekers to Zimbabwe, he should be entitled to support under section 4 without agreeing to return there voluntarily. However, the High Court held that, just because the Home Office had a 'generous' policy of not removing failed asylum-seekers to that country, that did not mean that it was reasonable for the applicant to refuse to return voluntarily.

Further challenges concerning Zimbabwean asylum-seekers were adjourned by the High Court on 4 August 2005 to await a decision of the AIT in a test case concerning the safety of removing failed asylum-seekers to Zimbabwe (*R (M, C & N) v SSHD*). Following hearings in early October 2005, the AIT determined that the process by which the UK enforces the involuntary return of failed asylum-seekers to Zimbabwe exposed them to risk at the hands of the Zimbabwean Central Intelligence Organisation (see *AA v SSHD*).

Iraq

In *R (Abdullah) v SSHD*, a failed Iraqi asylum-seeker was refused section 4 support because he had refused to sign an application to the International Organisation of Migration stating that he wished to make a 'voluntary' departure to Iraq (see requirement (1) above). He had refused to do so because he believed that the return journey was unsafe. Permission to apply for judicial review was granted in September 2004.

On 17 January 2005, NASS announced a change in policy in relation to failed Iraqi asylum-seekers. It accepted that it was arguable that there were risks in making the journey to Iraq and that, therefore, it would not continue to demand that an applicant sign up to return before they could get section 4 support. A large number of failed Iraqi asylum-seekers then became eligible for hard cases support.

However, by 1 August 2005, NASS announced that it considered that a safe route of return exists for Iraqis whose claims have been refused. From that date all such applicants who make an application for section 4 support have to show that they satisfy one of the requirements above e.g. by taking steps to leave. From September 2005, NASS is reviewing the cases of Iraqi nationals who had been provided with hard cases support.

The government initially stated its intention of beginning enforced returns to Iraq in February 2004. It states that the delay in doing so has been caused by

12

problems with practical arrangements. The latest chapter, as we go to press, is that, on 17 November 2005, the government stated that it had resolved the logistical difficulties and that it would be commencing removal straight away. The position paper issued by the government continues:

'We will only return people to those areas of the country assessed as sufficiently stable and where we are satisfied that the individual concerned will not be at risk'.

The government maintained its above position in relation to section 4 support and failed asylum-seekers from Iraq. Challenges are likely.

'Community activities' and other conditions

NASS can make it a condition of the accommodation provided as part of hard cases support that the applicant participates in 'community activities' (regs 4-5). These activities must not be for more than 35 hours per week. Before requiring that the asylum-seeker participates in these activities, NASS will consider whether the asylum-seeker is able to take part having regard to their physical, mental and medical condition and any responsibility they may have for dependent child/ren.

NASS will usually make it a condition of the accommodation that the applicant complies with certain standards of behaviour, that they report, live at a particular address and comply with steps taken to arrange their departure from the UK.

Failure to comply with community activities or any of these other conditions (which must all be properly notified) could lead to the withdrawal of the support. NASS will consider whether there is a reasonable excuse for failing to comply with the condition (Policy Bulletin 71, para. 8).

Applying for hard cases support and appeals

Applicants for hard cases support must complete the standard application form and return it to NASS. The form can be downloaded from the IND website in the section dealing with NASS. Applicants are asked to identify the ground upon which they say they qualify for support and provide the relevant evidence (see table above). Applicants are also told of the conditions on which any support is likely to be granted and they are asked to state that they understand and agree to them.

From 31 March 2005, an applicant who is refused hard cases support, or whose hard cases support is withdrawn, has been able to appeal to the Asylum Support Adjudicator (s103(2A) 2002 Act as added by s10(3) 2004 Act). Where the decision is to discontinue hard cases support, the support will normally continue during the period that the appeal is outstanding (NASS Policy Bulletin 71, para. 9.2).

Further applications for hard cases support

A person who has previously been refused hard cases support can make a further application which will be considered on its merits under the criteria set out in the table above. However, if the application was previously refused and there has been no change of circumstances since it was made, the application is likely to be refused again (Policy Bulletin 71, para. 10.2).

What is actually provided as hard cases support?

The support that is provided under section 4 is 'facilities for the accommodation of a person'. Support takes the form of 'board' (i.e. food and other essentials) and accommodation. Cash is not provided. As to the location of the accommodation, NASS states:

'Accommodation is provided in a number of locations across the UK. NASS shall endeavour to make support under section 4 available to a person in the region in which they were resident prior to the refusal of their asylum claim, or in the region in which they are resident at the time of their application. However, this will not always be possible and it may be necessary to provide a person with accommodation in another region.' (NASS Policy Bulletin 71, para. 6.2).

12

42 Asylum support appeals

This short chapter deals with appeals against decisions made by NASS concerning asylum support and hard cases support. For full details of both of these forms of support, see Chapter 41. For appeals against immigration decisions concerning immigration status, see Section 10.

In some cases where NASS makes a negative decision about asylum support or hard cases support, there is a right of appeal to the Asylum Support Adjudicators ('ASA'). Rights of appeal do not exist in all situations although there is legislation that is waiting to be brought into force, which will give some people the right of appeal who do not have it already.

Below we look first at which decisions allow a right of appeal and at the proposed changes to rights of appeal (immediately below). We then look at appeal procedures (▶1391 onwards). For quick reference on the timetable for NASS appeals, ▶see 1392–3.

Unless otherwise stated, references to 'rules' in this chapter are to the Asylum Support Appeals (Procedure) Rules 2000 (also referred to as the 'Asylum Support Appeals Rules').

WHEN CAN A PERSON APPEAL TO THE ASYLUM SUPPORT ADJUDICATORS?

Under the present legislation, a person who has had a negative decision from NASS can appeal to the ASA against a decision (see s103(1)(2)(2A) 1999 Act as amended by the 2004 Act):

- to refuse an application for NASS asylum support on the grounds that the applicant does not qualify for support under section 95 1999 Act;
- to stop providing NASS asylum support;
- to refuse an application for 'hard cases' support;
- to stop providing hard cases support;
- to either refuse an application for NASS asylum support or to stop providing such support on the grounds that the applicants are excluded from support as a failed asylum-seeking family that has not taken reasonable steps to leave the UK voluntarily or put themselves in a position where they will be able to leave (see s9(3)(4) 2004 Act making it clear that people in this 'fifth'

12

excluded class under Sch 3 2002 Act can appeal to the ASA; for further details about this excluded class, ▶see 1305–6, 1325–8, 1354–7).

The following two further points should be noted about the above rights of appeal.

1) The rights of appeal are against decisions to refuse to provide (or to stop providing) any support at all. At present, there are no appeal rights where support is being provided but the applicant disagrees with the *nature* of the support provided i.e. where the dispute is about the level or type of the support, or the location in which it is provided (but see under 'proposed changes' below).

   In *R (SSHD) v Chief Asylum Support Adjudicator and Ahmet Dogan (interested party)*, the Court of Appeal ruled there was no right of appeal where a family failed to travel to dispersed accommodation which was available and the temporary accommodation they had been staying in was withdrawn. The Court saw the dispute as really about the *location* of the accommodation being provided. Where the accommodation remains available to the asylum-seekers (as it generally does in 'failure to travel' cases) there will therefore be no right of appeal. Cases concerning harassment and other problems in the dispersal area (▶see 1363–4) may still reach the ASA where an applicant leaves accommodation and support is terminated as a result (see under 'exclusions from asylum support under the Asylum Support Regulations' at ▶1357–60).

2) In a badly drafted provision, the 1999 Act states that there is only a right of appeal against a decision to stop providing asylum support that is withdrawn 'before that support would otherwise have come to an end' (s103(2)). It is not clear what this means but it can perhaps be interpreted as meaning 'before the support would naturally terminate as a result of the applicant no longer being an asylum-seeker'. For when a person ceases to be an asylum-seeker, ▶see 1343–4.

There are also *no* rights of appeal against:

- decisions concerning interim asylum support made by local authorities;
- decisions about temporary (or 'emergency') asylum support – this is because this support is provided under section 98 rather than section 95 1999 Act;
- decisions that an applicant is excluded from support under section 55 2002 Act (s55(10) 2002 Act);
- decisions that an applicant is excluded from asylum support because they fall within excluded classes one to four in Schedule 3 2002 Act (see s9(3) 2004 Act).

It also *appears* that decisions to refuse to entertain an application for asylum support (▶see 1352–3, 1360), will not give rise to a right of appeal because they are not decisions that a person does not qualify for support under section 95 1999 Act.

In any case in which there is no right of appeal, the only means of challenging the decision of NASS (or the local authority where the decision concerns interim support) is judicial review. For judicial review procedures, ▶see 1213–22.

Proposed changes to rights of appeal

Section 53 2002 Act makes the following changes to rights of appeal to the ASA (some of which require further regulations to be made). It is not yet in force.

- Applicants will be able to appeal against decisions to refuse to provide asylum in an accommodation centre (this section is now unlikely to be brought in given that the project to set up accommodation centres has been abandoned).

- When NASS provides accommodation as asylum support or hard cases support, asylum-seekers will be able to appeal against a decision about *where* that support is provided. So, effectively, dispersal decisions will be subject to appeal.

The Asylum Support Adjudicators

The Asylum Support Adjudicators are based at Christopher Wren House in South London (▶see 1498 for address and telephone/fax numbers). Further information about how they operate can be obtained from their website (www.asylum-support-adjudicators.org.uk) which also contains copies of all of the decisions made by the adjudicators. Any appellant who wishes to contact the ASA about their appeal or to get further information about the appeals process can contact them on their freephone number: 0800 3897913.

The number of appeals dealt with by the ASA is much less than those heard by the AIT, which hears immigration and asylum appeals. The number of appeals is still, however, significant. According to ASA figures, they received 1172 appeals in the three months from July to September 2005.

APPEAL PROCEDURES

12

The appeal procedures operated by NASS and referred to below are set out in the Asylum Support Appeals (Procedure) Rules 2000 (referred to below as 'Asylum Support Appeals Rules' or simply the 'Rules') as amended by the Asylum Support Appeals (Procedure) (Amendment) Rules 2003. The 2003 Rules made changes to the timetable for appeals and they introduced a new notice of appeal form.

The emphasis in the Rules is to deal with appeals with the minimum of delay (see also s104(3) 1999 Act). Before the 2003 amendments the timetable was even tighter. The amendments built a number of additional days into the system. Appellants, for example, were given an extra day to lodge their notice of appeal and NASS was given a further day to serve the appeal bundle. In part quick time-limits benefit appellants because the ASA cannot order that temporary support is provided during the appeal process. If support is withdrawn pending an appeal, it may be possible to maintain it by seeking an injunction in judicial review proceedings.

The appeal procedures set out in the Rules are not detailed but the ASA have a general power to give directions on matters connected with the appeal where they consider that it is in the interests of justice to do so (rule 14). Although the procedures are not set out in detail, the ASA are under a duty to conduct proceedings fairly. This would be the case under domestic law but it is underlined also by the fact that the asylum support has been accepted as being a 'civil right' for the purposes of the ECHR (see *R (Husain) v Asylum Support Adjudicators and SSHD*, HC). This means that the fair trial requirements contained in Article 6 ECHR should be observed.

The timetable for the various stages of the hearing and determination of appeals is summarised in the table below.

TIMETABLE FOR APPEALS TO THE ASYLUM SUPPORT ADJUDICATORS

Asylum Support Appeals (Procedure) Rules 2000 as amended by the Asylum Support Appeals (Procedure) (Amendment) Rules 2003

ASA = Asylum Support Adjudicators

Day	Event
Day 1	Notice of appealable decision is *received* by the asylum-seeker (the appellant)
Day 4 (latest)	Notice of appeal must be received by ASA (rule 3(3))
Day 4 or Day 5	ASA faxes notice of appeal to NASS (rule 4(1))
Day 6	Assuming NASS fax notice of appeal on Day 4, NASS send appeal bundle to ASA by fax or hand and to the appellant by first-class post or by hand (rule 4(2))
Day 7	ASA (rules 4(3), 7): • decide whether to hold an oral hearing; • give notice of the date of any oral hearing to the parties; • if no oral hearing is to be held and if possible, ASA proceed to determine the appeal (rule 6(2)); • if there is no oral hearing and the appeal is determined, the appellant and NASS are each sent both the notice of decision and the statement of reasons for the decision (rule 13(2))
Days 8–12	On one of these days, the oral hearing must be held (rule 6(1)).

	The appeal is determined straight after the hearing. ASA notify the decision to the appellant and NASS at the hearing, or if they are not present, on the same day sends notice of the decision to the appellant and NASS (rule 13(1)(a)(b)(c))
	If there is no oral hearing and the appeal was not determined on day 7 (above), the appeal must be determined on day 12 at the latest (rule 6(1)). The notice of decision and the statement of reasons must both be sent to the parities on the day that the appeal is determined (rule 13(2))
Days 13, 14, 15	If the oral hearing was heard on day 12 (the last day), the reasons statement for the decision must be sent to the parties on one of these days (i.e. three days after day on which the appeal was determined) (rule 13(1)(d))

Note

However in applying the above table and the description of the procedures, which follows below (▶1393–6), it is important to remember that the following rules regarding timing and sending documents apply.

1) Unless otherwise stated in the table above or below, all notices or documents to be sent by either NASS or the appellant should be sent by first-class post, fax or given by hand (rule 17).

2) Where a notice or another document is sent by first-class post by NASS, or by the ASA, it will be assumed that it has been received by the appellant two days after the day on which it was sent, unless they can prove that they did not in fact receive it (rule 18(2)).

3) Where a notice or a document is sent other than by first-class post by NASS or the ASA, there is no assumption made about when it was received, it is treated as having been received on the day on which it was in fact received (rule 18(1)).

4) Where a time-limit expires a number of days after a particular event, time begins running at the end of the day on which the event occurs (rule 18(3)).

5) Where a time-limit covers a Saturday, Sunday, bank holiday, Christmas Day or Good Friday, that day is not counted for the purpose of the time-limit. Similarly, if the time-limit expires, or the rules say that a particular act is to be carried out on one of those days, the rules are still complied with if the act is carried out on the next working day (rule 18(4)(5) with reference to rule 2(1)).

12

Notice of appeal

Any decision against which an asylum-seeker has a right of appeal to the ASA must be communicated to that person in a letter from NASS. Notice of appeal must be sent to the ASA so that they receive it no later than three days after the day on which the notice of the decision was received (rule 3(3)). The notice of appeal is contained as a Schedule to the Asylum Support Appeals Rules and is a straightforward form. The grounds of the appeal should be stated. Among the other details requested by the form are: whether the appellant wants an oral hearing, whether the appellant will be represented and, if so, by whom and whether the appellant needs an interpreter and the relevant language. If an interpreter is requested, the ASA will provide one for the hearing.

The ASA can be requested to extend the time-limit for appealing and may do so either before or after the time-limit has expired but only if (rule 3(4)):

- it is in the interests of justice to extend the time-limit; and
- the appellant (or their representative) could not comply with the time-limit due to circumstances beyond their control.

Preparation of the appeal bundle

On the same day as the ASA receive the notice of appeal or, if that is not reasonably practicable, as soon as possible on the next day at the latest, the ASA must fax a copy of the notice of appeal and any supporting documents which have been sent in with the appeal form to NASS (rule 4(1)). The ASA may at this stage also make directions for the appeal.

Two days after the day that the ASA received the notice of appeal, NASS must fax or deliver by hand to the ASA, and either fax or send by first-class post to the asylum-seeker, copies of the following documents (known as the 'appeal bundle') (rule 4(2)):

- if the appeal is against a decision to refuse to provide support rather than a withdrawal of support, the form on which the appellant claimed support and any supporting documentation which is attached to that form;
- the decision letter refusing support;
- any other evidence which NASS took into account in refusing support.

Decision of the ASA whether to hold a hearing of the appeal

On the day after NASS sends to the ASA the above documents, the ASA must consider the documents and decide whether to hold an oral hearing of the appeal or whether the appeal is going to be determined without a hearing. Whether the ASA decide to hold an oral hearing or not, the ASA must set the date for when the appeal is going to be determined. If the ASA decide to hold an oral hearing, they must, on the same day, send a notice to NASS and to the appellant of the time, date and place of the hearing (rule 4(3)).

The ASA *must* decide to hold an oral hearing of the appeal if (rule 5(1)):

- the appellant has requested an oral hearing in their notice of appeal; or
- the ASA think that it is necessary, in order to fairly decide the appeal, that there is an oral hearing.

The ASA may also decide to hold an oral hearing of the appeal for any other reason. Where the ASA decide to hold an oral hearing, the hearing must be held and the appeal determined not later than five days after the day on which the ASA make the decision to hold a hearing. If the ASA decide not to hold an oral hearing, they should if possible proceed to determine the appeal straightaway, or at the very latest, no later than five days after the day on which they decide not to have an oral hearing (rule 6).

Further evidence before determination of the appeal

Prior to the determination of the appeal, the asylum-seeker or NASS may submit further evidence to the ASA. Copies of all such evidence should also be forwarded to the other party (rule 8). It should be noted that, if no oral hearing is to be held, the appeal will be determined quickly after notice of appeal was given which means that asylum-seekers and their representatives must act very quickly if they wish to provide further evidence. In particular, the appellant may wish to rely upon evidence, which shows a change in their circumstances after the date of the NASS decision.

If the appellant has not requested an oral hearing initially, but subsequently wishes to do so in the light of the bundle of evidence or further evidence submitted by NASS, the ASA should be notified of this as soon as possible by fax or telephone.

Oral hearings

If an oral appeal hearing is to take place, NASS may be asked to pay for the appellant's reasonable travelling expenses to the place of the hearing (s103(9) 1999 Act). NASS should send a travel warrant to the appellant at the address given on the appeal form. However, there is no public funding for legal representation at the hearing. A solicitor may be able to help with the preparation of the appeal and some legal advisers may be able to arrange free representation. For example the Asylum Support Appeals Project (ASAP) aims to provide free advice and representation to asylum-seekers and to provide advice and training for refugee community organisations who wish to provide advocacy on behalf of asylum-seekers (▶see 1499 for their contact details).

The Rules place no restrictions on who may represent an appellant (see rule 15). Therefore, an appellant could in principle ask a friend or relative to speak for them at the hearing although it will normally be necessary for the appellant themselves to give the actual evidence.

There are no rules that set out the procedure which must be adopted at the oral hearing of the appeal and the precise procedure will be for the ASA at the hearing to determine. Normally, however, appellants are able to give oral evidence and either they or their representative will have the

12

opportunity to directly address the ASA as to what decision should be made and to comment on all of the evidence which has been given or submitted.

If the ASA have decided to hold an oral hearing, the hearing may be heard in the appellant's absence in the following circumstances (rule 9):

- if the appellant stated in the notice of appeal that they did not want to be present or to be represented at an oral hearing; or
- the appellant did state in the notice of appeal that they wanted to be present or represented at an oral hearing, the appellant was notified of the date, time and place of the hearing but has not attended.

Hearings may also go ahead in the absence of a representative of NASS.

Decisions on appeals

Whether an appeal is dealt with orally or without a hearing, the ASA must give reasons for their decision in writing (see rule 13). Where an oral hearing is held, the ASA must state the decision that has been reached at the end of the hearing. If the appellant does not attend, notice of the decision will be sent out on the same day as the appeal is heard. In addition, whether the appellant attended the hearing or not, no later than three days after the day of the hearing, the ASA must send a written statement containing reasons for the decision. If the appeal is allowed, NASS should take immediate steps to comply with the decision.

Where the ASA do not hold an oral hearing, the notice of decision, together with the reasons for the decision, must be sent out on the same day as the appeal is determined.

Powers of ASA in deciding appeals

In deciding the appeal, the ASA are able to take into account any changes of circumstance which take place between the date on which the decision of NASS was made and the date of the determination of the appeal (rule 10(2)). There are, however, no rules that deal with who has the burden of proof in asylum support appeals. Applying ordinary legal principles, the person who makes a particular contention must prove it. So, while it may be for the asylum-seeker to demonstrate that they are destitute overall, if there are any particular contentions which NASS is making, then NASS may have the burden of proving them. For example, if NASS believes that the appellant has an income from other sources it may be for NASS to demonstrate this. If NASS is seeking to exclude someone from support on the basis, for example, that they have breached certain conditions, the burden will lie with NASS to demonstrate the necessary facts.

On deciding the appeal, the ASA can do one of three things (s103(3) 1999 Act):

- make NASS reconsider its decision;

- substitute their own decision for the decision which was made by NASS;
- dismiss the appeal so that the NASS decision stands.

In addition to the above powers, where appellants are appealing against a decision that they are excluded from asylum support as a failed asylum-seeking family that has failed to take reasonable steps to leave the UK, the ASA may 'annul' the certificate issued by the Home Office which put the family into this excluded class. The ASA may also specifically require the Home Office to reconsider whether the case should be so certified i.e. whether the family has indeed failed to take reasonable steps to leave (see s9(4) 2004 Act). This excluded class is set out in paragraph 7A Schedule 3 2002 Act and for further general details about policy and procedure relating to it, ▶see 1305–6, 1325–8, 1354–7.

There is no further right of appeal from a decision of the ASA. The only means of challenging the decision is judicial review.

Ending the appeal by withdrawal

The appellant may at any stage decide to withdraw the appeal. In addition, NASS may at any time decide that it wishes to withdraw the decision against which the appellant has appealed. If either party wishes to withdraw, they must notify the other party and the ASA straightaway. In either of these two circumstances, the appeal is treated as having come to an end (rule 16).

If NASS withdraws the decision, it is of course required to make a further decision on the application for support. If that decision is of a kind that is appealable (see above), and the person is dissatisfied with the second decision, they may of course appeal against the further decision.

12

Section 13 British nationality

Chapter 43
British nationality   1401

Development of nationality law   1402

Types of British nationality   1404

British nationality law and Hong Kong   1414

Right of abode   1417

Identifying British nationality from passports   1421

Obtaining a passport   1423

Chapter 44
Who is a British citizen?   1425

People who become 'British citizens' on
1 January 1983   1426

British citizens by birth (or adoption, or found
abandoned) in the UK on or after 1 January 1983   1428

BOTCs who become British citizens on
21 May 2002   1432

People born outside the UK who are British
citizens by birth   1433

Persons born stateless and persons born on ships
and aircraft   1437

Checking for British citizenship: a summary   1438

Renunciation of citizenship   1442

Deprivation of citizenship   1445

Chapter 45
Applying to be a British citizen   1447

Introduction   1447

Applications for British citizenship – general   1448

Naturalisation   1453

13

Registration of children   1473
Registration of adults   1485

43 British nationality

This section covers the law relating to British nationality. Nationality law is different from immigration law. It is not directly concerned with controlling who can enter and remain in the UK, but rather with the country of which a person is a citizen. Obviously there are direct links between the two, because most countries grant citizenship to their people, and those citizens are then able to leave the country and return with minimal fuss, and without the rigorous controls that generally apply to foreign nationals. This is true of 'British citizens', which is the prime status in British nationality law. However, British nationality law is complex, because it recognises not one but several forms of citizenship, each of which has different rights attached.

This chapter

This chapter begins by looking briefly at the development of British nationality law from its origin in feudal times to the British Nationality Act 1981 (▶see 1402–4). We then deal with the six existing kinds of British national, and describe each of them in turn (▶1404–14). In the course of this we look at the 'immigration' rights of those British nationals who do not have the right to enter the UK freely, but who nevertheless have rights over and above foreign nationals (▶see 1405). The critical concept dividing British nationals who can enter freely from those who cannot is the 'right of abode', which is still also retained by some Commonwealth citizens. The 'right of abode' is described at ▶1417–21. (For a list of countries whose nationals are 'Commonwealth citizens' ▶see 1525).

We then discuss how a person's British national status can be identified from the passport(s) they hold (▶1421–3) (although determining whether a person is a British citizen is addressed fully in Chapter 44).

The relationship between British nationality law and people from Hong Kong is complex and this is dealt with at ▶1414–7.

Finally, this chapter looks at the procedure for applying for a British passport (▶1423–4). This is subject to change at the time of writing, with the planned expansion of the UK Passport Service and the introduction of increased security procedures. We also look at the circumstances in which passports may be refused or withdrawn.

The further nationality chapters

The remaining two chapters in this section focus in much more detail on 'British citizenship', the most advantageous form of British nationality.

Chapter 44 deals with how British citizenship is acquired originally. So, it considers who is and who is not a British citizen. It also explains the provisions concerning the 'renunciation' and re-acquisition after renunciation of citizenship. It also looks at the process by which a person may be deprived of British citizenship.

Chapter 45 deals with the circumstances in which, and the procedures by which, people can apply to *become* British citizens, both by naturalisation and registration.

The Home Office provides detailed guidance on how it applies nationality law in the Nationality Instructions (NI), which can be found on its website. As the *Handbook* went to print, changes made by the Civil Partnership Act 2004 to the BNA 1981 were coming into force. The statutory changes are highlighted in the above two chapters, but changes to the NI have not been and these should be consulted.

DEVELOPMENT OF NATIONALITY LAW

The origins of nationality law lie in the allegiances owed, in English feudal society, by the people towards feudal lords, and by those lords to the monarch. This evolved into the concept of allegiance to the Crown. Allegiance to the Crown made a person a Crown 'subject'. The status of subject was given to those born within the Crown's territories. Over time, special arrangements were made both for the children of subjects who were born abroad and for foreigners to become subjects.

The Naturalization Act 1844 was the beginning of the modern process of 'naturalisation', the procedure through which foreigners can obtain national status by being granted it by the Secretary of State. During the remainder of the nineteenth and the first half of the twentieth centuries, further legislation was brought in concerning both the recognition and grant of British subject status. From 1847 onwards, a person naturalised in the UK obtained 'Imperial naturalisation'. This conferred British subject status throughout the British empire.

However, this idea of an empire-wide British subject status became unworkable in the twentieth century. Colonised peoples increased their resistance to colonialism, and Britain found it difficult to maintain political cohesion among so many territories overseas. Territories that had been settled by British people began to break away and become independent. At the same time, they established their own citizenship laws. For example, in 1946 Canada created its own Canadian citizenship, which was separate from the status of British subject.

British Nationality Act 1948

In the period 1948–83, new nationality and immigration laws restricted and defined citizenship rights. The 1948 Act created a citizenship of the United Kingdom and Colonies (CUKC) for those from the United Kingdom or from the colonies that were not yet independent. It also recognised two residual forms of British status: British Protected Persons (BPPs) and British Subjects Without Citizenship (BSWCs).

As the colonies gained independence, people from the newly independent countries would normally lose CUKC status and gain the citizenship of the new Commonwealth country, although there were some limited exceptions to this. At first, this development did not affect the right to enter the UK, as all Commonwealth citizens, as well as CUKCs, continued to be classed as 'British subjects'. British subject status was an overarching status carrying with it the 'right of abode' in the UK. A person with the 'right of abode' was generally free from immigration control, and had a right to enter, live and work in the UK.

'Commonwealth immigrants' legislation of the 1960s

In the 1960s the general right of abode for British subjects was restricted by new legislation. This began with the Commonwealth Immigrants Act 1962. These new laws restricted rights, not only for citizens from independent Commonwealth countries, but *also* for some CUKCs who did not have connections by birth or descent with the UK. Accordingly, holding a British passport no longer meant that a person had the automatic right to enter and live in Britain. Groups such as East African asians and people from Hong Kong found that they were unable to enter the country of their nationality, Britain, when they needed to do so.

However, some citizens of independent Commonwealth states, who were not CUKCs, retained the right of abode. This might be, for example, because they had a parent who had been born in the UK, or because they were married to a man who was British or who had the right of abode.

The British Nationality Act 1981

The British Nationality Act 1981 (which came into force on 1 January 1983) ('BNA 1981') set out to do a number of things. First, it changed the way people can obtain British nationality by birth, descent or grant. Second, it tried to bring nationality and immigration law into line. It abolished the status of 'CUKC' and replaced it with three new nationalities:

- CUKCs who had the right of abode became 'British citizens' (BCs);
- CUKCs who had gained that status because of a connection with an existing colony or dependency became 'British Dependent Territories citizens' (BDTCs);
- CUKCs who did not fit into either of these groups became 'British Overseas citizens' (BOCs).

13

Neither British Dependent Territories citizenship (BDTC), nor British Overseas citizenship (BOC) conferred the right of abode in the UK. However, some BDTCs were British citizens as well. For further details about BDTC status and the new British Overseas Territories citizenship (BOTC) that has since replaced it, ▶see 1406–8.

Citizens of independent Commonwealth countries who had the right of abode on 1 January 1983 will keep it for the rest of their lives. However, no one has been able to obtain the right of abode in the UK since that date without becoming a British citizen.

TYPES OF BRITISH NATIONALITY

There are now six types of British nationality which are set out in the table below.

PRESENT TYPES OF BRITISH NATIONAL STATUS

- British citizen (BC);
- British Overseas Territories citizen (BOTC);
- British Overseas citizen (BOC);
- British National (Overseas) (BN(O));
- British Protected Person (BPP);
- British subject (BS).

A person holding a British passport may have any of the above national statuses. A passport does not itself confer nationality. Passports are given to people who show that they are entitled to a particular nationality, and so, ultimately, they are *evidence* of a person's national status.

Each of the six types of nationality is considered in turn below (from ▶1406 onwards), together with examples of the main (but not the only) people who may hold them.

Only British citizens automatically have the right of abode, and can therefore freely enter the UK on proof of their status. Other kinds of British national *may* have obtained the right of abode. For example, anyone who was a BOTC immediately before 21 May 2002 was automatically granted British citizenship and obtained the right of abode in the UK, ▶1406 (see s3 British Overseas Territories Act 2002 and British Overseas Territories Act 2002 (Commencement) Order 2002). In addition, a person may have acquired the right of abode whilst retaining their original form of nationality, for example as a BS or a BPP.

British nationals who do not have the right of abode need leave to enter or remain in the UK, and therefore need to qualify under the immigration rules. Such nationals may have leave to be in the UK as students, spouses and so on, but their British nationality gives them no automatic right to be here. Generally speaking, therefore, British nationals without the right of abode are treated like other non-nationals when they seek admission. *However*, they do have some significant 'immigration' advantages (immediately below).

Immigration advantages of British nationals who do not have the right of abode

British nationals who do not have the right of abode, still have a number of advantages over and above foreign nationals, as follows.

1) BOCs who hold UK passports, wherever they were issued, and who satisfy an immigration officer at port that they have, since 1 March 1968, been given indefinite leave to enter or remain, may be admitted with indefinite leave to enter at any time (para. 17, HC 395). Such people are therefore exempt from the normal 'returning residents' rule, which generally requires those with indefinite leave to return within two years (▶see 112–6). BOCs who have been granted indefinite leave, and therefore admitted for settlement, may also have their passport endorsed by the UK Passport Agency so that it states that the 'holder has the right of re-admission to the UK'. This confirms that if they stay away from the UK for more than two years at a time, they cannot be refused indefinite leave to enter when they return. In practice this also applies to other British nationals, except BOTCs.

2) BDTCs (now BOTCs), BN(O)s, BOCs, BPPs and BSs may be admitted freely to the UK if they produce a UK passport issued in the 'UK and Islands' (see glossary) or the Republic of Ireland before 1 January 1973, *unless* the passport was endorsed to state that they were 'subject to immigration control' (para. 16, HC 395). Note that this only applies to a BS who has that status as a result of section 30(a) of the BNA 1981 – in other words, a person who would have been a British subject without citizenship (BSWC) immediately before the introduction of the BNA on 1 January 1983.

3) BOTCs, BOCs, BN(O)s, BPPs, and BSs may obtain entry without an entry clearance even if they intend to stay in the UK for more than six months (▶see 79–102). They do not require an entry clearance to come to the UK for work-permit employment (▶see 428), under the TWES scheme (▶see 442), or under the Science and Engineering Graduates Scheme (SEGS) (▶see 464–5).

4) Before 1 October 2004, those who arrived in the UK with a work permit and were refused leave to enter had an in-country right of appeal against the decision (see s92(3) 2002 Act). However, from that date, work-permit holders who are in the UK and are refused leave to enter only have an in-country right of appeal if they are one of the following: a BOTC, a BOC, a BN(O), a BPP, a BS (see s28 2004 Act).

13

In addition, as we discuss the various different British national statuses below, it will also be clear that specific arrangements are made for some to seek to register as British citizens.

British citizens

All British citizens have the right of abode in the UK and may, therefore, freely enter and remain without requiring leave. British citizens obtain their nationality by a connection with the UK itself, either by birth, descent, registration or naturalisation. The next two chapters in this section deal with British citizens. Chapter 44 sets out who is a British citizen (▶see in particular the flow-charts on 1440–1). Chapter 45 deals with applying to become a British citizen.

British Overseas Territories citizens (BOTCs) (formerly British Dependent Territories citizens (BDTCs))

BOTCs (formerly BDTCs) are people from the few remaining Overseas Territories (formerly 'Dependent Territories'). BDTC status came into being on 1 January 1983 for those CUKCs who had gained that status because of one of a number of connections with an existing colony or dependency. There have been substantial changes to their status. In addition, the British Overseas Territories Act 2002 (BOTA) adds one further category of people who became BDTCs after 1 January 1983 and later became BOTCs. This change applies to those who have a specific connection with the British Indian Ocean Territory (see s6 BOTA 2002).

People from the Falkland Islands (originally BDTCs) were made into full British citizens after the Falklands War under the British Nationality (Falkland Islands) Act 1983.

In an important development, the BOTA 2002 redesignated BDTCs as BOTCs. In addition, anyone who was a BOTC immediately before 21 May 2002 was automatically granted British citizenship, and obtained the right of abode in the UK (see s3 BOTA 2002 and British Overseas Territories Act 2002 (Commencement) Order 2002). BOTCs who became British citizens on 21 May 2002 are more fully discussed at ▶1432–3. The dependencies themselves were redesignated by the BOTA as 'British Overseas Territories'. They are: Anguilla, Bermuda, British Antarctica, British Indian Ocean Territory, British Virgin Islands, Cayman Islands, Falkland Islands, Gibraltar, Montserrat, Pitcairn Islands, St Helena and Dependencies, South Georgia and the South Sandwich Islands, Turks and Caicos Islands, and the Sovereign Base Areas of Akrotiri and Dhekelia, in Cyprus. However, the Act excludes BOTCs from the Cyprus Sovereign Base areas from obtaining the right of abode in the UK, on the basis that those territories have special status as military bases.

Born, adopted or found abandoned in the Overseas Territories

A person born, adopted or found abandoned in the Overseas Territories will be a BOTC by automatic acquisition. This is equivalent to the basis on which people become British citizens by having been born, adopted or found abandoned in the UK (▶see 1428–32).

Born outside the Overseas Territories

In certain circumstances, a person who was born outside the Overseas Territories after 1 January 1983 will automatically be a BOTC (see s16 of the BNA 1981; NI, Ch 24).

Registration

As with the provisions for the registration of minors born in the UK as British citizens by entitlement on grounds of a parent's status (▶see 1474), there are similar arrangements for registration as BOTCs by entitlement of minors born in an Overseas Territory. There are also arrangements for the registration of adults and minors as BOTCs by entitlement on grounds of residence, which are similar to the arrangements for the registration of adults and minors as British citizens on grounds of residence (▶see 1474).

There are also provisions for the registration of minors as BOTCs by entitlement for those born outside the Overseas Territories to a parent who was (or would have been) a BOTC by descent (see s7 of the BNA 1981; NI, Chs 29–30). For the difference between those who are citizens by 'descent' or 'otherwise than by descent', ▶see 1433–4. There is also a general discretion to register a minor as a BOTC (see s17 BNA 1981; NI, Ch 28; and ▶see the similar arrangements for discretionary registration of minors as British citizens at 1476–85).

Naturalisation

Adults may naturalise as BOTCs in a process very similar to that which applies to British citizens (see s18 BNA; NI, Ch 34). For naturalisation as a British citizen, ▶see 1453–73.

Statelessness and obtaining BOTC status

There are arrangements that allow for the acquisition of BOTC status by people who are stateless (Sch 2 BNA 1981; NI, Chs 25, 31).

Renunciation

A person may 'renounce' their BOTC status. Again, the provisions mirror those relating to the renunciation of British citizenship (▶see 1442–5) (see s24 BNA 1981; NI, Ch 35). However, a person who has renounced their CUKC, BDTC or BOTC status may apply to be registered once more as a BOTC (see ss22, 24 BNA; NI, Chs 32-33).

BOTCs' ability to register as British citizens

People who become BOTCs after the commencement of the BOTA on 21 May 2002 have been able to apply to be registered as British citizens under section 4A BNA 1981 (▶see 1488). A BOTC may also register as a

British citizen on grounds of time spent in Crown service (see s4(5) of the BNA 1981 and ▶see 1487). Both these forms of registration are *discretionary*. However, BOTCs may also register as British citizens as a matter of *entitlement* on either of the following two grounds:

- residence in the UK, if the requirements under section 4(2) BNA 1981 are satisfied (▶see 1486–7);
- if a BOTC is a UK national for European Community (EC) purposes (in practice, a person who acquired BOTC status as a result of a connection with Gibraltar) they may register under section 5 BNA 1981 (▶see 1488).

The need to go further than the BOTA

The 2002 Act is welcome, as it restores some citizenship rights that were taken away in 1962. However, JCWI believes that it does not go far enough: it does not restore the rights of British Overseas citizens, or bring the position of British Protected Persons, British subjects or British Nationals (Overseas) into line with that of British citizens. The explanatory notes to the legislation estimated a population of 200,000 for the Overseas Territories, and so extending rights at least to BOCs would not have had any major implications, given that there are estimated to be far fewer of them. The effect of the position has been felt particularly acutely in Kenya, where the conflicting policies of the British and Kenyan governments have resulted in the children of BOCs being rendered stateless, and the Kenyan government denying any form of responsibility towards them. However, stateless BOCs may have an entitlement to register as British citizens under section 4B of the BNA 1981 (▶see under BOCs, below).

British Overseas citizens

British Overseas Citizens ('BOCs') are people who were CUKCs but did not qualify as British citizens or BDTCs on 1 January 1983 (when the BNA came into force) because their CUKC status did not result from a connection with the UK or a British Dependent Territory. BOCs are mainly people from former colonies in East Africa ('East African Asians') and Malaysia who are from the minority ethnic communities in those countries. BOC status does not automatically carry the right of abode, nor can it be transmitted from parent to child.

The Commonwealth Immigrants Act 1968 removed rights of entry to the UK from CUKCs who were not born in the UK and who did not have a parent or grandparent who was born in the UK. These were essentially the people who later became BOCs. The number of people who are still suffering from this injustice is relatively small, but it is of obvious importance to them. Most BOCs outside the UK are in East Africa, India or Malaysia. Most of those in East Africa or India who qualified for special vouchers (▶see below 1409–10) and who wanted to come to the UK have already done so. In August 2000 the British High Commission in Malaysia estimated that there were 'up to 12,000' BOCs in Malaysia who were mainly elderly people of Indian descent, and who would not want to uproot themselves and go to the UK (letter to *JUSTICE*, 3 August 2000).

In the case of *Kaur*, the European Court of Justice was asked to rule on the position of BOCs who are unable to gain entry to the country of their only nationality. The Court found that the matter was outside EU law. At the hearing itself, however, the Court expressed concern at their position, describing them as 'Flying Dutchmen' – able to travel, but with no rights to settle anywhere. Deportation orders were enforced against two BOCs between 1994 and 1996, but the Home Office has not stated to which countries they were sent. Immigration officers have completed application forms for visas for countries to which the BOCs in question have made it clear they do not wish to go. It is important to monitor Home Office treatment of BOCs, and to challenge attempts to enforce controls against them.

British nationals with an East African connection: the special quota voucher scheme

The treatment of British nationals from East Africa, most of whom originated from the Indian subcontinent, is one of the most disreputable parts of British nationality law. When they came under pressure to leave countries such as Uganda and Kenya in the 1960s, the Commonwealth Immigrants Act 1968 was passed to deny them entry to the UK. After this, only a few were allowed entry to the UK every year, under the 'special voucher' scheme. When large-scale expulsions from Uganda took place in 1972, they had no right to live in any other country, and found it difficult or impossible to enter the UK. The European Commission on Human Rights held that this discrimination amounted to 'inhuman and degrading treatment' under the ECHR (*East African Asians v UK*).

As a result of the European Commission's judgment, the UK expanded the special voucher scheme, supposedly to 5,000 a year. However, the majority of expelled Ugandans had gone temporarily to India to await resettlement, and only 600 vouchers a year were allocated for them. The nominal quota was never reached; but during the 1980s an eight-year queue built up in India.

The special voucher scheme was abolished on 5 March 2002. Any new applications for special vouchers lodged on or after this date will presumably be refused without consideration. However, on 24 April 2002 the Home Secretary admitted that the UK has a moral obligation towards BOCs, and agreed to 'examine the possibility of an alternative arrangement'. A BOC may, in certain circumstances, now have an entitlement to register as a British citizen, under section 4B of the BNA 1981, following changes which came into force on 30 April 2003 (▶see 1411 and 1486).

The criteria for the voucher scheme were set outside the immigration rules, and administered at the discretion of the Home Secretary. Vouchers were issued only to British nationals with no other nationality, who were both:

13

- 'under pressure' to leave the country in which they were living; and
- 'heads of households'.

Under pressure to leave This criterion referred to people living in the countries of East and Central Africa (Uganda, Kenya, Tanzania, Malawi, Zambia) and people who had left those countries to go to India and await admission to the UK. Vouchers were not normally issued to people from East Africa who went to live in other countries (for example, to work in the Gulf States) or to British nationals living in other countries, even if their immigration or other status there was very insecure.

Heads of households Under the voucher scheme, married women were not regarded as 'heads of households' except in a few circumstances. Divorced or widowed women were eligible for vouchers if they fulfilled the other requirements. An attempt to challenge this blatant sex discrimination in the British courts failed (see *Amin*).

Voucher-holders' immediate family could qualify to accompany or join them in the UK. This included spouses and dependent children up to the age of 25. This upper age limit was introduced because the eight-year queue in India meant that children who were nearly 18 when their parents applied would reach 25 before the application had been considered. In order to remain dependent, however, children had to be unmarried and financially dependent on their parents (that is, not working). ECOs also investigated people to decide whether they were dependent 'by necessity', or had chosen to remain or become dependent in order to qualify to accompany the family.

BOCs from Malaysia

Besides East Africa and India, Malaysia is the place where there remain significant groupings of BOCs. Three areas of old Malaya – Penang, Malacca and Singapore – were ruled directly by Britain as the Straits Settlements and Malayan independence law provided that people who were born or whose father had been born in those areas before independence (31 August 1957) would retain their citizenship of the UK and Colonies. When Singapore became independent separately from Malaysia, this provision was lost for Singaporeans, but it still exists for people from Penang and Melaka. They are British nationals, but unless they have lived in the UK for five years and became settled before 1983, they are not British citizens, but BOCs. Since they had no connection with East Africa, they did not qualify for special quota vouchers. Malaysia does not permit people to gain any advantage from holding another nationality without forfeiting their Malaysian nationality, and many Malaysians do not know that they have British nationality. People with this connection with Penang or Melaka who wish to claim their British nationality should obtain specialist advice.

Obtaining BOC status

A person will automatically be a BOC if they were born in the UK or a British Overseas territory and would otherwise be stateless, provided that, at the time of birth, either of their parents was a BOC. There is also an entitlement to register as a BOC for a person born outside the UK and the British Overseas territories on or after 1 January 1983 where that person was born stateless and has remained stateless, provided that, at the time of their birth, their father or mother was a BOC. That person must also satisfy a residence requirement by demonstrating that they have been in the UK or a British Overseas Territory at the beginning of the period of three years ending with the date of application; and they were not absent from both the UK and the British Overseas territories for more than 270 days in that three-year period. There is a discretion to excuse some absences (NI, Ch 40).

There are also arrangements for the registration of a minor as a BOC. This broad discretion is normally exercised where all of the following criteria are satisfied (NI, Ch 39):

- the child has at least one parent who is a BOC;
- the child has no other nationality or citizenship, and cannot acquire one;
- the child is facing genuine difficulties through lack of a passport;
- the relevant government post confirms that the family's continued stay in the country in which they live is at risk to the point of deportation, and that there is no other country, other than the UK, to which the family could go were they to be deported.

BOCs may also renounce their status.

BOCs' ability to register as British citizens

A BOC is entitled to be registered as a British citizen if they have no other citizenship or nationality, and have not either renounced, voluntarily relinquished or lost through action or inaction any other citizenship after 4 July 2002 (see s4B BNA 1981 and ▶see 1486). BOCs are also entitled to be registered as British citizens on grounds of residence in the UK if the requirements under s4(2) BNA 1981 are satisfied (▶see 1486–7).

A BOC may also register as a British citizen on discretionary grounds on the basis of time they have spent in Crown service (see s4(5) of the BNA 1981 and ▶see 1487).

13

British Nationals (Overseas) (BN(O)s)

British Nationals (Overseas) ('BN(O)s') are people from Hong Kong who applied for this status before 1997, and who did not, or could not, register as British citizens under the 1990–97 Acts concerning Hong Kong (▶see 1416).

Under the Hong Kong (British Nationality) Order 1986, British Dependent Territories Citizens (BDTCs, as they then were) who had that status exclusively through a connection with Hong Kong, were entitled to be registered as BN(O)s (and to hold a passport in that status). BN(O) status was introduced at that time because when Hong Kong would revert to Chinese rule on 1 July 1997, people who had been BDTCs as a result of a connection with Hong Kong, would lose that status. BN(O) status cannot be transmitted from parent to child. Since 31 December 1997, it has not been possible to become a BN(O).

For further details about British nationality law and people from Hong Kong, ▶see below at 1414–7.

BN(O)s' ability to register as British citizens

A BN(O) is entitled to register as a British citizen on grounds of residence in the UK if the requirements under section 4(2) BNA 1981 are satisfied (▶see 1486–7). A BN(O) may also register as a British citizen, at the discretion of the Secretary of State, on grounds of time spent in Crown service (see s4(5) BNA 1981, and ▶see 1487).

British Protected Persons

British Protected Persons (BPPs) are people from places that were known generally as 'protectorates' (not colonies), which were mainly to be found in South Asia and Africa. These were countries or territories that were not part of the Crown's formal dominions, but were nevertheless under the control of Britain at least for some purposes, and were given the imperial protection of the Crown. These countries or territories are themselves sub-divided into 'protectorates', 'protected states', 'mandated territories' and 'trust territories'.

BPPs can be subdivided into those who derive that status from the exercise of the Royal Prerogative and those who derive it from legislation under the BNA 1948 (NI, Ch 54 describes who comes within each category). There are complicated provisions about keeping and losing BPP status as a result of the process of decolonisation. Many BPPs lost that status under legislation which was enacted when their countries became independent. BPP status which comes from the Royal Prerogative may be withdrawn at will (subject to international treaty obligations such as those on statelessness). BPP status under legislation is lost upon the acquisition of another nationality or citizenship, including BC, BOTC and BOC status.

Under the British Protectorates, Protected States and Protected Persons Order 1965, there is provision for certain categories of stateless person to register as BPPs.

BPPs' ability to register as British citizens

A BPP is entitled to be registered as a British citizen under section 4B BNA 1981 if they have no citizenship or nationality and have not renounced, voluntarily relinquished or lost any other citizenship through action or inaction after 4 July 2002 (▶see 1486). BPPs are also entitled to register as British citizens on the grounds of their residence in the UK if the requirements under section 4(2) BNA 1981 are satisfied (▶see 1486–7). BPPs may also register as British citizens on the grounds of time spent in Crown service, but this is at the discretion of the Secretary of State (see s4(5) BNA 1981 and ▶see 1487).

British subjects

British subjects (BSs) are mainly people who were previously British Subjects Without Citizenship (BSWCs) under sections 13 and 16 of the BNA 1948. This mainly applies to people who did not become CUKCs when the 1948 Act came into force on 1 January 1949, who were not citizens of Eire, and who did not acquire the citizenship of a Commonwealth state which became independent (for nationality purposes) after the 1948 Act. Such a person who, before 1 January 1983, did not become a CUKC, a citizen of Eire/Republic of Ireland, or a citizen of a Commonwealth state, and who did not make a 'declaration of alienage', became a BS on 1 January 1983 under the BNA 1981.

Most BSs are people from South Asia (India, Pakistan) who were born before 1948 and did not become CUKCs, or Indian or Pakistani citizens. However, there are also some other residual classes of British subject under the 1948 Act. Some women retained British subject status on the grounds that they had married a BSWC subsequently registered, and had not become CUKCs, or citizens of a Commonwealth country or of the Republic of Ireland. In addition, some Irish citizens who were British subjects on 31 December 1948 and had a relevant association with the UK may also have retained BS status.

BS status can be automatically obtained by a person born in the UK or a British overseas territory who would otherwise be stateless if, at the time of birth, either parent was a BS under the BNA 1981. As BS status does not give a right of abode in the UK, these arrangements are of limited use. There is also an entitlement to register as a BS if a person who is born outside the UK or an Overseas Territory on or after 1 January 1983 was born stateless and has remained stateless, provided that, at the time of their birth, their father or mother was a BS. The person wishing to register must also satisfy a residence requirement by showing that they were in the UK or a British Overseas Territory at the beginning of the period of three years ending with the date of the application; and that they were not absent from both the UK and the British Overseas Territories for more than 270 days in that three-year period. There is a discretion to excuse some absences (see NI, Ch 47).

There are also provisions for the registration of a minor as a BS. This broad discretion is normally exercised where all of the following criteria are satisfied (NI, Ch 45):

13

- at least one parent is a BS;
- the child has no other nationality or citizenship, and cannot acquire one;
- the child is facing genuine difficulties through lack of a passport;
- the relevant government post confirms that the family's continued stay in the country in which they live is at risk to the point of deportation, and there is no country other than the UK to which the family could go, were they to be deported.

A British subject, other than one who acquired the status as an Irish citizen, loses BS status on their acquisition of another nationality. A BS may also renounce that status.

British subjects' ability to register as British citizens

A BS under the BNA 1981 is entitled to register as a British citizen if they have no citizenship or nationality, and have not renounced, voluntarily relinquished or, through action or inaction, lost any other citizenship after 4 July 2002 (see s 4B of the BNA 1981 and ▶see 1486). BSs under the BNA 1981 are also entitled to register as British citizens as a result of their residence in the UK, provided that the requirements under section 4(2) BNA 1981 are satisfied (▶see 1486–7). A BS under the BNA 1981 may also register as a British citizen on the grounds of time spent in Crown service, but this is at the discretion of the Secretary of State (see s4(5) BNA 1981 and ▶see 1487).

BRITISH NATIONALITY LAW AND HONG KONG

The relationship between British nationality law and Hong Kong has been complex. Most British nationals from Hong Kong lost the right to live in the UK under the Commonwealth Immigrants Act 1962. The only CUKCs (as they then were) from Hong Kong who kept the right of abode at that time are the following groups:

- people born, registered or naturalised in the UK;
- people with a parent or grandparent who was born, registered or naturalised in the UK;
- people who had at any time before 1 January 1983 spent five years continuously and legally in the UK, and were settled in the UK at the end of that period;
- women married to men who fulfilled any of these conditions.

This means that most people of Chinese or other Asian origin in Hong Kong lost the right of abode in the UK. They became British Dependent Territories citizens. BDTC status was abolished for people from Hong Kong on 1 July 1997. Former BDTCs were only allowed to acquire the status of British National (Overseas) if they wished to retain British nationality. However, there are four ways in which such people may have been able, or may be able, to acquire the right of abode and become British citizens:

1) first, by living for five years or more in the UK before 1983. Some people from Hong Kong lived in the UK as students or workers in the 1950s or 1960s. At that time, people from Hong Kong and other Commonwealth countries were technically 'settled' in the UK, because no conditions could be put on their stay if they were admitted. It is therefore worth checking if Hong Kong British nationals have lived in the UK. If they lived in the UK for more than five years at any time before 1 January 1983, and had no time-limit on their stay at the end of that five-year period, they gained the right of abode and are therefore British citizens now;

2) second, by having registered under the quota for certain specified categories to become British Citizens under the British Nationality (Hong Kong) Act 1990 (▶see 1416);

3) third, by registering under the provisions for war wives and widows contained in the Hong Kong (War Wives and Widows) Act 1996 (▶see below at 1416);

4) fourth, by registering after 1 July 1997, under the provisions of the British Nationality (Hong Kong) Act 1997, for those who have no other nationality than British nationality (▶see 1416).

British Nationals (Overseas): the Hong Kong Act 1985

Under the 1985 agreement, Britain and China agreed that BDTCs would be able to apply for a new status, called British National (Overseas) (BN(O)). (▶See also 1412 for more details on BN(O) status and the Hong Kong (British Nationality) Order 1986.) The status of BDTC would no longer exist for people from Hong Kong. The status of BN(O) does not automatically carry the right of abode in the UK. The Chinese authorities do not regard it as a form of citizenship, but merely as a travel document facility.

BDTCs from Hong Kong could apply for BN(O) passports until September 1997. Anyone who had not applied by the relevant date lost British nationality altogether on 1 July 1997.

Most ex-BDTCs from Hong Kong are also considered by the Chinese authorities to be Chinese citizens, and now have Chinese citizenship. People who are not of Chinese ethnic origin may not be Chinese citizens – for example, people of Indian origin who have lived in Hong Kong for many years or generations. JCWI and others argued that they would be left with no real citizenship after 30 June 1997. The British government conceded that they needed special treatment, and they were finally allowed to register as British citizens, but only after Hong Kong was returned to China (▶see 1416).

13

Acquiring British citizenship: The British Nationality (Hong Kong) Acts 1990 and 1997 and the Hong Kong (War Wives and Widows) Act 1996

After a great deal of pressure, and on a piecemeal basis, the British government agreed to allow three categories of British nationals from Hong Kong to register as British citizens.

The British Nationality (Hong Kong) Act 1990

The British Nationality (Hong Kong) Act 1990 provided for British citizenship to be granted to 50,000 people in certain specified categories. They were people considered necessary to Hong Kong's future, but who might leave in the uncertainty leading up to the handover, particularly after the events in Tiananmen Square in 1989. Applications were decided on the basis of a points system, which set out to identify those considered most likely to emigrate, those who had been in sensitive government service, and some entrepreneurs. The final list of 2,400 registrations under this scheme was completed in 1997.

The Hong Kong (War Wives and Widows) Act 1996

This Act permitted around 50 women resident in Hong Kong, and whose husbands fought in the Second World War, to register as British citizens without the need to come to the UK. To be eligible, a woman must be able to show that the Home Office sent her a 'UK settlement letter' via the Hong Kong Immigration Department in 1994, confirming her right to enter the UK.

The British Nationality (Hong Kong) Act 1997

This legislation belatedly dealt with the position of Hong Kong British nationals who would not be eligible for any other nationality after 1 July 1997. It applied only to people who were ordinarily resident in Hong Kong on 3 February 1997. By this time many of those affected had already left, if they could, to find a more secure status.

A right to register as a British citizen was provided to people who met all of the following conditions. They had to be:

- ordinarily resident in Hong Kong at the time of application;
- ordinarily resident in Hong Kong immediately before 4 February 1997;
- BDTCs immediately before 4 February 1997;
- BDTCs only by virtue of their connection with Hong Kong (defined in the Schedule to the Act: in most cases due to their or their parents' birth, registration, naturalisation or adoption in Hong Kong), or alternatively BOCs, BPPs or BSs;
- stateless but for their British nationality.

For the meaning of 'ordinarily resident', ▶see 1274 and 1544–5. Applications can be made at any time after 1 July 1997.

People from Hong Kong who are living in the UK

The following check-list will help to decide the status of someone from Hong Kong who is living in the UK:

- Does the person have a (brown) certificate of identity? If so, the person is unlikely to be a British national of any kind. They were born in mainland China, and are probably entitled to Chinese citizenship. They may be able to obtain British citizenship by naturalisation, if they fulfil the requirements (▶see 1453–73).

- Does the person have a British passport?

- Does the passport state 'holder has the right of abode in the UK' or 'British citizen'? If so, the person is a British citizen, with the right of abode in the UK.

- Did the person, at any time before 1 January 1983, live legally in the UK for at least five years, without any conditions on their stay at the end of the period? If so, and provided that the person can prove this, they are a British citizen with the right of abode in the UK.

- Was the person born in the UK before 1983? Was the person born in the UK on or after 1 January 1983 to a parent who was British, or was settled in the UK at the time of the birth? If so, then in either case, the person is a British citizen.

If none of these apply, check the immigration stamp on the passport. This will show under what conditions, if any, the person has been admitted or allowed to remain. Only people with indefinite leave can apply for British citizenship. Students, visitors, work-permit holders, and so on, cannot apply and should not do so, as this may prejudice future applications to remain or return here.

RIGHT OF ABODE

The 'right of abode' is the most important benefit that British national status can bring. However, British nationality law does *not* confer the right of abode on all categories of British national. At present British citizens, and some Commonwealth citizens who, for the purposes of the Immigration Act 1971 are treated as 'British citizens', have the right of abode.

'Right of abode' is defined in section 1 1971 Act. It refers to people who are free to live in and come and go from the UK without let or hindrance, save for such controls as are necessary to establish their rights. A person who has the right of abode cannot be deported or removed from the UK. The burden of proof lies upon the person seeking to assert the right to show that they have the right of abode. Persons asserting a right of abode can therefore be asked to provide proof on entry. Proof is established by producing a British citizen passport or CUKC passport containing an endorsement that the person has the right of abode, or a 'certificate of entitlement' (see s3(8)(9) 1971 Act). These documents are available to

13

those who are entitled to them if they apply for them and support the application with the necessary documentation (▶see below at 1420–21 and 1423–4).

A person with the right of abode, whether a British citizen or Commonwealth citizen, may have lawful control placed on their movements. This may happen in the context, for example, of the criminal law, mental health legislation, restrictions on the movement of children in family and children proceedings and travel bans imposed on sports fans.

The right of abode is quite separate from the rights of other groups to whom only limited immigration controls apply: those with indefinite leave, those who are exempt from immigration controls (such as certain diplomats and members of armed forces), EEA nationals exercising rights of free movement, and those exercising rights of movement within the Common Travel Area.

We now look at the development of the right of abode.

Right of abode under the 1948 Act–1968 Act

Under the British Nationality Act 1948 all British subjects had the right of abode in the UK. This included CUKCs and Commonwealth citizens who were all British subjects. Restrictions on the right of abode were introduced by the Commonwealth Immigrants Act 1962, and further changed by the Commonwealth Immigrants Act 1968.

Right of abode under the 1971 Act

Under the 1971 Act (which was in force from 1 January 1973), the concept of the right of abode was defined so as to link it only indirectly to CUKC and Commonwealth citizen status. Between 1 January 1973 and the introduction of the BNA 1981 on 1 January 1983, the right of abode was determined by whether a person was a 'patrial'. Patriality was a new concept introduced by the 1971 Act. Certain CUKCs and certain Commonwealth citizens were defined as 'patrials'. During this period, section 2 1971 Act defined patrials (who had the right of abode) as those fitting into any of the following groups:

- CUKCs by birth, adoption, naturalisation, or registration in the UK;
- CUKCs with links to the UK through a parent or grandparent;
- CUKCs who had been ordinarily resident in the UK for five years;
- Commonwealth citizens who had a parent born in the UK;
- female Commonwealth citizens who became patrials through marriage.

Right of abode under the 1981 Act

The BNA 1981 replaced the existing section 2 1971 Act with a new section 2. This sought to anchor the concept of right of abode firmly to the new status of 'British citizenship'. Also, following the 1981 Act, certain Commonwealth citizens who were 'patrials' with the right of abode continued to have that right of abode, and were considered to be 'British citizens' for the purposes of the immigration controls under the 1971 Act. They are:

- Commonwealth citizens who had a parent born in the UK before 1 January 1983 (the date on which the BNA 1981 came into force); and

- female Commonwealth citizens who had become patrial through marriage to a man who was a patrial before 1 January 1983 and who still had that status on 31 December 1982.

In order to benefit from the new section 2 1971 Act, the above persons must not have ceased to be Commonwealth citizens in the meantime.

So, under the version of section 2 of the 1971 Act in force since 1 January 1983, the following people have the right of abode:

- British citizens (including former CUKCs who were born, adopted, registered or naturalised in the UK; those CUKCs with a relevant ancestral connection through a parent or grandparent to the UK under the previous section 2; and those CUKCs who obtained the right of abode through ordinary residence);

- Commonwealth citizens who, before 1 January 1983, had the right of abode as a result of having a parent born in the UK;

- female Commonwealth citizens who, before 1 January 1983, had the right of abode through marriage to a man with patrial status.

These changes were brought in at the same time as the status of 'CUKC' was replaced by the categories of British citizen, BDTC (now BOTC) and BOC. Prior to 1 January 1983, a CUKC who did not have the right of abode, and who wished to obtain it, could acquire it by five years' ordinary residence, free from immigration control. This possibility was removed by the BNA 1981. However, it is now possible for such people to register by entitlement as a British citizen on grounds of residence under section 4 BNA 1981 (▶see 1486–7).

As stated above, women who were Commonwealth citizens on 31 December 1982 and who were married on or before that date to British citizen men, or men with the right of abode, themselves have the right of abode in the UK. If they wish to travel to the UK, these women need to apply to a British post for a 'certificate of entitlement to the right of abode' and pay a fee (see below). This provision does not apply to men. Nor does it apply to non-Commonwealth-citizen women. So, for example, Camerounian, Mozambican, Namibian, Pakistani and South African citizen women cannot benefit from this, because these countries were not members of the Commonwealth in 1982.

Although the BNA 1981 allowed the two groups of Commonwealth citizens referred to above to continue to have the right of abode, it also ensured that the right of abode could no longer be *acquired* in that way.

13

So it provided that:

1) from 1 January 1983, a female Commonwealth citizen could no longer acquire the right of abode by marrying a man with the right of abode 'on or after 1 January 1983'. Women in this position must apply to be naturalised as British citizens under section 6 of the BNA 1981 (▶see 1455);

2) a Commonwealth citizen born on or after 1 January 1983 will not acquire the right of abode as a result of having a parent born in the UK.

However, a person falling under (2) above may still automatically be a British citizen (see s2(1) of the BNA 1981, ▶see 1436).

Applying for a Certificate of Entitlement to the right of abode

A person may apply for a certificate of entitlement to show that they have the right of abode. The certificate is a sticker fixed into a valid passport. If a person is living abroad, the application should be made to the nearest designated British Embassy, British High Commission or British Diplomatic Post. The Foreign and Commonwealth Office website (www.fco.gov.uk) contains a list of such posts. There are separate queues for people with a claim to the right of abode. In South Asian countries, this means that the queue should be much shorter.

If a female Commonwealth citizen applied by mistake for an entry clearance and paid the fee appropriate to the entry clearance application, then the difference should be refunded by the ECO, as they have a duty to identify which category a person falls into. In order to obtain the certificate of entitlement on the basis of marriage, the woman will need her original marriage certificate (to show the date of the marriage) and proof that her husband was either a British citizen or a Commonwealth citizen with the right of abode at the time of the marriage. It does not matter if the husband has since died.

A person living in the UK who wishes to apply should complete Form ROA and send it, together with original documents, the application form, two passport-size photographs and the fee (presently £20) to:

Home Office Nationality Group
(Right of Abode)
PO Box 12
Liverpool
L2 7XS

Further information and application forms can be found on the Home Office website (www.ind.homeoffice.gov.uk).

It is possible to apply for the transfer into a new passport, of a certificate of patriality (a certificate issued to those under the right of abode provisions that applied prior to 1 January 1983), or a certificate of entitlement to the right of abode, contained in an old passport.

When the certificate of entitlement is granted, it is valid for the same length of time as the passport, and the person is free to travel to the UK and to return at any time during the validity of the passport. A person with a certificate of entitlement who is not a British citizen may seek naturalisation as a British citizen once they have resided in the UK for the required period (▶see 1453–5).

Under section 82 of the Nationality, Immigration and Asylum Act 2002 there is a right of appeal to the AIT against a refusal to issue a certificate of entitlement.

IDENTIFYING BRITISH NATIONALITY FROM PASSPORTS

Establishing a person's nationality from their passport is relatively easy for those with current passports. All passports issued since 1 January 1983 will describe the citizenship status a person acquired under the 1981 Act. It is more complicated to establish the present citizenship of those British nationals who have pre-1983 passports, or no passports at all.

Passports issued on or after 1 January 1983

Passports issued on or after 1 January 1983 should describe the person's nationality status on the page containing their personal details as follows: 'British citizen', 'British Overseas citizen', 'British Dependent Territories citizen', 'British Overseas Territories citizen', 'British subject', 'British Protected Person' or 'British National (Overseas)'.

The following points should be noted.

- There is now no endorsement on British citizen passports stating that the holder has the right of abode. This is because British citizens all have the right of abode. This worries some people when they get a new passport, because they may think that their right of abode has been withdrawn. They should be reassured that this is not the case.

- Few other British nationals have the right of abode in the UK. These people should have passport endorsements called 'certificates of entitlement to the right of abode' (see above, and for an example ▶see 202). Certificates of entitlement have replaced the old 'certificates of patriality', which were issued before 1 January 1983.

- All British passports issued now are in the uniform EU passport format, which is maroon-coloured and computer-readable. Some people, wrongly, believe that they are of lower status than the old blue passports. Those issued to British citizens, British subjects with the right of abode in the UK, and BOTCs by virtue of a connection with Gibraltar, also bear the words 'European Union' (or 'European Community' if issued before December 1997).

Passports issued before 1 January 1983

Most British passports issued before 1 January 1983 describe the holder, on page 1, as a 'British subject: Citizen of the UK and Colonies'. If this is

13

the case, turn to page 5 of the passport. This usually says 'Holder has the right of abode in the UK'. If this is in the passport and has not been crossed out, it is almost certain that the holder is now a British citizen. He or she would automatically have become a British citizen on 1 January 1983 without needing to do anything about it.

If the wording on page 5 has been cancelled, then it is likely that the holder is a British Overseas citizen (BOC). The holder may also have been a BDTC, now a BOTC (▶see 1406 above for their status following the British Overseas Territories Act 2002, which gave BOTCs the right of abode in the UK as British citizens). Otherwise, if the wording has been cancelled, this will mean that the holder, including if they are a BOC, does not have the right of abode in the UK, and will need to fit into the immigration rules to come to or stay in the UK. However, it is still worth checking the points below, in case this status has changed since the passport was issued, or it was issued in error.

The statuses of British Protected Person and British subject were not changed by the British Nationality Act 1981. Passports issued before or after 1983 will show these statuses on the first page. A few British subjects (often married women) have the right of abode in the UK. If so, it will be signalled on page 5, or as a 'certificate of patriality' stamp. However, the majority of BPPs and BSs do not have the right of abode in the UK, and will need to fit into the immigration rules if they wish to come to or stay in the UK.

Further points to check where passport was issued before 1 January 1983

The following further points should be noted.

- Check that nothing has happened to change the person's status since the passport was issued. As stated above, a passport is not proof of present nationality; it is only evidence that a person had that status when the passport was issued. This is particularly relevant for people from Commonwealth countries who hold British passports which were issued before their countries became independent. At independence, moïst people from that country automatically lost their British nationality and gained nationality of the newly independent country. However, their British passports were not recalled, and they were usually not even told about their change of nationality. For people born outside the UK, without parents or grandparents born in Britain, it is therefore worth checking the date of issue of the passport against the date of independence of their country of origin (▶see 1525–6).

- People from Caribbean countries which gained their independence from 1981 onwards gain citizenship of the new country but also, if they had lived in the UK for more than five years and were settled before independence, keep their British citizenship. This has applied so far to people from Belize, St Christopher & Nevis, Antigua & Barbuda and Bermuda.

- Some people from Hong Kong are not any kind of British national, though they have travel documents which were issued by the Hong Kong government or the British Home Office. They are people born in the People's Republic of China who emigrated to Hong Kong, and may subsequently have come to the UK. They travel on brown documents called certificates of identity (or 'CIs' in Hong Kong). They are, in effect, stateless people (save for having a right to Chinese nationality), and have no special rights in British immigration and nationality law.

Checking for British citizenship

If people have current passports describing them as 'British citizens', then it is clear that they are British citizens. However, some people do not have British passports (for example, children born in the UK, or children born abroad who have been issued with certificates of entitlement to the right of abode endorsed on their foreign passport, rather than a British passport issued overseas), or may have changed their status since their British or foreign passport was issued. The flow-charts contained in the tables on ▶1440–1 will help to identify other people who are British citizens. The flow-charts do not cover all the ways of acquiring British citizenship. Details about who is already a British citizen and how British citizenship may be acquired are dealt with in the next two chapters.

OBTAINING A PASSPORT

Practical details about applying for a passport can be found on the UK Passport Service website at www.passport.gov.uk. Application forms and guidance notes ('How to fill in your passport application form', IL/12 10/04) are also available from Post Offices. There is also a 24-hour Passport Advice line on 0870 521 0410.

There is more than one type of application form, and the requirements for applying for passports are subject to frequent change. At the time of writing, there is a planned expansion of the UK Passport Agency to allow for the interview of all persons applying for passports. These changes are part of a programme of enhanced security checks. Up-to-the-minute information on forms, costs and procedures can be obtained from the website given above.

Refusal or withdrawal of a passport

In restricted circumstances, a passport may be withheld from someone even if they are accepted as being a British national. There is no statutory basis for a passport to be issued to British nationals other than British Nationals (Overseas), and the issue of a passport is derived from the royal prerogative. Under criteria issued by the government it seems that a passport may be refused or withdrawn in any of the following circumstances:

- where a minor is being taken out of the country illegally or without the permission of the parent, or the person with parental responsibility;

13

- where there is good evidence that a person wishes to avoid prosecution;
- where an applicant's conduct is so undesirable that the enjoyment of passport facilities is contrary to the public interest;
- where a person has been repatriated to the UK at public expense and has not repaid the cost;
- where a warrant for the person's arrest has been issued in the UK;
- where a person is wanted for a serious crime in the UK.

Where a person is refused a passport or a passport is withdrawn, reasons must be given. The decision-maker should also provide a warning that a passport is liable to be refused on a particular basis, so as to give the applicant an opportunity to make representations. A decision to refuse or to withdraw a passport can be challenged by judicial review (see *Everett*). The refusal to issue a passport may be unreasonable, may be based on a false premise, may fail to take a relevant consideration into account, or may take into account irrelevant considerations. In addition, it may hinder other lawful entitlements to move freely under statutory or common law of the UK and/or the EU. A decision to refuse a passport may also be disproportionate as a matter of human rights law and/or EU law. A person whose British nationality is not questioned but who is refused a passport should therefore seek specialist advice.

44 Who is a British citizen?

This chapter explains which people are automatically British citizens, i.e., without having to make any application to be British. 'British citizen' is a status established under the British Nationality Act 1981 (the 'BNA'), which came into force on 1 January 1983. It is the prime nationality status in UK law. All British citizens have the 'right of abode' in the UK (for an explanation of the 'right of abode' ▶see 1417–20). This means that, subject to proving their status (usually by producing a passport) they can come and go from the UK freely 'without let or hindrance' (see s1 1971 Act). However, British nationality law is complex and there are other kinds of British national whose status does not give them the right of abode. They are looked at in Chapter 43 (▶see 1404–14). There is also a small category of Commonwealth nationals who, although they are not British nationals, have the right of abode. They are also dealt with in Chapter 41 (▶see 1419–20).

This chapter

People born before 1 January 1983 who were classed 'British citizens' on that date In this chapter, we first look at who was 'classed' as a British citizen on 1 January 1983 when the BNA came into force and British nationality statuses were re-classified (▶immediately below 1426–8). The information here obviously deals with people who were born *before* 1 January 1983.

People born, adopted or found in the UK on or after 1 January 1983 We then move on to describe those categories of people who obtained British citizenship by being born, adopted or found in the UK (or in the Falkland Islands) *on or after* 1 January 1983 (▶1428–32). In considering who qualifies as a British citizen on this basis, we look at the important definitions of the word 'parent', and the circumstances in which it may or may not include 'father', and the word 'settled', which apply for nationality purposes.

BOTCs We then deal briefly with the category of British Overseas Territories citizens (BOTCs) who became British citizens on 21 May 2002.

People born abroad who are British citizens The chapter then moves on to consider which people born abroad are British citizens, as again the

13

situation changed as a result of the BNA (▶1433–6). In order to consider this category of people, we also deal with the important concept of who is a British citizen 'otherwise than by descent' and who is a British citizen 'by descent' (▶see 1433–4). We then look separately at those born outside the UK but in the British Overseas Territories on or after 21 May 2002 (▶1436–7) and at the position of people born stateless or on ships or aircraft (▶1437–8).

Flowcharts and summary of 'who is a British citizen' The answer to the general question asked by this chapter, 'who is a British citizen?' is then summarised at ▶1438–42 and we provide summary flowcharts dealing with this question (▶see at 1440) and the question of who becomes a British citizen 'by descent' only (▶see at 1441).

Renunciation of citizenship The chapter then covers 'renunciation' of British citizenship and also registration as a British citizen once more after a person has renounced either British citizenship or Citizenship of the United Kingdom and Colonies (CUKC status) (▶1442–5).

Deprivation of citizenship Finally, this chapter looks at the circumstances in which people can be deprived of their British citizenship and circumstances in which the Home Office may treat the grant of citizenship to a particular person as not having any effect (▶1445).

Chapter 45

The final chapter in this section, Chapter 45, also concerns 'British citizen' status. However, that chapter deals with the routes by which people who are not born British can *apply to become* British. There are two procedures for applying to become British: naturalisation and registration. Inevitably, there are strict requirements that need to be satisfied. Registration in particular is available in a variety of different circumstances.

PEOPLE WHO BECAME 'BRITISH CITIZENS' ON 1 JANUARY 1983

As stated above, 'British citizen' was a status introduced by the BNA 1981 when it came into force on 1 January 1983. Before that date, the most beneficial form of national status was to be a Citizen of the United Kingdom and Colonies (CUKC) with right of abode in the UK. The BNA re-classified British national statuses. Therefore, inevitably, on 1 January 1983, certain people were automatically re-classified as British citizens.

For the development of British nationality law up to and including 1 January 1983 and the previous forms of citizenship, see the previous chapter at ▶1402–4.

The general rule

Those people who, on 31 December 1982, were CUKCs with the right of abode in the UK under section 2 1971 Act *as it was then in force* were re-classified as British citizens under the BNA (see s11(1) BNA 1981). At that point, section 2 1971 Act defined who was 'patrial' and had the right of abode as a result. Two classes of CUKCs were patrial under this provision:

1) CUKCs by birth, adoption, naturalisation or registration in the UK;
2) CUKCs with a similar connection to the UK through a parent or grand-parent.

So, the general rule is that those who, on 31 December 1982, were CUKCs in either of the above two categories, automatically became British citizens on 1 January 1983. For a general summary of the position, ▶see 1438–9 and Flowchart 1 at ▶1440.

There is an exception to this rule (see s11(2) BNA). This is that any person who was registered as a CUKC under section 1(1)(a) British Nationality (No. 2) Act 1964 (stateless persons) did not become a British citizen on 1 January 1983 *unless*:

- their mother became, or but for her death would have become, a British citizen under section 11(1) on 1 January 1983 ; *or*
- they had the right of abode in the UK under section 2(1)(c) 1971 Act as it was then in force (that is as a result of settlement in the UK with five or more years of ordinary residence).

It should also be noted that a person would not have become a CUKC by their birth in the UK in the first place if, at the time of their birth, their father was either a diplomat or an enemy alien (see British Nationality and Status of Aliens Act 1914 and the British Nationality Act 1948).

Two other categories of people who became British citizens on 1 January 1983

In addition to the general rule above, there are two further categories of people who were born before 1 January 1983 and who became British citizens on that date. They are as follows.

Certain persons registered under the British Nationality Act 1948

Anyone who was registered under section 12(6) 1948 Act on the grounds of descent in the male line from a person who was born or naturalised in the UK, became a British citizen on 1 January 1983 whether or not they had the right of abode immediately before that date.

Falkland Islanders

A person, who on the re-classification of citizenship became a British Dependent Territories citizen under section 23 BNA 1981 on 1 January 1983, might also on that date become a British citizen if they had a connection with the Falkland Islands. This would be the case if they were, on 31 December 1982, a CUKC with any of the following connections to the Falkland Islands:

- they held CUKC status by birth, naturalisation or registration in the Falkland Islands;

- one of their parents or grandparents was a CUKC by birth, naturalisation or registration in the Falkland Islands (or but for death would have been a CUKC by any of those means);or

- she is a woman who was, or had previously been, married to a man who became a British citizen under either of the categories above (or would have been but for his death);

The person can benefit from the above *provided* they had not renounced or been deprived of British Dependent Territories Citizenship (BDTC) between 1 January 1983 and 27 March 1983.

BRITISH CITIZENS BY BIRTH (OR ADOPTION, OR FOUND ABANDONED) IN THE UK ON OR AFTER 1 JANUARY 1983

Under section 1 BNA 1981, certain people born in the UK on or after 1 January 1983, acquire British citizenship automatically at birth. A person born in the UK on or after 1 January 1983 is a British citizen at birth if, at the time of the birth:

- one of their parents is a British citizen; *or*

- one of their parents is settled in the UK.

Not all fathers count as a 'parent' for these purposes (see immediately below). For the meaning of 'settled', ▶see also below at 1429–30.

With very limited exceptions, applying for example to children of certain diplomats, people born in the UK before 1 January 1983 are British citizens.

Meaning of 'parent'

The definition of 'parent' and 'father' for the purposes of the BNA is found in sections 47 and 50 BNA 1981. A 'parent' does not yet include a father who is not married to the child's mother. The definition of 'parent' does however include the mother whether or not she is married to the natural father. So, a child born in the UK after 1 January 1983 to a mother (who is not settled or a British citizen) and a father (who is settled or is a British citizen) will not be British if the two of them are not lawfully married at the time of the child's birth. If the parents marry after the child's birth, the child may automatically become British from the date of the marriage, depending on the law of the country in which the father was domiciled at the time of the marriage. By section 47 BNA 1981, if the parents marry each other *in the UK* after the child is born then the child *will* be legitimate for all matters under the BNA provided the father is 'domiciled' (▶see 320 and 1540) in the UK, and in consequence is automatically British from the date of the marriage.

Section 9 2002 Act: an end to discrimination?

Despite the recommendations of the Law Commission as long ago as 1986 and the development of DNA testing, this discrimination against children whose parents are not married remains in place. A recent challenge to the rule under the HRA was unsuccessful in the Court of Appeal (*Montana*). Section 9 of the Nationality, Immigration and Asylum Act 2002 abolishes discrimination in nationality law against 'illegitimate' children but that measure has, at the time of writing, still not been brought into force despite indications that it would be by now.

Registration of 'illegitimate' children and children of parents who later became settled

However the Home Office does operate a policy under which 'illegitimate children' may be *registered* as British citizens by discretion under section 3(1) BNA 1981 (for details, ▶see 1482). It should also be noted that a child born in the UK to a parent who was not settled at the time of birth but who subsequently becomes settled, has an entitlement to register as a British citizen (s1(3) BNA 1981) (▶see 1474).

Meaning of 'settled'

For a person to be 'settled' in the UK they must be 'ordinarily resident' (▶1274 and 1544–5) in the UK, (or where relevant a British Overseas Territory), without being subject under the immigration laws to any restriction on the period for which they may remain. If a child is born to parents in the UK who are not settled but who have limited leave, an application can be made for the child to be granted leave in line with their parent/s (▶see 394–5). If the parent/s subsequently become settled, or the child lives in the UK for ten years, the child is entitled to be registered as a British citizen (▶see 1474). Where a child seeks to rely on a father who is not married to the child's mother, and the father becomes settled or naturalised as a British citizen, the child may apply to register as a British citizen at the discretion of the Secretary of State (s3(1) BNA 1981).

Are EEA nationals 'settled' for these purposes?

In the past, the Home Office accepted that children of EEA nationals born in the UK were born British. This was because EEA nationals have no formal time-limits on their stay under British immigration law because conventional immigration controls do not generally apply to them. However in 1994 in the case of *Gal*, the IAT decided that, where an EEA national's stay depends on their continuing in a particular activity, there is in practice a limit on their stay. Therefore, their children born in the UK would not auto-

13

matically be born British. Despite this case, the Home Office continued in practice to regard EEA nationals exercising free-movement rights as 'settled' and it therefore operated a policy, which considered their UK-born children automatically to be British citizens.

However, the Home Office view then changed. The European Economic Area Regulations 2000 (reg. 8) confirmed the revised Home Office view to the effect that most EEA nationals who are exercising free-movement rights are to be treated as having restrictions on the period of their leave and are therefore not settled. The only EEA nationals exercising free-movement rights who are regarded as 'settled' are those who EU law or the immigration rules say are entitled to permanent residence in the UK (►see 559–60 for details of EEA nationals who are treated as having a permanent right of residence). So, for example, an ordinary EEA national exercising free-movement rights as a worker who holds a residence permit valid for a limited period, or no residence permit at all, is not treated as 'settled' for nationality purposes. A child born to such a person is not born a British citizen.

However, the Home Office confirmed in a letter to the Immigration Law Practitioners' Association in September 2000, that the change in the law only applies to children born on or after 2 October 2000. Children born to parents exercising rights of free movement before that time are British citizens whether or not their parent had by that time established a right of permanent residence. This of course leads to the anomalous situation where a later child born to an EEA national in the UK is not British, whereas their brother or sister born before 2 October 2000 is British. It is obviously worth applying for registration of such children on the basis that they have a British citizen sibling (►see 1484).

What is the position of UK-born children who are not British citizens?

Children born in the UK on or after 1 January 1983 and who are not born British but whose parents have limited leave, can be granted leave in line with them (►see 393–5). If the parent/s settle in the UK, or the child remains in the UK for ten years or more, the child is entitled to register as a British citizen (►see 1474).

If the child was born in the UK but is not British because they were born 'illegitimate' to their settled or British citizen father and non-settled or non-British mother, and their parents marry, the child will become British by the parents' marriage provided the father is 'domiciled' in the UK (►320 and 1540). Where a child seeks to rely on a father who is not married to the child's mother, and the father is settled or a British citizen, the child may apply to register as a British citizen under section 3(1) BNA 1981; such a decision being at the discretion of the Secretary of State.

Where neither parent is settled and neither is a British citizen and one of them becomes settled or naturalises as a British citizen then the child is entitled to register as British where it is the mother or the *married* father who becomes settled or British (section 1(3) BNA 1981). Where the *unmarried* father is the one who becomes settled or British the child may apply to register as a British citizen at the discretion of the Secretary of State.

Can UK-born non-British children be removed?

If none of the above applies, or before they do apply, then the position for these UK-born children who are not born British is that they do not have any immigration status. There is no *independent* power to take enforcement action against them: they have not 'entered' the UK in an unlawful manner so they are not illegal entrants; they have not applied for and been refused leave to enter so they cannot be removed as 'port' cases; and they cannot be administratively removed as a result of overstaying or breaching conditions of leave because they have not been granted leave. *However*, this does not mean that they are free from immigration controls. They can be removed from the UK together with their parent/s as part of the family unit if their parent/s are:

- removed from the UK as 'port' cases or as 'illegal entrants' (this power has only existed from 10 February 2003, see para. 10A Sch 2 1971 Act as inserted by the 2002 Act); or
- administratively removed from the UK (as overstayers, people who have breached their conditions of leave, people who have obtained, or tried to obtain, leave to remain by deception or people who have 'ceased' to be refugees); or
- ordered to be deported from the UK.

For further details about the removal of children born in the UK who are not British, ▶see 386–90.

Also, if such a child leaves the UK then they will require leave to enter on their return. If they are travelling with parents who obtain leave to enter the UK and the child is re-admitted for the same time period and on the same conditions as their parents (as is normal), the child will then be subject to the usual sanctions if they overstay that leave. If the non-British citizen parents want to travel and to take the child with them, the child has no claim to a British passport. They may be entitled to the nationality of either parent, depending on the nationality laws of their parents' country and may be able to get a passport from the relevant High Commission or Embassy. Alternatively, the parent may be able to have the child's name inserted on their passport. If the child is not able to get a passport, the parent should try to obtain the refusal in writing, or confirmation that the child is not regarded as a citizen of that country. It may then be possible for the parent to obtain a stateless travel document (▶see 879) for the child from the Home Office.

13

Birth in Falkland Islands after 1 January 1983

A person born or adopted in the Falkland Islands on or after 1 January 1983 will automatically be a British citizen under the same criteria as those born or adopted in the UK.

Adoption in the UK after 1 January 1983

Adoptions which take place in *either* of the following circumstances result in the child being a British citizen from the date of the adoption order (see s1(5) BNA 1981). This is the case where the adoption is:

- authorised by order of a court in the UK *and* the adopter, or in the case of a joint adoption, one of the adopters, is a British citizen on the day of the adoption order; or

- a 'Convention' adoption under the Hague Convention on the Protection of Children and Cooperation in respect of Inter-Country Adoption 1993 *if* the adoption takes place on or after 1 June 2003, *and* the adopter, or in the case of a joint adoption, one of the adopters, is a British citizen on the date the Convention adoption is effected *and* the adopter, or in the case of a joint adoption, both of the adopters, are habitually resident in UK on the date of the Convention adoption. For a list of the countries in which the Hague Convention is in force, ▶see 1528. ▶See also 380–1

British citizenship which is obtained as a result of adoption is not lost if the adoption order ceases to have effect at a later date, for example on annulment (see s1(6) BNA 1981). However, where the order is set aside by a higher court on appeal by the Home Secretary, section 1(6) has no effect and the child will cease to be a British citizen.

Abandoned infants

A newborn infant found abandoned in the UK on or after 1 January 1983 is, unless the contrary is shown, assumed to have been born in the UK on or after 1 January 1983 to a parent who was either a British citizen or settled in UK at the time of birth (s1(2) BNA 1981). Such a child is therefore a British citizen.

BOTCS WHO BECAME BRITISH CITIZENS ON 21 MAY 2002

Under the British Overseas Territories Act 2002, British Overseas Territories citizens (BOTCs) (i.e. former British Dependent Territories citizens) became British citizens automatically on 21 May 2002, provided they had that citizenship by connection with a 'qualifying' overseas territory (see s3 BOTA 2002). The qualifying overseas territories are all of the British Overseas territories *except* the sovereign base areas of Dhekelia and Akrotiri both of which are in Cyprus. For a full list of the British Overseas Territories see ▶1406.

A person also became a British citizen automatically on 21 May 2002 if they met all of the following conditions (see s6 BOTA 2002):

- they were born on or after 26 April 1969 and before 1 January 1983;
- they were born to a woman who, at the time of the birth, was a CUKC (for the meaning of CUKC, ▶see 1403–4 and 1426–7) as a result of her birth in the British Indian Ocean Territory;
- immediately before 21 May 2002, they were neither a British citizen nor a BOC.

People who were only BOTCs by descent only became British citizens 'by descent', which means they cannot automatically transmit their citizenship on to their children (▶see below).

For the citizenship of persons born in the qualifying territories on or after 21 May 2002, ▶see below at 1436–7.

PEOPLE BORN OUTSIDE THE UK WHO ARE BRITISH CITIZENS BY BIRTH

Certain people who are born outside the UK or the Falkland Islands on or after 1 January 1983 may also be British citizens because their parents have transmitted their citizenship to them (see s2(1) BNA). Whether the parent/s can automatically transmit their citizenship to children born abroad depends on whether the parent/s are classed as British citizens 'otherwise than by descent' or 'by descent'. We therefore look first at this critical concept and then we look at the different categories of people born abroad (below at ▶1434–6).

For a general summary relating to those born outside the UK and who obtain citizenship by descent, ▶see below at 1438–41 and Flowchart 2 at 1441.

The meaning of British citizenship 'otherwise than by descent' and 'by descent'

British citizens divide into two categories. They are either:

- British citizens 'otherwise than by descent'; or
- British citizens 'by descent'.

For the purposes of freely entering and remaining in the UK, leaving and returning to the UK and all the other general rights of citizenship, the distinction between the two has no practical importance. The only area where the difference is important is in the ability of parents to automatically transmit their citizenship to their children who are born abroad. British citizens 'by descent' have the *less* favourable status. They can only transmit their citizenship if their parents are in Crown, designated or EC service ▶1436. British citizens 'otherwise than by descent' automatically transmit their citizenship to children born abroad.

13

Whether a person is a citizen 'otherwise than by descent' or 'by descent' depends upon how they obtained their citizenship in the first place. A person is a British citizen 'otherwise than by descent', in general, if they are a British citizen (NIs Ch 20 para. 20.1.4):

- by birth, adoption (▶see 380), registration or naturalisation in the UK or Falkland Islands (or a 'qualifying' territory on or after 21 May 2002);
- who immediately before 21 May 2002 were British Overseas Territories citizens by connection with a qualifying territory; or
- because they were adopted on or after 1 June 2003 in any country under the terms of the Hague Convention on the Protection of Children and Cooperation in Respect of Intercountry Adoption 1993, ▶see 380–1 and 1528.

However there are exceptions. There is a list of those classes of people who are British citizens 'by descent' in section 14 BNA 1981. This list includes many forms of registration and care should be taken to ascertain which forms of registration are by descent or otherwise than by descent. In the chapter on naturalisation and registration, for each way of becoming a British citizen we have indicated whether the process leads to citizenship by descent or otherwise than by descent.

A British citizen who holds a British passport will not be able to tell from that passport whether they are a British citizen 'otherwise than by descent' or 'by descent'. It has to be worked out separately. It is important because their status will affect whether they can automatically pass on British citizenship to their children or if such children will need to register in order to become British citizens.

Can a British citizen 'upgrade' their status to 'otherwise than by descent'?

'British citizen' is a single concept and so a person who is a British citizen 'by descent' cannot upgrade their status in order to become British 'otherwise than by descent' so as to be able to transmit their citizenship to children born abroad. This was confirmed by the Court of Appeal in *Ullah* in which it was held that a British citizen by descent could not upgrade their status by naturalisation.

People born outside the UK before 1 January 1983

Before 1 January 1983, British nationality by descent could pass only through fathers. Children born overseas to CUKC mothers and foreign fathers were not born British. Children born outside the UK to CUKC fathers automatically became CUKCs by descent with the right of abode (and therefore with full citizenship rights), provided their father obtained that status in one of the following ways:

- by being born, or being adopted by a CUKC father, in the UK; or
- by being registered or naturalised in the UK before the child was born.

If the father registered outside the UK it would give him, and possibly the child, some other kind of British nationality, but not CUKC status. If the father became a CUKC after a child's birth, this would not retrospectively make the child British. Note that 'father' here applies only to a man who was lawfully married to the child's mother.

British (CUKC) mother

Although children born outside the UK before 1 January 1983 to CUKC (British) mothers could not inherit their mother's citizenship, special arrangements were subsequently made for them. The Home Office stated that, if British-born mothers applied for their non-UK-born children to be registered as British citizens, this would be granted provided both of the following conditions were satisfied:

- if the parents were still married, the father of the child had no well-founded objection to the application; and
- the child was still under 18 at the time of application.

Because the child had to be under 18, this concession came to an end for practical purposes at the end of 2000 (by which time those born before 1 January 1983 would all have become 18). However, certain people who were born abroad to CUKC mothers between 8 February 1961 and 31 December 1982 may still be registered as British citizens by entitlement (see s4C BNA 1981 and ▶see 1485–6).

British grandfather

There are also some circumstances in which having a British grandfather could mean that a person born overseas before 1 January 1983 is a British citizen now. This applies if *all* of the following conditions are satisfied:

- the grandfather in question is the person's paternal grandfather (i.e. their father's father);
- the grandfather acquired his citizenship in the UK by birth, registration or naturalisation;
- the child was born in a non-Commonwealth country (▶see 1525–6 for a list of Commonwealth countries); and
- the child's birth was registered at a British consulate within a year of the birth.

People born outside the UK on or after 1 January 1983

A person born outside the UK on or after 1 January 1983 is a British citizen at birth if, at the time of the birth, either parent is a British citizen 'otherwise than by descent' (s2(1)(a) BNA 1981). For the distinction between 'otherwise than by descent' and 'by descent' and how to determine which category a British citizen falls into, ▶see above 1433–4. Again, 'parent' for these purposes does not include a father if the parents of the child were not married. If the parents marry each other in the UK after the child is born, then the child will be 'legitimate' for nationality purposes provided the father is 'domiciled' (▶320 and 1540) in the UK (▶see above 1428–9) and therefore, automatically British from the date of the marriage. Section 9 Nationality, Immigration and Asylum Act 2002 abolishes discrimination in nationality law against 'illegitimate' children but that measure has, at the time of writing, still not been brought into force.

A child who obtains British citizen status in this way will be British 'by descent' and therefore will *not* be able to pass on their citizenship automatically to their own children who are born outside the UK (▶see however, 1474–5 for the possibility of registration of these children as British citizens in such circumstances). So, the principle is that, where children of British citizens are born outside the UK, citizenship may only pass for one generation. After that, the link that provides automatic citizenship is broken.

Crown, designated or EC service

There are other ways in which children born abroad to a British citizen may automatically acquire British citizenship, and these will make them British citizens 'otherwise than by descent'.

A person born outside the UK on or after 1 January 1983 is a British citizen at birth if, at the time of the birth all the following requirements are met (section 2(1)(b) BNA 1981):

- either parent is a British citizen whether 'by descent' or 'otherwise than by descent';
- that parent is serving outside the UK in Crown Service under the government of the United Kingdom, or in any designated service under section 2(3) BNA 1981 (see NIs, Ch 4, Annex A); and
- was recruited in the UK for that service.

In addition, a person born outside the UK on or after 1 January 1983 is a British citizen at birth, if at the time of the birth all the following requirements are met (s 2(1)(c) BNA 1981):

- either parent is a British citizen whether 'by descent' or 'otherwise than by descent';
- the parent is serving outside the UK in service under a European Community institution (see NIs, Chapter 4, Annex B); and
- was recruited for that service in a country which at the time was a member of the European Community.

People born outside the UK but in the Overseas Territories on or after 21 May 2002

A person born in a 'qualifying' British Overseas Territory (i.e. a British Overseas territory other than the sovereign bases in Cyprus, see the definition at ▶1432 above) on or after 21 May 2002 may be a British citizen at birth.

This will be the case provided that *any one* of the following conditions is satisfied at the time of the birth (see s1(1) BNA 1981 as amended by Schedule 1 British Overseas Territories Act 2002), namely that either of the child's parents:

- is a British citizen;
- is settled in the UK; or
- is settled in the qualifying territory in which the child was born.

There are very similar provisions relating to children adopted in the Overseas Territories and for newborn infants found abandoned in the Overseas Territories as there are relating to adoption and abandonment in the UK (▶see above).

PERSONS BORN STATELESS AND PERSONS BORN ON SHIPS AND AIRCRAFT

Under the United Nations Convention on the Reduction of Statelessness 1961, the UK has certain obligations in international law to help reduce statelessness.

Born in the UK

A person born in the UK on or after 1 January 1983, who would otherwise have been stateless, will be either: a BOTC; a BOC; both a British citizen and a BOC; or a BS (see para. 1, schedule 2 BNA 1981), if, at the time of birth, either of their parents was, respectively, a British Overseas Territories citizen and/or a BOC, or if one of them was a BS under the BNA 1981 (▶see 1413–4).

Born in an Overseas Territory

A person born in a British Overseas Territory on or after 1 January 1983 who would otherwise have been stateless, will be either: a British citizen; a BOC; both a British citizen and a BOC; or a BS (see para. 2, schedule 2 BNA 1981), if either of their parents was, respectively, a British citizen and/or a BOC, or if one of them was a BS under the BNA 1981. However, a person cannot benefit from these provisions if, at birth, they are already a BOTC under section 15(1) BNA 1981 by being born in a British Overseas Territory at a time when their father or mother was a BOTC, or was settled in a British Overseas Territory. Nor can a person benefit if, at birth, they obtained British citizen status by descent as a person born outside the UK to parent/s who were British otherwise than by descent, or who were serving in Crown, designated or EC service (▶see above 1436) outside the UK. It obviously also does not apply to other British citizens either.

Registration OF stateless persons

There are also provisions for the registration of persons who would otherwise be stateless who were:

13

- born in the UK or an Overseas Territory on or after 1 January 1983 but lack a parent who is a British national (▶see 1488–9);
- born outside the UK and the Overseas Territories on or after 1 January 1983 but have a parent who is a British national (▶see 1489–90);
- born before commencement of the BNA 1981 on 1 January 1983 (▶see 1490).

Birth outside the UK on UK ship or aircraft

A person born on or after 1 January 1983 outside the UK aboard a ship, hovercraft or aircraft is regarded for nationality purposes as having been born in the UK provided that either parent was a British citizen, or the child would otherwise be stateless. In addition in either case, one of the two following conditions must be satisfied at the time of the birth in order for the child to be born British (see s50(7) BNA):

- the ship or aircraft was registered in the UK;
- the ship or aircraft was unregistered but belonged to the government of the UK.

There are similar provisions in force in relation to the Overseas Territories.

CHECKING FOR BRITISH CITIZENSHIP: A SUMMARY

This section provides a summary of the answer to the general question as to 'who is a British citizen?' which is set out in more detail above.

We first summarise the position for people born in the UK and then for people born overseas. We also use two flowcharts to illustrate the position. Obviously, the easiest way to check for a person's citizenship is to see their passport (for determining citizenship by looking at passports, see the previous chapter at ▶1421–3). However, a passport is only evidence of a person's citizenship, it is not the source of their status. People are only given passports when they have demonstrated their status. In some cases, people will be unsure as to their citizenship and often advice will need to be taken.

Flowchart 1 (▶1440) deals with 'who is a British citizen?'.

Flowchart 2 (▶1441) deals with 'who is a British citizen *by descent*?' (as opposed to being a British citizen 'otherwise than by descent') (▶see also at 1433–4 above).

Note that it is not definite that people are not British citizens just because they do not fit into the flowcharts. They do not deal with connections to the Overseas Territories or some of the exceptions referred to above. Also, nationality is a complex area and there are other minor ways of acquiring British citizenship. The flowcharts deal only with 'British citizens', the prime British nationality status, and not other kinds of British national.

People born in the UK

Before 1 January 1983, everyone born in the UK, and all children adopted in the UK by a British father, were Citizens of the United Kingdom and Colonies (CUKCs). These people are now British citizens. The only significant category of exception was the children of diplomats. The BNA 1981 changed the position concerning obtaining nationality by birth in the UK. People born in the UK on or after 1 January 1983 become British citizens at birth only if one of their parents is settled (for the meaning of 'parent' ▶see 1428 and for the meaning of 'settled' ▶see 1429–30).

Therefore children born in the UK on or after 1 January 1983, whose parents have only limited leave (for example: visitors, students, *au pairs*, work permit holders, refugees granted status after 30 August 2005 and who are granted limited leave initially), or who have a form of limited exceptional leave (for example humanitarian protection, discretionary leave, leave outside the rules), or who have no leave (for example asylum-seekers, overstayers, illegal entrants) are not born British citizens. Children born to parents with limited leave may be granted leave in line with their parent/s (▶see 394–5). If the parent/s subsequently become settled, or the child has lived in the UK for ten years, the child is entitled to be registered as a British citizen (▶see 1474).

The child may also become British automatically if the parents marry and the only reason why they were not born British is because the parents were not married (▶see 1428 above). 'Illegitimate' children may also apply to register even if their parents do not marry (▶see 1482). For the position for UK-born children of EEA nationals, ▶see above at 1429–30.

People born outside the UK

As with people born in the UK, the position for those born outside the UK also changed when the BNA came into force on 1 January 1983.

People born outside the UK before 1 January 1983

Before 1 January 1983, British nationality by descent to children born overseas could pass only through CUKC fathers who obtained their status by a connection with the UK. A policy was later put in place to enable children born abroad to CUKC mothers to inherit citizenship but only if the application to register was made before the child was 18 (all such children have now become 18). Certain people who were born abroad to CUKC mothers between 8 February 1961 and 31 December 1982 are still entitled to register as British citizens. There are also some circumstances in which having a British grandfather could mean that a person born overseas before 1 January 1983 is now a British citizen(▶see 1435).

People born outside the UK on or after 1 January 1983

From 1 January 1983, a child who is born abroad is a British citizen if they have a parent who is a British citizen 'otherwise than by descent' and is

13

FLOWCHART 1: WHO IS AUTOMATICALLY A BRITISH CITIZEN?

People born before 1 January 1983

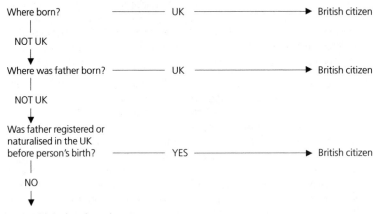

Where born? ————— UK ————————————▶ British citizen

NOT UK

Where was father born? ————— UK ————————————▶ British citizen

NOT UK

Was father registered or
naturalised in the UK
before person's birth? ————— YES ————————————▶ British citizen

NO

Not British (unless through
a connection with British
paternal grandfather ▶see 1435).

People born on or after 1 January 1983

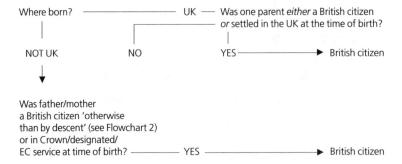

Where born? ————————————— UK — Was one parent *either* a British citizen
　　　　　　　　　　　　　　　　　　　　　　or settled in the UK at the time of birth?

NOT UK　　　　　　　NO　　　　　　　YES————————————▶ British citizen

Was father/mother
a British citizen 'otherwise
than by descent' (see Flowchart 2)
or in Crown/designated/
EC service at time of birth? ————— YES ————————————▶ British citizen

Note:

1) You cannot be sure that someone is *not* British on the basis of these flowcharts

2) Throughout, parent or father = father who is married to mother but the position for 'illegitimate' children will change when section 9 2002 Act is brought into force.

3) A person may be able to register or naturalise as a British citizen under various provisions (▶see Ch 45).

FLOWCHART 2: WHO IS A BRITISH CITIZEN BY DESCENT?

British citizenship 'by descent' is a *less* advantageous form of citizenship than British citizenship 'otherwise than by descent'. For the advantages of British citizenship 'otherwise than by descent', ►see 1433–4.

For children born outside the UK to a British parent on or after 1 January 1983

1 British father or mother ───────────────► British citizen by descent
  born in UK
  |
      NO
      ↓

2 Father or mother registered or naturalised in
  the UK before child's birth ───────────────► British citizen by descent
  |
      NO
      ↓

3 Father or mother was UK and Colonies
  citizen (CUKC) born overseas who gained
  right of abode by living for five years in
  UK prior to 1 January 1983 ───────────────► British citizen by descent
  |
      NO
      ↓

  i)   Father or mother a British citizen by descent; and
  ii) father or mother had a parent as in (1), (2) or (3) above; and
  iii) has spent at least three years in UK prior to child's birth
                                          ↓
          Right to register as British citizen
          within a year of birth (or up to ───────────────► British citizen by descent
          (six years by discretion)
          ↓
          Right to register in UK if at any
          time child and both parents live ───────────────► British citizen otherwise
          in UK for three years   than by descent

Note

1 You cannot be sure that someone is *not* British by descent on the basis of this flowchart.

2 Throughout, parent or father = father who is married to mother but the position for 'illegitimate' children will change when section 9 2002 Act is brought into force.

3 A person may be able to register as a British citizen under various other provisions (►see Ch 45).

13

---

therefore automatically able to pass on their citizenship to their children born abroad (►see further above at 1433 and 1435–7). Fathers can only do this if they count as a 'parent' within the definition at ►1428 above. The child will be British by descent, which means they themselves cannot transmit their citizenship to their own children born overseas. However, there are special arrangements for the registration of such children as

British citizens provided stringent conditions are met (►see 1474–6).

In addition, a child who is born abroad is a British citizen if born to a British citizen parent who is serving in either government service or a European Community institution (►see 1436). This latter form of automatic acquisition applies regardless of whether the parent is a British citizen 'by descent' or 'otherwise than by descent' (►see 1436)

Flowchart 2 explains who is British 'by descent' and the fact that such people cannot automatically transmit their citizenship on to their own children born overseas.

People born overseas who do not have a British parent (or in limited circumstances a grandparent) can normally only obtain British citizenship by living in the UK and meeting the residence and other requirements for registration or naturalisation, see Chapter 45.

RENUNCIATION OF CITIZENSHIP

A British citizen who is of full age and capacity can make a declaration renouncing that status (see s12 BNA 1981). For these purposes minors who have married or who have formed a civil partnership are treated as being of full age. At the point that the declaration is registered, the person ceases to be a British citizen. However, if a person makes a declaration in the belief that another citizenship or nationality will be acquired and this does not happen within six months of the registration of the renunciation, the person will be regarded as having remained a British citizen.

The Home Office is not obliged to register a declaration of renunciation if it is made while the UK is at war.

Renunciation declarations are made on Form RN1. They are made locally, so if the person is in a British Overseas Territory, they will normally be made to the governor of that territory. They can also be made to a consular official if the person is in a foreign country.

The Home Office has a policy of giving priority to declarations of renunciation. In situations where the authorities of another country have given a date by which the person should renounce their British citizenship, the Home Office will aim to register the declaration by that date. Where more than six months have passed since the declaration was made, it may still be registered if there is up-to-date evidence that the declarant is a citizen of another country, or is about to become one. In the absence of such evidence, the Home Office will return the form and invite the applicant to re-date and sign it and then resubmit it with the necessary evidence.

Although people should think very carefully before renouncing their British citizenship, there is a route back to British citizenship for persons who have renounced it. This is the case both for those who renounced their status as a 'British citizen' since 1 January 1983 (immediately below) and for those who renounced 'CUKC' status before that date (below at ►1443–4).

Registration as a British Citizen following renunciation of British Citizenship

A British citizen who has lost that status as a result of making a declaration of renunciation is entitled to be registered as a British citizen if they satisfy all of the following conditions (see s13(1) BNA 1981):

- they are of 'full capacity' (for the meaning of this, ►see 1455–6);
- they have made a declaration of resumption of British citizenship;
- the renunciation was necessary to enable them to retain or acquire some other form of citizenship or nationality.

A person who was a British citizen 'by descent' when they renounced their British citizenship will become a British citizen 'by descent' on registration under this provision. Everyone else will become a British citizen 'otherwise than by descent'.

A person is not entitled to register under section 13(1) BNA 1981 more than once. A person who registers under section 13(1) and then *again* renounces their British citizenship, can be registered again but only by discretion under section 13(3) BNA 1981 if the Secretary of State thinks fit. A person who would have been a British citizen on 1 January 1983 if they had not already renounced their CUKC status cannot be registered under section 13 BNA but may be eligible for registration under section 10 BNA 1981 (►see below).

Registration as a British Citizen following renunciation of CUKC status

Citizens of the United Kingdom and Colonies (CUKCs) who, *before* 1 January 1983, lost that status as a result of making a declaration of renunciation may be registered as British citizens (see s10 BNA 1981). Some may register by entitlement and some as a matter of discretion.

Entitled to be registered following renunciation

Those who satisfy *all* of the following conditions are *entitled* to be registered as a British citizen under section 10(1) BNA 1981, namely:

- they are of 'full capacity' (for the meaning of this, ►see 1455–6);
- they have ceased to be a CUKC as a result of making a declaration of renunciation;
- at the time of making their declaration, they were, or were about to become, a citizen of a country listed as a Commonwealth country as at 31 December 1982 (see NIs, Ch 16, Annex A for a list of such countries as of that date);
- they could not have remained or become a citizen of such a Commonwealth country unless they renounced CUKC citizenship *or* they reasonably believed that they would be deprived of citizenship of such a country unless they renounced CUKC citizenship; and

13

- on the date of application they had a 'qualifying connection' (see below for the meaning of this) with the UK or (if a woman) had been married to a person who had, or but for his death, would have had such a connection.

Discretionary registration following renunciation

A person may also be registered as a British citizen at the Secretary of State's *discretion* under section 10(2) BNA 1981 if they satisfy *all* of the following conditions:

- they are of full capacity;
- they had, before 1 January 1983, ceased to be a CUKC as the result of making a declaration of renunciation; and
- on the date of the application they had a 'qualifying connection' (see below for meaning) with the UK or had, at any time before the application, (if a woman) been married to or had formed a civil partnership with a person who had, or but for his death, would have had such a connection.

A person cannot be registered under section 10(1) more than once. A person who registers under section 10(1) and then renounces British citizenship can only be registered by discretion under section 10(2), or under section 13 BNA 1981 (see above).

Meaning of 'qualifying connection'

Under these provisions a 'qualifying connection' with the UK means that the person (man or woman), *or* that person's father *or* paternal grandfather meets *any* of the following conditions:

- they were born in the UK;
- they were naturalised in the UK; or
- they were registered as a CUKC either in the UK or in a country which has, as at any time, been listed in section 1(3) British Nationality Act 1948 (see Nls, Ch 16, Annex B).

For these purposes, 'father' does not include the father of a child whose parents were not married unless the parents subsequently marry each other.

Before 7 November 2002, only women could qualify on the basis of marriage to a person with a qualifying connection. However, since 7 November 2002 when section 5 2002 Act came into force, men who were married to CUKCs and made applications on or after that date, or had undetermined applications on that date, can use that marriage in order to help show a qualifying connection

Registration 'by descent' or 'otherwise than by descent'?

Registration as a British citizen by this method gives British citizenship 'otherwise than by descent' *unless*, had the person not renounced CUKC citizenship, they would on 1 January 1983 have become a British citizen 'by descent'. If they would have become a British citizen 'by descent' on 1 January 1983, then their registration will result in their becoming a British citizen 'by descent'.

DEPRIVATION OF CITIZENSHIP

People may only have their British nationality taken away from them in certain situations. The law about 'deprivation' of citizenship was changed on 1 April 2003 as a result of section 4 Nationality, Immigration and Asylum Act 2002, which amended section 40 BNA 1981. From that date a British citizen, a BOTC, a BOC, a BN(O), a BPP or a BS may be deprived of their citizenship if the Secretary of State is satisfied that they either:

- did anything seriously prejudicial to the vital interests of the UK or a British Overseas Territory (for example involvement in espionage, terrorism, or fighting for an enemy against UK or allied forces) *and* they would not become stateless as a result of deprivation; or

- acquired their citizenship status by registration or naturalisation and did so by using fraud, false representations or concealing material facts.

There is a right of appeal to the AIT against a decision to make a deprivation order (s40A BNA 1981). If the Secretary of State certifies that the deprivation decision was taken on the basis of information which should not be made public in the interests of national security, international relations or otherwise in the public interest, the right of appeal is to the Special Immigration Appeals Commission (SIAC).

Proposed changes

The Immigration, Nationality and Asylum Bill 2005 contains late amendments made by the government. In brief, these late amendments incorporate proposals to replace the current provision ('seriously prejudicial to the vital interests of the UK') with legislation that will deprive a person of their citizenship on the basis of grounds of 'conducive to the public good'. These grounds have already been expanded in August 2005 to incorporate widely defined 'unacceptable behaviour' criteria (►see 1019–20) under new anti-terror measures. JCWI is briefing strongly against these new proposals on the basis that citizenship is a fundamental right which should not be undermined on such vague criteria. Many members of the UK's ethnic minorities have dual (British and another) nationality and their British citizenship will effectively be demoted to a second-class form of citizenship if these proposals go through.

13

Registration or naturalisation not treated as having any effect

Aside from deprivation, there are certain situations in which the Secretary of State will treat registration or naturalisation as a British citizen as a nullity. This means that the registration or naturalisation is treated as though it never took place and has no effect. Examples of these situations are where (Nls Ch 55):

- the registration or naturalisation was obtained by impersonation;
- the person registered or naturalised already held the citizenship status which was conferred;
- the person was dead when the citizenship status was conferred;
- there was no application for citizenship;
- the application was made without the knowledge or consent of the person to whom it related.

45 Applying to be a British citizen

INTRODUCTION

This chapter explains how people who are not British citizens at birth may obtain British citizenship by applying to become British. In order to determine whether a person is automatically a British citizen (i.e. by their place of birth or by descent), see Chapter 44. There are two different processes by which people who do not automatically have British citizenship, can apply to obtain it.

Naturalisation Almost all adults (over 18) who apply to become British citizens must do so under the naturalisation process. Formally, naturalisation is always a discretionary decision but, in reality, provided all of the requirements are met, applications for naturalisation are granted.

Registration All children under 18 who apply to become British citizens must apply to 'register' as citizens (▶see1473–85). A very small number of adults may also apply to register (▶see below 1485–90). Registration is sometimes a right and so, provided the requirements are met, it cannot be refused. In most cases, however, registration is a discretionary decision.

This chapter describes the various requirements, which applicants have to meet in order to obtain citizenship in the above ways. Provisions to register or naturalise are set out in the British Nationality Act 1981 (referred to as the 'BNA 1981'). In most cases involving registration, the criteria for decisions are not fully set out in the legislation and discretion therefore plays a large part. Sometimes, when the requirements are set out in the BNA 1981, the Home Office has the power to waive those requirements. This chapter explains the factors that are taken into account by the Home Office in exercising its discretion.

In order that applications and representations are made together with all relevant information and evidence, we have set out both the formal requirements and the basis upon which discretion may be exercised in some detail. Guidance on the exercise of discretion can be found in the Nationality Instructions (NI) which are posted on the IND website, www.ind.homeoffice.gov.uk. They are divided into two volumes. Volume I is divided into six parts and contains instructions for caseworkers at the Home Office. Volume II contains other general and procedural informa-

13

tion. Where we have drawn upon them to explain the discretionary criteria, which the Home Office uses, we have generally given a reference. The NIs should also be consulted for up-to-date information.

We look first at general procedures concerning applications for citizenship (▶1448–53). Because the new citizenship ceremonies apply to both naturalisations and some registrations, they are also dealt with in this opening part.

The chapter then deals with naturalisation (▶1453–73) before turning to consider applications for registration by children (▶1473–85), and lastly registration by adults (▶1485–90).

Note that this chapter is concerned only with obtaining British citizenship, which of course carries with it the right of abode in the UK. It is not concerned with the other, less valuable, forms of British nationality, which are described in Chapter 43.

APPLICATIONS FOR BRITISH CITIZENSHIP – GENERAL

The application

Unlike applications for leave to remain in the UK (▶see 125 and 134), the forms listed below are not prescribed by legislation or rules, although applicants are strongly advised to use them. Therefore, the Home Office will treat as an application for British citizenship, any request, which sets out the applicant's full name, address, date and place of birth (unless this cannot be supplied), and contains the relevant documents and a declaration stating that the contents are true.

The forms contain a declaration, which has to be completed. If an application is received in the Home Office more than six months after the date on which it is declared, there is a possibility that an applicant's circumstances will have changed. The Home Office will therefore return the form to be re-declared to ensure that the information given is up-to-date.

The application must also be accompanied by an application fee. For a list of the present fees that are charged, ▶see 1509. The date of application is the date of its receipt in the Home Office or the relevant receiving authority abroad.

An application made by a person who, although they may not have known it, is already a British citizen, will not be treated as an application for citizenship but simply as a request for confirmation of status. In this situation the Home Office should refund the application fee. In considering an application, the Home Office should always recognise a right to British citizenship rather than grant British citizenship by discretion.

The forms

The forms upon which applications for citizenship are made are as follows.

Form AN (NEW) Application for naturalisation as a British citizen under section 6 BNA 1981.

Form B (OS) Application for registration as a British citizen by British Overseas citizens, British Subjects and British Protected Persons under section 4B BNA 1981.

Form B (OTA) Application for registration as a British citizen by British Overseas Territories citizens, British Nationals (Overseas), British Overseas citizens, British Subjects and British Protected Persons under sections 4 and 4A BNA 1981.

Form EM Application for registration as a British citizen under the British Nationality (Hong Kong) Act 1997.

Form G Application for registration as a British citizen by a British Overseas Territories citizen who is a United Kingdom national for EC purposes under section 5 BNA 1981. This form only applies to Gibraltarians.

Form MN1 Application for the registration of a minor as a British citizen under sections 1(3), 3(1), 3(2), 3(5) BNA 1981.

Form RS1 Application for registration as a British citizen by a person who either:
- renounced CUKC citizenship before 1 January 1983 (s10 BNA 1981); or
- renounced British citizenship under section 13 BNA 1981.

Form S1 Application for registration by a stateless person who had an entitlement to registration under the British Nationality (No. 2) Act 1964 under paragraph 5, Schedule 2 BNA 1981.

Form S2 Application for registration on grounds of residence by a stateless person who was born on or after 1 January 1983 outside the United Kingdom and the British Overseas Territories under paragraph 4, Schedule 2 BNA 1981.

Form S3 Application for registration on grounds of residence by a stateless person who was born on or after 1 January 1983 in the United Kingdom or a British Overseas Territory under paragraph 3, Schedule 2 BNA 1981.

Form T Application for registration as a British citizen on grounds of residence by a person aged ten or more, born in the United Kingdom on or after 1 January 1983 under section 1(4) BNA 1981.

Form UKM Application for registration as a British citizen by certain adult children of British mothers under section 4C BNA 1981.

Form WW Application for registration as a British citizen under the Hong Kong (War Wives and Widows) Act 1996.

Both the forms and detailed guidance notes in relation to each can be downloaded from the IND website (www.ind.homeoffice.gov.uk).

Where should the application be made?

In the UK Applications for naturalisation and registration should be sent to:

Home Office IND
Managed Migration Directorate (Nationality Group)
Casework Support Unit
PO Box 12
LIVERPOOL
L69 2UX

Abroad The power to determine applications for British citizenship rests solely with the Home Secretary. All applications for British citizenship wherever made, must eventually come to the Home Office to be determined. However, if someone is outside the UK, they should direct any enquiries and generally submit their application to the nearest British Embassy, Consulate or High Commission for their application to be valid. Those in the Channel Islands or the Isle of Man should contact the Lieutenant-Governor, and those in a British Overseas Territory should contact the Governor.

The decision

Once the application has been made, the Home Office should either grant or refuse citizenship and cannot treat an application as abandoned. Although there is no legal provision for applications to be withdrawn, the Home Office may regard an application as withdrawn upon receipt of a clear statement signed by the applicant (or responsible person who has declared a minor's application form) that they do not wish to continue with it.

Granting the application

Where the Home Office decides to grant an application and the applicant is 18 or over, the applicant will be informed that the Secretary of State proposes to grant the application and that a citizenship certificate may be issued provided that the applicant takes an oath or makes an affirmation. Those who applied on or after 1 January 2004 must attend a citizenship ceremony and make a pledge (▶see1451–3). Minors who become 18 before a decision is made may have to take an oath of allegiance and attend a ceremony.

Once a person has British citizenship, they are entitled to apply for a British passport (▶1423–4) or a Certificate of Entitlement to the right of abode.

Challenging decisions

If an application for British citizenship, by either naturalisation or registration, is refused there is no right of appeal. The only method of challenge is by judicial review. Of course, if on the facts of the case, the applicant simply cannot satisfy a requirement of the legislation, which the Home Office has no power to waive, then there can be no challenge to the decision. Before embarking on judicial review, in particular if there has been a clear misapplication of the law or policy, or the Home Office must have misunderstood the facts of the case, it may be worth trying to get the Home Office to reconsider the decision. A 'letter before action' setting out why an applicant disagrees with the decision is normally required in judicial review anyway. Basic judicial review procedures are covered at ▶1213–22 but anyone considering this action, should seek proper legal advice. Very few applications for judicial review are made in nationality cases. However, where there is an application for recognition of citizenship, an entitlement to registration, or an injustice arising out of the exercise of discretion in a registration or naturalisation case, then there may be scope for a challenge.

In considering whether a decision on nationality is lawful, it is worth bearing in mind the following points.

- From 7 November 2002, the Home Office should give reasons for refusing all nationality applications (s44 BNA 1981 as amended by s7 2002 Act).
- The Home Office cannot refuse to accept an application. In a discretionary case, even if the application does not meet the requirements of Home Office policy, the Home Office must be prepared to consider making an exception even to their own policy. This will particularly be so where a very strong case has been made. The reasons given must show that the grounds put forward have been considered on their own merits.
- Decisions must be made on the basis of the material put forward and consider the up-to-date circumstances, taking into account all relevant matters. Decisions cannot simply rest on a decision made in a previous application some time ago or on a decision made on an immigration application.
- Discretion in nationality decisions must be exercised without regard to the race, colour or religion of the person who may be affected by the decision (s41 BNA 1981).

The new oath and pledge and citizenship ceremonies

If an application for British citizenship is made on or after 1 January 2004 and granted, the applicant will be required to take an oath or make an affirmation and make a pledge at a citizenship ceremony before they are registered or naturalised as British citizens.

The wording of the oath is as follows:

'I, (name), swear by Almighty God that, on becoming a British citizen, I will be faithful and bear true allegiance to Her Majesty Queen Elizabeth the Second, Her Heirs and Successors according to law.'

For those who wish to affirm, the wording of the oath is changed by substituting *'…do solemnly and sincerely affirm…'* for the words *'…swear by Almighty God…'*.

13

In addition to making an oath or affirmation, a person must also make a pledge. The wording of the pledge is as follows:

'I will give my loyalty to the United Kingdom and respect its rights and freedoms. I will uphold its democratic values. I will observe its laws faithfully and fulfil my duties and obligations as a British citizen.'

In the special circumstances of a particular case, an applicant may be exempted from any of the following requirements:

- the requirement to attend a citizenship ceremony;
- the requirement to make an oath/affirmation of allegiance and pledge;
- the time-limit for attending a ceremony.

Exemptions will be granted only in exceptional circumstances.

In England, Scotland and Wales the registrar of a local authority will conduct the ceremony and administer the oath/affirmation and pledge. Elsewhere, the ceremony is conducted, and the oath and pledge are administered, by a person authorised by the Secretary of State.

The person conducting the ceremony will administer the oath/affirmation and pledge, and date the certificate of registration/naturalisation with the date of the ceremony. They will also issue it to the applicant at the ceremony, and notify the Secretary of State in writing within 14 days of the ceremony that the applicant has made the oath and pledge.

Time-limit and invitation

When applicants are required to attend a ceremony and make an oath or affirmation of allegiance and pledge, they must normally do so within a three-month time-limit. Otherwise, they cannot be registered or naturalised unless the Secretary of State decides to extend the period.

When the Home Office decides to grant an application for naturalisation or registration, the applicant will be issued with a 'ceremony invitation' letter and will be advised to contact the relevant local authority or consular post in order to arrange attendance at a citizenship ceremony within three months. The letter will include information on the appropriate local authority with whom to arrange attendance at a citizenship ceremony.

If the applicant asks for an extension of time and gives an acceptable reason, an extension of up to three months, or whatever longer period may be justified by the reason given for the request, may be allowed. An application for an extension will normally be granted where the applicant is temporarily abroad, the applicant has moved from one country to another, the local authority concerned has been unable to provide a ceremony within the time available, the applicant or a close family member is ill, or there has been some form of administrative error, either by the Home Office, a British post abroad or the local authority.

If an applicant does not attend a citizenship ceremony within the time-limit, the Home Secretary is not able to register or naturalise them. However, if the applicant still wishes to become a British citizen, and had a *right* through registration to such citizenship at the date of application, a certificate may be issued at any time on the basis of the original application, on payment of the balance of any fee and on attending the ceremony to make the oath and pledge.

Where an application was made involving the exercise of *discretion* by the Secretary of State (all naturalisation and some registration applications) it may be reconsidered where such an application was refused on the basis that the applicant failed to arrange to attend a citizenship ceremony but the Home Office is satisfied either that the applicant was genuinely unaware of the ceremony notification or that, although the applicant was aware of the notification, the lack of response was due to some failure on the part of an agent. In all other cases, the applicant will need to re-apply.

Further useful and up-to-date information on citizenship ceremonies may be found at www.ind.homeoffice.gov.uk/british_citizenship/english/home page.html.

NATURALISATION

This is the main way in which adults may become British citizens. Those who are under 18 cannot naturalise to become British citizens. An adult may be naturalised under section 6 BNA 1981. Naturalisation is formally at the discretion of the Secretary of State but, if the requirements set out in the legislation are met, it is generally granted. Refusals are normally based upon one or more of these requirements not being met.

An application for naturalisation is made on Form AN (NEW) and needs to be supported by two referees who are British citizens. If a certificate of naturalisation is to be granted, then the applicant will have to take an oath and pledge and participate in a citizenship ceremony (▶see above).

There are two routes for naturalisation:

- naturalisation based on five-years' residence in the UK;
- naturalisation based on marriage or civil partnership and residence in the UK.

A person who naturalises becomes a British citizen 'otherwise than by descent'. The main importance of this is that they can transmit their citizenship to their first generation children born abroad (for full details, ▶see 1433–4).

Some of the requirements for naturalisation, such as age, capacity and residence requirements, need to be satisfied at the date of application. The other requirements, such as good character, language skills and intentions, need to be satisfied at the date of consideration.

13

Minors applying at the same time Although minor children cannot be naturalised, they may apply for registration on the same application form as an adult who seeks naturalisation (Form AN (NEW)). Some children may have become British citizens at an earlier date, such as children born in the UK to a woman with indefinite leave who is herself applying for naturalisation. In such cases the Home Office will recognise the status of the children and take no further action in respect of them.

Naturalisation based on five-years' residence

The requirements for naturalisation based on residence are as follows (s6(1) BNA 1981).

On the date of application, the applicant must:

- be of full age (18 or over);
- be of 'full capacity' (▶1455–6); and
- either meet the 'residence requirement' (▶below), or be serving outside the UK in Crown Service (▶1471–3).

The 'residence requirement' that the applicant must also meet is that they were (for full details, ▶see 1457–63):

- in the UK at the beginning of the period of five years ending on the date of application;
- not absent from the UK for more than 450 days in that five-year period;
- not absent from the UK for more than 90 days in the period of 12 months ending on the day of application;
- not subject, under the immigration laws, to any restriction on their period of stay in the UK on the date of application (▶see1459–60), or at any other time in the 12 month period ending with the date of application (▶see1460–1); and
- not in breach of immigration laws at any time in the five years ending with the date of application in the United Kingdom (▶see1461–3).

As of the *date of consideration*, the applicant must *also* satisfy the following requirements:

- be of 'good character (▶1463–5);
- have a sufficient knowledge of the English, Welsh or Scottish Gaelic language and (from 1 November 2005) sufficient knowledge about life in the United Kingdom (▶1465–9);
- still be of 'full capacity'; and
- intend either to have their home or principal home in the UK (▶1469–70) if the application is granted; or to enter into or continue in either Crown service, service in an international organisation of which the UK is a member, or service in the employment of a company or association established in the UK (▶1471–3).

There are discretions as to the language requirement and some of the residence requirements. These are considered below.

Naturalisation based on marriage or civil partnership and residence

The main differences between this and the first route are that the applicant must be married to or have formed a civil partnership with a British citizen, the residence requirements are less demanding and the applicant does not have to intend to have the UK as their home or principal home.

The requirements for naturalisation based on marriage or civil partnership and residence are as follows (s6(2) BNA 1981).

On the date of application, the applicant must:

- be of full age (18 or over);
- be of 'full capacity' (▶below);
- be married to or have formed a civil partnership with a British citizen; and
- meet the residence requirement (▶below).

The applicant must also meet all of the following to satisfy the 'residence requirement' (for full details, ▶see 1457–63):

- they were in the UK at the beginning of the three years ending on the date of the application;
- they were not absent from the UK for more than 270 days in that three-year period;
- they were not absent from the UK for more than 90 days in the 12 months ending with the date of application;
- they were not subject under the immigration laws to any restriction on the period of stay in the UK on the date of application (▶see1459–60);
- they were not in breach of the immigration laws in the UK at any time in the three years ending with the date of the application(▶see1461–3).

In addition, applicants must satisfy all of the following requirements *as of the date of consideration*. Applicants must:

- be of 'good character' (▶1463–5);
- have a sufficient knowledge of the English, Welsh or Scottish Gaelic language and (from 1 November 2005) sufficient knowledge about life in the United Kingdom (▶1465–9); and
- still be of 'full capacity'.

There are discretions as to the language requirement and some of the residence requirements. These are considered below.

Full age and capacity

'Full age' is straightforward, applicants must be aged 18 or over. 'Full capacity' is defined as being 'not of unsound mind' (s50 BNA 1981). The Home Office expects an applicant to be able to grasp the purpose of the application. They do not expect a total understanding of citizenship and procedure or a continuing level of comprehension. The requirement is not intended to deny naturalisation to those whose mental disability makes it difficult for them to communicate. It is usually assumed that an applicant meets the requirement unless there is information that indicates otherwise.

Evidence of a mental illness or treatment is not in itself a ground for refusal. Where there is a doubt, an applicant should be given the opportunity to submit medical reports from the health care professionals responsible for their treatment. If there are conflicting professional opinions, an applicant will normally be given the benefit of the doubt.

In an application made on or after 1 January 2004 a successful applicant will have to make an oath and pledge to a registrar at a citizenship ceremony. The registrar will want to be satisfied that the applicant understands the significance of the oath. If there is a doubt, it should be made clear that the 'full capacity' requirement has been treated as satisfied by the Home Office and if necessary the Home Office should be asked to provide information on the full capacity requirement to the person administering the oath.

Absences

Only whole days' absences are counted (s50 BNA 1981). Days of departure and arrival are not to be counted as absences. In addition to actual absences from the UK, there are periods of time, which count as 'technical' absences and must be taken into account.

An applicant who was physically present is nevertheless regarded as 'absent' from the UK during any period that they were (para. 9, Sch 1 BNA 1981):

- entitled to an exemption from immigration control in their capacity as:
  - diplomats, save for locally engaged staff who are now considered to be subject to immigration control;
  - a member of the family and a part of the household of a person entitled to an exemption as a diplomat;
  - members of home, Commonwealth and visiting forces;
- detained as a result of a criminal sentence passed by a court in the UK or a court abroad;
- detained in hospital under a hospital order made in connection with a conviction for an offence;
- detained under any power of detention of the UK immigration laws; or
- liable to be detained for any of the reasons above but were unlawfully at large, or absent without leave and were liable to be arrested in consequence.

Although the BNA 1981 states that the above periods are all periods of 'absence', it also gives the Home Office a discretion to treat any of the same periods as periods when the applicant was present in the UK. There is a discretion under schedule 1 BNA 1981 to regard the periods of absence listed above as residence for naturalisation purposes. Full information on the policy can be found in the NI (Ch 18 Annex B para. 9.5 onwards).

Detention and temporary admission

A period of time spent in detention under the immigration laws or where a person is unlawfully at large and supposed to be detained, is a technical absence for the purposes of naturalisation. Any period spent on temporary admission should *not* be treated as a technical absence (para. 9 Sch 1 BNA 1981).

However, Home Office practice is different. If a person is granted leave to enter the UK following a period of detention, the period of detention *will* normally count as residence. If a person is removed or departs from the UK following a period of detention, this period of technical absence while in detention will *not* normally be counted as residence. Similarly, for a person on temporary admission who is not subsequently granted leave to enter but is removed or departs, then the period of temporary admission will normally be treated as a technical absence. Periods of time spent unlawfully at large, such as absconding while on temporary admission, or where a person ought to be in detention, will *not* normally count as residence for the purpose of naturalisation.

The residence requirements

The residence requirements for the two routes to naturalisation are different in terms of lengths of time (▶above at 1454, 1455) but the concepts are the same. The following explanations apply to *both* routes. The lengths of time given apply to the 'five-year residence' route (and those in brackets apply to the 'marriage or civil partnership and residence' route).

Presence in the UK at the beginning of the five or three-year qualifying period

There is generally no discretion to waive the requirement to be physically present in the UK on the date five (or three) years before the date of application. There is an exception for applicants in Crown service who apply under the five-year residence route. In addition, the spouses or civil partners of British citizens in Crown or 'designated service' (listed in NI Ch 4 Annex A) and applicants who are 'technically' absent from the UK (▶1456) can apply for discretion to be exercised so that they are exempted from the requirement of presence in the UK five (or three) years before the date of application (NI Ch 18 Annex B paras 6 and 9).

The qualifying period ends the day after the application date. Thus, if an application is made on 1 March 2004, and a three-year qualifying period is required, then the start date of the relevant qualifying period is 2 March

13

2001 and the applicant should have been physically present in the UK on that date.

Re-declaration If an applicant misses the requirement to have been in the UK on the date five (or three) years prior to the application date by three months or less either way, then the Home Office may consider asking the applicant to re-declare the application by re-signing and re-dating it if, subject to this three-month limit, the applicant could otherwise meet the residence requirement from the new date. The Home Office may also offer a re-declaration where the case is being considered within three months of application and the requirement of being in the UK on the date five (or three) years before the date of application would have been met within the three months after the application was submitted. If a form is re-declared, the original application date is superseded by the new application date, being the date on which the re-declared form is received at the Home Office (NI, Ch 18, Annex B para. 3.3).

Where a minor has been included for registration as a British citizen on a form for an adult's naturalisation and would be aged 18 on the date that the adult has had to re-declare the application, the minor should not be placed at a disadvantage by the new date. The original date of receipt will be retained for the minor so that they continue to be eligible for registration as a British citizen.

Excess absences in the five (or three) year qualifying period

There is a discretion to waive excess absences in the five (or three) years' residence qualifying periods (see the NI, Ch 18, Annex B, para. 4). The discretion will normally be exercised, according to the criteria set out below, provided the Home Office considers that the applicant has 'thrown in their lot' with the UK and meets the other requirements for naturalisation.

Absences of 480 (or 300) days in total will normally be disregarded.

Up to 900 (or 540) days' total absence may be disregarded only if the application is otherwise in order and if the applicant has established their home, family and a substantial part of their estate in the UK. *Additionally*, the Home Office will require that any *one* of the following conditions is satisfied:

- two (or one) year's residence (without substantial absences) immediately prior to the five (or three) year qualifying period. If the period to be disregarded is greater than 730 (or 450) days, the period of prior residence should be at least three (or two) years (without substantial absences) immediately prior to the five (or three) year qualifying period;
- excess absences were during a period in Crown service such as the army abroad, or accompanying a British citizen spouse or civil partner on an overseas appointment;
- excess absences were an unavoidable consequence of the nature of a career;

- there are exceptional compelling reasons of an occupational or compassionate nature to justify naturalisation now (e.g. a job where British citizenship is a requirement).

Absences of more than 900 (or 540) days will rarely be waived. Any application for such a waiver will be considered at a senior level in the Home Office.

Excess absences in the final year

In applications based on five-years' residence, excess absences in the final year of the qualifying period will only be overlooked, as a matter of policy, if the 'future intention' requirement is met. If this requirement is met, or if the application is based on marriage or civil partnership and residence, the following policy applies (NI, Ch 18, Annex B, para. 5).

- Absences not exceeding 100 days will normally be disregarded.
- For all absences of more than 100 days to be disregarded, the applicant must have demonstrated links to the UK by showing such links through the presence of their family, an established home in the UK, and a substantial part of their estate in the UK.
- *Additionally*, the absence must be justified by Crown service or compelling occupational or compassionate reasons; where:
  - the absences exceed 100 days but not more than 180 days, where the five (or three) year residence requirements are *not* met;
  - the absences exceed 180 days where the residence requirements over the five (or three) year period are met;
  - the absences exceed 180 days where the residence requirements over the five (or three) year qualifying period are *not* met only in the most exceptional circumstances.

'Not subject under the immigration laws to any restriction on period of stay'

Applicants for naturalisation must be free of immigration restrictions on the date of their application (para. 1(2)(c), Sch 1 BNA 1981). Persons falling into any of the following categories will be considered to be free from time restrictions on the date of application (NI, Ch 18, Annex B, para. 7):

- those with indefinite leave;
- those not in the UK and therefore not subject to a restriction on the date of application (there is no need to be physically present in the UK on the *date* of application itself);
- those exempt from immigration control as diplomats or their family members, and members of relevant armed forces;
- Irish nationals, by virtue of benefiting from the Common Travel Area provisions;

13

- EEA and Swiss nationals or their family members (who are considered to have no restriction on their right to remain in consequence of regulation 8 of the Immigration (European Economic Area) Regulations 2000) (▶see 559 and 519–21);
- people who have entered the UK illegally and have not been granted limited leave (although such a person will be in the UK in breach of immigration laws and thus will have a different hurdle to overcome; ▶see 1461–3 for when discretion may be exercised in respect of breaches);
- a person refused leave to remain before 2 October 2000 and not required to leave the UK by virtue of having an immigration appeal pending against refusal of leave (although such a person will be in the UK in breach of immigration laws and thus will have another hurdle to overcome; ▶see 1461–3 for when discretion may be exercised in respect of breaches).

A person is *not* regarded as being free of immigration time restrictions if they (NI, Ch 18, Annex B, para. 7.2):

- have limited leave;
- have overstayed limited leave to enter or remain;
- are on temporary admission;
- are in immigration detention; or
- have absconded from temporary admission or detention.

Not subject to any time restriction in the previous 12 months

In cases relying only on five-years' residence rather than marriage, applicants must also have been free from time restrictions for the period of 12 months ending with the date of their application. There is a discretion to waive this requirement, which will normally be favourably exercised if any of the following circumstances apply (NI, Ch 18, Annex B, para. 7.4):

- although at the date of application, the applicant had been free of conditions for less than 12 months, by the date of consideration the applicant has been free of conditions for 12 months or more, so long as the other requirements are met;
- the time-limit was imposed inappropriately on return to the UK after a visit abroad and the applicant has returning resident status or should be exempted from immigration control, for example, diplomats and serving members of armed forces;
- the applicant is an EEA or Swiss national who does not satisfy this requirement, and the Home Office is satisfied that they were genuinely unaware of the need to satisfy this requirement;
- consideration of an application for indefinite leave made more than 15 months before the citizenship application, was subject to delay through no fault of the applicant, provided that indefinite leave was eventually granted;

- the applicant had limited leave for a period of less than ten days at the beginning of the 12-month period and had no time restrictions for the remainder of the 12 months;
- the applicant had limited leave for a period between ten and 90 days at the beginning of the 12-month period if all the other requirements are met and the applicant has demonstrated established links through the presence in the UK of home, family and a substantial part of their estate;
- in the following circumstances the applicant has to show that they have established links through the presence in the UK of home, family and a substantial part of their estate; *and* there are compelling business or compassionate reasons to justify granting the application now:
  - they had limited leave for more than 90 days at the beginning of the 12-month period and all the other requirements are met;
  - they had limited leave, which exceeded ten days at the beginning of the 12-month period, and the other residence requirements are *not* met, and there are the most exceptional circumstances.

Breaches of the immigration laws during the five (or three) year residence period

Those applying for naturalisation under both the five-year residence, and marriage and residence routes, must show that they were not in breach of the immigration laws during the relevant five (or three) year period.

Persons are in the UK in breach of immigration laws unless (s11 2002 Act):

- they have the right of abode;
- they have leave to be in the UK;
- they are exercising rights of free movement within the meaning of the EEA 2000 Regulations (since 7 November 2002 when s11 2002 Act came into force) i.e. they are a 'qualified person' within the meaning of those regulations (▶Chapter 18), or they are the family member of such a person (▶see below for the position of EEA nationals who had been 'qualified persons' before 7 November 2002);
- they are entitled to enter or remain in the UK as a crew member of a ship or aircraft (▶475);
- they are exempt from immigration control as diplomats, soldiers and other special cases (set out in s8 1971 Act) (▶472–6).

Temporary admission Those on temporary admission may or may not be in breach of the immigration laws. In addition, in order to be 'in the UK in breach of the immigration laws', it is necessary first to count as being 'in the UK'. For the purposes of this particular definition, a person is not in the UK unless they have actually 'entered' the UK. So, people who apply for leave to enter at port and who are granted temporary admission (or who are detained under immigration powers at port), do not 'enter' the

13

UK provided that they do not breach their conditions of temporary admission (s11 1971 Act applied by s11(3) 2002 Act). This continues to apply even if they are refused leave to enter. Some people, in particular asylum-seekers, may have this status as a port applicant given temporary admission but deemed not to have entered, for years.

EEA nationals An EEA national who, on or before 7 November 2002, had been at any time since their last entry a 'qualified person' in that they had the right to reside under EU law as applied in UK law, or the family member of such a person, is not regarded as having been in the UK unlawfully unless they remained in the UK contrary to a deportation order or removal directions. Such a person continues to be considered as being lawfully in the UK after 7 November 2002 notwithstanding the intro-duction of section 11 of the 2002 Act on 7 November 2002.

Applications to extend leave Persons who apply 'in-time' (before their leave runs out) to extend their leave to remain are given automatic exten-sions of leave while their applications are considered and are not in the UK in breach of immigration laws during this time. However, the rules govern-ing automatic extensions of leave prior to, during and after appeals are different for those who received decisions before 2 October 2000, those who received decisions between 2 October 2000 and 31 March 2003, and those who received decisions from 1 April 2003. These and the proposals in the 2005 Bill are fully explained at ▶143–6.

Discretion There is a discretion to disregard a person being in the UK in breach of the immigration laws during the five (or three) year residence period. This particular discretion does not cover matters such as breaching a restriction on taking employment. It refers to breaches such as being in the UK without leave to enter or remain, that is being here unlawfully.

A breach of immigration laws will normally be disregarded where (NI, Ch 18, Annex B, para. 8.9):

- it was inadvertent, for example where a person forgot to apply for further leave to remain;
- it was due to a rejection of an 'in-time' application on an incorrectly completed but mandatory application form for leave to remain (so long as the form was submitted in good faith);
- it was outside the person's control (e.g. a minor reliant on parents to complete the form);
- in the case of applications for leave to remain before 2 October 2000, the period of unlawful residence was due to the expiry of leave pending an appeal to the (then) adjudicator or IAT, and indefinite leave was granted prior to the naturalisation application being made; or
- a person entered the UK clandestinely and presented themself without delay to the immigration authorities or was detected shortly afterwards. The normal period of delay that could be waived is usually one month but may be longer in extenuating circumstances. Where such a person applies

after clandestine entry in these circumstances they will not be regarded as being unlawfully in the UK during the whole period of their application.

If a person breaches immigration control, for example by overstaying without submitting an in-time application, the Home Office will not generally waive the breach if it arose because the applicant was considering whether to regularise their position. This is particularly so where the breach is both serious and deliberate (NI, Ch 18, Annex B, para. 8.10). But it is always worth making representations in meritorious cases because this is only Home Office policy and the Secretary of State must consider the merits of an individual application.

The 'good character' requirement

There is no statutory definition of 'good character'. An applicant will normally be accepted to be of good character if (NI, Ch 18, Annex D):

- the enquiries made reveal no 'relevant adverse matters';
- there are no unspent convictions;
- there is no information on the Home Office file to cast doubts on the applicant's character;
- the applicant is economically active (businessperson, self-employed, of independent means, or a sole trader) and there is written confirmation from the Inland Revenue that their business affairs are in order;
- the applicant is not an undischarged bankrupt.

A person who does not meet one of the above factors or who is obviously unsuitable in the eyes of the Home Office may be refused without the Home Office giving further thought to the application.

The Home Office has indicated that someone would not be considered to be of good character where there was evidence to suggest (NI Ch 18, Annex D, para. 2):

- they did not respect and were not prepared to abide by the law;
- their financial affairs were not in order, for example with the Revenue;
- their activities were notorious and cast doubt on their standing in the local community;
- they had practised deceit, for example in their dealings with government departments; or
- they had assisted in the evasion of immigration control.

Criminal activity

Where there is evidence of criminal convictions the Home Office will have regard to the Rehabilitation of Offenders Act 1974 to see if and when a conviction becomes 'spent'. Spent convictions should not be taken into account by the Home Office in assessing the good character requirement. Where a person has been sentenced to imprisonment for more than 30 months, the provisions allowing a conviction to be 'spent' do not apply. The NIs (Ch18, Annex D(i)) also list 'corrective training', 'preventative detention', and 'detention during Her Majesty's Pleasure' as measures where the provisions allowing a conviction to be spent do not apply. The rehabilitation periods, whereby a conviction becomes spent are set out in the NI at Chapter 18, Annex D(i). Where an applicant has an overseas conviction, the Home Office may take it and the circumstances surrounding it into account unless it would have been regarded as 'spent' if committed in the UK.

Where an applicant has a conviction that can never become spent, for example where a sentence of imprisonment is more than 30 months, the Home Office may disregard it where the applicant has remained free of conviction for a 'clear' period (set out in NI, Ch 18, Annex D(ii)); that is to say the period of time after which a sentence can be safely ignored. Where a person is subject to a 'hospital order' alone or with a restriction order following conviction in criminal proceedings, there are special provisions that apply as to good character and as to when a person is rehabilitated.

Serious allegations of criminal activity will normally be taken into account and investigated. In addition, an applicant who is listed on the Sex Offenders Register can expect to have this taken into consideration.

Financial soundness

Applicants who are bankrupt, those who are evading their tax responsibilities and those who are attempting to defraud the Department of Work and Pensions will be the subject of particularly careful consideration by the Home Office (see NI, Ch 18, Annex D, para. 4). Enquires will be made and an application for naturalisation may be refused. A debtor with heavy debts may be refused naturalisation but may be able to make representations that demonstrate that discretion ought still to be exercised in favour of naturalisation. Dishonesty in relation to public funds and non-payment of council tax may also lead to a refusal to naturalise an applicant. Any person subject to such an allegation should make careful submissions to explain the context, especially if the allegation is admitted.

Notoriety

In extreme cases the Home Office will take other aspects of an applicant's behaviour into account. In themselves the following aspects *should not* be relevant to a determination of whether a person has a *good character*: divorce/separation; promiscuity or sexual preference within the law; drinking or gambling; eccentricity, including beliefs, appearance and lifestyle; and unemployment, working habits and means of support.

However where an applicant has made themselves notorious in their local community by the scale and persistence of their behaviour, the Home Office will consider refusing the application (NI Ch 18, Annex D, para. 5).

Evidence of anti-social behaviour will also be taken into account. Where a naturalisation decision is likely to attract press reaction or public attention this may be taken into account.

Deception

An applicant who is found to have lied or concealed the truth will have that held against them in the determination of their application (NI, Ch 18, Annex D, para. 6). Minor matters may be overlooked. Where a matter is serious, deliberate and there is a failure to cooperate with enquiries, an application will normally be refused.

Evasion of immigration control

Where the Home Office has good reason to believe that an applicant is, or has recently been involved in an attempt to assist a person in the evasion of immigration control, the application will normally be refused (NI, Ch 18, Annex D, para. 7). Where an applicant has a history of evading immigration control they may still be naturalised if they meet the statutory requirements without requiring the exercise of discretion by the Secretary of State and there is no other evidence to cast doubt on their character and standing in the community during the full five (three) year qualifying period.

Language and knowledge of life in the UK

An applicant for naturalisation on grounds of five-years' residence and, since 28 July 2004, on grounds of marriage and residence, is required to have 'sufficient knowledge' of English, Welsh or Scottish Gaelic. For outstanding applications made before 28 July 2004 the Home Office has a policy to assume an adequate level of knowledge unless there is evidence to the contrary. If there is evidence to the contrary, the Home Office could still make enquiries from the referees and ask if the applicant can speak and understand the language so that they can undertake a simple conversation about themselves, their family and their way of life, and communicate sufficiently to deal with everyday situations such as shopping.

From 28 July 2004 new arrangements were put in place for all applicants for naturalisation to demonstrate their knowledge of English, Welsh or Scottish Gaelic. These arrangements changed again on 1 November 2005 when the Home Office added a new requirement that a person seeking naturalisation must demonstrate sufficient knowledge about life in the UK (discussed below). From that date applicants will have to pass only one test or language course with a citizenship syllabus (▶see below).

13

Applications made from 28 July 2004 to 31 October 2005

An applicant is deemed to have a sufficient knowledge of English if they have any of the following (British Nationality (General) (Amendment) Regulations 2004 and (Amendment No.2) Regulations 2004):

- a certificate showing that they have attained a qualification in 'English for Speakers of Other Languages (ESOL) skills for life Entry 3' approved by the Qualifications and Curriculum Authority;

- written confirmation from a 'designated person' (▶see below) that the applicant has a sufficient knowledge of the English language for the purpose of naturalisation. A designated person can certify that an applicant has sufficient knowledge of English where the applicant does not have an ESOL skills for life Entry Level 3 certificate but has a different qualification granted by an educational institution in the UK or elsewhere and the applicant claims that it is the equivalent or better than the ESOL certificate; or

- written confirmation from a 'designated person' that the applicant has a knowledge of the English language, which might reasonably be expected from a 'native English speaker of full age and capacity'. A designated person can certify that an applicant has sufficient knowledge of English where the applicant claims this to be the case and attends an interview with the designated person for the purpose of testing the truth of the claim.

These provisions apply to the English language. Special arrangements have to be made for testing language skills where a knowledge of Welsh or Scottish Gaelic is relied on.

If an applicant has an educational qualification that could only be obtained by someone who speaks good English then the Home Office will accept this for the purpose of naturalisation. This could include GCSEs, A-Levels, or a degree or diploma from a university or higher education institute in the UK or another English-speaking country. Degrees and diplomas from non-English speaking countries will also be accepted where there is evidence that the language of instruction was English.

Where a person is seeking to show that they speak English as well as a native speaker then the procedure for applying for certification to a 'designated person' can be used to establish that the language requirement is satisfied. The only people presently designated for this purpose are notaries and solicitors. At the interview an applicant will hold a brief conversation with the solicitor or notary in order for the solicitor or notary to satisfy themselves that the applicant has language skills that are as good as those of the average native speaker. A solicitor or notary who is asked to certify language skills is entitled to charge a fee for this service.

For a person who relies on an ESOL certificate at Entry level 3 or higher, a copy other than the original, should be sent with the rest of the application and the fee. In Scotland the equivalent to the ESOL certificate at Entry level 3 are two Scottish Qualifications Authority ESOL Units at Access 3 level.

A person who is learning English, and who does not have an ESOL certificate at Entry Level 3, but believes that they may be of sufficient standard for such a certificate, can apply for Initial Assessment in ESOL. The person monitoring the assessment can sign the assessment if they consider that the applicant has demonstrated language skills sufficient for the Entry 3 standard. An ESOL provider may be able to help with information on those teachers and tutors who undertake Initial Assessments. A fee can be charged by the assessor.

A person who does not yet have English at the standard of ESOL Entry 3 will need to attend language classes up to ESOL Entry 3. Details of colleges offering courses can be obtained through Learn Direct at www.learndirect.co.uk, or by phone on 0800 101 901.

An application will normally only be refused on the basis of non-satisfaction of the language requirements, where:

- there is conclusive evidence that the applicant does not have sufficient knowledge of Welsh or Scottish Gaelic, where one of those languages is relied upon; or
- an application was made on or after 28 July 2004 and the applicant has not satisfied one of the three ways of establishing sufficient knowledge of English.

There is a discretion for the Home Office to waive the language requirement due to age, or physical or mental condition under the BNA 1981. This is set out in the NI at Chapter 18, Annex E paragraph 2.6. The criteria are similar to those applying after 1 November 2005 and are discussed below.

Applications made from 1 November 2005; sufficient knowledge about life in the UK

All those applying for naturalisation from 1 November 2005 have to demonstrate sufficient knowledge of life in the UK as well as the language requirement (para. 1(1)(ca), Sch 1 BNA 1981). The new requirements are set out in the British Nationality (General) (Amendment) Regulations 2005. Certification by a designated person or the production of qualification certificates will not be accepted. There are two principal methods by which applicants based in the UK can demonstrate the necessary requirements (NI, Ch 18, Annex E, section 1):

- applicants have to pass a 'Life in the UK' test (▶see below) pitched at ESOL Entry level 3;
- those applicants who do not have sufficient knowledge of English to sit the above test have to successfully undertake an 'ESOL with citizenship' course.

13

Those who are unsure what their level of English is can receive an initial assessment at their local further education college or at a Learn Direct centre. Alternatively, they can take a tutorial online (see the 'Life in the UK' website below) to find out whether or not their standard of English may be sufficient.

'Life in the UK' test The test is based on the Home Office publication *Life in the United Kingdom: A Journey to Citizenship* which costs £9.99 and should be widely available to buy (it can be ordered online from www.tso.co.uk/bookshop). The test specifically focuses on chapters 2, 3 and 4 of that book and consists of 24 questions to be answered in 45 minutes. Ninety test centres across the UK, operated by UFI Ltd (University for Industry) administer the tests. Many of these centres are based in colleges and learning centres. The applicant will need to produce a letter from a test centre stating that they have successfully passed the test.

Those intending to take the test should telephone the Life in the UK test help line on 0800 0154245 or visit the website www.lifeintheuktest.gov.uk/ to find out where the centres are. A separate fee of £34 on top of the naturalisation application fee is payable.

ESOL with citizenship course Applicants who feel that they do not possess the required level of English (ESOL Entry 3) to pass the 'Life in the UK' test above can choose instead to take an ESOL course, which incorporates a citizenship syllabus. The course is intended to enable a student to gain sufficient knowledge of the UK at the same time as developing their knowledge of the English language. The course can be taken at various further education colleges across the UK. Those wishing to take the test should telephone Learn Direct on 0800 100 900 to establish their nearest college. The course should be free for applicants who have resided in the UK for three years or more.

The Home Office will want to see a certificate from the college confirming that the applicant has successfully passed the course 'Skills for Life ESOL' at Entry levels 1, 2 or 3. The certificate should be awarded by one of six awarding bodies (the NIs have the list at Ch 18, Annex E, para. 1.2.3.5). Additionally, the college should issue a letter confirming that the ESOL course contained citizenship material.

Discretion to waive the language and knowledge of life in the UK requirement

Where, because of age, physical or mental condition it would be un-reasonable to require the applicant to fulfil the language and knowledge of life in the UK requirements, they can be waived under the BNA 1981. Home Office policy is set out in the NI at Chapter 18, Annex E paragraphs 1.5.2 to 1.5.5 for applications made from 1 November 2005 and is summarised here. A similar discretion applies for applications made from 28 July 2004 to 31 October 2005 (see NI Ch 18, Annex E para. 2.6).

Age An applicant aged 65 will benefit from a waiver of the requirements. Those aged between 60 and 65 will normally benefit from a waiver if they specifically request it. Those under 60 should not expect to have the requirements waived on the ground of age alone.

Physical Condition If a person is suffering from a long term illness or disability which severely restricts mobility, preventing the ability to attend classes or take the test, or a person is deaf, mute or suffers from a speech impediment, discretion will normally be exercised.

Mental Condition Where an applicant has a mental impairment and is not able to speak or learn the relevant language, although they can meet the full capacity requirement, discretion should be exercised.

Referees

The form for naturalisation, Form AN(New), requires a person to provide two referees. While there is no statutory requirement for referees, they are used by the Home Office as a source of information for checks to be performed.

The Home Office may contact referees where there is a doubt as to full capacity, character, language or future intentions. Both referees must be British citizens, aged 25 or over, have known the applicant for at least three years, and not be a solicitor, agent or relative of the applicant. They must be someone who knows the applicant in a personal capacity. Referees must not be related to each other and not have been convicted of an imprisonable offence in the last ten years. A referee is asked how long they have known the applicant, how, when and for what reason they met the applicant, to confirm in their opinion that the applicant meets the statutory requirements other than the residence requirements, and to give any other relevant information.

Intention to make home in the UK

Those applying on the basis of five-years' residence have to demonstrate their future intentions with respect to the UK (see NI, Ch 18, Annex F).

In assessing future intentions the Home Office will look at past behaviour. If past behaviour is satisfactory then the Home Office will take this at face value. If an applicant states that it is their intention to have their home or principal home in the UK, past behaviour and other matters that satisfy the requirement will include:

- meeting the residence requirement without the need to exercise discretion to excuse excess absences, ignoring excess absences of up to 30 days;
- having an established, owned or rented home here;
- being or intending to be absent for not more than six months, the absence being temporary, intending to return (if they have not already

13

done so), and maintaining an established home here where any close family have remained and continuing to live with them;

- the lack of any information to cast doubt on their intention, such as a spouse who intends to become resident abroad, or a prolonged absence of more than six months.

If residence has not been established and there is evidence of a principal residence outside the UK, the Home Office may seek to find out whether the applicant or family member owns property abroad and whether the applicant's family live abroad. If the spouse or partner of the applicant lives abroad, the Home Office will take into account whether the couple are separated, whether the spouse or partner has applied for entry clearance, whether the Home Office is satisfied that the spouse or partner intends to join the applicant or it is apparent that the couple are content to live apart for the foreseeable future. The Home Office may also seek further information on where an applicant is domiciled for tax purposes.

Where it is apparent that an applicant does or intends to maintain their principal residence abroad, an application will normally be refused. Where an applicant is going abroad for more than six months the application will normally be refused (re-application will be possible on return). An exception will be made where the time spent abroad is more than six months but the applicant is undertaking voluntary work; or studies, training or employment necessary for a UK-based profession, vocation or occupation; or the absence is part of an established pattern (such as for a seaman) although the applicant is based in the UK. In these circumstances the Home Office will want to be satisfied that the applicant definitely intends to return to the UK after a fixed period of time.

Some applicants such as actors and musicians do not have a principal home. In such cases the Home Office will look at the position under UK tax law, what property if any is owned here, what personal connections there are with the UK, the length of time spent in the UK each year, and the extent to which the applicant identifies with the UK. An application will normally be accepted where an applicant is domiciled in the UK for tax purposes, where reasonable time when not working is spent in the UK, and where the applicant has some personal connections in the UK. Discretion will also be exercised if some factors are not made out but there are other strong links with the UK.

Crown service, employment in a relevant international organisation, or relevant private employment

The alternative to showing an intention to make one's main home in the UK for those applying under the five-year residence route for naturalisation (►see above), is to show an intention to enter into or continue in Crown service, in the service of an international organisation of which the UK is a member, or in the service of a company or association established in the UK.

An applicant will be considered to be in the service of an international organisation of which the UK is a member if they are an employee, or giving services on a full time basis without payment or for a nominal sum, and giving services direct to and for the benefit of the organisation. An applicant who intends to enter or continue in relevant international service may be able to meet the future intentions requirement. Evidence of service will be required from the organisation concerned. The list of relevant international organisations can be found in NI, Chapter 18, Annex F(i).

A person who is in the service of a company established in the UK may also meet the future intentions requirement. If an applicant is working outside the UK for such a company they will be accepted as doing so where they are an employee, self-employed and registered as a company, or self-employed as a partner in a going concern, or a company director. A company is considered to be established in the UK if it is described as an English, Scottish, Northern Irish or overseas company under the Companies Acts, the company is a going concern and it is not registered for convenience only. A company which does not meet one of these requirements or by the distribution of its workforce shows that it only has a notional presence in the UK will not be regarded as established in the UK. An applicant who intends to enter or continue in company service may meet the requirement if there is, or will be, an implied or express contract of employment; they are or will be in the direct employment of the company concerned, or employed by a seconding company as its own career staff, and can produce written confirmation of the service or intended service from the company concerned.

An applicant in the service of an association established in the UK, and working outside the UK, may be able to meet the future intentions requirement. An applicant will be regarded as in relevant service where they are in the direct employment of the organisation and have an implied or express contract of employment. An applicant who intends to enter or continue in the service of a relevant association will need to produce confirmation from the organisation concerned.

An applicant who intends to enter or to continue in Crown service or other relevant employment abroad for at least five years from the time the application is considered, will be regarded as meeting the future intentions requirement. If the applicant cannot show an intention to complete five years' further service, account will be taken of future intentions after service has been completed. If the applicant will be returning or remaining in the UK then the future intentions requirement will be met. If the applicant has bought property in the UK, or has strong family links in the UK, or has previously always returned to the UK after service abroad, has a stated intention to do so again and there is no information to suggest otherwise, then the future intentions requirement will be met.

13

An applicant who accompanies a spouse or partner on an overseas posting for more than six months will satisfy the requirement where the established spouse or partner would satisfy the home or principal home criteria.

An applicant will be considered to have an established spouse or partner when the application is being considered if they have been married to, or cohabited with, the relevant person for at least 12 months. Evidence such as a marriage certificate, where relevant, and documents that establish joint commitments may be required. This can take the form of joint bank account details or bills, evidence of children of the relationship, correspondence to the same address, official records or letters from third parties.

Crown Service as an alternative to the residence requirements

Where a person applies for naturalisation under the five-year residence route, there is an alternative to satisfying the residence requirement for those serving outside the UK in Crown Service under the government of the UK. Crown Service is defined in the NIs. Applications for naturalisation relying on Crown Service will require evidence from the relevant government department or branch of the armed forces.

Applicants will still have to meet the criteria of good character, language and future intentions. They will also have to demonstrate that their service and connection to the UK make it right for the Secretary of State to exercise discretion and naturalise them. The relevant criteria, with the most important first, are set out below. Therefore, an applicant who fails the 'quality of service' test is unlikely to be naturalised.

The criteria in relation to service and connection to the UK are (NI, Ch 18, Annex C, para. 2) as follows.

- Quality of service: the applicant must be the holder of a responsible post and have performed their duties to an exceptionally high standard.
- Connections with the UK. In order of importance (most important first): past residence in the UK; whereabouts of close family members; whereabouts of property, house, other property investments, savings accounts etc; and whereabouts of and contact with friends.
- Rank or grade: the more senior, the more likely an applicant will be considered to have performed outstanding service (although junior post holders will also be considered on their record).
- Loyalty, where this is shown, as 'tested and demonstrated beyond question'.
- Length of service: 'exceptional service' for a significant period of usually more than ten years.

Those in Crown Service who do not meet the above criteria may still be considered where it would be advantageous operationally for such persons to be British citizens. Where the Foreign and Commonwealth

Office submit an application on behalf of a Crown Servant and request priority, the Home Office should deal with that application as quickly as possible and out of turn.

REGISTRATION OF CHILDREN

Registration is a process similar to naturalisation. It is a means by which a person may become a British citizen. However only certain classes of persons are eligible to register as British citizens.

Firstly, there is registration as British citizens for children under 18 and those who are eligible through having been children of certain British nationals (▶see below).

Secondly, there is registration for those who are adults (and, in some cases, for children too) and who have a special or privileged status that enables them to register as British citizens rather than having to apply for naturalisation. For these adults registration provides a route to citizenship by registration by entitlement and/or by discretion with less stringent criteria than the route provided by naturalisation (▶see later at 1485–90). Naturalisation is only ever discretionary.

Children who automatically acquire British citizenship are discussed in Chapter 44. Those who are not British have to register as opposed to naturalise as British citizens. Some will have an *entitlement* or a right to register and they are set out immediately below (one group includes 'children' born to certain British nationals who are over 18). Others will only be able to apply at the discretion of the Secretary of State, as discussed at ▶1476–85.

Where an application for registration was made before 1 January 2004 by a minor who becomes 18 by the time the application is decided, the applicant may have to take an oath or make an affirmation of allegiance. If the application is made on or after 1 January 2004, they will have to attend a citizenship ceremony and make an oath of allegiance and a pledge. These are discussed at ▶1450–3.

Not all applications by minors require the consent of parents or guardians. Those minors who may register by entitlement, with one exception, do not require consent. Other minors do require the consent of parents or guardians in applying for registration (discussed at ▶1478–9 and 1485). Form MN1 appears to require the consent of parents or guardians in all applications but the NIs indicate where consent is not required. The issue of parental consent is considered on a case-by-case basis in this chapter.

Where a child is born 'illegitimate', a reference to parent or parents is generally only a reference to the mother alone.

13

Registration of children by entitlement

Registration of children born in the UK on grounds of their parent's status

Children under 18 (minors) are entitled to registration if: they were born in the UK on or after 1 January 1983; they were not British citizens at birth because at that time neither parent was a British citizen or settled here; and either parent has become a British citizen or settled in the UK since their birth (s1(3) BNA 1981). Registration under this provision gives British citizenship *otherwise* than by descent (▶see 1433–4 for the advantages of this type of citizenship).

Form MN1 should be used for the application if the child is not included on the parent's application. A child would be included on a parent's application if the parent was, for example, applying for naturalisation at the same time.

Registration of persons born in the UK on grounds of ten-years' residence

Adults or minors are entitled to registration as a citizen if they were born in the UK on or after 1 January 1983, they were not a British citizen at birth because at the time neither parent was a British citizen or settled here, they are aged ten years or more on the date of application, they have lived in the UK for the first ten years of their life, and during that ten years they were not out of the UK for more than 90 days in any one of those years (s1(4) BNA 1981). Registration under this provision gives British citizenship *otherwise* than by descent (▶see 1433–4 for the advantages of this type of citizenship).

There is a discretion to allow absences from the UK amounting to more than 90 days in any one or more of the first ten years of the person's life (see the NIs, Ch 8 para. 8.5). Form T should be used for the application if the applicant is a minor and not included on the parent's application.

Registration of children born outside the UK to British citizens by descent

Minors born abroad are entitled to register as British citizens if (s3(2) BNA 1981):

- either parent was a British citizen by descent at the time of the child's birth;
- the mother or father of the parent in question became or, but for their death, would have become a British citizen *otherwise* than by descent on 1 January 1983;
- the application is made within 12 months (but ▶see below for special circumstances) of the child's birth; and the parent in question satisfied *all* of the following criteria:

- had at any time before the child's birth lived in the UK (or a 'qualifying territory', ▶see 1432, if the child was born on or after 21 May 2002) for a continuous period of three years;
- was in the UK (or qualifying territory) at the beginning of that three-year period;
- was not absent from the UK (or qualifying territory) for more than 270 days in that three-year period.

The residence requirements do not apply if the child was born stateless. Registration under this provision gives British citizenship by descent only (▶see 1433–4 for an explanation of this type of citizenship). Some children may obtain British citizenship *otherwise* than by descent based on three-year's residence (▶see below 1476).

Special circumstances Applications may be made within six years of a child's birth rather than 12 months if there are special circumstances (s3(4) BNA 1981). These special circumstances include:

- if the parents received incorrect nationality advice from an official source, a solicitor, or a recognised advisory agency;
- there were domestic difficulties;
- the family had intended to come here and apply for registration under section 3(5) (discussed below) but had been prevented from returning to the UK due to:
  - the death of one of the parents; or
  - other unforeseen circumstances or a significant change in domestic circumstances such as a divorce;
- enquiries were made within 12 months, and this was followed up by an application no later than three months after the end of that period;
- the application is made up to a month late;
- the child has a brother or sister who has made a similar successful application; or
- the child would suffer significant and special hardship by not being a British citizen.

Hardship means a serious disadvantage to the family or to the child, which goes beyond the normal benefit and convenience of citizenship. This could include where the family's ability to remain depends upon the child receiving British citizenship. Evidence of the hardship alleged will be required. The broad discretion to consider an application for registration within six years of a child's birth is not limited by the factors listed above if a sufficiently compelling case can be made.

The absence of parental consent is not a reason for refusal. The child has an entitlement to registration if the other criteria are satisfied.

13

Registration of children born outside the UK to British citizens by descent on grounds of three-years' residence

A minor born abroad will be entitled to registration if (s3(5) BNA 1981):

- at the time of the birth they had a parent who was a British citizen by descent;
- they and both parents were in the UK (or a 'qualifying territory', ►see 1432, if the child was born on or after 21 May 2002) at the beginning of a three-year period ending with the date of the application;
- neither the child nor the parents were absent from the UK (or a qualifying territory) for more than 270 days in that three-year period; and
- the consent of both parents is given to the application.

If on or before the date of the application, the person's father or mother has died, the parent's marriage had ended in divorce or annulment or the civil partnership had terminated , or on the date of application the parents were legally separated, then the residence requirements need only be met by the child and either one of the parents. Where one parent has died, consent will only be required from the surviving parent. Parental consent of both parents (if alive) is a statutory requirement. There is no discretion to dispense with this requirement. If consent from the parents cannot be obtained, then another route to registration needs to be considered.

There is no discretion to accept a longer period of absence of more than 270 days in the three years before the date of application. Registration under this provision provides British citizenship *otherwise* than by descent (►see 1433–4 for the advantages of this type of citizenship). Form MN1 should be used where the minor is not included in a parent's application.

Registration of any child by discretion

Any child who is a minor may be registered as a British citizen if the Secretary of State thinks fit to register them (s3(1) BNA 1981). Registration is by discretion (not entitlement) and the exercise of this discretion is discussed below.

Registration under section 3 (1) gives British citizenship otherwise than by descent in most cases (►see 1433–4 for the advantages of this type of citizenship). However, it gives British citizenship by descent only if the father or the mother was a British citizen at the time of the child's birth. This will be relevant, for example, to children born abroad to a parent who is British by descent only. 'Father' or 'mother' in this context does not include an adoptive father or mother. Furthermore, the term 'father' does not include the father of an 'illegitimate' child. Children who were adopted by British citizens or born 'illegitimate' children of British citizen men will be British citizens otherwise than by descent if they are registered under section 3 (1) BNA 1981.

Form MN1 should be used if the child is not included on a parent's application or someone else's for registration or naturalisation. If the child turns out to have an automatic claim for British citizenship when they apply for registration, the Home Office should write to explain that the application is not necessary and refund in full the fees submitted with the application.

There are a number of policies in relation to the registration of children born abroad to certain British citizens who do not come within any category for registration by entitlement (above) and these are discussed further (▶see 1480–3).

All of the criteria set out below generally apply to most children applying at the Secretary of State's discretion. Specific policies for special classes of children modify the criteria and these are set out at ▶1480–5.

Future intentions

The child's future must be seen to lie in the UK. The past behaviour of the applicant and the family will be considered. The intention requirement will normally be satisfied if there is an established way of life in the UK that looks set to continue. A child who has a settled home in the UK, whose future intentions are confirmed on the application form and who meets the residence criteria below (▶1479–80), will normally be registered.

A child who is resident abroad is unlikely to be registered unless they are a second or subsequent generation child born abroad into a British citizen family on long term business or service overseas (▶see 1482–3). If the child or either of its parents has recently left the UK for more than six months, or the child is about to leave the UK, or one or both parents are resident abroad then further enquiries may be made by the Home Office. However an application may be accepted if the child is abroad with a parent in Crown service such as the armed forces or, if the child had an established home in the UK before going abroad to which they will be returning. The absence abroad should not total more than six months and it should be intended that the child will return by the end of the six months. Applications made abroad should be submitted to the appropriate local British official and not the Home Office, otherwise the application will not be valid.

Citizenship and immigration status of parents

If a child applies together with a parent for citizenship, then both parents will be expected to be settled in the UK. Refusal of a parent's application will normally lead to the child's application being refused. If a child applies on their own, then the Home Office will normally expect one parent to be British and both parents to be settled in the UK. If neither parent is, or will be, a British citizen then registration is unlikely. However there may be exceptional circumstances that can justify registration. An application that does not meet these criteria will normally be refused unless registration can be said to be in the child's best interest.

If there is a divorce or separation then it will be expected that the parent with day-to-day responsibility is a British citizen or that the parent is settled in the UK and there are good reasons why registration is appropriate.

Consent of the parent

Normally, the consent of both parents is required. In situations where a marriage has temporarily or permanently broken down, or the child is 'illegitimate', greater flexibility is shown. Where the parents are legally separated or divorced, and both parents have parental responsibility (▶see below) or residence orders, then both should be consulted. Where there is an informal separation, both parents should be asked for consent. Where the child is 'illegitimate', the mother will automatically have parental responsibility and the father may have acquired it.

Parental responsibility may be held by:

- the mother;
- the father, if the child was born legitimate;
- the father, if the child was 'illegitimate', and he has one of the following:
  - a residence order;
  - a parental responsibility order;
  - a parental responsibility agreement with the mother; or
  - he has since married the mother;
- a guardian of the child (▶1484);
- a person with a custody or residence order;
- a local authority which has a care order (▶1484);
- a person who holds an emergency protection order; or
- a person who has adopted the child (▶1481–2).

Where one parent applies for a child to be registered, steps will be taken to obtain the other parent's view. However the other parent's view may be dispensed with where the applicant parent has sole residence of the child, or the child is 'illegitimate' and there is no reason to believe that the father has parental responsibility, or the applicant parent or their solicitor states that the other parent has abandoned the child or states that the other parent's whereabouts are not known or that they cannot reasonably be traced, or the other parent has not responded to enquiries.

If the other parent objects to registration, then this will not usually be overridden where the child's home is in the country of the existing nationality which would be lost by registration as a British citizen, or if there was evidence that the child has been or would be brought here in contravention of a court order, or if there are outstanding court proceedings over the custody of the child, or if there is reason to believe that registration would not be in the child's interests.

An objection by the other parent may be overridden where the child is living in the UK with the applicant parent and registration would appear to be in the child's best interests. It may also be reasonable to override an objection where they are ill-founded, motivated by bad feeling between the parents, or the objecting parent appeared not to be acting in the child's best interests.

If a child who is 17 or over when the application is considered signifies a wish in writing to be registered, they may be registered despite any parental objections.

Residence in the UK

A child will normally be expected to have completed a period of residence in the UK. Where a child is over 13 the Home Office will normally expect them to have completed two years' residence in the UK before being registered. For children under 13 the length of residence will not be so important if the decision maker is satisfied that the child's future lies in the UK and that registration would otherwise be appropriate. Minors aged 16 or over on arrival will normally have their applications for registration refused, however each case will be considered on its merits.

The Home Office will also consider cases, which do not meet the normal residence requirements. Residence means continuous presence. Holidays and short visits abroad will not breach continuity but absences of six months or more may be considered to break the qualifying period of residence.

A minor of any age, who has less than two-years' residence, will be considered for registration where there are reasons for so doing. Such reasons could include situations:

- where the offer of a job in the UK to the child depends upon British citizenship or,
- where the minor is two months or less short of meeting the residence requirement and satisfies any of the following:
  - they would still be a minor at the end of the two-month period;
  - they would become 18 before the end of the two-month period but were prevented from coming here earlier through circumstances beyond the family's control;
  - there are compelling compassionate reasons for accepting a shorter period of residence or refusal would cause the child considerable hardship;
  - the child would be the only member of the family who would not become British;

- an application has been made on behalf of more than one child and at least one is under 13; or
- the child's residence is broken but periods of residence may still be aggregated.

Conditions of stay

The Home Office will expect a child who applies for registration to be free of conditions of stay such as time-limits on stay because the future of a child whose stay is restricted is not considered to lie in the UK. However if one or both parents are British citizens who have come to live permanently in the UK then this factor may be less important if the other criteria are met.

Character

The character of a child becomes a more important factor, the nearer they become to the age of 18. If a child is 16 or over, the Home Office will have regard to the same standards that it applies for an adult (►see 1463–5). Character will still be an issue if a child is under 16 and there are serious doubts about the child's character.

Special classes of children who may register by discretion

The general requirements that the Home Office has laid down for children to be registered at its discretion under section 3(1) BNA 1981 are set out above. However, there are special groups of children who may not be able to satisfy all of the above requirements but who may still be registered under section 3(1) as a matter of discretion. These are set out below.

Children born abroad to a parent in Crown, designated or Community service

A minor born abroad will normally be registered if all the following conditions are satisfied (NI, Ch 9, para. 9.7.6):

- they were born before the date of designation or admission as a European Community institution (see NI, Ch 4);
- the mother or father is, or was at their death, a British citizen by descent;
- a parent is, or but for their death would have been, in designated or European Community institution service on the date of application;
- at the time of the child's birth the parent was in that service before it was designated or admitted;
- where necessary both parents consent to the registration, or any objections by the non-applicant parent are ill-founded; and
- there is no reason to refuse on character grounds.

Children born abroad whose grandfather was in Crown, designated or Community service

A minor born abroad to a parent whose father was in Crown, designated or European Community institution service will normally be registered if all of the following conditions are satisfied (NI, Ch 9, para. 9.7.5):

- the child was born before the date of the designation of the service;
- the mother or father was a CUKC by birth or descent;
- the mother or father became or would but for their death have become a British citizen otherwise than by descent under s14(2) BNA 1981:
  - on 1 January 1983 because they (i.e. the parent of the child seeking registration) were born to a father who was in Crown, designated or Community Institution service at the time of the birth; or
  - on the date of designation because they (i.e. the parent of the child seeking registration) were born to a father who at the time of the birth was in service which has been designated since 1 January 1983; and
- where appropriate, both parents consent to registration, or any objections by the non applicant parent are ill founded; and
- there is no reason to refuse on character grounds.

Children born to a parent who renounces and then resumes British citizenship

A minor who is born to a parent who has renounced and subsequently resumed British citizenship will normally be registered if:

- the mother or father has renounced and subsequently resumed British citizenship;
- the parent became a British citizen otherwise than by descent, on resumption;
- the child was born before the date of resumption;
- when necessary, both parents consent to the registration, or any objections by the non applicant parent are ill-founded; and
- there is no reason to refuse on character grounds.

Children adopted abroad by British citizens

There is special consideration given to children adopted abroad by British citizens because of international obligations. It should be checked whether a child was adopted in a 'qualifying territory' (▶see 1432) or adopted under the Hague Convention, which is discussed at ▶1432 and 380–1. The countries in which the Hague Convention is in force are listed at ▶1528. Such children may have an automatic claim to British citizenship. In some cases involving British citizens who adopt children, the Hague Convention gives an automatic claim to British citizenship under section 1(5) BNA 1981. For adoption generally ▶see 379–85.

13

Children adopted abroad by British citizens do not have to be registered but the preference of the Home Office is to give an adopted child the nationality the child would have had had they been born to the adoptive parent.

A child adopted overseas will normally be registered if:

- at least one of the adoptive parents is a British citizen otherwise than by descent;
- if necessary, both adoptive parents have signified their consent to the registration;
- there is no reason to refuse on character grounds; and
- the Home Office is satisfied that the adoption is not one of convenience arranged to facilitate the child's admission to the United Kingdom; and *either*
  - the adoption was made under the law of a country which is specified in the Adoption (Designation of Overseas Adoption) Order 1973 (listed at ▶1528), *or*
  - the Home Office is satisfied that there has been a genuine transfer of parental responsibility on the grounds of the original parents' inability (or unwillingness) to care for the child.

'Illegitimate' children of British citizen fathers

Unlike mothers, fathers cannot transmit British citizenship to any 'illegitimate' children they may have (see s50(9) BNA 1981). In this situation the Home Office will normally register any 'illegitimate minor' of a British father if it is satisfied about the paternity of the child and the consent of all those with parental responsibility has been given. Section 9 2002 Act introduced a provision that removes the distinction between legitimate and 'illegitimate' children. However, section 9 has not yet come into force.

Second or subsequent generations born and brought into a British citizen family on long-term business abroad or service overseas

The Home Office will normally register a second or subsequent generation child born and living abroad if all the following conditions are satisfied:

- the child is part of a British citizen family on long-term business abroad; or at least one parent is a British citizen working overseas for an international organisation of which the UK is a member;
- if necessary, both parents consent to the registration or any objections by the non-applicant parent are ill-founded;
- there is no reason to refuse on character grounds;
- either, both the child and the family have strong links with the United Kingdom, or there are compassionate circumstances.

Mentally disturbed children

Sympathetic consideration is normally given to the registration of minors whose mental capacity is limited. This is because it may be impossible for them to acquire British citizenship once they reach 18. Where a child becomes 18 before the application is approved, they will be required to attend a citizenship ceremony to take an oath of allegiance before registration or naturalisation unless that requirement is waived. There is discretion to set aside the requirements to attend a citizenship ceremony and to take the oath and pledge, which should normally be exercised where it is known that the child's mental capacity is affected so that it might be impossible for the oath of allegiance to be taken.

A mentally disturbed minor should meet the general registration criteria set out above, save that in addition, the Home Office will normally register if:

- the child would be granted citizenship if applying as an adult;
- would otherwise be the only family member who was not a British citizen;
- would be unable to meet the normal two-year residence expectation before reaching majority but the child's future clearly lies in the UK; or
- the child would suffer hardship by not being registered.

Married children

Children under 18 who are married are assumed to have a family status on their own account and as such to be less a part of their parents' family. The Home Office need not normally take into account the parents' citizenship or immigration status and, if the minor is 17 or over when the application is considered, less weight will be given to the consent of the parents to registration. In addition, if the child is married to a British citizen, the decision maker need not normally consider where the child's future lies.

Children wishing to follow a particular career

If it is a requirement that a child be a British citizen in order to follow a career then Home Office policy is to try and facilitate that when considering applications for registration. This is particularly so where the child wishes to join the armed forces or the police. Normal criteria can be disregarded in these cases. The fact that neither parent is a British citizen will not normally be a sufficient reason for refusal. Credible evidence of an application for such a career and of a provisional offer will be required.

British citizen siblings

It is Home Office policy to register a minor as a British citizen if that applicant has a British brother or sister, regardless of how that brother or sister acquired their British citizenship.

Wards of court

Where a child is a ward of court or is subject to a 'prohibited steps order' on a question of nationality, the consent of the court to the nationality application must be obtained.

Guardianship orders

A guardian is appointed to look after a child's upbringing where nobody has parental responsibility for the child. A guardian may make an application for the registration of a minor as a British citizen. The Home Office will examine applications made by a guardian, to make sure that the guardianship is not a device to get around immigration control. The usual criteria set out at ▶1477–80 will also need to be satisfied.

A child will normally be registered if:

- the child's parents have died;
- at least one of them was a British citizen;
- the guardian or one guardian is a British citizen; and
- the child meets the residence and other normal expectations.

Custodianship and other parental responsibility orders

Custodianship orders are no longer made and are deemed to be parental responsibility orders. Where an application for registration of a minor is made by a person sharing parental responsibility for a child with the parents, the consent of all the parents will be sought. A person sharing a parental responsibility order with the natural parents does not take the place of the parents for the purposes of registration under section 3(1). The usual criteria will have to be met.

Children in care

An application for registration may be made on behalf of a child who is being looked after by a local authority. Where the local authority shares parental responsibility with the parents, the parents' consent must be sought. Where the application is made by the parents, the local authority will be asked for a report. If the local authority supports the application for registration, the child will normally be registered. If the local authority does not support the recommendation then the child will not be registered while the care order remains in force.

Where the local authority makes an application for registration, the Home Office will seek a report from them. For general details about children in care, ▶see 391–2.

Applications made by persons other than parents

Where an application is made by a person who is not a parent or a person with parental responsibility, it will normally be refused unless there are special circumstances. These could include where the child's parents are dead and the child is living permanently with the person making the application or where the child's parents have gone abroad for the long term and the child has been left in the permanent care of the person making the application.

Applications made by the minor

A minor may make an application for registration themselves but this will normally be refused unless there is consent from the parents or the person with parental responsibility. However if a minor is over 17 and has a good reason for making the application, it will be considered in the normal way.

The views of the minor

Where a minor opposes an application for their registration, then the Home Office will give consideration as to whether to refuse the application. The older the minor, the more likely the refusal.

REGISTRATION OF ADULTS

Adults normally obtain British citizenship through naturalisation, and registration is normally reserved for children. However, there are three groups of adults who can apply for registration and they are set out below. Certain minors can also be registered under these groups. Another group that includes both adults and children are those who are born in the UK and have lived here for the first ten years of their life. They are discussed at ▶1474.

Those born before 1983 to British mothers

Those born abroad before commencement of the BNA 1981 on 1 January 1983 could only inherit citizenship from their fathers and not their mothers (▶1434–5). Those born in the UK of course, before that date, automatically became British by birth. In an attempt to partly rectify this inequality, section 13 2002 Act amended the BNA 1981 to provide for the registration of the following class of people (s4C BNA 1981):

- those born after 7 February 1961 and before 1 January 1983;
- who would have been British (CUKCs) under the old British Nationality Act 1948 if that section had provided for citizenship by descent from a mother in the same terms as it provided for citizenship by descent from a father and which would have given them the right of abode in the UK.

Application Form UKM should be used. Registration under this provision gives British citizenship by descent only. If an applicant is also *entitled* to British citizenship by another route, that application should be considered first if it gives British citizenship *otherwise* than by descent. This could be the case where there is an entitlement to registration if the person is, for example a British Overseas citizen (BOC). In addition, applicants who

13

appear to be eligible for naturalisation should normally have the advantage of obtaining British citizenship otherwise than by descent, which naturalisation gives, explained to them.

Registration of BOCs, BSs, BN(O)s and BPPs

One small group of adults and minors who are able to obtain British citizenship by registration are British nationals who are not British citizens (BOCs, BPPs and others). The different methods of registration available to them are set out below. They have an entitlement to registration if they are settled in the UK (▶see below). However, it is difficult for most of these people to become settled in the UK as they must first obtain indefinite leave, usually under the ordinary immigration rules. After a long and sustained period of campaigning by organisations such as JCWI, the government introduced through the 2002 Act , a provision into the BNA 1981 for certain British nationals to register as British citizens if they do not have the citizenship of another country.

Registration by Entitlement for BOCs, BSs, and BPPs

On 4 July 2002, the government announced that certain British nationals, both adults and minors, would be *entitled* to be registered as British citizens if (s4B BNA 1981):

- they are a British Overseas citizen, a British subject (under the British Nationality Act 1981) or a British Protected Person;
- the Secretary of State is satisfied that they have no other citizenship or nationality; and
- the Secretary of State is satisfied that they have not, after 4 July 2002, renounced, voluntarily relinquished or lost 'through action or inaction' any citizenship or nationality.

Registration under this route gives British citizenship by descent only. Minors do not require the consent of their parents. Applicants will be expected to supply statements from the authorities in the country or countries concerned confirming that they do not have its citizenship or nationality. Applications may still be accepted if these cannot be obtained. The Home Office has some knowledge of the nationality laws of Commonwealth states and other states formerly under British rule. Applicants for registration should ensure that adequate information about the nationality laws applicable to them in other relevant countries is advanced in support of their claim. Form B(OS) should be used.

Registration of BOCs, BPPs, BSs BOTCs and BN(O)s, on grounds of residence

A person, adult or minor, who is a BOC, BPP, BS, BOTC or BN(O) and who has settlement rights in the UK will be *entitled* to register as a British citizen (s4(2) BNA 1981) if all of the following are satisfied:

- they were in the UK at the beginning of the period of five years ending with the date of application or they were settled in the UK immediately before 1 January 1983;
- they were not absent from the UK for more than 450 days in the five-year period ending with the date of the application;
- they were not absent from the UK for more than 90 days in the 12 months ending with the date of the application;
- they were not, on the date of application, subject under the immigration laws to any restriction on their stay in the UK;
- they were not subject, under the immigration laws, to any restriction on their stay in the UK in the 12 months immediately before the date of application;
- they were not, at any time in the five years ending with the date of application in the UK in breach of the immigration laws.

Registration by this method gives British citizenship *otherwise* than by descent. Minors can apply under this provision and do not require their parents' consent. There is a discretion to allow absences in excess of those set out above and this is set out in the NIs at Chapter 12, Annex A.

Registration on grounds of service

A person, adult or minor, who is a BOC, BPP, BS, BOTC or BN(O) *may* be registered at the discretion of the Secretary of State as a British citizen if the Secretary of State (s4(5) BNA 1981):

- is satisfied that the applicant has at any time served in a relevant service; and
- thinks it fitting in the special circumstances of the applicant's case.

This provision is designed to be used to reward those who serve the Crown in the British Overseas Territories in a particularly deserving way. It enables such people to avoid having to have been resident in the UK for five years before seeking registration, and is intended to be used sparingly. The Secretary of State will consider quality of service, connections with the UK, rank, loyalty and length of service (▶see 1472–3 for further discussion of these criteria).

'Relevant service' will include Crown service under the government of a British Overseas Territory and paid or unpaid service as a member of a body established by law in a British Overseas Territory, members of which are appointed by or on behalf of the Crown. Service could be in a statutory body, an education board, a trade advisory board, a military body or another relevant body. Registration under this route gives British citizenship otherwise than by descent.

13

Registration of BOTCs

Those who were BOTCs before 21 May 2002 (when the British Overseas Territories Act 2002 (BOTA) commenced) automatically gained British citizenship and the right of abode in the UK (►1432–3). Those who became BOTCs after that date, both adults and minors, have been able to apply to be registered as British citizens *at the discretion* of the Secretary of State if they (s4A BNA 1981):

- do not have that status only by virtue of a connection with the Sovereign Base Areas of Akrotiri and Dhekelia; and
- had not previously ceased to be a British citizen as a result of declaration or renunciation.

Registration by this route gives British citizenship *otherwise* than by descent. Minors will normally require the consent of their parents and the test for good character applies.

Registration of BOTCs who are UK nationals for EC purposes

A person of any age can register as a British citizen if they are a BOTC and a UK national for European Community purposes (s5 BNA 1981). A UK national for EC purposes is defined in a declaration made to the European Commission by the UK. This process of registration primarily concerns BOTCs who obtained that status through a connection with Gibraltar. For EC purposes a UK national is:

- a British citizen; or
- a person who is a British subject (under Part IV BNA 1981) and who has the right of abode in the UK and is therefore exempt from UK immigration control; or
- a BOTC who has acquired citizenship from a connection with Gibraltar.

The NIs set out in detail what is meant by a connection with Gibraltar at Chapter 13, Annex A. This statutory provision has ceased to be relevant for most BOTCs following the BOTA and is now of relevance to those BOTCs who acquired that citizenship on or after 21 May 2002 by naturalisation or registration. A person registered under this section is a British citizen by descent. Form G should be used.

Registration of stateless persons

British nationality law provides certain classes of people who do not have any other nationality with the right to register as British citizens and these are set out below.

Stateless persons aged between 10 and 22 born in the UK or in a British Overseas Territory

Those who are born in the UK or a British Overseas Territory and have no other nationality are entitled to registration if (sch 2, para. 3 BNA 1981):

- they were born on or after 1 January 1983;
- they were born and have remained stateless;
- on the date of application, they have reached ten years of age and are under 22 years of age;
- they were in the UK or a British Overseas Territory for five years ending with the date of application; and
- in that five years, they were not absent from the UK or a British Overseas Territory for more than 450 days.

A person who meets the above requirements is entitled to registration as a British citizen, if the number of days spent in the UK during the five-year qualifying period exceeds the number of days spent in the British overseas territories. If this criterion is not met, then subject to the other requirements being fulfilled, the person is entitled to be registered as a BOTC.

There is discretion to allow absences in excess of 450 days in the five-year qualifying period. Registration under this provision gives British citizenship *otherwise* than by descent (▶see 1433–4 for the advantages of this type of citizenship).

Stateless persons born to British nationals outside the UK and the British Overseas Territories

Those born abroad to parents who have some form of British nationality but who did not inherit that nationality and are otherwise stateless are *entitled* to register as a British citizen if (sch2, para. 4 BNA 1981):

- they were born on or after 1 January 1983;
- they were born outside the UK and the British overseas territories and were born and have remained stateless;
- at the time of their birth their father or mother was a British citizen, BOTC, BOC, or a BS under the BNA 1981;
- they were in the UK or a British Overseas Territory at the beginning of the three years ending with the date of application; and
- they were not absent from both the UK and the British Overseas territories for more than 270 days in that three-year period.

A person who meets these requirements is entitled to registration as a British citizen, a BOTC or a BOC, or a combination of all three depending on which status their father or mother possessed. Alternatively, if one parent was solely a BS (British subject) and neither parent held another form of British nationality (such as British Overseas Territories citizenship), then that person will be entitled to be registered as a BS.

Common with other nationality provisions, the term 'father' does not include a reference to the father of an 'illegitimate' child unless the parents have subsequently married. There is a discretion to allow absences in excess of 270 days in the three-year qualifying period. If British

13

citizenship or British Overseas Territories citizenship is granted, then this is citizenship *otherwise* than by descent. British Overseas citizenship and British subject status *cannot* be transmitted to descendants if granted.

Persons born before 1 January 1983

Under schedule 2, paragraph 5 BNA 1983 a person is entitled to registration under this provision if:

- they were born before 1 January 1983;
- they were born and have remained stateless; *and*
- either their mother was a CUKC at the time of the person's birth, or the person was born in a place that was at the date of application, within the UK or a British Overseas Territory, or the person meets the requirements (►see below) of parentage or residence and parentage under the British Nationality (No. 2) Act 1964, as amended by section 4 British Nationality Act 1965.

A person may be registered as: a British citizen; a BOTC; both of the former; or a BOC only. The requirements are more fully set out in the NIs at Chapter 40. The requirements for registration by reference to the British Nationality (No. 2) Act 1964, as amended by section 4 British Nationality Act 1965 are complicated. They are set out in the NIs at Chapter 15.

Section 14 **Information**

Useful addresses and telephone numbers   1493

Visa nationals and specified nationals   1507

Fees   1509

Entry clearance posts   1511

Work-related applications   1519

Commonwealth countries   1525

Registering with the police   1527

Countries whose adoption decisions are
recognised in the UK and Hague Convention
countries   1528

Abbreviations   1530

Other sources of information   1534

Glossary   1536

Alphabetical list of cases   1551

14

Useful addresses and telephone numbers

HOME OFFICE

Immigration and Nationality Directorate (IND)

General Enquiries
Lunar House
40 Wellesley Road
Croydon CR9 2BY
website: www.ind.homeoffice.gov.uk
tel   0870 606 7766

Applications accompanied by a payment should be sent to:
Initial Consideration Unit – [state type of form e.g. 'FLR (M)']
Immigration and Nationality Directorate
PO Box 3615
Walsall
Cannock WS11 0WS

For application forms:
tel   0870 241 0645

Asylum procedures
See Ch 22 for details of the various asylum processes operating throughout the UK.

SEFs must be submitted to:
Asylum Co-ordination Unit
PO Box 1234
Croydon CR9 1ZX

To book an appointment for an ARC to be issued:
Central Event Booking Unit
PO Box 222
Liverpool
L69 2TY

Nationality Directorate
3rd floor, India Buildings
Water Street, Liverpool L2 0QN
tel   0845 010 5200
fax   0151 237 5385
email enquiries to:

nationalityenquiries@ind.homeoffice.gsi.gov.uk

Complaints
IND Complaints Unit
PO Box 1384
Croydon CR9 3YJ
tel 0870 241 6523
fax 0208 760 4310
email: ind.cu@homeoffice.gsi.gov.uk

Complaints about conduct of a member of staff at:
IND: tel 0870 241 6523
Port or detention centre:
tel   020 8604 1822
Immigration Service operations:
020 8745 2350

Home Office Regional Public Enquiry Offices (PEOs)

Phone numbers to make appointment only

Croydon PEO
Lunar House
40 Wellesley Road
Croydon, CR9 2BY
tel   0870 606 7766

Birmingham Public Enquiry Office (PEO)
Dominion Court
41 Station Road
Solihull
Birmingham
B91 3RT
tel   0121 704 5450

Glasgow PEO
Festival Court
200 Brand Street
Govan, Glasgow
G51 1DH
tel   0141 555 1258

14

Liverpool PEO
Reliance House,
Water Street,
Liverpool L2 8XU
tel   0151 237 0405/73

WORK PERMITS (UK)

For general enquiries relating to Work
Permits, SAWS, HSMP and Sectors Based
Scheme write to
Customer Relations Team
Work Permits (UK)
PO Box 3468
Sheffield
tel   0114 259 4074
fax 0114 259 3776
website www.workingintheUK.gov.uk
email
wpcustomers@indhomeoffice.gsi.gov.uk

Submit work permit applications to:
Work Permits (UK)
PO Box 551
Heavens Walk
Doncaster Carr
Doncaster DN1 1XU
(►See 427 for faxing applications)

Submit (FLR(IED)) leave to remain
applications to:
Work Permits (UK) – FLR (IED)
Home Office
Walsall Road
Cannock WS11 0JA

Separate 'Business Teams' have been set up
to issue advice on business and commercial
work permit applications for employers. Full
details are contained in the *Business &
Commercial guidance note* on the Work
Permits UK website (above).

Separate 'Leave to Remain Teams' have
been set up to issue advice on in-country
leave to remain applications. Full details are
contained in the *Business & Commercial
guidance note* on the Work Permits UK
website (above).

Those who are pursuing or wish to request
a review of a work permit decision should
contact the:
Reviews Team
tel   0114 274 3188
fax 0114 274 3103

NATIONAL ASYLUM SUPPORT SERVICE

(►See also 1500–1 for voluntary sector
agencies)

Whitgift Centre
Block B
15 Wellesley Road
Croydon
CR9 1AT
tel   0845 602 1739 (general and
application enquiries)
tel   0845 600 0914 (sudden
termination/interruption of NASS support)
fax 020 8604 6842/020 8604 6795

NASS Regional Offices

Greater London
1st Floor, Quest House,
11 Cross Rd
Croydon CR9 6EL
tel   020 8633 0503
fax 020 8633 0896

South West
Unit 1, Greystoke Business Centre,
High Street,
Portishead,
Bristol, BS20 6PY
tel   01275 815300
fax 01275 815301

South East & Central
Units 4&6 Whitfield Court,
White Cliffs Business Park,
Honeywood Road,
Whitfield,
Dover CT16 3PX
tel   01304 873111
fax 01304 873133

East of England
Stuart House,
St John's Street,
Peterborough, PE1 1QF
tel   01733 847826
fax 01733 847800

East Midlands
Regus House,
Herald Way,
Pegasus Business Park,
Castle Donnington,
Derbyshire DE74 2TZ
tel   01332 638617
fax 01332 638290

West Midlands
NASS West Midlands,
3rd Floor Chadwick House,
Blenheim Court,
Warwick Road,
Solihull, B91 2AA
tel   0121 345 8000
fax 0121 345 8096/97

North West
PO Box 191,
Manchester Airport M90 3WZ
tel   0161 261 1307
fax 0161 261 1323

Yorkshire and Humberside
Waterside House,
Kirkstall Road,
Leeds LS4 2QB
tel   0113 386 5654
fax 0113 386 5700

North East
Rotterdam House,
116 Quayside House,
Newcastle, NE1 3DY
tel   0191 376 2856
fax 0191 206 4276

Wales
Room 216, Regus House,
Falcon Drive,
Cardiff Bay CF10 4RY
tel   02920 504001
fax 02920 504211

Scotland
c/o IS Scottish Enforcement Unit,
Festival Court,
200 Brand Street,
Glasgow G51 1DH
tel   0141 4191308
fax 0141 4191329

Northern Ireland
Room 514, 5th Floor,
Brookmount Buildings,
42 Fountain Street,
Belfast, BT1 2EE
tel   02870 251 999
fax 02890 547 835

NASS Complaints
PO Box 1384
Croydon CR9 3YT
Fax: 020 8760 8485

Home Office (Minister's Private Office)
3rd Floor Peel Building
2 Marsham Street
London
SW1P 4DF

IMMIGRATION SERVICE ENFORCEMENT UNITS
(some incorporated within Ports of Entry – see below)

Becket House
66–68 St Thomas' Street,
London SE1 3QU
tel   020 7238 1300
fax 020 7378 9107

Midlands Enforcement Unit
Sandford House
41 Homer Road,
Solihull, B91 3QT
tel   0121 606 7300
fax 0121 606 7325

North West Enforcement Unit
Units 1–2 Dallas Court
South Langworthy Road
Salford Quays
Salford, Manchester, M50 2GF
tel   0161 888 4100
fax 0161 888 4119

South East Ports Surveillance Team
Dover Hoverport
Dover, Kent
CT17 9TF
tel   01304 200 400
fax 01304 216 303

Eton House
581 Staines Road
Hounslow
TW4 5DL
tel   020 8814 5060
fax 020 8814 5345

PORTS OF ENTRY

Belfast International Airport
tel   02894 422500
fax 02894 459211

Birmingham International Airport
tel   0121 606 7350
fax 0121 782 0006

Bristol Airport
tel/fax 01275 472843

14

Cardiff Airport
tel   01446 710485
fax 01446 710606

Cheriton (Channel Tunnel)
tel   01303 282645
fax 01303 282610

City Airport (London)
tel   020 7474 1395
fax 020 7511 2363

Dover East Immigration
tel   01304 200400
fax 01304 216303

Dover Harbour Police Station
Detention Centre
tel   01304 216370
fax 01304 204316

East Midlands Airport
tel   01332 812000
fax 01332 817190

Edinburgh
tel   0131 344 3330
fax 0131 348 4029

Gatwick South Terminal
tel   01293 502019
fax 01293 501022

Gatwick North Terminal
tel   01293 507075
fax 01293 507097

Glasgow Airport
tel   0141 847 5300
fax 0141 887 1566

Harwich
tel   01255 509700
fax 01255 509718

Heathrow Terminal 1
tel   020 8745 6800
fax 020 8745 6828

Heathrow Terminal 2
tel   020 8745 6850
fax 020 8745 6867

Heathrow Terminal 3
tel   020 8745 6900
fax 020 8745 6943

Heathrow Terminal 4
tel   020 8745 4700
fax 020 8745 4705

Hull
tel   01482 577 342/343/344
fax 01482 577 350

Leeds
tel   0113 386 5680
fax 0113 386 5758

Liverpool
tel   0151 237 0444
fax 0151 237 0472

Luton
tel   01582 439030
fax 01582 405215

Manchester Airport Terminal 1
tel   0161 489 2653
fax 0161 489 2069

Manchester Airport Terminal 2
Tel   0161 489 6045/6232
Fax 0161 489 5779

Newcastle Aiport
tel   0191 214 2700
fax 0191 214 2707

Sheffield City Airport
tel   0114 201 5316
fax 0114 201 5317

Stansted Airport
tel   01279 680118
fax 01279 680145

Waterloo International Terminal
tel   020 7919 5916
fax 020 7919 5918

DETENTION CENTRES

Campsfield House
Langford Lane, Kiddlington,
Oxford, OX5 1RE
tel   01865 845700 (switchboard)
tel   01865 845 700 (detainees)
fax 01865 377723
Social visits 2pm–5pm, 6pm–9pm
Legal visits 9am–12pm, 1.30–5pm,
7pm–9pm

Dungavel Detention Centre
Dungavel House Immigration Centre
Strathaven
South Lanarkshire, ML10 6RF
tel   01698 395 000
fax 01698 395 067
Social visits: 1.30pm – 8.30pm
fax 9.30am – 9pm

Harmondsworth Detention Centre
Colnbrook Bypass
Longford, West Drayton
Middlesex UB7 0HB
tel   020 8283 3850

fax 020 8283 3851
Social visits 2pm–8.30pm
Legal visits 9am–9pm
(7 days a week)

Haslar Immigration Removal Centre
2 Dolphin Way, Gosport,
Hants PO12 2AW
tel 02392 604 000 (switchboard)
tel 02392 528 636 (immigration office)
fax 02392 604 001
Social and legal visits 2pm–4pm
Last admission 3.30pm
Thursday 9am-4pm (no access between
12.30pm-1.30pm)

Lindholme Removal Centre
Bawtry Road
Hatfield Woodhouse,
Doncaster DN7 6WZ
tel 01302 524666
fax 01302 848620
Social visits 9am-11.30am and
1.45–4.30pm (Mon-Fri)
1.45pm-4pm (Sat & Sun)
Legal visits Book a time in the morning or
afternoon except between
11.30am–1.45pm (Mon–Fri)

Tinsley House Detention Centre
Perimeter Road South
Gatwick Airport
West Sussex RH6 0PQ
tel 01293 434800
fax 01293 423221
Social visits 2pm–9pm (last admission 8.30)
Legal visits 9am–12.30pm, 2pm–9pm (last
admission 8.30)
Arrange by faxing letter in advance.
For a legal visit photo ID is required as well
as a copy of the fax which was sent for the
visit with names of all people attending

Yarls Wood Immigration Detention Centre
Twinwoods Road
Clapham
Bedfordshire MK41 6HL
tel 01234 821000
fax 01234 821196
Social visits 2pm–9pm
Legal visits 9am–9pm

HOME OFFICE PRESENTING OFFICERS AND JUDICIAL REVIEW
(for representatives at AIT appeal hearings
to contact prior to hearings)

Birmingham
1st Floor, 2308 Coventry Road,
Sheldon
Birmingham B26 3JS
tel 0121 700 1616
fax 0121 700 1696/1697/1694

Glasgow
10th Floor, Eagle Building
215 Bothwell Street, Glasgow G2 7ED
tel 0141 221 4218
fax 0141 204 5987

Hatton Cross
Hanover House, Plane Tree Crescent
Feltham, Middlesex TW13 7JJ
tel 020 8917 2039
fax 020 8890 6489

Leeds
2nd Floor, Springfield House,
76 Wellington Street, Leeds LS1 2AY
tel 0113 244 4205
fax 0113 245 3472

London
2nd floor, Building 1, Angel Square
1 Torrens Street, London EC1V 1NY
tel 020 7239 1701
fax 020 7239 1702/1616

Manchester
13th Floor West Point
501 Chester Road
Old Trafford
Manchester M16 9HU
tel 0161 261 0937
fax 0161 261 0980

Judicial Review Management Unit
Immigration and Nationality Directorate
Electric House
3 Wellesley Road
Croydon CR0 2AG

Treasury Solicitor
Queen Anne's Chambers
28 Broadway
London SW1H 9JS
tel 020 7210 3000
fax 020 7210 3397

14

COURTS

Royal Courts of Justice
Strand
London WC2A 2LL
tel 020 7947 6000
website www.hmcourts-service.gov.uk

ASYLUM AND IMMIGRATION TRIBUNAL

General queries
P. O. Box 6987
Leicester LE1 6ZX
tel 0845 600 0877
fax 0116 249 4130/1
website www.ait.gov.uk

Completed appeal forms and supporting
documentation should be sent to:
Asylum and Immigration Tribunal
P. O. Box 7866
Loughborough LE11 2XZ
fax 01509 221 699

APPEAL CENTRES

All calls have to go through the main AIT
number shown above

Birmingham
Sheldon Court
1 Wagon Lane
Birmingham B26 3DU

Bradford
Phoenix House
Rushton Avenue
Bradford, BD3 7BH

Bromley
Bromley Magistrates Court
1st Floor, 1 London Road,
Bromley
Kent BR1 1RA

Croydon
Croydon Magistrates Court
Barclay Road
Croydon
Surrey
CR9 3NG

Glasgow
4th floor, Eagle Building
215 Bothwell Street
Glasgow G2 7EZ

London
Taylor House
88 Rosebery Avenue
Islington, London EC1R 4QU

London
Field House
15 Bream's Buildings
London EC4A 1DZ
Tel 020 7073 4200

Hatton Cross
York House and Gloucester House
Duke's Green Avenue
Feltham
Middlesex TW14 0LS

Manchester
2 Piccadilly Plaza
Manchester M1 4AH

Newport
Columbus House
Chepstow Road
Langstone Business Park
Newport
Wales NP18 2LX

North Shields
Kings Court
Royal Quays
Earl Grey Way
North Shields NE29 6AR

Stoke
Bennett House
Town Road, Henley
Stoke-on-Trent ST1 2QB

Surbiton
Sessions House
17 Ewell Road
Surbiton
Surrey KT6 6AG

ASYLUM SUPPORT ADJUDICATORS

Christopher Wren House
113 High Street Croydon
CRO 1QG
tel 020 8588 2500
Freephone: 0800 389 7913
Fax: 020 8588 2519
www.asylum-support-adjudicators.org.uk

GOVERNMENT OFFICES

Department of Work and Pensions
Overseas Pensions Claim
Tyneview Park,
Whitley Road,
Benton,
Newcastle-upon-Tyne NE98 1BA
tel 0191 218 7777
website www.dwp.gov.uk

UK Visas

Foreign & Commonwealth Office
King Charles Street
London SW1A 2AH
tel 020 7008 8438 (general)
tel 020 7008 8308 (forms and leaflets)
fax 020 7008 8359
website www.ukvisas.gov.uk

Palace of Westminster

(House of Commons and House of Lords)
London SW1A 2PW
tel 020 7219 3000

Overseas Visitors' Records Office

Brandon House
180 Borough High Street,
London SE1 1LH
Metropolitan Police Service Information Line
020 7230 1208 (recorded information)

BRITISH HIGH COMMISSIONS AND EMBASSIES ABROAD

A full list of embassies and high
commissions with telephone, fax, email and
address contact details on the Foreign &
Commonwealth Office (FCO) website at
www.fco.gov.uk Click on *Directory / UK
Embassies overseas.*

Or telephone UK Visas
tel 020 7008 8438 (general)

ADVICE

▶See 62–3 for further details

England and Wales

Approved private solicitors' firms and not-
for-profit sector advice agencies that supply
legally aided immigration advice
Community Legal Service (CLS)
CLS Directory Call Centre
tel 0845 608 1122
website www.clsdirect.org.uk

Northern Ireland

Solicitors that operate the legal aid scheme
(not immigration specifically):
Northern Ireland Legal Services Commission
website www.nilsc.org.uk

Scotland

Solicitors' firms (not approved but usually
able to apply for legal aid funding):
The Law Society of Scotland
tel 0131 226 7411 (Records dept)
website www.lawscot.org.uk

Non-solicitor agencies

The OISC has a list of all non-solicitor
advisers (both private and not-for profit)
throughout the UK who are approved by
them to give out immigration advice. For
details:

OISC website www.oisc.org.uk
OISC helpline 0845 000 0046
Address (see immediately below)

Asylum Aid

Advice line 020 7247 8741 (Monday
afternoons and Thursday mornings)
28 Commercial Street,
London E1 6LS
tel 020 7377 5123
fax 020 7247 7789
email info@asylumaid.org.uk
website www.asylumaid.org.uk

Asylum Support Appeal Project (ASAP)

Cornerstone House
14 Willis Road
Croydon CR0 2XX

Citizens Advice

Citizens Advice bureaux (CABs) across the
UK offer advice on a wide range of issues.
Details of the various CABs can be obtained
from the CLS directory (see above) or from
the Citizens Advice main office:
Myddleton House
115–123 Pentonville Road
London N1 9LZ
tel 020 7833 2181
fax 020 7833 4371
website www.citizensadvice.org.uk

Immigration Advisory Service (IAS)

IAS has regional offices across the UK listed
below. They also have local surgeries that
operate from these offices. Full contact
details can be obtained from IAS's Head
Office (details below).
Or from their website www.iasuk.org
Or emailing them advice@ias.org

Head office (and central London office)
3rd Floor,
County House,
190 Great Dover Street,
London SE1 4YB
tel 020 7967 1200
fax 020 7403 5875

Regional IAS offices:
Birmingham
Bradford
Cardiff

14

Derby
Glasgow
Ebury, Hounslow
Hounslow Central
Leeds
Leicester
Liverpool
Manchester
Middlesbrough
Norwich
Oakington
Peterborough

Refugee Legal Centre (RLC)
Advice line 020 7780 3220 (9.30am to 4pm, closed 1–2pm, Monday, Tuesday, Wednesday and Friday)
Detention line 0800 592 398
The above lines are open from 9.30am to 4pm, closed 1-2pm, on Mondays, Tuesdays, Wednesdays and Fridays)
Removals outside hours: 07831 598 057 (6pm to 9am)

RLC provides legal advice for asylum-seekers at its offices in
London
Leeds
Dover
Contact the London office for details:
Nelson House
153–157 Commercial Road, London E1 2DA
tel   020 7780 3200 (administration)
tel   07831 598 057 (emergencies)
fax 020 7780 3201
email rlc@refugee-legal-centre.org.uk
website www.refugee-legal-centre.org.uk

COMPLAINTS ABOUT ADVISERS

Office of the Immigration Services Commissioner (OISC)
5th floor, Counting House
53 Tooley Street, London SE1 2QN

tel   020 7211 1500
fax 020 7211 1553

Complaints about solicitors in England and Wales only
The Law Society Consumer Complaints Service
Victoria Court, 8 Dormer Place,
Leamington Spa
Warwickshire CV32 5AE
tel   0845 608 6565

Solicitors in Scotland only
Law Society of Scotland
Client Relations Office
26 Drumsheugh Gardens
Edinburgh, EH3 7YR
tel   0131 476 8137

Solicitors in Northern Ireland only
Law Society of Northern Ireland
98 Victoria Street
Belfast BT1 3JZ
tel   028 90 23 16 14

Complaints about barristers
Write to:
The Complaints Department
General Council of the Bar
289 - 293 High Holborn
London WC1V 7HZ
tel   020 7242 0082
A complaints form can be downloaded from: www.barcouncil.org.uk

ACCOMMODATION AND SUPPORT FOR ASYLUM-SEEKERS
The following voluntary sector agencies are contracted to NASS to provide emergency accommodation and induction services across the UK. They can also provide initial advice and support to asylum-seekers.

Migrant Helpline
One stop services in Dover, Folkestone, Gravesend, Brighton, Hastings, Margate. Emergency accommodation in Kent and South London.
Contact main offices for contact details:
The Rendezous Building, Eastern Docks
Freight Services Approach Road
Dover
Kent CT16 1JA
tel   01304 203 977
fax 01304 203 995

45 Friends Road
Croydon
Surrey CD0 1ED
tel   020 8774 0002
fax 020 8774 0003

North of England Refugee Service
One stop services in the North East. Offices in Middlesbrough, Newcastle and Sunderland. Contact main office:
2 Jesmond Rd West
Newcastle upon Tyne NE2 4PQ
tel   0191 245 7311
fax 0191 245 7320
email info@refugee.org.uk
website refugee.org.uk

Northern Ireland Council for Ethnic Minorities (NICEM)
One-stop service, advice and support
3rd Floor
Ascot House
24-31 Shaftesbury Square
Belfast BT2 7DB
tel   028 9023 8645 / 028 9031 9666
tel   028 9024 2025 (24 hours emergency enquires only)
fax 028 9031 9485
info@nicem.org.uk
website www.nicem .org.uk

Refugee Action
One-stop, advice and reception services in Bristol, Leicester, Liverpool, London, Manchester, Nottingham and Plymouth. Contact head office for details:

The Old Fire Station
150 Waterloo Road
London SE1 8SB
tel   020 7654 7700
fax 020 7401 3699
website www.refugee-action.org.uk

Refugee Arrivals Project
Emergency accommodation and reception services at Heathrow, Gatwick, Stansted and Luton airports.
Contact main office for details:
41b Cross Lances Rd,
Hounslow, TW3 2AD
tel   020 8607 6888
fax 020 8607 6851

Heathrow Airport reception office
tel   (9.30am to 10pm) 020 8759 5740
fax 020 8759 7058
website www.refugee-arrivals.org.uk

Refugee Council
Emergency accommodation and one stop services in London, Birmingham, Leeds and Ipswich. Contact head office for details:
3 Bondway
London SW8 1SJ
tel   020 7820 3000
info 020 7820 3085
fax 020 7582 9929
email info@refugeecouncil.org.uk
website www.refugeecouncil.org.uk

The Refugee Council also provides support and advice for unaccompanied asylum-seeking children (▶see 688).

The Panel of Advisers for Unaccompanied Refugee Children
Refugee Council
240–250 Ferndale Road
Brixton
London SW9 5BB
tel   020 7346 1134
fax 020 7346 1140

Scottish Refugee Council
Support and advice services in Glasgow and Edinburgh.
Contact head office for details:
5 Cadogan Square
(170 Blythswood Court)
Glasgow G2 7PH
tel   0141 248 9799
freephone 0800 085 6087
fax 0141 243 2499

Welsh Refugee Council
Support and advice services in Cardiff, Swansea, Newport and Wrexham
Phoenix House
389 Newport Road
Cardiff CF24 1TP
tel   02920 489800
fax 02920 432980
email info@welshrefugeecouncil.org

UK NON-GOVERNMENTAL ORGANISATIONS

AIRE Centre (Advice on Individual Rights in Europe)
Advice line 020 7831 3850

3rd Floor, 17 Red Lion Square,
London WC1R 4QH
tel   020 7831 4276
fax 020 7404 7760
email info@airecentre.org
website www.airecentre.org.uk

Amnesty International UK
17-25 New Inn Yard
London EC2A 3EA
tel   020 7033 1500
fax 020 7033 1503
email info@amnesty.org.uk
website www.amnesty.org.uk

Anti-Slavery International
Thomas Clarkson House
The Stableyard
Broomgrove Road
London
tel   020 7501 8920
website www.antislavery.org

14

Association of Visitors to Immigration Detainees (AVID)
Coordinator
Box 7
Oxted RH8 0YT
tel/fax 01883 717 275
email avid.helenireland@btinternet.com
website www.aviddetention.org.uk

Asylum Rights Campaign
46 Francis Street,
London SW1P 1QN
tel 020 7798 7027
fax 020 7798 9010

Bail for Immigration Detainees (BID)
28 Commercial Street
London E1 6LS
tel 020 7247 3590
fax 020 7247 3550
email
bailforimmigrationdetainees@yahoo.co.uk

Bosnian Information & Refugee Centre
60–62 Mill Lane
London NW6 1NJ
tel 020 7433 3834

British Agencies for Adoption and Fostering (BAAF)
Skyline House, 200 Union Street
London SE1 0LX
tel 020 7593 2000
fax 020 7593 2001
email mail@baaf.org.uk
website www.baaf.org.uk

British Red Cross
See below

Child Poverty Action Group (CPAG)
(welfare benefits training)
94 White Lion St.
London N1 9PF
tel 020 7837-7979
fax 020 7837-6414

Children's Legal Centre
University of Essex
Wivenhoe Park
Colchester
Essex CO4 3SQ
Education advice line 0845 345 4345
Info line 0845 120 3747
admin 01206 872466
fax 01206 874026
email clc@essex.ac.uk
website www.childrenslegalcentre.com

Chinese Information Advice Centre
104-108 Oxford Street
London W1D 1LP
tel 020 7323 1538
fax 020 7436 7108
www.ciac.co.uk

Commission for Racial Equality
St Dunstan's House
201-211 Borough High Street
London, SE1 1GZ
tel 020 7939 0000
fax 020 7930 0001
email info@cre.gov.uk
website www.cre.gov.uk

Detention Advice Service
Unit B3, 62 Beechwood Road
London E8 3DY
tel 020 7254 6888
fax 020 7254 8555
email: das@detentionadvice.org.uk
website: www.detentionadvice.org.uk

East European Advice Centre
Room 209, Palingswick House
241 King Street
London W6 9LP
tel 020 8741 1288
fax 020 8741 8388
email info@eeac.gov.uk

Educational Grants Advisory Service
501–505 Kingsland Road
London E8 4AU
tel 020 7254 6251
fax 020 7249 5443
email egasenquiry@fwa.org.uk
www.fwa.org.uk

Education Action International (RETAS)
Advice on employment and training for asylum-seekers and refugees
Office in Leeds also
Advice line: 020 7426 5801
(Tue/Thu 2:30pm-5pm)
14 Dufferin Street
London EC1Y 8PD
tel 020 7426 5800
email info@education-action.org

Electronic Immigration Network
The Progress Centre
Charlton Place
Ardwick Green
Manchester M12 6HS
tel 0161 273 7515/0845 458 4151
fax 0161 274 3159/0845 458 0051
email info@ein.org.uk
website www.ein.org.uk

Foundation for Public Service Interpreting
1 St Clements Court
London EC4N 7HB
tel 020 7623 9191
fax 020 7283 3678
website www.nisuk.co.uk
Free Representation Unit
6th Floor, 289-293 High Holborn
London WC1V 7HZ
tel 020 7611 9555
fax 020 7611 9551

Gatwick Detainees Welfare Group
225 Three Bridges Road
Three Bridges
Crawley RH10 1LG
tel 01293 434 350
Freephone for detainees at Tinsley House
Detention Centre 0800 389 4367
fax 01293 434 351
email
GDWG@gatwickdetainees.freeserve.co.uk

Greater Manchester Immigration Aid Unit
1 Delaunays Road
Crumpsall Green
M8 4QS
tel 0161 740 7722
fax 0161 740 5172
email gmiau@ein.org.uk

Haslar Visitors Group
All Saints Centre
Commercial Road
Portsmouth PO1 4BT
tel/fax 0239 283 9222
email
mw@haslarvisitors.org.uk/coordinator@hasl
arvisitors.org.uk

Human Rights Watch
2nd floor, 2-12 Pentonville Road
London N1 9HF
tel 020 7713 1995
fax 020 7713 1800
email hrwuk@hrw.org
website www.hrw.org

**Immigration Law Practitioners'
Association (ILPA)**
Lindsey House
40/42 Charterhouse Street
London EC1M 6JN
tel 020 7251 8383
fax 020 7251 8384
email info@ilpa.org.uk
website www.ilpa.org.uk

Institute of Race Relations
2–6 Leeke Street
London WC1X 9HS
tel 020 7837 0041/020 7833 2010
fax 020 7278 0623
email info@irr.org.uk
website www.irr.org.uk

Interights
Lancaster House
33 Islington High Street
London N1 9LH
tel 020 7278 3230
fax 020 7278 4334
email ir@interights.org
website www.interights.org

International Social Service of UK
Cranmer House
39 Brixton Road
London SW9 6DD
tel 020 7735 8941
fax 020 7582 0696
email mark.issuk@btopenworld.com

Justice
59 Carter Lane
London EC4V 5AQ
tel 020 7329 5100
fax 020 7329 5055
email admin@justice.org.uk
website www.justice.org.uk

Kalayaan
St Francis Centre
Pottery Lane
London W11 4NQ
tel 020 7243 2942
fax 020 7792 3060

Law For All
PO Box 230
Brentford, TW8 9FL
tel 020 8758 0668
fax 020 8758 0669
email info@lawforall.org.uk

Legal Action Group
242 Pentonville Road
London N1 9UN
tel 020 7833 2931
fax 020 7837 6094
email lag@lag.org.uk
website www.lag.org.uk

Liberty
National Council for Civil Liberties
21 Tabard Street,
London SE1 4LA
tel 020 7403 3888
fax 020 7407 5354

14

email info@liberty-human-rights.org.uk
website www.liberty-human-rights.org.uk

London Advice Services Alliance
(Welfare benefits training in London)
LASA, Universal House
88/94 Wentworth St
London E1 7SA
tel   020 7377 9981
fax 020 7247 4725
email info@lasa.org.uk

London Detainee Support Group
77 Holloway Road
London N7 8JZ
tel   020 7700 0606
fax 020 7700 4433
email ldsg@lineone.net

Medical Foundation for the Care of Victims of Torture
111 Isledon Road
London N7 7JW
tel   020 7697 7777
fax 020 7697 7799
website www.torturecare.org.uk

Midlands Refugee Council
5th Floor Smithfield House
Digbeth
Birmingham B5 6BS
tel   0121 622 1515
fax 0121 622 4061
email info@refugeecouncil.org.uk

Migrants Resource Centre
24 Churton Street
London SW1V 2LP
tel   020 7834 6650
fax 020 7931 8187
email info@migrants.org.uk

Minority Rights Group
54 Commercial Street
London E1 6LT
tel   020 7422 4200
fax 020 7422 4201
email minority.rights@mrgmail.org
website www.minorityrights.org

National Coalition of Anti-Deportation Campaigns
110 Hamstead Road
Birmingham B20 2QS
tel   0121 554 6947
fax 0870 055 4570
email ncadc@ncadc.org.uk
website www.ncadc.org.uk

National Union of Students
2nd Floor, Centro 3
Mandela Street
London NW1 0DU
tel   0871 221 8221
fax 0871 221 8222
email nusuk@nusuk.org.uk
website www.nusonline.co.uk

Praxis
Pott Street
London E2 0EF
tel   020 7729 7985
fax 020 7729 0134
email admin@praxis.org.uk
website: www.praxis.org.uk

Royal College of Nursing Immigration Advice Service
20 Cavendish Square
London W1G 0RN
tel   020 7647 3874
email immigation.advice@rcn.org.uk
website www.rcn.org.uk

Runnymede Trust
Suite 106
The London Fruit and Wool Exchange
Brushfield Street
London E1 6EP
tel   0207 377 9222
fax 0207 377 6622
website www.runnymedetrust.org

Shelter
88 Old Street
London EC1V 9HU
tel   020 7490 6720
fax 020 7490 4844
website www.shelter.org.uk

Terrence Higgins Trust (THT)
THT has offices and advice centres across England and Wales. Details can be obtained from their national office:
52-54 Grays Inn Road
London WC1X 8JU
tel   020 7831 0330
fax 020 7242 0121
email info@tht.org.uk

UKCOSA (The Council for International Education)
Advice for international students wishing to study in the UK.
9–17 St Albans Place
London N1 0NX
tel   020 7288 4330
fax 020 7288 4360
website www.ukcosa.org.uk

UK Lesbian & Gay Immigration Group
(formerly Stonewall Immigration Group)
Advice line 020 7620 6010
P O Box 51524
London SE1 7ZW
email admin@uklgig.org.uk
website www.uklgig.org.uk

EUROPEAN AND INTERNATIONAL ORGANISATIONS

British Red Cross
60 offices across UK – contact freephone
no. below.
International Tracing and Message Service
UK Office
9 Grosvenor Crescent
London SW1X 7EJ
Freephone 0800 169 2030
website www.redcross.org.uk

International Labour Organisation (ILO)
Migration Branch
4 route des Morillons
CH-1211 Geneva 22
Switzerland
tel +41-22-7997854
fax +41-22-7916480
website www.ilo.org

International Organisation for Migration (IOM)
21 Westminster Palace Gardens
Artillery Row
London SW1P 1RR
Freephone 0800 783 2332
tel 020 7233 0001
fax 020 7233 2001
website www.iomlondon.org

Platform for International Cooperation on Undocumented Migrants (PICUM)
Gaucheretstraat 164
1030 Brussels
Belgium
tel + 32 (2) 274.14.39
fax + 32 (2) 274.14.48

December 18
Attention Ms Myriam De Feyter
Postbus 22
B–9820 Merelbeke (Belgium)
fax 0032 (9) 351.97.62
email info@december18.net
website www.december18.net

United Nations High Commission for Refugees
The Office of the Representative for the UK
Strand Bridge House
138–142 Strand
London WC2R 1HH
tel 020 7759 8090
fax 020 7759 8119
website www.unhcr.ch

STATUTORY INDEPENDENT REVIEW BODIES

Advisory Panel on Country Information (APCI)
PO Box 1539
Croydon CR9 3WR
email APCI@homeoffice.gsi.gov.uk

Parliamentary Ombudsman
For making a complaint and telephone
details, ▶see 1229 onwards
The Parliamentary and Health Service
Ombudsman
Millbank Tower
Millbank
London SW1P 4QP
fax 020 7217 4000
website www.ombudsman.org.uk

FREEDOM OF INFORMATION

Work Permits (UK)
Freedom of Information Team
PO Box 3468
Sheffield S3 8WA
fax 0114 207 4311
email freedomofinformation.workpermits@
ind.homeoffice.gsi.gov.uk.

Home Office
Information Access Manager
Record Management Service
Home Office
fax 020 7273 3592
email info.access@homeoffice.gsi.gov.uk

Home Office
Data Protection Act requests:
Immigration and Nationality Directorate
Subject Access Bureau
10th Floor, Sunley House
Bedford Park
Croydon CR0 2AP

Information Commissioner
Wycliffe House
Water Lane
Wilmslow
Cheshire SK9 5AP

14

Visa nationals and specified nationals

VISA NATIONALS

Visa nationals are people who always need to get entry clearance in advance of travelling to the UK, for whatever purpose. Countries whose citizens are visa nationals include (Appendix 1 HC 395, current at November 2005):

Afghanistan
Albania
Algeria
Angola
Armenia
Azerbaijan
Bahrain
Bangladesh
Belarus
Benin
Bhutan
Bosnia Herzegovina
Bulgaria
Burkina Faso
Burma
Burundi
Cambodia
Cameroon
Cape Verde
Central African Republic
Chad
China (except Hong Kong and Macao)
Colombia
Comoros
Congo
Republic of Croatia

Cuba
Democratic Republic of the Congo
Djibouti
Dominican Republic
Ecuador
Egypt
Equatorial Guinea
Eritrea
Ethiopia
Fiji
Gabon
Gambia
Georgia
Ghana
Guinea
Guinea Bissau
Guyana
Haiti
India
Indonesia
Iran
Iraq
Ivory Coast
Jamaica
Jordan
Kazakhstan

Kenya
Korea (North)
Kuwait
Kyrgyzstan
Laos
Lebanon
Liberia
Libya
Macedonia
Madagascar
Mali
Mauritania
Moldova
Mongolia
Morocco
Mozambique
Nepal
Niger
Nigeria
Oman
Pakistan
Peru
Philippines
Qatar
Romania
Russia
Rwanda
Sao Tome e Principe

Saudi Arabia
Senegal
Sierra Leone
Somalia
Sri Lanka
Sudan
Surinam
Syria
Taiwan
Tajikistan
Tanzania
Thailand
Togo
Tunisia
Turkey
Turkmenistan
Uganda
Ukraine
United Arab Emirates
Uzbekistan
Vietnam
Yemen
Zambia
Zimbabwe
Yugoslav former territories

14

The following are also visa nationals: persons who hold passports or travel documents issued by the former Soviet Union or by the former Socialist Federal Republic of Yugoslavia; stateless persons; persons who hold 'non-national documents'.

SPECIFIED NATIONALS

Specified nationals who are coming to the UK for more than six months must now have an entry clearance. From 13 November 2005, all foreign nationals coming to the UK for more than six months must obtain entry clearance (▶see 81–2).

Fees

The following list contains a selection of fees. The Home Office or UK Visas may raise fees at very short notice. It is advisable to check the current fees with them.

Applying to the Home Office for leave to remain

The Home Office introduced charging for leave to remain applications in April 2003. The fees were again revised for applications from 1 April 2005 as follows:

£335   all postal applications

£250   student postal applications only

£160   postal applications for transferring leave and endorsing No Time Limit stamps into new passports

£500   personal callers ('premium service)

▶See 126–7 for those who are exempt from paying the new fees.

Applying to the Home Office for nationality purposes

Fees for nationality applications were revised on 1 April 2005.

£268   naturalisation (includes ceremony fee)

£336   naturalisation (joint applications for those who are married) (includes two separate ceremony fees)

£188   registration for adults (includes ceremony fee)

£200   registration for minors (single applications and multiple applications by siblings)

£34   'Life in the UK' test fee. For a list of those who are exempt from the test, ▶see 1469. Those below ESOL entry level 3 have to undertake a language/citizenship course instead of the 'Life in the UK' test (▶see 1468).

Applying to the Home Office for travel documents

£42   Refugee Convention travel document (£25 for children under 16)

£42   Stateless Persons' document

£195   Certificate of Identity (£115 for children under 16)

For British passport applications, contact the UK Passport Service on 0871 521 0410 or see their website www.ukpa.gov.uk.

Applying to Work Permits (UK)

Work Permits (UK) charges a fee for applications for Immigration Employment Documents (IEDs). IEDs include various types of work permits (including Training and Work Experience

Scheme permits), Sectors Based Scheme permits and Seasonal Agricultural Scheme work cards. ▶See 418–20 for more details.

£153   IED

£315   Highly Skilled Migrant Scheme (HSMP)

A separate fee is payable for those in the UK applying for leave to remain (see above, £315 postal and £500 'premium' applications). Those applying from abroad will also have to pay a separate fee for entry clearance (see below).

Further guidance is available from Work Permits (UK) (▶see 420–1 for details on making general enquiries).

Applying abroad for entry clearance

All entry clearance fees are non-refundable and are usually payable in local currency. Check the fees with the local British embassy, consulate or high commission.

Visitors

£50	valid for six months
£85	valid up to ten years
£30	transit DAT

Settlement

£260	to accompany or join a relative settled in the UK, including spouses and fiancées
free	EEA/Swiss permit

Other

£85	other entry clearance applications, including those applying as a student or for work purposes
£85	certificate of entitlement

Entry clearance posts

Some British high commissions and embassies abroad are designated to offer a full entry clearance service and some only a partial service, mainly for diplomatic/official, medical and business visit visa, and refugee family reunion only.

Up-to-date details are available from UK Visas (▶see 1499 for details).

The following list was issued on 20 May 2004 and can be found in the DSPs at Volume 1, Annex 1.4:

A. Full entry clearance service

The following posts have been designated to offer a full entry clearance service:

Country	Post	Country	Post
Albania	Tirana	Colombia	Bogota
Angola	Luanda	Congo, Democratic Republic of	Kinshasa
Argentina	Buenos Aires		
Armenia	Yerevan	Croatia	Zagreb
Australia	Canberra	Cuba	Havana
Austria	Vienna	Cyprus	Nicosia
Bahrain	Bahrain	Czech Republic	Prague
Bangladesh*	Dhaka	Denmark	Copenhagen
Barbados	Bridgetown	Dominican Republic	Santo Domingo
Belarus	Minsk	Ecuador	Quito
Belgium	Brussels	Egypt	Cairo
Bolivia	La Paz	Eritrea	Asmara
Bosnia & Herzegovina	Sarajevo	Estonia	Tallinn
		Ethiopia	Addis Ababa
Botswana	Gaborone	Falkland Islands	Stanley (Falkland Islands Dept of Immigration)
Brazil	Rio de Janeiro		
Brunei	Bandar Seri Begawan		
		Fiji	Suva
Bulgaria	Sofia	Finland	Helsinki
Burma/Myanmar	Rangoon	France	Paris
Cameroon	Yaoundé	Gambia, The	Banjul
Canada	Ottawa	Germany	Dusseldorf
Chile	Santiago	Ghana	Accra
China	Beijing	Gibraltar	Gibraltar (Dept of Immigration)
" "	Shanghai		
" "	Guangzhou	Greece	Athens
" "	Hong Kong SAR	Hungary	Budapest

14

Country	Post	Country	Post
Iceland	Reykjavik	Philippines	Manila
India**	New Delhi	Poland	Warsaw
" "	Mumbai (Bombay)	Portugal	Lisbon
		Qatar	Doha
" "	Kolkata (Calcutta)	Romania	Bucharest
" "	Chennai (Madras)	Russian Federation	Moscow
		" "	St Petersburg
Indonesia	Jakarta	" "	Ekaterinburg
Iran	Tehran	Saudi Arabia	Jedda
Irish Republic	Dublin	" "	Riyadh
Israel	Tel Aviv	Senegal	Dakar
Italy	Rome	Serbia and Montenegro	Belgrade
Jamaica	Kingston		
Japan	Tokyo	Seychelles	Victoria
Jordan	Amman	Sierra Leone	Freetown
Kenya	Nairobi	Singapore	Singapore***
Korea (South)	Seoul	Slovak Republic	Bratislava
Kuwait	Kuwait	Solomon Islands	Honiara
Latvia	Riga	South Africa	Pretoria
Lebanon	Beirut	Spain	Madrid
Libya	Tripoli	Sri Lanka	Colombo
Lithuania	Vilnius	Sudan	Khartoum
Luxembourg	Luxembourg	Swaziland	Mbabane
Macedonia	Skopje	Sweden	Stockholm
Madagascar	Antananarivo	Switzerland	Geneva
Malawi	Lilongwe	Tanzania	Dar es Salaam
Malaysia	Kuala Lumpur	Thailand	Bangkok
Malta	Valletta	Tonga	Nuku'alofa
Mauritius	Port Louis	Trinidad and Tobago	Port of Spain
Mexico	Mexico City		
Mongolia	Ulaanbaatar	Tunisia	Tunis
Mozambique	Maputo	Turkmenistan	Ashgabat
Namibia	Windhoek	Uganda****	Kampala
Nepal	Kathmandu	Ukraine	Kiev
Netherlands	Amsterdam	UAE	Abu Dhabi
New Zealand	Wellington	" "	Dubai
Nigeria	Abuja	United States	Chicago
" "	Lagos	" "	Los Angeles
		" "	New York
Norway	Oslo	Uruguay	Montevideo
Oman	Muscat	Vanuatu	Port Vila
Palestine	Jerusalem	Venezuela	Caracas
Panama	Panama City	Vietnam	Hanoi
Papua New Guinea	Port Moresby	Zambia	Lusaka
Peru	Lima	Zimbabwe*****	Harare

* Applications are accepted at Visa Application Centre in Sylhet.

** Applications are accepted at Visa Application Centres in Ahmedabad, Bangalore, Cochin, Chandigarh, Chennai, Hyderabad, Jalandhar, Kolkata, Mumbai, New Delhi and Pune.

*** Applications are accepted at the Visa Application Centre in Singapore.

**** Applications are accepted at the Visa Application Centre in Kampala.

***** Applications are accepted at the Visa Application Centres in Harare, Bulawayo, Mutare, Gwen and Victoria Falls.

B: Limited service (diplomats & officials only)

The following posts are designated to offer a limited service to members of the Diplomatic and Consular Corps (including International Organisations) there and officials of the host country. Other applicants for visit visas may apply at *any* designated post (see list A above). Applicants for other categories of visa should apply at the designated post stipulated:

Country	Post	Other visa categories
Brazil	Brasilia	Rio de Janeiro
Cambodia	Phnom Penh	Bangkok
Germany	Berlin	Dusseldorf
Morocco	Rabat	Casablanca
Rwanda	Kigali	Kampala
Switzerland	Berne	Geneva

C: Limited service (others)

The following posts have been designated to offer a limited entry clearance service as indicated:

Country	Post	
Algeria	Algiers	Closed to personal callers. Restricted service for some categories. Applications are accepted by an agency.
Azerbaijan	Baku	Accepts only applications from Azeri nationals, diplomats, officials, and third country nationals resident in Azerbaijan. Other visa applications should be made in Moscow.
Georgia	Tbilisi	Only accepts applications from Georgian nationals; diplomats; officials of international organisations; third country nationals resident in Georgia for longer than six months.
Kazakhstan	Almaty	Accepts applications from nationals and residents of Kazakhstan and Kyrgyzstan. Other applicants should apply at the appropriate designated post (see list A).
Morocco	Tangier	Accepts applications for entry into Gibraltar only. Other applicants should apply at Casablanca.
Morocco	Casablanca	Closed to personal callers pending a move to a more suitable location. Applications can be made via drop box.
Pakistan	Islamabad	A limited service is operating, only through a courier service available in Islamabad, Mirpur (AK), Sialkot, Multan, Karachi, Hyderabad, Peshawar, Lahore, Faisalabad, Gujranwala and Quetta.

14

Syria	Damascus	Closed to personal callers. All applications must be submitted at the DHL office, Queen's Centre, Mezze.
Taiwan	BTCO Taipei	Accepts visit/student/business visa applications from Taiwanese nationals. Other categories of applicant should apply at any designated post.
Turkey	Ankara & Istanbul	Closed to personal callers. Limited interviewing capacity. Applications must be made through agents or by mail/courier.
Uzbekistan	Tashkent	Accepts applications from nationals resident in Uzbekistan for over six months. Also from resident diplomats and representatives of international organisations. Other applicants should apply at the appropriate designated post (see list A above).
Yemen	Sana'a	Closed to personal callers. Limited postal service in co-operation with FedEx offices throughout Yemen.

D: British posts not designated to offer an entry clearance service

Applicants for visit visas may apply at *any* designated post (see list A above). Applicants for other categories of visa should apply to the designated post stipulated:

Country	Post	Apply at
Afghanistan	Kabul	Islamabad or Dubai
Australia	Adelaide	Canberra
" "	Brisbane	Canberra
" "	Melbourne	Canberra
" "	Perth	Canberra
" "	Sydney	Canberra
Bahamas	Nassau	New York
Belize	Belmopan	New York
Bermuda	Hamilton	New York
Bhutan	(none)	Kolkata
Bosnia & Herzegovina	Banja Luka	Sarajevo
Brazil	Sao Paulo	Rio de Janeiro
Cameroon	Douala	Yaounde
Canada	Montreal	Ottawa
" "	Toronto	Ottawa
" "	Vancouver	Ottawa
" "	Calgary	Ottawa
Cayman Islands	Georgetown	Kingston
China	Chongqing	Any other Chinese post
Cost Rica	San Jose	New York
East Timor	Dili	Jakarta

Ecuador	Guauquil	Quito
Egypt	Alexandria	Cairo
France	Bordeaux	Paris
" "	Lille	Paris
" "	Lyon	Paris
" "	Marseille	Paris
" "	Strasbourg	Paris
Germany	Frankfurt	Dusseldorf
" "	Hamburg	Dusseldorf
" "	Leipzig	Dusseldorf
" "	Munich	Dusseldorf
" "	Stuttgart	Dusseldorf
Greece	Corfu	Athens
" "	Heraklion (Crete)	Athens
" "	Thessaloniki	Athens
Guatemala	Guatemala City	New York
Holy See	Rome	Rome
Iraq	Baghdad	Amman
Italy	Florence	Rome
" "	Milan	Rome
" "	Naples	Rome
Japan	Osaka	Tokyo
" "	Nagoya	Tokyo
" "	Fukuoka	Tokyo
Korea (North)	Pyongyang	Beijing
Lesotho	Maseru	Pretoria
Mexico	Guadalajara	Mexico City
" "	Monterrey	Mexico City
Moldova	Chisinau	Bucharest
Netherlands	The Hague	Amsterdam
New Zealand	Auckland	Wellington
Nicaragua	Managua	New York
Paraguay	Asuncion	Rio de Janeiro
Portugal	Oporto	Lisbon
Saudi Arabia	Al Khobar	Riyadh
Serbia & Montenegro	Pristina, Kosovo	Belgrade
Slovenia	Ljubljana	Zagreb
South Africa	CapeTown	Pretoria

14

" "	Durban	Pretoria
" "	Johannesburg	Pretoria
Spain	Alicante	Madrid
" "	Barcelona	Madrid
" "	Bilbao	Madrid
" "	Ibiza	Madrid
" "	Las Palmas	Madrid
" "	Malaga	Madrid
" "	Santa Cruz de Tenerife	Madrid
" "	Seville	Madrid
Sweden	Gothenburg	Stockholm
Tajikistan	Dushanbe	Tashkent
Turkey	Antalya	Istanbul or Ankara
" "	Izmir	Istanbul or Ankara
United States	Atlanta	New York
" "	Boston	New York
" "	Dallas	Los Angeles
" "	Denver	Los Angeles
" "	Houston	Los Angeles
" "	Miami	New York
" "	Orlando	New York
" "	Puerto Rico	New York
" "	San Francisco	Los Angeles
" "	Seattle	Los Angeles
" "	Washington	New York
Vietnam	Ho Chi Minh City	Hanoi
Yemen	Aden	Sana'a

*ECO Bridgetown visits the following islands periodically.

Anguilla	Anguilla	Bridgetown*
Antigua & Barbuda	St John's	Bridgetown*
British Virgin Islands	Tortola	Bridgetown*
Commonwealth of Dominica	Roseau	Bridgetown*
Grenada	St George's	Bridgetown*
Montserrat	Plymouth	Bridgetown*
St Kitts and Nevis	Basseterre	Bridgetown*
St Lucia	Castries	Bridgetown*
St Vincent & the Grenadines	Kingstown	Bridgetown*

E: British diplomatic/consular representation – non-resident

Country	Apply at
Andorra	Madrid
Benin	Lagos
Burkina Faso	Abidjan
Cape Verde	Dakar
Central African Republic	Yaoundé
Chad	Lagos or Abuja
Comoros	Antananarivo
Congo	Kinshasa
Djibouti	Addis Ababa
Dominica	Bridgetown
El Salvador	Panama City
Equatorial Guinea	Yaoundé or most accessible post
Gabon	Yaoundé or most accessible post
Guinea	Dakar
Guinea Bissau	Dakar
Haiti	Santo Domingo
Honduras	Panama City
Kiribati	Suva
Kyrgyzstan	Almaty
Laos	Bangkok
Liberia	Abidjan
Liechtenstein	Geneva
Macau	Hong Kong
Mali	Dakar
Marshall Islands	Suva
Mauritania	Casablanca
Micronesia	Suva
Monaco	Paris
Nauru	Suva
Netherlands Antilles	Amsterdam or Caracas
Niger	Abidjan
Palau	Apply to most accessible post
Samoa	Wellington
San Marino	Rome
Sao Tome and Principe	Luanda

14

Sikkim	Kolkata (Calcutta)
Suriname	Bridgetown or Port of Spain
Togo	Accra
Tuvalu	Suva
Western Samoa	Wellington

F: Posts temporarily closed

The following posts have temporarily been closed. Applicants for visit visas may apply at any designated post (see list A). Others should apply at the designated post stipulated.

Country	Post	Apply at
Guyana	Georgetown	Bridgetown or Port of Spain
Pakistan	Karachi	Islamabad
Somalia	Mogadishu	Nairobi or Addis Ababa

Work-related applications

SHORTAGE OCCUPATIONS LIST

The following occupations are acknowledged by Work Permits (UK) as being in short supply. Employers of prospective employees who qualify under the following list may obtain work permits under a simplified 'Tier 1' procedure ▶see 424–5. The following list is correct as at November 2005.

A current list is available from the Work Permits (UK) website www.workingintheuk.gov.uk

ENGINEERS

For jobs that are listed below the person must have a degree with at least 2 years relevant experience from a civil, structures or electrical background. Senior positions in these posts would be expected to have at least 5 years relevant experience.

Railways Planner or Engineer
Railways Modeller
Railway Track Design or Permanent Way Engineer
Communications Engineer
Power Supply Engineer or Electrification Engineer

Structural/bridge engineers

For jobs that are listed below the person must have a degree with at least 2 years relevant experience from a structures background. Senior posts in the jobs listed below would generally require appropriate chartered status and a minimum of 5 years relevant experience.

Structural Engineer
Infrastructure Engineer or Buildings Engineer
Bridge Engineer or Highways Structural Engineer

Transportation and highways engineers

For jobs that are listed below the person must have a transport related degree or a degree with at least 2 years relevant experience from a civil background.

Traffic Engineer or Transport Planner
Transport Modeller or Transport Economist (The applicant would be expected to have experience in multi-model studies & modelling software such as TRIPS, EMME2, QVIEW, SATURN, PEDROUTE or Microsimulation)
Traffic Signal Engineer
Highways Design Engineer or Highways Planning Engineer
Highways Maintenance Engineer

Ground Engineering

Geoenvironmental Engineer
Geotechnical Engineer
Geological Advisor
Geological Analyst

14

Geological Associate
Geological Engineer
Geologist / Hydrogeologist
Geology / Reservoir Engineer
Geomechanics Engineer
Geophysical Specialist
Geophysicist
Geoscientist
Geosupport Engineer.
Engineering Geologist
Ground Engineer
Contaminated Land Specialist

HEALTHCARE SECTOR

Doctors

Salaried GPs

Dentists

Salaried General Dental Practitioners
Salaried Assistant Dentists
Salaried Vocational Dental Practitioner
Consultants in Paediatric Dentistry
Consultants in Dental Specialities

Consultant posts in the following specialist areas:

Accident and Emergency	Intensive Care Medicine
Additional Dental Specialities	Medical Microbiology & Virology
Anaesthetics	Medical Oncology
Cardiology	Neurology
Cardiothoracic Surgery	Neurosurgery
Chemical Pathology	Nuclear Medicine
Child and Adolescent Psychiatry	Obstetrics and Gynaecology
Clinical Cytogenetics and Molecular Genetics	Occupational Health
	Old Age Psychiatry
Clinical Neurophysiology	Opthalmology
Clinical Oncology	Oral & Maxillo-facial Surgery
Clinical Radiology	Orthodontics
Dermatology	Otolaryngology
Endocrinology and Diabetes Mellitus	Paediatric Cardiology
Endodentics	Paediatrics
Forensic Psychiatry	Palliative Medicine
Gastroenterology	Plastic Surgery
General Adult Psychiatry	Psychiatry of Learning Disabilities
General Internal Medicine	Psychotheropy
General Surgery	Public Health Medicine
Genito-urinary medicine	Rehabilitation Medicine
Geriatric Medicine	Renal Medicine
Haematology	Respiratory Medicine
Histopathology	Rheumatology
Immunology	Trauma and Orthopaedic Surgery
Infectious Diseases	Urology

General
Audiologist
Audiological scientist
Clinical Psychologist
Dietician
Occupational Therapist
Pharmacist
Pharmacy Technician
Pre-Registration Cytogeneticist
Senior Physiotherapist
Speech and Language Therapist
Social Worker
State Registered Scientists In Cytogenetics
Biomedical Scientist / Medical Laboratory Scientific Officer (MLSO)
Qualified HPC registered Diagnostic and Therapeutic Radiographers, including ultrasonographers

Nurses
All registered nurses and midwives

OTHER OCCUPATIONS
Actuary
CAA Licensed Aircraft Engineers
Teacher – all posts in England covering compulsory schooling
Veterinary Surgeon

INFORMATION TECHNOLOGY

For jobs which are listed below, the person must have the relevant skills and experience listed on a separate webpage linked to the information technology list in the Work Permits (UK) web pages.

Occupation	*Technology area*
Architects in senior positions only	Java
	Java Script
Business Analyst	In any technology area
Network Specialist	In any technology area
Analyst Programmer	Active server Pages/Activex
Database Specialist	C and C++ programming languages
Software Engineer	Cool:gen
	Peoplesoft
	SQL Server
	XML
	DHTML
	Broadvision E-Commerce Tools
Software Engineer (cont.)	All customer relationship Management (CRM) and Computer technology (CTI) packages (especially Siebel, Clarify and Oracle CRM)

OTHER OCCUPATIONS
Actuary
CAA Licensed Aircraft Engineers
Teacher – all posts in England covering compulsory schooling
Veterinary Surgeon

HIGHLY SKILLED MIGRANT PROGRAMME
INCOME BAND/COUNTRY LIST

Code A countries

Income band 1: £40,000 (under 28, £27,000)
Income band 2: £100,000 (under 28, £40,000)
Income band 3: £250,000 (under 28, £60,000)

Andorra	Italy
Aruba	Japan
Australia	Kuwait
Austria	Liechtenstein
Belgium	Luxembourg
Bermuda	Monaco
Canada	Netherlands
Cayman Islands	Norway
Channel Islands	Qatar
Denmark	San Marino
Finland	Singapore
France	Sweden
French Polynesia	Switzerland
Germany	UAE
Gibraltar	United Kingdom
Guam	United States of
Hong Kong	America
Iceland	Vatican
Ireland	

Code B countries

Income band 1: £17,500 (under 28, £11,800)
Income band 2: £43,750 (under 28, £17,500)
Income band 3: £109,375 (under 28, £26,250)

American Samoa	Malaysia
Antigua and	Malta
Barbuda	Mauritius
Argentina	Mexico
Bahamas	Netherlands Antilles
Bahrain	New Caledonia
Barbados	New Zealand
Botswana	Northern Mariana
Brunei	Islands
Chile	Oman
Costa Rica	Palau
Croatia	Panama
Cyprus	Poland
Czech Republic	Portugal
Estonia	Puerto Rico
Faeroe Islands	Saudi Arabia
Greece	Seychelles
Greenland	Slovak Republic
Grenada	Slovenia
Hungary	Spain
Israel	St. Kitts and Nevis
Korea	St. Lucia
Rep. of (South	Taiwan (Territory of)
Korea)	Trinidad and Tobago
Latvia	Uruguay
Lebanon	Venezuela
Libya	Virgin Islands
Macao (China)	

Code C countries

Income band 1: £12,500 (under 28, £8,450)
Income band 2: £31,250 (under 28, £12,500)
Income band 3: £78,125 (under 28, £18,750)

Albania	Macedonia
Algeria	Maldives
Belarus	Marshall Islands
Belize	Micronesia
Bolivia	Morocco
Bosnia and	Namibia
Herzegovina	Nauru
Brazil	Paraguay
Bulgaria	Peru
Cape Verde	Philippines
China (excluding	Romania
Hong Kong)	Russian Federation
Colombia	Samoa
Dominica	South Africa
Dominican Republic	St. Vincent and the
Ecuador	Grenadines
Egypt	Suriname
El Salvador	Swaziland
Fiji	Syrian Arab Republic
Gabon	Thailand
Guatemala	Tonga
Honduras	Tunisia
Iran	Turkey
Jamaica	Turkmenistan
Jordan	Vanuatu
Kazakhstan	West Bank and Gaza
Lithuania	Yugoslavia

Code D countries

Income band 1: £7,500 (under 28, £5,000)
Income band 2: £18,750 (under 28, £7,500)
Income band 3: £46,875 (under 28, £11,250)

Angola	Iraq
Armenia	Kenya
Azerbaijan	Kiribati
Bangladesh	Lesotho
Benin	Mauritania
Bhutan	Moldova
Cameroon	Mongolia
Comoros	Myanmar
Congo, Republic of	Nicaragua
the	Pakistan
Cote d'Ivoire	Papua New Guinea
Cuba	Senegal
Djibouti	Solomon Islands
Equatorial Guinea	Sri Lanka
Gambia	Sudan
Georgia	Ukraine
Guinea	Uzbekistan
Guyana	Vietnam
Haiti	Yemen
India	Zambia
Indonesia	Zimbabwe

14

Code E countries
Income band 1: £3,500 (under 28, £2,350)
Income band 2: £8,750 (under 28, £3,500)
Income band 3: £21,875 (under 28, £5,250)

Afghanistan
Burkina Faso
Burundi
Cambodia
Central African
Republic
Congo,
Democratic Republic
of the
Chad
Eritrea
Ethiopia
Ghana
Guinea-Bissau
Korea (N)
Kyrgyz Republic
Lao PDR
Liberia

Madagascar
Malawi
Mali
Mayotte
Mozambique
Nepal
Niger
Nigeria
Rwanda
Sao Tome and
Principe
Sierra Leone
Somalia
Tajikistan
Tanzania
Togo
Uganda

Commonwealth countries

COMMONWEALTH COUNTRIES

Citizens of the following countries are Commonwealth citizens, as are British citizens, British Dependant Territories citizens and British Overseas citizens. The country names are followed by the dates of independence or – where relevant – dates of joining:

Antigua and Barbuda	1.11.81	India	15.8.47	St Christopher & Nevis	19.9.83
Australia	1.1.01	Jamaica	6.8.62	St Lucia	22.2.79
Bahamas	10.7.73	Kenya	12.12.63	St Vincent and the Grenadines	27.10.79
Bangladesh	26.3.71	Kiribati	12.7.79		
as East Pakistan	15.8.47	Lesotho	4.10.66	Samoa	1970
Barbados	30.11.66	Malawi	6.7.64	Seychelles	29.6.76
Belize	21.9.81	Malaysia	31.8.57	Sierra Leone	27.4.61
Botswana	30.9.66	Maldives	1982	Singapore	3.6.65
Brunei Darassalam	1984	Malta	21.9.64	Solomon Islands	7.7.78
		Mauritius	12.3.68	South Africa	1931
Cameroon joined 1.11.95		Mozambique joined 14.11.95			left 1961
Canada	1.7 31				rejoined 31.5.94
Cyprus	16.8.60	Namibia joined 21.3.90		Sri Lanka	4.2.48
	joined 13.3.61	Nauru	31.1.68	Swaziland	6.9.68
Dominica	3.11.78		joined 31.1.80	Tanzania	9.12.61
Fiji	left1987	New Zealand	26.9.07	Tonga	4.6.70
	rejoined 1997	Nigeria*	1.10.60	Trinidad and Tobago	31.8.62
	suspended from the		suspended 11.11.95		
	councils of the		rejoined 29.5.99	Tuvalu	1.10.78
	Commonwealth 2000	Pakistan*	15.8.47	Uganda	1962
The Gambia	18.2.65	left 1972,rejoined 1989		Vanuatu	30.7.80
Ghana	6.3.57	suspended from the		Zambia	24.10.64
Grenada	7.2.74	councils of the		Zimbabwe	18.4.80
		Commonwealth 1999			
Guyana	26.5.66	Papua New Guinea 16.9.75			

Commonwealth nationality is no longer as significant as it once was but remains relevant in immigration law in four circumstances:

14

- only Commonwealth citizens can have the right of abode ▶see 1401 and 1417–21;
- only Commonwealth nationals (plus citizens of the Republic of Ireland) can be exempt from deportation on the basis of their residence in Britain since before 1973;
- working holiday status is only available to Commonwealth nationals; and so is
- the right to work and to settle here on the basis of UK ancestry.

These categories are covered in more detail in the chapters of this book.

*Pakistan's withdrawal from the Commonwealth meant that Pakistani citizens were not considered as Commonwealth nationals for that period. They were unable to take any of the advantages of Commonwealth nationality, even if they had been ordinarily resident in the UK since before Pakistan's withdrawal. Nigeria's suspension, on the other hand means that Nigerians remain Commonwealth citizens and can, for example, qualify as working holidaymakers.

Registering with the police

REGISTERING WITH THE POLICE

Those who are required to register with the police as a condition of their entry or stay in the UK (paras 325-326) (▶see 1006–7) have been restricted to certain nationals of the following countries (Appendix 2 HC 395):

Afghanistan	Iran	Peru
Algeria	Iraq	Qatar
Argentina	Israel	Russia
Armenia	Jordan	Saudi Arabia
Azerbaijan	Kazakhstan	Sudan
Bahrain	Kuwait	Syria
Belarus	Kyrgyzstan	Tajikistan
Bolivia	Lebanon	Tunisia
Brazil	Libya	Turkey
China	Moldova	Turkmenistan
Colombia	Morocco	United Arab Emirates
Cuba	North Korea	Ukraine
Egypt	Oman	Uzbekistan
Georgia	Palestine	Yemen

Stateless persons and those holding non-national travel documents are also required to register.

14

Countries whose adoption decisions are recognised in the UK and Hague Convention countries

HAGUE CONVENTION COUNTRIES

The Hague Convention on the Protection of Children and Cooperation in Respect of Inter-country Adoption has entered into force in the following countries; children adopted in these countries may be British (▶see 380–81):

Albania	Cyprus	Latvia	Poland
Andorra	Czech Republic	Lithuania	Portugal
Australia	Denmark	Luxembourg	Romania
Austria	Ecuador	Madagascar	San Marino
Azerbaijan	El Salvador	Malta	Slovak Republic
Belarus	Estonia	Mauritius	Slovenia
Belgium	Finland	Mexico	South Africa
Bolivia	France	Moldova	Spain
Brazil	Georgia	Monaco	Sri Lanka
Bulgaria	Germany	Mongolia	Sweden
Burkino Faso	Guatamala	Netherlands	Switzerland
Burundi	Guinea	New Zealand	Thailand
Canada	Hungary	Norway	Turkey
Chile	India	Panama	UK
China	Ireland	Paraguay	Uruguay
Colombia	Israel	Peru	Venezuela
Costa Rica	Italy	Philippines	

COUNTRIES WHOSE ADOPTION DECISIONS ARE RECOGNISED IN THE UK

The following countries are designated under the Schedule to the Adoption (Designation of Overseas Adoptions) Order 1973 and adoptions in these countries may be recognised in the UK (▶see 383):

Commonwealth countries

Australia	Dominica	Malta	Sri Lanka
Bahamas	Fiji	Mauritius	Swaziland
Barbados	Ghana	Montserrat	Tanzania
Bermuda	Gibraltar	New Zealand	Tonga
Botswana	Guyana	Nigeria	Trinidad and Tobago
British Honduras	Hong Kong	Pitcairn	
British Virgin Islands	Jamaica	St. Christopher, Nevis and Anguilla	Uganda
	Kenya		Zambia
Canada	Lesotho	St. Vincent	Zimbabwe (listed as Southern Rhodesia)
Cayman Islands	Malawi	Seychelles	
The Republic of Cyprus	Malaysia	Singapore	

Other countries

Austria	The Federal Republic of Germany and Land Berlin (West Berlin)	Netherlands (including the Antilles)	Spain (including the Balearics and the Canary Islands)
Belgium			
Denmark (including Greenland and the Faroes)		Norway	
	Greece	Portugal (including the Azores and Madeira)	Surinam
Finland	Iceland		Sweden
France (including Reunion, Martinique, Guadeloupe and French Guyana)	The Republic of Ireland	South Africa and South West Africa	Switzerland
	Israel		Turkey
	Italy		USA
	Luxembourg		Yugoslavia

Abbreviations

GENERAL TERMS

AIT	Asylum and Immigration Tribunal
API	Asylum Policy Instructions (by name of instruction and paragraph)
ARC	application registration card
ASA	asylum support adjudicator
ASU	Asylum Screening Unit
A8/Accession 8	The eight countries that acceded to the EU on 1 May 2004 in respect of whose nationals restrictions have been imposed
BC	British citizen
BDTC	British Dependent Territories Citizen
BN(O)	British Nationals (Overseas)
BOC	British Overseas Citizen
BOTA	British Overseas Territories Act 2002
BOTC	British Overseas Territories Citizen
BPP	British Protected Persons
BS	British subjects
CA	Court of Appeal
CESC	Council of Europe Social Charter 1961
CIPU	Country Information and Policy Unit
CLR	Controlled Legal Representation
CLS	Community Legal Service
CTA	common travel area
CUKC	Citizens of the United Kingdom and Colonies
DL	discretionary leave
DSP	Diplomatic Services Procedures
EC	European Community
EC Treaty	Treaty of Rome (treaty establishing the EC)
EDI	European Directorate Instructions
EEA	European Economic Area
EU	European Union
ECHR	European Convention of Human Rights

ECO	entry clearance officer
ECom HR	European Commission on Human Rights
ECSMA	European Convention on Social and Medical Assistance 1953
ECtHR	European Court of Human Rights
EDI	European Directorate Instructions
EEA	European Economic Area
EIN	Electronic Immigration Network
ELR/ELE	exceptional leave to remain/exceptional leave to enter
EU	European Union
GB	Great Britain
GATS	General Agreement on Trade in Services
Hague Convention	Hague Convention on the Protection of Children and Cooperation in Respect of Inter-country Adoption
HC	High Court
HL	House of Lords
HMO	Houses in Multiple Occupation
HSMP	Highly Skilled Migrants Programme
HP	humanitarian protection
IAA	Immigration Appellate Authorities
IAT	Immigration Appeal Tribunal
IANL	Immigration, Asylum & Nationality Law
ISD	Immigration Status Document
IDI	Immigration Directorate Instructions (by Chapter, section and paragraph; and in some cases, annex)
ICD	Integrated Casework Directorate
IFA	internal flight alternative (also 'IPA' internal protection alternative)
IJ	Immigration Judge
IND	Immigration and Nationality Department
JECU	Joint Entry Clearance Unit (now UK Visas)
LSC	Legal Services Commission
NAM	New asylum model
NASS	National Asylum Support Service
NWP	North West Pilot
NI	Nationality Directorate Instructions (by Chapter, section and paragraph; and in some cases, annex)
OEM	Operation Enforcement Manual
OFSTED	Office for Standards in Education
OISC	Office of the Immigration Services Commissioner
PEO	Public Enquiry Office
Policy Bulletin	NASS Policy Bulletin
PTSD	post-traumatic stress disorder

14

SAL	standard acknowledgement letter
SBS	Sectors Based Scheme
SEF	statement of evidence form
SEF/NINO	SEF/National Insurance Number interviews
SEGS	Science and Engineering Graduate Scheme
TA	temporary admission
TEU	Maastrict Treaty on European Union
TWES	Training and Work Experience Scheme
UASC	unaccompanied asylum seeking child
UDHR	Universal Declaration of Human Rights
UK	United Kingdom
UKCOSA	The Council for International Education
UKRP	United Kingdom Residence Permit
UNHCR	United Nations High Commissioner for Refugees
2002 White Paper	*Secure Borders, Safe Haven: Integration with Diversity in Modern Britain*, 7 February 2002 (Home Office)
1951 Convention/ Refugee Convention	Convention Relating to the Status of Refugees 1951

LEGISLATION

Acts of Parliament

1971 Act	Immigration Act 1971
RRA	Race Relations Act 1976
BNA 1981	British Nationality Act 1981
PACE	Police and Criminal Evidence Act 1984
1988 Act	Immigration Act 1988
1993 Act	Asylum and Immigration Appeals Act 1993
1996 Act	Asylum and Immigration Act 1996
1997 Act	Special Immigration Appeals Commission Act 1997
HRA	Human Rights Act 1998
1999 Act	Immigration and Asylum Act 1999
2000 Act	Race Relations (Amendment) Act 2000
BOTA 2002	British Overseas Territories Act 2002
2002 Act	Nationality, Immigration and Asylum Act 2002
2004 Act	Asylum and Immigration (Treatment of Claimants, etc) Act 2004
2005 Bill	Immigration, Asylum and Nationality Bill

Immigration Rules

HC 395	Present statement of immigration rules made under the Immigration Act 1971
HC	House of Commons paper, amending main statement of immigration rules
Cmd	Command paper, amending main statement of immigration rules

Secondary Legislation

1972 Order	Control of Entry through Republic of Ireland Order 1972
2003 Regulations	Immigration (Leave to Remain)(Fees) Regulations 2003
2003 Regulations	Tax Credits (Immigration) Regulations 2003
Accession Regulations	Accession (Immigration and Worker Registration) Regulations 2004
Asylum Support Appeals Rules	Asylum Support Appeals (Procedure) Rules 2000
Asylum Support Regulations	Asylum Support Regulations 2000
CPR	Civil Procedure Rules
Detention Centre Rules	Detention Centre Rules 2001
EEA 2000 Regulations	Immigration (European Economic Area) Regulations 2000
Fast Track Order	Asylum and Immigration (Fast Track Time Limits) Order 2005
Fast Track Rules	Asylum and Immigration Tribunal (Fast Track Procedure) Rules 2005
Interim Provisions Regulations	Asylum Support (Interim Provisions) Regulations
Leave to Enter Order	Immigration (Leave to Enter and Remain) Order 2000
Notices Regulations	Immigration (Notices) Regulations 2003
Procedure Rules	Asylum and Immigration Tribunal (Procedure) Rules 2005
VOLO	Immigration (Variation of Leave) Order 1976
Withholding Regulations	Withholding and Withdrawal of Support (Travel Assistance and Temporary Accommodation) Regulations 2002

Note: Abbreviations for various welfare benefits and related secondary legislation are listed in a separate table in Ch 39 ▶1232-3

Note

Sometimes we have referred to 'Regulations' or 'Rules' to refer to certain pieces of secondary legislation rather than using the abbreviations above. This has been done to save space in the text – it should be clear from the context and the chapter as a whole which rules or regulations are being referred to when this is done.

14

Other sources of information

GENERAL: IMMIGRATION, NATIONALITY AND ASYLUM

Butterworths Immigration Law Service (Butterworths) (updated approx three times per year)(Butterworths)

Macdonald's Immigration Law & Practice 6th Edition (2005), Macdonald and Webber (Butterworths)

Immigration Law & Practice (2005), Jackson and Warr (Sweet & Maxwell) – now a service

Textbook on Immigration and Asylum Law (2004), Clayton (Oxford University Press)

2004 ACT

Blackstone's Guide to the Asylum and Immigration Act 2004 (2004), Doughty Street Chambers (Oxford University Press)

ASYLUM AND REFUGEES

The Law of Refugee Status (1991), Hathaway (Butterworths)

Asylum Law & Practice (2003), Symes and Jorro (Butterworths)

The Rights of Refugees under International Law (2005), Hathaway (Cambridge University Press)

The Refugee in International Law 2nd Edition (1996), Guy S. Goodwin-Gill (Clarendon)

The State of the World's Refugees: Fifty years of humanitarian action (2000) (UNHCR)

CHILDREN

Putting Children First: a guide for immigration practitioners (2002), Coker, Finch, Stanley (Legal Action Group)

CRIME AND IMMIGRATION

Immigration Advice at the Police Station 3rd Edition (2005), Brennan (The Law Society)

EUROPEAN FREE MOVEMENT

Free movement of persons in the enlarged European Union (2005), Rogers and Scannell (Sweet & Maxwell)

Free movement of persons in the European Union (1996), Martin & Guild (Butterworths)

The Legal Framework and Social Consequences of Free Movement of Persons in the European Union (1999), Guild (Kluwer Law International)

EXTRADITION

Jones and Doobay on extradition and mutual assistance (3rd Edn) (2005), Jones and Doobay (Sweet & Maxwell)

Blackstone's guide to the Extradition Act 2003 (2004), Knowles (Oxford University Press)

HUMAN RIGHTS

Human Rights Law and Practice (2nd Edn) (2004) Lester and Pannick (Butterworths)

The Law of Human Rights (2000) Clayton and Tomlinson (Oxford University Press)

European Human Rights Law (1999) Starmer (Legal Action Group)

HUMAN RIGHTS AND IMMIGRATION

Blake and Fransman: Immigration, Nationality and Asylum under the Human Rights Act 1998 (1999) Blake, Fransman (Butterworths)

Immigration, asylum & human rights (2003), Blake and Husain (Oxford University Press)

LEGISLATION

Immigration Law Handbook (4th Edn) (2005), Phelan and Gillespie (Blackstone Press)

NATIONALITY

Fransman: British Nationality Law (2nd Edn) (1998), Fransman (Butterworths)

STUDENTS

UKCOSA Manual 2005, A Guide to Regulations and Procedures for International Students (2005) (UKCOSA)

WELFARE

Housing Allocation and Homelessness: Law and Practice (2005/06), Luba and Davies (Jordan Publishing)

Homelessness and Allocations (6th Edn) (2002), Arden and Hunter (Legal Action Group)

Migration and Social Security Benefits Handbook (3rd Edn) (2002), Seddon, Fitzpatrick and Chatwin (CPAG) A further edition is expected shortly

Support for Asylum Seekers (2nd Edn) (2004), Willman, Knafler, Pierce (Legal Action Group)

Welfare Benefits and Tax Credits Handbook (7th Edn) (2005/2006), Osbourne & Others (CPAG)

CPAG's Housing Benefit and Council Tax Benefit Legislation (17th Edn) (2005), Wright & Others (CPAG)

PERIODICALS AND UPDATES

Bulletin (JCWI) – quarterly immigration policy review

Immigration, Asylum and Nationality Law (IANL) (Tolleys Publishing) – quarterly review

Immigration Law Digest (Immigration Advisory Service)

International Journal of Refugee Law (Oxford University Press)

Legal Action (Legal Action Group) – contains periodic 'recent developments' in immigration

14

LAW REPORTS

Immigration Appeal Reports (Imm AR) (HMSO)

Immigration and Nationality Law Reports (INLR) (Jordan Publishing)

Glossary

This section is intended for quick reference. It introduces many of the commonest and the most technical terms encountered in immigration and refugee law. Many of the items dealt with here are covered in more detail in the text, and may be found through the index. Terms found elsewhere in the glossary are marked with an asterisk. Note: not all the terms set out below are used in the *Handbook* but may be used by immigration officials or other advisers and are included for that reason.

Where a term referred to in the explanation of a phrase is given an asterisk **(*)** and is in bold, this means that that term is given its own explanation elsewhere in the glossary.

Accession: This is the term which is used to describe the process by which a non-EU country joins the EU. In particular, it has been used to refer to the joining of the EU by ten additional countries from 1 May 2004 under a 'Treaty of Accesssion' made on 16 April 2003. The ten states which joined are: Cyprus, Czech Republic, Estonia, Hungary, Latvia, Lithuania, Malta, Poland, Slovakia, Slovenia.

Accession 8 ('A8'): The Accession 8 countries eight of the countries listed above under *'Accession'* excluding Cyprus and Malta. The EU free movement rights of nationals of the A8 countries can be restricted until the end of a 'transitional period' in 2011. The UK has taken advantage of this to place certain limitations on the rights of A8 nationals, which include their rights to reside in the UK in order to look for work. This has been done mainly in order to prevent their access to forms of welfare support.

Accreditation scheme: All advisers who undertake legally-aided immigration work must be accredited by the Legal Services Commission and Law Society under a jointly-operated accreditation scheme. ▶See 73 for more details.

Accommodation centre: Accommodation centres are provided for by the 2002 Act as places where asylum-seekers may be required to reside under the terms of their temporary admission (they are not 'detained'). Support would be provided to asylum-seekers in the accommodation centre. The government has now abandoned the scheme to set up accommodation centres.

Adjudicator: the person who, before 4 April 2005, heard and decided an immigration appeal at first instance. Adjudicators heard cases on their own, in centres around the country. For many years they were appointed by the Home Office, subsequently they were appointed by the Lord Chancellor's Department. Immigration appeals are now heard by the *Asylum and Immigration Tribunal (AIT)*.

Administrative removal: This is the form of *enforcement used to remove those who have breached their conditions of leave, overstayed their leave, obtained leave by deception or whose indefinite leave has been revoked because they have ceased to be a refugee. Before the 1999 Act, people in these categories were *deported but they are now subject to a summary, quick form of removal like illegal entrants.

Appellant: a person who brings an appeal. In the first place this will always be an individual who has been refused something they were applying for (entry clearance, a certificate of entitlement, leave to enter, a variation of leave, asylum, a residence permit), or has been refused revocation of a deportation order, or against whom the Home Office has taken action (such as removing them as an illegal entrant or deciding to make a deportation order). An 'appellant' may also be the person who appeals to the AIT, the Asylum Support Adjudicator, the Court of Appeal or any other court.

Application forms: since November 1996 a change to the immigration rules meant that in most categories applications to the Home Office to extend 'leave' (stay) or to change the category of leave must be made on a standard form, supplied by the Home Office. This includes applications made outside the rules, and the exceptions are applications: for asylum, to stay as an *EEA national or family member under the terms of the European treaties or applications to vary leave made on entry to an immigration officer by a person who has leave when they arrive.

Application registration card (ARC): These are replacement forms of identification for those who have claimed asylum which have replaced *standard acknowledgement letters (SALs). They have been issued at the Home Office Asylum Screening Unit in Croydon since January 2002. They are biometric smart cards with personal details including fingerprints and employment status.

Assistants: This is the term used to refer to the various voluntary agencies (such as the Refugee Council and Refugee Action) who help asylum-seekers to complete their applications for asylum support and pass them to the *National Asylum Support Service (NASS). They also arrange for the provision of temporary accommodation for asylum-seekers on behalf of NASS until such time as a decision is made as to whether they qualify for *asylum support.

Association Agreement: a treaty signed between the European Community and another country, which gives the other country preferential access to the countries of the *EEA. Some only give advantages for trade, but the most important allow nationals of the other country to enter mainly as self-employed or business people.

Asylum: the leave to enter or remain given to a person recognised as a refugee under the 1951 United Nations Convention. The rights that go with it mostly also stem from the Convention. Asylum used to be granted with *indefinite leave to remain but now successful applicants are given five years' limited leave initially.

Asylum and Immigration Tribunal (AIT): This is the new 'single tier' immigration appeal court which, from 4 April 2005, has taken over from the 'two tier' immigration adjudicators and Immigration Appeal Tribunal. The people who sit to hear cases in the AIT are *immigration judges.

Asylum Screening Unit: the Home Office department which records people applying for asylum after entering the UK, and carries out fingerprinting, identity checks and screening.

Asylum-seeker: a person requesting asylum or refugee status in the UK, whose application has not yet been decided. For *asylum support purposes, 'asylum-seeker' also includes a person who has made a claim under Article 3 ECHR.

Asylum support: This is the form of support given to asylum seekers as a replacement for the old system of support through welfare benefits or under the National Assistance Act 1948. It was introduced in April 2000 under the 1999 Act. An *'interim' asylum support scheme has been in operation since December 1999 whereby local authorities provide asylum support under a similar framework to certain asylum seekers. Only asylum-seekers who are 'destitute' (without adequate accommodation or the means to meet their essential living needs) can obtain this support. The interim scheme comes to an end on 3 April 2006.

14

Asylum Support Adjudicator (ASA): Asylum support adjudicators hear appeals from decisions made by the *National Asylum Support Service (NASS) that a person is not entitled to *asylum support or *hard case support, or their support is terminated.

Benefits Agency: the administrative branch of the Department of Social Security (DSS), which makes benefits payments.

British citizens: there are two kinds of British citizens: British citizens otherwise than by descent and British citizens by descent. The difference is that the first group can pass British citizenship on automatically to their children born outside the UK and the second cannot.

British Dependent Territories citizens: these are people who are British because of their connection with a place that is not yet independent. They may have been born, adopted, registered or naturalised in that colony and can retain British Dependent Territories citizenship as long as the colony continues. When the colony gains independence or ceases to exist as a separate territory, people lose British Dependent Territories citizenship. This form of British nationality left people requiring leave to enter and remain in the UK, and gave no right of abode anywhere other than the particular dependent (or overseas) territory with which it is connected. However, under the British Overseas Territories Act 2002, BDTCs were re-designated as '*British Overseas Territories Citizens' (BOTCs) who became 'British citizens' with the *right of abode on 21 May 2002.

British Nationals (Overseas): this status was created for British Dependent Territories citizens from Hong Kong, who are able to keep this British nationality status now that Hong Kong is again part of China. However, the status no longer gives a right to anything more than a passport which functions as a travel document.

British Overseas citizens: these are people who were born in a place that used to be a British colony but who did not qualify for citizenship under the law of the new independent country or of any other country and therefore retained their British nationality. They require leave to enter or remain in the UK, and have no right of abode anywhere through this citizenship. Many were able to obtain *'Special Vouchers' but these have been abolished for those applying after 4 March 2002.

British Overseas Territories: These territories were previously known as British Dependent Territories, hence the name of the citizenship associated with them. The remaining territories under British rule are Anguilla, Bermuda, British Antarctica, British Indian Ocean Territory, Cayman Islands, Falkland Islands, Gibraltar, Montserrat, Pitcairn Island, St Helena, Turks and Caicos Islands, Virgin Islands, Cyprus sovereign base areas.

British Protected Persons: these are people who are from a country which used to be a British protectorate, protected state or trust territory rather than a colony, and who did not gain the citizenship of the new independent country or of any other country.

British subjects: these are people who are from a country which used to be a British colony, who never became citizens of the UK and Colonies under the British Nationality Act 1948 and who did not gain citizenship of the new independent country or of any other country. Before 1983, the term 'British subject' meant exactly the same as *'Commonwealth citizen' but it is now only used for this small group of people. This status (it is not strictly a form of citizenship) automatically ceases on acquisition of any other nationality.

Certificate of entitlement: Commonwealth citizens who have the *right of abode must prove their right either by obtaining a British citizen passport (if they are entitled to one, and depending on the rules about dual citizenship), or by having a certificate of entitlement placed in their passport. The certificate is a type of visa sticker, but unlike other entry clearances it can also be applied for within the United Kingdom.

Certified case: This can mean a number of things. A certificate issued by the Secretary of

State under s94 2002 Act that an asylum or human rights claim is 'clearly unfounded' prevents an in-country right of appeal. A certificate issued under s96 2002 Act prevents further appeals where there has been an earlier right of appeal. Where the Secretary of State certifies a case under section 97 2002 Act, the effect of this is to prevent the applicant from appealing to the ***AIT**. There is an appeal to the ***Special Immigration Appeal Commission** instead. Cases which are certified under s9 2004 Act (para 7A Sch 3 2002 Act) to the effect that a family has failed to take reasonable steps to voluntarily leave the UK, prevents the family from access to support. There are other certificates which can be issued in asylum and human rights cases which have a different effect. In ***third country cases**, the Home Office may issue a third-country certificate.

Civil partner: This is the term given those who, from 5 December 2005, can enter into a 'civil partnership' under the Civil Partnership Act 2004. In this way, the legislation allows same sex couples to give their relationship a legal status. From 5 December 2005, the immigration rules will allow civil partners to be treated in much the same way as spouses.

Commissioner's decisions: decisions made on social security appeals. They are cited as CIS (if an 'income support' case) /reference number/year. Other cases are listed by initials of the benefit (e.g. JSA). Cases which are considered particularly significant are known as starred decisions.

Common Travel Area: comprises the ***UK**, Republic of Ireland, Isle of Man and the Channel Islands. There are no immigration controls at the borders between them and people's passports are not stamped with leave to enter.

Commonwealth citizens: most ex-British colonies when they gained independence decided to join this loose group of countries, headed by the British monarch, to retain contacts, trade preferences etc. Commonwealth citizens still retain a few immigration-law advantages over others. All categories of British nationals, except ***British Protected Persons**, are Commonwealth citizens.

Community Legal Service: The Community Legal Service is a scheme established by the Access to Justice Act 1999 to co-ordinate and rationalise the provision of funds for civil legal and advice services in a way that will effectively meet the needs of individuals.

Convention: in refugee law 'the Convention' invariably means the United Nations Convention Relating to the Status of Refugees, Geneva, 1951, with its Protocol, New York, 1967. The original Convention was restricted in scope by reference to events that had occurred in Europe prior to 1951, but the Protocol removed both the geographical and historical restrictions, to apply the Convention conditions to any refugees. Not all countries have signed and ratified the Convention, and there are still a few of those that have which have not signed up to the Protocol, and so retain restrictions in their definition of refugees. Following the Human Rights Act 1998, 'the Convention' may also be used to refer to the ***'European Convention on Human Rights** and Fundamental Freedoms' (ECHR).

Convention grounds: an asylum-seeker will qualify for asylum under the Refugee Convention if they can show that their case fits within the criteria of the 1951 Convention. They must show (i) that they have a fear, which is (ii) objectively well-founded, that if they were returned to their country of origin (iii) they would face persecution, (iv) on grounds of their race, religion, nationality, membership of a particular social group, or political opinion. These motives for persecution are the only ones that count. If a person shows that they would face persecution for any other reason, or that they cannot be returned to their country for any other reason, the Home Office should normally grant ***humanitarian protection** instead.

Council of Europe: a larger and much looser grouping than the European Union or the EEA, the Council of Europe comprises over 40 member states. Best known in Britain as the source of the ***European Convention on Human Rights**.

Council of Europe Social Charter: although made in 1961, the significance of the

14

Charter on the benefit entitlement of nationals of its member states has only become apparent with the increasing restrictions on eligibility for income support and housing benefit/council tax benefit in recent years.

Curtailment of leave: The Home Office has certain powers to cut short a person's leave to enter or remain in the UK if, for example, a person no longer satisfies the requirements of the rules upon which leave was granted.

Deportation: sending a person out of the UK under an order signed by the Home Secretary. This process of *'enforcement is now only used if a person has been convicted of a serious criminal offence, or because the Home Secretary has decided on public policy or national security grounds that the person's presence is 'not conducive to the public good'. Family members of deportees can also be deported. The person cannot return unless the order has first been revoked.

Determination: the judgements of the *Asylum and Immigration Tribunal are known as determinations. It is common for written determinations to be sent out some weeks after the hearing.

Directions: this is used in at least two distinct senses:

i) **removal directions:** when people are to be expelled from the UK, the immigration authorities make arrangements for them to be sent either to the country of their nationality, the country which issued their travel document (if different), the country from which they embarked to come here, or another country where they would be admitted. A notice of these arrangements, specifying the destination and flight details (or ferry or Channel Tunnel train) is served in advance.

ii) **appeal directions:** before the full hearing of an *asylum or *human rights case it is usual for the *Asylum and Immigration Tribunal to issue standard directions that various procedural steps are completed within times specified. A standard form is usually given, dealing with the production of documentary evidence, a chronology of events, a 'skeleton argument' and other issues. Representatives complain that nearly all the burden of these falls on appellants, and the Home Office are rarely required to take similar steps.

Dis-benefitted asylum-seekers: This is the phrase often used to refer to asylum-seekers who were entitled to welfare benefits because they claimed asylum on arrival before 3 April 2000 and who then receive a negative decision on their asylum application after that time so that they are no longer entitled to asylum welfare benefits. They then become entitled to asylum support if they are destitute. Generally, if the asylum decision was made on or after 25 September 2000, they are entitled to *NASS support, otherwise, they are entitled to *'interim' asylum support from a local authority. By April 2006, NASS is intending to take direct responsibility for all such asylum-seekers.

Discretionary Leave (DL): This is a form of leave outside the immigration rules that can be granted to people who succeed in their human rights claims. Alternatively, *humanitarian protection may be granted to successful human rights applicants. In a small number of cases, it may also be granted to people who cannot establish an entitlement to remain in the UK on human rights grounds. From 1 April 2003, together with *humanitarian protection, discretionary leave replaces asylum-based *exceptional leave to enter/remain.

Dispersal: This is the government policy operated by NASS under which it attempts to place asylum-seekers in accommodation outside London and the South-East into 'cluster' areas of asylum-seekers where there is a ready supply of low-cost accommodation available. .

DNA: since 1989 the government has operated a scheme to provide DNA testing free of charge to first time applicants for settlement if there are doubts as to the relationship between applicant and sponsor. Entry clearance officers cannot force people to undergo tests, but are likely to refuse anyone who declines to do so, just because they 'can not be satisfied' about the relationship. The scheme is supposed to be self-financing by recovering costs through general visa fees. It is available world-wide but is mainly used in a few posts (Addis Ababa, Lagos, Istanbul and across the Indian sub-continent) and above all in Dhaka.

Domicile: the country to which people feel they belong and in which they intend to spend the rest of their life. Normally people are considered to have a 'domicile of origin', usually the country in which they were born and grew up. This can only be changed by a conscious decision to settle and stay in another country and thus acquire a 'domicile of choice'. Questions asked to determine the domicile of people who have left their countries of origin often include where they hope to die and be buried/cremated. Domicile is important in deciding which countries' laws affect a particular person, for example in deciding whether a person is capable of contracting a polygamous marriage, or of adopting a child in a particular country. People's immigration status has no direct connection with their domicile.

Dual citizenship: some people may qualify for the nationality of more than one country if for example they are born in one country to parents who hold the citizenship of another. Or they may marry, or live somewhere else, and become eligible to naturalize. Whether or not they can hold more than one nationality depends on the laws in each country. Britain expressly recognizes dual (or multiple) nationality, and so do all the commonwealth Caribbean states, Bangladesh and Pakistan. India, and most of the African commonwealth, do not. In many cases possession of more than one passport is tolerated, even though a country's law may not permit recognition. Children are generally permitted to retain dual nationality, and then opt for one or the other on becoming adults, if the law of one of those countries does not generally permit holding more than one passport. It is possible to be both a *British Overseas Citizen and a *British citizen at the same time.

Dublin Convention and Dublin 'II' Regulation: The Dublin Convention was negotiated between all the member states of the EU, but as an inter-governmental measure, rather than part of community law, so the institutions of the EU had no say in its operation. The purpose of the Convention was to determine which state should take the responsibility for dealing with an asylum claim, and it came into force on 1 September 1997. There is now a further 'Dublin' agreement in the form of an EC Council Regulation ((EC) No 343/2003) issued on 18 February 2003.

Electronic Immigration Network: after some years of development and lobbying for funds, the Electronic Immigration Network was launched in June 1998. It provides on-line access to a large number of links of interest to immigration advisers and others. It also carries, for subscribers, the full text of a large selection of immigration case judgements.

Enforcement: This is a term which, in the past has been used to refer to the *'deportation' and *illegal entry methods of requiring people to leave the UK. In the *Handbook* we use the term to refer to *all* of the standard ways in which people can be forced to leave, including those who are removed having been refused leave to enter the UK and those who are in breach of their conditions or who *overstay. The 1999 Act also uses the term 'enforcement' to refer to all of these methods of forced departure (see s28 inserting s24A 1971 Act).

Entry clearance officers: officials at British posts overseas who deal with immigration applications there. In a 'visa national' country, they may also be known as visa officers, in a non-visa Commonwealth country as entry certificate officers. In larger posts there will also be a senior rank of officer known as Entry Clearance Manager.

European Convention on Human Rights (ECHR): an international instrument agreed by the Council of Europe. It has now been largely incorporated into UK law by the Human

14

Rights Act 1998 (HRA). This has had a large impact upon immigration and asylum law in the UK.

European Economic Area: covers the countries of the European Union (EU – previously the European Community) plus three other European countries, Iceland, Liechtenstein and Norway. From 1 May 2004, ten further states acceded to the EU. The countries of the EU (including those that acceded on 1 May 2004) are listed at ▶505. Swiss nationals have the same free movement rights as EEA nationals.

EU Freedom of movement: the framework of the European Union is said to rest on four 'freedoms' – of goods, services, capital, and people. People are given the freedom to move around the countries of the European Union (and now the EEA) as workers, or to provide or receive services or for certain other well-defined reasons. The scope of these provisions, and the limitations on free movement, are not detailed in the Treaties, and much depends on interpretations from the European Court of Justice.

Exceptional leave to enter or remain: people who apply for refugee status in the UK and are refused used to be granted exceptional leave to enter or remain in the UK if the Home Office considers that it would not be safe for them to be returned to their country of origin. This form of leave outside the immigration rules has now been replaced by *humanitarian protection and *discretionary leave. 'Exceptional leave' is also used in a broader sense to refer to anyone who is granted leave outside the immigration rules even if no asylum application has been made. For details about exceptional leave ▶see 147–8. For an explanation of the development of humanitarian protection, discretionary leave and their relationship with exceptional leave ▶see 859–75 and 597–8.

Extradition: This procedure is not covered in the *Handbook*. It refers to the means by which a person can be sent to another country to stand trial for a criminal offence. It is a complex area and anyone who is being subject to extradition proceedings should be referred for specialist advice.

Extra-territorial effect: This is a term which has been used to describe an argument about the true extent of the *ECHR rights incorporated by the Human Rights Act 1998. The Home Office has tried to argue that, if a person is to be sent to another country, they can only complain about a breach of their human rights on the basis of what will happen to them in that country if they face treatment contrary to Article 3 (torture or inhuman or degrading treatment or punishment). This is because the Home Office say that the ECHR does not have 'extra-territorial' effect in relation to the other Articles under the Convention. In a starred decision (*Kacaj*), the IAT rejected this Home Office argument. The House of Lords considered the matter further in *Ullah & Do* (▶see 788–9).

Family life: This often refers to the 'right to respect for family life' under Article 8 ECHR which is one of the rights incorporated by the Human Rights Act. The House of Lords considered the matter further in *Ullah & Do*.

Family visitor: Under the 1999 Act, a right of appeal against refusal of entry clearance was re-introduced for 'family visitors'. The definition of 'family visitor' is contained in Regulations.

Fees: under the Consular Fees Act 1980 fees can be charged for all entry clearance applications and para 30 HC 395 states that an entry clearance application is not validly made until the fees are paid. The level of fees is set in sterling by the Consular Fees Orders, but they must be paid at the entry clearance post in the local currency. The Home Office also charges for *immigration employment document (IED) applications and in-country applications for leave to remain.

Great Britain: the UK excluding Northern Ireland, that is England, Scotland and Wales. It does not include the Isle of Man or the Channel Islands.

Green books: the popular name for the Immigration Appeals Reports.

Habeas Corpus: This is a High Court procedure under which a person who is detained can challenge their detention on the basis that there is *no legal power* to detain them.

Habitual residence: a term used in social security law in order to exclude some people from eligibility for certain welfare benefits and local authority provided housing.

Hard cases support: 'Hard cases' support is the support which, in certain cases, is made available to those who are no longer entitled to *asylum support because they have exhausted the appeals process. It is provided in the form of accommodation and board. The legal power to provide this support is contained in section 4 of the 1999 Act.

Highly Skilled Migrants Programme (HSMP): The Highly Skilled Migrants Programme was introduced by the government in January 2002 as part of its economic migration policy referred to in the 2002 White Paper. Applicants are allocated points based on their educational qualifications, work experience, past earnings, achievements in a chosen field and whether it is a 'priority' application.

HC 395: whenever *immigration rules are changed or replaced, completely or in part, the paper published is always entitled 'Statement of Changes in Immigration Rules'. What distinguishes them most easily is the issue number. The present rules are set out in HC 395 which was issued in May 1994 and in force from 1 October 1994; although it has been repeatedly amended since. The amending statements are also statements of immigration rules which are given a number prefixed with either 'HC' (House of Commons paper) or 'Cmd' (Command Paper).

Humanitarian Protection (HP): This is a form of leave outside the immigration rules that can be granted to people who succeed in their human rights claims. Alternatively, *discretionary leave may be granted to successful human rights applicants. From 1 April 2003, together with *discretionary leave, humanitarian protection replaces asylum-based *exceptional leave to enter/remain. For more details about the development of humanitarian protection and *discretionary leave ▶see 859–62.

Illegal entrant: a person who immigration officers believe has entered the UK illegally; either by bypassing immigration control altogether, by using false/forged or by deception as to his or her identity or reasons for coming to the UK, or by entering in breach of a current deportation order.

Immigration Appeal Tribunal (IAT): This used to be the second tier of the Immigration Appellate Authority (IAA) (the first being the adjudicators) to who people used to appeal if their immigration appeal was dismissed by the *adjudicator. When hearing appeals, it consisted of a two or three member panel. Before a person could appeal to the IAT, they had to obtain the IAT's 'leave' (permission) to appeal. Appeals are now made to the single tier *Asylum and Immigration Tribunal.

Immigration authorities: used in the *Handbook* to refer to those officials responsible for immigration control: Home Office officials, *immigration officers, *entry clearance officers.

Immigration officer: usually an official at a British port of entry dealing with on-entry immigration applications. They may also deal with *enforcement of immigration control.

Immigration Service: Any member of the Immigration Service may be referred to as an immigration officer. The operational ranks of the service are immigration officer, immigration Assistant (below immigration officer, and will not handle casework directly), Chief Immigration Officer, who will be required to approve refusal and detention decisions, and Inspector.

Immigration and Nationality Directorate: the department of the Home Office responsible for handling all applications concerning immigration, nationality and asylum, as well as for enforcement and developing policy in these areas of law.

14

Immigration Employment Document (IED): This term was introduced by the 2002 Act and refers to any document which 'relates to employment and is issued for a purpose of the immigration rules' (see s122 2002 Act, para 6 *HC 395). The term is often shortened to 'IED'. The IEDS are: *work permits, documents issued by the Home Office confirming that the person meets the criteria under the HSMP, a permit issued under the sectors-based-scheme and a Home Office 'work card' issued by an approved operator under the seasonal agricultural workers' scheme.

Immigration Judges: This is the name given to the people who, from 4 April 2005, sit in the new *Asylum and Immigration Tribunal to hear appeals in immigration, asylum and human rights cases. There is a hierarchy which includes immigration judges, senior immigration judges etc.

Immigration rules: the rules of practice, published by the Home Office as to the conditions which various different categories of applicant have to satisfy in order to be admitted to the UK. If they are published while Parliament is sitting, they are called House of Commons papers, such as *HC 395; if in a Parliamentary recess, they are Command papers, such as Cm 3365. They are frequently amended. It is always open to the immigration authorities to waive the rules and grant leave exceptionally.

Indefinite leave: leave to enter or remain in the UK without any time limit. If there is no time limit, no other immigration conditions can be put on the person's stay either. A person who has indefinite leave to enter or remain is generally accepted as being *settled in the UK.

Induction centre: Induction centres are initial places of residence for asylum-seekers in order to give them a basic introduction to and understanding of the asylum process when they arrive. Applicants will not be 'detained' there but can be required to reside there for a very limited period under the terms of their *temporary admission even if they do not require any support.

Innovators scheme: This scheme was introduced as a two-year pilot operation in September 2000 in order to attract entrepreneurs to the UK. It is particularly targeted at those in the field of 'e' business and other new technology fields.

Interim (asylum) support: This is a form of *asylum support (see above) provided to certain asylum-seekers by local authorities rather than by *NASS. It will shortly be brought to an end under the interim scheme project (▶see 1373–4).

Interim scheme project: This is the process under which it is intended that the *National Asylum Support Service will take over responsibility for all of those classes of asylum-seeker who are still the responsibility of local authorities under the *interim (asylum) support scheme. The process should be complete by 3 March 2006.

Internal flight: sometimes referred to as 'internal flight alternative', or 'IFA'. It is also sometimes known as the 'internal protection alternative' and reference is also made to an ability to 'internally relocate'. If an asylum seeker claims that they would be at risk in a particular region of their country of origin the Home Office may reply that they could be safe elsewhere in that country. So they may refuse a Tamil from the Jaffna area of Sri Lanka, saying that they would be safe in Colombo, or a Kurd from south eastern Turkey, on the assention that he or she could live peaceably in the west of the country. The issue may sometimes arise only in the course of an appeal.

International terrorists: 'International terrorists' is a term taken from the Anti-terrorism, Crime and Security Act 2001 to refer to certain people who are connected with international terrorism who could be detained by the immigration authorities even though they had not been charged with or convicted of an offence and even though they cannot (legally or practically) be *removed from the UK. Following a decision of the House of Lords the legislation has been replaced (▶see 901–2).

Judicial review: a means of asking the High Court to rule on the legal validity of decision-making by a public body. It may be the only way of contesting an immigration refusal when there is no right of appeal. It is also used as a means of challenging a range of decisions for which there is no alternative remedy.

Leave to enter/remain: Permission given by immigration officials for people to enter or remain in the UK. It may be *limited or *indefinite.

Legal Services Commission: The Legal Services Commission is a public body created by the Access to Justice Act 1999. It is responsible for carrying out functions in relation to the Community Legal Service and the Criminal Defence Service as required by statute.

Limited leave: permission to enter or remain in the UK which has a time limit, and may have other conditions attached to it.

Maintenance undertaking: A formal statement signed by a person living in the UK that he or she will support a relative applying to come to or to remain in the UK. It means that the relative is not eligible to claim non-contributory welfare benefits for five years after it was signed, or after the person was given leave to enter or remain in the UK on this basis, whichever is the later, unless the signatory to the undertaking dies.

National Asylum Support Service (NASS): This is the name of the part of the Home Office which is responsible for operating the national scheme of *asylum support.

Naturalisation: a process of applying for British nationality. The application is formally at the discretion of the Home Office and can be made on the basis of residence in the UK, marriage to a British partner or Crown service. Naturalisation and *registration are both ways of gaining British citizenship; the citizenship obtained is the same whichever process is used.

'One-stop' procedure: The one-stop system of appeals was introduced by the 1999 Act to ensure that people raise all of their grounds (particularly asylum and human rights grounds) for staying in the UK at the same time so that they can be considered altogether by the Home Office and determined in one appeal. There are penalties for not complying with the procedure. The system was simplified by the 2002 Act.

Ordinary residence: this is defined in the case of *Shah* in the House of Lords as the place where someone is normally living for the time being. If a person is not legally in a country, that period does not count as ordinary residence. Reasons for residence can include 'education, business or profession, employment, health, family or merely love of the place'. People can be ordinarily resident in the UK without being settled here, for example students, work permit holders and *au pairs*. It is not an immigration status and has no direct connection to this. The term is also used in relation to access to the National Health Service and some benefits. Ordinary residence may change; the Home Office could argue that several months' residence abroad, particularly if the person had taken a job or given up a home in the UK, had broken ordinary residence in the UK. However, it is possible to be ordinarily resident in more than one country at a time, so such decisions can be challenged.

Overseas Territories: see British Overseas Territories.

Overstayer: a person who was granted limited leave to enter or remain in the UK but who has remained longer than the time allowed.

Patriality: another word for *right of abode. It was first used in the Immigration Act 1971 but was replaced by the term 'right of abode' in the British Nationality Act 1981.

Permit-free employment: a list of jobs which people may come to the UK to do without the employers needing to get *work permits or anyother *immigration employment document.

14

Person from abroad: a term first used by the Department of Social Security Benefits Agency meaning a person who is not eligible to claim certain welfare benefits. It has now been largely replaced by the definition of persons who are *subject to immigration control under s115 of the 1999 Act. Those who are required to pass the 'habitual residence' test in order to obtain certain benefits, are excluded as being 'persons from abroad' if they cannot pass this test.

Pillars: one way of explaining the significance of the Maastricht Treaty on the European Union is to consider the Union as the roof of a building, supported by three pillars. One pillar is the European Community (which includes economic policy and the free movement of EEA nationals), the second is the Common Foreign and Security Policy (CFSP) and the third Justice and Home Affairs matters (which includes *third-country national migration).

Police registration certificate: the certificate provided by the police to those non-Commonwealth, non-EEA citizens who are required to register with them.

Political asylum: another term used for *refugee status (see below).

Pre-sift: at certain diplomatic posts which receive large numbers of applications for visit visas there has been a system of weeding out those applications which look likely to fail, and recommending to the person that they withdraw. The advantage to the applicant is that if they withdraw they keep the fee, but if they persist and are refused, they lose it. People cannot be obliged to withdraw an application, and must be told of their right to continue. They should also be given a notice explaining what has happened, but as their application has not been considered in full, this notice does not explain the reasons for the failure.

Private life: this refers to the 'right to respect for private life' under Article 8 *ECHR which is one of the rights incorporated by the Human Rights Act 1998.

Probationary period: this refers to the period which a spouse or *unmarried partner of a person settled in the UK has to serve with limited leave before becoming entitled to apply for settlement. From December 2005, it is also applied to *civil partnerships. The probationary period is 24 months.

Proportionality: this is a legal term which is used in various different contexts. For our purposes, it is most often used to describe the balancing exercise which must be carried out to determine whether a 'restricted' human right under the *ECHR (like Article 8) can be interfered with in the interests of the community so that the right as a whole is not violated by government action. For example, the Home Office will often try to justify some interference with the right to respect for family life under Article 8, on the grounds that the interference is 'proportionate' when measured against the need to maintain a proper immigration control.

Public funds: This is the term used in the immigration rules to describe those welfare benefits which applicants need to show that they will not have to claim but that they can be adequately maintained in the UK without them. Often a condition is attached to leave to prohibit recourse to public funds. A person who claims public funds when prohibited from doing so can be subject to *administrative removal.

Quality Mark: Quality Mark is a standard that all providers of legal and advice services must achieve in order to be part of the *Community Legal Service scheme.

Recommendations: When an appeal is dismissed by the *AIT but there are strong compassionate reasons why a person ought to be allowed to remain in the UK, representatives can ask the Immigration Judge to make a 'recommendation' to the Home Office that leave outside the rules is granted. Whether to make a recommendation and whether the Home Office will follow a recommendation are both discretionary decisions. Making recommendations in dismissed cases, is not part of the formal powers of the AIT.

Refoulement: the central obligation of the UN *Convention is that of 'non refoulement', in Article 33. This is the provision requiring a state not to 'expel or return a refugee in any manner whatsoever to the frontiers of territories where his life or freedom would be threatened on account of his race, religion, nationality, membership of a particular social group or political opinion', unless it can be shown that he or she is a danger to the security of that state.

Refugee: according to the UN Convention is a person who is unwilling or unable to return to the country of their nationality or former habitual residence because of a well-founded fear of persecution on specified grounds (the *'Convention grounds'). When the Home Office recognises people as refugees, it grants them *asylum in the UK.

Registration: there are three distinct immigration/nationality law uses of this term.

1 A process of applying for British nationality. The word is now used for any child and certain categories of adult applying for British nationality. Registration and *naturalisation are both ways of gaining British nationality.

2 Registering the birth of a child at a British post overseas. A child born outside the UK to a *British citizen parent who was not themself born in the UK may be registered within one year of birth to become a British citizen by descent.

3 Registering with the police. Nationals of some countries may be required to register with the police. This means going to the local police station, or the Aliens Registration Office in London, with the passport, two passport-sized photos and details of address and occupation, registering their details with the police and paying a fee.

Regularisation of overstayers scheme: This is the scheme by which people who were overstayers could make applications to the Home Office to 'regularise' their stay in the UK before 1 October 2000. If they made the application under the Immigration (Regularisation Period for Overstayers) Regulations 2000, then, if the application was later refused, they kept their rights of appeal which existed under the Immigration Act 1971 for those who were *deported as overstayers rather than those who are to be removed from the UK *administratively under section 10 of the 1999 Act. There were delays in making decisions for those who made these applications. Almost all of these decisions should now have been made.

Removal: the final process by which the *immigration authorities expel a person from the UK.

Residence document: the term used in European law to refer to the documents which must be provided to the family member of an EEA national where that member is not him or herself a national of the EEA but who is entitled to be in the UK as the family member of an EEA national who is exercising *EU rights of free movement.

Residence permit: a document issued by the Home Office to EEA nationals to confirm their right to live in the UK as persons exercising *EU rights of free movement.

Respondent: in an appeal, or in judicial review, the person against whom the case is brought is the respondent. Typically this will be the Secretary of State at the Home Office. Immigration officers at the ports and *entry clearance officers at posts abroad, however, can legally take decisions in their own names and so may become respondents (See also *appellant).

Returning residents: people who had indefinite leave when they last left the UK and are returning to the UK within two years of departure. They should be admitted for an indefinite period, provided the immigration officers are satisfied that they intend to return to stay permanently. If they are returning after they have been away from the UK for over two years, there is a discretion in the immigration rules to admit them.

14

Right of abode: being free of immigration control and able to enter the UK freely at any time, after no matter how long an absence. It is more than simply having the right to live in the UK, or the right to stay indefinitely. All *British citizens have the right of abode. So do some *Commonwealth citizens – people who were born before 1 January 1983 and had a parent born in the UK (when the parent is the father, he must have been married to the mother) and women who were Commonwealth citizens before 1 January 1983 and were married before that date to a man who was born, registered or naturalised in the UK, or who is a Commonwealth citizen with a parent born in the UK, as above.

Right to reside: The most common use of this term is under regulations introduced from 1 May 2004 which adds another layer to the *habitual residence test which restricts access to social security benefit and access to local authority provided housing. The intention is to restrict, in particular those EEA nationals (include *Accession 8 nationals) who are not present in the UK exercising *EU rights of free movement.

Schengen group: this comprises all EU countries except the UK, Ireland and Denmark. The group has planned since 1988 to establish a common immigration policy and common border controls, with no internal border checks. The agreement came into effect on 26 March 1995 for seven countries. The Schengen 'acquis' or agreement is now incorporated within the framework of the European Union by the Treaty of Amsterdam, except for those countries which have opted out.

Settled: someone who is *ordinarily resident in the UK without any restrictions on the time they are permitted to remain here. British citizens and those with indefinite leave who usually live in the UK are, therefore, all generally accepted as being 'settled'.

Special quota voucher: the permission granted to certain *British nationals, who are not *British citizens, to come to settle in the UK. The system was set up in 1968, after the Commonwealth Immigrants Act 1968 removed the rights of British people without a connection by birth or descent with Britain itself to come to Britain. In order to qualify under the scheme, people must have no other nationality but British; be 'heads of house-holds'; have some connection with East Africa and be under pressure to leave the country in which they are currently living. Special vouchers were abolished on 4 March 2002.

Special Immigration Appeals Commission: until 1998 whenever the Home Secretary decided to expel someone and cited reasons of national security there has been no right of appeal but only an opportunity for a very limited review. This procedure was considered inadequate by the European Court of Human Rights, leading to the creation of this Commission to provide a meaningful appeal.

Sponsor: a friend, relative or other person who supports an applicant's application to come to the UK. In some cases, they are asked to sign a *maintenance undertaking.

Standard acknowledgement letter (SAL): a letter which used to be issued by the Home Office or immigration service to people seeking asylum. People who applied for asylum on entry to the UK had a document called SAL1 and people who applied after entry had a SAL2. SALs are now being replaced by *Application Registration Cards.

Subject to immigration control: This is a term which advisers and the Home Office often use to refer to people who need *leave to enter or remain in the UK (i.e. people who do not have the *right of abode and who are not exercising European rights of free movement and are not exempt from immigration control). The 1996 Act (s13(2)) gives this definition to this term. The 1999 Act gives a different definition for this term which is used to define who is not able to access certain forms of welfare provision (s115(9) 1999 Act). To avoid confusion, in the *Handbook*, we have only used the term as it is used in the 1999 Act for welfare purposes (▶see 1249–58).

Switching: 'Switching' is a term used to describe applications made for people who have leave to be in the UK on one basis (for example as a visitor) and who then wish to apply for leave to remain in a different capacity (for example as a spouse) without leaving the UK. The *immigration rules severely restrict the circumstances in which people may 'switch' (see ▶Chapter 7).

Temporary admission (TA): a kind of limbo state, used as an alternative to detention. Technically these are different forms of temporary admission (▶see 950–5) but we have used the term to cover all forms (most lawyers and some Home Office officials generally do not distinguish). People can be on temporary admission for long periods of time and can, at any time be detained while they have temporary admission. Most people on 'TA' also have conditions attached: as to residence, reporting and a prohibition on working.

Temporary protection: one reason given by governments for the decline in the proportion of asylum-seekers granted asylum is the inflexibility of the status set up by the Refugee Convention. It is said that this makes it unsuitable as a response to emergencies. For some time, therefore, there was discussion in the EU about creating a more limited form of status. The intention was to create a status in which decisions could be made quickly to provide for whole groups of displaced people, but without considering individual cases in detail, and the rights that are to be given would be much more limited. In particular there is no expectation of eventual settlement.

Third country: This term is usually used to refer to a country, other than the one which an asylum applicant is a national of, but which the Home Office may wish to send an asylum applicant to, rather than considering their application for asylum in the UK. There are criteria set out in the *Dublin 'II' Regulation for determining which state in Europe is responsible for determining an asylum claim made by an asylum-seeker within their territories. 'Third country national' is also the term given in the free movement context to people who are not EEA nationals.

Travel documents: although this may refer to any document of identity provided for the purpose of international travel, it is generally used to mean the non-national documents issued to refugees, stateless persons and those granted *HP, *DL or *ELR.

UNHCR: the United Nations High Commission for Refugees maintains offices with responsibility for each country which is a signatory to the Convention. They have an interest in ensuring consistency in the application of the Convention, and can be joined to an asylum appeal as a party. They also produce the *Handbook on Procedures and Criteria for Determining Refugee Status*.

United Kingdom: comprises Great Britain together with Northern Ireland. British immigration law applies equally throughout the UK.

United Kingdom and Islands: this refers to the UK together with the Crown Dependencies of the Isle of Man and the Channel Islands. Certain provisions in law apply to this area as a whole. The Islands have their own immigration arrangements, but these are closely integrated with the UK controls.

Unmarried partners: This term is used in the immigration rules to refer to couples (heterosexual or same-sex) who have been together for two or more years and are in a relationship 'akin to marriage'. They are permitted to obtain leave on similar terms to spouses. From 5 December 2005, same sex couples are able to give their relationship legal status by becoming *'civil partners'. Civil partners will be able to apply as dependants in the same way as spouses.

Visa nationals: people who always need to get entry clearance in advance of travelling to the UK, for whatever purpose, unless they are *returning residents or are returning within a period of earlier leave granted for more than six months. Countries whose citizens are visa nationals are listed in an Appendix to the immigration rules, which is amended from time to time, usually to add fresh countries.

14

Voluntary departure: people liable to deportation may decide to leave before an order is signed. The Immigration Service will usually permit this if the person buys his or her own ticket.

Work permits: The permission gained by employers to employ a worker from overseas who does not otherwise qualify to come to live in the UK. Work Permits (UK) issues permits to employers, not to workers, to employ a named person in a specific job. Any change of job means the new employers must apply for a new permit. A work permit is also categorised as one of the *immigration employment documents.

Alphabetical list of cases

Case citations

Many of the cases which are listed in the case list below have been 'reported'. This means that the case has been put into a series of law reports (sometimes general law reports and sometimes specialist law reports). Listed immediately below is a guide to the abbreviations used in order to refer to a particular series of law reports. The citations given in the case list are the standard way of citing the case and referring to the law report.

In addition, all cases which are now decided in the High Court, Court of Appeal or House of Lords are given a 'neutral citation number'. This number is given to the case by the court itself and, when searching on an electronic database in particular, using this reference can be very useful. For these cases, as well as any law report citation, we have also tried to give the neutral citation number. Neutral citation numbers for the Administrative Court in the High Court are given as EWHC Admin [...]; in the Court of Appeal Civil Division, are EWCA Civ [...]; and for the House of Lords are UKHL [...].

For some cases we only have a neutral citation number. Other unreported decisions are: cases given as 'CO/.../...' (unreported cases in the High Court shown by their Crown Office reference number); cases given as 'Applcn No...' (decisions of the European Court of Human Rights); cases shown only as 'CIS/.../...' (Social Security Commissioners' decisions); named cases followed only by a number in round brackets (decisions of the Immigration Appeal Tribunal); and 'UKAIT' (decisions of the AIT which now has a much more detailed system for the citation of its decisions (▶see 1110).

Many of the unreported decisions of the IAT and AIT can be accessed by subscribing to the Electronic Immigration Network (EIN) (▶see 1502 for contact details).

At the end of the citation to the cases listed, we have indicated (in round brackets) the court in which the case was decided. These abbreviations are straightforward. 'HC' is High Court. 'CA' is Court of Appeal. 'CC' is County Court. 'HL' is House of Lords. 'ECtHR' is the European Court of Human Rights. 'E Comm HR' is the European Commission for Human Rights. 'IAT' is the Immigration Appeal Tribunal. 'AIT' is the Asylum and Immigration Tribunal. 'OH' is the Scottish Outer House.

References to law reports

AC – *Appeal Cases*

All ER – *All England Law Reports*

BHRC – *Butterworths Human Rights Cases*

CCLR – *Community Care Law Reports*

CMLR – *Common Market Law Reports*

DR – *Decisions and Reports series of European human rights cases*

14

ECR – *European Case Reports*

EHRR – *European Human Rights Reports*

HLR – *Housing Law Reports*

Imm AR – *Immigration Appeal Reports (the 'Green Books')*

INLP – *Immigration and Nationality Law & Practice*

INLR – *Immigration and Nationality Law Reports*

LS Gaz – *Law Society Gazette*

QB – *Queens Bench Law Reports*

Sol Jo – *Solicitor's Journal*

WLR – *Weekly Law Reports*

A

A v Australia
[1997] 4 BHRC 210   919

A v SSHD [2003] INLR 249, [2003]
EWCA Civ 175 (CA)   796

A (Nigeria) v ECO [2004]
UKIAT 00019 (IAT)   1157

A, R v SSHD CO/2858/2004,
Consent order signed on
8 October 2004 (HC)   691

A, R v NASS and Waltham Forest LBC
[2003] EWCA Civ 1473,
[2004] 1 All ER 15,
(2003) 6 CCLR 538 (CA   1328

A (Somalia) [2004]
UKIAT 00031 (IAT)   760

A W & G , R v Lambeth and Barnet LBC
[2003] UKHL 57 (HL) K,
R v Lambeth LBC
[2004] 1 WLR 272,
[2003] EWCA Civ 1150 (CA)   1328

A and A v Netherlands
(1992) 72 DR 118   824

A & Kanidagli, R v SSHD [2004]
All ER (D) 91 (Jul) [2004]
EWHC 1585 (Admin)
(settled at the Court of   1185, 1224,
Appeal hearing)   1283

A and others v SSHD [2005]
2 WLR 87, [2004]
UKHL 56 (HL)   778, 901-2,
   924, 1082

AA v SSHD AA/04507/2005,
[2005] UKAIT CG)   614

Abdadou v SSHD
[1998] SC 504, OH   341
Butterworths ILS Vol III,
section 3D, 91

Abdi (DS)   768, 1125
[1996] Imm AR 148, CA   1156

Abdi and Ismail v Barnet LBC
(pending appeal to the
Court of Appeal)   1296

Abdulaziz, Cabales and Balkandali v UK
Series A No 94,   791, 823
(1985) 7 EHRR 471 (ECtHR)   828, 845,
   886, 1189,
   1203

AC, R v IAT [2003] INLR 507, [2003]
EWHC 389 (Admin) (HC)   859

Ach-Charki v SSHD [1991]
Imm AR 162 (IAT)   318

Adam, Limbuela, Tesema,
R v SSHD ex p   1301,
[2005] UKHL 66 (HL)   1307-11,
   1326

Adan and Aitsegeur, R v SSHD ex p
[2001] INLR 44, HL   599, 601,
   605, 612,
   613, 753,
   797

Adebizi (15514)   1157

Adegbie v Austria
(Applcn No 26998/95)
(EComm HR)   847-8

Adesegun (Olusola A)v ECO, Lagos
[2002] UKIAT 02132 (IAT)   316

Adimi, Sorani & Kaziu
[2001] QB 667;   684, 702,
[2000] 3 WLR 434;   969, 1213,
[1999]Imm AR 560 (DC),   1235

Adoui and Cornuaille v Belgium:115-116/81
[1982] ECR 1665,
[1982] 3 CMLR 631   553

Abdulaziz & Others v [1985]
7 EHRR 471 (ECtHR)   1189, 1203

Abdullah, R v SSHD
(CO/3709/04) (HC)   1385

Advic v UK
[1995] 20 EHRR CD 125   825

AE & FE v SSHD [2003] INLR 475,
[2003] Imm AR 609,
[2003] EWCA Civ 1032 (CA)   622, 624,
                              798, 852

Ahmadi (Fawad) and another, R v SSHD
[2005] AllER (D)169(Dec)
12 December 2005(CA)   234

Ahmed v Austria
[1997] 24 EHRR 278   797

Ahmed (Iftikhar) v SSHD
[2000] INLR 1 (CA)   614

Ahmed (Ishaque) (CA) (12292) –
consent order not published   317

Ahmed and Patel, R v SSHD, ex p
[1998], INLR 570, CA   360

Ahmed (Kalem)
[1995] (12774) IAT   1157

Ahmed, Secretary of State for Work
and Pensions v,
[2005] EWCA Civ 535 (CA)   1253

Ahmed (Talha) v SSHD
[2002] UKIAT 01757 (IAT)   839

Ahmed (Tanveer) v SSHD
[2002] INLR 345,
[2002] Imm AR 318,
[2002] UKIAT00439 (IAT)   665

Ajayi v UK
Applcn 27663/95
20th June 1999 (unreported)   820

AK (Turkey) [2004]
UKIAT 00230 (IAT)   1157

Akaeke, SSHD v, [2005]
EWCA CIV 947 (CA)   842

AKB, R (1) Special Adjudicator (2)
Secretary of State ex p.
[1998] INLR 315   930, 977,
                   983, 1209

Akinde v SSHD
[1993] Imm AR 512, CA   1013

Akrich, C-109/01, 23 September 2003
[2004] INLR 36 (ECJ)   542, 543,
                        548, 549

Akyuz (see Ozturk)

Al-Ameri v Kensington & Chelsea
RLBC [2004] 2 AC 159,
[2004] UKHL 4 (HL)   286

Alexander v IAT [1982]
1 WLR 1076 (HL)   260

Ali (Arman), R v SSHD, ex p
[2000] Imm AR 134,
[2000] INLR 89   317, 886

Ali, Iqbal, R v IAT, ex p
[1994] Imm AR 295, CA   371

Ali v Switzerland
Applcn 24881/94 EComHR   924

Ali (Syed Tariq) v ECO Dhaka
[2002] UKIAT 02541 (IAT)   254

Alihajdaraj (Sadri) v SSHD
[2004] EWCA Civ 1084 (CA)   841

Amimim Mohammed
(Gibraltar Supreme Court)
[1992] 3 CMLR 481   590

Re Amin
[1983] 2 AC 818,
[1983] 2 All ER 864, HL   1189, 1410

Amin, R v IAT ex p
[1992] Imm AR 367   1156

Amirthanathan [2003]
EWHC 1107 (ADMIN) (HC)   930
(see also Nadarajah & Amirthanathan (CA))

Amuur v France
[1996] 22 EHRR 533, ECtHR   922

Antonissen, R v IAT, ex p: C-292/89
[1991] ECR I-745,
[1991] 2 CMLR 373, ECJ   519

Anufrijeva v Southwark London
Borough Council & others
[2004] 2 WLR 603,   1182, 1185,
[2004] QB 1124,   1186, 1187,
[2003] EWCA Civ 1406   1195, 1202,
(CA),   1203

Anufrijeva, R v SSHD
[2003] UKHL 36 (HL)   1256

Appellant S395/2002 v Minister for
Immigration [2004] INLR 233,
[2003] HCA 71 [S395]
(High Court of Australia)   616

Arif v SSHD [1999]
Imm AR 271 (CA)   628

Asante v SSHD
[1991] Imm AR 78 IAT   605

Askar v UK (Applcn No 26373/95)
(EcommHR)   1182

Assessment of damages –I
[Lord Brennan QC]
CCU 02 2/5/28   1208

Attafuah (Emmanuel), ECO
Accra v, [2002] UKIAT 05922
(IAT)   362, 844

14

Avon County Council, R v
Secretary of State for Education
and Science ex p,
[1991] 1 QB 558 (CA)   1221

Awuko (4220) IAT   371

Aydin v Turkey
[1997] 25 EHRR 251   795

Azam (Abrar) v ECO Islamabad)
(11704) (30/12/94) IAT   312

B

B, R v Merton LBC
[2003] 4 All ER 280,
[2003] EWHC 1689
(Admin)(HC)   691, 1324

B v SSHD [2003] Imm AR 591,
[2003] UKIAT 00020B (IAT)   619

B, R v SSHD [2002] All ER (D)
324 (Nov), [2002] EWCA
Civ 1797 (CA)   348,349

B, R v (1) Special Adjudicator (2)
Secretary of State ex p.
[1998] INLR 315   932

B(Ekaterina Padarina) v SSHD
[2001] EWHC Admin 775
(HC)   346

B and Hoxha, R v Special Adjudicator
[2005] UKHL 19 (HL)   613, 618,
628, 630,
631

B and others, R v Secretary of State
[2005] INLR 36,
[2004] EWCA Civ 1344 (CA)   697

Bagdanavicius, R v SSHD
[2005] UKHL 38 (HL)   611, 799

Bahar (R Othman) v Immigration Officer
[1998] Imm AR 534 IAT   1157

Bakir (Cafer), SSHD v,
[2002] UKIAT 01176 (IAT)   823

Balkandali, see Abdulaziz, Cabales and
Balkandali v UK

Barkoci & Malik, R v SSHD ex p,
C-257/99, [2001] All ER (EC)
903, ECR I-6557;
[2001] 3 CMLR 48;
[2002] INLR 152 (ECJ)   580

Barnett & Wilkinson v Chief
Constable of West Yorkshire
(CA) unreported, April 24,
1998 [1998]   1205, 1290

Barry, R v Gloucestershire CC ex p,
(1997) 1 CCLR 30
[1997] 2 All ER 1   1322

Bastiampillai, R v IAT, ex p
[1983] 2 All ER 844,
[1983] Imm AR 1   402

Batayav v SSHD
[2004] INLR 126,
[2003] EWCA Civ 1489 (CA)   797

Baumbast & R v SSHD, C-413/99
[2002] ECR I-7091;   359, 526,
[2002] 3 CMLR 23;   531-4, 536,
[2003] ICR 1347;   545,546,
[2003] INLR 1 (ECJ)   561

Bayar (12380) IAT   406

BB v France 9 March 1998,
RJD 1998-VI p2596
(EComm HR)   810, 812

Begum (Hasna) (15629) IAT   317

Begum (Husna)
[2001] INLR 115, CA   406

Begum (Manshoora) R v IAT, ex p
[1986] Imm AR 385   405

Begum (Momotaz) (18699) IAT   313

Begum, R v Social Security Commissioner
[2003] EWHC 3380 also
reported as R(IS) 11/04   1253

Begum (Zabeda) (16677) consent order
before the Court of Appeal   317

Behre & others, R v Hillingdon LBC
[2003] EWHC 2075 (Admin)
(HC)   1325

Belgian Linguistic Case (No 2)
[1968] 1 EHRR 252 ECtHR   781

Beldjoudi v France
[1992] 14 EHRR 801 ECtHR   828, 843

Bensaid v UK
[2001] INLR 325,   791, 805,
[2001] 33 EHRR 205 ECtHR   810, 816–7,
851–2

Beqaraj, R v Special Adjudicator
[2002] EWHC 1469(Admin)
(HC)   1157

Bernard, R (on the application of,)
v Enfield LBC [2002]
EWHC 2282   1179, 1187,
1190-1,
1203

Berrehab v Netherlands
[1988] 11 EHRR 322, ECtHR   372, 824,
829, 831
1182, 1203

Bhakta CIS/1840/2004   1263

Bibi [2000] Imm AR 385 CA   401

Bibi (Debin) v ECO, Dhaka,
17 August 2001 (IAT) 366

Bibi, R v SSHD ex parte
[2005] EWHC 386 (Admin)
(HC) 824, 891

Bibi (Shabbana) v ECO, Islamabad
[2002] UKIAT 06623 (IAT) 307

Bibi (Sonor) (19199) IAT 317

Bi (Nazia) ECO v [2002]
UKIAT 05214 (IAT) 311

Bidar ECJ C-209-03
(15 March 2005) 300

Binbasi, R v SSHD ex p
[1989] Imm AR 593 608

Boadi v ECO (Ghana) [2002]
UKIAT 01323, [2003]
INLR 54 (IAT) 384

Botta v Italy
[1998] 26 EHRR 241 ECtHR 846

Boughanemi v France
[1996] 22 EHRR 228 ECtHR 824, 825
844

Boukssid v SSHD
[1998] Imm AR 270,
[1998] INLR 275, CA 540

Boultif v Switzerland
[2001] 33 EHRR1179 ECtHR 830–1, 843

Bouzagou, R v Governer of Ashford
Remand Centre, ex p
[1983] Imm AR 69 106

Box (Shamim); ECO Dhaka v
[2002] UKIAT 0221 844

Boybeyi, R v SSHD ex p,[1997]
INLR 130, [1997]
Imm AR 491 (CA) 733

Boyle v UK
[1994] 19 EHRR 179 EComHR 826

Brezinski and Glowacka, R v SSHD ex p
19th July 1996, unreported 974, 983

Bugdaycay v SSHD, Musisi Re
[1987] AC 514,
[1987] 1 All ER 940,
[1987] WLR 606,
[1987] Imm AR 250 969

Bushati(Yilka) v SSHD
[2002] UKIAT 03625 (IAT) 807

C

C v Commissioner of Police for the
Metropolis [Feb 2003](CC) 1205

CA v SSHD [2004] INLR 453,
[2004] EWCA Civ 1165 (CA) 813, 1155

Cabales, see Abdulaziz, Cabales and
Balkandali v UK

Cabrera (17123) IAT 1156

Camenzind v Switzerland
16th December [1997]
ECtHR 816

Campbell and Cosans v UK
[1982] 4 EHRR 293 795

Caparo Industries plc v Dickman
[1990] 2 AC 605 (HL)] 1178

Carpenter v SSHD, C-60/00
[2003] QB 416,
[2003] 2 WLR 267,
[2003] All ER (EC) 577,
[2002] ECR I-6279,
[2002] 2 CMLR 64,
[2002] INLR 439 (ECJ) 543-4

CH/3801/2004 1283

Chahal v UK [1996] 23 EHRR 413
ECtHR 796, 787
624, 923–4,
926, 929

Chang (01 TH00100) [2001] IAT 551

Chavrimootoo, R v IAT, ex p
[1995] Imm AR 267 1128

Chen v SSHD, C-200/02
[2005] INLR 1 (ECJ) 359, 529,
534-7

Chiew, R v IAT ex p, [1981]
Imm AR 102, QBD 493

CI/3280/2003 1262, 1263

Cicek v Turkey (2001)
App No 25704/94
27 February 2001 ECtHR 793

Ciliz v The Netherlands
[2000] 2 FLR 469
(Applcn 29192/95) (ECtHR) 827, 844,
1182, 1203

CIS/0345/2003 1284

CIS/3797/2003 1285

CIS/3573/05, CH 2484/05 1268

CJSA/4065/1999 1261, 1264

CJSA/4383/2003 1285

Clavijo-Hoyos (00/TH/02131) IAT 661

Cole v Turner (1704) 6 Mod. 149 1183

Collins v Secretary of State for
Work and Pensions
(Case C-138/02) (ECJ) 1261

Commission v Netherlands (ECR) (C/68/89)
[1991] ECR-I-2637 550

14

Commissioner of Police for the
Metropolis v Gerald [1998]
(CA) 1205

Coskuner [1998] CC/52752/97
(IAT) 1157

D

D v Home Office HC
[February 2003] 1207

D v UK
[1997] 24 EHRR 423 809–10,
811, 892,
1852

Dabrowski, R v SSHD
[2003] Imm AR 454,
[2003] EWCA Civ 580 (CA) 388

Dadibhai, R v IAT, ex p 24th October 1983,
(unreported) 402

Danaie, R v SSHD ex p
[1988] Imm AR 84,
[1998] INLR 124 (CA) 1128

Danian
[2000] Imm AR 96
[1999] INLR 553, CA 715

Danian (Thomas) v SSHD
[1999] INLR 533 (CA) 614

Danino (Naomi); Immigration
Officer, Gatwick South v
[2002] UKIAT 04895 (IAT) 849

Danleu (21500) IAT 1157

Daraz (see El-Ali (Amer Mohammed))

Davila-Puga
[2001] EWCA Civ 931 (CA) 665

Dehwari v Netherlands 29
EHRR CD 74 (EComm HR) 793

Demirkaya
[1999] Imm AR 498,
[1999] INLR 441 CA 604, 628,
797

Desai
[2000] INLR 10, CA 501

Devaseelan [2003] Imm AR 1,
[2002] UKIAT 702
(IAT, starred) 790, 1123

Devaseelan (Justin Surendran) v SSHD
[2002] UKIAT 00702 787, 735,
*13/3/02 IAT 1069

D'Hoop (ECJ C-224/98
(11 July 2002) 299

Diatta v Land Berlin: 267/83
[1985] ECR 567,
[1986] 2 CMLR 164, ECJ 529

Di Paolo v Office National de L'Emploi
(Case 76/76) [1977] E.C.R.,
[1977] 2 C.M.L.R. 59 (ECJ) 1261

Djali (Sefer) v IAT
[2003] EWCA Civ 1371 (CA)

Djebbar v SSHD
[2004] INLR 466,
[2004] EWCA Civ 804 (CA)
ImmAR497 1123

DM (Proportionality – Article 8)
Croatia CG
[2004] UKIAT 00024,
[2004] Imm AR 211 (IAT) 841

Dogan (Ahmet) (interested party),
R (SSHD) v Chief Asylum
Support Adjudicator and,
[2003] EWCA Civ 1673 (CA) 1390

Dogan C-388/03,
7 July 2005 (ECJ) 587

Do v IAT see Ullah

DR (Morocco)
[2005] UKIAT 00038
(IAT, starred) 1120

DS v Home Office HC
[October 2001] 1209

Dube (Zanek), SSHD v,
[2002] UKIAT 01367 (IAT) 276

Dudy v Home Office (CC) 1206

Durojaiye (Remi Adekola) v SSHD
[1991] Imm AR 307 260, 1013

Dursun v SSHD
[1993] Imm AR 169 (CA) 747

Dzhygun (00 TH 00728) IAT 608

E

E & R v SSHD
[2004] 2 WLR 1351, 1151,
[2004] INLR 268, 1157,1159,
[2004] EWCA Civ 49 (CA) 1160

East African Asians v UK
[1973] 3 EHRR 76, EComHR 796, 1409

Echternach & Moritz C-389/87,
C-390/87 [1989] ECR 723,
[1990] 2 CMLR 237 (ECJ) 534

Ejon, R v SSHD, ex p
[1998] INLR 195 711, 733

Ekinci, R v SSHD
[2004] Imm AR 15,
[2003] EWCA Civ 765 (CA) 836-9

El-Ali (Amer Mohammed) v SSHD;
Daraz v SSHD [2002] INLR 468,
[2002] EWCA Civ 1103,
[2003] Imm AR 179 (CA)   626

El Yassini v SSHD: C-416/96
[1999] All ER (EC)
[1999] INLR 131, ECJ   590

Erdogan, R v SSHD
[2004] EWCA Civ 1087 (CA)   1344

European Roma Rights Centre
and others, R v Immigration Officer, Prague
Airport & another
(UNHCR intervening)
[2005] 2WLR1,
[2005] 1 All ER 527   49, 697,
[2004] UKHL55 (HL)   703, 892

Evans, R v Governor of Brockhill Prison
ex parte (No 2)
[2001] 2 AC 19 (HL)   922, 930,
                          1208

Everett, R v Secretary of State for
Foreign and Commonwealth
Affairs ex p [1989] QB 811,
[1989] 2 WLR 224,
[1989] Imm AR 155 CA   1424

EZ v Home Office HC
[January 2004]   1206

F

F v West Berkshire Health Authority
[1990] 2 AC 1 (HL)   1183

Fadele v UK
[1990] 1 CD 15, 70 DR
HRCL Digest Vol 1 (1) 15   818, 829

Fadli, R v SSHD, ex p
[2001] 02 LS Gaz 40, CA   793

Farah v MPC [1998] QB 65)   1190

Farrakhan (Louis), R v SSHD
[2002] 4 All ER 289,
[2002] INLR 257,
[2002] Imm AR 447,
[2002] EWCA Civ 606 (CA)   808

Fatemeh (Miriam)
(00 TH 00921) IAT   608

Ferko (Andrej), R v SSHD, ex p
(CO 4205/1997) (1997)   930

Fitzpatrick v Sterling Housing
Association Ltd
[2001] 1 AC 27   827

Fornah [2005] EWCA Civ 680
(CA)   608, 617

Foughali (00 TH 01513/4)
[2000] IAT   619

Fox v Stirk and Bristol Electoral
Registration Officer
[1970] 2 QB 463 (CA)   303

G

G & M, (R (G) v IAT and R (M) v IAT)
[2005] 1 WLR 1445,
[2004] EWCA Civ 1731   1151

Gaima v SSHD
[1989] Imm AR 205 CA   1157

Gal (10620) INLP Vol 8 (2)
[1994] p 69 IAT   1429

Gangadeen and Jurawan v SSHD
[1998] INLR 206,
[1998] Imm AR 106, CA   360

Ganidagli, R v SSHD
[2001] INLR 479,
[2001]EWHC (Admin)70 (HC) 1157

Gardi (Azad) v SSHD
[2002] 1 WLR 2755,
[2002] INLR 499,
[2003] Imm AR 39,
[2002] EWCA Civ 750 (CA)
(later declared to be nullity
in Gardi v SSHD (No 2)
Declaration of Nullity
[2002] 1 WLR 3282,
[2002] INLR 557,
[2002] EWCA Civ 1560 (CA)) 610, 621

Gashi, R v SSHD ex p
[1999] Imm AR 231
[1999] INLR 276 reversed
[1999] Imm AR 415 CA   753

Gaskin v UK
[1989] 12 EHRR 36   825

Gezer, R v SSHD
[2003] EWHC 860 (Admin),
[2003] HLR 972 (HC),
[2004] EWCA Civ 1730 (CA)   1191

Ghaidan v Godin-Mendoza
[2004] 2 AC 557,
[2004] UKHL 30   827

Gill (Sukhjit)
(01TH02884)
IAT 6th December 2001   848

Gingi v Secretary of State for Work
and Pensions R (IS) 5/02,
[2001] EWCA Civ 1685 (CA)   1263

Gloszczuk, R v SSHD ex p, C-63/99,
[2002] All ER (EC) 353,
[2001] ECR I-6369;
[2001] 3 CMLR 46;
[2002] INLR 357 (ECJ)   577, 580

14

Golder v UK
[1979-1980] 1 EHRR 524   781

Gomez
[2000] INLR 549 IAT   606

Gorenkin   1319

Goswell v Commissioner of Police
for the Metropolis (CA) April 7
[1998](unreported)   1205

Grant v London Borough of Lambeth
[2004] EWCA Civ 1711 (CA)   1311, 1312

Green, R v SSHD, ex p
(29 October 1996) unreported;
on appeal (31 January 1997,
unreported), CA   234

Grzelczyk and Centre Public
d'Aide Sociale d'Ottignies-
Louvain-la-Neuve C-184/99
[2003] All ER (EC) 385;
[2001] ECR I-6193;
[2002] 1 CMLR 19;
[2002] ICR 566 (ECJ)   523

Greenfield, R v SSHD ex p
[2005] 2 All ER 240,   1174, 1201,
[2005] UKHL 14   1202, 1203

Gul v Switzerland
[1996] 22 EHRR 93 (ECtHR)   824, 828,
    846

Gurgur v ECO, Istanbul
[2002] UKIAT 0246 (IAT)   217

Gurol C-374, 7 July 2005 (ECJ)   585

Gurung v SSHD [2003] INLR 133,
[2003] Imm AR 115,
[2002] UKIAT 04870 (IAT)   624, 1080

Gurung (Kham Bahadur)
[2002] UKIAT01953 (IAT)   438

Gusinsky v Russia, 19 May 2004,
Applcn 70276/01 (ECtHR)   802

Guveya v NASS [2004]
EWHC 2371 (Admin) (HC)   1385

H

H (Somalia)
[2004] UKIAT 00027 (IAT)   770

Haddad (Ali)
[2000] INLR 117 IAT   716, 1119

Hadiova (Alena) v SSHD
[2003] Imm AR 490,
[2003] EWCA Civ 701 (CA)   805-6

Hague v Deputy Governor of
Parkhurst Prison and others,
Weldon v Home Office
[1991] 3 All ER 733   1178

Harrison v SSHD
[2003] INLR CA,
[2003] EWCA Civ 432 (CA)   803

Hashim, R v An Immigration Officer, ex p
(CO/2052/1999)
12th June 2000   343

Haughton (4889) IAT   371

He (Jin Tao) v SSHD
[2002] EWCA Civ 1150 (CA)   603

Henao v Netherlands
(Applcn No 13669/03)
(ECtHR)   810, 820

HI [2004] UKIAT 00092 CG (IAT)   848

HLR v France
[1997] 26 EHRR 29, ECtHR   799

Hill v Commissioner for the
Metropolis (CA) unreported
November 4, [1998]   1205

Hoekstra (nee Unger) 75/63
[1964] ECR 177,
[1964] CMLR 319, ECJ   547

Holub and Holub v SSHD
[2001] INLR 219 CA   820

Horvath v SSHD (UNHCR intervening)
[1999] Imm AR 121,
[1999] INLR 7; affd
[2000] Imm AR 205,
[2000] INLR 15, CA; affd
[2000] 3 All ER 577,
[2000] 3 WLR 379,
[2000] Imm AR 552,   604, 611,
[2000] INLR 239, HL   799, 1157

Hoye v Bush (1840)
1 Man & G 775   1184

Huang, Abu-Qulbain, Kashmiri v SSHD
[2005] EWCA Civ 105 (CA)   792, 834-5,
    850

Humbel, Belgium v C-263/86
[1988] ECR 5365 (ECJ)   522

Husan, R v SSHD
[2005] EWHC 189
(Admin) (HC)   1075

Husain, R v Asylum Support
Adjudicators and SSHD [2001]
EWHC Admin 582 (HC)   1392

Huzzey v Brent, Kensington and
Chelsea NHS Trust (QBD)
[2001] 00LQ1441   1209

Hysi (CA)
[2005] EWCA CIV 711 (CA)   622

I

I [2004] (HC)	1210
I v Home Office [June 2004] (HC)	1206
I, R v SSHD [2003] INLR 196, [2002] EWCA Civ 888 (CA)	925, 926, 927-9, 983, 1175
I and O, R v SSHD [2005] EWHC 1025 (Admin)(HC)	690, 908, 930
Ibraheem (11788) IAT	406
Ibrahim [2001] Imm AR 430, [2001] EWCA Civ 519	744, 754
ID & Others v The Home Office [2005] EWCA Civ 38 (CA)	908, 920, 930, 932, 1175, 1176, 1188, 1189, 1193, 1196, 1200
Imoh; ECO Lagos v [2002] UKIAT 01967	844
Iran & Others, R v SSHD [2005] EWCA Civ 982 (CA)	1049, 1156, 1157, 1158
Ireland v UK [1978] 2 EHRR 25 ECtHR	794, 795
Isiko, R v S SSHD ex p [2001] INLR 109, CA	339, 359, 829, 840
Islam v SSHD, R v IAT & SSHD ex p Shah and – see 'Shah and Islam'	349
Ivanauskiene v SA and SSHD [2002] INLR 1, EWCA Civ 1271 (CA)	1156

J

J, R v Enfield LBC [2002] EWHC 432, [2003] 5 CCLR 434 (HC)	1318
J, Re [1998] INLR 424, CA	818–9, 996,
J (Serbia and Montenegro) [2004] UKIAT 00016 (IAT)	841
Jabari v Turkey [2001] INLR 136 (ECtHR)	793
Jagot, R v SSHD ex p [2001] INLR501 (HL)	389
Jain [2000] Imm AR 76, [2000] INLR 71, CA	608, 615, 805

Jakupovic v Austria [2003] INLR 499, Applcn No 36757/97, 38 EHRR 595 (ECtHR)	849, 850
Janjanin (Zrinka) & Obrad Musanovic v SSHD [2004] Imm AR 264, [2004] EWCA Civ 448 (CA)	842
Jama (Zainab Ali) R v ECO, Addis Ababa, ex p (CO 3338/1999)	878, 879
Jaramillo v UK Applcn 24865/94 [1995]	820
Jeyeanthan, R v IAT ex p, [2000] 1 WLR 354, [2000] Imm AR 10, [2000] INLR 241 (CA)	1062
Jeyakumaran, R v SSHD ex p [1994] Imm AR 45	612
Jobe (Giran Saliu) v SSHD [2002] UKIAT 05444 (IAT)	849
Johnson, R v SSHD [2004] EWHC 1550 (Admin) (HC)	678, 929, 932, 977, 1208
Johnston v Ireland [1986] 9 EHRR 203, ECtHR	824
Jonah, R v IAT ex parte [1985] Imm AR 7	797

K

K [2004] (HC)	1210
K v SSHD [2003] UKIAT00033 (IAT)	587
K (India) [2004] UKIAT 00020 (IAT)	241
K, R (Kimani) v Lambeth LBC [2004] 1 WLR 272, [2003] EWCA Civ 1150]	1312
Kaba (Arben) v SSHD, C-356/98 [2000] All ER (EC) 537; [2000] ECR I-2623; [2003] 1 CMLR 39	540
Kacaj, SSHD v (01/TH00634)* [2001] INLR [2002] Imm AR 281 IAT	604, 787–8 794, 797, 804, 820, 833, 1122
Kagema [1997] Imm AR 137, CA	604, 797
Kaja v SSHD [1995] Imm AR 1	1121, 1122

14

Kalashnikov v Russia
[2003] 36 EHRR 34
(Applcn No 47095/99)
(July 2002) (ECtHR)   797

Kandasamy, R v Special
Adjudicator ex parte,
[1994] Imm AR 333 (HC)   747

Karanakaran v SSHD
[2000] 3 All ER 449,   623, 709
[2000] Imm AR 271,   792, 1106,
[2000] INLR 122, CA   1122, 1156

Kariharan and Koneswaran,
R v SSHD
[2002] INLR 383,
[2003] Imm AR 163,
[2002] EWCA Civ 1102 (CA)   857

Karoaglan, Hadavi and Bashiri –
consent order; CO/4634/2000;
CO/409/2001 ; CO/1040/2001
3 May 2001   716

Kasolo (13190) [1996] IAT   1157

Kassam, R v Immigration
Appeal Tribunal, ex p
[1980] 1 WLR 1037   1189

Kasuji
[1988] Imm AR 587   314

Kaur v SSHD [2002]
UKIAT 01170 (IAT)   311

Kaur (Balvir) v SSHD
[2002] UKIAT003387 (IAT)   608

Kaur, Balwinder (IAT) (12838)   317

Kaur (Kartar) (IAT)11549
15 November 1994   401

Kaur (Manjit) R v SSHD, ex p,
ECJ (C-192-99)
20 March 2001, unreported   513, 1409

Kausar
[1998] INLR 141 (IAT)   316

Kaya v Haringey LBC
[2002] HLR1

Kazmi, R v SSHD ex parte,
[1995] Imm AR 73 (HC)   732

KB, R v Mental Health Review
Tribunal [2004] QB 936;
[2003] EWHC 193 (Admin)   1203

Keegan v Ireland
[1994] 18 EHRR 342,
[1994] 3 FCR 165, ECtHR   824

Kelso, R v SSHD, ex p
[1998] INLR 603   986

Kempf v Staatssecretaris van Justitie,
C-139/85 [1986] ECR 1741;
[1987] 1 CMLR 764 (ECJ)   518

Kerkhoven v Netherlands (Commission)
19th May 1992 (unreported) 827

Khadir, R v Secretary of State for
the Home Department ex p,
[2005] UKHL 39 (HL)   920, 921,
                           925, 951,
                           956-7, 986,
                           987

Khan (9416) IAT   307

Khan (Dewan) (00TH02531) IAT,
30th November 2000   312

Khan, R v Oxfordshire CC
[2003] 5 CCLR 611,
[2004] EWCA Civ 309 (CA)   1318, 1321

Kharrazi, R v CIO Gatwick Airport, ex p
[1980] 1 WLR 1396   258

Khawaja & Khera
[1984] AC 74 (HL)   1013, 1215

Khawaja, R v Home Secretary ex p,
[1984] AC 74 (HL)   987, 1010

Khokhar
[1981] Imm AR 56   113

Kidane v SSHD [2002]
UKIAT 04814 (IAT)   848

Kimani, (see K, R (Kimani))

Kimvono, R v Tower Hamlets LBC ex p,
[2001] 33 HLR 78 QBD (HC)   1298

Kinuthia (Pauline) v SSHD
[2002] INLR 133,
[2001] EWCA Civ 2100 (CA)   611

Kirkham v Chief Constable of
the Greater Manchester Police
[1989] 2 QB 283   1179

KK [2004] UKIAT 00268 (IAT)   368

KK (Article 1F(C) Turkey) v SSHD
[2004] Imm AR 284 (IAT)   625

Klip and Kurger v Netherlands,
91A DR 66 (ECom)   290

Konan R, v SSHD
[2004] EWHC 22 Admin   929, 932

Kondova, R v SSHD ex p, C-235/99,
[2001] ECR I-6427;
[2001] 3 CMLR 47 (ECJ)   580

Kotecha, R v IAT, ex p
[1983] 2 All ER 289,
[1983] 1 WLR 487,
[1982] Imm AR 88, CA   1156

Kroon v Netherlands
[1994] 19 EHRR 263 (ECtHR) 824

Krotov v SSHD [2004] INLR 304,
[2004] EWCA Civ 69 (CA)   620

Kuguthas v SSHD
[2003] INLR 170,
EWCA Civ 31 (CA)   825, 826,
844, 846

Kungwengwe, R v SSHD
EWHC Admin 1427 (HC)   154

Kurtolli v SSHD
[2004] INLR 198,
[2003] EWHC 2744
(Admin) (HC)   818, 996

Kus v Landeshauptstadt Wiesbaden: C-237/91
[1992] ECR I-6781,
[1993] 2 CMLR 887, ECJ   587

Kwong (Yee-Kee) (10661)
IAT, 11 February 1994   528

L

LA (section 83(2) appeals –
human rights) Eritrea
[2004] UKIAT 00113 (AIT)   1079

Ladd v Marshall
[1954] 1 WLR 1489,
[1954] 3 All ER 745 (CA)   1160, 1161

Lam (Tan Te) v Tai A Chau Detention
[1997] AC 97   921, 924,
926

Lawrie-Blum v Land Baden-Wurttemberg: 66/85
[1986] ECR 2121,
[1987] 3 CMLR 389,
[1987] ICR 483, ECJ   518

Lebbink v Netherlands
(Applcn No 45582/99)
1 June 2004 (ECtHR)   824

Lekstaka, R v IAT
[2005] EWHC 745
(Admin) (HC)   835, 850

Levin C-53/81   1261

Levin v Secretary of State for Justice: 53/81
[1982] ECR 1035,
[1982] 2 CMLR 454, ECJ   518

Liu [2005] EWCA CIV 249 (CA)   608

Livingstone (10964) [1994] IAT   343

Lizarzaburu (10848) IAT   343

Luisi & Carbone v Minstero del Tesoro,
C-286/82, C-726/83
[1984] ECR 377;
[1985] 3 CMLR 52 (ECJ)   522

Lunt v Liverpool City Justices
[1991] (CA)   1208

Lustig-Prean and Beckett v UK
[2000] 31 EHRR 601   1203

M

M, R (on the application of,) v
SSHD Admin [2004] (HC)   1208

M, R v Islington LBC
[2004] EWCA Civ 235,
[2004] 7 CCLR 230 (CA)   389-90,
1312-4,
1315

M v Secretary of State for Work
and Pensions
[2005] 2 WLR 740,
[2004] EWCA Civ 1343 (CA)   827

M v Secretary of State for
Social Security
[2001] UK HL 35,
(R(DLA) 7/01) (HL)   1258

M v SSHD [2003]EWCA Civ146,
[2003] INLR306(CA)   1019

M & A v SSHD [2004] Imm AR 4,
[2003] EWCA Civ 263 (CA)   364

M (Croatia)
[2004] INLR 327 (IAT)   834

M (Mambakasa joined to
Anufrijeva as M in the
Court of Appeal.
See 'Anufrijeva')   1182, 1186

M, C & N, R v SSHD
(CO/2805/2005) (HC)   1385

MA (DP3/96 – interpretation
Algeria [2005] UKAIT 00127   339

MA (Fresh Evidence) Sri Lanka v
SSHD [2004] Imm AR 460,
[2004] UKIAT 00161 (IAT)   1159,1160

Maaouia v France
[2001] 33 EHRR 1037
9 [2001] BHRC 205 ECtHR   803

Mahamed (Abdi Hussen) & others v ECO,
Addis Ababa TH02555-2002,
16 August 2004 (IAT)   762, 765

Maheshwaran (Balasingham),
SSHD v, [2004] Imm AR 176,
[2002] EWCA Civ 173 (CA)   1157

Mahmod (Wasfi Suleman), Re
[1995] Imm AR 311   925

Mahmood v SSHD
[2001] 1 WLR 840 CA,
[2001] INLR 1 (CA)   11, 337
[2001] ImmAR 229   822–3, 830,
834, 836–7,
838, 840

14

Mahmood (Amjad) v ECO Islamabad
[2002] UKIAT 018919 (IAT)   317

Mambakasa, R v SSHD
[2003] EWHC 319 (HC)   97, 718,
(later joined to Anufrijeva   1185, 1225,
in the Court of Appeal)   1226, 1283

Mani, R v Lambeth LBC
[2004] HLR 5,
[2003] EWCA Civ 836,
[2003 6 CCLR 376,
[2004] LGR (CA)   1318

Marchon, R v SSHD ex p
[1993] 2 CMLR 132
[1993] Imm AR 384 (CA)   552

Marckx v Belgium
[1979] 2 EHRR 330 ECtHR   826

Mario v SSHD
[1998] ImmAR281   1156

Martin v Watson (1996)
1 A.C. 74   1192

Massaquoi [2001] Imm AR 309
(affd (C/2000/0622))
[2001] Imm AR 309 CA   640

Mata Estevez v Spain
[2001] Reports of Judgments
and Decisions 2001-VI, p311
(ECtHR)   827

Mayisokele (13039)
(1996, unreported), IAT   1157

Mbanza
[1999] Imm AR 508, CA   715

McKenzie, R v SSHD
[2001] EWHC Admin 630
(HC)   346

Meharban (Mohd)
[1989] Imm AR 57   321

Mehemi v France
[2000] 30 EHRR 739 (ECtHR)   830, 846

Mendes (12183) IAT   1157

Mersin, R v SSHD ex p
[2000] INLR 511   718

Mersin, R v SSHD ex p
[2001] INLR 511 (HC)   1185

Miah (Kari Shahjad) v ECO, Dhaka
[2002] UKIAT 02533 (IAT)   307

Miftari v SSHD
[2005] EWCA Civ 481 (CA)   1139

Miller
[1988] Imm AR 358, CA   751

Mindoukna (Romouald Andela)
(01TH02635) IAT
8th November [2001]   848

Minteh, Lamin R v SSHD, ex p
(396/5400/D) (8 March 1996,
unreported), CA   974

Minton v SSHD
[1990] Imm AR 199;
[1989] Imm AR 496   104

MM (Section 8:
Commencement) Iran
[2005] UKIAT 00115 (AIT)   710

MN (Kenya)
[2005] UKIAT00021 (IAT)   615-6

MNM v SSHD
[2000] INLR 576   1158

Modi (9714) IAT   317

Modinos v Cyprus
[1993] 16 EHRR 485   805

Mohamed, R v SSHD
[2002] EWHC 1530 (Admin)
(HC)   931, 977

Mohammed, R (on the application of
Mohammed and Others) v SSHD
[2000] EWHC 57 (Admin)
22 January 2001   744

Mohammed (Swaleh) (12412)
(4 August 1995,
unreported), IAT   1157

Mongoto (Delo)
[2005] EWCA CIV 751   850

Montana
[2001] 1WLR 552, CA.   1429

Montoya v SSHD
[2002] INLR 399,
[2002] EWCA Civ 620 (CA)   609

Moon (Human rights, entry
clearance, proportionality) USA
[2005] 00112 (IAT)   845

Morris, Westminster City Council
& the First Secretary of State v,
[2005] EWCA Civ 1184 (CA)   1297

Moustaquim v Belgium   823, 830
[1991] 13 EHRR 802 ECtHR   843

MPAX, R v Westminster City Council
[1997] CCLR 85 (CA)   1299, 1317
see also Westminster

MRAX, Mouvement contre le
racisme, l'antisemitisme et
la xenophobie ASBL, C-459/99
[2003] 1 WLR 1073;
[2002] ECR I-6591;   528, 529,
[2002] 3 CMLR 25 (ECJ)   551

Mthokozisi, R v SSHD
[2004] EWHC 2964
(Admin) (HC)   842

'Mumin' case, R v IAT ex parte
Secretary of State for the
Home Department
[1992] Imm AR 554 QBD (DC) 1125

Mungu v SSHD
[2003] EWCA Civ 360 (CA)   665

Munjaz v Mersey Care National
Health Service Trust & S v
Airedale National Health
Service Trust [2003]
EWCA Civ 1036 (CA)   1178

Munjaz, R v Ashworth Hospital (now
Mersey Care NHS Trust) ex p,
[2005] UKHL (HL)   1178

Musisi, Re
[1987] AC 514,
[1987] 2 WLR 606,
[1987] Imm AR 250 (HL)   752

Musisi, Re; Bugdaycay v SSHD
[1987] AC 514
[1987] WLR 606,
[1987] Imm AR 250
[1987] 1All ER 940   641

Muwanguzi v SSHD
HR/50328/01,
30 November 2003 (IAT)   813

N

N v SSHD [2004] INLR 10,
[2003] EWCA Civ 1369 (CA),
[2005] UKHL 31 (HL)   809-14,
851

N v SSHD (see 'Anufrijeva')   1186-7

N v Home Office
[2004] HC pre issue   1209

Nadarajah & Amirthanathan v SSHD
[2003] EWCA Civ 1768,
[2004] INLR 139 (CA)   908, 909,
915, 929,
930, 931

Nazari, R v
[1980] 3 All ER 880   1016, 1017

Nazli [2000] ECRI – 957,
C-340/97 (ECJ)   587

Nela v Home Office [2001] (CC)   1207

Nessa v Chief Adjudication Officer
[1999] WLR 1937,
(R(IS) 2/00) (HL)   1262, 1263

Nigatu, R v SSHD
[2004] EWHC 1806 (HC)   1343

Nhundu and Chiwera
(01TH00613) IAT   826, 829,
1st June 2001   846

Nmaju [2000] 36 LS Gaz 41,
[2001] INLR 26, CA   370

NS (Relevance of children to removal
– Article 8) Sri Lanka
[2005] UKIAT 00081 (IAT)   859

Nylund v Finland (Applcn NO 27110/95)
29 June 1999 (ECtHR)   824

O

O [1995] Imm AR 494 CA   612

O v Home Office
[Feb 2004] (CC)   1180

O, R v Haringey LBC and SSHD
[2004] EWCA Civ 535,
[2004] 7 CCLR 310 (CA)   1318

O and Bhika
[2001] I WLR 2359 (CA)   1317

Odozi (9582) IAT   1125

Ogle v CC Thames Valley Police
[2001] EWCA Civ 598   1176

Ogunkola v ECO, Lagos
[2002] UKIAT 02238 (IAT)   217

O'Hara v Chief Constable of
the RUC [1997] AC 286 (HL)   922

Okot v Commissioner of Police
for the Metropolis (Central
London County Court)
(Unreported)   1177, 1188

Olofinusi, R v IAT
[2002] INLR 588,
[2002] EWHC 2106
Admin (HC)   306

Omoruyi
[2001] Imm AR 175, CA   609

Onen (TH/43596/94 (22101; R1450)
4 February 1997 (IAT)   1125

Onibiyo, R v SSHD ex p
[1996] QB 768
[1996] Imm AR 370 CA   731, 732

Orange v Chief Constable of
West Yorkshire Police
[2001] 3 WLR 736.   1179

O'Rourke v Camden LBC
[1998] AC 188 (HL)   1185

Osman v UK
[1998] 29 EHRR 245
5 BHRC 293 ECtHR   793

Ouanes v SSHD
[1998] INLR 230,
[1998] Imm AR 76, CA   608

14

Ozgur Gundem v Turkey
[2001] 31 EHRR 1082, ECtHR
Judgement 16/03/2000 808

Ozturk (CO/6657/2004) & Akyuz
(CO/5725/2004) (HC)
[2005] EWHC1433
(Admin) 6 July 2005 (HC) 586, 587

P

P v Home Office & Parole Board
[March 2001] (HC) 1209

Pardeepan
[2000] INLR 447 735

Patel, R v ex p
[1993] Imm AR 392 157

Patel (Virendrakumar) v IAT
[1983] Imm AR 76 (CA) 259

Pattuwearachchi
[1991] Imm AR 341 258

Paw (4328) IAT 406

Payir v SSHD [2005] EWHC 1426
(Admin), 7 July 2005 (ECJ) 586, 587

Pepushi, R v CPS
[2004] EWHC 798
(Admin) (HC) 1236

Perks v UK (ECHR)
[1999] 30 EHRR 33 1206

Pharis (Ben) v SSHD
[2004] EWCA Civ 654 (CA) 1220

Pini v Romania
(Applcn Nos 78028/01,
78030/01) 22 June 2004
(ECtHR) 825

Poku v UK
[1996] 22 EHRR CD 94
(ECommHR) 373, 830

Q

Q, R v SSHD [2004] QB 36,
[2003] EWCA Civ 364 (CA) 713

Q, R v SSHD CO/5162/2003 (HC) 1207

Q & Others, R v SSHD
[2003] EWHC 2507
Admin (HC) 1222

Quaquah, R v SSHD, ex p
[2000] 03 LS Gaz 36, 786, 847,
[2000] INLR 196 868

Quijano (Fabian Martinez)
[1997] Imm AR 227, CA 609

R

R (IS) 3/97) 1261

R (IS) 12/98 1261

R (IS) 9/99 1261

R (SB) 2/85 1253

Ramalingathathevar (Sinnasamy),
23 November 2001
(01/TH/2733) (IAT) 403

Ramos (Suzara) v IAT
[1989] Imm AR 148, CA 369

Raulin v Minister van Onderwijs en
Wetenschappen: C-357/89
[1992] ECR I-1027,
[1994] 1 CMLR 227, ECJ 518

Ravichandran ,R v SSHD ex p
(No 2) [1996] Imm AR 418 733

Ravichandran
[1996] Imm AR 97, CA 604, 797,
802, 1119,
1156

Razgar, R v SSHD
[2004] 3 WLR 58, 745, 746,
[2004] INLR 349, 791-2, 804,
[2004] Imm AR 381, 806, 809,
[2004] UKHL 27 (HL) 817-8, 820,
1077, 1119,
833, 834,
844, 996,
1077-8

Razgar & Others v SSHD)
[2003] EWCA Civ 840 (CA) 1215

Reed, A.F. v Netherlands 59/85
[1986] ECR 1283;
[1987] 2 CMLR 448 343

Reeves v Commissioner of Police
for the Metropolitan
[2000] 1 AC 360f 1179

Refugee Legal Centre, R v SSHD
[2004] EWCA Civ 1481 (CA) 641, 679-80,
1135

Rehal v SSHD
[1989] Imm AR 576, CA 1012

Roberts v Chief Constable of Cheshire
[1999] 1 WLR 66) 1205

Robinson v SSHD
[1997] Imm AR 568
[1997] INLR 182, CA 602, 621,
622, 1139

Roma Rights Centre (see European Roma
Rights Centre and others)

Royer, C-48/75
[1976] ECR 497,
[1976] CMLR 619 (ECJ) 544, 553

RS [2004] UKIAT 00226 (IAT) 384

Rudolph (Dilskish Antoinette Hayley)
[1984] Imm AR 84   369, 371

Rush Portuguesa Lda v ONI: C-113/89
[1990] ECR I-1417,
[1991] 2 CMLR 818, ECJ   525
Rutili v Minister for the Interior: 36/75
[1975] ECR 1219,
[1976] 1 CMLR 140, ECJ   552

S

S v Home Office HC
[November 2003]   1206
S v SSHD [2002] INLR 416,
[2002] EWCA Civ 539 (CA)
S v UK [1984] 40 DR 196
(EComm HR)   826
S, D and T, R v SSHD
[2003] EWHC Admin 1941,
[2004] 7 CCLR 32 (HC)   1352
S & K, SSHD v, [2002]
UKIAT 05613 (IAT, starred)   1119
S (Pakistan) [2004]
UKIAT 00006 (IAT)   314
Saad, Diriye & Osario v SSHD
[2002] INLR 34,
[2002] Imm AR 471,
[2001] EWCA Civ 2008 (CA)   598, 730,
                               792 1079
Saadi, R v SSHD
[2002] 1 WLR 3131 HL;
[2002] UKHL 41 (HL);
[2002] 1 WLR 356,
[2001] EWCA Civ 1512   677-8, 921,
(CA) reversing   923, 924,
[2001] EWHC 670   931, 932,
Admin (HC)   934, 1200
Saadi v UK, Applcn no. 13229/03,
27 September 2005 (ECtHR)   886
Sahota v IAT [1995] ImmAR 50 (CA)   1157
Sala (Maria Martinez) v Freistaat
Bayern (Case C-85/96)
[1998] ECR 1-2691
(ECJ)   1282
Saluguo (18815) IAT   371
Samaroo (Allan) & Sezek (Mehmed)
(Mehmed) v SSHD
[2001] EWCA Civ 1139,   389, 835,
[2002] INLR55(CA)   844, 1019
Santillo;R v SSHD, ex p
[1981] QB 778
[1981] 2 All ER 897 CA   1021

Saribal, R v SSHD
[2002] EWHC 1542 (Admin)
[2002] INLR 596 (HC)   1021
Satu v Hackney LBC
[2002] EWCA Civ 1843 (CA)   1377
Savas: C-37/98, R v SSHD, ex p
[2000] 1 WLR 1828,
[2000] All ER (EC) 627,
[2000] INLR 398, ECJ   588. 589
Savchenkov
[1996] Imm AR 28, CA   607
Savjani v Inland Revenue Commissioners
[1981] QB 458   1190
Schmelz, R v IAT
[2004] EWCA Civ 29 (CA)   552
Sedrati & Others
(High Court) – consent order   506, 915
Seidi (AS 03022/2005)   1154
Selmouni v France
[2000] 29 EHRR 403 ECtHR   795
Sen v Netherlands
[2003] 36 EHRR   845-6
Senga, R v IAT ex p
(9 March 1994, unreported)   715
Senthuran v SSHD
[2004] 4 All ER 365,
[2004] EWCA Civ 950 (CA)   825, 841-2
Sepet & Bulbul v SSHD & UNHCR
[2003] 1 WLR 856,
[2003] 3 All ER 304,
[2003] INLR 322,
[2003] Imm AR 428, Independent,
March 25 (2003),
Times March 21 (2003),   604, 605,
[2003] UKHL 15 (HL)   619
Sesay (14142) IAT   1156
Sevince v Staatsecretaris van Justitie: C-192/89
[1990] ECR 1-3461,
[1992] 2 CMLR 57, ECJ   588
Sezek, R (on the application of) v SSHD
[2002] 1 WLR 348,
[2001] INLR 675, CA   924
see also Samaroo & Sezek
Shabir v ECO (01/TH/2897) (IAT)   313
Shah v, Barnet LBC
[1983] 2 AC 309 (HL)   303
Shah and Islam, R v IAT & SSHD ex p,
[1999] 2 AC 629
[1999] INLR 144 HL,   349, 607–8
[1999] Imm AR 283   616

14

Shakeel (Mohammad),
ECO Islamabad v, IAT
[2002] UKIAT 00605 (IAT)   319

Shala v SSHD
[2003] INLR 349,
EWCA Civ 233 (CA)   838, 840-1,
   842

Sharma v ECO, (New Delhi)
[2005] EWCA Civ 89 (CA)   384

Sheich (Habiba) v Bristol,
5BS 03394, 4 April 2005,
(County Court)   1295

Shen, R v Immigration Appeal
Tribunal ex p [2000] INLR 389   1122

Shillova, R v SSHD
[2002], [2002] INLR 611 (HC)   852, 1128

Shirreh, R v SSHD
(CO2194/1997)
(15th August 1997,
unreported)   632

Singh v ECO, New Delhi
[2004] EWCA Civ 1075,
[2004] INLR 1515 (CA)   385

Singh, R v SSHD ex p
[1998] INLR 608 (CA)   1115

Singh (Pawandeep) v ECO,
New Delhi [2005] 2 WLR 325,
[2004] EWCA Civ 1075 (CA)   825, 827

Singh & Singh (Mukhtiar and Paramjit)
31 July 2000 (SIAC)
Butterworths ILS Vol II,
Section 81-148 [51]-[101]   625

Singh, Bakhtaur
[1986] WLR 910
[1986] Imm AR 352 (HL)   1010, 1125

Singh, Hardial
[1983] Imm AR 198;
[1984] 1 WLR 704   919–20,
   924–9, 956

Singh, Surinder
[1992] 3 All ER 798
[1992] Imm AR 565   294, 541–4,

Sisojeva & Others–v- Latvia,
APPLCN 60654/00,
16 JUNE 2005 (ECtHR)   847

Sivakumar, R v SSHD [2003]
1 WLR 840,
[2003] 2 All ER 1097,
Times March 24 (2003),
[2003] INLR 157,
[2003] Imm AR 411,   605, 606,
[2003] UKHL 14 (HL)   620

Sivakumaran, R v SSHD ex p
[1998] AC 958
[1998] Imm AR 147   599, 602,
[1997] NLJ Rep 1206 HL   623, 1121

Skenderaj v SSHD
[2002] 4 All ER 555,
[2002] INLR 323,
[2002] Imm AR 519,
[2002] EWCA Civ 567 (CA)   607,609

Slimani
(01 TH 00092),
unreported, IAT   666

Slivenko v Latvia
[2004] 2 FCR 28,
15 BHRC 660 (ECtHR)   847

SM and Others
(Kurds-Protection-Relocation)
Iraq CG [2005] UKIAT00111   610

SM (Section 8: Judge's process)
[2005] UKIAT 00116 (AIT)   710

Soering v UK
[1989] 11 EHRR 439   787, 793,
   803

Soloot (AHR)
(01TH01366) IAT
10th August 2001   839, 848

Sorabjee v UK Commission
Applcn 239938/93
[1995]   820

SS (ECO – Article 8)
Malaysia v SSHD
[2004] Imm AR 153,
[2004] UKIAT 00091   859

SS Sri Lanka
[2004] UKIAT 00126 (IAT)   828

Stephens v Myers (1830)
4 C. & P. 349   1183

Steymann v Staatssecretaris van Justitie: 196/87
[1998] ECR 6159,
[1989] 1 CMLR 449, ECJ   518

Stillwaggon
[1975] Imm AR 132 (IAT)   493

Stoke on Trent Council v
W & J Wass Ltd
[1998] 1 WLR 1406   1184

Storozhenko v SSHD
[2002] Imm AR 329,
[2001] EWCA Civ 896 (CA)   608

Strbac
[2005] EWCA CIV 848 (CA)   841

Subaskaran (18892) IAT   1156

Subramaniam, R v IAT, ex p
[1977] QB 190, Imm AR 155 143
Sultana (19228) (IAT) 314

Suthendran v IAT
[1977] AC 539, Imm AR 44 143
Svazas (Rolandas) v SSHD
[2002] INLR 197,
[2002] Imm AR 363,
[2002] EWCA Civ 74 (CA) 611
Swaddling v Adjudication Officer
(Case C-90/97)
[1999] All ER (EC) 217,
ECR 1-1075,
[1999] 2 C.M.L.R. 679,
[1999] C.E.C. 184,
[1999] 2.F.L.R. 184,
[1999] Fam. Law. 382, 1260, 1261,
(R(IS) 6/99)(ECJ) 1263

T

T v North Yorkshire CC
[1999] IRLR 98 (CA) 1196
Tamil Information Centre, R v SSHD
[2002] EWHC 2155
(Admin) (HC) 888
Tas v Turkey
[2001] 33 EHRR 15 793
Tekere (Violet) v SSHD
(01/TH/174) (IAT) 276
Thangarasa, R v SSHD
[2003] 1 AC 920,
[2002] INLR 620,
[2002] UKHL 36 (HL) 746
Thirukumar, R v SSHD ex p
[1989] Imm AR 270
[1989] Imm AR 402, CA 641
Thompson and Hsu (CA)
[1997] 2 All ER 762 1205
Three Rivers DC v Bank of
England (No 3) [2003] 2 AC 1 1182
TI v UK [2000] INLR 211
(ECtHR) 744, 746,
753
Tower Hamlets LBC, R v Secretary of State for
the Environment ex p
[1993] 3 All ER 439;
[1993] Imm AR 495 1031
Trojani v Centre public d'aide
sociale de Bruxelles
(Case C-456/02) (ECJ) 1282
Tum (Veli) and Dari, R v SSHD
[2004] EWCA Civ 788 (CA) 589

Turkoglu, R v SSHD, ex p
[1988] QB 398,
[1987] 2 All ER 823,
[1987] WLR 992,
[1987] Imm AR 484, CA 986

U

Ullah[2001] EWCA Civ 659 (CA) 1434
Ullah, R v Special Adjudicator;
Do v IAT [2004] 3 WLR 23,
[2004] INLR 381, 11, 604, 787,
[2004] Imm AR 419, 788-9,
[2004] UKHL 26 (HL) 790, 791,
793, 797,
801, 803,
804, 806-7,
810, 818,
820, 833,
864
Ursaff v Societe a Responsabilite
limitee Hostellerie le Manoir,
C-27/91, 21 November 1991
(ECJ) 518
Uvovo (00 TH 01450)
IAS 2000 Vol 3, No 15 313

V

V Home Office (HC)
(January 2004) 1296
VE (Racial discrimination) Nigeria
[2005] UKIAT00057 (IAT) 891
Vallaj & Canaj, R (on the application of) v
Special Adjudicator
[2001] INLR 455
[2001] INLR 342, CA
[2001] EWCA Civ 782, (CA) 610
Vander Elst v Office des Migrations
Internationales: C-43/93
[1994] ECR I-3803,
[1995] 1 CMLR 513, ECJ 525

W

Wang (Bei Bei)
[2005] EWCA 293 (CA) 686
Wanjugu, R v SSHD
[2003] EWHC Admin 3116
(HC) 1363
Weng (Da Hua) & Wang
(Guo Xing), R v, [2005]
EWCA Crim 2248 686
Westminster, NASS v,
[2002] UKHL 38 (HL) 1317
Williams
(16574) 15 February 1998 370

14

Winterwerp v Netherland
[1979] 2 EHRR 387, (ECtHR)   922

X

X and Y v UK
[1993] 16 EHRR CD, EComHR
(ECtHR)   827

X, Y and Z v UK
[1997] 24 EHRR 143 (ECtHR)   824

Y

Yambos (IAT) 00TH 21723,
22 June 1999   400

Yiadom, R v SSHD ex p, C-357/98
[2001] All ER (EC) 267 (ECJ)   558

Yildiz v Secretary of State for
Social Security
[2001] EWCA Civ 309, R(IS)
9/01 (CA)   1256

Yogathas & Thangarasa, R v SSHD
[2003] 1 AC 920,
[2002] INLR 620,
[2002] UKHL 36 (HL)   753, 1077

Young, James and Webster v UK
[1981] 4 EHRR 38
[1982] 5 EHRR 201 (ECtHR)   807

Yousaf (9190) IAT   317

Youssef v Home Office
[2004] EWHC 1884 (HC)   921, 926

Z

Z v SSHD
[2004] EWCA Civ 1578 (CA)   616, 806

Z, A, M v SSHD
[2002] Imm AR 560, (CA),
EWCA Civ 952 (CA)   805, 806

Zafiu v Home Office (CC) (c1999) 1206

Zaitz
[2000] INLR 346 CA   619

Zakrocki, R v SSHD, ex p
[1996] 32 BMLR 108,
[1996] COD 304,
[1996] 16 LS Gaz 31,
140 Sol Jo LB 110   234

Zhou, R v SSHD
[2003] EWCA Civ 51 (CA)   264, 1005

Zia v SSHD
[1993] Imm AR 404   314

ZL & VL
[2003] INLR 224;   742, 746,
[2003] EWCA Civ 25 (CA)   1075,
                            1077-8,
                            1215

Index

For cases referred to in the text please see Alphabetical list of cases, pages 1551–1568

A

ABWOR (Assistance By Way of Representation Scheme 61
accelerated 'non-detained procedures' (listed separately under 'asylum')
Accession 8 (A8) countries
 family members 571
 habitual residence test 570
 housing assistance 1295
 'right to reside' test 1268-73
 settlement 572
Accession 8 (A8) nationals 563, 565, 1295
 asylum family concession 573
 removal 571
 restrictions on rights 568
Access to Justice Act 1999 67
Accession (Immigration and Worker Registration) Regulations 2004 565
Accession 8 countries 22
Accession 8 (A8) nationals 507, 566
 asylum family concession 573
 eligibility for housing assistance 1295
 family members 569
 habitual residence test 570
 right to reside 1268
 'right to reside' test 568
 settlement 572
 welfare benefits 1269
 Worker Registration Scheme 573
accommodation
 adequate 313
 fiancé(e)s 316
 overcrowded, definition of 314
accommodation centres 32
Accreditation Scheme 1091
 representation at appeals 1091
actors (see work permits)
adjournments (see appeals)
administrative' removal 26, 990, 1002
 breach of conditions 1004
 family members 1009
 notice of 208
 overstaying 1003

adoption 385
 adopted children, immigration rights 379
 Adoption (Bringing Children into the UK) Regulations 380
 British nationality 1432
 de facto 383
 genuine transfer of parental responsibility 361, 381, 382, 384, 385
 Inter-country Adoption (Hague Convention) Regulations 380
 The Adoption (Intercountry Aspects) Act 1999 380
Adoption Act 1976 380
Adoption and Children Act 2002 383
Adoption (Designation of Overseas Adoptions) Order 1973 383, 1519
advice
 Community Legal Service (CLS) 62
 Advisory Panel on Country Information (APCI) 706
Afghanistan 41, 675, 707
age dispute
 unaccompanied minor asylum-seekers (also listed separately) 688-91
agents of persecution/non-state agents
 Article 3 799-800
Airline Liaison Officers (ALOs) 49, 703
Albania 41, 419, 590, 675, 1075
 Albanian UASC returns project 42
Algeria 590
Aliens Act 1905 5
Amnesty International 1109
Andorra 419, 462
Angola 707
Ankara' Agreement 22
 see Turkey 577
Anti-terrorism Crime and Security Act 2001 901, 924
Antigua & Barbuda 1422
appeals 37
 (see also Asylum and Immigration Tribunal)
 2005 Bill proposed changes (see Immigration and Asylum Bill 2005)

appeals *continued*
adjournments 1098, 1101-2
against refusal of entry clearance 1071
ASA (*see* Asylum Support Adjudicators)
asylum status appeals 1079
asylum support 1389
burden and standard of proof – human
rights cases 1122
certification as 'clearly unfounded' 1073-
8
certification under s96 2002 Act 1067-9
Court of Appeal following reconsideration
by AIT (*see* Court of Appeal)
determining without hearing 1102-3
error of law 1155
evidence 1105
exclusion from refugee status 1080-1
expert evidence 1108
explanatory statement/reasons 1094
family visitors
against refusal of enty clearance
1072-3
new proposals in 2005 Bill 1044
Review of Family Visitor Appeals 48
fast track 1129
froms (see forms and documents(
fresh claims 1069
grounds 1064
House of Lords 1149
legal aid 1091
non-suspensive (NSA) 643, 675, 1073
notice of appeal 1061
late 1062
one-stop appeals 1066
overview 1046
pending 1069
practice directions 1087
procedure 1086
refugee status appeals 1079
rights of appeal 1039-83
Special Immigration Appeals Commission
1081
standard directions 1095
submissions 1117
time-limits 1135, 1162-7
timetable 1088
transitional arrangements 1087
when people can appeal 1052
witness statements 1106-8
witness summons 1099
work permits – refusals to issues IEDs (*see*
Immigration Employment Documents)
applications
charging 125
exemptions from fees 126
application forms 127

dependants 127
multiple applications 130
Application Registration Cards (ARCs) 203,
651
applications 125
exemptions from fees 126
offences 1034
Approved Destination Status Agreement with
China 246
entry clearances 247
armed forces 150
Armenia 419
arrest 1032
assault and battery 1182
see also civil claims
Association Agreements 22, 505
application forms 131
applying for entry 578
applying to extend stay 580
business plans 584
Bulgaria and Romania 578
Chile 591
establishment 577, 583, 588, 590
family members 585
port applicants 582
settlement 585
switching 580-2
Stabilisation agreements 590
Turkey Association Agreement 585
Association of British Language Schools 254
asylum 19-20, 47, 595
accelerated 'non-detained' procedures
681
agents of persecution (*listed separately*)
appeals
non-suspensive (NSA) (*see* appeals)
under s83 2002 Act 1079
applying and applications
by post 647
delay 647, 711-2
late and opportunistic claims (*see* new
asylum model)
overseas 697
port 645
asylum refusals 728
backlog clearance 668
certification of asylum claim
third country 745-6
civil war 612
conscientious objection 619
credibility (*see* asylum-seekers)
Convention reason 605-9
imputed opinion 605
political opinion 606
race, religion and nationality 609
severity of ill-treatment 606

asylum *continued*
    social group 607
    concessions (*listed separately*)
    country evidence 706-8
        Advisory Panel on Country Information
            (APCI) 706
        Country Information and Policy Unit
            (CIPU) (listed under 'Home Office')
        country reports 707
    decisions
        delays 717-9
        group decisions 715
        refusals 715
    delays in claiming 711
    exceptional leave to remain (ELR) 597
    family concession 668-9
    fast-track detention (*see* fast-track
        detention)
    fear of persecution 602
    fresh claims 730-5
    humanitarian protection (HP) 597
    induction processes 655-7
    internal flight alternative (*listed separately*)
    interviews
        public funding for representatives
            659
        victims of torture 661
        interpreters 658
        tape-recording 659
        travel warrants/expenses 660
    last-minute claims 712
    National Asylum Support Service (NASS)
        654
    New Asylum Model 637, 641
    one-stop procedure (*see* one-stop
        procedure)
    refusals 728-20
    screening 649
    standard of proof 622
    Statement of Evidence Form (SEF) 669
    third country asylum cases 737
    UNHCR Handbook 640
Asylum Act 1999 7
Asylum and Immigration (Treatment of
    Claimants) Act 8, 293, 296, 600
    credibility, s8 709-712
    section 9 exclusion from support 1325
Asylum and Immigration Act 1996 6, 600
    third country cases 752
Asylum and Immigration Appeals Act 1993
    6, 19, 600
    third country cases 752
Asylum and Immigration Tribunal (AIT) 8, 32,
    1039, 1052
    burden and standard of proof – immigration
        cases 1122

Case management review (CMR) hearings
    1095
    country guidance cases 1111
    cross-examination 1115
    errors of law 1155
    evidence 1105
        appellant and witnesses 1099-100
        -in-chief 1114
    fast track appeals 1129
    fresh evidence to challenge AIT 1159-61
    hearings
        first instance 1112
    legal aid 1153
    legal panel of three 1149-50
    powers of 118
    practice directions 1087
    public funding/legal aid 65-71, 1091
    re-examination 1116
    reconsideration hearings 1134, 1143
    record of proceedings 1118
        applying for 1134
        High Court (see High Court) 1140
        out of time 1137
    starred decisions 1110-11
Asylum and Immigration Tribunal (Fast Track
    Procedure) Rules 2005 1087
Asylum and Immigration Tribunal (Procedure)
    Rules 2005 1086
Asylum and the Immigration (Treatment of
    Claimant 31-32
asylum claims
    Dublin Convention and Dublin II
        Regulations 748
Asylum Policy Instructions (API) 12, 600
asylum refusals 715, 728
Asylum Screening Units (ASUs) 647
asylum-seekers 19-20
    2004 Act 709-12
    accommodation centres 32
    credibility 708
    dependants 691
    discouraging 701
    EU minimum standards for reception
        1379
    hard cases support 1381
    immigration rules 714-5
    mixed households 1357
    permission to work 694
    social services support, exclusion from (*see*
        social services)
    temporary admission 652
    unaccompanied minors 644, 686
        age dispute cases 1324
    voluntary returns 667
Asylum Seekers (Reception Conditions)
    Regulations 1379

asylum support
  adequate accommodation   1348
  appeals   1389
  claim for asylum   1342
  dependants of asylum-seekers   1345
  destitution   1348
  emergency accommodation   654-5
  essential living needs   1348
  exclusions   1350
  families with children, exclusion from
      support (see Asylum and Immigration
      (Treatment of Claimants) Act 2004,
      section 9)
  fresh claims   1342
  hard cases support   1381
  interim asylum support   1338
  judicial review   1222
  mixed households   1340
  National Asylum Support Service ('NASS')
      1337, 1360
    applying to   655, 1367
    decision   1369
    rates   1364
  NASS Policy Bulletins   1340
  section 55 2002 Act   655, 1350
  transferring to welfare benefits   1282
Asylum Support Adjudicators (ASA)   29,
    1389, 1391
Asylum Support Regulations
  exclusions from support   1357
attendance allowance (see welfare benefits)
Austria   505, 506
Azerbaijan   419

B

backdated benefit claims (see welfare benefits)
bail   957
  Asylum and Immigration Tribunal   958-65
  applying for   965-78
  Bail Circle   977
  Chief Immigration Officer (CIO)   957
  EEA cases   964
  Guidance Notes for Adjudicators   965
  hearing   978-82
  police inspector   957
  powers to grant bail   958-61
  Special Immigration Appeals Commission
      (SIAC)   965
  summary   970, 977
  sureties and personal recognisance   958,
      974
Bail for Immigration Detainees (BID)   69, 966
  reports on detention   947-8
Bangladesh   675, 707, 1075
Bar Council in England   65
Bar Council of Northern Ireland   65

battery (see assault and battery. see also civil
      claims)
Belgium   505
Belize   1422
Benin   675
Bermuda   1422
Bolivia   675, 1075
bonds, financial   35, 45
Bosnia   590
Bosnia and Herzegovina   462
Botswana   675
Brazil   675, 1075
British Accreditation Council for Independent
      Further Education   254
British citizens   49, 1406
  applying to become   1447
  British Nationality Act 1981   1425
  deprivation   1445
  grandfathers   1435
  mothers   1435
  oath and pledge   1451
  naturalisation   1453
  registration 1447
    adults   1485
    children   1473
British Council   254
British Dependent Territories Citizens (BDTCs)
      110, 1406
British nationality   1401
  abandoned infants   1432
  adoption   1432
  applying   1448
  children
      guardianship orders   1484
      wards of court   1484
  citizenship ceremonies   1451
  Crown, designated or EC service   1436,
      1470
  illegitimate children   1429
  language and Life in the UK tests   1465
  naturalisation   1447
  oath and pledge   1451
  parent
      consent of   1478
      meaning of   1428
  qualifying connection   1444
  renunciation   1442
  stateless persons   1437
British Nationality Act 1948   1403, 1427
British Nationality Act 1981   10, 15, 1403
  right of abode   1418
British Nationality (Hong Kong) Acts 1990
      1416
British Nationals (Overseas) (BN(O)s)   110,
      1415, 1411
  entry clearance   83

British Overseas Citizens (BOCs)   110,
   1408
   entry clearance   83
   long residence concession   157
British Overseas Territories citizens (BOTCs)
   1406, 1432
   entry clearance   83
British passports (*see* passports)
British Protected Persons   110, 1412
   entry clearance   83
British Red Cross   698, 1502
British Subjects   5, 110, 1413
   entry clearance   83
Bruegel and Natamba report
   Maintaining Contact   946
Bulgaria   419, 462, 508, 675, 1075
   Association Agreement   577
   au pairs   462
Burkina Faso   675
BUNAC students   468
Business Cases Unit (BCU)   583
business person   477-8
business purposes   477

C
Cameroon   675
Campsfield House   935
   fast track   1129
   inspection   943
Canada   675
carers   232-4
   allowance (*see* welfare benefits)
   of EEA national children   534-7
   visitors   232
case-law   11
Case management review hearings (CMR) (*see*
   Asylum and Immigration Tribunal)
categories of entry   15
Central African Republic   675
Central and Eastern European Countries
   (CEECs)   577
Certificate of approval, marriage   886
   human rights (*see* human rights)
certificate of entitlement to the right of abode
   85, 202
certificate of identity   881
certification
   appeals under s96 2002 Act (*see* appeals)
   asylum claims (*see* asylum)
   'clearly unfounded' (*see* appeals)
Chad   675
Channel Islands
   Common Travel Area (CTA)   26
   entry clearance   105
charging (*see* fees)
child benefit   1273

child tax credit   1258
children   357
   abandoned, nationality (*see* British
      nationality)
   access to   372
   adopted children   379-81, 383-5
   age dispute cases   1324
   aged 18 and over   348
   and asylum seeking families, exclusion
      from support (*see* Asylum and
      Immigration (Treatment of Claimants)
      Act 2004)
   born in the UK   393
   born in the UK and not born British   393
   Children Act 1989   1322
   citizenship (*see* British nationality,
      registration)
   DNA profiling   365
   DP/069/99   388
   EEA national children and parents   359
   enforcement against parents   386
   entry clearance   366
   European rights of free movement   531
   family court procedures   392
   guardianship order   1484
   human rights   359
      and Article 8   385, 387
   illegitimate children   1482
   joining a lone parent   367
   joining both parents   360
   joining parents who have limited leave
      376
   local authority care   391, 1484
   maintenance and accommodation   363
   married   363
   not leading an independent life   363
   registration as British citizen   1473
   seven-year policy   388
   sole-responsibility rule   368
   unaccompanied asylum-seeking children
      390, 686
   'under-12' concession   367
   wards of court   1484
   who are British citizens   358
   with right of abode   359
Children Act 1989   1322
Chile
   Association Agreement   591
China   41, 675, 707
   Approved Destination Status Agreement
      246
Chronically Sick and Disabled Persons Act
   1970
   Section 2   1320
Citizen of the United Kingdom and Colonies
   (CUKC)   5, 1426

citizenship ceremonies 1451
civil claims 29, 1171
  Adimi – see compensation and *Adimi*
    1235
  Article 5 breach 1178
  assault and battery 1182
  conviction, unlawful (*see* compensation and
    Adimi)
  damages 1201-10
  delay in issuing documents 1184-7
  detention
    poor conditions 1178
    removal from association 1179
    unlawful 1175
  discrimination
    Race Relations Act and Sex Discrimination
      Act 1189-90, 1194
  dispersal, separation and conditions
    1190
  family separation, unlawful 1182
  judicial review 1193
  making a claim 1172, 1192
  maladministration 1184
  malicious prosecution 1191
  misfeasance in public office 1181
  negligence 1178
  pre-action protocol 1210
  race discrimination 891-2
  removal, unlawful 1181-2
  search, unlawful 1183
  time-limits 1196
Civil Partnership Act 2004 31, 55, 344
Civil Procedure Rules (CPR) 1210
clinical attachment or dental observer post
  283
cohabitees (*see* unmarried partners)
Colnbrook House immigration removal centre
  935
  fast track 1129
Common Market 4
Common Travel Area (CTA) 26, 105
Commonwealth citizens
  women – wives of British citizens 294
Commonwealth Immigrants Act 1962 5,
  1403
Commonwealth Immigrants Act 1968 5
community activities 1386
community care assessments 1322
Community Legal Service (CLS) 59
  General Help 60
  General Help including Casework 60
  Quality Mark 59
  Specialist Help 60
Community Legal Service Fund 67
  CLS Directory 60
compensation and *Adimi* 1235

compensation schemes 1224
complaints 1223
  against advisers 65
  Home Office IND, about 1223
  Work Permits, about 1223
concessions
  1998 concession 717
  ILR family exercise 668-9
  DP/069/99 67-8, 390-3, 865, 870-1
  DP/4/95 67-8, 390-3, 865, 870-1
  DP/4/96 67-8, 390-3, 865, 870-1
  DP/2/93 337-41
  DP/3/96 337-41
  under-12 367
conducive to public good
  rights of appeal 1058
Congo (Brazzaville) 675
consanguineous relationships 323
consolatory payments 1225
control zones 106
Controlled Legal Representation (CLR)
  71-3, 1091
*Controlling our borders: Making migration
  work for Britain* 33, 934
conviction, unlawful, and compensation (*see*
  compensation and *Adimi*)
Cooperation Agreements 505
  Algeria, Morocco and Tunisia 590
Cotonou Agreement 591
Council of Europe 774
  Social Charter (CESC) 1259
  Revised Social Charter (*see* European
    Revised Social Charter)
council tax benefit 1279
country evidence and information (*see* under
  asylum)
country guidance cases 1111
country material for appeals 1108-10
Court of Appeal
  applying to and renewing, following
    reconsideration 1147-9
Court of Session (Scotland) 1140
credibility (*see* under asylum-seekers)
crews of ships and aircrafts 961
criminal activities, nationality 1464
criminal convictions, Article 8 and
  proportionality 843-4
criminal court
  power to release from detention 964
Croatia 419, 462, 590, 1293, 1295
Crown, designated or EC service 1470
Crown Proceedings Act 1947 1195
Croydon Asylum Screening Unit (ASU) 643,
  681
A Crying Shame 948
Cyprus 505, 512, 565

CUKC (see Citizens of the UK and Colonies)
Czech Republic 505, 565
    Roman Rights Centre case 892

D

damages (see civil claims)
Data Protection Act 1998 (DPA) 1174, 1176,
    1194, 1208
death penalty 793
Deciding to Detain 946
degrading treatment or punishment 795
delays
    in issuing documents (see civil claims)
Democratic Republic of Congo 707
Denmark 505
Department for Constitutional Affairs 68
Department for Education and Skills Register
        of education providers 263
Department of Trade and Industry
    1998 White Paper 414
Department of Work and Pensions 24
dependants
    dependent relatives 397
    of EEA nationals 398
    of those in temporary categories 355
    parents and grandparents 399
    retired persons of independent means 398
deportation 26, 141, 990
    conducive to the public good 1018
    criminal convictions 1020
    deportation orders 208, 1022
        revocation of 1024
    family members 1021
    notices of intention to deport 1017, 1021
    recommendations – appeals 1017
    removal 1026
    terrorism 1019
deprivation of citizenship 1445
    appeal 1055
    proposed changes 1445
designated post 89
detained fast-track processes (see fast-track)
detention 18-19, 898
    association, removal from (see civil claims)
    Article 5 ECHR 922
    conditions 942
    Detention Centre Rules 936
    EEA nationals 554-6
    families 947
    family members 907
    five-year strategy 908
    habeas corpus 987
    health needs 947
    Home Office policy 905
    human rights 973

    inspection 942
    international guidelines 917
    judicial review 986
    Operational Enforcement Manual (OEM)
        905
    places of detention 934
    pregnant asylum-seekers and those with
        babies 947
    removal from association 1179
    restriction orders 950
    risk of absconding 946
    short-term holding facilities 944
    sureties (see bail)
    suspected international terrorists 901
    temporary admission 950
    temporary release 950
    transfers, (see civil claims)
    unlawful 985, 1175
    who can be detained 899
Detention Centre Rules 19, 936, 939, 1179
diplomats
    locally recruited staff 470
    private servants 456
Diplomatic Service Procedures (DSP) 12
Direct Airside Transit Visa (DATV) 243, 703
    applying for 245
    exemptions 244
disability benefit 1273
disability living allowance 1242, 1245, 1257
discretionary leave (DL) 17, 598, 853, 859,
        864-5
    dependants 875-6
    family members 875
    leave granted 868
    upgrading to HP 872
discrimination 885-93
    Article 14 776-7, 886-7
    damages (see civil claims)
    race (see race discrimination)
dispersal
    conditions (see civil claims)
    separation and Article 8 (see civil claims)
divorce overseas 321
Djibouti 675
DNA testing 365
domestic workers rules 457
domestic violence 346-50
    concession 295
    European rights of free movement 529
domicile, marriage 320
Dover Enforcement Unit (DEU) 644
Dover immigration removal centre 935
Dover pilot scheme 681
Dungavel House 935
    inspection 944

E

East Africa
British nationals with an East African
connection   1409
EC Association Agreements (*see* Association
Agreements)
EC Directives/Regulations
1251/70   515, 520, 556
1612/68   514, 525, 531-2
73/148   548
73/148/EEC   514
75/34/ EEC   515
75/34/EEC   520
90/364/EEC   515
90/365/EEC   515
93/96/EEC   515, 525
asylum procedures (minimum standards)
641
Reception Conditions Directive   656,
1380
ECHR (*see* European Convention on Human
Rights)
ECSMA (*see* European Convention on Social
and Medical Assistance)
EC Treaty
Article 18(1)   514
Ecuador   675, 1075
education
access to   1335
EEA   136
EEA 2000 Regulations   507, 515
EEA Association Agreements
switching   188
EEA nationals   22, 136, 512, 1429 (*see also*
European rights of free movement)
and human rights   815
appeal rights   556-9
bail, right to   964
children of   359, 531
citizenship (*see* naturalisation)
detain, powers to   554-6
eligibility for housing assistance   1295
exclusion on public policy, security and
health grounds   552-3
exclusions from social services support (*see*
social services)
family members   294, 526
fiancé(e)s of   530
housing   563, 1295-6
involuntary unemployment   521
naturalisation   1462
relatives of   398
revoking rights of free movement   554
'settled' (nationality)   1429
social services   1306
temporary incapability   521

welfare benefits   563, 1281
EEA Residence Permits   202
electronic monitoring   652, 953
tagging   954
tracking   955
voice recognition   954
emergency accommodation (*see* asylum
support)
Empire Windrush   5
employers
code of practice   500
defences   497
EEA family members   500
offences   496
s8 1996 Act   496
employment
discrimination   500
unlawful (*see* unlawful work or business)
endorsements   189
by entry clearance officers   192
by immigration officers   194
cancellation of leave   197
Code 2 stamp   200
Code 8 stamp   198
date stamp   196
entry clearance   192
exit stamps   198
indefinite leave to enter   197
indefinite leave to remain   201
no longer issued   199
old style   193
open date stamp   196
refugees   204
refusal of leave to enter   193
refusals   201
variation of leave   196
enforcement   26
administrative removal   990, 1002
against parents whose child is British
389
criminal offences   1031
deportation   990, 1015
detention of EEA nationals   554-6
exemptions   991
extradition   1029
families   998
health problems   995-6
in the workplace   46
Mental Health Act   1028
over 65 policy   994
port removal   990, 1000
recent developments   991
removal   990, 1026
voluntary and supervised departures
1023, 1028
workplace/employers   1035

entertainers 445
  actors 445
  cultural artists 445
  unit companies 445
entry
  categories of 15
entry clearance 12, 24-25, 78-79
  appeals against refusal 93, 1071
  applying for 89
  Approved Destination Agreement 88
  Article 8 835-9, 844-6
  children 366
  decisions 93
  endorsements 192
  fingerprinting 91
  for returning residents 111
  forms for applying (table) 90
  from Channel Islands 105
  from Isle of Man 105
  from Republic of Ireland 105
  general grounds of refusal 93
    (table) 98
  old style passport endorsement 193
  red 192
  refusal stamp 193
  students 251, 260
  visit 192
Entry Clearance Monitor 48, 51, 216
Entry clearance officers (ECOs) 12, 24
Equatorial Guinea 675
Eritrea 707
  Eritrean nationals, permitted race
    discrimination 890
errors of law and AIT reconsideration (see
    Asylum and Immigration Tribunal)
Estonia 505, 565
Euro-Mediterranean Association Agreements
    590
European Asylum Procedures Directive
    641
European Commission 508
European Communities Act 1972 507
European Convention of Human Rights (ECHR)
    10, 20, 595, 773-4
  absolute rights 779
  Article 2 (the right to life) 775, 789
  Article 3 (prohibition on torture and
    inhuman or degrading treatment
    20-21, 136, 138, 775, 794, 809
    claims for protection 792, 855
    derogations 778
    detention of suspected international
      terrorist 901
    detrimental effect of return 809
    extra-territorial effect 787
    family or other connections 820

    memoranda of understanding 1020
  Article 4 (prohibition on slavery and forced
    labour) 775, 789
  Article 5 (right to liberty and security) 775,
    789
    damages (see civil claims)
    detention 922
    detention of suspected international
      terrorists 901
  Article 6 (right to a fair trial) 775, 789
  Article 7 (protection from retrospective
    punishment 776, 789
  Article 8 (respect for private and family life,
    home and correspondence) 20, 49,
    234, 294, 359, 776, 789-90, 803,
    809, 816, 821, 1182
    Article 8 and family reunion 769
    sexuality 804-6
    withdrawal of support 1327
  Article 9 (freedom of thought, conscience
    and religion) 776, 789
  Article 10 (freedom of expression) 776,
    789
  Article 11 (freedom of assembly and
    association) 776, 789
  Article 12 (right to marry and found a
    family) 776
  Article 14 (prohibition on discrimination)
    776, 789, 885
  Article 16 777
  Article 17 777
  Article 18 777
  Article 35 782
  discretionary leave 869-70
  extra-territorial effect and flagrant breaches
    787-92
  limitations on ECHR rights 778-81
  Protocol 1 776
  Protocol 13 776
  reservations 778
  restrictions on rights 779
  third country cases 858
  third country challenges 745
  torture 795
European Convention on Social and Medical
    Assistance (ECSMA) 1259
European Council 508
European Court of Human Rights (ECtHR)
    773, 774, 781
  procedure 783
  taking a case to Europe 781
European Court of Justice (ECJ) 509
European Directorate Instructions (EDI) 12,
    512
European Economic Area (EEA) 21, 503,
    506-7

European Economic Area Act 1993   507
European Economic Community (EEC)   503
European Free Trade Association (EFTA)   506
European Parliament   508
European rights of free movement   21-22,
    511 (see also EEA nationals)
  enforcement and detention   554
  family members of EEA nationals   526
  family permits   548
  overstayers and others irregularly in UK
    528
  port and temporary admission   528
  posted workers   525
  residence documents   544
  residence permits   544
  retired persons   523-4
  revoking rights   551
  rights of appeal   556
  self-employed – right of establishment   519
  self-sufficient persons   522
  spouses
    domestic violence   530
    marriages of convenience   527
  students   523
  welfare benefits entitlement   1281
  workers   518
European Union (Accession) Act 2003   507,
    565
European Union (EU)   503
  (see also European right of free movement
    and EEA nationals)
  Accession 8 nationals   507
  Association Agreements   505
  institutions   508
  law   504
    directives   506
    regulations   506
  Maastricht Treaty   504
  Single European Act (SEA)   503
  Treaty of Accession   504, 565
evidence
  asylum (see asylum)
  fresh evidence to challenge AIT (see Asylum
    and Immigration Tribunal)
examination of passengers
  permitted race discrimination   889
exceptional leave   17, 597
  family reunion   878
  transitional arrangements   873-5
exclusion
  from refugee status (see appeals)
exempt from immigration control   23, 472
  ceasing to be   475
explanatory statements   1094-5
expression, freedom of (Article 10)   807-8
extradition   1029

F

Faculty of Advocates in Scotland   65
Fairer, Faster, Firmer (1998)   44, 906, 936
Falkland Islands   1427, 1432
false imprisonment (see civil claims)
families
  detention of   947
  deportation of (see deportation)
  enforcement   998
  removals of (see removals)
  separation   1182
family life
  Article 8 principles   822-44
family permits   548
family reunion
  discretionary leave and humanitarian
    protection   876-7
  exceptional leave   877-8
  fees waiver   878-9
  refugees   697, 757-70
    entry clearance refusals and appeals
      768
    immigration rules   758-62
    Refugee Convention principle of family
      unity   764-7
    Somali policy   767
family separation, unlawful (see civil claims)
family visitors (see also visitors)   225-6,
    1071-3
Faroes   462
fast track procedures and processes
  appeals   1129-32
    reconsideration hearings   1146
  legal representation   676
  Harmondsworth (see Harmondsworth)
  Oakington Reception Centre (see
    Oakington)
  Suitability List   673
  Yarls Wood (see Yarls Wood)
Federal Republic of Yugoslavia   590
fiancé(e)s   303-4
  children of   361
  European rights of free movement   530
film crew on location   468
fingerprinting   91
  asylum screening   650
  entry clearance posts   40, 91
Finland   505-6
five-year strategy   31, 33
  appeals   48
  bonds   45
  detention   909
  five tiers   45
  removal   992
  return agreements   992
  sponsors   43

five-year strategy *continued*
  summary of changes (table) 34
  work permit auctions 43
forms and documents
  AIT-1 1063-4, 1066
  AIT-1-FT 1063, 1066
  AIT-2 1063
  AIT-3 1063-4
  AN (NEW) 1449, 1453
  AN(New) 1469
  B (OS) 1449
  B (OTA) 1449
  BUS 129, 132-133
  COA (Marriage) 130, 132-133, 297
  COA Multiple 130
  ECAA (Dep) 131
  ECAA Main 131, 582
  EEC1 131, 137, 545
  EEC2 131, 137
  EEC3 131, 549
  ELR 129, 132-133
  EM 1449
  FLR (FT: WISS) 128, 132
  FLR (IED) 129, 132, 136, 419, 431, 446,
    450, 452
  FLR (M) 128, 132, 344
  FLR (O) 128, 132, 228,
  FLR (S) 128, 132, 273-4
  FLR (SEGS) 128, 132
  G 1449
  HPDL 132-3
  HPDL 129
  ICD.1070 208
  ICD.1076 208
  ICD.1914 208
  IS 101 1015
  IS 101 (asylum) 1015
  IS 151A 208
  IS 151B 209
  IS 82 210
  IS 91R 908
  IS 96 207
  IS 96 NW 208
  IS118 210
  MN1 1449, 1473
  N461 1218
  NASS 1 1367
  NTL 129, 132
  NTL/TOC Multiple 130
  PF244 1142
  Postal LTR Multiple 130
  Premium Multiple 130
  RS1 1449
  S1 1449
  S2 1449
  S3 1449
  SB1X 450
  SET (F) 129, 132
  SET (M) 128, 132
  SET (O) 129, 136
  Student Multiple 130
  T 1449
  TOC 129, 132, 198
  Turkish ECAA (Main) 131
  UKM 1449
  VAF1 223
  WP3 446
  WP3X 446
  WRS 574
  WW 1449
France 505
Freedom of Information Act 1198
fresh human rights claims 857-9
Fresh Talent: Working in Scotland Scheme
  160, 453

G

Gabon 675
Gambia 675
gangmasters
  Gangmasters (Licensing) Act 2004 41
Gateway Protection Programme (*see* refugees)
General Agreement on Trades in Services
  (GATS) (*see* work permits)
general practitioners (*see* GPs)
Germany 505
Ghana 675
government representatives 474
GPs, access to services 1333-4
grandparents 399
  and human rights 826
Greece 505
Greenland 462
guardian's allowance 1274
Guardianship order (*see* British nationality,
  registration)
Guinea-Bissau 675
Gurkhas 150
GV3 'declaration of identity' 207, 760

H

habeas corpus 987
habitual residence test 1260
  accession 8 nationals 570
Hague Convention on the Protection of
  Children and Cooperation in Respect
  of Inter-country Adoption 1434
hard cases support 1381
  applications 1386
  exclusions 1382
Harmondsworth Immigration Removal Centre
  7, 639, 643, 673, 935

Harmondsworth Immigration Removal Centre *continued*
   fast track   1129
   flexibility policy   679
Haslar, HMP   935
   inspection   943
health
   Article 3   809-16
   Article 8   816-7
   enforcement (*listed separately*)
health care   53. 1328
   consultation paper   54
   free treatment and exemption from charges
      1330-3
   hospital treatment   1329
   primary health care, GPs   1333
Health Services and Public Health Act 1968
   Section 45   1321
hearings before the AIT (*see* Asylum and
      Immigration Tribunal)
Herzegovina   590
High Court
   applying for review of AIT decision
      1140-3
   reference   1149
   statutory application   1151
High Court in Northern Ireland   1140
Highly Skilled Migrant Programme   136
   MBA graduates   488
   points system   485
   settlement   490
   'significant' achievement   487
   switching   490
Highly Skilled Migrants' Programme   136
HIV/AIDS   814
   and human rights   851
HJT Country database   1109
HM Chief Inspector of Prisons   942
Home Office
   Advisory Panel on Country Information
      (APCI)   706
   Certificate of Identity   207
   country reports   707
   Country and Information Policy Unit (CIPU)
      706
   decisions on applications   138
   detention policy   905
   Operational Guidance Notes (OGNs)
      708
   Public Enquiry Offices   133
homelessness   1291, 1296
Hong Kong   1414
Hong Kong (War Wives and Widows) Act 1996
      1416
Hong Kong Act 1985   1415
hospital treatment (*see* health care)

hotel and catering SBS   449
   (*see also* SBS)
House of Lords
   appeals to (*see* appeals)   1149
housing   1289
   allocation schemes   1289
   homelessness   1296
   housing benefit   1279, 1289
human rights
   appeals   857
   certification   857
   civil claims – damages   1202
   damages for breach   1174
   discretionary leave   853, 859, 864-5
   fresh claims   858
   maladministration   1186
   making a claim   854
Human Rights Act 1998   7, 20
human rights applications
   switching   188
Human Rights Watch   1109
humanitarian protection (HP)   17, 597, 853,
      859
   dependants   875-6
   exclusions   863
   extensions   866-9, 875
   family members   875
   health (*see* health)
   leave granted   859-73
   third country (*see* third country)
   travel documents (*listed separately*)
Hungary   505, 565

I

Iceland   506
identity cards
   Identity Cards Bill   54
IED
   fees for   419
illegal entrants   208, 386, 647-8, 873, 1010-
      5, 1024, 1031-3, 1054, 1079, 1251,
      1314
   removal of   1010-5
Illegal entry   990, 1010
   deception   1013
   notice of   208
illegitimate children   1429
   discrimination against   1429
Immigration Act 1971   6, 78
immigration advice
   complaints about   65
Immigration and Asylum Accre ditation
      Scheme   63
Immigration and Asylum Act 1999   7, 78, 94,
      107, 600
   regulation of legal advisers   63

Immigration and Asylum Act 1999 *continued*
  third country cases   753-5
  who can provide legal advice   63
Immigration, Asylum and Nationality Bill 2005
    9, 31, 50, 124, 942
  appeals   1041-6
  offences   1035
Immigration and Asylum (Provision of
    Accommodation to Failed Asylum-
    Seekers Regulations) 2005   1392
Immigration and Nationality Directorate (IND)
    12, 24
  Initial Consideration Unit   132, 135
  Passport Hotline   134
Immigration Appeal Tribunal (IAT)   27
Immigration (Carriers' Liability) Act 1987
    703
Immigration Employment Documents (IEDs)
    24, 44, 85, 136, 418
  appeal against refusal to issue   439-40
Immigration Employment Document (Fees)
    Regulations 2003   419
Immigration (European Economic Area)
    Regulations   22, 515
immigration judges   1049-50
immigration law
  criminal offences   1033
Immigration Law Practitioners' Association
    (ILPA)   13, 1109
Immigration (Leave to Enter and Remain)
    Order   78, 85, 107
Immigration (Leave to Remain) (Fees)
    Regulations 2003   125
Immigration (Leave to Remain) (Prescribed
    Forms and Procedure) (No.2)
    Regulations 2005   34
Immigration (Notices) Regulations 2003
    1087
immigration officers
  powers of arrest and search   1032
immigration rules   10 *and throughout*
  third country cases   738, 747-8
Immigration Services Tribunal   67
Immigration Status Documents (ISDs)   140,
    204
Immigration (Variation of Leave) Order 1976
    (VOLO   143
  anti-terror measures   52
  appeal rights   50
  appeals   1041
  deprivation of citizenship   53
  enforcement   993
  penalties against employers   51
  powers to gather information   52
imprisonment, false (*see* civil claims)
incapacity benefit (*see* welfare benefits)

indefinite leave   17, 110
  returning residents   114
Independent Race Monitor   888-90
India   41, 675, 707, 1075
induction centres
  EC Reception Conditions Directive (*listed
    separately*)
  processes (*see* asylum support)
industrial injuries benefit (*see* welfare
    benefits)
inhuman treatment   795
injunctions (see judicial review)
innovators   481-3
  self-assessment   482
  switching   483
'Insight' Work Permits UK newsletter   421,
    440
integration loan (*see* refugees)
Integration Matters: A National Strategy for
    Refugee Integration   32
intention to make home in UK (*see* British
    nationality, naturalisation)
interim asylum support   1371
  accommodation   1375
  destitution   1377
  essential living needs   1375
  exclusions   1377
  procedures   1378
interim support   1338
internal relocation/flight
  Article 3   798
International Covenant on Civil and Political
    Rights (ICCPR)
  detention   919
international officials   474
interviews
  asylum (*see* asylum)
Iran   707
Iraq   707
Ireland   505
  entry through   1012
  Irish nationals   23
Isle of Man
  Common Travel Area   26
Italy   505
Ivory Coast   675

J

Jamaica   675, 707, 1075
JCWI proposals for change   53-5
jobseeker's allowance (*see* welfare benefits)
Joint Entry Clearance Unit   24
judicial review   29 1213
  civil claims   1193
  detention   986
  grounds for   1214

judicial review *continued*
   permission   1219
   pre-action protocol   1217
   removals, imminent   1220
   substantive hearing   1219
   time-limits   1218
   urgent cases   1217, 1221
Justice Denied, Asylum and Immigration Legal
     Aid, A System in Crisis   69
juxtaposed controls   102

K

Kenya   5, 675
Kosovo   633

L

landing cards   194
language analysis   889
Latvia   505, 565
Law Society Accreditation Scheme (*see*
     Accreditation Scheme)
Law Society of Northern Ireland   61
Law Society of Scotland   61
lawyers   480
Learning and Skills Council   287
leave   15
   automatic extension   653-6
   cancellation of   100, 108
   conditions of   18, 189
     for students   263
   discretionary Leave   17
   exceptional leave   17
   from Channel Islands   105
   from Republic of Ireland   105
   general grounds of refusal   97
     (table)   98
   granting or refusing before arrival in UK   94
   indefinite   17, 197
   leave to remain   25
   limited   17
   limited leave to remain   47
   non-lapsing leave   26
   outside the immigration rules   16
   refusals   197
   temporary admission   104
   variation on entry to the UK   102
Leave to Enter Order (*see* Immigration (Leave
     to Enter & Remain) Order 2000)
leave to remain   25
   automatic extension of   146
   extension of   146
   general grounds for refusal of   140
Leave Outside the Rules   148, 598
legal aid funding
   age dispute, unaccompanied minors   689
   AIT (*see* Asylum and Immigration Tribunal)

certificated work   73
civil claims (*see* civil claims)
Controlled Legal Representation   71-3,
     1091
Funding Code   67
Justice Denied, A System in Crisis
     (BID/Asylum Aid publication)   69
Legal Help   69-70
Legal Services Commission (LSC)   59-60, 67
   Accreditation Scheme   59
   General Civil Contract   67
   Specialist Quality Mark   67
Liberia   707
liberty, right to (*see* European Convention,
     Article 5)   800
Liechtenstein   506, 1293, 1295
limited leave   17, 116-117
limited leave to remain   47
Lindholme HMP   935
   inspection   943
Lithuania   505, 565
Local Government Act 2000
   Section 2   1321
long residence rules   151-153
   14-year long residence rule   155, 157
Luxembourg   505

M

Maastricht Treaty on European Union   504,
     513
Macedonia   419, 462, 590, 675, 1075, 1293,
     1295
Making immigration work for everyone   55
   JCWI's recommendations   56
Making Migration Work for Britain   31, 33,
     42, 45
   Consultation   416
maintenance and accommodation   308-318
   third-party support   317
maladministration (*see* civil claims)
Malawi   675
Malaysia   675
   BOCs from   1410
Mali   675
malicious prosecution (*see* civil claims)
Malta   505, 512, 565
marriage
   Article 8 and discretionary leave   294,
     875-9
   bigamy   319
   certificate of approval   297
   civil registration   300
   customary   319
   discrimination   886-7
   domicile   320
   DP/2/93   338, 340-1

marriage *continued*
DP3/96 339
entry clearance for 297
Immigration (Procedure for Marriage)
Regulations 296
in other countries 319
naturalisation for British citizenship 1455
of convenience, EEA rights
Article 8 824
polygamous (*see* polygamous marriages)
procedures 298
registrars, designated 299
relationship breakdown 351
same-sex 300, 318, 320, 323, 342-3
'sham' marriages 335
switching status 332
visitors 229
mandate refugees (*see* refugees)
Maternity Alliance report on detention
948
maternity allowance (*see* welfare benefits)
maternity pay (*see* welfare benefits)
Mauritania 675
Mauritius 675
media representatives 455
medical examination 99
Medical Foundation for the Care of Victims of
Torture 671
Members of Parliament
contacting 1227
Memoranda of Understanding 1020
Mental Health Act 1983 1028
Section 117 1320
mental ill health
and human rights 851-2
Migrant Workers: A TUC Guide 46
Minority Rights Group 1109
misfeasance in public office 1181
Moldova 419, 675, 1075
Monaco 462
Mongolia 675
Montenegro 707
Morocco 590
Mozambique 675

N

Namibia 675
NASS Policy Bulletins 1340
No.64 accommodation after release from
detention 971
National Asylum Support service (NASS) 12,
28, 654, 1337
National Health Service Act 1977
Schedule 8 1321
National Strategy for Refugee Integration 48
Nationality Instructions (NI) 12

Nationality, Immigration and Asylum Act 2002
7, 31-32, 600, 753-5
exclusions from support under schedule 3
1301
third country cases 755
Nationality, Immigration and Asylum Act 2002
(Juxtaposed Controls) Order 2003
naturalisation 1447, 1453
based on civil partnership 1455
based on marriage 1455
EEA nationals 1462
five-years' residence 1454
good character 1463
intention to make home in the UK 1469
knowledge of life in the UK 1465
'Life in the UK' test 1468
marriage 1455
referees 1469
residence requirements 1457
temporary admission 1461
Naturalization Act 1844 1402
negative resolution (immigration rules) 9
negligence 1178
maladministration 1185
Netherlands 505
New Asylum Model (NAM) 48, 637, 641
late and opportunistic 643
potential NSA 643
segmentation 642
Niger 675
Nigeria 675, 707
British posts in Lagos and Abuja 85
non-asylum in-country applications
charging 125
non-compliance refusals of asylum (*see* asylum
refusals)
non-lapsing leave 26, 107, 118
non-suspensive appeals (NSA) 643, 673,
675, 1073
non-visa nationals 25
North West Consortia Induction Service
656
North West Project (NWP) 643, 681
Northern Ireland 26
Legal aid and advice 61
Norway 506

O

Oakington Reception Centre 7, 19, 639,
643, 673, 907, 935, 942
fast-track timetable 677
fast-track legality 677
inspection 943
oath of allegiance and pledge (*see* British
nationality)
Office of the European Ombudsman 509

Office of the Immigration Services
    Commissioner (OISC)   59, 60, 62,
    419
  complaints   65
  disciplinary action by   66
  immigration advice and services   63
  rules and code of standards   64
Ombudsman
  Local Government (*listed separately*)
  Parliamentary (*listed separately*)
off-shore workers   470
one-stop
  additional grounds   663-4
  appeals   1066-7
  notices   139, 662, 664
Operational Enforcement Manual (OEM)   12,
    905, 908
Operational Guidance Notes (OGNs)   708
over 65 removals policy (*see* enforcement)
overseas government employees   459
Overseas Territories   1406
overstayers   1003, 1033
  Article 8   838-9

P

PACE (Police and Criminal Evidence Act 1984)
    659, 685
Pakistan   675, 707
parents   361
  access to children at school   375
  adoptive parents   361
  and grandparents   399
  definition of   1428
  joining a person who is not a parent   371
  of EEA national children   531-4
Parliamentary Commissioner for
    Administration (*see* Parliamentary
    Ombudsman)
Parliamentary Joint Committee on Human
    Rights   54
Parliamentary Ombudsman   30, 1229
partners (*see* unmarried partners)
passports
  endorsements   139, 192
  entering the UK without a passport
    1035
  identifying British nationality from   1421
  issued before 1 January 1983   1421
  obtaining a passport   1423
  refusal or withdrawal   1423
  return of passport while appeal of
    application is taking place   119
pension
  state pension credit (*see* welfare benefits)
  state retirement (*see* welfare benefits)

permit-free employment
  long term   453
persecution (*see* asylum *see also* refugees)
points system   34-42, 43, 45
Poland   505, 565
police detention   938
  lawfulness, civil claim   1177
policy instructions   9
port removal   26, 990, 1000
Portugal   505
posted workers   525-6
pre-action protocol   1210, 1217
  civil claims (*see* civil claims)
  judicial review (*see* judicial review)
pregnant women
  detention of   947
premises, unlawful searches (*see* civil claims)
Prevention of Terrorism Act 2005   902
  detention   901
prisons
  HM Chief Inspector   942-3
proportionality and Article 8   832-44
prosecution
  asylum-seekers, of   683-6
  malicious (*see* civil claims)
public funds   15
  definition of   309
  exemptions   309-11
  tax credits   310

Q

Qualifications and Curriculum Authority
    423
quota-based schemes   35, 45
Quota refugee resettlement programme (*see*
    refugees)

R

race discrimination   887-93
  damages (*see* civil claims)
  ministerial authorisations   888
  Race Monitor   888-90
  Stephen Lawrence Inquiry   887
Race Relations Act 1976   887
Race Relations (Amendment) Act 2000   887
Reception Conditions Directive (*see* EC
    Directives)
reconsideration orders and hearings (*see*
    Asylum and Immigration Tribunal)
Refugee Convention 1951   10, 47, 597
  and human rights   852
  Article 31   19
  Article 33   19
  family unity   764
  third country challenges   743-5

Refugee Council
  Panel of Advisers for Unaccompanied
    Refugee Children 698
Refugee Integration Loan 32
Refugee Legal Centre 1109
refugees 597-8
  active review 721, 725, 730
  benefit claims, backdating (see welfare
    benefits)
  ceasing to be a refugee 1008
  ceasing to qualify 627
  children of 758
  exclusion from Convention protection
    624
  family members, status of 760
  family reunion 757
  Gateway Protection Programme 697
  group refugees 699
  integration loans (see welfare benefits)
  limited leave 720-7
  Mandate refugees 698
  persecution 602
  qualifying for refugee status 601
  Quota refugee resettlement programme
    697
  refugee integration loans 1286
  refugees 'sur place' 712
  revocation of indefinite leave 627
  social services support, exclusion from (see
    social services)
  spouse of 758
  standard of proof 622
  'Sunrise' project 719, 727-8
  temporary protection 633
  'Ten or more' plan 699
  terrorism 627
  transfer of refugee status 699-700
  travel 631
  welfare benefits – backdating 1284
  well-founded fear 602
  women 607, 608, 616-9
registration
  children
    mentally disturbed 1483
  for nationality (see British nationalilty)
  registration with police
  passport endorsement 196
regularisation schemes (see concessions)
relatives
  human rights and Article 8 826
religion
  freedom of (Article 9) 807
removal
  appeals 1094
  breach of human rights 809-20
  families, of 998-1000

  judicial review (see judicial review)
  suicide /self-harm 996
  unlawful (see civil claims)
removal directions 209
renunciation of citizenship 1442
reporting centres 654
reporting conditions (see temporary
  admission)
Republic of Ireland 26
researchers, sponsored 425
residence documents 544-5
residence permits 544-5
restriction orders 950
retired persons, EEA free movement 524
retirement pension 1273
returning resident 17
  appeal against refusal of entry 116
  indefinite leave 114
  limited leave 115
  public funds 115
  refusal of entry 115
  settlement 114
returning residents rule 111
Review of Family Visitor Appeals 48
revocation
  deporation order 1024
  indefinite leave 1008, 1025-6
  of refugee status 1008
right of abode 13, 1417
  1971 Act 1418
  British Nationality Act 1948 1418
  British Nationality Act 1981 1418
  Certificate of Entitlement 109, 202, 1420
  children with 359
  Commonwealth citizens 110
  Commonwealth Immigrants Act 1968
    1418
right to reside 1264
rights of family reunion 20
Rochester, HMP 936, 945
Roma
  race discrimination 892
Romania 419, 462, 508, 675, 1075, 1293,
    1295
  Association Agreement 577
  au pairs 462

S

same sex partners
  Civil Partnership Act 2004 300
  EU free movement rights 343
  and human rights 827
San Marino 462
Save The Children report on detention 947
Science and Engineering Graduates Scheme
  (SEGS) 453

Science and Engineering Graduates Scheme
    continued
    switching 160
Scotland 'Fresh Talent' scheme 26
    legal aid and advice 61
Scottish Executive 415
screening (asylum) 649-50
search, entry and seizure 1032
search of premises
    unlawful 1183
    warrants 1184
Seasonal Agricultural Workers' Scheme
    (SAWS) 450
    switching 227
    work card 418, 451-2
Secretary of State for the Home Department
    Officers of 24
Sectors Based Scheme (SBS) 448
    dependants 450
    hotel and catering work 449
    permitted race discrimination 889
    switching 173
secure borders 49
Secure Borders, Safe Haven 7, 44, 235, 906
self-employed
    EEA – family members 519-20
self-sufficient persons 522-4
Senegal 675
Serbia 707
Serbia and Montenegro 675, 1075
service standards 417
settlement 17, 48
    'present and settled' 302
    'settled' 1429-30
    settled in the United Kingdom 302
severe disablement allowance (*see* welfare
    benefits)
Sex Discrimination Act
    damages (*see* civil claims)
sexuality
    asylum claim (*listed separately*)
    Article 8 804-6
Singapore 1410
Skills Advisory Body (SAB) 42
slavery, protection from (*see* European
    Convention, Article 4) 800
Slovakia 505, 565
Slovenia 505, 565
Social Charter and Revised Social Charter (*see*
    Council of Europe and European)
social fund 1275
Social Security Contribution and Benefits Act
    1992 1244, 1280
Social Security (Immigration and Asylum)
    Consequential Amendments
    Regulations 2000 1247

social services 1299
    community care assessments 1322
    exclusions 1301
        asylum-seekers 1304
        EEA nationals 1303, 1314-5
        human rights exception 1306
Social Work (Scotland) Act 1968 1302
sole traders 478
Somalia 707
    Somali travel documents, permitted race
        discrimination 889
Somaliland 41, 675
South Africa 675, 1075
Southall Black Sisters 345
Spain 505
Special Immigration Appeals Commission
    (SIAC) 965, 1081
    detention 965
Special Immigration Appeals Commission Act
    1997 10
special quota voucher scheme 1409
    heads of households 1410
'specified' nationals 55
sponsored researcher 415
spouses/partners 303-4, 318
    access to children 352
    divorce overseas 321
    'Domestic Violence Concession' 295
    EU free movement rights 343
    maintenance undertakings 318
    present and settled 305
    probationary period 295, 329
    recent developments 295
    switching status 332
    third-party support 317
Sri Lanka 41, 675, 1075
St Christopher & Nevis 1422
St Lucia 675
Standard Acknowledgement Letter (SAL)
    203-204, 651
starred decisions (*see* Asylum and Immigration
    Tribunal)
stateless persons
    registration as British citizens 1488
Statement of Changes in Immigration Rules
    11
Statement of Evidence Form (SEF) 669
    procedure 642
State Pension Credit Act 2002 1244
statutory review 1141-2, 1150-3
Stephen Lawrence Inquiry 887
students 249, 262
    ability to follow the course 257
    ability to meet the costs of the course
        256
    architectural students 263

students *continued*
  Association of British Language Schools 254
  bona fide private education institutions 253
  British Council 254
  BUNAC students 468
  City Technology Colleges 254
  clinical attachment / dental observer degree-level 272
  dental students 279, 283
  Department for Education and Skills Register 253
  EEA students 288
  employment (*see* permission to work)
  entry clearance 251, 260
  exchange students 255
  extending leave – how to apply 273
  fees 284
  foundation course 263
  full-time study 255
  independent fee-paying schools 254, 262
  intention to leave the UK 258
    concession relating to students 259
  internship work permits 265
  maintenance and accommodation 256
  medical students 250, 279, 283
  PLAB test 250, 282-3
  Prime Minister's Initiative 249, 270
  prospective students 252
  publicly funded institutions of further or higher 253
  re-sitting examinations 250
  recent developments 249
  regular attendance 271
  resitting examinations 276
  sabbatical students 250, 276, 278
  sandwich courses 265
  satisfactory progress 271
  self-sufficient, European rights of free movement 522-4
  short courses 263, 272
    spouses and children of 266
  student support 284, 286-7
  switching
    transitional arrangements 274-275
  technical 472
  transitional arrangements 270, 272
  undertakings, breaches 276
  work 257
  work experience 472
  writing up a thesis 276
subject to immigration control 14
Sudan 707
suicide/self-harm removals policy (*see* removal)
'Sunrise' project (*see* refugees)

support (*see* asylum support and *see* social services support')
sureties 974
  checklist 981
Swaziland 675
Sweden 505-6
switching 24
  human rights applications 188
Switzerland 506-7, 1293, 1295
  Immigration (Swiss Free Movement of Persons) (No. 515
  Swiss nationals 562

T

Tanzania 675
tax credits 311, 1273
  working tax credit (*see* welfare benefits)
Tax Credits Act 2002 310, 1244, 1269
Tax Credits (Immigration) Regulations 2003 310, 1247
teachers 419, 422, 425, 445
  and language assistants 463
  gap-year 468
temporary admission 18, 950
  citizenship (*see* naturalisation)
  conditions , 652-4, 952
    electronic monitoring (EM) 652, 953
  reporting 652-4
temporary protection 21, 633
Temporary Protection Directive 21
temporary release 950
ten-year long residence rules 154, 156
terrorism
  asylum-seekers and refugees 624, 627, 650
  deportation for unacceptable behaviour 1019
  memoranda of understanding 1020
Terrorism Act 2000 627
tests
  English language 48
  knowledge of life in the UK 48
third country
  1993 and 1996 Acts 752
  appeals and challenges 739-43
  asylum claims
    1993 and 1996 Acts 752-3
    1999 and 2002 Acts 753-5
    2004 Act 739
    certificates 'clearly unfounded' 745-6
    Dublin Convention and Dublin II Regulation 748-9
    family links 750
    immigration rules 747-8
  civil claims 1196
  detention 746, 915

third country *continued*
  human rights   745
third-country cases   20
third-country nationals   513
time-limits (appeals)   28
Tinsley House   935
  inspection   944
Togo   675
torts   1173
torture   795
Tough as Old Boots? Asylum, immigration and the paradox of New Labour policy   418
trafficking   1034
Training and Work Experience Scheme (TWES)
  approved training   441
  families of   279, 443
  work experience   441
transfer of refugee status (*see* refugees)
transit visitors   243, 245
travel
  before an appeal is decided   121
  before an application is decided   121
  embarkation controls   121
  GV3 'declaration of identity' document   207
  while appeal or application is outstanding   119
travel documents
  Certificates of Identity for those with DL, HP or ELE/R   880-3
Treaty establishing the European Community (EC Treaty)   503-4
  Article 17(1)   513
Treaty of Rome   507
trespass   1173, 1183-4, 1199
Trinidad and Tobago   675
Tunisia   590
Turkey   41, 419, 462, 508, 675, 707, 1293, 1295
  'Ankara Agreement'   577
Turkey Association Agreement   585

U

Uganda   5, 675, 707
UK nationals   513
UKCOSA (The Council for International Education)   284
Ukraine   675, 1075, 1293, 1295
unaccompanied minor asylum-seekers
  Children Act 1989   1322
  humanitarian protection and discretionary leave   870-1
  Refugee Council Panel of Advisers   688
  (*see also* children)
United Nations Convention on the Status of Refugees   19, 588

United Nations High Commission for Refugees (UNHCR)   1109
  Guidelines on the Detention of Asylum Seekers   917
  Quality Initiative   641
  UNHCR Handbook   601, 640
Uniform Format Visa (UFV)   192
United Kingdom Residence Permit (UKRP)   139
  Guidelines on detention   917
United States State Department   1109
unmarried partners
  Article 8   824
  'consanguineous' relationship   323
  EU free movement rights   343

V

Vietnam   675, 707
visa nationals   79
visitors   118, 213
  academic visitors   221
  amateur entertainers and sportspersons   222
  appeals
    against refusal of entry   226
      at the port   227
  applying for entry   214
  carers   232
  change of status   228
  dependant relatives   388
  entry clearance   117, 224
  excavations   222
  family visitors – appeals (*see* appeals)   226
  genuinely seeking entry   215
  intention to leave   216
  intention to work   216
  job interviewees   223
  lorry drivers   220
  maintenance and accommodation   219
  marriage visitors   229
  medical visitors   230
  monteurs   221
  sponsors   218
  switching status   227
  tour group couriers   220
  transit   243, 245

W

Wales   26
welfare   28
welfare benefits   1241, 1280
  'subject to immigration control'   1249
  Accession 8 nationals   1269
  bereavement benefits   1246, 1276
  child benefit   1273, 1280
  child tax credit   1258

welfare benefits *continued*
  contributory benefits   1276
  council tax benefit   1279
  dependants, claiming for   1276
  disability benefit   1273
  disability living allowance   1242, 1245,
    1257
  EEA nationals   563
  guardian's allowance   1274
  habitual residence test   1260
  housing benefit   1279
  income support   1277
  job-seekers allowance – income-based
    1277
  public funds   1243
  reciprocal agreements   1282
  refugee integration loans   1286
  retirement pension   1273
  right to reside   1264
    Accession 8 nationals   1268
  social fund   1275
  state pension credit   1279
  tax credits   1273, 1280
  widow's parent's allowance and widow's
    payment   1246, 1276
  working tax credit   1258
well-founded fear (*see* persecution)
Withholding and Withdrawal of Support
    (Travel Assistance and Temporary
    Accommodation) Regulations 2002
    1301, 1313-5
witness summons (*see* appeals)
work
  discrimination   500
  permission to   411
  permit-free employment   453
work permits   12, 418
  actors   445
  appeals   439
  business and commercial   421
  Business and Commercial Internal
    Caseworker Guidance   421
  children   436
  employees   422
  General Agreement on Trade in Services
    (GATS)   421, 447
  genuine vacancy   422
  IED 'appeals'   439
  intra-company transfers   424
  inward investment posts   424
  multiple applications   432
  scheme   420
  Seasonal Agricultural Workers' Scheme
    (SAWS)   450
  Sectors Based Scheme (SBS)   448
  senior board-level posts   424

    settlement of holders   437
  scheme   420
  sportspeople and entertainers   421, 444
    dependants of   421, 444, 447
  student interns   421, 447
  Tier 1 applications   424
  Tier 2 applications   425
  training and work experience (TWES)   421
Worker Registration Scheme   573
  employer sanctions   575
  refusal   575
  registration cards and certificates   574
working holidaymakers   235
  changes   235
  children of   242
  dependants of   355
  transitional arrangements   242
working tax credit   1258
work permit
  appeals   439-40
  children   436
  employees   422
  genuine vacancy   422
  intra-company transfers   424
  inward investment posts   424
  multiple applications   432
  multiple entry   435-6
  resident worker   422
  reviews   430-40
  senior board level posts   424
  student internships
  supplementary work   435
Work Permits (UK)   1494
  Business Case Unit address   132
  food processing   449

Y

Yugoslavia (former Socialist Federal Republic)
    Stabilisation and Association Agreement
    590
Yarls Wood Immigration Removal Centre
    639, 643, 673, 935

Z

Zambia   675
Zimbabwe   675, 707

 **membership services**

JCWI's strength is rooted in the diversity and support of its membership. JCWI is the only national organisation in this field which has never sought, nor accepted, central government funding, and can therefore claim to be truly free of government influence. We are needed now, more than ever, in an environment highly charged with debates on immigration and race, and we depend strongly on the support of our members in order to continue lobbying for justice and the elimination of discrimination in immigration policy. Currently our members range from legal practitioners through to refugee community organisations and individuals.

Key membership benefits:

• free quarterly JCWI Bulletins

• 10% discount on issues of JCWI Handbook

• substantial discounts on training of up to £260 per course (see overleaf).

To become a member, download a form from the JCWI website
www.jcwi.org.uk

Membership fees are as follows:

Individuals	Unwaged	£20
	Others (excluding practising lawyers)	£30
	Practising lawyer	£50
Commercial organisations (inc. solicitors' practices and barristers' chambers)		£100
Voluntary/Non-profit organisations	Small	£40
	Medium	£75
	Large	£200

Contact JCWI Membership and Publications on 020 7608 7307

 **publications**

Redesigned in early 2005, JCWI's Bulletin is a comprehensive journal targeted at everyone who needs to keep up to date in this rapidly changing field. The Bulletin is published quarterly and is FREE for members.

The Bulletin includes:

- Leading articles & features on important topical matters
- Digest of important legal decisions
- Articles on campaigns and actions

The Bulletin is published quarterly and is free for members.

For membership or subscription details visit www.jcwi.org.uk

Contact JCWI Membership and Publications on 020 7608 7307.

 **training**

Substantial discounts of up to £260 on course fees are available for JCWI members.

The latest training programme is available on the JCWI website www.jcwi.org.uk

Expert skills training in immigration, nationality and refugee law and practice to advisers and practitioners for nearly 25 years.

Some of the popular areas that we train on:

- The new appeals system
- Human rights law
- Working in the UK
- Family immigration
- OISC Levels of Competence and LSC Accreditation Courses

All courses are accredited by the Law Society and the Bar Council for continuing professional development (CPD) points. The courses are recommended by the Legal Services Commission and the Office of the Immigration Services Commissioner.

Contact: JCWI Training on 0207 608 7306

Or email: training@jcwi.org.uk